HTML

Comprehensive Concepts and Techniques, Fifth Edition

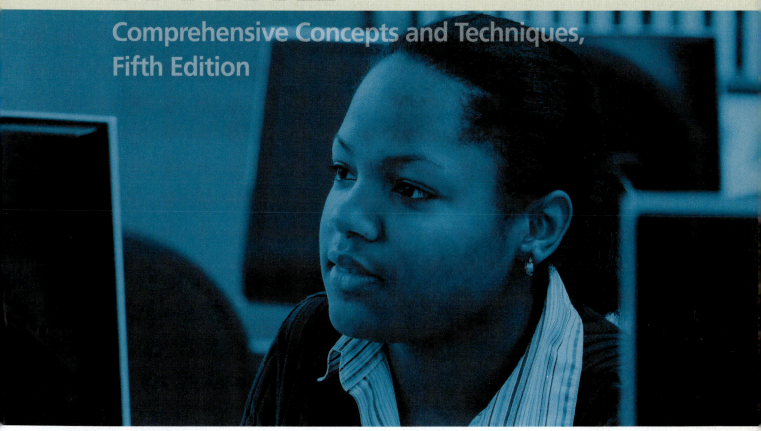

Gary B. Shelly
Denise M. Woods
William J. Dorin

Shelly Cashman Series®

An imprint of Course Technology, Cengage Learning

COURSE TECHNOLOGY
CENGAGE Learning™

Australia • Brazil • Japan • Korea • Mexico • Singapore • Spain • United Kingdom • United States

HTML
Comprehensive Concepts and Techniques, Fifth Edition
Gary B. Shelly, Denise M. Woods, William J. Dorin

Vice President, Publisher: Nicole Jones Pinard
Executive Editor: Kathleen McMahon
Senior Product Manager: Mali Jones
Product Manager: Klenda Martinez
Associate Product Manager: Jon Farnham
Editorial Assistant: Lauren Brody
Print Buyer: Julio Esperas
Content Project Manager: Heather Furrow
Developmental Editor: Deb Kaufmann
Executive Director of Marketing: Cheryl Costantini
Marketing Manager: Tristen Kendall
Marketing Coordinator: Julie Schuster
QA Manuscript Reviewers: John Freitas, Serge Palladino, Danielle Shaw, Marianne Snow, Susan Whalen
Art Director: Marissa Falco
Cover Design: Joel Sadagursky
Cover Photo: Jon Chomitz
Compositor: GEX Publishing Services
Printer: RRD Menasha

For product information and technology assistance, contact us at
Cengage Learning Customer & Sales Support, 1-800-354-9706

For permission to use material from this text or product, submit all requests online at **cengage.com/permissions**
Further permissions questions can be emailed to
permissionrequest@cengage.com

ISBN-13: 978-1-4239-2722-8

ISBN-10: 1-4239-2722-2

Course Technology
25 Thomson Place
Boston, Massachusetts 02210
USA

Cengage Learning is a leading provider of customized learning solutions with office locations around the globe, including Singapore, the United Kingdom, Australia, Mexico, Brazil, and Japan. Locate your local office at: **international.cengage.com/region**

Cengage Learning products are represented in Canada by Nelson Education, Ltd.

To learn more about Course Technology, visit **www.cengage.com/coursetechnology**
To learn more about Cengage Learning, visit **www.cengage.com**
Purchase any of our products at your local college bookstore or at our preferred online store **www.ichapters.com**

Printed in the United States of America
3 4 5 6 7 12 11 10

HTML

Comprehensive Concepts and Techniques, Fifth Edition

Contents

CHAPTER THREE

Creating Web Pages with Links, Images, and Formatted Text

CHAPTER FOUR
Creating Tables in a Web Site

CHAPTER FIVE
Creating an Image Map

CHAPTER EIGHT
Creating Style Sheets

CHAPTER NINE
Integrating JavaScript and HTML

CHAPTER ELEVEN
Using DOM to Enhance Web Pages

CHAPTER TWELVE

Creating and Using XML Documents

Appendices

APPENDIX A
HTML Quick Reference

APPENDIX B
Browser-Safe Color Palette

APPENDIX C
Accessibility Standards and the Web

APPENDIX D
CSS Properties and Values

APPENDIX E
JavaScript Quick Reference

APPENDIX F
XML Quick Reference

Preface

The Shelly Cashman Series® offers the finest textbooks in computer education. We are proud of the fact that our previous HTML books have been so well received. With each new edition of our HTML books, we have made significant improvements based on the comments made by instructors and students. The *HTML, Fifth Edition* books continue with the innovation, quality, and reliability you have come to expect from the Shelly Cashman Series.

In 2006 and 2007, the Shelly Cashman Series development team carefully reviewed our pedagogy and analyzed its effectiveness in teaching today's student. An extensive customer survey produced results confirming what the series is best known for: its step-by-step, screen-by-screen instructions, its project-oriented approach, and the quality of its content.

We learned, though, that students entering computer courses today are different than students taking these classes just a few years ago. Students today read less, but need to retain more. They need not only to be able to perform skills, but to retain those skills and know how to apply them to different settings. Today's students need to be continually engaged and challenged to retain what they're learning.

As a result, we've renewed our commitment to focusing on the user and how they learn best. This commitment is reflected in every change we've made to our HTML book.

Objectives of This Textbook

HTML: Comprehensive Concepts and Techniques, Fifth Edition is intended for use in a three-unit course that presents an in-depth coverage of HTML and basic Web design techniques. No experience with Web page development or computer programming is required. Specific objectives of this book are as follows:

- To teach the fundamentals of developing Web pages
- To acquaint students with the HTML language and creating Web pages suitable for course work, professional purposes, and personal use
- To acquaint students with the XHTML guidelines
- To expose students to common Web page formats and functions
- To illustrate how to add functionality to Web pages using JavaScript and DHTML using the Document Object Model (DOM)
- To show the benefits of XML
- To promote curiosity and independent exploration of World Wide Web resources
- To develop an exercise-oriented approach that allows students to learn by example
- To encourage independent study and help those who are learning how to create Web pages in a distance education environment

The Shelly Cashman Approach

Features of the Shelly Cashman Series HTML books include:

- **Project Orientation** Each chapter in the book presents a project with a practical problem and complete solution in an easy-to-understand approach.
- **Plan Ahead Boxes** The project orientation is enhanced by the inclusion of Plan Ahead boxes. These new features prepare students to create successful projects by encouraging them to think strategically about what they are trying to accomplish before they begin working.
- **Step-by-Step, Screen-by-Screen Instructions** Each of the tasks required to complete a project is clearly identified throughout the chapter. Now, the step-by-step instructions provide a context beyond point-and-click. Each step explains why students are performing a task, or the result of performing a certain action. Found on the screens accompanying each step, call-outs give students the information they need to know when they need to know it. Now, we've used color to distinguish the content in the call-outs. The Explanatory call-outs (in black) summarize what is happening on the screen and the Navigational call-outs (in red) show students where to click.

Q&A

What is a maximized window?

A maximized window fills the entire screen. When you maximize a window, the Maximize button changes to a Restore Down button.

- **Q&A** Found within many of the step-by-step sequences, Q&As raise the kinds of questions students may ask when working through a step sequence and provide answers about what they are doing, why they are doing it, and how that task might be approached differently.

Other Ways

1. In Windows Explorer, double-click HTML file name to open in default browser
2. In Windows Explorer, right-click HTML file name, click Open With, click browser name
3. Click Tools, Menu Bar if menu is not displayed; on Menu bar click File, Open and browse to desired file

- **Experimental Steps** These new steps, within our step-by-step instructions, encourage students to explore and experiment with HTML code. These steps are not necessary to complete the projects, but are designed to increase the confidence with the language and build problem-solving skills.
- **Thoroughly Tested Projects** Unparalleled quality is ensured because every screen in the book is produced by the author only after performing a step, and then each project must pass Course Technology's Quality Assurance program.
- **Other Ways Boxes** The Other Ways boxes displayed at the end of most of the step-by-step sequences specify the other ways to do the task completed in the steps. Thus, the steps and the Other Ways box make a comprehensive reference unit.

BTW

Tables
Tables are useful for a variety of purposes. They can store information in tabular form or create a layout on a Web page. Layouts created with tables give the Web developer more flexibility. You have more control over the placement of information or images. Many popular Web sites use tables.

- **BTW** These marginal annotations provide background information, tips, and answers to common questions that complement the topics covered, adding depth and perspective to the learning process.
- **Integration of the World Wide Web** The World Wide Web is integrated into the HTML learning experience by (1) BTW annotations that send students to Web sites for up-to-date information and alternative approaches to tasks; (2) an HTML Quick Reference Summary Web page that summarizes HTML tags and attributes; and (3) the Learn It Online section at the end of each chapter, which has chapter reinforcement exercises, learning games, and other types of student activities.
- **End-of-Chapter Student Activities** Extensive student activities at the end of each chapter provide the student with plenty of opportunities to reinforce the materials learned in the chapter through hands-on assignments. Several new types of activities have been added that challenge the student in new ways to expand their knowledge, and to apply their new skills to a project with personal relevance.

Organization of This Textbook

HTML: Comprehensive Concepts and Techniques, Fifth Edition consists of twelve chapters on HTML, and six appendices. The Chapters and Appendices are organized as follows:

Chapter 1 – Introduction to HTML This introductory chapter provides students with an overview of the Internet, World Wide Web, Web pages, HTML, and Web development. Topics include the types and purposes of Web sites; Web browsers; HTML standards; Dynamic Hypertext Markup Language (DHTML) and Extensible Hypertext Markup Language (XHTML) and their relationship to HTML. Additionally, Web editors, the five phases of the Web development life cycle, and the importance of usability testing are defined.

Chapter 2 – Creating and Editing a Web Page In Chapter 2, students are introduced to basic HTML tags and the various parts of a Web page. Topics include starting and quitting Notepad and a browser; entering headings and text into an HTML file; creating a bulleted list with HTML; adding an image, background color, and a horizontal rule; saving the HTML file and viewing it in the browser; validating the HTML code; viewing the HTML source code for a Web Page; printing the HTML file and the Web page; and Web page design.

Chapter 3 – Creating Web pages with Links, Images, and Formatted Text In Chapter 3, students are introduced to linking terms and definitions. Topics include adding an e-mail link; linking to another page on the same Web site; linking to another Web site; setting link targets within a page; linking to targets; using absolute and relative paths; types of image files; alternative text for images; defining image size; wrapping text around an image; and inserting images onto Web pages.

Chapter 4 – Creating Tables in a Web Site In Chapter 4, students learn how to create tables using HTML tags. First, students assess table needs and then plan the table. Topics include table definitions and terms; table uses; creating borderless tables; inserting images into tables; vertical and horizontal alignment within a table; adding color to a cell; adding links to another page; adding an e-mail link; using the rowspan and colspan attributes; adding captions; and spacing within and between cells.

Chapter 5 – Creating an Image Map In Chapter 5, students learn how to use an image map to create more advanced Web page navigation. Topics include image mapping purpose and considerations; selecting appropriate images for mapping; dividing an image into hotspots; creating links from those hotspots; and using text links in conjunction with image links.

Chapter 6 – Using Frames in a Web Site In Chapter 6, students are introduced to the use of frames in Web development. Topics include purpose and considerations when using frames; resizing frames; frame headers and scroll bars; frame navigation; and creating two-, three-, and four-frame structures.

Chapter 7 – Creating a Form on a Web Page In Chapter 7, students create a form for collecting user input. Topics include form purposes and basics; selecting check boxes, text boxes, and other controls on a form; using textareas for free-form text; and creating an e-mail link to submit the form information back to the Web page data collector. Students also are introduced to using advanced selection menus and fieldset tags to segregate groups of information.

Chapter 8 – Creating Style Sheets In Chapter 8, students are introduced to the three different types of Cascading Style Sheets (CSS) — embedded, external, and inline. Topics include adding an embedded style sheet to change the link styles, adding an external style sheet to format a Web page, and adding an inline style sheet to change the style of a small component of a Web page.

Chapter 9 – Integrating JavaScript and HTML In Chapter 9, students are introduced to integrating JavaScript into HTML files. Topics include JavaScript tags and comments within the HTML; placing HTML tags within JavaScript statements; introducing the document objects; defining variables; writing user-defined functions; extracting the current system date and using it to calculate the number of days to a future date; writing dynamic messages to a Web page; changing the color of the browser scroll bar track; and using the setTimeout() method.

Chapter 10 – Creating Pop-up Windows, Adding Scrolling Messages, and Validating Forms In Chapter 10, three common uses of JavaScript are presented; creating pop-up windows, adding scrolling messages, and validating forms. Topics include using JavaScript to conduct data entry validation on the client computer; working with the Document Object Model (DOM), forms, string lengths, and the Math object pow() method; using the if... else control structure with the parseInt(), is NaN(), and parseFloat() built-in functions to validate user input forms; and writing user-defined functions called by event handlers.

Chapter 11 – Using DOM to Enhance Web Pages In Chapter 11, students use DHTML in Web page development. Topics include defining the Document Object Model (DOM); creating layers using divisions (<div> tag); writing the code to make text or image objects scroll across or down a Web page using the JavaScript setTimeout() and clearTimeout() methods to start and stop scrolling; using JavaScript to create rotating banners on a Web page; using onmouseover and onmouseout event handlers to execute pop-up ScreenTips; using the <span> tag as a container for embedded style sheet code to format Web pages text and the ScreenTips; and calling user-defined functions directly with the JavaScript command.

Chapter 12 – Creating and Using XML Documents In Chapter 12, students develop an understanding of XML documents, the W3C design goals for creating XML tags, and real-world uses for XML. Topics include learning the syntax rules for well-formed and valid XML documents; defining document prolog, document instance, and recordset; describing the purpose of processing instructions, Document Type Definitions (DTD) and XSL style sheets; binding a CSS file to an XML document, an XML style sheet to an XML document, and an XML document to an HTML Web page; using the built-in table element methods; and creating a JavaScript user-defined function to search for specific data in an XML document.

Appendix A – HTML Quick Reference Appendix A includes an HTML quick reference that contains the most frequently used tags and their associated attributes.

Appendix B – Browser-Safe Color Palette Appendix B summarizes the 216 browser-safe colors that appear equally well on different monitors, operating systems, and browsers — including both the Windows and Mac OS operating systems and Internet Explorer and Netscape browsers.

Appendix C – Accessibility Standards for the Web Appendix C provides an overview of Web accessibility issues and the Section 508 Web accessibility guidelines used by developers to create accessible Web sites.

Appendix D – CSS Properties and Values Appendix D provides a listing of Cascading Style Sheet (CSS) properties and values together with a description of use.

Appendix E – JavaScript Quick Reference Appendix E is a JavaScript quick reference of statements, objects, properties, methods, and event handlers.

Appendix F – XML Quick Reference Appendix F is an XML quick reference that contains syntax rules, XML applications, element definitions and attributes, coding examples, and brief summary of XLS style sheet notation.

End-of-Chapter Student Activities

A notable strength of the Shelly Cashman Series HTML books is the extensive student activities at the end of each chapter. Well-structured student activities can make the difference between students merely participating in a class and students retaining the information they learn. The activities in the Shelly Cashman Series books include the following.

CHAPTER SUMMARY A concluding paragraph, followed by a listing of the tasks completed within a chapter together with the pages on which the step-by-step, screen-by-screen explanations appear.

LEARN IT ONLINE Every chapter features a Learn It Online section that is comprised of six exercises. These exercises include True/False, Multiple Choice, Short Answer, Flash Cards, Practice Test, and Learning Games.

APPLY YOUR KNOWLEDGE This exercise usually requires students to open and manipulate a file from the Data Files that parallels the activities learned in the chapter. To obtain a copy of the Data Files for Students, follow the instructions on the inside back cover of this text.

EXTEND YOUR KNOWLEDGE This exercise allows students to extend and expand on the skills learned within the chapter.

MAKE IT RIGHT This exercise requires students to analyze a document, identify errors and issues, and correct those errors and issues using skills learned in the chapter.

IN THE LAB Three in-depth assignments per chapter require students to utilize the chapter concepts and techniques to solve problems on a computer.

CASES AND PLACES Five unique real-world case-study situations, including Make It Personal, an open-ended project that relates to student's personal lives, and one small-group activity.

Instructor Resources Disc

The Shelly Cashman Series is dedicated to providing you with all of the tools you need to make your class a success. Information about all supplementary materials is available through your Course Technology representative or by calling one of the following telephone numbers: Colleges, Universities, Continuing Education Departments, Post-Secondary Vocational Schools, Career Colleges, Business, Industry, Government, Trade, Retailer, Wholesaler, Library and Resellers, 800-648-7450; K-12 Schools, Secondary Vocational Schools, Adult Education and School Districts, 800-354-9706; Canada, 800-268-2222.

The Instructor Resources disc for this textbook includes both teaching and testing aids. The contents of each item on the Instructor Resources disc (ISBN 1-4239-2723-0) are described in the following text.

INSTRUCTOR'S MANUAL The Instructor's Manual consists of Microsoft Word files, which include chapter objectives, lecture notes, teaching tips, classroom activities, lab activities, quick quizzes, figures and boxed elements summarized in the chapters, and a glossary page. The new format of the Instructor's Manual will allow you to map through every chapter easily.

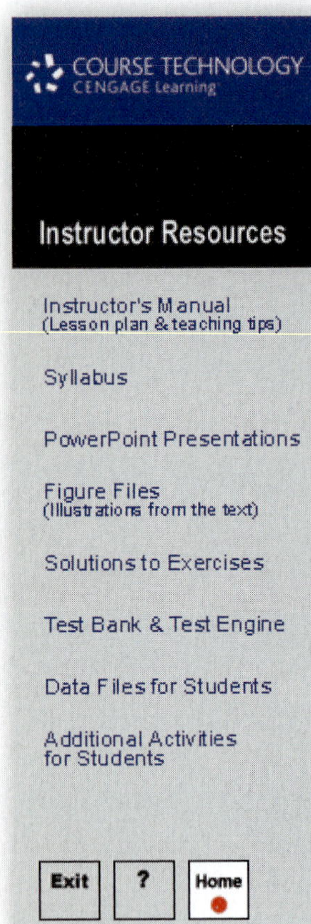

SYLLABUS Sample syllabi, which can be customized easily to a course, are included. The syllabi cover policies, class and lab assignments and exams, and procedural information.

FIGURE FILES Illustrations for every figure in the textbook are available in electronic form. Use this ancillary to present a slide show in lecture or to print transparencies for use in lecture with an overhead projector. If you have a personal computer and LCD device, this ancillary can be an effective tool for presenting lectures.

POWERPOINT PRESENTATIONS PowerPoint Presentations is a multimedia lecture presentation system that provides slides for each chapter. Presentations are based on chapter objectives. Use this presentation system to present well-organized lectures that are both interesting and knowledge based. PowerPoint Presentations provides consistent coverage at schools that use multiple lecturers.

SOLUTIONS TO EXERCISES Solutions are included for the end-of-chapter exercises, as well as the Chapter Reinforcement exercises.

TEST BANK & TEST ENGINE In the ExamView test bank, you will find a variety of question types (40 multiple-choice, 25 true/false, 20 completion, 5 modified multiple-choice, 5 modified true/false and 10 matching), including Critical Thinking questions (3 essays and 2 cases with 2 questions each). Each test bank contains 112 questions for every chapter with page number references, and when appropriate, figure references. A version of the test bank you can print also is included. The test bank comes with a copy of the test engine, ExamView, the ultimate tool for your objective-based testing needs. ExamView is a state-of-the-art test builder that is easy to use. ExamView enables you to create paper-, LAN-, or Web-based tests from test banks designed specifically for your Course Technology textbook. Utilize the ultra-efficient QuickTest Wizard to create tests in less than five minutes by taking advantage of Course Technology's question banks, or customize your own exams from scratch.

DATA FILES FOR STUDENTS All the files that are required by students to complete the exercises are included. You can distribute the files on the Instructor Resources disc to your students over a network, or you can have them follow the instructions on the inside back cover of this book to obtain a copy of the Data Files for Students.

ADDITIONAL ACTIVITIES FOR STUDENTS These additional activities consist of Chapter Reinforcement Exercises, which are true/false, multiple-choice, and short answer questions that help students gain confidence in the material learned.

Online Content

Blackboard is the leading distance learning solution provider and class-management platform today. Course Technology has partnered with Blackboard to bring you premium online content. Instructors: Content for use with *HTML: Comprehensive Concepts and Techniques* is available in a Blackboard Course Cartridge and may include topic reviews, case projects, review questions, test banks, practice tests, custom syllabi, and more.

Course Technology also has solutions for several other learning management systems. Please visit http://www.course.com today to see what's available for this title.

CourseCasts Learning on the Go. Always Available...Always Relevant.

Want to keep up with the latest technology trends relevant to you? Visit our site to find a library of podcasts, CourseCasts, featuring a "CourseCast of the Week," and download them to your portable media player at http://coursecasts.course.com.

Our fast-paced world is driven by technology. You know because you are an active participant — always on the go, always keeping up with technological trends, and always learning new ways to embrace technology to power your life.

Ken Baldauf, a faculty member of the Florida State University (FSU) Computer Science Department, is responsible for teaching technology classes to thousands of FSU students each year. He knows what you know; he knows what you want to learn. He is also an expert in the latest technology and will sort through and aggregate the most pertinent news and information so you can spend your time enjoying technology, rather than trying to figure it out.

Visit us at http://coursecasts.course.com to learn on the go!

CourseNotes

Course Technology's CourseNotes are six-panel quick reference cards that reinforce the most important and widely used features of a software application in a visual and user-friendly format. CourseNotes will serve as a great reference tool during and after the student completes the course. CourseNotes for Microsoft Office 2007, Word 2007, Excel 2007, Access 2007, PowerPoint 2007, Windows Vista, and more are available now!

To the Student . . . Getting the Most Out of Your Book

Welcome to *HTML: Comprehensive Concepts and Techniques, Fifth Edition*. You can save yourself a lot of time and gain a better understanding of HTML if you spend a few minutes reviewing the figures and callouts in this section.

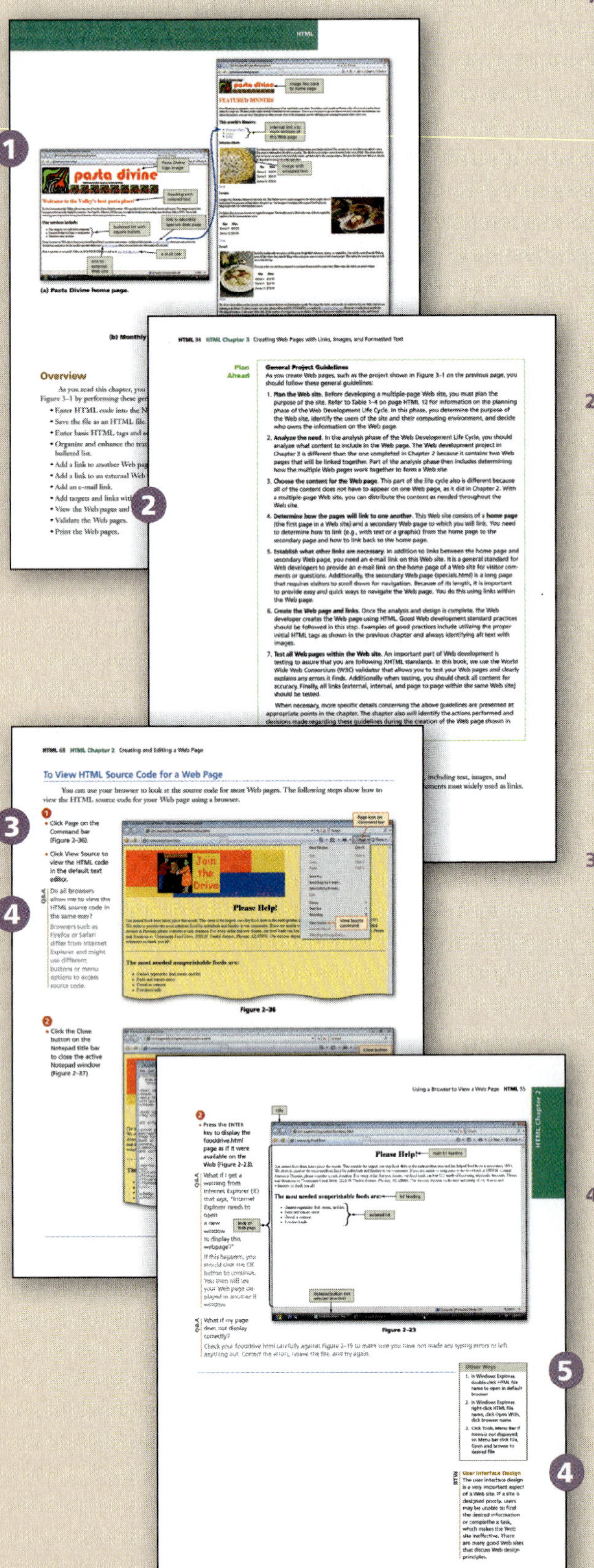

1 PROJECT ORIENTATION
Each chapter's project presents a practical problem and shows the solution in the first figure of the chapter. The project orientation lets you see firsthand how problems are solved from start to finish using up-to-date HTML coding practices and strategies.

2 PROJECT PLANNING GUIDELINES AND PLAN AHEAD BOXES
Overall planning guidelines at the beginning of a chapter and Plan Ahead boxes throughout encourage you to think critically about how to accomplish the next goal before you actually begin working.

3 CONSISTENT STEP-BY-STEP, SCREEN-BY-SCREEN PRESENTATION
Chapter solutions are built using a step-by-step, screen-by-screen approach. This pedagogy allows you to build the solution on a computer as you read through the chapter. Generally, each step includes an explanation that indicates the result of the step.

4 MORE THAN JUST STEP-BY-STEP
BTW annotations in the margins of the book, Q&As in the steps, and substantive text in the paragraphs provide background information, tips, and answers to common questions that complement the topics covered, adding depth and perspective. When you finish with this book, you will be ready to use HTML to create basic Web pages on your own. Experimental steps provide you with opportunities to step out on your own to try features of the programs, and pick up right where you left off in the chapter.

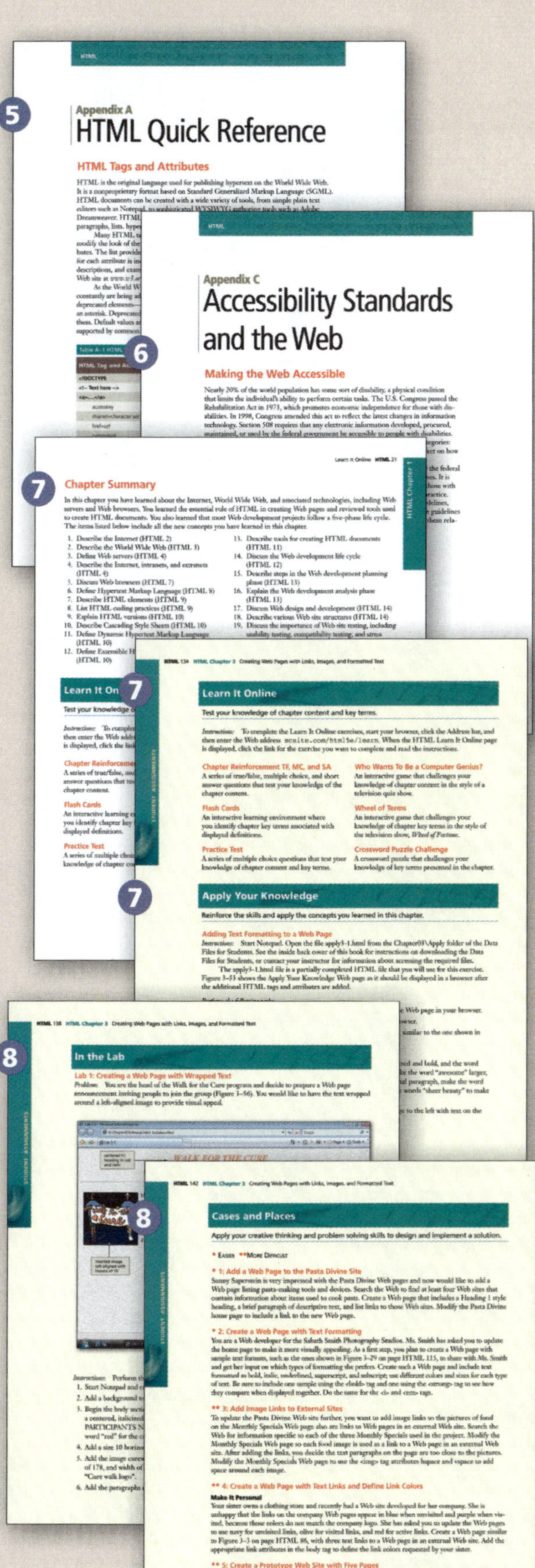

5 OTHER WAYS BOXES AND QUICK REFERENCE APPENDIX
Other Ways boxes follow many of the step sequences and show alternative ways to accomplish tasks. An HTML Quick Reference (Appendix A) at the back of the book summarizes common HTML tags and attributes and how they can be used.

6 EMPHASIS ON GETTING HELP WHEN YOU NEED IT
Appendices A through F provide you with reference materials for commonly reviewed material, such as tags, attributes, color selection and accessibility.

7 REVIEW, REINFORCEMENT, AND EXTENSION
After you successfully step through a project in a chapter, a section titled Chapter Summary identifies the tasks with which you should be familiar. Terms you should know for test purposes are bold in the text. The Learn It Online section at the end of each chapter offers reinforcement in the form of review questions, learning games, and practice tests. Also included are exercises that require you to extend your learning beyond the book.

8 LABORATORY EXERCISES
If you really want to learn how to develop Web pages, then you must design and implement solutions to problems on your own. Every chapter concludes with several carefully developed laboratory assignments that increase in complexity.

About Our New Cover Look

Learning styles of students have changed, but the Shelly Cashman Series' dedication to their success has remained steadfast for over 30 years. We are committed to continually updating our approach and content to reflect the way today's students learn and experience new technology.

This focus on the user is reflected in our bold new cover design, which features photographs of real students using the Shelly Cashman Series in their courses. Each book features a different user, reflecting the many ages, experiences, and backgrounds of all of the students learning with our books. When you use the Shelly Cashman Series, you can be assured that you are learning computer skills using the most effective courseware available.

We would like to thank the administration and faculty at the participating schools for their help in making our vision a reality. Most of all, we'd like to thank the wonderful students from all over the world who learn from our texts and now appear on our covers.

HTML

1 Introduction to HTML

Objectives

You will have mastered the material in this chapter when you can:

- Describe the Internet and its associated key terms
- Describe the World Wide Web and its associated key terms
- Identify the types and purposes of Web sites
- Discuss Web browsers and identify their purpose
- Define Hypertext Markup Language (HTML) and the standards used for Web development
- Discuss the use of Cascading Style Sheets in Web development
- Define Dynamic Hypertext Markup Language (DHTML) and describe its relationship to HTML
- Define Extensible Hypertext Markup Language (XHTML) and describe its relationship to HTML
- Describe tools used to create HTML documents
- Discuss the five phases of the Web development life cycle
- Describe Web site design and the purpose of each Web site structure
- Describe the importance of testing throughout the Web development life cycle

1 Introduction to HTML

Introduction

Connectivity has made a huge impact on our daily lives. In the United States alone, close to 200 million people have access to the Internet. According to Google, a popular search engine, over four billion Web pages are currently available on the World Wide Web. Today, computers and networks allow people to gather, analyze, and use information to make informed decisions and to communicate with others around the world. The world's largest network is the Internet — a worldwide network of computers that houses information on a multitude of subjects.

Without Hypertext Markup Language (HTML) and its associated technologies, the Web could not exist. In order to utilize these technologies effectively, you need to understand the main concepts behind the Internet and HTML. In this chapter, you will gain a better understanding of the Internet, the World Wide Web, and intranets. You are introduced to Web browsers, definitions of HTML and associated key terms, the five phases of the Web development life cycle, and the tasks that are involved in each phase.

What Is the Internet?

The **Internet** is a worldwide collection of computer networks that links millions of computers used by businesses, the government, educational institutions, organizations, and individuals using modems, phone lines, television cables, satellite links, and other communications devices and media (Figure 1–1). A **network** is a group of two or more computers that are connected to share resources and information. Today, high-, medium-, and low-speed data lines connect networks. These data lines allow data to move from one computer to another. The **Internet backbone** is a collection of high-speed data lines that connect major computer systems located around the world. An **Internet service provider (ISP)** is a company that has a permanent connection to the Internet backbone. ISPs utilize high- or medium-speed data lines to allow individuals and companies to connect to the backbone for access to the Internet. An Internet connection at home generally is a DSL or cable data line that connects to the ISP.

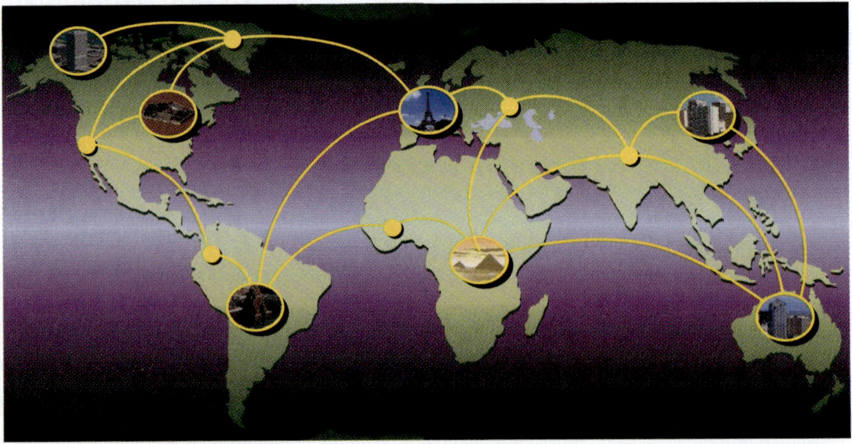

Figure 1–1 The Internet is a worldwide collection of computer networks.

More than 950 million people in 240 countries connect to the Internet using computers in their homes, offices, schools, and public locations such as libraries. Users with computers connected to the Internet can access a variety of services, including e-mail, social networking, online shopping, and the World Wide Web (Figure 1–2).

Figure 1–2 The Internet makes available a variety of services such as e-mail and the World Wide Web.

What Is the World Wide Web?

The **World Wide Web**, also called the **Web**, is the part of the Internet that supports multimedia and consists of a collection of linked documents. To support multimedia, the Web relies on the **Hypertext Transfer Protocol (HTTP)**, which is a set of rules for exchanging text, graphic, sound, video, and other multimedia files. The linked documents, or pages of information, on the Web are known as **Web pages**. Because the Web supports text, graphics, sound, and video, a Web page can include any of these multimedia elements. The Web is ever-changing and consists of hundreds of millions of Web pages. Because of the ease of creating Web pages, more are being added all the time.

BTW

Internet and WWW History
The World Wide Web Consortium (W3C or w3c.org), the de facto organization that governs HTML, provides a particularly rich history of the Internet and the World Wide Web. Search on "Internet history" or "WWW history" in your browser for many additional sources.

A **Web site** is a related collection of Web pages that is created and maintained by an individual, company, educational institution, or other organization. For example, as shown in Figure 1–3, many organizations, such as the Smithsonian, publish and maintain Web sites. Each Web site contains a **home page**, which is the first document users see when they access the Web site. The home page often serves as an index or table of contents to other documents and files stored on the site.

Figure 1–3 A Web site is a related collection of Web pages that is created and maintained by an individual, company, educational institution, or other organization.

Web Servers

Web pages are stored on a **Web server**, or **host**, which is a computer that stores and sends (serves) requested Web pages and other files. Any computer that has Web server software installed and is connected to the Internet can act as a Web server. Every Web site is stored on, and runs from, one or more Web servers. A large Web site may be spread over several servers in different geographic locations.

Publishing is copying Web pages and other files to a Web server. Once a Web page is published, anyone who has access to the Internet can view it, regardless of where the Web server is located. For example, although the Smithsonian Web site is stored on a Web server somewhere in the United States, it is available for viewing by anyone in the world. Once a Web page is published, it can be read by almost any computer: whether you use Mac, Windows, or Linux, you have access to millions of published Web pages.

Web Site Types and Purposes

The three general types of Web sites are Internet, intranet, and extranet. Table 1–1 lists characteristics of each of these three types of Web sites.

Table 1–1 Types of Web Sites

Type	Users	Access	Applications
Internet	Anyone	Public	Share information (personal information, product catalogs, course information, etc.) with the public
Intranet	Employees or members	Private	Share information (forms, manuals, organization schedules, etc.) with employees or members
Extranet	Select business partners	Private	Share information (inventory updates, product specifications, financial information, etc.) with partners and customers

An **Internet site**, also known as a **Web site**, is a site generally available to the public. Individuals, groups, companies, and educational institutions use Internet sites, or Web sites, for a variety of purposes. An individual, for example, might create a personal Web site that includes his or her résumé to make it easily accessible to any interested employers. Families also can share photographs of special events, schedules, or other information with each other through Web sites (Figure 1–4).

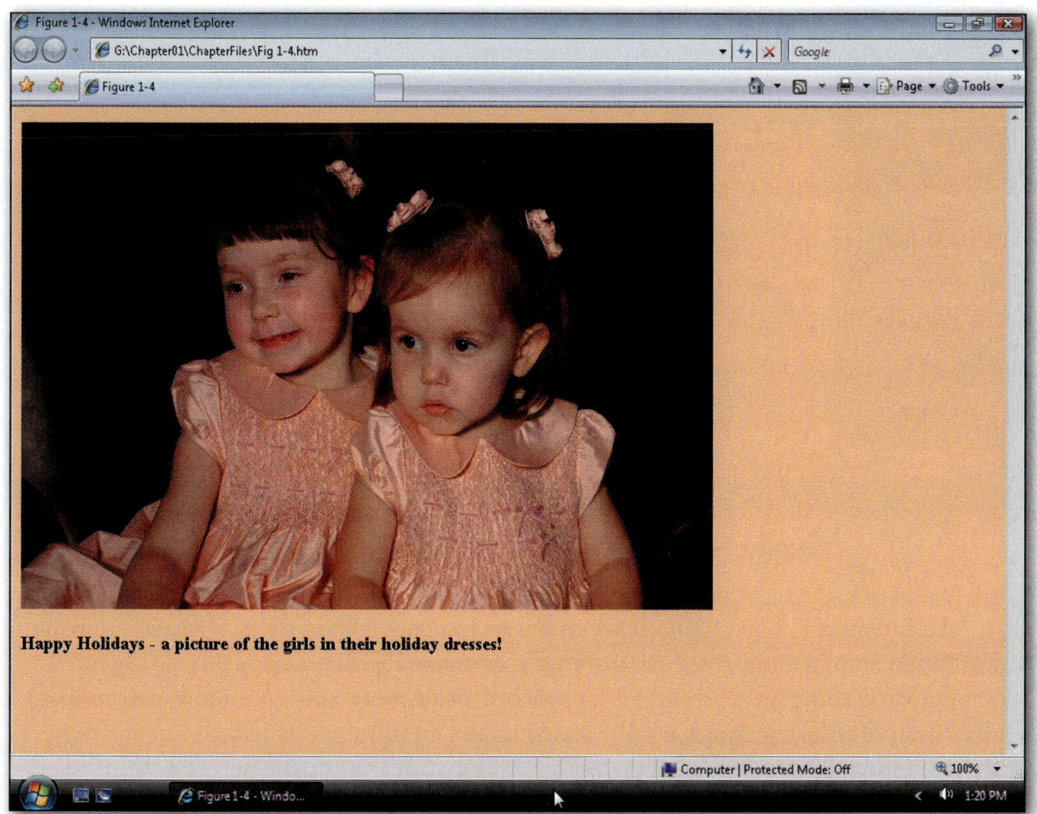

Figure 1–4 Web page on a personal Web site.

Companies use Web sites to advertise or sell their products and services worldwide, as well as to provide technical and product support for their customers. Many company Web sites also support **electronic commerce (e-commerce)**, which is the buying and selling of goods and services on the Internet. Using e-commerce technologies, these Web sites allow customers to browse product catalogs, comparison shop, and order products online. Many company Web sites also provide job postings and announcements, a frequently asked questions (FAQs) section, customer feedback links to solicit comments from their customers, and searchable technical support databases.

BTW

E-Commerce

Today, e-commerce is a standard part of doing business. E-commerce technologies, however, continue to change, offering new applications and potential uses. Several online magazines are dedicated to providing an in-depth look at e-commerce. Many print magazines also provide useful information about this important way to do business.

Colleges, universities, and other schools use Web sites to distribute information about areas of study, provide course information, or register students for classes online as shown in Figure 1–5. Instructors use their Web sites to issue announcements, post questions on the reading material, list contact information, and provide easy access to their lecture notes and slides. Many instructors today use the course management software adopted by their school to upload their course content. Many course management tools allow instructors to develop their own HTML Web content to display information within the course.

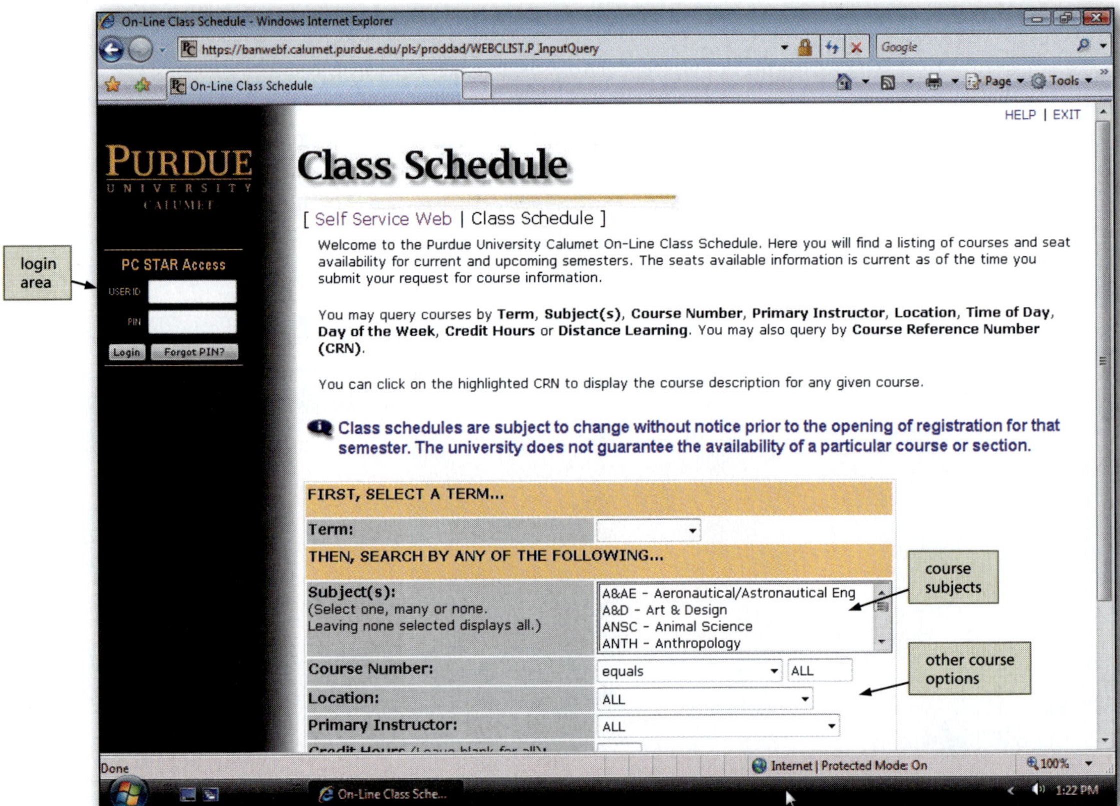

Figure 1–5 Web page from a university's Web site.

BTW

Intranets and Extranets
There are many Web sites that discuss ideas for intranets and exrranets. Many companies are already using these technologies and share their "best practice" techniques. The CIO Intranet/Extranet Research Center provides valuable information on building and maintaining an intranet or extranet, along with additional resources.

An **intranet** is a private network that uses Internet technologies to share company information among employees. An intranet is contained within a company or organization's network; some intranets also are password-protected to provide additional security. Policy and procedure manuals usually are found on an intranet, in addition to a variety of forms. Other documents, such as employee directories, company newsletters, product catalogs, and training manuals, often are distributed through an intranet. An intranet also can be used to facilitate working in groups and collecting feedback from employees.

An **extranet** is a private network that uses Internet technologies to share business information with select corporate partners or key customers. Most extranets are password-protected to restrict access to specific suppliers, vendors, partners, or customers. Companies and organizations can use an extranet to share product manuals, training modules, inventory status, and order information. An extranet also might support e-commerce to allow retailers to purchase inventory directly or to pay bills online, which is more efficient than calling partners to check on inventory levels or account status.

Web Browsers

To display a Web page on any type of Web site, a computer needs to have a Web browser installed. A **Web browser**, also called a **browser**, is a program that interprets and displays Web pages and enables you to view and interact with a Web page. Three popular browsers today are Microsoft Internet Explorer, Mozilla Firefox, and Apple Safari. Browsers provide a variety of features, including the capability to locate Web pages, to move forward and backward between Web pages, to bookmark favorite Web pages, and to choose security settings.

To locate a Web page using a browser, you type its Uniform Resource Locator (URL) in the browser's Address, or Location, bar. A **Uniform Resource Locator (URL)** is the address of a document or other file accessible on the Internet. An example of a URL on the Web is:

http://www.scsite.com/html5e/index.htm

The URL indicates to the browser to use the HTTP to locate a Web page named index.htm in the html5e folder on a Web server named scsite.com. Web page URLs can be found in a wide range of places, including school catalogs, business cards, product packaging, and advertisements.

A **hyperlink**, also called a **link**, is an element used to connect one Web page to another Web page on the same, or a different, Web server located anywhere in the world. Clicking a hyperlink allows you to move quickly from one Web page to another. You also can click hyperlinks to move to a different section of the same Web page.

Hyperlinks are an essential part of the World Wide Web. With hyperlinks, a Web site user does not have to view information linearly. Instead, he or she can click the available hyperlinks to view the information in a variety of ways. Many different Web page elements, including text, graphics, and animations, can serve as hyperlinks. Figure 1–6 shows examples of several different Web page elements used as hyperlinks.

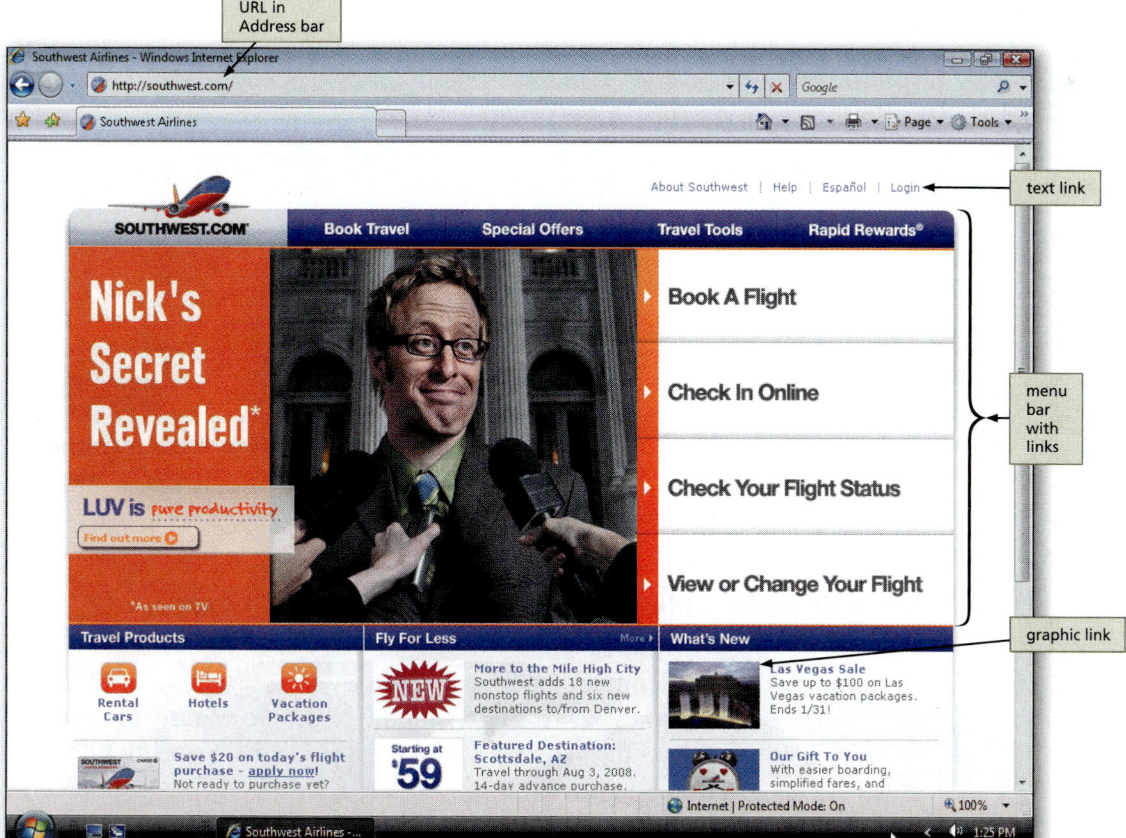

Figure 1–6 A Web page can use several different Web page elements as hyperlinks.

What Is Hypertext Markup Language?

Web pages are created using **Hypertext Markup Language (HTML)**, which is an authoring language used to create documents on the World Wide Web. HTML uses a set of special instructions called **tags** or **markup** to define the structure and layout of a Web document and specify how the page is displayed in a browser.

A Web page is a file that contains both text and HTML tags. HTML tags mark the text to define how it appears when viewed as a page on the Web. HTML includes hundreds of tags used to format Web pages and create hyperlinks to other documents or Web pages. For instance, the HTML tags <strong> and </strong> are used to indicate bold text, <p> and </p> are used to indicate a new paragraph, and <hr /> is used to display a horizontal rule across the page. Figure 1–7a shows the HTML tags needed to create the Web page shown in Figure 1–7b. You also can enhance HTML tags by using attributes as shown in Figure 1–7a. Attributes define additional characteristics for the HTML tag.

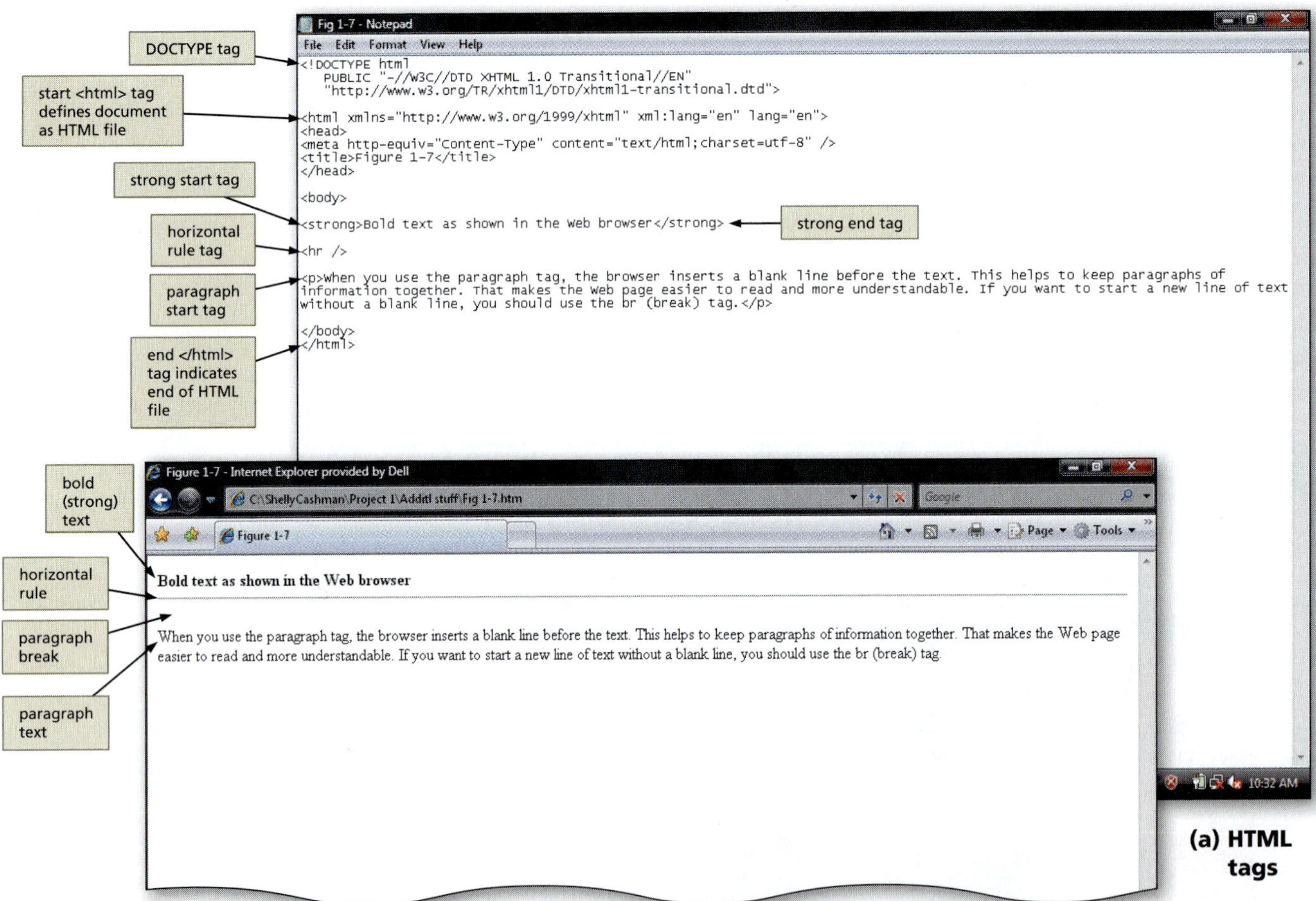

(a) HTML tags

(b) Resulting Web page

Figure 1–7 A Web page is a file that contains both text and HTML tags.

HTML is **platform independent**, meaning you can create, or code, an HTML file on one type of computer and then use a browser on another type of computer to view that file as a Web page. The page looks the same regardless of what platform you are using.

HTML Elements

HTML combines descriptive tags with special tags that denote formatting styles for how a document should appear in a Web browser. HTML elements include headings, paragraphs, hyperlinks, lists, images, and more. Most HTML elements consist of three parts: a start tag, content, and an end tag. For example, to specify that text should appear in bold on a Web page, you would enter the following HTML code:

```
<strong>sample text</strong>
```

where <strong> is the start tag, the phrase, "sample text" is the content that will appear in bold, and </strong> is the end tag. Table 1–2 shows examples of some HTML elements.

Table 1–2 HTML Elements

Element	Tag	Purpose
Title	<title>...</title>	Indicates title to appear on the title bar on the Web page
Body	<body>...</body>	Specifies what appears on the Web page; all Web page content is inserted within the start <body> tag and end </body> tag
Paragraph	<p>...</p>	Inserts a blank line before paragraph text
Line Break	 	Inserts a line break before the next element (no blank line)

BTW

HTML Elements
Numerous sources of information about HTML elements are available. The World Wide Web Consortium (w3c.org) provides the most comprehensive list of tags and attributes together with examples of their use. One of the main goals of the W3C is to help those building Web sites understand and utilize standards that make the Web accessible to all.

HTML Coding Practices

Similar to all programming languages, HTML has a set of coding practices designed to simplify the process of creating and editing HTML files and to ensure that Web pages appear correctly in different browsers.

When creating an HTML file, you should separate sections of the HTML code with spaces. Adding spaces between sections gives you an immediate view of the sections of code that relate to one another and helps you view the HTML elements in your document more clearly. HTML browsers ignore spaces that exist between the tags in your HTML document, so the spaces inserted within the code will not appear on the Web page. Figure 1–8 shows an example of an HTML file with code sections separated by blank lines. Another developer looking at this code can see immediately where the table and bulleted list are located in the code.

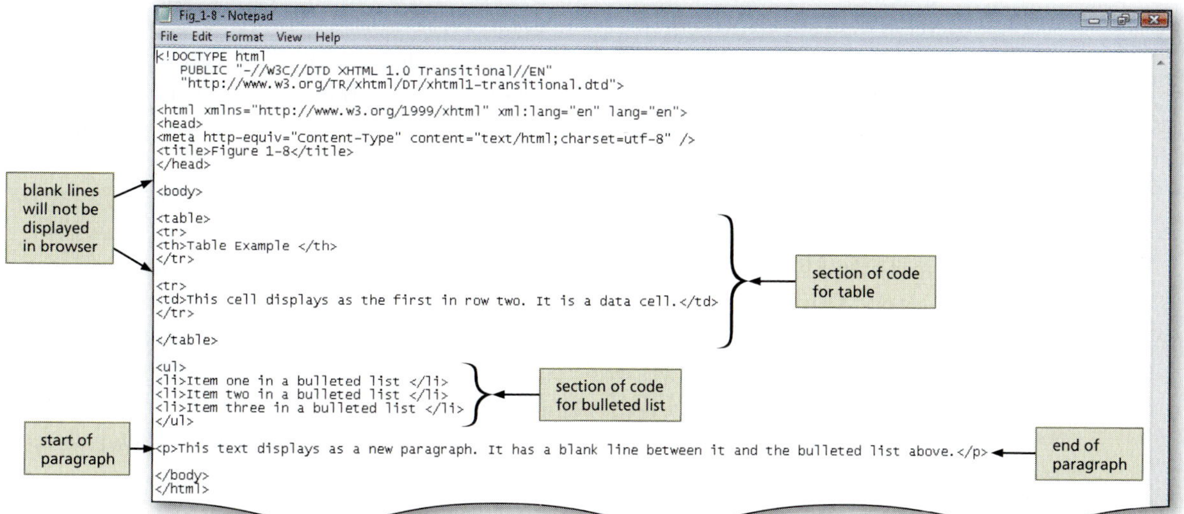

Figure 1–8 Adding spaces to HTML code separates sections to make reading easier.

HTML Versions

HTML has gone through several versions, each of which expands the capabilities of HTML. The most recent version of HTML is HTML 4.01, although most browsers still support HTML versions 3.2 and 2.0. To ensure that browsers can interpret each new version of HTML, the World Wide Web Consortium (W3C) maintains HTML standards, or specifications, which are publicly available on its Web site.

Cascading Style Sheets

In the early chapters of this book, you will use various HTML tags to alter the **style** (or look) of a Web page. Altering the style of individual elements on a Web page is an easy Web development technique to use. Appendix A at the back of this book and available online provides a list of HTML tags and corresponding attributes that will allow you to alter the Web page elements as needed. With large Web sites, however, it is better to use Cascading Style Sheets to change the style of the Web page elements. With **Cascading Style Sheets** (**CSS**) you write code that allows you to control an element within a single Web page or throughout an entire Web site. For example, changing a headline style from bold to italic in a Web site that contains hundreds of pages is much easier to do using a CSS instead of recoding the individual headline links.

Dynamic Hypertext Markup Language (DHTML)

HTML can be used with other Web technologies to provide additional Web page functionality. For example, the term **Dynamic HTML** (**DHTML**) describes a combination of HTML tags, CSS, and a scripting language such as JavaScript. DHTML allows users to create interactive, animated Web pages. CSS, JavaScript, and DHTML are covered in later chapters in this book.

Extensible Hypertext Markup Language (XHTML)

BTW **CSS, DHTML, and XHTML**
The W3C.org Web site has an extensive amount of information and tutorials about Cascading Style Sheets (CSS), Dynamic HTML (DHTML), and Extensible HTML (XHTML). The standards suggested in the W3C Web site are the ones that most Web developers follow.

Extensible Markup Language (XML) is a markup language that uses tags to describe the structure and content of a document, not the format. **Extensible Hypertext Markup Language (XHTML)** is a reformulation of HTML so it conforms to XML rules. As you have learned, HTML uses tags to describe how a document should appear in a Web browser. By incorporating HTML and XML, XHTML combines the display features of HTML and the stricter coding standards required by XML.

If you create a Web page in HTML and do not follow XHTML coding standards exactly (for example, by not using an end </p> tag), the Web browser on your computer can still interpret and display the Web page correctly. However, newer types of browsers, such as those for mobile phones or handheld computers, cannot interpret HTML code that does not meet the XHTML standards. Because XHTML has such strict coding standards, it helps ensure that Web pages created in XHTML will be readable by many different types of applications. An important step in Web development is to check that your Web pages are XHTML compliant. You will validate your Web pages in Chapter 2.

Table 1–3 lists some of the XHTML coding rules that Web developers should follow to ensure that their HTML code conforms to XHTML standards. All of the projects in this book follow XHTML standards (as discussed in Chapter 2) and adhere to the rules outlined in Table 1–3. The specifics of each rule are explained in detail as the rule is used in a project.

Table 1–3 XHTML Coding Practices

Practice	Invalid Example	Valid Example
HTML file must include a DOCTYPE statement	<html> <head><title>sample Web page</title>	<!DOCTYPE html PUBLIC "-//W3C//DTD XHTML 1.0 Transitional//EN" "http://www.w3.org/TR/xhtml1/DTD/xhtml1-transitional.dtd"> <html> <head><title>sample Web page</title>
All tags and attributes must be written in lowercase	<TABLE WIDTH="100%">	<table width="100%">
All attribute values must be enclosed by single or double quotation marks	<table width=100%>	<table width="100%">
All tags must be closed, including tags such as img, hr, and br, which do not have end tags, but which must be closed as a matter of practice	 <hr> <p>This is another paragraph	 <hr /> <p>This is another paragraph</p>
All elements must be nested properly	<p><strong>This is a bold paragraph</p></strong>	<p><strong>This is a bold paragraph</strong></p>

Tools for Creating HTML Documents

You can create Web pages using HTML with a simple text editor, such as Notepad, WordPad, or SimpleText. A **text editor** is a program that allows a user to enter, change, save, and print text, such as HTML. Text editors do not have many advanced features, but they do allow you to develop HTML documents easily. For instance, if you want to mark text to be displayed in italics on a Web page, type the text in the text editor and then surround the text with the start (<em>) and end (</em>) tags, as shown in Figure 1–9.

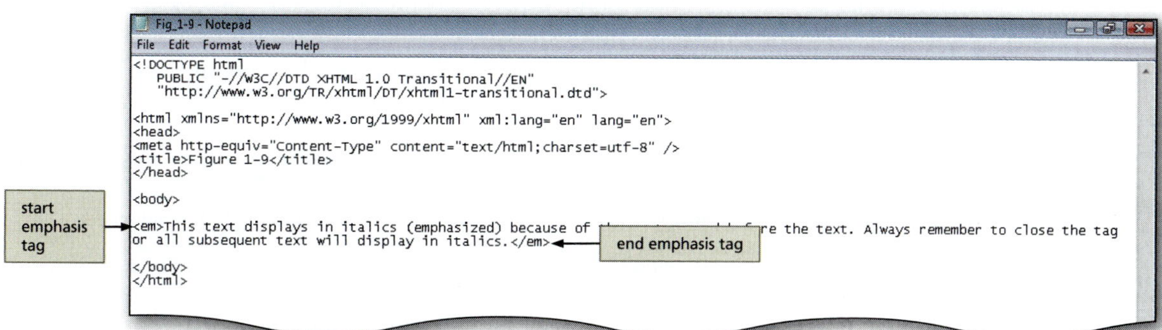

Figure 1–9 With a text editor such as Notepad, you type HTML tags directly in the documents.

You also can create Web pages using an HTML text editor, such as Macromedia HomeSite (now owned by Adobe) or BBEdit (for Macintosh). An **HTML text editor** is a program that provides basic text-editing functions, as well as more advanced features such as color-coding for various HTML tags, menus to insert HTML tags, and spell checkers. An **HTML object editor**, such as Adobe GoLive, provides the additional functionality of an outline editor that allows you to expand and collapse HTML objects and properties, edit parameters, and view graphics attached to the expanded objects.

Many popular software applications also provide features that enable you to develop Web pages easily. Microsoft Word, Excel, and PowerPoint, for example, have a Save as Web Page feature that converts a document into an HTML file by automatically adding HTML tags to the document. Using Microsoft Access, you can create a Web page that allows you to view data in a database. Adobe Acrobat also has an export feature that creates HTML files. Each of these applications also allows you to add hyperlinks, drop-down boxes, option buttons, or scrolling text to the Web page.

These advanced Web features make it simple to save any document, spreadsheet, database, or presentation to display as a Web page. Corporate policy and procedures manuals and PowerPoint presentations, for example, easily can be saved as Web pages and published to the company's intranet site. Extranet users can be given access to Web pages that allow them to view or update information stored in a database.

BTW

Free HTML WYSIWYG Editors

There are a number of popular WYSIWYG editors that are being used by many novice Web developers to create well-designed, interactive Web sites. You can find these by searching for "WYSIWYG HTML Editor" in most search engines.

You also can create Web pages using a WYSIWYG editor, such as, Adobe Dreamweaver, Amaya, Adobe's GoLive, or CoffeeCup HTML Editor. A **WYSIWYG editor** is a program that provides a graphical user interface that allows a developer to preview the Web page during its development. WYSIWYG (pronounced wizzywig) is an acronym for What You See Is What You Get. A WYSIWYG editor creates the HTML code for you as you add elements to the Web page, which means that you do not have to enter HTML tags directly.

Regardless of which type of program you use to create Web pages, it is important to understand the specifics of HTML so you can make changes outside of the editor. It also is important to understand the Web development life cycle so the Web pages in your Web site are consistent and complete.

Web Development Life Cycle

In any software development project, a systematic methodology, or process, should be followed through the life cycle of the project to ensure consistency and completeness. The Web development life cycle outlined in this section is one that can be utilized for any type or size of Web development project. The life cycle includes the following phases: planning, analysis, design and development, testing, and implementation and maintenance. Table 1–4 lists several questions that should be asked during each phase in the Web development life cycle.

Table 1–4 Web Development Phases and Questions

Web Development Phase	Questions To Ask
Planning	• What is the purpose of this Web site? • Who will use this Web site? • What are the users' computing environments? • Who owns and authors the information on the Web site? • Who decides if/where the information goes on the Web site?
Analysis	• What tasks do the users need to perform? • What information is useful to the users? • What process considerations must be made?
Design and Development	• How will the Web pages be organized? • What type of Web site structure is appropriate for the content? • What forms of multimedia contribute positively to the Web site? • How can accessibility issues be addressed without limiting usability? • Do we need to design for an international audience?

Table 1–4 Web Development Phases and Questions (continued)

Web Development Phase	Questions To Ask
Testing	• Do the Web pages pass the World Wide Web Consortium (W3C) validation process as XHTML compliant? • Is the Web site content correct? • Does the Web site function correctly? • Are users able to find the information they need to complete desired tasks? • Is navigation easy?
Implementation and Maintenance	• How is the Web site published? • How is the Web site updated? • Who is responsible for content updates? • Who is responsible for structure updates? • How will users be notified about updates to the Web site? • Will the Web site be monitored?

Web Site Planning

Web site planning, which is the first phase of the Web development life cycle, involves identifying the goals or purpose of the Web site. The first step in the Web site planning phase is to answer the question "What is the purpose of this Web site?" As you have learned, individuals and groups design and publish Web sites for a variety of purposes. Individuals develop Web sites to share their hobbies, to post résumés, or just to share ideas on personal interests. Organizations create Web sites to keep members informed of upcoming events or to recruit new members. Businesses create Web sites to advertise and sell products or to give their customers 24-hour online support. Instructors publish Web sites to inform students of course policies and requirements. Until you adequately can identify the intended purpose of the Web site, you should not proceed with the Web development project.

In addition to understanding the Web site's purpose, you also should understand who will use the Web site and the computing environments of most of the users. Knowing the makeup of your target audience — including age, gender, general demographic background, and level of computer literacy — will help you design a Web site appropriate for all users. Understanding their computing environments will determine what types of Web technologies to use. For example, if most users have low-speed Internet connections, you would not want to create pages with large graphics or multimedia elements.

A final aspect to the Web site planning phase is to identify the content owners and authors. To determine this, you need to ask the questions:

- Who owns and authors the information on the Web site?
- Who decides if/where the information goes on the Web site?

Once you have identified who will provide and authorize the Web site content, you can include those individuals in all aspects of the Web development project.

Web Site Analysis

During the analysis phase, you make decisions about the Web site content and functionality. To help define the appropriate Web site content and functionality, you first should identify the tasks that users need to perform. Answering that question allows you to define necessary content to facilitate those tasks and determine useful information for the users. Extraneous content should be eliminated from the Web site, because it does not serve any purpose.

In the analysis phase, it also is important to consider the processes required to support Web site features. For example, if you determine that users should be able to order products through the Web site, then you also need to define the processes or actions to be taken each time an order is submitted. For instance, after an order is submitted, how will that order be processed throughout the back-office business applications, such as inventory control and accounts payable? Will users receive e-mail confirmations with details about their orders?

The analysis phase is one of the more important phases in the Web development life cycle. Clearly understanding and defining the desired content and functionality of the Web site will direct the type of Web site that you design and reduce changes during Web site development.

Web Site Design and Development

BTW

Accessibility Standards

Creating a Web site that is accessible to all users allows your Web site to reach the widest audience. Further, under Section 508 law, any Web site or technology used by a U.S. federal agency must be usable by people with disabilities. See Appendix C for Section 508 guidelines.

After determining the purpose of the Web site and defining the content and functionality, you need to consider the Web site's design. Some key considerations in Web site design are defining how to organize Web page content, selecting the appropriate Web site structure, determining how to use multimedia, addressing accessibility issues, and designing pages for an international audience.

Many ways to organize a Web page exist, just as many ways to organize a report or paper exist. Table 1–5 lists some organizational standards for creating a Web page that is easy to read and navigate.

Web sites can use any of several different types of structures, including linear, hierarchical, and webbed. Each structure links, or connects, the Web pages in a different way to define how users navigate the site and view the Web pages. You should select a structure for the Web site based on how users will navigate the site to complete tasks and view the Web site content.

Table 1–5 Web Page Organizational Standards

Element	Organizational Standard	Reason
Titles	Use simple titles that clearly explain the purpose of the page	Titles help users understand the purpose of the page; a good title explains the page in the search engine results lists
Headings	Use headings to separate main topics	Headings make a Web page easier to read; simple headlines clearly explain the purpose of the page
Horizontal Rules	Insert horizontal rules to separate main topics	Horizontal rules provide graphical elements to break up Web page content
Paragraphs	Use paragraphs to help divide large amounts of text	Paragraphs provide shorter, more-readable sections of text
Lists	Utilize bulleted or numbered lists when appropriate	Lists provide organized, easy-to-read text that readers can scan
Page Length	Maintain suitable Web page lengths	Web users do not always scroll to view information on longer pages; appropriate page lengths increase the likelihood that users will view key information
Information	Emphasize the most important information by placing it at the top of a Web page	Web users are quick to peruse a page; placing critical information at the top of the page increases the likelihood that users will view key information
Other	Incorporate a contact e-mail address; include the date of the last modification	E-mail addresses and dates give users a way to contact a Web site developer with questions; the date last modified helps users determine the timeliness of the site information

A **linear** Web site structure connects Web pages in a straight line, as shown in Figure 1–10. A linear Web site structure is appropriate if the information on the Web pages should be read in a specific order. For example, if the information on the first Web page is necessary for understanding information on the second Web page, you should use a linear structure. Each page would have links from one Web page to the next, as well as a link to the home page.

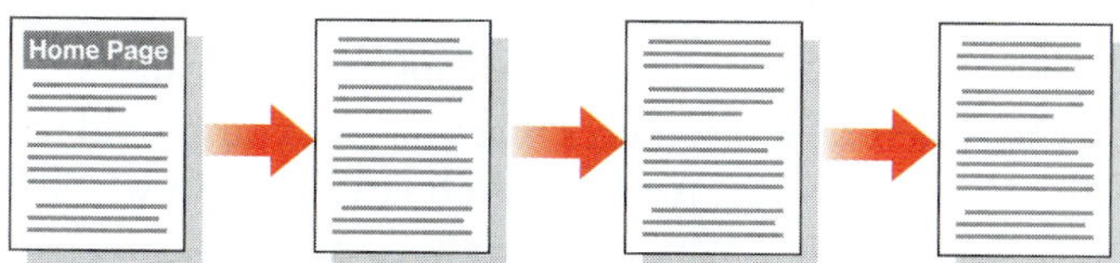

Figure 1–10 Linear Web site structure.

A **hierarchical** Web site structure connects Web pages in a tree-like structure, as shown in Figure 1–11. A hierarchical Web site structure works well on a site with a main index or table of contents page that links to all other Web pages. With this structure, the main index page would display general information, and secondary pages would include more detailed information. A **webbed** Web site structure has no set organization, as shown in Figure 1–12.

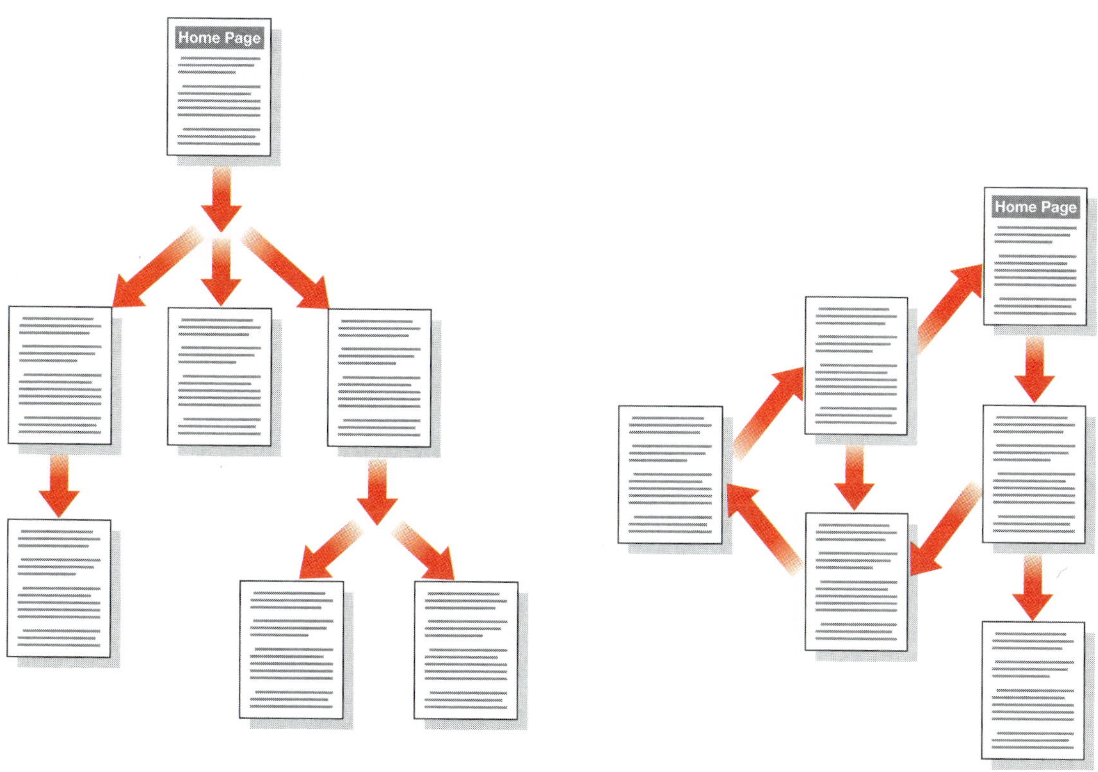

Figure 1–11 Hierarchical Web site structure.

Figure 1–12 Webbed Web site structure.

A webbed Web site structure works best on Web sites with information that does not need to be read in a specific order and with many navigation options users can select. The World Wide Web uses a webbed structure, so users can navigate among Web pages in any order they choose.

Most Web sites are a combination of the linear, hierarchical, and webbed structures. Some information on the Web site might be organized hierarchically from an index page, other information might be accessible from all areas of the site, and still other information might be organized linearly to be read in a specific order. Using a combination of the three structures is appropriate if it helps users navigate the site easily.

Regardless of the structure or structures that you use, you should balance the narrowness and depth of the Web site. A **broad Web site** is one in which the home page is the main index page, and all other Web pages are linked individually to the home page (Figure 1–13). By making the other Web pages accessible only through the home page, a broad Web site forces the user to return to the home page to move from one Web page to another. The structure makes navigation time-consuming and limiting for users. A better structure would present a user with navigation alternatives that allow for direct movement between the Web pages.

A **deep Web site** is one that has many levels of pages, requiring the user to click many times to reach a particular Web page (Figure 1–14). By requiring a visitor to move through several Web pages before reaching the desired Web page, a deep Web site forces a user to spend time viewing interim pages with little or no useful content.

Figure 1–13 Broad Web site.

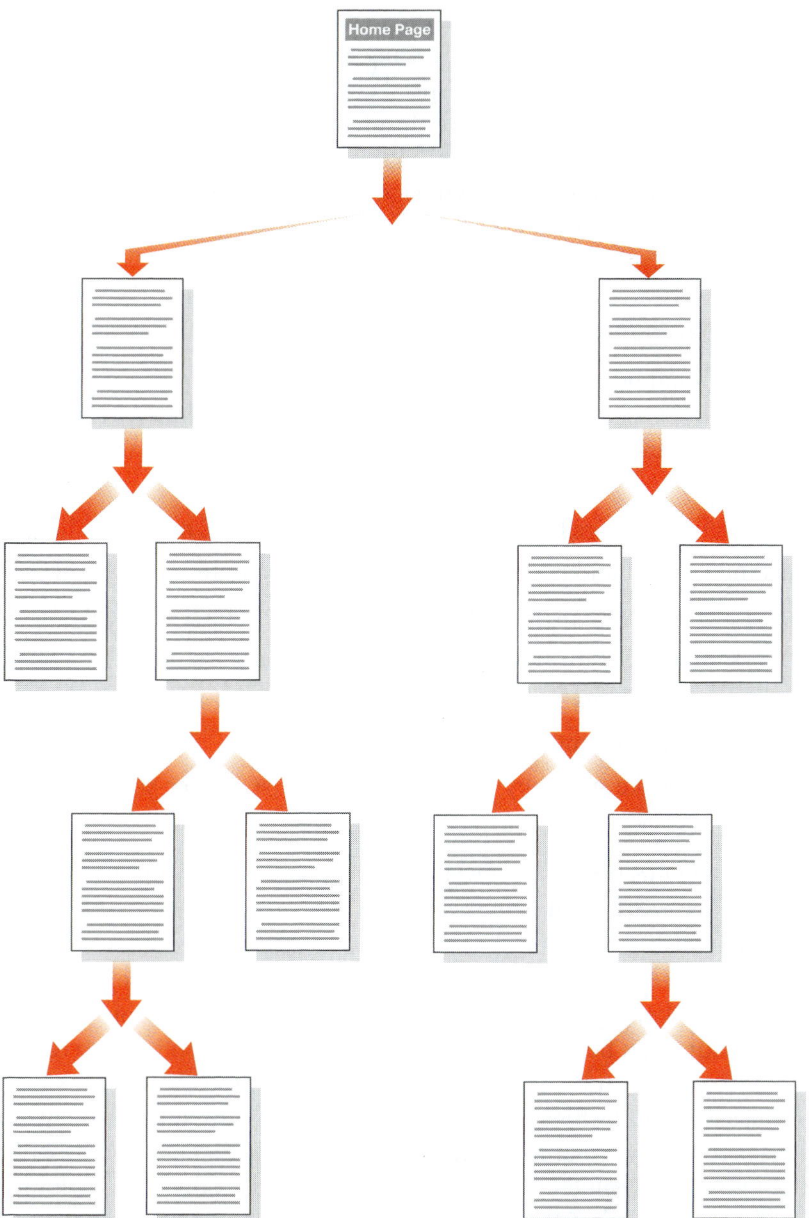

Figure 1–14 Deep Web site.

> **BTW**
> **User Interface Design**
> The user interface design is an important aspect of a Web site. If a site is designed poorly, users may be unable to find the desired information or complete a task, which makes the Web site ineffective.

As a Web developer, you must select an appropriate structure for the Web site and work to balance breadth and depth. Users go to a Web site looking for information to complete a task. Good design provides ease of navigation to allow users to find content quickly and easily.

During the design and development phase, you also should consider what, if any, types of multimedia could contribute positively to the Web site experience. For instance, adding a video message from the company CEO might be useful, but if the computing environment of your users cannot accommodate video playback, then the video serves no purpose. In general, do not use advanced multimedia technologies in a Web site unless they make a positive contribution to the Web site experience.

Finally, consider accessibility issues and internationalization. A Web developer should always design for viewing by a diverse audience, including physically impaired and global users. A key consideration is that the software used by physically impaired individuals does not work with some Web features. For instance, if you use graphics on the Web site, always include alternative text for each graphic. To support an international audience, use generic icons that can be understood globally, avoid slang expressions in the content, and build simple pages that load quickly over lower-speed connections.

The design issues just discussed are only a few of the basic Web page design issues that you need to consider. Throughout this book, design issues will be addressed as they relate to each project. Many excellent Web page design resources also are available on the Internet.

Web Site Testing

A Web site should be tested at various stages of the Web design and development processes. The testing process should be comprehensive and include a review of Web page content, functionality, and usability. Some basic steps to test content and functionality include:

- Validating each Web page by running it through the W3C markup validation service
- Proofreading content and page titles to review for accurate spelling and grammar
- Checking links to ensure they are not broken and are linked correctly
- Checking graphics to confirm they appear properly and are linked correctly
- Ensuring that accessibility and internationalization issues are addressed
- Testing forms and other interactive page elements
- Testing pages to make sure they load quickly, even over lower-speed connections
- Printing each page to check how printed pages look

Usability is the measure of how well a product, such as a Web site, allows a user to accomplish his or her goals. **Usability testing** is a method by which users of a Web site or other product are asked to perform certain tasks in an effort to measure the product's ease-of-use and the user's perception of the experience. Usability testing for a Web site should focus on three key aspects: content, navigation, and presentation.

Usability testing can be conducted in several ways. One good way to test a Web site's usability is to observe users interfacing with (or using) the Web site. As you observe users, you can track the links they click and record their actions and comments. You even can ask the users to explain what tasks they were trying to accomplish while navigating the site. The information gained by observing users can be invaluable in helping identify potential problem areas in the Web site. For example, if you observe that users have difficulty finding the Web page that lists store locations and hours of operation, you may want to clarify the link descriptions or make the links more prominent on the Web page.

Another way to conduct usability testing is to give users a specific task to complete (such as finding the product price list) and then observe how they navigate the site to complete the task. If possible, ask them to explain why they selected certain links. Both of these observation methods are extremely valuable, but require access to users in order to conduct this type of testing.

Usability testing also can be completed using a questionnaire or survey. When writing a questionnaire or survey, be sure to write open-ended questions that can give you valuable information. For instance, asking the yes/no question "Is the Web site visually appealing?" will not gather useful information. If you change that question to use a scaled response, such as, "Rate the visual appeal of this Web site, using a scale of 1 for low and 5 for high," you can get more valuable input from the users. A usability testing questionnaire always should include space for users to write additional explanatory comments.

Figure 1–15 shows some examples of types of questions and organization that you might include in a Web site usability testing questionnaire.

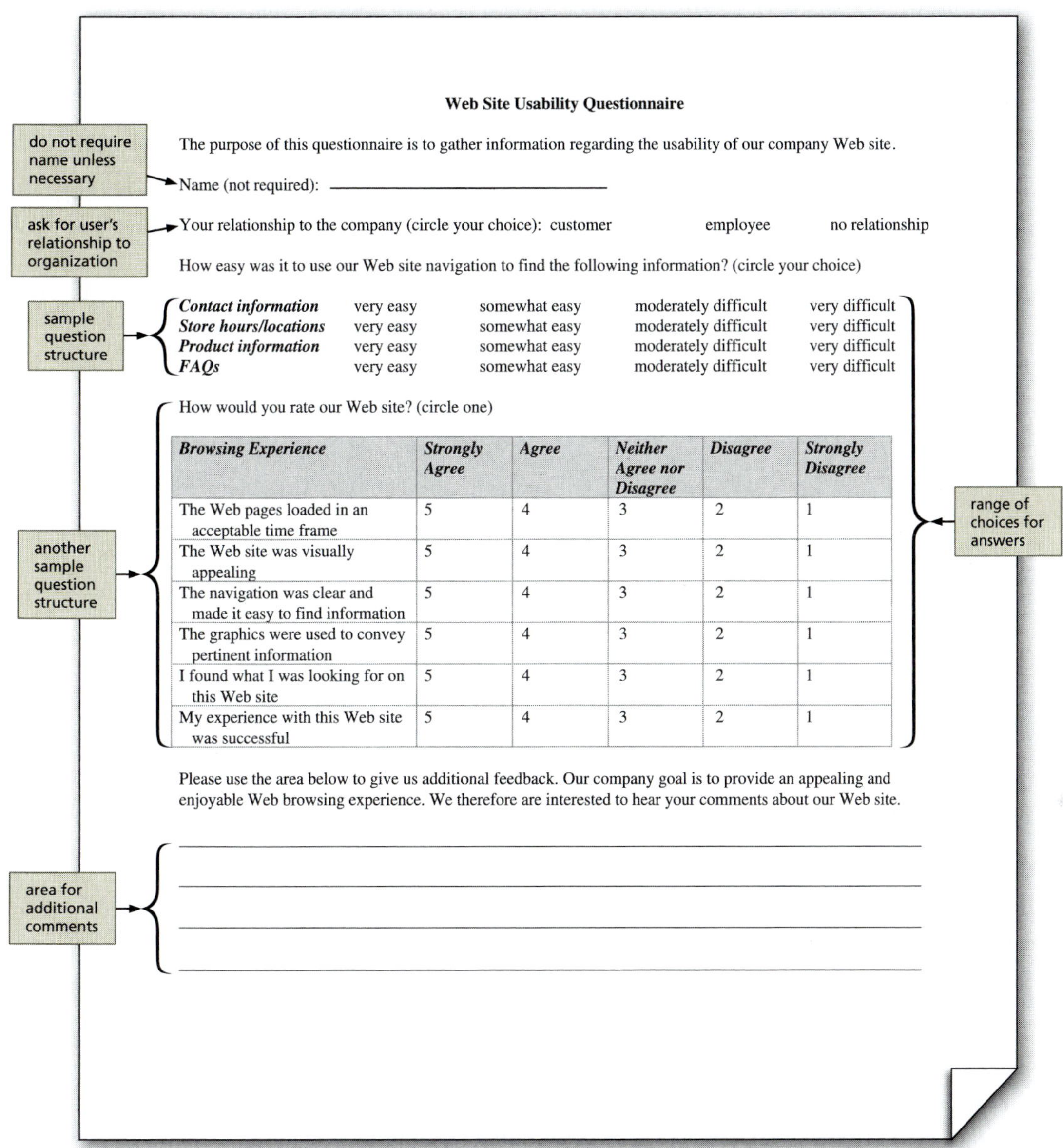

Web Site Usability Questionnaire

The purpose of this questionnaire is to gather information regarding the usability of our company Web site.

Name (not required): ____________________

Your relationship to the company (circle your choice): customer employee no relationship

How easy was it to use our Web site navigation to find the following information? (circle your choice)

Contact information	very easy	somewhat easy	moderately difficult	very difficult
Store hours/locations	very easy	somewhat easy	moderately difficult	very difficult
Product information	very easy	somewhat easy	moderately difficult	very difficult
FAQs	very easy	somewhat easy	moderately difficult	very difficult

How would you rate our Web site? (circle one)

Browsing Experience	***Strongly Agree***	***Agree***	***Neither Agree nor Disagree***	***Disagree***	***Strongly Disagree***
The Web pages loaded in an acceptable time frame	5	4	3	2	1
The Web site was visually appealing	5	4	3	2	1
The navigation was clear and made it easy to find information	5	4	3	2	1
The graphics were used to convey pertinent information	5	4	3	2	1
I found what I was looking for on this Web site	5	4	3	2	1
My experience with this Web site was successful	5	4	3	2	1

Please use the area below to give us additional feedback. Our company goal is to provide an appealing and enjoyable Web browsing experience. We therefore are interested to hear your comments about our Web site.

Figure 1–15 Web site usability testing questionnaire.

In addition to content, functionality, and usability testing, there are other types of testing. For a newly implemented or maintained Web site, two other types of tests should be conducted: compatibility testing and stress testing. **Compatibility testing** is done to verify that the Web site works with a variety of browsers and browser versions. Initially, test using the browsers that your audience is most likely to use. Different browsers display some aspects of Web pages differently, so it is important to test Web pages in several different browsers to verify they appear correctly in each browser. If you have used technologies that are not supported by older browsers or that require plug-ins, consider changing the content or providing alternative Web pages for viewing in older browsers. If your audience uses both PC and Macintosh computers, you need to test the Web pages using browsers on both platforms. You also may want to test the Web pages in several versions of the same browser (usually the two most recent versions), in the event users have not yet upgraded.

Stress testing determines what happens on your Web site when greater numbers of users access the site. A Web site with 10 users hitting it simultaneously may be fine. When 100 users use the Web site at once, it may operate at an unacceptably slow speed. Stress testing verifies that a Web site runs at an acceptable speed with many users.

Web Site Implementation and Maintenance

Once Web site testing is complete and any required changes have been made, the Web site can be implemented. Implementation of a Web site involves the actual publishing of the Web pages to a Web server. Many HTML editors and WYSIWYG editors provide publishing capabilities. You also can use FTP software, such as WS_FTP, to publish your Web pages to a Web server. After you publish a Web site, you should test the Web pages again to confirm no obvious errors exist, such as broken links or missing graphics.

Once a site is implemented, develop a process to maintain the Web site. The one constant about Web development is that users will request changes and content will require updates. You need to ensure, however, that updates to the Web site do not compromise the site's integrity and consistency. For example, if you have several different people updating various Web pages on a large Web site, you might find it difficult to maintain a consistent look on pages across the Web site. You should plan to update your Web site on a regular basis to keep content up-to-date. This could mean hourly, daily, weekly, or less often, depending on the site's purpose. Do not allow your content to become stale, outdated, or include links to Web pages that no longer exist.

To help manage the task of Web site maintenance, first determine who is responsible for updates to content, structure, functionality, and so on. Then, limit update responsibilities to specific users. Be sure the implementation is controlled by one or more Web developers who can verify that pages are tested thoroughly before they are published.

As updates and changes are made to a Web site, consider notifying users with a graphic banner or a "What's New" announcement, explaining any new features and how the features will benefit them. This technique not only keeps users informed, but also encourages them to come back to the Web site to see what is new.

Finally, Web site monitoring is another key aspect of maintaining a Web site. Usually, the Web servers that host Web sites keep logs of information about Web site usage. A **log** is the file that lists all of the Web pages that have been requested from the Web site. Web site logs are an invaluable source of information for a Web developer. Obtaining and analyzing the logs allows you to determine such things as the number of visitors, browser types and versions, connection speeds, pages most commonly requested, and usage patterns. With this information, you can design a Web site that is effective for your targeted audience, providing them with a rich and rewarding experience.

BTW

Quick Reference
For a list of HTML tags and their associated attributes, see the HTML Quick Reference (Appendix A) at the back of this book, or visit the HTML Quick Reference Web page (scsite.com/HTML5e/qr).

Chapter Summary

In this chapter you have learned about the Internet, World Wide Web, and associated technologies, including Web servers and Web browsers. You learned the essential role of HTML in creating Web pages and reviewed tools used to create HTML documents. You also learned that most Web development projects follow a five-phase life cycle. The items listed below include all the new concepts you have learned in this chapter.

1. Describe the Internet (HTML 2)
2. Describe the World Wide Web (HTML 3)
3. Define Web servers (HTML 4)
4. Describe the Internet, intranets, and extranets (HTML 4)
5. Discuss Web browsers (HTML 7)
6. Define Hypertext Markup Language (HTML 8)
7. Describe HTML elements (HTML 9)
8. List HTML coding practices (HTML 9)
9. Explain HTML versions (HTML 10)
10. Describe Cascading Style Sheets (HTML 10)
11. Define Dynamic Hypertext Markup Language (HTML 10)
12. Define Extensible Hypertext Markup Language (HTML 10)
13. Describe tools for creating HTML documents (HTML 11)
14. Discuss the Web development life cycle (HTML 12)
15. Describe steps in the Web development planning phase (HTML 13)
16. Explain the Web development analysis phase (HTML 13)
17. Discuss Web design and development (HTML 14)
18. Describe various Web site structures (HTML 14)
19. Discuss the importance of Web site testing, including usability testing, compatibility testing, and stress testing (HTML 18)
20. Discuss Web site implementation and maintenance (HTML 20)

Learn It Online

Test your knowledge of chapter content and key terms.

Instructions: To complete the Learn It Online exercises, start your browser, click the Address bar, and then enter the Web address `scsite.com/html5e/learn`. When the HTML Learn It Online page is displayed, click the link for the exercise you want to complete and read the instructions.

Chapter Reinforcement TF, MC, and SA

A series of true/false, multiple choice, and short answer questions that test your knowledge of the chapter content.

Flash Cards

An interactive learning environment where you identify chapter key terms associated with displayed definitions.

Practice Test

A series of multiple choice questions that test your knowledge of chapter content and key terms.

Who Wants To Be a Computer Genius?

An interactive game that challenges your knowledge of chapter content in the style of a television quiz show.

Wheel of Terms

An interactive game that challenges your knowledge of chapter key terms in the style of the television show *Wheel of Fortune*.

Crossword Puzzle Challenge

A crossword puzzle that challenges your knowledge of key terms presented in the chapter.

Apply Your Knowledge

Reinforce the skills and apply the concepts you learned in this chapter.

Understanding Web Page Organizational Standards

Instructions: Start your word-processing program. Open the file apply1-1.doc from the Chapter01\Apply folder of the Data Files for Students. See the inside back cover of this book for instructions for downloading the Data Files for Students, or contact your instructor for information on accessing the required files for this book. As shown in Table 1–6, the apply1-1.doc file lists Web page elements, organizational standards, and related reasons. It also contains blanks in all three columns.

Table 1–6 Web Page Organizational Standards

Element	Organizational Standard	Reason
Titles	Use to explain purpose of page clearly	
	Use to separate main topics	Makes a Web page easier to read; clearly explains what the page is about
Horizontal rules		Provides a graphic to break up Web page content
	Use to help divide large amounts of text	Provides shorter, more-readable sections of text
	Utilize these elements to organize text, when appropriate	Provides organized, easy-to-read text that readers can scan easily
Page length		Increases likelihood that users view key information on a page, without needing to scroll

Perform the following tasks:

1. Without referring to Table 1–5 (on page HTML 14), determine the correct elements, organizational standards, and reasons that are not listed.
2. Add the correct elements in the respective columns.
3. Save the document using the file name apply1-1solution.doc and then submit it in the format specified by your instructor.

Extend Your Knowledge

Extend the skills you learned in this chapter and experiment with new skills. You may need to use Help to complete the assignment.

Evaluating a User Survey

Instructions: Start your word-processing program. Open the document extend1-1.doc from the Chapter01\Extend folder of the Data Files for Students. See the inside back cover of this book for instructions on downloading the Data Files for Students, or contact your instructor for information about accessing the required files. This sample Web site survey shows various questions that could be asked in gathering feedback on Web site usability. It is important to assess the usability of your Web site, as mentioned in the chapter.

You will evaluate the user survey and modify the questions or add new questions that apply to the Web site that you have chosen. You then will ask five people to take the survey that you have modified.

Perform the following tasks:

1. Connect to the Internet and identify one Web site that you think is cumbersome to use.
2. Make changes to the user survey by following some of the guidelines provided in Figure 1–15. Add questions to the survey that will help you to improve the selected Web site.
3. Distribute your survey to at least five family members or friends and collect their responses.
4. Determine what you learned from the results of the surveys.
5. Identify what you can do to improve the Web site that you chose. Using a word processor, type your analysis, save it as extend1-1solution.doc, and then submit it in the format specified by your instructor.

Make It Right

Analyze a document and correct all errors and/or improve the design.

Correcting the Web Site Type Table

Instructions: Start your word-processing program. Open the file makeitright1-1.doc from the Chapter01\MakeItRight folder of the Data Files for Students. See the inside back cover of this book for instructions on downloading the Data Files for Students, or contact your instructor for information about accessing the required files. The document is a modified version of Table 1–1 (on page HTML 5), shown in Table 1–7. The table, which contains errors, lists information relative to the three types of Web sites discussed in Chapter 1: Internet, intranet, and extranet. Without referring to Table 1–1, make the necessary corrections to Table 1–7 by identifying the correct users, access, and applications for the three types of Web sites: Internet, intranet, and extranet. Save the revised document as makeitright1-1solution.doc and then submit it in the form as specified by your instructor.

Table 1–7 Types of Web Sites

Type	Users	Access	Applications
Internet	Select business partners	Private	Share information (inventory updates, or customers product specifications, financial information, etc.) with partners and customers
Intranet	Anyone	Public	Share information (personal information, product catalogs, course information, etc.) with the public
Extranet	Anyone	Public	Share information (forms, manuals, organization schedules, etc.) with employees or members

In the Lab

Design and/or create a document using the guidelines, concepts, and skills presented in this chapter. Labs are listed in order of increasing difficulty.

Lab 1: Redesigning a Web Site

Problem: Figure 1–16 shows the Web site of a popular retailer, Target. As you learned in this chapter, three common Web site structures include linear, hierarchical, and webbed. Based on that information, determine the structure used in the Target.com Web site. Review other similar Web sites and determine which Web site design features are beneficial to a user. Incorporate those ideas into a new Web site design for Target.com. Use paper to sketch the new Web site design for the Target.com Web site.

Continued >

In the Lab *continued*

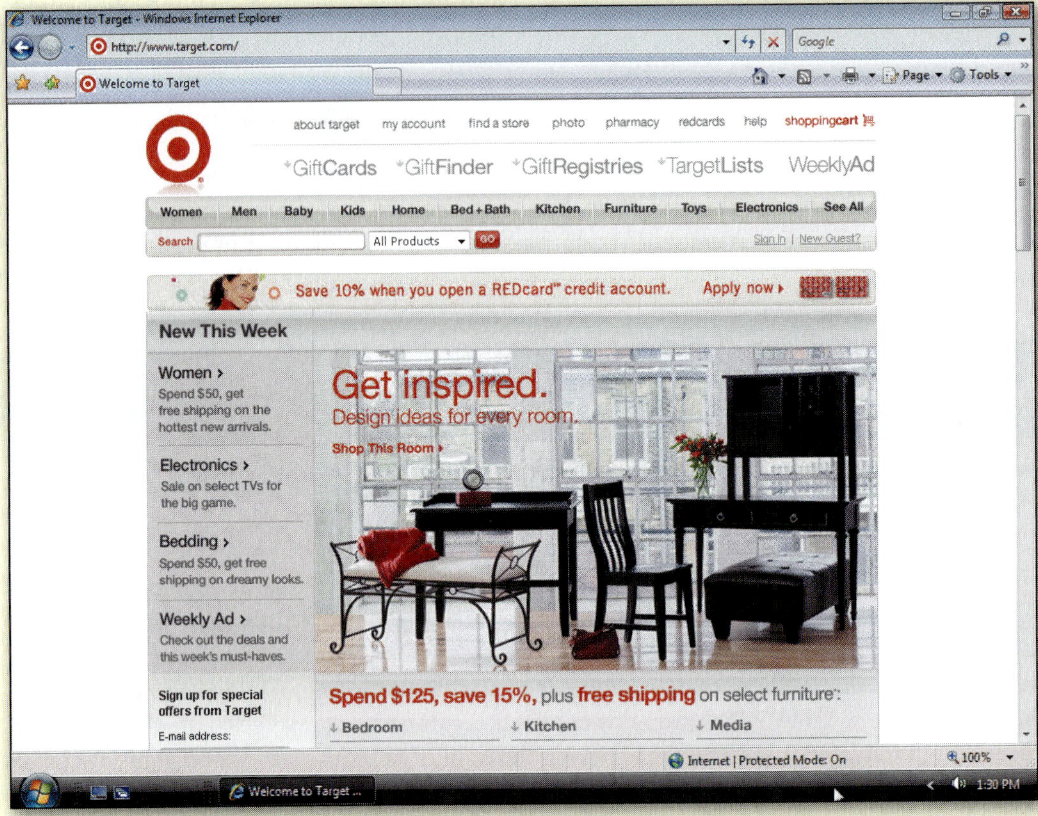

Figure 1–16

Instructions: Perform the following steps using your browser and paper.

1. Start your browser. Open the Target.com Web site in your browser. Print the home page by clicking Print on the File menu or by clicking the Print icon.
2. Navigate the Target.com Web site, determine the structure that the Web site utilizes (linear, hierarchical, or webbed), and then write that on the printout.
3. Find two other online department store Web sites. Print the home pages for each of those sites. Navigate these Web sites to identify any Web site design features that are beneficial to a user.
4. Using ideas from the online department store Web sites that you found in Step 3, sketch a new Web site structure and design for the Target.com site on paper.
5. Write your name on the printouts and the sketch and hand them in to your instructor.

In the Lab

Lab 2: Designing a City Fire Department Web Site

Problem: Your uncle is a fireman with your city's fire department, and he has asked you to design a Web site to link to from the city's main Web site. To do this, you must complete the planning and analysis phases by answering such questions as:

- What tasks will city residents want to complete on the Web site?
- What tasks will fire department personnel want to complete on the Web site?
- What types of information should be included?
- Who will provide information on the Web site content?

Interview several residents of the city in which you live and determine the answers to these questions. Based on that information, you will draw a sketch of a design for the home page of the fire department Web site, such as the design shown in Figure 1–17.

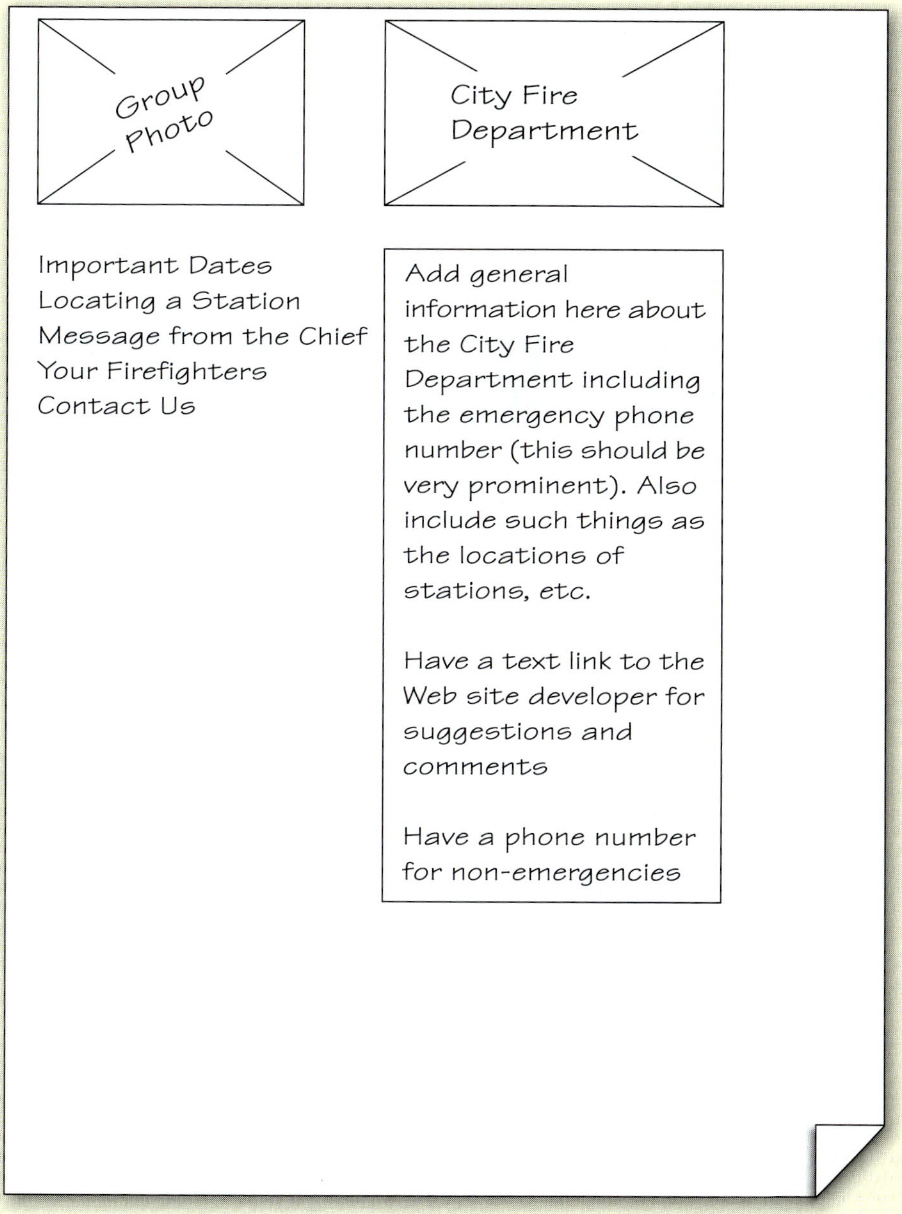

Figure 1–17

Instructions: Perform the following tasks using your word-processing program and paper.

1. Review the questions in the planning and analysis phases of the Web development life cycle, as shown in Table 1–4 on page HTML 12.
2. Assess the value of those questions listed in the table. Add other questions that you think are relevant to the planning and analysis of a fire department Web site.
3. Start your word-processing program. If necessary, open a new document. Enter the questions you will use for planning and analysis. Save the document using the file name lab1-2solution.doc. Print the document.

Continued >

In the Lab *continued*

4. Using the questions that you developed, interview fire department members to determine what information should be included in the Web site, who will provide the information, and so on.
5. After gathering the required information, sketch a design for the home page of the Web site on paper.
6. Share your design sketch with residents of the city and get their opinions on your design.
7. Redraw the design on paper, making any changes based on the input from the residents.
8. Write Original Design on the first design sketch.
9. Write Second Design on the second design sketch.
10. Write your name on the lab1-2solution printout and sketches and hand them in to your instructor.

In the Lab

Lab 3: Asking Planning Phase Questions: Internet, Intranet, and Extranet Designs

Problem: Three different types of Web sites were discussed in this chapter — Internet, intranet, and extranet. Each type of Web site is designed for a different target audience. Think of a business (for example, a restaurant, library, or ice cream shop) that you frequently visit and how that business might use an Internet, intranet, and extranet site. Using the Planning phase questions found in Table 1–4 on page HTML 12, determine the answers to the questions listed in Table 1–8. Enter your ideas in the table. If there are questions that are difficult/impossible to answer directly (for example, What are users' computing environments?), list ways that you can find the answers to those questions.

Table 1–8 Planning Phase Questions

Type Of Business			
Planning Question	**Internet**	**Intranet**	**Extranet**
What is the purpose of this Web site?			
Who will use this Web site?			
What are users' computing environments?			
Who owns and authors the information on the Web site?			
Who decides if/where the information goes on the Web site?			

Instructions: Start your word-processing program. Open the file lab1-3.doc from the Chapter01\IntheLab folder of the Data Files for Students. See the inside back cover of this book for instructions for downloading the Data Files for Students, or contact your instructor for information on accessing the required files. Perform the following tasks using your word-processing program.

1. Enter the type of business in the first row. Determine the answers to the first question for all three types of Web sites and then enter the answers in the appropriate table cells.
2. Continue answering the other four questions.
3. Save the file using the file name lab1-3solution.doc and then submit it in the format specified by your instructor.

Cases and Places

Apply your creative thinking and problem solving skills to design and implement a solution.

• Easier •• More Difficult

• 1: Learn More About Web Access Issues

A local job placement office wants to offer several of your company's online courses to their employees. A requirement of the job placement contract, however, is that the online courses must be accessible to users with physical challenges. Your manager has asked you to learn more about accessibility guidelines to determine what changes are needed to get the current online courses accessible to those with physical challenges. Research accessibility issues on the Web and determine what needs to be considered to satisfy accessibility requirements. Consider the following questions when doing your research: What types of physical challenges do you have to consider when developing Web pages? What recommendations do the Web sites make for accessibility? What does this mean for the Web page developer?

• 2: Determine Web Site Structure

As a Web developer at D2 Design, you often are asked to restructure clients' existing Web sites to make them more user friendly and easier to navigate. Find a Web site that utilizes more than one Web site structure (linear, hierarchical, and/or webbed). Is the information conveyed on the Web site displayed in the appropriate structure? Does the structure effectively support the information communicated? Print the home page of the Web site that you found. On a blank sheet of paper, sketch a design that you think might be more appropriate for the message. Use a word-processing program to create a document that explains why your new design is more effective.

•• 3: Learn More About XHTML Standards

You are hoping to update your university's Web site to XHTML, but first want to learn more about how XHTML differs from HTML. Visit the W3Schools Web site (w3schools.com) to learn more about HTML and XHTML. Using a word-processing program, create a document that briefly describes HTML and XHTML, how they are related, and how they differ.

•• 4: Design a Web Site for Your Aunt

Make It Personal

Your aunt recently opened a new art gallery. You would like to develop a Web site for her that can display her art for viewing and for sale. Thoroughly investigate the Web sites of other art galleries. Before starting on the design, you decide to create a list of Web design principles to which the Web site will adhere. Search the Web for more information about Web site design. Find three Web sites that give information about Web design principles. In a word-processing document, take the ideas presented in this chapter together with the ideas presented in the other Web sites and make a comprehensive list of Web design principles. Where appropriate, identify any conflicting design principles discussed in the Web sites.

•• 5: Create a Usability Survey

Working Together

Your school recently updated its Web site. The school counselors have selected a team to develop a usability survey or questionnaire that you can give to a group of users (including students, parents, and teachers) to evaluate the new Web site. What types of information do you hope to gain by distributing this survey or questionnaire? How can you convey information on the survey or questionnaire so it clearly identifies what you are asking? Create a usability survey using your word-processing program. Give the survey or questionnaire to at least five people, including at least one from each group identified above. Allow them to complete the survey or questionnaire and then look at the results. If possible, ask the users what they thought the various questions conveyed. Is that what you wanted to convey? If not, think of other ways to gather the information that you need in a format that is self-explanatory.

2 Creating and Editing a Web Page

Objectives

You will have mastered the material in this chapter when you can:

- Identify elements of a Web page
- Start Notepad and describe the Notepad window
- Enable word wrap in Notepad
- Enter the HTML tags
- Enter a centered heading and a paragraph of text
- Create an unordered, ordered, or definition list
- Save an HTML file
- Use a browser to view a Web page
- Activate Notepad
- Identify Web page image types and attributes
- Add an image, change the background color of a Web page, and add a horizontal rule
- View the HTML source code in a browser
- Print a Web page and an HTML file
- Quit Notepad and a browser

2 Creating and Editing a Web Page

Introduction

With an understanding of the Web development life cycle, you should have a good idea about the importance of proper Web site planning, analysis, and design. After completing these phases, the next phase is the actual development of a Web page using HTML. As discussed in Chapter 1, Web pages are created using HTML, which uses a set of special tags to define the structure, layout, and appearance of a Web page. In this chapter, you create and edit a Web page using basic HTML tags.

Project — Community Food Drive Web Page

Chapter 2 illustrates how to use HTML to create a Web page for the Community Food Drive, as shown in Figure 2–1a. The Student Theater Club is trying to devote more time to community service activities. Because you are the only Web development major in the group, they have asked your help in developing a Web page to advertise the upcoming food drive. The Community Food Drive Web page will include general information about the food drive, along with donation information and the list of foods that are most needed.

To enter text and HTML tags used to create the Web page, you will use a program called Notepad, as shown in Figure 2–1b. **Notepad** is a basic text editor you can use for simple documents or for creating Web pages using HTML. You also will use the Microsoft Internet Explorer browser to view your Web page as you create it. By default, Notepad and Internet Explorer are installed with Windows. If you do not have Notepad or Internet Explorer available on your computer, other text editor or browser programs will work.

Overview

As you read this chapter, you will learn how to create the Web page shown in Figure 2–1 by performing these general tasks:

- Enter HTML code into the Notepad window.
- Save the file as an HTML file.
- Enter basic HTML tags and add text to the file.
- Organize the text by adding headings and creating a bulleted list.
- Enhance the Web page's appearance.
- View the Web page and HTML code in your browser.
- Validate the Web page.
- Print the Web page.

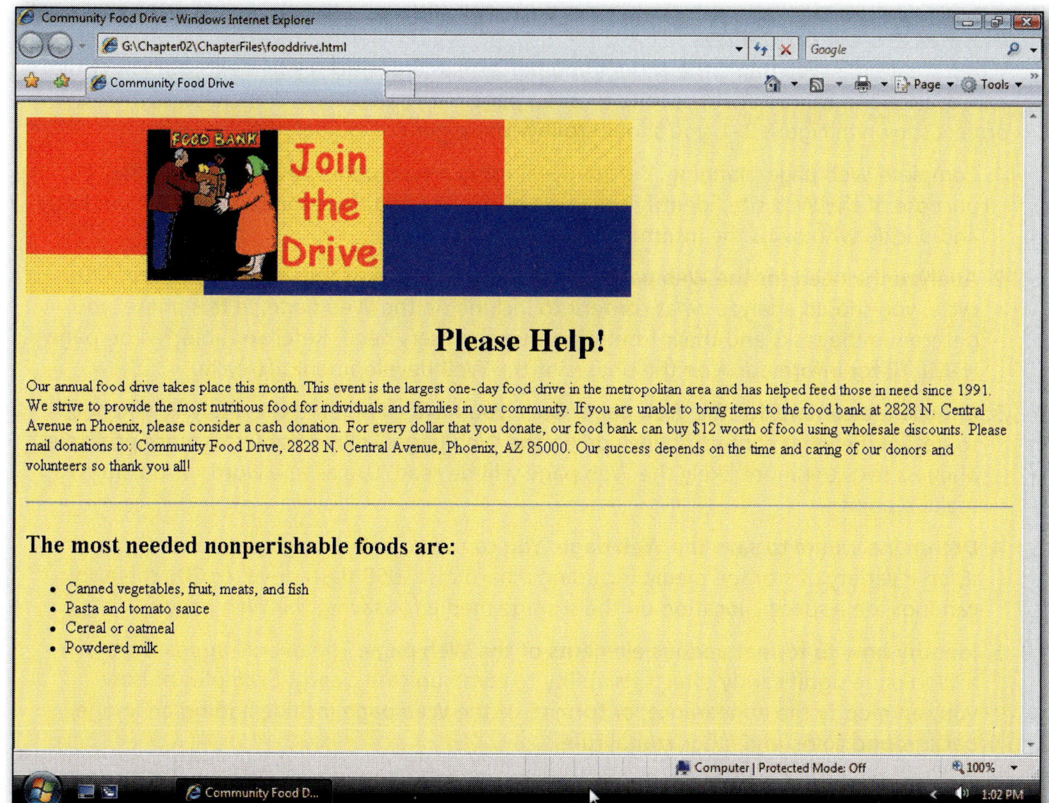

(a) Community Food Drive Web page.

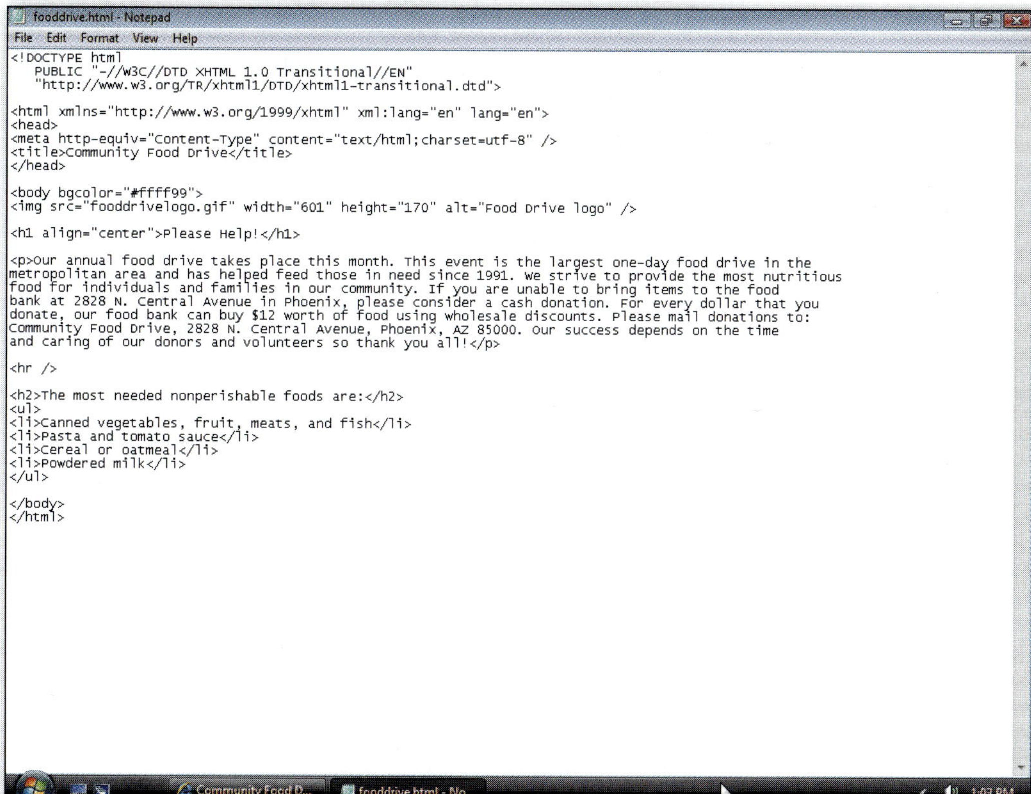


```
<!DOCTYPE html
   PUBLIC "-//W3C//DTD XHTML 1.0 Transitional//EN"
   "http://www.w3.org/TR/xhtml1/DTD/xhtml1-transitional.dtd">

<html xmlns="http://www.w3.org/1999/xhtml" xml:lang="en" lang="en">
<head>
<meta http-equiv="Content-Type" content="text/html;charset=utf-8" />
<title>Community Food Drive</title>
</head>

<body bgcolor="#ffff99">
<img src="fooddrivelogo.gif" width="601" height="170" alt="Food Drive logo" />

<h1 align="center">Please Help!</h1>

<p>Our annual food drive takes place this month. This event is the largest one-day food drive in the
metropolitan area and has helped feed those in need since 1991. We strive to provide the most nutritious
food for individuals and families in our community. If you are unable to bring items to the food
bank at 2828 N. Central Avenue in Phoenix, please consider a cash donation. For every dollar that you
donate, our food bank can buy $12 worth of food using wholesale discounts. Please mail donations to:
Community Food Drive, 2828 N. Central Avenue, Phoenix, AZ 85000. Our success depends on the time
and caring of our donors and volunteers so thank you all!</p>

<hr />

<h2>The most needed nonperishable foods are:</h2>
<ul>
<li>Canned vegetables, fruit, meats, and fish</li>
<li>Pasta and tomato sauce</li>
<li>Cereal or oatmeal</li>
<li>Powdered milk</li>
</ul>

</body>
</html>
```


(b) HTML code used to create the Web page.

Figure 2–1

Plan Ahead

General Project Guidelines

When creating a Web page, the actions you perform and decisions you make will affect the appearance and characteristics of the finished page. As you create a Web page, such as the project shown in Figure 2–1, you should follow these general guidelines:

1. **Complete Web page planning.** Before developing a Web page, you must know the purpose of the Web site, identify the users of the site and their computing environment, and decide who owns the information on the Web page.
2. **Analyze the need for the Web page.** In the analysis phase of the Web development life cycle, you should analyze what content to include on the Web page. In this phase, you determine the tasks and the information that the users need. Refer to Table 1–4 on page HTML 12 for information on the phases of the Web development life cycle.
3. **Choose the content for the Web page.** Once you have completed the analysis, you need to determine what content to include on the Web page. Follow the *less is more* principle. The less text, the more likely the Web page will be read. Use as few words as possible to make a point.
4. **Determine where to save the Web page.** You can store a Web page permanently, or **save** it, on a variety of storage media including a hard disk, USB flash drive, or CD. You also can indicate a specific location on the storage media for saving the Web page.
5. **Identify how to format various elements of the Web page.** The overall appearance of a Web page significantly affects its ability to communicate clearly. Examples of how you can modify the appearance, or **format**, of the Web page include adding an image, background color, and a horizontal rule.
6. **Find appropriate graphical images.** Eye-catching graphical images help to convey the Web page's overall message and add visual interest. Graphics could show a product, service, result, or benefit, or visually convey a message that is not expressed easily with words.
7. **Establish where to position and how to format the graphical images.** The position and format of the graphical images should grab the attention of passersby and draw them into reading the Web page.
8. **Test the Web page for XHTML compliance.** An important part of Web development is testing to assure that your Web page follows XHTML standards. The World Wide Web Consortium (W3C) has a validator available that allows you to test your Web page and clearly explains any errors that you have.

When necessary, more specific details concerning the above guidelines are presented at appropriate points in the chapter. The chapter also will identify the actions performed and decisions made regarding these guidelines during the creation of the Web page shown in Figure 2–1.

Elements of a Web Page

Today, many people — individuals, students, teachers, business executives, Web developers, and others — are developing Web pages for personal or professional reasons. Each person has his or her own style and the resulting Web pages are as diverse as the people who create them. Most Web pages, however, include several basic features, or elements, as shown in Figure 2–2.

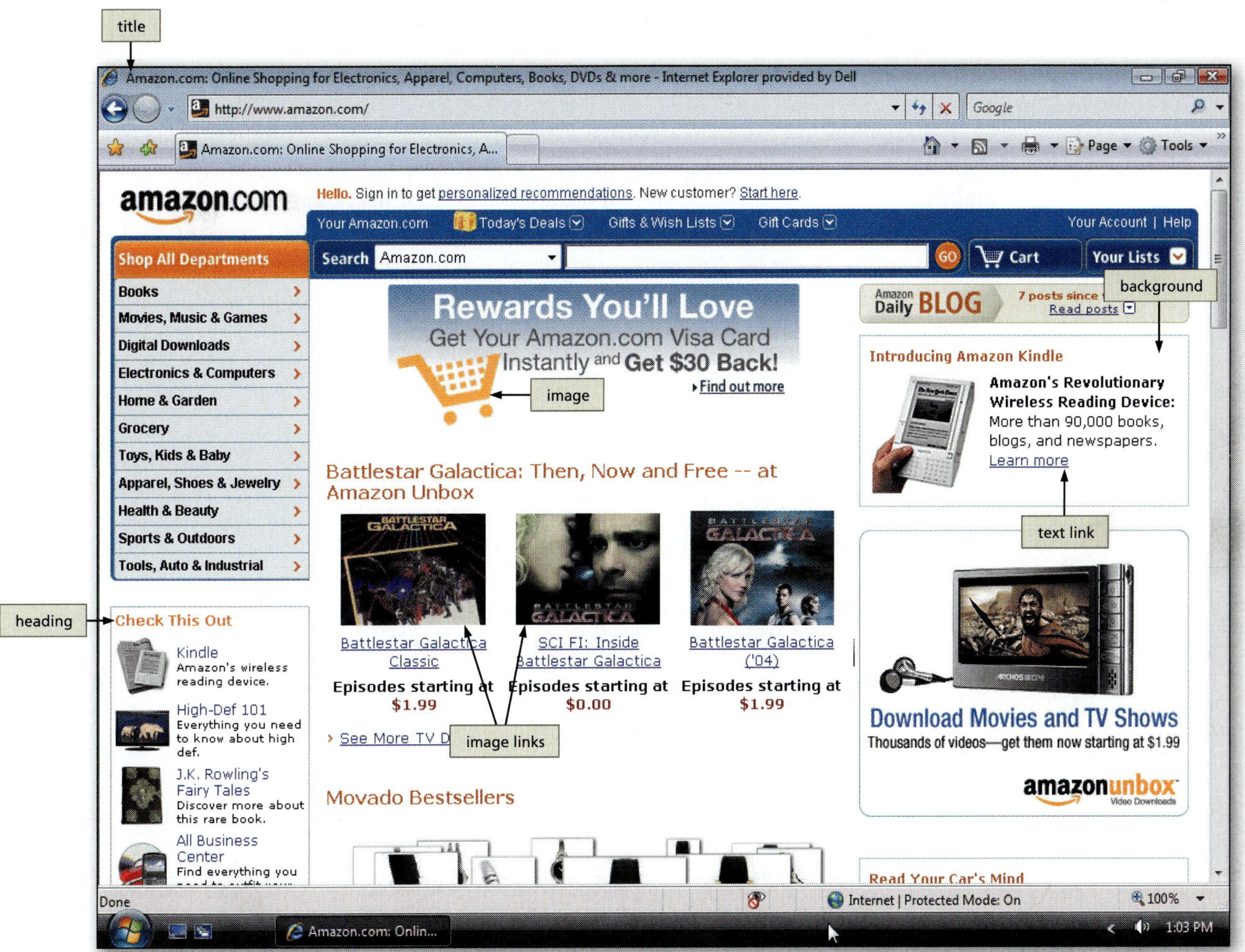

Figure 2–2 Elements of a Web page.

Window Elements

The **title** of a Web page is the text that appears on the title bar of the browser window when the Web page appears. The title also is the name assigned to the page if a user adds the page to the browser's list of **favorites**, or **bookmarks**. Because of its importance, you always should include a title on your Web page. The title, which usually is the first element you see, should identify the subject or purpose of the page. The title should be concise, yet descriptive, and briefly explain the page's content or purpose to the visitor.

The **body** of the Web page contains the information that is displayed in the browser window. The body can include text, graphics, and other elements. The **background** of a Web page is a solid color, a picture, or a graphic against which the other elements on the Web page appear. When choosing your background, be sure it does not overpower the information on the Web page. If you use an image for the background, the image is tiled, or repeated across and down the page.

BTW

Favorites and Bookmarks

Internet Explorer and Mozilla Firefox have a feature that allows you to add Web pages to a list, so you quickly can access them in the future. Internet Explorer refers to these as Favorites, while Firefox calls them Bookmarks. Web developers need to make sure that they include a descriptive title on their Web pages because that is the title that is shown in the bookmark or favorite.

Text Elements

Normal text is the default text format used for the main content of a Web page. Normal text can be used in a standard paragraph or formatted to appear as: bold (<strong>), italic (<em>), or underlined (<u>); in different colors; and so on. Normal text also can be used in a series of text items called a **list**. Typically, lists are bulleted or numbered.

Headings are used to set off paragraphs of text or different sections of a page. Headings are a larger font size than normal text and often are bold or italic or a different color than normal text.

Image Elements

Web pages typically use several different types of graphics, or images, such as an icon, bullet, line, photo, illustration, or other picture. An image used in a Web page also is called an **inline image**, which means the image or graphic file is not part of the HTML file. Instead, the Web browser merges the separate graphic file into the Web page as it is displayed in the browser window. The HTML file contains <img> tags that tell the browser which graphic file to request from the server, where to insert it on the page, and how to display it.

Web pages typically use several different types of inline images. An **image map** is a special type of inline image in which you define one or more areas as hotspots. A **hotspot** is an area of an image that activates a function when selected. For example, each hotspot in an image map can link to a different Web page. Some inline images are **animated**, meaning they include motion and can change in appearance.

Horizontal rules are lines that are displayed across a Web page to separate different sections of the page. Although the appearance of a horizontal rule can vary, many Web pages use an inline image as a horizontal rule. Alternatively, you can use the horizontal rule tag (<hr />) to add a simple horizontal rule, such as the one used in this project.

Hyperlink Elements

One of the more important elements of a Web page is a hyperlink, or link. A **link** is text, an image, or another Web page element that you click to instruct the browser to go to a location in a file or to request a file from a server. On the Web, links are the primary way to navigate between Web pages and among Web sites. Links point not only to Web pages, but also to graphics, sound, video, program files, e-mail addresses, and parts of the same Web page. Text links, also called hypertext links, are the most commonly used hyperlinks. When text identifies a hyperlink, it usually appears as underlined text, in a color different from the rest of the Web page text.

Defining Web Page Structure

To create an HTML document, you use a text editor to enter information about the structure of the Web page, the content of the Web page, and how that content should be displayed. This book uses the Notepad text editor that comes with Windows.

Before you begin entering the content, you must start by entering tags that define the overall structure of the Web page. You do this by inserting a <!DOCTYPE> tag and five tags (<html>, <head>, <meta />, <title>, and <body>). These tags define the structure of a standard Web page and divide the HTML file into its basic sections, such as the header information and the body of the page that contains text and graphics.

BTW

HTML Resources
The Web has many wonderful sources of information on HTML and Web page development. One of the better sources is the HTML Goodies Web site, which has primers and tutorials on a variety of topics as well as free downloads and discussion areas. To learn more about this Web site, search for "HTML Goodies" in a search engine.

The **<!DOCTYPE>** tag is used to tell the browser which HTML or XHTML version and type the document uses. The W3C supports three document types for HTML or XHTML: strict, transitional, and frameset. The **strict** document type is specified when you want to prohibit the use of deprecated tags. **Deprecated tags** are tags that the W3C has earmarked for eventual removal from their specifications, because those tags have been replaced with newer, more functional tags. The **transitional** document type allows the use of deprecated tags. The **frameset** document type, which is used to support frames on a Web page, also allows the use of deprecated tags. The <!DOCTYPE> tag includes a URL that references a Document Type Definition found on the W3C Web site. A **Document Type Definition** (**DTD**) is a file containing definitions of tags and how they should be used in a Web page. The project in this chapter uses the transitional document type.

BTW

The DOCTYPE Tag
The W3Schools Web site provides additional information about the DOCTYPE tags used for the strict, transitional, and frameset document types. To learn more about the DOCTYPE tag, visit the W3C Web site. It provides a wealth of information on this and other HTML tags.

Defining the HTML Document

The first set of tags beyond the <!DOCTYPE> tag, **<html>** and **</html>**, indicates the start and end of an HTML document. This set of tags contains all of the content of the Web page, the tags that format that content, and the tags that define the different parts of the document. Software tools, such as browsers, use these tags to determine where the HTML code in a file begins and ends.

The Header The next set of tags, **<head>** and **</head>**, contains the Web page title and other document header information. The **<meta />** tag has several functions. In this chapter, it is used to declare the character encoding UTF-8. When the browser encounters this meta tag, it will display the Web page properly, based on that UTF-8 encoding. The encoding chosen also is important when validating the Web page. The meta tag has other purposes that are described in subsequent chapters of the book. The **<title>** and **</title>** tags indicate the title of the Web page, which appears on the browser title bar when the Web page is displayed in the browser window. The title also is the name given to the page when a user adds the page to a favorites or bookmarks list.

BTW

XHTML Compliance
To make your HTML files compliant with XHTML standards, always enter tags in lowercase (with the exception of the <!DOCTYPE> tag, which is always uppercase). Throughout this book, the project directions follow these standards to help you learn good HTML and XHTML coding practices.

The Body The final set of tags, **<body>** and **</body>**, contains the main content of the Web page. All text, images, links, and other content are contained within this final set of tags. Table 2–1 lists the functions of the tags described so far as well as other tags that you use in this chapter.

Table 2–1 HTML Tags and Their Functions

HTML Tag	Function
<!DOCTYPE>	Indicates the version and type of HTML used; includes a URL reference to a DTD
<html> </html>	Indicates the start and end of an HTML document
<head> </head>	Indicates the start and end of a section of the document used for the title and other document header information
<meta />	Indicates hidden information about the Web page
<title> </title>	Indicates the start and end of the title. The title does not appear in the body of the Web page, but appears on the title bar of the browser.
<body> </body>	Indicates the start and end of the Web page body
<hn> </hn>	Indicates the start and end of the text section called a heading; sizes range from <h1> through <h6>. See Figure 2–8a on page HTML XX for heading size samples.
<p> </p>	Indicates the start of a new paragraph; inserts a blank line above the new paragraph
<ul> </ul>	Indicates the start and end of an unordered (bulleted) list

BTW

WordPad
WordPad is another text editor that you can use to create HTML files. To start WordPad, click the Start button on the taskbar, point to All Programs on the Start menu, point to Accessories on the All Programs submenu, and then click WordPad on the Accessories submenu. WordPad help provides tips on how to use the product.

Table 2–1 HTML Tags and Their Functions (continued)

HTML Tag	Function
<li> </li>	Indicates that the item that follows the tag is an item within a list
<hr />	Inserts a horizontal rule
 	Inserts a line break at the point where the tag appears

Most HTML start tags, such as <html>, <head>, <title>, and <body>, have corresponding end tags, </html>, </head>, </title>, and </body>. Note that, for tags that do not have end tags, such as <meta />, <hr />, and <br />, the tag is closed using a space and a forward slash.

To Start Notepad

With the planning, analysis, and design of the Web page complete, you can begin developing the Web page by entering HTML using a text editor. The following steps, which assume Windows Vista is running, start Notepad based on a typical installation. You may need to ask your instructor how to start Notepad for your computer.

- Click the Start button on the Windows Vista taskbar to display the Start menu.
- Click All Programs at the bottom of the left pane on the Start menu to display the All Programs list.
- Click Accessories in the All Programs list (Figure 2–3).

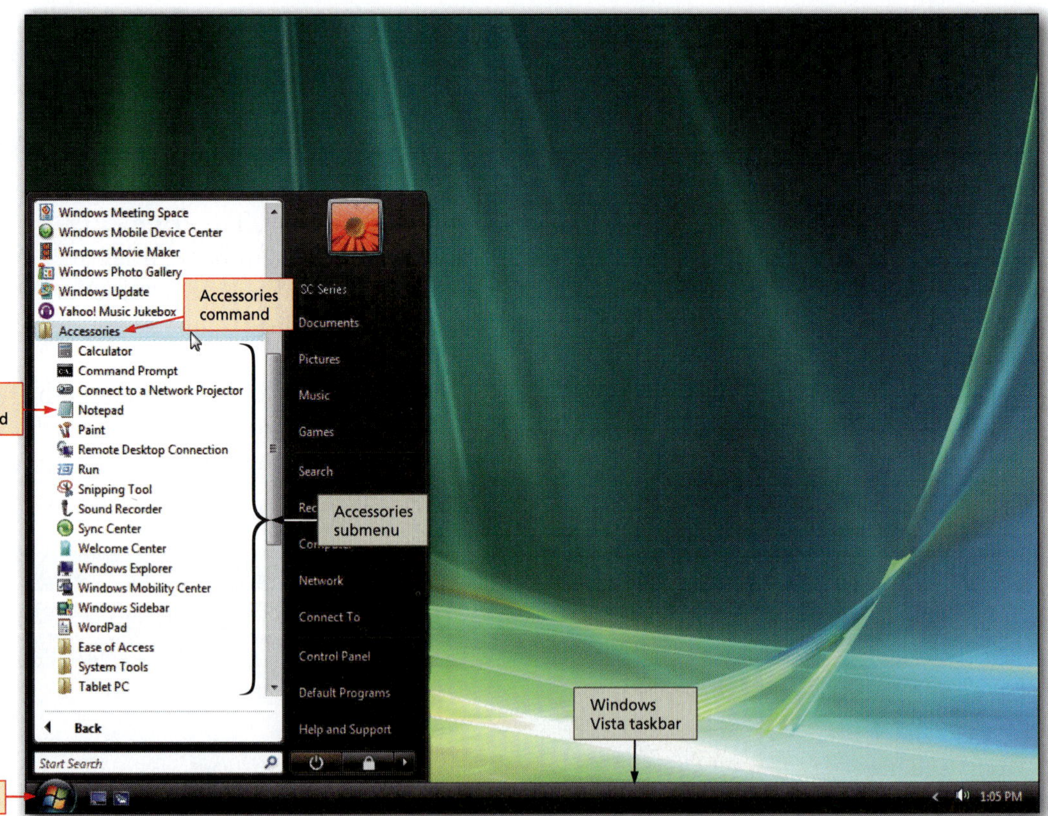

Figure 2–3

2

- Click Notepad in the Accessories list to display the Notepad window (Figure 2–4).
- If the Notepad window is not maximized, click the Maximize button on the Notepad title bar to maximize it.

Q&A What is a maximized window?

A maximized window fills the entire screen. When you maximize a window, the Maximize button changes to a Restore Down button.

Untitled – Notepad window

title bar

menu bar

Maximize button changed to a Restore Down button because window is maximized

text area

scroll bar

Figure 2–4

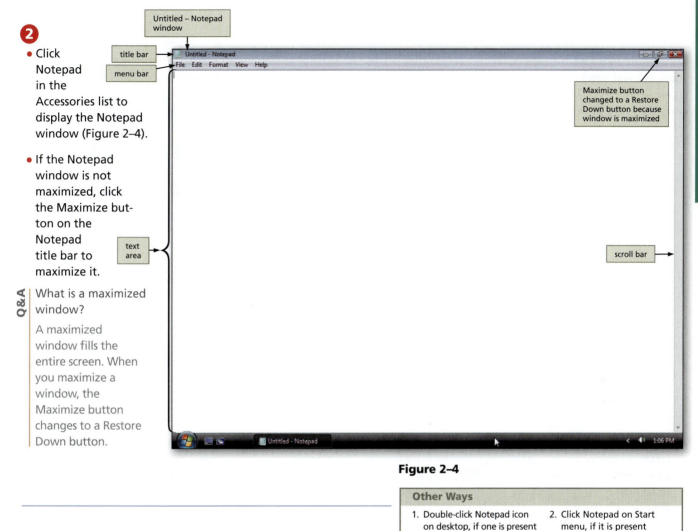

Other Ways	
1. Double-click Notepad icon on desktop, if one is present	2. Click Notepad on Start menu, if it is present

To Enable Word Wrap in Notepad

In Notepad, the text entered in the text area scrolls continuously to the right unless the Word Wrap feature is enabled, or turned on. **Word wrap** causes text lines to break at the right edge of the window and appear on a new line, so all entered text is visible in the Notepad window. Word wrap does not affect the way text prints. The following step shows how to enable word wrap in Notepad.

1

- Click Format on the menu bar (Figure 2–5).
- If the Word Wrap command does not have a check mark next to it, click Word Wrap.

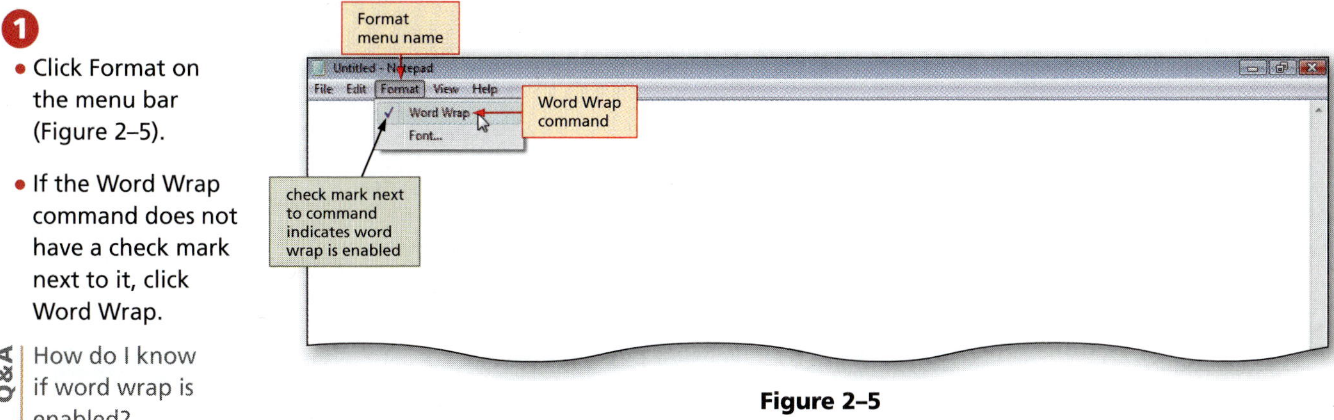

Figure 2–5

Q&A How do I know if word wrap is enabled?

When word wrap is enabled, a check mark precedes the Word Wrap command on the Format menu, and when you type, your words remain on the screen.

To Define the Web Page Structure Using HTML Tags

The first task is to enter the initial tags that define the Web page structure. Table 2–2 contains the HTML tags and text used to create the Web page shown in Figure 2–1. In this chapter and throughout this book, where large segments of HTML code or text are to be entered, you will find this code or text in tables with line number references, rather than within the steps. The steps will direct you to enter the text shown in the tables.

Table 2–2 Initial HTML Tags

Line	HTML Tag and Text
1	`<!DOCTYPE html`
2	`PUBLIC "-//W3C//DTD XHTML 1.0 Transitional//EN"`
3	`"http://www.w3.org/TR/xhtml1/DTD/xhtml1-transitional.dtd">`
4	
5	`<html xmlns="http://www.w3.org/1999/xhtml" xml:lang="en" lang="en">`
6	`<head>`
7	`<meta http-equiv="Content-Type" content="text/html;charset=utf-8" />`
8	`<title>Community Food Drive</title>`
9	`</head>`

The following steps illustrate how to enter the initial tags that define the structure of the Web page.

1

- Enter the HTML code shown in Table 2–2 (Figure 2–6). Press ENTER at the end of each line. If you make an error as you are typing, use the BACKSPACE key to delete all the characters back to and including the incorrect characters, and then continue typing.
- Press the ENTER key once more, leaving one blank line after the </head> tag.
- Compare what you typed to Figure 2–6. If you notice errors, use your mouse pointer or arrow keys to move the insertion point to the right of each error and use the BACKSPACE key to correct the error.

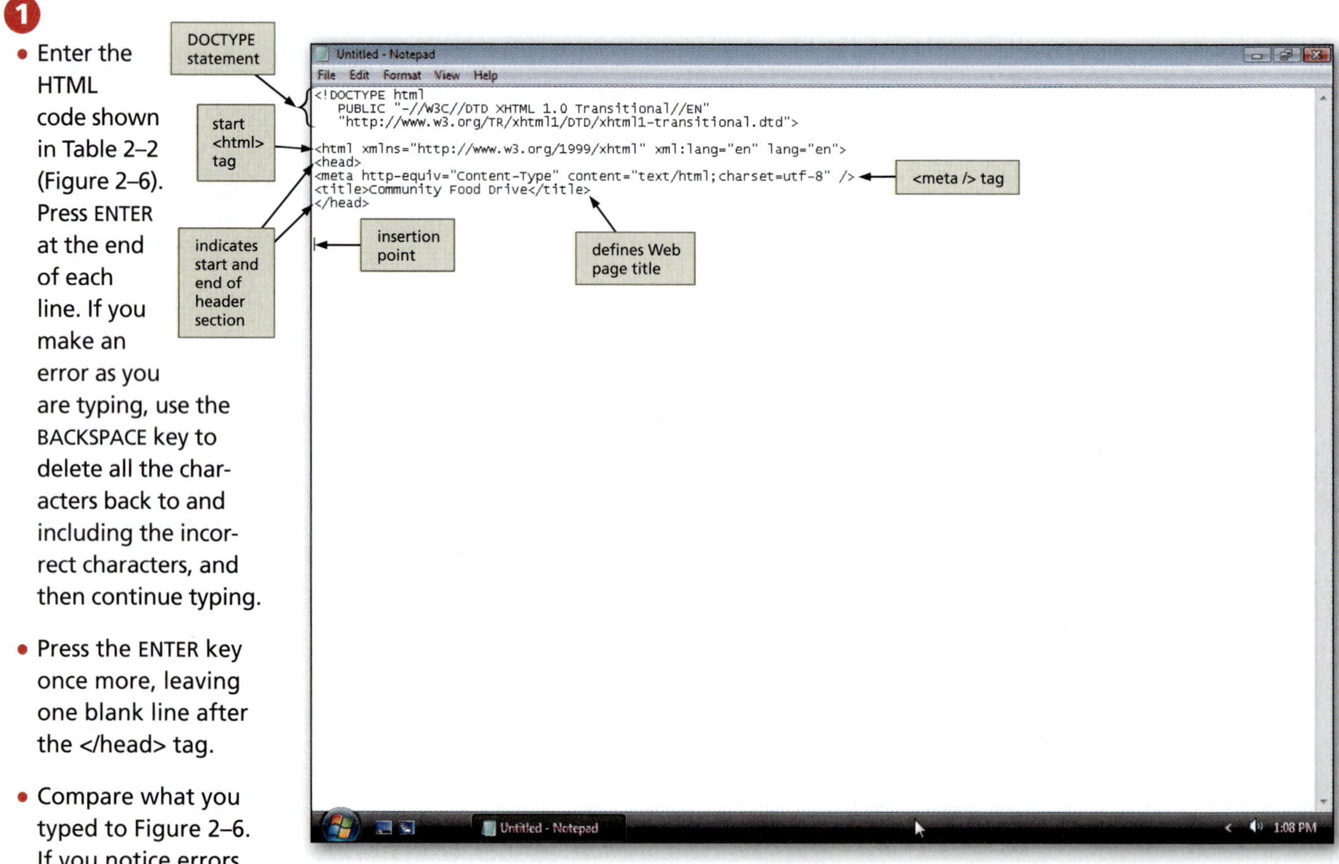

Figure 2–6

- Type <body> and then press the ENTER key twice.
- Type </body> and then press the ENTER key.
- Type </html> as the end tag (Figure 2–7).
- Compare what you typed to Figure 2–7 and correct errors in your typing if necessary.

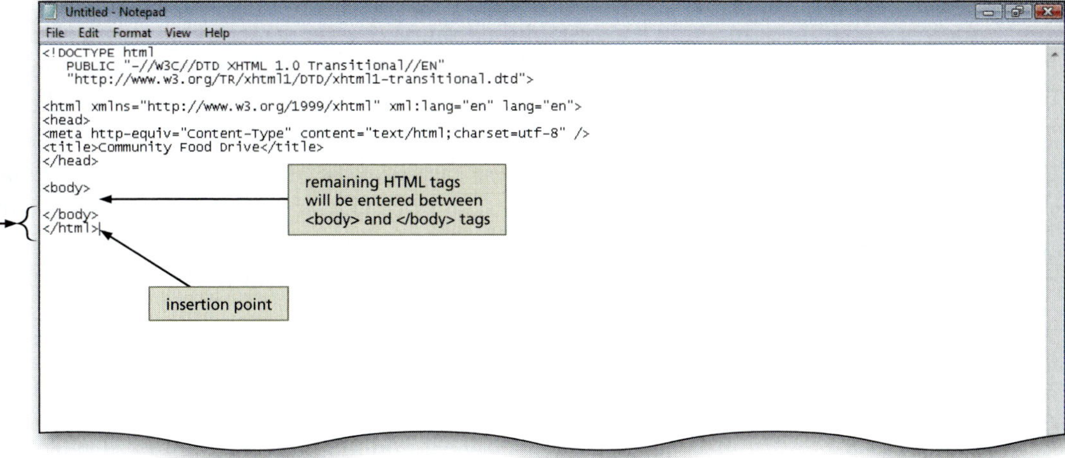

Figure 2–7

Q&A What is the difference between the <title> and <body> tags?

The text contained within the <title> </title> tags is what appears on the browser title bar when the Web page is displayed in the browser window. The text and graphics contained within the <body> </body> tags is what is displayed in the browser window.

Q&A Do I have to type the initial HTML tags for every Web page that I develop?

The same initial HTML tags are used in many other chapters. To avoid retyping these tags, you can save the code that you just typed in, and give it a new file name, something like structure.html or template.html. If you save this file at the root level of your folders, you will have easy access to it for other chapters.

Q&A Can I use either uppercase or lowercase letters for my HTML code?

To make your HTML files compliant with XHTML standards, always enter tags in lowercase (with the exception of the <!DOCTYPE> tag, which is always uppercase). In this book, the project directions follow these standards to help you learn good HTML and XHTML coding standards.

Plan Ahead

Identify how to format various elements of the text.

By formatting the characters and paragraphs on a Web page, you can improve its overall appearance. On a Web page, consider the following formatting suggestions.

- **Effectively utilize headings.** The main heading is generally the first line of text on the Web page. It conveys the purpose of the Web page, such as asking for help with the food drive. Heading size standards should be followed as shown in Figure 2–8. The main heading should be size 1, and subtopics or headings should be size 2.
- **Use default text size when appropriate.** The body text consists of all text between the heading and the bottom of the Web page. This text highlights the key points of the message in as few words as possible. It should be easy to read and follow. While emphasizing the positive, the body text must be realistic, truthful, and believable. The default font size and style is appropriate to use for the body of text.
- **Highlight key paragraphs with bullets.** A **bullet** is a dot or other symbol positioned at the beginning of a paragraph. The bulleted list contains specific information that is more clearly identified by a list versus a paragraph of text.

Entering Web Page Content

> **BTW**
> **Headings for Organization**
> When using headings to organize content and emphasize key points on a Web page, be sure to use headings consistently. That is, if you use a Heading 2 (<h2>) style for a specific level of text, you always should use a Heading 2 style to break up information at that level. Also, do not skip levels of headings in your document. For example, do not start with a Heading 1 (<h1>) style and then use a Heading 3 (<h3>) style.

Once you have established the Web page structure, it is time to enter the content of the Web page, including headings, informational text paragraphs, and a bulleted list.

Headings are used to separate text or add new topics on the Web page. Several styles and sizes of headings exist, indicated by the tags <h1> through <h6>, with <h1> being the largest. Generally, you use the Heading 1 style for the main heading. Figure 2–8a shows a Web page using various sizes of headings. A Web page usually has only one main heading; therefore, the HTML file for that Web page usually has only one set of <h1> </h1> tags. One method of maintaining a consistent look on a Web page is to use the same heading size for headings at the same topic level (Figure 2–8b). Notice that the paragraphs of text and the bullet lists are all separated by size 2 headings in Figure 2–8b. This separation indicates that the text (i.e., two paragraphs plus one bullet list) is all at the same level of importance on the Web page.

Web pages generally contain a significant amount of text. Breaking the text into paragraphs helps to separate key ideas and make the text easier to read. Paragraphs are separated with a blank line by using a <p> tag.

Sometimes text on a Web page is easier for users to read and understand when it is formatted as a list, instead of as a paragraph. HTML provides several types of lists, but the most popular are unordered (bullet) and ordered (numbered) lists. During the design phase of the Web development life cycle, you decide on the most effective way to structure the Web content and format the text on the Web page.

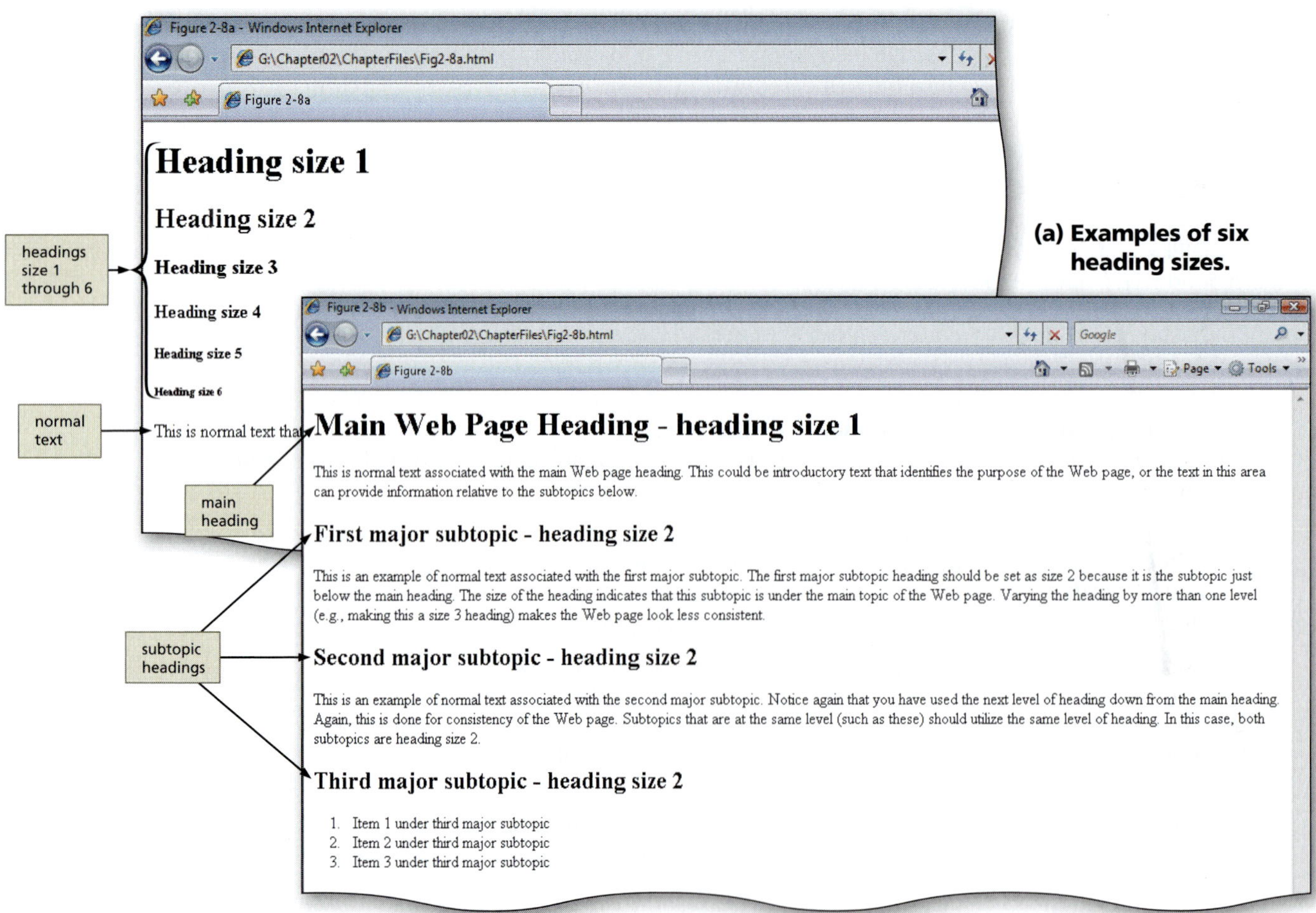

(a) Examples of six heading sizes.

(b) A consistent use of headings can help organize Web page content.

Figure 2–8

To Enter a Centered Heading

The heading, Please Help!, is the main heading and indicates the main message of the Web page. To draw attention to this heading, you will use the <h1> tag and center the heading. The following step illustrates how to enter a centered heading on the Web page.

1

- Click the blank line below the <body> tag and type `<h1 align="center">Please Help!</h1>` in the text area, and then press the ENTER key twice (Figure 2–9).

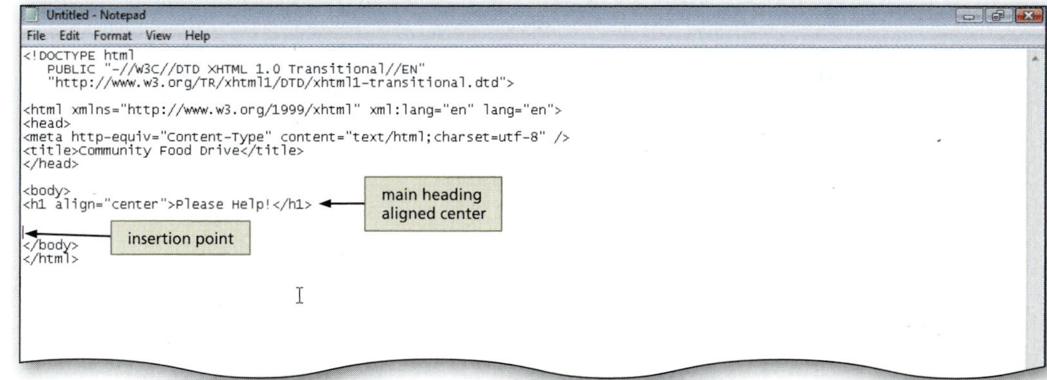

Figure 2–9

Q&A What is the purpose of using the align="center" attribute?

Using the **align** attribute, you can specify left-, right-, or center-alignment with the statements align="left", align="right", or align="center" in any heading tag. By default, headings are left-aligned; if an alignment is not specified, a heading is left-aligned.

Q&A Why did you put an additional line in the HTML code after the heading?

An additional space line was inserted for readability. This blank line will not be displayed on the Web page.

To Enter a Paragraph of Text

After you enter the heading, the next step is to add a paragraph of text using the <p> tag. When the browser finds a <p> tag in an HTML file, it starts a new line and inserts a blank line above the new paragraph. The </p> end tag indicates the end of the paragraph. Table 2–3 contains the HTML tags and text used in the paragraph.

Table 2–3 Adding a Paragraph of Text

Line	HTML Tag and Text
14	`<p>Our annual food drive takes place this month. This event is the largest one-day food drive in the`
15	`metropolitan area and has helped feed those in need since 1991. We strive to provide the most nutritious`
16	`food for individuals and families in our community. If you are unable to bring items to the food`
17	`bank at 2828 N. Central Avenue in Phoenix, please consider a cash donation. For every dollar that you`
18	`donate, our food bank can buy $12 worth of food using wholesale discounts. Please mail donations to:`
19	`Community Food Drive, 2828 N. Central Avenue, Phoenix, AZ 85000. Our success depends on the time`
20	`and caring of our donors and volunteers so thank you all!</p>`

The following step illustrates how to enter a paragraph of text in an HTML file.

1

- With the insertion point on line 14, enter the HTML code as shown in Table 2–3 on the previous page. Press ENTER at the end of each line in Table 2–3 and use only one space after periods.
- Press the ENTER key once more (Figure 2–10).

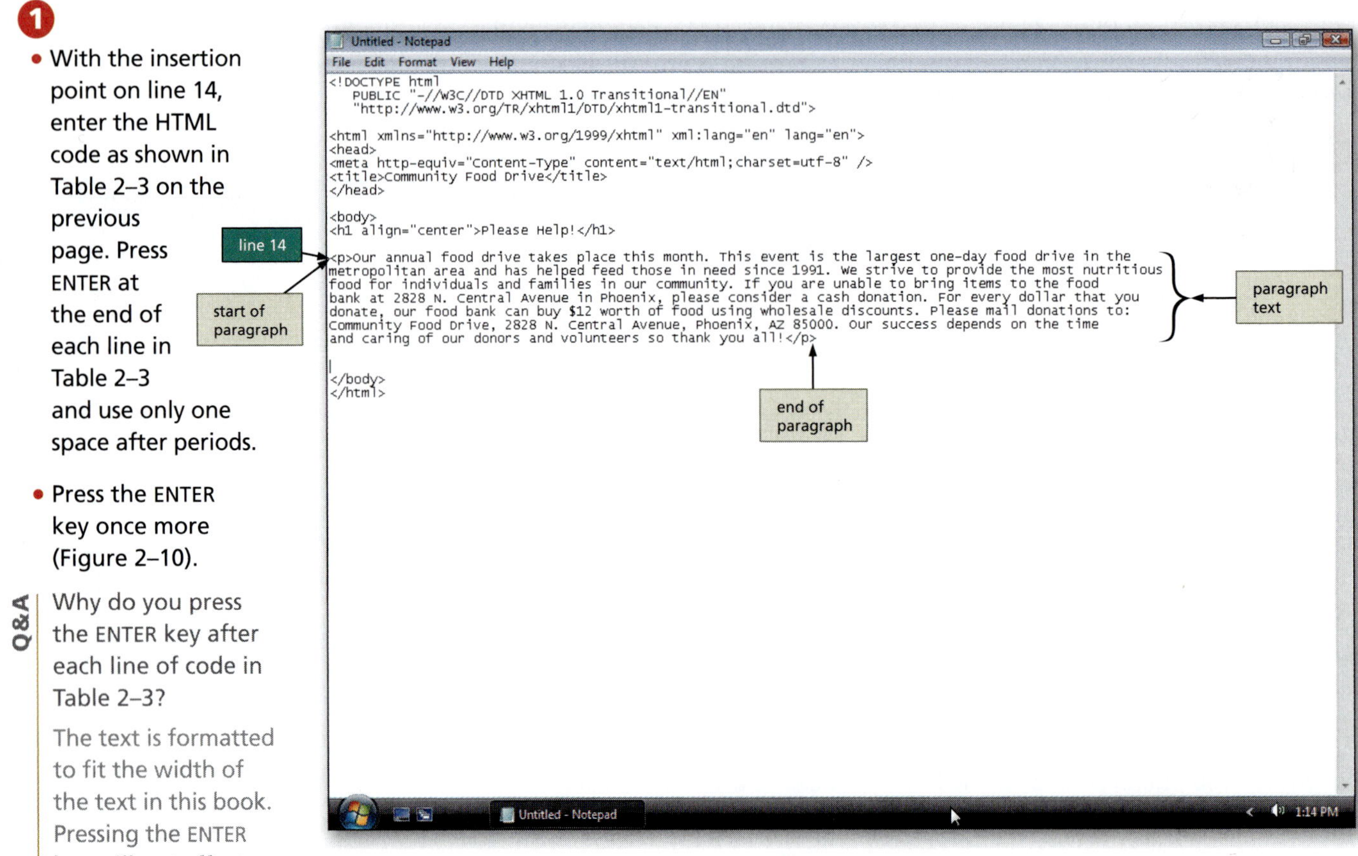

Figure 2–10

Q&A Why do you press the ENTER key after each line of code in Table 2–3?

The text is formatted to fit the width of the text in this book. Pressing the ENTER key will not affect the way that the page displays in the browser window. It is the <p> tag that affects the layout of the text in the browser. The <p> tag inserts a blank line between paragraphs of text.

Q&A What other tag can be used to break text on a Web page?

The <br /> tag also is used to break a line of text. As soon as the browser encounters a <br /> tag, it starts a new line with the text that follows the tag. Unlike the <p> tag, using the <br /> tag does not insert a blank line above the new line of text. The <br /> tag is used later in the book.

Using Lists to Present Content

Lists structure text into an itemized format. Typically, lists are bulleted (unordered) or numbered (ordered). An **unordered list**, which also is called a **bulleted list,** formats information using small images called bullets. Figure 2–11 shows Web page text formatted as unordered, or bulleted, lists and the HTML code used to create the lists.

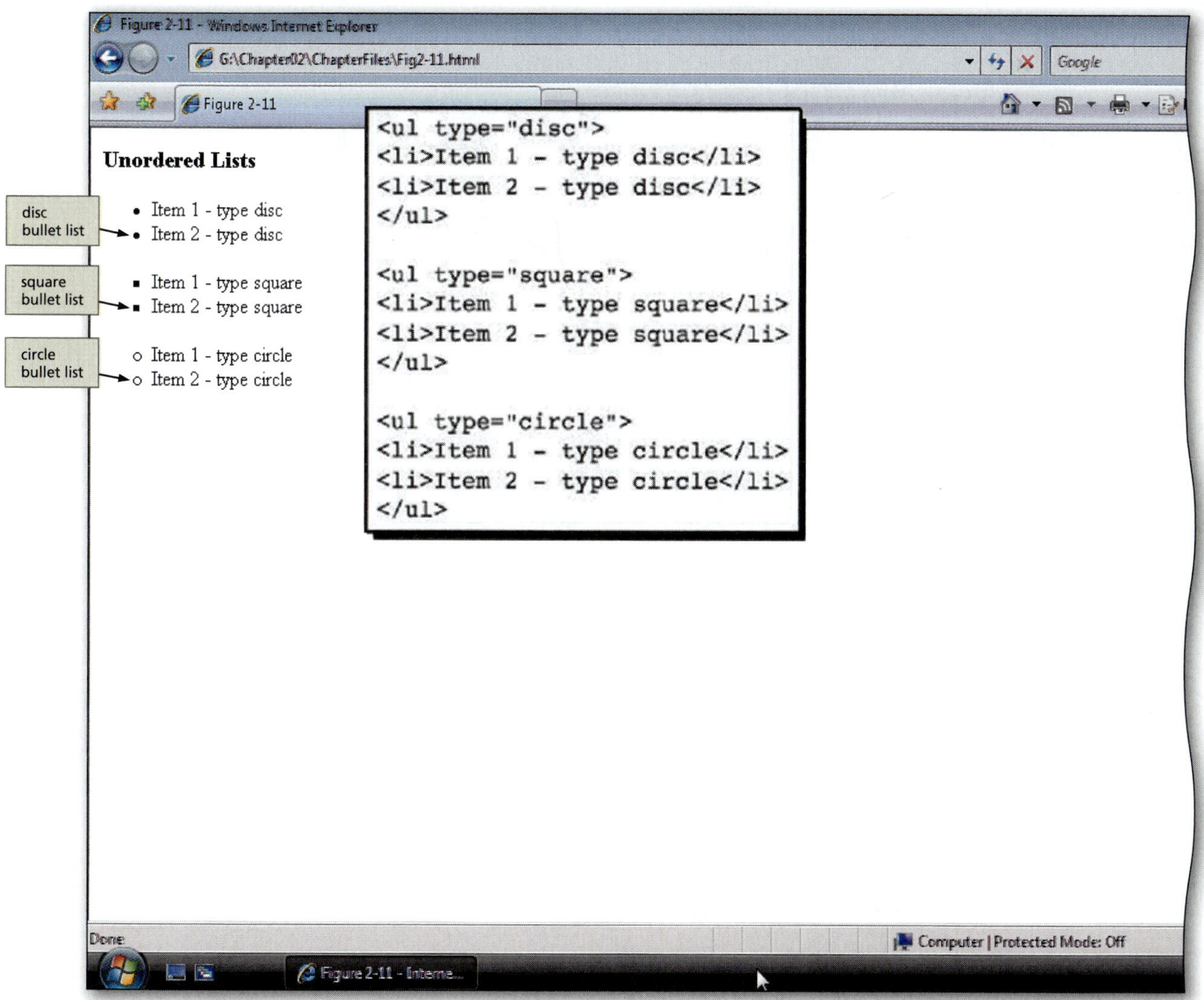

Figure 2–11

An **ordered list**, which also is called a **numbered list**, formats information in a series using numbers or letters. An ordered list works well to organize items where order must be emphasized, such as a series of steps. Figure 2–12 shows Web page text formatted as ordered, or numbered, lists and the HTML tags used to create the lists.

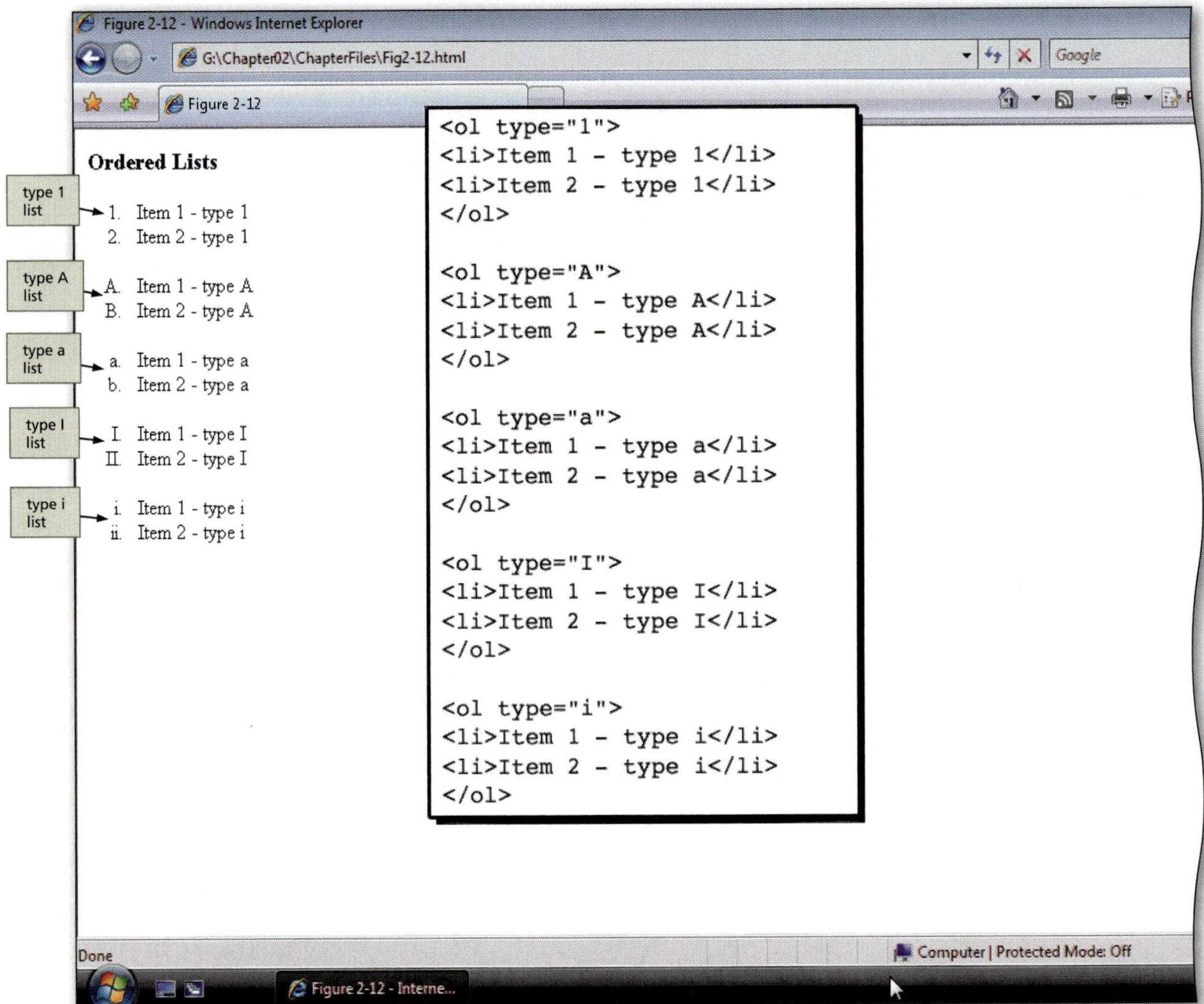

Figure 2–12

The **<ul>** and **</ul>** tags must be at the start and end of an unordered or bulleted list. The **<ol>** and **</ol>** tags are used at the start and end of an ordered or numbered list. Unordered and ordered lists have optional bullet and number types. As shown in Figure 2–11, an unordered list can use one of three different bullet options: disc, square, or circle. If no type is identified, the default, disc, is used. An ordered list can use numbers, letters, or Roman numerals, as shown in Figure 2–12. The default option is to use Arabic numbers, such as 1, 2, and 3.

After the <ul> or <ol> tag is entered to define the type of list, the **<li>** and **</li>** tags are used to define a list item in an ordered or unordered list.

To Create an Unordered List

To highlight the items needed at the Food Pantry, you will create a bulleted (unordered) list using the HTML tags and text shown in Table 2–4. Remember that each list item must start with <li> and end with </li>.

Table 2–4 Adding an Unordered List

Line	HTML Tag and Text
22	`<h2>The most needed nonperishable foods are:</h2>`
23	`<ul>`
24	`<li>Canned vegetables, fruit, meats, and fish</li>`
25	`<li>Pasta and tomato sauce</li>`
26	`<li>Cereal or oatmeal</li>`
27	`<li>Powdered milk</li>`
28	`</ul>`

The following step illustrates how to create an unordered, or bulleted, list using the default bullet style.

1

- With the insertion point on line 22, enter the HTML code as shown in Table 2–4. Press ENTER at the end of each line and use only one space after periods.
- Press the ENTER key after typing line 28 (Figure 2–13).

Q&A What types of bullets will this list contain?

Because the code does not specify a type attribute, the list uses the default disc bullet.

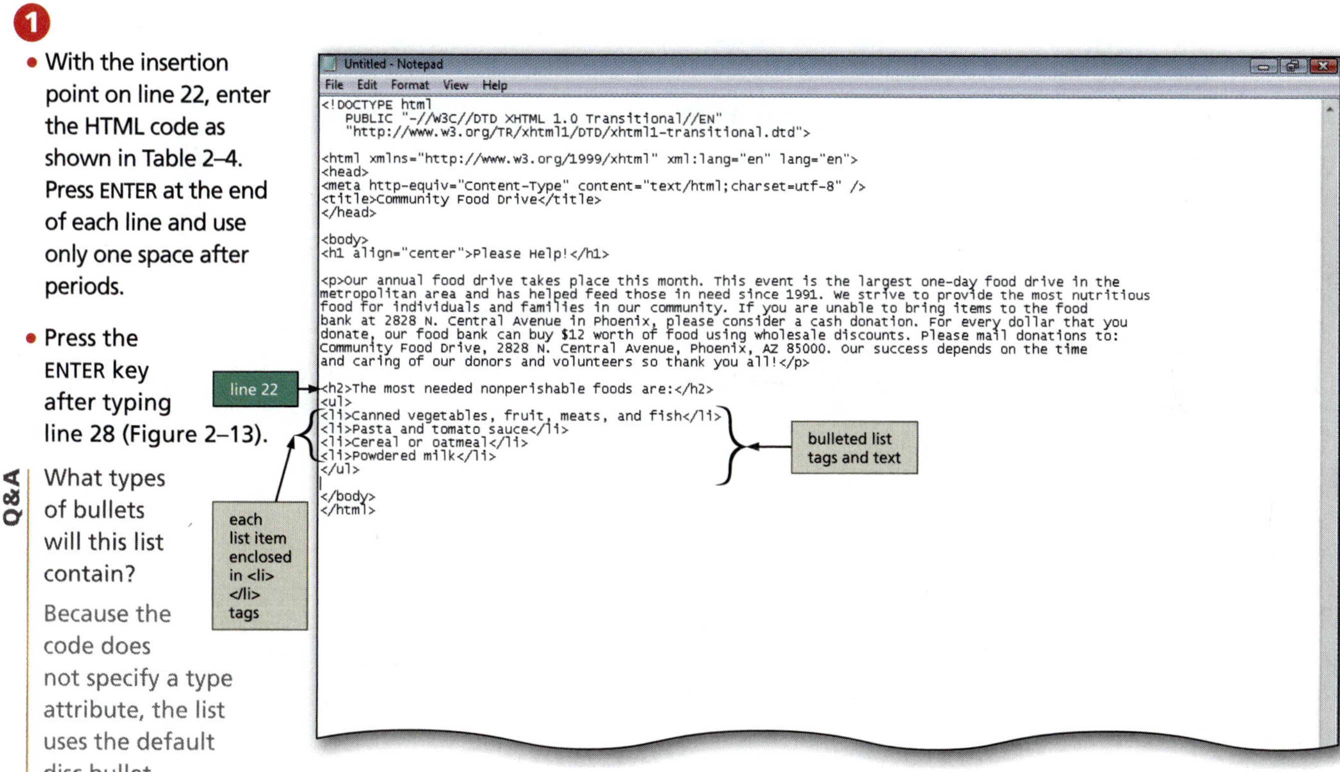

Figure 2–13

More About List Formats

If you use the <ul> or <ol> start tags without attributes, you will get the default bullet (disc) or number style (Arabic numerals). To change the default bullet or number type, the **type** attribute is entered within the <ol> or <ul> tags. The tags <ul type=" "> or <ol type=" "> create lists that use a specific bullet and number type, where the specified type is entered within the quotation marks.

By default, all numbered lists start with the number 1. You can change the starting number of an ordered list by using the **start** attribute. As an example, to begin a numbered list with the number "2" you would type:

```
<ol start="2">
```

as the tag. You also can use the **value** attribute in the <li> tag to indicate the value of the bullet. This is done by typing:

```
<li value="3">
```

as the tag. Both of these options are deprecated by the W3C, however. If you use these tags, you need to therefore use the transitional DOCTYPE.

In addition to ordered and unordered lists, there is a third kind of list, called a **definition list**, which offsets information in a dictionary-like style. Although they are used less often than unordered or ordered lists, definition lists are useful to create a glossary-like list of terms and definitions, as shown in Figure 2–14a. Figure 2–14b shows the HTML code used to create the definition list.

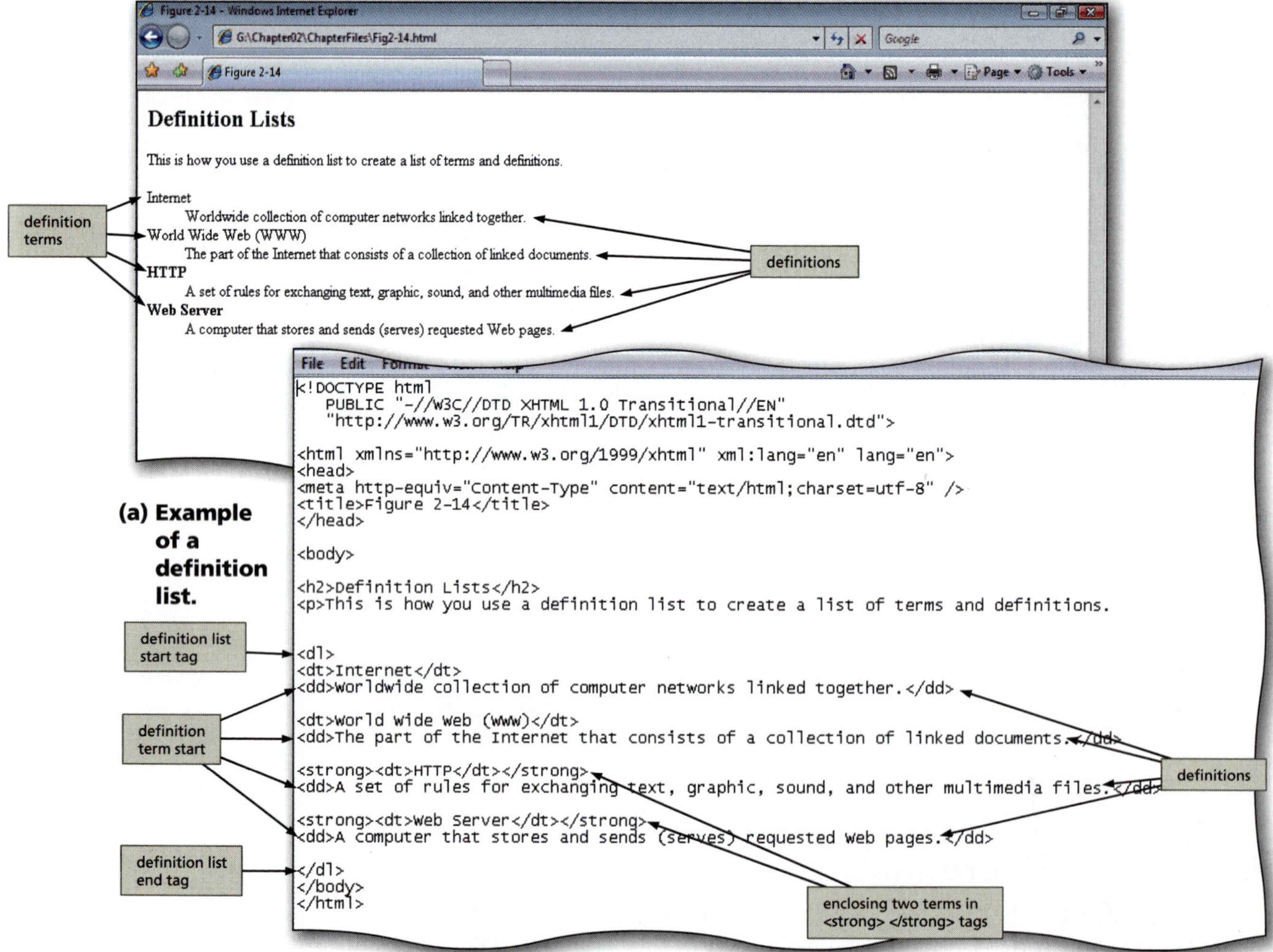

(a) Example of a definition list.

(b) HTML code used to create a definition list.

Figure 2–14

The syntax for definition lists is not as straightforward as the <ul>, <ol>, or <li> structure that is used in the unordered and ordered list styles. With definition lists, you use the **<dl>** and **</dl>** tags to start and end the list. A **<dt>** tag indicates a term, and a **<dd>** tag identifies the definition of that term by offsetting the definition from the term. Table 2–5 lists the elements of a definition list and their purposes.

Table 2–5 Definition List Elements and Purposes

Definition List Element	Purpose
<dl> </dl>	Start and end a definition list
<dt>	Identify a term
<dd>	Identify the definition of the term directly above

As shown in Figure 2–14, by default, the definition term is left-aligned on the line and the definition for each term is indented so it is easily distinguishable as the definition for the term above it. In order to more clearly identify the definition term, you may want to make the term bold as shown in the last two definitions (HTTP and Web Server) in Figure 2–14. You would do this by putting a <strong> tag before the <dt> tag and a </strong> after the </dt> tag.

Saving and Organizing HTML Files

Before you can see how your HTML file looks in a Web browser, you must save it. It also is important to save your HTML file for the following reasons:

- The document in memory will be lost if the computer is turned off or you lose electrical power while the text editor is open.
- If you run out of time before completing your project, you may finish your document at a future time without starting over.

HTML files must end with an extension of **.htm** or **.html**. HTML files with an extension of .html can be viewed on Web servers running an operating system that allows long file names. Web servers with Windows Server 2003, Windows XP, Windows 2000, Windows NT, or Macintosh operating systems all allow long file names. For Web servers that run an operating system that does not accept long file names, you need the .htm extension. In this book, all files are saved using the .html extension.

It is also important to organize your files in folders so that all files for a project or end-of-chapter exercise, including HTML code and graphical images, are saved in the same folder. We use a very simple folder structure with all the projects in this book. If you correctly downloaded the files from the Data Files for Students (see the inside back cover of this book), you will have the file structure required. When you initially save the fooddrive.html file, you will save it in the ChapterFiles subfolder of the Chapter02 folder. The graphical image used in Chapter 2, fooddrivelogo.gif, will be stored in that same folder—Chapter02\ChapterFiles. Because the chapter projects in this book are relatively simple and use few images, images and HTML code are stored in the same folder. In real-world applications, though, there may be hundreds or thousands of files in a Web site, and it is more appropriate to separate the HTML code and graphical images into different subfolders. You will learn more about organizing HTML files and folders in Chapter 3.

BTW

HTML File Names

HTML files have an extension of .html or .htm. Generally, the home page of a Web site is called index.html or index.htm. Sometimes the home page is called default.html or default.htm. Many service providers default to one of these file names as the first page of a Web site to display. Check with the service provider to find out which name they use.

Plan Ahead

Determine where to save the Web page.

When saving a Web page, you must decide which storage medium to use.

- If you always work on the same computer and have no need to transport your projects to a different location, then your computer's hard drive will suffice as a storage location. It is a good idea, however, to save a backup copy of your projects on a separate medium in case the file becomes corrupted or the computer's hard disk fails.
- If you plan to work on your projects in various locations or on multiple computers, then you should save your projects on a portable medium, such as a USB flash drive or CD. The projects in this book use a USB flash drive, which saves files quickly and reliably and can be reused. CDs are easily portable and serve as good backups for the final versions of projects because they generally can save files only one time.

To Save an HTML File

You have performed many steps in creating this project and do not want to risk losing the work you have done so far. Also, to view HTML in a browser, you must save the file. The following steps show how to save an HTML file.

1

- With a USB flash drive connected to one of the computer's USB ports, click File on the Notepad menu bar (Figure 2–15).

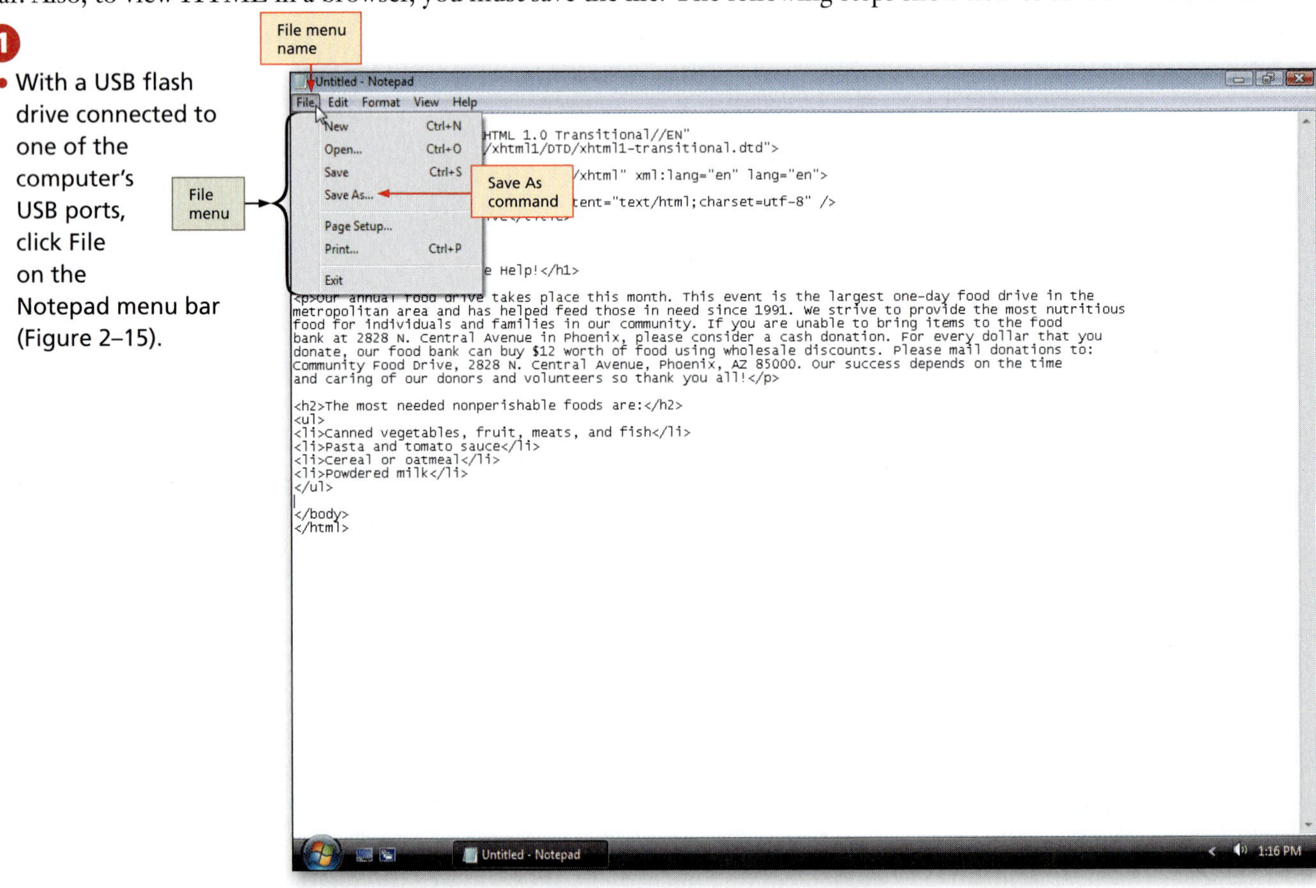

Figure 2–15

- Click Save As on the File menu to display the Save As dialog box (Figure 2–16).
- If the Navigation pane is not displayed in the Save As dialog box, click the Browse Folders button to expand the dialog box.
- If a Folders list is displayed below the Folders button, click the Folders button to remove the Folders list.

Q&A

Do I have to save to a USB flash drive?

No. You can save to any device or folder. A folder is a specific location on a storage medium. Use the same process, but select your device or folder.

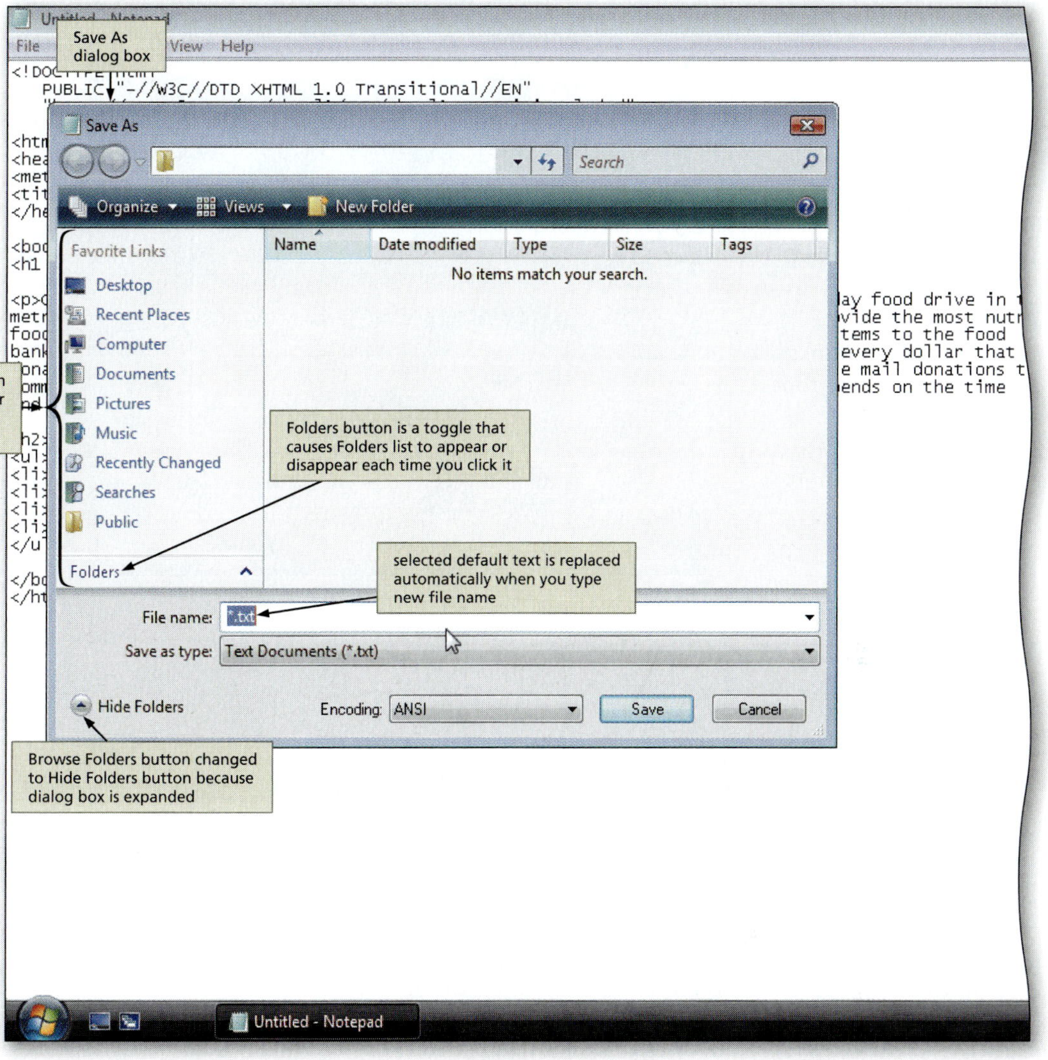

Figure 2–16

BTW

Saving Your File

It is a good idea to save your html file periodically as you are working to avoid the risk of losing your work completed thus far. You could get into the habit of saving your file after any large addition (i.e., a paragraph) of information. You might also want to save the file after typing in several HTML tags that would be difficult to redo.

- Type `fooddrive.html` in the File name text box to change the file name. Do not press ENTER after typing the file name.
- If Computer is not displayed in the Favorite Links section, drag the top or bottom edge of the Save As dialog box until Computer is displayed.
- Click Computer in the Favorite Links section to display a list of available drives (Figure 2–17).
- If necessary, scroll until UDISK 2.0 (G:) appears in the list of available drives.

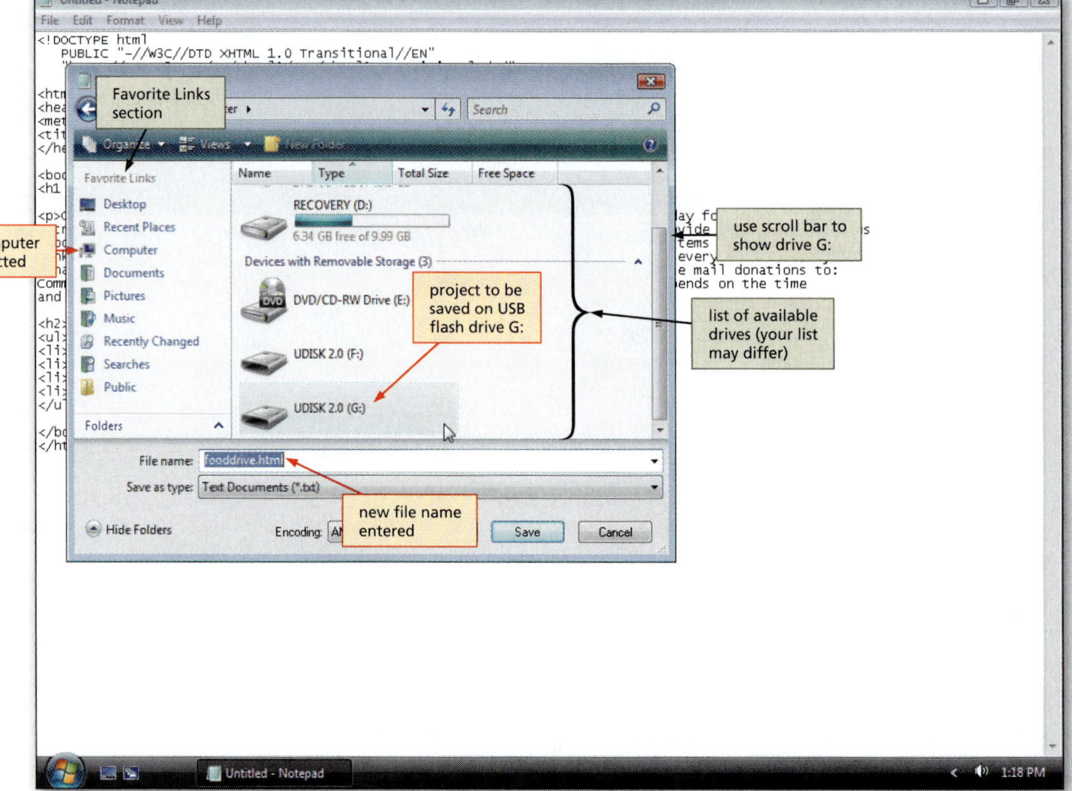

Figure 2–17

Q&A Why is my list of files, folders, and drives arranged and named differently from those shown in the figure?

Your computer's configuration determines how the list of files and folders is displayed and how drives are named. You can change the save location by clicking shortcuts on the **My Places bar**.

Q&A How do I know the drive and folder in which my file will be saved?

Notepad displays a list of available drives and folders. You then select the drive and/or folder into which you want to save the file.

4

- Double-click UDISK 2.0 (G:) in the Computer list to select the USB flash drive, drive G in this case, as the new save location.

Q&A What if my USB flash drive has a different name or letter?

It is likely that your USB flash drive will have a different name and drive letter and be connected to a different port. Verify that the device in your Computer list is correct.

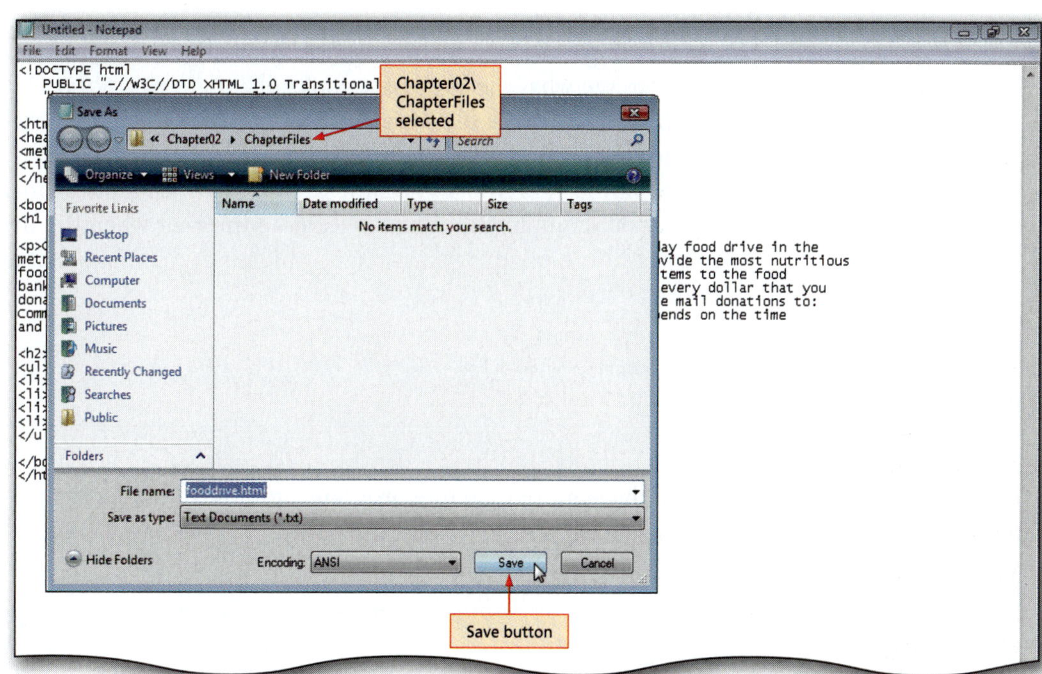

Figure 2–18

- If necessary, open the Chapter02\ChapterFiles folder (Figure 2–18).

Q&A What if my USB flash drive does not have a folder named Chapter02\ChapterFiles?

If you followed the steps to download the chapter files from the Data Files for Students, you should have a folder named Chapter02\ChapterFiles. If you do not, check with your instructor.

5

- Click the Save button in the Save As dialog box to save the file on the USB flash drive with the name fooddrive.html (Figure 2–19).

Q&A Is my file only on the USB drive now?

Although the HTML file is saved on a USB drive, it also remains in memory and is displayed on the screen (Figure 2–19). Notepad displays the new file name on the title bar.

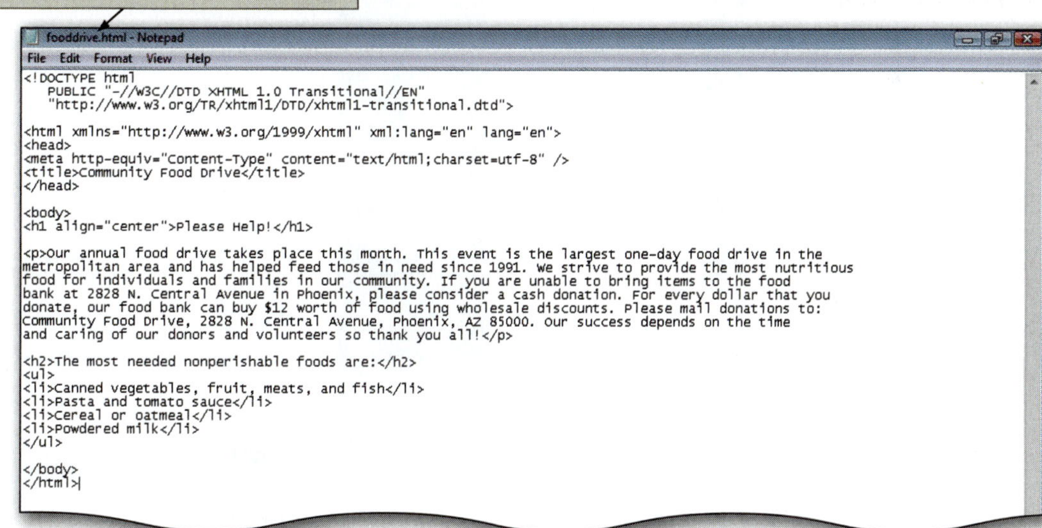

Figure 2–19

Other Ways

1. Press CTRL+S, type the file name, click Computer, select drive or folder, click Save button

Using a Browser to View a Web Page

After entering code in the HTML file and saving it, you should view the Web page in a browser to see what the Web page looks like up to this point. The HTML file is displayed in the browser as if the file were available on the Web. In general, viewing the Web page periodically during development is good coding practice, because it allows you to see the effect of various HTML tags on the text and to check for errors in your HTML file.

If your computer is connected to the Internet when the browser window opens, it displays a **home page**, or **start page**, which is a Web page that appears each time Internet Explorer starts.

To Start a Browser

With the HTML file saved on the USB drive, the next step is to view the Web page using a browser. Because Windows is **multitasking**, you can have more than one program running at a time, such as Notepad and your browser. The following steps illustrate how to start a browser to view a Web page.

1

- Click the Start button on the Windows Vista taskbar to display the Start menu.
- Click the Internet icon in the pinned items list on the Start menu to start Internet Explorer (Figure 2–20).

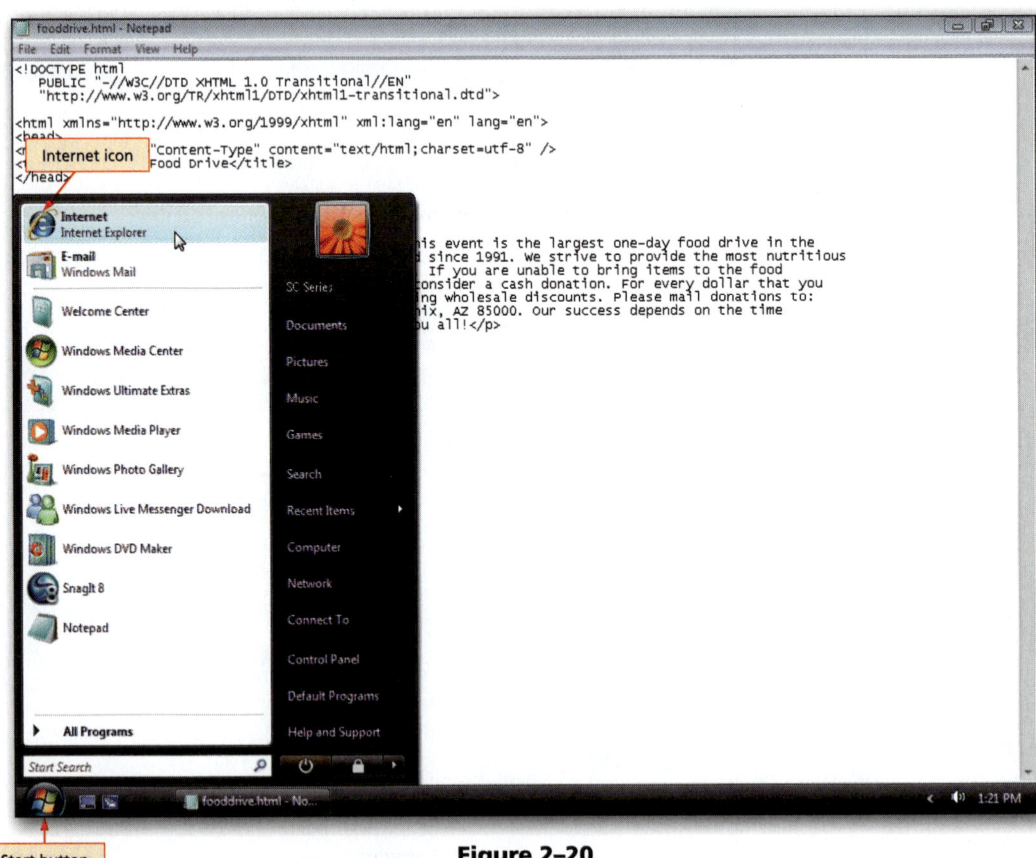

Figure 2–20

2

- If necessary, click the Maximize button to maximize the browser window (Figure 2–21).

Q&A Why does my browser display a different window?

Because it is possible to customize browser settings to change the Web page that appears as the home page, the home page that is displayed by your browser may be different. Schools and organizations often set a main page on their Web sites as the home page for browsers installed on lab or office computers.

Figure 2–21

Other Ways
1. Click Start, All Programs, Internet Explorer 2. Double-click Internet icon on desktop, if one is present 3. Click Internet icon on Quick Launch Toolbar at bottom of screen

BTW

Developing Web Pages for Multiple Browsers

When developing Web pages, you must consider the types of browsers visitors will use, including Internet Explorer and Mozilla Firefox for Windows or Safari or Internet Explorer fohr Mac OS. The Apple Web site provides suggestions for creating Web pages that will work in a wide range of browsers. Part of thorough testing includes bringing your Web pages up in different versions of different browsers.

To View a Web Page in a Browser

A browser allows you to open a Web file located on your computer and have full browsing capabilities, as if the Web page were stored on a Web server and made available on the Web. The following steps use this technique to view the HTML file, fooddrive.html, in a browser.

1

- Click the Address bar to select the URL on the Address bar.
- Type `g:\Chapter02\ChapterFiles\fooddrive.html` to display the new URL on the Address bar (Figure 2–22). The Web page does not display until you press the ENTER key as shown in the next step.

Q&A How can I correct the URL on the Address bar?

The URL is displayed on the Address bar. If you type an incorrect letter or symbol on the Address bar and notice the error before moving to the next step, use the BACKSPACE key to erase all the characters back to and including the one that is incorrect and then continue typing.

Figure 2–22

Q&A What if my file is in a different location?

You can type in the path to your file in the Address bar, or browse to your file as shown in Other Ways.

2

- Press the ENTER key to display the fooddrive.html page as if it were available on the Web (Figure 2–23).

Q&A What if I get a warning from Internet Explorer (IE) that says, "Internet Explorer needs to open a new window to display this webpage?"

If this happens, you should click the OK button to continue. You then will see your Web page displayed in another IE window.

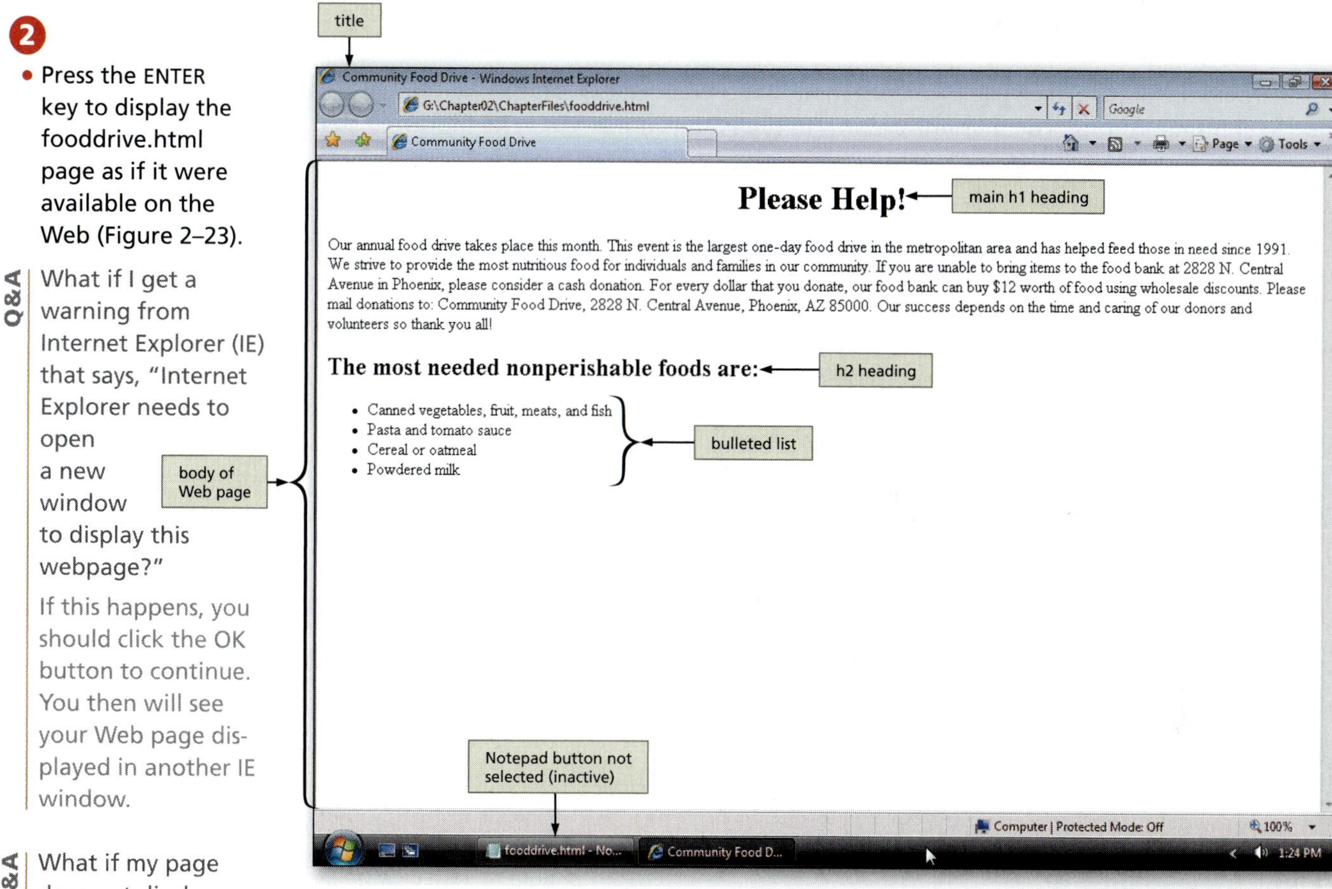

Figure 2–23

Q&A What if my page does not display correctly?

Check your fooddrive.html carefully against Figure 2–19 to make sure you have not made any typing errors or left anything out. Correct the errors, resave the file, and try again.

Other Ways

1. In Windows Explorer, double-click HTML file name to open in default browser
2. In Windows Explorer, right-click HTML file name, click Open With, click browser name
3. Click Tools, Menu Bar if menu is not displayed; on Menu bar click File, Open and browse to desired file

BTW

User Interface Design

The user interface design is a very important aspect of a Web site. If a site is designed poorly, users may be unable to find the desired information or complethe a task, which makes the Web site ineffective. There are many good Web sites that discuss Web design principles.

To Activate Notepad

After viewing the Web page, you can modify the Web page by adding additional tags or text to the HTML file. To continue editing, you first must return to the Notepad window. The following step illustrates how to activate Notepad.

- Click the fooddrive.html - Notepad button on the taskbar to maximize Notepad and make it the active window (Figure 2–24).

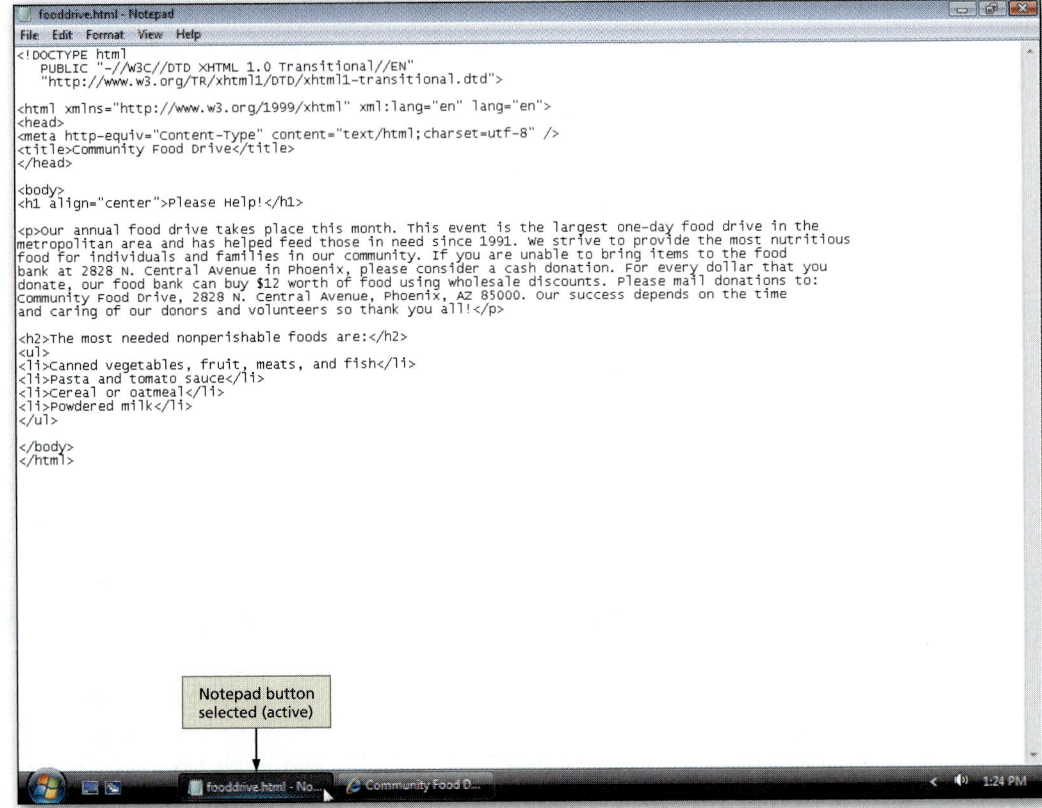

Figure 2–24

Plan Ahead

Find appropriate graphical images. **To use graphical images, also called graphics, on a Web page, the image must be stored digitally in a file. Files containing graphical images are available from a variety of sources:**

- Microsoft has free digital images on the Web for use in a document. Other Web sites also have images available, some of which are free, while others require a fee.
- You can take a picture with a digital camera and **download** it, which is the process of copying the digital picture from the camera to your computer.
- With a scanner, you can convert a printed picture, drawing, or diagram to a digital file.

If you receive a picture from a source other than yourself, do not use the file until you are certain it does not contain a virus. A **virus** is a computer program that can damage files and programs on your computer. Use an antivirus program to verify that any files you use are virus free.

Establish where to position and how to format the graphical image. The content, size, shape, position, and format of a graphic should capture the interest of passersby, enticing them to stop and read the Web page. Often, the graphic is the center of attraction and visually the largest element on a page. If you use colors in the graphical image, be sure they are part of the Web page's color scheme.

(continued)

Plan Ahead

(continued)

Identify the width and height of the image. The width and height of an image should always be identified in the <img> tag. These dimensions are used by the browser to determine the size to display the image. If you do not identify those attributes, the browser has to determine the size. This slows the process down for the browser.

Provide alternate text for the image. Alternate text should always be used for each image. This text is especially useful to vision-impaired users who use a screen reader, which translates information on a computer screen into audio output. The length of the alternate text should be reasonable.

Improving the Appearance of Your Web Page

One goal in Web page development is to create a Web page that is visually appealing and maintains the interest of the visitors. The Web page developed thus far in the chapter is functional, but lacks visual appeal. The following steps illustrate how to improve the appearance of the Web page from the one shown in Figure 2–25a to the one shown in Figure 2–25b by adding an image, adding a background color, and adding a horizontal rule.

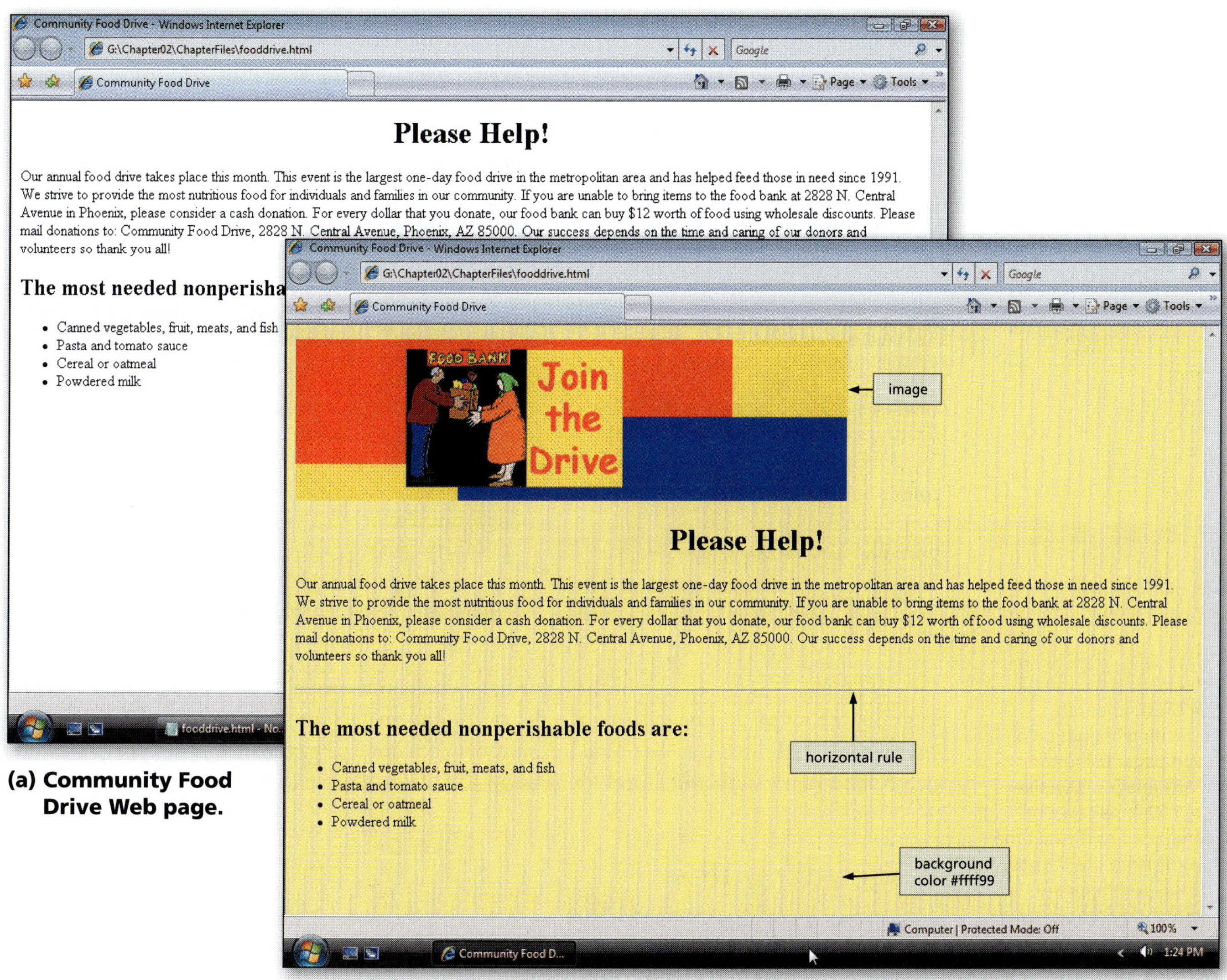

(a) Community Food Drive Web page.

(b) Community Food Drive Web page formatted to improve appearance.

Figure 2–25

Web Page Images

BTW

Images
Images on Web pages are viewed in a variety of environments, including slow connections to the Internet and slower computers. Optimizing your images is important to increase the speed of download for all of your Web page visitors. Search the Web for more information on image optimization.

Images are used in many ways to enhance the look of a Web page and make it more interesting and colorful. Images can be used to add background color, to help organize a Web page, to help clarify a point being made in the text, or to serve as links to other Web pages. Images also are often used to break up Web page sections (such as with a horizontal rule) or as directional elements that allow a visitor to navigate a Web site.

Image Types

Web pages use three types of files as images: GIF, JPEG, and PNG (Table 2–6). **Graphics Interchange Format** (**GIF**) files have an extension of .gif. A graphic image saved as a GIF (pronounced *jiff* or *giff*) uses compression techniques, called LZW compression, to make it smaller for download on the Web. Standard (or noninterlaced) GIF images are displayed one line at a time when loading. Interlaced GIF images load all at once, starting with a blurry look and becoming sharper as they load. Using interlaced GIFs for large images is a good technique, because a Web page visitor can see a blurred outline of the image as it loads.

Joint Photographic Experts Group (**JPEG**) files have an extension of .jpg, .jpe, or .jpeg. A JPEG (pronounced *JAY-peg*) is a graphic image saved using a compression technique other than LZW. JPEG files often are used for more complex images, such as photographs, because the JPEG file format supports more colors and resolutions than the other file types.

A third type of image file is **Portable Network Graphics** (**PNG**), which has a .png or .ping extension. The PNG (pronounced *ping*) format also is a compressed file format that supports multiple colors and resolutions. The World Wide Web Consortium developed the PNG format as a graphics standard and patent-free alternative to the GIF format. Most newer browsers support PNG images.

Table 2–6 Image Types and Uses

Image Type	Use
Graphics Interchange Format (GIF)	• Use for images with few colors (< 256) • Allows for transparent backgrounds
Joint Photographic Experts Group (JPEG)	• Use for images with many colors (> 256), such as photographs
Portable Network Graphics (PNG)	• Newest format for images • Use for all types of images • Allows for variation in transparency

BTW

Overusing Images
Be cautious about overusing images on a Web page. Using too many images may give your Web page a cluttered look or distract the visitor from the purpose of the Web page. An image should have a purpose, such as to convey content, visually organize a page, provide a hyperlink, or serve another function.

If an image is not in one of these formats, you can use a paint or graphics-editing program to convert an image to a .gif, .jpg, or .png format. Some paint programs even allow you to save a GIF image as interlaced. A number of paint and graphics-editing programs, such Adobe Photoshop and Corel Paint Shop Pro, are available in the marketplace today.

Image Attributes

You can enhance HTML tags by using attributes. **Attributes** define additional characteristics for the HTML tag. For instance, you should use the width and height attributes for all <img> tags. Table 2–7 lists the attributes that can be used with the <img> tag. In this chapter, the src and alt attributes are used in the <img> tag. Image attributes will be explained in detail because they are used in later chapters.

Table 2–7 Image Attributes

Attribute	Function
align	• Controls alignment • Can be set to bottom, middle, top, left, or right
alt	• Alternative text to display when an image is being loaded • Especially useful for screen readers, which translate information on a computer screen into audio output • Should be a brief representation of the purpose of the image • Generally should stick to 50 characters or fewer
border	• Defines the border width
height	• Defines the height of the image • Improves loading time
hspace	• Defines the horizontal space that separates the image from the text
src	• Defines the URL of the image to be loaded
vspace	• Defines the vertical space that separates the image from the text
width	• Defines the width of the image • Improves loading time

To Add an Image

In the early days when the Web was used mostly by researchers needing to share information with each other, having purely functional, text-only Web pages was the norm. Today, Web page visitors are used to a more graphically-oriented world, and have come to expect Web pages to use images that provide visual interest. The following step illustrates how to add an image to a Web page by entering an <img> tag in the HTML file.

1

- Click after the > symbol in <body> on line 11 and then press the ENTER key.
- Type `<img src="fooddrivelogo.gif" width="601" height="170" alt="Food Drive logo" />` and press ENTER to insert the image tag for the logo (Figure 2–26).

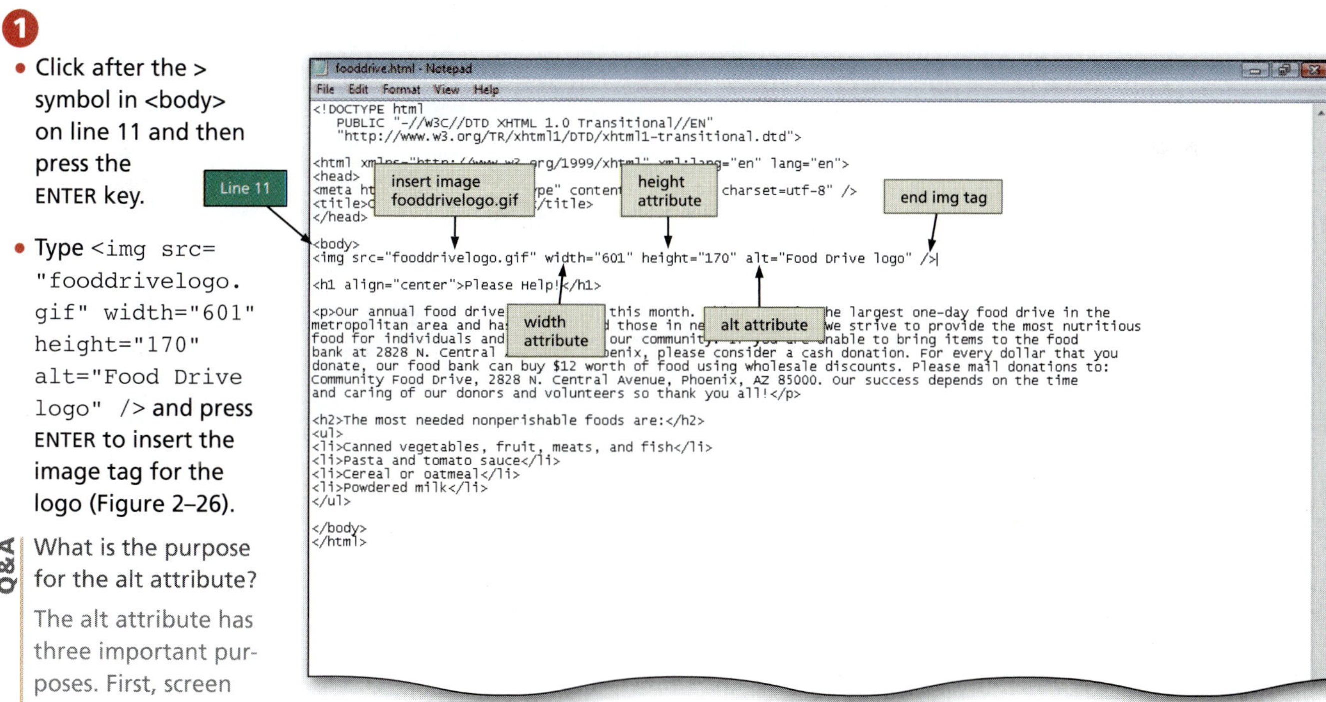

Figure 2–26

Q&A What is the purpose for the alt attribute?

The alt attribute has three important purposes. First, screen readers used by visually impaired users read the alternate text out loud. Second, the alternate text displays while the image is being loaded. Finally, the alt tag is required for XHTML compliance.

Plan Ahead

Add background color. Web developers often use background colors to call attention to a Web page. The color selected should coordinate with the images selected for the page. It also should allow the Web page text to be read easily. Some colors, such as dark colors, may not be appropriate because the default black text can not be displayed effectively on a dark background.

Insert a horizontal rule. It is useful to use a horizontal rule to break text up on a Web page. A horizontal rule is used as a divider for a page to separate text sections.

Other Visual Enhancements

BTW

Colors
Figure 2–27 does not list all possible Web colors. Many other colors are available that you can use for Web page backgrounds or text fonts. For more information about colors, see Appendix B or search the Web for browser colors.

One way to help capture a Web page visitor's attention is to use color. Many colors are available for use as a Web page background, text, or link. Figure 2–27 shows colors often used on Web pages, with the corresponding six-digit number codes. The six-digit number codes can be used to specify a color for a background, text, or links. The Community Food Drive Web page uses a pale yellow color (#ffff99) for the background.

COLORS IN HEX

Here is a table of common colors with their hexadecimal equivalents. Use the codes to define the desired color for the background, text, or links.

#ffc6a5	#ff9473	#ff6342	#ff3118	#ff0000	#d60000	#ad0000	#840000	#630000
#ffe7c6	#ffce9c	#ffb573	#ff9c4a	#ff8429	#d66321	#ad4a18	#844d18	#632910
#ffffc6	#ffff9c	#ffff6b	#ffff42	#ffff10	#d6c610	#ad9410	#847308	#635208
#f7ffce	#efef ad	#e7f784	#def763	#d6ef39	#b5bd31	#8c9429	#6b6b21	#524a18
#de93bd	#c6ef8c	#adde63	#94d639	#7bc618	#639c18	#527b10	#425a10	#314208
#ceefbd	#a5de94	#7bc66b	#52b552	#299c39	#218429	#186321	#184a18	#103910
#c6e7de	#94d6ce	#63bdb5	#31ada5	#089494	#087b7b	#006363	#004a4a	#003139
#c6eff7	#94d6e7	#63c6de	#31b5d6	#00a5c6	#0084a5	#006b84	#005263	#00394a
#bdc6de	#949cce	#6373b5	#3152a5	#083194	#082984	#08296b	#08215a	#00184a
#c6b5de	#9c7bbd	#7b52a5	#522994	#31007b	#29006b	#21005a	#21004a	#180042
#debdde	#ce84c6	#b552ad	#9c2994	#8c007b	#730063	#5a0052	#4a0042	#390031
#f7bdde	#e78cc6	#de5aad	#d63194	#ce007b	#a50063	#840052	#6b0042	#520031
#ffffff	#e0e0e0	#bfbfbf	#a1a1a1	#808080	#616161	#404040	#212121	#000000

THE SIXTEEN PREDEFINED COLORS

(Because these colors belong to the RGB spectrum, they will look a bit different on-screen.)

silver	gray	maroon	green	navy	purple	olive	teal
white	black	red	lime	blue	magenta	yellow	cyan

Figure 2–27

BTW

Browser-Safe Colors
Web developers used to have to make sure that they used browser-safe colors (Appendix B). The trend for monitors today is to display "true color" which means that any of 16 million colors can be displayed on the monitor. So few people use 8-bit monitors anymore that you generally do not have to limit yourself to browser-safe colors.

The color codes and names shown in Figure 2–27 can be used for background, text, and link colors. The bgcolor attribute is used in the <body> tag to specify the background color for the Web page. In later chapters, the text and link attributes are used in the <body> tag to change colors for those elements.

Another way to visually enhance the Web page is to add horizontal rules. As discussed earlier in the chapter, horizontal rules are lines that act as dividers on a Web page to provide a visual separation of sections on the page. You can use an inline image to add a horizontal rule, or you can use the horizontal rule tag (<hr />) to add a simple horizontal rule, as shown in the following steps. Figure 2–28 shows examples of a variety of horizontal rules and the HTML code used to add them. The default horizontal rule is shown in the first line of the page. Dimension is added to a horizontal rule by increasing the number of pixels that are displayed.

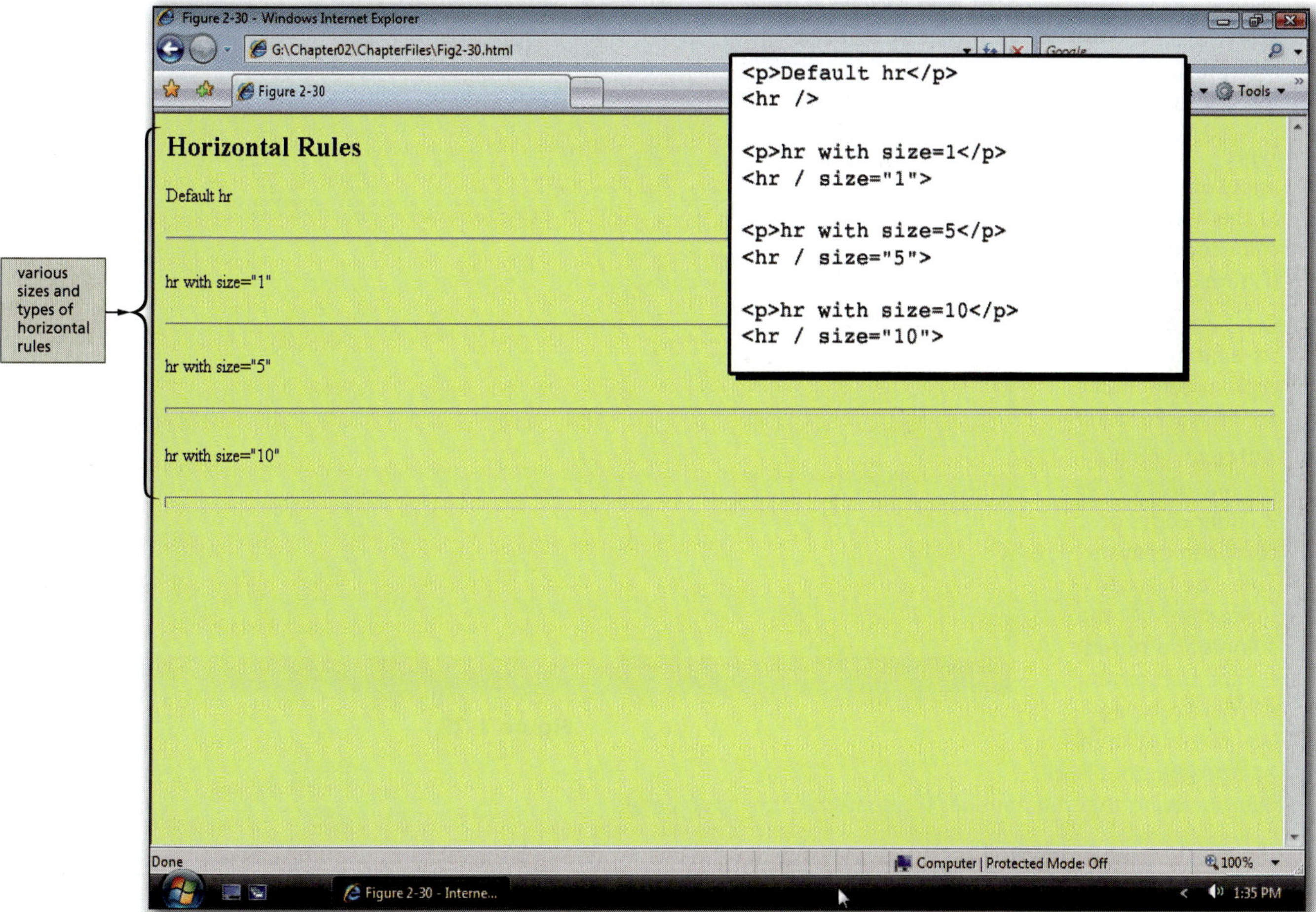

Figure 2–28 Examples of horizontal rules.

To Add a Background Color

To change the background color on a Web page, the bgcolor attribute must be added in the <body> tag of the HTML file. The **bgcolor** attribute lets you change the background color of the Web page. The following step shows how to add a background color using the bgcolor attribute.

1

- Click after the "y" but before the closing bracket in <body> on line 11 and then press the SPACEBAR.
- Type `bgcolor="#ffff99"` as the background color code (Figure 2–29).

Q&A Can I use any six-digit number code or color name for my background?

Although you may use any of the number codes or color names available, you have to make sure that the color is appropriate for the background of your Web page. You do not want a background that is so overpowering that it diminishes the content of the Web page.

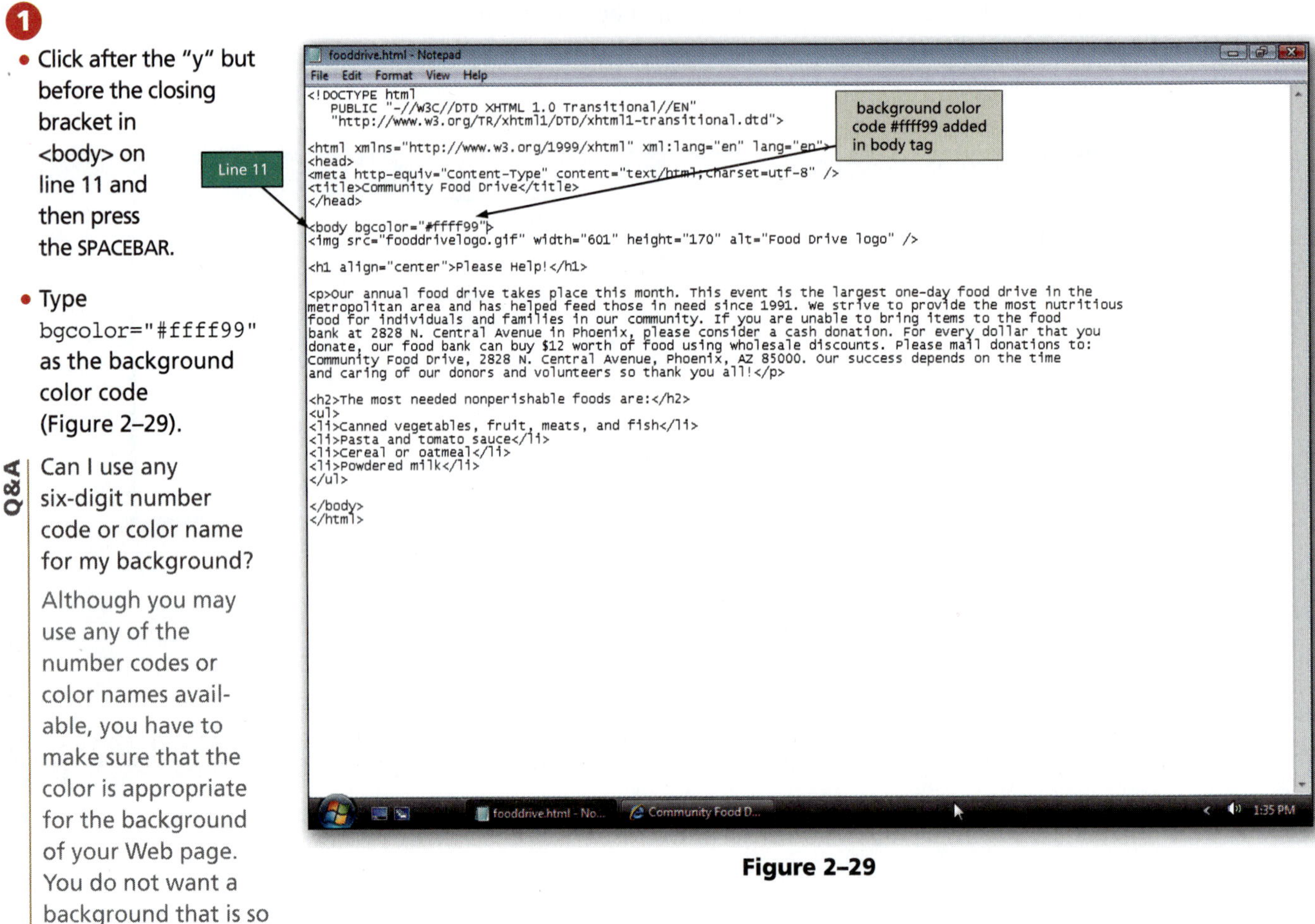

Figure 2–29

To Add a Horizontal Rule

The following step illustrates how to add a horizontal rule to a Web page.

1

- Click the blank line 23 and then press the ENTER key.
- Type <hr /> as the HTML tag and then press the ENTER key.
- Click File on the menu bar and then click Save (Figure 2–30).

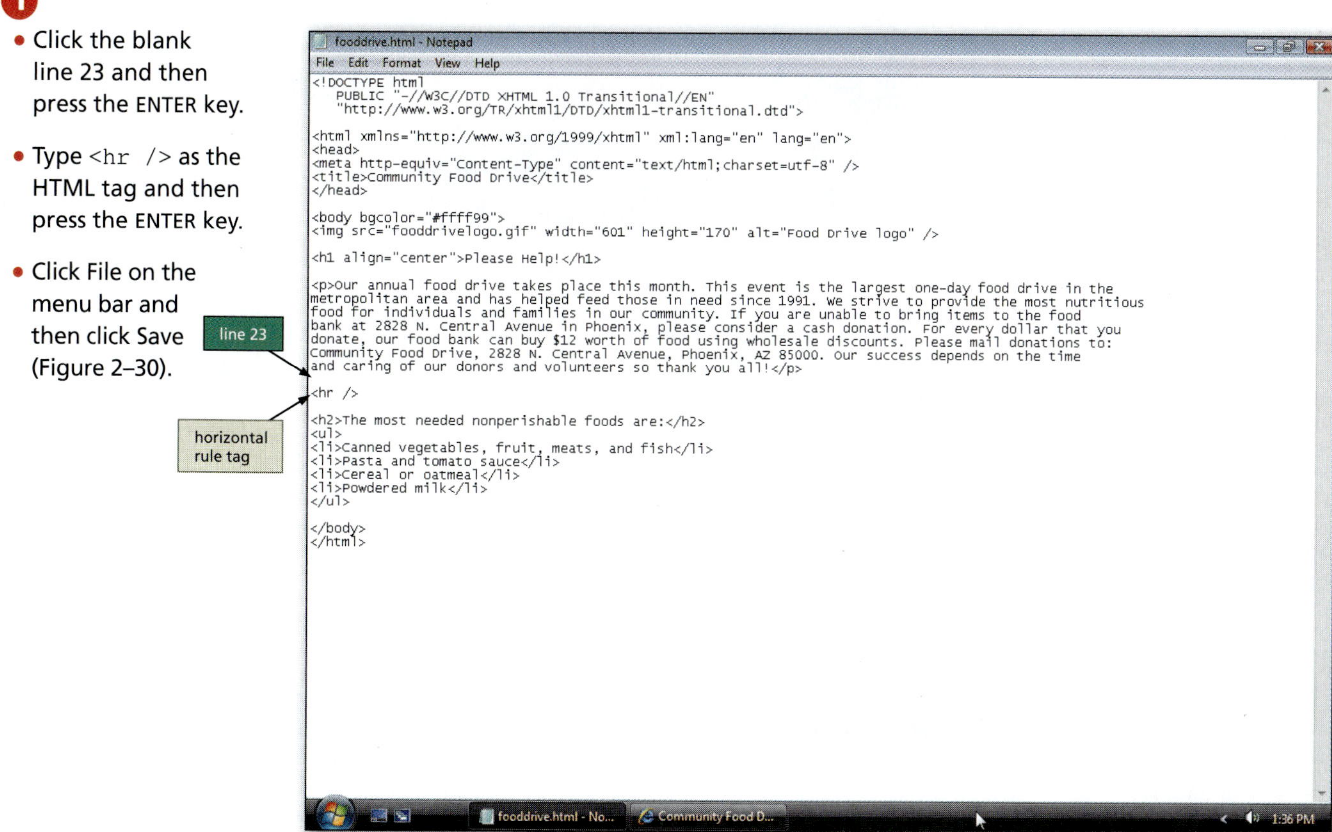

Figure 2–30

To Refresh the View in a Browser

As you continue developing the HTML file in Notepad, it is a good idea to view the file in your browser as you make modifications. Be sure to click the Refresh button when viewing the modified Web page in the browser, to ensure the latest version of the Web page is displayed. The step on the next page shows how to refresh the view of a Web page in a browser in order to view the modified Web page.

1

- Close the Notepad window.
- If necessary, click the Community Food Drive Home Page button on the taskbar to display the home page.
- Click the Refresh button on the Standard toolbar to display the modified Web page (Figure 2–31).

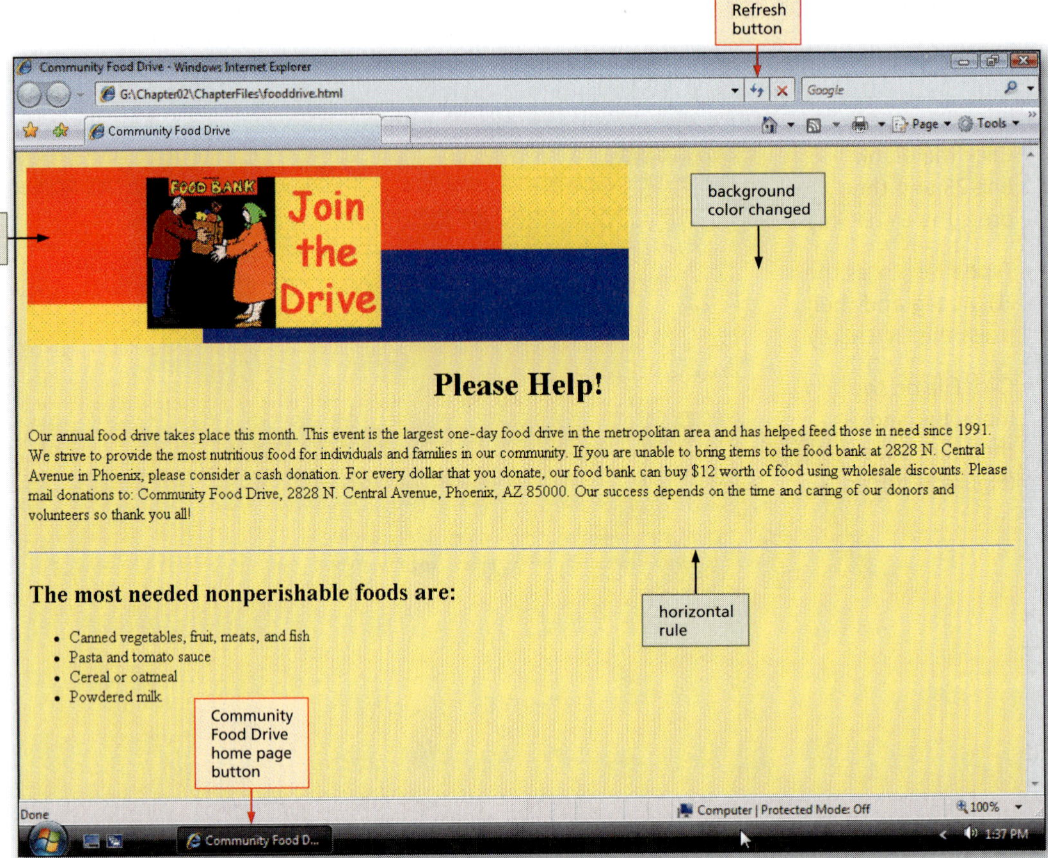

Figure 2–31

Other Ways

1. In Internet Explorer, press F5 to refresh the page

BTW

HTML and XHTML Tags
The Web has excellent sources that list HTML and XHTML tags. For more about HTML and XHTML, search for information on the Web.

Validating and Viewing HTML Code

In Chapter 1, you read about validating your HTML code. Many validation services are available on the Web that can be used to assure that your HTML code follows standards. This should always be a part of your Web page testing. The validation service used in this book is the W3C Markup Validation Service (validator.w3.org). The XHTML validator looks at the DOCTYPE statement to see which version of HTML or XHTML you are using, and then checks to see if the code is valid for that version. In this chapter, the project uses Transitional code.

If validation detects an error in your HTML code, you see the warning “This page is not Valid XHTML 1.0 Transitional!” in the header bar (Figure 2–32a). You also see in the Result area of the validation that the code failed validation and the number of errors that you have.

It is important to note that one error can result in more errors. As an example, the <hr /> tag in the fooddrive.html file was changed to <hr> to show code with an error (Figure 2–32a). You can scroll down the page or click the Jump To: Validation Output link to see detailed comments on each error. Figure 2–32b shows that in this case, one initial error resulted in a total of four errors.

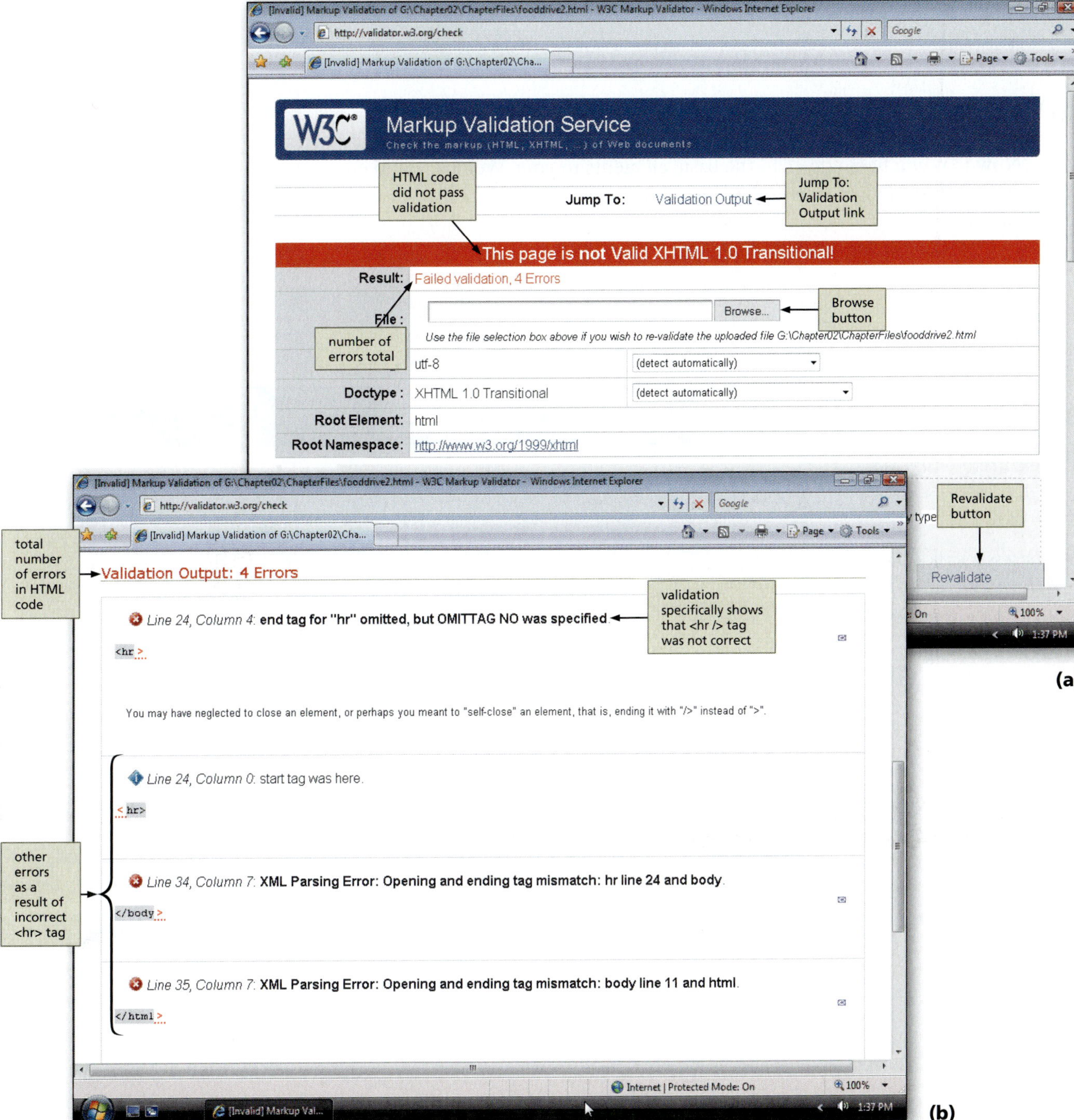

Figure 2–32

Source code is the code or instructions used to create a Web page or program. For a Web page, the source code is the HTML code, which then is translated by a browser into a graphical Web page. You can view the HTML source code for any Web page from within your browser. This feature allows you to check your own HTML source code, as well as to see the HTML code other developers used to create their Web pages. If a feature on a Web page is appropriate or appealing for your Web page, you can view the source to understand the HTML required to add that feature and then copy sections of the HTML code to put on your own Web pages.

To Validate HTML Code

Now that you have added all the basic elements to your Web page and enhanced it with images, color, and rules, you need to validate your code. The following steps illustrate how to validate your HTML code using the W3C validator.

1

- Click the Address bar on the browser to highlight the current URL.
- Type `validator.w3.org` to replace the current entry then press the ENTER key.
- If necessary, click OK if the browser asks to open a new window.
- Click the Validate by File Upload tab (Figure 2–33).

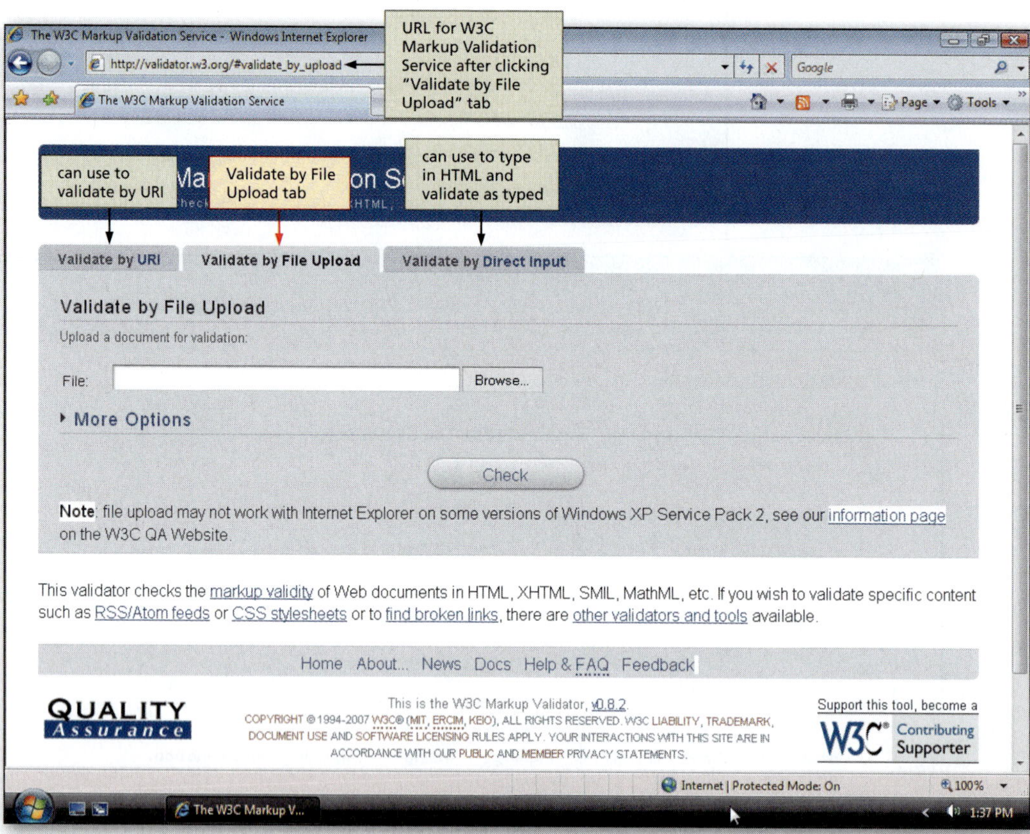

Figure 2–33

- Click the Browse button.
- Locate the fooddrive.html file on your storage device and then click the file name.
- Click the Open button on the Choose file dialog box and the file name will be inserted into the File box as shown in Figure 2–34.

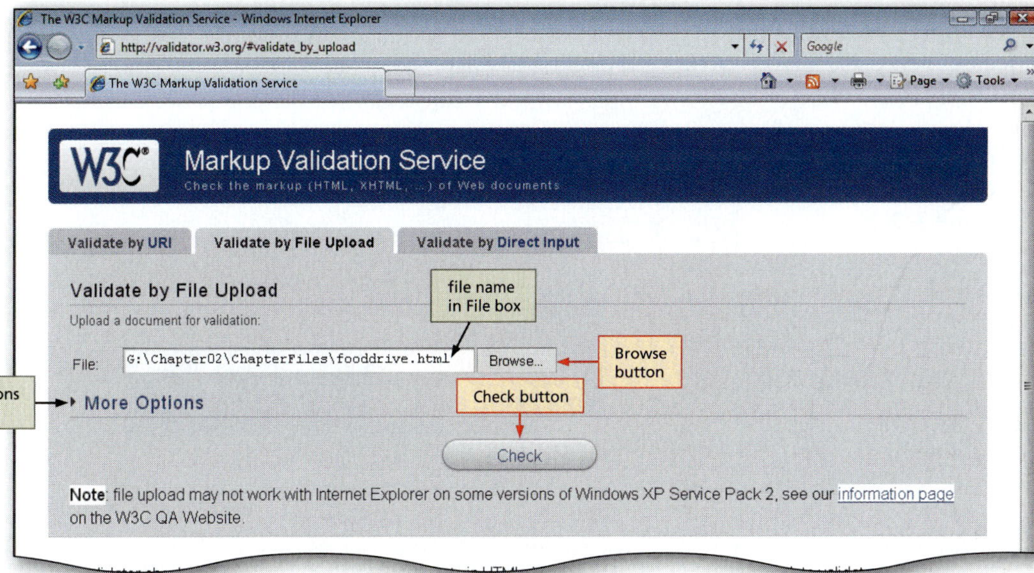

Figure 2–34

- Click the Check button (Figure 2–34). The resulting validation should be displayed as shown in Figure 2–35.
- Return to the Community Food Drive Web page, either by clicking the Back button on your browser or by clicking the Community Food Drive button in the task bar.

Q&A How do I know if my HTML code is valid?

In the Result area, you should see the words "Passed validation."

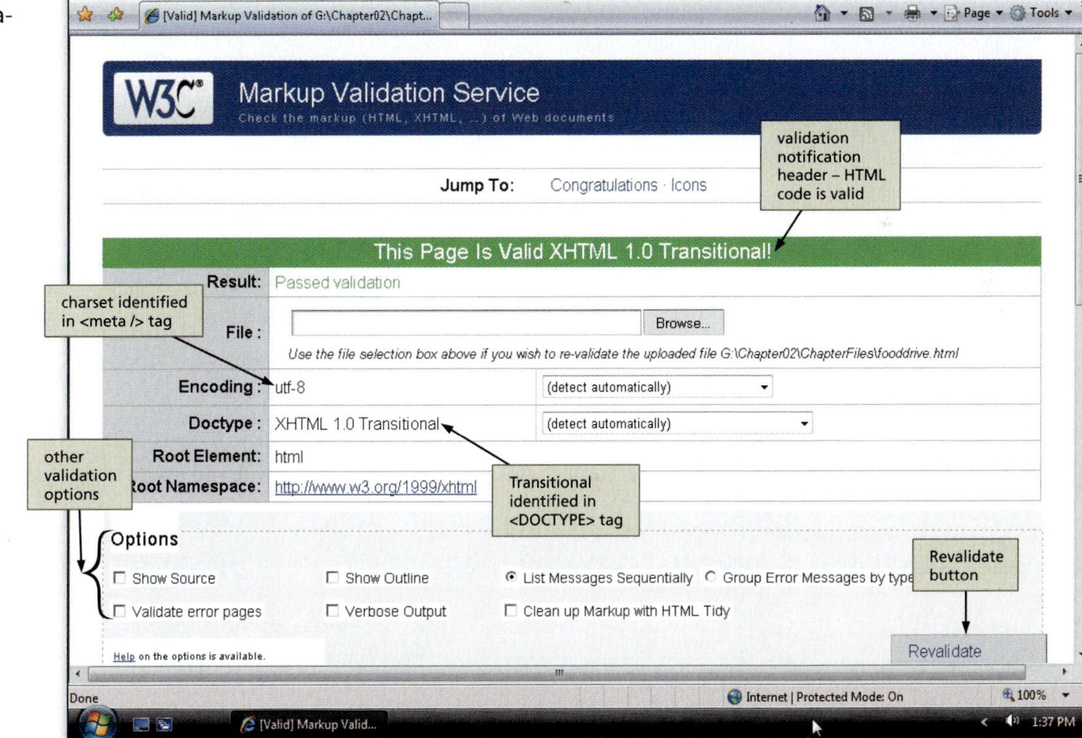

Figure 2–35

Q&A What can I do if my HTML code does not validate?

If your code has errors, edit your HTML file to correct the errors. The Markup Validation Service report lists clearly what is wrong with your code. Once you make the necessary changes and save the file, you can use the Browse button to open the corrected HTML file, then click the Revalidate button (Figure 2–35) to validate the changed code.

To View HTML Source Code for a Web Page

You can use your browser to look at the source code for most Web pages. The following steps show how to view the HTML source code for your Web page using a browser.

1

- Click Page on the Command bar (Figure 2–36).
- Click View Source to view the HTML code in the default text editor.

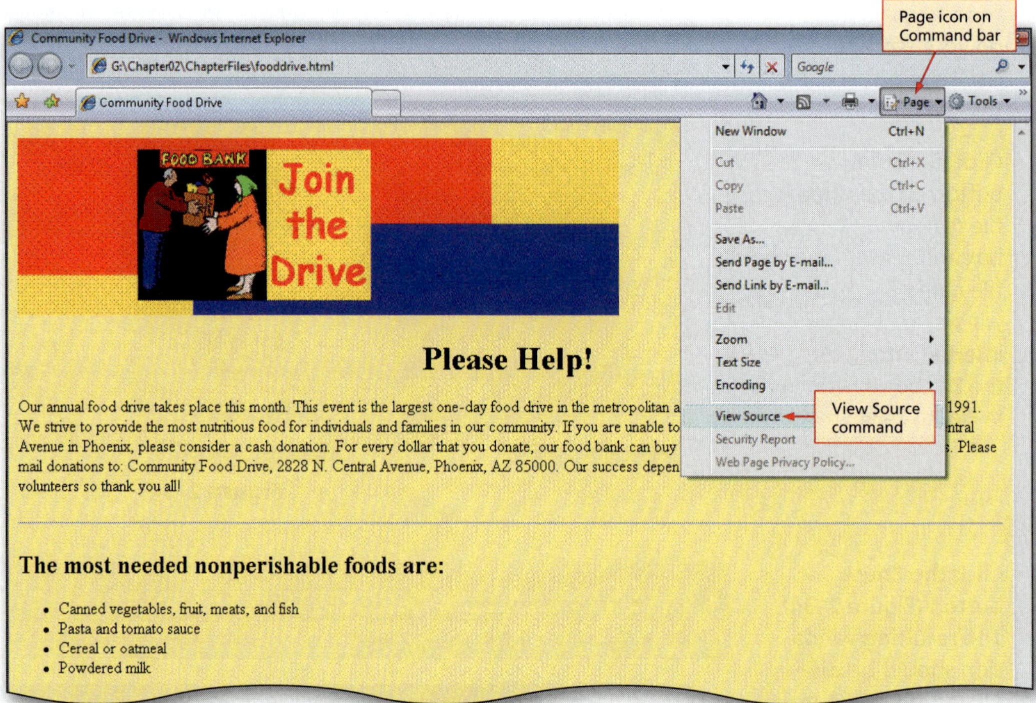

Figure 2–36

Q&A Do all browsers allow me to view the HTML source code in the same way?

Browsers such as Firefox or Safari differ from Internet Explorer and might use different buttons or menu options to access source code.

2

- Click the Close button on the Notepad title bar to close the active Notepad window (Figure 2–37).

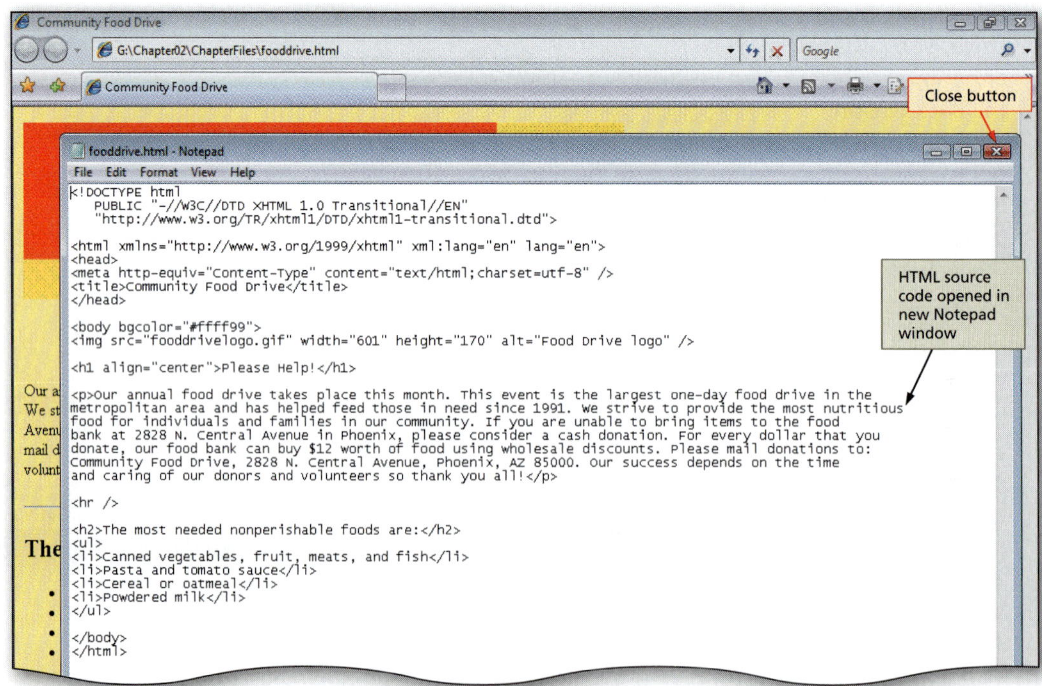

Figure 2–37

To Print a Web Page and an HTML File

After you have created the HTML file and saved it, you might want to print a copy of the HTML code and the resulting Web page. A printed version of a file, Web page, or other document is called a **hard copy** or **printout**. Printed copies of HTML files and Web pages can be kept for reference or to distribute. In many cases, HTML files and Web pages are printed and kept in binders for use by others. The following steps show how to print a Web page and its corresponding HTML file.

- Ready the printer according to the printer instructions.
- With the Community Food Drive Web page open in the browser window, click the Print icon on the Command bar.
- When the printer stops printing the Web page, retrieve the printout (Figure 2–38). Notice that the background color does not print as part of the document.

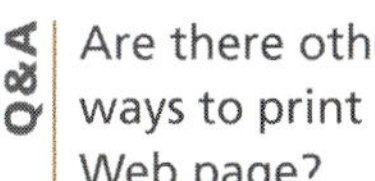

Are there other ways to print a Web page?

Notepad and Internet Explorer both provide other ways to print a document or Web page. Pressing CTRL+P in Notepad or Internet Explorer opens the Print dialog box, where you can select print options. You can also use the File menu, Print option.

Please Help!

Our annual food drive takes place this month. This event is the largest one-day food drive in the metropolitan area and has helped feed those in need since 1991. We strive to provide the most nutritious food for individuals and families in our community. If you are unable to participate by bringing items to the food bank, please consider a cash donation. For every dollar that you donate, our food bank can buy $12 worth of food using wholesale discounts. Please mail donations to: Community Food Drive, 2828 N. Central Avenue, Phoenix, AZ 85000. Our success depends on the time and caring of our donors and volunteers so thank you all!

The most needed nonperishable foods are:

- Canned vegetables, fruit, meats, and fish
- Pasta and tomato sauce
- Cereal or oatmeal
- Powdered milk

Figure 2–38

- Click the Notepad button on the taskbar to activate the Notepad window.
- Click File on the menu bar and then click the Print command, and then click the Print button to print a hard copy of the HTML code (Figure 2–39).

Q&A

Why do I need a printout of the HTML code?

Having a hardcopy printout is an invaluable tool for beginning developers. A printed copy can help you immediately see the relationship between the HTML tags and the Web page that you view in the browser.

```
                                   fooddrive.html
<!DOCTYPE html
  PUBLIC "-//W3C//DTD XHTML 1.0 Transitional//EN"
  "http://www.w3.org/TR/xhtml1/DTD/xhtml1-transitional.dtd">

<html xmlns="http://www.w3.org/1999/xhtml" xml:lang="en" lang="en">
<head>
<meta http-equiv="Content-Type" content="text/html;charset=utf-8" />
<title>Community Food Drive</title>
</head>

<body bgcolor="#f9fc05"
>

<img src="fooddrivelogo.gif" width="601" height="170" alt="Food Drive Logo" />
<h1 align="center">Please Help!</h1>
<p>Our annual food drive takes place this month. This event is the largest one-day
food drive in the
metropolitan area and has helped feed those in need since 1991. We strive to provide
the most nutritious
food for individuals and families in our community. If you are unable to participate
by bringing items
to the food bank, please consider a cash donation. For every dollar that you donate,
our food bank can
buy $12 worth of food using wholesale discounts. Please mail donations to: Community
Food Drive,
2828 N. Central Avenue, Phoenix, AZ 85000. Our success depends on the time and
caring of our donors and

volunteers so thank you all!</p>

<hr />

<h2>The most needed nonperishable foods are:</h2>
<ul>
<li>Canned vegetables, fruit, meats, and fish</li>
<li>Pasta and tomato sauce</li>
<li>Cereal or oatmeal</li>
<li> Powdered milk </li>
</ul>


</body>
</html>

                                   Page 1
```

Figure 2–39

To Quit Notepad and a Browser

The following step shows how to quit Notepad and a browser.

- Click the Close button on the Notepad title bar.
- Click the Close button on the Community Food Drive Home Page title bar.

BTW

Quick Reference
For a list of HTML tags and their associated attributes, see the HTML Quick Reference (Appendix A) at the back of this book, or visit the HTML Quick Reference Web page (scsite.com/HTML5e/qr).

Chapter Summary

In this chapter, you have learned how to identify the elements of a Web page, define the Web page structure, and enter Web page content using a text editor. You enhanced Web page appearance, saved and validated your code, and viewed your Web page and source code in a browser. The items listed below include all the new HTML skills you have learned in this chapter.

1. Start Notepad (HTML 36)
2. Enable Word Wrap in Notepad (HTML 37)
3. Define the Web Page Structure Using HTML Tags (HTML 38)
4. Enter a Centered Heading (HTML 41)
5. Enter a Paragraph of Text (HTML 41)
6. Create an Unordered List (HTML 45)
7. Save an HTML File (HTML 48)
8. Start a Browser (HTML 52)
9. View a Web Page in a Browser (HTML 54)
10. Activate Notepad (HTML 56)
11. Add an Image (HTML 59)
12. Add a Background Color (HTML 62)
13. Add a Horizontal Rule (HTML 63)
14. Refresh the View in a Browser (HTML 63)
15. Validate HTML Code (HTML 66)
16. View HTML Source Code for a Web Page (HTML 68)
17. Print a Web Page and an HTML File (HTML 69)
18. Quit Notepad and a Browser (HTML 71)

Learn It Online

Test your knowledge of chapter content and key terms.

Instructions: To complete the Learn It Online exercises, start your browser, click the Address bar, and then enter the Web address `scsite.com/html5e/learn`. When the HTML Learn It Online page is displayed, click the link for the exercise you want to complete and read the instructions.

Chapter Reinforcement TF, MC, and SA

A series of true/false, multiple choice, and short answer questions that test your knowledge of the chapter content.

Flash Cards

An interactive learning environment where you identify chapter key terms associated with displayed definitions.

Practice Test

A series of multiple choice questions that test your knowledge of chapter content and key terms.

Who Wants To Be a Computer Genius?

An interactive game that challenges your knowledge of chapter content in the style of a television quiz show.

Wheel of Terms

An interactive game that challenges your knowledge of chapter key terms in the style of the television show, *Wheel of Fortune*.

Crossword Puzzle Challenge

A crossword puzzle that challenges your knowledge of key terms presented in the chapter.

Apply Your Knowledge

Reinforce the skills and apply the concepts you learned in this chapter.

Editing the Apply Your Knowledge Web Page

Instructions: Start Notepad. Open the file apply2-1.html from the Chapter02\Apply folder of the Data Files for Students. See the inside back cover of this book for instructions for downloading the Data Files for Students, or contact your instructor for information about accessing the required files for this book.

The apply2-1.html file is a partially completed HTML file that you will use for this exercise. Figure 2–40 shows the Apply Your Knowledge Web page as it should be displayed in a browser after the additional HTML tags and attributes are added.

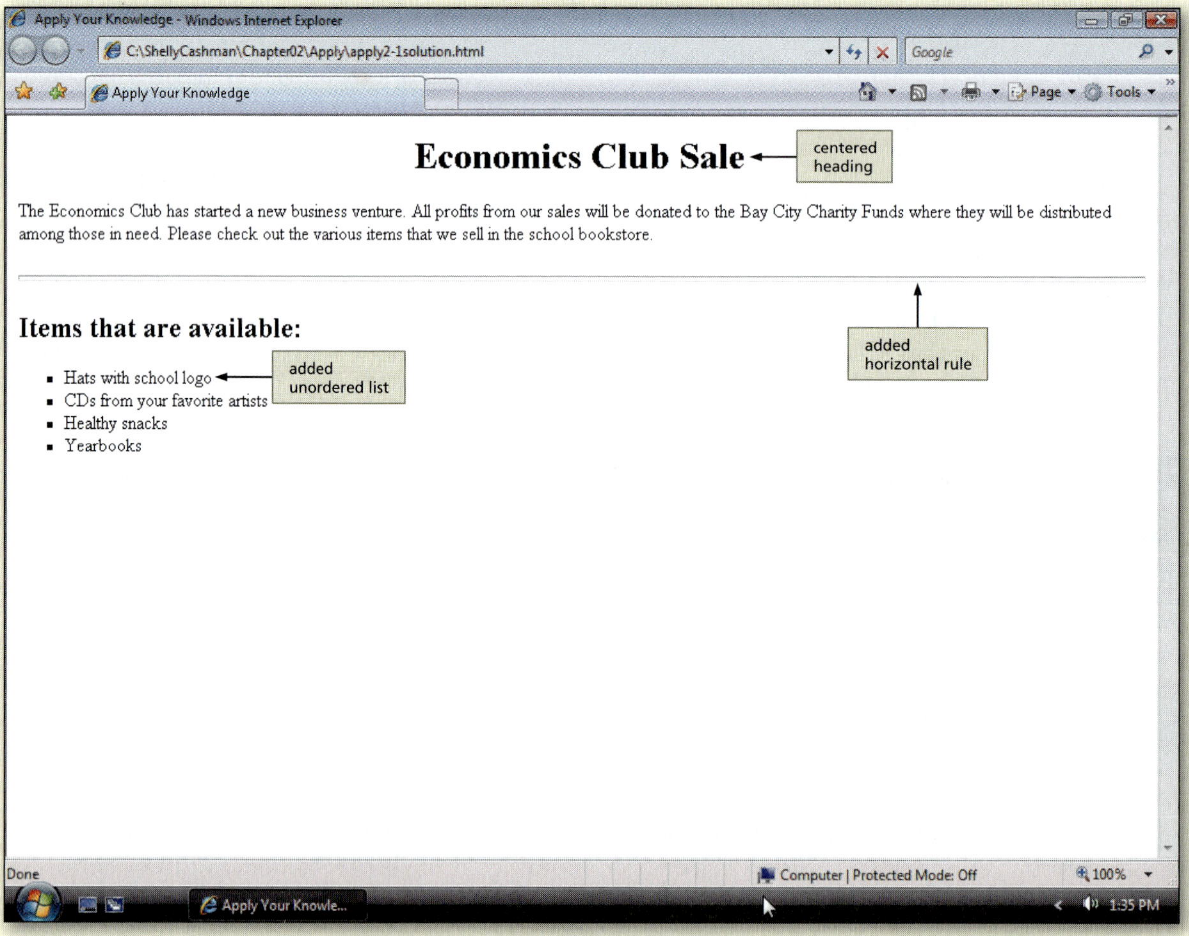

Figure 2–40

Perform the following tasks:

1. Enter g:\Chapter02\Apply\apply2-1.html as the URL to view the Web page in your browser.
2. Examine the HTML file and its appearance in the browser.
3. Using Notepad, change the HTML code to make the Web page look similar to the one shown in Figure 2–40. The hr shown on the Web page is size 5.
4. Save the revised HTML file in the Chapter02\Apply folder using the file name apply2-1solution.html.
5. Validate your HTML code at http://validator.w3.org/.

6. Enter g:\Chapter02\Apply\apply2-1solution.html as the URL to view the revised Web page in your browser.
7. Print the Web page.
8. Submit the revised HTML file and Web page in the format specified by your instructor.

Extend Your Knowledge

Extend the skills you learned in this chapter and experiment with new skills.

Creating a Definition List

Instructions: Start your browser. Open the file, extend2-1.html from the Chapter02\Extend folder of the Data Files for Students. See the inside back cover of this book for instructions on downloading the Data Files for Students, or contact your instructor for information about accessing the required files. This sample Web page contains all of the text for the Web page in bullet list format.

You will add the necessary tags to make this a definition list with terms that are bold as shown in Figure 2–41. (Note also that there are blank lines between the terms.)

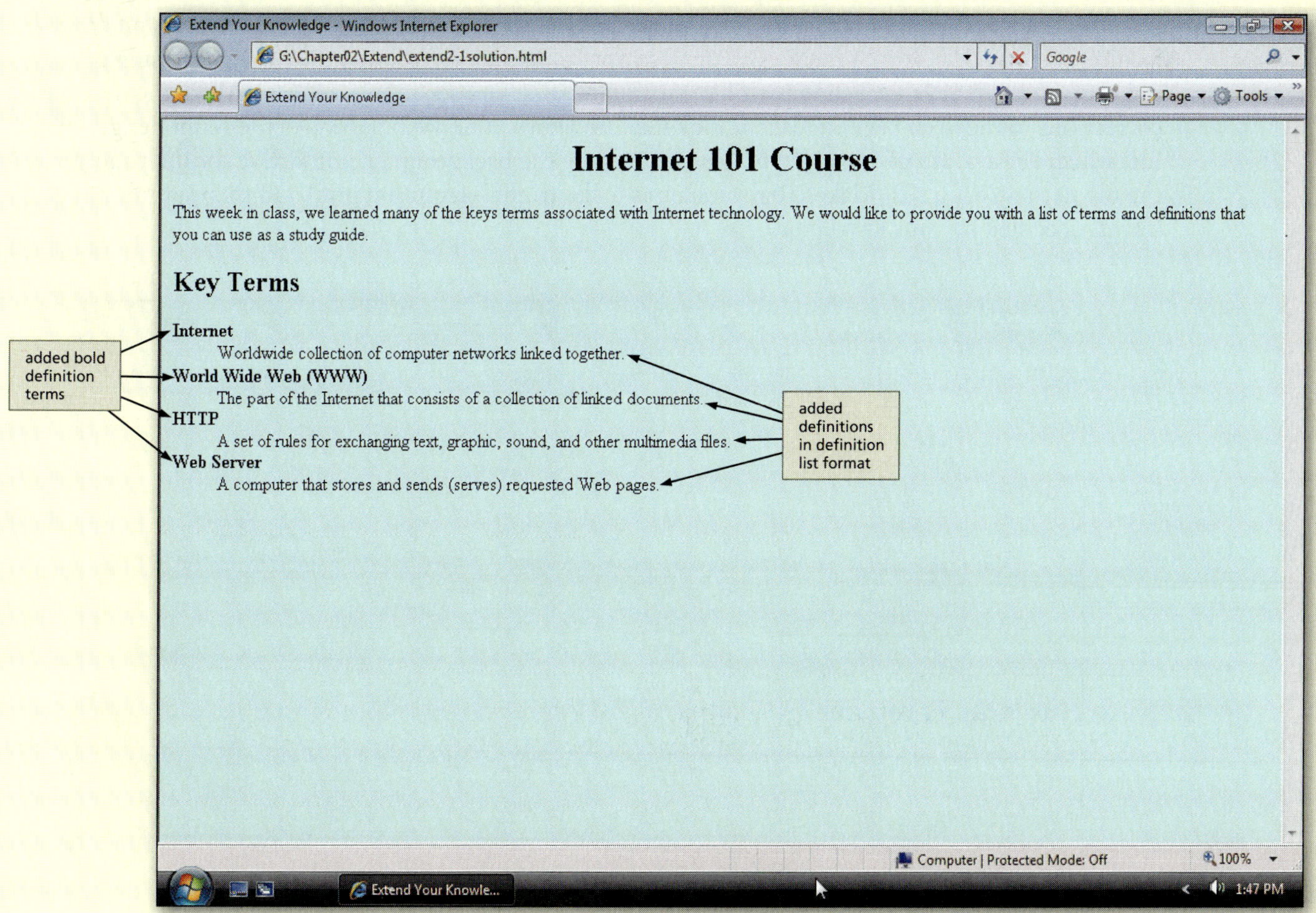

Figure 2–41

Continued >

Extend Your Knowledge *continued*

Perform the following tasks:

1. Using the text given in the file extend2-1.html, make changes to the HTML code to change the Web page from a bullet list to a definition list by following the definition list code shown in Figure 2–14 on page HTML 46.
2. Add the additional HTML code necessary to make the terms bold and have a blank line between terms.
3. Save the revised document in the Chapter02\Extend folder with the file name extend2-1solution.html and then submit it in the format specified by your instructor.

Make It Right

Analyze a document and correct all errors and/or improve the design.

Correcting the Friendly Reminder Web Page

Instructions: Start your browser. Open the file makeitright2-1.html from the Chapter02\MakeItRight folder of the Data Files for Students. See the inside back cover of this book for instructions on downloading the Data Files for Students, or contact your instructor for information about accessing the required files. The Web page is a modified version of what you see in Figure 2–42. Make the necessary corrections to the Web page to make it look like the figure. The Web page uses the reminder.gif image file, which has a width of 256 and a height of 256. Use the background color #ffff9c for the page. Save the file in the Chapter02\MakeItRight folder as makeitright2-1solution.html and then submit it in the format specified by your instructor.

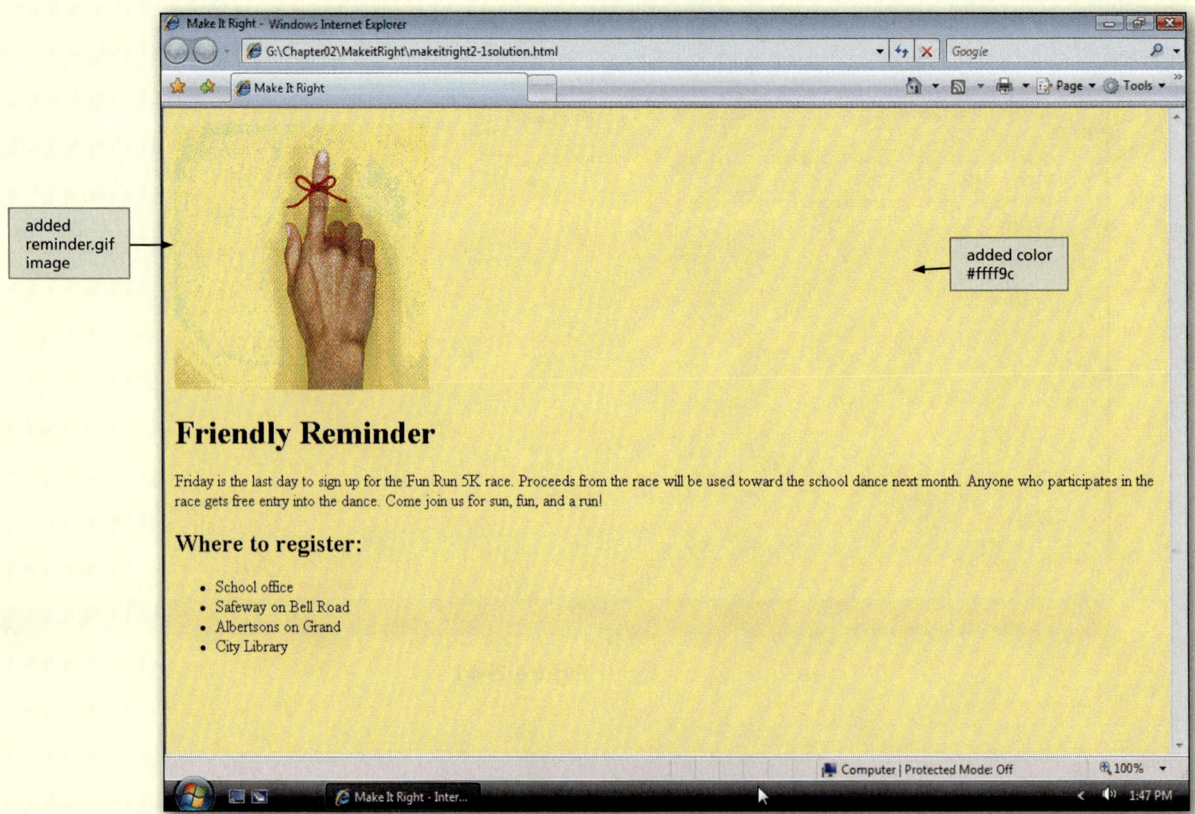

Figure 2–42

In the Lab

Lab 1: Creating a Personal Web Page

Problem: You did volunteer work for the Community Food Drive discussed in this chapter. You would like to recruit other friends to volunteer for community service. You have been asked to create a Web page to display information about why you choose to volunteer and let people know how they also can help, as shown in Figure 2–43.

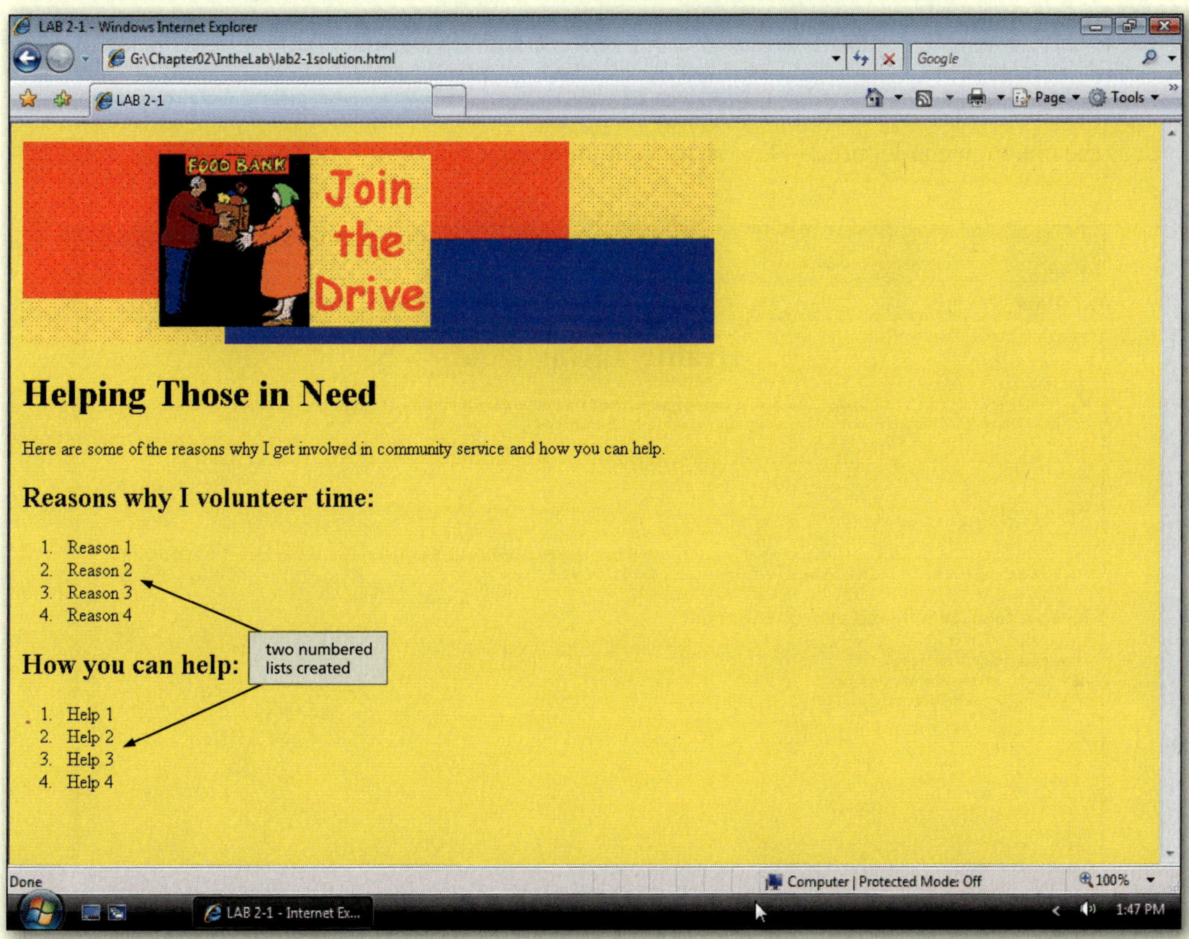

Figure 2–43

Instructions: Perform the following steps:

1. Start Notepad and create a new HTML file with the title, LAB 2-1, within the <title> </title> tags. For the initial HTML tags, you can use the structure.html file if you created one at the start of this project, otherwise type in the initial tags.
2. Begin the body section by adding the fooddrivelogo.gif image as well as the heading, Helping Those in Need. Format the heading to use the Heading 1 style left-aligned on the Web page.
3. Add two left-aligned headings, Reasons why I volunteer time and How you can help, using the Heading 2 style.
4. Add a background color to the Web page using the #f9fc05 color code.
5. Add two numbered lists of topics as shown in Figure 2–43.
6. Save the file in the Chapter02\IntheLab folder as lab2-1.html.

Continued >

In the Lab *continued*

7. Print the lab2-1.html file.
8. Enter g:\Chapter02\IntheLab\lab2-1.html as the URL to view the Web page in your browser.
9. Print the Web page.
10. Write your name on the printouts and hand them in to your instructor.

In the Lab

Lab 2: Creating an Information Web Page

Problem: You are learning more about healthy living and decide to prepare a Web page announcement, such as the one shown in Figure 2–44, to share your knowledge.

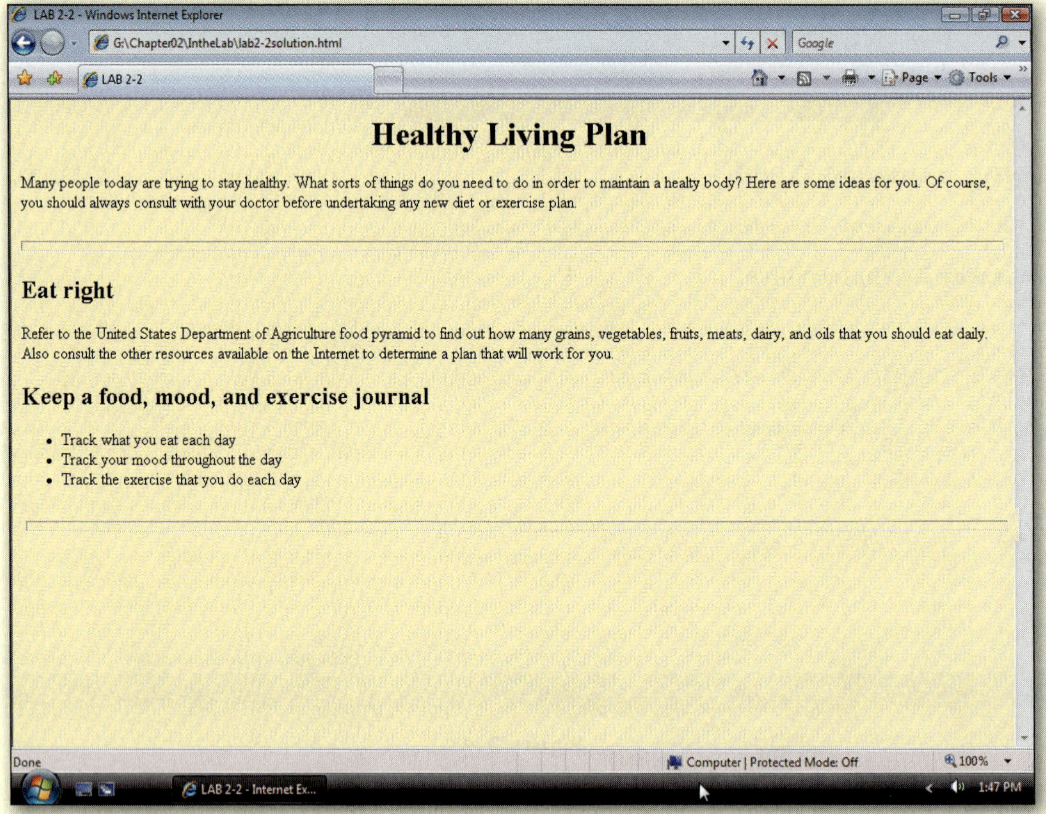

Figure 2–44

Instructions: Perform the following steps:

1. Start Notepad and create a new HTML file with the title LAB 2-2 within the <title> </title> tags.
2. Add a background color to the Web page using the #ffffcc color code.
3. Begin the body section by adding the heading Healthy Living Plan. Format the heading to use the Heading 1 style center-aligned on the Web page.
4. Add two size 10 horizontal rules as shown in Figure 2–44.
5. Add two headings, Eat right and Keep a food, mood, and exercise journal, using left-aligned Heading 2 styles.
6. Add the paragraphs of text, as shown in Figure 2–44.

7. Create one bullet list with the information shown.
8. Save the file in the Chapter02\IntheLab folder using the file name lab2-2.html.
9. Print the lab2-2.html file.
10. Enter g:\Chapter02\IntheLab\lab2-2.html as the URL to view the Web page in your browser.
11. Print the Web page.
12. Write your name on the printouts and hand them in to your instructor.

In the Lab

Lab 3: Composing a Personal Web Page

Problem: Your Aunt Betty is the director of the Campus Tutoring Service. She would like to have a Web page developed that explains the benefits of using the Campus Tutoring Service. You plan to use a paragraph of text (change the current paragraph to explain the purpose of the Campus Tutoring Service) and a bulleted list, as shown in Figure 2–45.

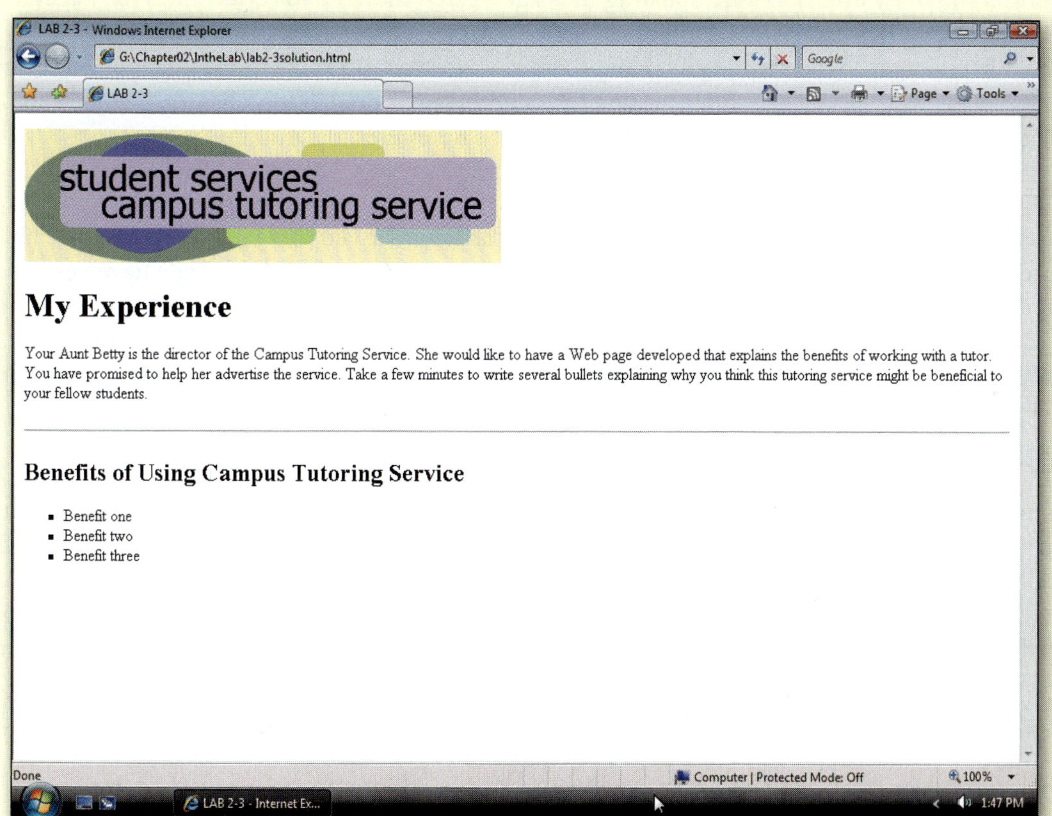

Figure 2–45

Instructions: Perform the following steps:

1. Start Notepad and create a new HTML file with the title LAB 2-3 within the <title> </title> tags.
2. Include a short paragraph of information and a bulleted list, using a format similar to the one shown in Figure 2–45, to provide information about your tutoring experience.
3. Insert the image file cts_clip8.gif, stored in the Chapter02\IntheLab folder.
4. Save the HTML file in the Chapter02\IntheLab folder using the file name lab2-3.html.

Continued >

In the Lab *continued*

5. Enter g:\Chapter02\IntheLab\lab2-3.html as the URL to view the Web page in your browser.
6. Print the Web page from your browser.
7. Write your name on the printout and hand it in to your instructor.

Cases and Places

Apply your creative thinking and problem solving skills to design and implement a solution.

• Easier ••More Difficult

• 1: Add to the Food Drive Web Site

Mr. Wattigney, the director of the Community Food Bank, likes the Web page you created in Chapter 2. Now that the Food Drive is over, he would like you to update the Web page with new information on upcoming community events. Before updating the page, search the Web to review the Web pages at other food banks or departments of community services for ideas on content to include or formatting to change. What do their Web sites look like? Are there changes you can make to the Chapter 2 Web page that reflect what other places have done? Using the concepts presented in this chapter, include additional information or change the formatting to make the page more interesting and timely.

• 2: Create an Artist Web Site

You are creating a new Web site for a local artist. The artist has asked that you use descriptive alt attributes for images on the Web page, because many of the viewers of his Web page have very slow Internet connections and images often do not load quickly. Search the Web for information on adding useful, descriptive alt attributes for images. Create a document with a brief paragraph explaining the various purposes of alt attributes. Include three examples of good, descriptive alt attributes and three examples of less descriptive alt attributes.

•• 3: Create a Web Page of HTML Definitions

As an instructor at the Maricopa Community College, you often update your Web site with information to help students in your classes. For an upcoming HTML class, you have decided to create a Web page with a definition list of HTML tags and their usage. Using the concepts presented in this chapter, use Notepad to create a Web page with the information listed in Table 2–1 on pages HTML 35 and 36. Add the heading HTML Tags and Their Functions at the top of the page. Use the HTML tag as the term (<dt>) and function as the definition of the term (<dd>). You may want to format your definition list so that it is more readable, using bold text and blank lines.

• • 4: Create a Personal Web Page

Make It Personal

Your class instructor wants to post all of the students' Web pages on the school server to show what his or her students have learned in class. Create a Web page of personal information, listing items such as your school major, jobs that you have had in the past, and your hobbies and interests. To make your personal Web page more visually interesting, search the Web for images that reflect your interests. (Remember that if the image is copyrighted, you cannot use it on a personal Web page unless you follow the guidelines provided with the image.) Insert an image or two onto the Web page to help explain who you are.

• • 5: Create Web Pages with Different Background Colors

Working Together

You are part of a Web usability team for Web-It, a local Web design firm. As part of a new project on the use of color on the Web, your team is doing research on which background colors are more appealing to users. Search the Web for information about browser-safe colors on the Web. Create three Web pages with the same information, but vary the background color. Be sure to save each different page as a different file name. Show those pages to some friends or family members to have them evaluate which background color they like and explain why they prefer one color to another. View these three Web pages on different computers used by members of the team. Do the colors look different? Why do you think they would? What factors contribute to the way in which a colored background would be displayed?

3 Creating Web Pages with Links, Images, and Formatted Text

Objectives

You will have mastered the material in this chapter when you can:

- Describe linking terms and definitions
- Create a home page and enhance a Web page using images
- Align and add bold, italics, and color to text
- Change the bullet type used in an unordered list
- Add a text link to a Web page in the same Web site
- Add an e-mail link
- Use absolute and relative paths
- Save and view an HTML file and test the links
- Open an HTML file
- Add an image with wrapped text
- Add a text link to a Web page on another Web site
- Add links to targets within a Web page
- Copy and paste HTML code
- Add an image link to a Web page in the same Web site

3 Creating Web Pages with Links, Images, and Formatted Text

Introduction

One of the most useful and important aspects of the World Wide Web is the ability to connect (link) one Web page to other Web pages — on the same server or on different Web servers — located anywhere in the world. Using hyperlinks, a Web site visitor can move from one page to another, and view information in any order. Many different Web page elements, including text, graphics, and animations, can serve as hyperlinks. In this chapter, you will create Web pages that are linked together. Before starting on this project, you would have already completed the Web site planning, analysis, and design phases of the Web Development Life Cycle.

Project — Pasta Divine Web Site

Chapter 3 illustrates how to use HTML to create a home page for the Pasta Divine Web site (Figure 3–1a) and to edit the existing specials.html Web page (Figure 3–1b) to improve its appearance and function. Your Uncle Mark recently opened an Italian restaurant in the city and named it Pasta Divine. He would like to advertise his monthly pasta carry-out specials on the Web. He knows that you have studied Web development in college and asked you to develop two Web pages that are linked together: a home page, and a Web page with the monthly specials. During your analysis, you determined that there are four basic types of links to use. The first type is a link from one Web page to another in the same Web site. The second type is a link to a Web page on a different Web site. The third type is a link within one Web page. The fourth type is an e-mail link. You plan to utilize all four of these types of links for your uncle's Web site.

The Pasta Divine home page (Figure 3–1a), which shows information about Pasta Divine and its services, includes a logo image, headings, an unordered (bulleted) list, an e-mail link, and a text link to a Web page on another Web site. This page also includes a link to the specials.html Web page. The specials.html Web page (Figure 3–1b) contains images with text wrapped around them and internal links that allow visitors to move easily from section to section within the Web page. The Web page also has an image link back to Pasta Divine's home page.

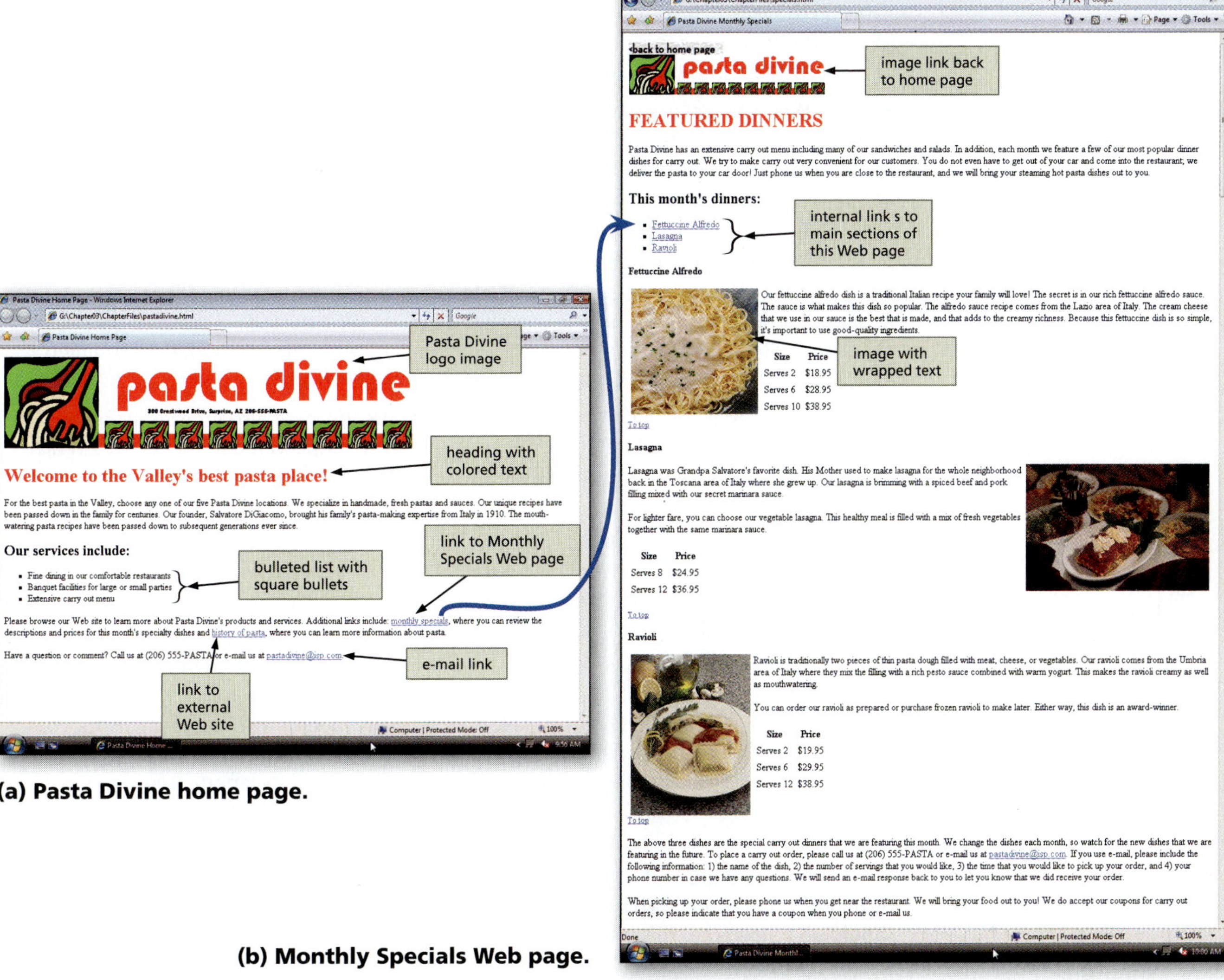

(a) Pasta Divine home page.

(b) Monthly Specials Web page.

Figure 3–1

Overview

As you read this chapter, you will learn how to create the Web page shown in Figure 3–1 by performing these general tasks:

- Enter HTML code into the Notepad window.
- Save the file as an HTML file.
- Enter basic HTML tags and add text to the file.
- Organize and enhance the text by adding colored headings and creating a bulleted list.
- Add a link to another Web page in the same Web site.
- Add a link to an external Web site.
- Add an e-mail link.
- Add targets and links within the same Web page.
- View the Web pages and HTML code in your browser.
- Validate the Web pages.
- Print the Web pages.

Plan Ahead

General Project Guidelines

As you create Web pages, such as the project shown in Figure 3–1 on the previous page, you should follow these general guidelines:

1. **Plan the Web site**. Before developing a multiple-page Web site, you must plan the purpose of the site. Refer to Table 1–4 on page HTML 12 for information on the planning phase of the Web Development Life Cycle. In this phase, you determine the purpose of the Web site, identify the users of the site and their computing environment, and decide who owns the information on the Web page.
2. **Analyze the need**. In the analysis phase of the Web Development Life Cycle, you should analyze what content to include in the Web page. The Web development project in Chapter 3 is different than the one completed in Chapter 2 because it contains two Web pages that will be linked together. Part of the analysis phase then includes determining how the multiple Web pages work together to form a Web site.
3. **Choose the content for the Web page**. This part of the life cycle also is different because all of the content does not have to appear on one Web page, as it did in Chapter 2. With a multiple-page Web site, you can distribute the content as needed throughout the Web site.
4. **Determine how the pages will link to one another**. This Web site consists of a **home page** (the first page in a Web site) and a secondary Web page to which you will link. You need to determine how to link (e.g., with text or a graphic) from the home page to the secondary page and how to link back to the home page.
5. **Establish what other links are necessary**. In addition to links between the home page and secondary Web page, you need an e-mail link on this Web site. It is a general standard for Web developers to provide an e-mail link on the home page of a Web site for visitor comments or questions. Additionally, the secondary Web page (specials.html) is a long page that requires visitors to scroll down for navigation. Because of its length, it is important to provide easy and quick ways to navigate the Web page. You do this using links within the Web page.
6. **Create the Web page and links**. Once the analysis and design is complete, the Web developer creates the Web page using HTML. Good Web development standard practices should be followed in this step. Examples of good practices include utilizing the proper initial HTML tags as shown in the previous chapter and always identifying alt text with images.
7. **Test all Web pages within the Web site**. An important part of Web development is testing to assure that you are following XHTML standards. In this book, we use the World Wide Web Consortium (W3C) validator that allows you to test your Web pages and clearly explains any errors it finds. Additionally when testing, you should check all content for accuracy. Finally, all links (external, internal, and page to page within the same Web site) should be tested.

When necessary, more specific details concerning the above guidelines are presented at appropriate points in the chapter. The chapter also will identify the actions performed and decisions made regarding these guidelines during the creation of the Web page shown in Figure 3–1.

Using Links on a Web Page

As you have learned, many different Web page elements, including text, images, and animations, can serve as links. Text and images are the elements most widely used as links. Figure 3–2 shows examples of text and image links.

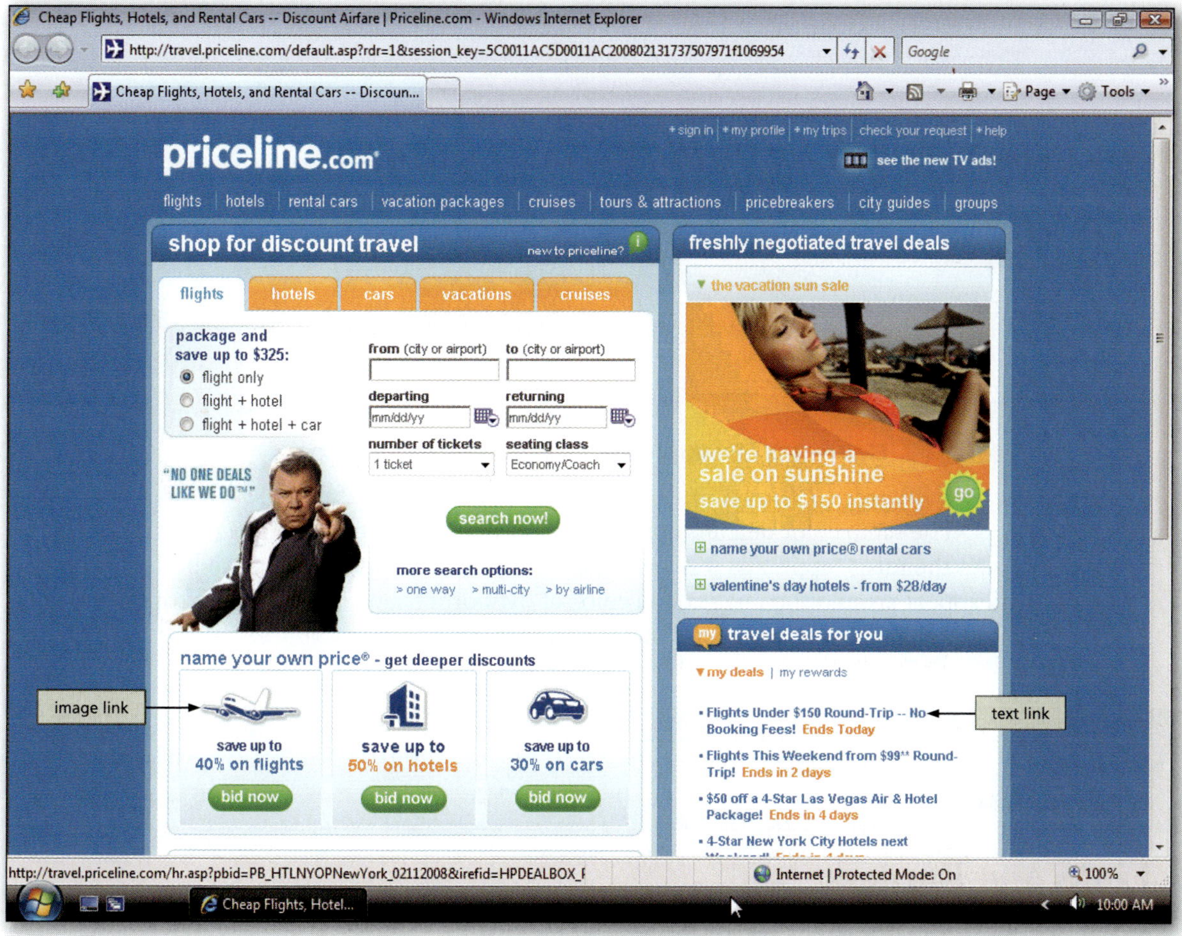

Figure 3–2 Text and image links on a Web page.

When using text links on a Web page, use descriptive text as the clickable word or phrase. For example, the phrase "Click here" does not explain the purpose of the link to the visitor. By contrast, the phrase "Save up to 40% on flights" indicates that the link connects to a Web page with discounted airline tickets.

When text identifies a link, it often appears as underlined text, in a color different from the main Web page text. Unless otherwise coded in the <body> tag, the browser settings define the colors of text links throughout a Web page. For example, with Internet Explorer, the default color for a normal link that has not been clicked (or visited) is blue, a visited link is purple, and an active link (a link just clicked by a user) varies in color. Figure 3–3 on the next page shows examples of text links in all three states (normal, visited, and active). Generally, as shown in Figure 3–3, moving the mouse pointer over a link causes the mouse pointer to change to a pointing hand. This change notifies the user that a link is available from that text or image.

BTW

Link Help

Many Web sites provide help for new HTML developers. For more information about links, search for key words such as "HTML Tutorials" or "HTML Help" in any good search engine.

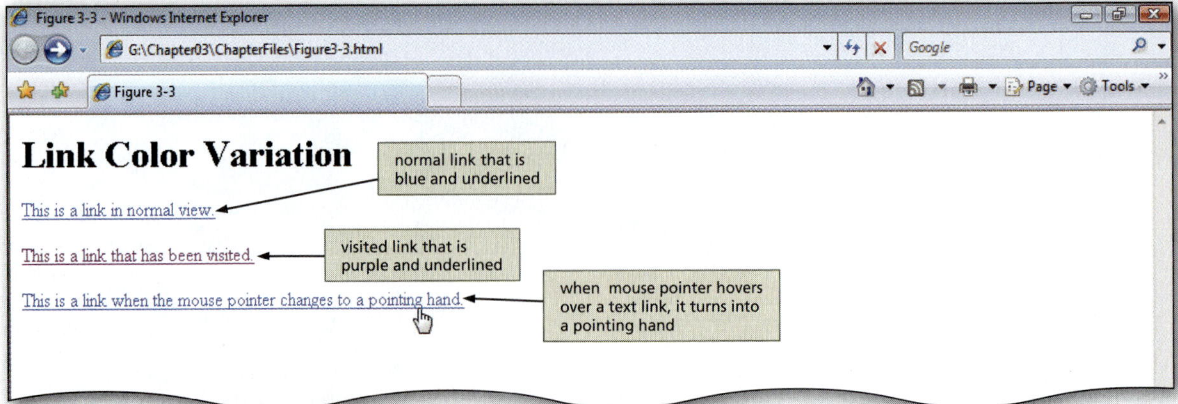

Figure 3–3 Examples of text link color variations.

The same color defaults apply to the border color around an image link. A border makes the image appear as if it has a frame around it. If the image has no border, no frame will appear around the image. The color of the border shows whether the border is a link, and whether the link has been visited (Figure 3–4).

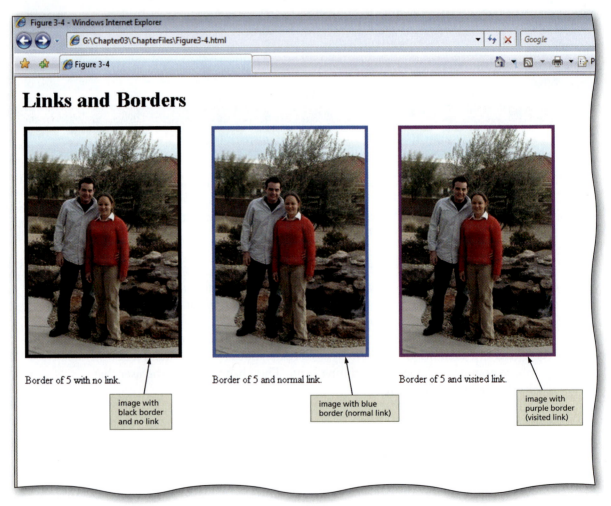

Figure 3–4

If you want to change the colors of text links or image link borders to override the browser defaults, you must enter attributes and values in the <body> tag. The format of the tag used to change normal, visited, and active link colors from the default is:

```
<body link="color" vlink="color" alink="color">
```

where color is a designated color code, such as #6633CC. Table 3–1 lists the link color attributes that can be specified in the <body> tag.

BTW

Link Colors
You can change the link colors in popular browsers. In Microsoft Internet Explorer, you find color selection on the Tools menu using Internet Options. In Netscape Communicator, click Preferences on the Edit menu. In both browsers, you change colors by clicking the color bars.

Table 3–1 Link Color Attributes for <body> Tag

Attribute	Function
link	• Normal link • Controls the color of a normal unvisited link and/or link without mouse pointer pointing to it • Default color usually is blue
vlink	• Visited link • Controls the color of a link that has been clicked or visited • Default color usually is green or purple
alink	• Active link • Controls the color of a link immediately after the mouse clicks the hyperlink • Default color usually is green or red

Linking to Another Web Page within the Same Web Site

Web pages often include links to connect one Web page to another page within the same Web site. For example, a visitor can click a link on the home page of a Web site (Figure 3–5a on the next page) to connect and view another Web page on the same Web site (Figure 3–5b). The Web pages created in this project include links to other pages in the same Web site: (1) the Pasta Divine home page includes a text link to the specials.html Web page; and (2) the Monthly Specials Web page includes an image link back to the Pasta Divine home page.

BTW

Links on a Web Page
An anchor tag also allows visitors to move within a single Web page. Use the name attribute to allow movement from one area to another on the same page. This linking technique is useful particularly on long pages. An index of links also can provide easy access to various areas within the Web page.

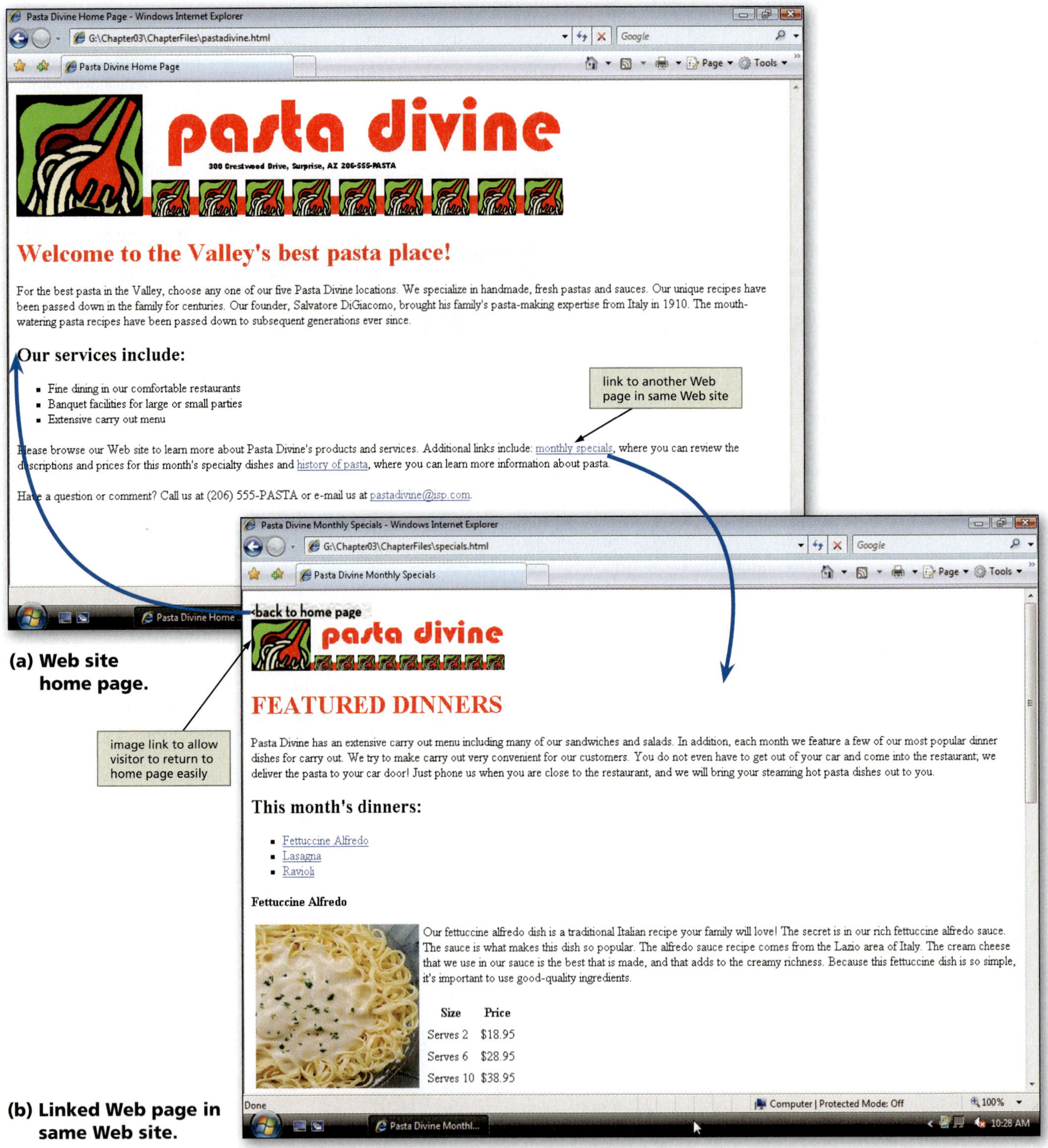

(a) Web site home page.

(b) Linked Web page in same Web site.

Figure 3–5

Linking to a Web Page in Another Web Site

A very important feature of the Web is the capability of linking to an external Web site. Web developers use these links to connect their Web pages to other Web pages with information on the same topic. The links are what give the Web its value as an interconnected resource and provide its "webbiness." In this project, the home page (Figure 3–6a) includes a link to a page on another Web site where the visitor can find additional information about the history of pasta (Figure 3–6b).

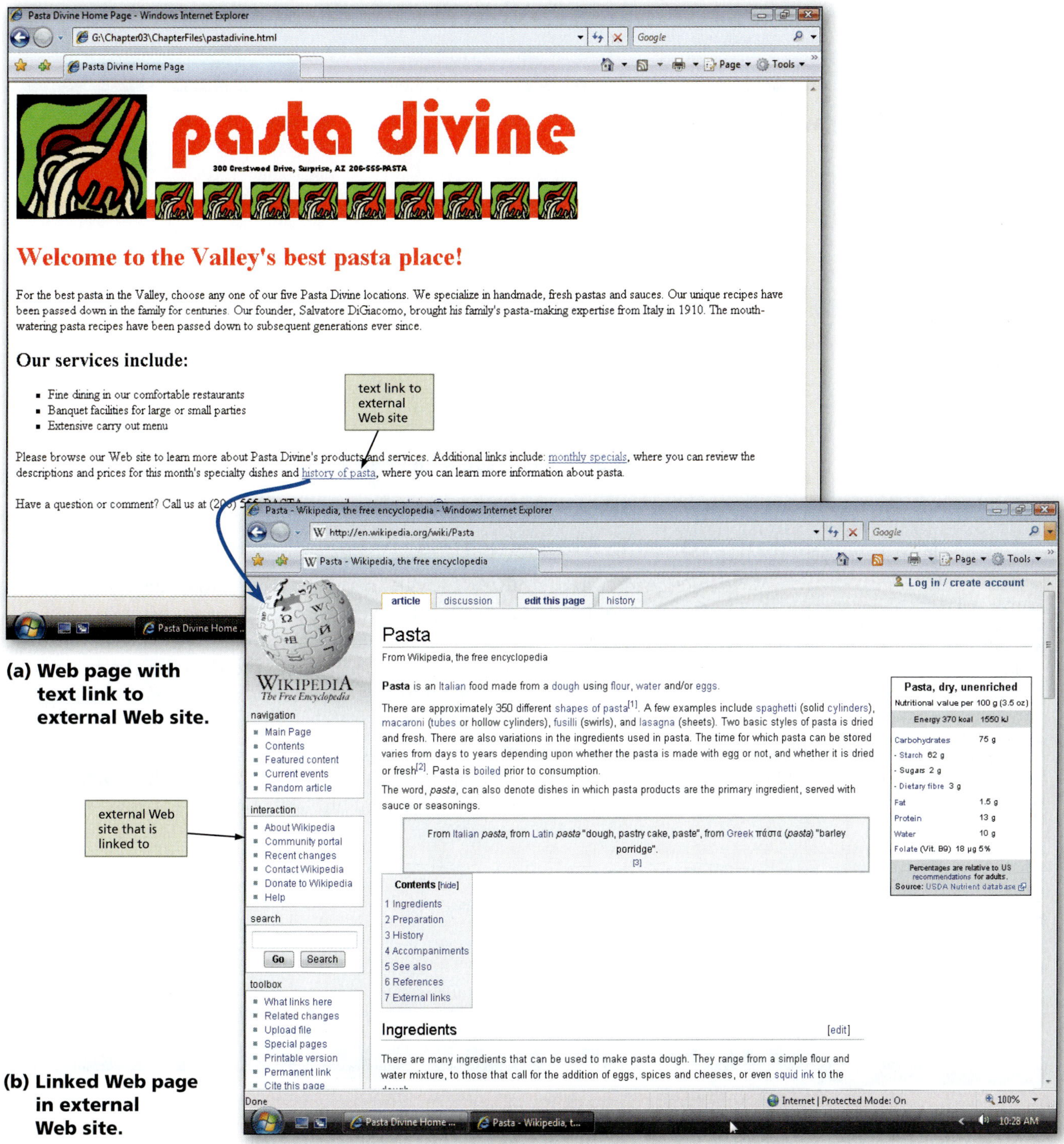

(a) Web page with text link to external Web site.

(b) Linked Web page in external Web site.

Figure 3–6

Linking within a Web Page

Links within a Web page allow visitors to move quickly from one section of the Web page to another. This is especially important in Web pages that are long and require a visitor to scroll down to see all of the content. Many Web pages contain a list of links like a menu or table of contents at the top of the page, with links to sections within the Web page (Figure 3–7 on the next page). In this project, the Monthly Specials Web page includes links from the top section of the Web page to other sections within the page, as well as links back to the top of the Web page.

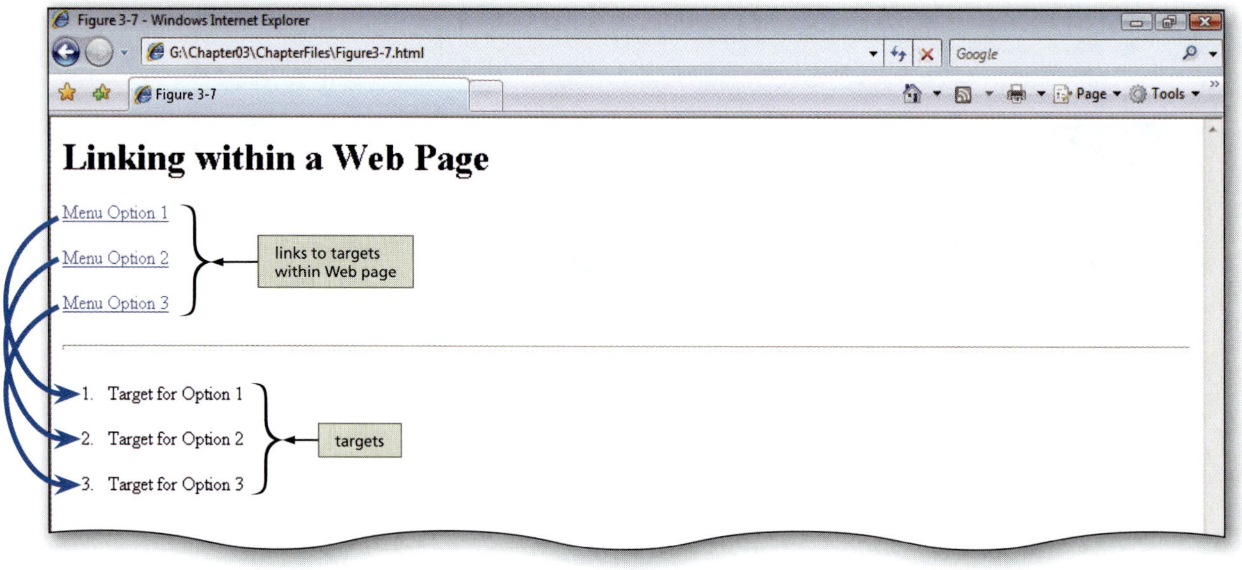

Figure 3–7 Web page with internal links.

Linking to an E-Mail Address

BTW

E-Mail Links
Although it is not common, you can assign more than one e-mail address to a mailto: tag. Use the form "mailto:first@isp.com, second@isp.com" in the <a href=> tag. Some older browsers may not support this tag.

A well-designed Web page always provides a way for visitors to contact the person at the company responsible for maintaining the Web site or addressing customer questions and comments. An easy way to provide contact information is to include an e-mail link on the Web site's home page, as well as on other pages in the Web site. As shown in Figure 3–8 , when a visitor clicks the **e-mail link**, it automatically opens a new message in the default e-mail program and inserts the appropriate contact e-mail address in the To field. Visitors then can type and send an e-mail to request additional information, comment on the Web site, or notify the company of a problem with its Web site. (*Note*: If your browser is not configured to send e-mail, the e-mail link will not work.)

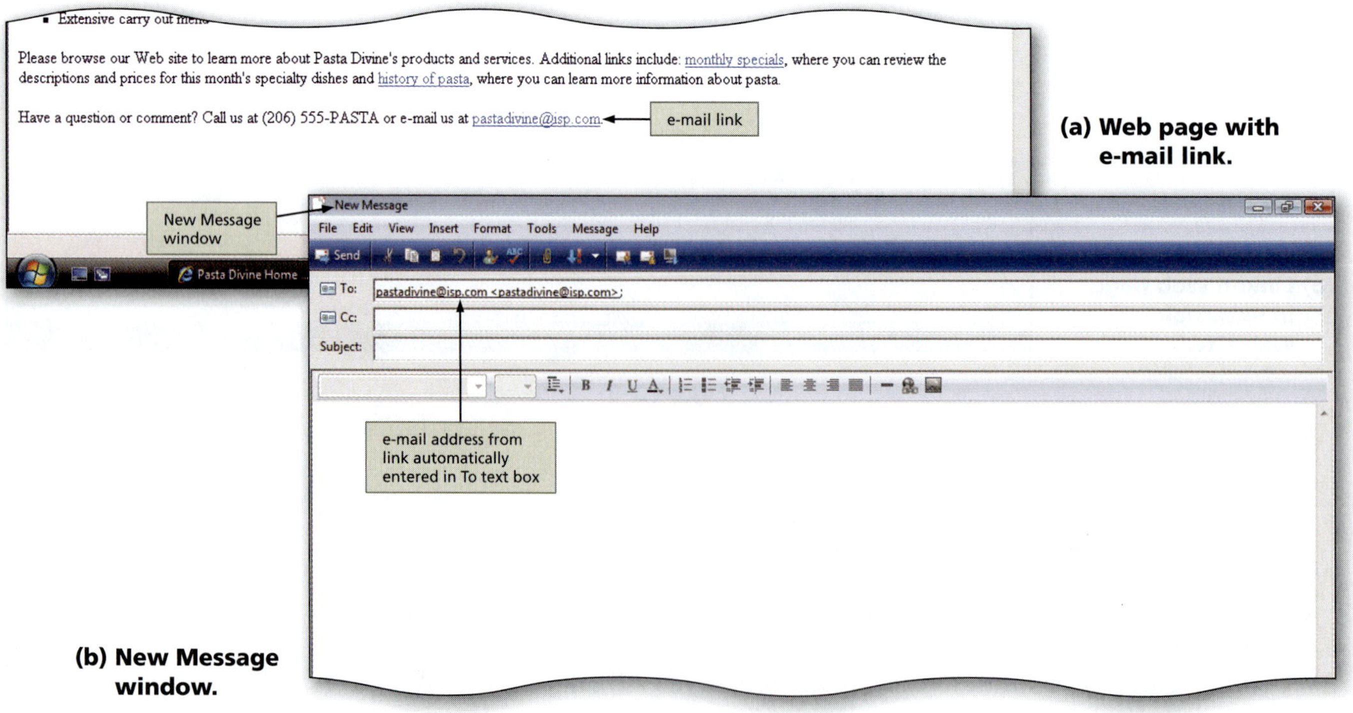

(a) Web page with e-mail link.

(b) New Message window.

Figure 3–8

Creating a Home Page

The first Web page developed in this chapter is the home page of the Pasta Divine Web site. A home page is the main page of a Web site, which visitors to a Web site generally will view first. A Web site home page should identify the purpose of the Web site by briefly stating what content, services, or features it provides. The home page also should indicate clearly what links the visitor should click to move from one page on the site to another. A Web developer should design the Web site in such a way that the links from one Web page to another are apparent and the navigation is clear. The Web site home page also should include an e-mail link, so visitors easily can find contact information for the individual or organization.

You begin creating the home page by starting Notepad and entering the initial HTML tags. Then you add an image, heading, text, and an unordered list to your home page. Finally, you add text and e-mail links, and then test the links.

To Start Notepad

The following step, which assumes Windows Vista is running, starts Notepad based on a typical installation. You may need to ask your instructor how to start Notepad for your computer.

- Click the Start button on the Windows Vista taskbar to display the Start menu.
- Click All Programs at the bottom of the left pane on the Start menu to display the All Programs list.
- Click Accessories in the All Programs list.
- Click Notepad in the Accessories list to display the Notepad window.
- If the Notepad window is not maximized, click the Maximize button on the Notepad title bar to maximize it.
- Click Format on the menu bar.
- If the Word Wrap command does not have a check mark next to it, click Word Wrap.

To Enter Initial HTML Tags to Define the Web Page Structure

Just as you did in Chapter 2, you start your file with the initial HTML tags that define the structure of the Web page. Table 3–2 contains the tags and text for this task.

Table 3–2 Initial HTML Tags

Line	HTML Tag and Text
1	`<!DOCTYPE html`
2	`PUBLIC "-//W3C//DTD XHTML 1.0 Transitional//EN"`
3	`"http://www.w3.org/TR/xhtml1/DTD/xhtml1-transitional.dtd">`
4	
5	`<html xmlns="http://www.w3.org/1999/xhtml" xml:lang="en" lang="en">`
6	`<head>`
7	`<meta http-equiv="Content-Type" content="text/html;charset=utf-8" />`
8	`<title>Pasta Divine Home Page</title>`

BTW

Copy Initial Structure
You can type in the initial HTML tags and save that code in a file (such as structure.html) to use as the basis for all HTML files, so you don't have to type this same code each time. Just remember to save the file immediately with a new name.

Table 3–2 Initial HTML Tags (continued)

Line	HTML Tag and Text
9	</head>
10	
11	<body>
12	
13	</body>
14	</html>

The following step illustrates how to enter the initial tags that define the structure of the Web page.

- Enter the HTML code shown in Table 3–2. Press ENTER at the end of each line. If you make an error as you are typing, use the BACKSPACE key to delete all the characters back to and including the incorrect characters, then continue typing.

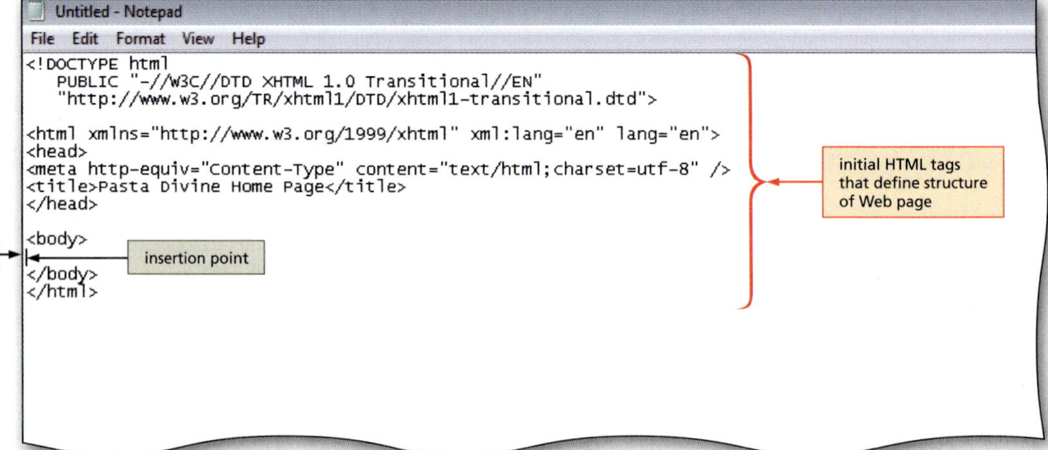

Figure 3–9

- Compare what you typed to Figure 3–9. If you notice errors, use your mouse pointer or ARROW keys to move the insertion point to the right of each error and use the BACKSPACE key to correct the error.

- Position the insertion point on the blank line between the <body> and </body> tags (line 12).

Plan Ahead

Identify how to format various elements of the text.

Before inserting the graphical and color elements on a Web page, you should plan how you want to format them. By effectively utilizing graphics and color, you can call attention to important topics on the Web page without overpowering it. Consider the following formatting suggestions.

- **Effectively utilize graphics.** An important part of Web development is the use of graphics to call attention to a Web page. Generally, companies utilize the same logo on their Web site as they use on print material associated with the company, such as business cards and letterheads. Using the same graphical image on all marketing materials, including the Web site, is a good way to provide a consistent visual and brand message to customers.

- **Utilize headings that connect to the graphics.** It is sometimes good to coordinate the color of the main heading to the graphics contained on the Web page. This can bring attention to the main heading, which is generally the first line of text on the Web page after a graphic. The main heading calls attention to the purpose of the Web page. Heading size standards should be followed as shown in Figure 3–1a on page HTML 83 with the main heading as size h1, and subtopics or headings as size h2.

To Add an Image

The Pasta Divine home page includes an image logo to provide visual appeal, catch the visitor's interest, and promote the company's brand. The following step illustrates how to add an image to a Web page by entering an <img> tag in the HTML file.

- Click the blank line below the <body> tag (line 12) and type `<img src="pdlogo.gif" width="711" height="155" alt="Pasta Divine logo" />` and then press the ENTER key (Figure 3–10).

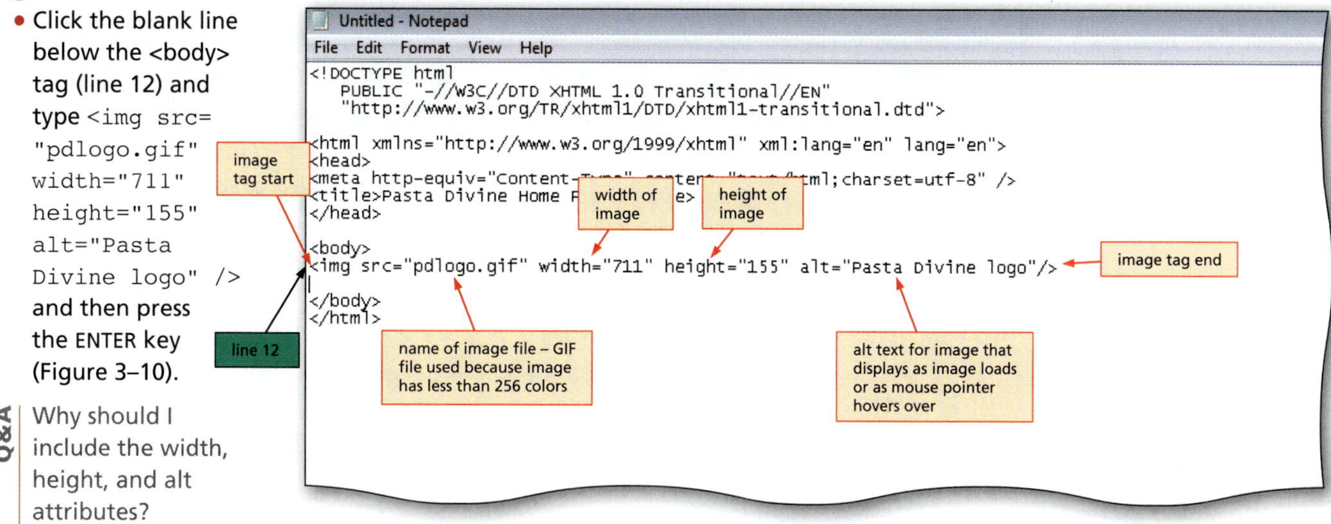


```
<!DOCTYPE html
   PUBLIC "-//W3C//DTD XHTML 1.0 Transitional//EN"
   "http://www.w3.org/TR/xhtml1/DTD/xhtml1-transitional.dtd">

<html xmlns="http://www.w3.org/1999/xhtml" xml:lang="en" lang="en">
<head>
<meta http-equiv="Content-Type" content="text/html;charset=utf-8" />
<title>Pasta Divine Home Page</title>
</head>

<body>
<img src="pdlogo.gif" width="711" height="155" alt="Pasta Divine logo"/>

</body>
</html>
```

Figure 3–10

Q&A Why should I include the width, height, and alt attributes?

Adding width and height attributes can improve page loading time because the browser does not have to figure the width and height before loading the image. The alt attribute provides information about the purpose of the image when the user's mouse hovers over the image and while the image is loading.

Q&A Why is this image a GIF file and not a JPG file?

This image contains a limited number of colors, which makes it a good candidate for a GIF file. If the image had many colors and features like shadowing, a JPG image would be a better choice. JPG supports more colors and resolutions than GIF or PNG.

Plan Ahead

Identify how to format text elements of the home page.
You should always make a plan before inserting the text elements of a Web page. By formatting the characters and paragraphs on a Web page, you can improve its overall appearance. On a Web page, consider the following formatting suggestions.

- **Use default text size when appropriate**. The body text consists of all text between the heading and the bottom of the Web page. This text is the main content of the Web page and should be used to highlight the key points of your message. You can vary your content by utilizing both paragraphs of text and lists.
- **Highlight key text with ordered or unordered lists**. An ordered or unordered list contains specific information that is more clearly identified by a list versus a paragraph of text. In this project, you use a bulleted (i.e., unordered) list but vary it by changing the type of bullet used. The square bullet has a nice look on a Web page and is different than the standard (i.e., default) disc bullet for unordered lists.
- **Determine other information suitable for the home page**. Other information that is suitable for a home page includes: the company address (often found in the logo), a phone number, and an e-mail link.

Adding Interest and Focus with Font Color and Size

BTW

Font Sizes
The most frequently used font attribute is size. The values of font sizes range from 1 to 7, with 3 being the default. You also can specify the font size as a relative value using a + (plus) or – (minus) sign. These relative values range from –3 to +4.

In Chapter 2, you learned how to vary the size of headings with the <h1> through <h6> tags. Any text on a Web page, including headings, can be formatted with a different color or style to make it stand out by using attributes of the <font> tag. Table 3–3 lists the different font attributes that can be used to enhance standard text on a Web page.

Table 3–3 Font Attributes and Values

Attribute and Value	Function
color="#xxxxxx"	• Changes the font color • Value inside quotation marks is a six-digit color code or color name
face="fontname"	• Changes the font face or type • Value inside quotation marks is the name of a font, such as Verdana or Arial; text appears using the default font if the font face is not specified
size="x"	• Changes the font size • Value inside quotation marks is a number that represents size • Values can be an actual font size of 1 (smallest) to 7 (largest) or a relative font size, such as +2 or -1, which specifies a number of sizes larger or smaller than the preset font size

Figure 3–11 lists several of these attributes and shows how they affect the text.

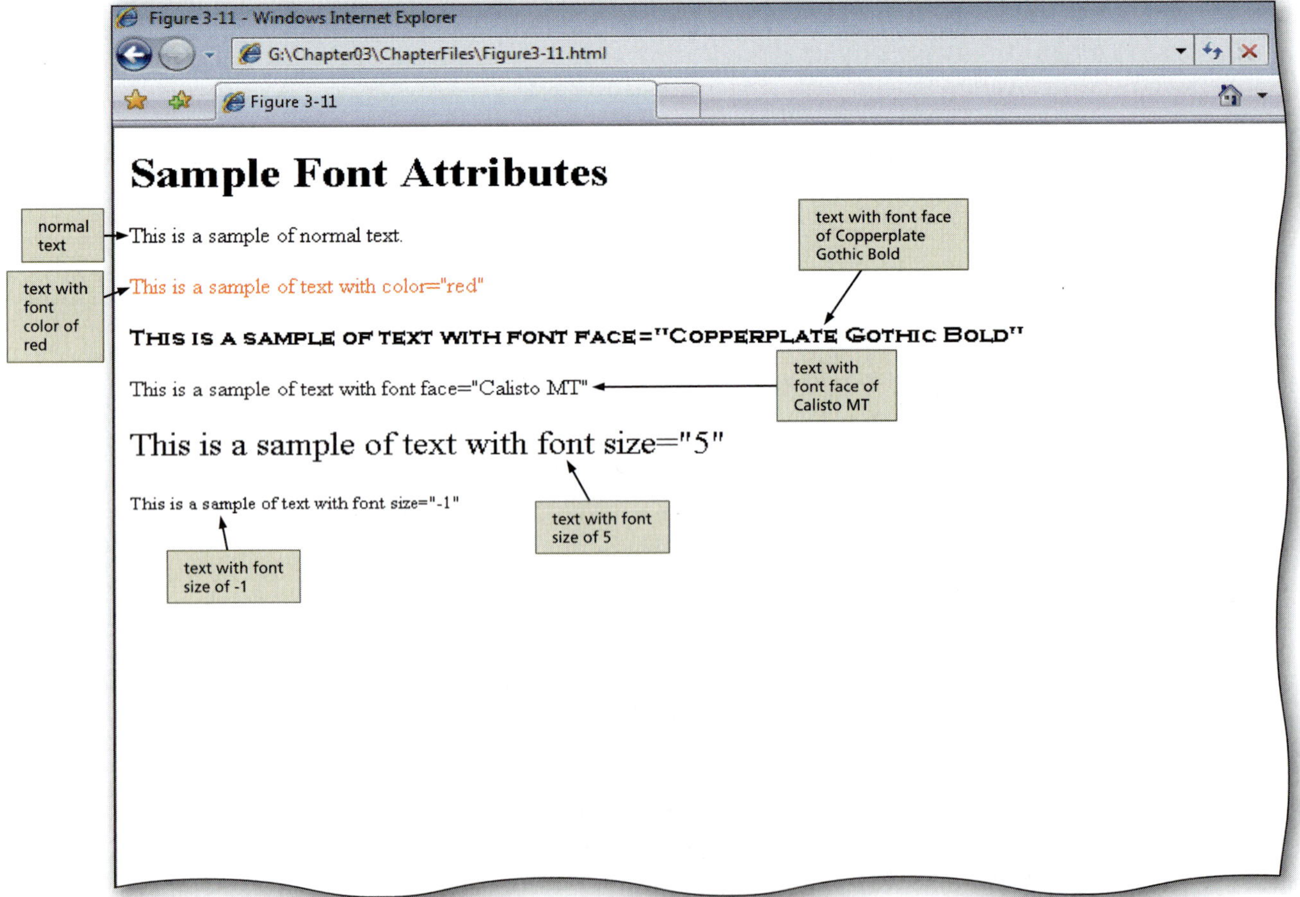

Figure 3–11 Examples of various font attributes.

To Add a Left-Aligned Heading with a Font Color

The following step shows how to enter HTML code to add a left-aligned heading formatted in red to provide visual impact.

- With the insertion point on line 13, type `<h1><font color="#ff0000">Welcome to the Valley's best pasta place!</font></h1>` and then press the ENTER key (Figure 3–12).

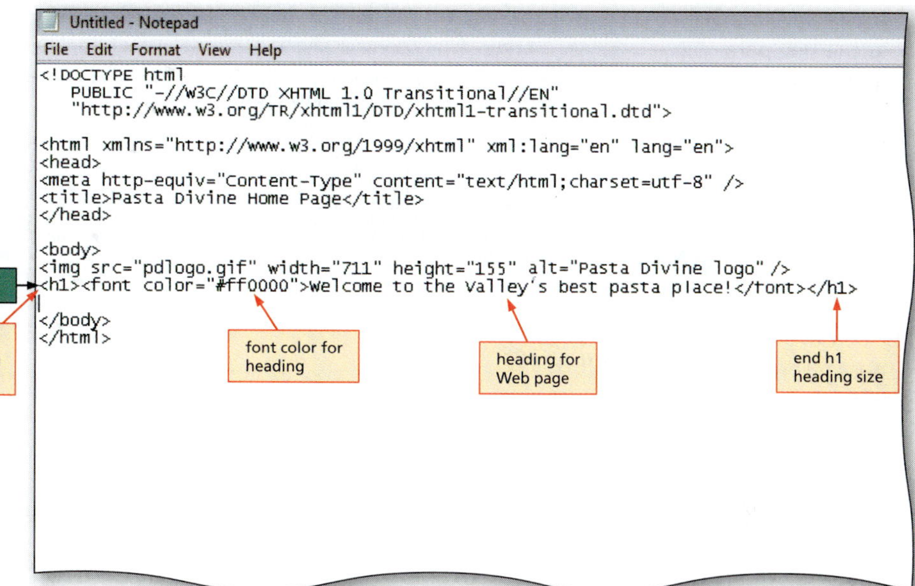

Figure 3–12

Q&A Why did I not have to use the align="left" attribute in this heading tag to left-align my heading?

The default alignment for a heading is left-aligned. If you do not specify an alignment, it will align left by default.

Q&A Can I insert tags in a different order?

When using these font attributes, remember that XHTML coding standards require that tags be nested properly. Nesting tags properly means that you always must enter end tags in an order opposite from the start tags. For example, as shown in Figure 3–12, the HTML code starts with the start <h1> heading tag, followed by the start <font> tag. The end tags are entered in the opposite order, with the end </font> tag first, followed by the end </h1> heading tag. Although a Web page with improper nesting tags might display in the browser correctly, it would not pass validation.

To Enter a Paragraph of Text

After the colored h1 heading for the Pasta Divine home page is entered, you need to add a paragraph of text introducing Pasta Divine. Table 3–4 shows the tags and text to enter.

Table 3–4 Paragraph of Text

Line	HTML Tag and Text
14	`<p>For the best pasta in the Valley, choose any one of our five Pasta Divine`
15	`locations. We specialize in handmade, fresh pastas and sauces. Our unique recipes`
16	`have been passed down in the family for centuries. Our founder, Salvatore`
17	`DiGiacomo, brought his family's pasta-making expertise from Italy in 1910.`
18	`The mouth-watering pasta recipes have been passed down to subsequent generations`
19	`ever since.</p>`

The following step illustrates how to enter a paragraph of text in an HTML file.

- With the insertion point on line 14 enter the HTML code shown in Table 3–4 as the first paragraph in the HTML file. Press ENTER at the end of each line (Figure 3–13).
- Press the ENTER key again.

Q&A Do I have to end all paragraphs of text with the </p> tag?

A Web page without </p> tags would display in the browser correctly. This Web page would not pass validation using the W3C Markup Validation Service, however. One missed </p> tag will result in many errors during validation.

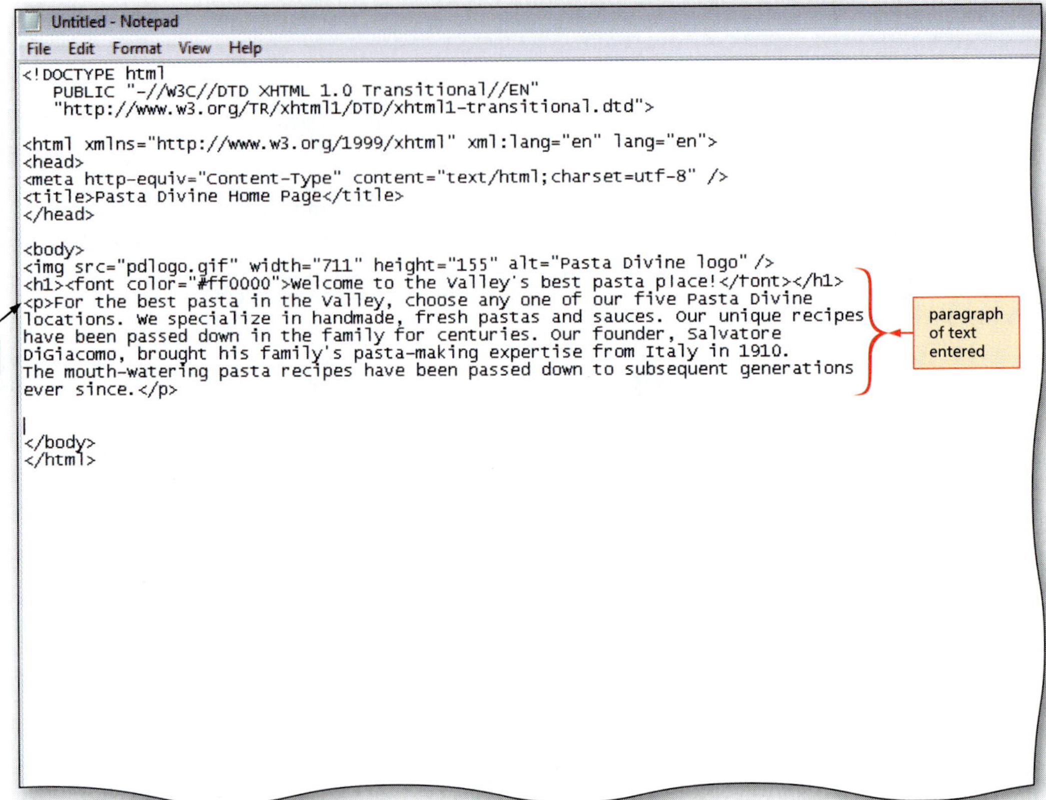

Figure 3–13

To Create an Unordered (Bulleted) List

The next step is to add an unordered list. An h2 heading above the unordered list visually separates the list from other elements on the Web page and indicates what the items in the list describe. Square bullets are used to identify items in the lists and to give the page a more distinctive look. Table 3–5 shows the HTML code used to create an unordered (bulleted) list for the Pasta Divine home page.

Table 3–5 HTML Code for Creating Unordered (Bulleted) Lists

Line	HTML Tag and Text
21	`<h2>Our services include:</h2>`
22	`<ul type="square">`
23	`<li>Fine dining in our comfortable restaurants</li>`
24	`<li>Banquet facilities for large or small parties</li>`
25	`<li>Extensive carry out menu</li>`
26	`</ul>`

The following step shows how to create the unordered (bulleted) list that appears on the Pasta Divine home page.

- If necessary, click line 21.
- Enter the HTML code shown in Table 3–5.
- After the </ul> in line 26, press the ENTER key twice to insert a blank line on line 27 and end on line 28 (Figure 3–14).

Q&A

What if I wanted to use a different bullet type?

For an open circle bullet, use "circle" for the ul type attribute. To use the default disc (filled circle) bullet, the type attribute does not need to be included.

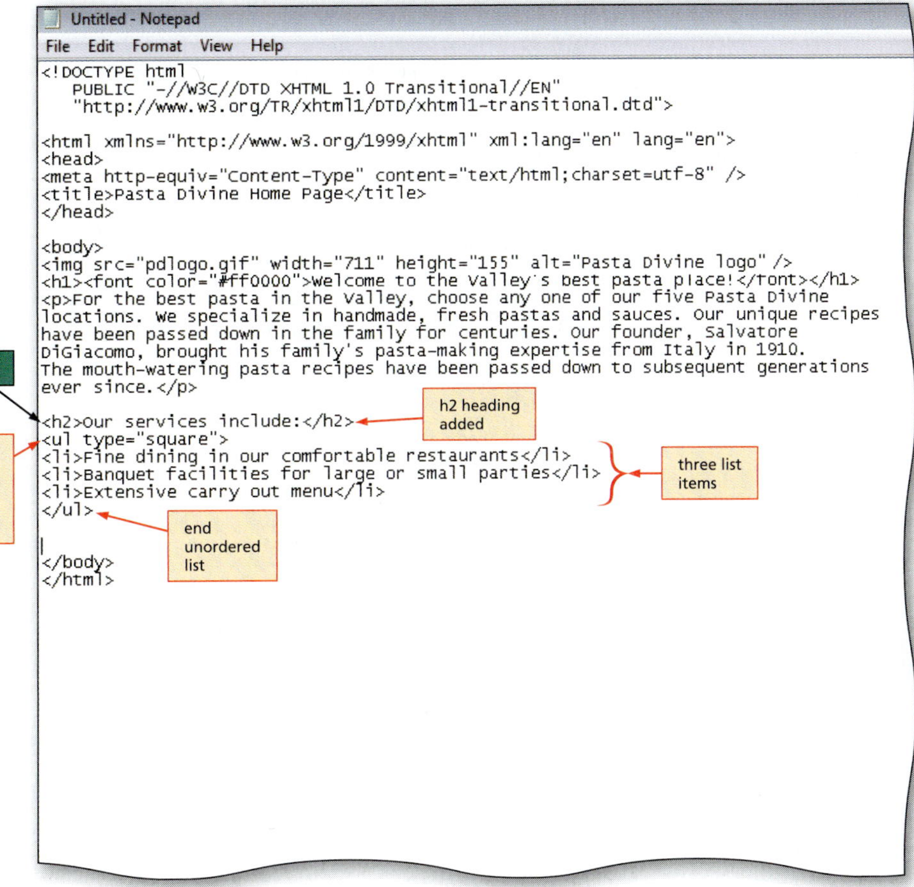

Figure 3–14

To Add Paragraphs of Text

Two other short paragraphs of text (as shown in Table 3–6) are now added to the home page. Because you want a blank line to display on the Web page between paragraphs, you will use a <p> tag at the start of the second paragraph.

Table 3–6 Other Paragraphs of Text

Line	HTML Tag and Text
28	`<p>Please browse our Web site to learn more about Pasta Divine's products and`
29	`services. Additional links include: monthly specials,`
30	`where you can review the descriptions and prices for this month's specialty dishes`
31	`and history of pasta, where`
32	`you can learn more information about pasta.</p>`
33	
34	`<p>Have a question or comment? Call us at (206) 555-PASTA or e-mail us at`
35	`pastadivine@isp.com.</p>`

The following step shows how to add the other paragraphs of text to the Pasta Divine home page.

- If necessary, click line 28.
- Enter the HTML code shown in Table 3–6 to insert the additional paragraphs of text. Press the ENTER key at the end of each line (Figure 3–15).

Q&A What if I wanted the second paragraph to start without a blank line above it?

If you wanted the second paragraph to move to the next line without a blank line in between, you would use the <br /> tag instead.

```
Untitled - Notepad
File Edit Format View Help
<!DOCTYPE html
   PUBLIC "-//W3C//DTD XHTML 1.0 Transitional//EN"
   "http://www.w3.org/TR/xhtml1/DTD/xhtml1-transitional.dtd">

<html xmlns="http://www.w3.org/1999/xhtml" xml:lang="en" lang="en">
<head>
<meta http-equiv="Content-Type" content="text/html;charset=utf-8" />
<title>Pasta Divine Home Page</title>
</head>

<body>
<img src="pdlogo.gif" width="711" height="155" alt="Pasta Divine logo" />
<h1><font color="#ff0000">Welcome to the Valley's best pasta place!</font></h1>
<p>For the best pasta in the valley, choose any one of our five Pasta Divine
locations. We specialize in handmade, fresh pastas and sauces. Our unique recipes
have been passed down in the family for centuries. Our founder, Salvatore
DiGiacomo, brought his family's pasta-making expertise from Italy in 1910.
The mouth-watering pasta recipes have been passed down to subsequent generations
ever since.</p>

<h2>Our services include:</h2>
<ul type="square">
<li>Fine dining in our comfortable restaurants</li>
<li>Banquet facilities for large or small parties</li>
<li>Extensive carry out menu</li>
</ul>

<p>Please browse our Web site to learn more about Pasta Divine's products and
services. Additional links include: monthly specials,
where you can review the descriptions and prices for this month's specialty dishes
and history of pasta, where
you can learn more information about pasta.</p>

<p>Have a question or comment? Call us at (206) 555-PASTA or e-mail us at
pastadivine@isp.com.</p>

</body>
</html>
```

last two paragraphs of text added

Figure 3–15

Plan Ahead

Planning how and where to use the four types of links is an important part of Web page design.

- **Identify how to link from the home page to another page in the Web site.** Linking to another Web page in a Web site is often done with text links. When determining what words to use, make sure that the text links are clear and easy to understand. Using a phrase such as "click here" is not one that clearly identifies where the link will go. Choosing words such as "monthly specials" tells the Web site visitor to click that link if they want to review the monthly specials.
- **Use an e-mail link on the home page.** A good standard practice is to include an e-mail link on the home page. Again, using words such as "click here" are not as effective as using a company's actual e-mail address (pastadivine@isp.com in this case) as the e-mail link text.
- **Use internal links on long Web pages.** Another good standard practice is to include links within a Web page when the page is long (i.e., when you have to press the PAGE DOWN key several times to get to the end of the Web page). Internal links help visitors navigate more easily within long Web pages. Also consider using links back to the top of a long Web page for ease of use.
- **Determine external links for the home page.** Visitors to a Web site might want additional information on a topic, so a link also can be included on the home page. Linking to an external Web site (i.e., one that is outside of the boundaries of the current Web site) is appropriate to provide additional information. Again, it is important to select words or phrases that make sense for that link.

Adding a Text Link to Another Web Page within the Same Web Site

The <a> and </a> tags are used to create links on a Web page. The <a> tag also is called the **anchor tag** because it is used to create anchors for links to another page in the same Web site, to a Web page in an external Web site, within the same Web page, and for e-mail links. The basic form of the tag used to create a link is:

```
<a href="URL">linktext</a>
```

where linktext is the clickable word or phrase that is displayed on the Web page and the value for href (hypertext reference) is the name or URL of the linked page or file. Table 3–7 shows some of the <a> tag attributes and their functions.

Table 3–7 <a> Tag Attributes and Functions

Attribute	Function
href	Specifies the URL of the linked page or file.
name	Defines a name for the current anchor so it may be the target or destination of another link. Each anchor on a Web page must use a unique name.
rel	Indicates a forward relationship from the current document to the linked document. The value of the rel attribute is a link type, such as prev, next, index, or copyright. For example, the Web page chapter3.html might include the tag <a rel="next" href="chapter4.html"> to indicate a link to the Web page for the next chapter, chapter4.html.
rev	Indicates a reverse (backward) relationship from the current document to the linked document. The value of the rev attribute is a link type, such as prev, next, index, or copyright. For example, the chapter3.html Web page might include the tag <a rev="prev" href="chapter2.html"> to indicate a link to the Web page for the previous chapter, chapter2.html.
type	Specifies the content type (also known as media types or MIME types) of the linked page or file to help a browser determine if it can handle the resource type. Examples of content types include text/html, image/jpeg, video/quicktime, application/java, text/css, and text/javascript.

Before creating a link, be sure you know the URL or name of the file to be linked and the text that will serve as the clickable word or phrase. The words should be descriptive and tell the Web page visitor the purpose of the link. For the Pasta Divine home page, the text link is a phrase in a paragraph at the bottom of the Web page.

BTW

Other Links

You also can create links to non-http Web pages such as FTP sites and newsgroups. To link to an FTP site, type ftp://URL rather than http://URL used in this project. For a newsgroup, type news:newsgroup name, and for any particular article within the newsgroup, type news:article name as the entry.

To Add a Text Link to Another Web Page within the Same Web Site

The Pasta Divine home page includes a text link to the Monthly Specials Web page, which is part of the same Web site. The following step illustrates how to add a text link to another Web page within the same Web site.

- Click immediately to the left of the m in the word monthly on line 29.
- Type `<a href="specials.html">` to start the link, setting the Web page specials.html as the linked Web page.
- Click immediately to the right of the s in specials and before the comma on line 29. Type `</a>` to close the link (Figure 3–16).

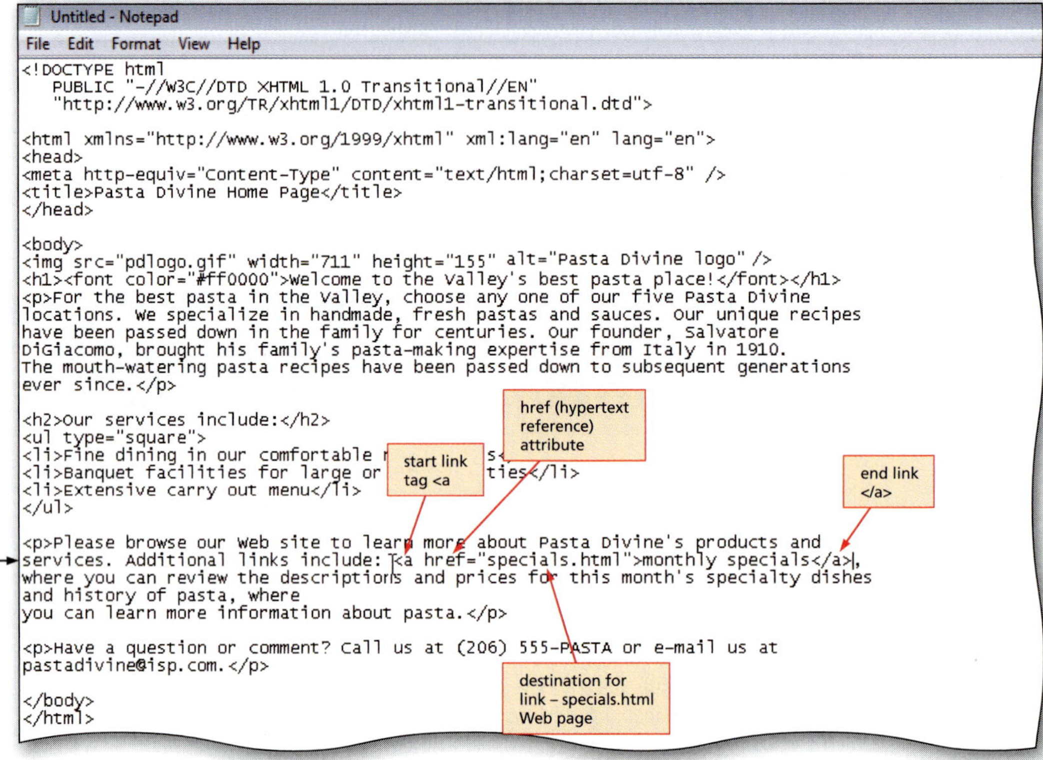

```
<!DOCTYPE html
   PUBLIC "-//W3C//DTD XHTML 1.0 Transitional//EN"
   "http://www.w3.org/TR/xhtml1/DTD/xhtml1-transitional.dtd">

<html xmlns="http://www.w3.org/1999/xhtml" xml:lang="en" lang="en">
<head>
<meta http-equiv="Content-Type" content="text/html;charset=utf-8" />
<title>Pasta Divine Home Page</title>
</head>

<body>
<img src="pdlogo.gif" width="711" height="155" alt="Pasta Divine logo" />
<h1><font color="#ff0000">Welcome to the Valley's best pasta place!</font></h1>
<p>For the best pasta in the Valley, choose any one of our five Pasta Divine
locations. We specialize in handmade, fresh pastas and sauces. Our unique recipes
have been passed down in the family for centuries. Our founder, Salvatore
DiGiacomo, brought his family's pasta-making expertise from Italy in 1910.
The mouth-watering pasta recipes have been passed down to subsequent generations
ever since.</p>

<h2>Our services include:</h2>
<ul type="square">
<li>Fine dining in our comfortable r...s</li>
<li>Banquet facilities for large or...ties</li>
<li>Extensive carry out menu</li>
</ul>

<p>Please browse our Web site to learn more about Pasta Divine's products and
services. Additional links include: <a href="specials.html">monthly specials</a>,
where you can review the descriptions and prices for this month's specialty dishes
and history of pasta, where
you can learn more information about pasta.</p>

<p>Have a question or comment? Call us at (206) 555-PASTA or e-mail us at
pastadivine@isp.com.</p>

</body>
</html>
```


Figure 3–16

Q&A What is the href attribute for?

The href stands for "hypertext reference" and is the URL of the destination Web page.

Q&A How will I know if my text is a link when it is displayed in the browser?

In the browser, you will immediately see that the text is a link because it will all be blue in color and underlined.

Q&A What happens if I forget to insert the </a> tag on a link?

A text link without the </a> tag would not display correctly in the browser. If you forget to use the </a> tag to end this text link, all of the text beyond the <a href=""> tag will serve as that link. In this example, all of the text that follows the m in monthly will link to the specials.html Web page, which is certainly not what you want.

Adding an E-Mail Link

Adding an e-mail link is similar to adding a text link, but instead of using a URL as the href attribute value, the href attribute value for an e-mail link uses the form:

```
<a href="mailto:address@email.com">linktext</a>
```

where the href attribute value uses the word *mailto* to indicate it is an e-mail link, followed by a colon and the e-mail address to which to send the e-mail message. When the browser recognizes a **mailto** URL in a clicked link, it automatically opens a new message in the default e-mail program and inserts the appropriate contact e-mail address in the To field.

The clickable text used for an e-mail link typically is the e-mail address used in the e-mail link. The Web page also should provide some information before the link, so visitors know the purpose of the e-mail link.

To Add an E-Mail Link

The Pasta Divine home page includes an e-mail link so customers can contact Pasta Divine for additional information or to comment on the Web page. The <a> and </a> tags used to create a text link to a Web page also are used to create an e-mail link. The following step shows how to add an e-mail link to a Web page.

- With the insertion point at the beginning of line 35, to the left of the p in pastadivine, type `<a href="mailto:pastadivine@isp.com">` as the start of the e-mail link. This will link to the e-mail address pastadivine@isp.com when the link is clicked.
- Click immediately after the m in isp.com and before the period in the e-mail address text on line 35.
- Type `</a>` to end the e-mail link as shown in Figure 3–17.

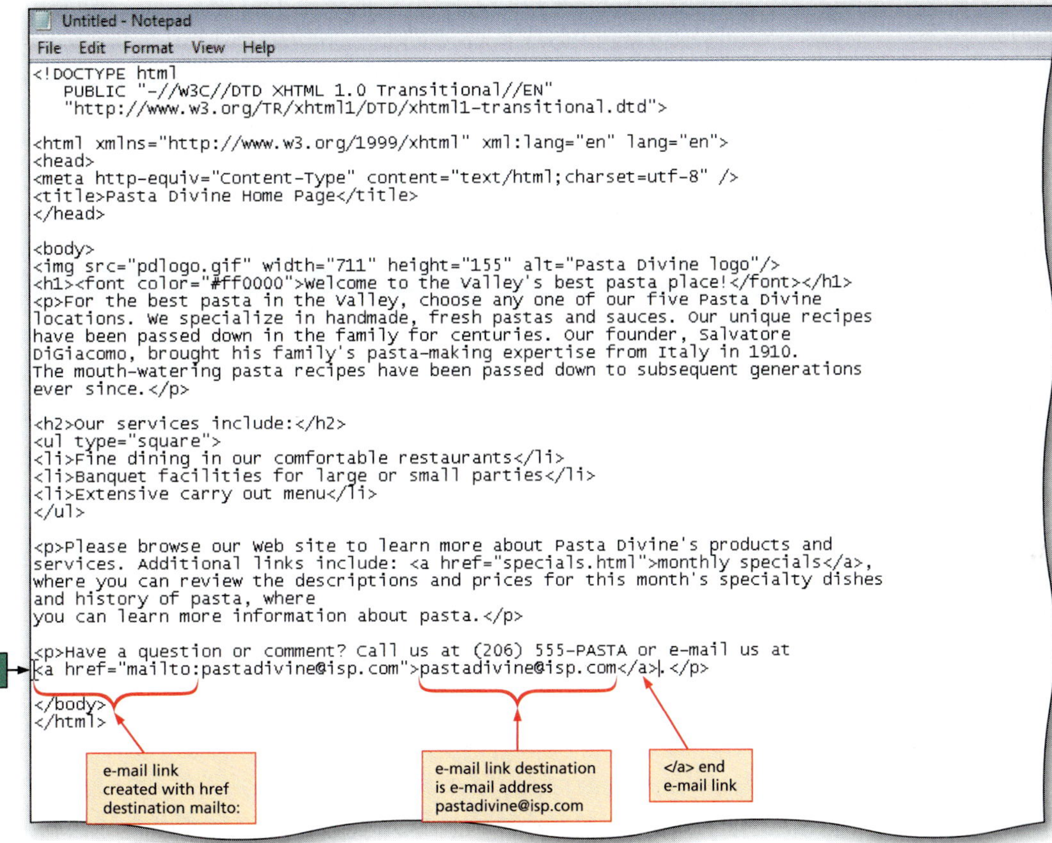


```
<!DOCTYPE html
   PUBLIC "-//W3C//DTD XHTML 1.0 Transitional//EN"
   "http://www.w3.org/TR/xhtml1/DTD/xhtml1-transitional.dtd">

<html xmlns="http://www.w3.org/1999/xhtml" xml:lang="en" lang="en">
<head>
<meta http-equiv="Content-Type" content="text/html;charset=utf-8" />
<title>Pasta Divine Home Page</title>
</head>

<body>
<img src="pdlogo.gif" width="711" height="155" alt="Pasta Divine logo"/>
<h1><font color="#ff0000">Welcome to the Valley's best pasta place!</font></h1>
<p>For the best pasta in the Valley, choose any one of our five Pasta Divine
locations. We specialize in handmade, fresh pastas and sauces. Our unique recipes
have been passed down in the family for centuries. Our founder, Salvatore
DiGiacomo, brought his family's pasta-making expertise from Italy in 1910.
The mouth-watering pasta recipes have been passed down to subsequent generations
ever since.</p>

<h2>Our services include:</h2>
<ul type="square">
<li>Fine dining in our comfortable restaurants</li>
<li>Banquet facilities for large or small parties</li>
<li>Extensive carry out menu</li>
</ul>

<p>Please browse our Web site to learn more about Pasta Divine's products and
services. Additional links include: <a href="specials.html">monthly specials</a>,
where you can review the descriptions and prices for this month's specialty dishes
and history of pasta, where
you can learn more information about pasta.</p>

<p>Have a question or comment? Call us at (206) 555-PASTA or e-mail us at
<a href="mailto:pastadivine@isp.com">pastadivine@isp.com</a>.</p>

</body>
</html>
```

Figure 3–17

Q&A

I see two occurrences of pastadivine@isp.com on line 35. Why do I need two?

The first occurrence of pastadivine@isp.com (the one within the link tag following the mailto:) is the destination of the link. The second occurrence of pastadivine@isp.com is the text link itself that will be displayed in the browser.

Adding Other Information to an E-Mail link

Sometimes, you need to add a message in the body of the e-mail in addition to the subject. This technique can be very helpful when more than one e-mail link is positioned on a Web page, and each link has a different purpose. For instance, one e-mail might be used for general questions, whereas another link might be used for specific information. You also can include a carbon-copy (cc) address. For instance, to include just a subject or to include a subject and body message text in the above mailto:, you would complete the steps on the next page.

To Add a Subject to an E-Mail Link

1. Type <a href=mailto:pastadivine@isp.com?subject=Monthly Specials> as the tag.

Sometimes, you need to add a message in the body of the e-mail in addition to the subject. This technique can be very helpful when more than one e-mail link is positioned on a Web page, and each link has a different purpose. For instance, one e-mail might be used for general questions, whereas another link might be used for specific information. Using the subject and body attributes can be helpful for this scenario. Notice that the two attributes (subject and body) are separated by an ampersand in the following example. The following step shows how to add the subject "Monthly Specials" to the e-mail together with the message text "What are the specials?" as shown in Figure 3–18.

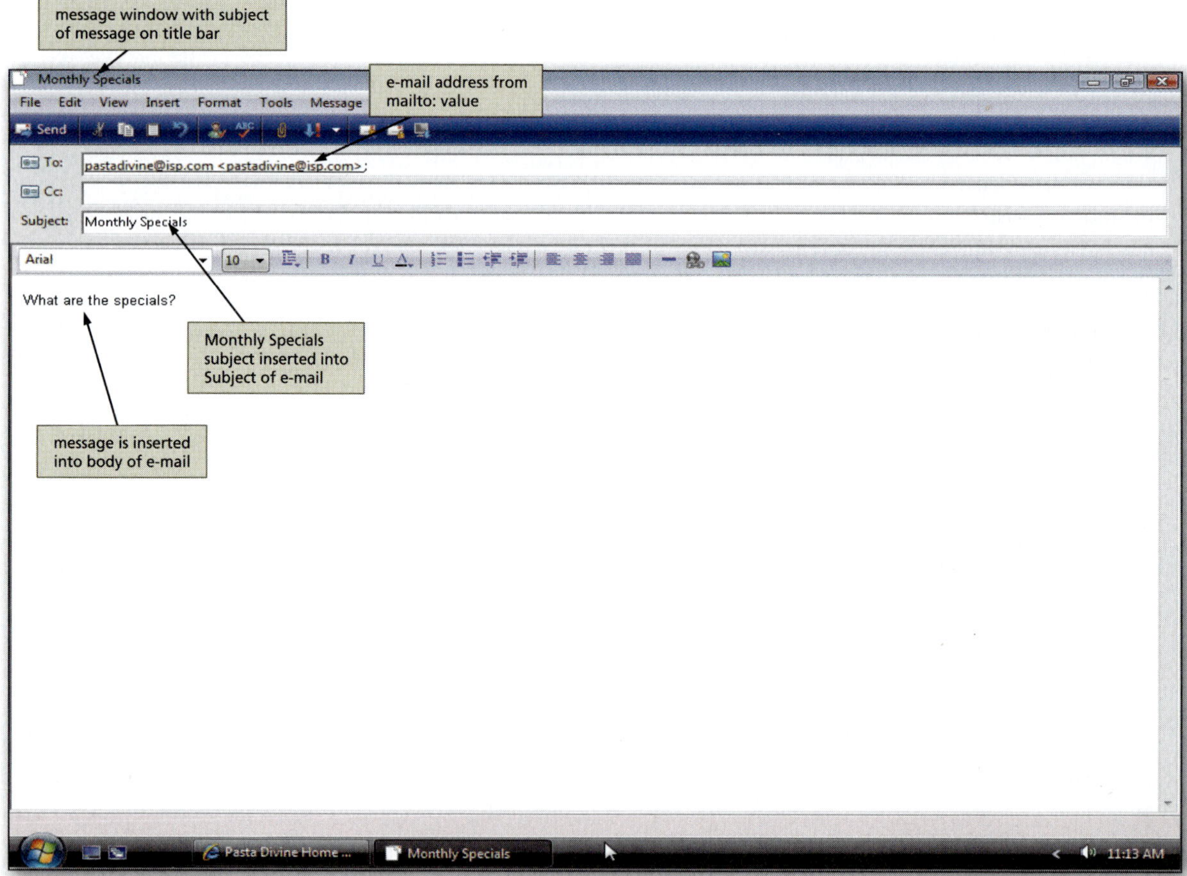

Figure 3–18

To Add a Subject Together with Body Message Text

1. Type <a href=mailto:pastadivine@isp.com?subject=Monthly Specials&body=What are the specials?> as the tag.

To Add a Text Link to a Web Page in Another Web Site

The <a> and </a> tags used to create a text link to a Web page within the same Web site also are used to create a link to a Web page in another Web site. The following step illustrates how to add a text link on the Monthly Specials Web page to an external Web page that describes the history of pasta.

- Click immediately to the left of the h in history on line 31 and type `<a href="http://en.wikipedia.org/wiki/Pasta">` to add the text link that will connect to the external Web site when clicked.
- Click immediately to the right of the a in pasta on line 31 and type `</a>` to end the tag as shown in Figure 3–19.

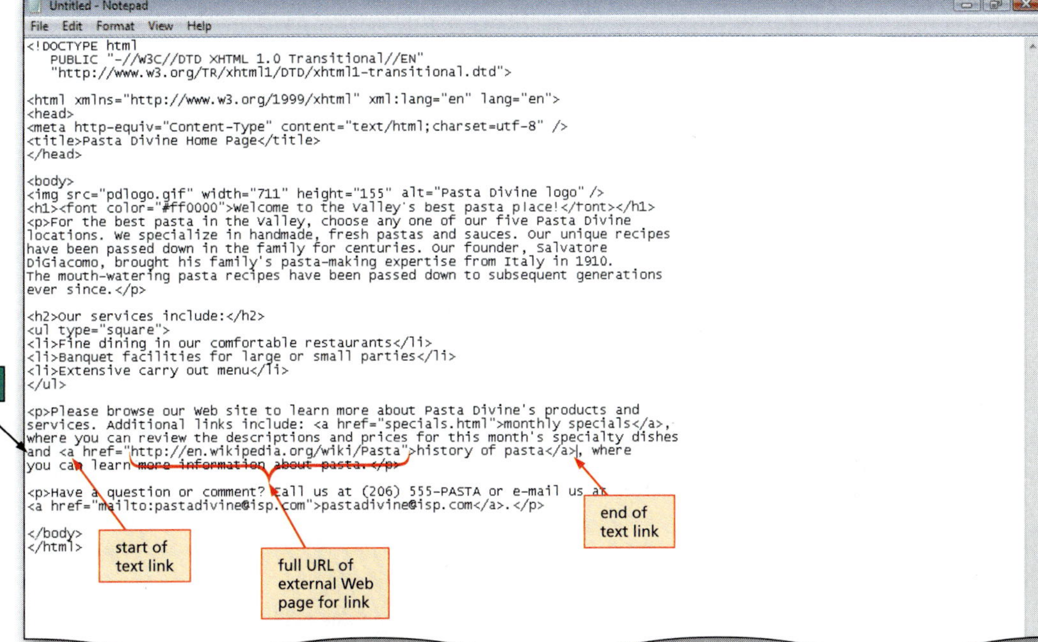


```
<!DOCTYPE html
     PUBLIC "-//W3C//DTD XHTML 1.0 Transitional//EN"
     "http://www.w3.org/TR/xhtml1/DTD/xhtml1-transitional.dtd">

<html xmlns="http://www.w3.org/1999/xhtml" xml:lang="en" lang="en">
<head>
<meta http-equiv="Content-Type" content="text/html;charset=utf-8" />
<title>Pasta Divine Home Page</title>
</head>

<body>
<img src="pdlogo.gif" width="711" height="155" alt="Pasta Divine logo" />
<h1><font color="#ff0000">Welcome to the Valley's best pasta place!</font></h1>
<p>For the best pasta in the Valley, choose any one of our five Pasta Divine
locations. We specialize in handmade, fresh pastas and sauces. Our unique recipes
have been passed down in the family for centuries. Our founder, Salvatore
DiGiacomo, brought his family's pasta-making expertise from Italy in 1910.
The mouth-watering pasta recipes have been passed down to subsequent generations
ever since.</p>

<h2>Our services include:</h2>
<ul type="square">
<li>Fine dining in our comfortable restaurants</li>
<li>Banquet facilities for large or small parties</li>
<li>Extensive carry out menu</li>
</ul>

<p>Please browse our Web site to learn more about Pasta Divine's products and
services. Additional links include: <a href="specials.html">monthly specials</a>,
where you can review the descriptions and prices for this month's specialty dishes
and <a href="http://en.wikipedia.org/wiki/Pasta">history of pasta</a>, where
you can learn more information about pasta.</p>

<p>Have a question or comment? Call us at (206) 555-PASTA or e-mail us at
<a href="mailto:pastadivine@isp.com">pastadivine@isp.com</a>.</p>

</body>
</html>
```

Figure 3–19

Q&A How do these links appear when displayed in the browser?

The text link is displayed in a blue, underlined font to indicate it is a link. The mouse pointer also changes to the pointing hand when moved over the link text.

Q&A When I type in the URL in the Address box of my browser, I never type in the http:// part of the URL. Why do I have to add the http:// in the link?

Although you do not need to type the http:// into the URL on the browser, you always must include that as part of the href when creating external links.

Q&A Why did I need the http:// part of the URL for this external link, but I did not need that for the Monthly Specials link?

The Monthly Specials Web page is stored in the same folder as the home page from which you are linking. You, therefore, do not need to include any information other than the name of the Web page file.

Using Absolute and Relative Paths

Before saving the HTML file, it is appropriate to revisit the overall concept of how the files are organized and saved. As noted in the last chapter, we use a very simple folder structure for projects in this book. In this book, the graphical images are stored in the same folder as the HTML files, for example, in the Chapter03\ChapterFiles folder. For most real-world applications, however, it would be more appropriate to separate the HTML code and the graphical images into different folders. Figure 3–20 on the next page shows an example of a more complex file structure that could be used for this book.

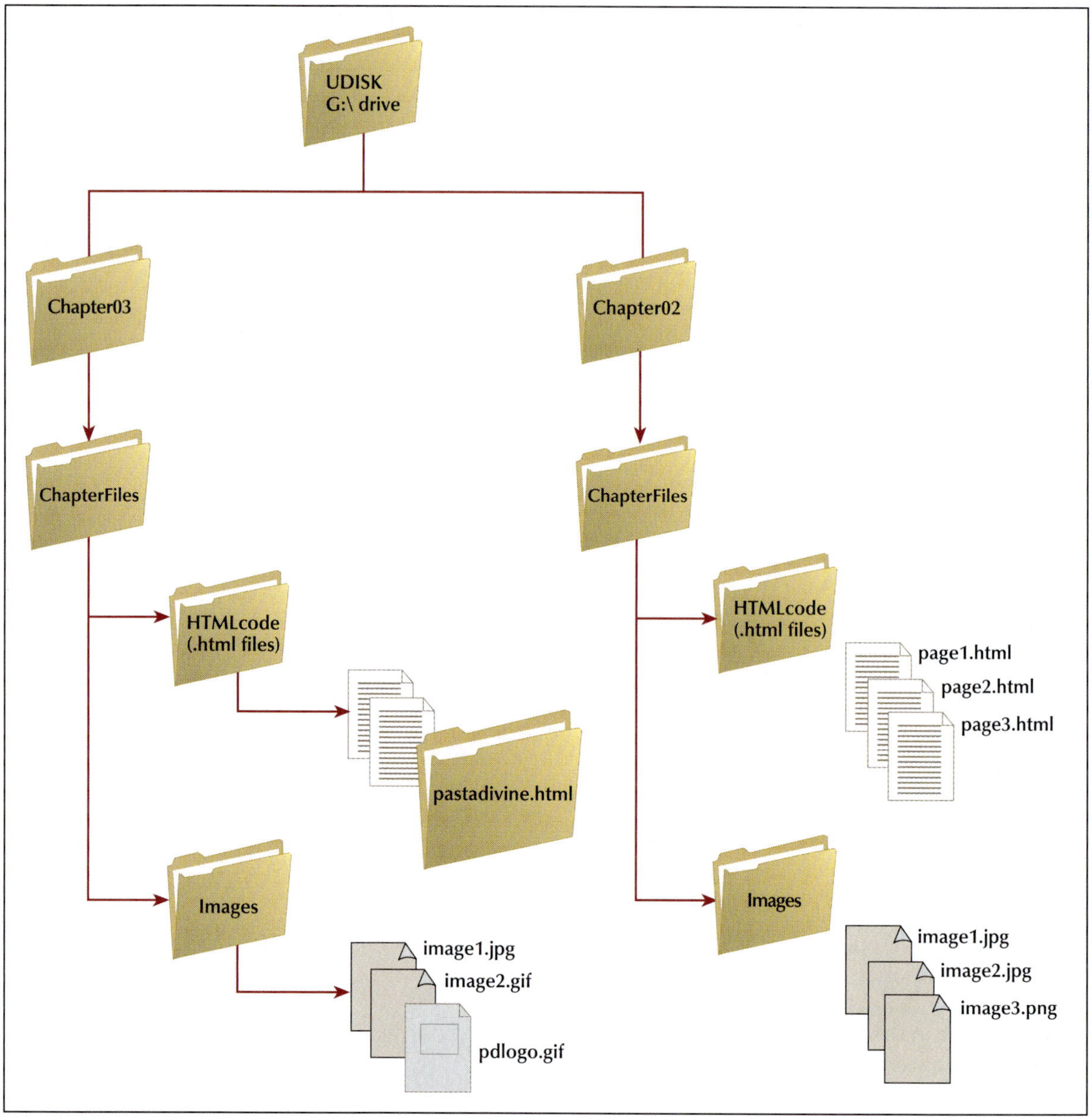

Figure 3–20

BTW

Logical vs. Physical Styles
For more information on the differences between logical and physical styles, search on the Web for "HTML logical style" and "HTML physical style". Many HTML tutorials also discuss this subject at length.

To understand how to use this sort of folder structure, you need to identify the folder location, or path, to the files. A **path** describes the location (folder or external Web site) where the files can be found, beginning with the UDISK G:\ drive (or another drive on your computer). This beginning location also is known as root. You can use either an absolute or relative path when identifying the location of the files. An **absolute path** specifies the exact address for the file to which you are linking or displaying a graphic. Looking at Figure 3–20, you would store the image pdlogo.gif in the Images folder and store the Web page itself, the pastadivine.html file, in the HTMLcode subfolder. If you moved to the HTMLcode subfolder and viewed the pastadivine.html file, the image pdlogo.gif would not appear because it is not in the same subfolder. To display the pastadivine.html file, you would use the following absolute path structure:

Chapter03\ChapterFiles\HTMLcode\pastadivine.html

Although absolute paths indicate the specific addresses of files, they can be cumbersome. If you have to move any of the files to a different folder or a different Web server, then all absolute paths would have to change.

Relative paths specify the location of a file, relative to the location of the file that is currently in use. A relative path utilizes the double period (..) symbol to move up or down the folder structure. So in the example in which you want to display the image pdlogo.gif (stored in the Images subfolder) from the Web page pastadivine.html (stored in the HTMLcode subfolder) within the Chapter03\ChapterFiles folders, you would use the following relative path structure:

..\Images\pdlogo.gif

It is better to use relative paths for flexibility wherever feasible. If the root folder must change for some reason, you would not have to change all addressing if you used relative paths. With absolute addressing, all paths would have to be changed.

To Save and Print an HTML File

With the HTML code for the Pasta Divine home page complete, you should save and print the file as a reference. The following step illustrates how to save and print an HTML file.

- With a USB flash drive connected to one of the computer's USB ports, click File on the Notepad menu bar and then click Save As. Type `pastadivine.html` in the File name text box (do not press ENTER).
- If Computer is not displayed in the Favorite Links section, drag the top or bottom edge of the Save As dialog box until Computer is displayed. If necessary, collapse the Folders pane to see the Computer link.
- Click Computer in the Favorite Links section to display a list of available drives.

```
<!DOCTYPE html
   PUBLIC "-//W3C//DTD XHTML 1.0 Transitional//EN"
   "http://www.w3.org/TR/xhtml1/DTD/xhtml1-transitional.dtd">

<html xmlns="http://www.w3.org/1999/xhtml" xml:lang="en" lang="en">
<head>
<meta http-equiv="Content-Type" content="text/html;charset=utf-8" />
<title>Pasta Divine Home Page</title>
</head>

<body>
<img src="pdlogo.gif" width="711" height="155" alt="Pasta Divine logo" />
<h1><font color="#ff0000">Welcome to the Valley's best pasta place!</font></h1>
<p>For the best pasta in the Valley, choose any one of our five Pasta Divine
locations. We specialize in handmade, fresh pastas and sauces. Our unique recipes
have been passed down in the family for centuries. Our founder, Salvatore
DiGiacomo, brought his family's pasta-making expertise from Italy in 1910.
The mouth-watering pasta recipes have been passed down to subsequent generations
ever since.</p>

<h2>Our services include:</h2>
<ul type="square">
<li>Fine dining in our comfortable restaurants</li>
<li>Banquet facilities for large or small parties</li>
<li>Extensive carry out menu</li>
</ul>

<p>Please browse our Web site to learn more about Pasta Divine's products and
services. Additional links include: <a href="specials.html">monthly specials</a>,
where you can review the descriptions and prices for this month's specialty dishes
and <a href="http://en.wikipedia.org/wiki/Pasta">history of pasta</a>, where
you can learn more information about pasta.</p>

<p>Have a question or comment? Call us at (206) 555-PASTA or e-mail us at
<a href="mailto:pastadivine@isp.com">pastadivine@isp.com</a>.</p>

</body>
</html>
```

Figure 3–21

- If necessary, scroll until UDISK 2.0 (G:) is displayed in the list of available drives.
- If necessary, open the Chapter03\ChapterFiles folder.
- Click the Save button in the Save As dialog box to save the file on the USB flash drive with the name pastadivine.html.
- Click File on the menu bar, click Print on the File menu, and then click the Print button in the Print dialog box to print a hard copy of the pastadivine.html file (Figure 3–21).

Validating and Viewing the Web Page and Testing Links

After you save and print the HTML file for the Pasta Divine home page, it should be validated to ensure that it meets current XHTML standards and viewed in a browser to confirm the Web page is displayed as desired. It also is important to test the two links in the Pasta Divine home page to verify they function as expected.

To Validate a Web Page

The following step illustrates how to validate an HTML file.

- Click the Start button on the Windows Vista taskbar to display the Start menu.
- Click the Internet icon in the pinned items list on the Start menu to start Internet Explorer. If necessary, click the Maximize button to maximize the browser window.
- Click the Address bar to select the URL in the Address bar.
- Type `validator.w3.org` to replace the current entry then press the ENTER key.
- Click the Validate by File Upload tab.

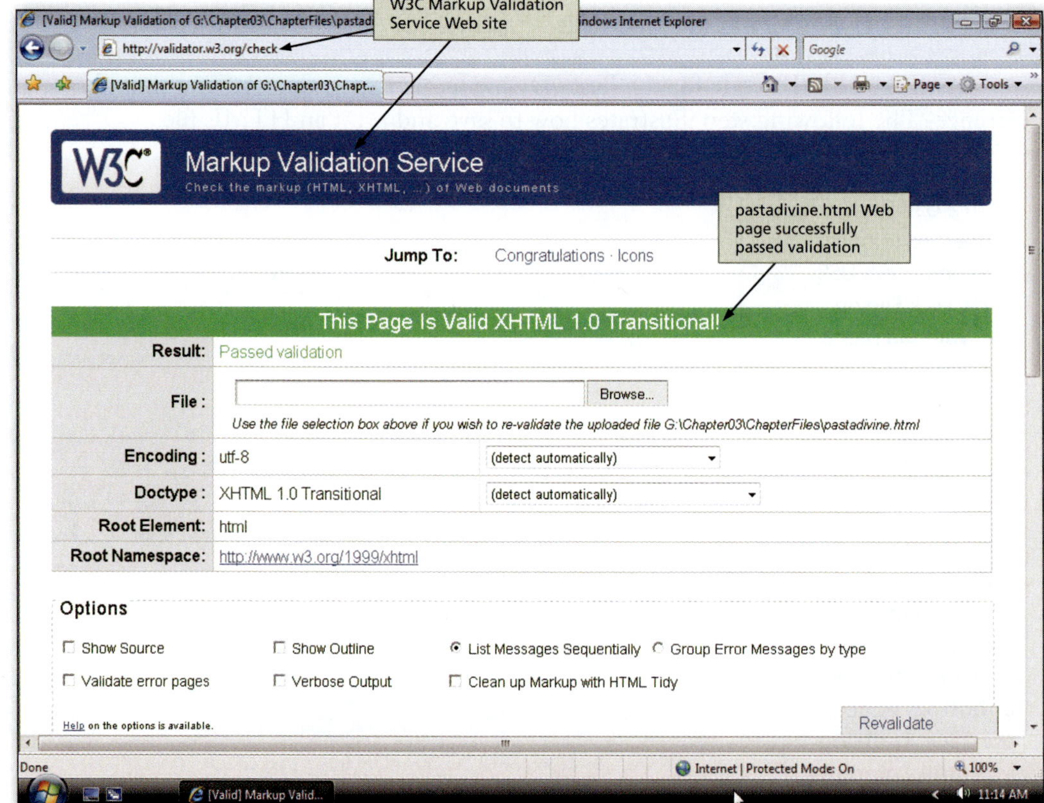

Figure 3–22

- Click the Browse button.
- Locate the pastadivine.html file on your storage device and click the file name.
- Click the Open button in the Choose file dialog box and the file name will be inserted into the File box.
- Click the Check button. The resulting validation should be displayed as shown in Figure 3–22.

Q&A

What if my HTML code does not validate?

If your code has errors, you should edit your HTML file to correct the errors. The Markup Validation Service report lists clearly what is wrong with your code. Once you make the necessary changes and save the file, you can again use the Browse button to open the corrected HTML file. You then use the Revalidate button to validate the changed code.

To View a Web Page

The following step illustrates how to view the HTML file in a browser.

1

- In Internet Explorer, click the Address bar to select the URL in the Address bar.
- Type `g:\Chapter03\ChapterFiles\pastadivine.html` to display the new URL in the Address bar and then press the ENTER key (Figure 3–23).

Q&A What if my page does not display correctly?

Check your pastadivine.html code carefully in Notepad to make sure you have not made any typing errors or left anything out. Correct the errors, resave the file, and try again.

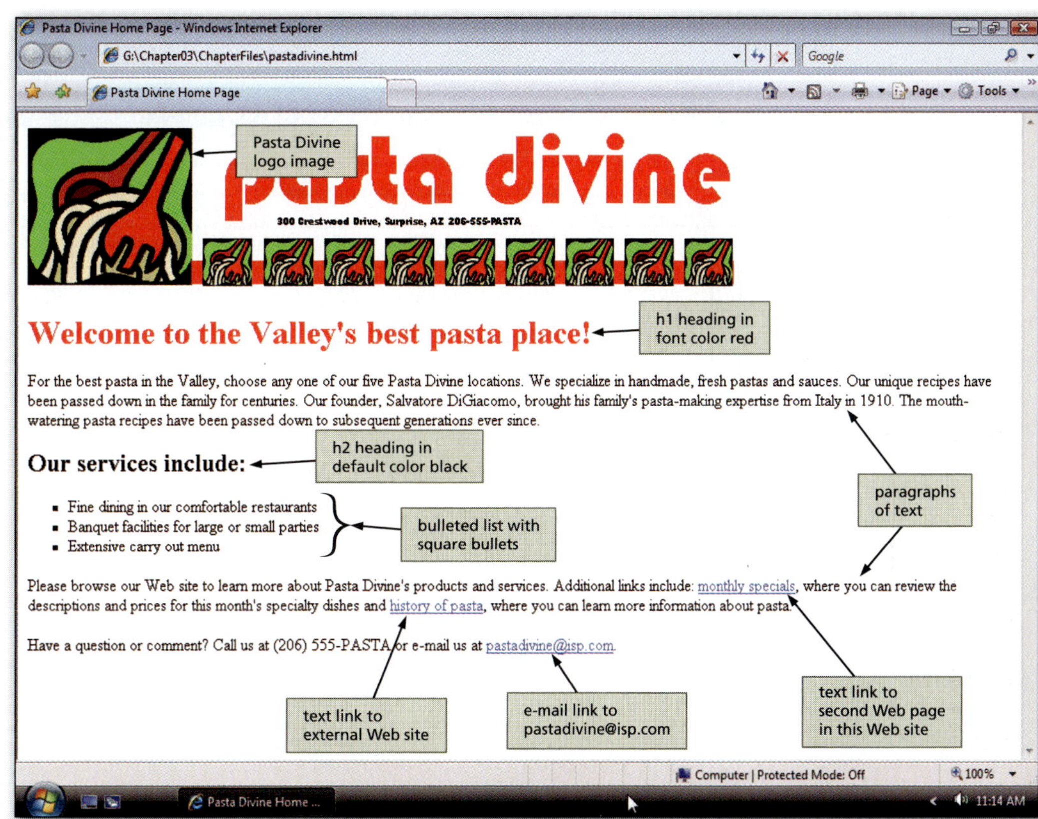

Figure 3–23

Plan Ahead

- **Determine what you need to test.** It is important to have a test plan when you test your Web pages. Planning what to test assures that all functionality of the Web page is tested. You should specifically test the display of the Web page itself together with testing that all of the links on the Web page work correctly.
- **Test the Web page as displayed in the browser.** Certainly the first part of testing is to verify that your Web page is displayed in the browser as intended. Ask the following questions: (1) Are the images all displayed where they should be? (2) Is the text presented as intended? (3) Are the links displayed as intended?
- **Test the links.** In your testing plan, you need to address all of the links that you have inserted into the Web page. It helps to create a matrix that includes three columns for information. The first column contains information about all of the links on the Web page. The second column contains information about the intended results of those links. The third column is the one that you complete during testing. If the link tests as it should, you can note that by putting a check mark in the third column. If the link test result is not as it should be, you can note in the third column what the result was. Using a technique such as this makes it easier to do thorough testing. When you know what the results of the test should be, it helps you verify valid links. This is an excellent technique to use when there are different people developing and testing the Web pages. The matrix will notify the developers of the test results clearly.

To Test Links on a Web Page

The following steps show how to test the links in the Pasta Divine home page to verify that they work correctly.

1

- With the Pasta Divine home page displayed in the browser, point to the e-mail link, pastadivine@isp.com and then click the link to open the default e-mail program with the address pastadivine@isp.com in the To: text box as shown in Figure 3–24.
- Click the Close button in the New Message window. If a dialog box asks if you want to save changes, click No.

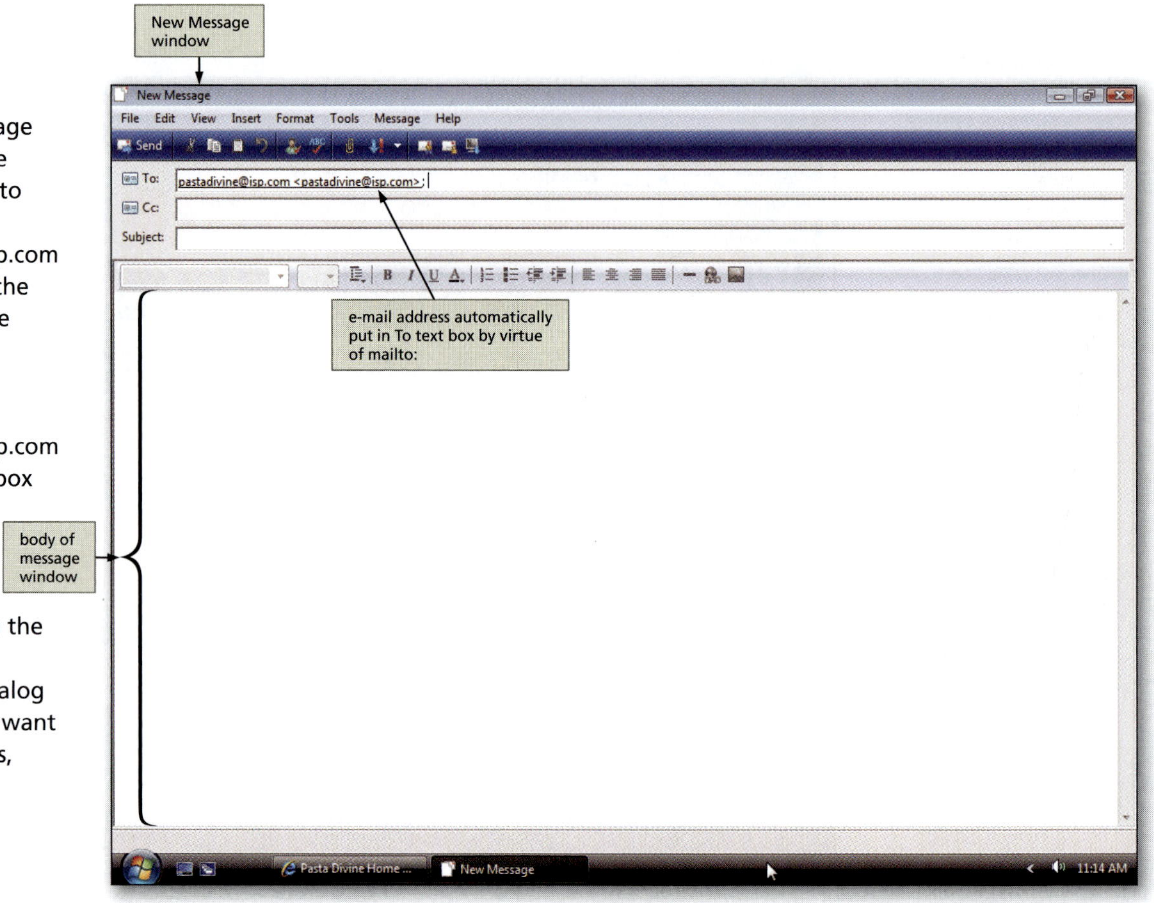

New Message window

e-mail address automatically put in To text box by virtue of mailto:

body of message window

Figure 3–24

BTW

Web Page Testing
An important part of Web page development is testing Web page links. For more information about link testing, search the Web for key words such as "HTML testing" or look at the World Wide Web Consortium (W3C) Web site.

2

- Click the history of pasta link to test the external link in the Web page. Close the browser window or use the Back button to return to the Pasta Divine home page.

- With the USB flash drive in drive G, point to the monthly specials link and click the link. The secondary Web page, specials.html, is displayed (Figure 3–25), although it is not completed.

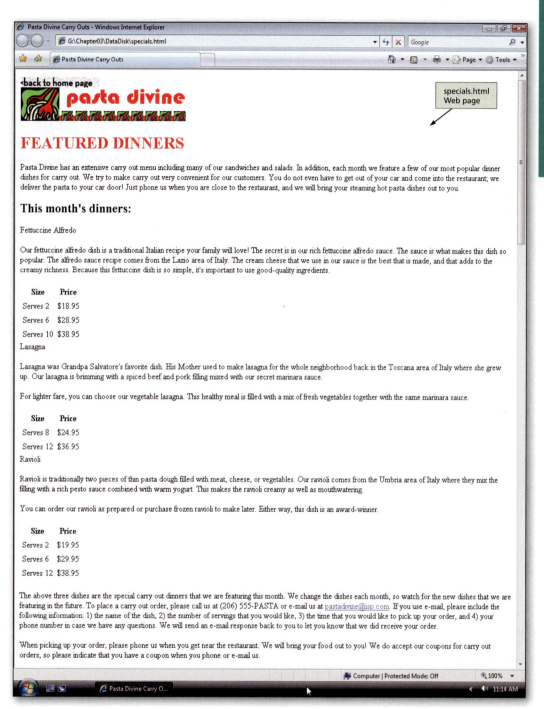

Pasta Divine Carry Outs - Windows Internet Explorer

G:\Chapter03\DataDisk\specials.html

Google

Pasta Divine Carry Outs

Page Tools

‹back to home page

pasta divine

specials.html Web page

FEATURED DINNERS

Pasta Divine has an extensive carry out menu including many of our sandwiches and salads. In addition, each month we feature a few of our most popular dinner dishes for carry out. We try to make carry out very convenient for our customers. You do not even have to get out of your car and come into the restaurant; we deliver the pasta to your car door! Just phone us when you are close to the restaurant, and we will bring your steaming hot pasta dishes out to you.

This month's dinners:

Fettuccine Alfredo

Our fettuccine alfredo dish is a traditional Italian recipe your family will love! The secret is in our rich fettuccine alfredo sauce. The sauce is what makes this dish so popular. The alfredo sauce recipe comes from the Lazio area of Italy. The cream cheese that we use in our sauce is the best that is made, and that adds to the creamy richness. Because this fettuccine dish is so simple, it's important to use good-quality ingredients.

Size	Price
Serves 2	$18.95
Serves 6	$28.95
Serves 10	$38.95

Lasagna

Lasagna was Grandpa Salvatore's favorite dish. His Mother used to make lasagna for the whole neighborhood back in the Toscana area of Italy where she grew up. Our lasagna is brimming with a spiced beef and pork filling mixed with our secret marinara sauce.

For lighter fare, you can choose our vegetable lasagna. This healthy meal is filled with a mix of fresh vegetables together with the same marinara sauce.

Size	Price
Serves 8	$24.95
Serves 12	$36.95

Ravioli

Ravioli is traditionally two pieces of thin pasta dough filled with meat, cheese, or vegetables. Our ravioli comes from the Umbria area of Italy where they mix the filling with a rich pesto sauce combined with warm yogurt. This makes the ravioli creamy as well as mouthwatering.

You can order our ravioli as prepared or purchase frozen ravioli to make later. Either way, this dish is an award-winner.

Size	Price
Serves 2	$19.95
Serves 6	$29.95
Serves 12	$38.95

The above three dishes are the special carry out dinners that we are featuring this month. We change the dishes each month, so watch for the new dishes that we are featuring in the future. To place a carry out order, please call us at (206) 555-PASTA or e-mail us at pastadivine@isp.com. If you use e-mail, please include the following information: 1) the name of the dish, 2) the number of servings that you would like, 3) the time that you would like to pick up your order, and 4) your phone number in case we have any questions. We will send an e-mail response back to you to let you know that we did receive your order.

When picking up your order, please phone us when you get near the restaurant. We will bring your food out to you! We do accept our coupons for carry out orders, so please indicate that you have a coupon when you phone or e-mail us.

Computer | Protected Mode: Off 100%

Pasta Divine Carry O... 11:14 AM

Figure 3–25

To Print a Web Page

The following step shows how to print the Web page for future reference.

- Close the browser window or click the Back button on the Standard toolbar to return to the Pasta Divine home page.
- Click the Print icon on the Command bar.
- Once the Pasta Divine home page is printed (Figure 3–26), click the monthly specials link to return to that Web page.

Welcome to the Valley's best pasta place!

For the best pasta in the Valley, choose any one of our five Pasta Divine locations. We specialize in handmade, fresh pastas and sauces. Our unique recipes have been passed down in the family for centuries. Our founder, Salvatore DiGiacomo, brought his family's pasta-making expertise from Italy in 1910. The mouth-watering pasta recipes have been passed down to subsequent generations ever since.

Our services include:

- Fine dining in our comfortable restaurants
- Banquet facilities for large or small parties
- Extensive carry out menu

Please browse our Web site to learn more about Pasta Divine's products and services. Additional links include: monthly specials, where you can review the descriptions and prices for this month's specialty dishes and history of pasta, where you can learn more information about pasta.

Have a question or comment? Call us at (206) 555-PASTA or e-mail us at pastadivine@isp.com.

Figure 3–26

Editing the Second Web Page

With the home page complete, the next step is to create the Monthly Specials page. For this part of the project, you will download an existing Web page file and edit the HTML code to create the Web page as shown in Figure 3–27. You will enhance text by making it bold (i.e., strong), add an image, and set text to wrap around the image. You also will add two additional types of links: links within the same Web page and an image link to a Web page in the same Web site.

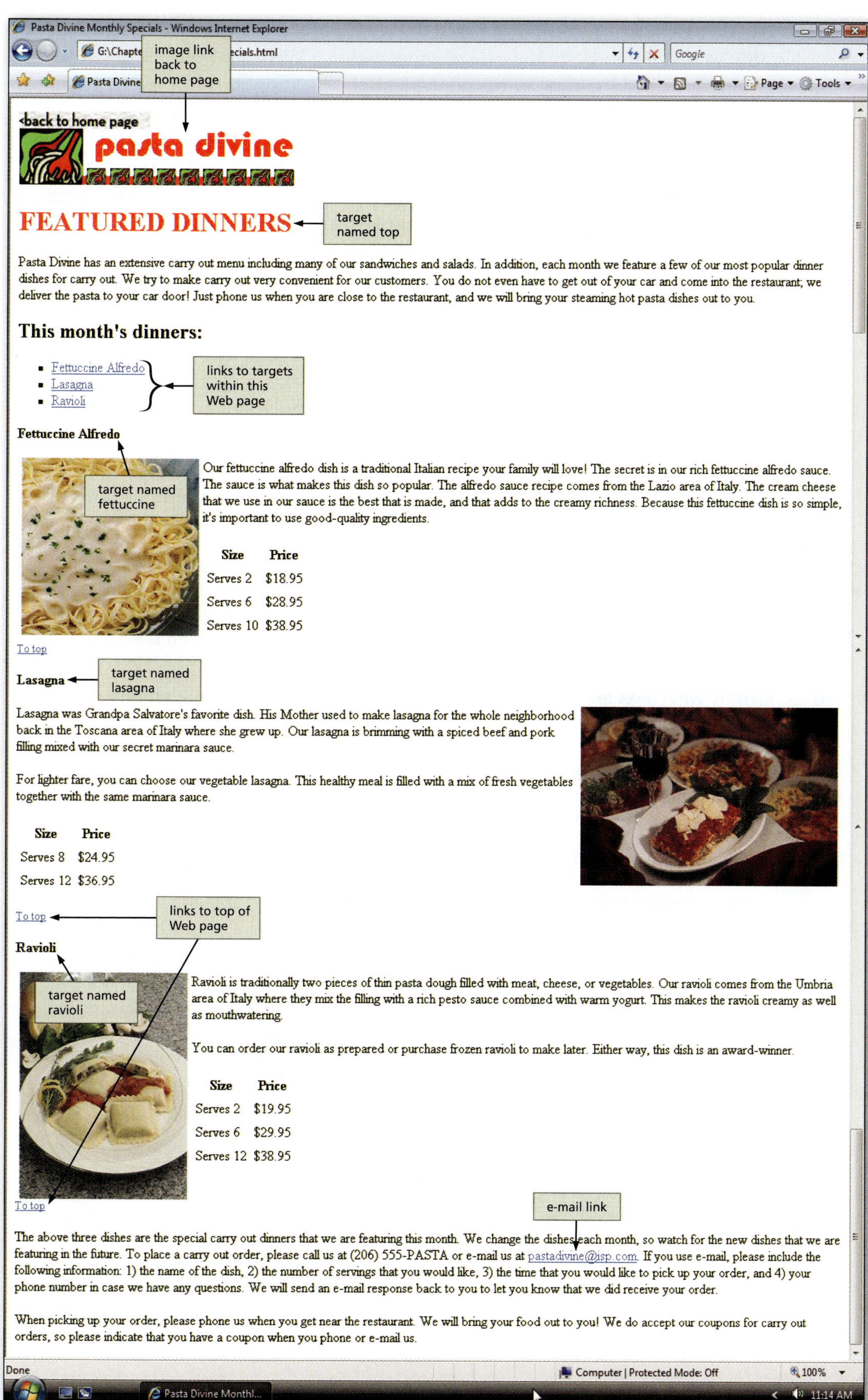

Pasta Divine Monthly Specials - Windows Internet Explorer
image link back to home page
back to home page
pasta divine
FEATURED DINNERS
target named top
Pasta Divine has an extensive carry out menu including many of our sandwiches and salads. In addition, each month we feature a few of our most popular dinner dishes for carry out. We try to make carry out very convenient for our customers. You do not even have to get out of your car and come into the restaurant; we deliver the pasta to your car door! Just phone us when you are close to the restaurant, and we will bring your steaming hot pasta dishes out to you.
This month's dinners:
Fettuccine Alfredo
Lasagna
Ravioli
links to targets within this Web page
Fettuccine Alfredo
target named fettuccine
Our fettuccine alfredo dish is a traditional Italian recipe your family will love! The secret is in our rich fettuccine alfredo sauce. The sauce is what makes this dish so popular. The alfredo sauce recipe comes from the Lazio area of Italy. The cream cheese that we use in our sauce is the best that is made, and that adds to the creamy richness. Because this fettuccine dish is so simple, it's important to use good-quality ingredients.
Size Price
Serves 2 $18.95
Serves 6 $28.95
Serves 10 $38.95
To top
Lasagna
target named lasagna
Lasagna was Grandpa Salvatore's favorite dish. His Mother used to make lasagna for the whole neighborhood back in the Toscana area of Italy where she grew up. Our lasagna is brimming with a spiced beef and pork filling mixed with our secret marinara sauce.
For lighter fare, you can choose our vegetable lasagna. This healthy meal is filled with a mix of fresh vegetables together with the same marinara sauce.
Size Price
Serves 8 $24.95
Serves 12 $36.95
To top
links to top of Web page
Ravioli
target named ravioli
Ravioli is traditionally two pieces of thin pasta dough filled with meat, cheese, or vegetables. Our ravioli comes from the Umbria area of Italy where they mix the filling with a rich pesto sauce combined with warm yogurt. This makes the ravioli creamy as well as mouthwatering.
You can order our ravioli as prepared or purchase frozen ravioli to make later. Either way, this dish is an award-winner.
Size Price
Serves 2 $19.95
Serves 6 $29.95
Serves 12 $38.95
To top
e-mail link
The above three dishes are the special carry out dinners that we are featuring this month. We change the dishes each month, so watch for the new dishes that we are featuring in the future. To place a carry out order, please call us at (206) 555-PASTA or e-mail us at pastadivine@isp.com. If you use e-mail, please include the following information: 1) the name of the dish, 2) the number of servings that you would like, 3) the time that you would like to pick up your order, and 4) your phone number in case we have any questions. We will send an e-mail response back to you to let you know that we did receive your order.
When picking up your order, please phone us when you get near the restaurant. We will bring your food out to you! We do accept our coupons for carry out orders, so please indicate that you have a coupon when you phone or e-mail us.
Done
Computer | Protected Mode: Off
100%
11:14 AM

Figure 3–27

As you have learned, the <a> tag used to create a link must specify the page, file, or location to which it links. In the case of a link within a Web page, the <a> tag specifies a **target**, or named location, in the same file. Before adding the links and targets in the Monthly Specials Web page, an unordered (bulleted) list that contains three items — Fettuccine Alfredo, Lasagna, and Ravioli — must be added to the page. The list items will serve as the links that are directed to the heading at the top of each major section of the Monthly Specials Web page. When clicked, these links will move the Web page visitor to the targets, which are named fettuccine, lasagna, and ravioli, respectively.

Because the Web page is so long, it is a good design practice to provide users with a quick way to move back to the top of the Web page without scrolling back. For this purpose, the Web page includes three text links named To top. These links are located just above the Lasagna and Ravioli headings, and at the bottom of the page above the last two paragraphs of text. When clicked, any To top link takes the Web page visitor back to the top of the page.

To complete the Monthly Specials Web page, you will create an image link, so users can click the back to home page link to return to the Pasta Divine home page. It is always important to provide a link back to the home page from subsequent Web pages. Your visitors should not have to use the Back button on the browser to return to the home page.

Plan Ahead

- **Determine what text formatting to use.** It helps to vary your text in a long Web page to break information up between headings. Using bold or italicized text sparingly gives the Web page a more interesting look. Make sure not to overdo the formatting of text because you can make the page look cluttered. It is more difficult to find the content that you are searching for in a cluttered Web page.
- **Identify what links are needed on a long Web page.** When you have an especially long Web page (one in which the visitor has to use the PAGE DOWN key), you should provide links within the Web page for easier navigation. You need to decide where it makes sense to put page breaks. Often it is best to put a link to major topics within the Web page. Make sure that the Web page visitor can easily move to those areas by providing links toward the top of the Web page.
- **Use links back to the top of the page.** Another good technique for long Web pages is to allow visitors to link back to the top of the Web page easily from several places on the page. Providing links back to the top of a long Web page makes browsing more enjoyable.
- **Create a link back to the home page.** If possible, you should always provide a link from secondary Web pages back to the home page. Your visitors should not have to use the Back button on the browser to get back to the home page of the Web site. A common Web development practice is to use a company logo (often a smaller version) to navigate back to the home page. Again, the purpose of this image link as well as other links mentioned here is to make your Web site easy to navigate.

BTW

Web Page Improvement

Web page development is an ongoing process. In Web page development, you create a Web page, view it in a browser, and then look for ways to improve the appearance of the page.

To Open an HTML File

The following step illustrates how to open the specials.html file in Notepad.

1

- Click the pastadivine Notepad button on the taskbar.
- With a USB flash drive connected to one of the computer's USB ports, click File on the menu bar and then click Open.
- If Computer is not displayed in the Favorite Links section, drag the top or bottom edge of the Open dialog box until Computer is displayed.
- Click Computer in the Favorite Links section to display a list of available drives.
- If necessary, scroll until UDISK 2.0 (G:) is displayed in the list of available drives.

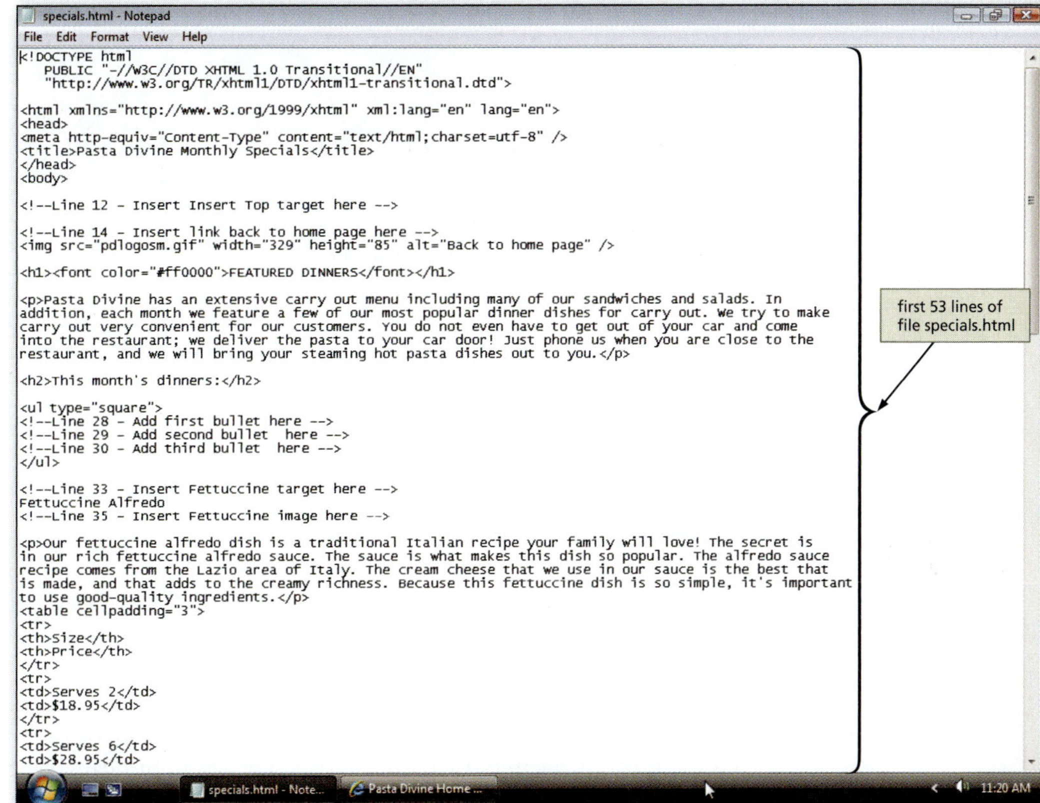

```
<!DOCTYPE html
    PUBLIC "-//W3C//DTD XHTML 1.0 Transitional//EN"
    "http://www.w3.org/TR/xhtml1/DTD/xhtml1-transitional.dtd">

<html xmlns="http://www.w3.org/1999/xhtml" xml:lang="en" lang="en">
<head>
<meta http-equiv="Content-Type" content="text/html;charset=utf-8" />
<title>Pasta Divine Monthly Specials</title>
</head>
<body>

<!--Line 12 - Insert Insert Top target here -->

<!--Line 14 - Insert link back to home page here -->
<img src="pdlogosm.gif" width="329" height="85" alt="Back to home page" />

<h1><font color="#ff0000">FEATURED DINNERS</font></h1>

<p>Pasta Divine has an extensive carry out menu including many of our sandwiches and salads. In
addition, each month we feature a few of our most popular dinner dishes for carry out. We try to make
carry out very convenient for our customers. You do not even have to get out of your car and come
into the restaurant; we deliver the pasta to your car door! Just phone us when you are close to the
restaurant, and we will bring your steaming hot pasta dishes out to you.</p>

<h2>This month's dinners:</h2>

<ul type="square">
<!--Line 28 - Add first bullet here -->
<!--Line 29 - Add second bullet  here -->
<!--Line 30 - Add third bullet  here -->
</ul>

<!--Line 33 - Insert Fettuccine target here -->
Fettuccine Alfredo
<!--Line 35 - Insert Fettuccine image here -->

<p>Our fettuccine alfredo dish is a traditional Italian recipe your family will love! The secret is
in our rich fettuccine alfredo sauce. The sauce is what makes this dish so popular. The alfredo sauce
recipe comes from the Lazio area of Italy. The cream cheese that we use in our sauce is the best that
is made, and that adds to the creamy richness. Because this fettuccine dish is so simple, it's important
to use good-quality ingredients.</p>
<table cellpadding="3">
<tr>
<th>Size</th>
<th>Price</th>
</tr>
<tr>
<td>Serves 2</td>
<td>$18.95</td>
</tr>
<tr>
<td>Serves 6</td>
<td>$28.95</td>
```


Figure 3–28

- If necessary, navigate to the USB drive (G:). Click the Chapter03 folder, and then click the ChapterFiles folder in the list of available folders.
- If necessary, click the file type box arrow, and then click All Files. Click specials.html in the list of files.
- Click the Open button in the Open dialog box to display the HTML code for the specials.html Web page as shown in Figure 3–28.

Q&A

If I open another file in Notepad, will I lose the pastadivine file?

The last saved version of pastadivine.html will still be on the USB drive, even though another HTML file is loaded in Notepad. Just remember always to save a file if you make changes to it.

Formatting Text

BTW **Text Formatting**
You can indent entire blocks of text by using the <blockquote> </blockquote> tags. Most popular browsers indent the text on either side by 40 pixels with these tags. You can use <p> and <br /> tags within the blockquote tags to control line breaking within the text.

Earlier in the project, the color attribute of the <font> tag was used to change the color of text on the Web page. HTML provides a number of other tags to format text, several of which are listed in Table 3–8.

Table 3–8 Text Formatting Tags

HTML Tag	Function
<b> </b>	Physical style tag that displays text as bold
<big> </big>	Increases the font size in comparison to the surrounding text
<blockquote> </blockquote>	Designates a long quotation; indents margins on sections of text
<em> </em>	Logical style tag that displays text with emphasis (usually appears as italicized)
<i> </i>	Physical style tag that displays text as italicized
<pre> </pre>	Sets enclosed text as preformatted material, meaning it preserves spaces and line breaks; often used for text in column format in another document pasted into HTML code
<small> </small>	Decreases the font size in comparison to the surrounding text
<strong> </strong>	Logical style tag that displays text with strong emphasis (usually appears as bold)
	Displays text as subscript (below normal text)
	Displays text as superscript (above normal text)
<tt> </tt>	Displays text as teletype or monospace text
<u> </u>	Displays text as underlined

BTW **Specifying Alternative Fonts**
If a Web page font is not available on users' computers, you can create a list of fonts and the browser will determine the font to use. For example, if the Web page uses a Geneva font, but Arial or Helvetica would also work well, you create a comma-separated list of acceptable fonts, using <font face="geneva, arial,helvetica"> *your text*</font> as the code. If a Web page uses a font that Web page visitors do not have on their computers, the Web page appears using a default font (usually Times New Roman).

Figure 3–29 shows a sample Web page with some of the text format tags. These tags fall into two categories: logical style tags and physical style tags. **Logical style tags** allow a browser to interpret the tag based on browser settings, relative to other text on a Web page. The <h2> heading tag, for example, is a logical style that indicates the heading text should be larger than regular text but smaller than text formatted using an <h1> heading tag. The <strong> tag is another logical style, which indicates that text should have a strong emphasis, and which most browsers interpret as displaying the text in bold font. **Physical style tags** specify a particular font change that is interpreted strictly by all browsers. For example, to ensure that text appears as bold font, you would enclose it between a start <b> and end </b> tag. The <strong> tag is a better fit for XHTML standards, and it does not dictate how the browser displays the text. In practice, the <strong> and <b> tags usually have the same result when the Web page is displayed.

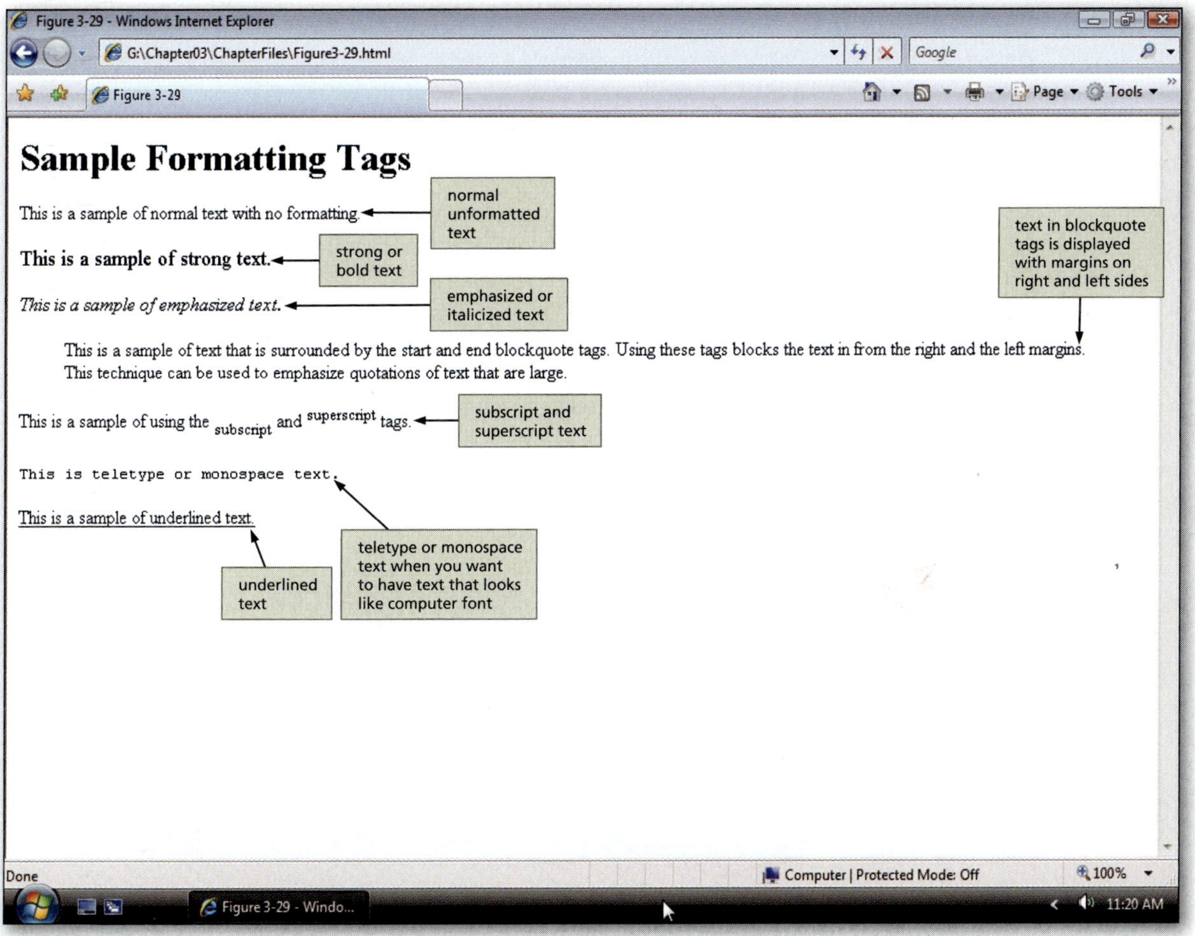

Figure 3–29 Examples of various text-formatting tags.

To Format Text in Bold

On the Monthly Specials Web page, you use the <strong> tag to bold the Fettuccine Alfredo, Lasagna, and Ravioli section heads. The steps on the next page illustrate how to format text using the <strong> tag.

- Click immediately to the left of the F in Fettuccine on line 34. Type `<strong>` as the start tag (Figure 3–30).
- Click immediately to the right of the o in Alfredo on line 34, and then type `</strong>` as the end tag to end the logical bold formatting style.

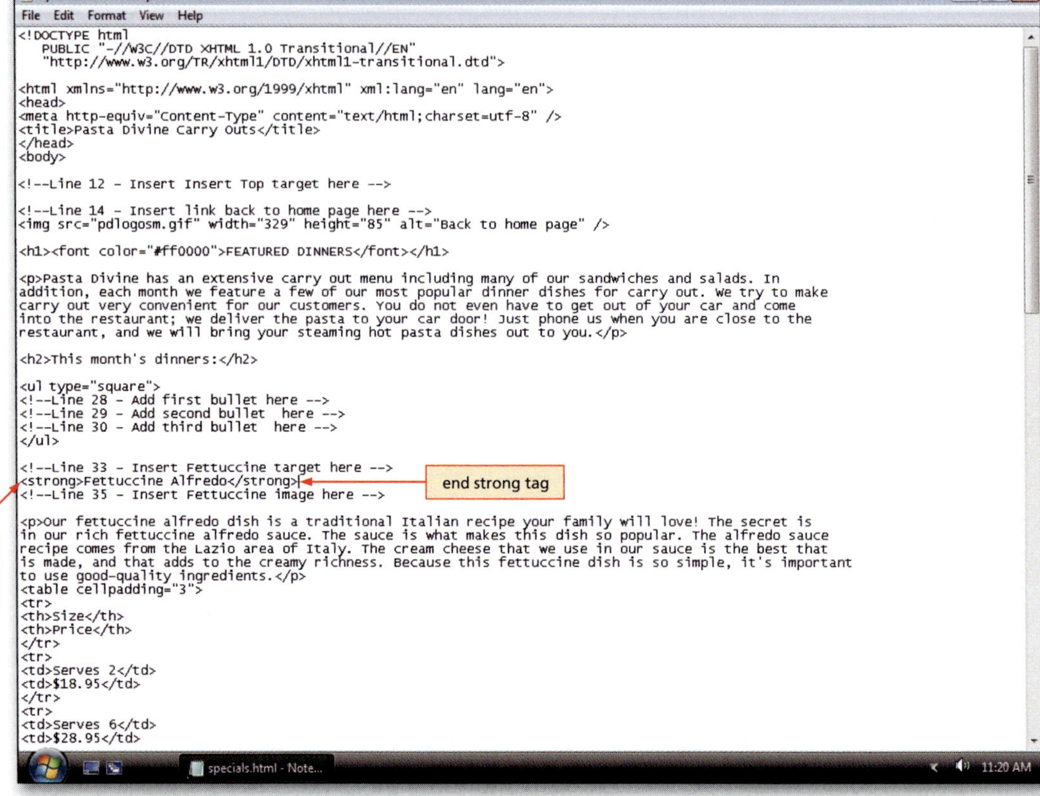

Figure 3–30

2

- Repeat Step 1 to bold the other two occurrences of section headers for the words Lasagna and Ravioli on lines 65 and 92 to surround the words with a logical bold style (Figure 3–31).

```
<!--Line 62 - Insert first To Top link here -->

<!--Line 64 - Insert Lasagna target here -->
<strong>Lasagna</strong>
<!--Line 66 - Insert Lasagna image here -->

<p>Lasagna was Grandpa Salvatore's favorite dish. His Mother used to make lasagna for the whole
neighborhood back in the Toscana area of Italy where she grew up. Our lasagna is brimming with a
spiced beef and pork filling mixed with our secret marinara sauce.</p>
<p>For lighter fare, you can choose our vegetable lasagna. This healthy meal is filled with a
mix of fresh vegetables together with the same marinara sauce.</p>
<table cellpadding="3">
<tr>
<th>Size</th>
<th>Price</th>
</tr>
<tr>
<td>Serves 8</td>
<td>$24.95</td>
</tr>
<tr>
<td>Serves 12</td>
<td>$36.95</td>
</tr>
</table>
<!--Line 87 - Insert Clear right here -->

<!--Line 89 - Insert second To Top link here -->

<!--Line 91 - Insert Ravioli target here -->
<strong>Ravioli</strong>
<!--Line 93 - Insert Ravioli image here -->

<p>Ravioli is traditionally two pieces of thin pasta dough filled with meat, cheese, or vegetables.
Our ravioli comes from the Umbria area of Italy where they mix the filling with a rich pesto sauce
combined with warm yogurt. This makes the ravioli creamy as well as mouthwatering.</p>
<p>You can order our ravioli as prepared or purchase frozen ravioli to make later. Either way, this
dish is an award-winner.</p>
<table cellpadding="3">
<tr>
```

start strong tag inserted at line 65

end strong tags inserted at lines 65 and 92

start strong tag inserted at line 92

Figure 3–31

Q&A

Would the <b> tag have resulted in the same look in the browser as that displayed by using the <strong> tag?

The look might have been the same (i.e., bold text), depending on the browser. You use the <strong> tag because it is browser independent. It is a logical style tag.

Adding an Image with Wrapped Text

As shown in Table 2–7 on page HTML 59, the <img> tag has many attributes, including attributes to specify height, width, alignment, alternative text, and so on. In Chapter 2, the HTML code used the height and width attributes to identify the size of the image to the browser and the alt attribute to define the text that appears when the user moves the mouse over the image. Alternative text also appears when the site visitor is using a screen reader.

Alignment also is a key consideration when inserting an image. Alignment can give an image and the surrounding text completely different looks. Figure 3–32 shows two images, the first of which is left-aligned, which wraps any text to the right of the image. The format of the HTML code to add the left-aligned image is:

```
<img src="fettuccine.jpg" width="308" height="205"
alt="Fettuccine" align="left" />
```

whereas the HTML code to add the right-aligned image is:

```
<img src="lasagna.jpg" width="308" height="205" alt="Lasagna"
align="right" />
```

The src attribute indicates the file name of the image file, align="left" aligns the image to the left of the text, while align="right" aligns the image to the right of the text. In both cases, the height and width are in number of pixels, and the alt attribute shows the alternative text as the image is loading.

The hspace and vspace attributes control the amount of horizontal and vertical space around an image in pixels. If you do not use these attributes, the text will line up right on the border of the image, as shown in Figure 3–32.

BTW

Obtaining Images on the Web

The Web contains many sites with thousands of image files on countless subjects that can be downloaded for free and used for noncommercial purposes. Using a search engine, enter a search for the phrases "free GIFs" or "free Web images" to find collections of images for use on a Web site. If you find a graphic you want to use, right-click the image, click Save Picture As on the shortcut menu, and then save the image to your computer. Regardless of where you get the images, always be aware of copyright rules and regulations.

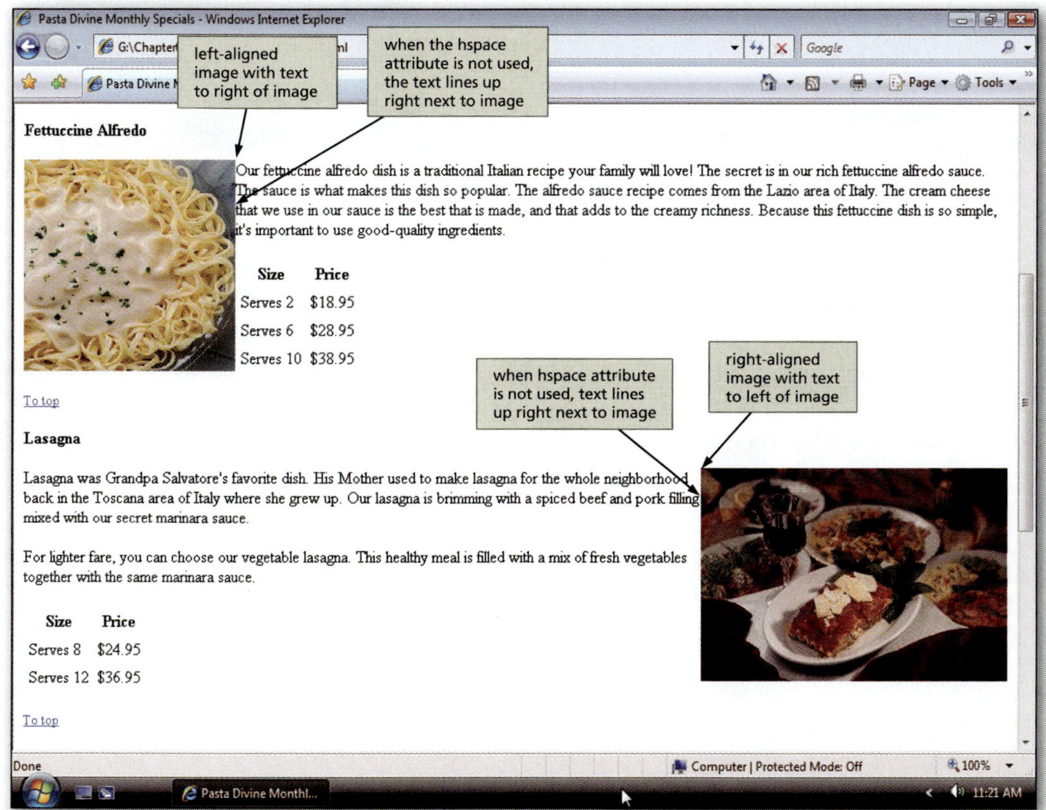

Figure 3–32 Left- and right-aligned images.

It is also good design practice to add space around images so they are easy to see and are not too close to the surrounding text. Figure 3–33 shows images on the Monthly Specials Web page with hspace="5" attributes, which adds 5 pixels of space horizontally (on either side) around the image.

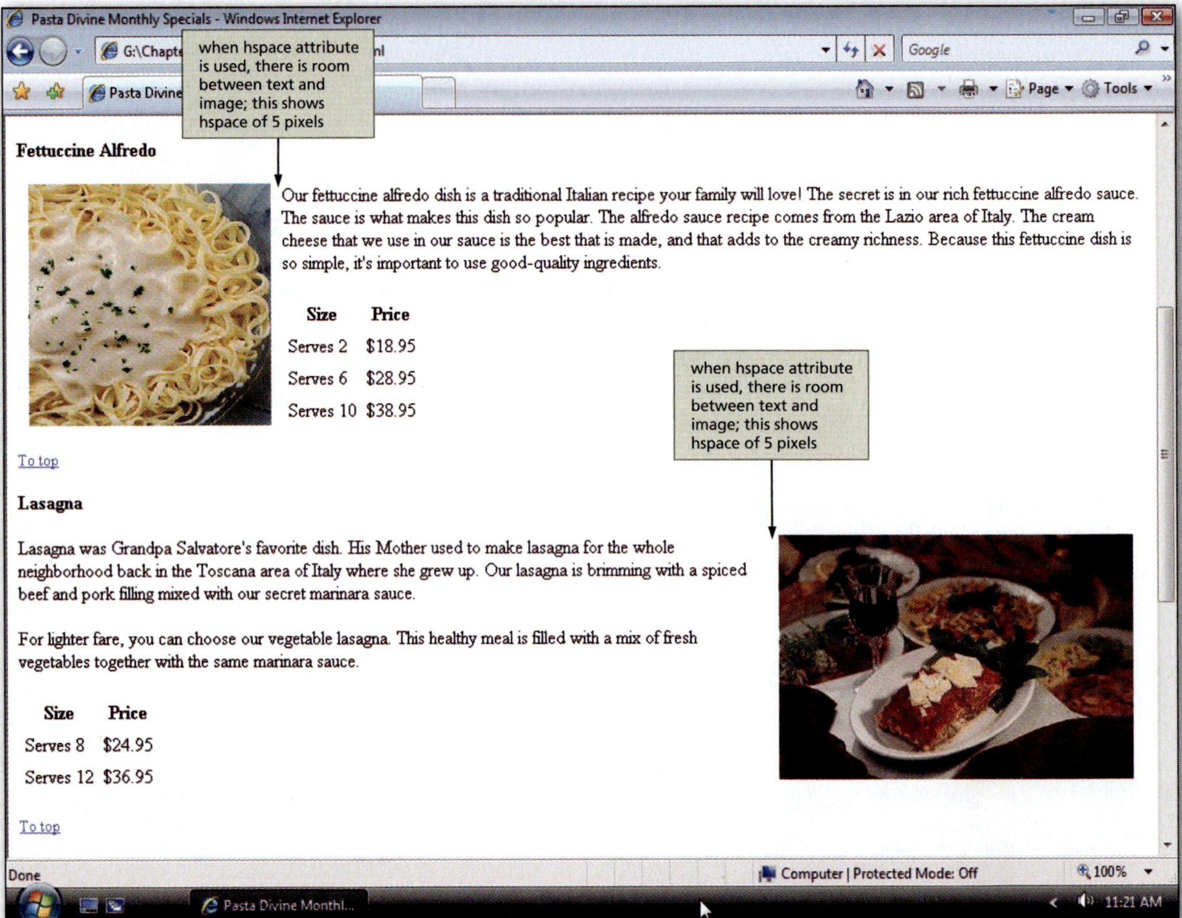

Figure 3–33 Images and text with hspace attribute used.

> **BTW**
> **Other Sources of Images**
> Many applications come with clip art that can be used on Web pages. Other types of digital images, such as images scanned by a scanner or pictures taken with a digital camera, also can be included on a Web page. You also can create images using a paint or image-editing program.

Another way to control space around images is to use the paragraph <p> tag. Remember that a paragraph tag inserts a blank line above the next object (text or image) after the paragraph tag. Figure 3–34a shows an example of using a <p> tag before inserting the Fettuccine image, whereas Figure 3–34b shows an example of not using a <p> tag before the <img> tag. In this project, we will use the paragraph tag before the <img> tag to give more space between the image and the heading.

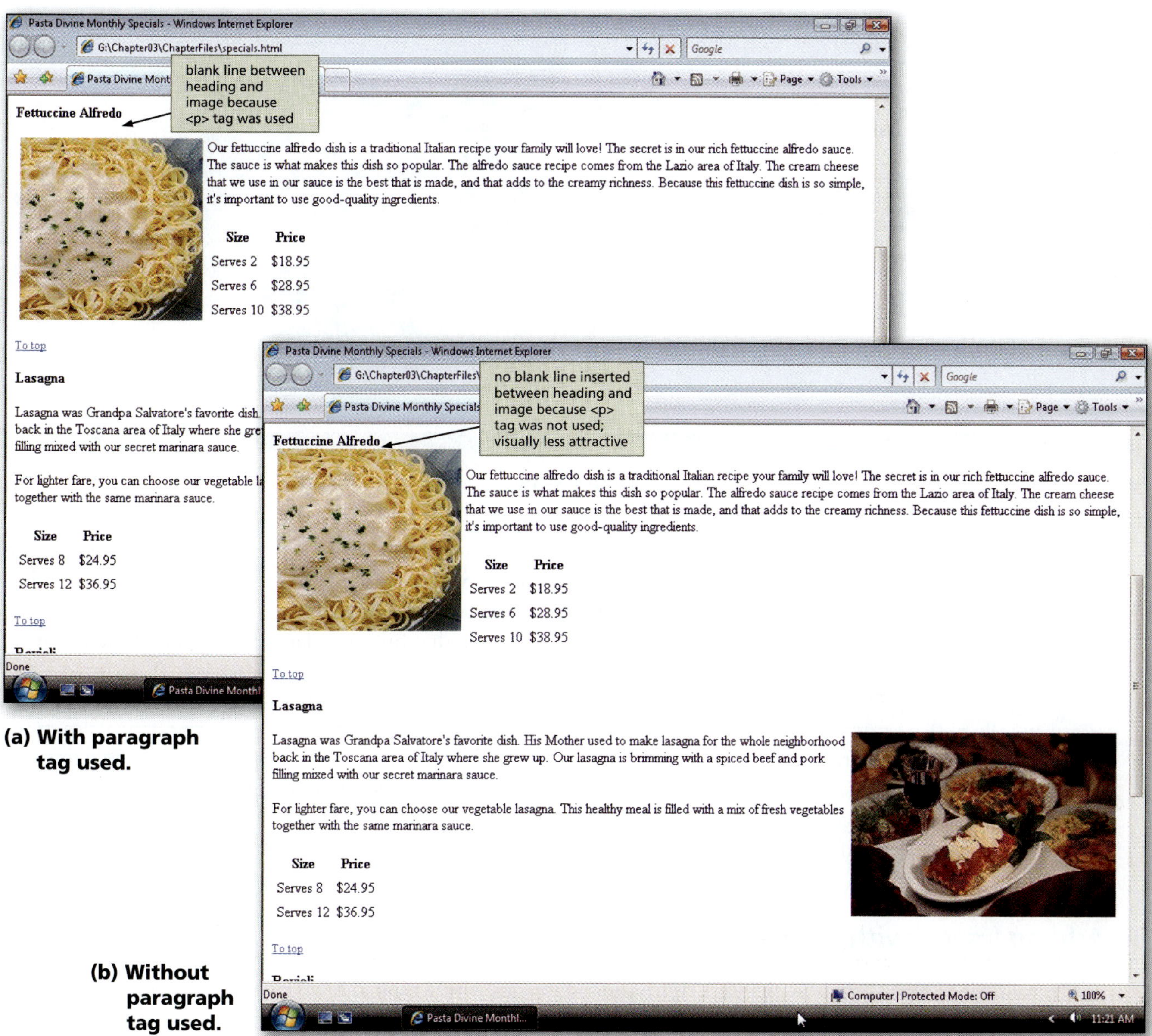

Figure 3–34

Using Thumbnail Images

Many Web developers use thumbnail images to improve page loading time. A **thumbnail image** is a smaller version of the image itself. The thumbnail is used as a link that, when clicked, will load the full-sized image. Figure 3–35a on the next page shows an example of a thumbnail image. When the image is clicked, the browser loads the full-sized image (Figure 3–35b). Loading images can take a long time, depending on the size and the complexity of the image. Using a thumbnail image gives a visitor the opportunity to decide whether to view the full-sized image.

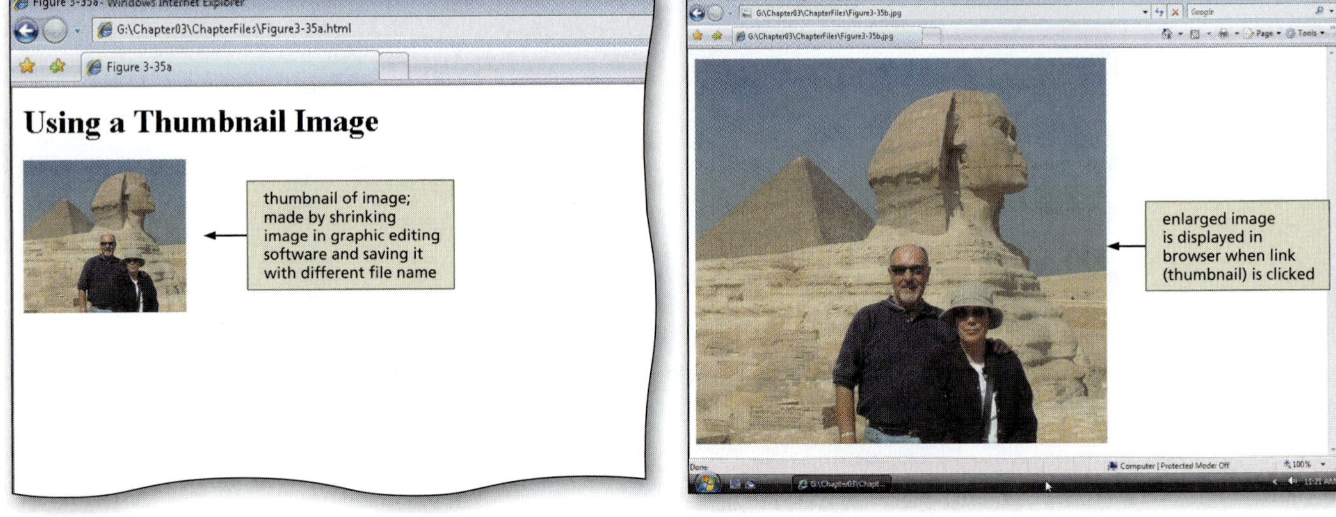

(a) **Figure 3–35** (b)

To create a thumbnail version of an image, the image can be resized to a smaller size in a paint or image-editing project and then saved with a different file name. The thumbnail image then is added to a Web page as an image link to the larger version of the image. The HTML code to add a thumbnail image that links to a larger image takes the form:

```
<a href="largeimage.gif"><img src="thumbnail.gif" /></a>
```

where largeimage.gif is the name of the full-sized image and thumbnail.gif is the name of the smaller version of the image. If a visitor clicks the thumbnail image to view the larger image, he or she can use the Back button on the browser's Standard toolbar to return to the original Web page displaying the thumbnail image.

To Add an Image with Wrapped Text

The following steps show how to insert right-aligned images with wrapped text.

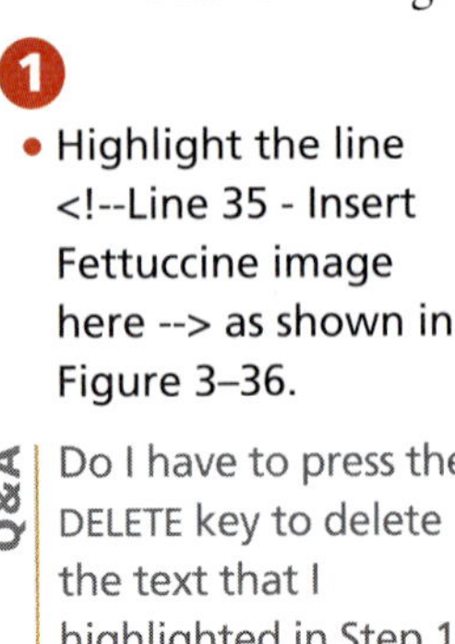

1

- Highlight the line <!--Line 35 - Insert Fettuccine image here --> as shown in Figure 3–36.

Q&A Do I have to press the DELETE key to delete the text that I highlighted in Step 1?

No, you do not have to press the DELETE key to delete the text on line 35. As long as the text is highlighted, the text is automatically deleted as soon as you start typing the HTML code in Step 2.

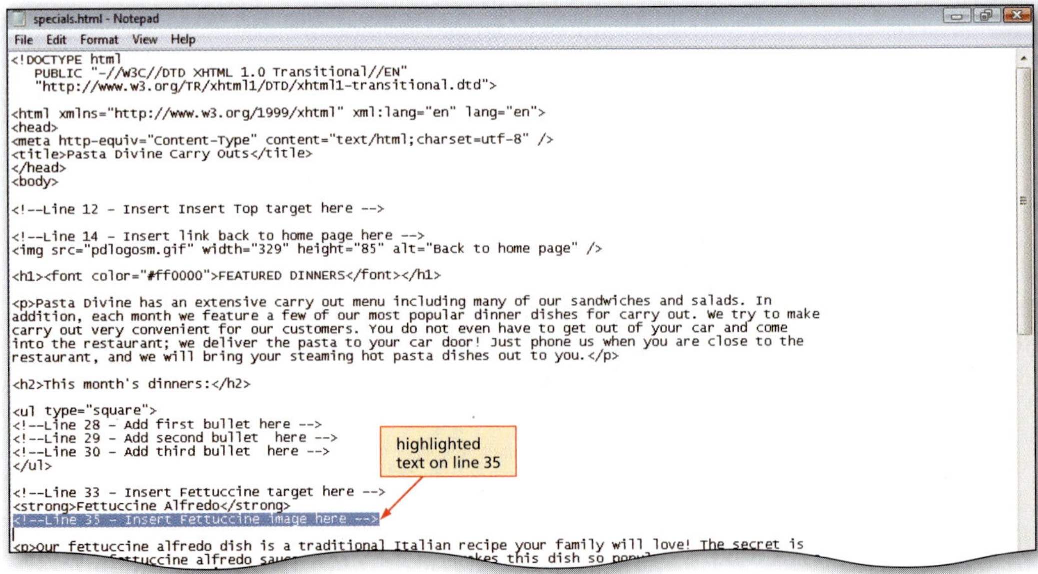

Figure 3–36

2

- Type <p><img src="fettuccine.jpg" width="212" height="203" alt="Fettuccine" align="left" hspace="5" /></p> and do not press the ENTER key. This HTML code inserts an image named fettuccine.jpg that is left-aligned on the Web page, with text wrapped to its right and with five pixels of space around the image horizontally (Figure 3–37).

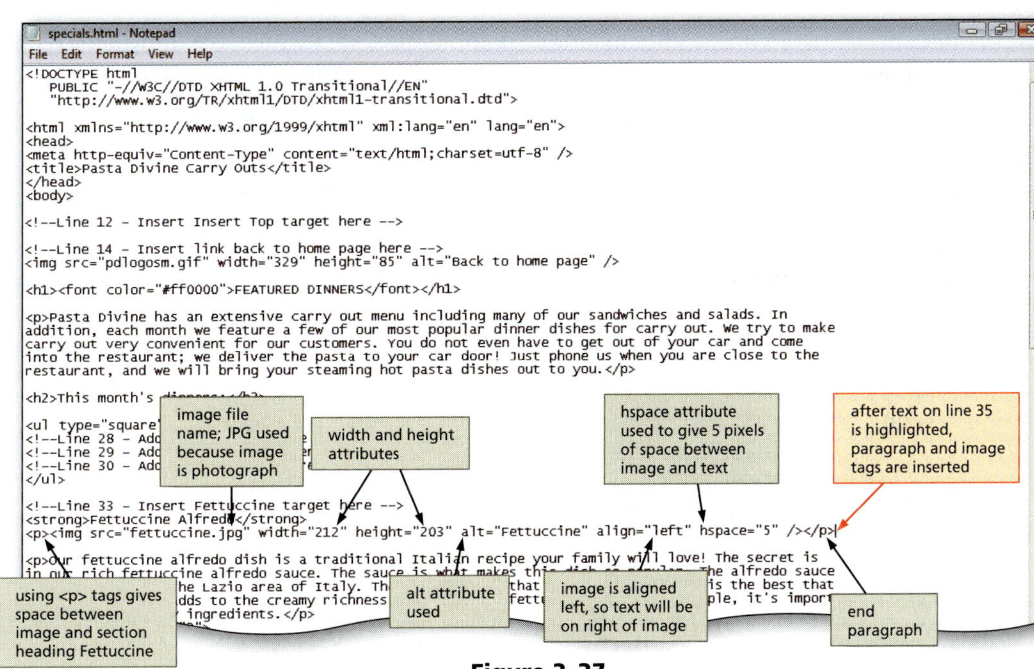

Figure 3–37

3

- Highlight the line <!--Line 66 - Insert Lasagna image here --> on line 66.
- Type <p><img src="lasagna.jpg" width="308" height="205" alt="Lasagna" align="right" hspace="5" /> </p> (do not press ENTER) to insert a right-aligned image with wrapped text.
- Highlight the line <!--Line 93 - Insert Ravioli image here --> on line 93.

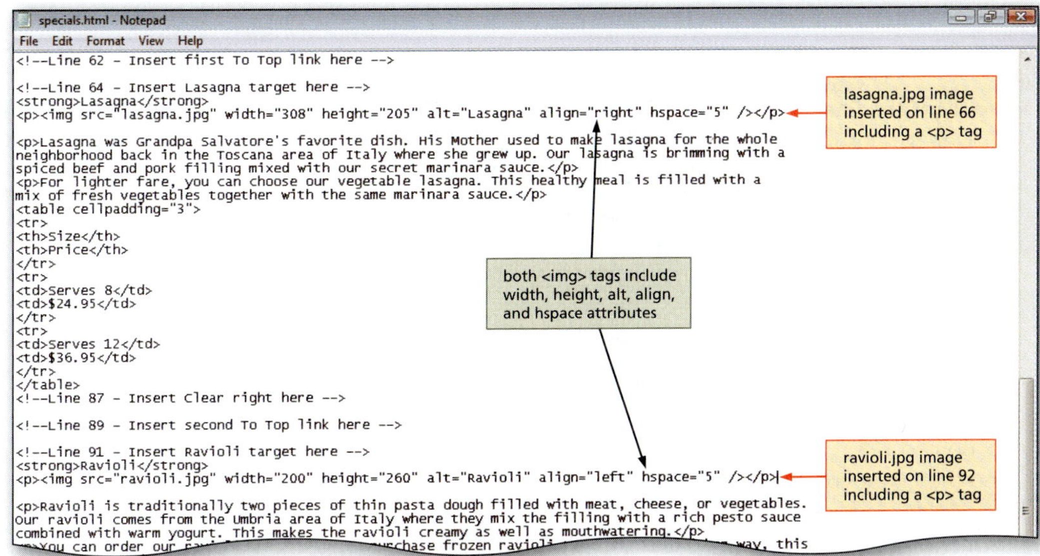

Figure 3–38

- Type <p><img src="ravioli.jpg" width="200" height="260" alt="Ravioli" align="left" hspace="5" /></p> (do not press ENTER) to insert a left-aligned image with wrapped text (Figure 3–38).

Q&A Why are JPG files used for these images rather than GIF files?

The images used for this Web page are photographs. JPG files are better suited for photographs in which there are many colors, shadowing, etc.

Q&A Why are we using the hspace attribute for these images?

Using hspace (horizontal space) adds room around the image horizontally. That puts space between the image and the text wrapped around the image. Experimenting with different hspace and vspace sizes is worthwhile when developing Web pages.

To Clear the Text Wrapping

After specifying an image alignment and defining how text wraps, you must enter a break (<br />) tag to stop the text wrapping. You use the <br clear="left" /> and <br clear="right" /> tags to show where the text should stop wrapping. The following steps show how to enter code to clear the text wrapping.

- Highlight the line <!--Line 60 - Insert Clear left here --> on line 60, and then type `<br clear="left" />` as the tag (Figure 3–39).

```
specials.html - Notepad
File  Edit  Format  View  Help
<!--Line 33 - Insert Fettuccine target here -->
<strong>Fettuccine Alfredo</strong>
<p><img src="fettuccine.jpg" width="212" height="203" alt="Fettuccine" align="left" hspace="5" /></p>

<p>Our fettuccine alfredo dish is a traditional Italian recipe your family will love! The secret is
in our rich fettuccine alfredo sauce. The sauce is what makes this dish so popular. The alfredo sauce
recipe comes from the Lazio area of Italy. The cream cheese that we use in our sauce is the best that
is made, and that adds to the creamy richness. Because this fettuccine dish is so simple, it's important
to use good-quality ingredients.</p>
<table cellpadding="3">
<tr>
<th>Size</th>
<th>Price</th>
</tr>
<tr>
<td>Serves 2</td>
<td>$18.95</td>
</tr>
<tr>
<td>Serves 6</td>
<td>$28.95</td>
</tr>
<tr>
<td>Serves 10</td>
<td>$38.95</td>
</tr>
</table>
<br clear="left" />

<!--Line 62 - Insert first To Top link here -->

<!--Line 64 - Insert Lasagna target here -->
<strong>Lasagna</strong>
<p><img src="lasagna.jpg" width="308" height="205" alt="Lasagna" align="right" hspace="5" /></p>
```

break clear tag inserted; must be clear="left" because image was aligned to left

Figure 3–39

- Highlight the line <!--Line 87 - Insert Clear right here --> on line 87, and then type `<br clear="right" />` as the tag.
- Highlight the line <!--Line 118 - Insert Clear left here --> on 118, and then type `<br clear="left" />` as the tag to clear the text wrapping for both left- and right-aligned images as displayed in Figure 3–40.

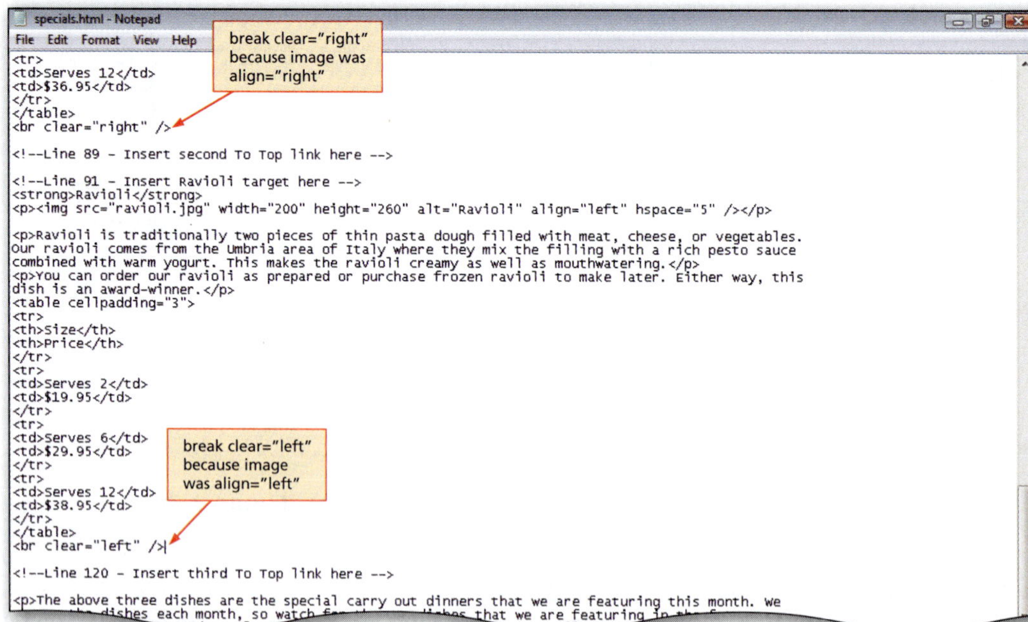


```
<tr>
<td>Serves 12</td>
<td>$36.95</td>
</tr>
</table>
<br clear="right" />

<!--Line 89 - Insert second To Top link here -->

<!--Line 91 - Insert Ravioli target here -->
<strong>Ravioli</strong>
<p><img src="ravioli.jpg" width="200" height="260" alt="Ravioli" align="left" hspace="5" /></p>

<p>Ravioli is traditionally two pieces of thin pasta dough filled with meat, cheese, or vegetables.
Our ravioli comes from the Umbria area of Italy where they mix the filling with a rich pesto sauce
combined with warm yogurt. This makes the ravioli creamy as well as mouthwatering.</p>
<p>You can order our ravioli as prepared or purchase frozen ravioli to make later. Either way, this
dish is an award-winner.</p>
<table cellpadding="3">
<tr>
<th>Size</th>
<th>Price</th>
</tr>
<tr>
<td>Serves 2</td>
<td>$19.95</td>
</tr>
<tr>
<td>Serves 6</td>
<td>$29.95</td>
</tr>
<tr>
<td>Serves 12</td>
<td>$38.95</td>
</tr>
</table>
<br clear="left" />

<!--Line 120 - Insert third To Top link here -->

<p>The above three dishes are the special carry out dinners that we are featuring this month. We
```

Figure 3–40

Q&A What happens if you do not use the <br clear="direction" /> tag?

Your text following the wrapped image will not be displayed as you intended. The following text will continue to wrap beyond the end of the text and image combination.

Q&A Is there one tag to clear all alignments?

Yes. The <br clear="all" /> tag clears all text alignments.

Adding Links within a Web Page

The final links to be added in this project are links within the Monthly Specials Web page. Because the Monthly Specials Web page is quite long, it would be easier for the visitors to have a menu or list at the top of the Web page that facilitates immediate movement to another section. Figure 3–41a on the next page shows how clicking the text link Fettuccine Alfredo at the top of the page links to the Fettuccine Alfredo section in another part of the Web page (Figure 3–41b). When the mouse pointer is moved over the words Fettuccine Alfredo and clicked, the browser repositions, or links, the page to the target named fettuccine.

To create links within the same Web page, the targets for the links first must be created. Link targets are created using the <a> tag with the name attribute, using the form:

```
<a name= "targetname"></a>
```

where targetname is a unique name for a link target within that Web page. Notice that the tag uses the name attribute, rather than the href attribute, and that no text is included between the start <a> and end </a> tag, because the target is not intended to appear on the Web page as a clickable link. Instead, the link target is intended to mark a specific area of the Web page, to which a link can be directed.

Links to link targets are created using the <a> tag with the name attribute, using the form:

```
<a href="#targetname">
```

where targetname is the name of a link target in that Web page. Notice that the tag uses the href attribute, followed by the pound sign (#) and the target name enclosed in quotation marks.

Another type of link within a Web page is an image link. The last step in editing the Monthly Specials Web page is to add an image link from the Monthly Specials Web page back to the Pasta Divine home page.

BTW **Web Page Size**
The file size of a Web page is the total file size of all elements, including the HTML file and any images. The more images a Web page contains, the longer it takes to download. When adding images, test the download time; if it takes more than 10 seconds, most users will not wait to view the page.

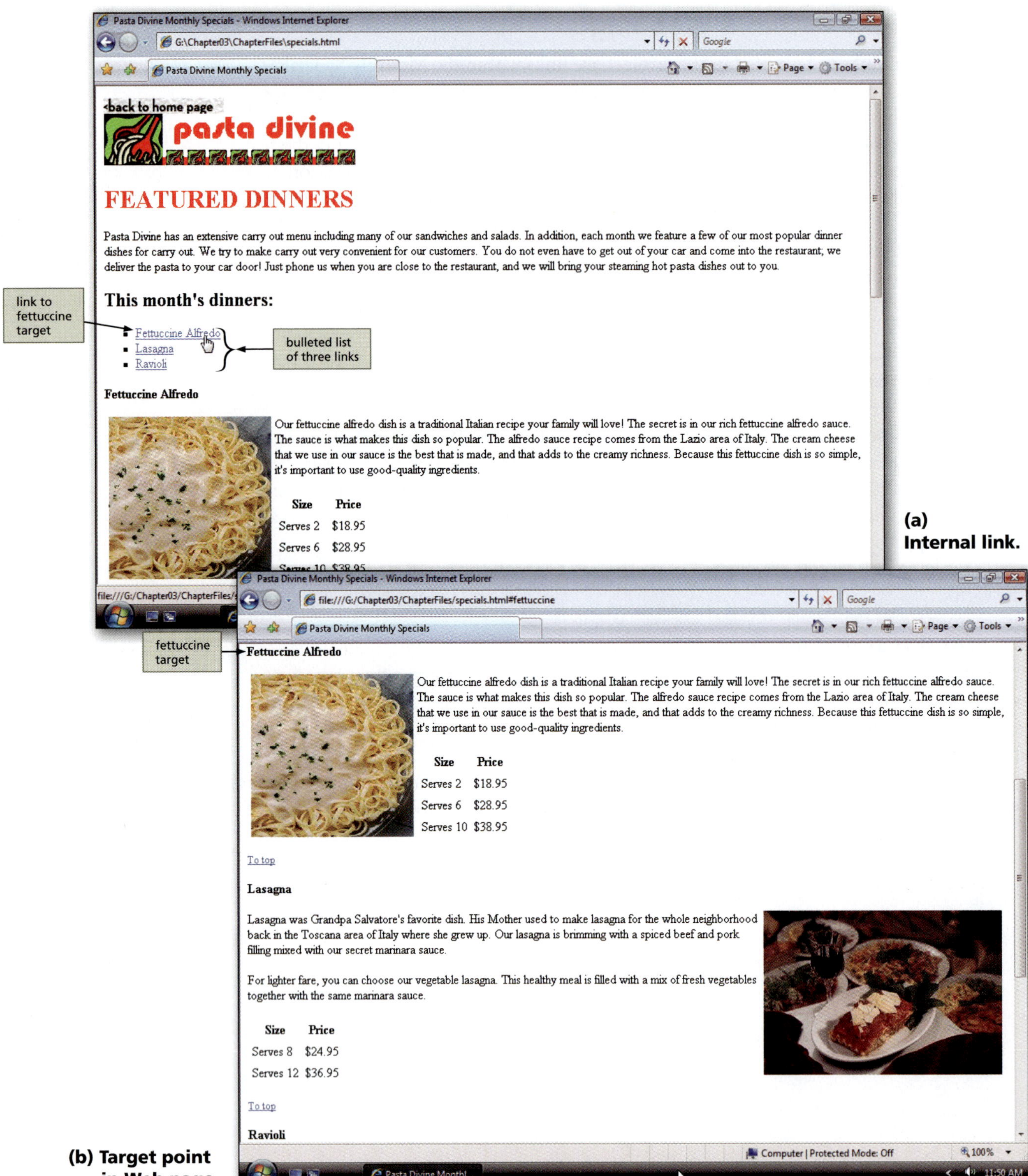
Pasta Divine Monthly Specials - Windows Internet Explorer
G:\Chapter03\ChapterFiles\specials.html
<back to home page
pasta divine
FEATURED DINNERS
Pasta Divine has an extensive carry out menu including many of our sandwiches and salads. In addition, each month we feature a few of our most popular dinner dishes for carry out. We try to make carry out very convenient for our customers. You do not even have to get out of your car and come into the restaurant; we deliver the pasta to your car door! Just phone us when you are close to the restaurant, and we will bring your steaming hot pasta dishes out to you.
This month's dinners:
link to fettuccine target
Fettuccine Alfredo
Lasagna
Ravioli
bulleted list of three links
Fettuccine Alfredo
Our fettuccine alfredo dish is a traditional Italian recipe your family will love! The secret is in our rich fettuccine alfredo sauce. The sauce is what makes this dish so popular. The alfredo sauce recipe comes from the Lazio area of Italy. The cream cheese that we use in our sauce is the best that is made, and that adds to the creamy richness. Because this fettuccine dish is so simple, it's important to use good-quality ingredients.
Size Price
Serves 2 $18.95
Serves 6 $28.95
(a) Internal link.
file:///G:/Chapter03/ChapterFiles/specials.html#fettuccine
fettuccine target
Serves 10 $38.95
To top
Lasagna
Lasagna was Grandpa Salvatore's favorite dish. His Mother used to make lasagna for the whole neighborhood back in the Toscana area of Italy where she grew up. Our lasagna is brimming with a spiced beef and pork filling mixed with our secret marinara sauce.
For lighter fare, you can choose our vegetable lasagna. This healthy meal is filled with a mix of fresh vegetables together with the same marinara sauce.
Size Price
Serves 8 $24.95
Serves 12 $36.95
To top
Ravioli
Computer | Protected Mode: Off
100%
11:50 AM
(b) Target point in Web page.

Figure 3–41

To Set Link Targets

The next step is to set link targets to the Fettuccine Alfredo, Lasagna, and Ravioli sections of the Web page. The following steps show how to set the three link targets in the Monthly Specials Web page.

1

- Highlight the line <!--Line 33 - Insert Fettuccine target here --> on line 33.
- Type `<a name="fettuccine"></a>` to create a link target named fettuccine (Figure 3–42).

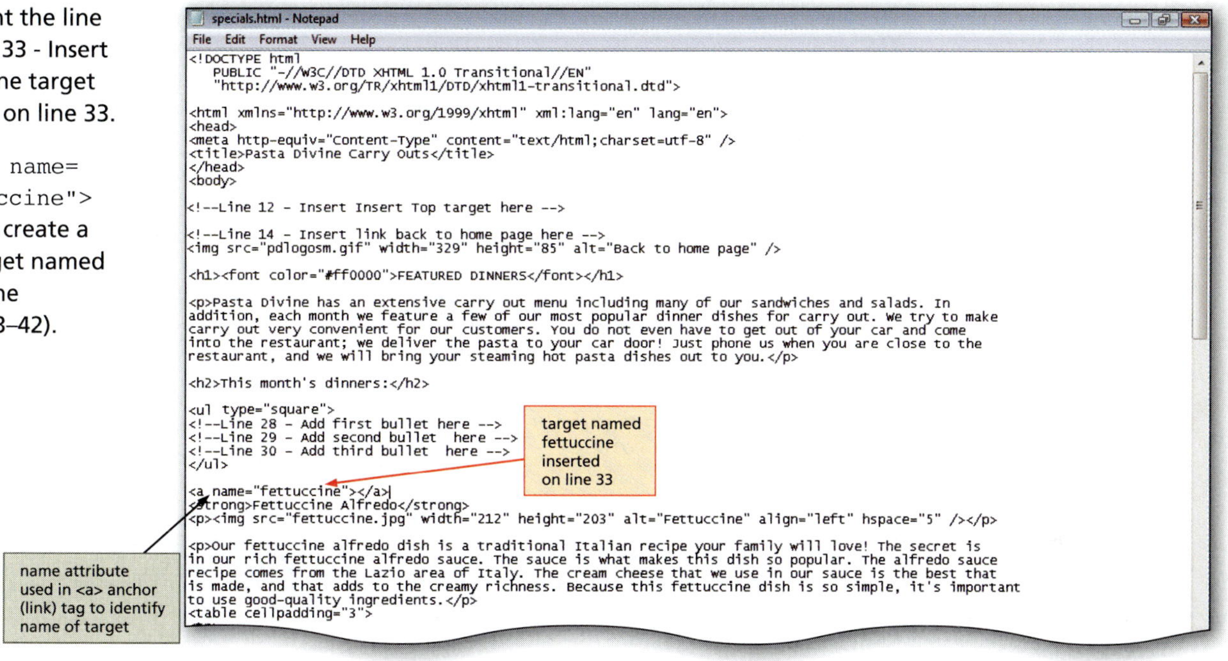

```
specials.html - Notepad
File  Edit  Format  View  Help
<!DOCTYPE html
   PUBLIC "-//W3C//DTD XHTML 1.0 Transitional//EN"
   "http://www.w3.org/TR/xhtml1/DTD/xhtml1-transitional.dtd">

<html xmlns="http://www.w3.org/1999/xhtml" xml:lang="en" lang="en">
<head>
<meta http-equiv="Content-Type" content="text/html;charset=utf-8" />
<title>Pasta Divine Carry Outs</title>
</head>
<body>

<!--Line 12 - Insert Insert Top target here -->

<!--Line 14 - Insert link back to home page here -->
<img src="pdlogosm.gif" width="329" height="85" alt="Back to home page" />

<h1><font color="#ff0000">FEATURED DINNERS</font></h1>

<p>Pasta Divine has an extensive carry out menu including many of our sandwiches and salads. In
addition, each month we feature a few of our most popular dinner dishes for carry out. We try to make
carry out very convenient for our customers. You do not even have to get out of your car and come
into the restaurant; we deliver the pasta to your car door! Just phone us when you are close to the
restaurant, and we will bring your steaming hot pasta dishes out to you.</p>

<h2>This month's dinners:</h2>

<ul type="square">
<!--Line 28 - Add first bullet here -->
<!--Line 29 - Add second bullet  here -->
<!--Line 30 - Add third bullet  here -->
</ul>

<a name="fettuccine"></a>
<strong>Fettuccine Alfredo</strong>
<p><img src="fettuccine.jpg" width="212" height="203" alt="Fettuccine" align="left" hspace="5" /></p>

<p>Our fettuccine alfredo dish is a traditional Italian recipe your family will love! The secret is
in our rich fettuccine alfredo sauce. The sauce is what makes this dish so popular. The alfredo sauce
recipe comes from the Lazio area of Italy. The cream cheese that we use in our sauce is the best that
is made, and that adds to the creamy richness. Because this fettuccine dish is so simple, it's important
to use good-quality ingredients.</p>
<table cellpadding="3">
```

target named fettuccine inserted on line 33

name attribute used in <a> anchor (link) tag to identify name of target

Figure 3–42

2

- Highlight the line <!--Line 64 - Insert Lasagna target here --> on line 64.
- Type `<a name="lasagna"></a>` to create a link target named lasagna.
- Highlight the line <!--Line 91 - Insert Ravioli target here -->.
- Type `<a name="ravioli"></a>` to create a link target named ravioli (Figure 3–43).

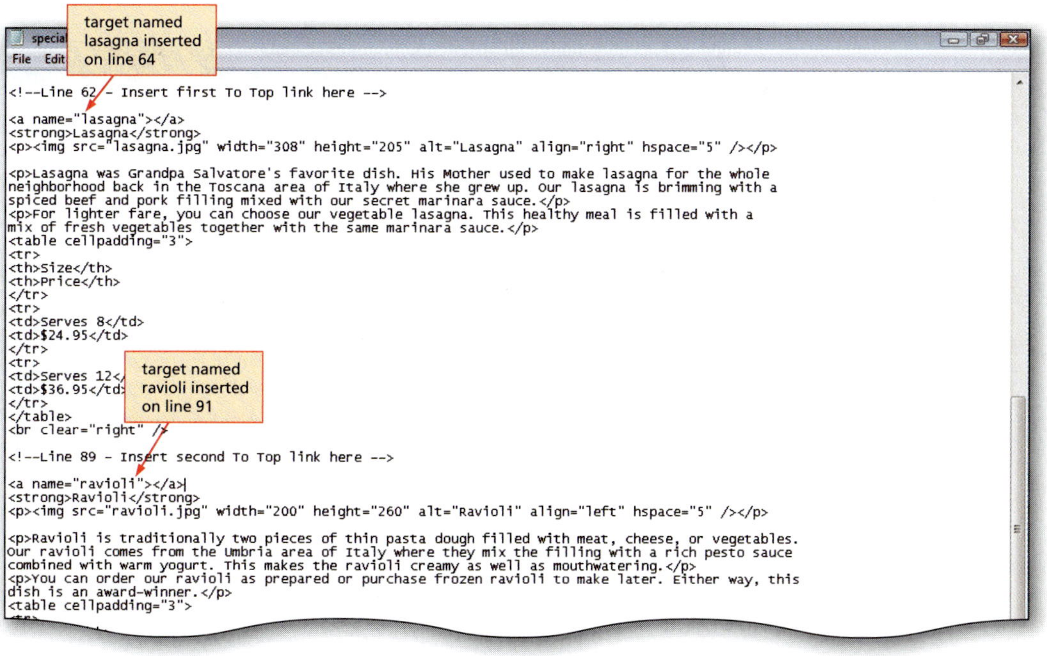

```
<!--Line 62 - Insert first To Top link here -->

<a name="lasagna"></a>
<strong>Lasagna</strong>
<p><img src="lasagna.jpg" width="308" height="205" alt="Lasagna" align="right" hspace="5" /></p>

<p>Lasagna was Grandpa Salvatore's favorite dish. His Mother used to make lasagna for the whole
neighborhood back in the Toscana area of Italy where she grew up. Our lasagna is brimming with a
spiced beef and pork filling mixed with our secret marinara sauce.</p>
<p>For lighter fare, you can choose our vegetable lasagna. This healthy meal is filled with a
mix of fresh vegetables together with the same marinara sauce.</p>
<table cellpadding="3">
<tr>
<th>Size</th>
<th>Price</th>
</tr>
<tr>
<td>Serves 8</td>
<td>$24.95</td>
</tr>
<tr>
<td>Serves 12</td>
<td>$36.95</td>
</tr>
</table>
<br clear="right" />

<!--Line 89 - Insert second To Top link here -->

<a name="ravioli"></a>
<strong>Ravioli</strong>
<p><img src="ravioli.jpg" width="200" height="260" alt="Ravioli" align="left" hspace="5" /></p>

<p>Ravioli is traditionally two pieces of thin pasta dough filled with meat, cheese, or vegetables.
Our ravioli comes from the Umbria area of Italy where they mix the filling with a rich pesto sauce
combined with warm yogurt. This makes the ravioli creamy as well as mouthwatering.</p>
<p>You can order our ravioli as prepared or purchase frozen ravioli to make later. Either way, this
dish is an award-winner.</p>
<table cellpadding="3">
```

target named lasagna inserted on line 64

target named ravioli inserted on line 91

Figure 3–43

Q&A

There is nothing between the start anchor and end anchor tags for these targets. Will they work?

These targets are just placeholders, so they do not need any words or phrases; they only need a target name as shown in the anchor tag.

To Add Links to Link Targets within a Web Page

The following step shows how to create an unordered (bulleted) list and then to use the list items as links to link targets within the Web page.

- Highlight the line <!--Line 28 - Add first bullet here -->.
- Type `<li><a href="#fettuccine">Fettuccine Alfredo</a></li>` to create a link target named fettuccine.
- Highlight the line <!--Line 29 - Add second bullet here -->.
- Type `<li><a href="#lasagna">Lasagna</a></li>` to create a link target named lasagna.
- Highlight the line <!--Line 30 - Add third bullet here -->.
- Type `<li><a href="#ravioli">Ravioli</a></li>` to create a link target named ravioli (Figure 3–44).

```
specials.html - Notepad
File Edit Format View Help
<!DOCTYPE html
   PUBLIC "-//W3C//DTD XHTML 1.0 Transitional//EN"
   "http://www.w3.org/TR/xhtml1/DTD/xhtml1-transitional.dtd">

<html xmlns="http://www.w3.org/1999/xhtml" xml:lang="en" lang="en">
<head>
<meta http-equiv="Content-Type" content="text/html;charset=utf-8" />
<title>Pasta Divine Carry Outs</title>
</head>
<body>

<!--Line 12 - Insert Insert Top target here -->

<!--Line 14 - Insert link back to home page here -->
<img src="pdlogosm.gif" width="329" height="85" alt="Back to home page" />

<h1><font color="#ff0000">FEATURED DINNERS</font></h1>

<p>Pasta Divine has an extensive carry out menu including many of our sandwiches and salads. In
addition, each month we feature a few of our most popular dinner dishes for carry out. We try to make
carry out very convenient for our customers. You do not even have to get out of your car and come
into the restaurant; we deliver the pasta to your car door! Just phone us when you are close to the
restaurant, and we will bring your steaming hot pasta dishes out to you.</p>

<h2>This month's dinners:</h2>

<ul type="square">
<li><a href="#fettuccine">Fettuccine Alfredo</a></li>
<li><a href="#lasagna">Lasagna</a></li>
<li><a href="#ravioli">Ravioli</a></li>
</ul>

<a name="fettuccine"></a>
<strong>Fettuccine Alfredo</strong>
<p><img src="fettuccine.jpg" width="212" height="203" alt="Fettuccine" align="left" hspace="5" /></p>

<p>Our fettuccine alfredo dish is a traditional Italian recipe your family will love! The secret is
in our rich fettuccine alfredo sauce. The sauce is what makes this dish so popular. The alfredo sauce
recipe comes from the Lazio area of Italy. The cream cheese that we use in our sauce is the best that
is made, and that adds to the creamy richness. Because this fettuccine dish is so simple, it's important
to use good-quality ingredients.</p>
<table cellpadding="3">
<tr>
<th>Size</th>
<th>Price</th>
</tr>
<tr>
<td>Serves 2</td>
<td>$18.95</td>
</tr>
<tr>
<td>Serves 6</td>
<td>$28.95</td>
```

three list items inserted starting on line 28 for links to three targets; note use of # symbol; this indicates link destination is section of same Web page
specials.html - Note...
12:08 PM

Figure 3–44

Q&A

Do I have to use a bullet list for the links?

No, you can use any text for the links to the targets created in the step above. The bullet list makes the links easy to use and keeps the links in one area of the Web page.

To Add Links to a Target at the Top of the Page

In this step, you add three "To top" links to provide a quick way to move back to the top of the Web page. To make these links, you first set the target at the top of the page, and then create the links to that target. The following steps illustrate how to add links to a target at the top of the page.

1

- Highlight the line <!--Line 12 - Insert Top target here --> on line 12.
- Type `<a name="top"></a>` as the tag that will create a target at the top of the Web page named top (Figure 3–45).

```
specials.html - Notepad
File  Edit  Format  View  Help
<!DOCTYPE html
   PUBLIC "-//W3C//DTD XHTML 1.0 Transitional//EN"
   "http://www.w3.org/TR/xhtml1/DTD/xhtml1-transitional.dtd">

<html xmlns="http://www.w3.org/1999/xhtml" xml:lang="en" lang="en">
<head>
<meta http-equiv="Content-Type" content="text/html;charset=utf-8" />
<title>Pasta Divine Monthly Specials</title>
</head>
<body>

<a name="top"></a>

<!--Line 14 - Insert link back to home page here -->
<img src="pdlogosm.gif" width="329" height="85" alt="Back to home page" />

<h1><font color="#ff0000">FEATURED DINNERS</font></h1>

<p>Pasta Divine has an extensive carry out menu including many of our sandwiches and salads. In
addition, each month we feature a few of our most popular dinner dishes for carry out. We try to make
carry out very convenient for our customers. You do not even have to get out of your car and come
into the restaurant; we deliver the pasta to your car door! Just phone us when you are close to the
restaurant, and we will bring your steaming hot pasta dishes out to you.</p>

<h2>This month's dinners:</h2>

<ul type="square">
<li><a href="#fettuccine">Fettuccine Alfredo</a></li>
<li><a href="#lasagna">Lasagna</a></li>
<li><a href="#ravioli">Ravioli</a></li>
</ul>

<a name="fettuccine"></a>
<strong>Fettuccine Alfredo</strong>
<p><img src="fettuccine.jpg" width="212" height="203" alt="Fettucine" align="left" hspace="5" /></p>

<p>Our fettuccine alfredo dish is a traditional Italian recipe your family will love! The secret is
in our rich fettuccine alfredo sauce. The sauce is what makes this dish so popular. The alfredo sauce
recipe comes from the Lazio area of Italy. The cream cheese that we use in our sauce is the best that
is made, and that adds to the creamy richness. Because this fettuccine dish is so simple, it's important
```

inserted target named top takes visitors to top of Web page when link is clicked; inserted just after <body> tag

Figure 3–45

2

- Highlight the line <!--Line 62 - Insert first To Top link here --> to position the insertion point on the line 62.
- Type `<p><a href="#top"><font size="-1">To top</font></a></p>` as the tag (Figure 3–46).

Q&A Why do you use a -1 for the font size for this link?

The link back to the top of the page should be subtle yet noticeable as distinguished from the other text on the page.

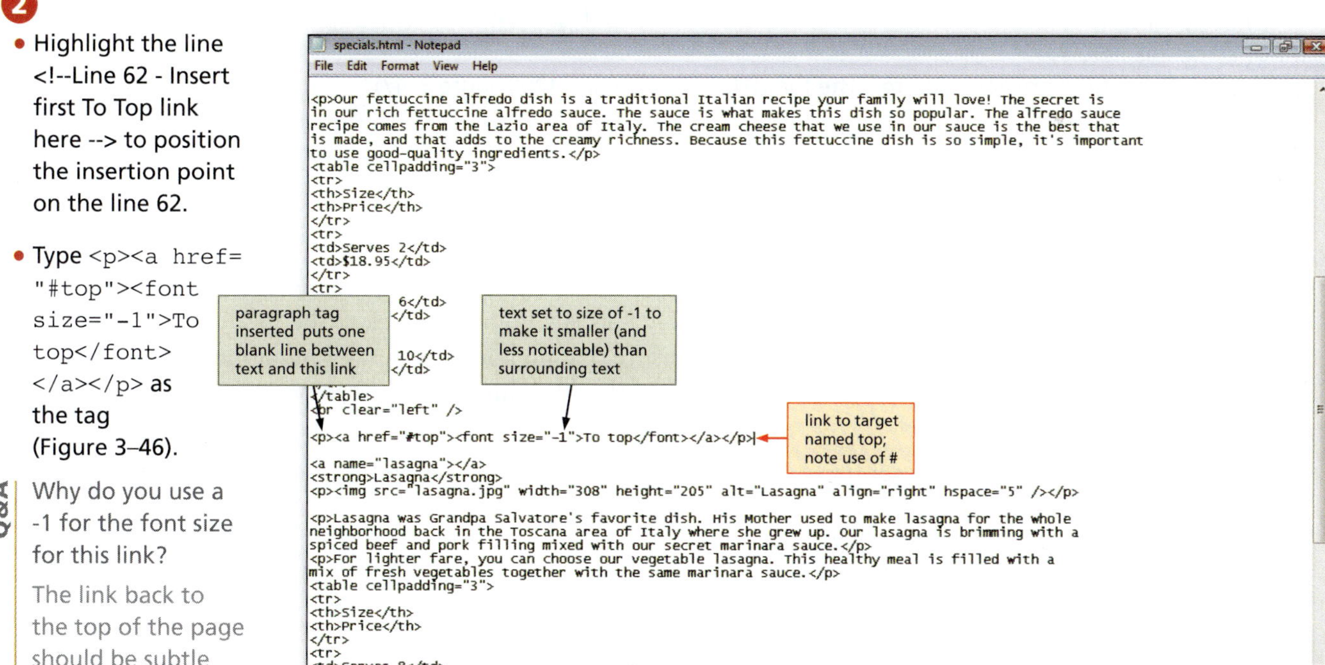

```
specials.html - Notepad
File  Edit  Format  View  Help

<p>Our fettuccine alfredo dish is a traditional Italian recipe your family will love! The secret is
in our rich fettuccine alfredo sauce. The sauce is what makes this dish so popular. The alfredo sauce
recipe comes from the Lazio area of Italy. The cream cheese that we use in our sauce is the best that
is made, and that adds to the creamy richness. Because this fettuccine dish is so simple, it's important
to use good-quality ingredients.</p>
<table cellpadding="3">
<tr>
<th>Size</th>
<th>Price</th>
</tr>
<tr>
<td>Serves 2</td>
<td>$18.95</td>
</tr>
<tr>
   6</td>
</td>
   10</td>
</td>
</table>
<br clear="left" />
<p><a href="#top"><font size="-1">To top</font></a></p>

<a name="lasagna"></a>
<strong>Lasagna</strong>
<p><img src="lasagna.jpg" width="308" height="205" alt="Lasagna" align="right" hspace="5" /></p>

<p>Lasagna was Grandpa Salvatore's favorite dish. His Mother used to make lasagna for the whole
neighborhood back in the Toscana area of Italy where she grew up. Our lasagna is brimming with a
spiced beef and pork filling mixed with our secret marinara sauce.</p>
<p>For lighter fare, you can choose our vegetable lasagna. This healthy meal is filled with a
mix of fresh vegetables together with the same marinara sauce.</p>
<table cellpadding="3">
<tr>
<th>Size</th>
<th>Price</th>
</tr>
<tr>
<td>Serves 8</td>
```


Figure 3–46

To Copy and Paste HTML Code

The copy and paste feature can be very useful for entering the same code in different places. The following step shows how to copy and paste the link code to three other lines in the HTML code.

- Highlight the HTML code `<p><a href="#top"><font size="-1"> To top</font></a></p>` on line 62.
- Click Edit on the menu bar and then click Copy.
- Highlight the line <!--Line 89 - Insert second To Top link here --> on line 89 to position the pointer.
- Click Edit on the menu bar and then click Paste to paste the HTML code that you copied above.
- Highlight the line <!--Line 120 - Insert third To Top link here --> on line 120. Repeat the previous step to paste the HTML code on line 120 (Figure 3–47).

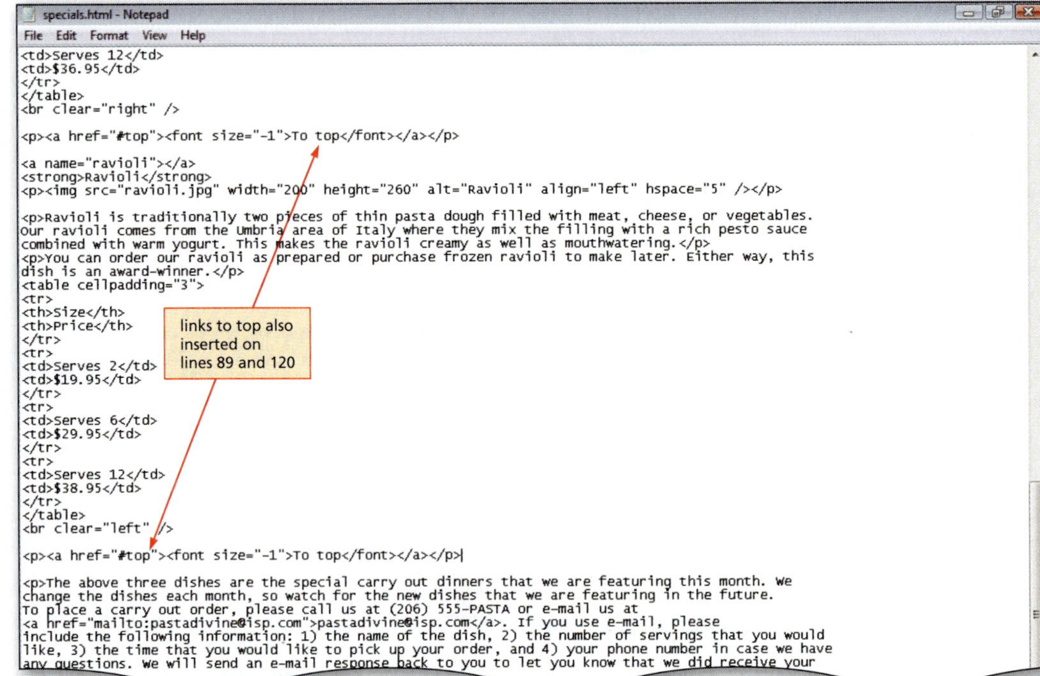

Figure 3–47

To Add an Image Link to a Web Page

The last step is to add an image link from the Monthly Specials Web page back to the Pasta Divine home page. You set the image border attribute value to zero to ensure that no border appears around the image. The following steps show how to create an image link at the top of the Monthly Specials Web page.

- Highlight the line <!--Line 14 - Insert link back to home page here --> on line 14.
- Type `<a href="pastadivine.html">` as the tag to start a link that will use the image pdlogosm.gif to link back to the home page as shown in Figure 3–48.

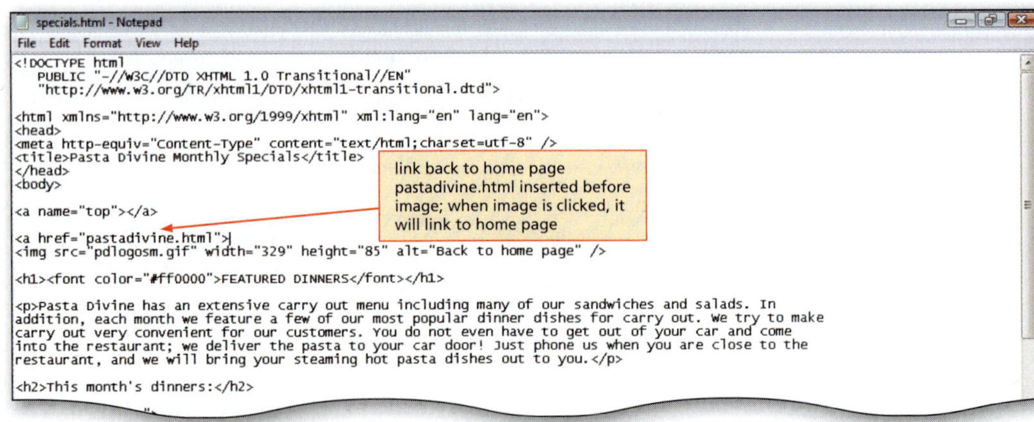

Figure 3–48

2

- Click immediately to the right of the > in the attribute alt="Back to home page" /> on line 15.
- Type </a> as the tag to end the link as shown in Figure 3–49.

specials.html - Notepad

File Edit Format View Help

```
<!DOCTYPE html
   PUBLIC "-//W3C//DTD XHTML 1.0 Transitional//EN"
   "http://www.w3.org/TR/xhtml1/DTD/xhtml1-transitional.dtd">

<html xmlns="http://www.w3.org/1999/xhtml" xml:lang="en" lang="en">
<head>
<meta http-equiv="Content-Type" content="text/html;charset=utf-8" />
<title>Pasta Divine Monthly Specials</title>
</head>
<body>

<a name="top"></a>

<a href="pastadivine.html">
<img src="pdlogosm.gif" width="329" height="85" alt="Back to home page" /></a>

<h1><font color="#ff0000">FEATURED DINNERS</font></h1>

<p>Pasta Divine has an extensive carry out menu including many of our sandwiches and salads. In
addition, each month we feature a few of our most popular dinner dishes for carry out. We try to make
carry out very convenient for our customers. You do not even have to get out of your car and come
into the restaurant; we deliver the pasta to your car door! Just phone us when you are close to the
restaurant, and we will bring your steaming hot pasta dishes out to you.</p>

<h2>This month's dinners:</h2>

<ul type="square">
<li><a href="#fettuccine">Fettuccine Alfredo</a></li>
<li><a href="#lasagna">Lasagna</a></li>
<li><a href="#ravioli">Ravioli</a></li>
</ul>

<a name="fettuccine"></a>
<strong>Fettuccine Alfredo</strong>
<p><img src="fettuccine.jpg" width="212" height="203" alt="Fettucine" align="left" hspace="5" /></p>

<p>Our fettuccine alfredo dish is a traditional Italian recipe your family will love! The secret is
in our rich fettuccine alfredo sauce. The sauce is what makes this dish so popular. The alfredo sauce
recipe comes from the Lazio area of Italy. The cream cheese that we use in our sauce is the best that
```

</a> end link to home page

Figure 3–49

3

- Click immediately to the right of the second " in alt="Back to home page" /> to position the insertion point.
- Press the SPACEBAR, then type `border="0"` as the attribute to create a borderless link as shown in Figure 3–50.

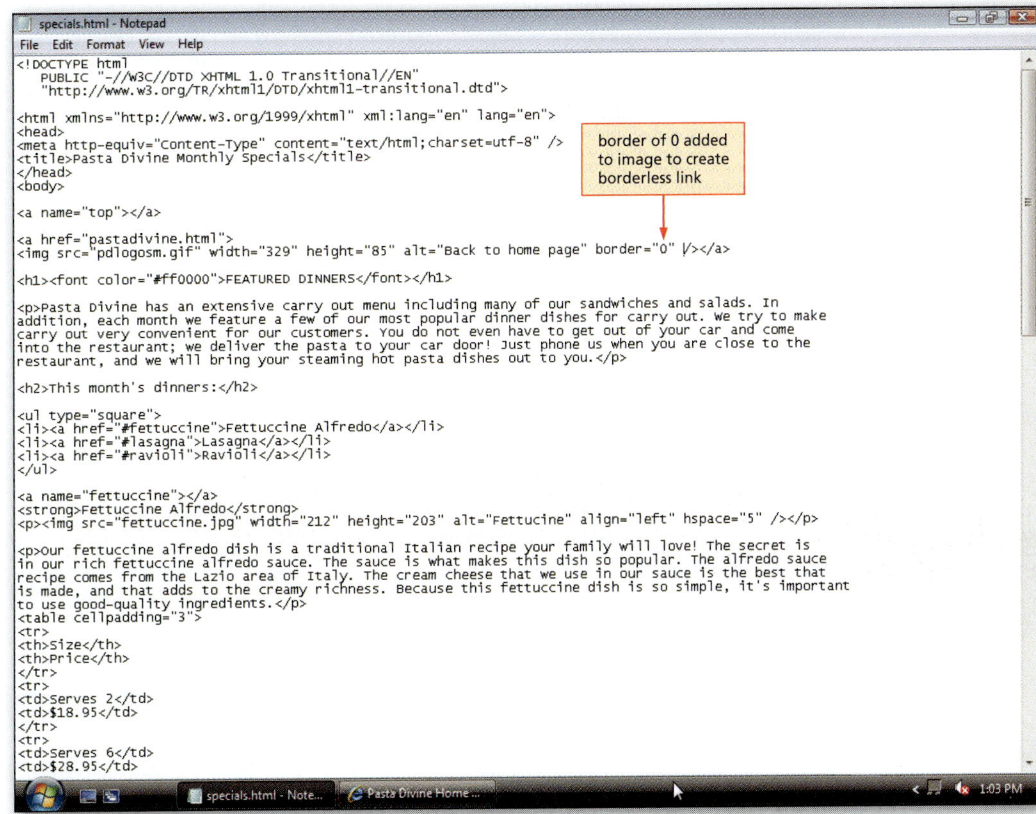
specials.html - Notepad

File Edit Format View Help

```
<!DOCTYPE html
   PUBLIC "-//W3C//DTD XHTML 1.0 Transitional//EN"
   "http://www.w3.org/TR/xhtml1/DTD/xhtml1-transitional.dtd">

<html xmlns="http://www.w3.org/1999/xhtml" xml:lang="en" lang="en">
<head>
<meta http-equiv="Content-Type" content="text/html;charset=utf-8" />
<title>Pasta Divine Monthly Specials</title>
</head>
<body>

<a name="top"></a>

<a href="pastadivine.html">
<img src="pdlogosm.gif" width="329" height="85" alt="Back to home page" border="0" /></a>

<h1><font color="#ff0000">FEATURED DINNERS</font></h1>

<p>Pasta Divine has an extensive carry out menu including many of our sandwiches and salads. In
addition, each month we feature a few of our most popular dinner dishes for carry out. We try to make
carry out very convenient for our customers. You do not even have to get out of your car and come
into the restaurant; we deliver the pasta to your car door! Just phone us when you are close to the
restaurant, and we will bring your steaming hot pasta dishes out to you.</p>

<h2>This month's dinners:</h2>

<ul type="square">
<li><a href="#fettuccine">Fettuccine Alfredo</a></li>
<li><a href="#lasagna">Lasagna</a></li>
<li><a href="#ravioli">Ravioli</a></li>
</ul>

<a name="fettuccine"></a>
<strong>Fettuccine Alfredo</strong>
<p><img src="fettuccine.jpg" width="212" height="203" alt="Fettucine" align="left" hspace="5" /></p>

<p>Our fettuccine alfredo dish is a traditional Italian recipe your family will love! The secret is
in our rich fettuccine alfredo sauce. The sauce is what makes this dish so popular. The alfredo sauce
recipe comes from the Lazio area of Italy. The cream cheese that we use in our sauce is the best that
is made, and that adds to the creamy richness. Because this fettuccine dish is so simple, it's important
to use good-quality ingredients.</p>
<table cellpadding="3">
<tr>
<th>Size</th>
<th>Price</th>
</tr>
<tr>
<td>Serves 2</td>
<td>$18.95</td>
</tr>
<tr>
<td>Serves 6</td>
<td>$28.95</td>
```


Figure 3–50

Q&A

Why is there a border="0" attribute in the <img> tag?

If the border="0" is not used, then there would be a default blue border around the image link at startup. Once the link was clicked, the border would change to purple. You make this a borderless link so that the border colors do not conflict with the colors in the image itself.

To Save and Print the HTML File

With the HTML code for the Monthly Specials Web page complete, the HTML file should be saved and a copy should be printed as a reference. The following step illustrates how to save and print the HTML file.

If necessary, activate the Notepad window.

- Click File on the menu bar, and then Save on the File menu to save the HTML file as specials.html.
- Click File on the menu bar, click Print on the File menu, and then click the Print button in the Print dialog box to print the HTML code (Figure 3–51).

```
<!DOCTYPE html
   PUBLIC "-//W3C//DTD XHTML 1.0 Transitional//EN"
   "http://www.w3.org/TR/xhtml1/DTD/xhtml1-transitional.dtd">

<html xmlns="http://www.w3.org/1999/xhtml" xml:lang="en" lang="en">
<head>
<meta http-equiv="Content-Type" content="text/html;charset=utf-8" />
<title>Pasta Divine Monthly Specials</title>
</head>
<body>

<a name="top"></a>

<a href="pastadivine.html">
<img src="pdlogosm.gif" width="329" height="85" alt="Back to home page" border="0" /></a>

<h1><font color="#ff0000">FEATURED DINNERS</font></h1>

<p>Pasta Divine has an extensive carry out menu including many of our sandwiches and salads. In
addition, each month we feature a few of our most popular dinner dishes for carry out. We try to make
carry out very convenient for our customers. You do not even have to get out of your car and come
into the restaurant; we deliver the pasta to your car door! Just phone us when you are close to the
restaurant, and we will bring your steaming hot pasta dishes out to you.</p>

<h2>This month's dinners:</h2>

<ul>
<li><a href="#fettuccine">Fettucine Alfredo</a></li>
<li><a href="#lasagna">Lasagna</a></li>
<li><a href="#ravioli">Ravioli</a></li>
</ul>

<a name="fettuccine"></a>
<strong>Fettuccine Alfredo</strong>
<p><img src="fettuccine.jpg" width="212" height="203" alt="Fettucine" align="left" hspace="5" /></p>

<p>Our fettuccine alfredo dish is a traditional Italian recipe your family will love! The secret is
in our rich fettuccine alfredo sauce. The sauce is what makes this dish so popular. The alfredo sauce
recipe comes from the Lazio area of Italy. The cream cheese that we use in our sauce is the best that
is made, and that adds to the creamy richness. Because this fettuccine dish is so simple, it's important
to use good-quality ingredients.</p>
<table cellpadding="3">
<tr>
<th>Size</th>
<th>Price</th>
</tr>
<tr>
<td>Serves 2</td>
<td>$18.95</td>
</tr>
<tr>
<td>Serves 6</td>
<td>$28.95</td>
</tr>
<tr>
<td>Serves 10</td>
<td>$38.95</td>
</tr>
</table>
<br clear="left" />

<p><a href="#top"><font size="-1">To top</font></a></p>

<a name="lasagna"></a>
<strong>Lasagna</strong>
<p><img src="lasagna.jpg" width="308" height="205" alt="Lasagna" align="right" hspace="5" /></p>

<p>Lasagna was Grandpa Salvatore's favorite dish. His Mother used to make lasagna for the whole
neighborhood back in the Toscana area of Italy where she grew up. Our lasagna is brimming with a
spiced beef and pork filling mixed with our secret marinara sauce.</p>
<p>For lighter fare, you can choose our vegetable lasagna. This healthy meal is filled with a
mix of fresh vegetables together with the same marinara sauce.</p>
```

(a)

Figure 3–51

```
<table cellpadding="3">
<tr>
<th>Size</th>
<th>Price</th>
</tr>
<tr>
<td>Serves 8</td>
<td>$24.95</td>
</tr>
<tr>
<td>Serves 12</td>
<td>$36.95</td>
</tr>
</table>
<br clear="right" />

<p><a href="#top"><font size="-1">To top</font></a></p>

<a name="ravioli"></a>
<strong>Ravioli</strong>
<p><img src="ravioli.jpg" width="200" height="260" alt="Ravioli" align="left" hspace="5" /></p>

<p>Ravioli is traditionally two pieces of thin pasta dough filled with meat, cheese, or vegetables.
Our ravioli comes from the Umbria area of Italy where they mix the filling with a rich pesto sauce
combined with warm yogurt. This makes the ravioli creamy as well as mouthwatering.</p>
<p>You can order our ravioli as prepared or purchase frozen ravioli to make later. Either way, this
dish is an award-winner.</p>
<table cellpadding="3">
<tr>
<th>Size</th>
<th>Price</th>
</tr>
<tr>
<td>Serves 2</td>
<td>$19.95</td>
</tr>
<tr>
<td>Serves 6</td>
<td>$29.95</td>
</tr>
<tr>
<td>Serves 12</td>
<td>$38.95</td>
</tr>
</table>
<br clear="left" />

<p><a href="#top"><font size="-1">To top</font></a></p>

<p>The above three dishes are the special carry out dinners that we are featuring this month. We
change the dishes each month, so watch for the new dishes that we are featuring in the future.
To place a carry out order, please call us at (206) 555-PASTA or e-mail us at
<a href="mailto:pastadivine@isp.com">pastadivine@isp.com</a>. If you use e-mail, please
include the following information: 1) the name of the dish, 2) the number of servings that you would
like, 3) the time that you would like to pick up your order, and 4) your phone number in case we have
any questions. We will send an e-mail response back to you to let you know that we did receive your
order.</p>
<p>When picking up your order, please phone us when you get near the restaurant. We will bring
your food out to you! We do accept our coupons for carry out orders, so please indicate that you have
a coupon when you phone or e-mail us.</p>

</body>
</html>
```

(b)

Figure 3–51 (continued)

To Validate, View, and Test a Web Page

- Open a new browser window and go to validator.w3.org.
- Click the Validate by File Upload tab, browse to the specials.html Web page, and then click Open.
- Click the Check button to determine if the Web page is valid. If the file is not valid, make corrections and revalidate.
- Click the Pasta Divine Monthly Specials button on the taskbar to view the page in your browser.
- Click the Refresh button on the Standard toolbar to display the changes made to the Web page, which should now look like Figure 3–27 on page HTML 111.

- Verify that all internal links work correctly by clicking the three links in the bulleted list at the top of the Web page. Also make sure to check the three "To top" links. Finally, verify that the image link to the home page works.

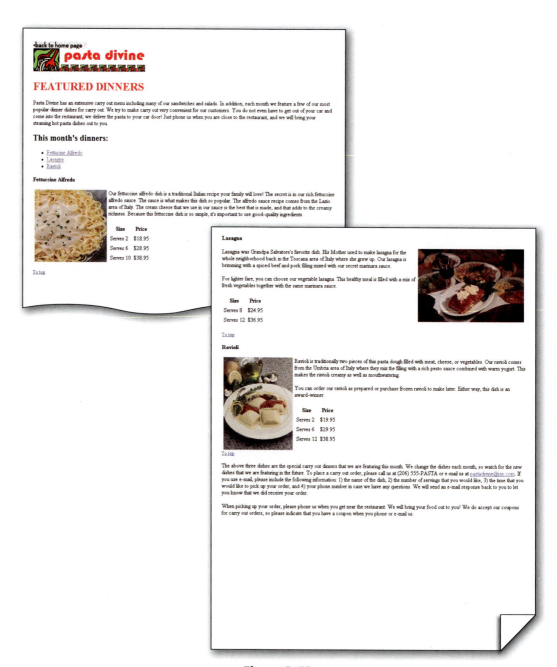

How can I tell if internal links are working when the link and target are displayed in the same browser window?

To see movement to a link, you might need to restore down and resize the browser window so that the target is not visible, then click the link.

To Print a Web Page

1

- Click the Print icon on the Command bar. The printed page is shown in Figure 3–52.

Figure 3–52

To Quit Notepad and a Browser

- Click the Close button on all open browser windows.
- Click the Close button on the Notepad window.

Chapter Summary

In this chapter, you have learned how to develop a two-page Web site with links, images, and formatted text. The items listed below include all the new HTML skills you have learned in this chapter.

1. Enter Initial HTML Tags to Define the Web Page Structure (HTML 91)
2. Add an Image (HTML 93)
3. Add a Left-Aligned Heading with a Font Color (HTML 95)
4. Create an Unordered (Bulleted) List (HTML 96)
5. Add Paragraphs of Text (HTML 97)
6. Add a Text Link to Another Web Page within the Same Web Site (HTML 100)
7. Add an E-Mail Link (HTML 101)
8. Add a Text Link to a Web Page in Another Web Site (HTML 103)
9. Test Links on a Web Page (HTML 108)
10. Format Text in Bold (HTML 115)
11. Add an Image with Wrapped Text (HTML 120)
12. Clear the Text Wrapping (HTML 122)
13. Set Link Targets (HTML 125)
14. Add Links to Link Targets within a Web Page (HTML 126)
15. Add Links to a Target at the Top of the Page (HTML 127)
16. Copy and Paste HTML Code (HTML 128)
17. Add an Image Link to a Web Page (HTML 128)

Learn It Online

Test your knowledge of chapter content and key terms.

Instructions: To complete the Learn It Online exercises, start your browser, click the Address bar, and then enter the Web address `scsite.com/html5e/learn`. When the HTML Learn It Online page is displayed, click the link for the exercise you want to complete and read the instructions.

Chapter Reinforcement TF, MC, and SA

A series of true/false, multiple choice, and short answer questions that test your knowledge of the chapter content.

Flash Cards

An interactive learning environment where you identify chapter key terms associated with displayed definitions.

Practice Test

A series of multiple choice questions that test your knowledge of chapter content and key terms.

Who Wants To Be a Computer Genius?

An interactive game that challenges your knowledge of chapter content in the style of a television quiz show.

Wheel of Terms

An interactive game that challenges your knowledge of chapter key terms in the style of the television show, *Wheel of Fortune*.

Crossword Puzzle Challenge

A crossword puzzle that challenges your knowledge of key terms presented in the chapter.

Apply Your Knowledge

Reinforce the skills and apply the concepts you learned in this chapter.

Adding Text Formatting to a Web Page

Instructions: Start Notepad. Open the file apply3-1.html from the Chapter03\Apply folder of the Data Files for Students. See the inside back cover of this book for instructions on downloading the Data Files for Students, or contact your instructor for information about accessing the required files.

The apply3-1.html file is a partially completed HTML file that you will use for this exercise. Figure 3–53 shows the Apply Your Knowledge Web page as it should be displayed in a browser after the additional HTML tags and attributes are added.

Perform the following tasks:

1. Enter g:\Chapter03\Apply\apply3-1.html as the URL to view the Web page in your browser.
2. Examine the HTML file in Notepad and its appearance in the browser.
3. In Notepad, change the HTML code to make the Web page look similar to the one shown in Figure 3–53.
4. Center the h1 heading, Chinese Garden, and make it red.
5. In the first paragraph, make the words "Chinese garden" emphasized and bold, and the word "China" strong. In the second paragraph, use the <big> tag to make the word "awesome" larger, and use the <strong> tag to make the word "none" bold. In the final paragraph, make the word "love" red, the word "relax" italic, and use the <strong> tag on the words "sheer beauty" to make the words appear as bold text.
6. Add align and hspace attributes in the <img> tag to align the image to the left with text on the right, with hspace of 10 pixels between the image and text.

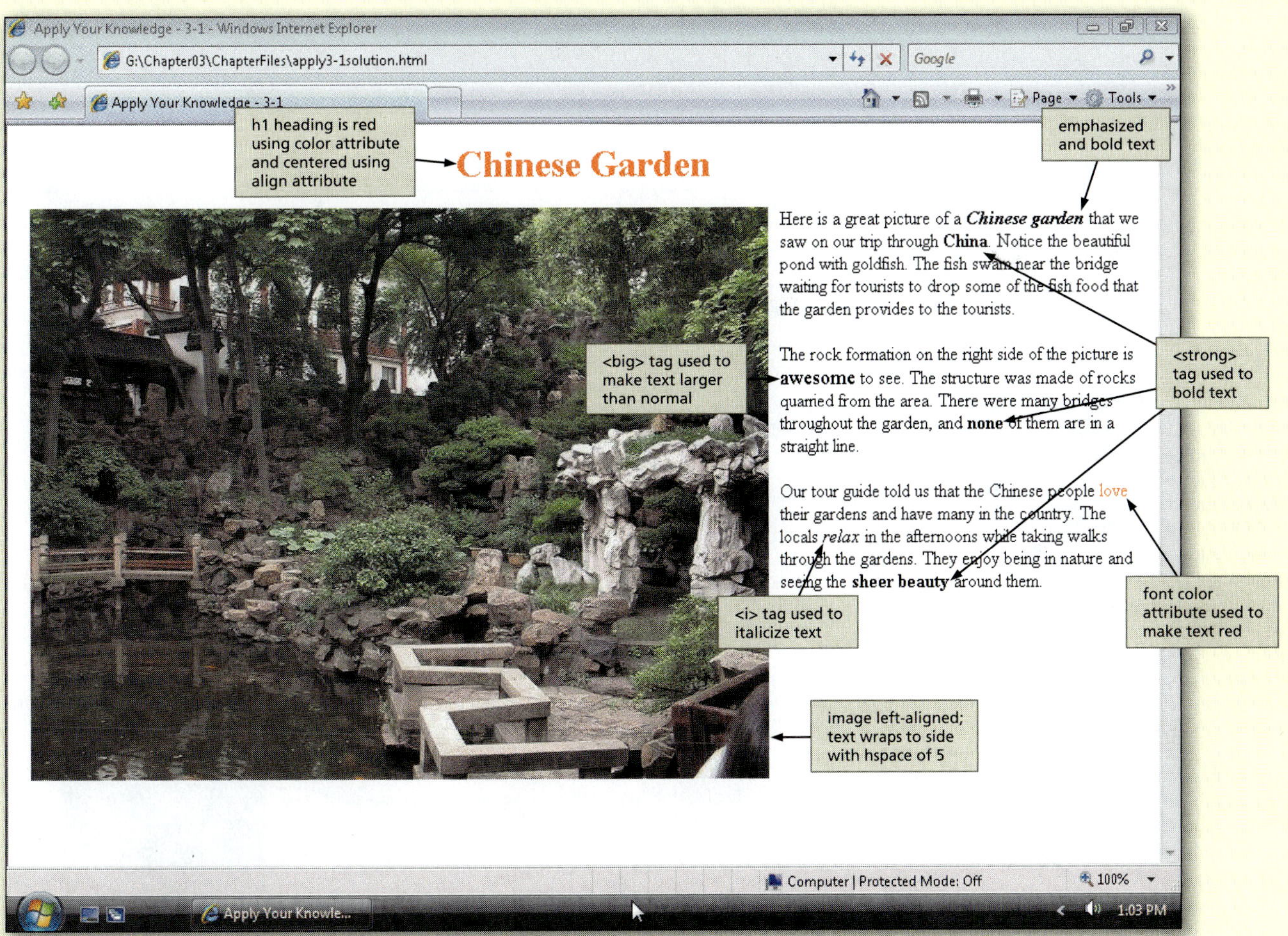

Figure 3–53

7. Save the revised HTML file in the Chapter03\Apply folder using the file name apply3-1solution.html.
8. Validate your code and test all links.
9. Print the revised HTML file.
10. Enter g:\Chapter03\Apply\apply3-1solution.html as the URL to view the revised Web page in your browser.
11. Print the Web page.
12. Submit the revised HTML file and Web page in the format specified by your instructor.

Extend Your Knowledge

Extend the skills you learned in this chapter and experiment with new skills.

Creating Targets and Links

Instructions: Start Notepad. Open the file extend3-1.html from the Chapter03\Extend folder of the Data Files for Students. See the inside back cover of this book for instructions on downloading the Data Files for Students, or contact your instructor for information about accessing the required files. This sample HTML file contains all of the text for the Web page shown in Figure 3–54 on the next page. You will add the necessary tags to make this Web page appear with left- and right-aligned images, text formatting, and links as shown in Figure 3–54.

Continued >

Extend Your Knowledge *continued*

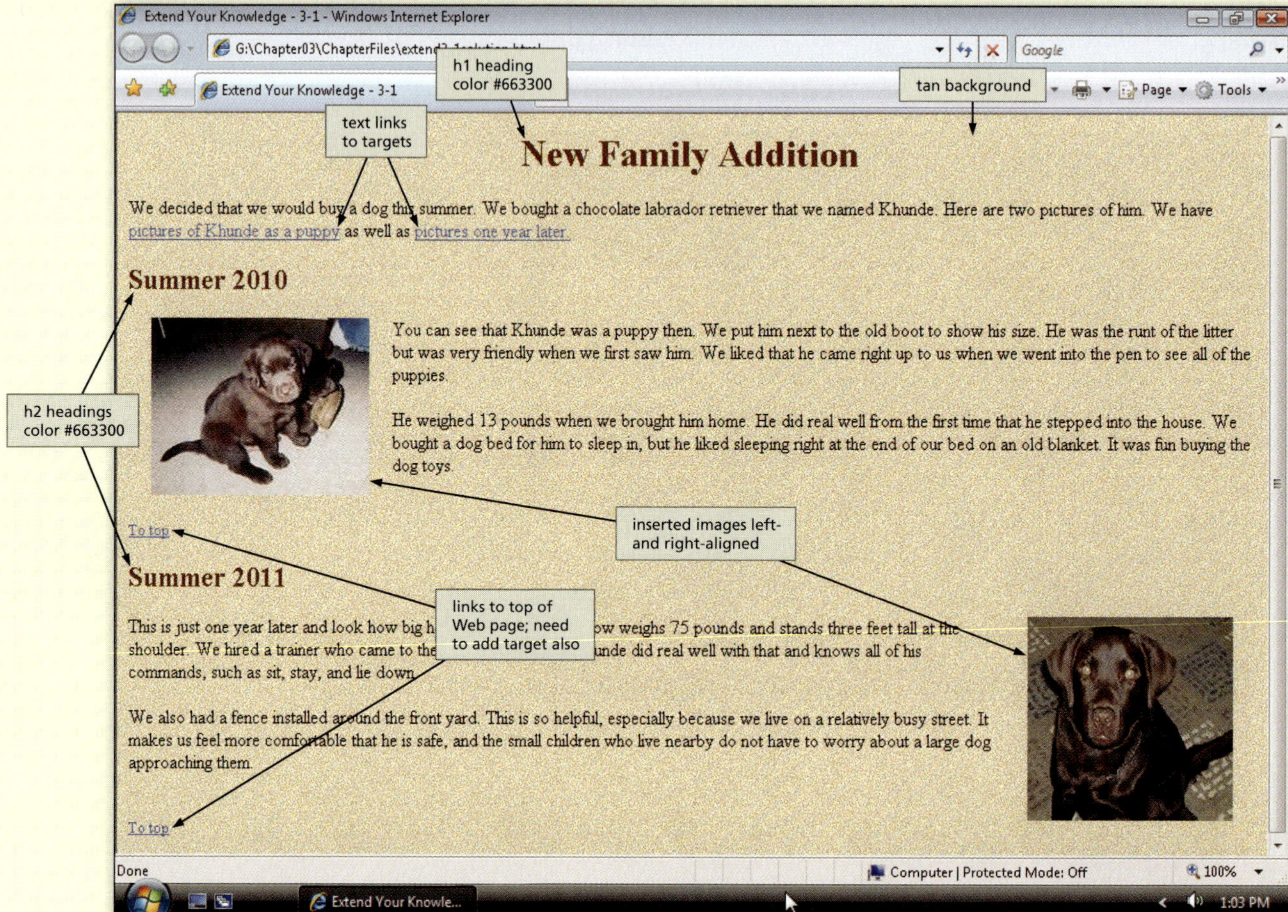

Figure 3–54

Perform the following tasks:

1. Use the tanbkgrnd.gif image as the background for the Web page. (*Hint*: Review the HTML Quick Reference in Appendix A for more information on doing this.)
2. Apply the color #663300 to the h2 text for Summer 2010 and Summer 2011.
3. Add code to align the first picture on the left with hspace of 20. Add code to align the second picture on the right, also with an hspace of 20. (*Hint*: Remember to clear alignment for both images.)
4. Add the HTML code to create three targets (one at the top of the Web page, one near the first h2 heading, and the last near the second h2 heading). Also create two link(s) back to the top with font size -1 as shown in Figure 3–54.
5. Save the revised document as extend3-1solution.html and submit it the format specified by your instructor.
6. Validate your HTML code and test all links.

Make It Right

Analyze a document and correct all errors and/or improve the design.

Correcting the Grand Canyon Web Page

Instructions: Start Notepad. Open the file makeitright3-1.html from the Chapter03\MakeItRight folder of the Data Files for Students. See the inside back cover of this book for instructions on downloading the Data Files for Students, or contact your instructor for information about accessing the required files. The Web page is a modified version of what you see in Figure 3–55. Make the necessary corrections to the Web page to make it look like the figure. The Web page uses the images grandcanyon1.jpg and grandcanyon2.jpg, which have widths and heights of 346 × 259 and 321 × 288, respectively.

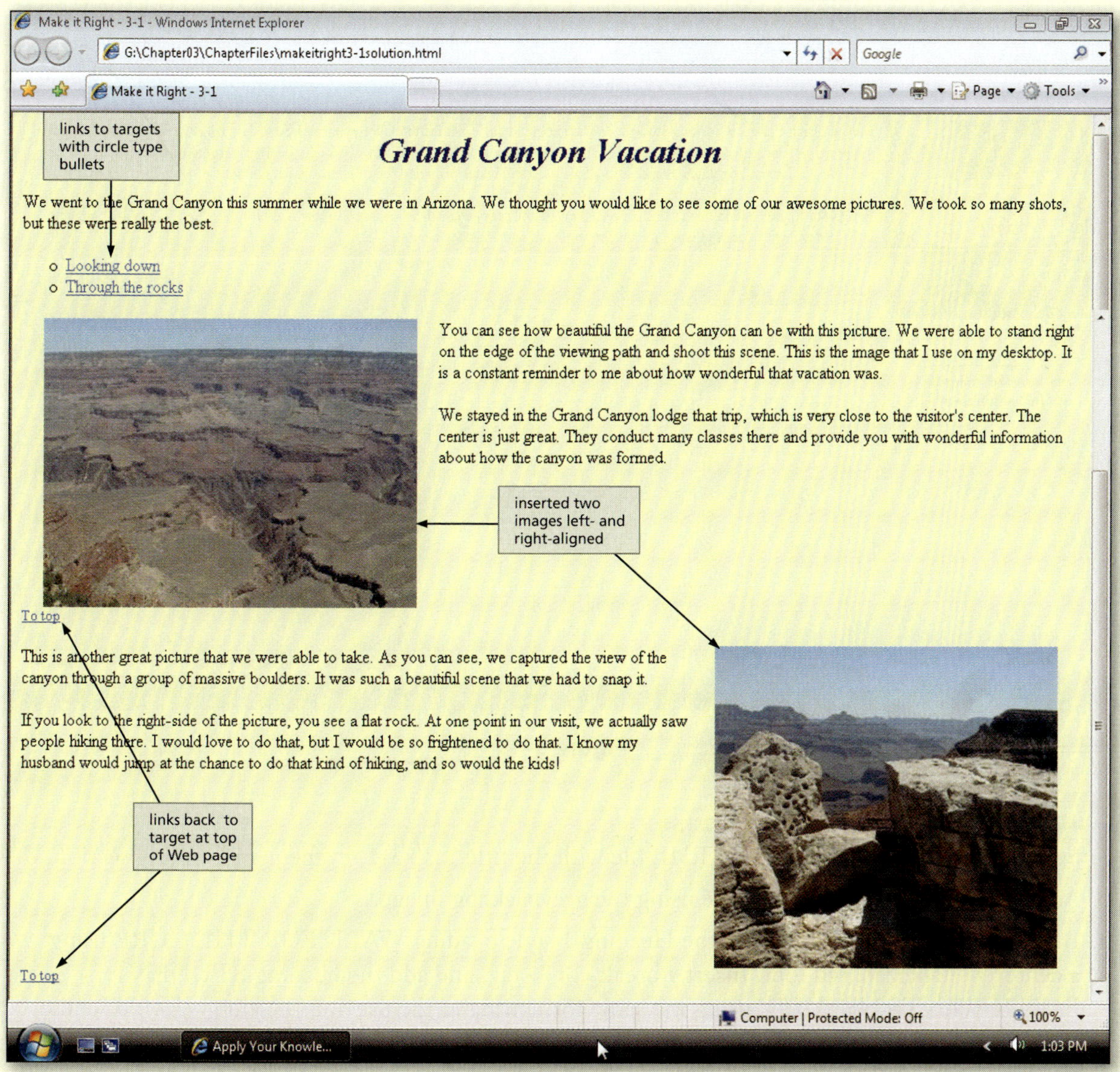

Figure 3–55

In the Lab

Lab 1: Creating a Web Page with Wrapped Text

Problem: You are the head of the Walk for the Cure program and decide to prepare a Web page announcement inviting people to join the group (Figure 3–56). You would like to have the text wrapped around a left-aligned image to provide visual appeal.

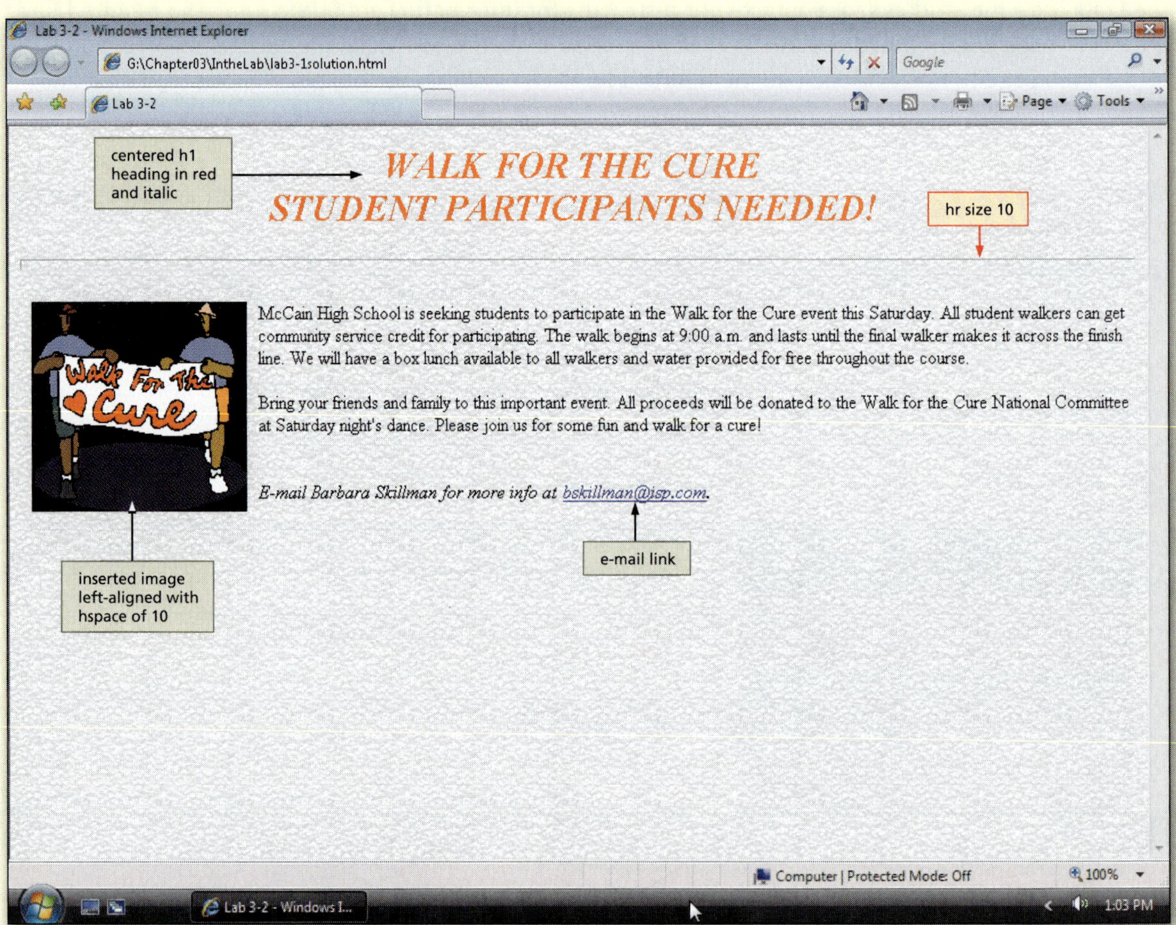

Figure 3–56

Instructions: Perform the following tasks:

1. Start Notepad and create a new HTML file with the title, Lab 3-1, in the main heading section.
2. Add a background to the Web page using the greyback.jpg image.
3. Begin the body section by adding the Heading 1 style heading WALK FOR THE CURE using a centered, italicized, red font. Insert a break <br /> tag, and add the heading STUDENT PARTICIPANTS NEEDED! using the same formatting as the previous heading. (*Hint*: Use the word “red” for the color code.)
4. Add a size 10 horizontal rule below the heading.
5. Add the image curewalk.gif using attributes so it is left-aligned with horizontal space of 10, height of 178, and width of 190. Left-alignment will wrap text to the right of the image. Add alt text for “Cure walk logo”.
6. Add the paragraphs of information as shown in Figure 3–56.

7. Add an italicized e-mail sentence at the bottom of the page, and create the e-mail link as shown in Figure 3–56.
8. Save the HTML file in the Chapter03\IntheLab folder using the file name lab3-1solution.html.
9. Validate the HTML code and test all links.
10. Print the lab3-1solution.html file.
11. Enter the URL g:\Chapter03\IntheLab\lab3-1solution.html to view the Web page in your browser.
12. Print the Web page.
13. Write your name on the printouts and hand them in to your instructor.

In the Lab

2: Creating a Web Page with Links

Problem: Your instructor wants you to create a Web page demonstrating your knowledge of link targets. You have been asked to create a Web page to demonstrate this technique, similar to the one shown in Figure 3–57.

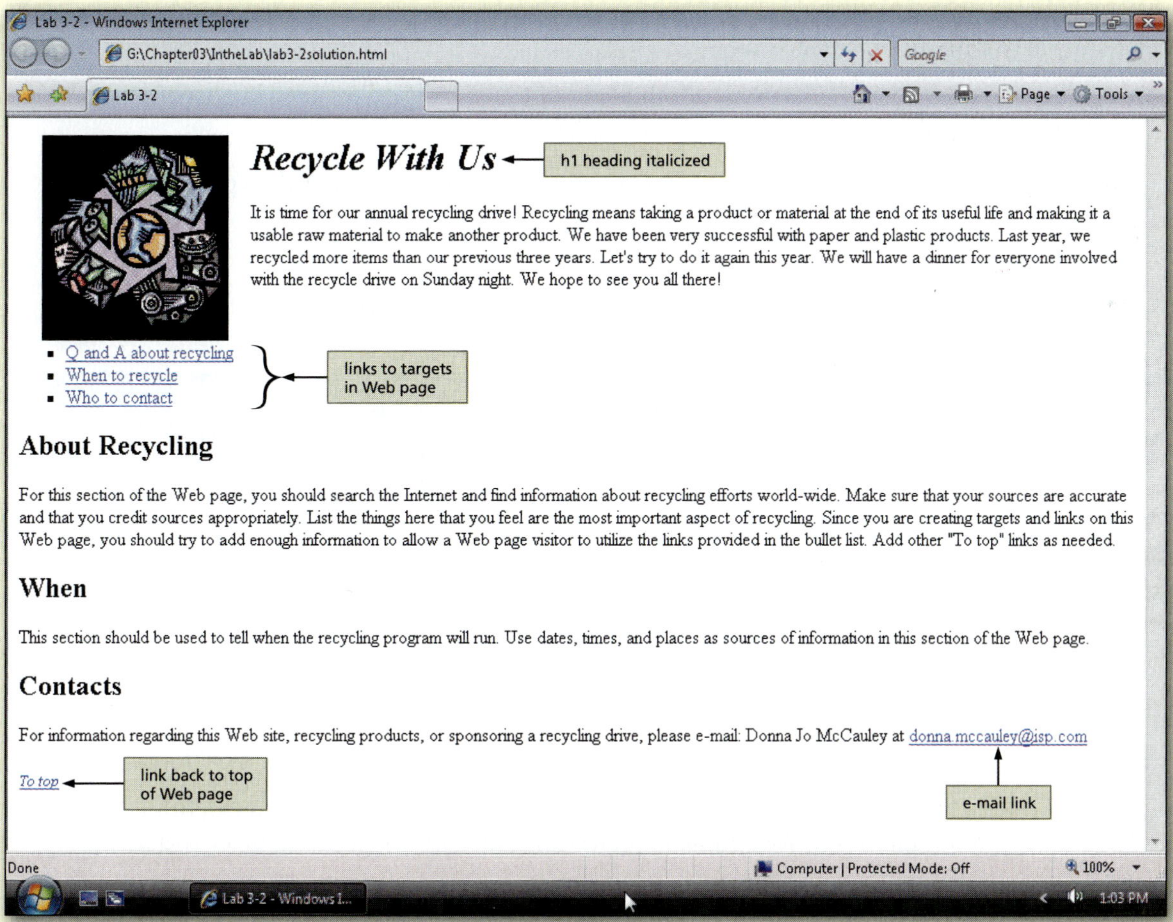

Figure 3–57

Instructions: Perform the following steps:

1. Start Notepad and create a new HTML file with the title, Lab 3-2, in the main heading section.

Continued >

In the Lab *continued*

2. Begin the body section by adding the image recycle.gif and aligning it to the left. Use the hspace attribute with a value of 20.
3. Add the heading Recycle With Us. Format the heading to use the Heading 1 style, left-aligned, italic, with the font color black.
4. Add an unordered list with the three list items, as shown in Figure 3–57. Use a square bullet type for the bullets. These three items will be used to link to the three sections of text below them.
5. Add a Heading 2 style heading, About Recycling, and set a link target named about. Type a paragraph of text based on your research of the topic, as shown in Figure 3–57 on the previous page.
6. Add a Heading 2 style heading, When, and set a link target named when. Type a paragraph based on your research of the topic, as shown in Figure 3–57.
7. Add a Heading 2 style heading, Contacts, and set a link target named contact. Type the paragraph as shown in Figure 3–57.
8. Create a link target at the top of the page named top.
9. Create a top link at the bottom of the page, as shown in Figure 3–57. Set the link to direct to the top target at the top of the page.
10. Create links from the bulleted list to the three targets.
11. Create an e-mail link as shown in Figure 3–57.
12. Save the HTML file in the Chapter03\IntheLab folder using the file name lab3-2solution.html.
13. Print the lab3-2solution.html file.
14. Enter the URL g:\Chapter03\IntheLab\lab3-2solution.html to view the Web page in your browser.
15. Print the Web page.
16. Write your name on both printouts and hand them in to your instructor.

In the Lab

3: Creating Two Linked Web Pages

Problem: Your Communications instructor has asked each student in the class to create a two-page Web site to help students in the class get to know each other. She suggested using the basic template shown in Figures 3–58a and 3–58b as a starting point. The first Web page (Figure 3–58a) is a home page that includes basic personal information and a link to the second Web page. The second Web page (Figure 3–58b) includes a paragraph of text and numbered lists with links.

Instructions: Perform the following steps:

1. Start Notepad and create a new HTML file with the title Lab 3-3 in the main heading section.
2. In the first Web page, include a Heading style 1 heading, similar to the one shown in Figure 3–58a, and a short paragraph of text. Experiment and use any color for the heading (navy is shown).
3. Create a text link to the second Web page, lab3-3favorites.html.
4. Save the HTML file in the Chapter03\IntheLab folder using the file name lab3-3solution.html. Print the lab3-3solution.html file.
5. Start a new HTML file with the title Lab 3-3 Favorites in the main heading section.
6. In the second Web page, include a Heading style 1 heading, similar to the one shown in Figure 3–58b, a short paragraph of text, and two Heading style 2 headings. Use any color for the heading (navy is shown).

7. Create two ordered (numbered) lists with at least two items that serve as links to Web pages on another Web site. Add a link back to the first Web page, as shown in Figure 3–58b.
8. Save the HTML file in the Chapter03\IntheLab folder using the file name lab3-3favorites.html. Print the lab3-3favorites.html file.
9. Enter the URL g:\Chapter03\IntheLab\lab3-3solution.html to view the Web page in your browser. Click the text link to the second Web page. Click the links in the lists to test them.
10. Print the Web pages.
11. Write your name on the printouts and hand them in to your instructor.

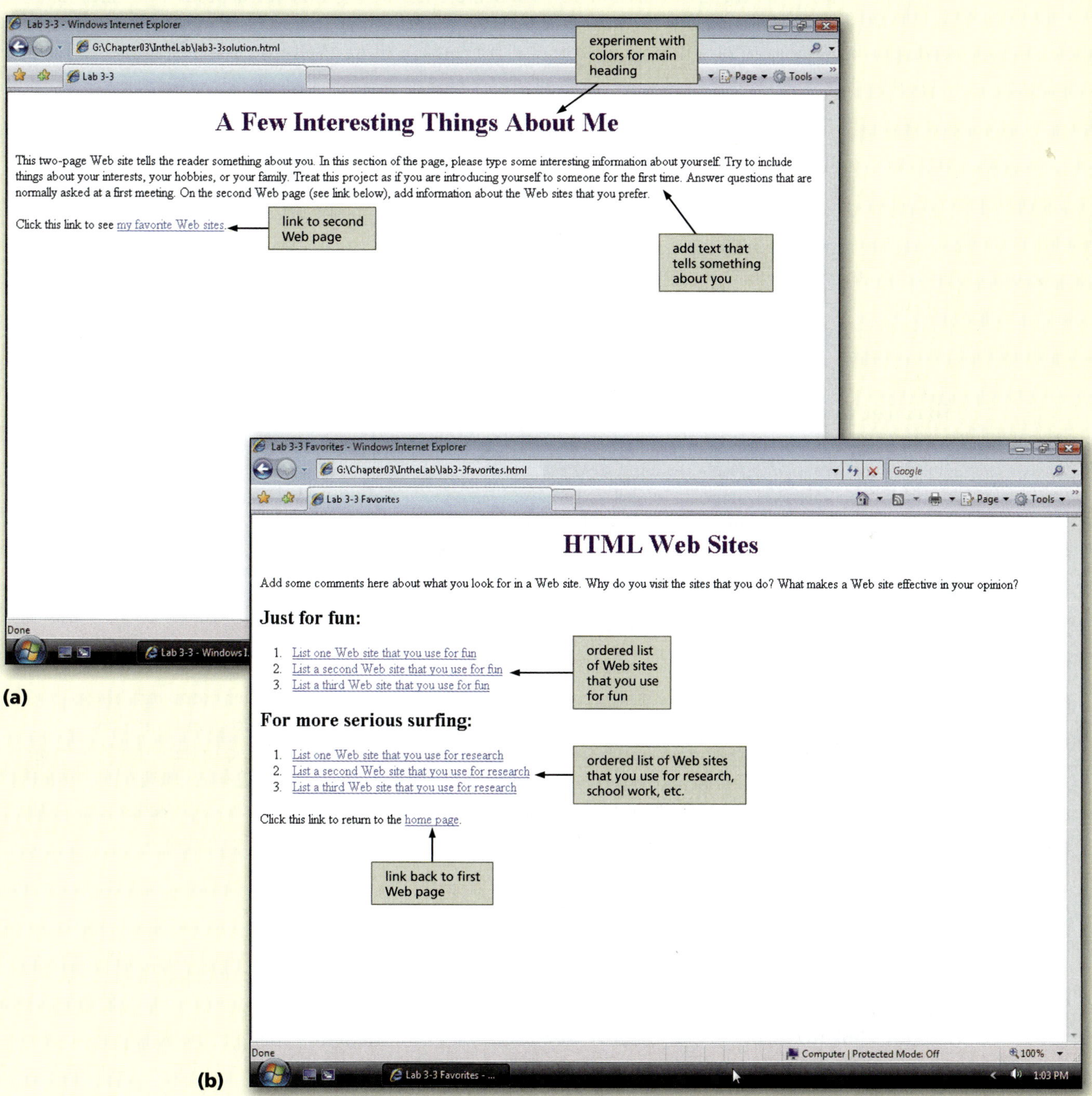

Figure 3–58

Cases and Places

Apply your creative thinking and problem solving skills to design and implement a solution.

• Easier ••More Difficult

• 1: Add a Web Page to the Pasta Divine Site

Sunny Saperstein is very impressed with the Pasta Divine Web pages and now would like to add a Web page listing pasta-making tools and devices. Search the Web to find at least four Web sites that contain information about items used to cook pasta. Create a Web page that includes a Heading 1 style heading, a brief paragraph of descriptive text, and list links to those Web sites. Modify the Pasta Divine home page to include a link to the new Web page.

• 2: Create a Web Page with Text Formatting

You are a Web developer for the Sabath Smith Photography Studios. Ms. Smith has asked you to update the home page to make it more visually appealing. As a first step, you plan to create a Web page with sample text formats, such as the ones shown in Figure 3–29 on page HTML 115, to share with Ms. Smith and get her input on which types of formatting she prefers. Create such a Web page and include text formatted as bold, italic, underlined, superscript, and subscript; use different colors and sizes for each type of text. Be sure to include one sample using the <bold> tag and one using the <strong> tag to see how they compare when displayed together. Do the same for the <i> and <em> tags.

•• 3: Add Image Links to External Sites

To update the Pasta Divine Web site further, you want to add image links so the pictures of food on the Monthly Specials Web page also are links to Web pages in an external Web site. Search the Web for information specific to each of the three Monthly Specials used in the project. Modify the Monthly Specials Web page so each food image is used as a link to a Web page in an external Web site. After adding the links, you decide the text paragraphs on the page are too close to the pictures. Modify the Monthly Specials Web page to use the <img> tag attributes hspace and vspace to add space around each image.

•• 4: Create a Web Page with Text Links and Define Link Colors

Make It Personal

Your sister owns a clothing store and recently had a Web site developed for her company. She is unhappy that the links on the company Web pages appear in blue when unvisited and purple when visited, because those colors do not match the company logo. She has asked you to update the Web pages to use navy for unvisited links, olive for visited links, and red for active links. Create a Web page similar to Figure 3–3 on page HTML 86, with three text links to a Web page in an external Web site. Add the appropriate link attributes in the body tag to define the link colors requested by your sister.

•• 5: Create a Prototype Web Site with Five Pages

Working Together

Your manager at Uptown Enterprises has asked your team to create a simple five-page prototype of the Web pages in the new Entertainment section for the online magazine CityStuff. The home page should include headings and brief paragraphs of text for Arts, Music, Movies, and Dining. Within each paragraph of text is a link to one of the four detailed Web pages for each section (for example, the Arts link should connect to the Arts Web page). The home page also includes an e-mail link at the bottom of the page. Add a To top link that connects to a target at the top of the page. The four detailed Web pages should include links to external Web sites of interest and a link back to the home page. If possible, also find appropriate images to use as a background or in the Web page, and set text to wrap around the images.

4 Creating Tables in a Web Site

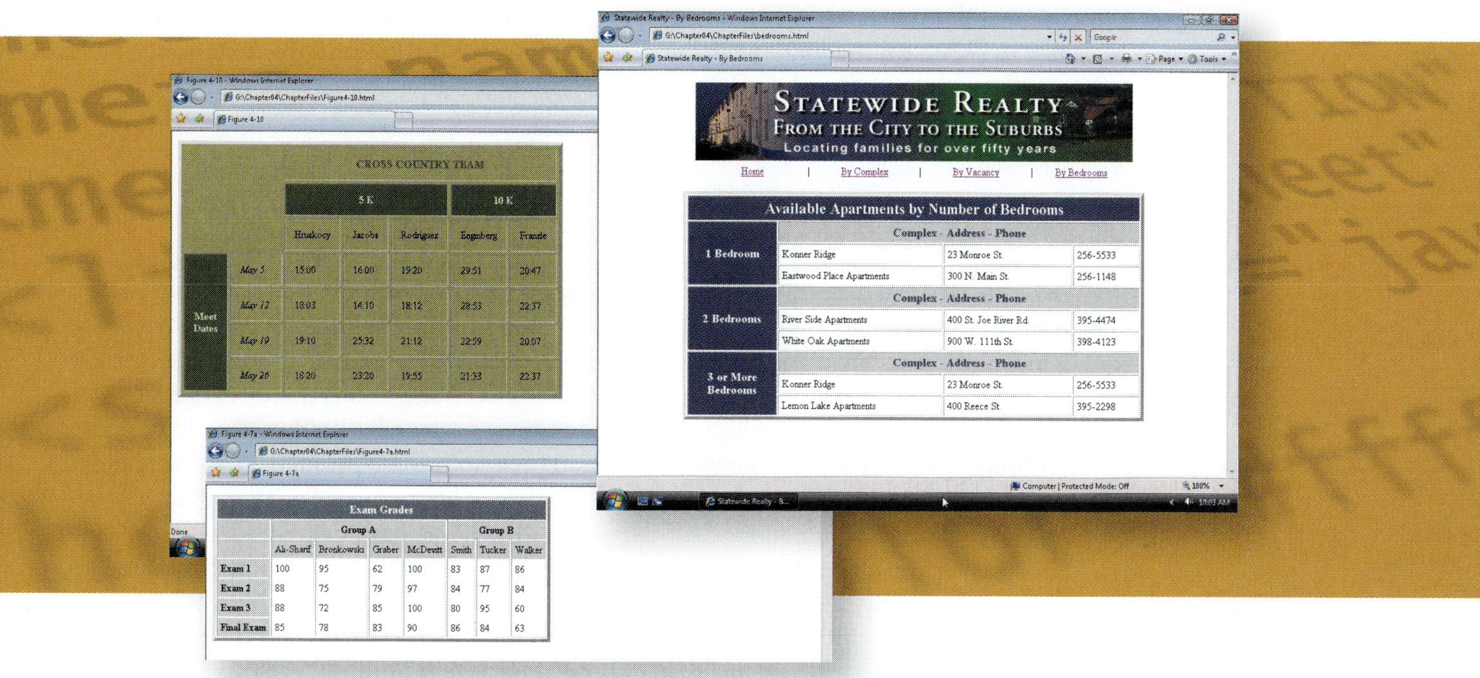

Objectives

You will have mastered the material in this chapter when you can:

- Define table elements
- Describe the steps used to plan, design, and code a table
- Create a borderless table to position images
- Create a horizontal menu bar with text links
- Copy and paste HTML code to a new file
- Create a borderless table to organize text
- Create a table with borders and insert text
- Change the horizontal alignment of text
- Add background color to rows and cells
- Alter the spacing between and within cells using the cellspacing and cellpadding attributes
- Insert a caption below a table
- Create headings that span rows and columns using the rowspan and colspan attributes

4 Creating Tables in a Web Site

Introduction

The project in Chapter 4 adds to your HTML knowledge by teaching you how to organize and present information on a Web page using tables with rows and columns. In this chapter, you learn about the elements used in a table and how to plan, design, and code a table. You also learn how to create tables to organize text and images and to use a table to create a horizontal menu bar with text links. You also learn how to enhance tables by using a variety of attributes and formats, such as borders, colors, spacing, spanning cells, and by adding a caption.

Project — Statewide Realty Web site

Many articles and case studies indicate that having a solid Web site makes it easier for companies' customers to find them, provides a way to communicate the company's brand, and allows the company to provide additional services. As advertising director for Statewide Realty, you want to enhance Statewide's Web site to increase the company's exposure to current and new customers, and to incorporate ideas gathered from customer feedback surveys. The new site will allow customers to browse through an apartment database by complex name, vacancy, or the number of bedrooms needed.

As shown in Figure 4–1a, the Statewide Realty home page includes two borderless tables to position an image and a menu bar at the top of the Web page. The By Complex, By Vacancy, and By Bedrooms Web pages (Figures 4–1b, 4–1c, and 4–1d) each include two borderless tables at the top as well as one table with borders that displays the contents of the Web pages. You will edit the vacancy.html Web page (Figure 4–1c) to add cellspacing and cellpadding attributes, thereby adjusting the spacing between cells, and to add a caption with information about the table. The bedrooms.html Web page file (Figure 4–1d) is edited to use the colspan and rowspan attributes to create headings that span several columns and rows.

As you read through this chapter and work on the project, you will learn how to plan, design, and code tables to create a user-friendly Web site. You also will learn to format tables and to combine table features to make the pages more readable. In addition, you will learn to create a menu bar with text links.

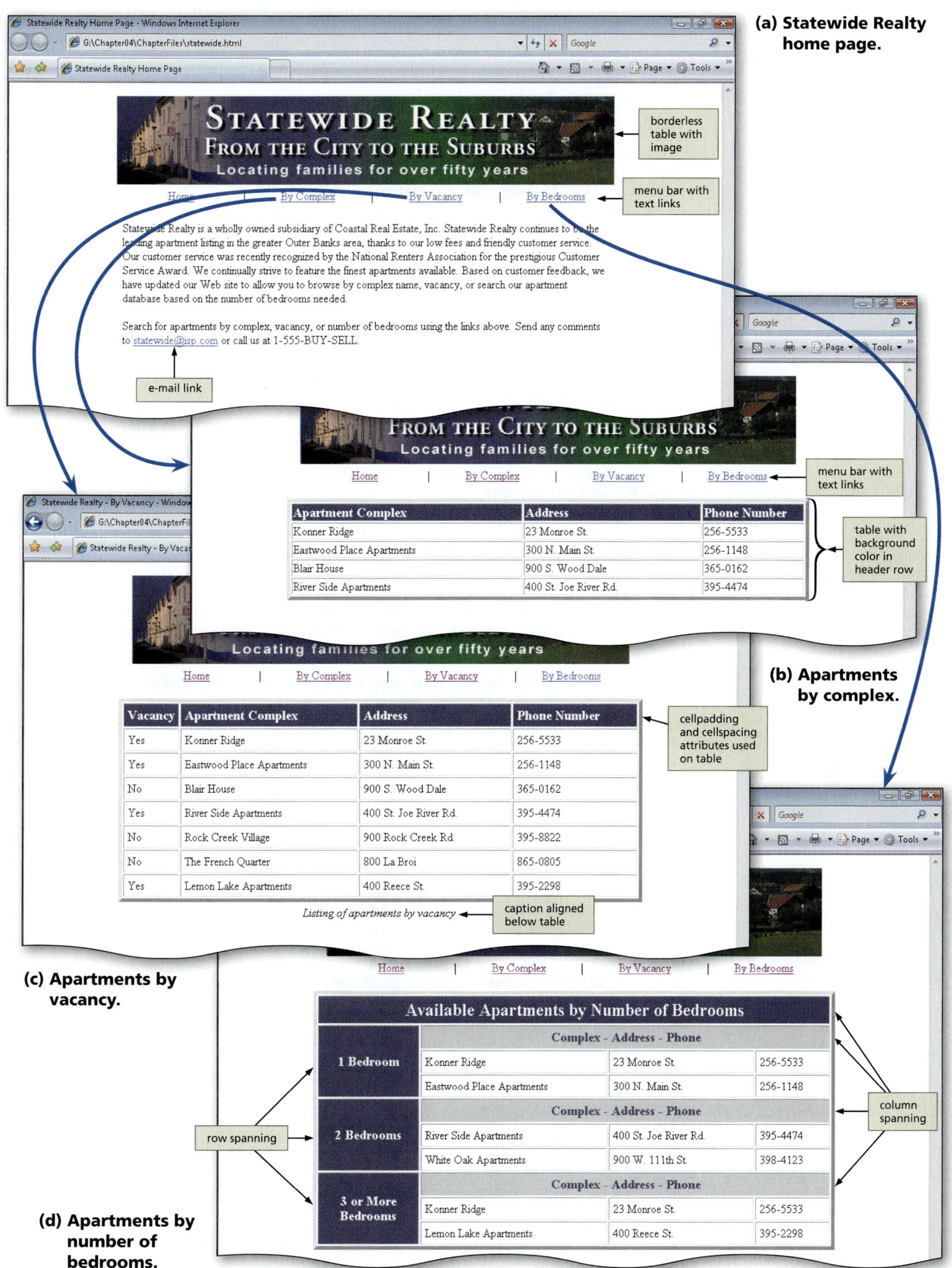

(a) Statewide Realty home page.
borderless table with image
menu bar with text links
e-mail link
Statewide Realty is a wholly owned subsidiary of Coastal Real Estate, Inc. Statewide Realty continues to be the leading apartment listing in the greater Outer Banks area, thanks to our low fees and friendly customer service. Our customer service was recently recognized by the National Renters Association for the prestigious Customer Service Award. We continually strive to feature the finest apartments available. Based on customer feedback, we have updated our Web site to allow you to browse by complex name, vacancy, or search our apartment database based on the number of bedrooms needed.
Search for apartments by complex, vacancy, or number of bedrooms using the links above. Send any comments to statewide@isp.com or call us at 1-555-BUY-SELL.
(b) Apartments by complex.
menu bar with text links
table with background color in header row
(c) Apartments by vacancy.
cellpadding and cellspacing attributes used on table
caption aligned below table
Listing of apartments by vacancy
(d) Apartments by number of bedrooms.
row spanning
column spanning
Available Apartments by Number of Bedrooms

Figure 4–1

Overview

As you read this chapter, you will learn how to create the Web pages shown in Figures 4–1a through 4–1d by performing these general tasks:

- Enter HTML code into the Notepad window.
- Save the file as an HTML file.
- Enter basic HTML tags and add text to the file.
- Create a borderless table that contains both text and graphical images.
- Create a table with borders to display information in an organized manner.
- Add a horizontal menu bar with text links.
- Add HTML tags that enhance a table with cellpadding and cellspacing.
- Enhance a Web table with row- and column-spanning.
- View the Web pages and HTML code in your browser.
- Validate the Web pages.
- Print the HTML code and Web pages.

Plan Ahead

General Project Guidelines
When creating a Web page, the actions you perform and decisions you make will affect the appearance and characteristics of the finished page. As you create a Web page, such as those shown in Figures 4–1a through 4–1d on the previous page, you should follow these general guidelines:

1. **Complete Web page planning**. Before developing a Web page, you must know the purpose of the Web site, identify the users of the site and their computing environment, and decide who owns the information on the Web page.
2. **Analyze the organization of the Web page**. In the analysis phase of the Web development life cycle, you should analyze what content to include on the Web page and how to organize that information. In this phase, you need to determine what information you want specifically to convey so that you can highlight that information on the Web page using different techniques. Refer to Table 1–4 on page HTML 12 for information on the phases of the Web development life cycle.
3. **Choose the organization for the Web page**. Once you have completed the analysis, you need to determine what content to include on the Web page. With tables, you are able to display the Web page content in a very organized manner. Tables can be used to display text only as well as for graphical images or combinations of text and images. Some text is better highlighted by using different colors for column or row headings. Other information is displayed more effectively with row- and column-spanning techniques. This should all be determined before coding the Web pages.
4. **Identify how to format various elements of the Web page**. The overall appearance of a Web page significantly affects its ability to communicate clearly. Additionally, you want to provide easy navigation for your Web site visitors. Adding images and color helps to communicate your message and adding a menu bar with links to the other Web pages within the Web site makes it easy to navigate the Web site.
5. **Determine where to save the Web page**. You can store a Web page permanently, or **save** it, on a variety of storage media including a hard disk, USB flash drive, CD, or DVD. You also can indicate a specific location on the storage media for saving the Web page.
6. **Create the Web page and links**. After analyzing and designing the Web site, you need to develop the individual Web pages. It is important to maintain a consistent look throughout the Web site. Use graphics and links consistently so that your Web site visitor does not become confused.

(continued)

Plan Ahead

(continued)

7. **Test all Web pages within the Web site.** An important part of Web development is testing to assure that you are following XHTML standards. In this book, we use the World Wide Web Consortium (W3C) validator that allows you to test your Web page and clearly explains any errors you have. Additionally when testing, you should check all content for accuracy. Finally, all links should be tested.

When necessary, more specific details concerning the above guidelines are presented at appropriate points in the chapter. The chapter also will identify the actions performed and decisions made regarding these guidelines during the creation of the Web pages shown in Figures 4–1a through 4–1d on page HTML 145.

Creating Web Pages with Tables

Tables allow you to organize information on a Web page using HTML tags. Tables are useful when you want to arrange text and images into rows and columns in order to make the information straightforward and clear to the Web page visitor. You can use tables to create Web pages with newspaper-type columns of text or structured lists of information. Tables can be complex, using the rowspan and colspan attributes to span rows and columns, background colors in cells, and borders to provide formatting (Figure 4–2a). Tables also can be simple, with a basic grid format and no color (Figure 4–2b). The purpose of the table helps to define what formatting is appropriate.

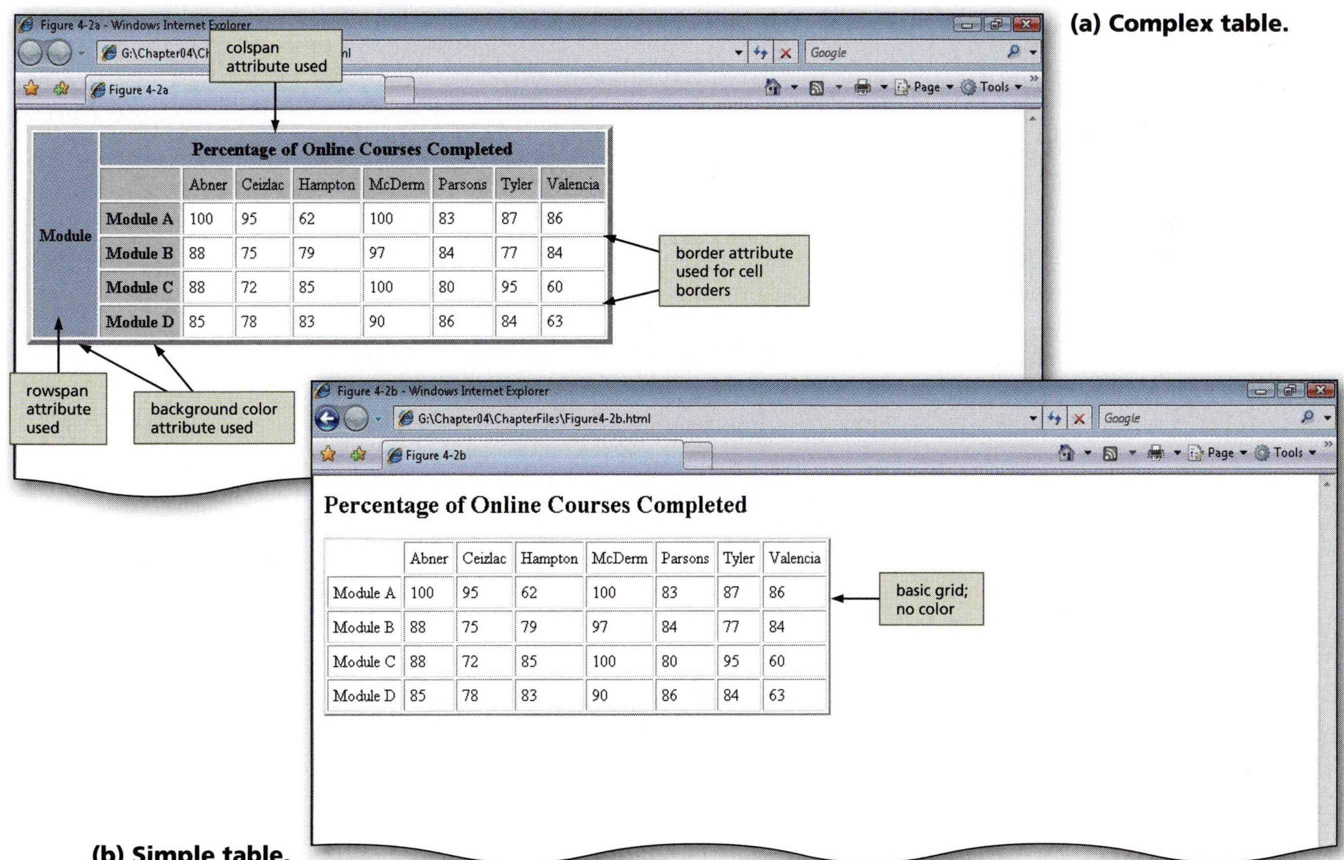

(a) Complex table.

(b) Simple table.

Figure 4–2

In Chapter 3, you learned how to wrap text around an image. You also can use tables to position text and images, such as the one shown in Figure 4–3, which uses a borderless table to position text to the left of the map images. An advantage of using a table to position text and images instead of just wrapping the text around the image is that you have more control over the placement of the text and image.

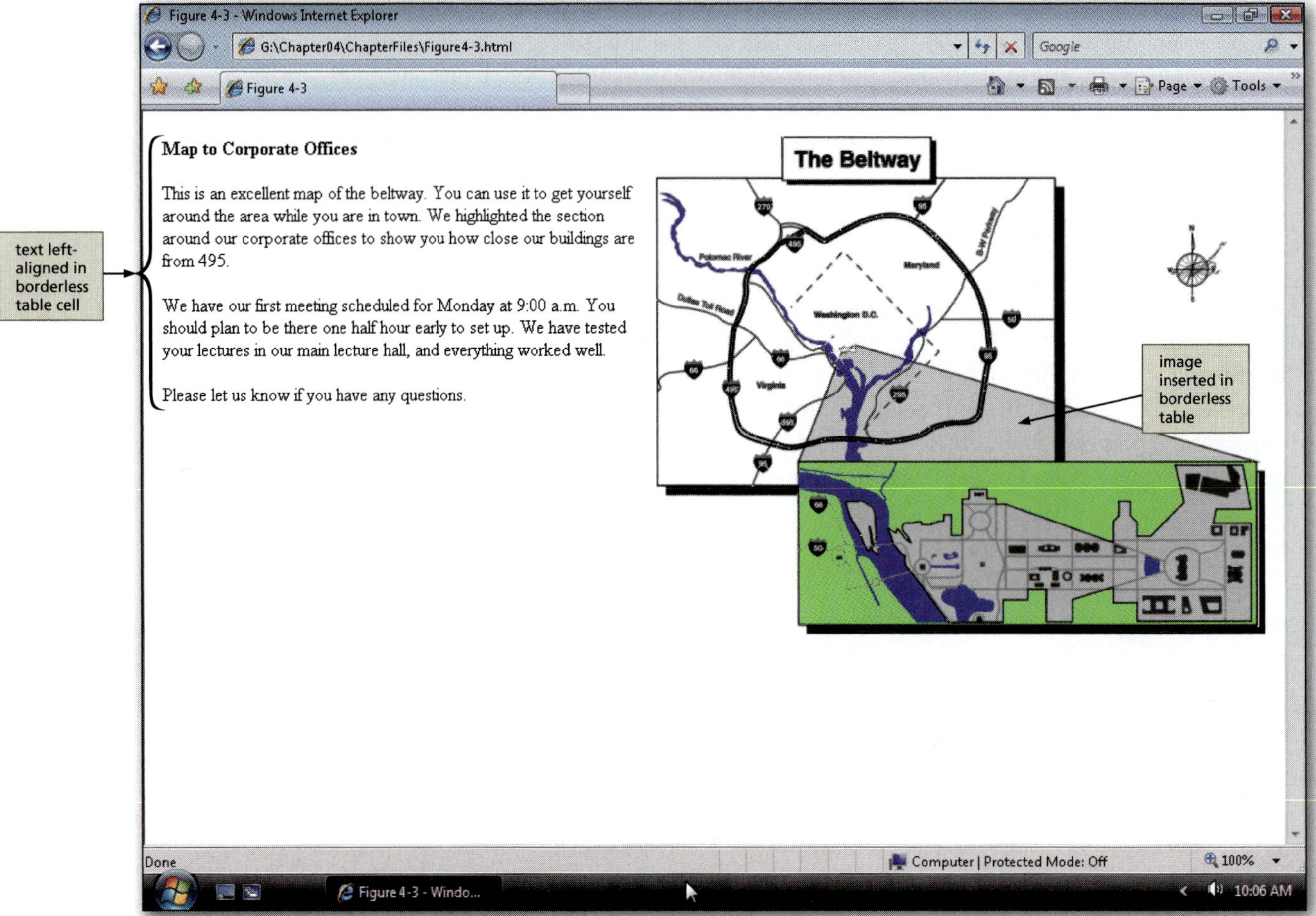

Figure 4–3 Image and text positioned in table.

Tables also can be used to create a border or frame around an image. Figure 4–4 shows a Web page with an image inserted into a table with one row and one cell. The border is set to a pixel width of 15 to create the appearance of a frame. Using a table to create a frame is a simple technique that gives an image a polished look and highlights the image.

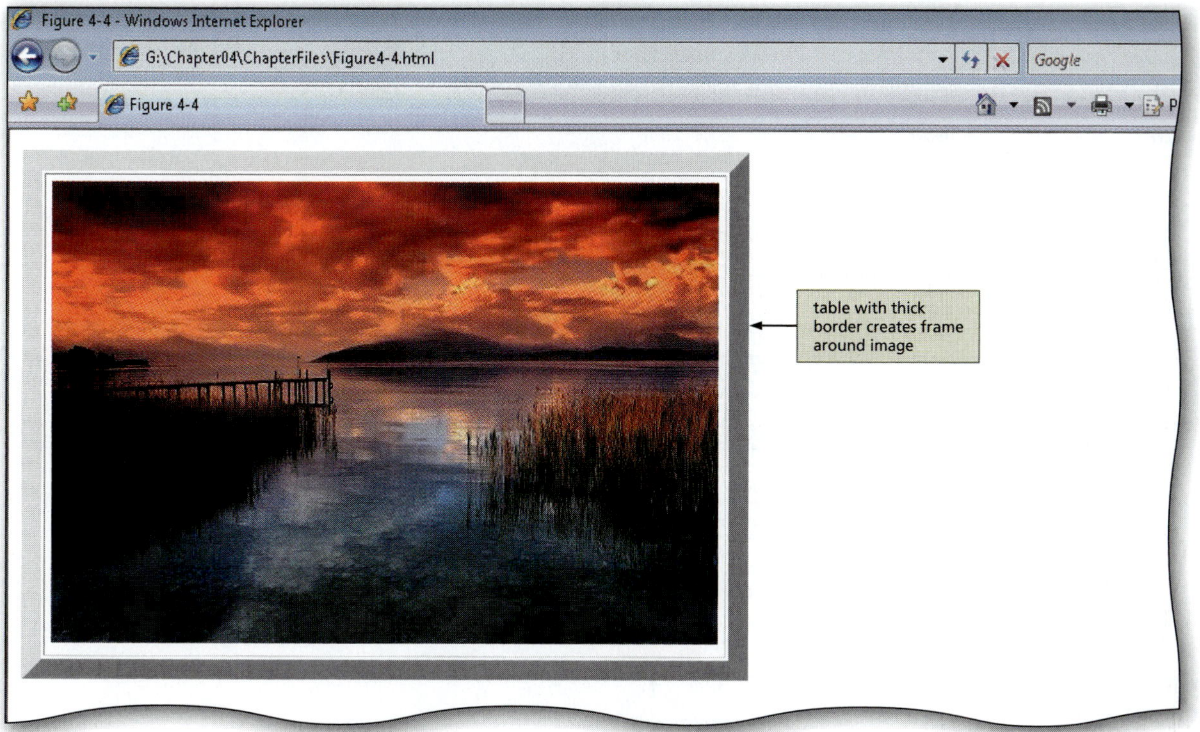

Figure 4–4 Table used as image frame.

Table Elements

Tables consist of rows, columns, and cells, much like spreadsheets. A **row** is a horizontal line of information. A **column** is a vertical line of information. A **cell** is the intersection of a row and a column. Figure 4–5 on the next page shows examples of these three elements. In Figure 4–5a, the fifth row in the table has a gray background. In Figure 4–5b, the fourth column has a peach background. In Figure 4–5c, the cell at the intersection of column 2 and row 6 has a gold background.

As shown in Figure 4–5c, a cell can be one of two types: a heading cell or a data cell. A **heading cell** displays text as bold and center-aligned. A **data cell** displays normal text that is left-aligned.

Understanding the row, column, and cell elements is important as you create a table using HTML. Attributes are set relative to these table elements. For example, you can set attributes for an entire row of information, for a single cell, or for one or more cells within a row.

BTW

Tables

Tables are useful for a variety of purposes. They can store information in tabular form or create a layout on a Web page. Layouts created with tables give the Web developer more flexibility. You have more control over the placement of information or images. Many popular Web sites use tables.

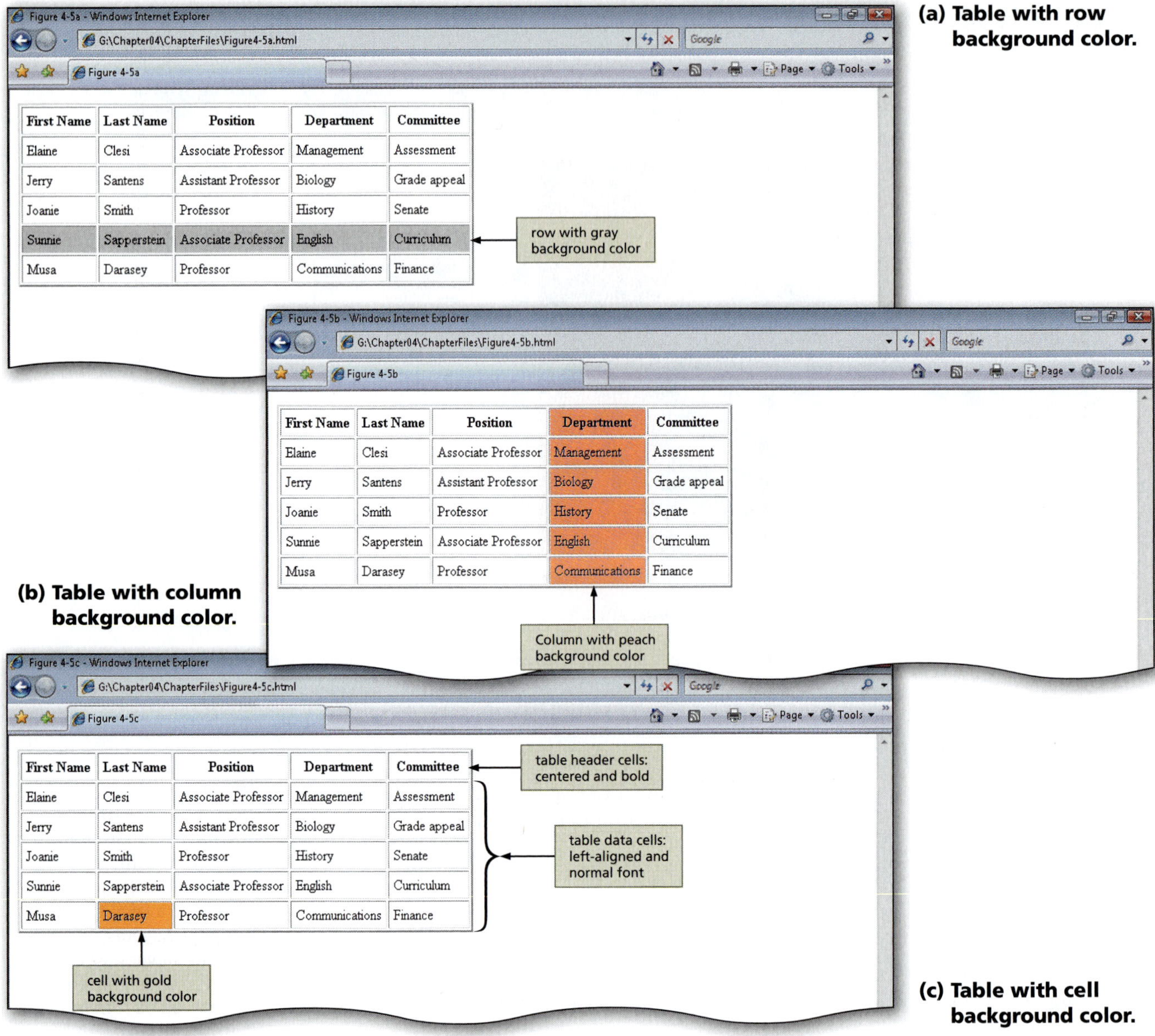

(a) Table with row background color.

(b) Table with column background color.

(c) Table with cell background color.

Figure 4–5

Table Borders, Headers, Captions, and Rules

> **BTW**
> **Table Elements**
> Many Web sources discuss table parts, giving numerous examples and tips. For more information about HTML table parts, search the Web for key terms such as HTML Table Elements or HTML Table Properties.

Tables include features such as table borders, table headers, table captions, and rules (Figure 4–6). A **table border** is the line that encloses the perimeter of the table. A **table header** is the same as a heading cell — it is any cell with bold text that indicates the purpose of the row or column. A header row is used to identify the meaning of the numbers in each column, and headings that span columns and rows are used to provide additional information. Headers also are used by non-visual browsers to identify table content. A **table caption** is descriptive text located above or below the table that further describes the purpose of the table.

Tables can use these features individually or in combination. The purpose for the table dictates which of these features are used. For example, the table shown in Figure 4–6 lists columns of numbers. A header row is used to identify the meaning of the numbers in each column, and headings that span columns and rows are used to provide additional information. Finally, the table caption explains that each number is based on thousands (that is, the 10 listed in the table represents 10,000).

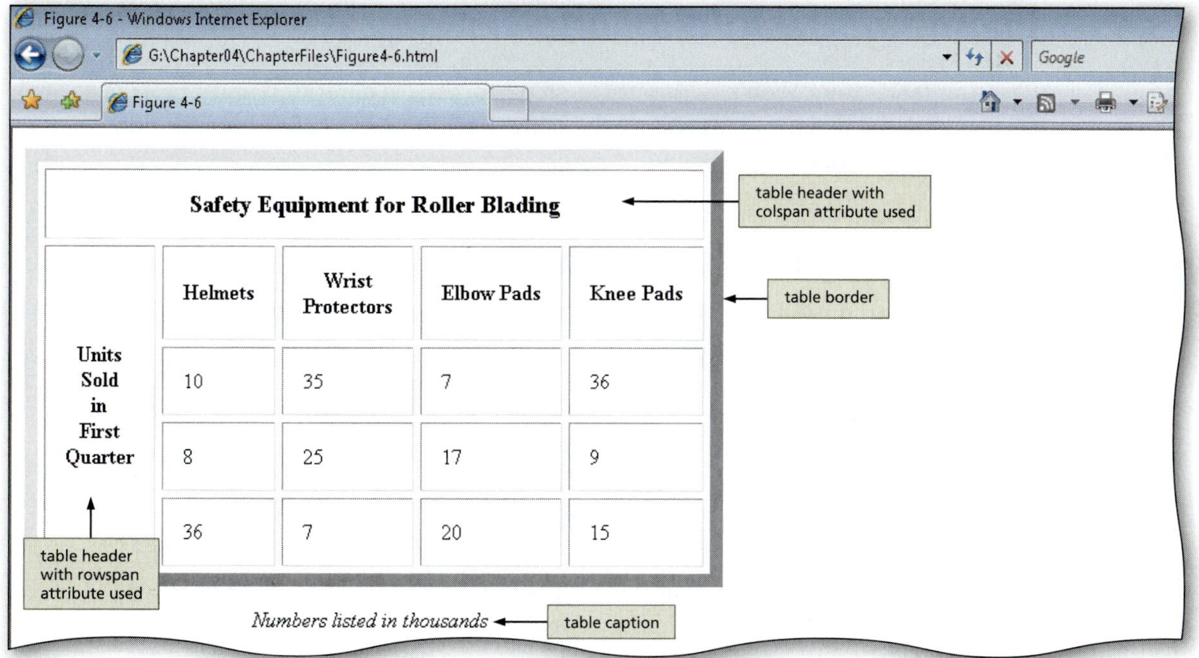

Figure 4–6 Table headers, border, and caption.

Another useful table attribute is the rules attribute, which creates horizontal or vertical lines in a table. The **rules attribute** allows a Web developer to select which internal borders to show in a table. It supports several values to provide different formatting options. For example, using rules="none" creates a table with no internal rules. Using rules="cols" creates a table with vertical rules between each column in the table (Figure 4–7a), while rules="rows" creates a table with horizontal rules between each row in the table (Figure 4–7b). Appendix A provides additional information on values supported by the rules attribute.

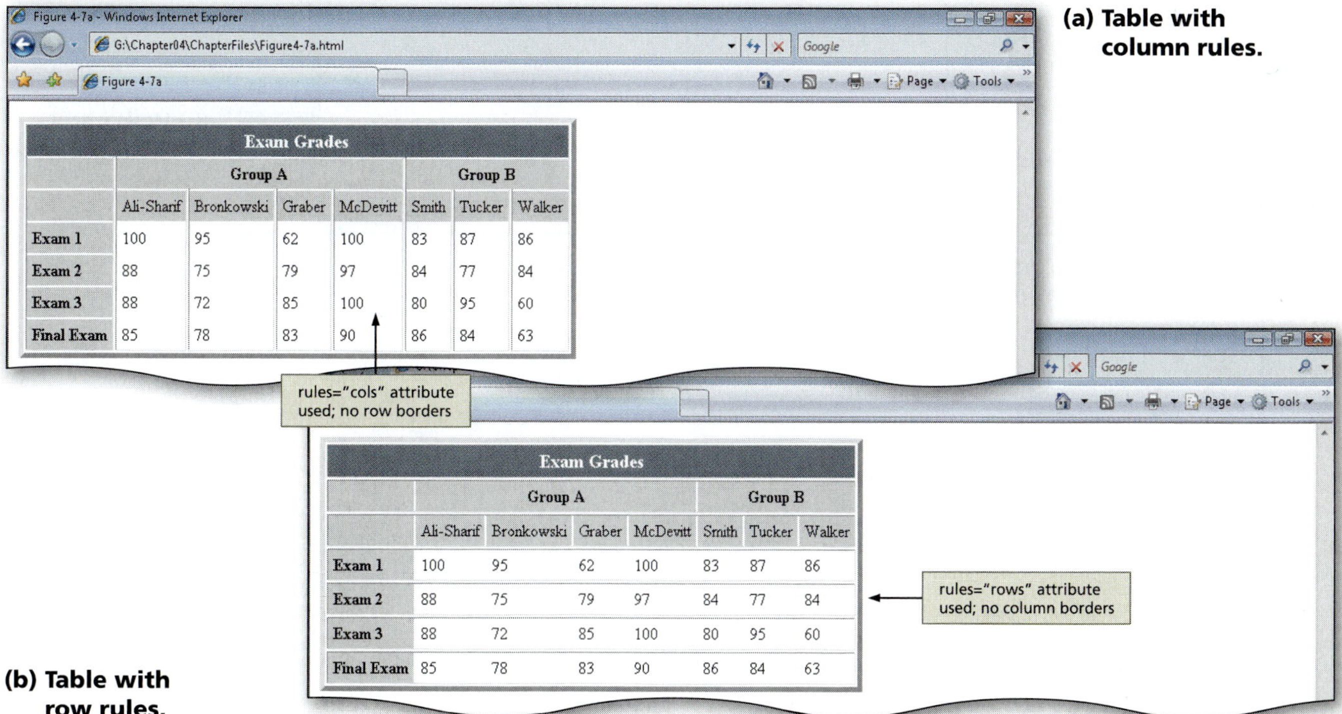

(a) Table with column rules.

Exam Grades							
	Group A				Group B		
	Ali-Sharif	Bronkowski	Graber	McDevitt	Smith	Tucker	Walker
Exam 1	100	95	62	100	83	87	86
Exam 2	88	75	79	97	84	77	84
Exam 3	88	72	85	100	80	95	60
Final Exam	85	78	83	90	86	84	63

(b) Table with row rules.

Exam Grades							
	Group A				Group B		
	Ali-Sharif	Bronkowski	Graber	McDevitt	Smith	Tucker	Walker
Exam 1	100	95	62	100	83	87	86
Exam 2	88	75	79	97	84	77	84
Exam 3	88	72	85	100	80	95	60
Final Exam	85	78	83	90	86	84	63

Figure 4–7 Table with row rules.

Planning, Designing, and Coding a Table

Creating tables for a Web page is a three-step process: (1) determining if a table is needed; (2) planning the table; and (3) coding the table. Each of these steps is discussed in detail in the following sections.

Determining If a Table Is Needed

First, you must determine whether a table is necessary. Not all Web pages require the use of tables. A general rule is that a table should be used when it will help organize information or Web page elements in such a way that it is easier for the Web page visitor to read. Tables generally are useful on a Web page if the Web page needs to display a structured, organized list of information or includes text and images that must be positioned in a very specific manner. Figures 4–8a and 4–8b show examples of information displayed as text in both a table and a bulleted list. To present this information, a table (Figure 4–8a) would be the better choice. The bulleted list (Figure 4–8b) might give the Web page an acceptable look, but the table presents the information more clearly.

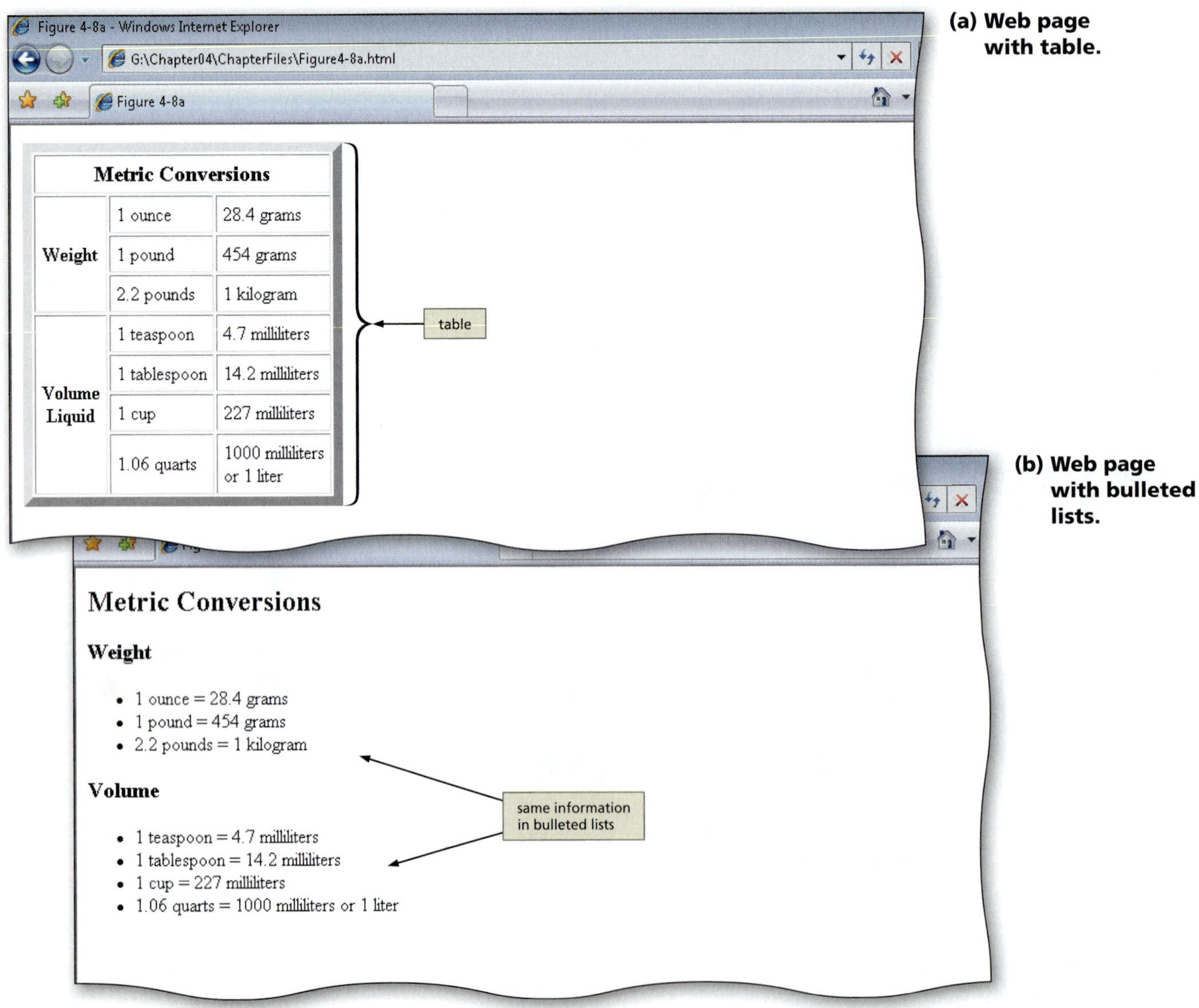

Figure 4–8

Planning the Table

To create effective tables, you must plan how the information will appear in the table and then create a good design. Before writing any HTML code, sketch the table on paper. After the table is sketched on paper, it is easier to see how many rows and columns to create, if the table will include headings, and if any of the headings span rows or columns. Conceptualizing the table on paper first saves time when you try to determine which HTML table tags to use to create the table.

For example, to create a simple table that lists the times run by various cross-country team members, you might sketch the table shown in Figure 4–9a. If runners participate in two different race lengths, such as 5K and 10K, that information can be included in a table designed as shown in Figure 4–9b. If the table needs to include different race dates for each race length, that information can be included in a table such as the one shown in Figure 4–9c. Finally, to make the table easier for the Web page visitor to understand, the table should include headings that span rows and columns and a caption. For instance, in Figure 4–9b, the headings 5K and 10K each span two columns of data. Because column spanning is used, you can easily see which runners ran in the 5K or 10K races. In Figure 4–9c, because of row spanning, you can easily tell what date each race was run. Design issues such as these should be considered while planning the table, before any HTML code is entered. Figure 4–10 on the next page shows how the table might look after it his coded.

NAME1	NAME2	NAME3	NAME4
TIME	TIME	TIME	TIME

(a) Simple table.

5K		10K	
NAME1	NAME2	NAME3	NAME4
TIME	TIME	TIME	TIME

(b) Column spanning added.

		5K		10K	
		NAME1	NAME2	NAME3	NAME4
Meet Dates	MAY 5	TIME	TIME	TIME	TIME
	MAY 12	TIME	TIME	TIME	TIME
	MAY 19	TIME	TIME	TIME	TIME
	MAY 26	TIME	TIME	TIME	TIME

(c) Row spanning added.

Figure 4–9

BTW

Table Tutorials
Table tutorials are available through online sources. Tutorials take you step-by-step through a creation process. Search the Web for the phrase HTML Table Tutorial to find excellent sources of information.

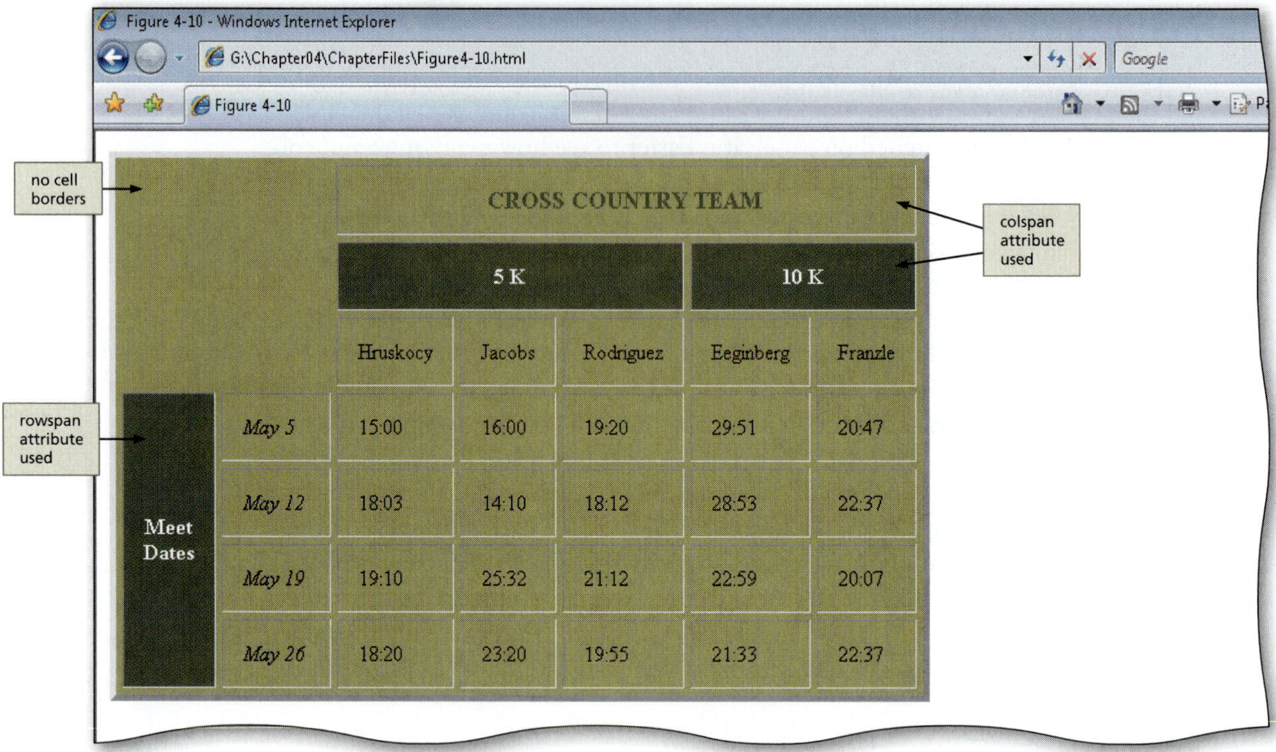

Figure 4–10 Table with row and column spanning.

Coding the Table

After you have completed the table design, you can begin coding the table using HTML tags. Table 4–1 shows the four main HTML tags used to create a table. Each of these tags has a number of attributes, which are discussed later in this chapter.

Table 4–1 HTML Table Tags

Tag	Function
<table></table>	• Indicates the start and end of a table • All other table tags are inserted within these tags
<tr> </tr>	• Indicates the start and end of a table row • Rows consist of heading or data cells
<th> </th>	• Indicates the start and end of a table heading (also called a heading cell) • Table headings default to bold text and center alignment
<td> </td>	• Indicates the start and end of a data cell in a table • Data cells default to normal text and left-alignment

Figure 4–11a shows an example of these tags used in an HTML file, and Figure 4–11b shows the resulting Web page. As shown in Figure 4–11b, the table has four rows (a table header and three rows of data cells) and two columns. The rows are indicated in the HTML file in Figure 4–11a by the start **<tr>** tags and the end **</tr>** tags. For this simple table, the number of columns in the table is determined based on the number of cells within each row. As shown in Figure 4–11b, each row has two cells, which results in a table with two columns. (Later in this chapter, you will learn how to indicate the number of columns within the <table> tag.)

As shown in the HTML in Figure 4–11a, the first row includes table heading cells, as indicated by the start **<th>** tag and end **</th>** tag. In the second, third, and fourth rows, the cells contain data, indicated by the start **<td>** tag and end **</td>** tag. In the resulting table, as shown in Figure 4–11b, the table header in row 1 appears as bold and centered text. The text in the data cells in rows 2 through 4 is left-aligned and normal text. The table in Figure 4–11b has a border, and cellspacing of 5 pixels was added to highlight further the differences between the cells. You learn about cellspacing later in the chapter.

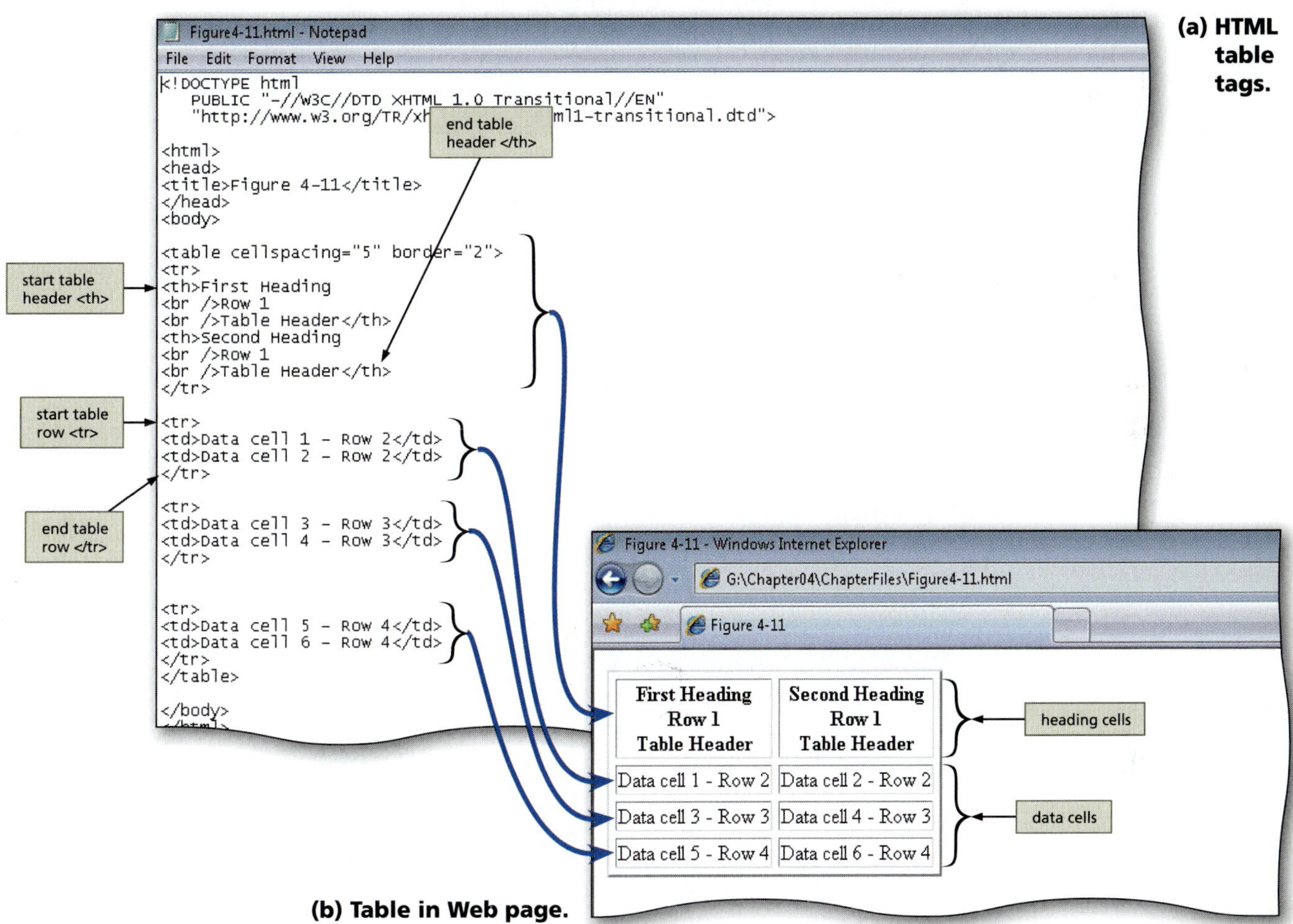


```
<!DOCTYPE html
   PUBLIC "-//W3C//DTD XHTML 1.0 Transitional//EN"
   "http://www.w3.org/TR/xhtml1/DTD/xhtml1-transitional.dtd">

<html>
<head>
<title>Figure 4-11</title>
</head>
<body>

<table cellspacing="5" border="2">
<tr>
<th>First Heading
<br />Row 1
<br />Table Header</th>
<th>Second Heading
<br />Row 1
<br />Table Header</th>
</tr>

<tr>
<td>Data cell 1 - Row 2</td>
<td>Data cell 2 - Row 2</td>
</tr>

<tr>
<td>Data cell 3 - Row 3</td>
<td>Data cell 4 - Row 3</td>
</tr>


<tr>
<td>Data cell 5 - Row 4</td>
<td>Data cell 6 - Row 4</td>
</tr>
</table>

</body>
</html>
```

(a) HTML table tags.

(b) Table in Web page.

Figure 4–11

Table Tag Attributes

Each of the four main table tags listed in Table 4–1 on page HTML 154 has different attributes. Table 4–2 on the next page lists these tags and the main attributes associated with each tag. The <th> and <td> tags, which are both used to specify the contents of a cell, have the same attributes. Many of the table tags and attributes listed in Table 4–2 are used in creating the Statewide Realty Web site.

Table 4–2 Table Tag Attributes and Functions

Tag	Attribute	Function
<table> </table>	align bgcolor border cellspacing cellpadding cols width	• Controls table alignment (left, center, right) • Sets background color for table • Defines width of table border in pixels • Defines space between cells in pixels • Defines space between a cell's contents and its border in pixels • Defines number of columns • Sets table width relative to window width
<tr> </tr>	align bgcolor valign	• Horizontally aligns row (left, center, right, justify) • Sets background color for row • Vertically aligns row (top, middle, bottom)
<th> </th> and <td> </td>	align bgcolor colspan rowspan valign	• Horizontally aligns cell (left, center, right, justify) • Sets background color for cell • Sets number of columns spanned by a cell • Sets number of rows spanned by a cell • Vertically aligns cell (top, middle, bottom)

Creating a Home Page with a Borderless Table

The first Web page developed in this chapter's project is the home page of the Statewide Realty Web site. As you have learned, the home page is the main page of a Web site, and is what Web site visitors generally view first. Visitors then click links to move from the home page to the other Web pages in the site. The Statewide Realty home page includes three links to other pages: the By Complex Web page, the By Vacancy Web page, and the By Bedrooms Web page. The home page also provides an e-mail link, so visitors can contact Statewide Realty easily.

To Start Notepad

The first step in creating the Statewide Realty Web site is to start Notepad and ensure that word wrap is enabled. The following step, which assumes Windows Vista is running, starts Notepad based on a typical installation. You may need to ask your instructor how to start Notepad for your computer.

- Click the Start button on the Windows Vista taskbar to display the Start menu.
- Click All Programs at the bottom of the left pane on the Start menu to display the All Programs list.
- Click Accessories in the All Programs list.
- Click Notepad in the Accessories list to display the Notepad window.
- If the Notepad window is not maximized, click the Maximize button on the Notepad title bar to maximize it.
- Click Format on the menu bar.
- If the Word Wrap command does not have a check mark next to it, click Word Wrap.

To Enter Initial HTML Tags to Define the Web Page Structure

Just as you did in Chapters 2 and 3, you start your file with the initial HTML tags that define the structure of the Web page. Table 4–3 contains the tags and text for this task.

Table 4–3 Initial HTML Tags

Line	Html Tag And Text
1	<!DOCTYPE html
2	PUBLIC "-//W3C//DTD XHTML 1.0 Transitional//EN"
3	"http://www.w3.org/TR/xhtml1/DTD/xhtml1-transitional.dtd">
4	
5	<html xmlns="http://www.w3.org/1999/xhtml" xml:lang="en" lang="en">
6	<head>
7	<meta http-equiv="Content-Type" content="text/html;charset=utf-8" />
8	<title>Statewide Realty Home Page</title>
9	</head>
10	
11	<body>
12	
13	</body>
14	</html>

The following step illustrates how to enter the initial tags that define the structure of the Web page.

- Enter the HTML code shown in Table 4–3. Press ENTER at the end of each line. If you make an error as you are typing, use the BACKSPACE key to delete all the characters back to and including the incorrect characters, then continue typing.
- Compare what you typed to Figure 4–12. If you notice errors, use your mouse pointer or ARROW keys to move the insertion point to the right of each error and use the BACKSPACE key to correct the error.
- Position the insertion point on the blank line between the <body> and </body> tags (line 12).

Untitled - Notepad

File Edit Format View Help

```
<!DOCTYPE html
   PUBLIC "-//W3C//DTD XHTML 1.0 Transitional//EN"
   "http://www.w3.org/TR/xhtml1/DTD/xhtml1-transitional.dtd">

<html xmlns="http://www.w3.org/1999/xhtml" xml:lang="en" lang="en">
<head>
<meta http-equiv="Content-Type" content="text/html;charset=utf-8" />
<title>Statewide Realty Home Page</title>
</head>

<body>

</body>
</html>
```

initial HTML tags to define Web page structure

line 12

Figure 4–12

Plan Ahead

Identify how to format various elements of the text.

Before inserting tables or graphical elements on a Web page, you should plan how you want to format them. By effectively utilizing tables and graphics, you can better organize the most important topics on the Web page. Consider the following formatting suggestions.

- **Format tables to organize Web page content.** Sometimes it is better to have no border around the table, while other times borders enhance the look of the table, depending on the content and purpose of the table. In this chapter, you will use both bordered and borderless tables. Another consideration is where to place the table (left-, right-, or center-aligned).
- **Effectively utilize graphics.** An important part of Web development is the use of graphics to call attention to a Web page. Generally, companies utilize the same logo on their Web site as they use on print material associated with the company, such as business cards and letterheads. Using the same graphical image on all marketing materials, including the Web site, is a good way to provide a consistent visual and brand message to customers. Colorful company logos add an attention-grabbing element to a Web page.

Creating a Borderless Table and Inserting an Image

The HTML code to create a borderless table to hold the Statewide Realty logo image as shown in Figure 4–13 is as follows:

```
<table align="center">
```

where the align="center" attribute creates a table centered on the Web page. This is to be a borderless table, so you do not need to add the border attribute.

BTW

Table Borders

Table borders frame an image. You can insert a single image into a one-row, one-column table. Using a border gives the image a 3-D appearance, making the image appear to have a frame around it. A border of 1 pixel (border="1") is too small to use as a frame, but border="25" is too large.

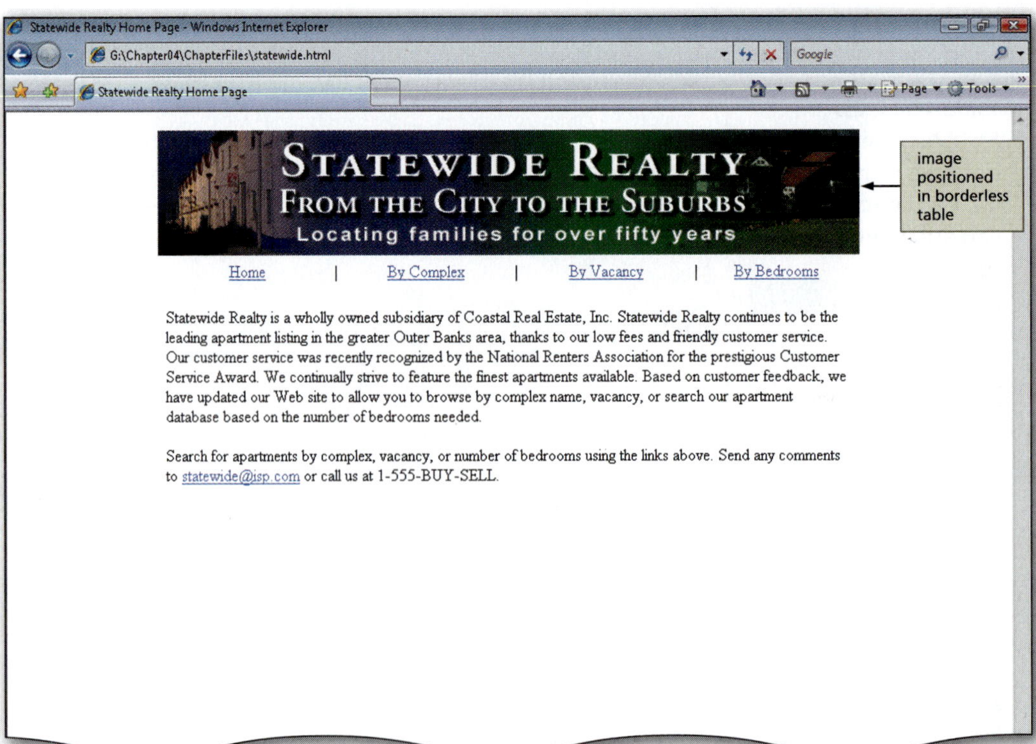

Figure 4–13

The table shown in Figure 4–13 contains one row with one data cell in the row. The data cell contains the logo image statewidebanner.jpg. To create data cells in a row, the HTML tags must include one or more sets of <td> </td> (table data) tags between the <tr> </tr> (table row) tags. Data cell (<td> </td>) tags are used rather than header cell (<th> </th>) tags, so that the image files can be left-aligned in the cell, instead of using the default center-alignment for heading cells.

To Create a Borderless Table to Position Images

- If necessary, click line 12 to position the insertion point.
- Type `<table align="center">` and then press the ENTER key to center the table (Figure 4–14).

Figure 4–14

Q&A I see many other table tag attributes in Table 4–2 on page HTML 156. Why am I not using more of those?

The first table is a very simple table that only contains the graphic for the top of the Web page. In later steps, you will utilize other attributes, as necessary, in the table tag.

Q&A What kind of border will this table have because I have not identified a border size?

When you do not specifically identify the border size, the table will be borderless. You can identify the size of a table border (see Appendix A) in number of pixels, which you will do in subsequent steps.

Q&A Is there another way to define table attributes?

You can define table attributes (for example, colors and alignment) by using style sheets. This is the preferred technique when defining specific characteristics of a table. This project concentrates on table basics, which must be understood to utilize style sheets effectively for those characteristics.

To Insert Images in a Table

The following step shows how to enter HTML code to add a left-aligned image at the top of the Web page.

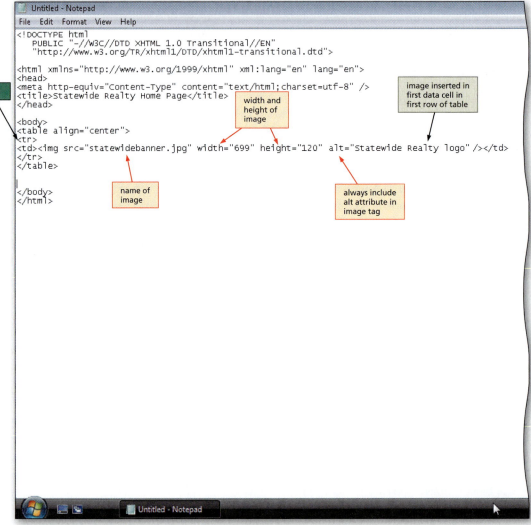

- If necessary, click line 13, type `<tr>` as the table row tag, and then press the ENTER key.
- Type `<td> <img src="statewidebanner.jpg" width="699" height="120" alt="Statewide Realty logo" /> </td>` to enter the image as table data, and then press the ENTER key.
- Type `</tr>` to end the table row and then press the ENTER key.
- Type `</table>` to end the table and then press the ENTER key twice (Figure 4–15).

```
<!DOCTYPE html
   PUBLIC "-//W3C//DTD XHTML 1.0 Transitional//EN"
    "http://www.w3.org/TR/xhtml1/DTD/xhtml1-transitional.dtd">

<html xmlns="http://www.w3.org/1999/xhtml" xml:lang="en" lang="en">
<head>
<meta http-equiv="Content-Type" content="text/html;charset=utf-8" />
<title>Statewide Realty Home Page</title>
</head>

<body>
<table align="center">
<tr>
<td><img src="statewidebanner.jpg" width="699" height="120" alt="Statewide Realty logo" /></td>
</tr>
</table>

</body>
</html>
```


Figure 4–15

Q&A How can I determine the height and width of an image?

You can determine the height and width of an image using a paint or image editing program. Once you know the height and width, you also can adjust the width and height by using the width and height attributes in the <img> tag. Be aware that, in doing so, you might cause the image to look distorted on the Web page.

Q&A Why do I need both the <tr> and the <td> tags for a one-cell row? It seems that I could use one or the other, rather than both tags.

Although the one-cell table would display in the browser with only the <tr> or <td> tags, you should always use both the row and cell tags when creating a table. Good Web development techniques include using the tags that are required whether or not eliminating some of them allows them to display in the browser.

Plan Ahead

- **Determine what table formatting to use.** When using a table to organize text links, it is important to first decide how to format the table. Although you may not want to distract from the text links by creating a table with a heavy border, you need to separate the text links in such a way that they are easy to find. Creating a borderless table with separators (e.g., pipe symbols) between the text links helps organize but not distract from the links.
- **Identify what links are needed.** Each Web page in a multipage Web site should have a link back to the home page of the Web site. Web developers often use the company logo to link back to the home page. In this project, the logo is also the central image of the Web pages. Because of that, a better option might be to provide a text link called "Home" that visitors can use to return to the home page. There also should be links to the other pages on the Web site from each Web page. Putting these links in a table at the top of each Web page helps visitors navigate easily. If a Web page is very long, it also might be a good idea to put the same text link table at the bottom of the Web page. Again, the purpose of providing links is to make it easy to navigate the Web site.

BTW

Navigation
Studies have been conducted to assess the best location on a Web page for navigation bars and lists. The research indicated that navigation options on the top, side, and bottom of a Web page show slight differences in visitor usability. The most important aspect of Web page navigation is to make the options easy to locate so visitors do not have to search for them.

Creating a Horizontal Menu Bar with Text Links

The Web site created in this project consists of four Web pages. Visitors should be able to move easily from one Web page to any of the other three Web pages. Providing a menu bar prominently across the top of the Web page (Figure 4–16) gives the visitor ready access to navigation links.

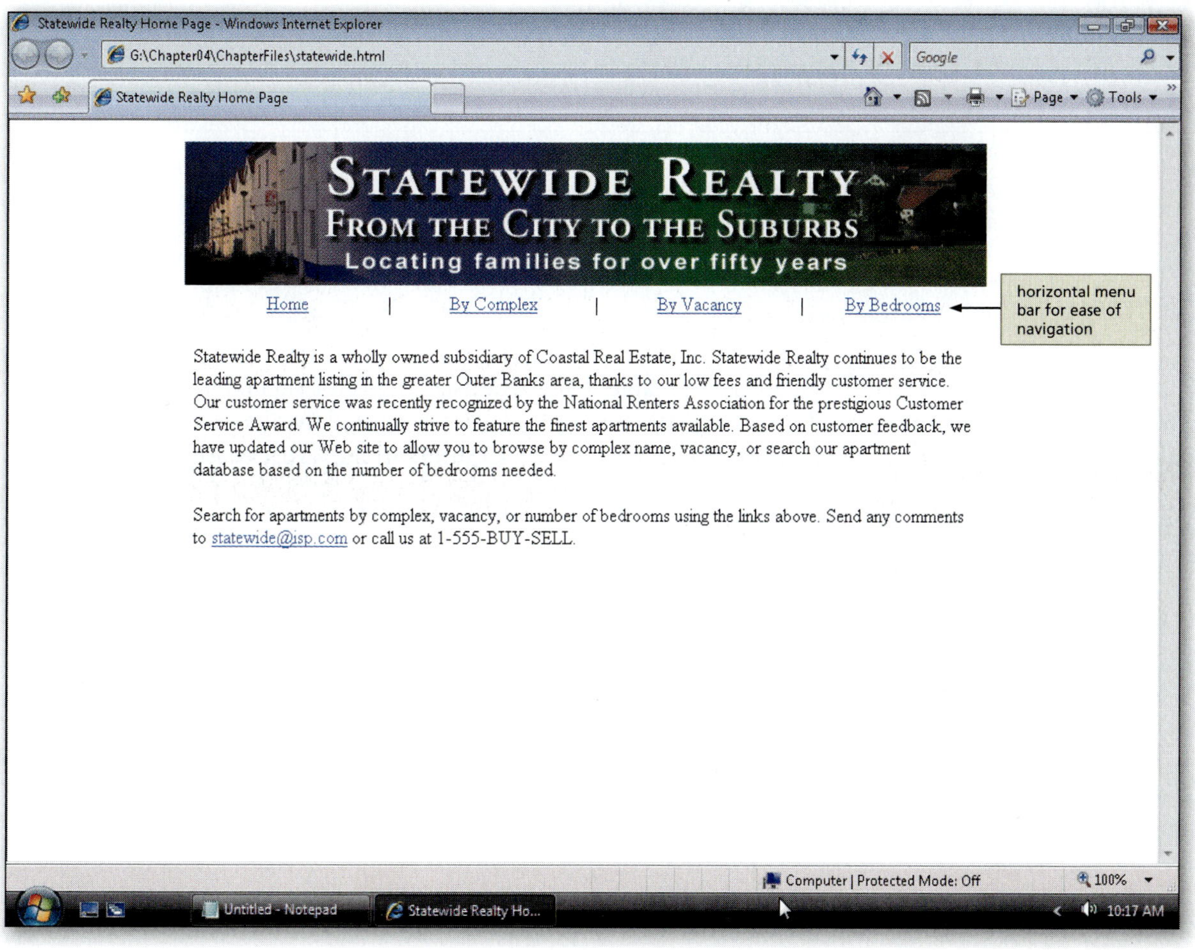

Statewide Realty Home Page - Windows Internet Explorer
G:\Chapter04\ChapterFiles\statewide.html
Statewide Realty Home Page
STATEWIDE REALTY
FROM THE CITY TO THE SUBURBS
Locating families for over fifty years
Home | By Complex | By Vacancy | By Bedrooms
horizontal menu bar for ease of navigation
Statewide Realty is a wholly owned subsidiary of Coastal Real Estate, Inc. Statewide Realty continues to be the leading apartment listing in the greater Outer Banks area, thanks to our low fees and friendly customer service. Our customer service was recently recognized by the National Renters Association for the prestigious Customer Service Award. We continually strive to feature the finest apartments available. Based on customer feedback, we have updated our Web site to allow you to browse by complex name, vacancy, or search our apartment database based on the number of bedrooms needed.
Search for apartments by complex, vacancy, or number of bedrooms using the links above. Send any comments to statewide@isp.com or call us at 1-555-BUY-SELL.
Computer | Protected Mode: Off
100%
Untitled - Notepad
Statewide Realty Ho...
10:17 AM

Figure 4–16

The table created for the horizontal menu bar is a borderless (no border attribute used), one-row, seven-column table. To better align the menu bar with the Statewide Realty logo, the table is set to 70% of the window's width, so that it is not as wide as the logo table. The menu bar consists of four links — Home, By Complex, By Vacancy, and By Bedrooms — that link to the Web pages statewide.html, complex.html, vacancy.html, and bedrooms.html, respectively. Each link is inserted in a single column (cell). The | (pipe) symbol is included in a column between each of the four links to separate them visually.

The width of each column in the table is specified using the width attribute of the <td> tag. For the four cells with text links, the column widths are set to a width of 25%. The column widths for the cells with the | (pipe) symbols are set to 1%, because the symbol does not require much space in the menu bar.

To Create a Horizontal Menu Bar with Text Links

Table 4–4 shows the HTML code for the horizontal menu bar.

Table 4–4 HTML Code to Insert a Menu Bar

<table>
<tr><th>Line</th><th>HTML Tag and Text</th></tr>
<tr><td>18</td><td><table width="70%" align="center"></td></tr>
<tr><td>19</td><td><tr align="center"></td></tr>
<tr><td>20</td><td><td width="25%"><a href="statewide.html">Home</a></td></td></tr>
<tr><td>21</td><td><td width="1%">|</td></td></tr>
<tr><td>22</td><td><td width="25%"><a href="complex.html">By Complex</a></td></td></tr>
<tr><td>23</td><td><td width="1%">|</td></td></tr>
<tr><td>24</td><td><td width="25%"><a href="vacancy.html">By Vacancy</a></td></td></tr>
<tr><td>25</td><td><td width="1%">|</td></td></tr>
<tr><td>26</td><td><td width="25%"><a href="bedrooms.html">By Bedrooms</a></td></td></tr>
<tr><td>27</td><td></tr></td></tr>
<tr><td>28</td><td></table></td></tr>
</table>

The following step shows how to create a borderless table that contains a horizontal menu bar that is 70% of the width of the window, and contains text links to four pages on the Web site, separated by pipe symbols. The pipe symbol is usually found above the ENTER key; it is inserted when you press Shift and the \ (backslash) key.

1

- If necessary, click line 18 (Figure 4–17).
- Enter the HTML code as shown in Table 4–4, pressing ENTER after each line.
- Press the ENTER key once.

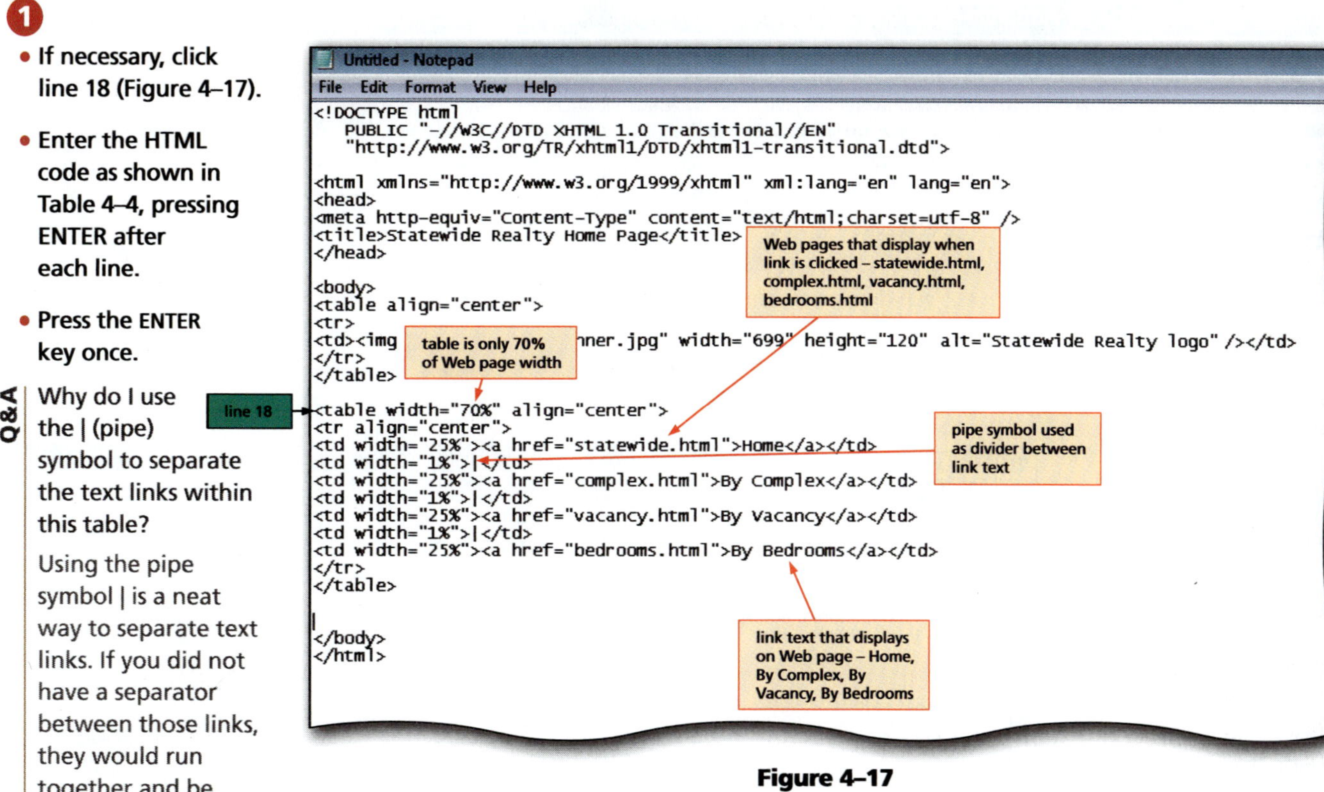

Figure 4–17

Q&A

Why do I use the | (pipe) symbol to separate the text links within this table?

Using the pipe symbol | is a neat way to separate text links. If you did not have a separator between those links, they would run together and be difficult to read. Having a separator between them makes it easy to see that there are four distinct text links on the menu bar. You also could have used a table with borders to separate the text links, but that might not be as attractive an option directly underneath the banner.

To Add Text to a Table Cell

Next, paragraphs of text must be added to the Web page. A separate, borderless table is used to display that text so that the width of the table can be controlled. This allows the table with the horizontal menu bar and the table with the paragraph of text to display as the same width on the Web page to give the page a more cohesive look. Table 4–5 contains the code to add the paragraphs of text.

Table 4–5 HTML Code to Add Paragraphs of Text

Line	HTML Tag and Text
30	` <table width="70%" align="center">`
31	`<tr>`
32	`<td>Statewide Realty is a wholly owned subsidiary of Coastal Real Estate, Inc.`
33	`Statewide Realty continues to be the leading apartment listing in the greater Outer Banks area,`
34	`thanks to our low fees and friendly customer service. Our customer service was recently`
35	`recognized by the National Renters Association for the prestigious Customer Service Award.`
36	`We continually strive to feature the finest apartments available. Based on customer feedback,`
37	`we have updated our Web site to allow you to browse by complex name, vacancy, or search our`
38	`apartment database based on the number of bedrooms needed.`
39	

Table 4–5 HTML Code to Add Paragraphs of Text *(continued)*

Line	HTML Tag and Text
40	<p>Search for apartments by complex, vacancy, or number of bedrooms using the links above.
41	Send any comments to <a href="mailto:statewide@isp.com">statewide@isp.com</a> or call us at
42	1-555-BUY-SELL.</p></td>
43	</tr>
44	</table>

The following step illustrates how to add text to a table cell.

- If necessary, click line 30.
- Enter the HTML code as shown in Table 4–5 to specify the table width and add text to the table, pressing the ENTER key after each line (Figure 4–18).

```
Untitled - Notepad
File Edit Format View Help
<!DOCTYPE html
   PUBLIC "-//W3C//DTD XHTML 1.0 Transitional//EN"
   "http://www.w3.org/TR/xhtml1/DTD/xhtml1-transitional.dtd">

<html xmlns="http://www.w3.org/1999/xhtml" xml:lang="en" lang="en">
<head>
<meta http-equiv="Content-Type" content="text/html;charset=utf-8" />
<title>Statewide Realty Home Page</title>
</head>

<body>
<table align="center">
<tr>
<td><img src="statewidebanner.jpg" width="699" height="120" alt="Statewide Realty logo" /></td>
</tr>
</table>

<table width="70%" align="center">
<tr align="center">
<td width="25%"><a href="statewide.html">Home</a></td>
<td width="1%">|</td>
<td width="25%"><a href="complex.html">By Complex</a></td>
<td width="1%">|</td>
<td width="25%"><a href="vacancy.html">By Vacancy</a></td>
<td width="1%">|</td>
<td width="25%"><a href="bedrooms.html">By Bedrooms</a></td>
</tr>
</table>

<br /><table width="70%" align="center">
<tr>
<td>Statewide Realty is a wholly owned subsidiary of Coastal Real Estate, Inc.
Statewide Realty continues to be the leading apartment listing in the greater Outer Banks area,
thanks to our low fees and friendly customer service. Our customer service was recently
recognized by the National Renters Association for the prestigious Customer Service Award.
We continually strive to feature the finest apartments available. Based on customer feedback,
we have updated our Web site to allow you to browse by complex name, vacancy, or search our
apartment database based on the number of bedrooms needed.

<p>Search for apartments by complex, vacancy, or number of bedrooms using the links above.
Send any comments to <a href="mailto:statewide@isp.com">statewide@isp.com</a> or call us at
1-555-BUY-SELL.</p></td>
</tr>
</table>

</body>
</html>
```

make table only 70% of Web page to match menu bar table

paragraphs of text added

line 30

end table

e-mail link

Figure 4–18

Q&A **How would the paragraphs of text display if I had not put them in another borderless table?**

The text would have displayed across the whole Web page from left to right. The text would not have been centered under the Statewide Realty banner image and the horizontal menu bar. This would have given the Web page a less consistent look. By using borderless tables that are both 70% of the Web page, the page looks neat and clean.

Q&A **Why did I use only one table data cell for the two paragraphs of text? Could I have used two data cells and put one paragraph in each?**

Using two data cells would not have given you the same effect as using one data cell with a paragraph tag (<p>) between the two paragraphs. Two data cells would have positioned the second paragraph directly under the first paragraph with no blank line. Using a paragraph tag within one data cell separates the two paragraphs with a blank line in between.

To Save and Print the HTML File

With the HTML code for the Statewide Realty home page complete, you should save and print the file as a reference. The following step illustrates how to save and print the HTML file.

- With a USB flash drive connected to one of the computer's USB ports, click File on the Notepad menu bar and then click Save As. Type `statewide.html` in the File name text box (do not press ENTER).
- Navigate to the g:\Chapter04\ChapterFiles folder, or the folder where you store your chapter files.
- Click the Save button in the Save As dialog box to save the file with the name statewide.html.
- Click File on the menu bar, click Print on the File menu then click the Print button in the Print dialog box (Figure 4–19).

```
<!DOCTYPE html
   PUBLIC "-//W3C//DTD XHTML 1.0 Transitional//EN"
   "http://www.w3.org/TR/xhtml1/DTD/xhtml1-transitional.dtd">

<html xmlns="http://www.w3.org/1999/xhtml" xml:lang="en" lang="en">
<head>
<meta http-equiv="Content-Type" content="text/html;charset=utf-8" />
<title>Statewide Realty Home Page</title>
</head>

<body>
<table align="center">
<tr>
<td><img src="statewidebanner.jpg" width="699" height="120" alt="Statewide Realty logo" /></td>
</tr>
</table>

<table width="70%" align="center">
<tr align="center">
<td width="25%"><a href="statewide.html">Home</a></td>
<td width="1%">|</td>
<td width="25%"><a href="complex.html">By Complex</a></td>
<td width="1%">|</td>
<td width="25%"><a href="vacancy.html">By Vacancy</a></td>
<td width="1%">|</td>
<td width="25%"><a href="bedrooms.html">By Bedrooms</a></td>
</tr>
</table>

<br /><table width="70%" align="center">
<tr>
<td>Statewide Realty is a wholly owned subsidiary of Coastal Real Estate, Inc.
Statewide Realty continues to be the leading apartment listing in the greater Outer Banks area,
thanks to our low fees and friendly customer service. Our customer service was recently
recognized by the National Renters Association for the prestigious Customer Service Award.
We continually strive to feature the finest apartments available. Based on customer feedback,
we have updated our Web site to allow you to browse by complex name, vacancy, or search our
apartment database based on the number of bedrooms needed.

<p>Search for apartments by complex, vacancy, or number of bedrooms using the links above.
Send any comments to <a href="mailto:statewide@isp.com">statewide@isp.com</a> or call us at
1-555-BUY-SELL.</p></td>
</tr>
</table>

</body>
</html>
```

Figure 4–19

Validating and Viewing the Web Page and Testing Links

After you save and print the HTML file for the Statewide Realty home page, it should be validated to ensure that it meets current XHTML standards, and viewed in a browser to confirm the Web page appears as desired. It also is important to test the four links on the Statewide Realty home page to verify they function as expected.

To Validate a Web Page

The following step illustrates how to validate an HTML file.

- Open Internet Explorer and navigate to the Web site `validator.w3.org`.
- Click the Validate by File Upload tab.
- Click the Browse button.
- Locate the statewide.html file on your storage device and click the file name.
- Click the Open button in the Choose file dialog box and the file name will be inserted into the File box.
- Click the Check button.

Q&A What if my HTML code does not pass the validation process?

If your file does not pass validation, you need to make changes to the file to correct your errors. You should then revalidate the file.

To View a Web Page

The following step illustrates how to view the HTML file in a browser.

- In Internet Explorer, click the Address bar to select the URL on the Address bar.
- Type `g:\Chapter04\ChapterFiles\statewide.html` on the Address bar of your browser and press ENTER to display the Web page (Figure 4–20).

Q&A What if my page does not display correctly?

Check your statewide.html code carefully in Notepad to make sure you have not made any typing errors or left anything out. Correct the errors, resave the file, and try again.

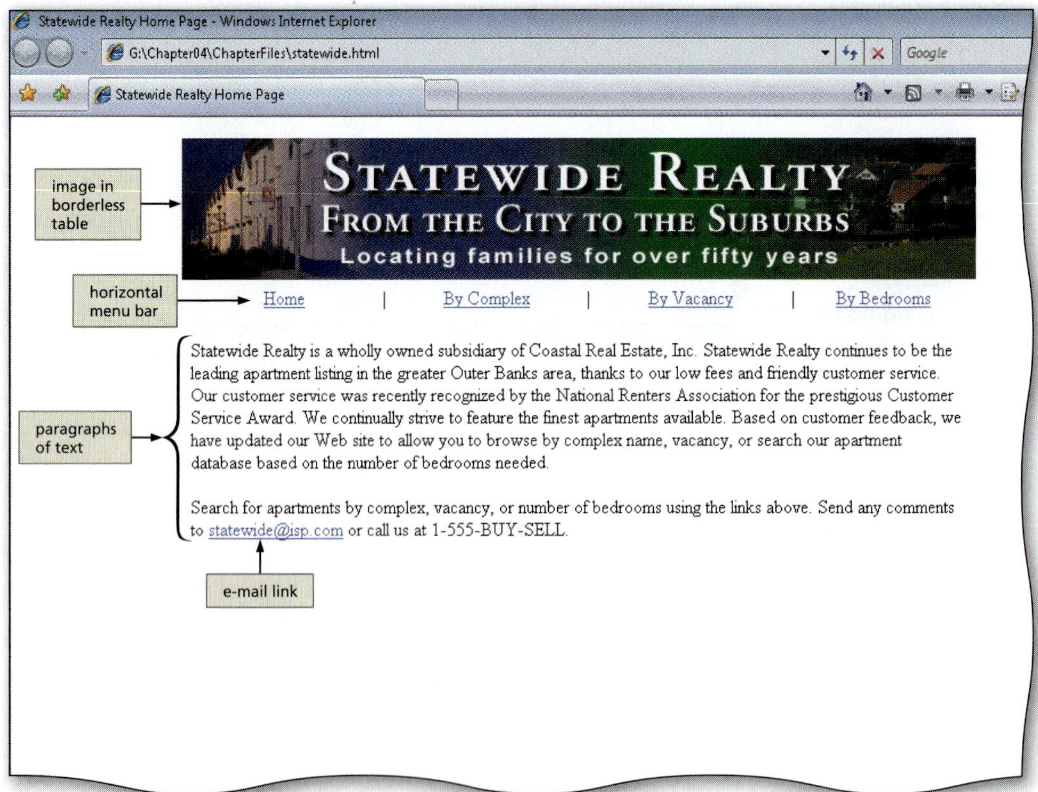

Figure 4–20

To Test Links on a Web Page

The following step shows how to test the links on the Statewide Realty home page to verify that they work correctly.

- With the home page displayed in the browser, point to the e-mail link, statewide@isp.com and click the link to open the default e-mail program with the address statewide@isp.com in the To: text box.
- Click the Close button in the New Message window. If a dialog box asks if you want to save changes, click No.
- With the USB flash drive in drive G, click the By Vacancy link and the By Bedrooms link to test these links to the additional Web pages provided on the Data Disk for Students (vacancy.html and bedrooms.html). Test the link to the home page from each of those Web pages. (The link for the By Complex Web page will not work because that Web page is not yet created; you will create it in the next section of this chapter.)

To Print a Web Page

The following step shows how to print the Web page for future reference.

- Return to the Statewide Realty home page.
- Click the Print icon on the Command bar to print the Web page (Figure 4–21).

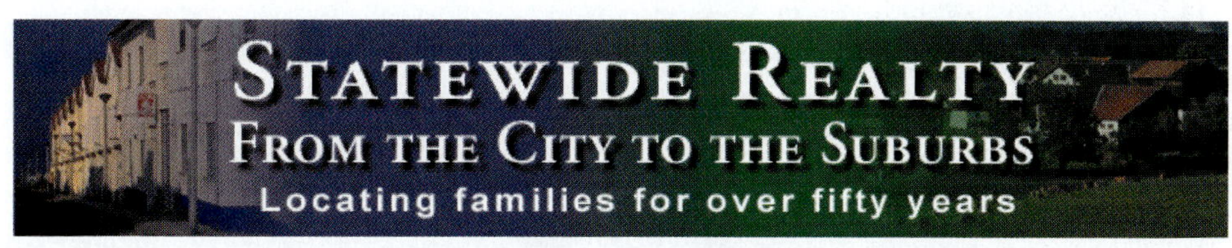

Figure 4–21

Creating a Second Web Page

Now that you have created the Statewide Realty home page with a horizontal menu bar of text links for easy navigation to other pages in the site, it is time to create one of those linked pages — the By Complex page (Figure 4–22). Like the home page, the By Complex page includes the logo image and a horizontal menu bar of text links. Having the Statewide Realty logo and the horizontal menu bar at the top of each page provides consistency throughout the Web site. The menu bar lists the four Web pages — Home, By Complex, By Vacancy, and By Bedrooms — with a | (pipe) symbol between links. Beneath the menu bar is a table listing available apartments by apartment complex.

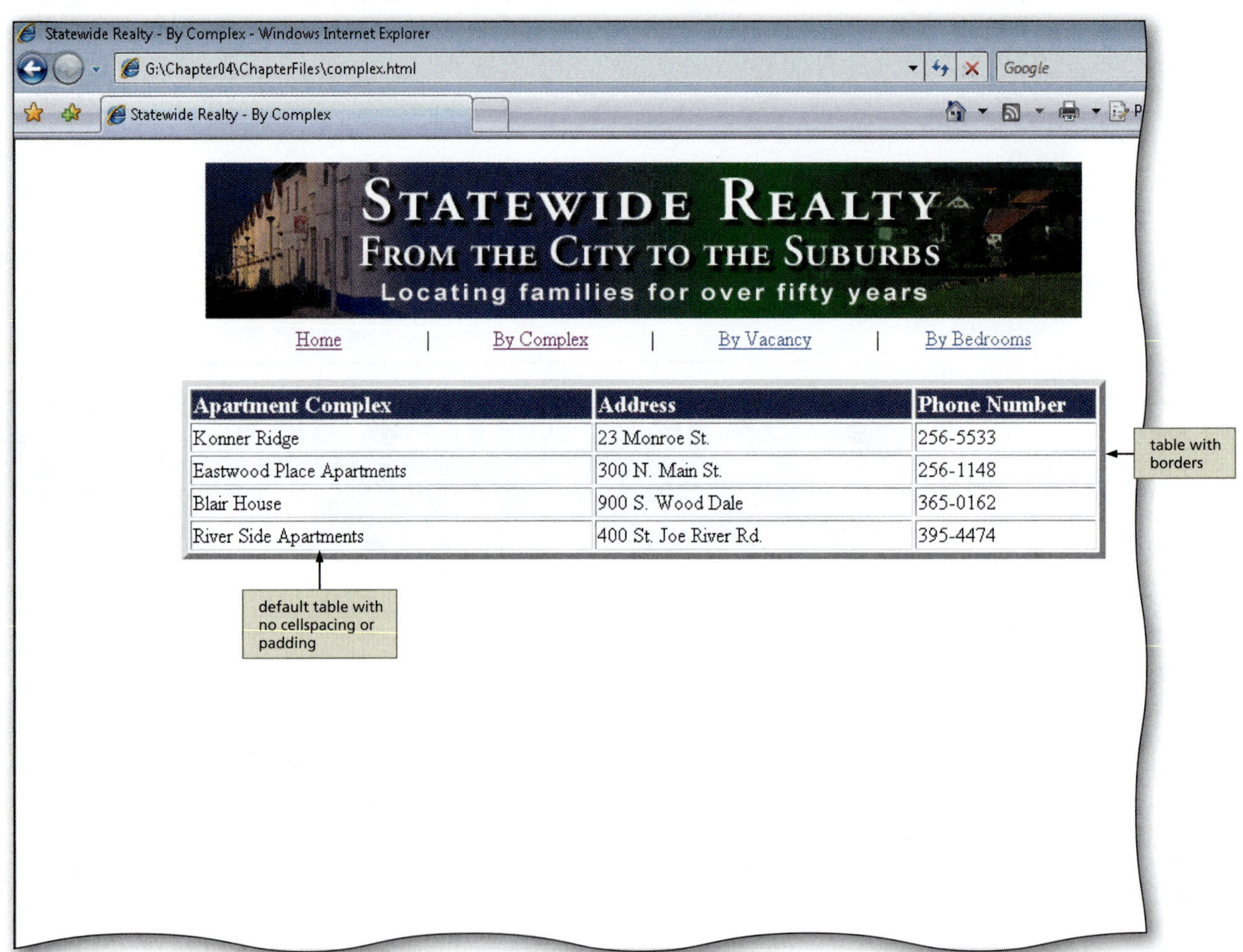

Figure 4–22 By Complex Web page.

The first step in creating the By Complex Web page is to add the HTML tags to define the Web page structure and the two borderless tables with the Statewide Realty banner image and the horizontal menu bar. Because the logo image and menu bar are the same as on the home page, you can copy and paste HTML code from the home page and then edit it for the By Complex page.

To Copy and Paste HTML Code to a New File

The following step shows how to copy the HTML tags to define the Web page structure and the two borderless tables from the HTML file, statewide.html, to a new HTML file.

1

- Click the statewide - Notepad button on the taskbar.
- Click immediately to the left of the < in the <!DOCTYPE html tag on line 1.
- Drag through the second </table> tag on line 28 to highlight lines 1 through 28.
- Press CTRL+C to copy the selected lines to the Clipboard.
- Click File on the Notepad menu bar and then click New.
- Press CTRL+V to paste the contents from the Clipboard into a new file (Figure 4–23).

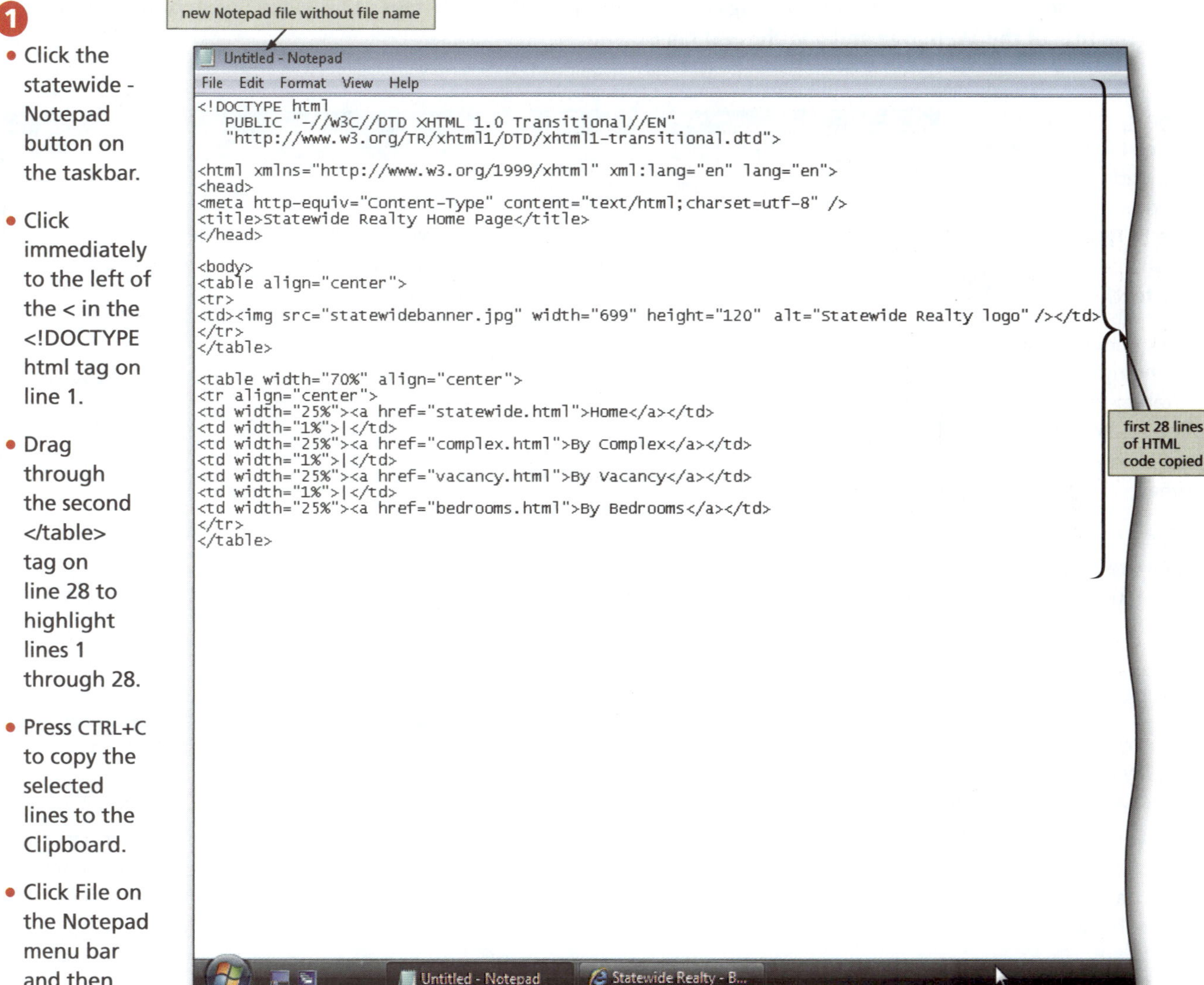

Figure 4–23

To Change the Web Page Title

The next step is to edit the copied HTML to change the title of the Web page from Statewide Realty Home Page to Statewide Realty - By Complex, so that the title of the current Web page is displayed on the title bar of the Web browser. You also need to add end tags for the <body> and <html> tags. The following step shows how to change the title of the Web page and add the end tags.

- Highlight the words Home Page between the <title> and </title> tags on line 8. Type `- By Complex` as the text.
- Click immediately to the right of the </table> tag on line 28. Press the ENTER key three times.
- Type `</body>` and then press the ENTER key.
- Type `</html>` as the end tag (Figure 4–24).

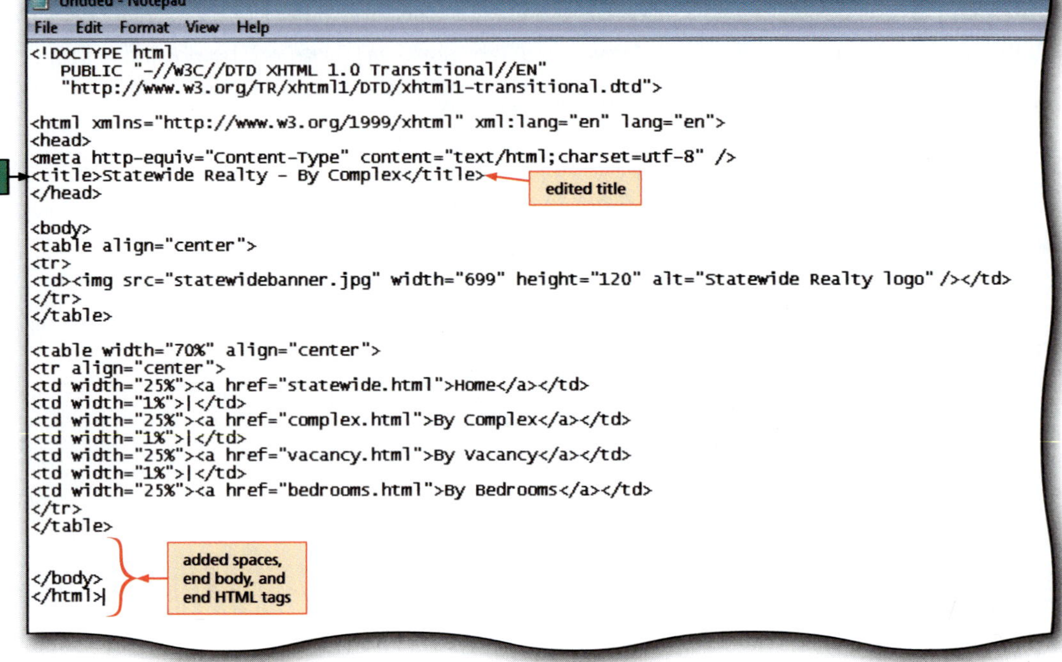

Figure 4–24

Q&A

Will my Web page display correctly without changing the title?

Yes, your Web page will display correctly, but the wrong information will show on the title bar of the browser. The title tag is used to display information about the Web page to the visitor. If you had not changed this title, the By Complex Web page would have shown Home Page in the title. The title also is what displays in the Favorites or Bookmarks section of the browser.

Plan Ahead

- **Determine what table formatting to use.** Borderless tables often are appropriate when the tables are used to position text and image elements. In other instances, such as when a table is used to structure columns and rows of information, borders are appropriate. For example, the By Complex Web page lists three columns and five rows of information about available apartments by apartment complex. Figure 4–25a shows this information in a table with borders. Figure 4–25b shows the same information in a table without borders. As shown in this figure, using a table with borders makes the information on the By Complex Web page easier to read and provides a frame that gives the table a three-dimensional appearance.
- **Identify what color schemes work and do not distract from the purpose.** It is important to add an element of color to your Web pages in order to make the appearance attractive. You need to make sure, though, that the color does not distract from the message of the content. In the case of the By Complex table, you will add background color to the table header cell <th> to bring attention to the text in the header, using a color from the banner image to tie the table together with the image. Because the background color is so dark, you need to change the text to white (or a lighter color) to make reading easier. The default black text does not show up well on very dark background colors.

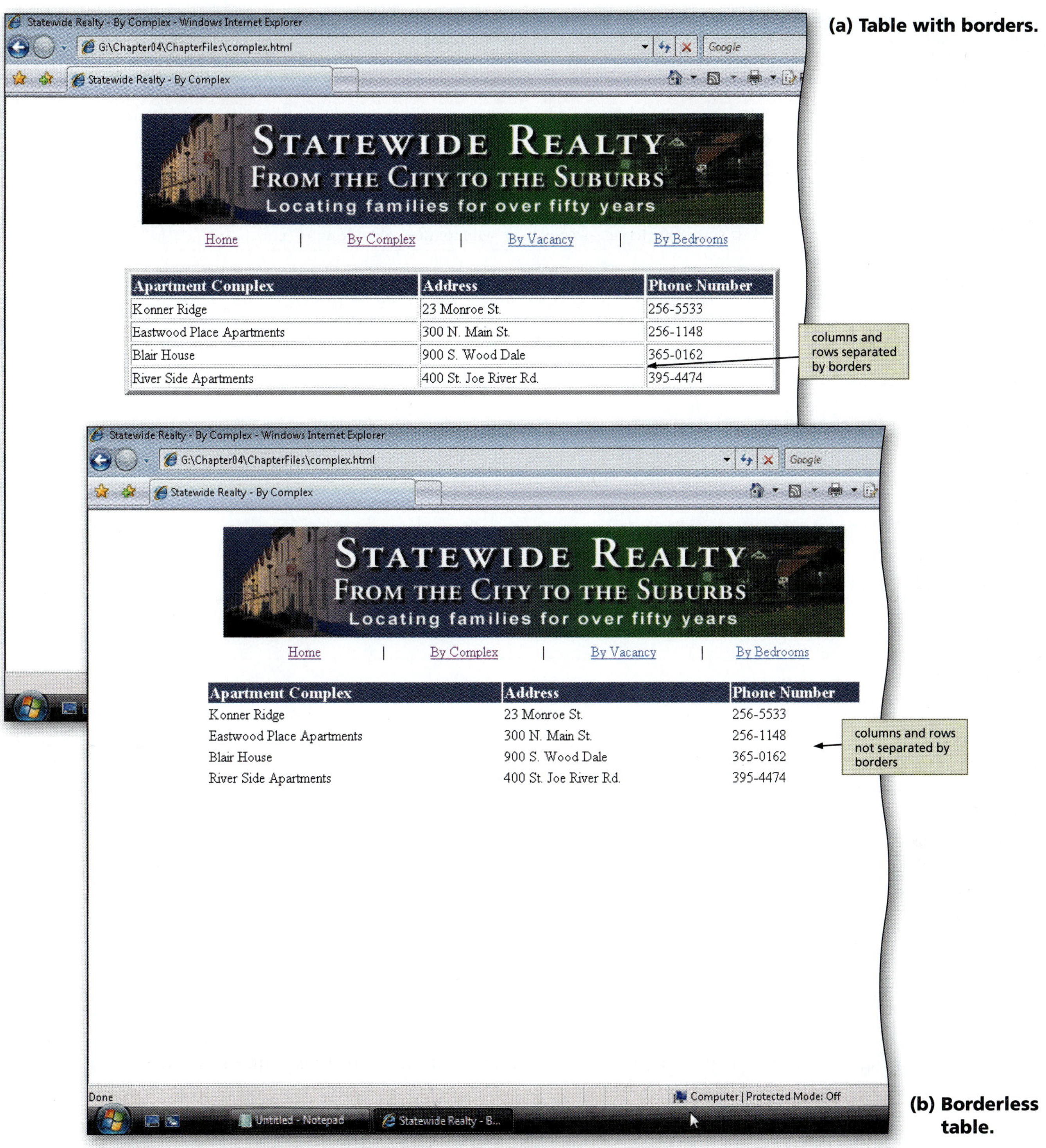

(a) Table with borders.

(b) Borderless table.

Figure 4–25

To Create a Table with Borders and Insert Text

Creating the table shown in Figure 4–25a involves first creating a table with three columns and five rows. The first row of the table is for column headings; the other rows are for data. As you have learned, heading cells differ from data cells in their appearance. Text in a heading cell appears as bold and centered, while text in a data cell appears as normal and left-aligned. Table 4–6 on the next page contains the HTML tags and text used to create the table of apartment complexes on the By Complex Web page.

Table 4–6 HTML Code to Create a Table with Borders and Insert Text into Cells

HTML Tag and Text

```
<br /><table border="5" width="75%" align="center">
<tr bgcolor="#4b5781">
<th align="left"><font color="white" size="+1">Apartment Complex</font></th>
<th align="left"><font color="white" size="+1">Address</font></th>
<th align="left"><font color="white" size="+1">Phone Number</font></th>
</tr>

<tr>
<td width="45%">Konner Ridge</td>
<td width="35%">23 Monroe St.</td>
<td width="20%">256-5533</td>
</tr>

<tr>
<td>Eastwood Place Apartments</td>
<td>300 N. Main St.</td>
<td>256-1148</td>
</tr>

<tr>
<td>Blair House</td>
<td>900 S. Wood Dale</td>
<td>365-0162</td>
</tr>

<tr>
<td>River Side Apartments</td>
<td>400 St. Joe River Rd.</td>
<td>395-4474</td>
</tr>
</table>
```

The following step illustrates how to create a table with borders and insert text into heading and data cells.

- Click line 29 (blank line immediately above the </body> tag) to position the insertion point.
- Enter the HTML code as shown in Table 4–6, pressing ENTER after each line except the last line (Figure 4–26).

Q&A When you set the table border, what does the number represent?

It represents the number of pixels that you want the border to be. The higher the number you use, the wider the border will be. You need to analyze how large or small the border should be based on the other elements of your Web page and the content in the table.

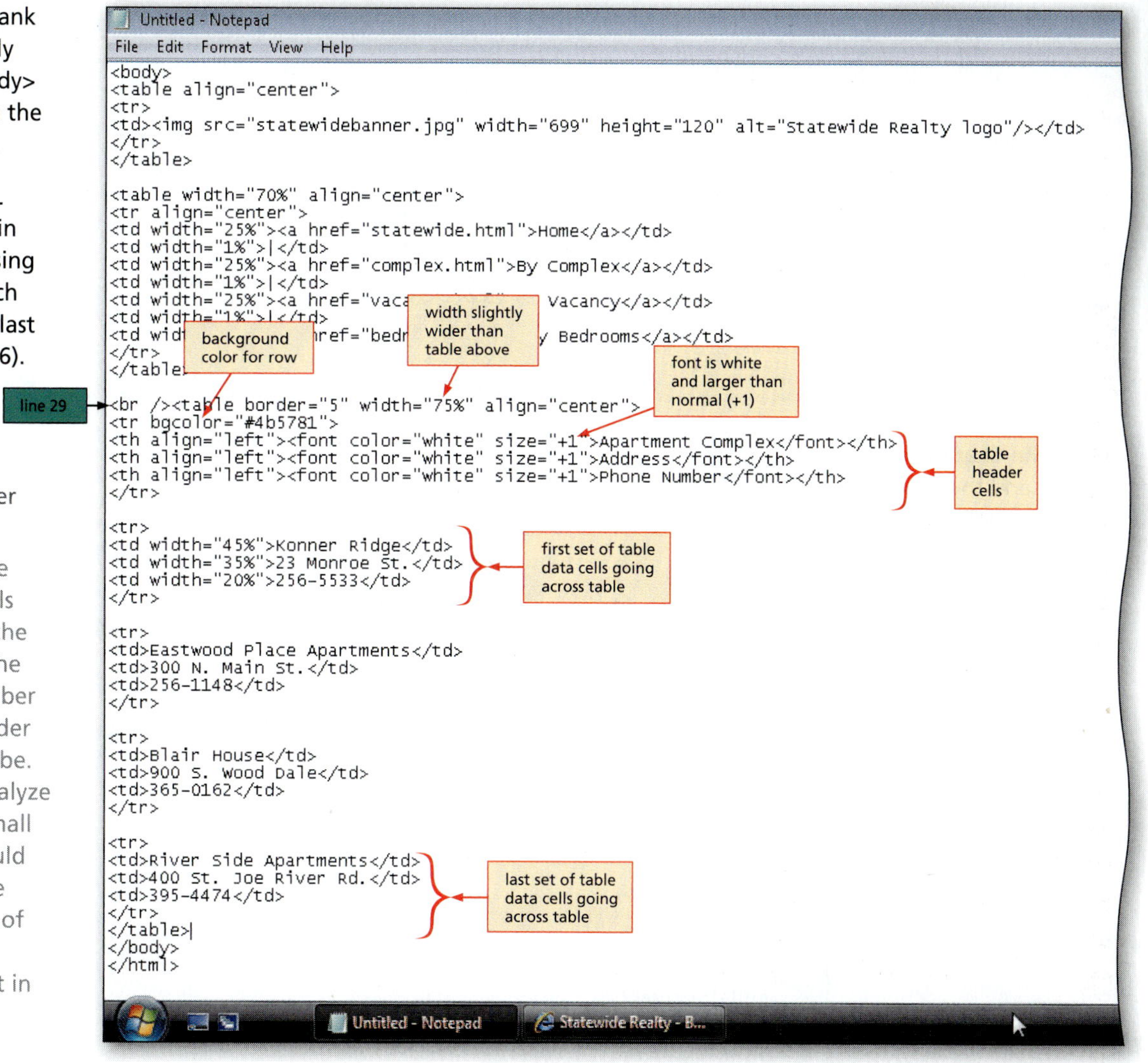

```
<body>
<table align="center">
<tr>
<td><img src="statewidebanner.jpg" width="699" height="120" alt="Statewide Realty logo"/></td>
</tr>
</table>

<table width="70%" align="center">
<tr align="center">
<td width="25%"><a href="statewide.html">Home</a></td>
<td width="1%">|</td>
<td width="25%"><a href="complex.html">By Complex</a></td>
<td width="1%">|</td>
<td width="25%"><a href="vaca          Vacancy</a></td>
<td wid
<td wid           ref="bedr          y Bedrooms</a></td>
</tr>
</table

<br /><table border="5" width="75%" align="center">
<tr bgcolor="#4b5781">
<th align="left"><font color="white" size="+1">Apartment Complex</font></th>
<th align="left"><font color="white" size="+1">Address</font></th>
<th align="left"><font color="white" size="+1">Phone Number</font></th>
</tr>

<tr>
<td width="45%">Konner Ridge</td>
<td width="35%">23 Monroe St.</td>
<td width="20%">256-5533</td>
</tr>

<tr>
<td>Eastwood Place Apartments</td>
<td>300 N. Main St.</td>
<td>256-1148</td>
</tr>

<tr>
<td>Blair House</td>
<td>900 S. Wood Dale</td>
<td>365-0162</td>
</tr>

<tr>
<td>River Side Apartments</td>
<td>400 St. Joe River Rd.</td>
<td>395-4474</td>
</tr>
</table>
</body>
</html>
```

Figure 4–26

Q&A Are there other attributes that can be used in the <table> tag?

Many other attributes can be used in the <table> tag (see Appendix A). The frame and rules attributes can be used to vary the look of your table significantly.

Q&A Are there other attributes that can be used in the <tr>, <th>, and <td> tags?

Other attributes also can be used in the <tr>, <th>, and <td> tags (see Appendix A). The best way to review these attributes is to try them in simple tables to see the effect. Viewing tables with various attributes designated side by side on a Web page helps you to determine which attributes to use.

To Save and Print the HTML File

With the HTML code for the table with borders added, the By Complex Web page is complete. The HTML file now should be saved and a copy printed as a reference.

- With a USB drive plugged into the computer, click File on the menu bar and then click Save As. Type `complex.html` in the File name text box.
- If necessary, click USB (G:) in the Save in list. Click the Chapter04 folder and then click the ChapterFiles folder in the list of available folders. Click the Save button in the Save As dialog box.
- Click File on the menu bar, click Print on the File menu, and then click the Print button in the Print dialog box (Figure 4–27).

```
<!DOCTYPE html
   PUBLIC "-//W3C//DTD XHTML 1.0 Transitional//EN"
   "http://www.w3.org/TR/xhtml1/DTD/xhtml1-transitional.dtd">

<html xmlns="http://www.w3.org/1999/xhtml" xml:lang="en" lang="en">
<head>
<meta http-equiv="Content-Type" content="text/html;charset=utf-8" />
<title>Statewide Realty - By Complex</title>
</head>

<body>
<table align="center">
<tr>
<td> <img src="statewidebanner.jpg" width="699" height="120" alt="Statewide Realty logo" /></td>
</tr>
</table>

<table width="70%" align="center">
<tr align="center">
<td width="25%"><a href="statewide.html">Home</a></td>
<td width="1%">|</td>
<td width="25%"><a href="complex.html">By Complex</a></td>
<td width="1%">|</td>
<td width="25%"><a href="vacancy.html">By Vacancy</a></td>
<td width="1%">|</td>
<td width="25%"><a href="bedrooms.html">By Bedrooms</a></td>
</tr>
</table>|

<br /><table border="5" width="75%" align="center">
<tr bgcolor="#4b5781">
<th align="left"><font color="white" size="+1">Apartment Complex</font></th>
<th align="left"><font color="white" size="+1">Address</font></th>
<th align="left"><font color="white" size="+1">Phone Number</font></th>
</tr>

<tr>
<td width="45%">Konner Ridge</td>
<td width="35%">23 Monroe St.</td>
<td width="20%">256-5533</td>
</tr>

<tr>
<td>Eastwood Place Apartments</td>
<td>300 N. Main St.</td>
<td>256-1148</td>
</tr>

<tr>
<td>Blair House</td>
<td>900 S. Wood Dale</td>
<td>365-0162</td>
</tr>

<tr>
<td>River Side Apartments</td>
<td>400 St. Joe River Rd.</td>
<td>395-4474</td>
</tr>
</table>
</body>
</html>
```

Figure 4–27

To Validate, View, and Print the Web Page Using the Browser

After saving and printing the HTML file, perform the following step to validate, view, and print the Web page.

1

- Click the Internet Explorer button on the taskbar.
- Use the W3C validator service to validate the complex.html Web page.
- Use the Back button or click the Statewide Realty Home Page button on the taskbar to return to the Statewide Realty home page.
- Click the By Complex link to display the By Complex page (Figure 4–28).
- Click the Print button on the Command bar to print the Statewide Realty - By Complex Web page.

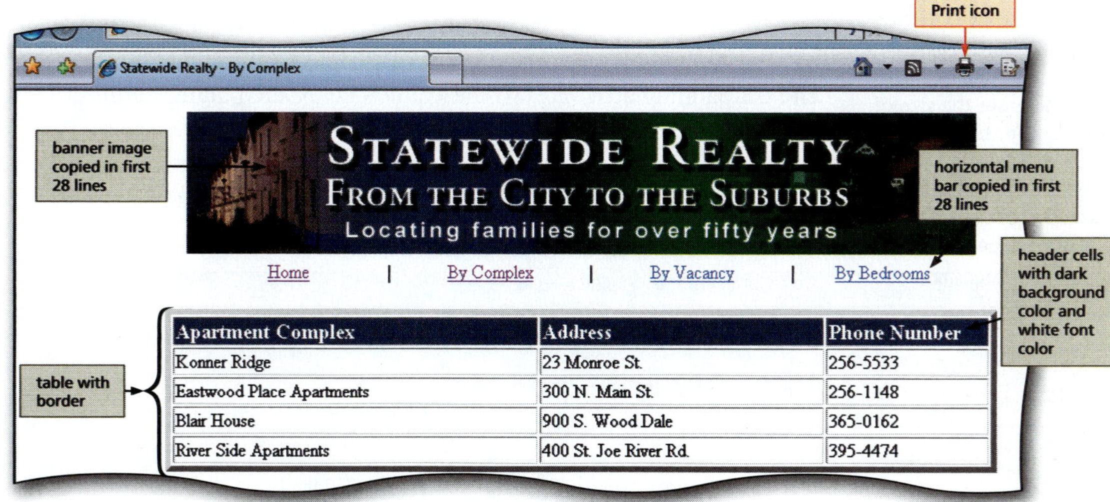

Figure 4–28

To Test Links on a Web Page

After confirming that the Web page appears as desired, the four links on the horizontal menu bar should be tested to verify that they function as expected. The following step shows how to test the links on the complex.html Web page.

1

- Click the Home link to change to the Statewide Realty home page.
- Click the By Complex link to return to the complex.html Web page.
- Click the By Bedrooms link. (You will add a heading to the By Bedrooms page later in the project.)
- Click the By Vacancy link. (Figure 4–29).

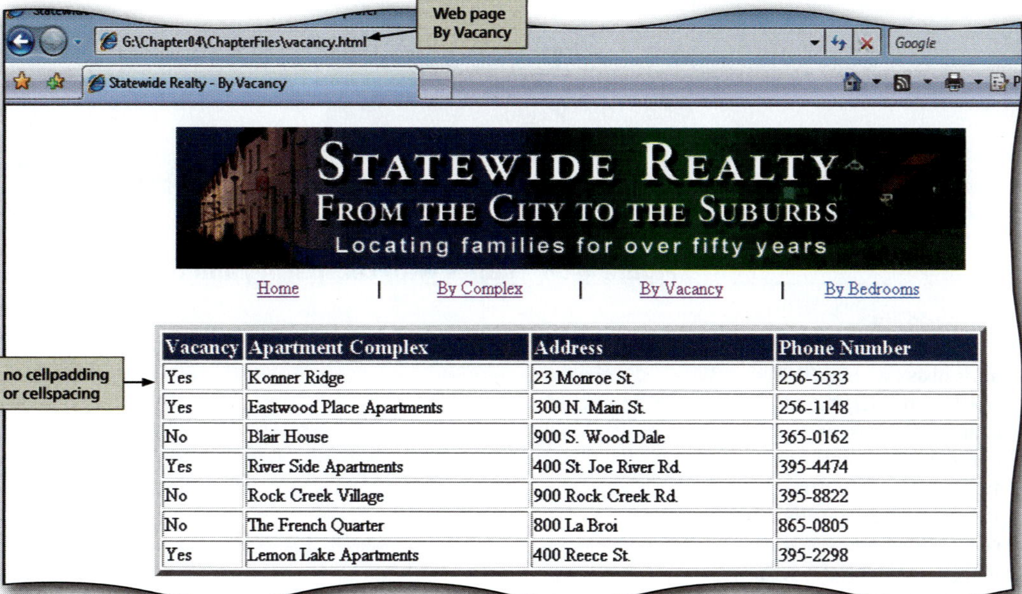

Figure 4–29

BTW

Cellspacing
The cellspacing attribute adds pixels between cells. The purpose of cellspacing is to add space between cells, whether or not a border exists. With a border, cellspacing increases the size of the border between the cells. Without a border, cellspacing increases the amount of white space between the cells.

Adding Cellspacing, Cellpadding, and a Caption

The table of information on the By Complex Web page did not use the cellspacing or cellpadding attributes. The size of each data cell, therefore, automatically was set to the minimum size needed for the text inserted in the data cell. The vacancy.html Web page, however, should be modified to use cellspacing and cellpadding by adding the cellspacing and cellpadding attributes to the <table> tag. **Cellspacing** defines the number of pixels of space between cells in a table. **Cellpadding** defines the number of pixels of space between a cell's contents and its border. Figures 4–30a through 4–30c illustrate how using the cellspacing and cellpadding <table> tag attributes can affect a table's appearance.

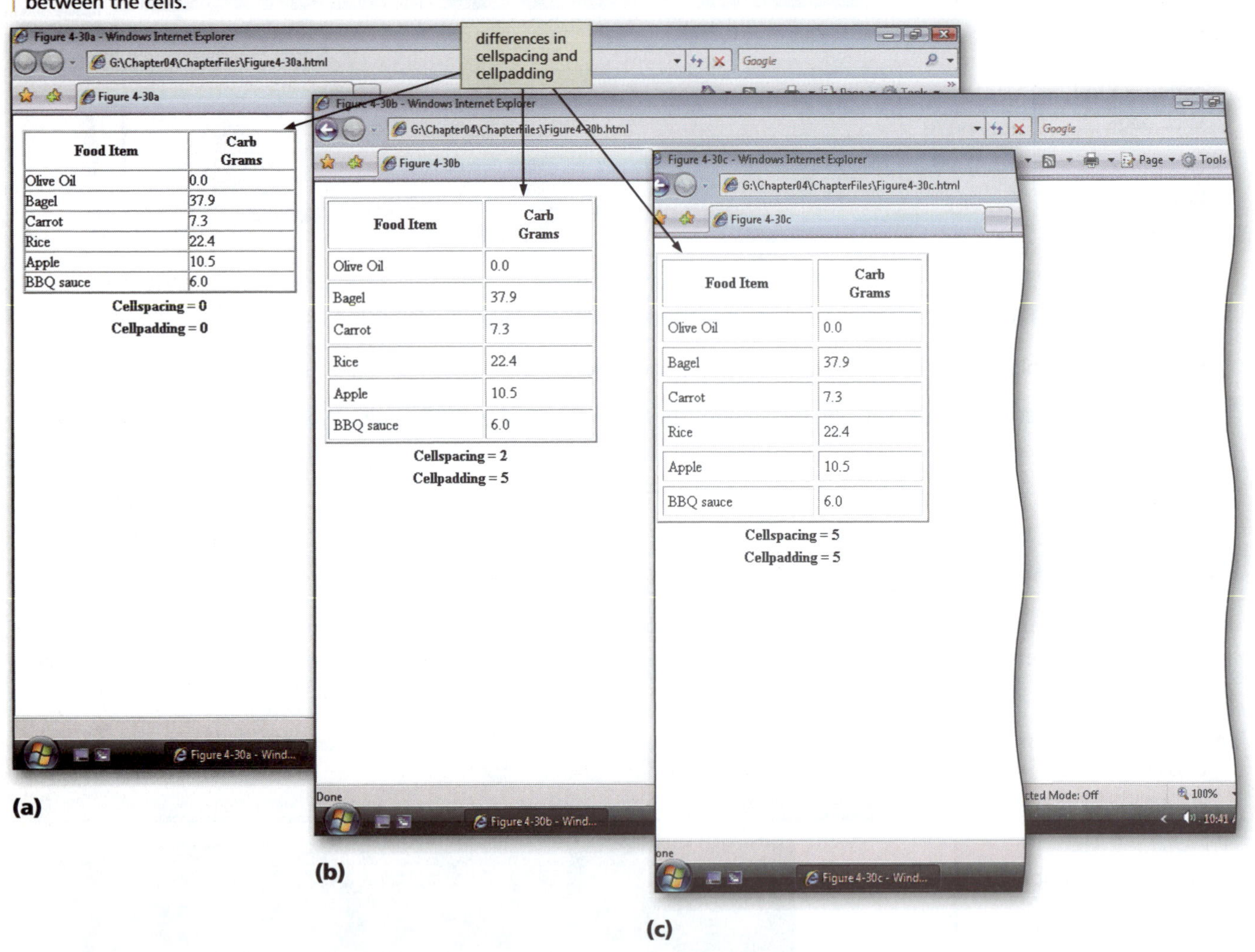

Figure 4–30 Tables with cellspacing and cellpadding.

BTW

Cellpadding
The cellpadding attribute adds pixels within a cell border. The purpose of cellpadding is to keep the content within each cell from looking too close to the content of another cell. Cellpadding sets a margin for the right, left, top, and bottom of the cell with the specification of one tag.

Figure 4–31a shows how the vacancy.html file from the Student Data Files looks as currently designed. Figure 4–31b shows how the Vacancy Web page will appear after cellspacing, cellpadding, and a caption are added.

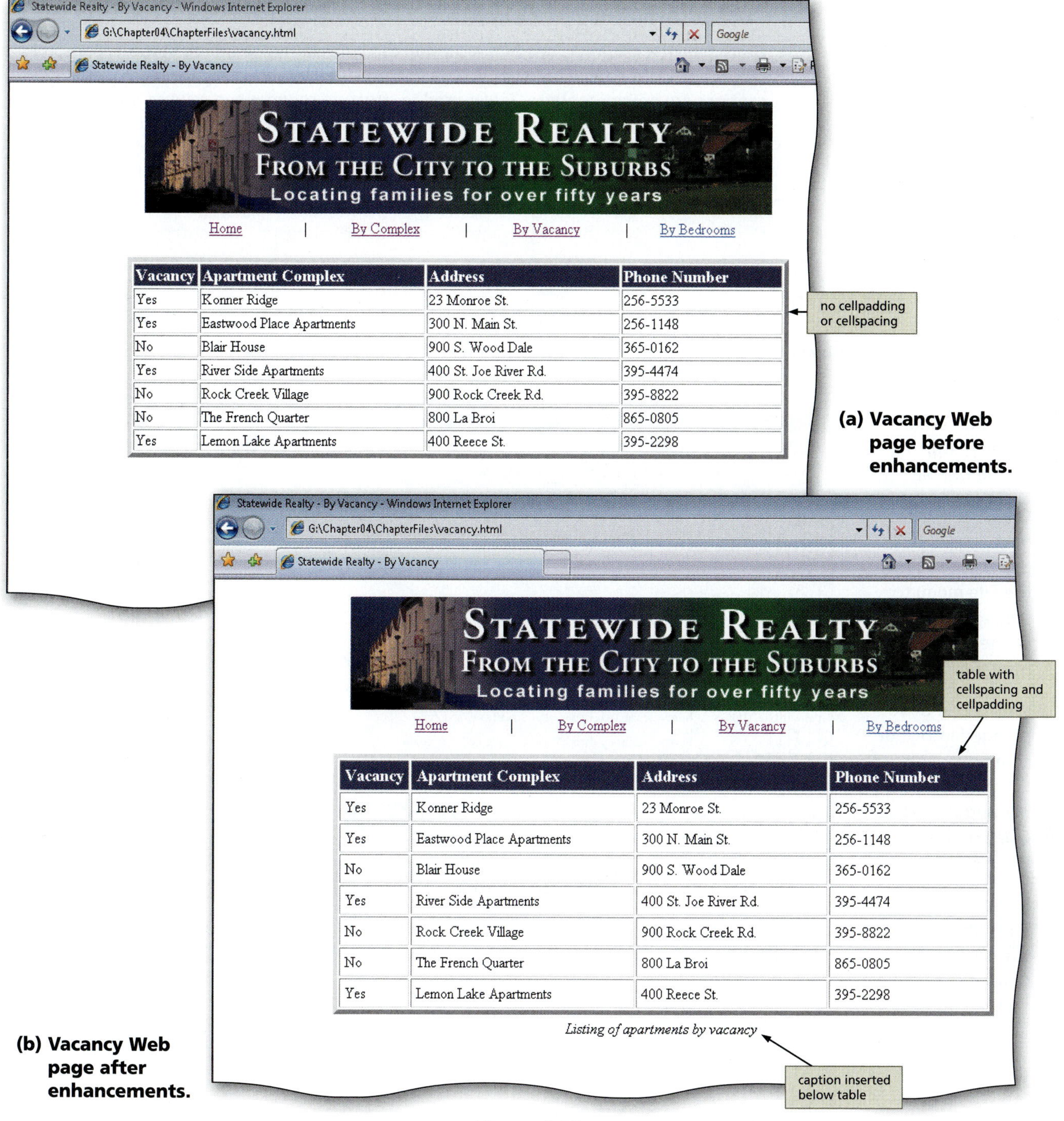

(a) Vacancy Web page before enhancements.

(b) Vacancy Web page after enhancements.

Figure 4–31

Plan Ahead

- **Determine what table spacing to use.** Another consideration to make when designing tables is how much space to provide within the table. Cellspacing is the space between the borders of each cell. Cellpadding is the space between a cell's content and its border. Both attributes serve the purpose of making the table of information easier to read. No rule of thumb says how much cellpadding or cellspacing should be used. Try various values to see the effect on the table.
- **Determine if a caption is needed.** A caption can help clarify the table's purpose. For some tables, such as the table used to position images and the tables used to create menu bars, captions are not appropriate. Tables used to structure columns and rows of information, such as the vacancy table, can benefit from having a caption to clarify the contents of the table. Captions can run above, below, to the left, or to the right of the table. The placement of the caption depends on the purpose of the caption, but captions often appear below the table.

To Open an HTML File

In the following step you activate Notepad and open the vacancy.html Web page file.

1

- Click the complex - Notepad button on the taskbar.
- Click File on the menu bar and then click Save on the File menu to save any changes to the complex. html file.
- With a USB drive plugged into your computer, click File on the menu bar and then click Open on the File menu.
- If necessary, navigate to the Chapter04\ChapterFiles folder on the USB drive.
- If necessary, click the Files of type box arrow and then click All Files to display all files in the g:\Chapter04\ChapterFiles folder.
- Click vacancy.html in the list of files.
- Click the Open button to open the vacancy.html file in Notepad (Figure 4–32).

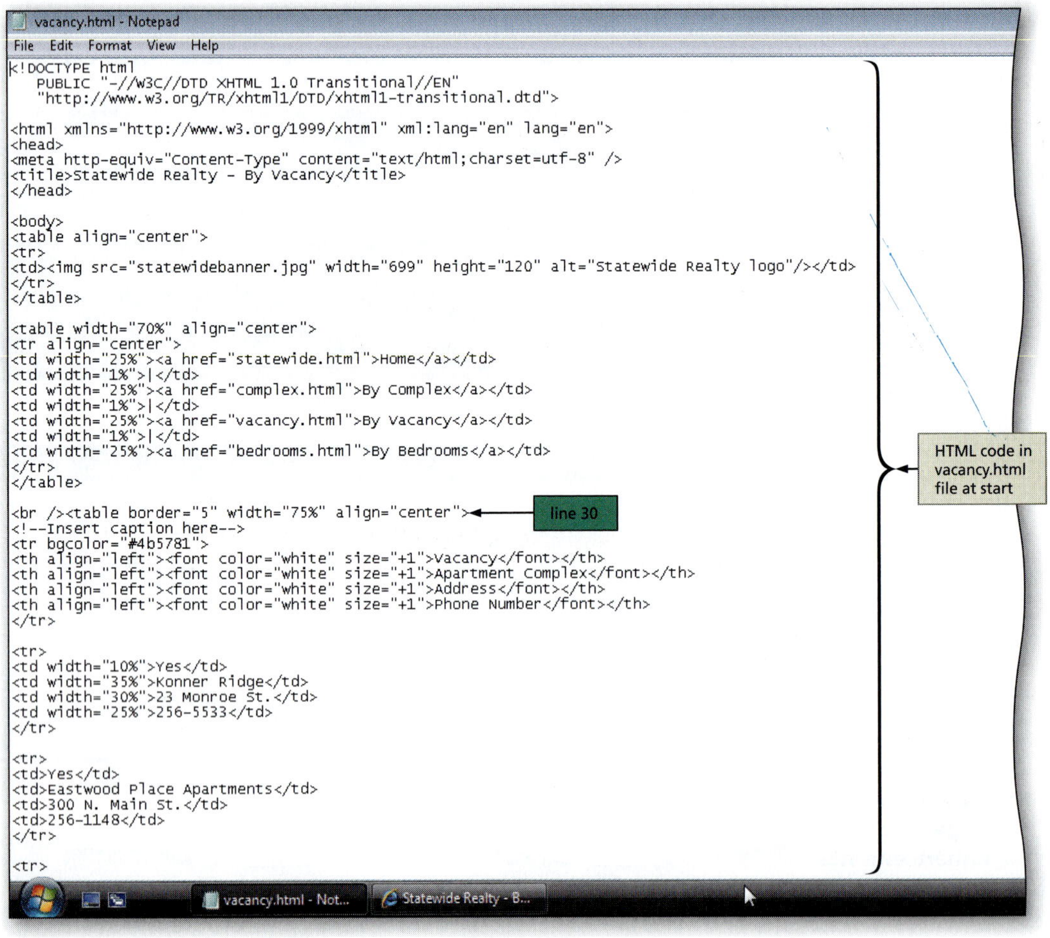

vacancy.html - Notepad

File Edit Format View Help

```
<!DOCTYPE html
   PUBLIC "-//W3C//DTD XHTML 1.0 Transitional//EN"
   "http://www.w3.org/TR/xhtml1/DTD/xhtml1-transitional.dtd">

<html xmlns="http://www.w3.org/1999/xhtml" xml:lang="en" lang="en">
<head>
<meta http-equiv="Content-Type" content="text/html;charset=utf-8" />
<title>Statewide Realty - By Vacancy</title>
</head>

<body>
<table align="center">
<tr>
<td><img src="statewidebanner.jpg" width="699" height="120" alt="Statewide Realty logo"/></td>
</tr>
</table>

<table width="70%" align="center">
<tr align="center">
<td width="25%"><a href="statewide.html">Home</a></td>
<td width="1%">|</td>
<td width="25%"><a href="complex.html">By Complex</a></td>
<td width="1%">|</td>
<td width="25%"><a href="vacancy.html">By Vacancy</a></td>
<td width="1%">|</td>
<td width="25%"><a href="bedrooms.html">By Bedrooms</a></td>
</tr>
</table>

<br /><table border="5" width="75%" align="center">
<!--Insert caption here-->
<tr bgcolor="#4b5781">
<th align="left"><font color="white" size="+1">Vacancy</font></th>
<th align="left"><font color="white" size="+1">Apartment Complex</font></th>
<th align="left"><font color="white" size="+1">Address</font></th>
<th align="left"><font color="white" size="+1">Phone Number</font></th>
</tr>

<tr>
<td width="10%">Yes</td>
<td width="35%">Konner Ridge</td>
<td width="30%">23 Monroe St.</td>
<td width="25%">256-5533</td>
</tr>

<tr>
<td>Yes</td>
<td>Eastwood Place Apartments</td>
<td>300 N. Main St.</td>
<td>256-1148</td>
</tr>

<tr>
```

line 30

HTML code in vacancy.html file at start

vacancy.html - Not... Statewide Realty - B...

Figure 4–32

To Add Cellspacing and Cellpadding to a Table

With the vacancy.html file open, the HTML code to add cellspacing and cellpadding can be added. The following step shows how to add cellspacing and cellpadding to a table.

- Click immediately to the right of the width="75%" on line 30 and then press the SPACEBAR.
- Type `cellspacing="2" cellpadding="5"` as the attributes and values (Figure 4–33).

Q&A Is there another way to set the cellpadding and cellspacing attributes for a Web page?

You can set padding and border-spacing styles with Cascading Style Sheets (CSS), but that is not yet supported by all browsers.

Q&A What is the amount of cellpadding and cellspacing if I do not specify this in the table tag?

The default value for cellpadding is 1, while the default value for cellspacing is 2.

vacancy.html - Notepad

File Edit Format View Help

```
<!DOCTYPE html
   PUBLIC "-//W3C//DTD XHTML 1.0 Transitional//EN"
   "http://www.w3.org/TR/xhtml1/DTD/xhtml1-transitional.dtd">

<html xmlns="http://www.w3.org/1999/xhtml" xml:lang="en" lang="en">
<head>
<meta http-equiv="Content-Type" content="text/html;charset=utf-8" />
<title>Statewide Realty - By Vacancy</title>
</head>

<body>
<table align="center">
<tr>
<td><img src="statewidebanner.jpg" width="699" height="120" alt="Statewide Realty logo"/></td>
</tr>
</table>

<table width="70%" align="center">
<tr align="center">
<td width="25%"><a href="statewide.html">Home</a></td>
<td width="1%">|</td>
<td width="25%"><a href="complex.html">By Complex</a></td>
<td width="1%">|</td>
<td width="25%"><a href="vacancy.html"></a></td>
<td width="1%">|</td>
<td width="25%"><a href="bedrooms.html ms</a></td>
</tr>
</table>

<br /><table border="5" width="75%" cellspacing="2" cellpadding="5" align="center">
<!--Insert caption here-->
<tr bgcolor="#4b5781">
<th align="left"><font color="white" size="+1">Vacancy</font></th>
<th align="left"><font color="white" size="+1">Apartment Complex</font></th>
<th align="left"><font color="white" size="+1">Address</font></th>
<th align="left"><font color="white" size="+1">Phone Number</font></th>
</tr>

<tr>
<td width="10%">Yes</td>
<td width="35%">Konner Ridge</td>
<td width="30%">23 Monroe St.</td>
<td width="25%">256-5533</td>
</tr>

<tr>
<td>Yes</td>
<td>Eastwood Place Apartments</td>
<td>300 N. Main St.</td>
<td>256-1148</td>
</tr>

<tr>
```


Figure 4–33

Q&A Can I set the cellpadding and cellspacing differently for different cells?

No, you cannot set cellpadding and cellspacing differently for various cells. This attribute is only available for the <table> (whole table) tag.

To Add a Table Caption

Captions are added to tables using the <caption> </caption> tags to enclose the caption text. You add formatting to make the caption italic, and the align attribute to place the caption at the bottom of the table.

The following step shows how to add a caption below the vacancy table.

- Highlight the text <!--Line 31 - Insert caption here -->.
- Type `<caption align="bottom"><em>Listing of apartments by vacancy</em></caption>` as the tag to add the italic caption below the table (Figure 4–34).

Experiment

- Substitute align="top", align="left", or align="right" for align="bottom" and display the page in a browser to see different caption placements. End with align="bottom".

Q&A

Why would I use the caption tag?

You might use the caption to further explain the main purpose of the table. In the example above, you are further notifying the visitors that the table shows a listing of apartments by vacancy. Other uses are shown earlier in the chapter where the caption is added to identify the unit of measure used in the table.

vacancy.html - Notepad

File Edit Format View Help

```
<!DOCTYPE html
   PUBLIC "-//W3C//DTD XHTML 1.0 Transitional//EN"
   "http://www.w3.org/TR/xhtml1/DTD/xhtml1-transitional.dtd">

<html xmlns="http://www.w3.org/1999/xhtml" xml:lang="en" lang="en">
<head>
<meta http-equiv="Content-Type" content="text/html;charset=utf-8" />
<title>Statewide Realty - By Vacancy</title>
</head>

<body>
<table align="center">
<tr>
<td><img src="statewidebanner.jpg" width="699" height="120" alt="Statewide Realty logo"/></td>
</tr>
</table>

<table width="70%" align="center">
<tr align="center">
<td width="25%"><a href="statewide.html">Home</a></td>
<td width="1%">|</td>
<td width="25%"><a href="complex.html">By Complex</a></td>
<td width="1%">|</td>
<td width="25%"><a href="vacancy.html">By Vacancy</a></td>
<td width="1%">|</td>
<td width="25%"><a                   ms.html">By Bedrooms</a></td>
</tr>
</table>

<br /><table border="5" width="75%" cellspacing="2" cellpadding="5" align="center">
<caption align="bottom"><em>Listing of apartments by vacancy</em></caption>
<tr bgcolor="#4b5781">
<th align="left"><font color="white" size="+1">Vacancy</font></th>
<th align="left"><font color="white" size="+1">Apartment Complex</font></th>
<th align="left"><font color="white" size="+1">Address</font></th>
<th align="left"><font color="white" size="+1">Phone Number</font></th>
</tr>

<tr>
<td width="10%">Yes</td>
<td width="35%">Konner Ridge</td>
<td width="30%">23 Monroe St.</td>
<td width="25%">256-5533</td>
</tr>

<tr>
<td>Yes</td>
<td>Eastwood Place Apartments</td>
<td>300 N. Main St.</td>
<td>256-1148</td>
</tr>

<tr>
```


Figure 4–34

To Save, Validate, Print, and View the HTML File and Print the Web Page

1

- With the USB drive plugged into your computer, click File on the menu bar and then click Save to save the vacancy.html file.
- Click File on the menu bar, click Print on the File menu, and then click the Print button to print the file.
- Click the Internet Explorer button on the taskbar to display the Statewide Realty - By Vacancy page (Figure 4–35).
- Validate the Web page using the W3C validator service.
- Use the Back button or taskbar to return to the Statewide Realty - By Vacancy page.
- Click the Refresh icon on the Address bar to show the most recent file.
- Click the Print button on the Command bar to print the Web page.

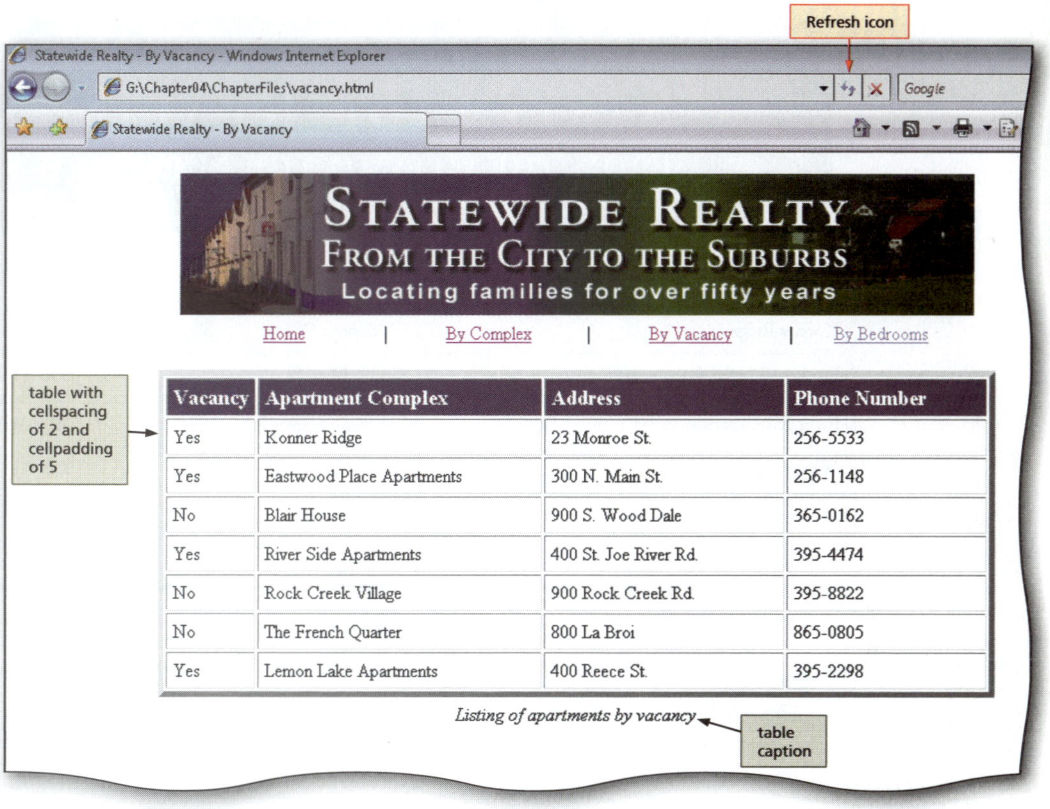

Refresh icon

Statewide Realty - By Vacancy - Windows Internet Explorer

G:\Chapter04\ChapterFiles\vacancy.html

STATEWIDE REALTY
FROM THE CITY TO THE SUBURBS
Locating families for over fifty years

Home | By Complex | By Vacancy | By Bedrooms

table with cellspacing of 2 and cellpadding of 5

Vacancy	Apartment Complex	Address	Phone Number
Yes	Konner Ridge	23 Monroe St.	256-5533
Yes	Eastwood Place Apartments	300 N. Main St.	256-1148
No	Blair House	900 S. Wood Dale	365-0162
Yes	River Side Apartments	400 St. Joe River Rd.	395-4474
No	Rock Creek Village	900 Rock Creek Rd.	395-8822
No	The French Quarter	800 La Broi	865-0805
Yes	Lemon Lake Apartments	400 Reece St.	395-2298

Listing of apartments by vacancy

table caption

Figure 4–35

Spanning Rows and Columns

If you need to merge several cells into one, you can use row or column spanning. You can span rows or columns anywhere in a table. Generally, row and column spanning is used to create headings in tables. The **colspan attribute** of the <th> or <td> tag sets a number of columns spanned by a cell. The **rowspan attribute** of the <th> or <td> tag sets a number of rows spanned by a cell. Figure 4–10 on page HTML 154 shows examples of both column and row spanning. Notice that the heading 5K spans (or goes across) three columns, while the heading 10K spans (or goes across) two columns. The heading Meet Dates spans (or goes across) four rows of information.

Figure 4–36 on the next page shows what the bedrooms.html Web page looks like at the start of the process. All of the table content is there, but no row or column spanning is done yet . You will enter the HTML code to complete the row and column spanning (Figure 4–37). In Figure 4–37, the heading Complex - Address - Phone is an example of column spanning. In this case, this heading spans three columns. In the same figure, the words “1 Bedroom,” “2 Bedrooms,” and “3 or More Bedrooms” are used as headings that span rows of information. All of these headings span three rows in the table.

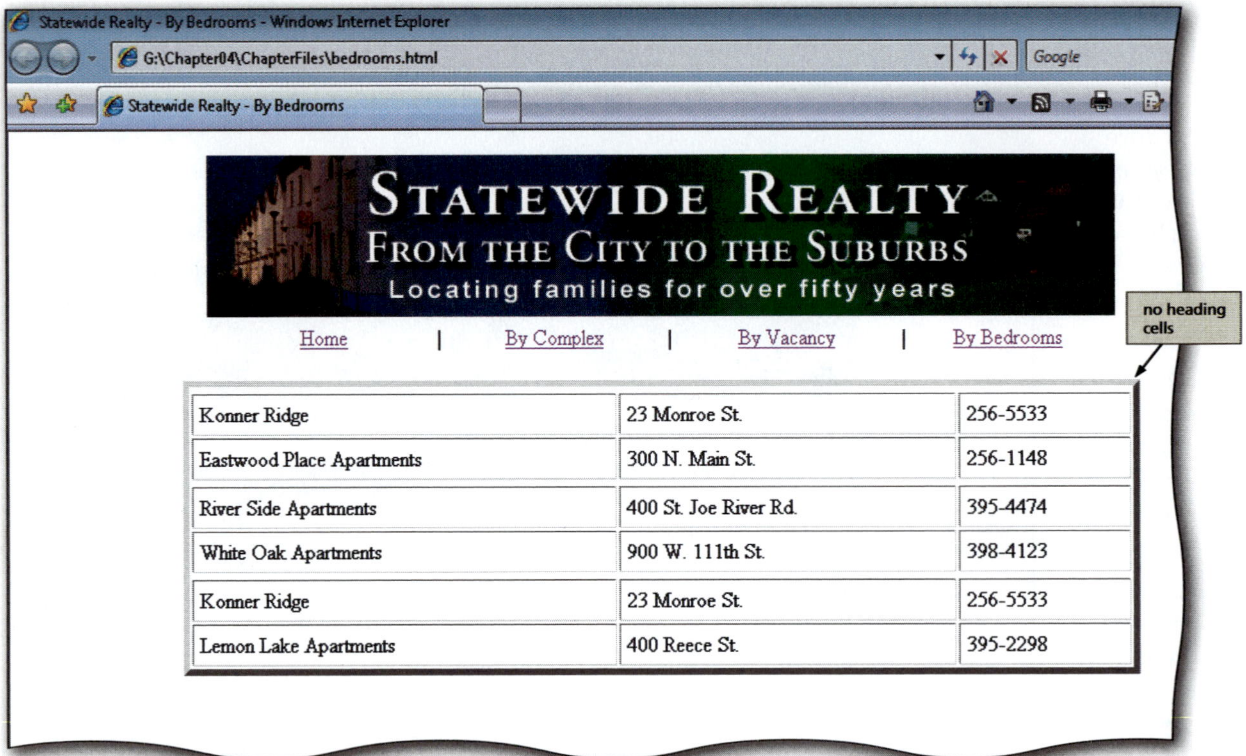

Figure 4–36 By Bedrooms Web page before enhancements.

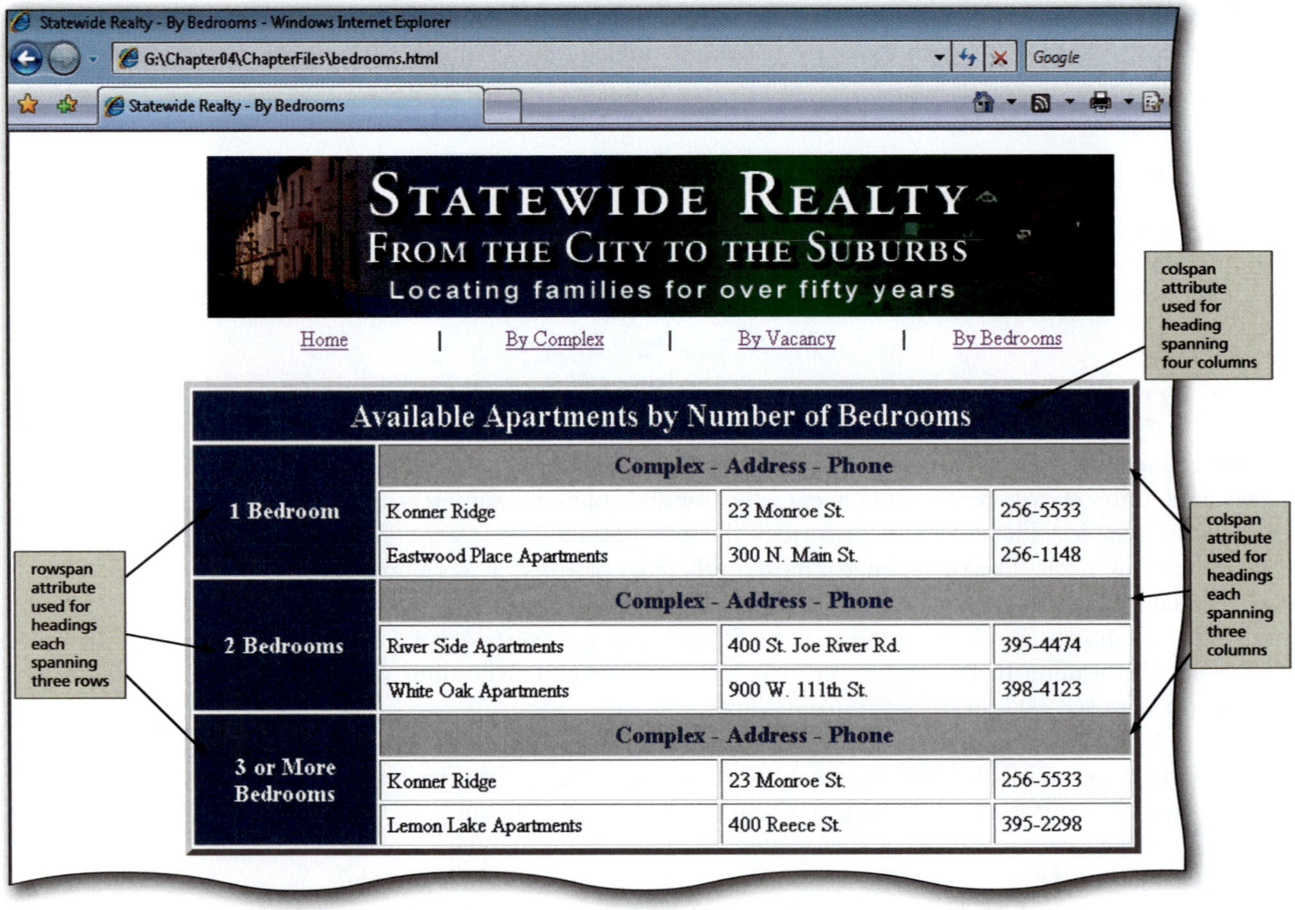

Statewide Realty - By Bedrooms - Windows Internet Explorer

G:\Chapter04\ChapterFiles\bedrooms.html

Google

Statewide Realty - By Bedrooms

STATEWIDE REALTY

FROM THE CITY TO THE SUBURBS

Locating families for over fifty years

Home | By Complex | By Vacancy | By Bedrooms

colspan attribute used for heading spanning four columns

Available Apartments by Number of Bedrooms			
1 Bedroom	Complex - Address - Phone		
	Konner Ridge	23 Monroe St.	256-5533
	Eastwood Place Apartments	300 N. Main St.	256-1148
2 Bedrooms	Complex - Address - Phone		
	River Side Apartments	400 St. Joe River Rd.	395-4474
	White Oak Apartments	900 W. 111th St.	398-4123
3 or More Bedrooms	Complex - Address - Phone		
	Konner Ridge	23 Monroe St.	256-5533
	Lemon Lake Apartments	400 Reece St.	395-2298

rowspan attribute used for headings each spanning three rows

colspan attribute used for headings each spanning three columns

Figure 4–37 By Bedrooms Web page after enhancements.

The first step when deciding to span rows or columns is to sketch the table design on a piece of paper, as shown in Figure 4–38. The table organizes available apartments by number of bedrooms and thus should have a main heading, such as Available Apartments by Number of Bedrooms. Three different numbers of bedrooms are represented by the information in the rows: 1 Bedroom, 2 Bedrooms, and 3 or More Bedrooms. The columns in the table also require subheadings to indicate what information is included about each apartment.

Row and Column Spanning
Creating headings that span rows and columns defines tables more clearly. For more information about row and column spanning, search the Web. Many HTML tutorials have good suggestions for the use of column and row spanning.

Available Apartments by Number of Bedrooms			
1 Bedroom	Complex - Address - Phone		
	Konner Ridge	23 Monroe St.	256-5533
	Eastwood Place Apartments	300 N. Main St.	256-1148
2 Bedrooms	Complex - Address - Phone		
	River Side Apartments	400 St. Joe River Rd.	395-4474
	White Oak Apartments	900 W. 111th St.	398-4123
3 or More Bedrooms	Complex - Address - Phone		
	Konner Ridge	23 Monroe St.	256-5533
	Lemon Lake Apartments	400 Reece St.	395-2298

Figure 4–38

After defining the main sections of a table, you must determine how many rows or columns each heading should span. For example, the title heading for the table (Available Apartments by Number of Bedrooms) should span all four table columns. The heading for the first main section (1 Bedroom) should span three rows, while the heading for the second section (2 Bedrooms) also should span three rows. Finally, the heading for the third main section (3 or More Bedrooms) should span three rows. The row headings, Complex - Address - Phone, should span three columns.

In the following steps you open the file, bedrooms.html, and add rowspan and colspan attributes to create table headings that span rows and columns.

Plan Ahead

- **Determine whether to use row and column spanning.** The purpose of the table determines whether you need to add row or column spanning. If the content is broken into logical segments of information, you may need to include row or column spanning in order to make the content clear. If you decide to add row or column spanning, it is best to sketch your ideas on paper first. This could help you understand more clearly what tags you need to use where.
- **Determine if different colors are needed for backgrounds.** You can help visitors more easily read a table full of information by varying the background colors effectively. If you use the same color background for the same level (or type) of information, it can help visually organize the information. Again, you may have to use a light font color if the background color is very dark.

To Open an HTML File

- Click the vacancy - Notepad button on the taskbar.
- With the USB drive plugged into your computer, click File on the menu bar and then click Open on the File menu.
- If necessary, navigate to the Chapter04\ChapterFiles folder on the USB drive.
- If necessary, click the Files of type box arrow, click All Files, and then double-click bedrooms.html in the list of files to open the file in Notepad.

To Create the First Heading That Spans Columns

The first step is to create three headings that span three rows each in the body of the table. Figure 4–37 on page HTML 183 shows three occurrences of the (Complex - Address - Phone headings.) You use the colspan attribute to span three columns of the table for each heading. Table 4–7 lists the HTML code required to create a heading column that spans three columns.

Table 4–7 HTML Code for Headings

```
<th colspan="3" bgcolor="gainsboro">
<font color="#4b5781" size="+1">Complex - Address - Phone</font>
</th>
</tr>
```

The step on the next page illustrates how to enter HTML code to create a heading column that spans three columns.

1

- Highlight <!--Insert first colspan heading here --> on line 35.
- Enter the code as shown in Table 4–7 on the previous page (Figure 4–39).

Q&A I see that the new column heading has a background color exactly like one of the colors in the banner image. How did you figure out which color code to use?

Using advanced graphic editing software, you can select a color within an image by clicking with an editing tool on the color you want. You can then review the color code for the color selected and use that in your HTML code as the font color as shown in line 36. This same color code will be used later as the cell background color.

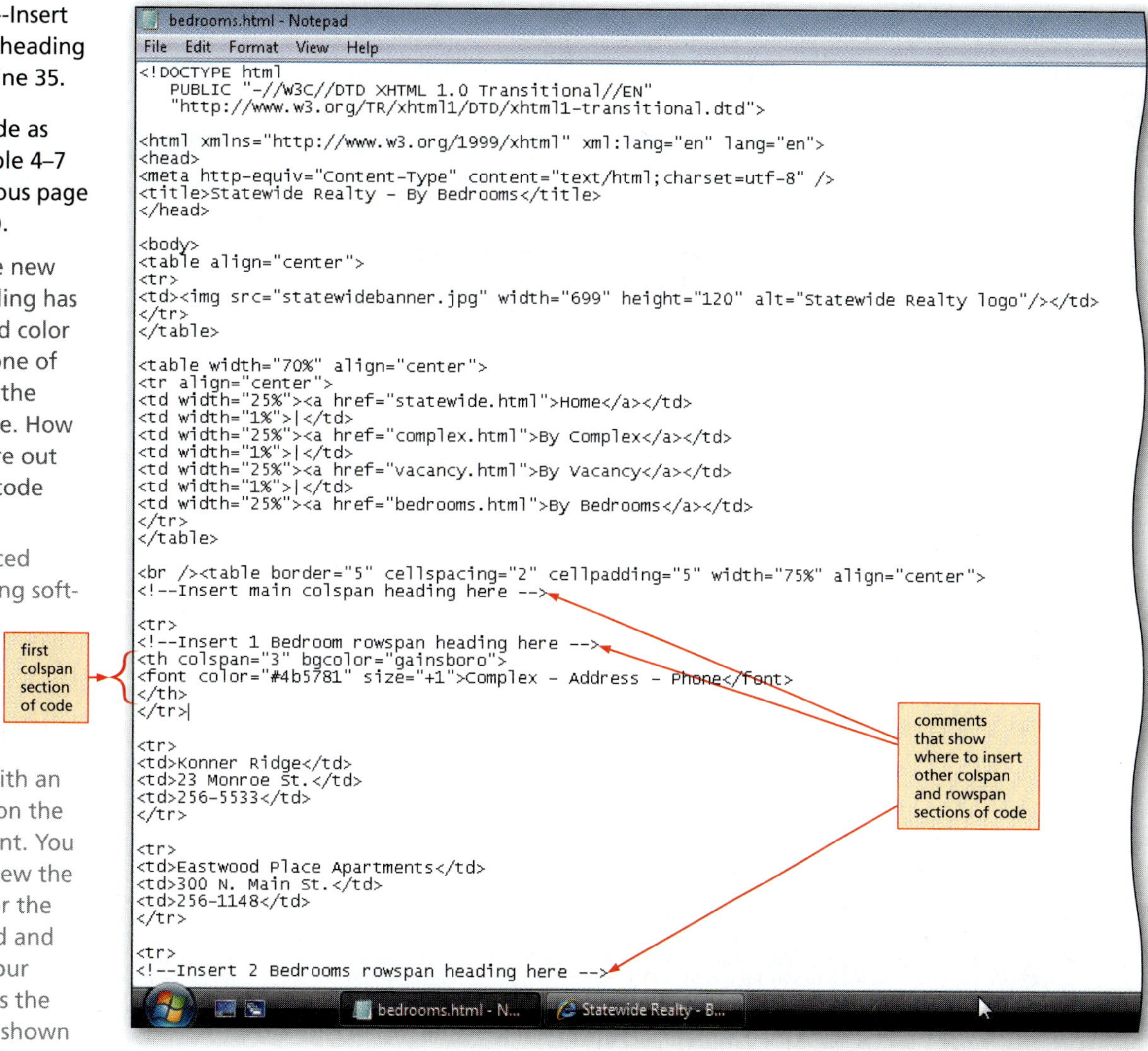

```
<!DOCTYPE html
   PUBLIC "-//W3C//DTD XHTML 1.0 Transitional//EN"
   "http://www.w3.org/TR/xhtml1/DTD/xhtml1-transitional.dtd">

<html xmlns="http://www.w3.org/1999/xhtml" xml:lang="en" lang="en">
<head>
<meta http-equiv="Content-Type" content="text/html;charset=utf-8" />
<title>Statewide Realty - By Bedrooms</title>
</head>

<body>
<table align="center">
<tr>
<td><img src="statewidebanner.jpg" width="699" height="120" alt="Statewide Realty logo"/></td>
</tr>
</table>

<table width="70%" align="center">
<tr align="center">
<td width="25%"><a href="statewide.html">Home</a></td>
<td width="1%">|</td>
<td width="25%"><a href="complex.html">By Complex</a></td>
<td width="1%">|</td>
<td width="25%"><a href="vacancy.html">By Vacancy</a></td>
<td width="1%">|</td>
<td width="25%"><a href="bedrooms.html">By Bedrooms</a></td>
</tr>
</table>

<br /><table border="5" cellspacing="2" cellpadding="5" width="75%" align="center">
<!--Insert main colspan heading here -->

<tr>
<!--Insert 1 Bedroom rowspan heading here -->
<th colspan="3" bgcolor="gainsboro">
<font color="#4b5781" size="+1">Complex - Address - Phone</font>
</th>
</tr>

<tr>
<td>Konner Ridge</td>
<td>23 Monroe St.</td>
<td>256-5533</td>
</tr>

<tr>
<td>Eastwood Place Apartments</td>
<td>300 N. Main St.</td>
<td>256-1148</td>
</tr>

<tr>
<!--Insert 2 Bedrooms rowspan heading here -->
```

bedrooms.html - Notepad
File Edit Format View Help
first colspan section of code
comments that show where to insert other colspan and rowspan sections of code
bedrooms.html - N...
Statewide Realty - B...

Figure 4–39

Q&A What does the “size= +1” attribute in the <font> tag do?

The +1 is a relative value for the font size that makes the font for the heading slightly larger than normal. This helps to call attention to the words in the heading.

To Create the Second and Third Headings That Span Columns

The simplest way to create the second and third column spans is to copy the code that you entered above and paste that code into the remaining sections designated for colspans.

- Highlight lines 35 through 38 (the lines that you entered above) and press CTRL+C to copy the selected lines to the Clipboard.
- Highlight <!--Insert second colspan heading here --> on line 55 and press CTRL+V to paste the selected lines from the Clipboard as shown in Figure 4–40.

```
bedrooms.html - Notepad
File  Edit  Format  View  Help
</tr>

<tr>
<td>Konner Ridge</td>
<td>23 Monroe St.</td>
<td>256-5533</td>
</tr>

<tr>
<td>Eastwood Place Apartments</td>
<td>300 N. Main St.</td>
<td>256-1148</td>
</tr>

<tr>
<!--Insert 2 Bedrooms rowspan heading here -->
<th colspan="3" bgcolor="gainsboro">
<font color="#4b5781" size="+1">Complex - Address - Phone</font>
</th>
</tr>

<tr>
<td>River Side Apartments</td>
<td>400 St. Joe River Rd.</td>
<td>395-4474</td>
</tr>

<tr>
<td>White Oak Apartments</td>
<td>900 W. 111th St.</td>
<td>398-4123</td>
</tr>

<tr>
<!--Insert 3 or More Bedrooms rowspan heading here -->
<!--Insert third colspan heading here -->

<tr>
<td>Konner Ridge</td>
<td>23 Monroe St.</td>
<td>256-5533</td>
</tr>

<tr>
<td>Lemon Lake Apartments</td>
<td>400 Reece St.</td>
<td>395-2298</td>
</tr>
</table>

</body>
</html>
```

second colspan section of code inserted

insert third colspan section of code here

bedrooms.html - N... | Statewide Realty - B...

Figure 4–40

2

- Highlight <!--Insert third colspan heading here --> on line 74 and press CTRL+V to paste the selected lines from the Clipboard. If the HTML file was saved and viewed in a browser at this point, the table would appear as shown in Figure 4–41.

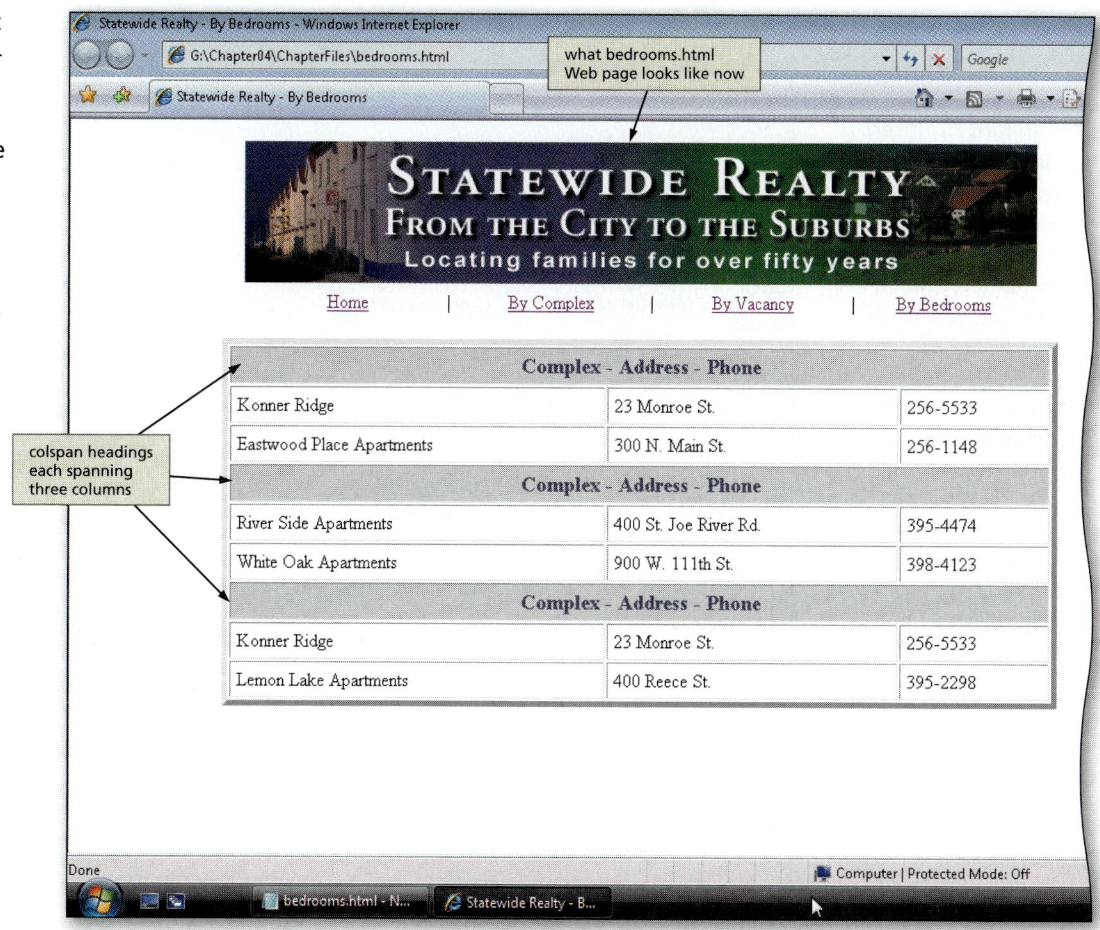

Figure 4–41

To Create the Headings That Span Rows

The following steps illustrate how to enter HTML code to create a heading that spans three rows.

- Highlight <!--Insert 1 Bedroom rowspan heading here --> on line 34.
- Type `<th rowspan="3" width="20%" bgcolor="#4b5781">` and then press the ENTER key.
- Type `<font color="#ffffff" size="+1"> 1 Bedroom</font>` and then press the ENTER key.
- Type `</th>` and then press the ENTER key (Figure 4–42).

```
bedrooms.html - Notepad
File Edit Format View Help
<!DOCTYPE html
   PUBLIC "-//W3C//DTD XHTML 1.0 Transitional//EN"
   "http://www.w3.org/TR/xhtml1/DTD/xhtml1-transitional.dtd">

<html xmlns="http://www.w3.org/1999/xhtml" xml:lang="en" lang="en">
<head>
<meta http-equiv="Content-Type" content="text/html;charset=utf-8" />
<title>Statewide Realty - By Bedrooms</title>
</head>

<body>
<table align="center">
<tr>
<td><img src="statewidebanner.jpg" width="699" height="120" alt="Statewide Realty logo"/></td>
</tr>
</table>

<table width="70%" align="center">
<tr align="center">
<td width="25%"><a href="statewide.html">Home</a></td>
<td width="1%">|</td>
<td width="25%"><a href="complex.html">By Complex</a></td>
<td width="1%">|</td>
<td width="25%"><a href="vacancy.html">By Vacancy</a></td>
<td width="1%">|</td>
<td width="25%"><a href="bedrooms.html">By Bedrooms</a></td>
</tr>
</table>

<br /><table border="5" cellspacing="2" cellpadding="5" width="75%" align="center">
<!--Insert main colspan heading here -->

<tr>
<th rowspan="3" width="20%" bgcolor="#4b5781">
<font color="#ffffff" size="+1">1 Bedroom</font>
</th>
<th colspan="3" bgcolor="gainsboro">
<font color="#4b5781" size="+1">Complex - Address - Phone</font>
</th>
</tr>

<tr>
<td>Konner Ridge</td>
<td>23 Monroe St.</td>
<td>256-5533</td>
</tr>

<tr>
<td>Eastwood Place Apartments</td>
<td>300 N. Main St.</td>
<td>256-1148</td>
</tr>
bedrooms.html - N...   Statewide Realty - B...
```

first of three rowspan headings

Figure 4–42

2

- Highlight <!--Insert 2 Bedrooms rowspan heading here -->.
- Type `<th rowspan="3" width="20%" bgcolor="#4b5781">` and then press the ENTER key.
- Type `<font color="#ffffff" size="+1">2 Bedrooms</font>` and then press the ENTER key.
- Type `</th>` and then press the ENTER key.

3

- Highlight <!--Insert 3 or More Bedrooms rowspan heading here --> .
- Type `<th rowspan="3" width="20%" bgcolor= "#4b5781">` and then press the ENTER key.
- Type `<font color= "#ffffff" size="+1">` `3 or More` and then press the ENTER key.
- Type `<br /> Bedrooms </font>`and then press the ENTER key.
- Type `</th>` as the end tag. If you save the file now, the Web page looks like that shown in Figure 4–43.

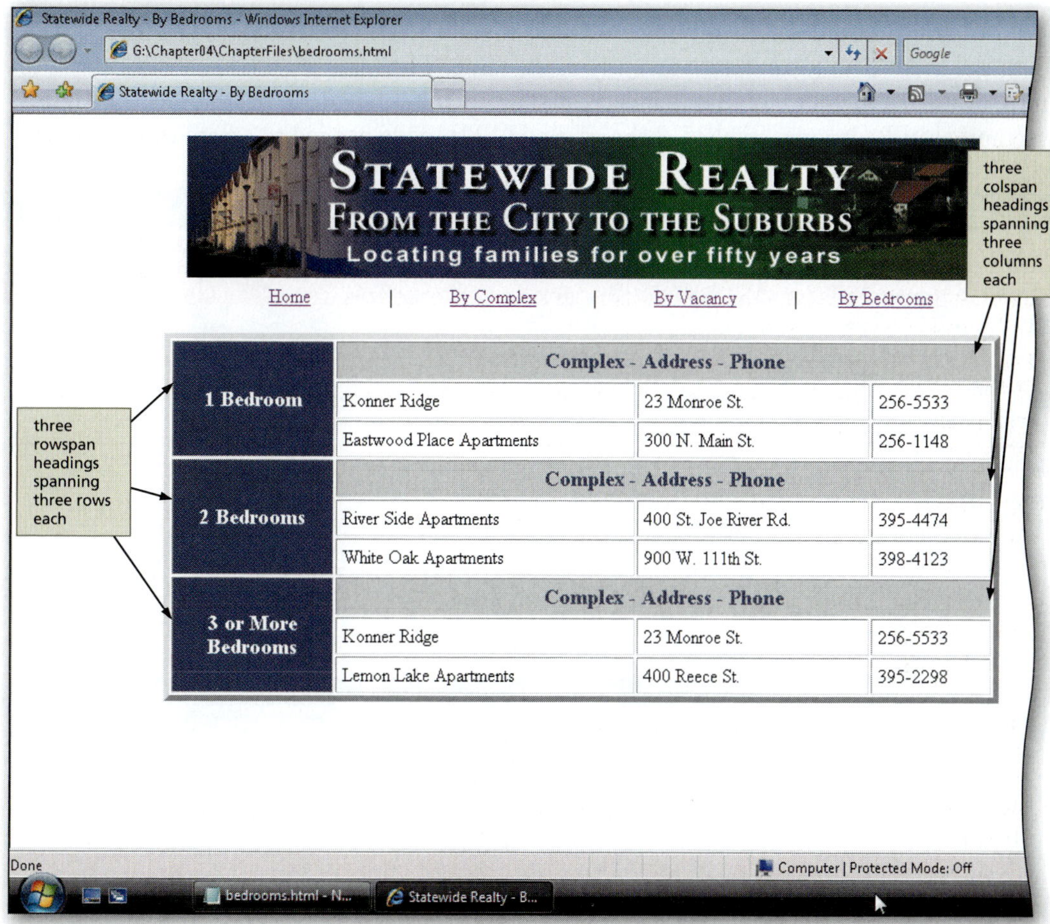

Figure 4–43

Q&A Why are we using a white font color (#ffffff) for the headings?

Because the background color is so dark (#4b5781), you could not easily read the heading if it was the default color of black. Changing the font color to white on a dark background color makes it easier to read.

Q&A Why did we use a <br /> tag in Step 3 above?

We wanted to maintain a consistent look in the rowspan text. Because the first two cells contain approximately the same number of characters (i.e., 1 Bedroom and 2 Bedrooms), we wanted to maintain that width for the cell. By using the <br /> tag, you move the word Bedrooms to the second line of the third heading cell.

To Span the Main Heading Across All Columns

As shown in the sketch in Figure 4–38 on page HTML 183, the main heading for the table is in a new row above the first row of text that is currently in the table. The main heading spans across all three of the existing columns, as well as the new column that is created on the left. The main heading has one line — Available Apartments by Number of Bedrooms. Table 4–8 shows the HTML code needed to create this heading.

Table 4–8 HTML Code for Additional Headings

Line	HTML Tag and Text
31	`<tr>`
32	`<th colspan="4" bgcolor="#4b5781">`
33	`<font color="white" face="chaucer" size="+2">Available Apartments by Number of Bedrooms</font>`
34	`</th>`
35	`</tr>`

The following step illustrates how to enter HTML code to create a main heading that spans all columns.

1

- If necessary, click bedrooms - Notepad on the taskbar.
- Highlight the <!--Insert main colspan heading here --> text on line 31.
- Enter the code as shown in Table 4–8 (Figure 4–44).

Q&A Why do we need the <tr> tag at the start of this code?

Entering the <tr> tag in Step 1 created a new row that contains the overall heading for this table.

Q&A I notice that all rowspan and colspan headings use <th> tags. Could we have had the same effect using <td> tags?

Because these are all used as headings, we wanted them to be bold and centered. Text contained within <th> tags default to bold and centered. If we had used <td> tags, the text would have been left-aligned and normal font.


```
<!DOCTYPE html
   PUBLIC "-//W3C//DTD XHTML 1.0 Transitional//EN"
   "http://www.w3.org/TR/xhtml1/DTD/xhtml1-transitional.dtd">

<html xmlns="http://www.w3.org/1999/xhtml" xml:lang="en" lang="en">
<head>
<meta http-equiv="Content-Type" content="text/html;charset=utf-8" />
<title>Statewide Realty - By Bedrooms</title>
</head>

<body>
<table align="center">
<tr>
<td><img src="statewidebanner.jpg" width="699" height="120" alt="Statewide Realty logo"/></td>
</tr>
</table>

<table width="70%" align="center">
<tr align="center">
<td width="25%"><a href="statewide.html">Home</a></td>
<td width="1%">|</td>
<td width="25%"><a href="complex.html">By Complex</a></td>

<br /><table border="5" cellspacing="2" cellpadding="5" width="75%" align="center">
<tr>
<th colspan="4" bgcolor="#4b5781">
<font color="white" face="chaucer" size="+2">Available Apartments by Number of Bedrooms</font>
</th>
</tr>

<tr>
<th rowspan
<font color
</th>
<th colspan="3" bgcolor="gainsboro">
<font color="#4b5781" size="+1">Complex - Address - Phone</font>
</th>
</tr>
```

Figure 4–44

To Save and Print the HTML File and View and Print the Web Page

1

- With the USB drive plugged into your computer, click File on the menu bar and then click Save to save the bedrooms.html file.
- Click File on the menu bar. Click Print on the File menu, and then click the Print button (Figure 4–45).

```
<!DOCTYPE html
   PUBLIC "-//W3C//DTD XHTML 1.0 Transitional//EN"
   "http://www.w3.org/TR/xhtml1/DTD/xhtml1-transitional.dtd">

<html xmlns="http://www.w3.org/1999/xhtml" xml:lang="en" lang="en">
<head>
<meta http-equiv="Content-Type" content="text/html;charset=utf-8" />
<title>Statewide Realty - By Bedrooms</title>
</head>

<body>
<table align="center">
<tr>
<td><img src="statewidebanner.jpg" width="699" height="120" alt="Statewide Realty logo"/></td>
</tr>
</table>

<table width="70%" align="center">
<tr align="center">
<td width="25%"><a href="statewide.html">Home</a></td>
<td width="1%">|</td>
<td width="25%"><a href="complex.html">By Complex</a></td>
<td width="1%">|</td>
<td width="25%"><a href="vacancy.html">By Vacancy</a></td>
<td width="1%">|</td>
<td width="25%"><a href="bedrooms.html">By Bedrooms</a></td>
</tr>
</table>

<br /><table border="5" cellspacing="2" cellpadding="5" width="75%" align="center">
<tr>
<th colspan="4" bgcolor="#4b5781">
<font color="white" face="chaucer" size="+2">Available Apartments by Number of Bedrooms</font>
</th>
</tr>

<tr>
<th rowspan="3" width="20%" bgcolor="#4b5781">
<font color="#ffffff" size="+1">1 Bedroom</font>
</th>
<th colspan="3" bgcolor="gainsboro">
<font color="#4b5781" size="+1">Complex - Address - Phone</font>
</th>
</tr>
```

Figure 4–45

- Click the Statewide Realty- By Bedrooms button on the taskbar.
- Click the Refresh button on the Standard Buttons toolbar. With this final colspan entered, the Web page now looks like that shown in Figure 4–46.
- Click the Print button on the Standard Buttons toolbar to print the Web page.

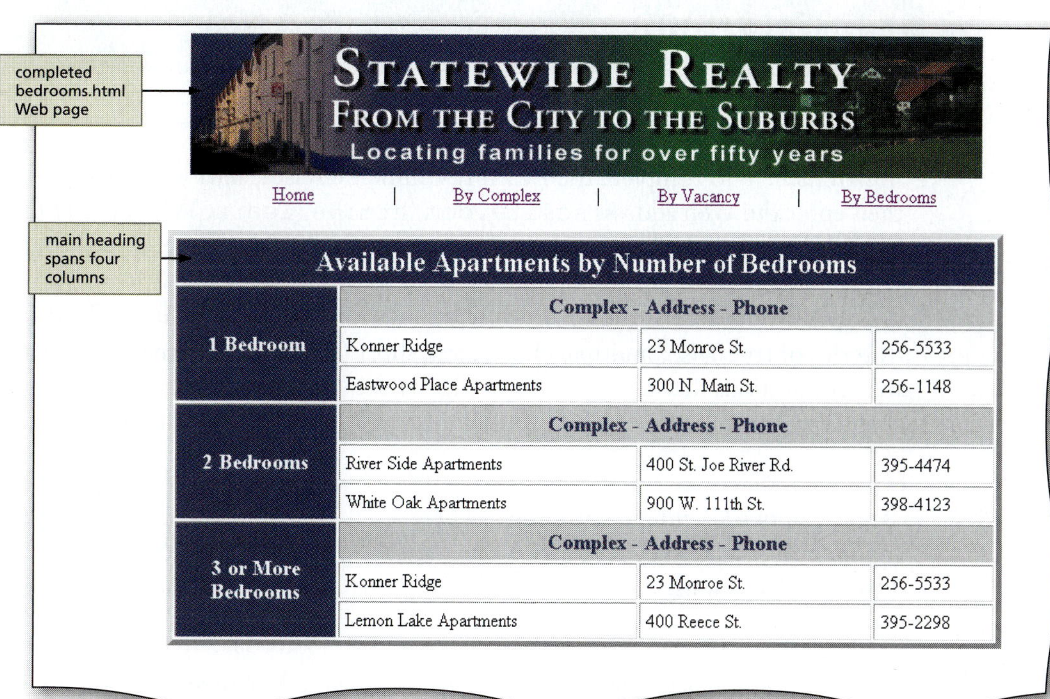

Figure 4–46

To Quit Notepad and a Browser

- Click the Close button on the browser title bar.
- Click the Close button on the Notepad window title bar.

Chapter Summary

In this chapter, you learned about table elements and the steps to plan, design, and code a table in HTML. You learned to enhance a table with background color, cellspacing, cellpadding, a caption, and headers that span rows and columns. The items listed below include all the new HTML skills you have learned in this chapter.

1. Create a Borderless Table to Position Images (HTML 159)
2. Insert Images in a Table (HTML 160)
3. Create a Horizontal Menu Bar with Text Links (HTML 162)
4. Add Text to a Table Cell (HTML 163)
5. Copy and Paste HTML Code to a New File (HTML 169)
6. Change the Web Page Title (HTML 170)
7. Create a Table with Borders and Insert Text (HTML 171)
8. Add Cellspacing and Cellpadding to a Table (HTML 179)
9. Add a Table Caption (HTML 180)
10. Create the First Heading That Spans Columns (HTML 184)
11. Create the Second and Third Headings That Span Columns (HTML 186)
12. Create the Headings That Span Rows (HTML 188)
13. Span the Main Heading Across All Columns (HTML 190)

Learn It Online

Test your knowledge of chapter content and key terms.

Instructions: To complete the Learn It Online exercises, start your browser, click the Address bar, and then enter the Web address `scsite.com/html5e/learn`. When the HTML Learn It Online page is displayed, click the link for the exercise you want to complete and read the instructions.

Chapter Reinforcement TF, MC, and SA

A series of true/false, multiple choice, and short answer questions that test your knowledge of the chapter content.

Flash Cards

An interactive learning environment where you identify chapter key terms associated with displayed definitions.

Practice Test

A series of multiple choice questions that test your knowledge of chapter content and key terms.

Who Wants To Be a Computer Genius?

An interactive game that challenges your knowledge of chapter content in the style of a television quiz show.

Wheel of Terms

An interactive game that challenges your knowledge of chapter key terms in the style of the television show, *Wheel of Fortune*.

Crossword Puzzle Challenge

A crossword puzzle that challenges your knowledge of key terms presented in the chapter.

Apply Your Knowledge

Reinforce the skills and apply the concepts you learned in this chapter.

Editing a Table on a Web Page

Instructions: Start Notepad. Open the file apply4-1.html from the Chapter04\Apply folder of the Data Files for Students. See the inside back cover of this book for instructions on downloading the Data Files for Students, or contact your instructor for information about accessing the required files.

The apply4-1.html file is a partially completed HTML file that you will use for this exercise. Figure 4–47 shows the Apply Your Knowledge Web page as it should be displayed in a browser after the additional HTML tags and attributes are added.

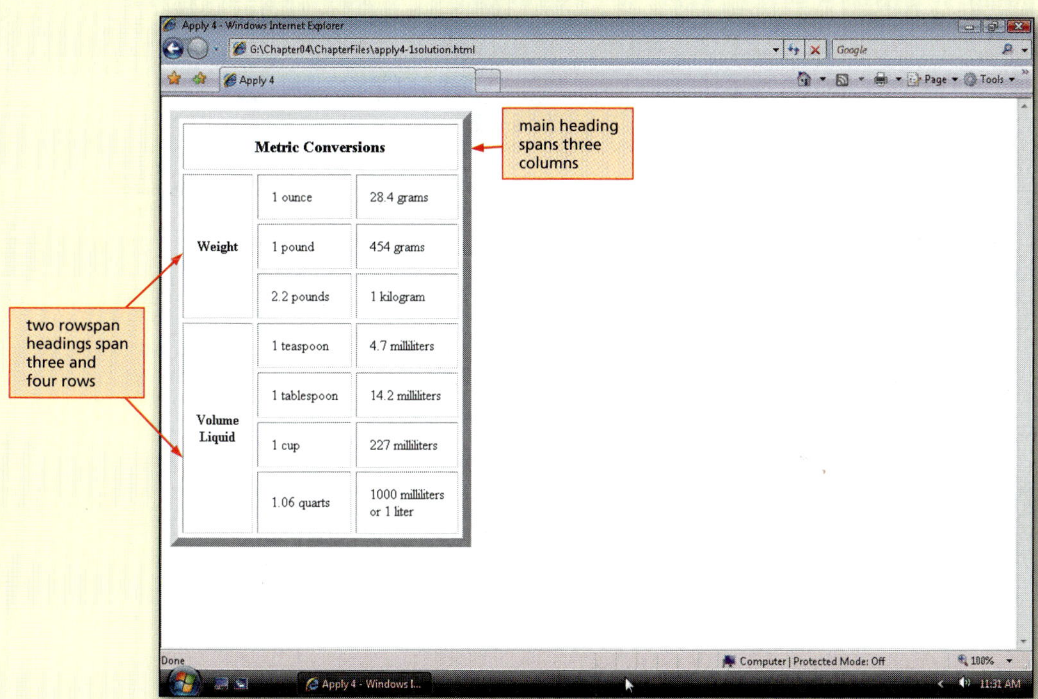

Figure 4–47

Perform the following tasks:

1. Enter the URL g:\Chapter04\Apply\apply4-1.html to view the Web page in your browser.
2. Examine the HTML file and its appearance as a Web page in the browser.
3. Add a border of 10, cellspacing of 5, and cellpadding of 15 to the table.
4. Add any HTML code necessary for additional features shown on the Web page in Figure 4–47. Your changes should include a main colspan heading that spans three columns of information and two rowspan headings that span three and four rows, respectively.
5. Save the revised file in the Chapter04\Apply folder using the file name apply4-1solution.html.
6. Print the revised HTML file.
7. Enter the URL g:\Chapter04\Apply\apply4-1solution.html to view the Web page in your browser.
8. Print the Web page.
9. Write your name on both printouts and hand them in to your instructor.

STUDENT ASSIGNMENTS

Extend Your Knowledge

Extend the skills you learned in this chapter and experiment with new skills.

Creating a Table with Rules

Instructions: Start Notepad. Open the file extend4-1.html from the Chapter04\Extend folder of the Data Files for Students. See the inside back cover of this book for instructions on downloading the Data Files for Students, or contact your instructor for information about accessing the required files. This sample HTML file contains all of the text for the Web page shown in Figure 4–48. You will add the necessary tags to make this Web page display the table as shown in Figure 4–48.

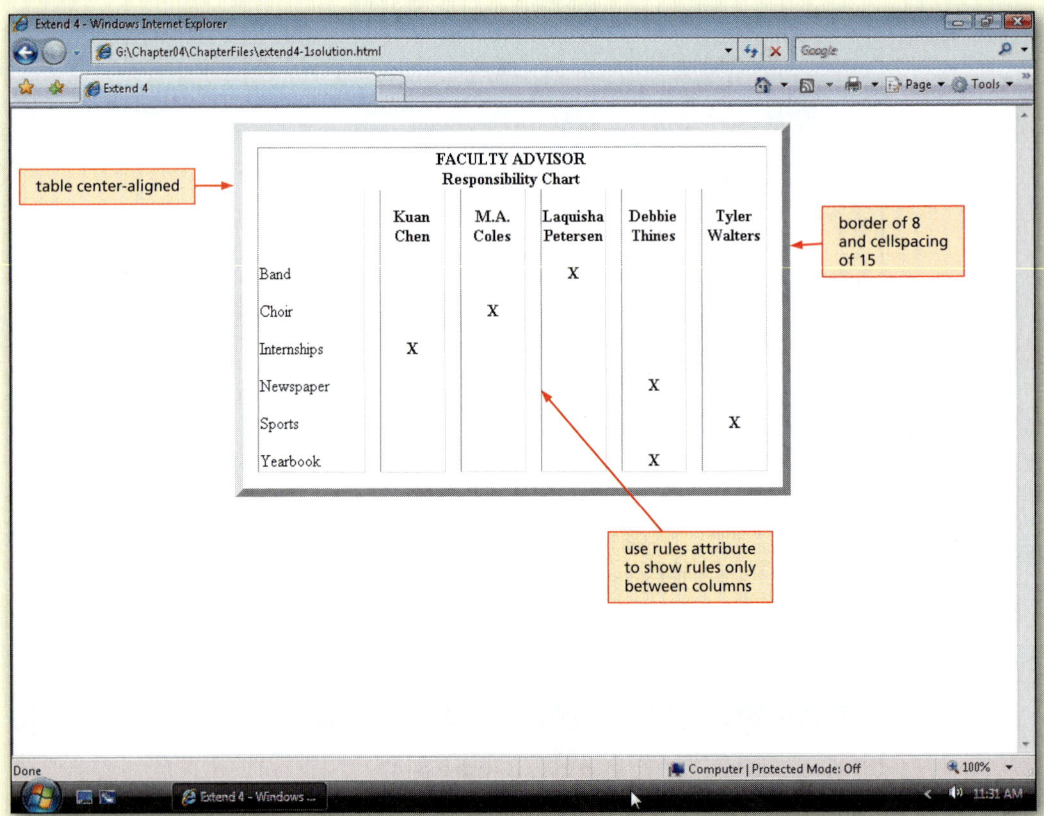

Figure 4–48

Perform the following tasks:

1. Add HTML code to align the table in the center of the Web page. Also give it a border of 8 with cellspacing of 15.
2. Insert the additional HTML code necessary to change the "rules" (see Appendix A) to only display columns. Add other table attributes not used in this chapter to further enhance the table.
3. Save the revised document as extend4-1solution.html and then submit it in the format specified by your instructor.

Make It Right

Analyze a document and correct all errors and/or improve the design.

Correcting the Golf Course Tournament Schedule

Instructions: Start your browser. Open the file makeitright4-1.html from the Chapter04\MakeitRight folder of the Data Files for Students. See the inside back cover of this book for instructions on downloading the Data Files for Students, or contact your instructor for information about accessing the required files. The Web page is a modified version of what you see in Figure 4–49. Make the necessary corrections to the Web page to make it look like the figure. The Web page should include the six columns of information with a main heading that spans across all six columns. The second row has a line break between the person's first and last name. (*Hint*: Use the <br /> tag.)

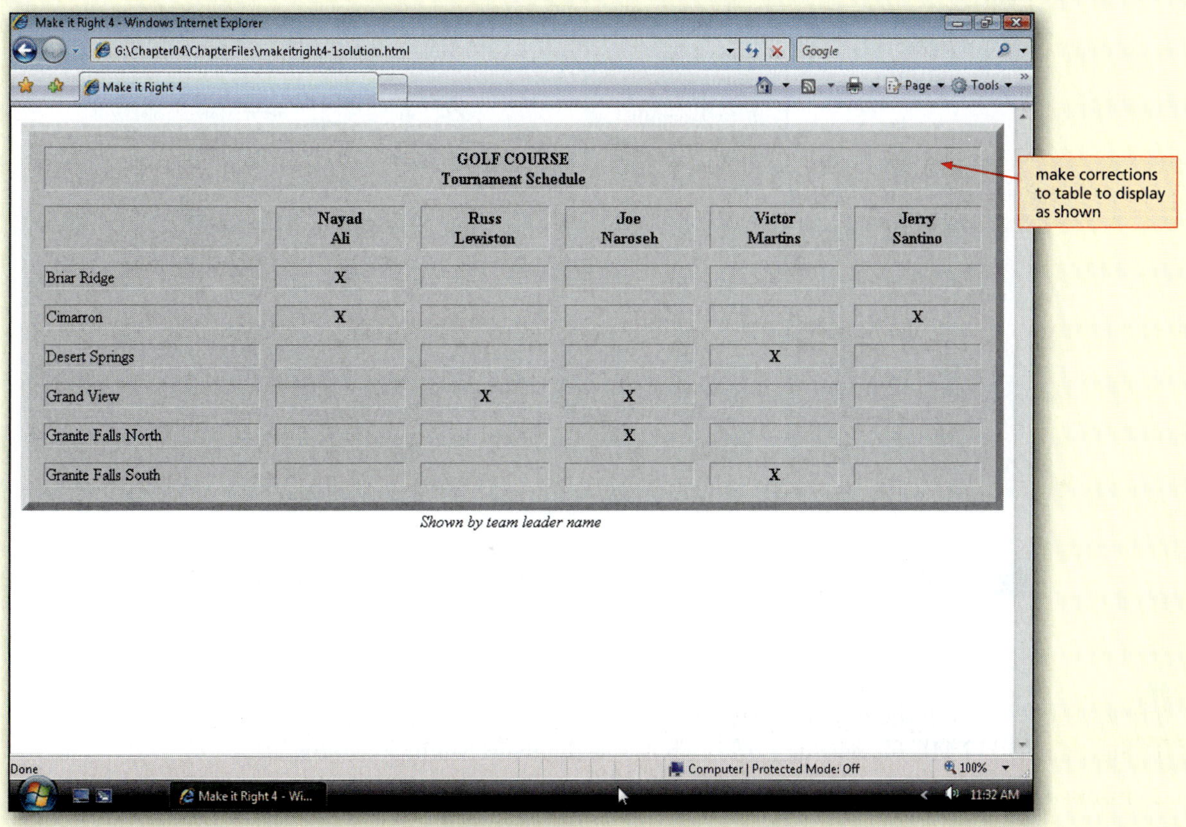

Figure 4–49

In the Lab

Lab 1: Creating a Table with Multiple Images

Problem: Statewide Realty wants to review customer service award logos for potential use on the home page and compare them with the Web page without an image. You have been asked to create a Web page that shows the four logo samples, similar to the one shown in Figure 4–50.

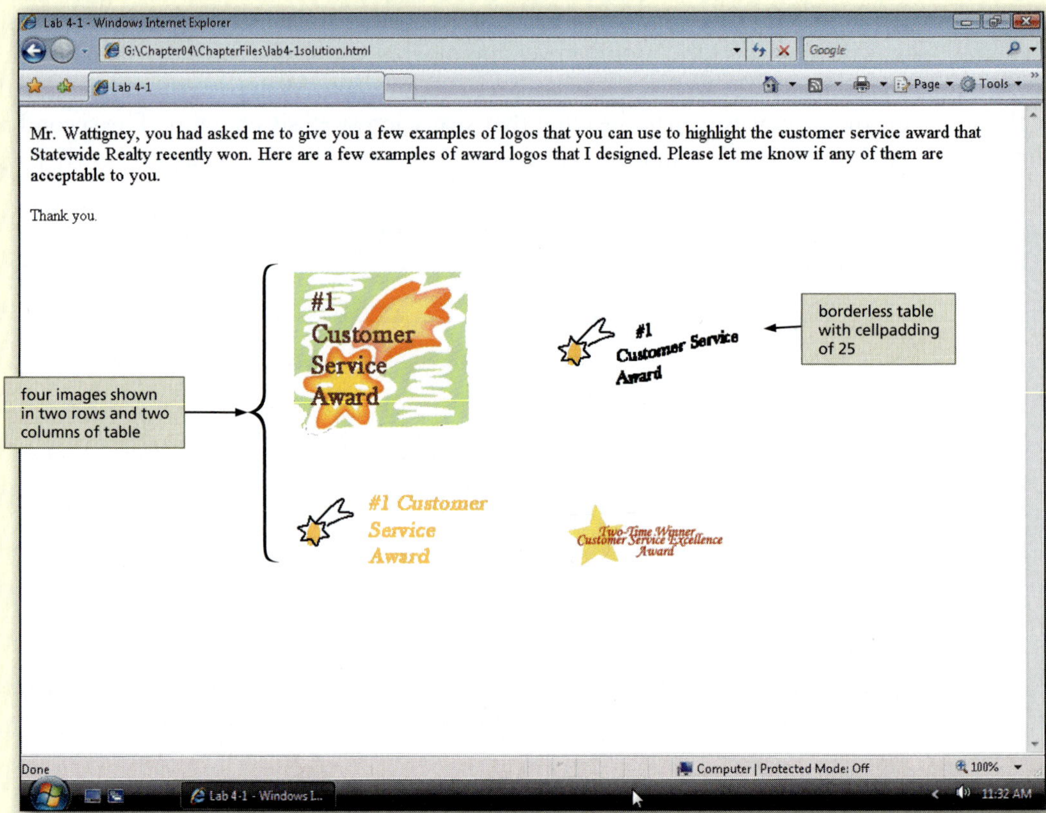

Figure 4–50

Instructions: Perform the following steps:

1. Start a new HTML file with the title Lab 4-1 in the main heading section.
2. Insert the text shown in the top lines of the Web page using a font size of +1.
3. Add a centered borderless table with two columns and two rows and cellpadding of 25.
4. Insert the image award1.gif in the first column of the first row. (*Hint*: You can use Microsoft Paint to determine the width and height of each image.)
5. Add the second image award2.gif to that same row in a second column.
6. Start a new row and add the images award3.gif and award4.gif.
7. Save the HTML file in the Chapter04\IntheLab folder using the file name lab4-1solution.html. Validate the Web page using the W3C validator service.
8. Print the lab4-1solution.html file.
9. Open the file lab4-1solution.html in your browser to view it as a Web page.
10. Print the Web page.
11. Write your name on the printouts and hand them in to your instructor.

In the Lab

Lab 2: Creating Two Linked Pages

Problem: Your manager at Voytkovich Antiquities has asked you to create two Web pages, similar to the ones shown in Figures 4–51a and 4–51b on the next page. The first Web page is a home page that presents information about Voytkovich Antiquities, together with two links. The Prices link on the first page will be linked to a price list of items found at the antiquities store. The second link, called Links, should direct the Web page visitor to another Web page of your choosing that has to do with antiquities. You may select a museum or another similar site of your choosing.

Instructions: Perform the following steps:

1. Start a new HTML file with the title Lab 4-2a in the main heading section.
2. Create a 50% wide, one-row, two-column borderless table with the image mask.jpg in the left-hand data cell and the words Voytkovich Antiquities (use the <br /> tag between those words) in an olive color and size 7 in the right-hand data cell.
3. Create a second one-row, two-column borderless table. Make the first column 20% wide with a background color of dark khaki and then add two links to the column: Prices (lab4-2bsolution.html) and Links (which links to an antiquity Web site of your choosing). Make the second column 80% wide and include the text and an e-mail link as shown in Figure 4–51a.
4. Save the HTML file using the file name lab4-2asolution.html in the Chapter04\IntheLab folder. Print the HTML file.
5. Start a new HTML file with the title [Your name] Lab 4-2b in the main heading section.
6. Create a five-row, two-column table with a five-pixel border, cellpadding of 15, and cellspacing of 5. Use dark khaki for the background color of the top row.
7. Span the first heading across both columns, as shown in Figure 4–51b.
8. Enter the headings, Item and Price, and additional information in the appropriate table cells, as shown in Figure 4–51b. Make sure to include a link (font size of -1) back to the home page.
9. Save the HTML file in the Chapter04\IntheLab folder using the file name lab4-2bsolution.html. Print the HTML file. Validate the file using the W3C validator service.
10. Open the file lab4-2asolution.html in your browser and test the Prices link to verify it links to the lab4-2bsolution.htm Web page.
11. Print both Web pages.
12. Write your name on all printouts and hand them in to your instructor.

Continued >

In the Lab *continued*

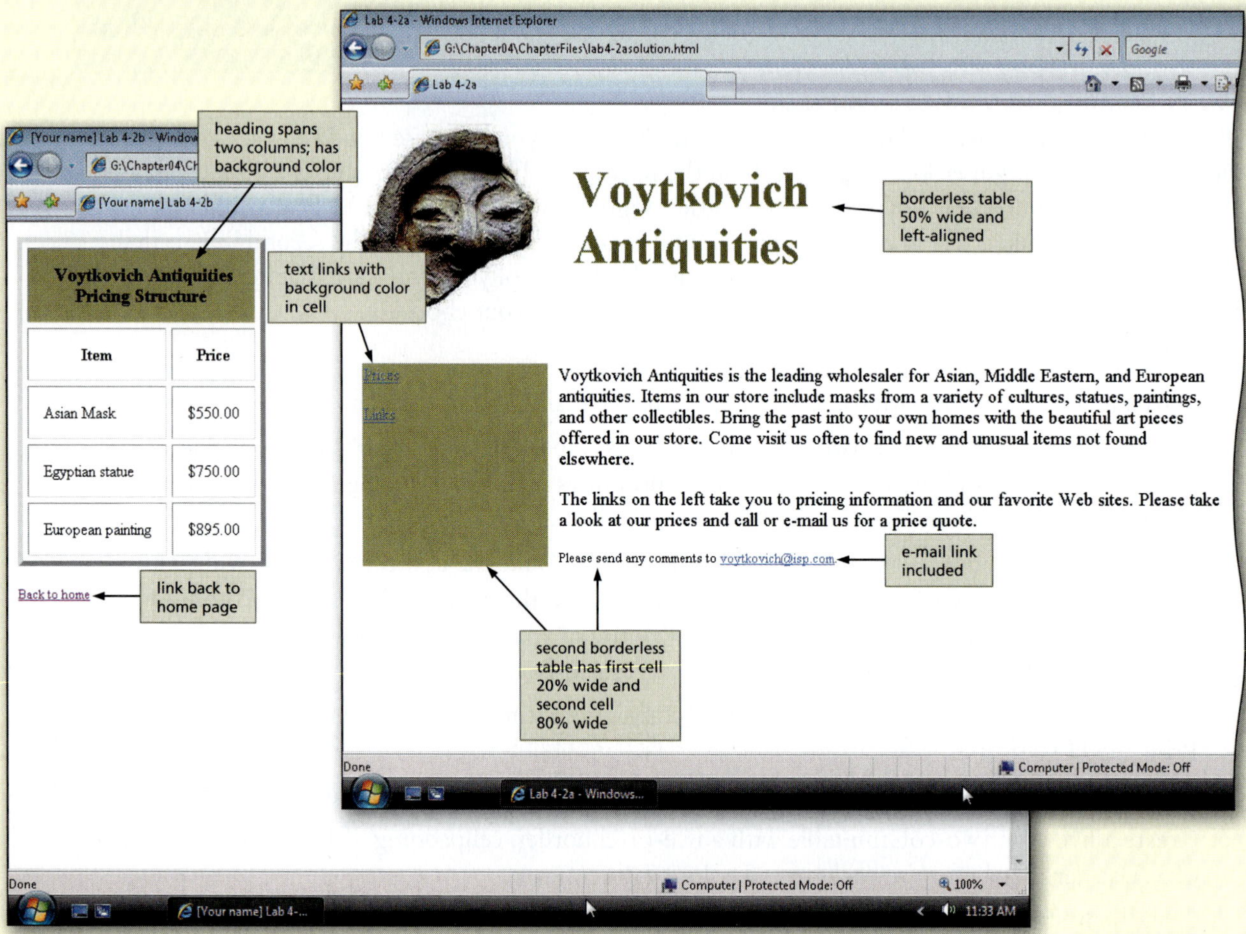

Figure 4–51

In the Lab

Lab 3: Creating Linked Schedules

Problem: You want to create two Web pages that list your school, study, volunteer, and work schedule, similar to the ones shown in Figures 4–52a and 4–52b. The Web pages will use tables with headings that span several rows and columns to organize the information and will include links from one page to the other.

Instructions: Perform the following steps:

1. Start two new HTML files with the titles Lab 4-3a and Lab 4-3b, respectively, in the main heading section.
2. In the Lab 4-3a file (School), create a bordered table with a menu bar as shown in Figure 4–52a. In the Lab 4-3b file (Work), create a borderless table in which only rows display (Figure 4–52b). (*Hint:* see the rules attribute.)
3. Include the headings and data cells as shown in both pages, with valid information in the data cells.
4. Add background colors for cells, as you see fit.
5. Save the HTML files in the Chapter04\IntheLab folder using the file names lab4-3asolution.html and lab4-3bsolution.html, respectively. Print the HTML files. Validate the file using the W3C validator service.

6. Open the file, lab4-3asolution.html, in your browser and test the Work link to verify it links to the lab4-3bsolution.html Web page. Test the School link to verify it links to the lab4-3asolution.html Web page. Print both Web pages from your browser.
7. Write your name on all printouts and hand them in to your instructor.

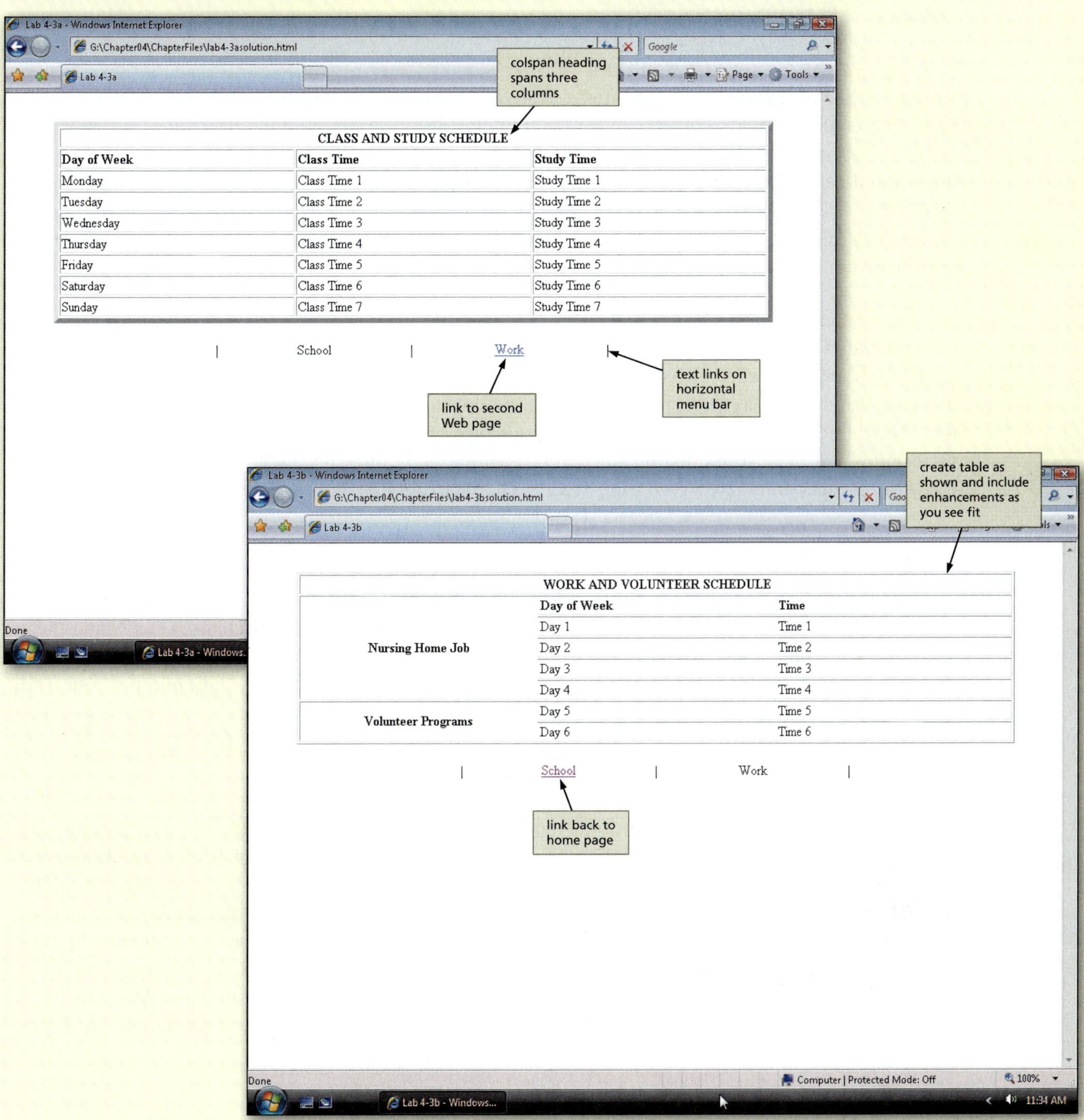

Figure 4–52

Cases and Places

Apply your creative thinking and problem-solving skills to design and implement a solution.

• Easier ••More Difficult

• 1: Add to the Statewide Realty Web Site

In the In the Lab 1 exercise, you created a Web page that includes four new customer service award logos that could be used on the Statewide Realty home page. After seeing the new logos, the management staff at Statewide Realty has asked you to modify the Statewide Realty home page to test the new logos and determine if one of them is a good fit. They also have asked you to insert a logo image on the three other Statewide Realty Web pages, so they can review how that would look. After modifying the Statewide Realty Web pages, have other students evaluate the new pages, comparing them with what was created in the chapter.

• 2: Finding Tables on the Web

Browse the Web to find three Web pages that contain borderless tables and three Web pages that contain tables with borders. To verify, you can check the Web page source code from within the browser. Print all six pages and indicate if these are appropriate uses of each type of table and why. Next, find three Web pages that do not use tables currently but that should, in your opinion. Determine how these pages might display their content more effectively with the use of tables. Print those three pages and sketch Web page designs that incorporate tables.

•• 3: Locating Color Charts on the Web

Chapter 2 and Appendix B contain charts of colors that can be used for Web pages. They both list the six-digit number codes for colors. Browse the Web to find Web pages with color charts that are created using tables. To verify, you can check the Web page source code from within the browser. Using these Web pages and Figure 2–27 on page HTML 60 as a reference, create a Web page with a table that shows at least 12 colors not listed in this chapter. For each cell, include the six-digit number code as the text and set the background color of that cell to the same six-digit number code.

•• 4: Creating a Time Schedule

Make It Personal

Your computer club wants you to create a table that lists meeting, open lab, and lab class times for the computer labs. Sketch a basic table format to use for this purpose and ask a few friends (or classmates) what they think. Once you have determined a good design for the Web page, begin to code the table needed. As you begin to build the Web page, you start thinking about other table attributes that could make the Web pages look even better. Create a Web page with a basic five-row, two-column table with a one-pixel border. Review the additional table attributes listed in Appendix A, including the rules attribute. Find information on those attributes on other Web sites, including the W3C Web site (*www.w3.org*). Modify the basic table on your Web page to incorporate at least four of these attributes.

•• 5: Creating a Gift Shop Web Site

Working Together

Double-D Web Design recently was hired to build a new Web site for a local gift shop. Your team is working on creating a basic four-page Web site to share with the owners for their input. On the home page, include a menu of items (Gifts, Cards, Engraving) and link those items to subsequent Web pages with more detailed information about each topic. On each linked Web page, use a table to organize lists of information related to each topic (Gifts, Cards, Engraving). Format each table slightly differently to demonstrate topics learned in this project, such as the use of the cellspacing and cellpadding attributes, the rowspan and colspan attributes, captions, background colors, and so on.

5 Creating an Image Map

Objectives

You will have mastered the material in this chapter when you can:

- Define terms relating to image mapping
- List the differences between server-side and client-side image maps
- Name the two components of an image map and describe the steps to implement an image map
- Distinguish between appropriate and inappropriate images for mapping
- Sketch hotspots on an image
- Describe how the x- and y-coordinates relate to vertical and horizontal alignment
- Open an image in Paint and use Paint to map the coordinates
- Create the home page and additional Web pages
- Create a table, insert an image into a table, and use the usemap attribute to define an image map
- Add text to a table cell and create a horizontal menu bar with text links
- Use the <map> </map> tags to start and end a map
- Use the <area> tag to indicate the shape, coordinates, and URL for a mapped area
- Change link colors

5 Creating an Image Map

Introduction

Many of the Web pages in Chapters 2 through 4 used the <img> tag to add images. In Chapter 3, an image also was used as a link back to the home page, by using the <a> </a> tags to define the image as the clickable element for the link. When an image is used as a link, as in Chapter 3, the entire image becomes the clickable element, or hotspot. With an image map, the entire image does not have to be clickable. Instead, one or more specific areas serve as hotspots. An image map is a special type of inline image in which you define one or more areas as hotspots. For example, each hotspot in an image map can link to another part of the same Web page or to a different Web page. Using an image map in this way gives Web page developers significant flexibility, as well as creative ways to include navigation options. Instead of using only text links, a Web page can include an image map that highlights key sections of a Web site and allows a user to navigate to that section by clicking the appropriate area of the image map.

Project — Southwest Map

Chapter 5 illustrates how to create an image map with links to other Web pages within the Southwest Map Web site. The Southwest Map Web site includes four Web pages, each linked to the home page using an image map and text links, as shown in Figure 5–1. In Chapter 5, you will create two of the four Web pages on the Web site: the home page (Figure 5–1a) and the Arizona Web page (Figure 5–1b). The Web pages shown in Figures 5–1c and 5–1d are included in the Data Files for Students. HTML tags are used to create the image map that supports the three clickable areas in the image. One of the key features of the Web is its support for graphics, so Web visitors expect to view many images on the Web pages that they visit. Images make Web pages more exciting and interesting to view and, in the case of image maps, provide a creative way to make navigational elements available to users.

BTW

Image Maps

Image maps are used frequently for Web site navigation. Many online HTML sources address the purposes of image maps and give suggestions for their use. An online style guide produced by the World Wide Web Consortium is available for use by Web developers at www.w3c.org.

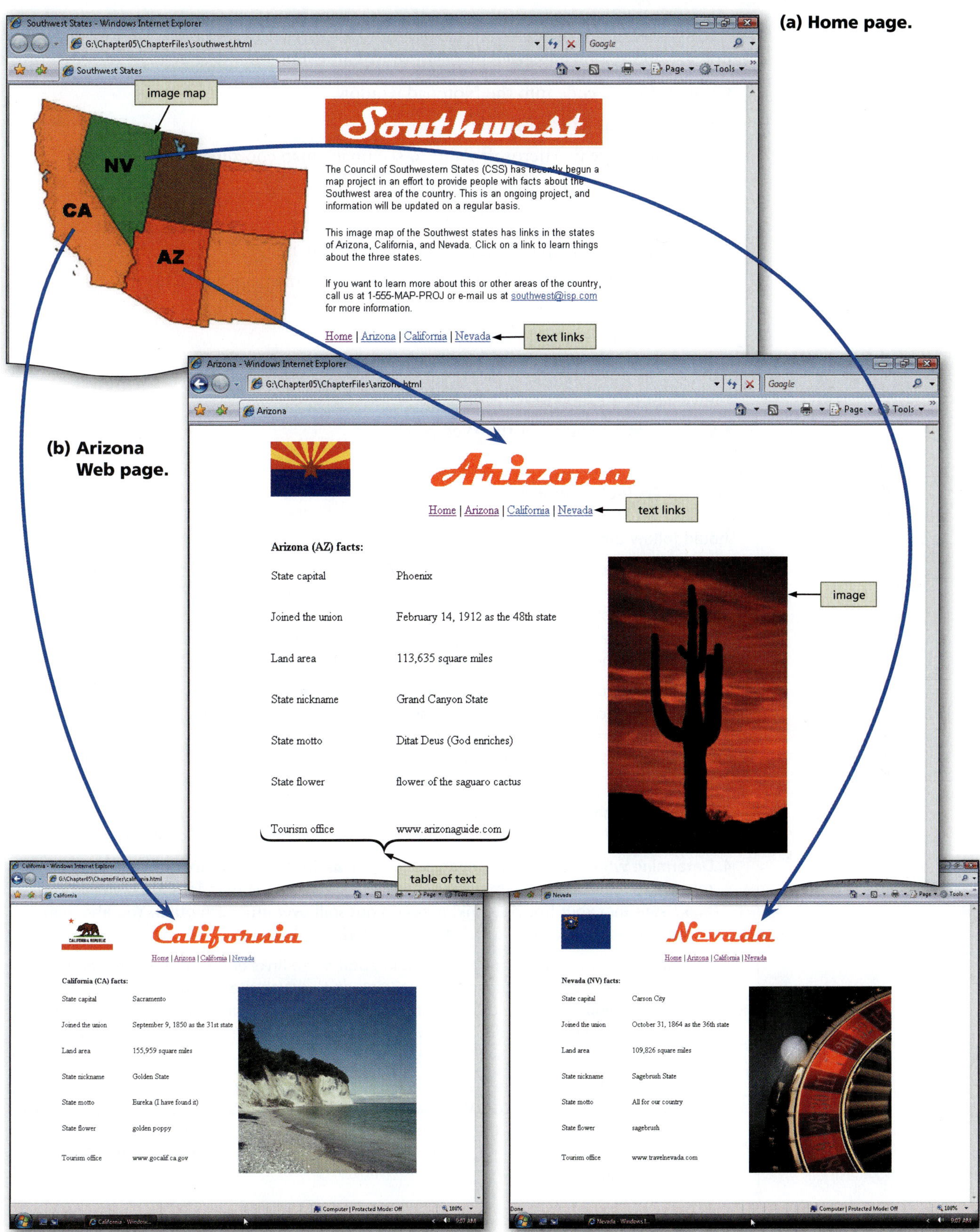

(a) Home page.

(b) Arizona Web page.

(c) California Web page.

(d) Nevada Web page.

Figure 5–1

Overview

As you read this chapter, you will learn how to create the Web pages shown in Figure 5–1 on the previous page by performing these general tasks:

- Enter HTML code into the Notepad window.
- Save the file as an HTML file.
- View the image in Microsoft Paint to see image map coordinates.
- Enter basic HTML tags and add text to the file.
- Insert an image to be used as an image map.
- Create an image map by mapping hotspots on the image.
- Create links to the other Web pages and to the home page with a horizontal menu bar.
- Add an e-mail link.
- Create a new Web page with tables of information.
- Save and print the HTML code.
- Validate, view, and print the Web pages.

Plan Ahead

General Project Guidelines

As you create Web pages, such as the project shown in Figure 5–1 on page HTML 203, you should follow these general guidelines:

1. **Plan the Web site.** As always, you should plan a multiple-page Web site before your begin to write your HTML code. Refer to Table 1–4 on pages HTML 12 and 13 for information on the planning phase of the Web Development Life Cycle. In this phase, you determine the purpose of the Web site, identify the users of the site and their computing environment, and decide who owns the information on the Web page.
2. **Analyze the need.** In the analysis phase of the Web Development Life Cycle, you should analyze what content to include on the Web page. The Web development project in Chapter 5 is different than the one completed in other chapters because it contains an image map. Part of the analysis phase then includes determining what image to use and where to put links within the image map.
3. **Choose the image.** You need to select an image that has distinguishable areas that can be used as links. Not all images are conducive to image mapping, as described in the chapter.
4. **Determine what areas of the image map to use as links.** Once an appropriate image is selected, you need to determine how to divide up the image map for links. You want to make sure that your hotspot (link) areas do not spill over into each other. You also want to make sure that the links are clearly separated.
5. **Establish what other links are necessary.** In addition to links between the home page and secondary Web pages, you need an e-mail link on this Web site. It is a general standard for Web developers to provide an e-mail link on the home page of a Web site for visitor comments or questions. Additionally, you need to provide links to all other Web pages on the Web site (arizona.html, california.html, and nevada.html).
6. **Create the Web page, image map, and links.** Once the analysis and design is complete, the Web developer creates the Web pages using HTML. Good Web development standard practices should be followed, such as utilizing the initial HTML tags as shown in previous chapters, providing text links for all hotspots in the image map, and always identifying alt text with images.

(continued)

Plan Ahead

(continued)

7. **Test all Web pages within the Web site.** An important part of Web development is testing to assure that you are following XHTML standards. In this book, we use the World Wide Web Consortium (W3C) validator that allows you to test your Web page and clearly explains any errors you have. Additionally when testing, you should check all content for accuracy. Finally, all links (image map hotspots, text links, and page to page within the same Web site) should be tested.

When necessary, more specific details concerning the above guidelines are presented at appropriate points in the chapter. The chapter also will identify the actions performed and decisions made regarding these guidelines during the creation of the Web pages shown in Figure 5–1 on page HTML 203.

Introduction to Image Maps

In this chapter, you use an image map to create three clickable areas within a single image, each with a link to a different Web page. All three of the clickable areas have a polygon shape. Figure 5–2a shows the borders of the three clickable areas, each of which encloses a specific area of the map. These outlines, although visible in the figure, are not visible on the Web page. A Web page visitor clicking anywhere within one of the polygonal shaped clickable areas will link to the associated Web page. Figure 5–2b shows areas that are not part of the clickable areas. Any area outside those clickable areas is not linked to another Web page.

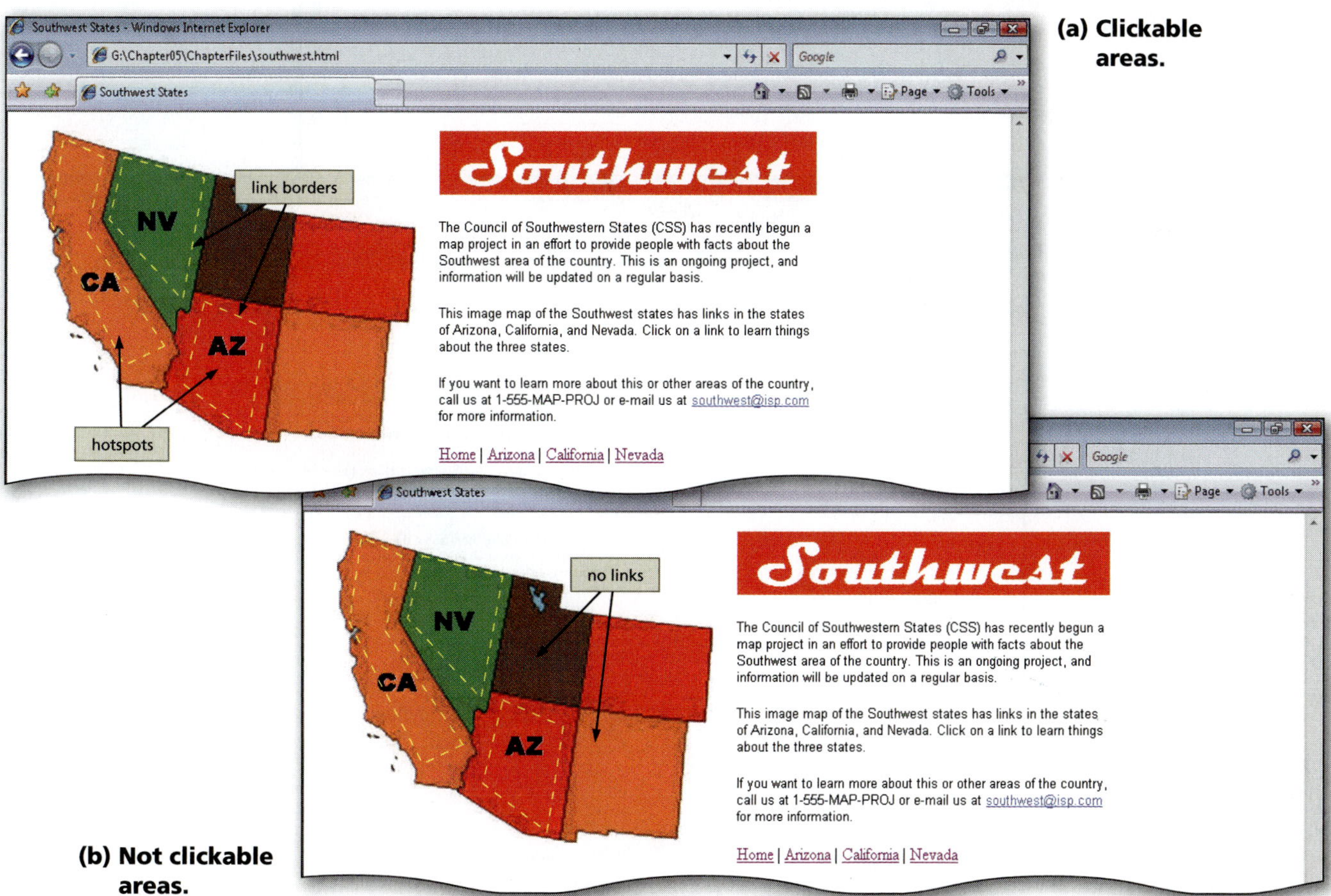

(a) Clickable areas.

(b) Not clickable areas.

Figure 5–2

Using Image Maps

One of the risks in using image maps to provide navigational elements is that if the image does not load, a user will not have the ability to navigate to other linked Web pages. Another potential issue is that using a large image for an image map can increase the amount of time required for pages to download over lower-speed connections. To avoid such performance issues, some people turn off the viewing of images when they browse Web pages, electing to display only text in their browsers. These users, and users of text-based browsers, also will not be able to navigate a Web page that relies on an image map. For these reasons, a Web page that uses an image map for navigation also should include text links to the URLs reflected in the image map, as shown in Figure 5–3a. Using text links in conjunction with the image map ensures that if the image does not download or a Web page visitor has images turned off, as shown in Figure 5–3b, a user still can navigate to other Web pages using the text links.

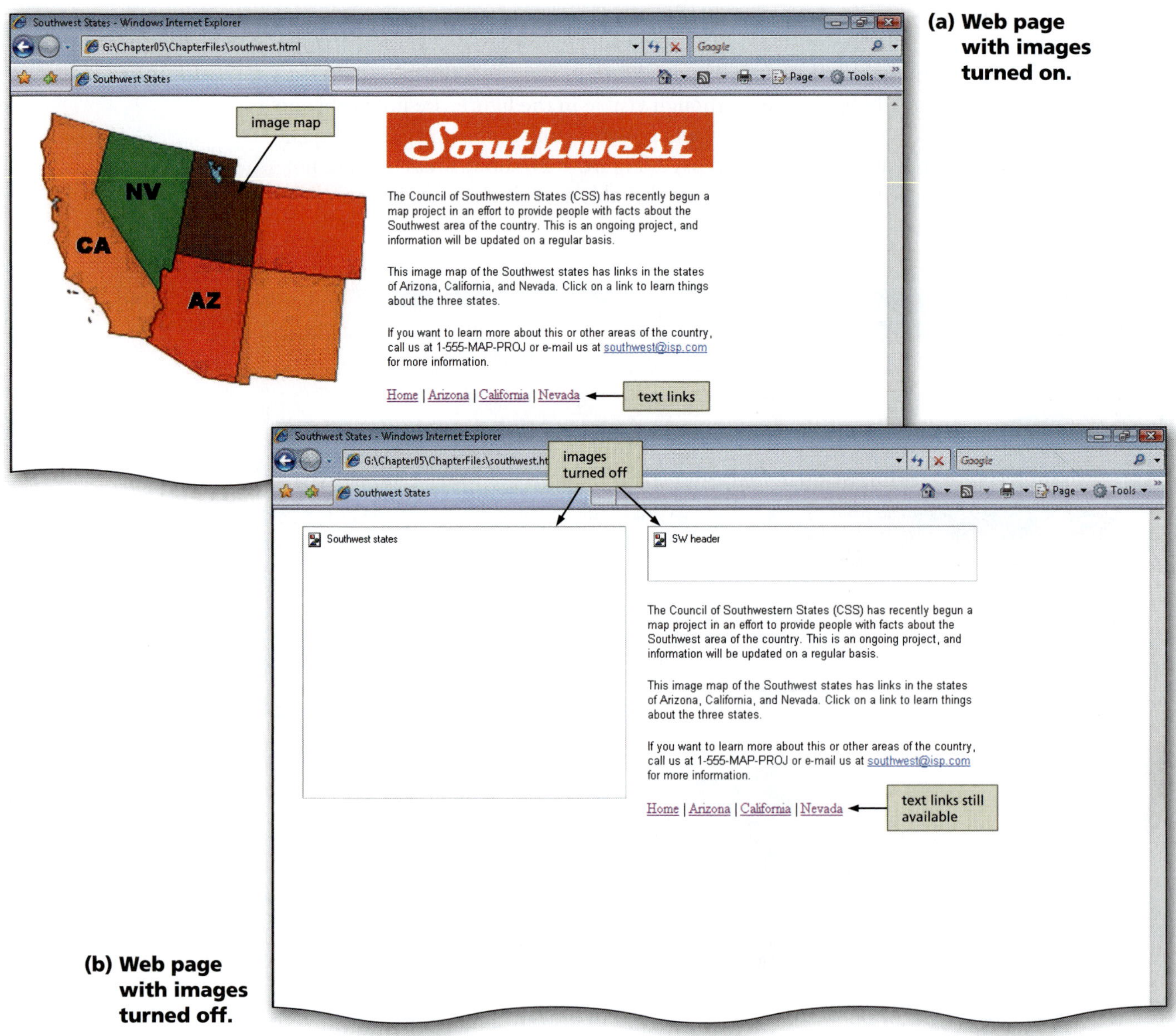

Figure 5–3

Image maps can enhance the functionality and appeal of Web pages in many ways. For example, an image map can be used as an **image map button bar**, which is a menu bar that uses graphical images, as shown in Figure 5–4. This makes the menu bar a more attractive feature of the Web page.

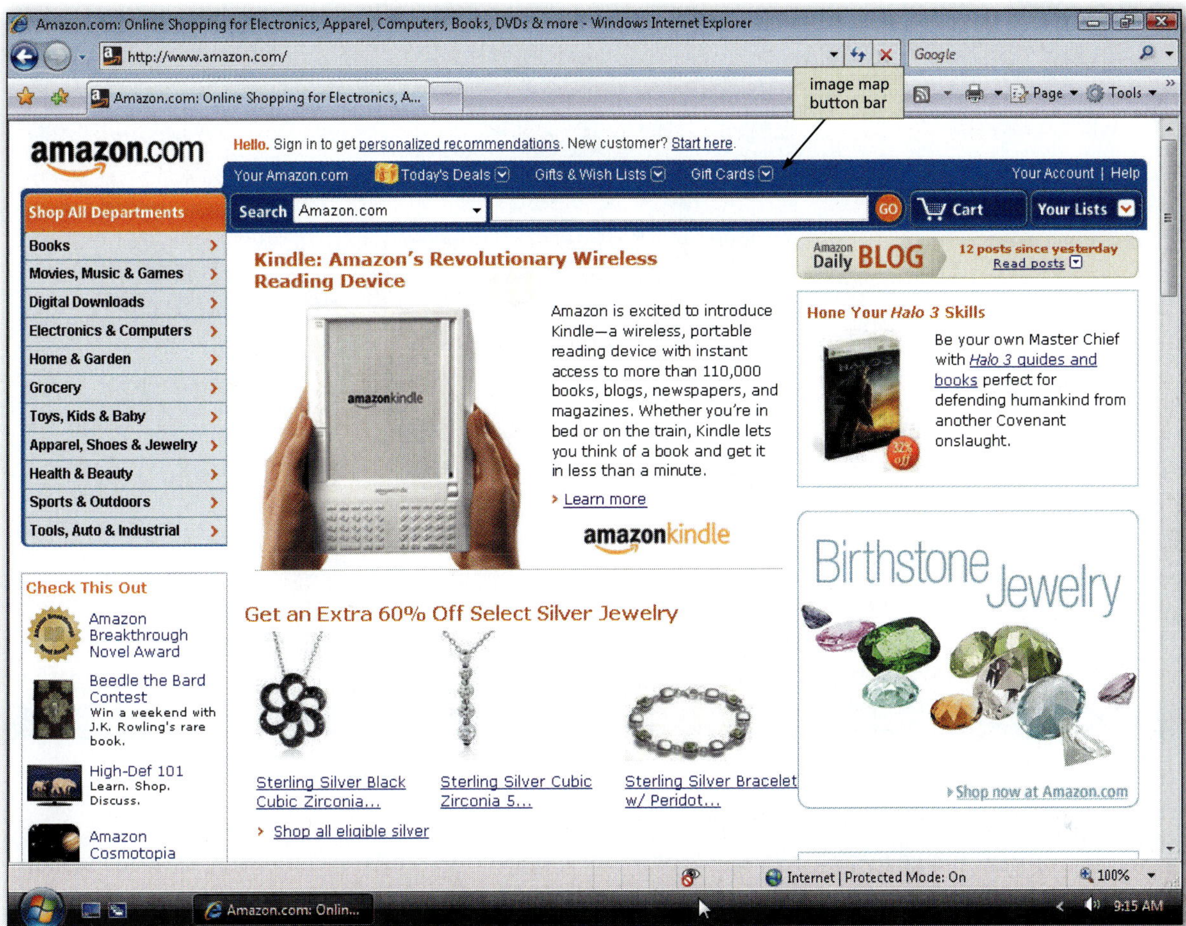

Figure 5–4 Image map on e-commerce site.

Image maps are also utilized to divide a geographical map into hotspots, as shown in Figure 5–5 on the next page. A Web page visitor can click a geographical area on the map and be linked to additional information about that location.

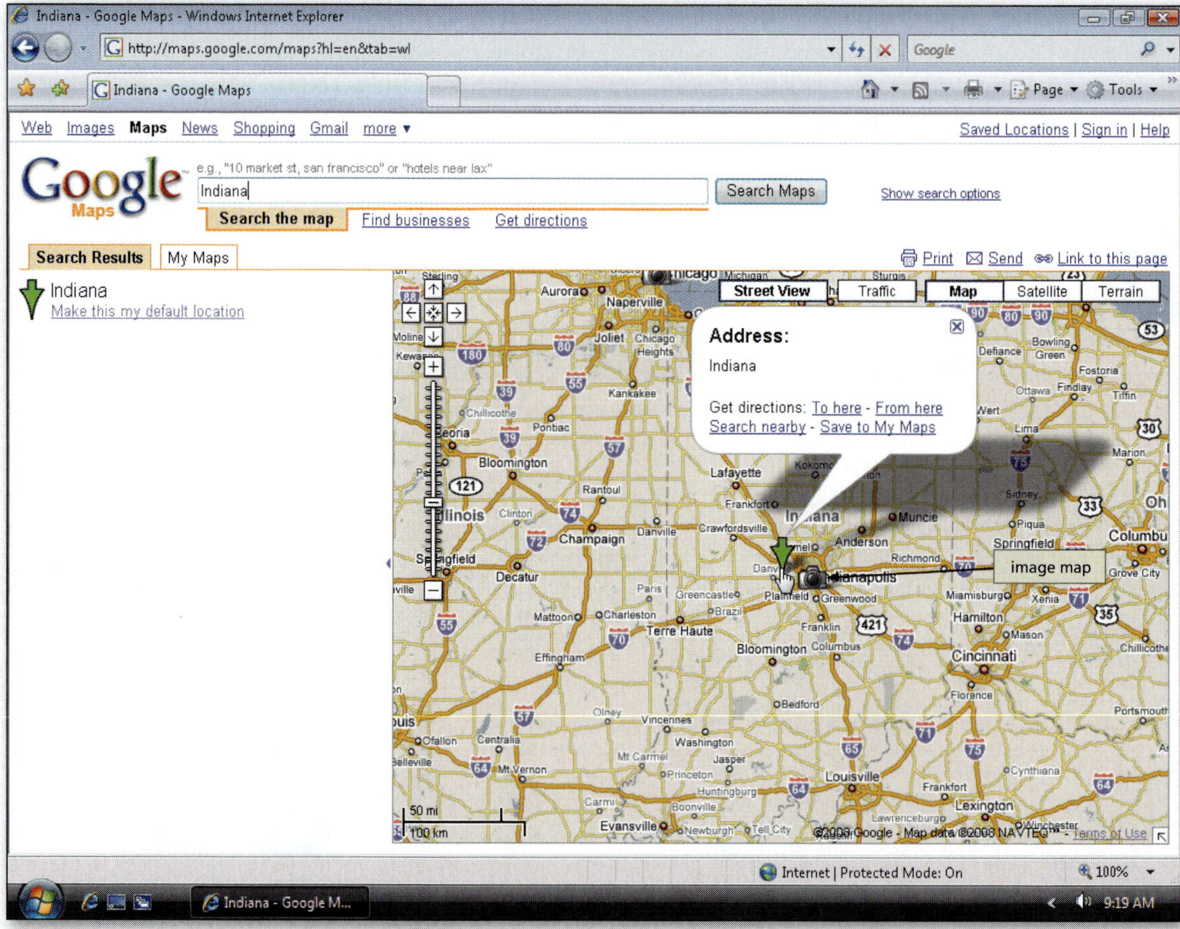

Figure 5–5 Image map on map Web page.

Image maps can be used for many applications. The travel industry uses image maps for many of their applications. For instance, the levels on a cruise ship (Figure 5–6a) can be used to link to the floor plan of a particular deck (Figure 5–6b).

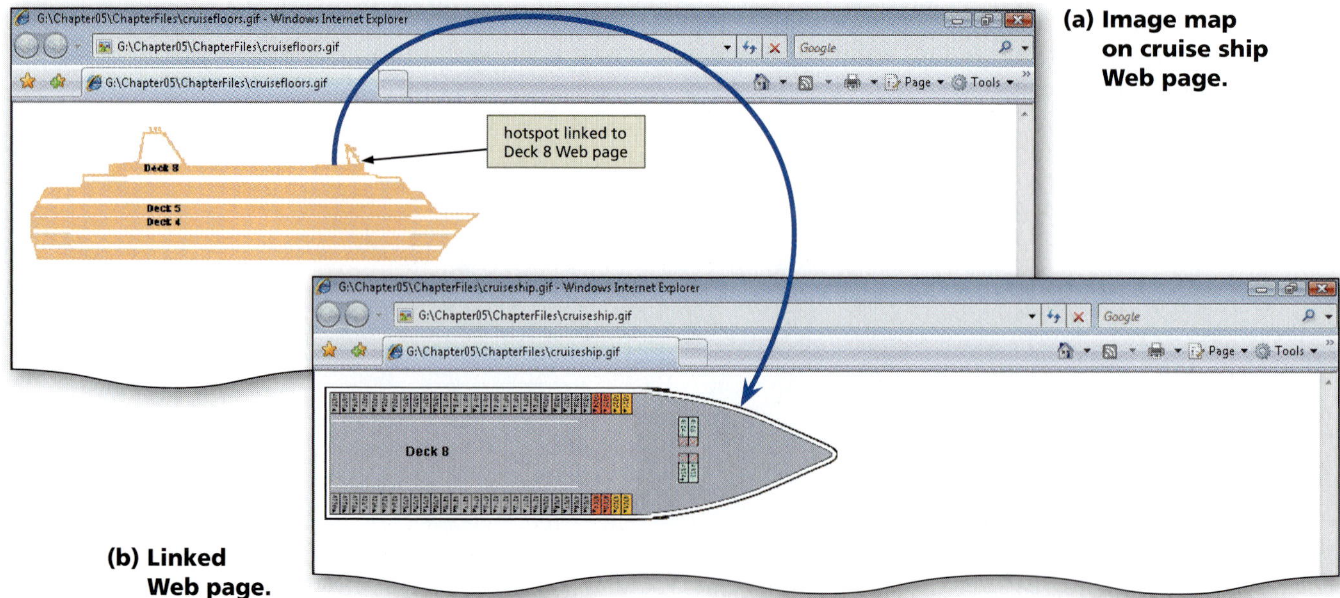

Figure 5–6

Organizations also use image maps to create hotspots that link different functional areas within a business or organization, as shown in Figure 5–7, to Web pages that contain more information about that specific area or department.

A company with several products or services can use an image map as a creative way to provide links to more specific information about those products or services (Figure 5–8).

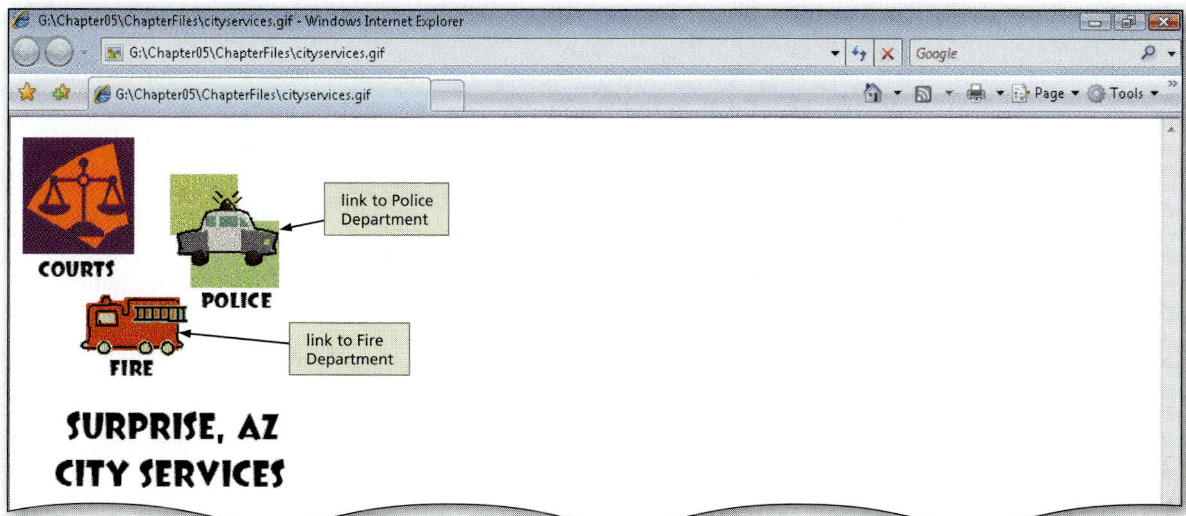

Figure 5–7 Image map on municipal Web page.

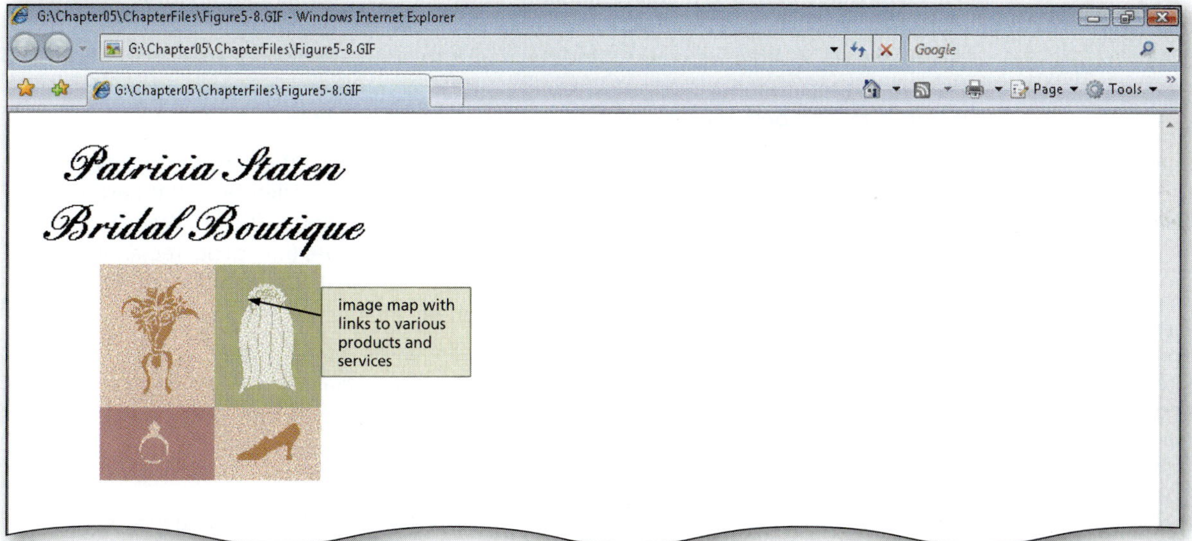

Figure 5–8 Image map on products and services Web page.

Server-Side vs. Client-Side Image Maps

Two types of image maps exist: server-side and client-side. In a **server-side image map**, the image is displayed by the client (browser) and implemented by a program that runs on the Web server. When a Web page visitor clicks a link on a server-side image map, the browser sends the x- and y-coordinates of the mouse click to the Web server, which interprets them and then links the visitor to the correct Web page based on those coordinates. Thus, with a server-side image map, the Web server does all the work.

BTW

Server-Side vs. Client-Side Image Maps
Web sites exist that provide information about server-side versus client-side image maps. To see an example of how image maps can be used for Web pages and which type is more efficient, search on "HTML image maps" in a Web browser search engine.

With a **client-side image map**, the browser does all the work. Most Web developers prefer to work with client-side image mapping, which does not have to send the x- and y-coordinates of the mouse click to the Web server to be interpreted. Instead, the coordinates are included in the HTML file along with the URL to which to link. When a visitor to a Web page clicks within a client-side image map, the browser processes the data without interaction with the Web server.

One advantage of server-side image mapping is that most, if not all, browsers support server-side image maps, while some older browsers do not support client-side image maps. Server-side image maps have disadvantages, however. They require additional software to be running on the Web server. That would then require that the server administrator maintain and update that server software on a regular basis. Also, an image map available on a particular Web site's server must be registered to the server before it can be used. Although this process is simple, it must be done. Further, all changes to that registered image map must be coordinated on the Web server, which does not allow for quick updates. Client-side image maps help reduce the load on the Web server, generally download faster, and provide faster response when a user clicks a link. In this chapter's project, you will create a client-side image map with three links on the home page of the Southwest Map Web site.

Plan Ahead

Understand the image map process.
Before inserting the graphical and color elements on a Web page, you should plan how you want to format them. By effectively utilizing graphics and color, you can call attention to important topics on the Web page without overpowering it. Creating a client-side image map for a Web page is a four-step process:

1. **Select an image to use as an image map.** Not all images are appropriate for good image mapping. Those images without distinct boundaries are not easy to map. Besides causing difficulty to the Web developer to find the points to plot, non-distinct areas make it difficult for visitors to see where one link might end and another begins. When choosing an image to map, choose wisely.
2. **Sketch in the hotspots on the image.** It is sometimes good to print a copy of the image and draw the hotspot areas on top of the paper image. You can then take that hardcopy and review it while working with the image in the image editing software. When sketching (either on paper or in the software), determine what shapes (i.e., circle, rectangle, or polygon) make sense for the specific area that you want to link. Based on this determination, start the next step of plotting those areas on the image.
3. **Map the image coordinates for each hotspot**. This chapter explains what x- and y-coordinates you need to provide for every linkable area. One thing to consider is making sure that the linkable areas do not run over one another. This overrun ends up confusing your Web site visitors because they think they will link to one area, and the coordinates take them somewhere else.
4. **Create the HTML code for the image map**. Writing HTML code for an image map is different than anything that you have done thus far in the book. When you create an image map, you first insert the image itself and then identify the name of the map that you use later in the HTML code. Further down in the code, you actually use that name and identify the map areas that form the boundaries around the hotspot.

BTW

Server-Side Image Maps
When a hotspot on an image map is clicked, a special image map program that is stored on the Web server runs. In addition, the browser also sends the x- and y-coordinates to the Web server for the position of the link on the image map. Most, if not all, browsers support server-side image maps.

Creating an Image Map

An image map consists of two components: an image and a map definition that defines the hotspots and the URLs to which they link.

Selecting Images

Not all images are appropriate candidates for image mapping. An appropriate image, and a good choice for an image map, is one that has obvious visual sections. The USA map image shown in Figure 5–9a, for example, has distinct, easy-to-see sections, which serve as ideal hotspots. A user easily could select an individual area on the map to link to more information about each region. The image in 5-9b, however, would not be a good choice because the boundaries of the states are indistinct.

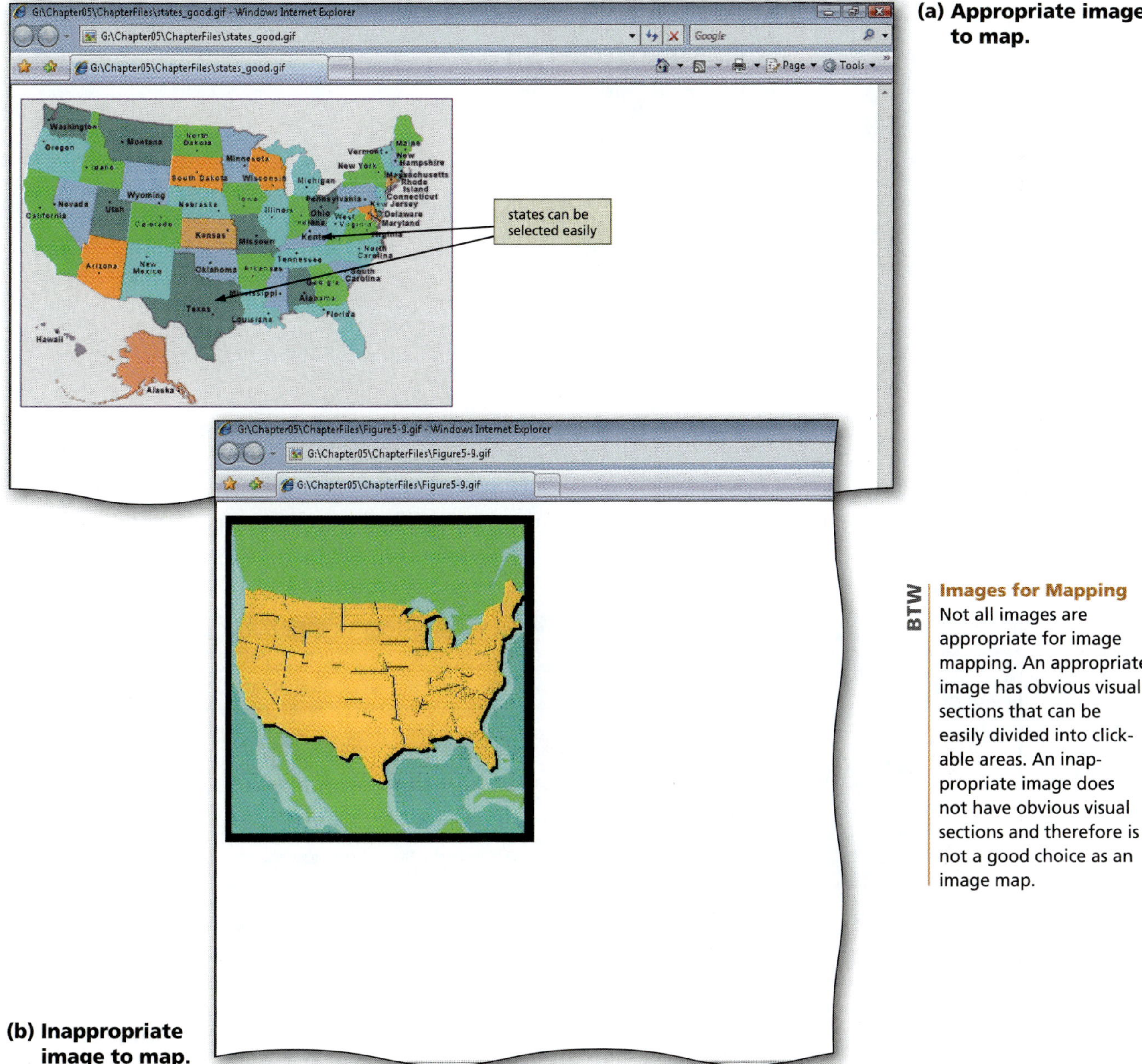

(a) Appropriate image to map.

(b) Inappropriate image to map.

Figure 5–9

> **BTW**
>
> **Images for Mapping**
>
> Not all images are appropriate for image mapping. An appropriate image has obvious visual sections that can be easily divided into clickable areas. An inappropriate image does not have obvious visual sections and therefore is not a good choice as an image map.

Sketching the Borders of Hotspots

After an appropriate image is selected for the image map, the next step is to sketch the hotspots (clickable areas) within the image. Figure 5–10 shows an example of an image map with the borders of the hotspots sketched on the image. A map of Europe is used, with two countries (Spain and Sweden) defined as hotspots. The image map thus will include a hotspot for two countries, each of which can link to a different Web page.

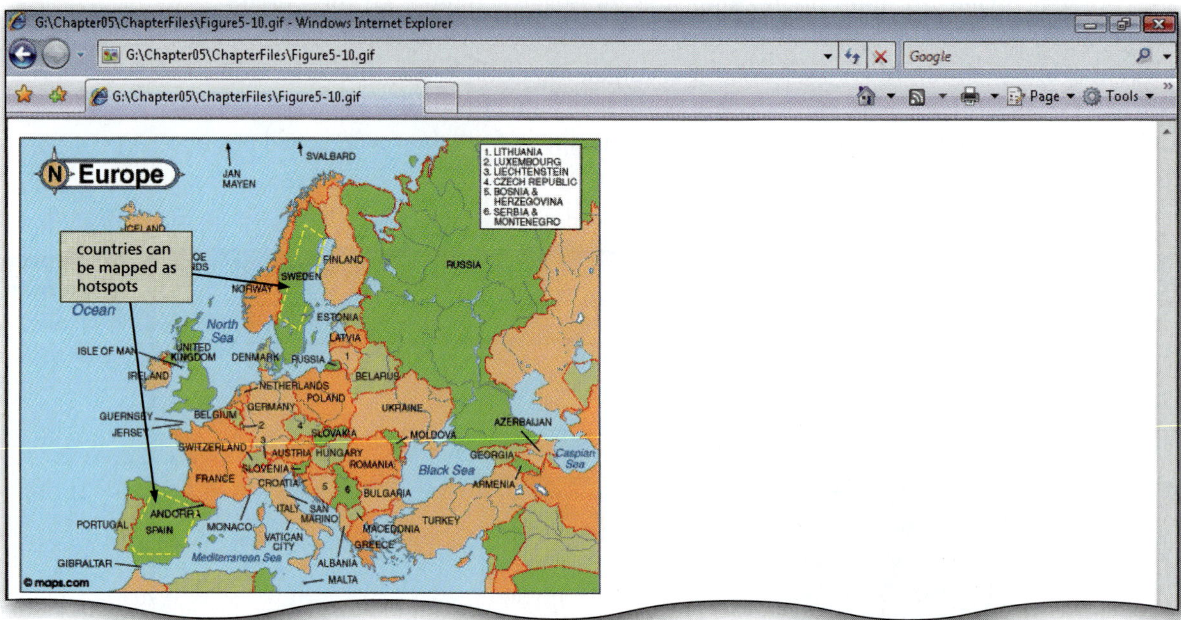

Figure 5–10 Sketched areas for image map hotspots.

Figure 5–11 shows the southwestern states image used as an image map in this chapter, with the hotspots sketched in. This image, southwest.jpg, is included in the Data Files for Students. Three states are defined as hotspots, which will link to other Web pages that contain information about each state. The process of mapping the image coordinates for each hotspot is based on this initial sketch.

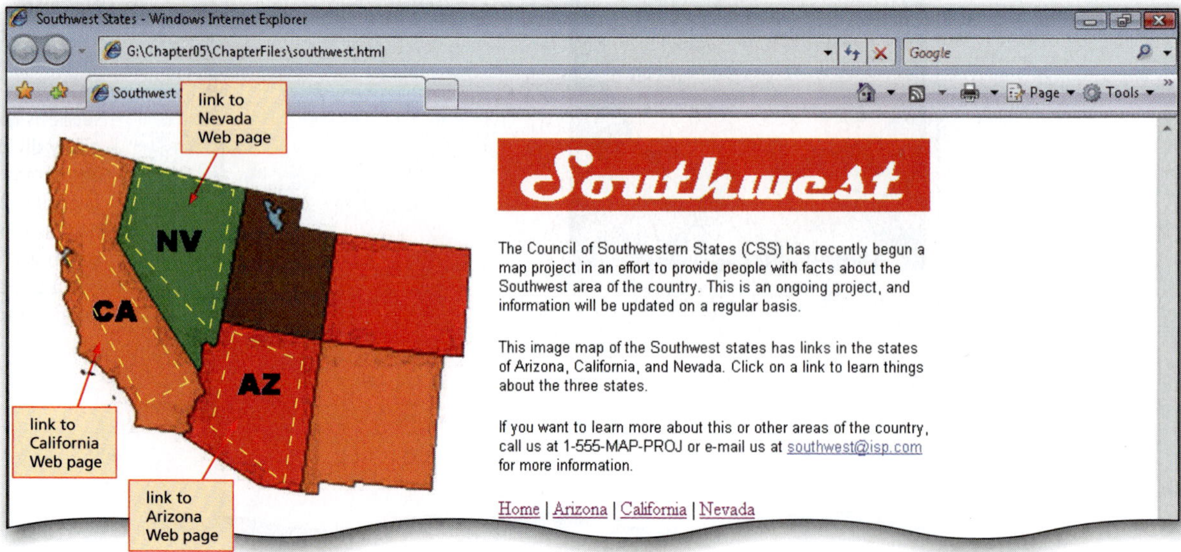

Figure 5–11 Sketched areas for southwestern states image map.

Mapping Image Coordinates

After you have determined how to divide the image into areas, you must determine the x- and y-coordinates for those sections. The x- and y-coordinates are based on a position relative to the x- and y-axes. The **x-axis** runs horizontally along the base of the image, while the **y-axis** runs vertically along the left of the image. The top-left corner of an image thus is the coordinate point (0,0), as shown in Figure 5–12. The first number of a **coordinate pair** is the x-coordinate, and the second number is the y-coordinate. Figure 5–12 shows some sample x- and y-coordinates in a Paint window that contains the image southwest.jpg. The y-coordinate numbers increase as you move the mouse pointer down the image, and the x-coordinate numbers increase as you move the mouse pointer to the right on the image. As you move the mouse pointer, the coordinates of its position are displayed on the status bar.

You can use a simple or a sophisticated image editing or paint program to determine the x- and y-coordinates of various image points. In this project, the Paint program is used to find the x- and y-coordinates that you will use in the map definition that divides a single image into several areas.

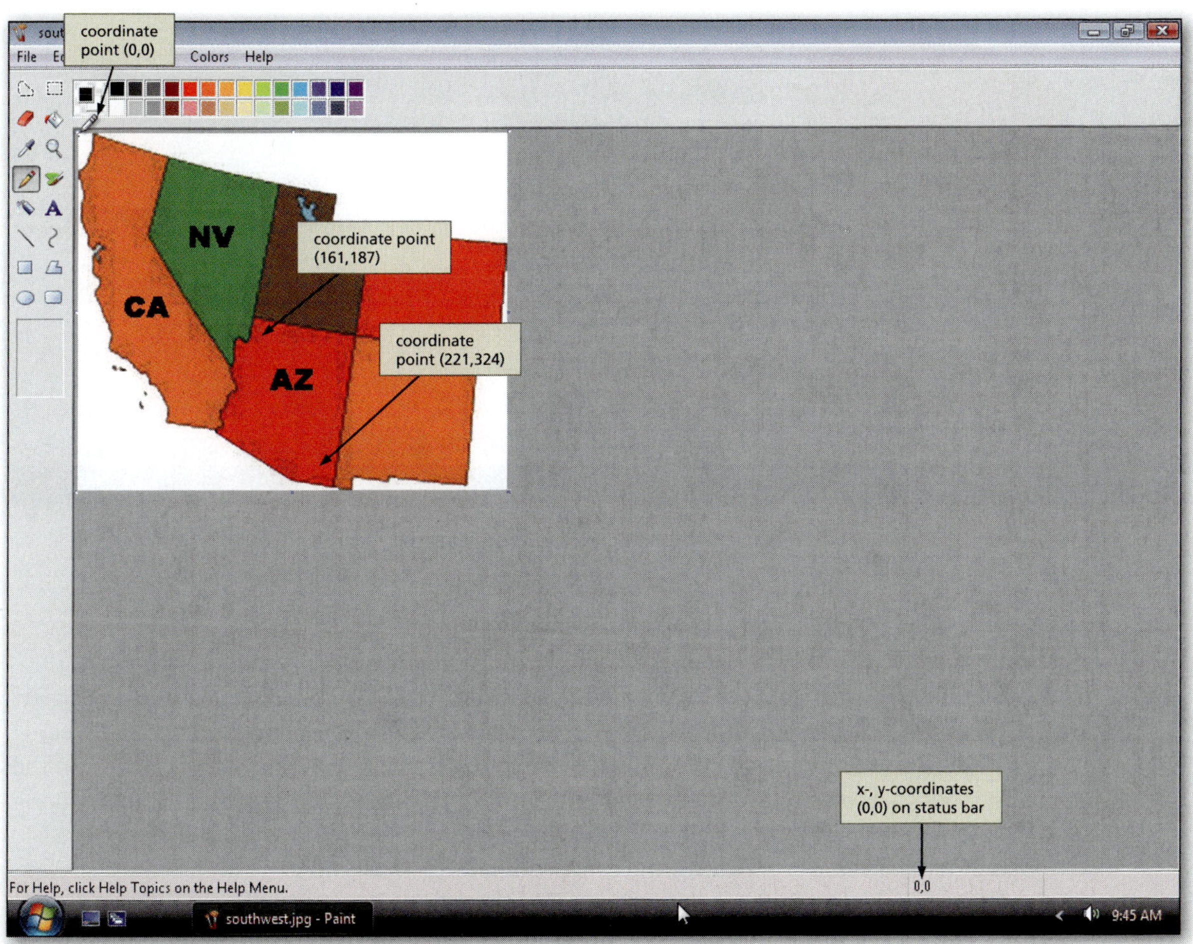

Figure 5–12 Southwest map open in Paint.

Map areas can use one of three shapes: rectangle, circle, or polygon. These shapes are shown in Figure 5–13. To define a map area of an image, you must determine the x- and y-coordinates for that shape and then insert the coordinates for the various map shapes in the HTML code.

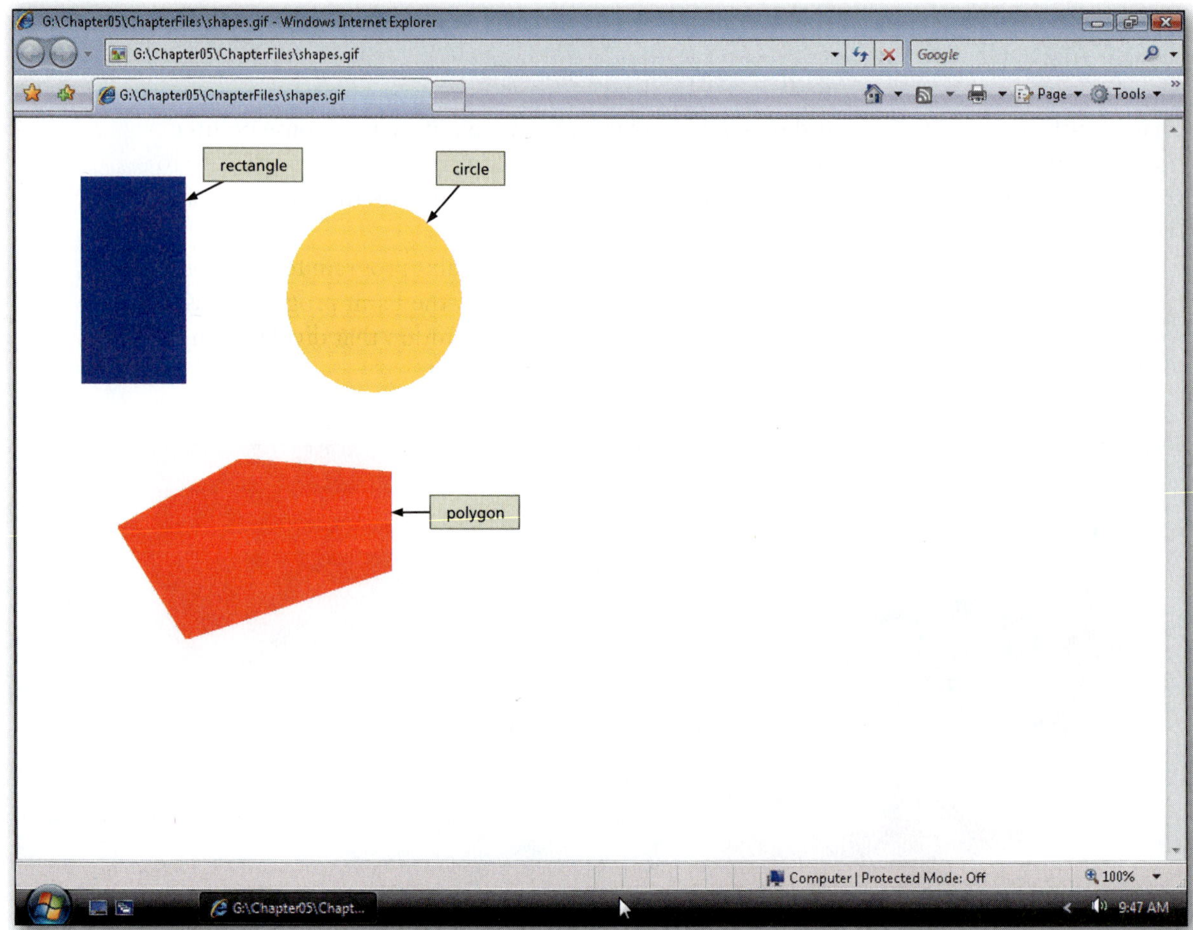

Figure 5–13 Shapes of map areas.

For a rectangular map area, you use the coordinates of the top-left and the bottom-right corners. For example, as shown in Figure 5–14, the rectangle's x- and y-coordinates are (46,35) for the top-left corner and (137,208) for the bottom-right corner. You use "rect" as the value for the shape attribute for rectangles. For a circular map area, you use the center point and the radius as the coordinates. The x- and y- coordinates of the center point of the circle in Figure 5–14 are (308,113). If the mouse pointer is moved along the y-axis (113) to the border of the circle, the x-axis is 380. The radius can be calculated by subtracting the x-axis value of the center point (308) from the x-axis value of the circle's right border (380), which gives a radius of 72 (380 - 308). For circles, you use "circle" as the value for the shape attribute. For a polygonal map area, you must use the coordinates for each corner of the shape. For example, in Figure 5–14, the polygon has five corners with the coordinates (78,309), (183,251), (316,262), (317,344), and (136,402). For polygonal shapes, you use "poly" as the value for the shape attribute.

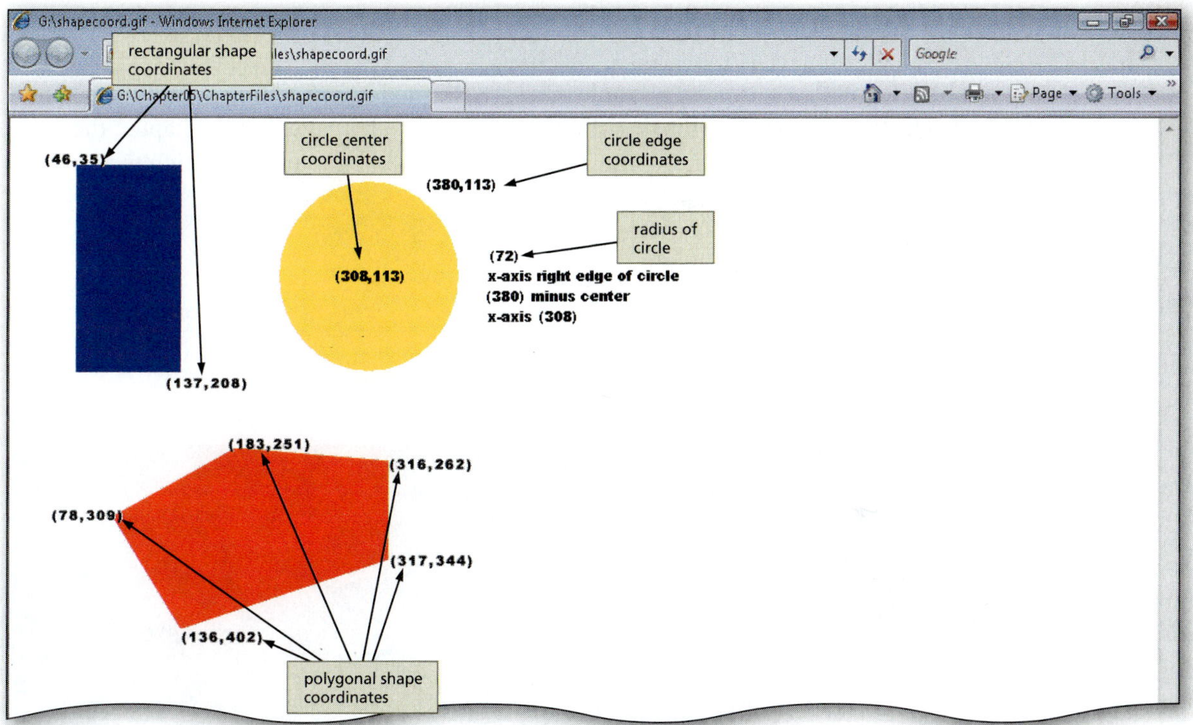

Figure 5–14 Coordinates of map areas.

In the Southwest map image (southwest.jpg), the image map will use three polygon shapes for the three hotspots, as sketched in Figure 5–11 on page HTML 212. Clickable areas are mapped in polygon shapes enclosing the following areas: Arizona, California, and Nevada.

Coding the Map

The final step in creating an image map is writing the HTML code for the map. To create a client-side image map, the tags <map> </map> and <area> are used. The map start tag (**<map>**) and map end tag (**</map>**) create the client-side image map. The **<area>** tag defines the specific areas of the map and the links and anchors for those areas. The x- and y-coordinates for each map area are inserted into the <area> tag with the **coords** attribute, within quotation marks and separated by commas.

Plan Ahead

Working with the image.
In order to determine the x- and y-coordinates for image map points, you need to open the image in the chosen software tool.

- **Select a software tool.** Computers running the Windows operating system already have an image editing tool available, Paint. This chapter shows you how to work with your image within Paint. For other suggested editing software products, see Table 5–2 on page HTML 222.
- **Edit the image.** It is sometimes necessary to alter the image before using it on the Web page. In the case of the project in this chapter, the images were all too large for the page. Microsoft Paint was used to scale down the size of the image (Image menu, Resize/Skew). Paint also gives you the image dimensions (i.e., width and height) you need for the <img> tag.
- **Make other changes to the image.** In Paint, you can make other changes to the image such as flipping the image horizontally or vertically, or altering the colors of the image. Other graphic editing software provides a variety of tools to alter an image slightly or significantly.

Using Paint to Locate X- and Y-Coordinates

As you have learned, you can use a simple or a sophisticated image editing or paint program to determine the x- and y-coordinates of various points on an image. In this chapter, the Paint program is used to find the x- and y-coordinates used in the map definition that divides a single image into several areas.

To Start Paint

The following steps illustrate how to start Paint.

- Click the Start button on the taskbar.
- Point to All Programs on the Start menu, click Accessories on the All Programs submenu, and then point to Paint on the Accessories submenu (Figure 5–15).
- Click Paint.

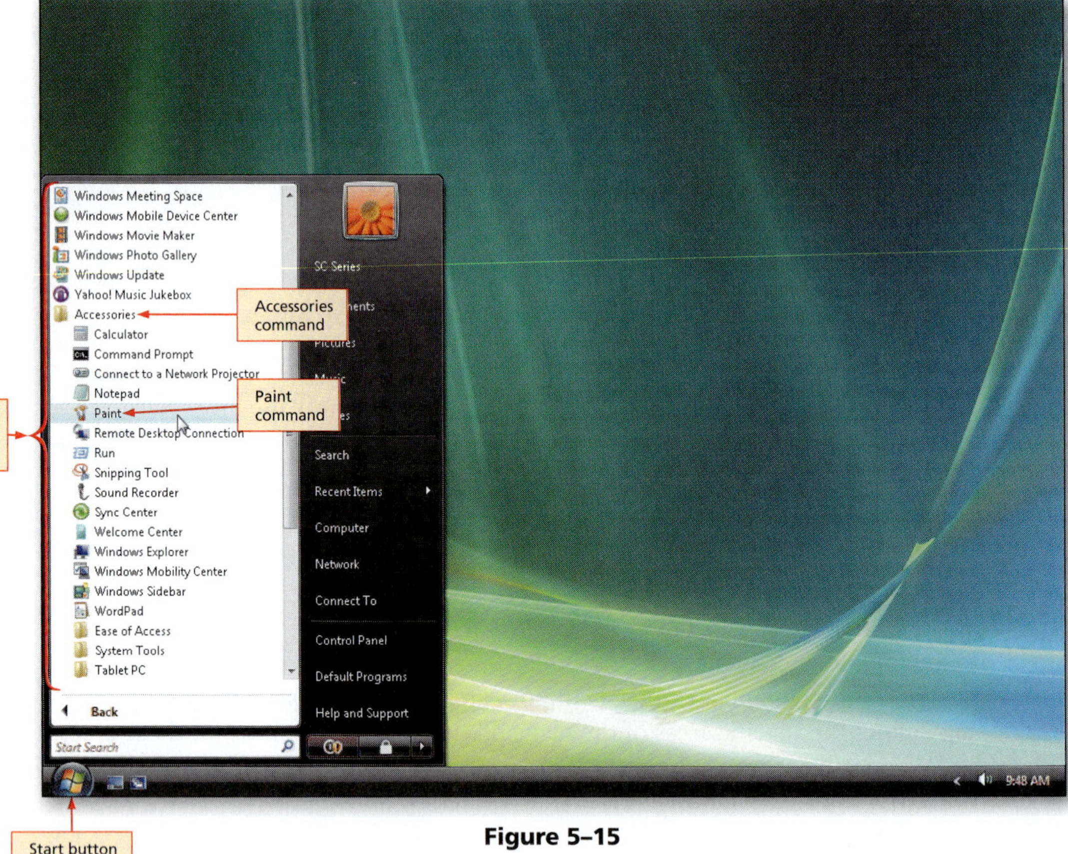

Figure 5–15

BTW

Using Paint

The Help feature of Paint can answer your questions about the use of this popular tool. Paint can be used to identify the x- and y-coordinates in an image used as an image map. It also can be used to create images that are used as image maps.

2

- If necessary, click the Maximize button on the right side of the title bar to maximize the window (Figure 5–16).

Q&A Do all computers running Windows include Paint?

Yes, Paint should be included with all Windows operating systems.

Q&A How can I find out more about using Paint?

The Paint Help utility is quite good. You can search for information using its Search option or the Index. Paint Help gives step-by-step instructions for many tasks.

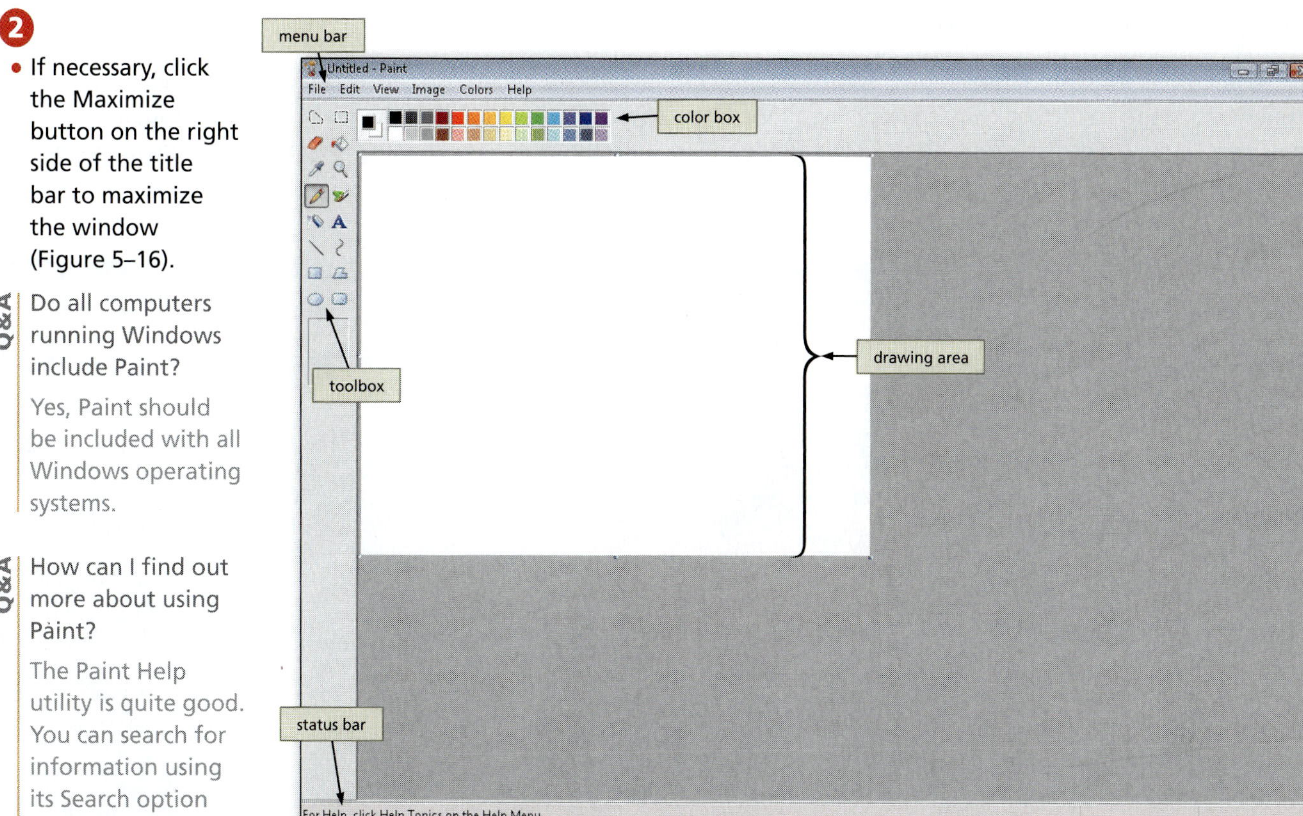

Figure 5–16

The Paint Window

The Paint window contains several elements similar to the document windows in other applications. The main elements of the Paint window are the drawing area, the toolbox, the color box, the menu bar, and the status bar, as shown in Figure 5–16.

Drawing area The **drawing area** is where the image is displayed.

Toolbox The **toolbox** displays tools that are used to edit or draw an image. In this project, the Pencil tool in the toolbox is used to find the x- and y-coordinates of the southwestern states image.

Color Box The **color box** displays a palette of colors that can be used to set the colors of the foreground, the background, or other elements in a drawing.

Menu Bar The **menu bar** is at the top of the window just below the title bar and shows the Paint menu names. Each menu name contains a list of commands that can be used to: open, save, and print the image in a file; edit the image; change the view of the Paint window; and perform other tasks.

Status Bar The **status bar** displays the coordinates of the center of the mouse pointer at its current position on the image.

To Open an Image File in Paint

The Southwest states image file (southwest.jpg) used for the image map is stored in the Data Files for Students. See the inside back cover of this book for instructions for downloading the Data Files for Students or see your instructor for information about accessing the files required for this book. The following step illustrates how to open an image file in Paint.

- With a USB drive plugged into your computer, click File on the Paint menu bar and then click Open on the File menu.
- If Computer is not displayed in the Favorite Links section, drag the top or bottom edge of the Open dialog box until Computer is displayed.
- Click Computer in the Favorite Links section to display a list of available drives.
- If necessary, scroll until UDISK 2.0 (G:) appears in the list of available drives.
- If necessary, click the Look in box arrow, and then double-click USB drive (G:). Double-click the Chapter05 folder, and then double-click the ChapterFiles folder in the list of available folders.
- Click the southwest.jpg image, then click the Open button in the Open dialog box to display the image that will be used for image mapping in this chapter as shown in Figure 5–17.

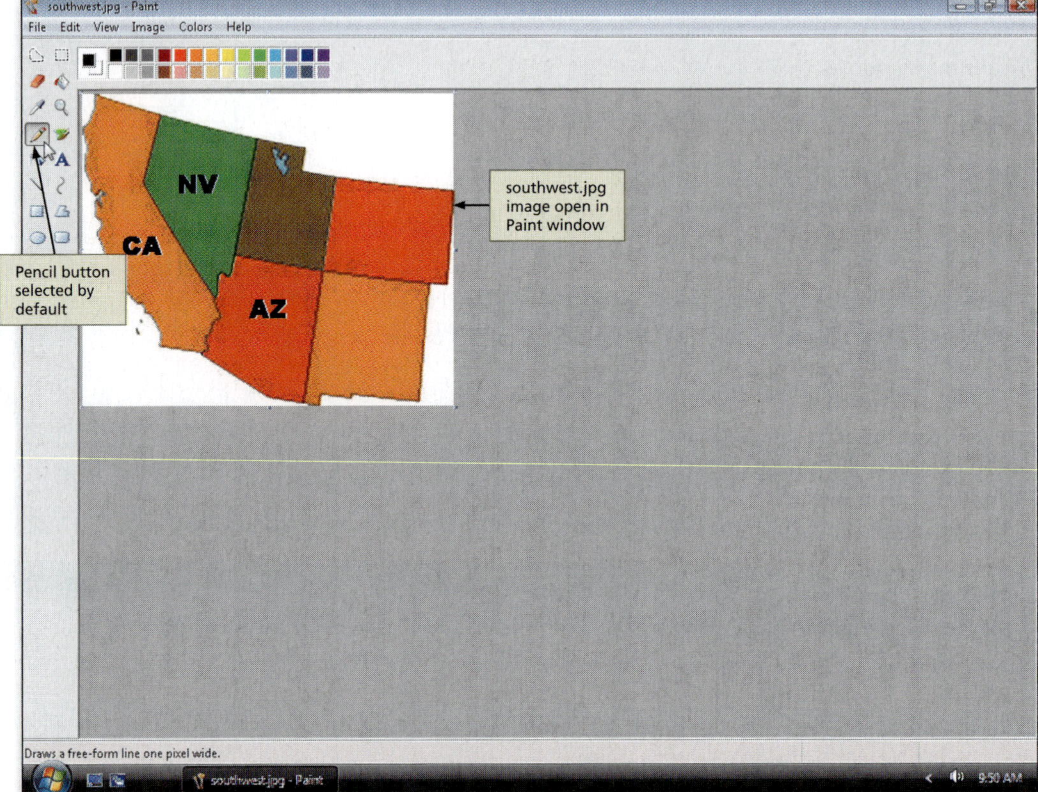

Figure 5–17

Locating X- and Y-Coordinates of an Image

The next step is to locate the x- and y-coordinates of the areas that should be mapped on the image. As shown in Figure 5–18, the image map should include three clickable polygonal areas that will link to other Web pages. For each of the three linkable map areas, every x- and y-coordinate pair corner must be determined.

As you have learned, the x- and y-coordinates begin with (0,0) in the top-left corner of the image, as shown in Figure 5–18. Moving the mouse pointer to the right (horizontally) increases the x-coordinate, and moving the mouse pointer down (vertically) increases the y-coordinate. Because all three clickable areas sketched on the southwest.jpg image are polygon shaped, the map definition must include the x- and y-coordinates of each point in each polygon. You use the poly attribute for all hotspot areas in this project.

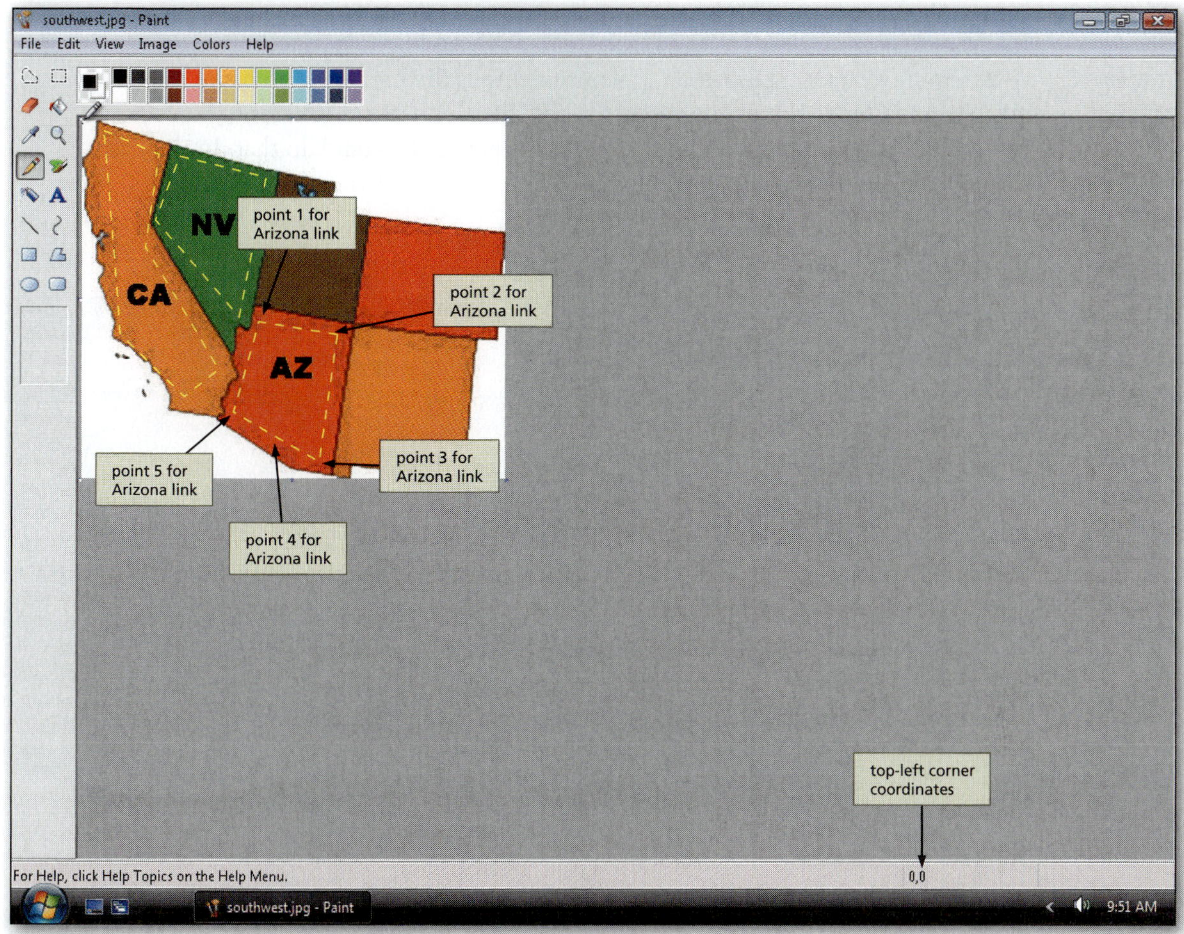

Figure 5–18

Table 5–1 shows the x- and y-coordinates for of all three polygon-shaped map areas. The first number is the x-coordinate, and the second number is the y-coordinate. For example, the Arizona polygon consists of five pairs of x- and y-coordinates. The first x-coordinate is 157 and the first-left y-coordinate is 162. The next set of x- and y-coordinates in the Arizona map shape is 234 and 177; the third set is 217 and 288; the fourth set of coordinates is 187 and 285; and the final set of coordinates is 128 and 250. These x- and y-coordinates are used in the <area> tag to create the map definition for an image map.

Table 5–1 X- and Y- Coordinates

	Pairs of X- and Y-Coordinates
Arizona (five points)	157,162 and 234,177 and 217,288 and 187,285 and 128,250
California (seven points)	16,10 and 69,25 and 51,85 and 129,204 and 114,242 and 34,167 and 6,67
Nevada (five points)	81,24 and 169,47 and 144,166 and 126,175 and 68,85

To Locate X- and Y-Coordinates of an Image

The following steps illustrate how to locate the x- and y-coordinates of the boundary points of each clickable polygon area by moving the mouse pointer to the various points to see the x- and y-coordinates of those points. Although you do not need to record the coordinates for this project, you generally would do that. In this case though, you will compare the coordinates with those shown in Table 5–1, which lists the exact coordinates used in the <area> tags for this project.

- If necessary, click the Pencil button in the toolbox (Figure 5–19).

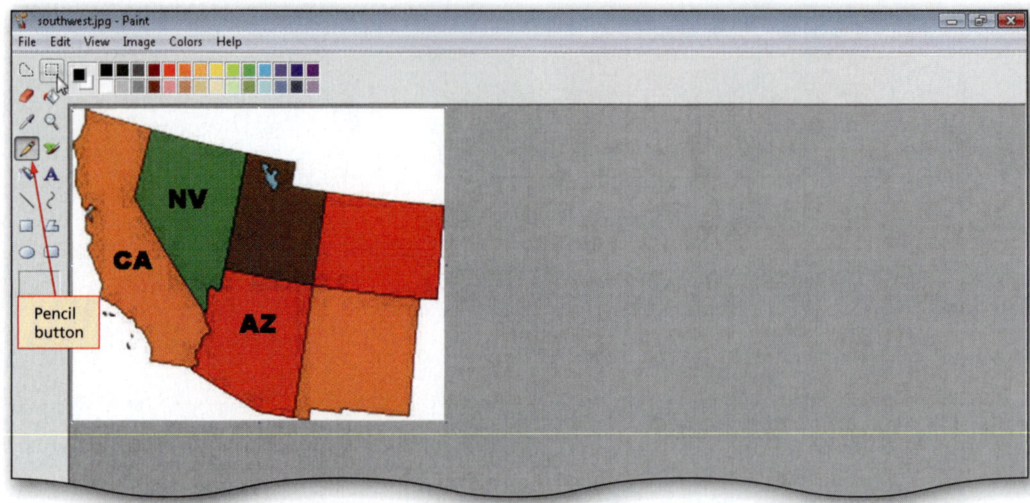

Figure 5–19

- Move the mouse pointer near the top-left corner of Arizona and note the x- and y-coordinates for that point as indicated in the status bar. Move the mouse until the coordinates read (157,162) (Figure 5–20). (Do not click the mouse button.)

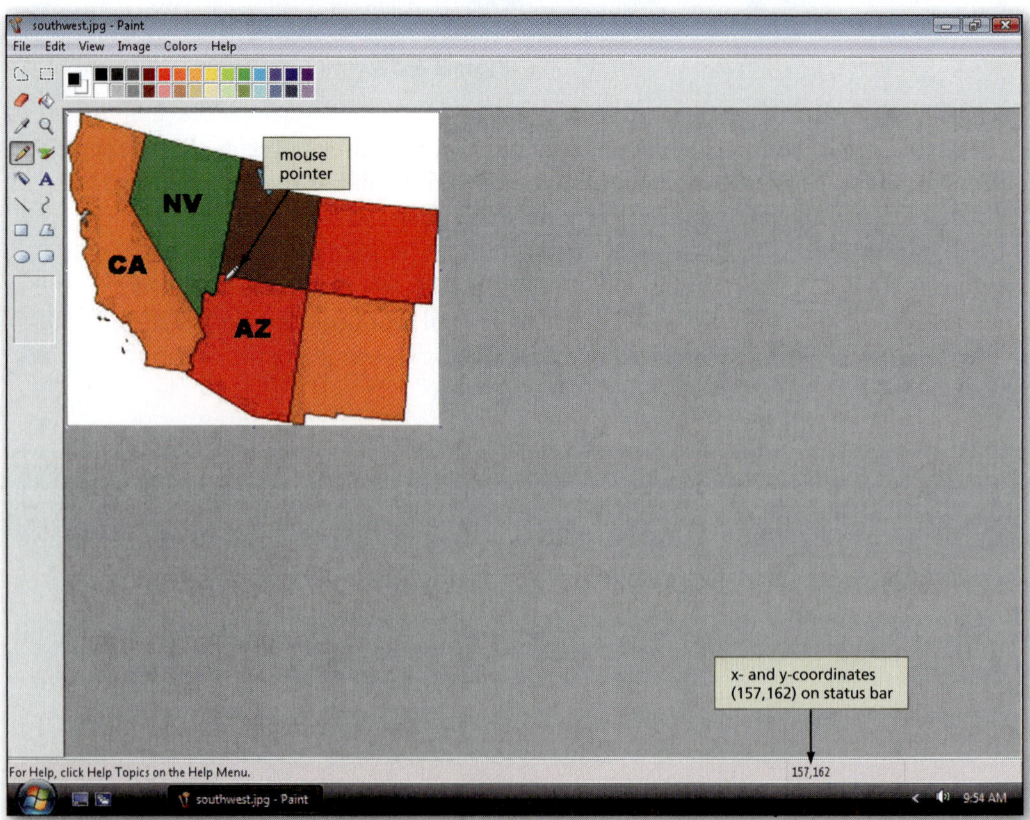

Figure 5–20

- Move the mouse pointer near the top-right corner of Arizona. The coordinates should read (234,177) (your coordinates may differ slightly) as indicated on the status bar (Figure 5–21). (Do not click the mouse button.)
- Move the mouse pointer to other points in the Arizona, California and Nevada hotspots by following the x- and y-coordinates in Table 5–1 on page HTML 219.
- After you have finished, click the Close button on the right side of the title bar. If prompted, do not save any changes to the file.

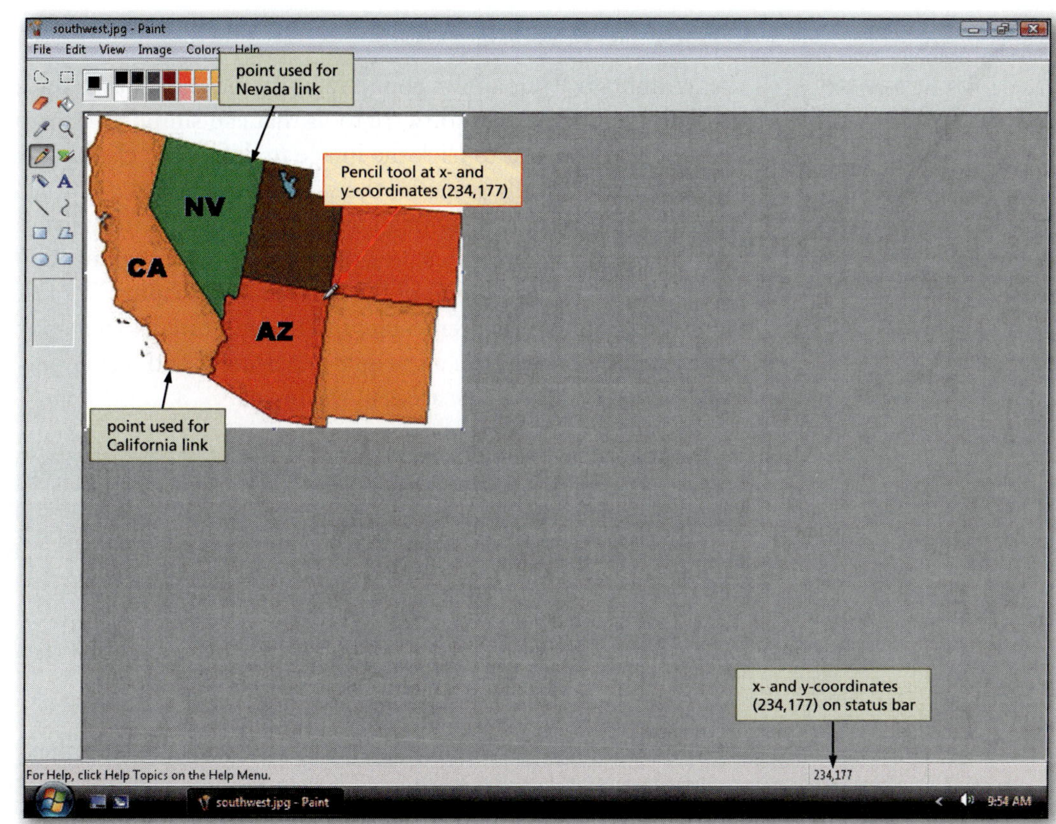

Figure 5–21

Q&A

I am not sure of the purpose of this exercise because the coordinates are already given to us for the project. Why am I doing these steps using Paint?

For the purpose of the project, we give you the coordinates to use. The normal image mapping process, however, consists of: finding an appropriate image, sketching out where you think the boundaries will be, and finding the coordinates on your own using a software tool that shows that information. The purpose of this exercise is to get you familiar with using Paint to find the coordinates.

Q&A

I notice that in addition to the Pencil tool, I can use the Free-Form Select and the Select tools to show the x- and y-coordinates on the status bar. Is it OK to use them?

It is fine to use any of the three tools for this purpose. You are only trying to see the x- and y-coordinates for the hotspot areas.

Experiment

- Play with the Image and Colors menu items. They give you many options to alter the image.

BTW

Graphics Software
Many graphics tools are available for advanced image creation and maintenance. One of the more popular tools is Adobe Photoshop. Photoshop allows you to create images that can be used as image maps or crop sections out of existing images.

Other Software Tools

Although Paint allows you to identify the coordinates for a map area manually, there are dedicated image map software tools that can simplify this process (see Table 5–2). These tools allow you to click the image to define the clickable areas of the image map and then automatically generate the x- and y-coordinates and HTML code needed for the image map. If possible, download one of the software tools listed in Table 5–2 and use that software to map the clickable areas in the southwest.jpg image. As further practice, open the file shapecoord.gif found in the Chapter05\ChapterFiles folder in Paint (Figure 5–22) and use your mouse pointer to identify the coordinates to map the clickable areas in the shapecoord.gif image. You also could experiment with using one or more of the tools in Table 5–2 to map clickable areas in the image.

Table 5–2 Image Map Software Tools

Tool	Platform
Mapedit	Windows, UNIX, Mac OS
CoffeeCup Image Mapper	Windows
Imaptool	Linux/X-Window

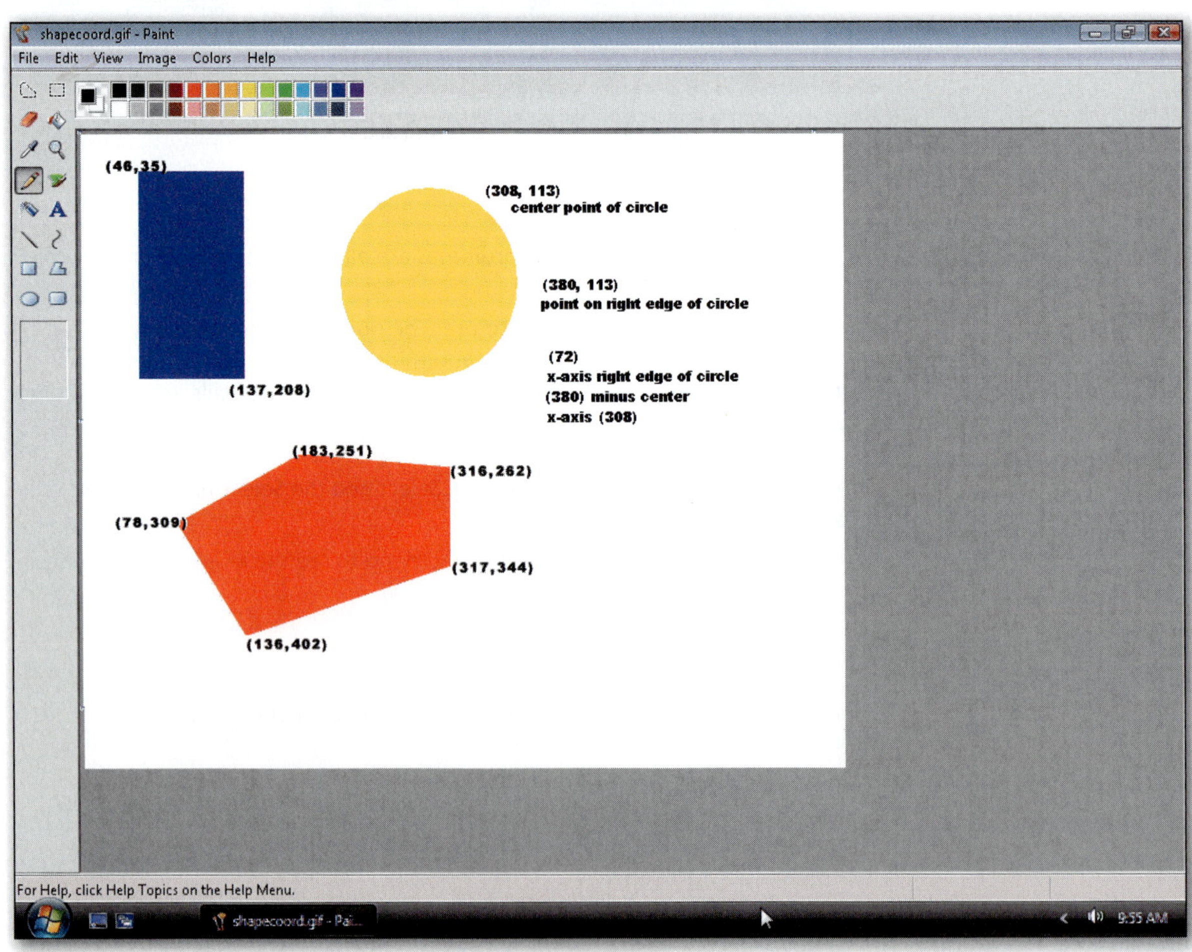

Figure 5–22

Plan Ahead

Starting the home page.

Just as with the other projects in previous chapters, you need to review good Web development standards before you start a new Web page.

- **Use the HTML structure tags required.** You will validate your Web pages for this project, so make sure that you use the HTML tags needed to make the page XHTML compliant. This includes using the <meta> tag and a DOCTYPE statement.
- **Copy what you can.** In earlier chapters, you copied HTML code from one completed page to another to make it easier. You should do the same in this project. Once a Web page is validated, you know that the initial HTML tags are correct. It makes sense then to copy/paste those lines of code to the next Web page file. If you are utilizing the same menu bar throughout a Web site, it also makes sense to copy that code from one Web page to another.

Creating the Home Page

Before the image map can be added to the home page of the Southwest Map Web site, the home page must be created. The home page includes a borderless table, a logo image, and paragraphs of text, along with a table of text links to other pages on the Web site (arizona.html, california.html, and nevada.html).

To Start Notepad and Enter Initial HTML Tags

The first steps in creating the home page are to start Notepad and enter the initial HTML tags to define the overall structure of the Web page, as shown in Table 5–3.

Table 5–3 HTML Code to Define Web Page Structure

Line	HTML Tag and Text
1	<!DOCTYPE html
2	PUBLIC "-//W3C//DTD XHTML 1.0 Transitional//EN"
3	"http://www.w3.org/TR/xhtml1/DTD/xhtml1-transitional.dtd">
4	
5	<html xmlns="http://www.w3.org/1999/xhtml" lang="en" xml:lang="en">
6	<head>
7	<meta http-equiv="Content-Type" content="text/html;charset=utf-8" />
8	<title>Southwest States</title>
9	</head>
10	<body>
11	
12	
13	</body>
14	</html>

The following step illustrates how to start Notepad and enter HTML tags to define the Web page structure.

1

- Click the Start button on the taskbar and then point to All Programs on the Start menu.
- Click Accessories on the All Programs submenu and then click Notepad on the Accessories submenu.
- If necessary, click the Maximize button.
- If necessary, click Format on the menu bar and click Word Wrap to turn on Word Wrap.
- Enter the HTML code as shown in Table 5–3 on page HTML 223.

Creating a Table

The next task in developing the home page is to create a left-aligned, borderless table with one row and two columns, as shown in Figure 5–23. The first data cell contains the image southwest.jpg, which will be used for the image map. The second data cell contains the logo and paragraphs of information about Southwest mapping project, along with the text links on the bottom of the Web page.

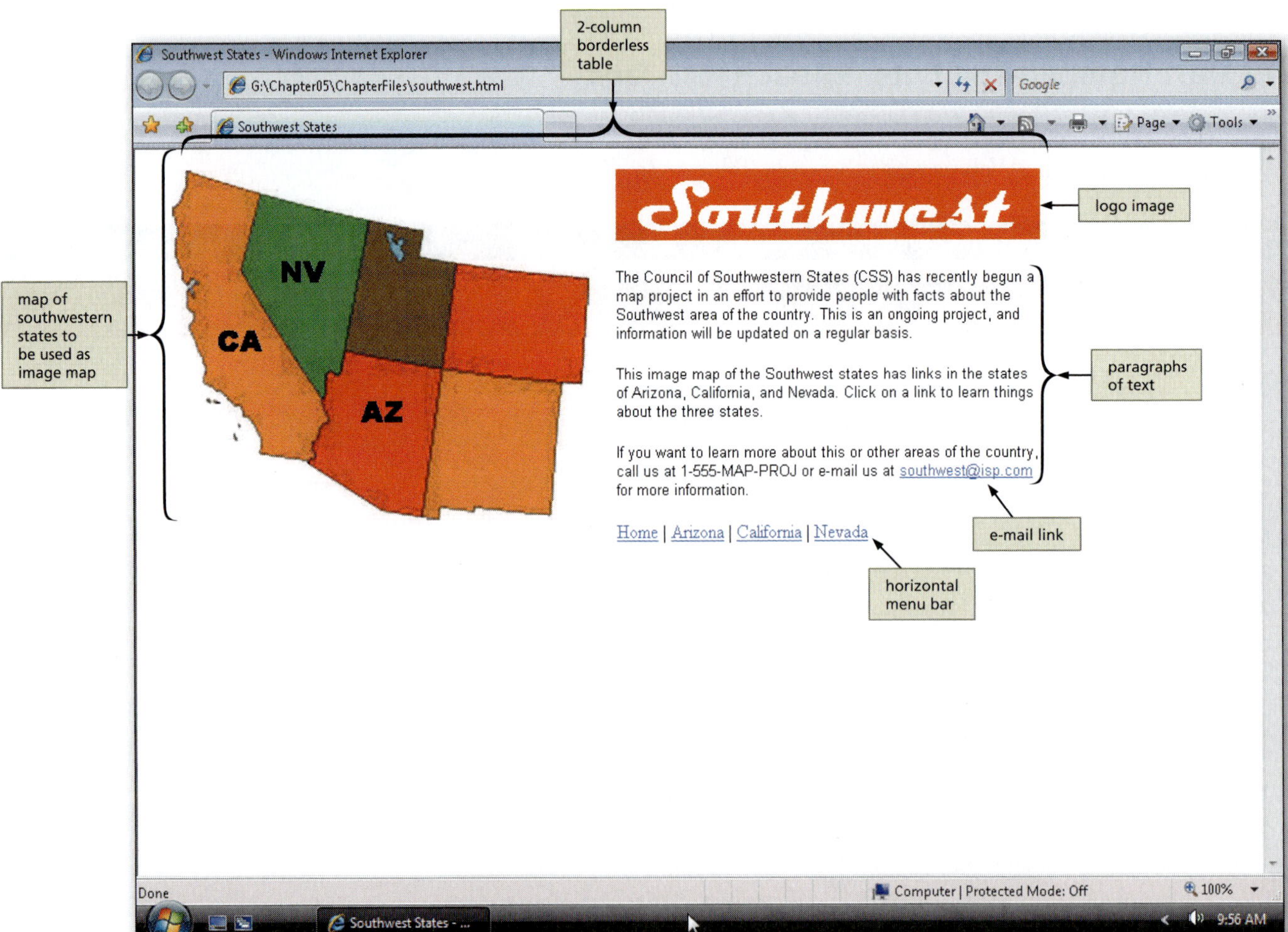

Figure 5–23

The two cells of the table are created using <td> tags that create table data cells. As you learned in Chapter 4, the <td> tag aligns the contents of a cell in the center of the cell vertically and to the left horizontally, by default. As shown in Figure 5–23, the table should use a vertical alignment so the contents of all cells are aligned with the top of the cell. The HTML code thus should use a <tr> tag with the valign="top" attribute to create a table row that uses vertical alignment. Using this tag eliminates the need to set each table data cell to use vertical alignment.

To Create a Table

The following step creates a one-row, two-column borderless table, with a table row that uses vertical alignment.

1

- With the insertion point on line 12, type `<table width="75%">` and then press the ENTER key.
- Type `<tr valign="top">` and then press the ENTER key twice as shown in Figure 5–24.

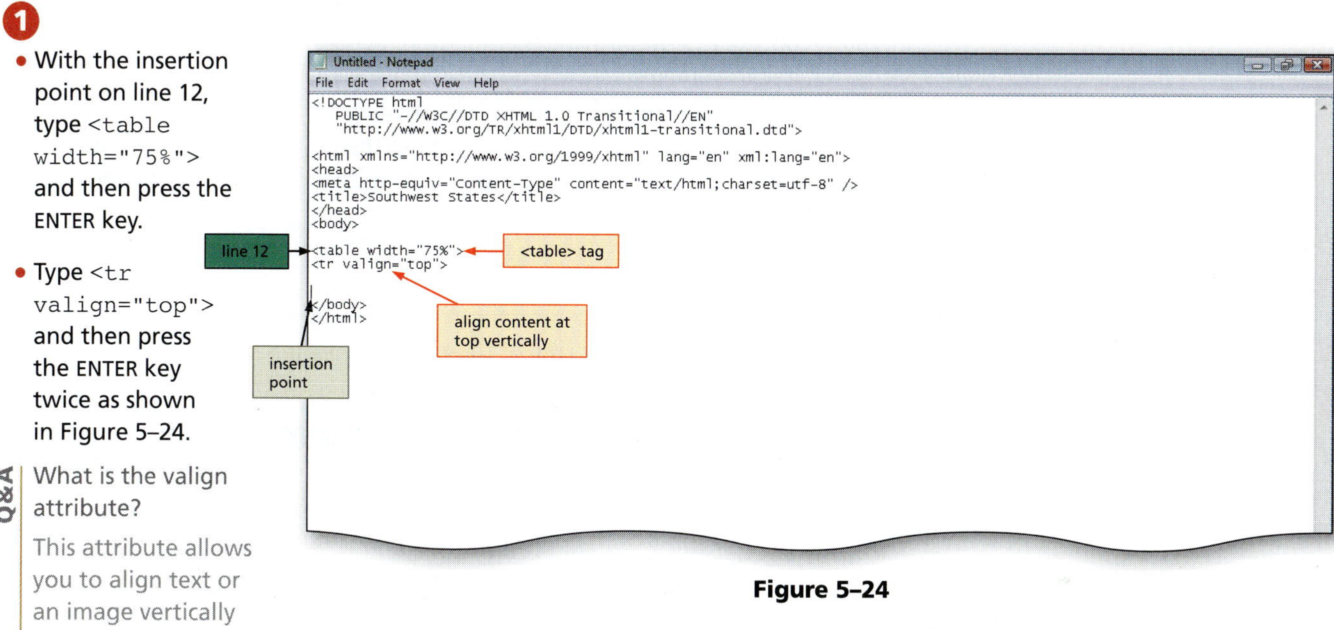

Figure 5–24

Q&A What is the valign attribute?

This attribute allows you to align text or an image vertically in the table. In this example, you align the first row of the table at the top.

Inserting an Image to Use as an Image Map

The next step in creating the home page is to add the image, described in Table 5–4, which is used as the image map. The image, southwest.jpg, is stored in the Data Files for Students.

BTW **Image Map Tutorials**
Many great resources on the Web discuss image maps. For more information about tutorials, search for the term "image map tutorials" with any good search engine.

Table 5–4 Tag Attributes Used to Create Image Maps

Tag	Attribute	Function
<img>	usemap ismap	• Indicates the URL of a client-side image map • Indicates a server-side image map

> **BTW**
> **Image Width and Height**
> As you have learned in earlier projects, specifying the width and height attributes helps improve page loading time because the browser does not have to determine the width and height of the image.

The Southwest Map home page will use a client-side image map. The HTML code to add the image thus will use attributes of the <img> tag — src, width, height, border, hspace, and usemap — as follows:

```
<img src="southwest.jpg" width="374" height="300" border="0"
alt="Southwest states" hspace="20" usemap="#states" />
```

where the src attribute identifies the image, the width and height attributes define the image size, and the border attribute makes the image borderless. The hspace attribute adds 20 pixels of horizontal space between the image and the text, so the text does not run right up against the image.

The usemap attribute indicates to the browser which client-side image map will be used for that image. The client-side image map is placed within the <map> tag and defines the x- and y-coordinates of the areas on the image being used for the image map. Later in this chapter, a map named states will be created using the <map> tag. When adding the image to use as an image map, the value of the usemap attribute — in this case, usemap="#states" — indicates that the browser should use the image map named states as its image map source. The following steps show how to add an image to use as an image map.

To Insert an Image to Use as an Image Map

The following step shows how to insert an image in the first row of the table.

1

- If necessary, click line 15.
- Type `<td>` and then press the ENTER key.
- Type `<img src="southwest.jpg" width="374" height="300" border="0" alt="Southwest states" hspace="20" usemap="#states" />` and then press the ENTER key.
- Type `</td>` and then press the ENTER key twice (Figure 5–25).

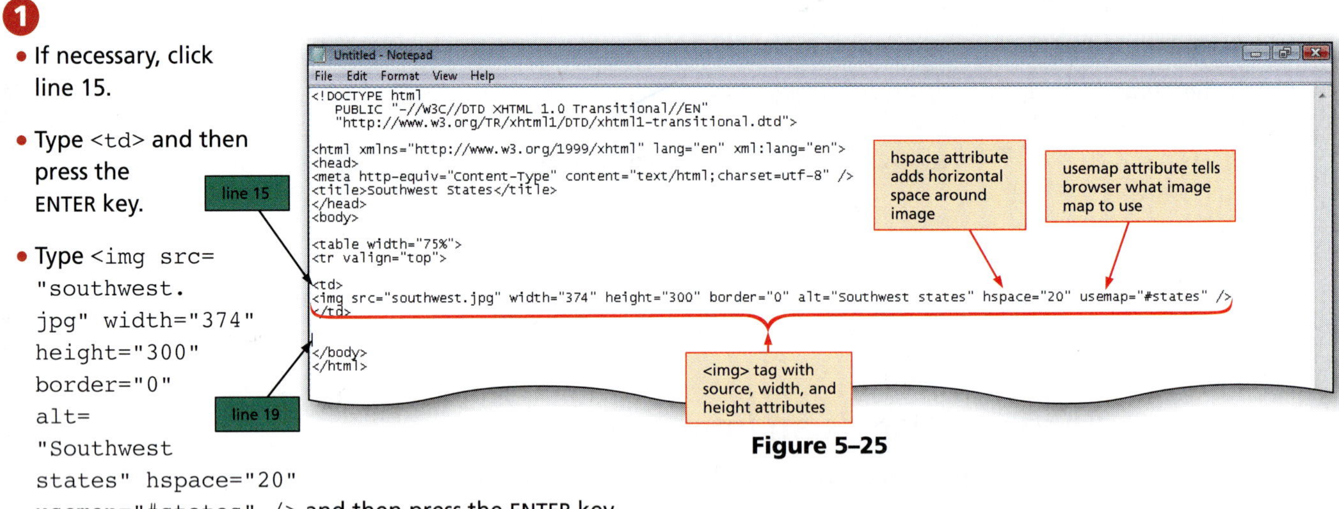

Figure 5–25

> **Q&A**
> I do not understand the purpose of the usemap attribute. Can you explain it?
>
> The usemap attribute is what identifies the image with the map that will be inserted at the end of this Web page. The value (i.e., #states) in the usemap attribute tells the browser that this is an image map, and that it needs to look at the <map> tag name and id with that name (states) for the mapping.

> **Q&A**
> If I want to speed up the download of a large image, can I change the dimensions of the image using the width and height attributes to make it smaller?
>
> Although you can do this, you should not. Making a change to an image with these attributes still forces the browser to download the entire image and then display it as you indicate in the width and height attributes. If you want to speed up the download by making the image smaller, you should use Paint (or some other image editing software) to change the dimensions and then save the image. In Paint, look under Image and then Resize/Skew.

To Add a Header and Text to a Table Cell

The home page also contains three paragraphs of text in the right column of the first row. The HTML code for this text is shown in Table 5–5. Entering the HTML code shown in Table 5–5 adds three paragraphs of text describing the company and an e-mail link. As you have learned, a Web page always should include an e-mail address on the home page for visitor contact.

Table 5–5 HTML Code for Inserting Paragraphs

Line	HTML Tag and Text
19	`<td><img src="swheader.gif" width="376" height="61" alt="SW header" />`
20	`<p><font size="2" face="arial">The Council of Southwestern States (CSS) has recently begun a map`
21	`project in an effort to provide people with facts about the Southwest area of the country. This is`
22	`an ongoing project, and information will be updated on a regular basis.</font></p>`
23	
24	`<p><font size="2" face="arial">This image map of the Southwest states has links in the states of Arizona,`
25	`California, and Nevada. Click on a link to learn things about the three states.</font></p>`
26	
27	`<p><font size="2" face="arial">If you want to learn more about this or other areas of the country, call`
28	`us at 1-555-MAP-PROJ or e-mail us at <a href="mailto:southwest@isp.com">southwest@isp.com</a>`
29	`for more information.</font></p>`

The following step shows how to enter the tags for the paragraphs of text.

1

- If necessary, click line 19.
- Enter the HTML code shown in Table 5–4 and then press the ENTER key twice (Figure 5–26).

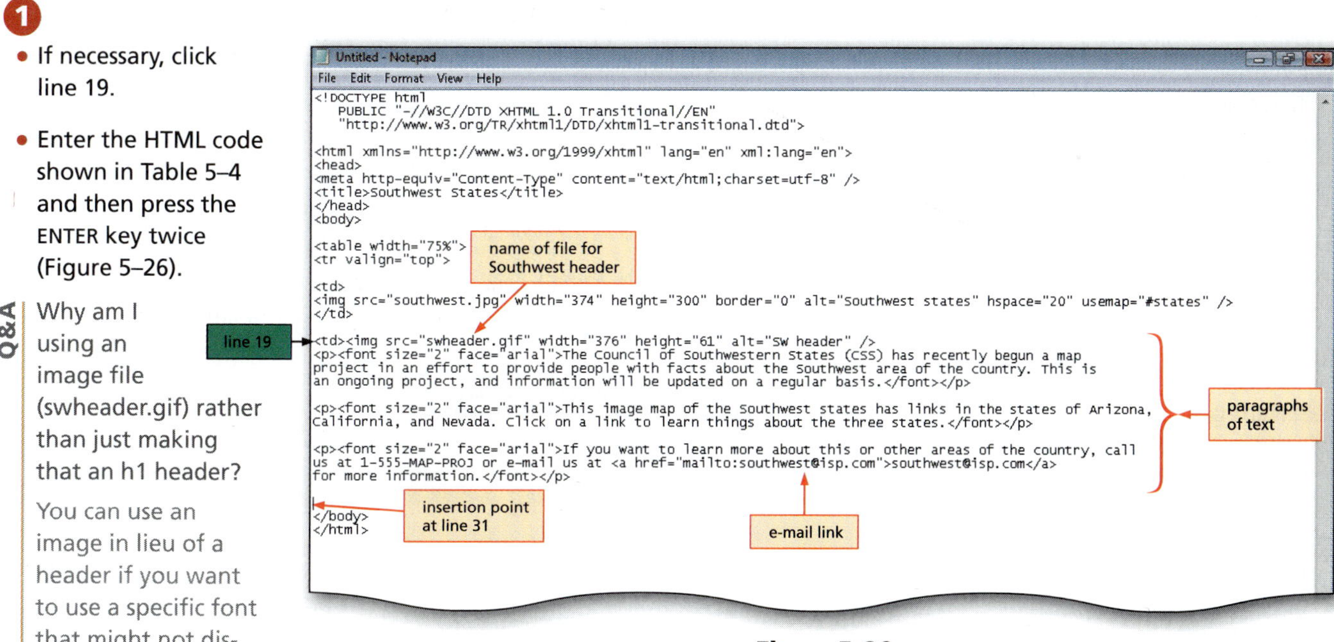

Figure 5–26

Q&A

Why am I using an image file (swheader.gif) rather than just making that an h1 header?

You can use an image in lieu of a header if you want to use a specific font that might not display properly on all computers. In this case, we created the header using the Text tool and Magneto font in Paint and saved it as a .gif file. Make sure to display the Text Toolbar (look under View) to do this.

To Create a Horizontal Menu Bar with Text Links

The next step is to create a horizontal menu bar of text links at the bottom of the page that mirror the image map links. As previously discussed, it is important that a Web page include text links to all URLs in the image map, in the event the image does not download, a user is using a text reader of some sort, or a user's browser is set to not display images.

Table 5–6 shows the HTML code used to create the horizontal menu bar. As shown in lines 31 through 35, the HTML code adds the menu bar to the existing data cell in the table.

Table 5–6 HTML Code for Creating a Horizontal Menu Bar

<table>
<tr><th>Line</th><th>HTML Tag and Text</th></tr>
<tr><td>31</td><td><p><a href="southwest.html">Home</a> |</td></tr>
<tr><td>32</td><td><a href="arizona.html">Arizona</a> |</td></tr>
<tr><td>33</td><td><a href="california.html">California</a> |</td></tr>
<tr><td>34</td><td><a href="nevada.html">Nevada</a></p></td></tr>
<tr><td>35</td><td></td></td></tr>
</table>

The following step shows how to create the text links at the bottom of the home page.

1

- If necessary, click line 31.
- Enter the HTML code shown in Table 5–6 and then press the ENTER key twice (Figure 5–27).

Q&A I notice that we use a horizontal menu bar for many projects in the book. Are there other ways to display a menu?

Many different ways exist to display your menu. The horizontal menu bar is used because it makes sense aesthetically in these projects. A great idea is to review other menu bar options on the Internet and view the HTML source. You can get a lot of ideas by looking at the Web pages and source code from other Web developers. Remember that the whole point of the menu bar is to allow easy navigation access to your Web site visitors.

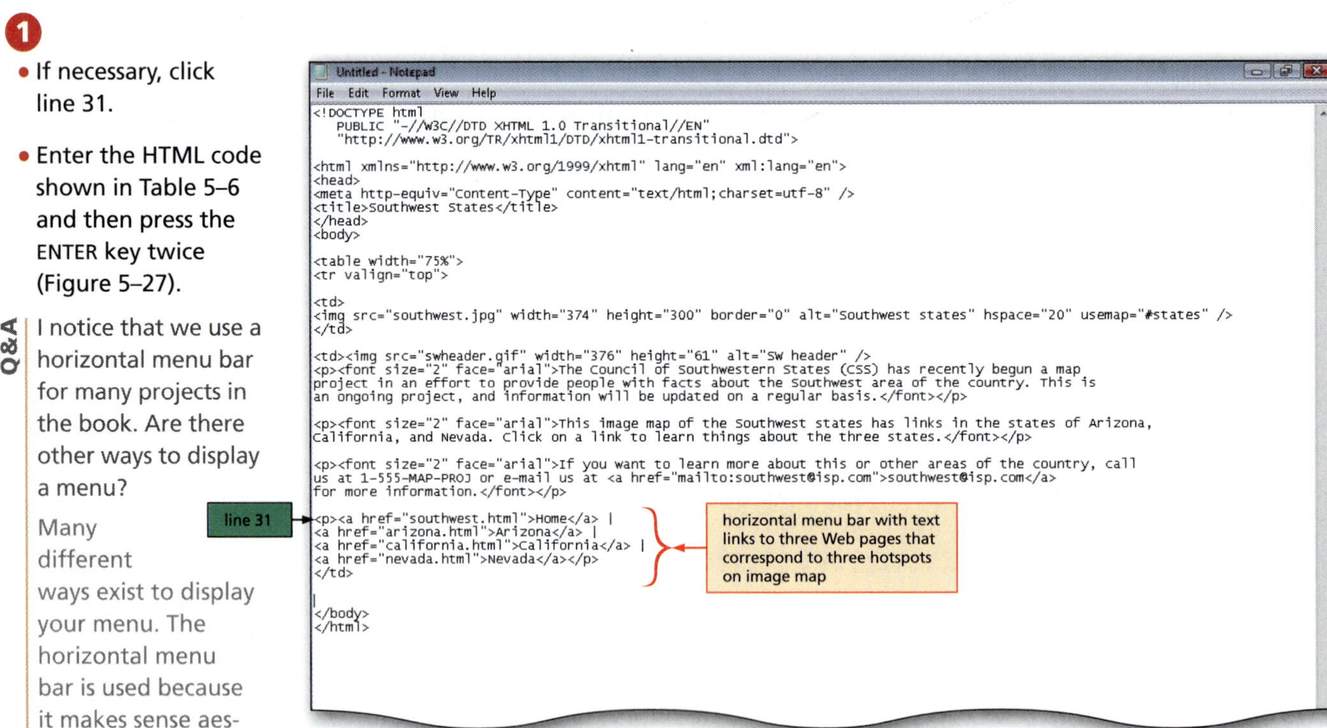

Figure 5–27

To End the Table

To complete the table, you add the closing tags for the table row and table.

- If necessary, click line 37.
- Type </tr> and then press the ENTER key.
- Type </table> and then press the ENTER key twice as shown in Figure 5–28.

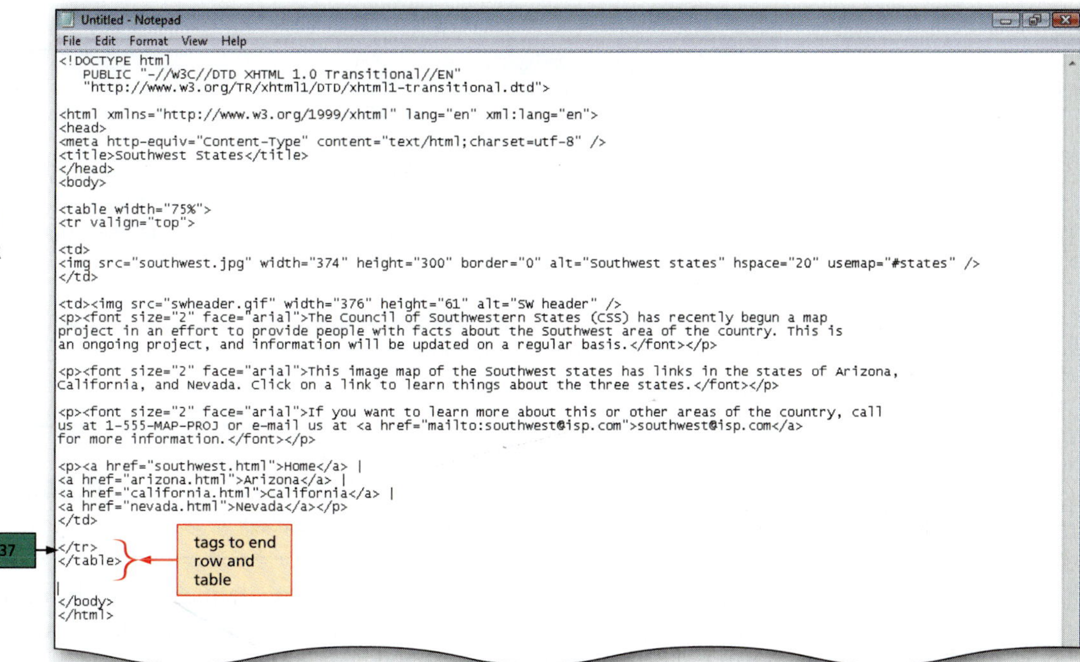

Figure 5–28

> **Plan Ahead**
>
> **Creating an image map.**
> This is the final step in the four-step process of image mapping. The HTML code is very specific about what is required for image mapping. It only takes one coordinate that is not correct or one shape that is wrong for the image map not to work as intended.
>
> - **Use the <map> tag.** The <map> tag identifies the name and ID for the image map. It is important that the name is spelled correctly, and that the same name is used in the usemap attribute in the <img> tag.
> - **Use the <area> tag.** The <area> tag also is very important in image mapping. You identify the area shape and the x- and y-coordinates in this tag. Again, if even one number is typed incorrectly, it can make the image map nearly unusable. Image mapping software (described on page HTML 230) makes this a moot point because it inserts the coordinates for you into the HTML code.

BTW

Text Links
It is important to use text links on all Web pages in addition to using an image map. Some people turn graphics off while browsing the Web. If you did not have text links, those people could not access your other Web pages with graphics turned off. With text links, all your Web site visitors have access to all pages in the Web site.

Coding the Image Map Using HTML Tags and Attributes

Thus far, the chapter has addressed three of the four steps in creating an image map: the southwest.jpg image to use as an image map has been selected and added to the home page, the hotspots have been sketched on the southwest.jpg image, and Paint was used to locate the x- and y-coordinates for each map area on the image that serves as a hotspot. With these steps completed, the final step is to code the image map using HTML. Table 5–7 shows the two HTML tags used to create an image map, along with several key attributes of each.

Table 5–7 Tags and Tag Attributes Used to Create Image Maps

Tag	Attribute	Function
<map> </map>		• Creates a client-side image map
	name	• Defines the map's name
<area>		• Defines clickable areas within a <map> element, as well as links and anchors
	shape	• Indicates the shape of the map area; possible values are rect, poly, and circle
	coords	• Indicates the x- and y-coordinates of the points bounding the map area
	href	• Indicates the link (URL) used for a map area
	alt	• Indicates the alternate text for the image

BTW

Accessibility
Developers should use accessibility guidelines when developing Web pages. It is important that the Web page content is understandable and navigable. The W3C gives some good suggestions for Web site accessibility issues that should be reviewed. For more information about accessibility, visit the W3C Web site, or refer to Appendix C in this book.

The start <map> tag and end </map> tag define the section of code that includes the client-side image map. The <area> tag is used to define the clickable areas on the image map. An example of the <area> tag is:

```
<area shape="poly"
coords="157,162,234,177,217,288,187,285,128,250"
href="arizona.html" alt="AZ shape" />
```

where the **shape** attribute with the **poly** value defines the clickable map area as a polygon. Other possible values for the shape attribute are circle and rect (rectangle). The alt attribute defines alternate text for the image. The **coords** attribute indicates the pairs of x- and y-coordinates of the polygon that serve as the boundaries of the linkable area. In a polygon, all pairs of x- and y-coordinates must be included. Finally, the href attribute designates the URL of the link. In this example, a Web page visitor clicking anywhere within the polygon bordered by x,y (157,162,234,177,217,288,187,285,128,250) will link to the Web page arizona.html.

To insert the <area> tag for the circle and polygon shapes, such as those shown in Figure 5–14 on page HTML 215, the HTML code would be as follows:

```
<area shape="circle" coords="308, 113, 72" href="circle.html">
<area shape="poly"
coords="78, 309, 183, 251, 316, 262, 317, 344, 136, 402"
href="poly.html">
```

To Create an Image Map

For the image map on the Southwest Map home page, three clickable areas are created, one for each state: Arizona, California, and Nevada. All three clickable areas are polygonal in shape. Table 5–8 shows the HTML code used to create the image map for the southwest.jpg image on the home page. Line 40 defines the name of the image map as states, which is the name referenced in the usemap attribute of the <img> tag that added the southwest.jpg image. Lines 41 through 43 define the three polygonal map areas for the image map, based on the x- and y-coordinates listed in Table 5–1 on page HTML 219. Each polygonal map area links to one of the three other Web pages on the Web site.

Table 5–8 HTML Code for Creating an Image Map

Line	HTML Tag and Text
40	`<map name="states" id="states">`
41	`<area shape="poly" coords="157,162,234,177,217,288,187,285,128,250" href="arizona.html" alt="AZ shape" />`
42	`<area shape="poly" coords="16,10,69,25,51,85,129,204,114,242,34,167,6,67" href="california.html" alt="CA shape" />`
43	`<area shape="poly" coords="81,24,169,47,144,166,126,175,68,85" href="nevada.html" alt="NV shape" />`
44	`</map>`

The following step illustrates how to enter the HTML code to create the image map for the southwest.jpg image.

1

- If necessary, click line 40.
- Enter the HTML code shown in Table 5–8 (Figure 5–29).

Q&A For this project, I am using all polygon shapes. Could I have used other shapes for these three states?

A rectangle shape could have been appropriate for the state of Arizona, but it would not have included the slight southward dip at the bottom of the state. To include as much of the states' area in the hotspots, we used polygons.

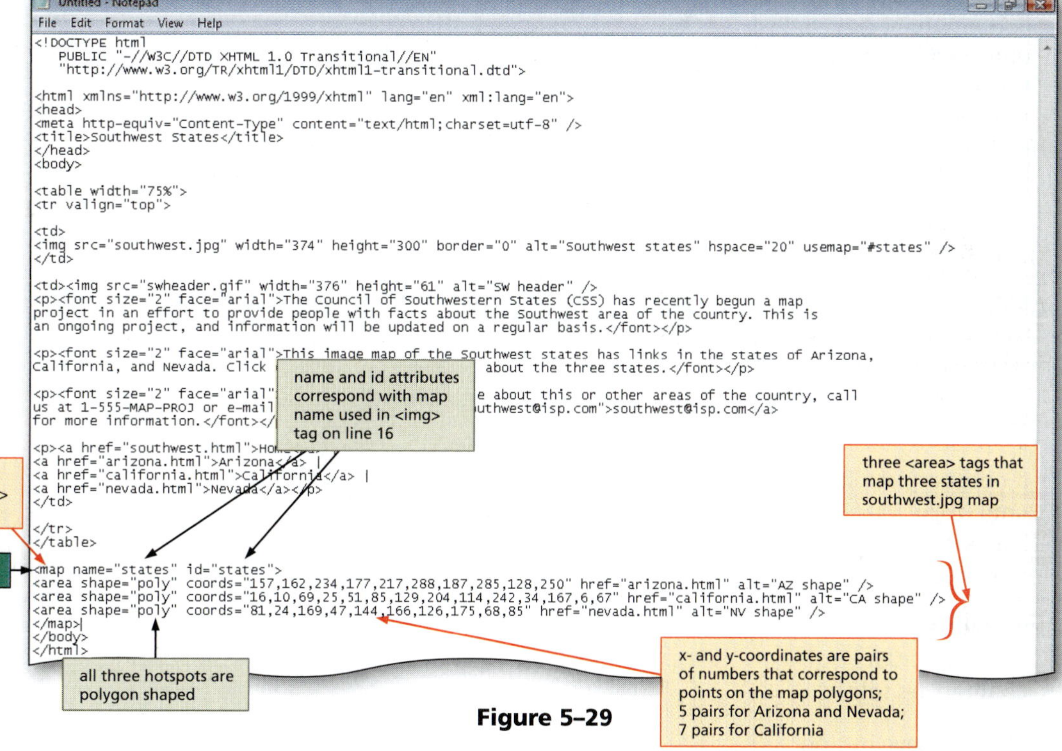

Figure 5–29

Q&A Could I have used other x- and y-coordinates for this image map?

Sure, this is a very subjective part of image mapping. You need to select the points in the boundaries that make sense to you. Just make sure that the points also will make sense to your Web page visitors. Also, take care not to overlap the points or you will end up with false results.

To Save and Print the HTML File

- With a USB drive plugged into your computer, click File on the Notepad menu bar and then click Save As. Type `southwest.html` in the File name text box (do not press ENTER).
- If Computer is not displayed in the Favorite Links section, drag the top or bottom edge of the Save As dialog box until Computer is displayed.
- Click Computer in the Favorite Links section to display a list of available drives.
- If necessary, scroll until UDISK 2.0 (G:) appears in the list of available drives.
- If necessary, open the Chapter05\ChapterFiles folder.
- Click the Save button in the Save As dialog box to save the file on the USB flash drive with the name southwest.html.

```
<!DOCTYPE html
   PUBLIC "-//W3C//DTD XHTML 1.0 Transitional//EN"
   "http://www.w3.org/TR/xhtml1/DTD/xhtml1-transitional.dtd">

<html xmlns="http://www.w3.org/1999/xhtml" lang="en" xml:lang="en">
<head>
<meta http-equiv="Content-Type" content="text/html;charset=utf-8" />
<title>Southwest States</title>
</head>
<body>

<table width="75%">
<tr valign="top">

<td>
<img src="southwest.jpg" width="374" height="300" border="0" alt="Southwest states" hspace="20" usemap="#states" /
</td>

<td><img src="swheader.gif" width="376" height="61" alt="SW header" />
<p><font size="2" face="arial">The Council of Southwestern States (CSS) has recently begun a map
project in an effort to provide people with facts about the Southwest area of the country. This is
an ongoing project, and information will be updated on a regular basis.</font></p>

<p><font size="2" face="arial">This image map of the Southwest states has links in the states of Arizona,
California, and Nevada. Click on a link to learn things about the three states.</font></p>

<p><font size="2" face="arial">If you want to learn more about this or other areas of the country, call
us at 1-555-MAP-PROJ or e-mail us at <a href="mailto:southwest@isp.com">southwest@isp.com</a>
for more information.</font></p>

<p><a href="southwest.html">Home</a> |
<a href="arizona.html">Arizona</a> |
<a href="california.html">California</a> |
<a href="nevada.html">Nevada</a></p>
</td>

</tr>
</table>

<map name="states" id="states">
<area shape="poly" coords="157,162,234,177,217,288,187,285,128,250" href="arizona.html" alt="AZ shape" />
<area shape="poly" coords="16,10,69,25,51,85,129,204,114,242,34,167,6,67" href="california.html" alt="CA shape" />
<area shape="poly" coords="81,24,169,47,144,166,126,175,68,85" href="nevada.html" alt="NV shape" />
</map>
</body>
</html>
```

Figure 5–30

- Click File on the menu bar, and then click Print on the File menu (Figure 5–30).

To Validate, View, and Print a Web Page

After the HTML file for the Southwest Map home page is saved and printed, you should validate it, view it in a browser to confirm that the Web page appears as desired, and test that the links function as expected. The following steps illustrate how to validate, view, and print a Web page.

1

- Open your browser and browse to the `validator.w3.org` link.
- Click the Validate by File Upload tab.
- Click the Browse button.
- Locate the southwest.html file on your storage device and click the file name.
- Click the Open button in the File Upload dialog box and the file name will be inserted into the File box.
- Click the Check button. The resulting validation should display as shown in Figure 5–31.

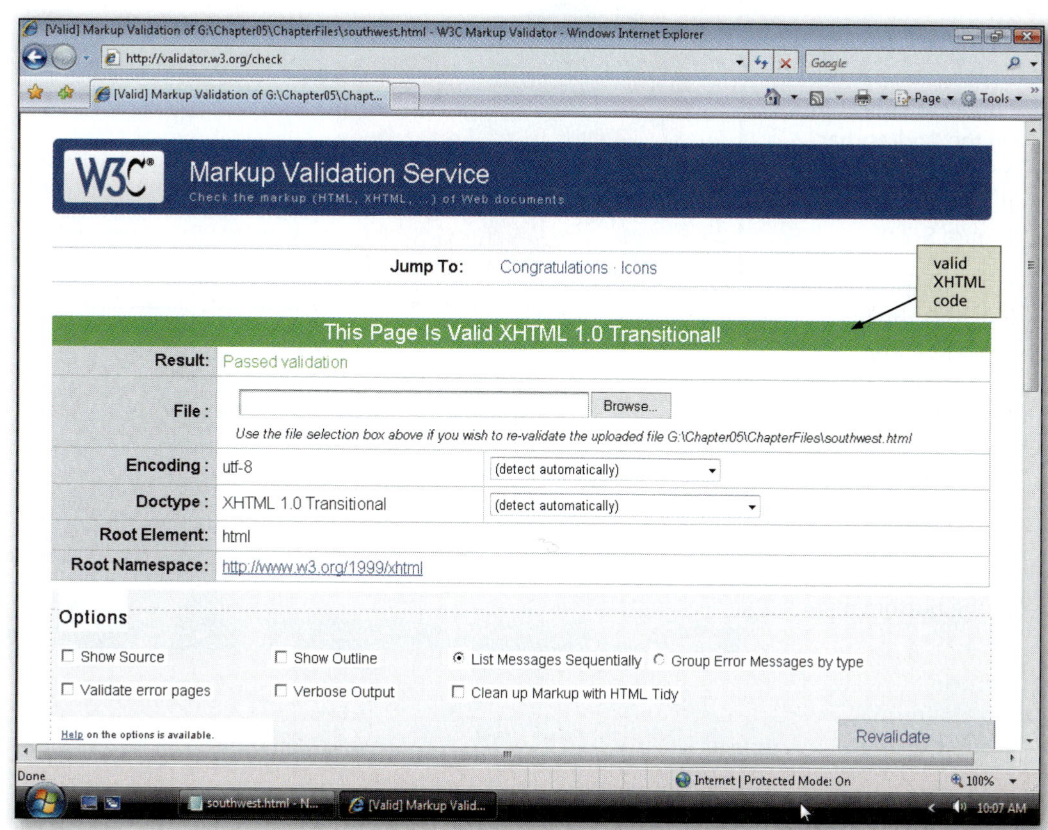

Figure 5–31

2

- In Internet Explorer, click the Address bar to select the URL on the Address bar.
- Type `g:\Chapter05\ChapterFiles\southwest.html` to display the new URL on the Address bar and then press the ENTER key (Figure 5–32).
- Click the e-mail link to verify that it works correctly. Next, test the links to the California and Nevada pages by clicking the corresponding mapped areas of the image and the text links at the bottom of the page.

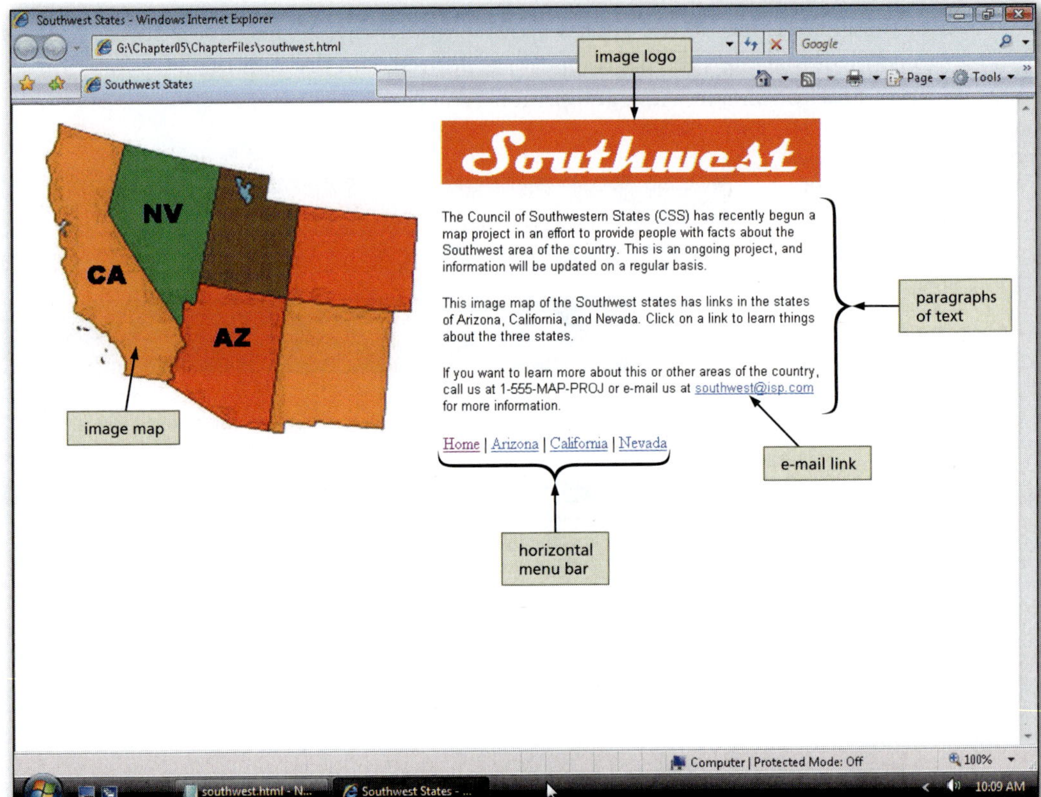

Figure 5–32

Q&A Why do the Nevada and California links work, but not the Arizona link?

These links work because the files nevada.html and california.html are stored in the Chapter05\ChapterFiles folder of the Data Files for Students. The Arizona hotspot and text link cannot be tested yet because the Arizona Web page has not been created.

BTW

Testing Image Maps

It is important to test the Web page thoroughly in the browser, especially with image maps. If one incorrect number is typed as an x- or y-coordinate, the entire image map can be wrong. Make sure that the clickable area is exactly where you want it to be by testing your Web pages.

3

- Click the Print button on the Standard Buttons toolbar to print the Web page (Figure 5–33).

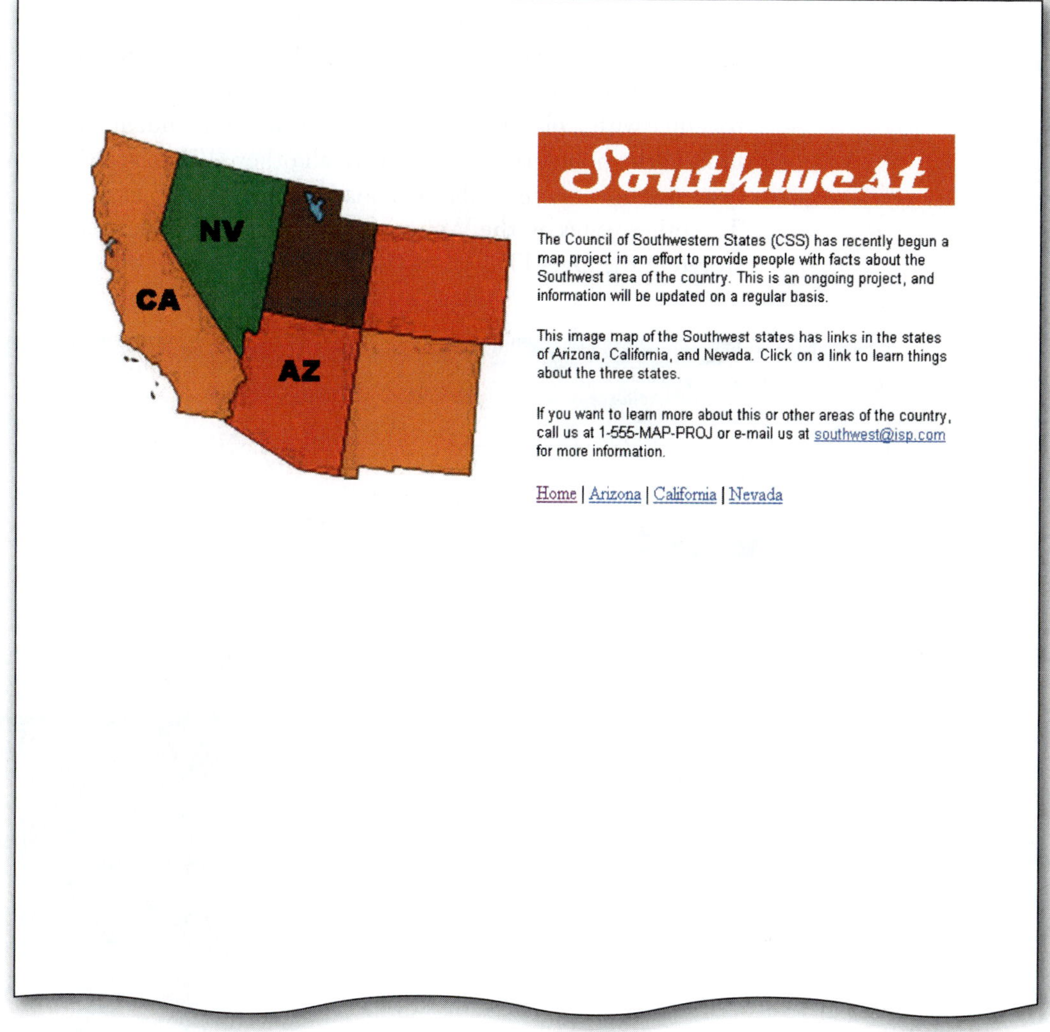

Figure 5–33

Plan Ahead

Planning subsequent Web pages.

The content for secondary Web pages is very important because these pages are generally what the visitor is searching for. The home page gives a good introduction to a Web site, but the main site content is generally found in the subsequent Web pages.

- **Determine content and organization.** The way in which the Web page is organized is important as well. For the subsequent Web pages in this project (i.e., Arizona, California, and Nevada), we need to determine a Web page layout that works well for all three states. Using tables for the Web pages allows us to organize the pages in a readable manner.
- **Make the Web page attractive.** Color and images used on a Web page help to make it attractive to your Web site visitor. In the case of the secondary Web pages, we used an image of the state flag together with a picture that is relevant to that state. If we had just displayed the text content in tables alone, it would not have been as attractive.

Creating a Second Web Page

With the home page complete, the next step is to create the Arizona Web page. As shown in Figure 5–1 on page HTML 203, each area represented in the image map (Arizona, California, and Nevada) has a separate Web page that contains text that describes the area, together with a picture relevant to the state. The individual area Web pages also have text links to the home page, as well as to all other Web pages on the Web site. This section discusses how to create the Arizona Web page (arizona.html), as shown in Figure 5–34. The other pages on the Web site (california.html and nevada.html) are completed and stored in the Data Files for Students.

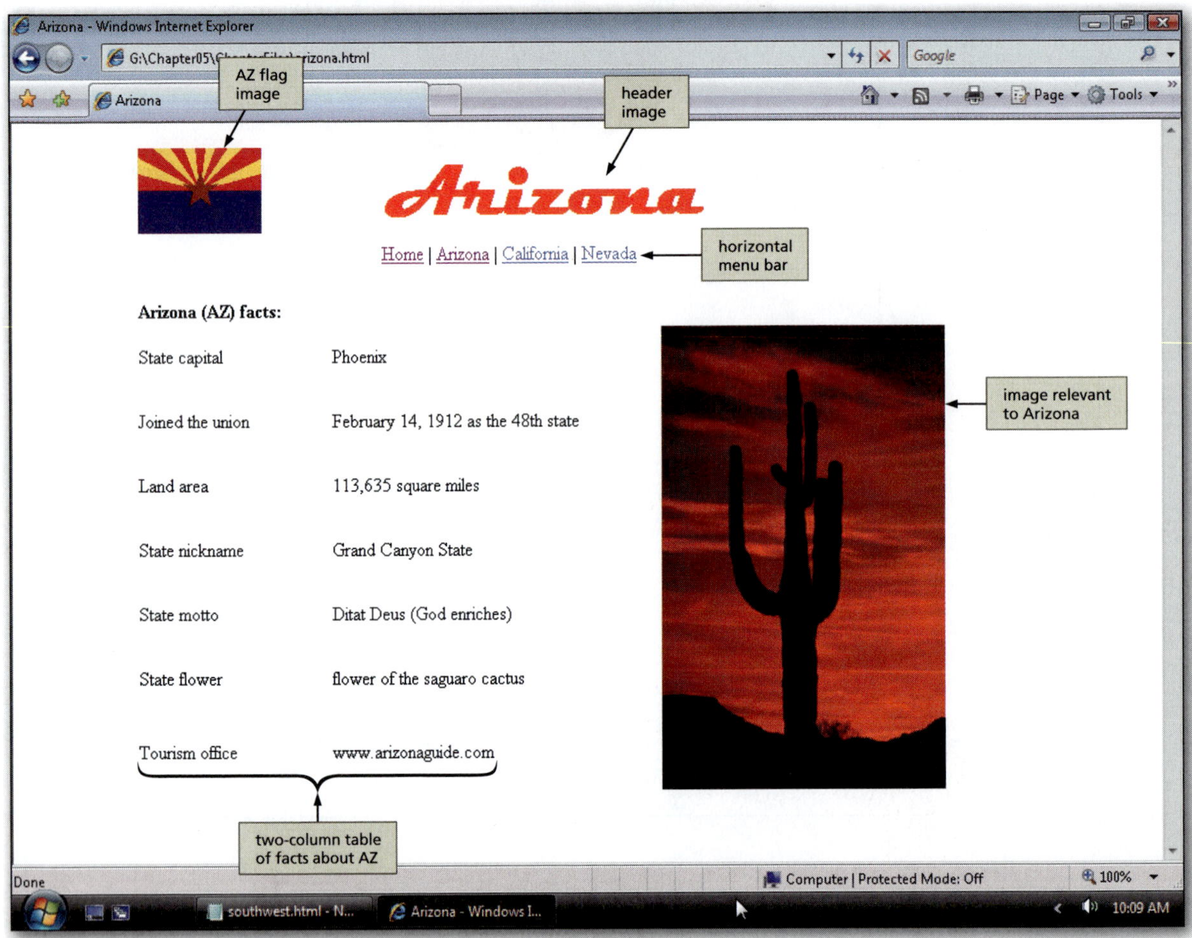

Figure 5–34

To Copy and Paste HTML Code to a New File

The easiest way to start creating the Arizona Web page is to reuse code from the home page, wherever possible. For example, the first ten lines of HTML code on the home page, which are used to describe the Web page structure, can be used on the Arizona Web page. The following step illustrates how to copy the first ten lines of HTML code from the HTML file for the home page and then paste the lines in the HTML file for the Arizona Web page.

- Click the southwest - Notepad button on the taskbar.
- When the southwest.html file is displayed in the Notepad window, click immediately to the left of the < in the <!DOCTYPE html tag on line 1. Drag through the <body> tag on line 10 to highlight lines 1 through 10.
- Press CTRL+C to copy the selected lines to the Clipboard.
- Click File on the menu bar and then click New.
- Press CTRL+V to paste the contents of the Clipboard into the new file (Figure 5–35).

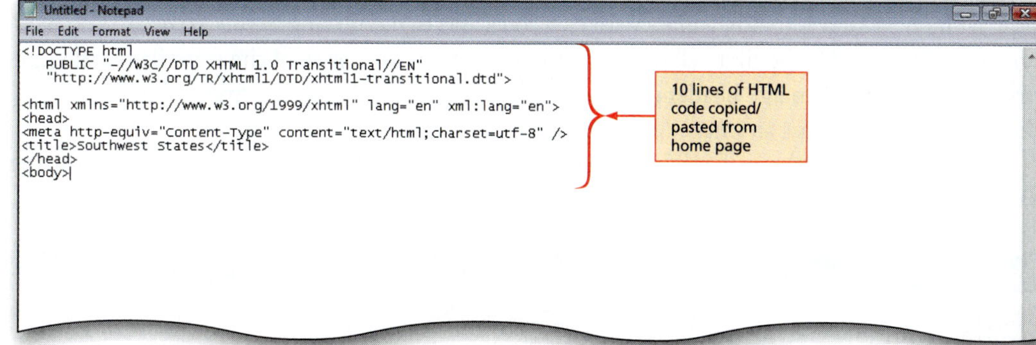

Figure 5–35

To Change the Web Page Title

The next step is to edit the pasted code to change the title of the Web page. The title of the Web page should be changed to Arizona, so the title of the current Web page is displayed on the title bar of the Web browser. The following step shows how to change the title of the Web page.

- Highlight the words Southwest States between the <title> and </title> tags on line 8. Type `Arizona` as the title to replace the words Southwest States.
- Click immediately to the right of the <body> tag on line 10 and then press the ENTER key three times.
- Type `</body>` and then press the ENTER key.
- Type `</html>`.
- Return the insertion point to line 12 (Figure 5–36).

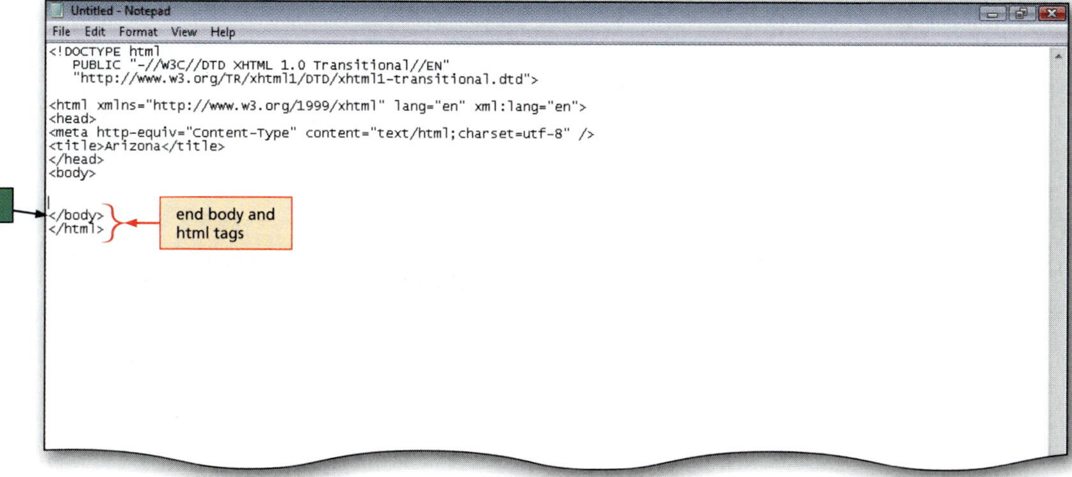

Figure 5–36

To Add a Heading

The next step is to add a table with two rows and two columns to the Arizona Web page. As shown in Figure 5–34 on page HTML 236, the first cell of the first row contains an image of the state flag (azflag.gif). The second cell of the first row contains an image header (azheader.gif). In the second row, the first cell contains a table of information, while the second cell contains an image (arizona.jpg).

Table 5–9 lists the HTML code used to create the first row of the table and enter the heading to identify the Web page.

Table 5–9 HTML Code for Adding a Heading

Line	HTML Tag and Text
12	`<table width="80%" align="center">`
13	`<tr>`
14	`<td><img src="azflag.gif" width="108" height="72" alt="Arizona flag" /></td>`
15	`<td><img src="azheader.gif" width="293" height="79" alt="Arizona header" /></td>`
16	`</tr>`

The following step illustrates how to enter the HTML code to create a table and then add a heading in the first cell of the first row.

1

- If necessary, click line 12.
- Enter the HTML code shown in Table 5–9, pressing the ENTER key twice after the last line (Figure 5–37).

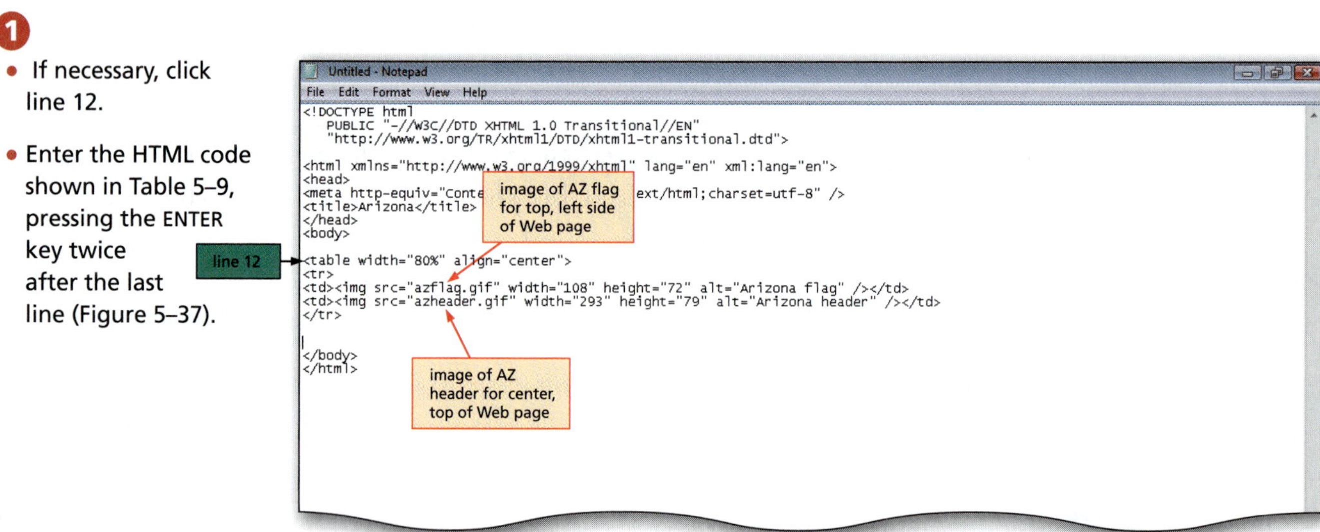

Figure 5–37

To Add a Horizontal Menu Bar

Next, you will add navigation that allows visitors to link to any Web page quickly on the Web site. Table 5–10 shows the HTML code used to add a horizontal menu bar to the Arizona Web page.

Table 5–10 HTML Code to Add Paragraphs of Text

Line	HTML Tag and Text
18	`<tr>`
19	`<td> </td>`
20	`<td><a href="southwest.html">Home</a> |`
21	`<a href="arizona.html">Arizona</a> |`
22	`<a href="california.html">California</a> |`
23	`<a href="nevada.html">Nevada</a>`
24	`</td>`
25	`</tr>`
26	`</table>`

The following step shows how to add paragraphs of text.

1

- If necessary, click line 18.
- Enter the HTML code shown in Table 5–10, pressing the ENTER key twice after the last line (Figure 5–38).

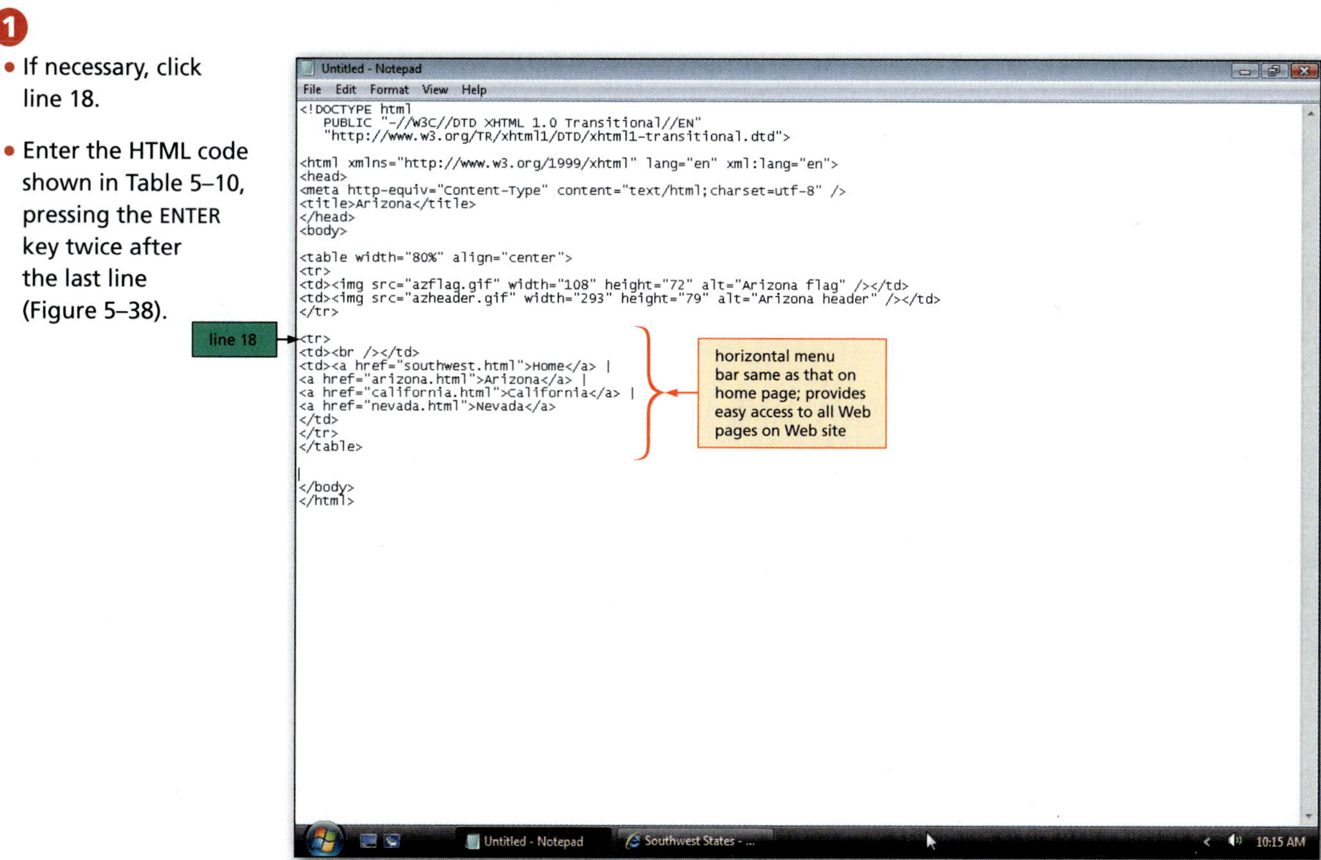

Figure 5–38

To Add Information and an Image

The next step in creating the Arizona Web page is to create a second table for information and an image relevant to Arizona, as shown in Figure 5–34 on page HTML 236. The image that is used, arizona.jpg, is stored in the Data Files for Students. Table 5–11 shows the HTML code to add a photo of a cactus and information about Arizona to the Arizona Web page. In line 42, you insert an image into the table. Because the image is large, you want it to span across all rows of data.

Table 5–11 HTML Code for Adding Information and an Image

Line	HTML Tag and Text
28	`<table width="80%" align="center">`
29	`<tr>`
30	`<td> </td>`
31	`<td> </td>`
32	`</tr>`
33	
34	`<tr>`
35	`<td><b>Arizona (AZ) facts:</b></td>`
36	`<td> </td>`
37	`</tr>`
38	
39	`<tr>`
40	`<td>State capital</td>`
41	`<td>Phoenix</td>`
42	`<td rowspan="9"><img src="cactus.jpg" width="246" height="389" alt="AZ cactus" /></td>`
43	`</tr>`
44	
45	`<tr>`
46	`<td>Joined the union</td>`
47	`<td>February 14, 1912 as the 48th state</td>`
48	`</tr>`
49	
50	`<tr>`
51	`<td>Land area</td>`
52	`<td>113,635 square miles</td>`
53	`</tr>`

1

- If necessary, click line 28.
- Enter the HTML code shown in Table 5–11, pressing the ENTER key twice after the last line (Figure 5–39).

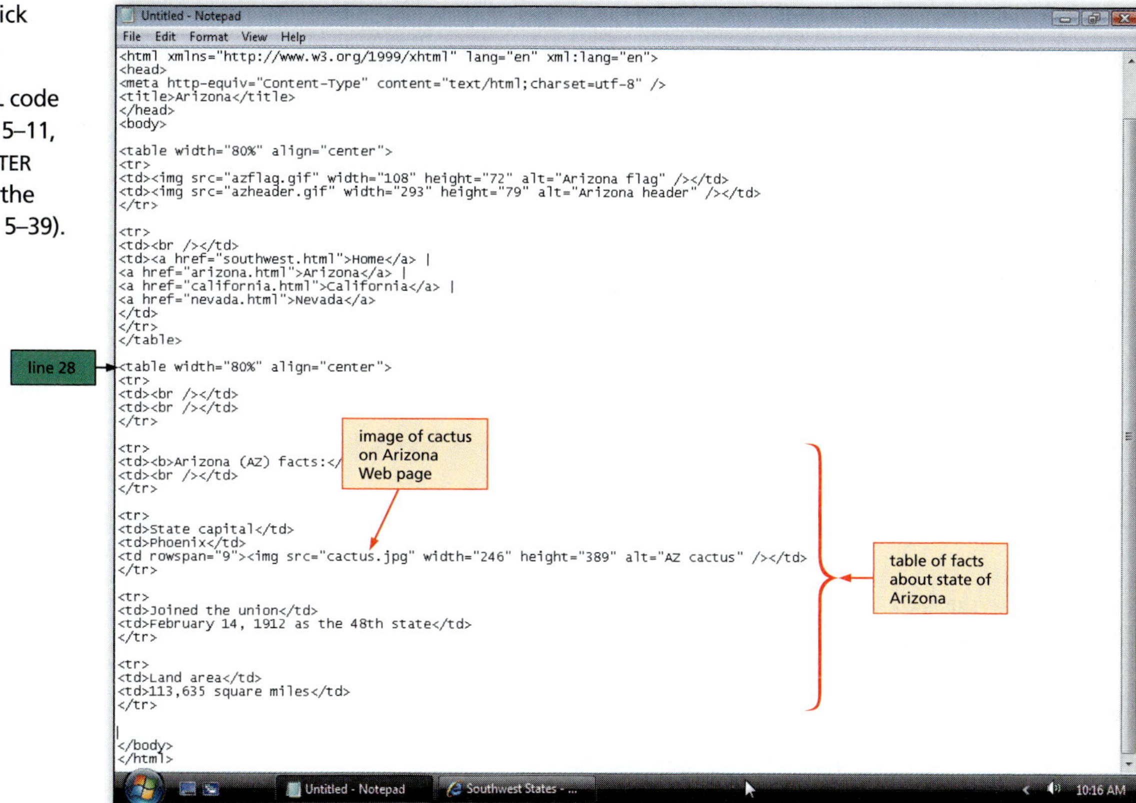

Figure 5–39

To Add Additional Information

The remainder of information (as shown in Figure 5–34 on page HTML 236) is added next. Table 5–12 shows the HTML code used to add the additional information on the Arizona Web page.

Table 5–12 HTML Code for Adding the Remaining Information

Line	HTML Tag and Text
55	<tr>
56	<td>State nickname</td>
57	<td>Grand Canyon State</td>
58	</tr>
59	
60	<tr>
61	<td>State motto</td>
62	<td>Ditat Deus (God enriches)</td>
63	</tr>
64	
65	<tr>
66	<td>State flower</td>

Table 5–12 HTML Code for Adding the Remaining Information *(continued)*

Line	HTML Tag and Text
67	<td>flower of the saguaro cactus</td>
68	</tr>
69	
70	<tr>
71	<td>Tourism office</td>
72	<td>www.arizonaguide.com</td>
73	</tr>
74	</table>

The following step shows how to enter the code to create the horizontal menu bar.

1

- If necessary, click line 55.
- Enter the HTML code shown in Table 5–12 (Figure 5–40).

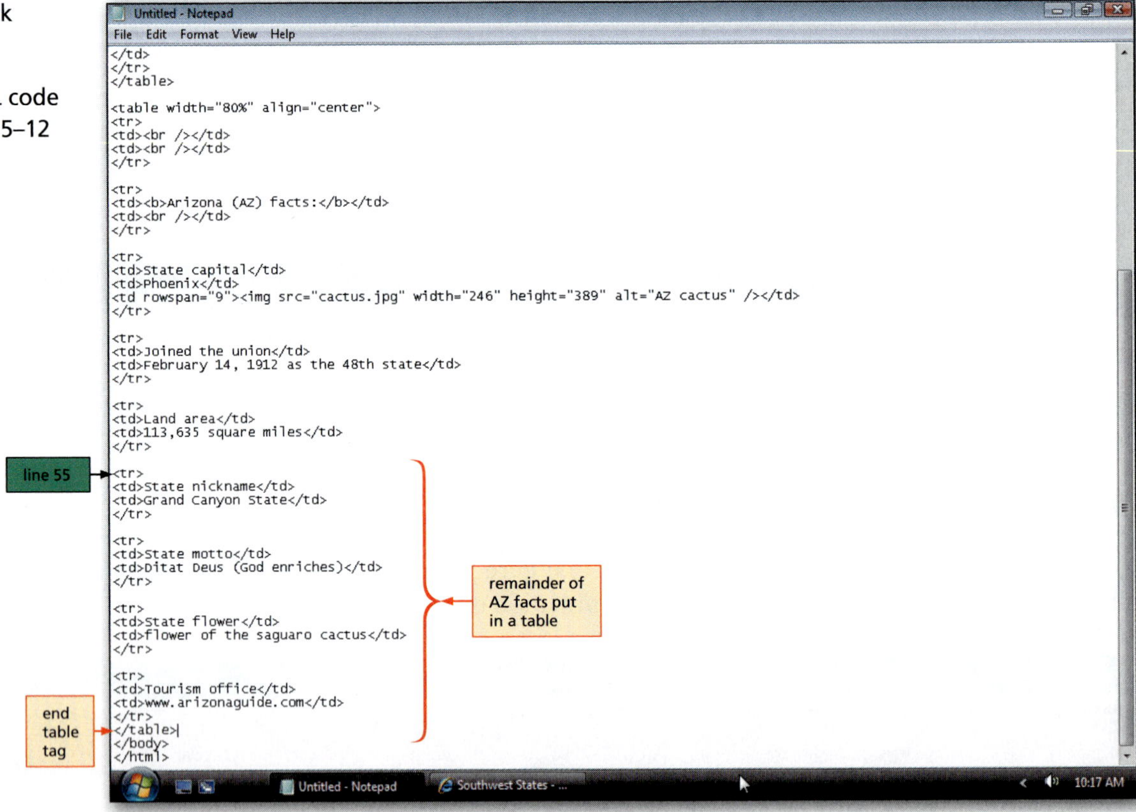

Figure 5–40

To Save and Print the HTML File

- With a USB drive plugged into your computer, click File on the menu bar and then click Save As. Type `arizona.html` in the File name text box.
- If necessary, click UDISK (G:) in the Save in list. Click the Chapter05 folder and then double-click the ChapterFiles folder in the list of available folders. Click the Save button in the Save As dialog box.
- Click File on the menu bar and then click Print on the File menu (Figure 5–41).

```
<html xmlns="http://www.w3.org/1999/xhtml" lang="en" xml:lang="en">
<head>
<meta http-equiv="Content-Type" content="text/html;charset=utf-8" />
<title>Arizona</title>
</head>
<body>

<table width="80%" align="center">
<tr>
<td><img src="azflag.gif" width="108" height="72" alt="Arizona flag" /></td>
<td><img src="azheader.gif" width="293" height="79" alt="Arizona header" /></td>
</tr>

<tr>
<td><br /></td>
<td><a href="southwest.html">Home</a> |
<a href="arizona.html">Arizona</a> |
<a href="california.html">California</a> |
<a href="nevada.html">Nevada</a>
</td>
</tr>
</table>

<table width="80%" align="center">
<tr>
<td><br /></td>
<td><br /></td>
</tr>

<tr>
<td><b>Arizona (AZ) facts:</b></td>
<td><br /></td>
</tr>

<tr>
<td>State capital</td>
<td>Phoenix</td>
<td rowspan="9"><img src="cactus.jpg" width="246" height="389" alt="AZ cactus" /></td>
</tr>

<tr>
<td>Joined the union</td>
<td>February 14, 1912 as the 48th state</td>
</tr>

<tr>
<td>Land area</td>
<td>113,635 square miles</td>
</tr>

<tr>
<td>State nickname</td>
<td>Grand Canyon State</td>
</tr>

<tr>
<td>State motto</td>
<td>Ditat Deus (God enriches)</td>
</tr>

<tr>
<td>State flower</td>
<td>flower of the saguaro cactus</td>
</tr>

<tr>
<td>Tourism office</td>
<td>www.arizonaguide.com</td>
</tr>
</table>
</body>
</html>
```

Figure 5–41

To Validate, View, and Print the Web Page

- Click the Internet Explorer button on the taskbar.
- Validate the Arizona Web page using the W3C validation service.
- Click the Arizona area on the Southwest states image map to display the Web page as shown in Figure 5–42.

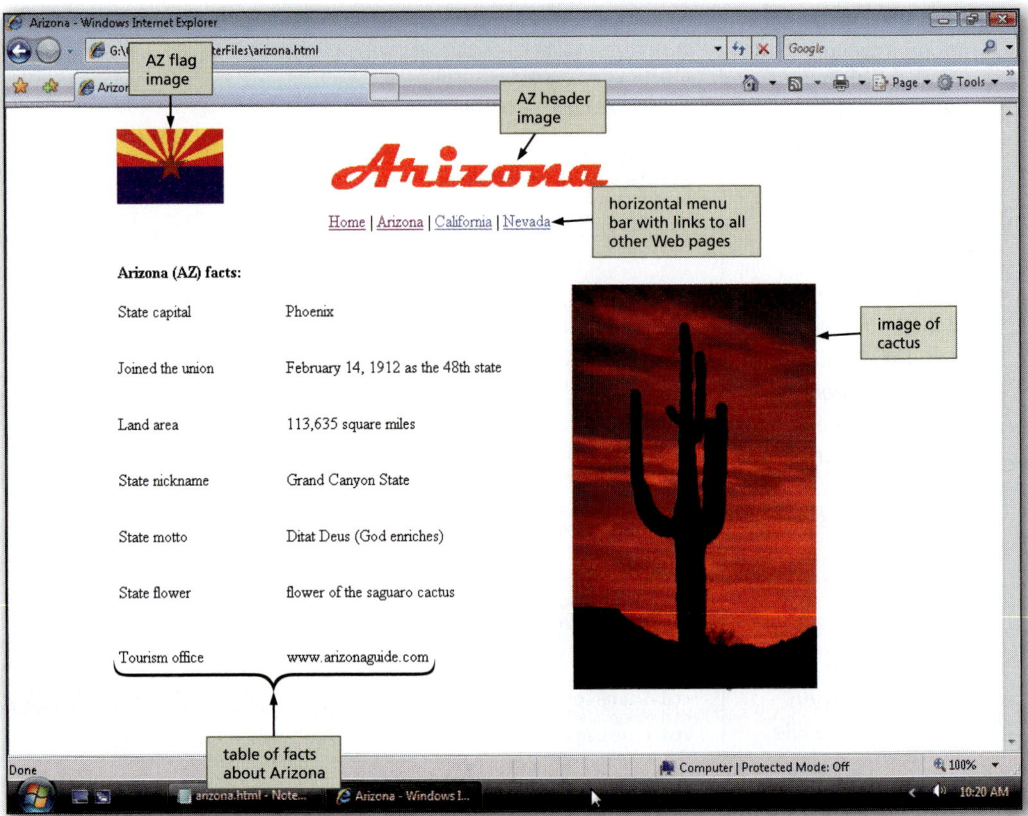

Figure 5–42

- Click the Print button on the Standard Buttons toolbar to print the Web page (Figure 5–43).

Home | Arizona | California | Nevada

Arizona (AZ) facts:

State capital	Phoenix
Joined the union	February 14, 1912 as the 48th state
Land area	113,635 square miles
State nickname	Grand Canyon State
State motto	Ditat Deus (God enriches)
State flower	flower of the saguaro cactus
Tourism office	www.arizonaguide.com

Figure 5–43

To Test the Links

The next step is to test the links on the various pages on the Web site to verify that each link connects to the appropriate Web page. If possible, view all of the Web pages in more than one browser type or version to ensure that the Web pages appear correctly in different browsers. Links must be tested from the image map on the home page, as well as from the horizontal menu bar on each of the Web pages. If any of the links do not work correctly, return to Notepad to modify the HTML code, save the changes, and then retest the links in the browser.

- Click the Home link on the Arizona Web page.
- Click the Nevada area on the image map on the home page.
- Click the California link on the Nevada Web page.
- Click the Home link on the California Web page (Figure 5–44).
- If any of the links do not work correctly, return to Notepad to modify the HTML code, save the changes, and then retest the links in the browser.

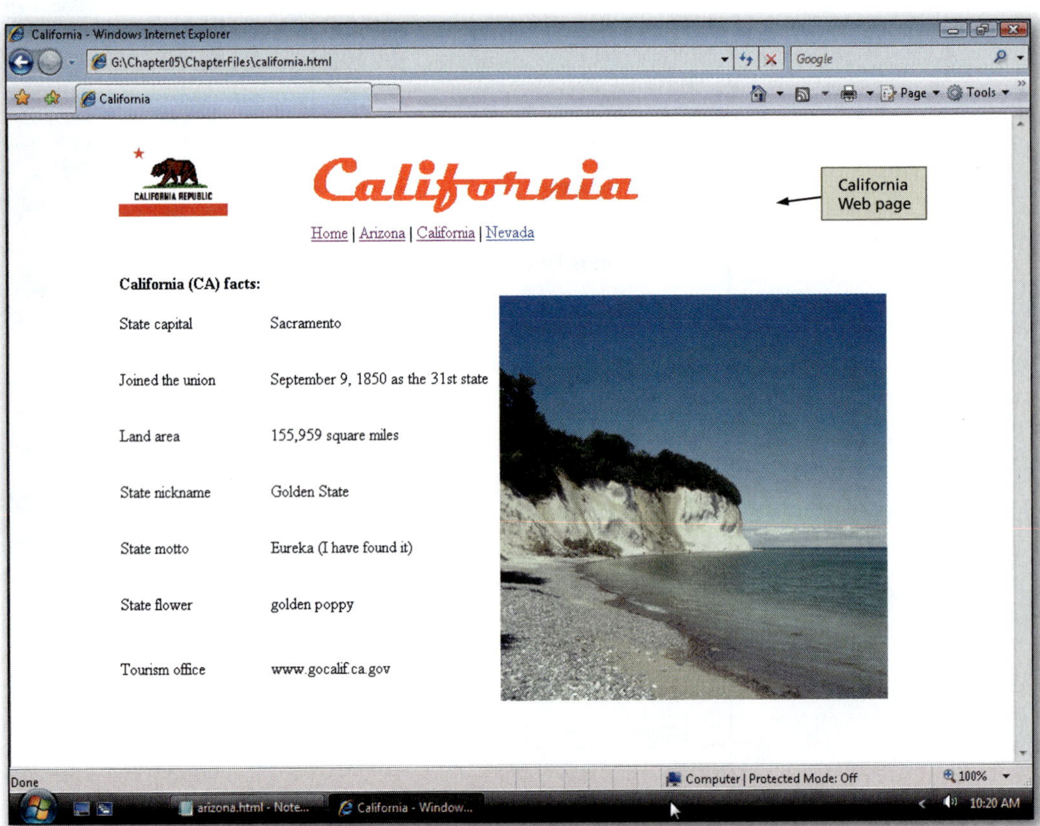

Figure 5–44

To Quit Notepad and a Browser

- Click the Close button on the browser title bar.
- Click the Close button on the Notepad window title bar.

Chapter Summary

In this chapter, you have learned how to develop a Web site that utilizes image mapping from the home page to create three clickable areas. The items listed below include all the new HTML skills you have learned in this chapter.

1. Start Paint (HTML 216)
2. Open an Image File in Paint (HTML 218)
3. Locate X- and Y-Coordinates of an Image (HTML 220)
4. Create a Table (HTML 225)
5. Insert an Image to Use as an Image Map (HTML 226)
6. Add a Header and Text to a Table Cell (HTML 227)
7. Create a Horizontal Menu Bar with Text Links (HTML 228)
8. End the Table (HTML 229)
9. Create an Image Map (HTML 230)
10. Validate, View, and Print a Web Page (HTML 233)
11. Copy and Paste HTML Code to a New File (HTML 236)
12. Change the Web Page Title (HTML 237)
13. Add a Heading (HTML 238)
14. Add a Horizontal Menu Bar (HTML 239)
15. Add Information and an Image (HTML 240)
16. Add Additional Information (HTML 241)

Learn It Online

Test your knowledge of chapter content and key terms.

Instructions: To complete the Learn It Online exercises, start your browser, click the Address bar, and then enter the Web address `scsite.com/html5e/learn`. When the HTML Learn It Online page is displayed, click the link for the exercise you want to complete and read the instructions.

Chapter Reinforcement TF, MC, and SA

A series of true/false, multiple choice, and short answer questions that test your knowledge of the chapter content.

Flash Cards

An interactive learning environment where you identify chapter key terms associated with displayed definitions.

Practice Test

A series of multiple choice questions that test your knowledge of chapter content and key terms.

Who Wants To Be a Computer Genius?

An interactive game that challenges your knowledge of chapter content in the style of a television quiz show.

Wheel of Terms

An interactive game that challenges your knowledge of chapter key terms in the style of the television show, *Wheel of Fortune*.

Crossword Puzzle Challenge

A crossword puzzle that challenges your knowledge of key terms presented in the chapter.

STUDENT ASSIGNMENTS

Apply Your Knowledge

Reinforce the skills and apply the concepts you learned in this chapter.

Adding an Image Map to a Web Page

Instructions: Start Notepad. Open the file apply5-1.html from the Chapter05\Apply folder of the Data Files for Students. See the inside back cover of this book for instructions on downloading the Data Files for Students, or contact your instructor for information about accessing the required files. The apply5-1.html file is a partially completed HTML file that needs to be completed. Figure 5–45 shows the Apply Your Knowledge Web page as it should appear in your browser after the errors are corrected.

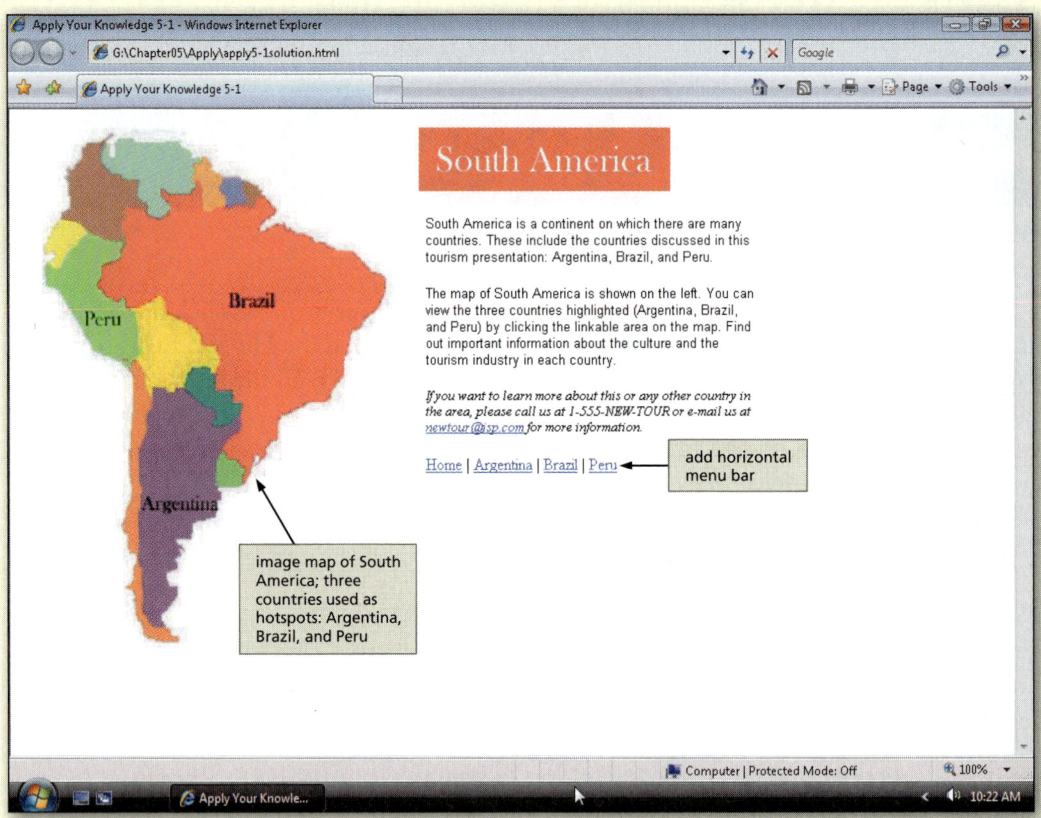

Figure 5–45

1. Enter the URL G:\Chapter05\Apply\apply5-1.html to view the Web page in your browser.
2. Examine the HTML file and its appearance as a Web page in the browser.
3. Using Paint, open the file samerica.jpg from the Chapter05\Apply folder. Determine the x- and y-coordinates necessary to create three clickable areas on the map image, one each for Argentina, Brazil, and Peru. You may either use rectangle or polygon shapes for the three areas.
4. Add HTML code to the apply5-1.html file to create an image map that links each clickable area on the map image to an external Web page of your choice.
5. Create a Web page for one of the countries. Research information about the country and include some interesting facts. Include some images on the secondary Web page, but be aware of copyright laws governing their use.

6. Add code to create a horizontal menu bar as shown in Figure 5–45.
7. Save the revised file in the Chapter05\Apply folder using the file name apply5-1solution.html.
8. Validate the Web pages to assure that you are in compliance with current standards.
9. Test the links completely.
10. Print the revised HTML file.
11. Enter the URL G:\Chapter05\Apply\apply5-1solution.html to view the Web page in your browser.
12. Print the Web page.
13. Submit the completed HTML file and Web page in the format specified by your instructor.

Extend Your Knowledge

Extend the skills you learned in this chapter and experiment with new skills.

Creating an Image Map

Instructions: Start Notepad. Open the file extend5-1.html from the Chapter05\Extend folder of the Data Files for Students. See the inside back cover of this book for instructions on downloading the Data Files for Students, or contact your instructor for information about accessing the required files. This sample HTML file contains all of the text for the Web page shown in Figure 5–46. You will add the necessary tags to make the familytree.jpg image an image map with at least three hotspots.

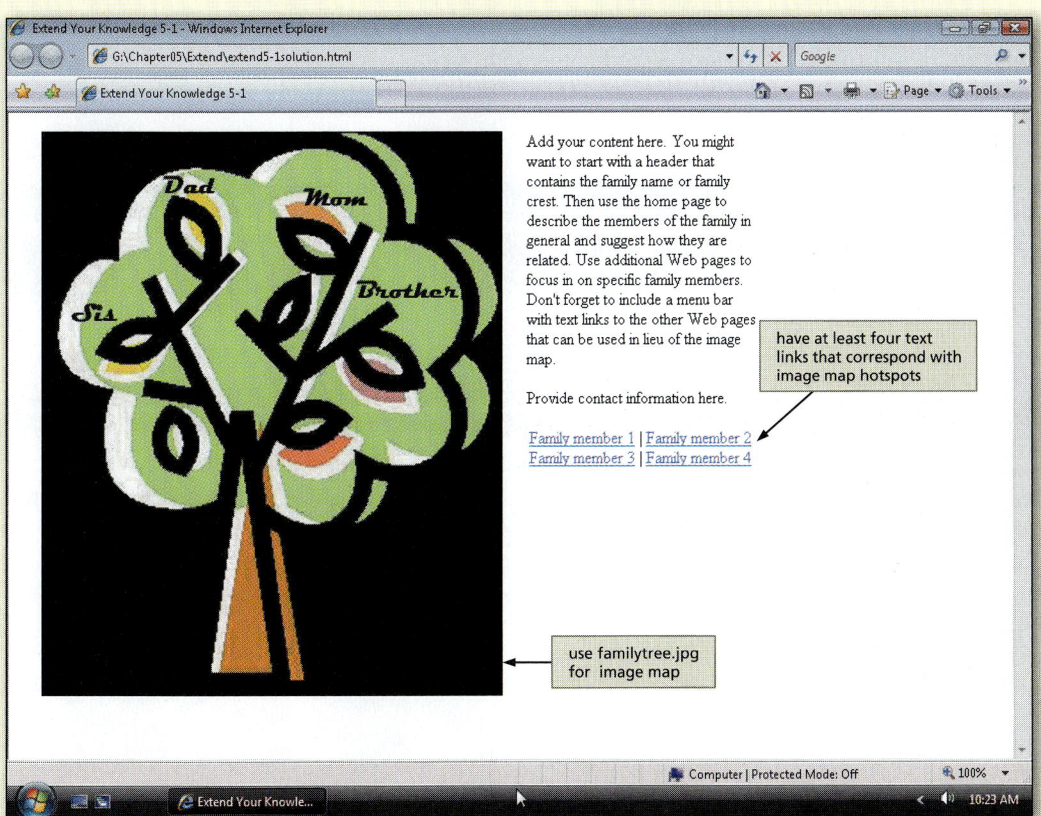

Figure 5–46

Continued >

Extend Your Knowledge *continued*

Perform the following tasks:

1. Use the familytree.jpg image for the image map on this Web page.
2. Using Paint, determine several (at least three) linkable areas in the tree. Use those links to connect to secondary Web pages that contain information about family members. If you have a digital camera, take pictures of the family members to include on the secondary Web pages. Include text that describes their interests or occupations.
3. Add HTML code to align the first picture on the left with hspace of 20.
4. Save the revised document as extend5-1solution.html.
5. Validate your HTML code and test all links.
6. Submit the completed HTML file and Web page in the format specified by your instructor.

Make It Right

Analyze a document and correct all errors and/or improve the design.

Correcting the Travel Agency Web Page

Instructions: Start Notepad. Open the file makeitright5-1.html from the Chapter05\MakeItRight folder of the Data Files for Students. See the inside back cover of this book for instructions on downloading the Data Files for Students, or contact your instructor for information about accessing the required files. The Web page is a modified version of what you see in Figure 5–47. Make the necessary corrections to the Web page to make it look like the figure. The Web page uses the image getaway.gif. Add four text links at the bottom of the Web page as shown in Figure 5–47, using Table 5–13 for link name suggestions and URLs. Submit the completed HTML file and Web page in the format specified by your instructor.

Table 5–13 Image Map Coordinates, URLs, and Text Links

Text Link	Image Map Coordinates	URLS
Ski & Snow	55,96,253,134	http://www.coloradoski.com/
Surf & Sun	301,93,497,134	http://www.nationalgeographicexpeditions.com/
Golf & Spa	55,161,244,201	http://www.seasidegolf.com/
Adventure	283,158,498,195	http://www.abercrombiekent.com/index.cfm

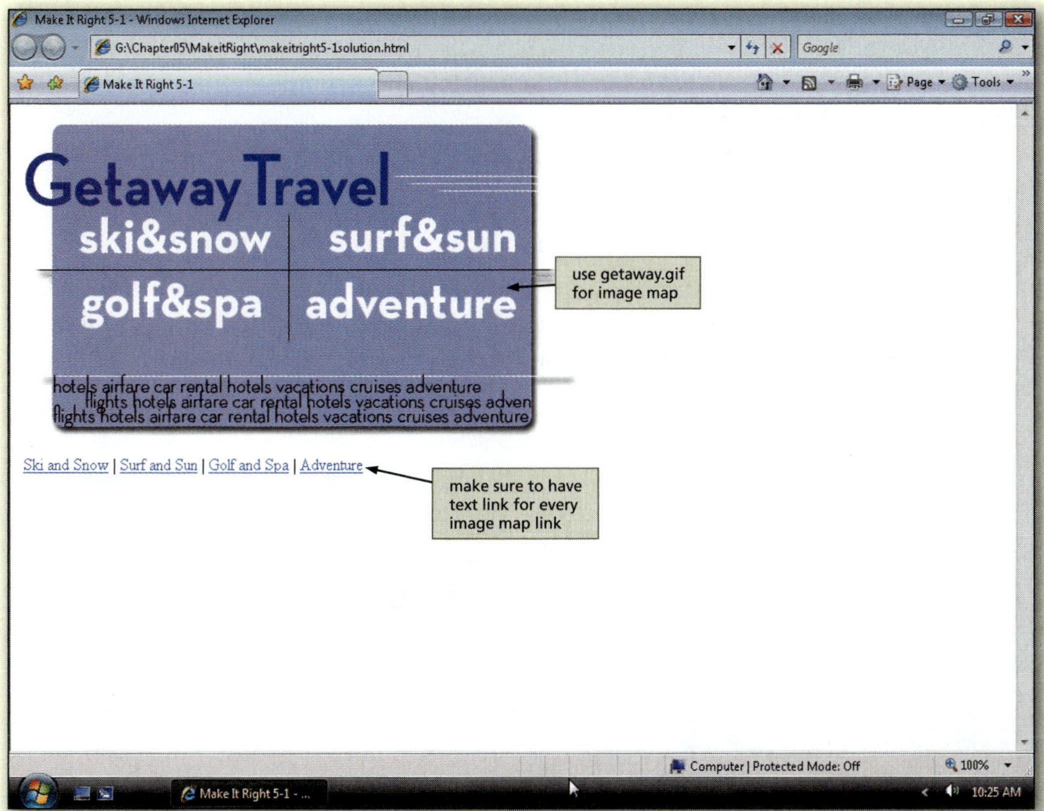

Figure 5–47

In the Lab

Lab 1: Creating a Donation Analysis Page

Problem: Your school has held a donation drive, and you have been asked to create a Web page to show the results. You decide to create a Web page similar to the Web page in Figure 5–48, with the file money.gif as an image map that links to three Web pages of your choosing.

Instructions: Start Paint and Notepad. Perform the following steps:

1. Using Paint, open the file money.gif from the Chapter05\IntheLab folder.
2. Determine the x- and y-coordinates necessary to create three rectangular clickable areas on the graphical image, one for each of the three areas, including Theater Club, Computer Club, and Future Teachers of America Club. Write down those coordinates for later use.

Continued >

In the Lab *continued*

3. Using Notepad, create a new HTML file with the title Lab 5-1 in the title section. Add the heading and text as shown in Figure 5–48.
4. Insert the image money.gif after the heading. Use the usemap attribute usemap="#money" in the <img> tag.
5. Enter the <map> </map> tags required to create the image map named money.
6. Enter the <area> tags required to define three rectangular clickable areas on the image money.gif. Use the x- and y-coordinates determined in Step 2 and set the href attribute to display the three gifs included in the Chapter05\IntheLab folder of the Data Files for Students (ccdonations.gif, tcdonations.gif, and ftadonations.gif).

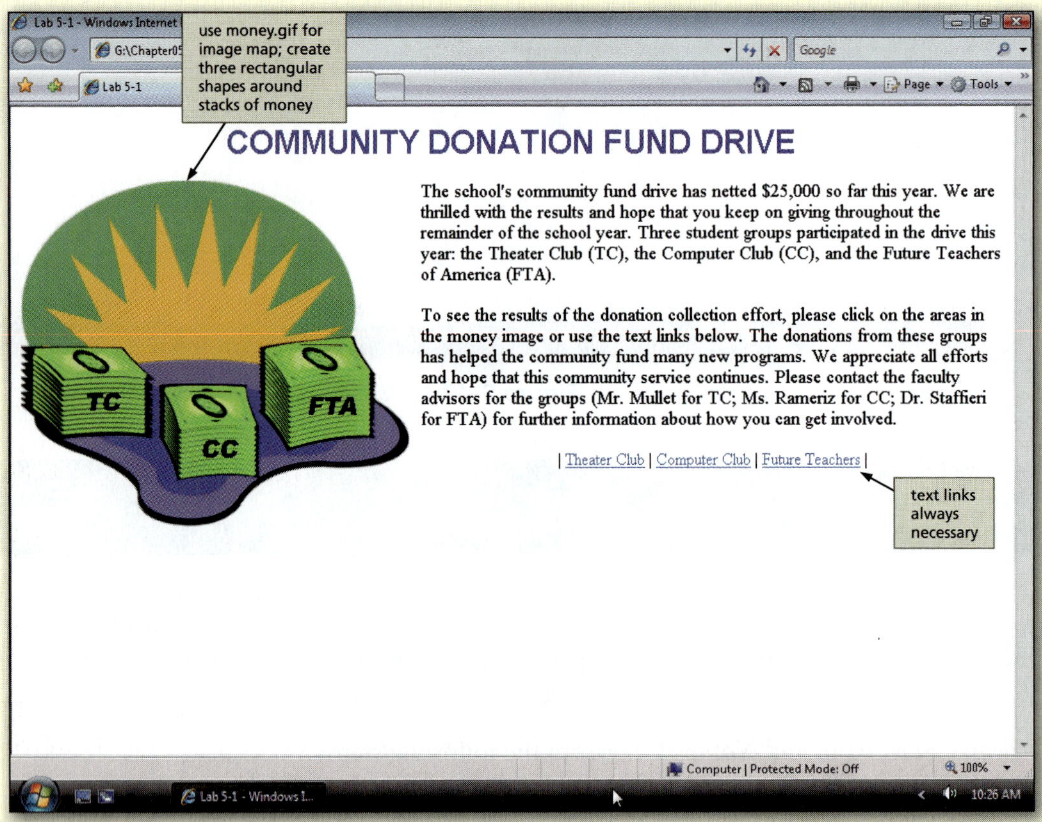

Figure 5–48

7. For a bonus project, create three Web pages and use those for your links, rather than the three gifs provided.
8. Save the HTML file in the Chapter05\IntheLab folder using the file name lab5-1solution.html. Validate the Web page using W3C. Print the HTML file.
9. Open the file lab5-1solution.html in your browser and test the image map and text links to verify they link to the correct Web pages.
10. Print the main Web page and the three linked Web pages.
11. Submit the completed HTML files and Web pages in the format specified by your instructor.

In the Lab

Lab 2: Mapping Sales Figures

Problem: You decide to use your image mapping skills to create a Web page that describes your company's sales figures for the year. You plan to create a Web page similar to the one shown in Figure 5–49, with the file barchart.png (note the different image type) as an image map that links to four Web pages with information on the various sales for the four quarters of the year.

Instructions: Start Paint and Notepad. Perform the following steps using a computer:

1. Using Paint, open the file barchart.png from the Chapter05\IntheLab folder.
2. Each area on the bar chart image has a rectangular shape. Use good judgment when planning those shapes, ensuring that no areas overlap and that the shape makes sense for that area of the image. Using Paint, estimate the x- and y-coordinates necessary to create four clickable areas on the barchart.png image.
3. Using Notepad, create a new HTML file with the title Lab 5-2 in the title section. Add the heading and text as shown in Figure 5–49.
4. Begin the body section by adding a header with #000064 as the color. Use Paint to determine the dimensions of the image for the <img> tag. Align the image so that it is to the right of the text.
5. Use the usemap attribute usemap="#chart" in the <img> tag.
6. Enter the <map> </map> tags required to create the image map named chart.
7. Enter the <area> tags required to define four clickable areas on the image barchart.png. Use the x- and y-coordinates determined in Step 2 and set the href attribute to link to the sample.html file from the Data Files for Students or create your own secondary Web page.
8. Save the HTML file in the Chapter05\IntheLab folder using the file name lab5-2solution.html. Validate the Web page(s) using W3C. Print the HTML file.
9. Open the file lab 5-2solution. html, in your browser and test the image map and text links to verify they link to the correct Web pages.
10. Print the main Web page and the three linked Web pages.
11. Submit the completed HTML files and Web pages in the format specified by your instructor.

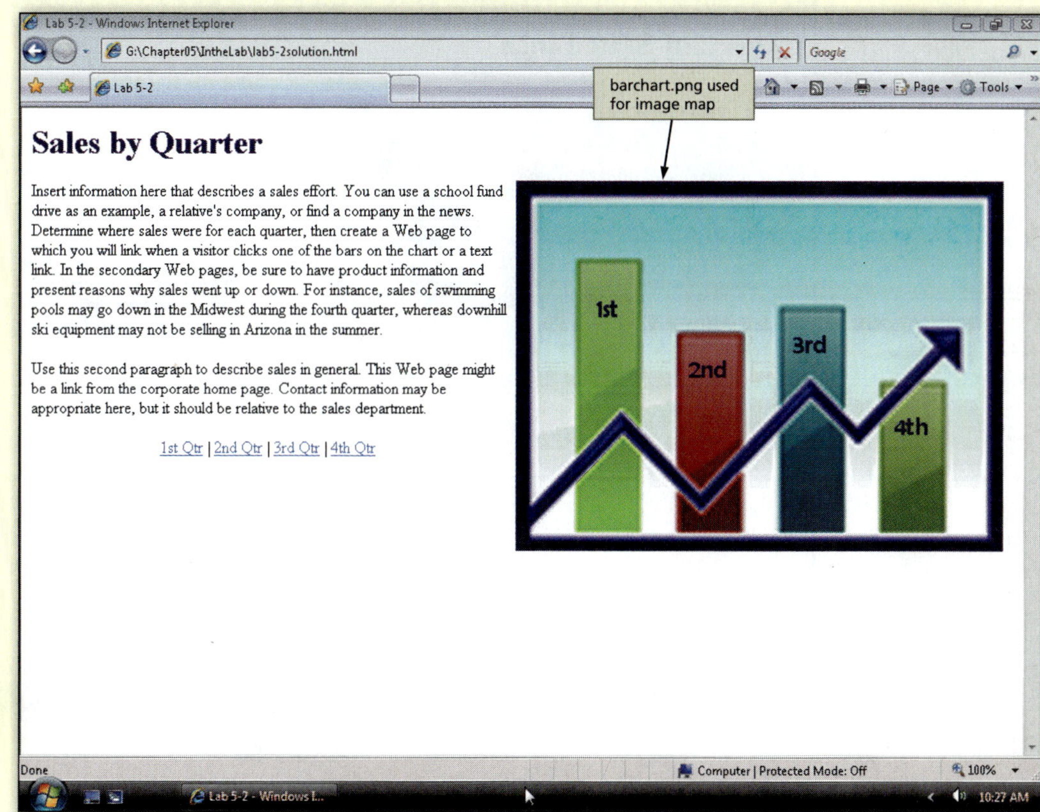

Figure 5–49

In the Lab

Lab 3: Creating a Government Services Web Page

Problem: Your manager at the City Hall has asked you to create a Web page that provides easy access to important Web sites within your state and two other states of your choice. You plan to create a Web page similar to the one shown in Figure 5–50, with the file states_good.gif, as an image map that links to three government Web sites. Browse the Web to find government Web sites that are common throughout three different states (for example, Department of Education, tax information, and state departments) and then use these links in the image map.

Instructions: Start Paint and Notepad. Perform the following tasks:

1. Using Paint, open the file states_good.gif from the Chapter05\IntheLab folder of the Data Files for Students.
2. Using Paint, determine the x- and y-coordinates necessary to create three clickable areas on the map image, using a circle, a rectangle, and a polygon shape for one state each. Write down those coordinates for later use.
3. Using Notepad, create a new HTML file with the title Lab 5-3 in the main heading section.
4. Begin the body section by adding the Important State Links heading, as shown in Figure 5–50.
5. Insert the image states_good.gif after the heading. Use the usemap attribute usemap="#states" in the <img> tag.
6. Enter the <map> </map> tags required to create the image map named states.

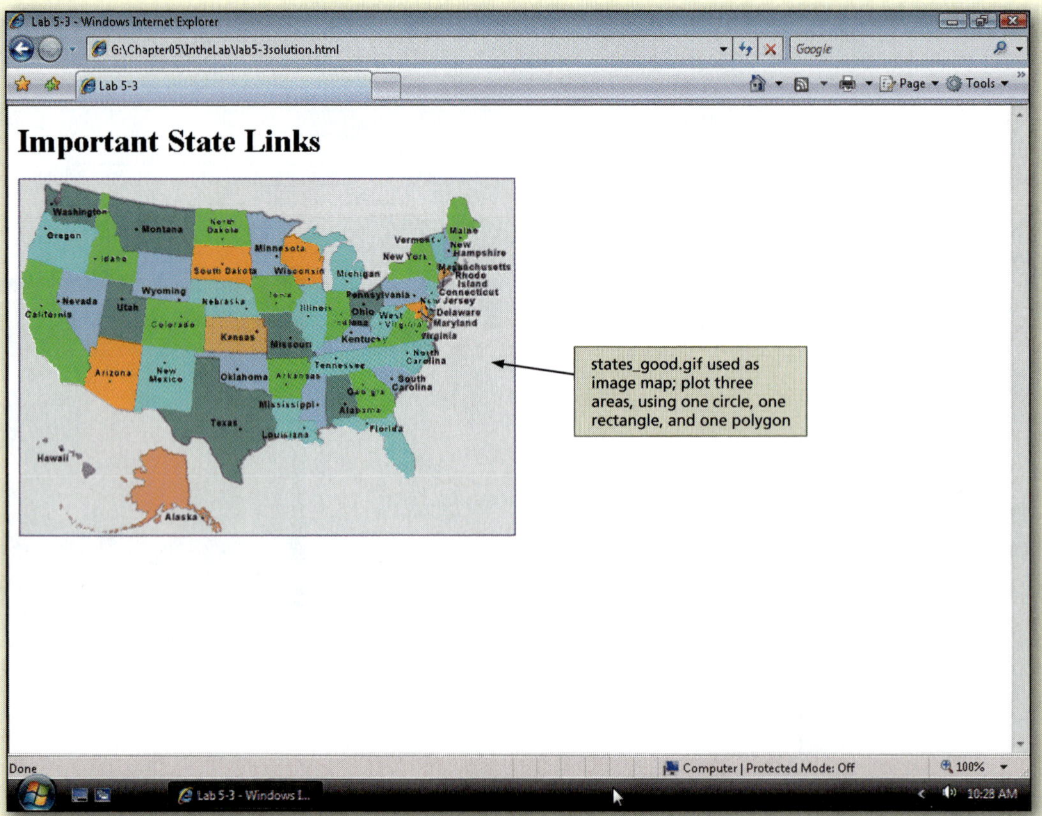

Figure 5–50

7. Enter the <area> tags required to define three clickable areas on the image states_good.gif. Use the x- and y-coordinates determined in Step 2 and set the href attribute to use the URLs for the three government Web sites you have identified for three different states.
8. Save the HTML file in the Chapter05\IntheLab folder using the file name lab5-3solution.html. Validate the Web page. Print the HTML file.
9. Open the file lab 5-3solution.html in your browser and test the image map and text links to verify they link to the correct Web pages.
10. Print the main Web page and the four linked Web pages.
11. Submit the completed HTML files and Web pages in the format specified by your instructor.

Cases and Places

Apply your creative thinking and problem solving skills to design and implement a solution.

• Easier ••More Difficult

• 1: Completing Southwest States

The head of the Council of Southwestern States (CSS) was so excited by this project that she wants you to finish up with the remaining states. Find information about the remaining Southwest states and create Web pages for them. Don't forget to add those states to the horizontal menu bar and to the image map. You can use an image editing software package (even Paint will work) to add the two-letter state abbreviations to the image map. A good idea is to make a copy of the original image and save it under a different name so that you can play with the image and still reserve the original. Magneto font size 16 was used for the font.

• 2: Library Services

The marketing director of your community library wants to create a new graphical home page that highlights the different services that the library provides, including: book reserve, video rentals, available meeting rooms, and computers with Internet access. Using the books.jpg image from the Chapter05\CasesandPlaces folder of the Data Files for Students, create a Web page. First, open the books.jpg image in Paint to determine hotspots that you can use as three or four links. For a higher level of difficulty, use the Text tool in Paint to add relevant words onto the books for those links. (*Hint*: Search the Paint Help utility for the word Text.) From those hotspots, create links to subsequent Web pages that describe the services. Be sure to include text links at the bottom of the page to mirror the links in the image map.

•• 3: Browsing with Images Turned Off

As discussed in this chapter, some Web site visitors turn graphics off while browsing. Determine in your Web development (or any other) class how many students do turn off graphics. With this information in hand, search the Web to find three Web sites that utilize image maps. Track the time that it takes to load the three Web pages with image maps. Turn off graphics in your browser (in Internet Explorer, click the Tools button and click Internet Options, and then click the Advanced tab; scroll down and click Show pictures under Multimedia to deselect it). Next, clear the browser's history (in Internet Explorer, click the Tools button and Internet Options, and then click the Delete button under Browsing history). Reload each of the three Web pages and again track the time it takes for the pages to load, this time without images. Determine if the Web pages load more quickly with images off. Review each Web page and determine if you can use all of the links despite having graphics turned off.

•• 4: Create an Image Map Using Available Software

Make It Personal

The Graphics Design Director at Axcelent has asked you to search the Web to learn more about the image mapping software tools listed in Table 5–2 on page HTML 222, as well as additional software tools not listed in this chapter. Read the information about each tool, including its costs, free trial version availability, platform(s) supported, and ease of use. If a free trial version is offered at any of the Web sites and you are using your own computer (or your instructor or lab coordinator allows it), download the software and use it to create an image map. Compare the technique of using these tools to the technique used in this chapter using Paint. Write a synopsis of the available products, including cost, free trial version availability, platform(s) supported, and ease of use.

• • 5: Creating a Travel Journal

Working Together

Each member of your team should think of a hobby, sport, or interest that they have. Search the Internet or available free clip art for an image that depicts this interest. (*Hint:* Microsoft has clip art available that you can use to practice your image mapping skills. Visit www.microsoft.com and search for Clip Art.) Use graphic editing software (Paint is fine for this purpose) to combine your images together to create one image map. The Web site should use this image map to create links that will route visitors to each team member's Web page. The team should sketch the overall plan for the Web site and then have each team member create at least one Web page that describes their area of interest. On each Web page, include at least one or more text paragraphs, and relevant graphical images.

6 Using Frames in a Web Site

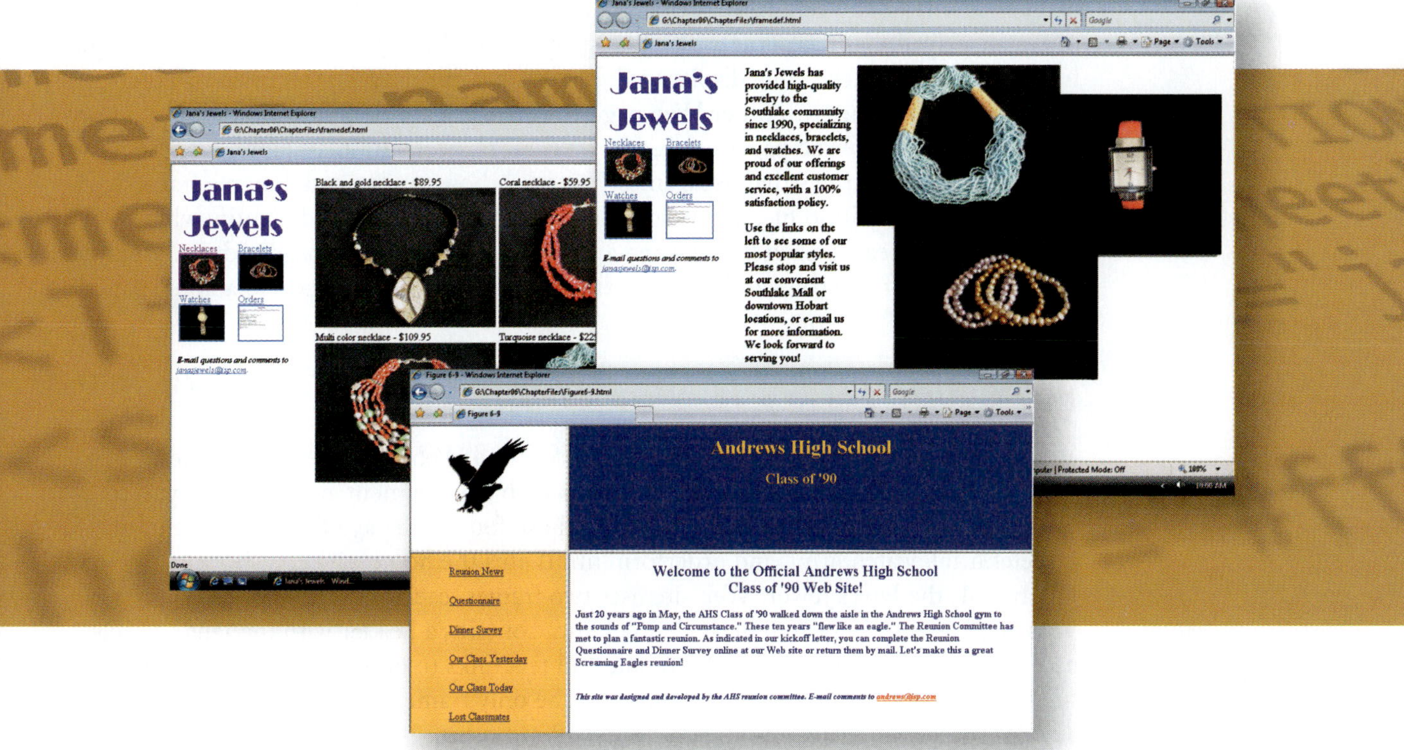

Objectives

You will have mastered the material in this chapter when you can:

- Define terms related to frames
- Describe the steps used to design a frame structure
- Plan and lay out a frameset
- Create a frame definition file that defines three frames
- Use the <frameset> tag
- Use the <frame /> tag
- Change frame scrolling options
- Name a frame content target
- Identify Web pages to display at startup
- Set frame rows and columns
- Create a navigation menu page with text links
- Create a home page

6 Using Frames in a Web Site

Introduction

Chapter 6 introduces frames and their use in Web page development. A **frame** is a rectangular area of a Web page — essentially, a window — in which a separate Web page can be displayed. Frames allow a user to display several Web pages at one time in a single browser window. Each frame displays a different, individual Web page, each of which is capable of interacting with other Web pages. Web pages that include frames look and act differently from the Web pages created in previous projects. In this chapter, you learn how to create Web pages that use frames. You learn how to plan and design a frameset, create a frame definition file, define scrolling options for frames, and identify which Web pages should appear in each frame when a user first visits the Web page address. Finally, you learn to set frame rows and columns and create a navigation page and a home page.

Project — Jana's Jewels Web Site

Your best friend's Mom, Jana Alvarez, wants to have a Web site developed for her jewelry store. She knows that you are taking a class in Web development and has asked you to create the site. The Jana's Jewels Web site will use four Web page files (necklace.html, bracelet.html, watch.html, and orderform.html) plus the home page. As shown in Figure 6–1, the Jana's Jewels Web site uses two frames, each of which displays a different Web page. Frame 1, located in the left column, contains a header with the Jana's Jewels name and a navigation menu with graphic and text links to other Web pages in the Web site. Frame 2, located in the right column, is the only frame in which content changes. The Web page, home.html, appears in frame 2 at startup — that is, when the site first is accessed by a visitor (Figure 6–1a). When a link in frame 1 is clicked, frame 2 displays the content of the linked Web page, thus replacing the previous content of the frame. The Web page to define the frames and the two Web pages that are displayed in the frames at startup — menu.html and home.html — are created in the chapter. The other files you will need can be found in the Data Files for Students.

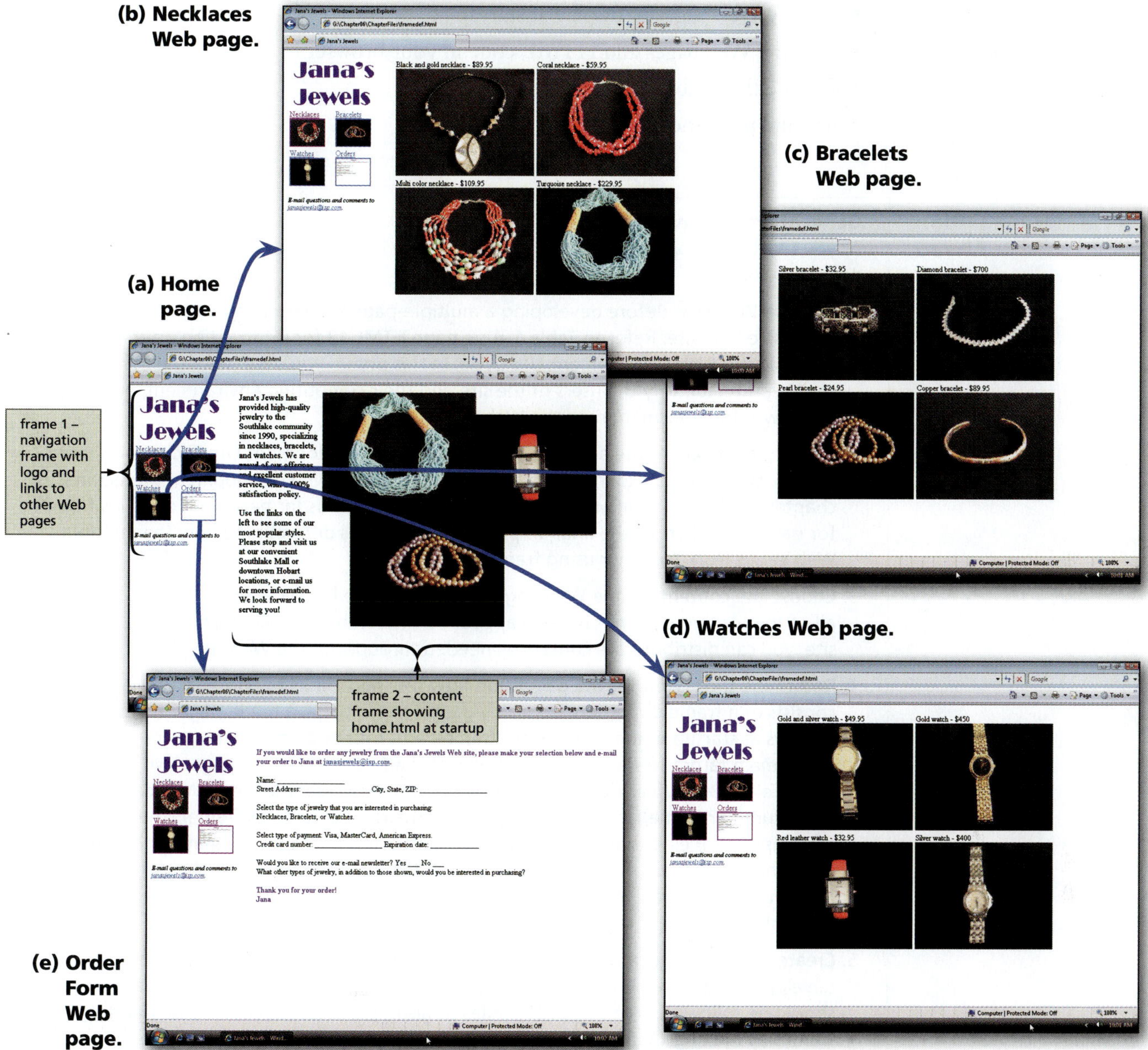

Figure 6–1

Overview

As you read this chapter, you will learn how to create the Web pages shown in Figure 6–1 by performing these general tasks:

- Plan and lay out a frameset
- Enter HTML code into the Notepad window
- Save the file as an HTML file
- Enter basic HTML tags and add text to the file
- Create a frame definition file that defines two frames
- Use the <frameset> tag

- Use the <frame /> tag
- Identify Web pages to display at startup
- View the Web pages and HTML code in your browser
- Validate the Web pages
- Test and print the Web pages

Plan Ahead

General Project Guidelines

As you create Web pages, such as the project shown in Figure 6–1, you should follow these general guidelines:

1. **Plan the Web site.** Before developing a multiple-page Web site, you must plan the purpose of the site. Refer to Table 1–4 on page HTML 12 for information on the planning phase of the Web Development Life Cycle. In this phase, you determine the purpose of the Web site, identify the users of the site and their computing environment, and decide who owns the information on the Web page.
2. **Analyze the need.** In the analysis phase of the Web Development Life Cycle, you should analyze what content to include on the Web page. The Web development project in this chapter is different than any other project completed thus far because it contains frames for navigation. Part of the analysis phase then includes determining how the multiple Web pages work together using frames.
3. **Choose the content for the Web page.** This part of the life cycle also is different because all of the content does not have to appear on one Web page. With a multiple-page Web site, you can distribute the content as needed throughout the Web site.
4. **Determine the layout for the pages and how one page links to another.** This Web site consists of a frame definition file, a navigation menu page, a home page (the page that displays at startup in the main target frame), and four additional Web pages that display in the main target frame when their link is clicked from the menu page. Two Web pages are visible at startup as defined in the frame definition file: the menu Web page (in the left column or frame) and the home page (in the right column or frame). The menu page remains static (i.e., it is always visible) in the left-hand frame (or column) of the Web site. The other Web pages display one at a time in the main target frame (the right frame or column) when clicked. With frames, navigation is easy because the menu is always available.
5. **Create the Web page and links.** Once the analysis and design is complete, the Web developer creates the Web page using HTML. Good Web development standard practices should be followed in this step. Examples of good practices include: identifying target frames by naming them, and always creating a frame definition file.
6. **Test all Web pages within the Web site.** An important part of Web development is testing to assure that you are following XHTML standards. In this book, we use the World Wide Web Consortium (W3C) validator that allows you to test your Web page and clearly explains any errors you have. Additionally when testing, you should check all content for accuracy. Finally, all links (from the menu frame or any e-mail links available) should be tested.

When necessary, more specific details concerning the above guidelines are presented at appropriate points in the chapter. The chapter also will identify the actions performed and decisions made regarding these guidelines during the creation of the Web page shown in Figure 6–1 on the previous page.

Using Frames

When frames are used, the browser window contains multiple Web page or image files. Frames can be used:

- To allow a Web site visitor to view more than one Web page at a time
- To create a navigation menu, as a replacement for such objects as menu lists and menu bars
- To display headers, navigation menus, or other information that needs to remain on the screen as other parts of the Web page change

The HTML code to use frames is a little different from the code you have used in projects so far in this book. To use frames, you must:

- Create a frame definition file to define the layout of frames
- Add frameset tags to define the columns and rows of frames
- Define other frame attributes, such as borders, margins, and scrolling

BTW

Framesets

A frameset can be thought of as a window with various panes. Within each windowpane is a separate Web page. The frame definition file is the HTML file that defines the Web pages that are displayed in the individual panes. Every Web page used in a frameset can be viewed independently in the browser as well as within the frameset.

Creating a Frame Definition File

The first step in creating frames for a Web site is to create a frame definition file. A **frame definition file** defines the layout of the frames in a Web site and specifies the Web page contents of each frame. The frame definition file is loaded when the visitor enters the URL of the Web site in the Address box. The information in the frame definition file defines the Web pages to be displayed in each frame when the page first is loaded and when a user clicks a link.

For the Jana's Jewels Web site, the frame definition file is named framedef.html. The frame definition file specifies that the Web site will use two frames — one to provide a navigation menu and one to display the main Web page with the pictures of jewelry.

A frame definition file uses a combination of three HTML tags and attributes, as shown in Table 6–1.

Table 6–1 Frame Tags

Tag	Function
`<frameset>` `</frameset>`	• Defines the structure of the frames within a window • Required end tag when creating frames
`<frame />`	• Defines a given frame; required for each frame
`<noframes>` `</noframes>`	• Defines alternative content that appears if the browser does not support frames • Supported by multiple types and versions of browsers

A **frameset** is used to define the layout of the frames that are displayed. A start <frameset> tag and end </frameset> tag are used to enclose the content and structure of the frame definition file. Within these tags a <frame /> tag is used to define each frame. No end </frame> tag is used. The start <noframes> and end </noframes> tags are used to specify alternative text that appears on a visitor's screen if the visitor's browser does not support frames.

A frame definition file also contains additional information, specified in attributes and values. Table 6–2 on the next page summarizes the attributes for each frame-related tag.

Figure 6–2a on the next page shows the HTML code for the frame definition file, framedef.html, which is used in the Jana's Jewels Web site. The HTML code uses the <frame /> tag to define two frames within the start <frameset> and end </frameset> tags.

For each frame, the src attribute is used to define which Web page should be displayed in the frame at startup. These two Web pages (menu.html and home.html) are shown in Figures 6–2b and 6–2c. When the frame definition file, framedef.html, is displayed in the browser window, it will appear as shown in Figure 6–1a on page HTML 261.

Table 6–2 Frame Tag Attributes

Tag	Attribute	Function
<frameset>	cols rows	• Indicates the number of columns • Indicates the number of rows
<frame />	frameborder marginwidth marginheight noresize name scrolling src	• Turns frame borders on or off (1 or 0) • Adjusts the margin on the left and right of a frame • Adjusts the margin above and below a document within a frame • Locks the borders of a frame to prohibit resizing • Defines the name of a frame that is used as a target • Indicates whether a scroll bar is present • Indicates the Web page or other file to be displayed in the frame

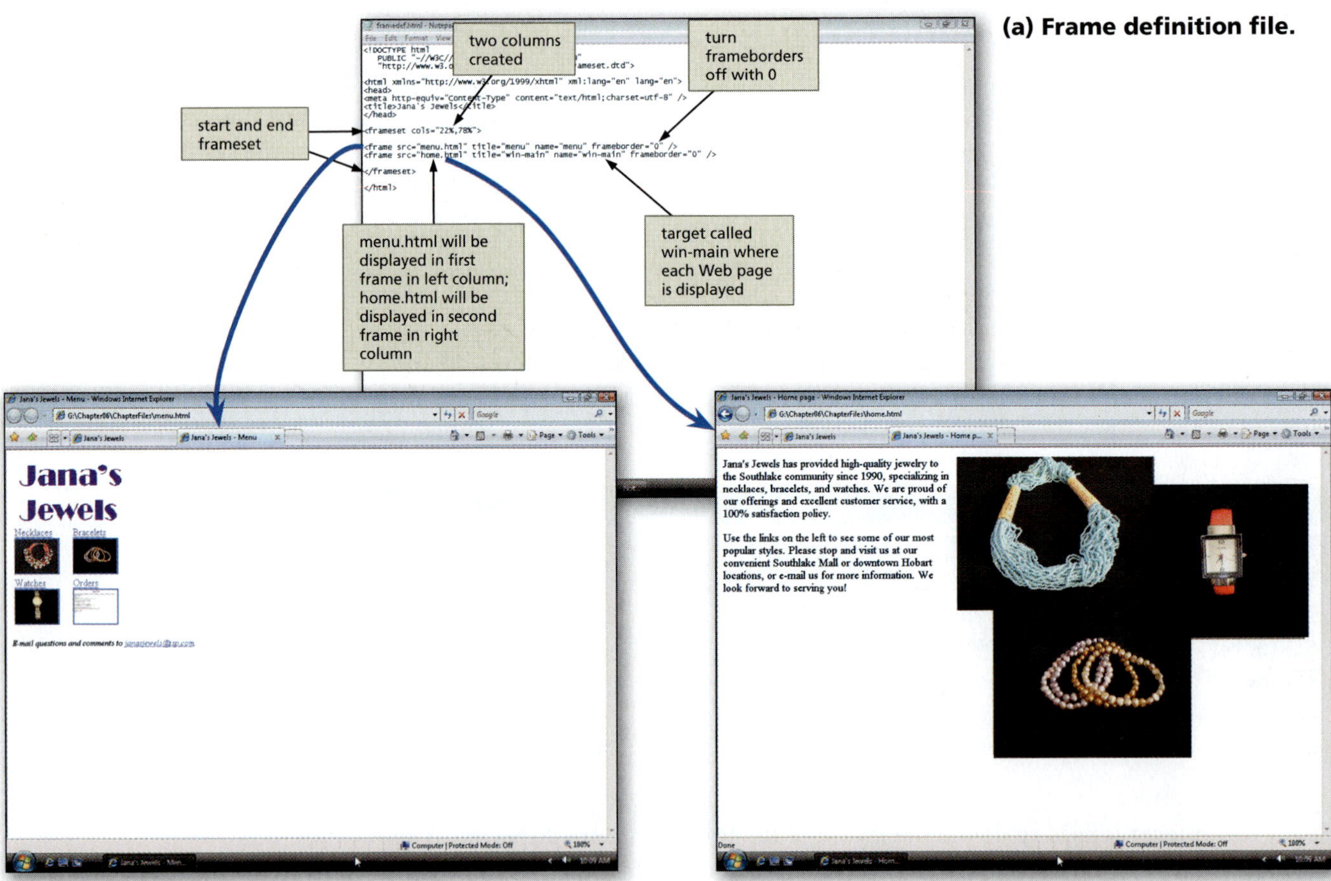

(a) Frame definition file.

(b) Navigation Web page menu.html.

(c) Home Web page home.html.

Figure 6–2

Defining Columns and Rows in a Frameset

Within the <frameset> tag you specify the number of columns and rows in the display area with the cols and rows attributes. For example, Figure 6–3a shows a frameset with two rows, and Figure 6–3b shows a frameset with two columns.

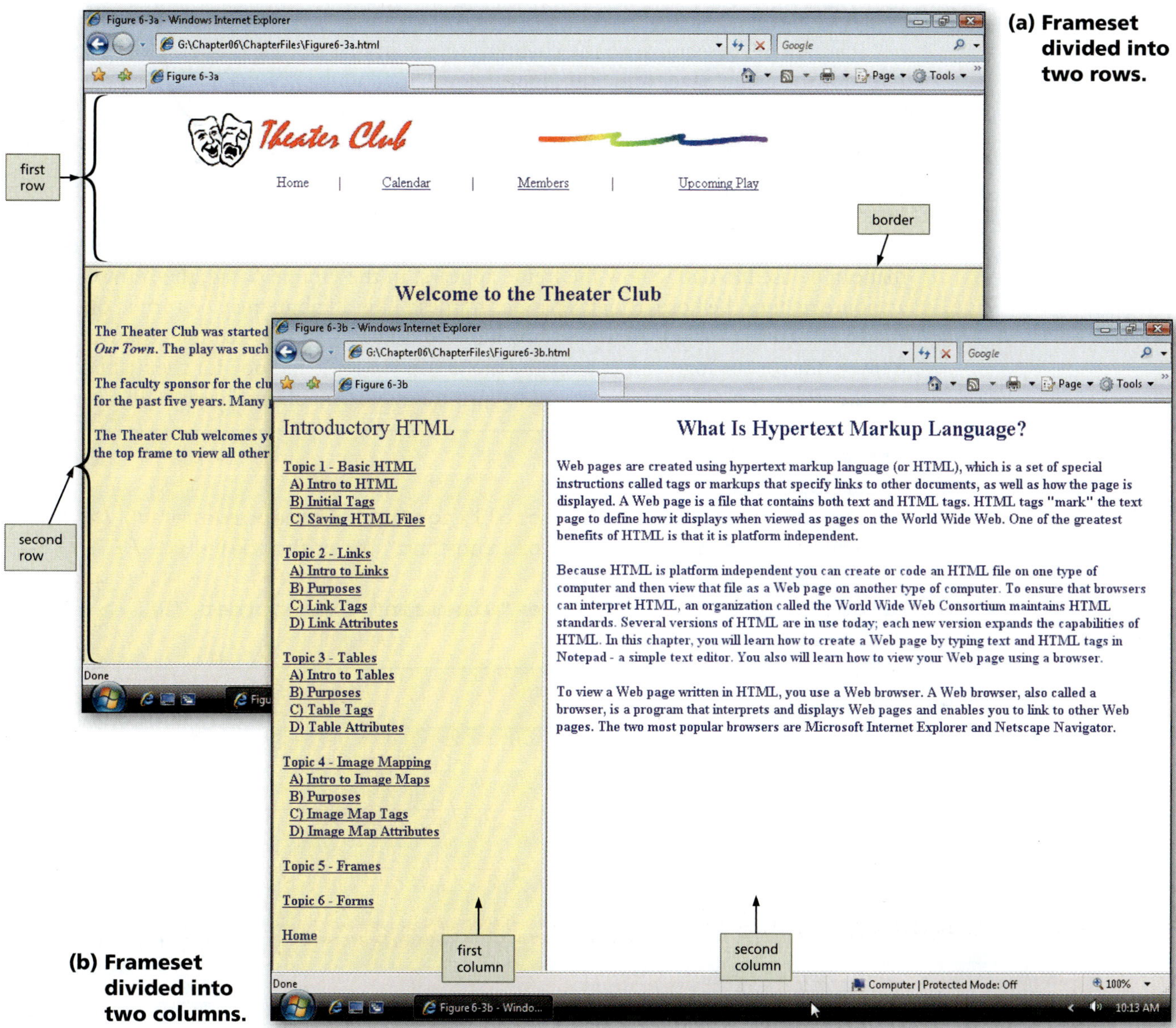

(a) Frameset divided into two rows.

(b) Frameset divided into two columns.

Figure 6–3

The HTML code used to create the Web page shown in Figure 6–3a is:

```
<frameset rows="30%,70%">
<frame src="menu2.html"/>
<frame src="home2.html" name="win-main" />
</frameset>
```

BTW

Frames
You can find a thorough discussion of frames on the World Wide Web Consortium Web site. The document contains an introduction to frames as well as frame layouts. All possible frame tags and attributes are discussed. For more information on frames, search on "HTML Frames" in a search engine.

The HTML code used to create the Web page shown in Figure 6–3b is:

```
<frameset cols="18%,82%">
<frame src="menu1.html" />
<frame src="home1.html" name="win-main" />
</frameset>
```

Figure 6–3b is similar to the chapter project, in that the left frame is used as the frame for the menu page, while the right frame is used to display the main Web page content, including the home page and additional Web pages.

Defining Frame Attributes

As shown in Table 6–2 on page HTML 264, the <frame /> tag has several attributes that can be used to define how the frame appears. In the <frame /> tag, the **frameborder** attribute defines the border that separates frames. This attribute may be turned on (1), as shown in Figure 6–4a, or off (0), as shown in Figure 6–4b. In this example, there are three frames; one for the logo and one for the menu (on the left), and one for the main content (on the right). The HTML code used to turn frameborders off in Figure 6–4b is:

```
<frameset cols="25%,75%">
<frameset rows="18%,82%">
<frame src="header.html" scrolling="no" frameborder="0" />
<frame src="menu.html" scrolling="no" frameborder="0" />
</frameset>
<frame src="home.html" name="win-main" frameborder="0" />
</frameset>
```

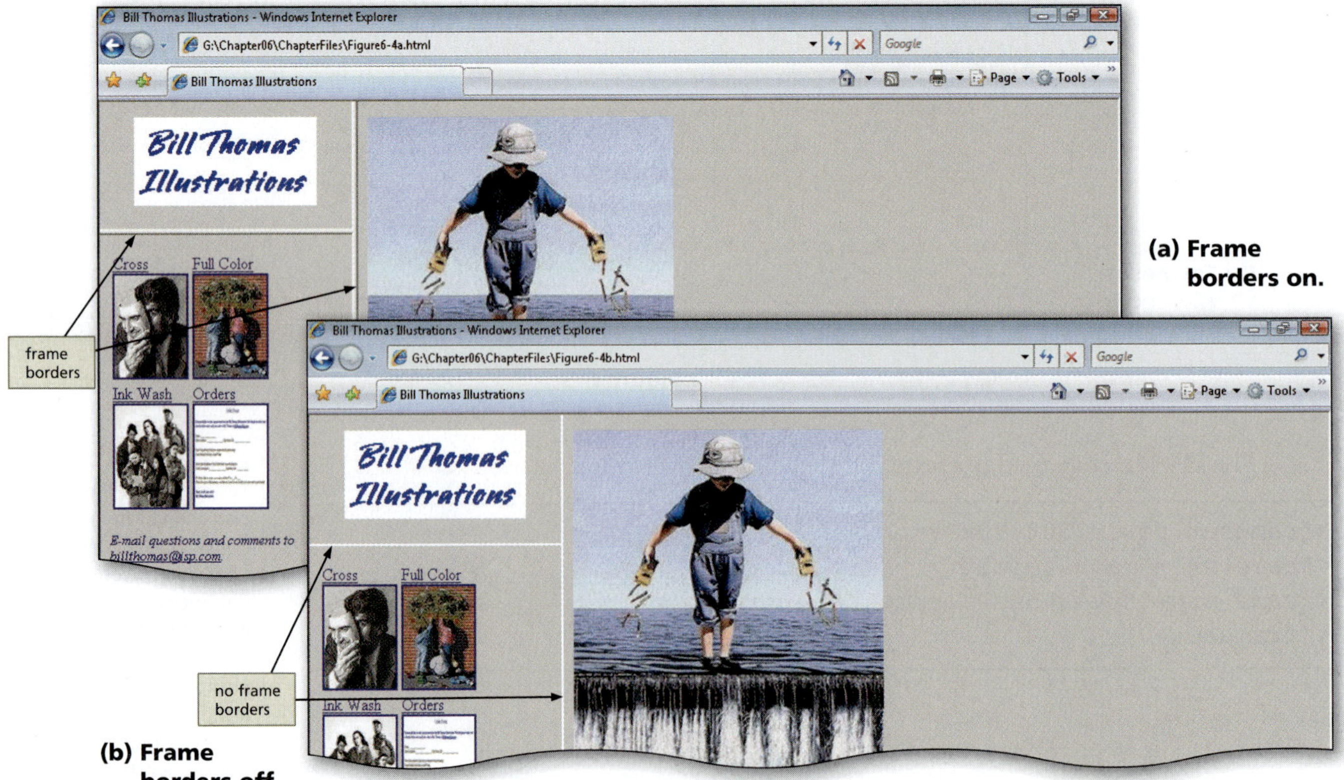

Figure 6–4

If the border is turned off, the browser automatically inserts five pixels of space to separate the frames. The amount of space, in pixels, can be increased or decreased.

The **marginwidth** attribute lets you change the margin on the left and/or right of a frame. The **marginheight** attribute lets you change the margin above and below a document within a frame. In both cases, you specify the size of the margin in number of pixels. In Figure 6–5, the marginwidth and marginheight of both the menu and header frames are set to 40 by using the attributes and values marginwidth="40" and marginheight="40" in the <frame /> tags. You can see the effect that this gives to those frames by putting 40 pixels of space in the margins.

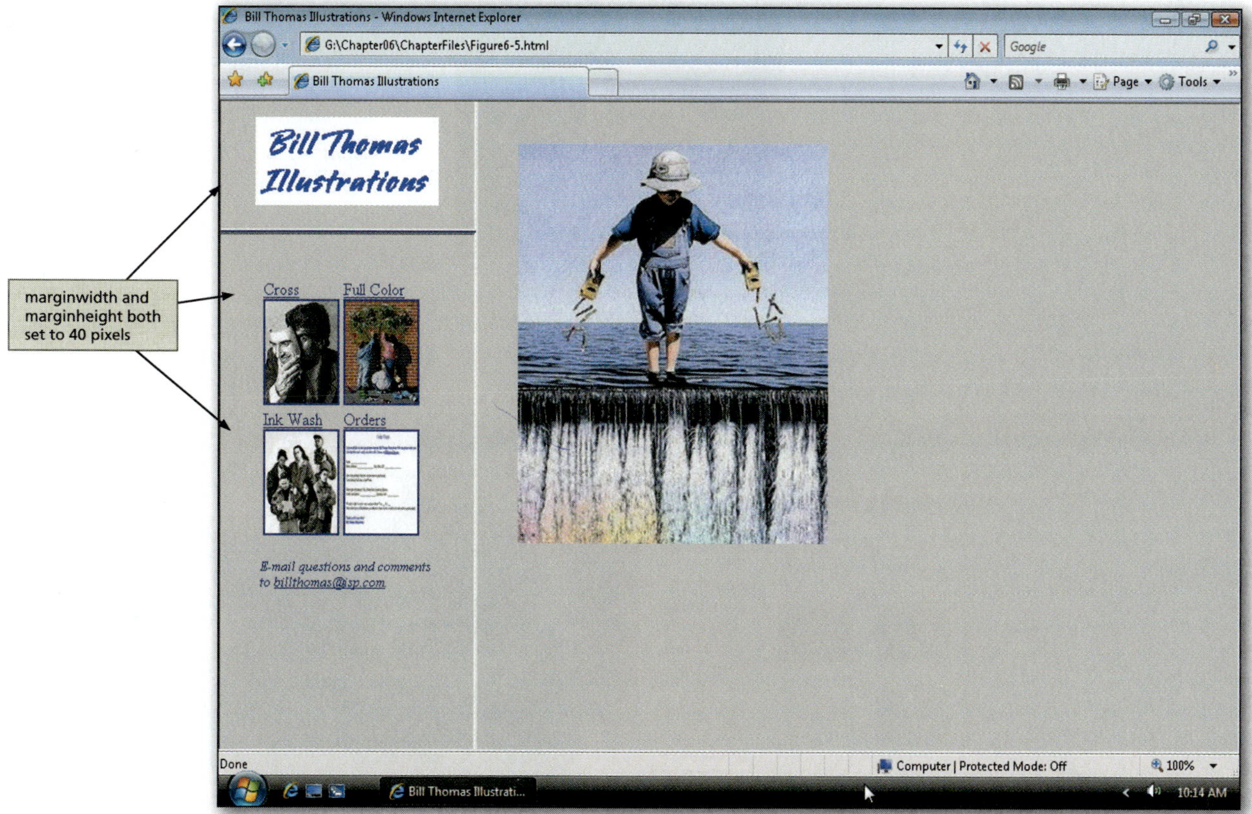

Figure 6–5 Frames with marginwidth and marginheight used.

As you have learned in previous chapters, scroll bars allow a Web page visitor to scroll vertically or horizontally through a Web page when the page is longer or wider than the screen. By default, the browser window is displayed with a horizontal or vertical scroll bar, or both, that is added automatically whenever the content of a Web page exceeds the length or width of the frame area. The **scrolling** attribute of the <frame /> tag instructs the browser that scroll bars should not be displayed. Turning off scrolling prevents the user from being able to scroll the page. For example, as shown in Figure 6–6a on the next page, scrolling in frame 1 is not necessary because all the information appears in the frames without the need to scroll. Frame 2, however, may need a scroll bar. In Figure 6–6a, no scroll bar is needed for that frame, but in Figure 6–6b, a scroll bar is needed because the Web page content exceeds the length of the frame area. If scroll bars should appear in a frame, no HTML code is required; by default, scroll bars will appear in the frame as needed. To turn off scroll bars, the <frame /> tag must include the **scrolling="no"** attribute and value.

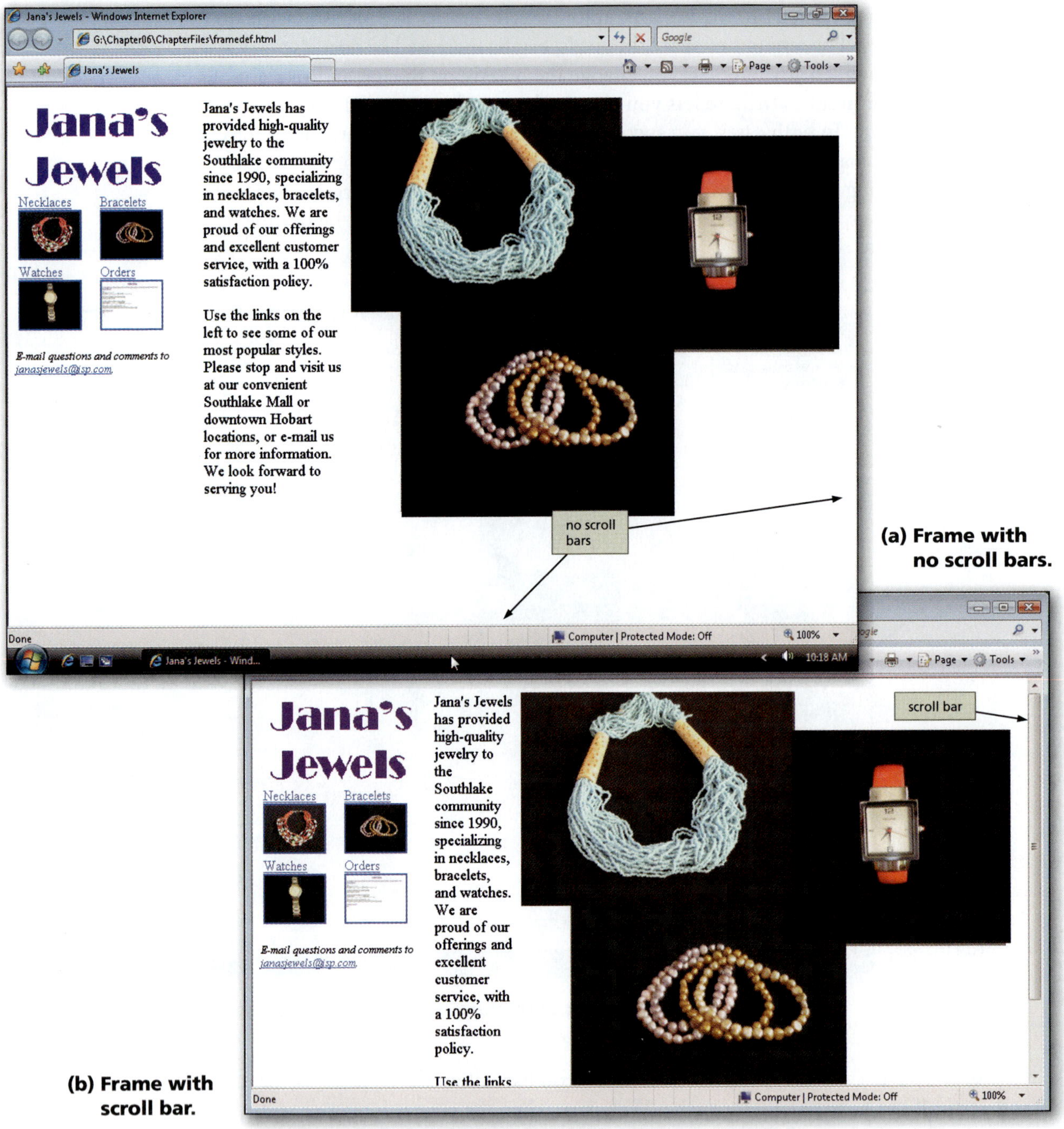

(a) Frame with no scroll bars.

(b) Frame with scroll bar.

Figure 6–6

> **BTW**
> **Margin Width and Height**
> By default, most browsers display a frame's contents with margins of 8 pixels on each side of the frame. Use the marginwidth and marginheight attributes within the <frame /> tag to adjust those margins.

One important frame attribute not used in this chapter project is noresize. By default, Web page visitors can resize any frame on the screen by moving the mouse pointer to the frame's border and dragging the border (Figure 6–7). In many cases, however, a Web developer may want to restrict a user's ability to resize frames. For instance, if the developer wants to ensure that the Web page is displayed exactly as created, the **noresize** attribute could be used to prevent Web site visitors from resizing the frame.

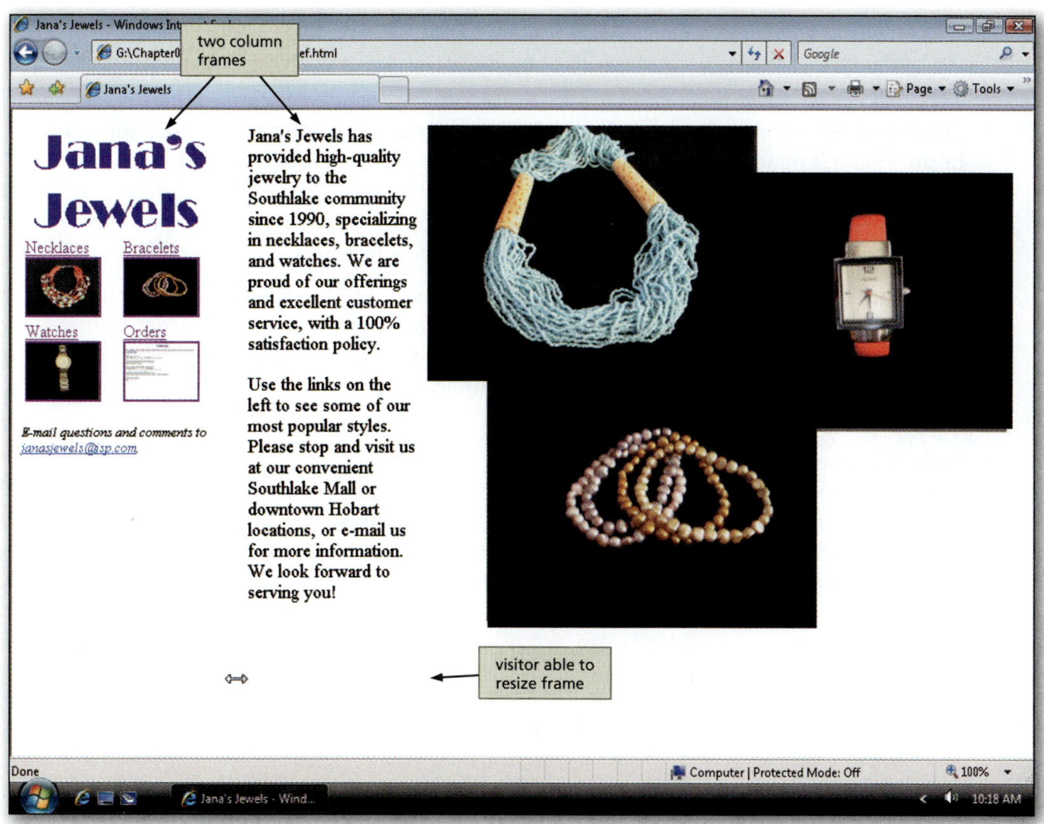

Figure 6–7 Sample layout for two-frame structure.

For example, to eliminate resizing for the frames in this chapter project, the noresize attribute would be added to the <frame /> tags in the frame definition file, as follows:

```
<frame src="menu.html" title="menu" name="menu"
noresize="noresize" />
<frame src="home.html" title="win-main" name="win-main"
noresize="noresize"/>
```

If the noresize attribute is not specified, visitors are able to resize a frame. The frame returns to its original size when the Web page is refreshed in the browser.

Additional frame attributes, such as name and src, are discussed later in the project when they are used.

Plan Ahead

Identify what frame layout to use for the Web pages.

The first step to consider when designing a frame structure is how to lay out the Web pages. A number of layouts are available for use. You need to determine where to put the navigation frame so that it is convenient but not distracting. You also need to determine where to put the main target frame so that you give it enough space to contain the necessary content. Consider the following formatting suggestions.

- **Effectively place the navigation frame.** An important part of using frames for Web page layout is to make navigation (i.e., a menu bar) convenient but not distracting to the overall look of the Web page. Most often you find the navigation on the left side of a Web page or on top.

(continued)

Plan Ahead

(continued)

- **Effectively place the main target frame.** This step is equally important because the main target frame is generally the only frame in which the content changes. In this chapter project as well as many other Web sites, the Web pages with content are displayed in the main target frame. The frame needs to be large enough to contain the content and convenient enough for the visitor to see immediately where it is.
- **Add other frames as necessary.** Depending on the layout of the Web page, you may need to have more than two frames (i.e., a navigation frame and a main target frame). Looking at the examples listed in the chapter, a three- or four-frame structure may be appropriate to your purpose. This is all determined during the design and planning of the frame structure.
- **Code the frame definition file.** Once you have determined the frame layout, you need to code the frame definition file. This step is crucial to the successful implementation of the frame structure. It helps to write code, save it, and then view it in the browser to see the effect. If you need to make changes because the structure is not what you expected, you can easily change the code, save it, and refresh it in the browser.

Planning and Laying Out Frames

The most important step in creating an effective frame structure is planning and laying out a good frame design. Sketching the frame structure on paper before writing the HTML code, as shown in Figure 6–8, can help save time when determining which HTML <frameset> and <frame /> tags and attributes to use. Once the structure is on paper, the number of rows and columns required, as well as whether scrolling is needed, is more apparent.

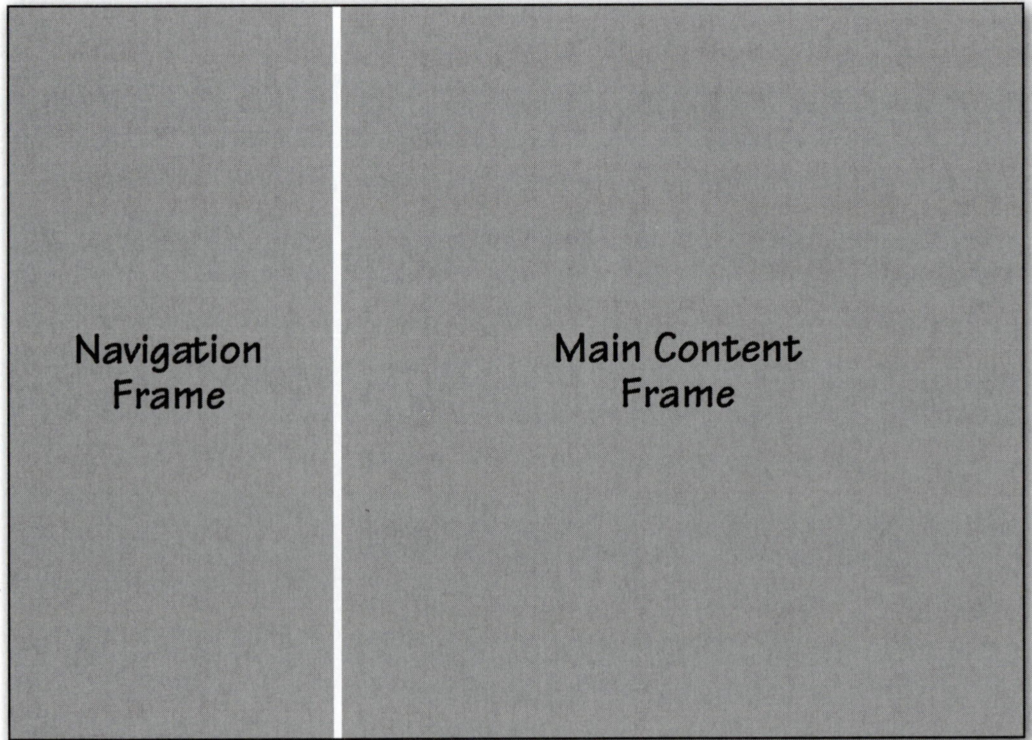

Figure 6–8

Frame layouts can be designed in a variety of ways. The goal and purpose of the Web site is to determine which layout is appropriate. For example, as shown in Figure 6–1a on page HTML 261, the Jana's Jewels Web site uses a basic two-frame structure. This frame layout is appropriate for a Web site that needs to display a company, school, or personal logo or banner on the Web page and needs to provide stable navigation. In addition, the content frame is the only frame whose content changes. An example of the HTML code to define a two-frame structure is as follows. Note that there will always be one frame for each <frame /> tag that is used.

BTW

Frame Design

Whether you are using frames or any other navigation technique, design is very important. Many Web sites are available that provide information about the use of frames and link to example Web sites that talk about advanced Web design issues and topics. Many design tips also are available that can help you create a Web site that is informative as well as attractive.

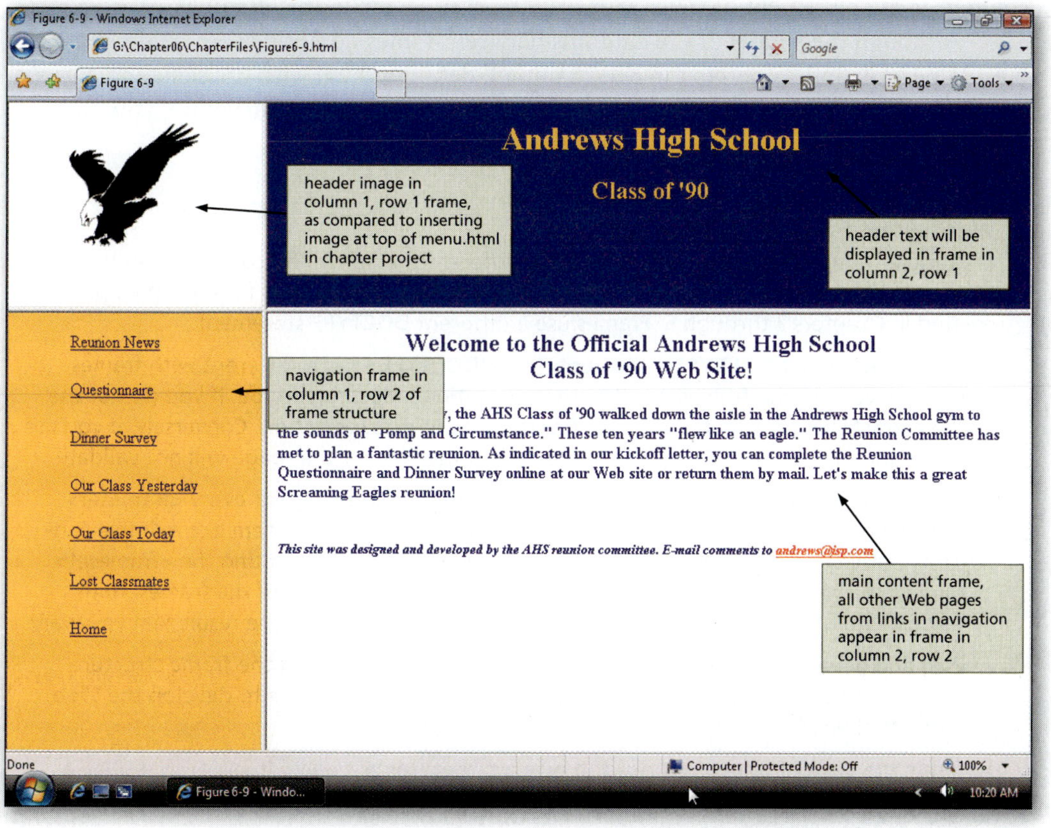

```
<frameset cols="30%,70%">
<frame src="menu.html" title="menu" name="menu" />
<frame src="home.html" title="win-main" name="win-main" />
</frameset>
```

A four-frame structure, as shown in Figure 6–9, can be used to split a header image from the header text.

Figure 6–9 Sample layout for four-frame structure.

BTW

Noframes
Most browsers, including Internet Explorer, Netscape, and Firefox, support frames. A small number of browsers, however, do not support frames. To create alternative text that appears in lieu of frames for such browsers, use a <noframes> tag after the last </frameset> tag. You must end this section of HTML code with the </noframes> tag.

An example of the HTML code to define a four-frame structure is as follows. Note the four <frame /> tags that are used to divide a Web page into four different frames.

```
<frameset rows="30%,70%">
<frameset cols="25%,75%">
<frame src="logo.html" title="logo" name="logo" scrolling="no" />
<frame src="header.html" title="header" name="header"
scrolling="no" />
</frameset>
<frameset cols="25%,75%">
<frame src="menu.html" title="menu" name="menu" scrolling="no" />
<frame src="home.html" title="win-main" name="win-main" />
</frameset>
</frameset>
```

Notice that the four-frame structure includes additional <frameset> tags to increase the number of frames to four. The most important task to manipulate multiple rows and columns is the placement of the </frameset> tags, as shown in this example.

Although the widths of the columns between frames do not have to be the same (i.e., 25 percent and 75 percent in this example), defining them with the same dimensions maintains a border that is straight down the page. Using this basic structure, you can define any number of rows and columns in a frame structure.

Plan Ahead

Writing the frame definition code.
Creating a frame definition file is completely different than anything completed so far in this book. You have been able to copy and paste the initial HTML tags for each Web page created in Chapters 2 through 5. Frames use a different DOCTYPE statement.

- **Utilize the correct DOCTYPE statement.** The <!DOCTYPE> tag is different with frames because you use the frameset rather than transitional document type. If you do not use the correct DOCTYPE statement, the frames will not pass validation. Conversely, if you use the frameset type on a Web page that does not use frames, that page will not validate.
- **Match and nest your <frameset> and </frameset> tags correctly.** For every <frameset> tag, you have to have a corresponding </frameset> tag. This may seem like a simple concept relative to the projects that you have completed so far, but nesting the <frameset> tags can be very tricky. Once you determine the physical structure of the frames, think through your HTML code carefully. If you do not, you will not get the result that you want.
- **Plan and develop the Web pages used in each frame.** Developing the frame structure is only one part of dividing a Web page into frames. You also have to develop the Web pages that will be displayed in each frame.
- **Name the target frames.** You need to give a target frame a name in order to display a Web page in it. You will utilize the "name" later on in the process when you create links from the navigation frame.

BTW

Why Noframes?
Because Web page visitors use so many different browsers, it is difficult to plan for all browser types and versions. The noframes tag allows you to accommodate those visitors who cannot otherwise see your Web page in frames.

Creating a Frame Definition File

After the design of the frame structure is complete, the first step in creating the Web page is to code the frame definition file using HTML tags. The frame definition file created in this chapter project (framedef.html) is used to define a two-frame structure and to indicate the names of the HTML files that will be displayed in the frames.

To Enter Initial HTML Tags to Define the Web Page Structure

Table 6–3 shows the initial HTML tags used in the frame definition file.

Table 6–3 Code for Initial HTML Tags in a Frame Definition File

Line	HTML Tag and Text
1	`<!DOCTYPE html`
2	`PUBLIC "-//W3C//DTD XHTML 1.0 Frameset//EN"`
3	`"http://www.w3.org/TR/xhtml1/DTD/xhtml1-frameset.dtd">`
4	
5	`<html xmlns="http://www.w3.org/1999/xhtml" xml:lang="en" lang="en">`
6	`<head>`
7	`<meta http-equiv="Content-Type" content="text/html;charset=utf-8" />`
8	`<title>Jana's Jewels</title>`
9	`</head>`
10	
11	
12	
13	`</html>`

The following step illustrates how to start Notepad and enter HTML tags to define the Web page structure for a frame definition file.

- Open a new file in Notepad and enter the HTML code shown in Table 6–3. Press ENTER at the end of each line of code. If you make an error as you are typing, use the BACKSPACE key to delete all the characters back to and including the incorrect characters, and then continue typing.

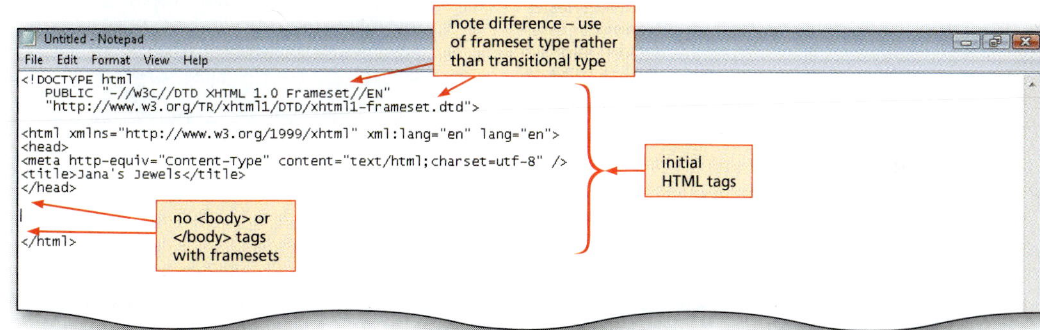

Figure 6–10

- Compare what you typed to Figure 6–10. If you notice errors, use your mouse pointer or ARROW keys to move the insertion point to the right of each error and use the BACKSPACE key to correct the error.
- Position the insertion point on the blank line two lines below the </head> tag and two lines above the </html> tag (line 11).

Q&A Why am I using the frameset type in the <!DOCTYPE> tag in this chapter project?

The frameset type tells the browser that this Web page contains a frame structure. For this chapter project, you have to use the frameset type.

Q&A Other than using the frameset type in the <!DOCTYPE> tag in this chapter project, are there other differences in the initial HTML tags?

The only other difference in developing a frame structure versus creating a Web page is that you do not use the <body> and </body> tags in the frame definition file. The remainder of the initial HTML tags are the same for a frameset structure.

Defining the Frameset Columns and Rows

After the document type is declared for the Jana's Jewels Web site, the next step in creating the frame definition file is to enter <frameset> tags to define the frame structure — that is, the number of columns and rows of the display area. As shown in Figure 6–11, the frame definition file (framedef.html) used in the Jana's Jewels Web site includes two columns that divide the screen vertically. When the framedef.html file is opened in a browser, the navigation menu (menu.html) appears in the left frame. While the content of the left frame remains constant, the Web page displayed in the right frame changes. At startup, it contains the Web page home.html.

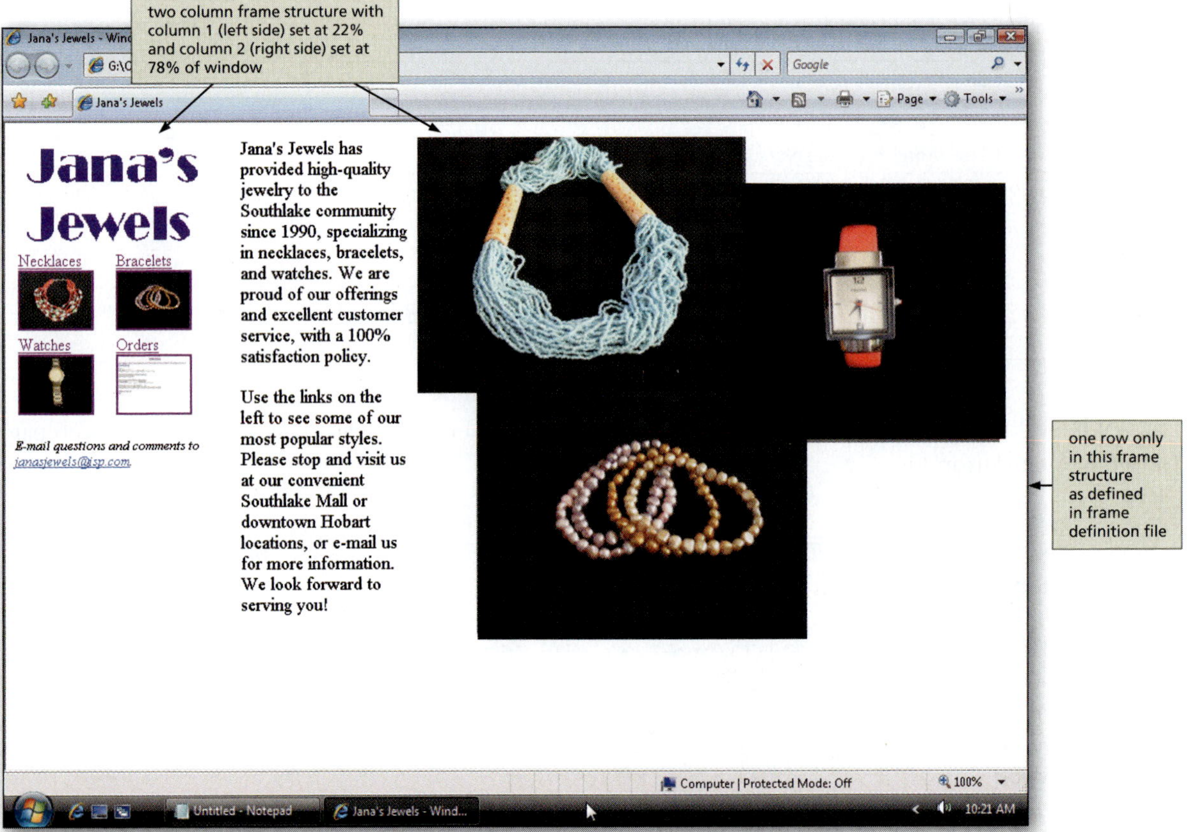

Figure 6–11 Two-frame structure for Web site.

The cols attribute of the <frameset> tag is used to set the number and sizes of columns. For example, entering the HTML code:

```
<frameset cols="22%,78%">
```

creates two columns in the frameset. The cols="22%,78%" attribute indicates that the page consists of two columns, which will fill 22 percent and 78 percent of the screen, respectively, as shown in Figure 6–11.

If a frame structure needs more than two frame columns, additional column widths can be specified in the cols attribute of the <frameset> tag. For example, the HTML code:

```
<frameset cols="20%,65%,15%">
```

is used to create three columns, with widths of 20 percent, 65 percent, and 15 percent, respectively. (Note that the total of all percentages always should be 100 percent.)

The size of a frame column or row may be specified as a percentage of the total screen size, as a number of pixels, or with an asterisk (*). Using a percentage has an advantage in that the width and height of the column or row will change as the browser window is resized. This maintains the set proportion of the frames. By contrast, if the frame column width or row height is defined in pixels, the size of the frame is fixed and does not resize when the browser window is resized. If you use an asterisk, the browser determines how much space is necessary for the frame based on information you include in the attribute. For example, an asterisk can be used to split a screen into three equal-sized column frames by indicating cols="*,*,*". In this case, each column will be 33.3 percent of the total screen size. An asterisk also can be used to set a row to split equally whatever space is left for the unspecified frames, as in rows="*,25,*". Here, the first and third rows each would be 37.5 percent of the total screen size.

To Define Columns and Rows in the Frameset

The following step shows how to enter HTML code to define the columns and rows for the two-column frame structure in this project.

- If necessary, click line 11.
- Type `<frameset cols="22%,78%">` to define the two columns and then press the ENTER key twice (Figure 6–12).

```
Untitled - Notepad
File  Edit  Format  View  Help
<!DOCTYPE html
   PUBLIC "-//W3C//DTD XHTML 1.0 Frameset//EN"
   "http://www.w3.org/TR/xhtml1/DTD/xhtml1-frameset.dtd">

<html xmlns="http://www.w3.org/1999/xhtml" xml:lang="en" lang="en">
<head>
<meta http-equiv="Content-Type" content="text/html;charset=utf-8" />
<title>Jana's Jewels</title>
</head>

<frameset cols="22%,78%">


</html>
```

start frameset tag with two columns set at 22% and 78%, respectively

Figure 6–12

Q&A I do not understand what it means to set one column to 22 percent and another to 78 percent. Can you explain that further?

If you think of your Web page as 100 percent when viewing it, setting one column to 22% means that the column will only take up 22 percent (or almost one quarter) of the window in the browser. The other Web page will display in the remaining 78 percent (100–22) of the window in the browser.

Q&A How do you determine what percentage to set any frame?

This is something that is not hard science and must be tested. You may have an especially wide navigation bar (maybe with long words for the links) that might need more room than 25 percent of the window. Or, the company logo may be such a size that more space is needed. You want to be able to see everything needed in a frame, so you sometimes have to play with the numbers when testing.

Specifying Attributes of the Menu and Main Frame

Now that you have defined the overall layout of the frameset, it is time to add the specific attributes of each frame. A <frame /> tag is used to define each frame in a frame definition file. The src attribute of the <frame /> tag is used to identify the Web page that will appear in this frame.

For the Jana's Jewels Web site, two frames must be defined using <frame /> tags. The first <frame /> tag specifies the frame in the first column. This frame displays the navigation menu page, menu.html, which is used for navigation of the Web site. (The file, menu.html,

> **BTW**
> **Frame Sizes**
> The size of a frame should be determined by the content that it displays. If a frame is too small, the visitor has to scroll vertically or horizontally to read the content. If the frame is too large, the excess space around the text makes the page look unattractive. When you create your frame size, think about effectively using the space.

is created later in this project.) The menu.html Web page will remain constant as users browse through the Web site; no other Web page appears in that frame. Borders should be turned off (frameborder="0") for this frame, but scrolling should be allowed. It is important for Web page visitors to have access to all links on the menu frame. If you turn scrolling off, visitors may not have access to all links when the screen is resized. To be compliant with accessibility guidelines (see Appendix C), you should always use the title and name attributes to identify each frame.

The second <frame /> tag specifies the main frame in the second column. This frame will display variable content. At startup, the main frame displays the Web page home.html. When a user clicks a link in the navigation menu (i.e., the left frame), the Web page in the main frame changes to display the linked content. For example, if a user clicks the Order Form link in the menu frame, the Web page orderform.html will be displayed in the main frame.

The name attribute name="win-main" is used to assign the target name win-main to the main frame. The links in the navigation menu will use the target name win-main to indicate that all linked Web pages should be displayed in the main frame. Note that any frame may be named using the name attribute of the <frame /> tag. For example, if you needed to display additional Web pages in the menu frame, you could specify a target name for that frame.

Finally, borders will be turned off for the main frame, to match the other frames. Scrolling will not be turned off for this frame, because this frame may require scroll bars to view all of the content.

To Specify Attributes of the Menu Frame

The following step shows how to enter HTML code to specify attributes of the menu frame.

1

- If necessary, click line 13.
- Type `<frame src="menu.html" title="menu" name="menu" frameborder= "0" />` and then press the ENTER key to insert the HTML code for the menu frame as shown in Figure 6–13.

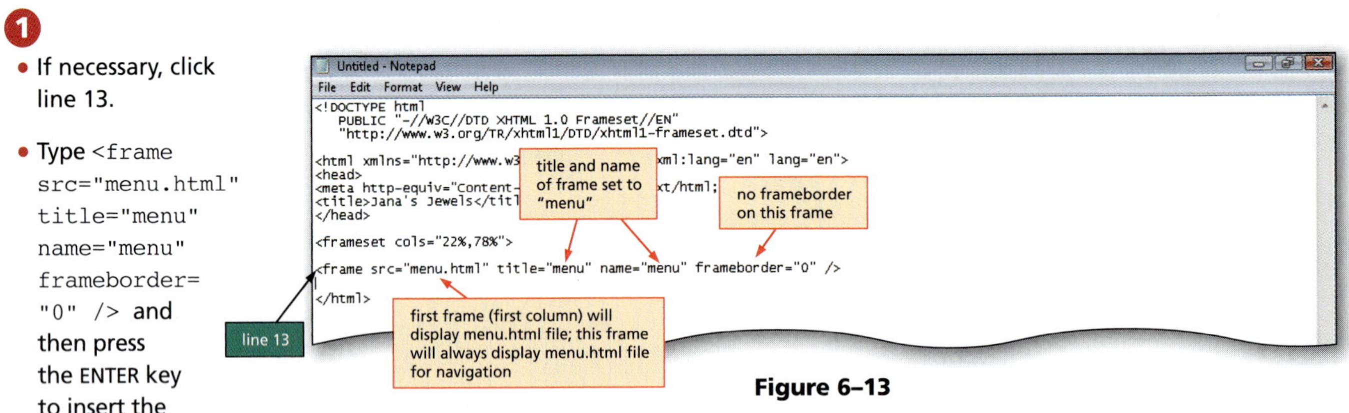

Figure 6–13

> **Q&A**
> How will I use the name attribute in the frame that contains the navigation page?
>
> For this chapter project, you will not use the name attribute for this frame. It is a good practice to give each frame a name, though. If your Web site expands, you may need to display a different Web page in that frame. If you have given the frame a name, you can vary the content of the frame.

> **Q&A**
> I can see why I need scrolling to be turned on for the main content frame, but why should I not turn scrolling off for this navigation page?
>
> Generally, it would be acceptable to have scrolling turned off for this page, but just in case the page gets longer (i.e., you insert more links), it is best to leave scrolling on. Look at the amount of space that you have available at the bottom of the menu.html Web page in the browser. If you had scrolling turned off, you can still get to the lowest portion of the Web page (i.e., the e-mail link). If the visitor shrinks the view in the browser, however, or if you add another group of links, then it is important to leave scrolling on so visitors can easily access all the links.

To Specify Attributes of the Main Frame

The following step shows how to enter HTML code to specify attributes of the main frame.

1

- If necessary, click line 14.
- Type `<frame src="home.html" title="win-main" name="win-main" frameborder="0" />` and then press the ENTER key twice to insert the HTML code for the main frame as shown in Figure 6–14.

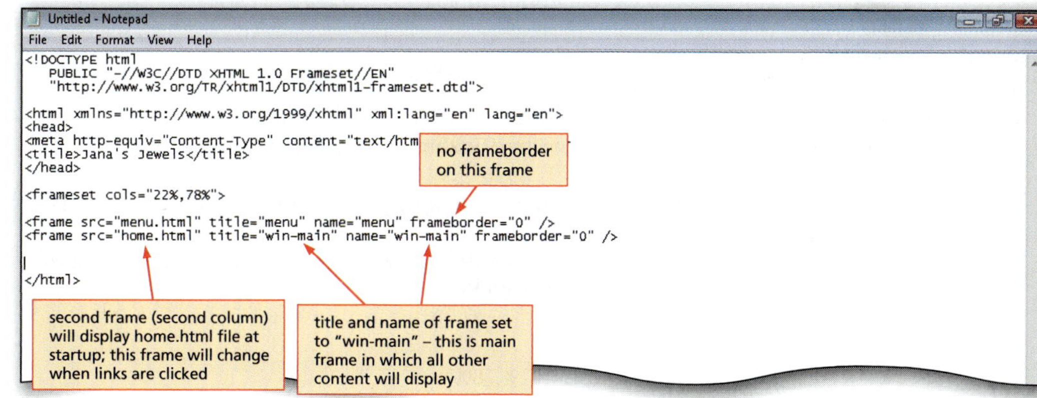

```
<!DOCTYPE html
   PUBLIC "-//W3C//DTD XHTML 1.0 Frameset//EN"
   "http://www.w3.org/TR/xhtml1/DTD/xhtml1-frameset.dtd">

<html xmlns="http://www.w3.org/1999/xhtml" xml:lang="en" lang="en">
<head>
<meta http-equiv="Content-Type" content="text/htm
<title>Jana's Jewels</title>
</head>

<frameset cols="22%,78%">

<frame src="menu.html" title="menu" name="menu" frameborder="0" />
<frame src="home.html" title="win-main" name="win-main" frameborder="0" />

</html>
```

Untitled - Notepad
File Edit Format View Help
no frameborder on this frame
second frame (second column) will display home.html file at startup; this frame will change when links are clicked
title and name of frame set to "win-main" – this is main frame in which all other content will display

Figure 6–14

Q&A Do I always have to name my main frame "win-main"?

No, you can name the frame what you want. The title "win-main" is a convention from programming in other languages, and the author's choice here.

Q&A Why do we not leave frameborders on (i.e., 1) in this chapter project?

You could leave the frameborders on; it is a matter of aesthetic taste. You could try it to see how you like it: take the attribute/value frameborders="0" out, save the file under another name (i.e., try framedef2.html), and open that file. What do you think?

Q&A I have seen Web pages in which you code frameborders="no" to turn borders off. Why is this different?

You can use frameborders="no" to turn frame borders off, but this statement will not validate correctly. You should always use frameborders="0" to turn frame borders off and frameborders="1" to turn frame borders on.

To End the Frameset

- If necessary, click line 16.
- Type `</frameset>` as the ending tag and then press the ENTER key (Figure 6–15).

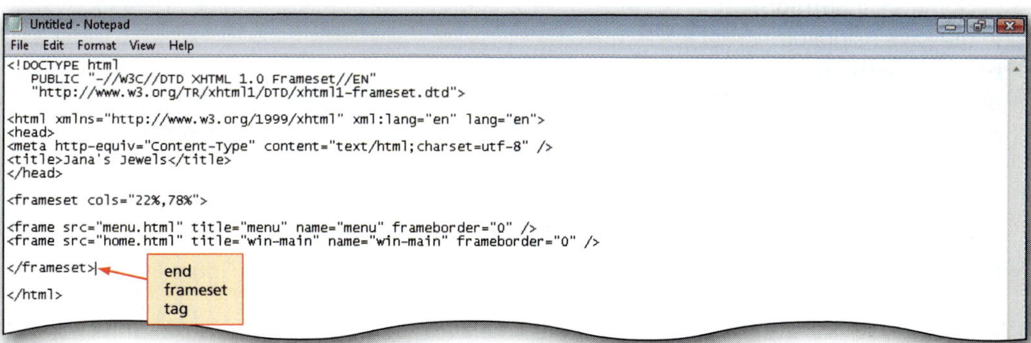

```
<!DOCTYPE html
   PUBLIC "-//W3C//DTD XHTML 1.0 Frameset//EN"
   "http://www.w3.org/TR/xhtml1/DTD/xhtml1-frameset.dtd">

<html xmlns="http://www.w3.org/1999/xhtml" xml:lang="en" lang="en">
<head>
<meta http-equiv="Content-Type" content="text/html;charset=utf-8" />
<title>Jana's Jewels</title>
</head>

<frameset cols="22%,78%">

<frame src="menu.html" title="menu" name="menu" frameborder="0" />
<frame src="home.html" title="win-main" name="win-main" frameborder="0" />

</frameset>

</html>
```

Untitled - Notepad
File Edit Format View Help
end frameset tag

Figure 6–15

To Save, Validate, and Print the HTML File

With the HTML code for the frame definition file complete, the file should be saved, validated, and printed.

- With a USB flash drive connected to one of the computer's USB ports, click File on the Notepad menu bar and then click Save As. Type `framedef.html` in the File name text box (do not press ENTER).
- If Computer is not displayed in the Favorite Links section, drag the top or bottom edge of the Save As dialog box until Computer is displayed.
- Click Computer in the Favorite Links section to display a list of available drives.
- If necessary, scroll until UDISK 2.0 (G:) appears in the list of available drives.
- If necessary, open the Chapter06\ChapterFiles folder.
- Click the Save button in the Save As dialog box to save the file on the USB flash drive with the file name `framedef.html`.
- Validate the Web page.
- Click framedef.html – Notepad on the taskbar and print the HTML file (Figure 6–16).

```
<!DOCTYPE html
  PUBLIC "-//W3C//DTD XHTML 1.0 Frameset//EN"
  "http://www.w3.org/TR/xhtml1/DTD/xhtml1-frameset.dtd">

<html xmlns="http://www.w3.org/1999/xhtml" xml:lang="en" lang="en">
<head>
<meta http-equiv="Content-Type" content="text/html;charset=utf-8" />
<title>Jana's Jewels</title>
</head>

<frameset cols="22%,78%">

<frame src="menu.html" title="menu" name="menu" frameborder="0" />
<frame src="home.html" title="win-main" name="win-main" frameborder="0" />

</frameset>

</html>
```

Figure 6–16

BTW

Saving Files

In the projects in this book, you save HTML files after inserting all of the HTML tags and text. When developing Web pages, it is a good idea to save your files more frequently so that you do not accidentally lose anything that you have entered. That way, if there is a power outage or other unforeseen interruption, your work is not lost. Give the file a name that makes sense and identifies the purpose of the Web page.

Creating the navigation menu frame.

Creating a navigation menu frame uses a different technique than what you have developed so far. With frames, you need to make sure the linked Web page will be displayed correctly.

- **Utilize the target frames correctly.** You already named the target frame when you developed the frame definition file. Now, when creating the Web page for the navigation frame, you need to add one additional attribute. When you create a link to another Web page within a frame structure, you need to identify the target frame where you want the Web page to display.

Plan Ahead

Creating the Navigation Menu Page

As previously discussed, the menu frame of the Jana's Jewels Web site always will display the menu Web page, menu.html. This Web page contains the Jana's Jewels logo together with graphic and text links that are used as a navigation menu. Now you will create this page that includes the links to display the various pages in the main frame. Remember that you should always include text links with every graphic link in the event that the Web page visitor turns graphics off.

To Start a New Notepad Document and Enter Initial HTML Tags

As with other Web pages, an initial set of HTML tags defines the overall structure of the Web page. Table 6–4 shows the initial HTML tags used on the menu page. Note that the menu page also uses the transitional document type.

Table 6–4 Code for Initial HTML Tags for Menu Page

Line	HTML Tag and Text
1	<!DOCTYPE html
2	PUBLIC "-//W3C//DTD XHTML 1.0 Transitional//EN"
3	"http://www.w3.org/TR/xhtml1/DTD/xhtml1-transitional.dtd">
4	
5	<html xmlns="http://www.w3.org/1999/xhtml" xml:lang="en" lang="en">
6	<head>
7	<meta http-equiv="Content-Type" content="text/html;charset=utf-8" />
8	<title>Jana's Jewels - Menu</title>
9	</head>
10	<body>
11	
12	
13	</body>
14	</html>

The following step illustrates how to open a new document in Notepad and then enter HTML tags to define the Web page structure for the menu page.

- Click File on the Notepad menu bar and then click New.
- Enter the HTML code in Table 6–4 to enter the initial tags.
- Position the insertion point on line 12 (Figure 6–17).

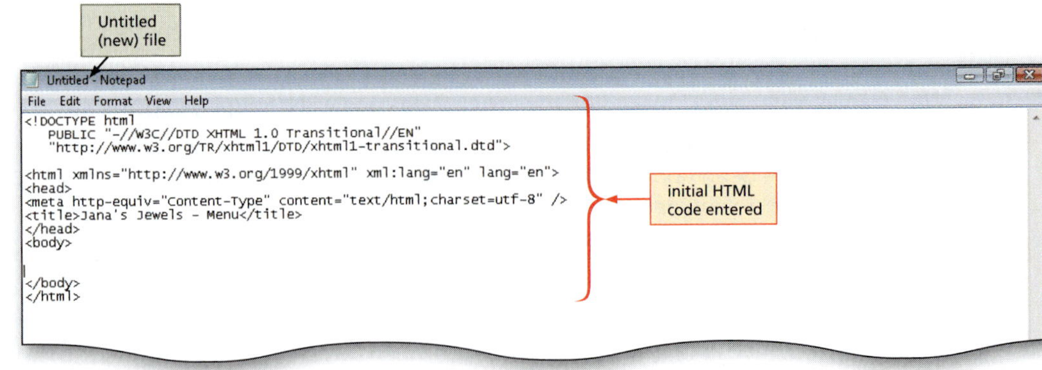

Figure 6–17

To Add Links with Targets to the Menu Page

The next step is to add a logo with a link to the home page together with graphic and text links to the menu page within a table structure. The menu page should contain four links that correspond to the four Web pages in the Jana's Jewels Web site: necklace.html, bracelet.html, watch.html, and orderform.html. The Web site visitor can return to the Home page by clicking the logo in the top-left corner of the menu.html Web page. This image spans two columns in the table. Table 6–5 lists the HTML code used to create the links in the menu page. In previous steps, the main frame was assigned the name win-main using the name attribute of the <frame /> tag. As shown in lines 14 through 28, each link on the menu page has the target attribute, target="win-main", to indicate that all linked Web pages or images should be displayed in the main frame.

Table 6–5 HTML Code for Creating Links

Line	HTML Tag and Text
12	`<table border="0">`
13	`<tr>`
14	`<td colspan="2"><a href="home.html" target="win-main">`
15	`<img src="jewelslogo.gif" width="192" height="101" alt="Link to home" border="0" /></a></td>`
16	`</tr>`
17	
18	`<tr>`
19	`<td><a href="necklace.html" target="win-main">Necklaces`
20	` <img src="necklacesm.jpg" width="72" height="54" alt="Small necklace" /></a></td>`
21	`<td><a href="bracelet.html" target="win-main">Bracelets`
22	` <img src="braceletsm.jpg" width="72" height="54" alt="Small bracelet" /></a></td>`
23	`</tr>`
24	
25	`<tr>`
26	`<td><a href="watch.html" target="win-main">Watches`
27	` <img src="watchsm.jpg" width="72" height="54" alt="Small watch" /></a></td>`
28	`<td><a href="orderform.html" target="win-main">Orders`
29	` <img src="orderformsm.jpg" width="72" height="54" alt="Small order form" /></a></td>`
30	`</tr>`
31	`</table>`

The following step shows how to add links with targets to the menu page.

1

- If necessary, click line 12.
- Enter the HTML code shown in Table 6–5, and then press the ENTER key twice after the last line (Figure 6–18).

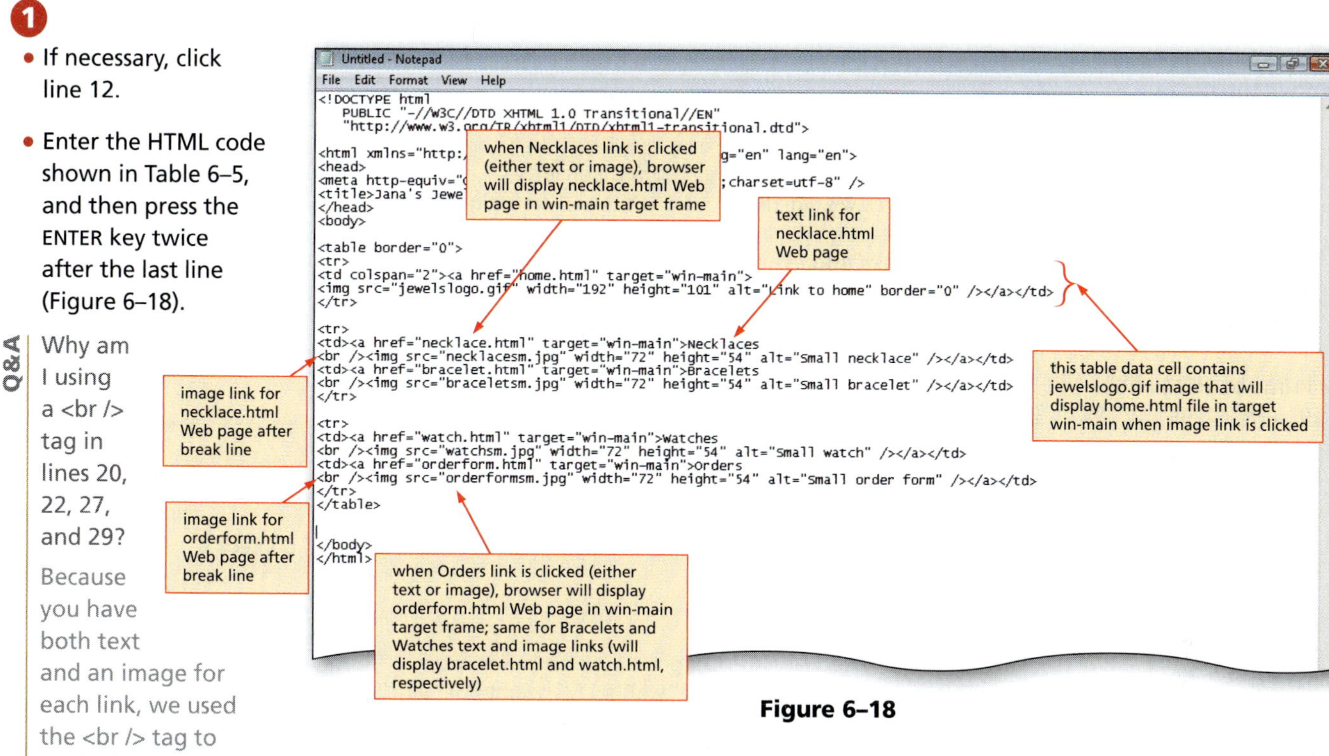

Figure 6–18

Q&A **Why am I using a <br /> tag in lines 20, 22, 27, and 29?**

Because you have both text and an image for each link, we used the <br /> tag to stack them one on top of the other without creating a blank line in between (as the <p> tag would do). This is something that you can play with and determine how it looks to you.

To Add an E-mail Link

The next step is to add an e-mail link to the menu page.

1

- If necessary, click line 33.
- Type `<p><em><font size="-1">E-mail questions and comments to` as the code and press the ENTER key.
- Type `<a href="mailto:janasjewels@isp.com">janasjewels@isp.com</a>.</font></em></p>` to complete the e-mail link as shown in Figure 6–19 (do not press ENTER).

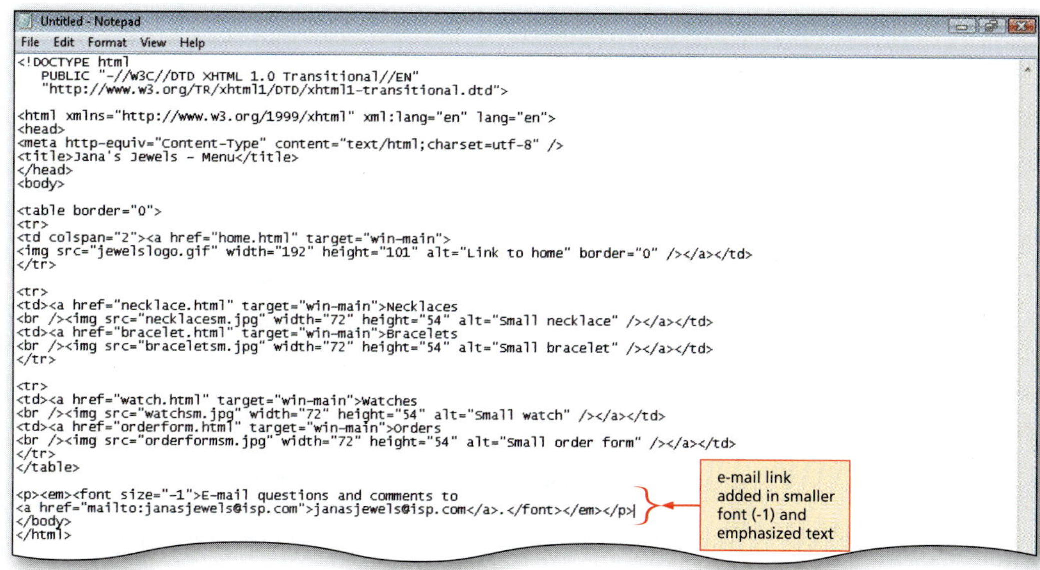

```
<!DOCTYPE html
   PUBLIC "-//W3C//DTD XHTML 1.0 Transitional//EN"
   "http://www.w3.org/TR/xhtml1/DTD/xhtml1-transitional.dtd">

<html xmlns="http://www.w3.org/1999/xhtml" xml:lang="en" lang="en">
<head>
<meta http-equiv="Content-Type" content="text/html;charset=utf-8" />
<title>Jana's Jewels - Menu</title>
</head>
<body>

<table border="0">
<tr>
<td colspan="2"><a href="home.html" target="win-main">
<img src="jewelslogo.gif" width="192" height="101" alt="Link to home" border="0" /></a></td>
</tr>

<tr>
<td><a href="necklace.html" target="win-main">Necklaces
<br /><img src="necklacesm.jpg" width="72" height="54" alt="Small necklace" /></a></td>
<td><a href="bracelet.html" target="win-main">Bracelets
<br /><img src="braceletsm.jpg" width="72" height="54" alt="Small bracelet" /></a></td>
</tr>

<tr>
<td><a href="watch.html" target="win-main">Watches
<br /><img src="watchsm.jpg" width="72" height="54" alt="Small watch" /></a></td>
<td><a href="orderform.html" target="win-main">Orders
<br /><img src="orderformsm.jpg" width="72" height="54" alt="Small order form" /></a></td>
</tr>
</table>

<p><em><font size="-1">E-mail questions and comments to
<a href="mailto:janasjewels@isp.com">janasjewels@isp.com</a>.</font></em></p>
</body>
</html>
```


Figure 6–19

To Save, Validate, and Print the HTML File

- Save the file in the Chapter06\ChapterFiles folder on your USB drive with the file name `menu.html`.
- Validate the Web page.
- Print the HTML file (Figure 6–20).

```
<!DOCTYPE html
  PUBLIC "-//W3C//DTD XHTML 1.0 Transitional//EN"
  "http://www.w3.org/TR/xhtml1/DTD/xhtml1-transitional.dtd">

<html xmlns="http://www.w3.org/1999/xhtml" xml:lang="en" lang="en">
<head>
<meta http-equiv="Content-Type" content="text/html;charset=utf-8" />
<title>Jana's Jewels - Menu</title>
</head>
<body>

<table border="0">
<tr>
<td colspan="2"><a href="home.html" target="win-main">
<img src="jewelslogo.gif" width="192" height="101" alt="Link to home" border="0" /></a></td>
</tr>

<tr>
<td><a href="necklace.html" target="win-main">Necklaces
<br /><img src="necklacesm.jpg" width="72" height="54" alt="Small necklace" /></a></td>
<td><a href="bracelet.html" target="win-main">Bracelets
<br /><img src="braceletsm.jpg" width="72" height="54" alt="Small bracelet" /></a></td>
</tr>

<tr>
<td><a href="watch.html" target="win-main">Watches
<br /><img src="watchsm.jpg" width="72" height="54" alt="Small watch" /></a></td>
<td><a href="orderform.html" target="win-main">Orders
<br /><img src="orderformsm.jpg" width="72" height="54" alt="Small order form" /></a></td>
</tr>
</table>

<p><em><font size="-1">E-mail questions and comments to
<a href="mailto:janasjewels@isp.com">janasjewels@isp.com</a>.</font></em></p>
</body>
</html>
```

Figure 6–20

Plan Ahead

Creating a home page with frames.

- **Develop an attractive and logical home page.** With frames, a home page is just one part of a frame structure. The home page in a frame structure is the Web page that displays at startup. This usually contains general information about the company or service.
- **Provide a way for visitors to return easily to the home (startup) page.** One common way of doing this is to utilize the logo as a link back to the home page.

Creating the Home Page

Two HTML files now are complete: the frame definition file (framedef.html) and the menu page that will be used for navigation (menu.html). The next step is to create the home page (home.html) that will be displayed in the main frame at startup.

The first step in creating the home.html Web page is to add the HTML tags that define the Web page structure for the page. Because the structure is the same as on the menu.html page, you can copy and paste HTML code from the menu page and then edit it for the home page.

To Copy and Paste HTML Code to a New File

The following step shows how to copy the HTML tags to define the Web page structure from menu.html to a new HTML file.

1

- Click menu.html – Notepad on the taskbar, if necessary.
- Click immediately to the left of the < in the <!DOCTYPE html tag on line 1.
- Drag through the <body> tag on line 10 to highlight lines 1 through 10.
- Press CTRL+C to copy the selected lines to the Clipboard.
- Click File on the Notepad menu bar and then click New.
- Press CTRL+V to paste the contents from the Clipboard into a new file.
- Press the ENTER key three times.
- Type `</body>` and then press the ENTER key.
- Type `</html>` and then press the ENTER key.
- Change the title on line 8 to say Home page (rather than Menu).
- Click line 12 to position the insertion point (Figure 6–21).

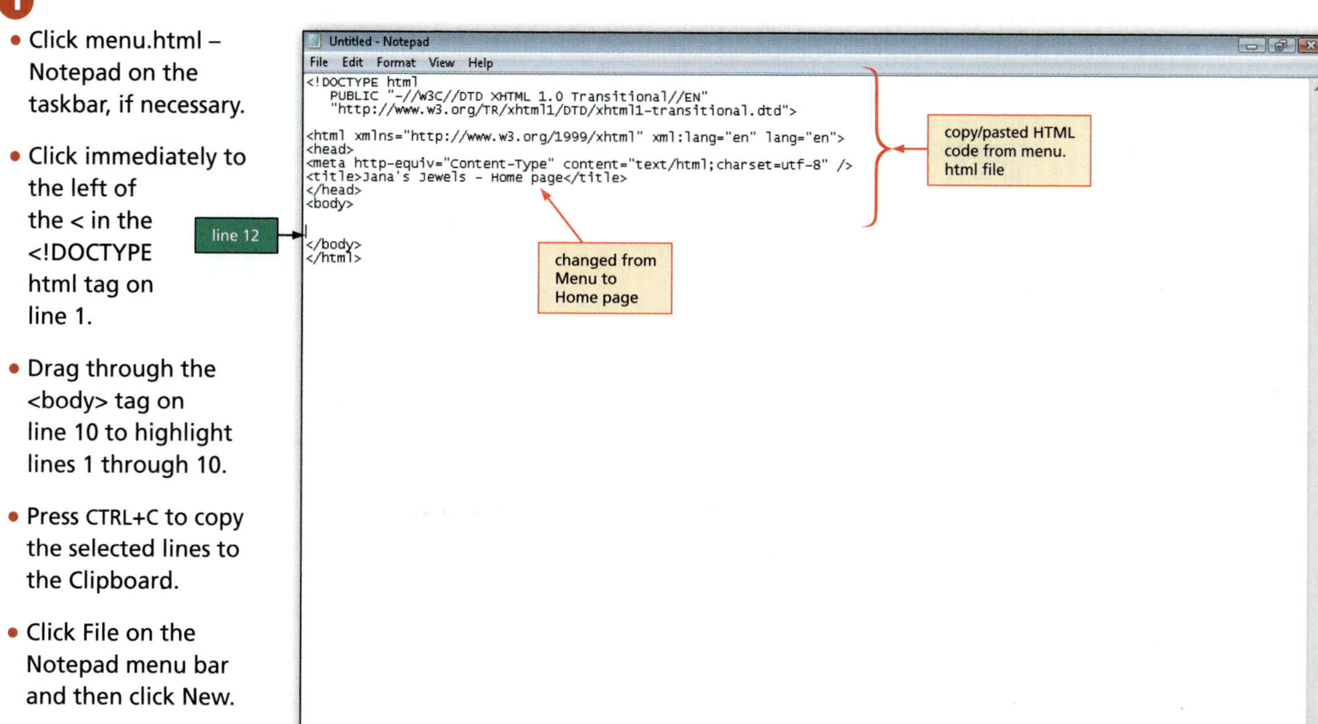

Figure 6–21

To Create the Home Page

Table 6–6 contains the HTML code you will enter to create the home page with a jewelry collage image and text.

Table 6–6 HTML Code to Create the home page

Line	HTML Tag and Text
12	<img src="homeimage.jpg" width="585" height="483" alt="Jewelry collage" align="right" hspace="10" />
13	
14	<p><font size="+1">Jana's Jewels has provided high-quality jewelry to the Southlake community since
15	1990, specializing in necklaces, bracelets, and watches. We are proud of our offerings and excellent
16	customer service, with a 100% satisfaction policy.</font></p>
17	
18	<p><font size="+1">Use the links on the left to see some of our most popular styles. Please stop and
19	visit us at our convenient Southlake Mall or downtown Hobart locations, or e-mail us for more
20	information. We look forward to serving you!</font></p>

- If necessary, click line 12.
- Enter the HTML code shown in Table 6–6, pressing the ENTER key after each line (Figure 6–22).

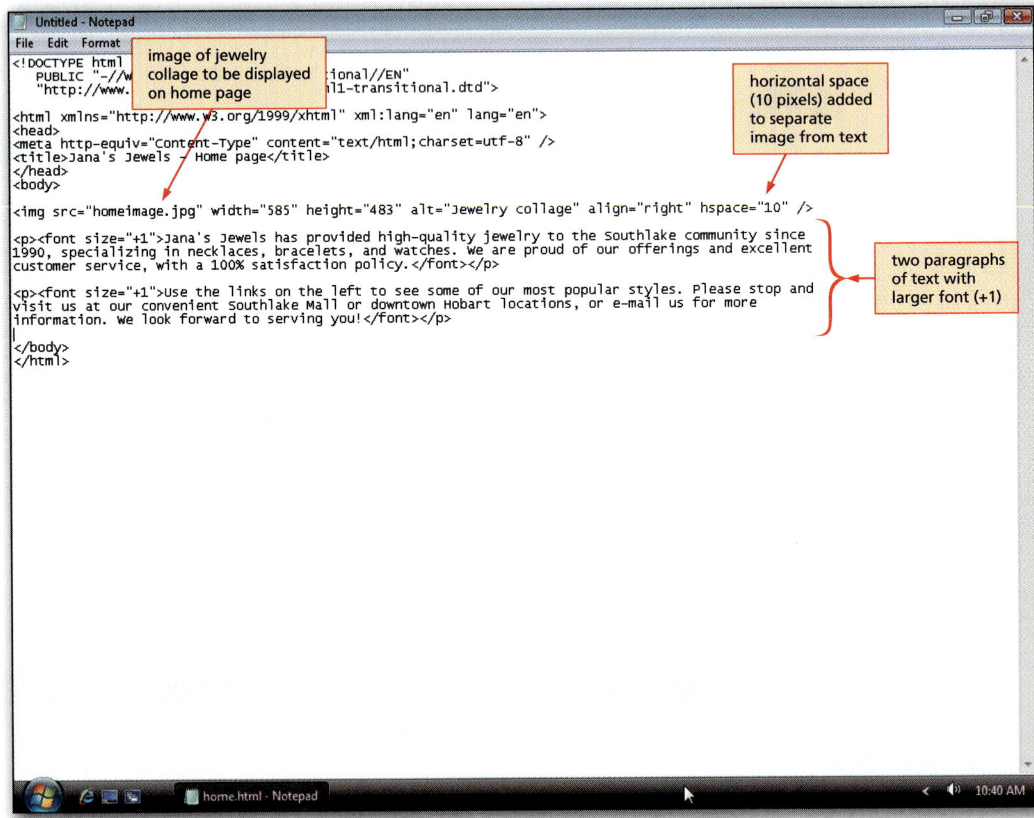

Figure 6–22

To Save, Validate, and Print the HTML File

1

- Save the file in the Chapter06\ChapterFiles folder of your USB drive as `home.html`.
- Validate the Web page.
- Print the HTML file (Figure 6–23).

Q&A Do I have to develop, save, and validate each Web page as I go, or can I just create them all and then validate them together? That seems easier to me.

You could do all of the Web page development first and then validate all Web pages. This may seem easier. If you validate each page as you have the HTML file open in Notepad, however, it is easier to correct validation errors. If you get an error during validation, you can just click the Notepad window, make changes, and re-validate.

```
<!DOCTYPE html
  PUBLIC "-//W3C//DTD XHTML 1.0 Transitional//EN"
  "http://www.w3.org/TR/xhtml1/DTD/xhtml1-transitional.dtd">

<html xmlns="http://www.w3.org/1999/xhtml" xml:lang="en" lang="en">
<head>
<meta http-equiv="Content-Type" content="text/html;charset=utf-8" />
<title>Jana's Jewels - Home page</title>
</head>
<body>

<img src="homeimage.jpg" width="585" height="483" alt="Jewelry collage" align="right"
hspace="10" />

<p><font size="+1">Jana's Jewels has provided high-quality jewelry to the Southlake community
since 1990, specializing in necklaces, bracelets, and watches. We are proud of our offerings and
excellent customer service, with a 100% satisfaction policy.</font></p>

<p><font size="+1">Use the links on the left to see some of our most popular styles. Please stop
and visit us at our convenient Southlake Mall or downtown Hobart locations, or e-mail us for more
information. We look forward to serving you!</font></p>

</body>
</html>
```

Figure 6–23

BTW

Noresize

If the noresize attribute is not used, Firefox and Netscape display a small hash mark in the middle of the border. This indicates that the frame can be resized. If noresize is used, the hash mark does not appear. Internet Explorer does not display a hash mark for frames that allow resizing. You would use the noresize attribute when you do not want the Web page visitor to resize the frame. You can allow visitors to resize some of the frames and not others by using noresize in the various <frame /> tags.

Plan Ahead

Testing Your Web pages.

- **Determine what you need to test.** It is important to have a test plan when you test your Web pages. Planning what to test assures that all functionality of the Web page is tested. You should specifically test the display of the Web page itself together with testing that all of the links on the Web page work correctly.
- **Test the Web page as displayed in the browser.** The first part of testing is to verify that your Web page displays properly in the browser. Ask the following questions: (1) Are the images all displayed where they should be? (2) Is the text presented as intended? (3) Are the links displayed as intended? And, for this chapter, (4) Are the frames laid out as you expected?
- **Test the links.** With a frame structure, when you test the links you also have to test that each linked Web page displays in the frame that you intended. If you do not name a frame target in your link, the Web page will display in the same frame as the link.

Viewing, Testing, and Printing Web Pages

With the Jana's Jewels Web site complete, you should view each of the Web pages in the Web site in a browser to confirm that the Web page appears as desired and that the links function as expected. After testing the links, the Web pages and HTML code for each Web page should be printed for future reference. Because the Web site home page is divided into frames, three printing options are available. You can print the Web page as it appears on the screen or print individual framed Web pages separately. The Options tab of the browser's Print dialog box includes these three options:

- As laid out on screen
- Only the selected frame
- All frames individually

The default is to print only the selected frame. To print all frames of the frame definition file in one printout, the As laid out on screen option should be used. Your purpose for printing the page determines which option you should select. If the Web page does not contain frames, these options are not available in the Print dialog box Options tab.

To View and Print the Frame Definition File Using a Browser

To test the Web pages in the Jana's Jewels Web site, you first open the framedef.html page in the browser to verify that the correct pages are displayed in the frame structure at startup. After verifying that the correct pages are displayed, the Web page should be printed for future reference.

- Start your browser.
- Type `G:\Chapter06\ChapterFiles\framedef.html` in the Address box and then press the ENTER key to view the two Web pages defined in the frame definition file and verify that the correct pages are displayed at startup (Figure 6–24).
- Click the drop-down arrow on the Print icon on the Command bar, and then click Print.

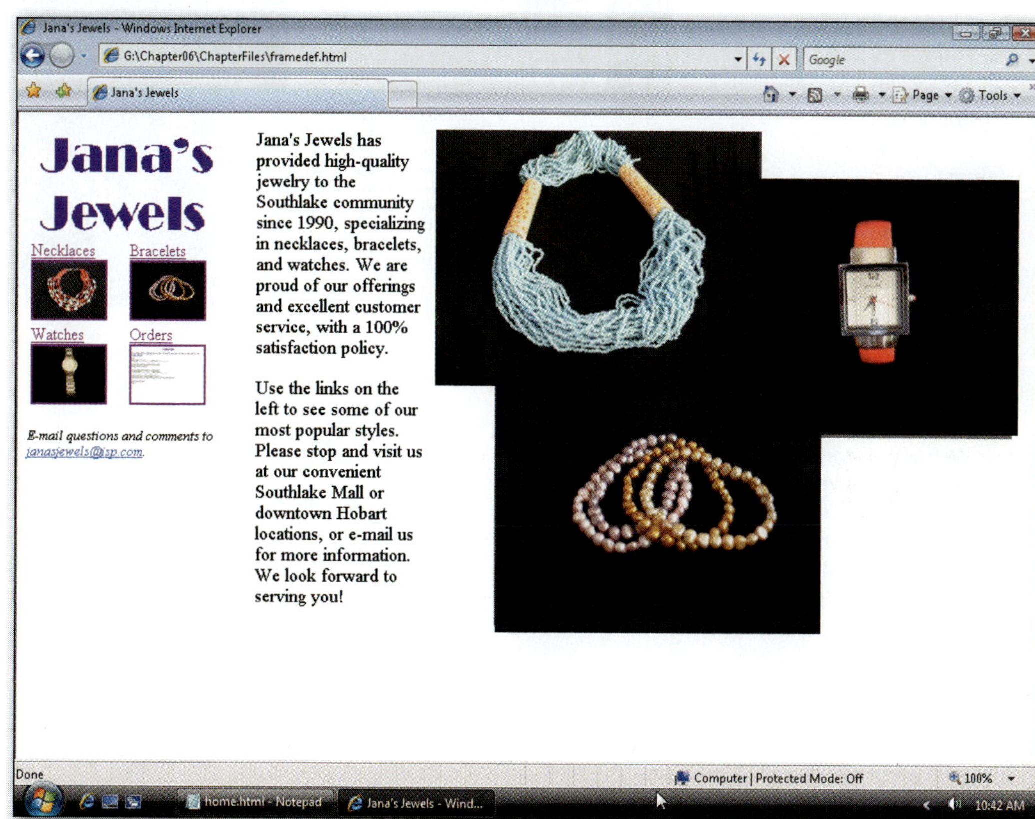

Figure 6–24

- Click the Options tab in the Print dialog box.
- Click As laid out on screen to select it, and then click the Print button to print the frames as laid out on screen (Figure 6–25).

BTW

Frameset Tags

Be sure to use the </frameset> tag when developing Web pages with frames. If you do not add this tag, some older browsers will display a blank page. The Web server log collects statistics about your Web site visitors' browser types and versions. These statistics are an excellent source of information about what types of browsers are visiting your Web site.

BTW

Scrolling in Frames

Be careful when deciding to turn frame scrolling off. The menu frame is generally used to provide links to all of the Web pages in the Web site. If you turn off scrolling in that frame, and a visitor has very low screen resolution settings, all of the menu options might not display. A visitor also may shrink the size of the browser window, which may not show all menu options.

Figure 6–25

To Test and Print the Links

The next step is to test the links by clicking each link on the menu bar to ensure the correct Web page is displayed in the main frame. If you like, you can print each page as you test the links. Finally, test the e-mail address link to ensure it works correctly. If any of the links do not work correctly, return to Notepad to modify the HTML code, save the changes, and then retest the links in the browser. When you are satisfied that the links are functioning properly, print each file as laid out in the browser.

- Click the Necklaces link on the navigation menu and ensure that the Necklaces page shows in the main frame.
- Click the drop-down arrow on the Print icon on the Command bar and click Print. Click the Options tab in the Print dialog box, click As laid out on screen, and then click the Print button to print a copy of the necklace.html Web page as laid out in the browser (Figure 6–26).
- Click the Bracelets link on the navigation menu and ensure that the Bracelets page shows in the main frame. If you want a copy of the Web page as shown in the browser, print the Web page using the As laid out on screen option.

Figure 6–26

- Click the Watches link on the navigation menu and ensure that the Watches page shows in the main frame. If you want a copy of the Web page as shown in the browser, print the Web page using the As laid out on screen option.
- Click the Orders link on the navigation menu to ensure that the order form appears in the main frame. If you want a copy of the Web page as shown in the browser, print the Web page using the As laid out on screen option.
- Click the Home link on the navigation menu by clicking the Jana's Jewels logo.
- Click the e-mail link and verify that the New Message window shows janasjewels@isp.com as the address. Click the Close button to close the New Message window and quit the e-mail program.

To Quit Notepad and a Browser

- Click the Close button on the browser title bar.
- Click the Close button on the Notepad window title bar.

Chapter Summary

In this chapter, you have learned how to develop a frame definition file that displays two individual Web pages when opened in the browser. The left frame contains the navigation menu, while the right frame contains the content as linked. The items listed below include all the new HTML skills you have learned in this chapter.

1. Enter Initial HTML Tags to Define the Web Page Structure (HTML 273)
2. Define Columns and Rows in the Frameset (HTML 275)
3. Specify Attributes of the Menu Frame (HTML 276)
4. Specify Attributes of the Main Frame (HTML 277)
5. End the Frameset (HTML 277)
6. Add Links with Targets to the Menu Page (HTML 280)
7. Create the Home Page (HTML 284)
8. View and Print the Frame Definition File Using a Browser (HTML 287)

Learn It Online

Test your knowledge of chapter content and key terms.

Instructions: To complete the Learn It Online exercises, start your browser, click the Address bar, and then enter the Web address `scsite.com/html5e/learn`. When the HTML Learn It Online page is displayed, click the link for the exercise you want to complete and read the instructions.

Chapter Reinforcement TF, MC, and SA

A series of true/false, multiple choice, and short answer questions that test your knowledge of the chapter content.

Flash Cards

An interactive learning environment where you identify chapter key terms associated with displayed definitions.

Practice Test

A series of multiple choice questions that test your knowledge of chapter content and key terms.

Who Wants To Be a Computer Genius?

An interactive game that challenges your knowledge of chapter content in the style of a television quiz show.

Wheel of Terms

An interactive game that challenges your knowledge of chapter key terms in the style of the television show, *Wheel of Fortune*.

Crossword Puzzle Challenge

A crossword puzzle that challenges your knowledge of key terms presented in the chapter.

Apply Your Knowledge

Reinforce the skills and apply the concepts you learned in this chapter.

Completing a Web Page with Frames

Instructions: Start Notepad. Open the file apply6-1.html from the Chapter06\Apply folder of the Data Files for Students. See the inside back cover of this book for instructions on downloading the Data Files for Students, or contact your instructor for information about accessing the required files. The apply6-1.html and apply6-1menu.html files are partially completed HTML files for a Theater Club Web page. Figure 6–27 shows the Web page as it should appear in your browser after the additional tags and attributes are inserted. With the Web page completed, a user should be able to click a link in the top frame to display a sample linked page in the bottom frame.

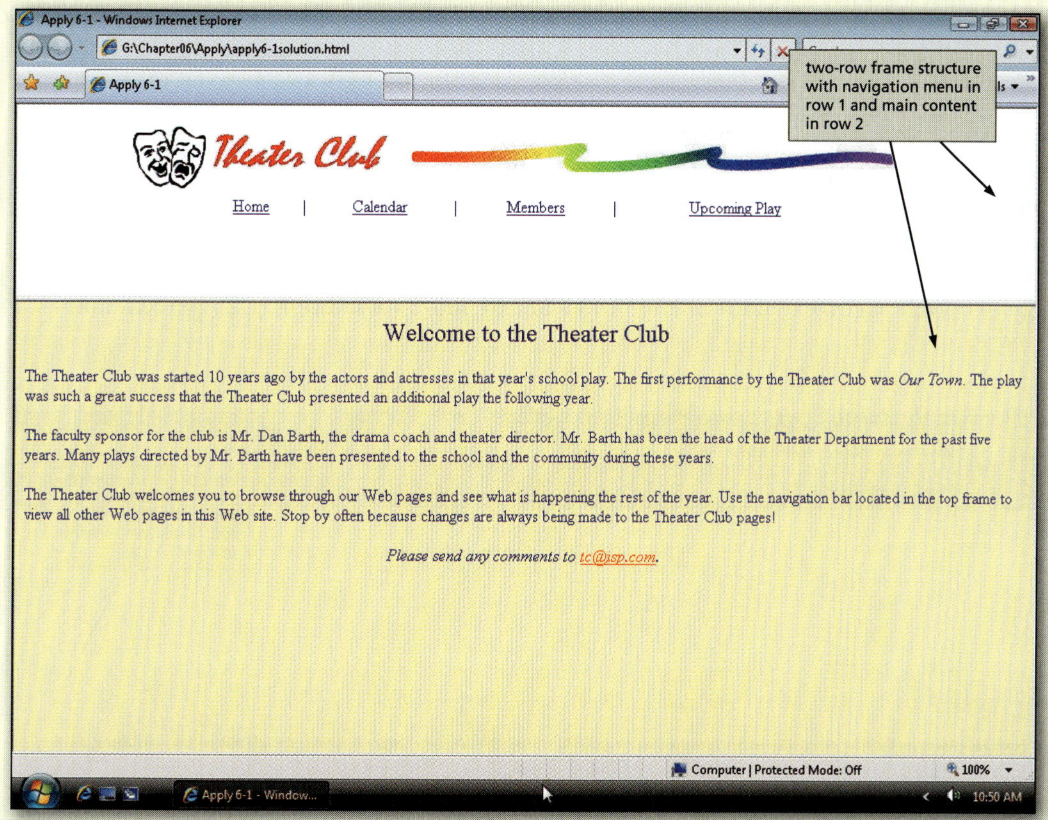

Figure 6–27

Perform the following tasks:

1. With the apply6-1.html file open in Notepad, add the HTML tags and attributes needed to make the Web page look similar to the one shown in Figure 6–27. The frames should be divided into 30 percent and 70 percent rows. The first row should display the apply6-1menu.html file, and the second row should display the apply6-1home.html file.
2. Save the revised file in the Chapter06\Apply folder using the file name apply6-1solution.html.
3. Open the apply6-1menu.html file in Notepad. The first borderless table should be centered and display in 80 percent of the window. The second menu bar table also should be centered and borderless but display in 65 percent of the window.

Continued >

Apply Your Knowledge *continued*

4. Return to the apply6-1solution.html file and make sure that the Home link works correctly. All other links display the sample.html Web page.
5. Print the revised HTML files.
6. Validate your HTML code and test all links.
7. Enter the URL G:\Chapter06\Apply\apply6-1solution.html to view the Web page in your browser.
8. Print the Web page.
9. Submit the files in the format specified by your instructor.

Extend Your Knowledge

Extend the skills you learned in this chapter and experiment with new skills.

Creating a Web Page with Frames

Instructions: Start Notepad. Open the file extend6-1.html from the Chapter06\Extend folder of the Data Files for Students. See the inside back cover of this book for instructions on downloading the Data Files for Students, or contact your instructor for information about accessing the required files. This is the frame definition file for the Web page shown in Figure 6–28. You will add the necessary tags to display two Web pages, extend6-1menu.html and extend6-1home.html, in 25 percent and 75 percent frames.

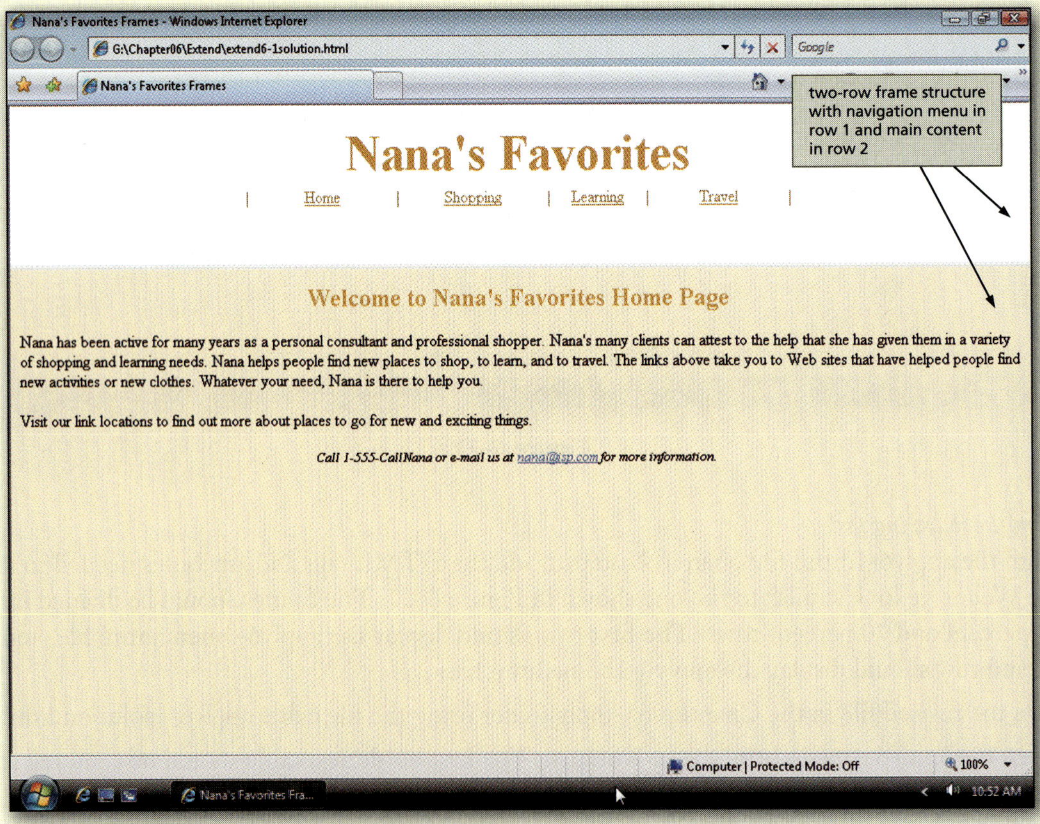

Figure 6–28

Perform the following tasks:

1. With the extend6-1.html file open in Notepad, create a two-row frame structure in which extend6-1menu.html displays in the top 25 percent of the Web page and extend6-1home.html displays in the lower 75 percent of the Web page.
2. Save the file as extend6-1solution.html. Validate the code. Print the file.
3. Open the extend6-1menu.html file in Notepad. Add the HTML code necessary to display the Home page (provided in the Data Files in the Chapter06\Extend folder) when the Home link is clicked. Also add three other URLs of your choice for the Shopping, Learning, and Travel links.
4. Save the revised document and print the file.
5. Validate your HTML code and test all links.
6. Submit the solution in the format specified by your instructor.

Make It Right

Analyze a document and correct all errors and/or improve the design.

Correcting the Greyhound Adoption Web Page

Instructions: Start Notepad. Open the file makeitright6-1.html from the Chapter06\MakeItRight folder of the Data Files for Students. See the inside back cover of this book for instructions on downloading the Data Files for Students, or contact your instructor for information about accessing the required files. The Web page is a modified version of what you see in Figure 6–29, which has 28 percent and 72 percent columns, respectively. Make the necessary corrections to the Web page to make it look like the figure. You also need to modify the makeitright6-1menu.html file. In addition to inserting the HTML code that links to the Home page (makeitright6-1home.html file provided in the Chapter06\ MakeitRight folder), you need to insert the image greyhound.gif that has a width of 212 and a height of 97. The other three links on the menu can link to the sample.html Web page.

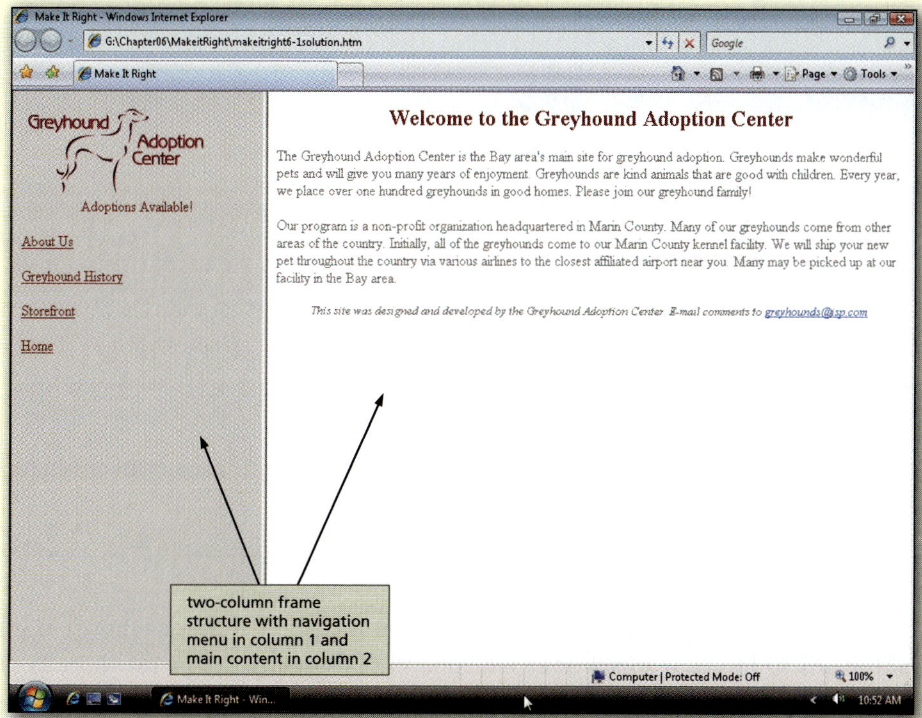

Figure 6–29

STUDENT ASSIGNMENTS

In the Lab

Lab 1: Creating a Two-Frame Structure for a Soccer Web Site

Problem: The Director of the Schererville Soccer league has asked you to create a new Web site with information on the upcoming soccer season. After reviewing the content with the Director, you suggest using a two-frame structure with two horizontal frames, as shown in Figure 6–30. The top frame will display a header and menu bar for navigation, while the bottom frame will display schedules, standings, rules, and other information.

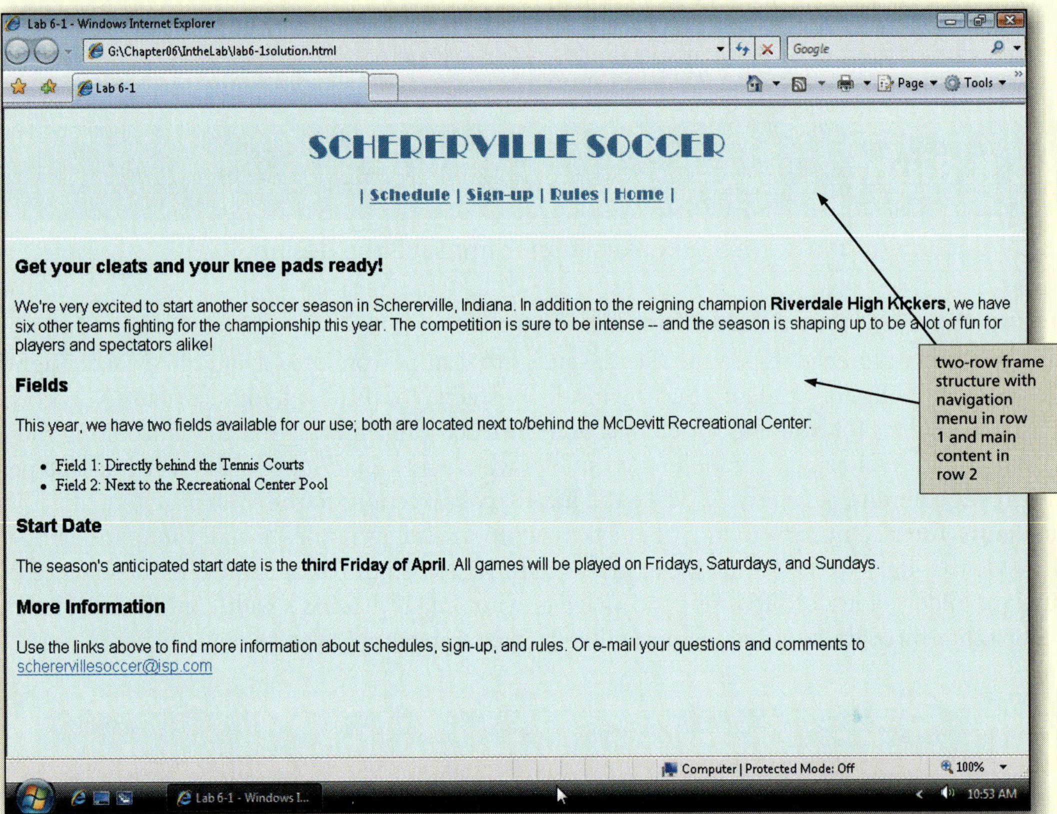

Figure 6–30

Instructions: Perform the following steps:

1. Using Notepad, create a new HTML file with the title Lab 6-1 in the main title section.
2. Begin the frame definition file by specifying two rows. The first row should be 20 percent of the total screen width and the second row should be 80 percent of the screen width.
3. For the top frame named menu, set the frame to display the Web page lab6-1menu.html at startup. Turn off scrolling and borders.
4. For the bottom frame, set the frame to display the Web page lab6-1home.html at startup. Turn off borders. Assign the frame the name win-main.
5. Save the HTML file in the Chapter06\IntheLab folder using the file name lab6-1solution.html. Print the HTML file.
6. Open lab6-1solution.html in your browser to verify that the pages appear as shown in Figure 6–30. Verify that the link to Home works. For an added level of difficulty, create the three Web pages that can be linked from the menu (Schedule, Sign-up, and Rules) in your browser and test the menu bar links to verify they link to the correct Web pages.

7. Click the Home link on the menu bar and then print the file lab6-1solution.html using the As laid out on screen option.
8. Validate all of your code using the W3C validator.
9. Submit the files in the format specified by your instructor.

In the Lab

Lab 2: Bright Idea, LLC Web Site

Problem: The nonprofit organization, Bright Idea, LLC, has decided to advertise on the Internet. You have been asked to create a Web site with a two-frame structure, as shown in Figure 6–31. First, you need to create a frame definition file that specifies a two-column structure, with columns set to 20 percent and 80 percent. At startup, the left frame displays the Web page, lab6-2menu.html, which includes links to additional Web pages about the company. At startup, the right frame displays the Web page, lab6-2home.html, which serves as a home page.

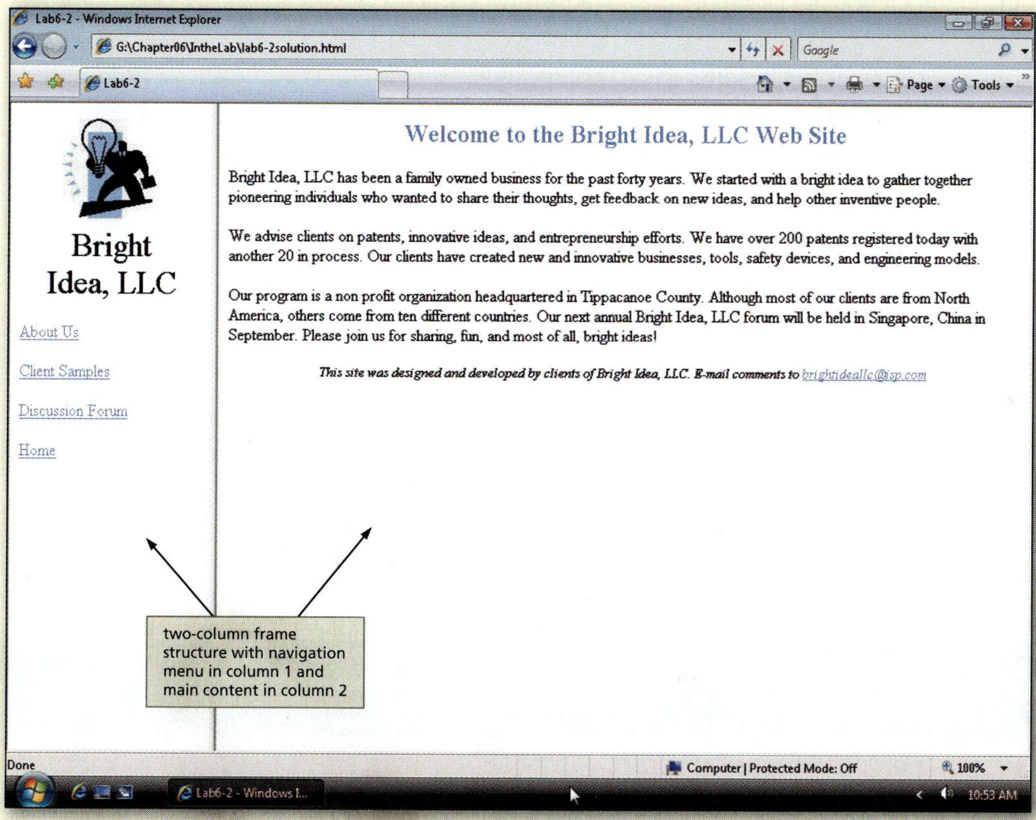

Figure 6–31

Instructions: Perform the following steps:

1. Using Notepad, create a new HTML file with the title [Your name] Lab 6-2 in the main title section.
2. Create a frame definition file that specifies a two-frame structure with two columns set to 20 percent and 80 percent, respectively. Save the HTML file in the Chapter06\IntheLab folder using the file name lab6-2solution.html. Print the HTML file.

Continued >

In the Lab *continued*

3. Create a menu page to appear in the left frame by completing the following steps:
   a. Create a new file in Notepad.
   b. Set all links (normal, visited, active) to be displayed in dodgerblue color text.
   c. Add the image, brightidealogo.jpg, from the Chapter06\IntheLab folder.
   d. Add the text, Bright Idea, LLC, in font size +3, below the image. Center both the image and the text.
   e. Create four text links, as shown in Figure 6–31. Set the Home text link to link to the Web page, lab6-2home.html. Set the other three links — About Us, Client Samples, and Discussion Forum — to link to any Web page in the Data Files for Students. For a higher level of difficulty create a page for the About Us link, find information online about patents or new inventions for the Client Samples link, and find an online discussion area for the Discussion Forum link.
   f. Save the HTML file in the Chapter06\IntheLab folder using the file name lab6-2menu.html. Print the HTML file.
4. Create a home page that contains the text shown in Figure 6–31 and appears in the right frame, by completing the following steps:
   a. Enter and format the heading to be center-aligned and bold, with a font size of +2 and a font color of dodgerblue.
   b. Enter and format the remaining Web page text with a font color of black.
   c. Format the last paragraph and e-mail address to be italic.
   d. Make the link colors (normal, active, and visited) dodgerblue.
   e. Save the HTML file in the Chapter06\IntheLab folder using the file name lab6-2home.html. Print the HTML file.
5. Open the HTML file lab6-2solution.html in your browser and test the menu bar links to verify they link to the correct Web pages.
6. Click the Home link on the menu bar and then print the file lab6-2solution.html using the As laid out onscreen option.
7. Validate all of your code using the W3C validator.
8. Submit the files in the format specified by your instructor.

In the Lab

Lab 3: Creating a Four-Frame Structure

Problem: You recently have started doing freelance Web development work for a few local companies. You want to create a Web site with a four-frame structure, as shown in Figure 6–32, to promote the Web development work you have done in previous projects. After creating the frame definition file, use any image stored in the Data Files for Students as your logo. Use any of the Web pages previously created and stored in the Data Files for Students to appear in the bottom-right frame.

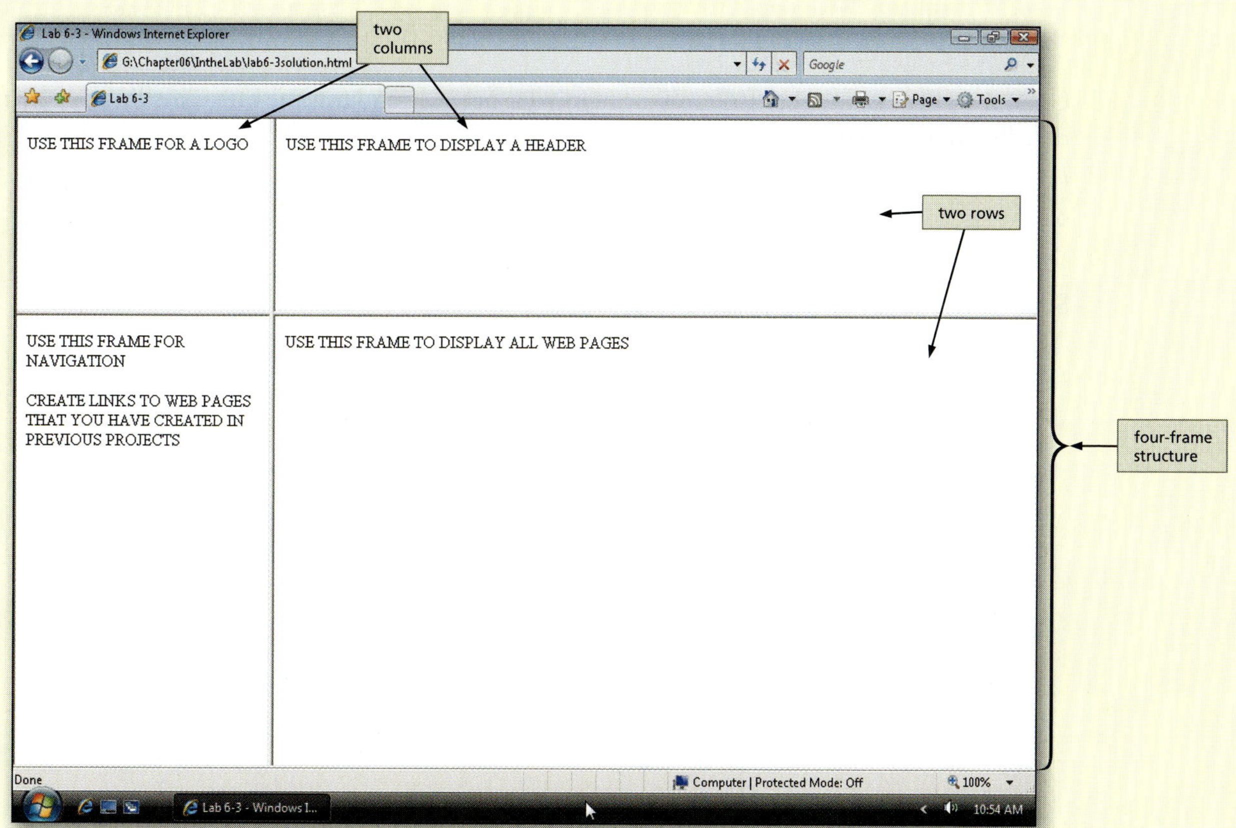

Figure 6–32

Instructions: Perform the following steps:

1. Using Notepad, create a new HTML file with the title Lab 6-3 in the main title section. Enter code to create a frame definition file that specifies a four-frame structure, similar to the one in Figure 6–32. For each frame, set the Web page to be displayed at startup lab6-3logo.html for the logo frame, lab6-3header.html for the header frame, lab6-3menu.html for the navigation menu frame, and lab6-3home.html for the main frame. Turn scrolling and borders for each frame on or off, as you think is appropriate.
2. Save the HTML file in the Chapter06\IntheLab folder using the file name lab6-3solution.html. Print the HTML file.
3. Create a logo page to appear in the logo frame. Using any image stored in the Data Files for Students, add a logo to the Web page. Save the HTML file in the Chapter06\IntheLab folder using the file name lab6-3logo.html. Print the HTML file.
4. Create a header page to appear in the header frame. Include a text heading that has a unique color and font face. Save the HTML file in the Chapter06\IntheLab folder using the file name lab6-3header.html. Print the HTML file.
5. Create a menu page to appear in the navigation menu frame. Include text links to several Web pages created in this or previous projects, as well as a text link to the home page (lab6-3home.html). Save the HTML file in the Chapter06\IntheLab folder using the file name lab6-3menu.html. Print the HTML file.
6. Create a home page to appear in the navigation (or main) frame. Include text that describes your HTML and Web page development skills, along with contact information and an e-mail link. Save the HTML file in the Chapter06\IntheLab folder using the file name lab6-3home.html. Print the HTML file.

Continued >

In the Lab *continued*

7. Open the HTML file lab6-3solution.html in your browser and test the menu bar links to verify they link to the correct Web pages.
8. Click the Home link on the menu bar and then print the file lab6-3solution.html using the As laid out onscreen option.
9. Validate all of your code using the W3C validator.
10. Submit the files in the format specified by your instructor.

Cases and Places

Apply your creative thinking and problem solving skills to design and implement a solution.

• EASIER ••MORE DIFFICULT

• 1: Frames for a Good Cause

In the Make It Right exercise on page HTML 293, you created a two-frame structure for a greyhound adoption Web site. Think of another organization such as this that could use a nice Web site to promote the good works that they do. Create a simple prototype of a Web site for this organization. How would you restructure this Web site so the e-mail link is always available? What other changes could you make to the Web site design or frame structure to make the Web site more effective or easier to navigate? Make these changes to the Web site, open the frame definition file in a browser, and then print the Web page using the As laid out onscreen option. Turn that printout in to your instructor with a synopsis of why your design is a better solution than the previous two-frame structure used in the Make It Right exercise.

• 2: Frame Standards

In preparation for a design planning session, the Manager of Web Development at Axcelent has asked you to locate two Web sites that use frames in their page structures, and view the HTML source code for the pages and see what frame options were used on the pages. Is the scrolling turned off, or is the default used? How many frames allow scrolling? Is the noresize attribute utilized? As part of this research, he has asked you to write a brief assessment of the intended purpose for using a frame structure, discussing whether the Web site is more or less effective because of the frames. Print each overall Web page (remember to use the As laid out onscreen option in the Print dialog box) and then sketch a design for each Web page using a different frame structure or no frames. How does your structure compare with the originals? Which Web site layout is more effective?

•• 3: Melanie's Web Page Frames

The manager of Melanie's Collectibles Store, Melanie McDevitt, saw the Web site that you developed for Jana's Jewels and likes what she sees. She has asked you to design a prototype for a similar Web site she can use to sell the jewelry (all kinds) and small statues that she sells in her store. Because they have numerous pictures available, they want to utilize the thumbnail technique discussed in Chapter 3. Use a digital camera to take pictures of small items that may be sold in a store such as Melanie's. If you do not have a digital camera, find images on the Web that you can use as samples. You can use some of the jewelry pictures used in the chapter project as well. Be sure to save those images as thumbnails with a different file name. Note all width and height values for all images so that you can use them in your <img> tags. Create a structure to display the items (and prices if required) in an easy-to-use manner.

•• 4: Frames for Reference

Make It Personal

The instructor for your Web development class has asked if you can create a reference Web site that can be used by students taking the Introductory HTML course. You suggest a Web site similar to the one shown in Figure 6–3b on page HTML 265, which is a Web site with a two-frame structure that provides an excellent reference Web site for information about HTML. Create a similar Web site using a two-frame structure, with the table of contents in the left frame and the content in the right frame. Include at least four topics in the table of contents and create Web pages that contain information about the topics shown in the table of contents.

•• 5: Frame Usability

Working Together

LightWorks Design recently has contracted with several customers who want to use frames on their Web sites. Having read several articles suggesting that frames limit Web site usability, the Senior Web Developer has some concerns about using frames — and has asked everyone on the team to help research the pros and cons of using frames in a Web site. Find at least five Web sites (be sure to include the W3C Web site) that discuss the use of frames. Develop a matrix that describes when or if Web sites could be made more effective with the use of frames. Find some research that describes ways in which you can determine whether or not a browser supports frames. What do you need to do from a coding standpoint to display a Web site in browsers that do not support frames? From a Web site maintenance perspective, what would be the ramifications of this decision? Write a paper discussing the information that you find about using frames.

7 Creating a Form on a Web Page

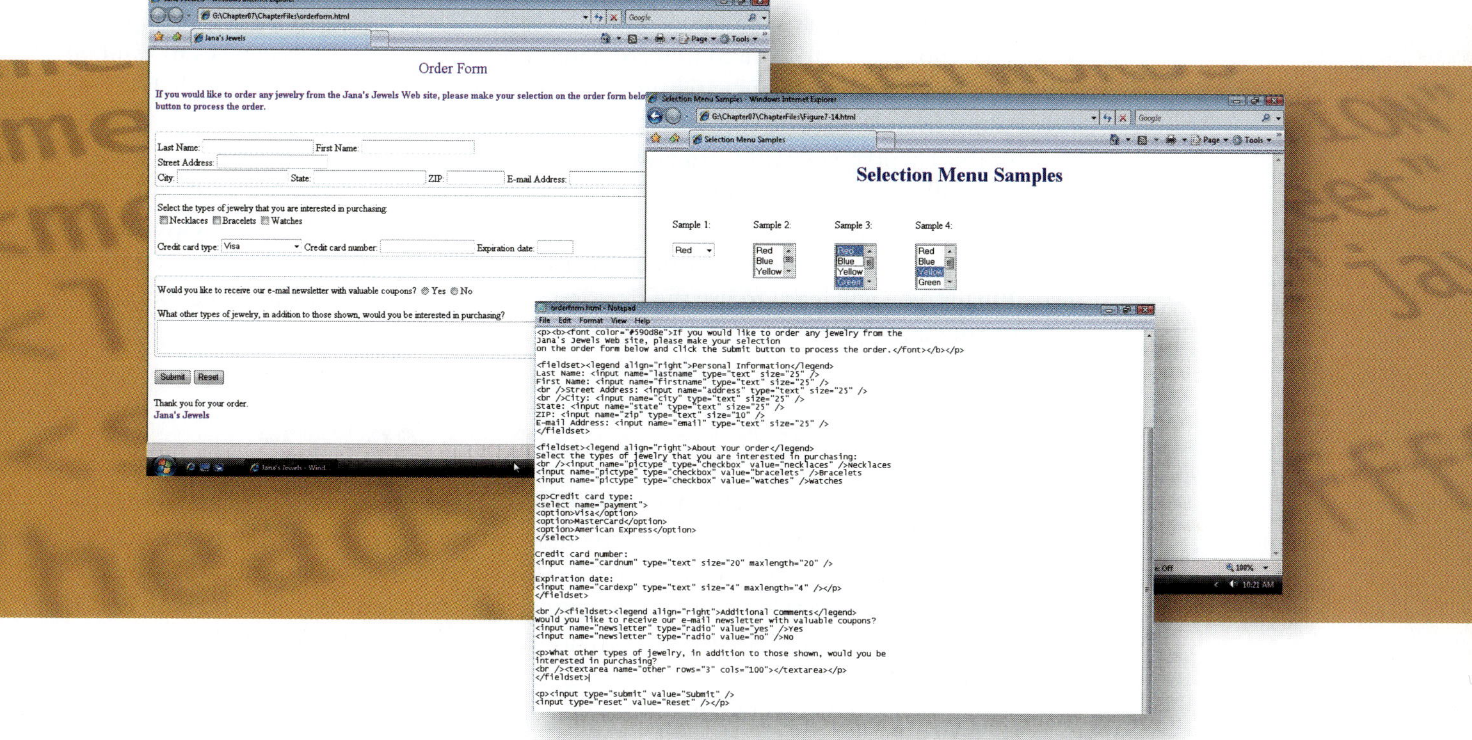

Objectives

You will have mastered the material in this chapter when you can:

- Define terms related to forms
- Describe the different form controls and their uses
- Use the <form> tag
- Use the <input /> tag
- Create a text box
- Create check boxes
- Create a selection menu with multiple options
- Use the <select> tag
- Use the <option> tag
- Create radio buttons
- Create a textarea box
- Create a Submit button
- Create a Reset button
- Use the <fieldset> tag to group form information

7 Creating a Form on a Web Page

Introduction

The goal of the projects completed thus far has been to present information *to* Web page visitors. In this chapter, you learn how to get information *from* Web site visitors by adding a form for user input.

Using a Web page form for user input reduces the potential for errors, because customers enter data or select options from the form included directly on the Web page. A form has input fields to remind users to enter information and limits choices to valid options to avoid incorrect data entry. Forms provide an easy way to collect needed information from Web page visitors.

In this chapter, you will learn how to use HTML to create a form on a Web page. The form will include several controls, including check boxes, a drop-down list, radio buttons, and text boxes. You also will learn to add Submit and Reset buttons that customers can use to submit the completed form or clear the information previously entered into the form. Finally, you will learn to use the <fieldset> tag to group information on a form in a user-friendly way.

Project — Creating Forms on a Web Page

The Jana's Jewels Web site has been a great success. Many customers have viewed the jewelry on the Web site, followed the instructions on the Order Form Web page, and have sent e-mail requests to purchase jewelry. Although most of the e-mails are complete, Jana discovered that several e-mails are missing key information. She asks you if an easier, less error-prone way exists for customers to notify her of their selections and purchase information.

In Chapter 6, you created the Order Form Web page for the Jana's Jewels Web site as a text-based Web page that listed the information needed to place an order. To place an order, customers had to type all of their order information into an e-mail and then send it to a specific e-mail address. While such an approach to information gathering does work, it is inefficient and prone to error. Users easily can forget to include required information or request options that are not available.

In this project, you enter HTML tags to modify the text-based Order Form Web page on the Jana's Jewels Web site (Figure 7–1a) and to create an Order Form Web page with a form, as shown in Figure 7–1b. This page requests the same information as the text-based Web page, but includes a form that allows users to enter data, select options, and then submit the form to an e-mail address.

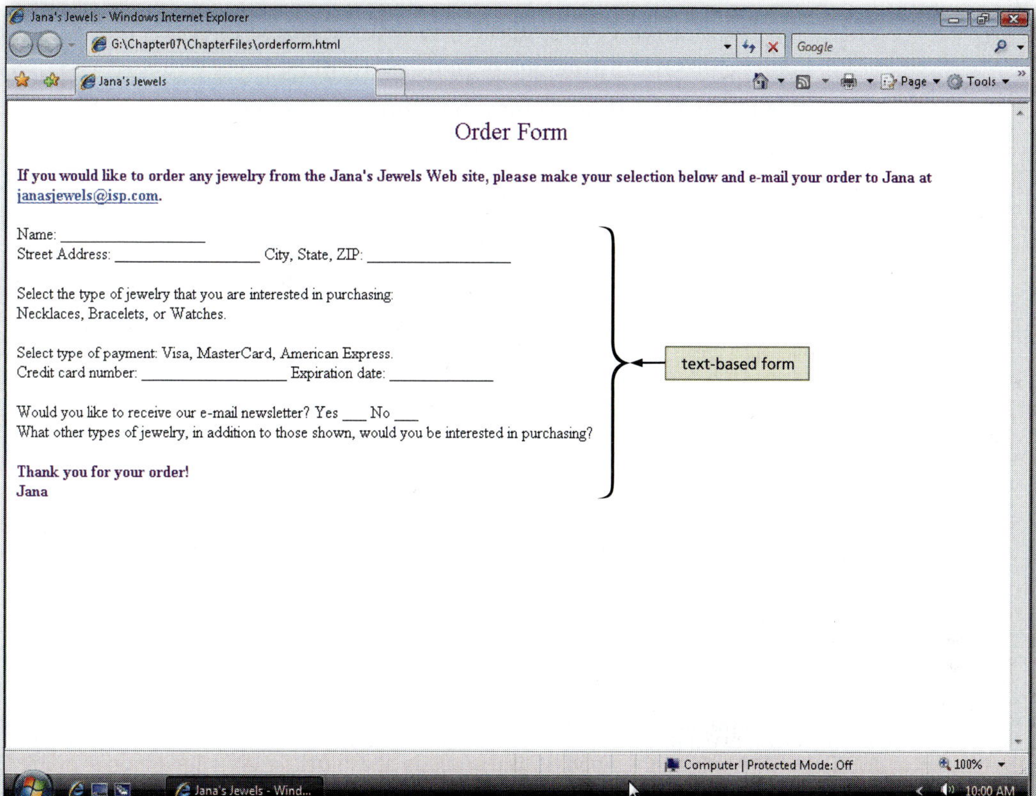

(a) Order Form Web page in text format.

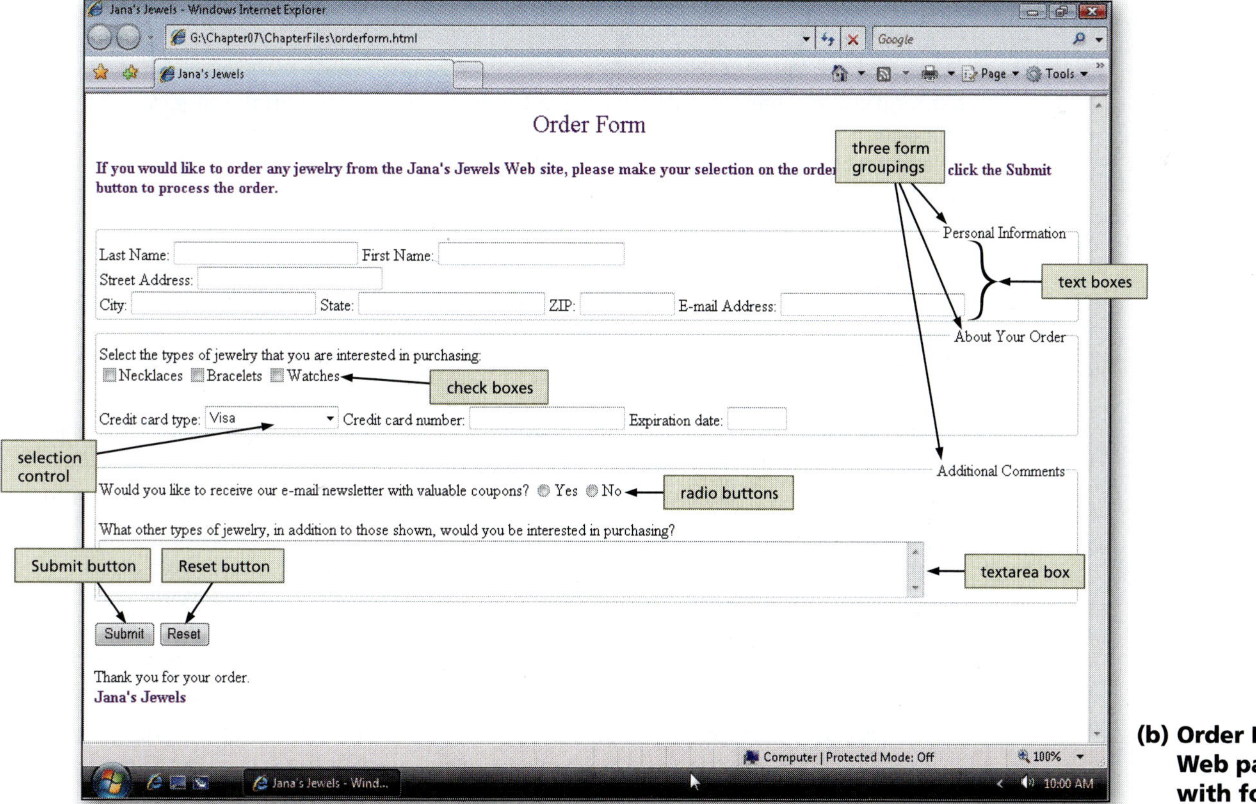

(b) Order Form Web page with form.

Figure 7–1

Overview

As you read this chapter, you will learn how to create the Web pages shown in Figure 7–1 on the previous page by performing these general tasks:

- Enter HTML code into the Notepad window.
- Save the file as an HTML file.
- Enter basic HTML tags and add text to the file.
- Insert tags to create a form with several input controls.
- Create Submit and Reset buttons on the form.
- Add interest and organization to the form using fieldset tags.
- Save and print the HTML code.
- Validate, view, and print the Web pages.

Plan Ahead

General Project Guidelines

As you create Web pages, such as the project shown in Figure 7–1 on the previous page, you should follow these general guidelines:

1. **Plan the Web site.** You should plan the information that you hope to collect before you begin to write your HTML code. Refer to Table 1–4 on page HTML 12 for information on the planning phase of the Web Development Life Cycle. In this phase, you determine the purpose of the Web form, identify the users of the form and their computing environment, and decide how best to capture the information sought using a Web page.
2. **Analyze the need.** In the analysis phase of the Web Development Life Cycle, you should analyze what content to include in the Web page form. The Web development project in Chapter 7 is different than the one completed in other chapters because it contains a form. Part of the analysis phase then includes determining what information to collect and the best form input controls to use for this collection.
3. **Determine the types of controls to use.** The type of information a form is intended to gather dictates what controls are used in the form. For instance, in the case in which only one option from a list can be selected, you should use the radio button control. In the case in which more than one option can be selected, you can use check boxes or selection controls. If you want users to be able to add their own comments, you can use a textarea box. Most forms use a combination of controls, not just a single type.
4. **Establish what other form options are necessary.** Form organization is an important aspect of Web page form development. You want to be sure that the user understands what information to provide. You also want the form to be attractive and easy to use. Consider using fieldset tags to divide the form attractively and segregate information into logical subsets.
5. **Create the Web page form and links.** Once the analysis and design is complete, the Web developer creates the Web page form using HTML. Good Web development standard practices should be followed in this step. Examples of good practices include utilizing the form controls that are appropriate for specific needs.
6. **Test the Web page form.** An important part of Web development is testing to assure that you are following XHTML standards. In this book, we use the World Wide Web Consortium (W3C) validator that allows you to test your Web page and clearly explains any errors you have. Additionally when testing, you should verify that all controls work as intended. Finally, both the Submit and the Reset buttons should be tested.

When necessary, more specific details concerning the above guidelines are presented at appropriate points in the chapter. The chapter also will identify the actions performed and decisions made regarding these guidelines during the creation of the Web page shown in Figure 7–1.

Web Page Forms

The Order Form Web page shown in Figure 7–1b on page HTML 303 shows an example of a Web page form designed to request specific information from the Web page visitor. A Web page form has three main components:

1. Input controls
2. A <form> tag, which contains the information necessary to process the form
3. A Submit button, which sends the data to be processed

BTW

Forms

Several HTML guides on the Internet discuss the use of forms on Web pages. Many of these sites are created and maintained at universities. The guides give practical tips on the purpose and use of HTML tags and attributes. To view an HTML guide, use a search engine to search for the phrase "HTML Guide" or a related phrase.

Input Controls

An **input control** is any type of input mechanism on a form. A form may contain several different input controls classified as data or text input controls. A **data input control** can be a radio button (radio), a check box (checkbox), a Submit button (submit), a Reset button (reset), or a selection menu (select). A **text input control** allows the user to enter text through the following:

- a **text box** (text), for small amounts of text
- a **textarea box** (textarea), for larger amounts of text
- a **password text box** (password), for entering a password

As shown in Figure 7–1b, the form developed in this chapter uses several different data and text input controls.

Of the available input controls, the eight listed in Table 7–1 are used most often in form creation.

Table 7–1 Form Input Controls

Control	Function	Remarks
text	• Creates a single-line field for a relatively small amount of text	• Indicates both the size of the field and the total maximum length
password	• Identical to text boxes used for single-line data entry	• Echoes (or masks) the entered text as bullets
textarea	• Creates a multiple-line field for a relatively large amount of text	• Indicates the number of rows and columns for the area
select	• Creates a drop-down list or menu of choices from which a visitor can select an option or options	• Indicates the length of the list in number of rows
checkbox	• Creates a list item	• More than one item in a list can be chosen
radio	• Creates a list item	• Indicates only one item in a list can be chosen
submit	• Submits a form for processing	• Tells the browser to send the data on the form to the server
reset	• Resets the form	• Returns all input controls to the default status

A **text control** creates a text box that is used for a single line of input (Figure 7–2 on the next page). The text control has two attributes:

1. **Size**, which determines the number of characters that are displayed on the form
2. **Maxlength**, which specifies the maximum length of the input field

BTW

Form Tutorial
What better way to learn more about the HTML form tag than using a tutorial on the Web? Many Web sites have lessons grouped by topic, starting with initial HTML tags. An index is generally provided for ease of use. To find HTML tutorials, search the Web using a popular search engine.

The maximum length of the field may exceed the size of the field that appears on the form. For example, consider a field size of three characters and a maximum length of nine characters. If a Web page visitor types in more characters than the size of the text box (three characters), the characters scroll to the left, to a maximum of nine characters entered.

A **password control** also creates a text box used for a single line of input (Figure 7–2), except that the characters entered into the field can appear as asterisks or bullets. A password text box holds the password entered by a visitor. The password appears as a series of characters, asterisks, or bullets as determined by the Web developer, one per character for the password entered. This feature is designed to help protect the visitor's password from being observed by others as it is being entered.

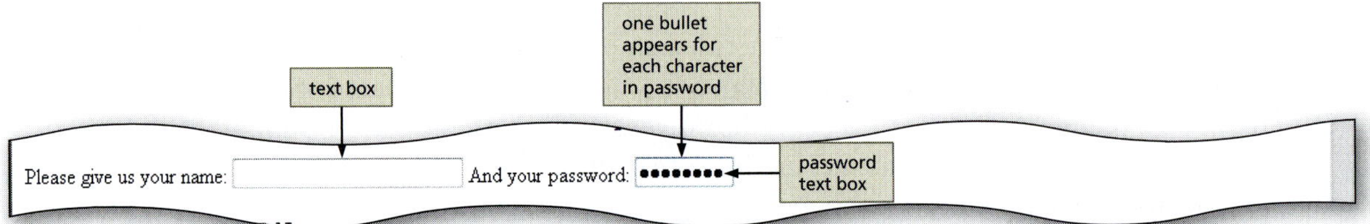

Figure 7–2 Text and password text controls.

A **radio control** limits the Web page visitor to only one choice from a list of choices (Figure 7–3). Each choice is preceded by a **radio button**, or option button, which typically appears as an open circle. When the visitor selects one of the radio buttons, all other radio buttons in the list automatically are deselected. By default, all radio buttons are deselected. To set a particular button as the default, you use the checked value within the <input /> tag.

Figure 7–3 Radio button and checkbox controls.

A **checkbox control** allows a Web page visitor to select more than one choice from a list of choices (Figure 7–3). Each choice in a check box list can be either on or off. By default, all check boxes are deselected. The default can be changed so a particular check box is preselected as the default, by using the checked value within the <input /> tag.

A **select control** creates a selection menu from which the visitor selects one or more choices (Figure 7–4). This prevents the visitor from having to type information into a text or textarea field. A select control is suitable when a limited number of choices are available. The user clicks the list arrow to view all the choices in the menu. When clicked, the default appears first and is highlighted to indicate that it is selected.

Figure 7–4 Different options for selection controls.

A **textarea control** creates a field that allows multiple lines of input (Figure 7–5). Textarea fields are useful when an extensive amount of input is required from, or desired of, a Web page visitor. The textarea control has two primary attributes:

1. **Rows,** which specifies the number of rows in the textarea field
2. **Cols,** which specifies the number of columns in the textarea field

The **fieldset control** (Figure 7–5) helps to group related form elements together. This makes the form easier to read and complete. The form segment in Figure 7–5 shows two groupings: one with a left-aligned legend and the other with a right-aligned legend. Using fieldset tags to segregate information allows the Web page visitor immediately to see that two (or more) categories of information are included in the form. The easier that it is for a user to complete a form, the more likely it is that he or she will complete it.

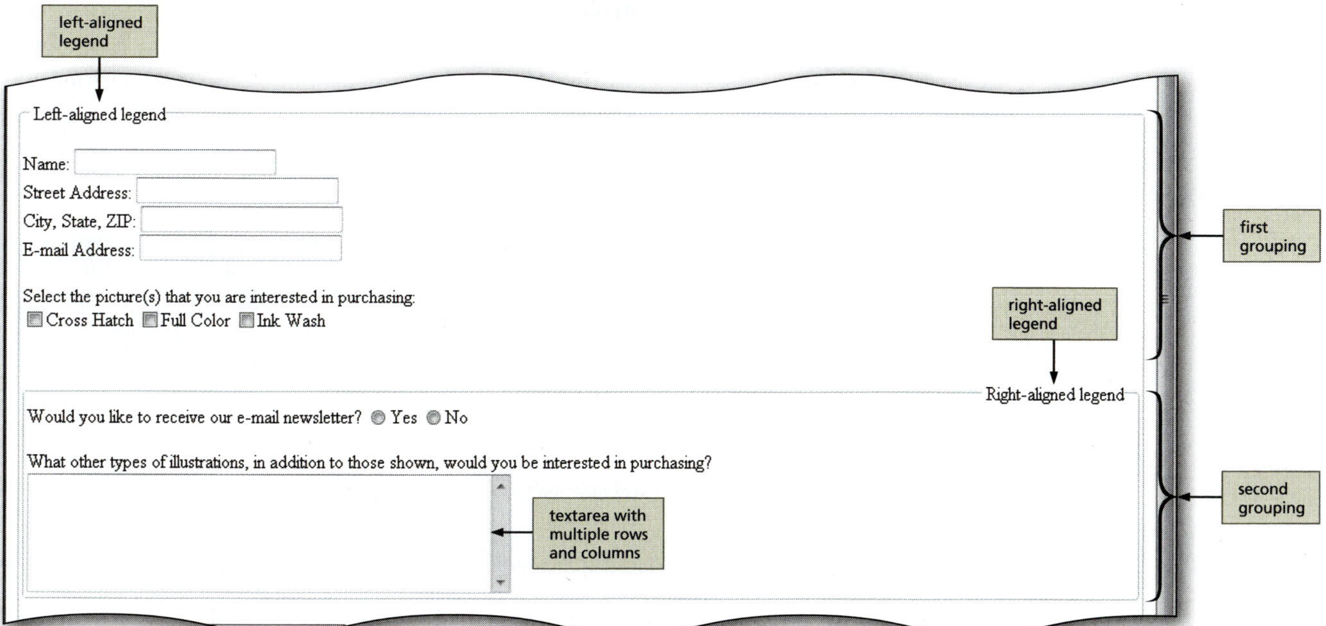

Figure 7–5 Fieldset control.

The **submit control** and the **reset control** create the Submit and Reset buttons, respectively (Figure 7–6 on the next page). The **Submit button** sends the information to the appropriate location for processing. The **Reset button** clears any input that was entered in the form, resetting the input controls back to the defaults. A Web page form must include a Submit button, and most also include a Reset button.

Figure 7–6 Submit and Reset button controls.

Regardless of the specific type, each input control has one or two attributes:

1. Name — the **name** attribute identifies the specific information that is being sent when the form is submitted for processing. All controls have a name.
2. Value — all controls except textarea also have a **value** attribute. The value attribute is the type of data that is contained in the named input control (that is, the data that the Web page visitor enters). For a textarea field, no value attribute is possible because of the variability of the input.

When a Web page visitor clicks the Submit button on the form, both the control name and the value of the data contained within that control are sent to be processed.

HTML Tags Used to Create Forms

Form statements start with the <form> tag and end with the </form> tag. The input controls in a form are created using either HTML tags or attributes of HTML tags. For example, the select and textarea controls are created using the HTML tags <select> and <textarea>, respectively. Other input controls are created using attributes of HTML tags. For example, the text boxes, check boxes, radio buttons, and Submit and Reset buttons all are created using the type attribute of the <input /> tag. Table 7–2 lists the HTML tags used to create the order form in this chapter. Any combination of these elements can be used in a Web page form.

Table 7–2 HTML Tags Used to Create Forms

Tag	Function	Remarks
<fieldset> </fieldset>	Groups related controls on a form	Optionally used for readability
<form> </form>	Creates a form that allows user input	Required when creating forms
<input />	Defines the controls used in the form, using a variety of type attribute values	Required for input controls
<legend> </legend>	Defines the text that is displayed in the grouping borders	Optionally used when using <fieldset> tags
<select> </select>	Creates a menu of choices from which a visitor selects	Required for selection choices
<option> </option>	Specifies a choice in a <select> tag	Required, one per choice
<textarea> </textarea>	Creates a multiple-line text input area	Required for longer text inputs that appear on several lines

Attributes of HTML Tags Used to Create Forms

Many of the HTML tags used to create forms have several attributes. Table 7–3 lists some of the HTML tags used to create forms, along with their main attributes and functions.

Table 7–3 Attributes of HTML Tags Used to Create Forms

Tag	Attribute	Function
<form> </form>	action	• URL for action completed by the server
	method	• HTTP method (post)
	target	• Location at which the resource will be displayed
<input />	type	• Type of input control (text, password, checkbox, radio, submit, reset, file, hidden, image, button)
	name	• Name of the control
	value	• Value submitted if a control is selected (required for radio and checkbox controls)
	checked	• Sets a radio button to a checked state (only one can be checked)
	disabled	• Disables a control
	readonly	• Used for text passwords
	size	• Number of characters that appear on the form
	maxlength	• Maximum number of characters that can be entered
	src	• URL to the location of an image stored on the server
	alt	• Alternative text for an image control
	tabindex	• Sets tabbing order among control elements
<legend> </legend>	align	• Indicates how a legend should be aligned
<select> </select>	name	• Name of the element
	size	• Number of options visible when Web page is first opened
	multiple	• Allows for multiple selections in select list
	disabled	• Disables a control
	tabindex	• Sets the tabbing order among control elements
<option> </option>	selected	• Specifies whether an option is selected
	disabled	• Disables a control
	value	• Value submitted if a control is selected
<textarea> </textarea>	name	• Name of the control
	rows	• Height in number of rows
	cols	• Width in number of columns
	disabled	• Disables a control
	readonly	• Used for text passwords
	tabindex	• Sets the tabbing order among control elements

BTW

Radio Buttons
Old-time car radios were operated by a row of large black plastic buttons. Push one button, and you would get one preset radio station. You could push only one button at a time. Radio buttons on forms work the same way as the old-time radio buttons—one button at a time. With check boxes, more than one option can be selected at a time.

Creating a Form on a Web Page

In this chapter, you will modify the text-based Order Form Web page (orderform.html) used in the Jana's Jewels Web site. The file, orderform.html, currently contains only text and does not utilize a form or form controls (Figure 7–1a on page HTML 303). Using this text-based order form is inconvenient for the user, who must retype the required order information into an e-mail message and then e-mail that information to the address listed in the opening paragraph of text.

The file, orderform.html, is stored in the Data Files for Students for this chapter. After opening this file in Notepad, you will enter HTML code to convert this text-based Web page into the Web page form shown in Figure 7–1b on page HTML 303.

BTW

Textareas
To create a textarea, the Web developer specifies the number of rows and columns in which the Web page visitor can enter information. The maximum number of characters for a textarea is 32,700. It is a good rule to keep the number of columns in a textarea to 50 or fewer. Using that as a limit, the textarea will fit on most screens.

Plan Ahead

Processing form information.

One of the most important issues to determine when creating a Web page form is what to do with the information once it is entered. One way to process the information is to use a CGI script, which is code that has been previously written in a language other than HTML. Another way to process the information is to post the information to an e-mail address.

- **Using a CGI script.** This action is beyond the scope of this book, but it is the more efficient way to handle the information input into the Web page form. A Web developer would have to find out what script capabilities reside on the server in order to utilize it.
- **Posting to an e-mail address.** Because we do not know what CGI scripts are available on the Web servers at your location, we will utilize the e-mail posting technique in this chapter. The information posted to an e-mail address is not readily usable, so other steps will have to be taken to utilize the data coming in via e-mail.

To Start Notepad and Open an HTML File

The following step illustrates how to start Notepad and open the HTML file, orderform.html.

1

- Start Notepad and, if necessary, maximize the window.
- With a USB drive plugged into your computer, click File on the menu bar and then click Open on the File menu.
- If necessary, navigate to the Chapter07\ChapterFiles folder on the USB drive.
- If necessary, click the Files of type box arrow and then click All Files to display all files in the g:\Chapter07\ChapterFiles folder.

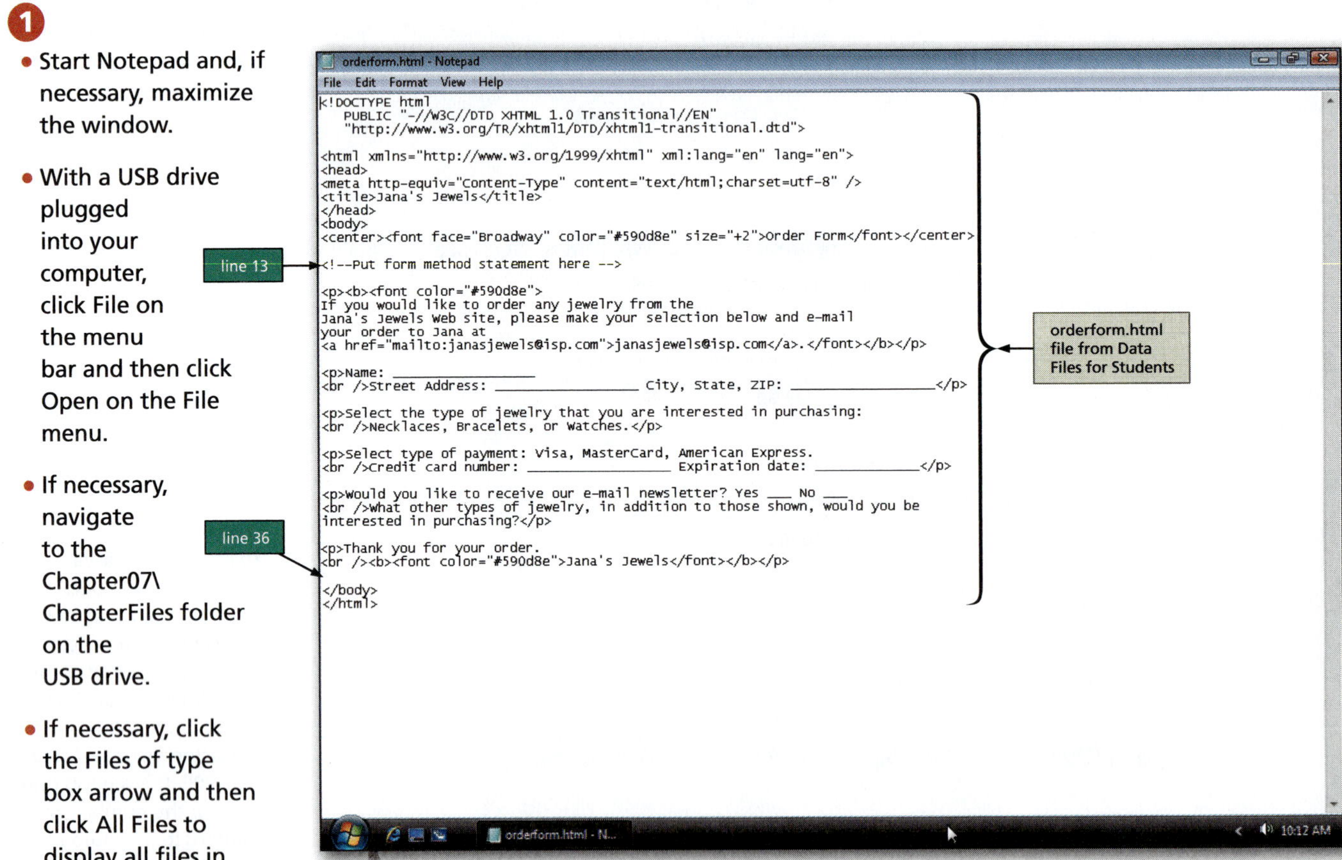

Figure 7–7

- Click orderform.html in the list of files.
- Click the Open button to open the orderform.html file in Notepad (Figure 7–7).

Creating a Form and Identifying the Form Process

When adding a form to a Web page, the first steps are creating the form and identifying how the form is processed when it is submitted. The start <form> and end </form> tags designate an area of a Web page as a form. Between the <form> and </form> tags, form controls can be added to request different types of information and allow the appropriate input responses. A form can include any number of controls.

The **action attribute** of the <form> tag specifies the action that is taken when the form is submitted. Information entered in forms can be sent by e-mail to an e-mail address or can be used to update a database. Although the e-mail option is functional, many Web sites process information from forms using Common Gateway Interface (CGI) scripting. A **CGI script** is a program written in a programming language (such as PHP or Perl) that communicates with the Web server. The CGI script sends the information input on the Web page form to the server for processing. Because this type of processing involves programming tasks that are beyond the scope of this book, the information entered in the order form created in this chapter will be submitted in a file to an e-mail address. The e-mail address will be specified as the action attribute value in the <form> tag.

BTW

CGI Scripts
Using CGI scripts to process forms is a much more efficient way to handle the data that is sent from a form. Many Web sites have free sample CGI scripts for Web developers to use. Search the Web for relevant CGI information and free samples.

The **method attribute** of the <form> tag specifies the manner in which the data entered in the form is sent to the server to be processed. Two primary ways are used in HTML: the get method and the post method. The **get method** sends the name-value pairs to the end of the URL indicated in the action attribute. The **post method** sends a separate data file with the name-value pairs to the URL (or e-mail address) indicated in the action attribute. Most Web developers prefer the post method because it is much more flexible. You need to be cautious when using the get method. Some Web servers limit a URL's size, so you run the risk of truncating relevant information when using the get method. The post method is used for the forms in this chapter.

The following HTML code creates a form using the post method and an action attribute to indicate that the form information should be sent to an e-mail address in an attached data file:

```
<form method="post" action="mailto:janasjewels@isp.com">
```

When the form is submitted, a file containing the input data is sent as an e-mail attachment to the e-mail address janasjewels@isp.com.

To Create a Form and Identify the Form Process

The following step shows how to enter HTML code to create a form and identify the form process.

1

- Highlight the words <!--Put form method statement here --> on line 13.
- Type `<form method="post" action="mailto:janasjewels@isp.com">` to replace the highlighted words with the new tag.
- Click on the blank line 36 and press the ENTER key.
- Type `</form>` but do not press the ENTER key (Figure 7–8).

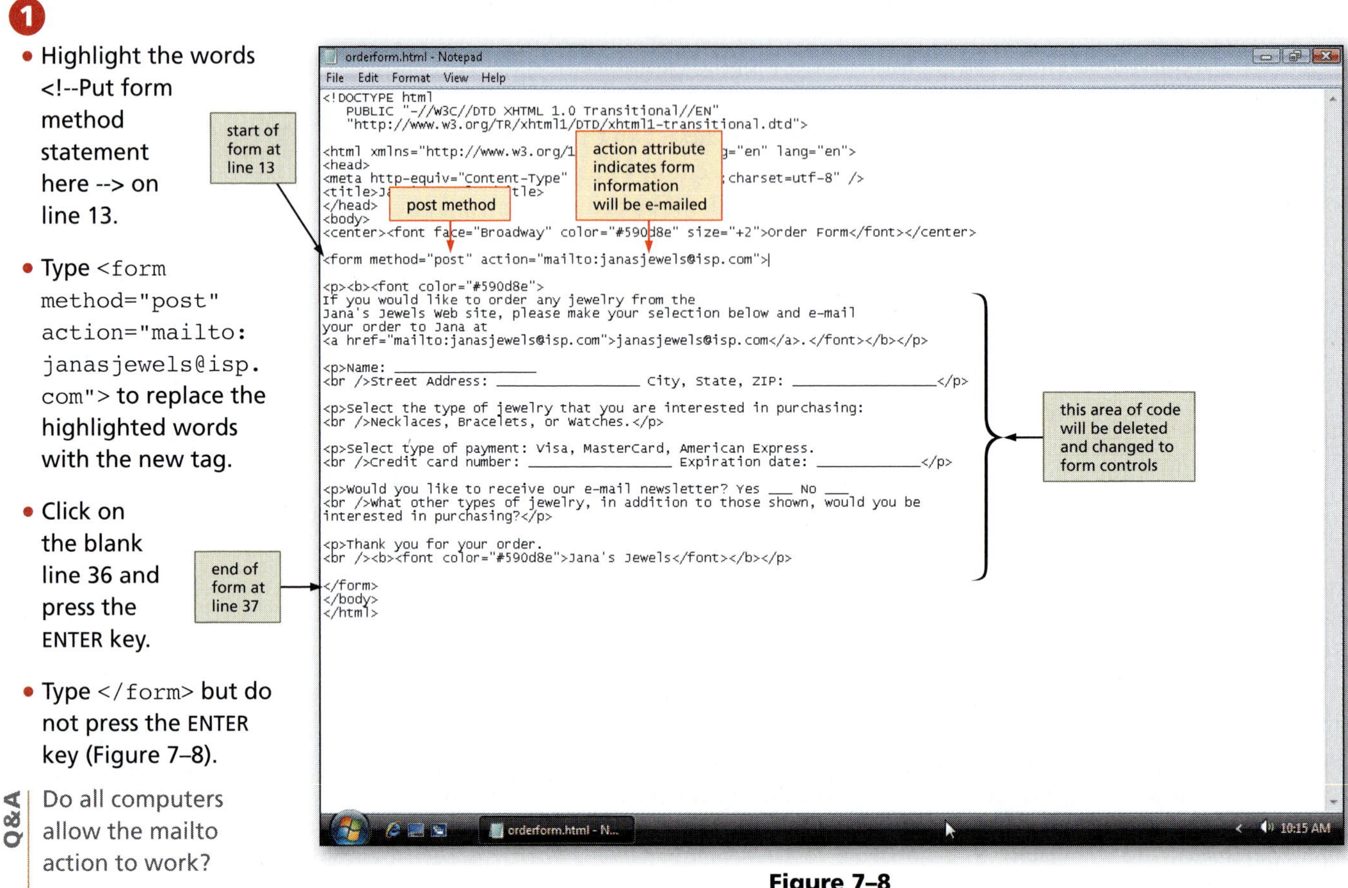

Figure 7–8

Q&A Do all computers allow the mailto action to work?

Some schools and organizations restrict the use of the mailto action. This is something that you need to test in order to determine whether or not it will work in your situation.

Q&A What do I need in order to utilize a CGI script for processing?

Most ISPs provide generic form-processing scripts. These scripts are designed to process the data coming in through the form immediately and give you easier access to usable information. Find out from the ISP what CGI scripts are available and how you can use them.

To Change the Text Message

The next step in updating the text-based Order Form Web page is to modify the text that tells the user to submit the questionnaire by e-mail. Table 7–4 shows the new HTML code used to provide instructions to users on how to submit the information on the order form.

Table 7–4 HTML Code to Change the Text Message

Line	HTML Tag and Text
17	`on the order form below and click the Submit button to process the order.</font></b></p>`

The following step illustrates how to change the text message to provide instructions on how to use the order form.

1

- Highlight lines 18 through 32 (starting with the word "below" and ending above <p>Thank you for your order) and then press the DELETE key.
- With the insertion point on line 18, enter the HTML code shown in Table 7–4 and then press the ENTER key twice (Figure 7–9).

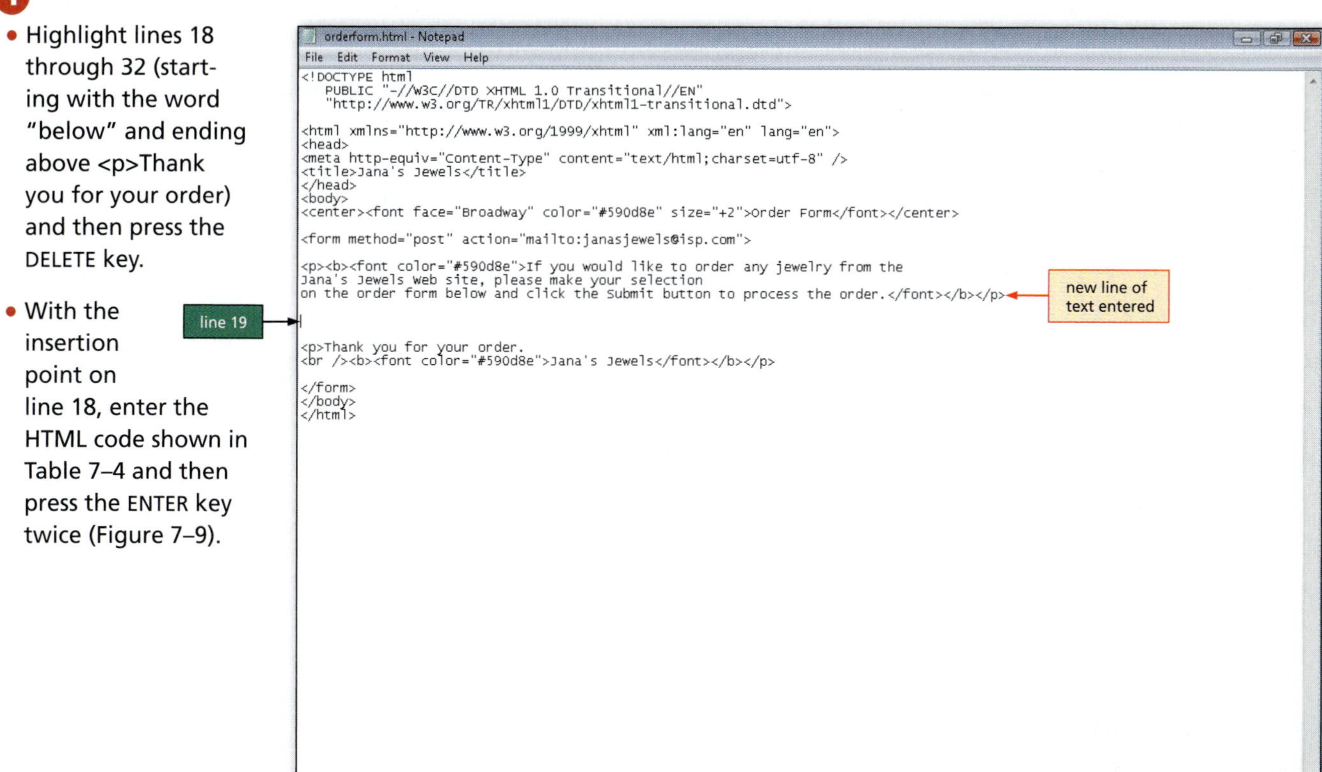

Figure 7–9

Plan Ahead

Form controls.
Before creating a Web page form, you should plan how you want to format it. By effectively utilizing input controls, you can call attention to important data collection areas on the Web page without overpowering it. Creating an effective form includes:

1. **Determine what data to collect.** In the case of a form designed to sell a product, you need the visitor's name and address information. Make sure to provide enough space for each field so that you do not cut out important information. For instance, an address field only 10 characters long may cut out much of the street name.
2. **Determine what types of control to use.** For data such as name and address, you need text input areas. For data such as credit card type, there is a limited subset (i.e., American Express, Visa, and MasterCard), so a selection control is appropriate. When you ask what types of jewelry the visitor is interested in buying, you can use check boxes, which allow multiple selection. In the case of a Yes/No answer (i.e., Do you want the newsletter?), a radio button is more appropriate.
3. **Lay out the input areas effectively.** One of the first input items you may want is the visitor's name and address information. That should go to the top of the page. Also, you can group information together on the same line if it makes sense to make the Web page form short enough that visitors do not have to scroll much. Notice in our order form that the city/state/ZIP are on one line of the Web page.
4. **Use grouping techniques for clarity.** The last thing that you may want to do on a Web page form is group like input items together. We use the fieldset tag to segregate personal information from order information and from other comments that the visitor might make.

Adding Text Boxes

As previously discussed, a text box allows for a single line of input. The HTML code below shows an example of the code used to add a text box to a form:

```
<input name="address" type="text" size="25" maxlength="25" />
```

The <input /> tag creates an input control, while the attribute and value type="text" specifies that the input control is a text box. The name attribute of the input control is set to the value address, to describe the information to be entered in this text box. When the form is submitted, the name is used to distinguish the value associated with that field from other fields.

The size attribute indicates the size of the text box that appears on the form. In the following HTML code, size="25" sets the text field to 25 characters in length, which means that only 25 characters will appear in the text box. The maxlength attribute maxlength="25" limits the number of characters that can be entered in the text box to 25 characters. The maxlength attribute specifies the same number of characters (25) as the size attribute (25), so all characters entered by a user will appear in the text box. If you specify a maximum number of characters that is greater than the number of characters specified in the size attribute, the additional characters scroll to the right in the text box as the user enters them.

To Add Text Boxes

The next step in creating the order form is to add seven text boxes to the form for users to enter first name, last name, street address, city, state, ZIP, and e-mail address. Table 7–5 shows the HTML code to add seven text boxes to the form. Each text box has a size of 25 characters, except the ZIP text box, with only 10 characters. No maxlength attribute is specified, which means users can enter text items longer than 25 characters, but only 25 characters will display in the text box.

Table 7–5 HTML Code to Add Text Boxes

Line	HTML Tag and Text
19	Last Name: <input name="lastname" type="text" size="25" />
20	First Name: <input name="firstname" type="text" size="25" />
21	 Street Address: <input name="address" type="text" size="25" />
22	 City: <input name="city" type="text" size="25" />
23	State: <input name="state" type="text" size="25" />
24	ZIP: <input name="zip" type="text" size="10" />
25	E-mail Address: <input name="email" type="text" size="25" />

The following step illustrates how to add text boxes to the form.

1

- If necessary, click line 19.
- Enter the HTML code shown in Table 7–5 and then press the ENTER key twice (Figure 7–10).

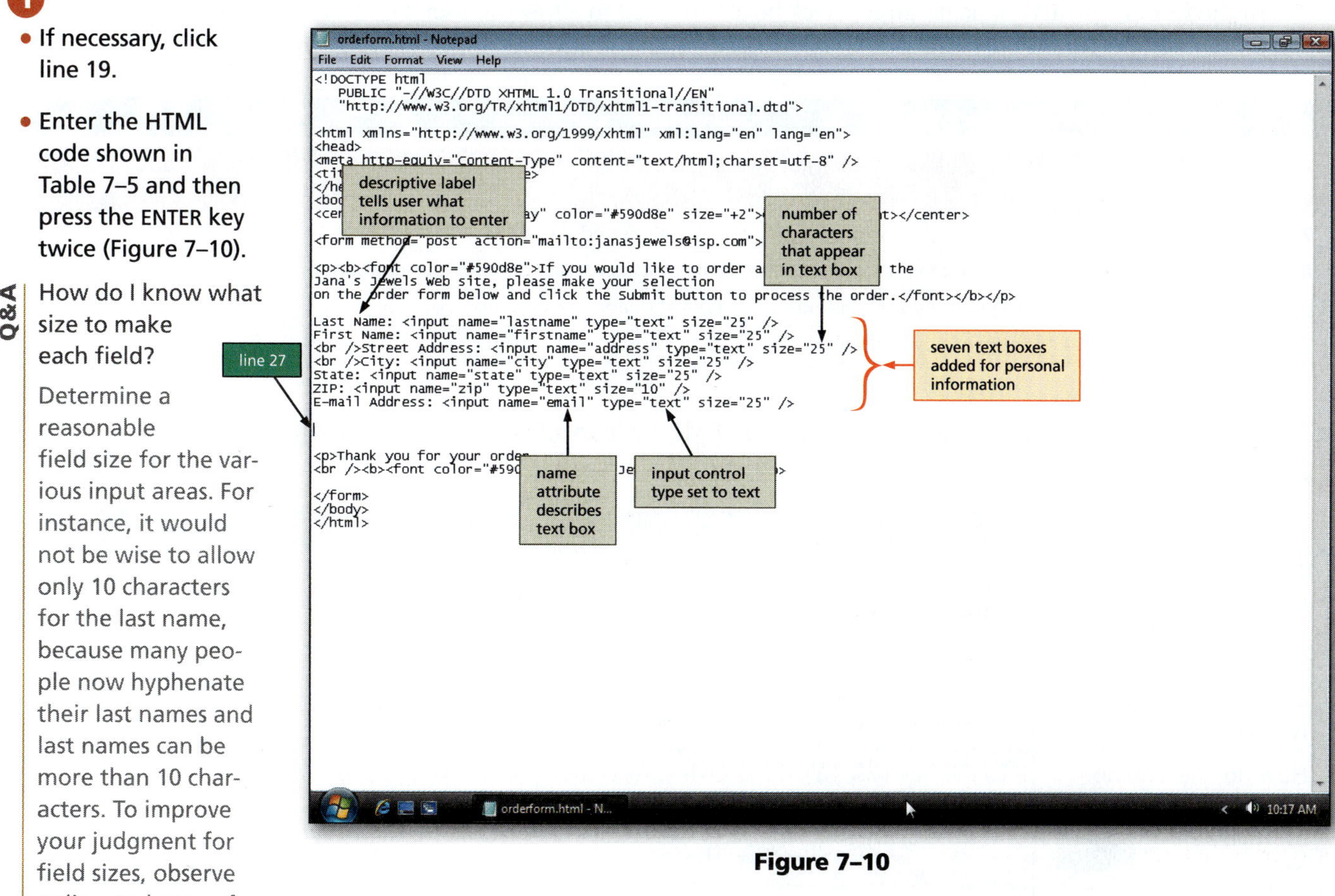

Figure 7–10

Q&A

How do I know what size to make each field?

Determine a reasonable field size for the various input areas. For instance, it would not be wise to allow only 10 characters for the last name, because many people now hyphenate their last names and last names can be more than 10 characters. To improve your judgment for field sizes, observe online and paper forms that you complete. Also, think of long street or city names and try those in the forms that you create.

Q&A

What is the default value if I do not specify the type in my <input /> tag?

The default type for the <input /> tag is a text box. Therefore, if the type attribute is not used in the <input /> tag, it creates a text box.

Adding Check Boxes

Check boxes are similar to radio buttons, except they allow multiple options to be selected. Radio buttons should be used when only one option can be selected, while check boxes should be used when the user can select more than one option.

The HTML code below shows an example of the code used to add a check box to a form:

```
<input name="pictype" type="checkbox" value="watches" />Watches
```

The <input /> tag creates an input control, while the attribute and value type="checkbox" specifies that the input control is a check box. The name attribute of the input control is set to the value pictype. When the form is submitted, the name is used to distinguish the values associated with these checkbox fields from other fields. The value attribute watches indicates the value submitted in the file, if this check box is selected.

To Add Check Boxes

In the Order Form Web page, three check boxes are used to allow the user to select one or more types of pictures to purchase. Table 7–6 shows the HTML code to add three check boxes to the form.

Table 7–6 HTML Code to Add Check Boxes

Line	HTML Tag and Text
27	`Select the types of jewelry that you are interested in purchasing:`
28	` <input name="pictype" type="checkbox" value="necklaces" />Necklaces`
29	`<input name="pictype" type="checkbox" value="bracelets" />Bracelets`
30	`<input name="pictype" type="checkbox" value="watches" />Watches`

The step that follows illustrates how to enter HTML code to add check boxes to the form.

1

- If necessary, click line 27.
- Enter the HTML code shown in Table 7–6 and then press the ENTER key twice (Figure 7–11).

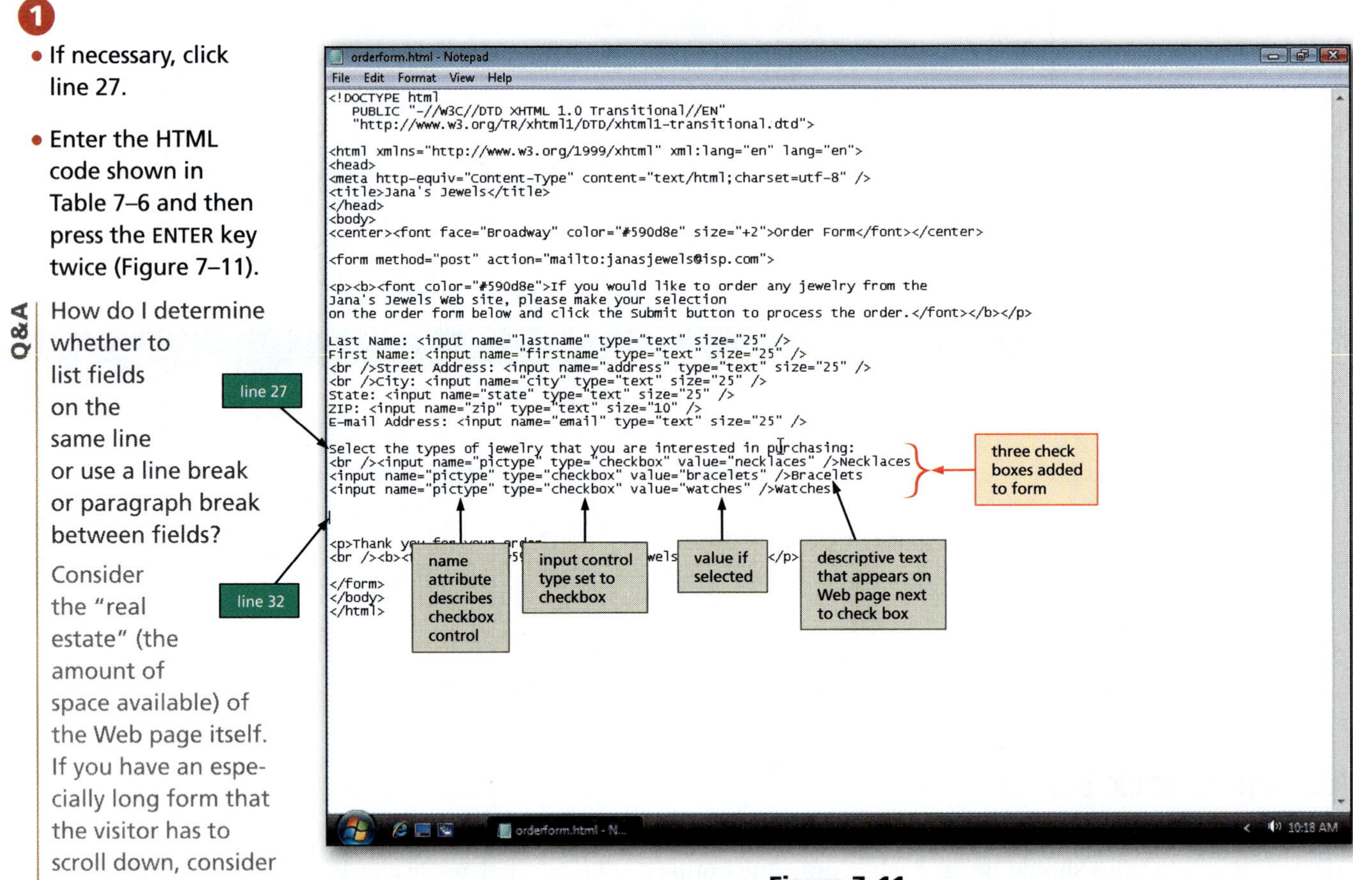

Figure 7–11

Q&A

How do I determine whether to list fields on the same line or use a line break or paragraph break between fields?

Consider the "real estate" (the amount of space available) of the Web page itself. If you have an especially long form that the visitor has to scroll down, consider positioning the fields across, rather than down the form. You do not want to crowd the information, but you also do not want to force the visitor to scroll excessively.

Adding a Selection Menu

A select control is used to create a selection menu from which the visitor selects one or more choices. A select control is suitable when a limited number of choices are available. Figure 7–12 shows the basic selection menu used in the order form, with three credit card types (Visa, MasterCard, and American Express) as the choices in the list.

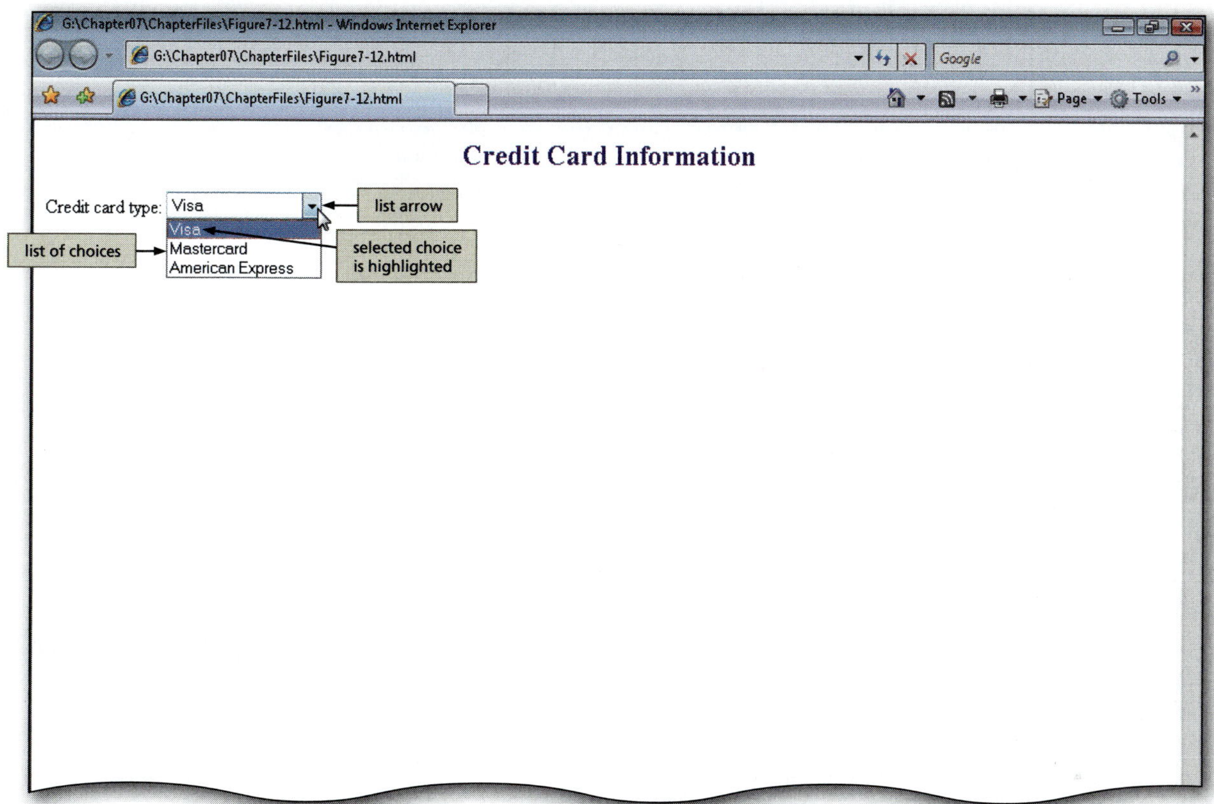

Figure 7–12

If you do not specify a size attribute, only one option is displayed, along with a list arrow, as shown in Figure 7–12. When the list arrow is clicked, the selection menu displays all selection options. When the user selects an option, such as Visa, in the list, it appears as highlighted.

To Add a Selection Menu

Table 7–7 shows the HTML code used to create the selection menu shown in Figure 7–12.

Table 7–7 HTML Code to Add a Selection Menu

Line	HTML Tag and Text
32	`<p>Credit card type:`
33	`<select name="payment">`
34	`<option>Visa</option>`
35	`<option>MasterCard</option>`
36	`<option>American Express</option>`
37	`</select>`

The following step illustrates how to add a selection menu to the Web page form.

1

- If necessary, click line 32.
- Enter the HTML code shown in Table 7–7 and then press the ENTER key twice (Figure 7–13).

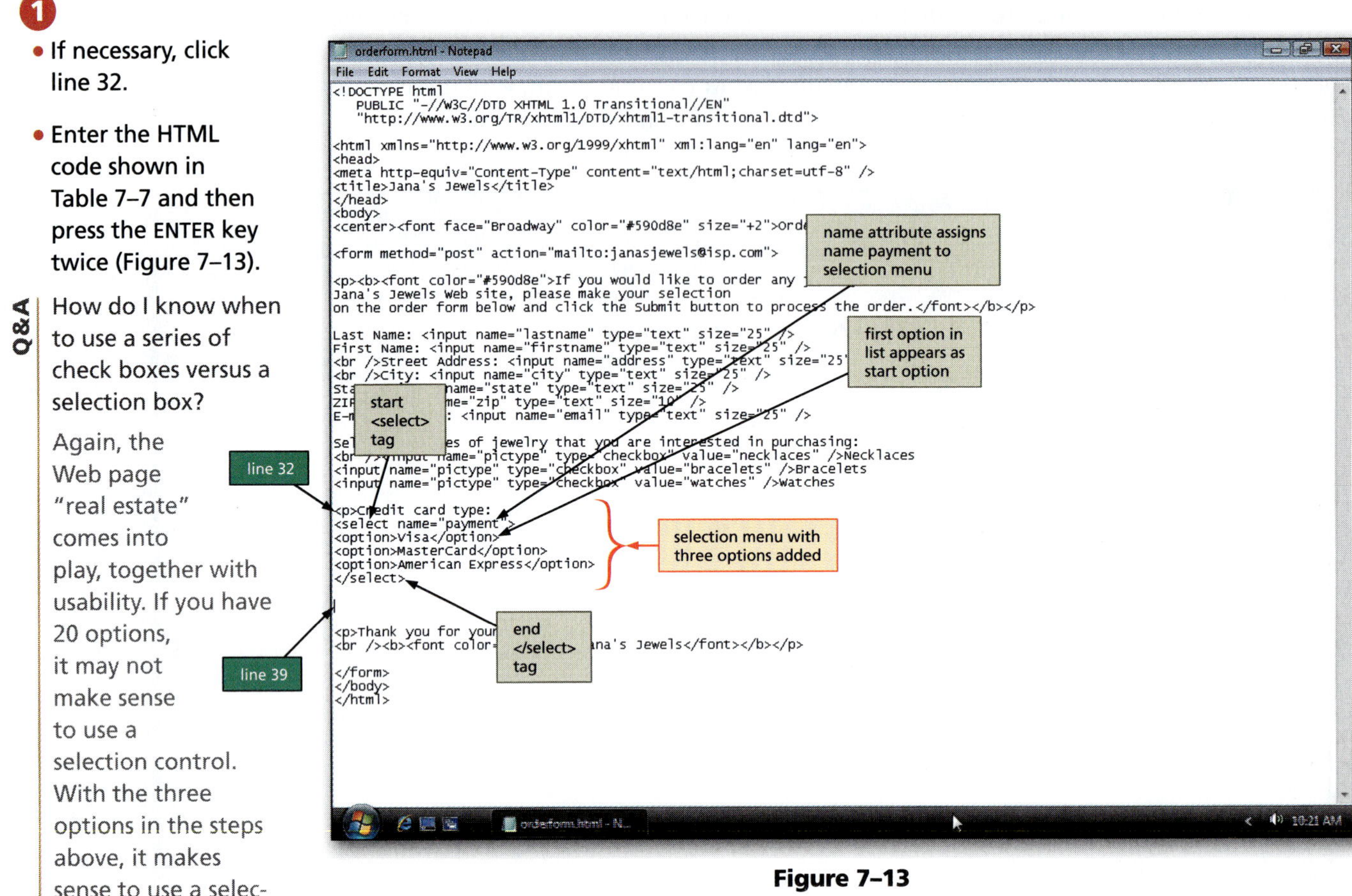

Figure 7–13

Q&A How do I know when to use a series of check boxes versus a selection box?

Again, the Web page "real estate" comes into play, together with usability. If you have 20 options, it may not make sense to use a selection control. With the three options in the steps above, it makes sense to use a selection control rather than a check box. Those three options (e.g., Visa, MasterCard, American Express) are standard credit card types. Most online forms put those three standard types in a selection box, so users are familiar with the model. Whereas in the previous steps (i.e., adding check boxes), you can easily increase the number of check boxes by adding more types of jewelry.

Q&A How do I know what control type, such as text box, check box, radio button, to use?

Again, one way to enhance your Web development skills is to use the Web and be mindful of the different techniques that Web developers use. If you see a technique or control that makes great sense, or one that seems counter-intuitive, note those things and apply (or do not apply) them to your own Web development.

Adding More Advanced Selection Menus

Selection menus have many variations beyond the simple selection menu used in the Order Form Web page. Table 7–3 on page HTML 309 lists several attributes for the <select> tag. Using these attributes, a selection menu can be set to display multiple choices or only one, with a drop-down list to allow a user to select another choice. A selection menu also can be defined to have one choice preselected as the default.

Figure 7–14 shows samples of selection menus. The HTML code used to create each selection menu is shown in Figure 7–15.

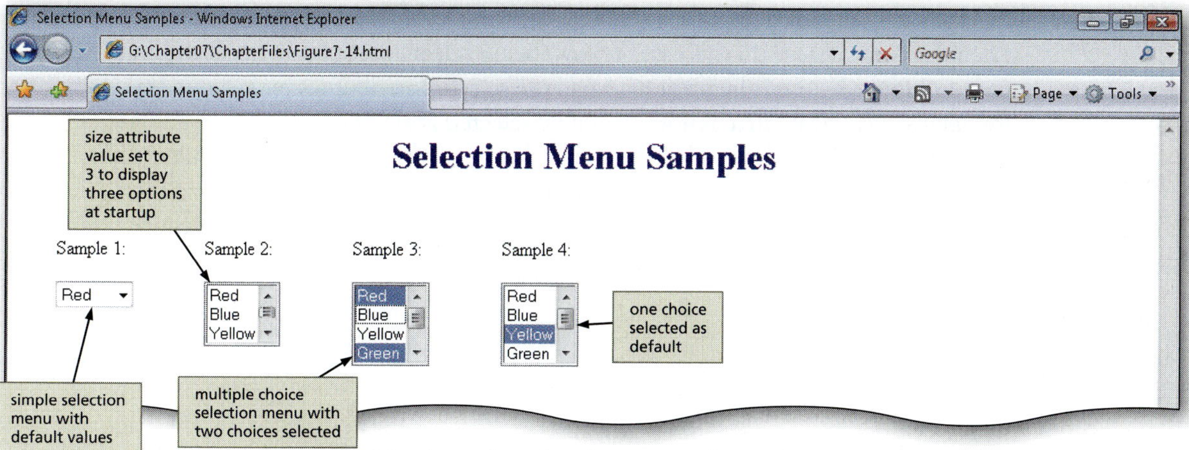

Figure 7–14 Sample selection controls with variations.

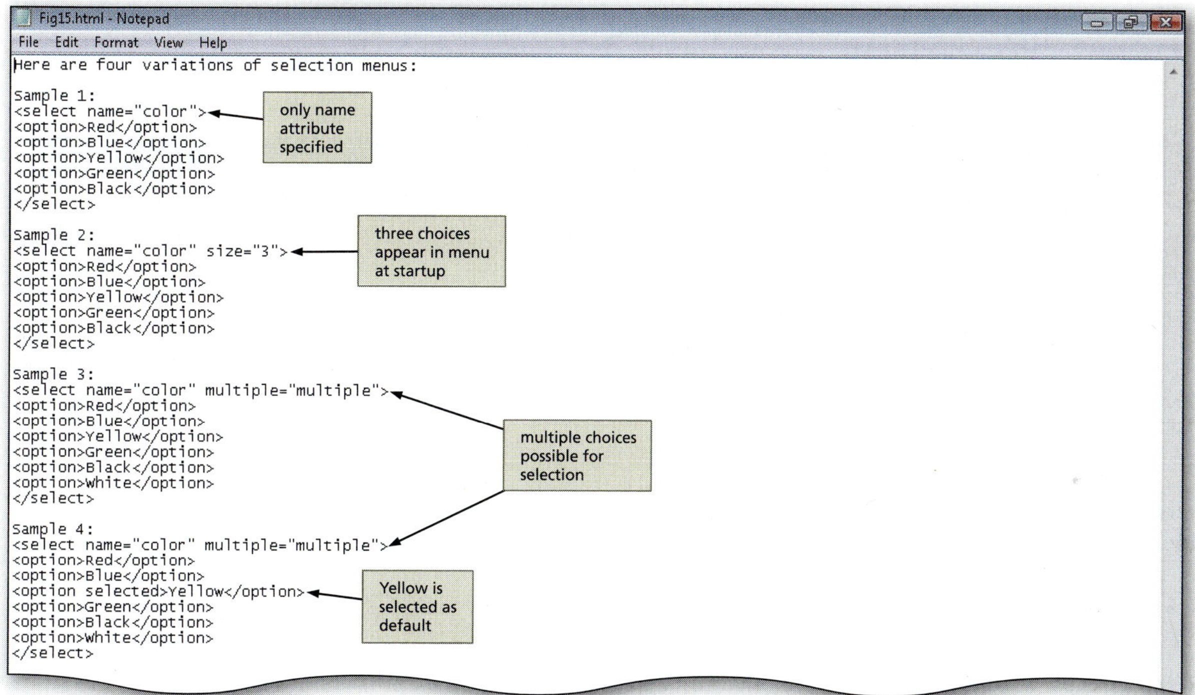


```
Here are four variations of selection menus:

Sample 1:
<select name="color">
<option>Red</option>
<option>Blue</option>
<option>Yellow</option>
<option>Green</option>
<option>Black</option>
</select>

Sample 2:
<select name="color" size="3">
<option>Red</option>
<option>Blue</option>
<option>Yellow</option>
<option>Green</option>
<option>Black</option>
</select>

Sample 3:
<select name="color" multiple="multiple">
<option>Red</option>
<option>Blue</option>
<option>Yellow</option>
<option>Green</option>
<option>Black</option>
<option>White</option>
</select>

Sample 4:
<select name="color" multiple="multiple">
<option>Red</option>
<option>Blue</option>
<option selected>Yellow</option>
<option>Green</option>
<option>Black</option>
<option>White</option>
</select>
```

Figure 7–15 HTML code to create selection menus.

The selection menu in Sample 1 is a basic selection menu, with no attributes specified other than the name and the list options. This resulting selection menu uses a list menu that allows users to select one choice from the list. No choice is selected by default. The selection menu in Sample 2 uses a size attribute value of 3 to indicate that three choices should appear in the menu at startup. A user can use the up and down scroll arrows to view other choices in the list. The selection menu in Sample 3 uses the multiple attribute to allow a user to select more than one choice in the list. To select multiple choices, a user first must select one choice and then press and hold the CTRL key while clicking other choices in the list. If a user wants to select several consecutive choices, he or she can select the first choice and then press and hold the SHIFT key while selecting the last choice. All choices between the first choice and last choice automatically will be selected. The selection menu in Sample 4 also contains the

BTW

Options

The <select> and <option> tags are useful when you have a limited number of choices from which a Web page visitor can select. If the number of options becomes too large, a better choice might be to use the <optgroup> tag before the first <option> tag in the first group that you want to use in a submenu. After the last option in that group, use the </optgroup> tag.

> **BTW**
> **Fonts**
> The Broadway font was selected for the titles in this project by using the <font face> tag and attribute. Not all Web page visitors have the Broadway font on their computers, however. If a visitor does not have the font used by the Web developer for a Web page, the text is displayed in the default font.

multiple attribute, so one or more choices can be selected. In addition, Sample 4 provides an example of one choice (in this case, Yellow) being selected at startup. As shown in the HTML code in Figure 7–15 on the previous page, the selected attribute is included in the <option> tag for Yellow, to indicate that Yellow should be selected at startup.

The purpose of the selection menu dictates the type of selection menu that should be used and the HTML code required to create that select control. Using the basic tags and attributes shown in Figure 7–15, you can create a wide variety of selection menus to suit almost any purpose.

To Add Additional Text Boxes

The next step in creating the Order Form Web page is to add two more text boxes for credit card number and expiration date. Table 7–8 shows the HTML code used to add the additional text boxes. A text field is used rather than a textarea field because the user needs to enter only one row of characters.

Table 7–8 HTML Code to Add Additional Text Boxes

Line	HTML Tag and Text
39	`Credit card number:`
40	`<input name="cardnum" type="text" size="20" maxlength="20" />`
41	
42	`Expiration date:`
43	`<input name="cardexp" type="text" size="4" maxlength="4" /></p>`

The following step illustrates how to add two additional text boxes to the Web page form.

1

- If necessary, click line 39.
- Enter the HTML code shown in Table 7–8 and then press the ENTER key twice (Figure 7–16).

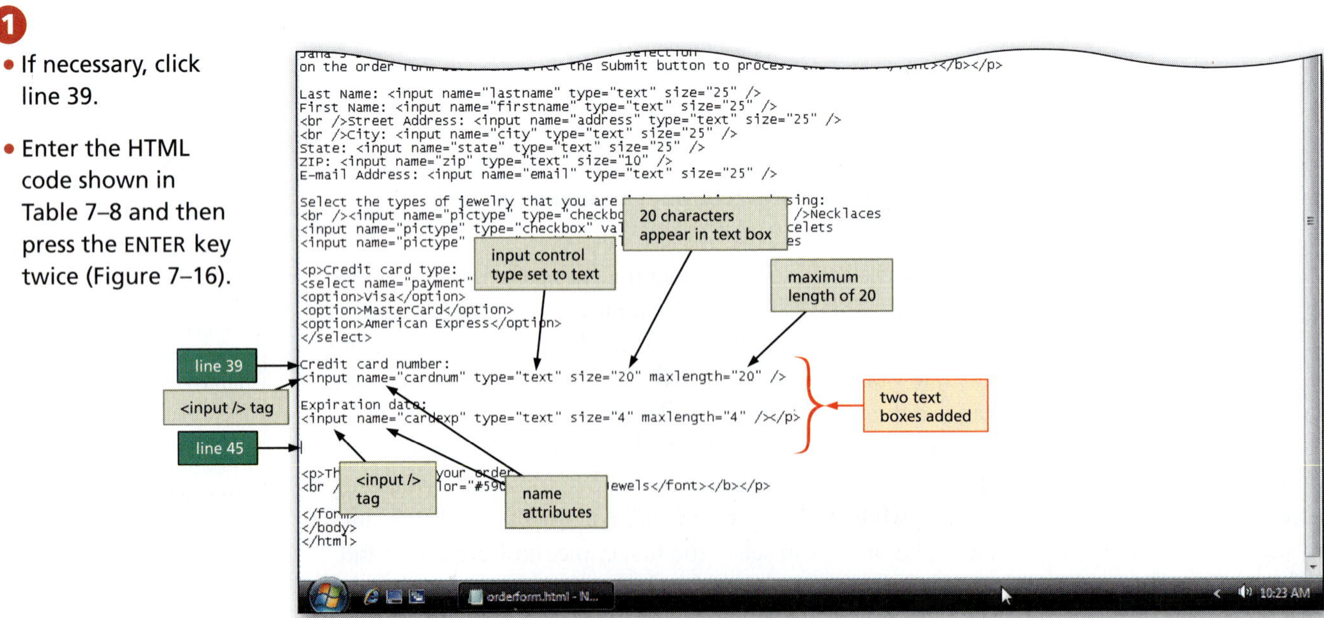

Figure 7–16

Adding Radio Buttons and a Textarea

The next step is to add radio buttons and a textarea to the form. Remember that radio buttons are appropriate to use when a user can select only one choice from a set of two or more choices. Questions with a Yes or No answer are perfect for the use of radio buttons. On the Order Form Web page, radio buttons allow users to select a Yes or No answer to a question about receiving an e-mail newsletter.

The order form also includes a textarea that allows the user to add additional comments about other types of jewelry he or she might be interested in purchasing. Because the response can be longer than just one line, a textarea control is used.

To Add Radio Buttons

Table 7–9 contains the HTML code to add a set of radio buttons to the Order Form Web page.

Table 7–9 HTML Code to Add Radio Buttons

Line	HTML Tag and Text
45	`Would you like to receive our e-mail newsletter with valuable coupons?`
46	`<input name="newsletter" type="radio" value="yes" />Yes`
47	`<input name="newsletter" type="radio" value="no" />No`

The following step illustrates how to add a set of two radio buttons to the form.

1

- If necessary, click line 45.
- Enter the HTML code shown in Table 7–9 and then press the ENTER key twice (Figure 7–17).

Q&A Could I have used check boxes for this control, rather than radio buttons?

You could have used check boxes, but it would not make sense for this information. In this case, this is a clear yes or no answer. With check boxes, you are assuming that they can make multiple selections. Again, look at the standards used in most Web development.

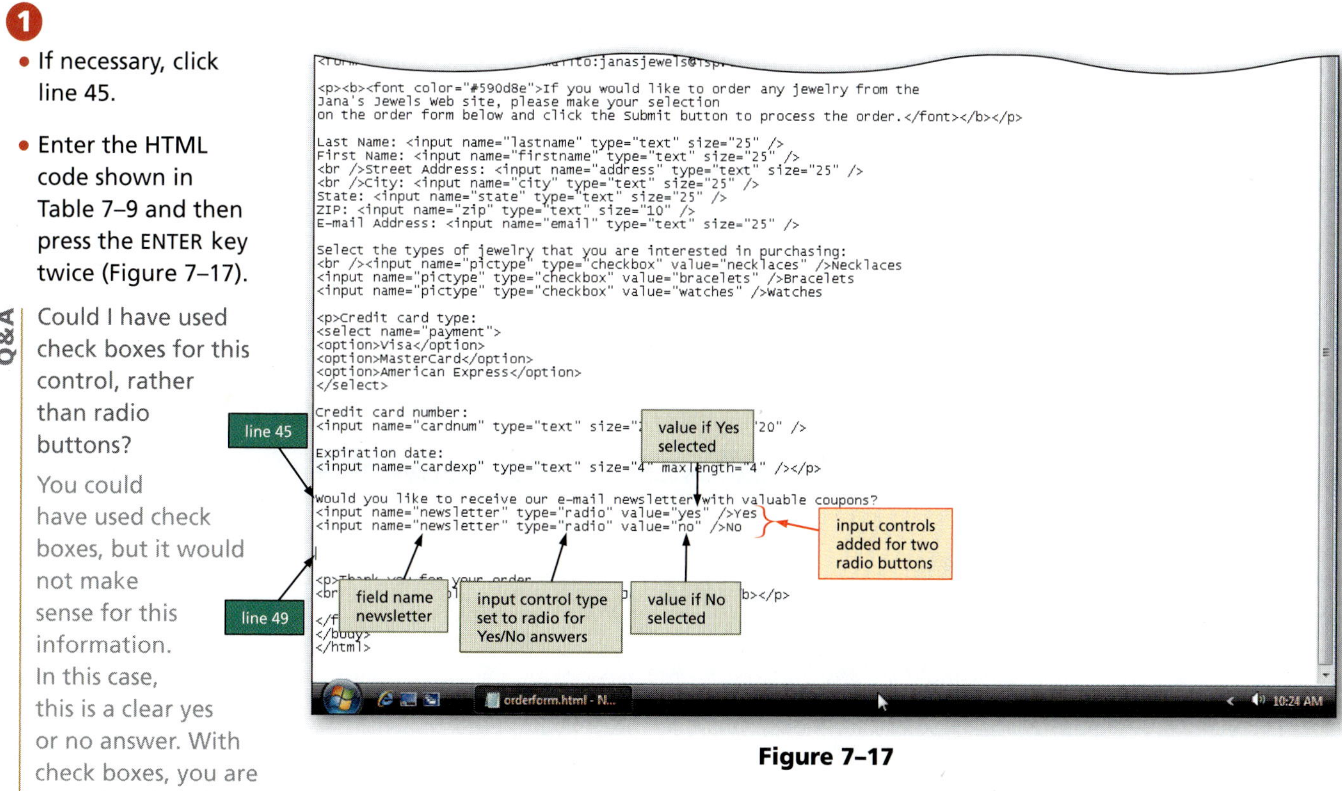

Figure 7–17

To Add a Textarea

The next step is to add a textarea to the form. You use a textarea because you want the user to be able to input more than one line. Table 7–10 contains the tags and text to specify a textarea for multiple-line input.

Table 7–10 HTML Code to Add a Textarea

Line	HTML Tag and Text
49	`<p>What other types of jewelry, in addition to those shown, would you be`
50	`interested in purchasing?`
51	` <textarea name="other" rows="3" cols="100"></textarea></p>`

The following step illustrates how to add a textarea to the order form.

- If necessary, click line 49.
- Enter the HTML code shown in Table 7–10 and then press the ENTER key twice (Figure 7–18).

```
<title>Jana's Jewels</title>
</head>
<body>
<center><font face="Broadway" color="#590d8e" size="+2">Order Form</font></center>

<form method="post" action="mailto:janasjewels@isp.com">

<p><b><font color="#590d8e">If you would like to order any jewelry from the
Jana's Jewels Web site, please make your selection
on the order form below and click the Submit button to process the order.</font></b></p>

Last Name: <input name="lastname" type="text" size="25" />
First Name: <input name="firstname" type="text" size="25" />
<br />Street Address: <input name="address" type="text" size="25" />
<br />City: <input name="city" type="text" size="25" />
State: <input name="state" type="text" size="25" />
ZIP: <input name="zip" type="text" size="10" />
E-mail Address: <input name="email" type="text" size="25" />

Select the types of jewelry that you are interested in purchasing:
<br /><input name="pictype" type="checkbox" value="necklaces" />Necklaces
<input name="pictype" type="checkbox" value="bracelets" />Bracelets
<input name="pictype" type="checkbox" value="watches" />Watches

<p>Credit card type:
<select name="payment">
<option>Visa</option>
<option>MasterCard</option>
<option>American Express</option>
</select>

Credit card number:
<input name="cardnum" type="t                    ength="20" />

Expiration date:
<input name="cardexp" type="t                    ngth="4" /></p>

Would you like to receive our                    with valuable coupons?
<input name="newsletter" type="radio" value="yes" />Yes
<input name="newsletter" type="radio" value="no" />No

<p>What other types of jewelry, in addition to those shown, would you be
interested in purchasing?
<br /><textarea name="other" rows="3" cols="100"></textarea></p>


<p>Thank you for
<br /><b><font co          Jana's Jewels</font></b></p>

</form>
</body>
```


Figure 7–18

Q&A How do I know how big to make the textarea box?

Again, you need to look at the standards used in most Web development. You also have to view the textarea box in the browser to see how the size affects the Web page form. For instance, if we had made the number of rows 4, rather than 3, the Web page visitor would not have seen the "Thank you for your order. Jana's Jewels" message on the bottom of the page. That is something that you want the visitor to see without scrolling.

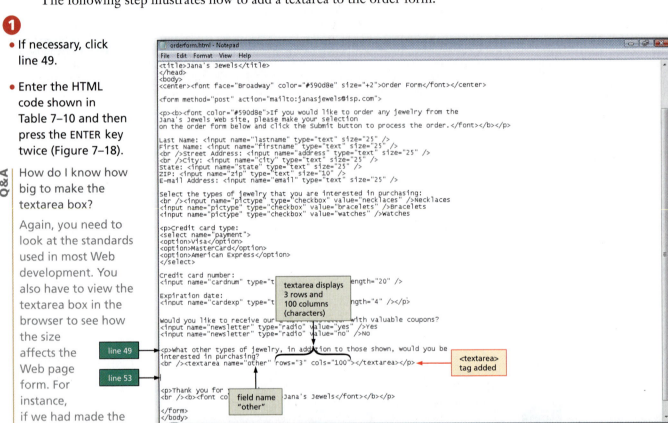

Adding Submit and Reset Buttons

The form controls are useless unless the information entered in the form can be submitted for processing. The next step in creating the order form is to add two buttons at the bottom of the Web page form. The first button, Submit, is for submitting the form. When the visitor clicks this button, the data entered into the form is sent to the appropriate location for processing. The second button, Reset, clears any data that was entered in the form.

The HTML code below shows the <input /> tags used to create the Submit and Reset buttons on a Web page form:

```
<p><input type="submit" value="Submit" />
<input type="reset" value="Reset" /></p>
```

The first line of HTML code creates a Submit button on the Web page form. A Submit button is created by using the attribute type="submit" in an <input /> tag. The value attribute is used to indicate the text that should appear on the button face — in this case, Submit.

When a user clicks the Submit button, all data currently entered in the form is sent to the appropriate location for processing. The action taken when a form is submitted is based on the method and action attributes specified in the <form> tag. In the <form> tag at the start of this form, the HTML code set the form attributes to method="post" and action="mailto:janasjewels@isp.com". Thus, when a user clicks the Submit button, a data file that contains all the input data automatically is sent as an e-mail attachment to the e-mail address janasjewels@isp.com. By default, the data file is named Postdata.att.

The code below shows a sample of the data file that is sent to the e-mail address, when using the post method:

```
payment=American Express&newsletter=yes&other=I would be
interested in more Southwest jewelry
```

The data entered in the form appears in the data file as name-value pairs — the name of the control as specified in the name attribute, followed by the value entered or selected in the control. In the above example, the user selected American Express in the selection menu named payment and clicked the Yes radio button named newsletter. The user also entered a comment in the textarea control named other indicating that he or she would be interested in more Southwest jewelry. An ampersand (&) strings together all of the name-value pairs to make them easier to read.

The Reset button also is an important part of any form. Resetting the form clears any information previously typed into a text box or textarea and resets radio buttons, check boxes, selection menus, and other controls to their initial values. As shown in the second line of the HTML code above, a Reset button is created by using the attribute type="reset" in an <input /> tag. The value attribute is used to indicate the text that should appear on the button face — in this case, Reset.

BTW

Feedback

One good use of forms is to get feedback from your visitors. Suggestions from visitors not only can help improve the Web site, but can give your visitors the sense that you care about their opinions. Taking visitor feedback into account provides for better customer satisfaction.

BTW

Submit Buttons

A simplistic, default button is created when you use the type="submit" attribute and value within the <input> tag. The <button> tag also can be used to create a submit button. The <button> tag gives you the option of using an image for the button, rather than using the default button style. The appearance of the button text can be changed with the <style> tag. These tags give you more flexibility when creating Submit or Reset buttons.

To Add Submit and Reset Buttons

The following step illustrates how to add a Submit button and a Reset button to the form.

1

- If necessary, click line 53.
- Type `<p><input type="submit" value="Submit" />` to create the Submit button and then press the ENTER key.
- Type `<input type="reset" value="Reset" /></p>` to create the Reset button. Do not press the ENTER key (Figure 7–19).

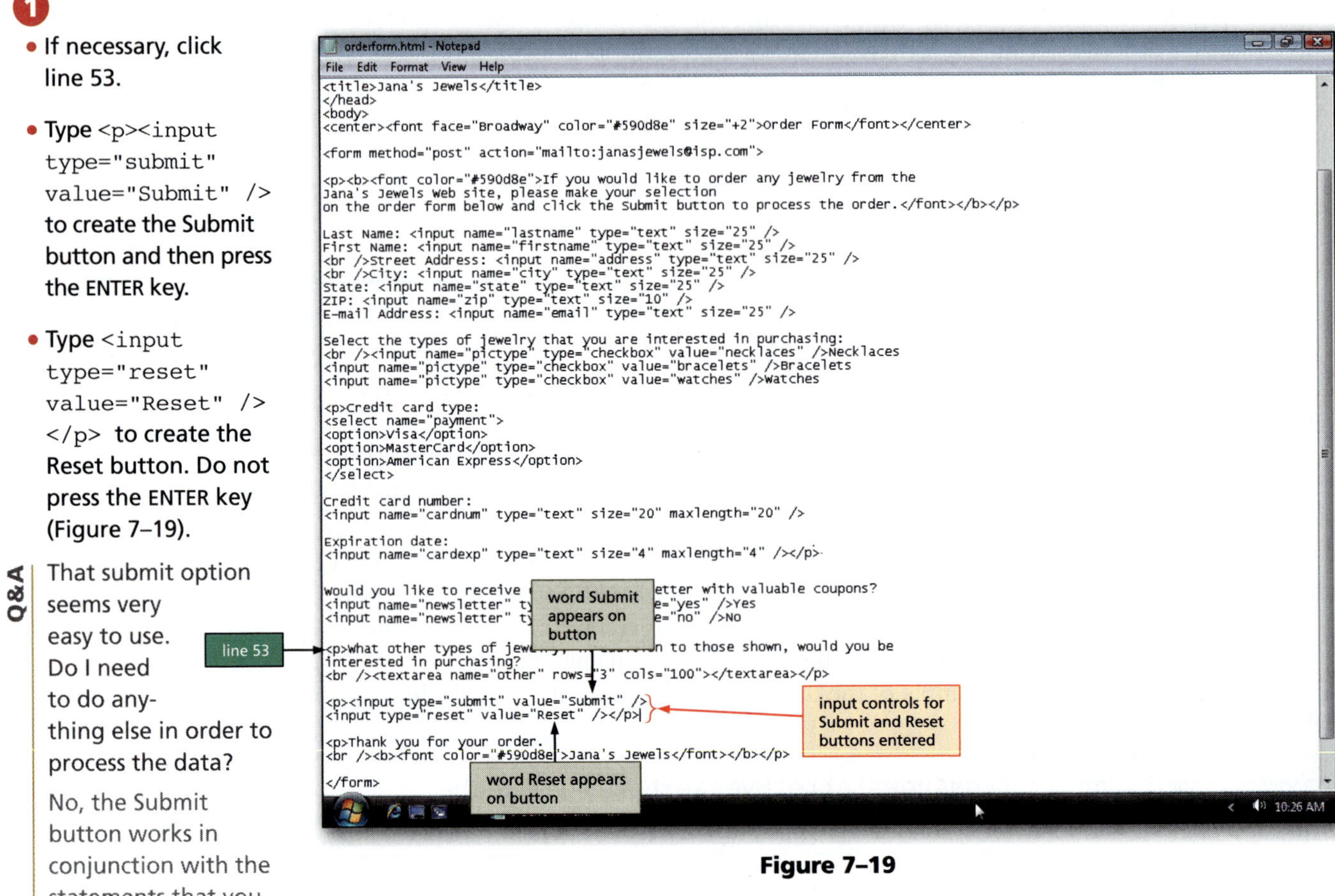

Figure 7–19

Q&A That submit option seems very easy to use. Do I need to do anything else in order to process the data?

No, the Submit button works in conjunction with the statements that you provided in your form tag in order to process the data entered.

Q&A Why do I need the Reset button?

It is best always to provide a Reset button next to the Submit button. This is useful to clear all of the data entered in case your visitors want to start over or if they change their minds or make mistakes.

Q&A If a visitor uses the Reset button, what does that do to default values that I have included in the tags?

Reset will set those default values back to the original values included in the tags. In other words, if you use a default value, Reset does not clear that value.

Plan Ahead

Organizing a form.
When using fieldset tags to separate and organize information on a form, consider the following:

- **Required vs. optional information.** You can group all required information into one section of the form and place all optional information into another grouping. By doing this, you call attention immediately to the required information on the form.
- **General organization.** It can be helpful to enhance the look and feel of the form with groupings. Especially in the case of a long form, using separators helps direct the visitors' attention.

Organizing a Form Using Form Groupings

An important aspect of creating a Web page form is making the form easy for Web site visitors to understand. Grouping similar information on a form, for example, makes the information easier to read and understand — and, as a result, easier to complete. Grouping is especially helpful in cases where some information is required and some is optional. In the order form, for example, all the personal information is required (for example, name, address, and credit card number). The final questions on the form, however, are optional (for example, do they want to receive the newsletter and additional comments). The form thus should be modified to group required and optional information.

A **fieldset** control is used to group similar information on a form. The HTML code below shows the <fieldset> tag used to add a fieldset control to a Web page form:

```
<fieldset><legend align="left">Required Information</legend>
</fieldset>
```

The <legend> tag within the fieldset tag is optional. Using the <legend> tag creates a legend for the fieldset, which is the text that appears in the grouping borders, as shown in the example in Figure 7–20. The align attribute is used to align the legend to the left or right of the fieldset control.

BTW

Groupings
An important part of good Web design is to make a form easy to use. Your Web site visitors are more likely to complete a form if they readily understand the information that is being requested. You can use the fieldset tag to group similar information together.

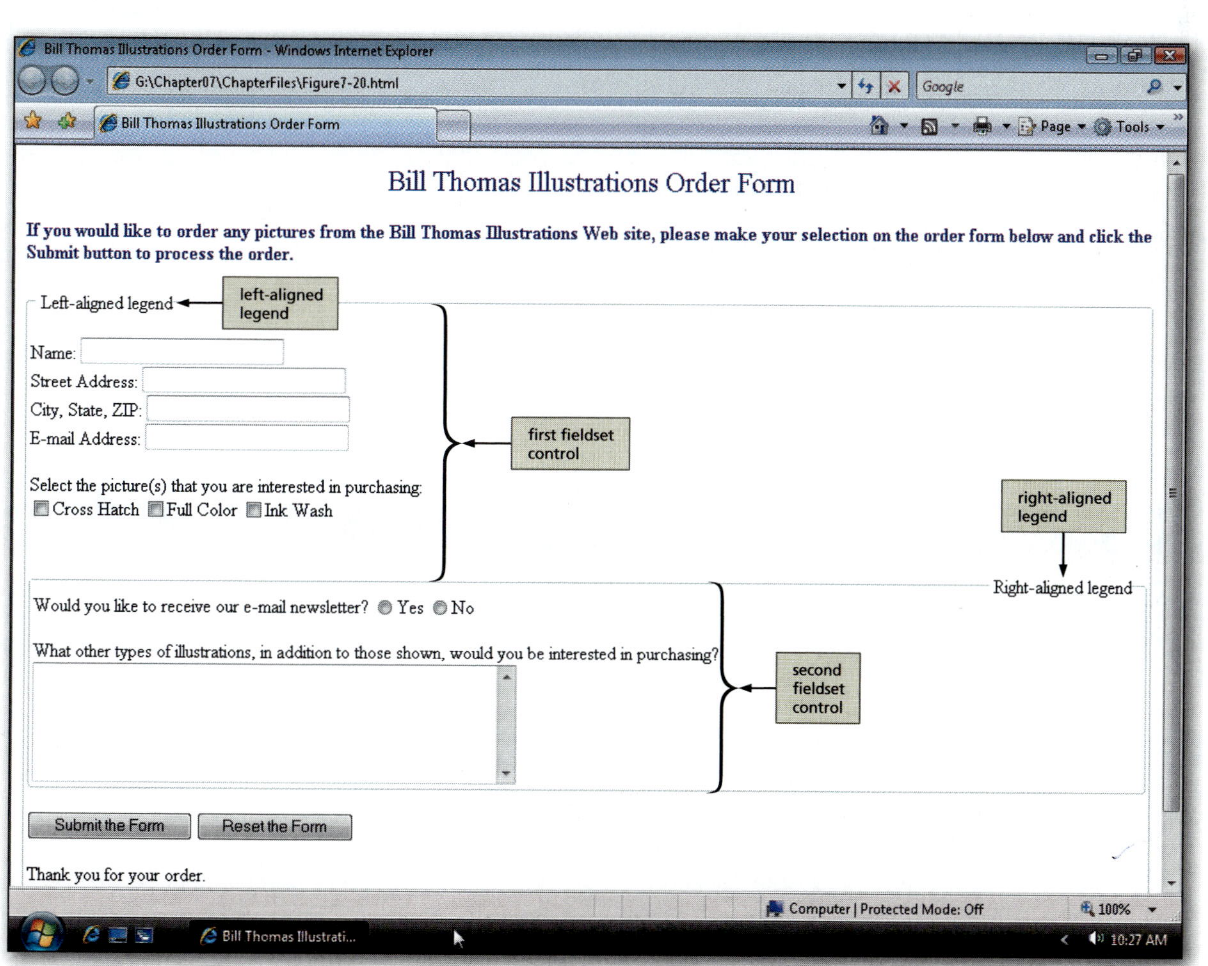

Figure 7–20

In the Order Form Web page that you will create, three fieldset controls are added to group similar information on the form. The first fieldset control is used to group personal information on the form, as shown in Figure 7–21. The second fieldset control is used to group order information. The first fieldset control has the legend, Personal Information, aligned to the right. The second fieldset control has the legend, About Your Order, aligned to the right. The third fieldset control has the legend, Additional Comments, aligned to the right. These groupings nicely divide the form so it is more readable and clearly defines what information is required and what is optional, or additional.

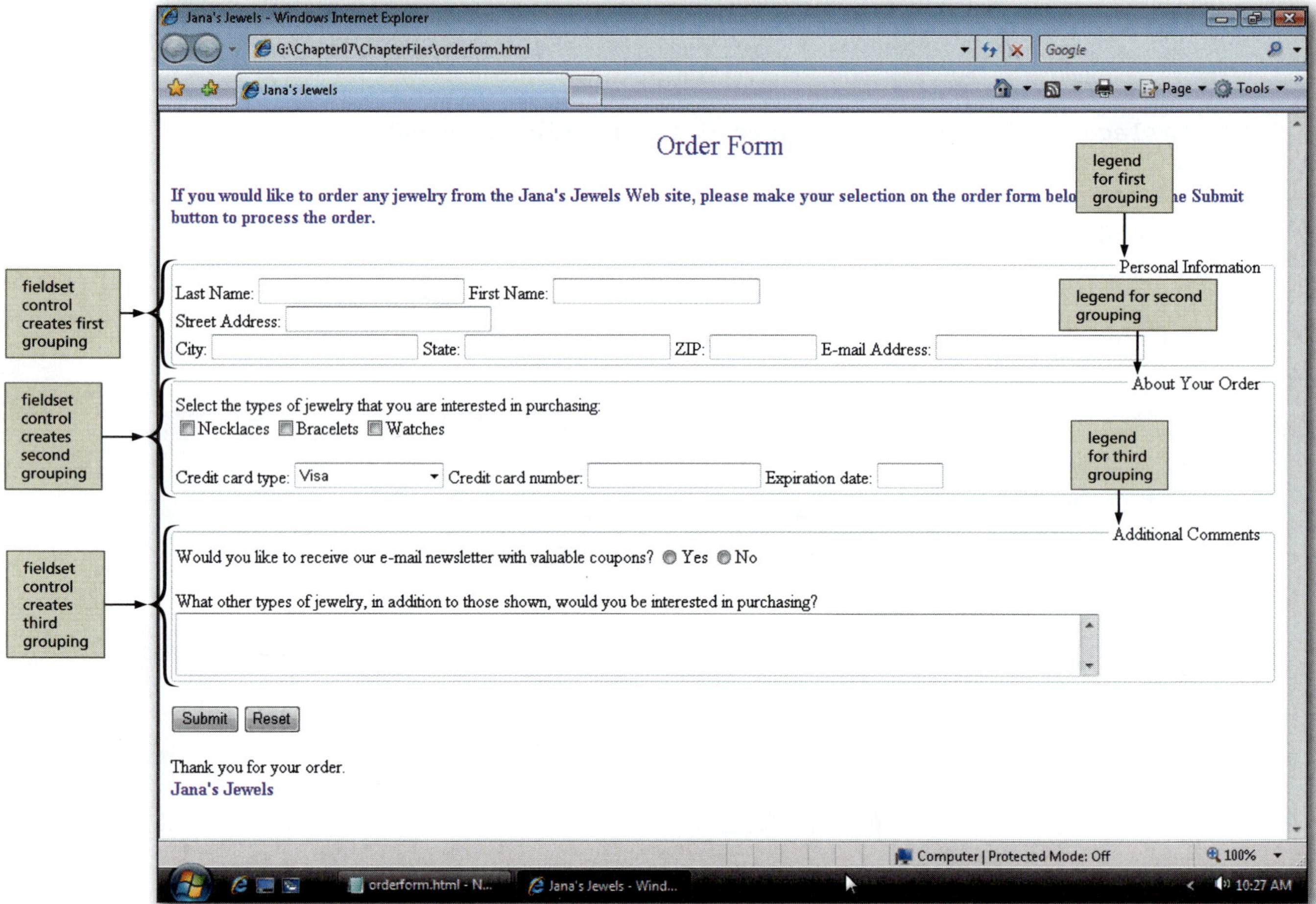

Figure 7–21

To Add Fieldset Controls to Create Form Groupings

The following step shows how to add three sets of fieldset tags to create information groupings on the Web page form.

1

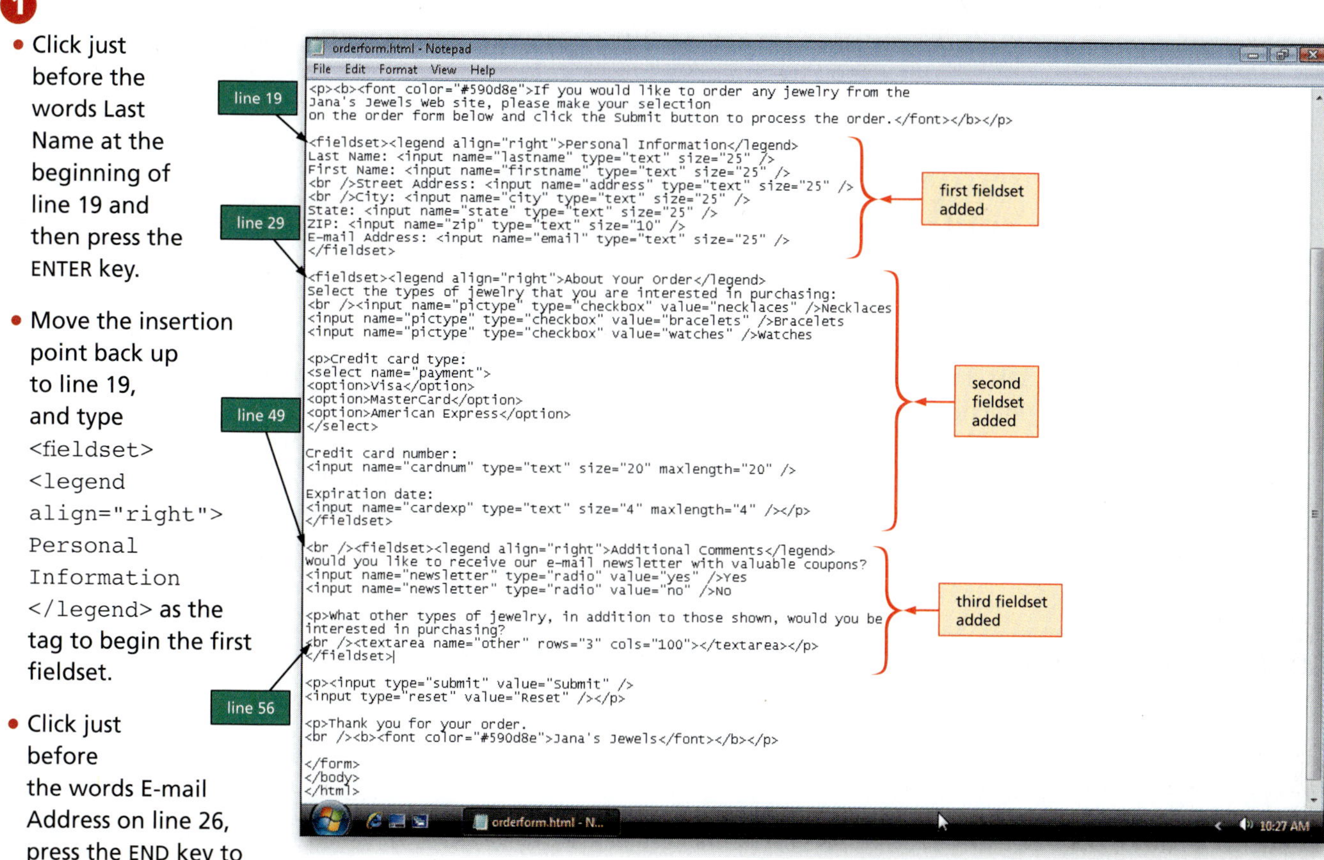

```
orderform.html - Notepad
File Edit Format View Help
<p><b><font color="#590d8e">If you would like to order any jewelry from the
Jana's Jewels web site, please make your selection
on the order form below and click the Submit button to process the order.</font></b></p>

<fieldset><legend align="right">Personal Information</legend>
Last Name: <input name="lastname" type="text" size="25" />
First Name: <input name="firstname" type="text" size="25" />
<br />Street Address: <input name="address" type="text" size="25" />
<br />City: <input name="city" type="text" size="25" />
State: <input name="state" type="text" size="25" />
ZIP: <input name="zip" type="text" size="10" />
E-mail Address: <input name="email" type="text" size="25" />
</fieldset>

<fieldset><legend align="right">About Your Order</legend>
Select the types of jewelry that you are interested in purchasing:
<br /><input name="pictype" type="checkbox" value="necklaces" />Necklaces
<input name="pictype" type="checkbox" value="bracelets" />Bracelets
<input name="pictype" type="checkbox" value="watches" />Watches

<p>Credit card type:
<select name="payment">
<option>Visa</option>
<option>MasterCard</option>
<option>American Express</option>
</select>

Credit card number:
<input name="cardnum" type="text" size="20" maxlength="20" />

Expiration date:
<input name="cardexp" type="text" size="4" maxlength="4" /></p>
</fieldset>

<br /><fieldset><legend align="right">Additional Comments</legend>
Would you like to receive our e-mail newsletter with valuable coupons?
<input name="newsletter" type="radio" value="yes" />Yes
<input name="newsletter" type="radio" value="no" />No

<p>What other types of jewelry, in addition to those shown, would you be
interested in purchasing?
<br /><textarea name="other" rows="3" cols="100"></textarea></p>
</fieldset>

<p><input type="submit" value="Submit" />
<input type="reset" value="Reset" /></p>

<p>Thank you for your order.
<br /><b><font color="#590d8e">Jana's Jewels</font></b></p>

</form>
</body>
</html>
```


Figure 7–22

- Click just before the words Last Name at the beginning of line 19 and then press the ENTER key.
- Move the insertion point back up to line 19, and type `<fieldset><legend align="right">Personal Information</legend>` as the tag to begin the first fieldset.
- Click just before the words E-mail Address on line 26, press the END key to move to the end of the line, and then press the ENTER key.
- Type `</fieldset>` to end the first fieldset and then press the ENTER key twice.
- With the insertion point on line 29, type `<fieldset><legend align="right">About Your Order</legend>` to start the second fieldset.
- Click to the right of the </p> on line 46 (at the end of the <input name= "cardexp" line) and then press the ENTER key.
- Type `</fieldset>` and then press the ENTER key twice.
- Type `<br /><fieldset><legend align="right">Additional Comments</legend>` on line 49 to start the third fieldset.
- Click to the right of the </p> on line 56 (at the end of the line with textarea tags) and then press the ENTER key.
- Type `</fieldset>` to end the third fieldset (Figure 7–22).

Q&A What is the default value for the <legend> alignment?

If you do not indicate otherwise, the legend will align left.

Q&A Are there other options such as colored borders that I can use with the <fieldset> tag?

Yes, you can set the margins, font, colors, etc. for the <fieldset> tag, but you would have to use Cascading Style Sheets (CSS), discussed in the next chapter, for that capability.

To Save the HTML File

With the Order Form Web page complete, the HTML file should be saved. The following step illustrates how to save the orderform.html file on the USB drive.

- With a USB drive plugged into your computer, click File on the menu bar and then click Save to save the orderform.html file.

Validating, Viewing, Testing, and Printing the Web Page and HTML Code

After completing the Order Form Web page, you should validate the code, and view and test it in a browser to confirm that the Web page appears as desired and that the controls function as expected.

Note that you cannot test the Submit button because it automatically generates an e-mail message to janasjewels@isp.com, which is a nonexistent e-mail address. After testing the controls, the Web page and HTML code for each Web page should be printed for future reference.

To Validate, View, Test, and Print a Web Page and HTML

The following steps illustrate how to validate, view, test, and print a Web page.

- Validate the orderform.html file by file upload at `validator.w3.org`.
- In Internet Explorer, click the Address bar to select the URL on the Address bar.
- Type `g:\Chapter07\ChapterFiles\orderform.html` and then press the ENTER key to display the completed Order Form for Jana's Jewels (Figure 7–23).
- Review the form to make sure all spelling is correct and the controls are positioned appropriately.

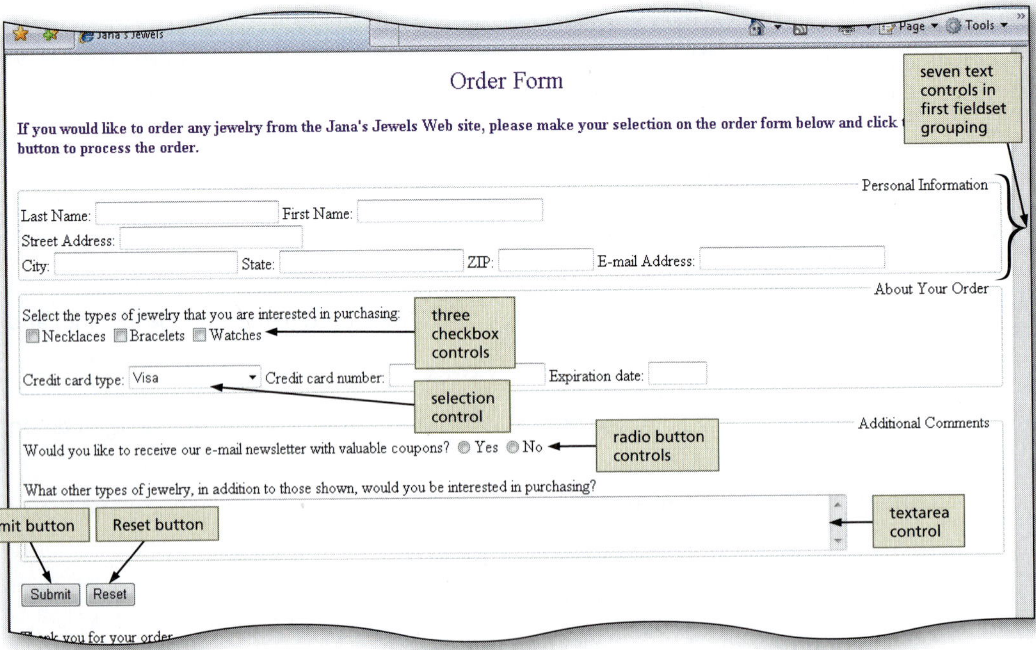

Figure 7–23

- Test all of the text boxes on the form. Try to type more than the maximum number of allowable characters in the cardnum and cardexp boxes.

- Click the check boxes to test them. You should be able to choose one, two, or three of the boxes at the same time because check boxes are designed to select more than one option.
- Test the selection control by clicking the list arrow and selecting one of the three options.
- Click the radio buttons to test them. You should be able to choose only one choice (Yes or No).
- Test the textarea by entering a paragraph of text. Verify that it allows more characters to be entered than are shown in the textarea.
- Click the Reset button. It should clear and reset all controls to their original (default) state.

- Click the Print icon on the Command bar to print the Web page (Figure 7–24).

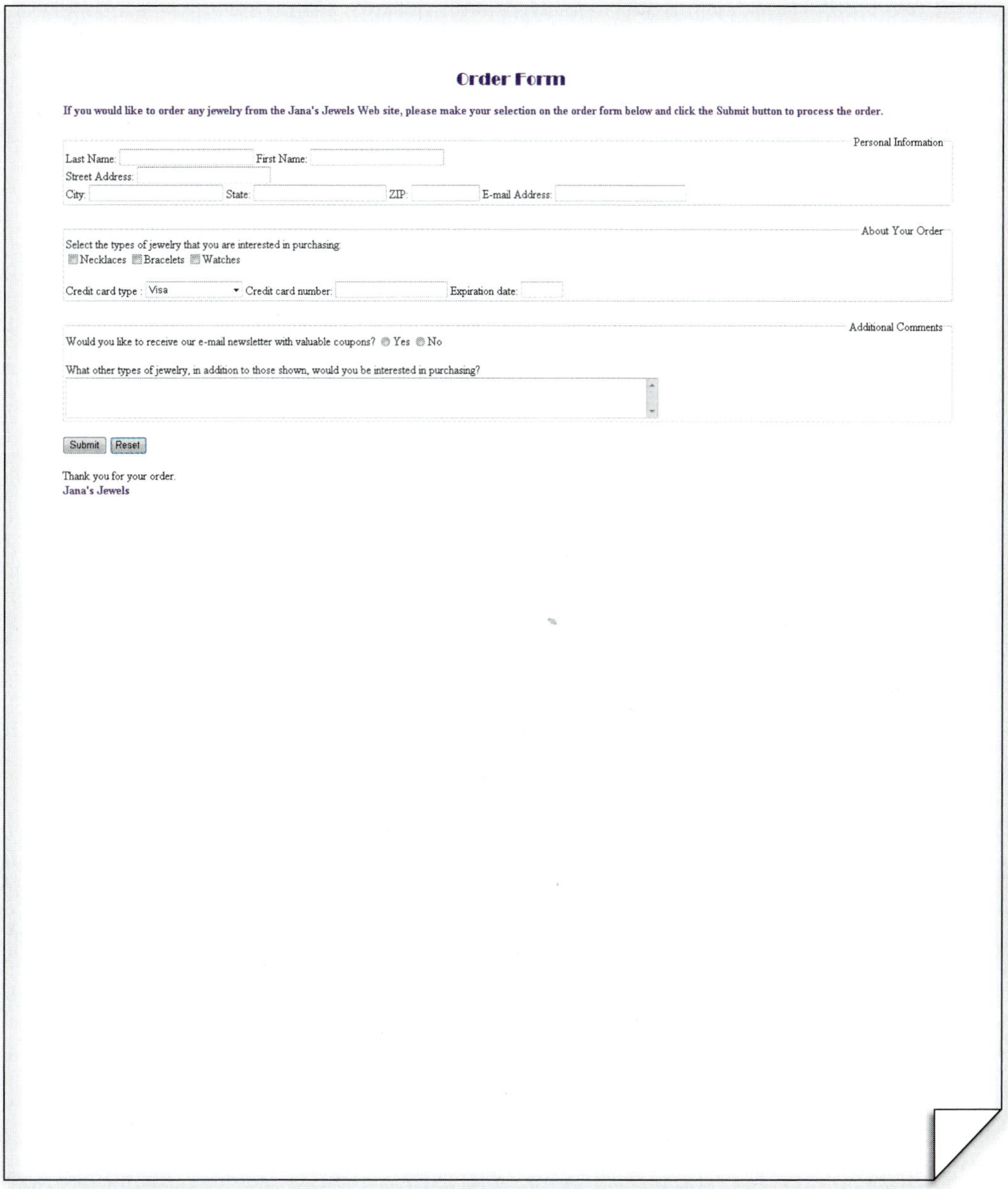

Figure 7–24

- Click the orderform.html - Notepad button on the taskbar.
- Click File on the menu bar and then click Print. Click the Print button in the Print dialog box to print the HTML file (Figure 7–25).

```
<!DOCTYPE html
   PUBLIC "-//W3C//DTD XHTML 1.0 Transitional//EN"
   "http://www.w3.org/TR/xhtml1/DTD/xhtml1-transitional.dtd">

<html xmlns="http://www.w3.org/1999/xhtml" xml:lang="en" lang="en">
<head>
<meta http-equiv="Content-Type" content="text/html;charset=utf-8" />
<title>Jana's Jewels</title>
</head>
<body>
<center><font face="Broadway" color="#590d8e" size="+2">Order Form</font></center>

<form method="post" action="mailto:janasjewels@isp.com">

<p><b><font color="#590d8e">If you would like to order any jewelry from the
Jana's Jewels Web site, please make your selection
on the order form below and click the Submit button to process the order.</font></b></p>

<fieldset><legend align="right">Personal Information</legend>
Last Name: <input name="lastname" type="text" size="25" />
First Name: <input name="firstname" type="text" size="25" />
<br />Street Address: <input name="address" type="text" size="25" />
<br />City: <input name="city" type="text" size="25" />
State: <input name="state" type="text" size="25" />
ZIP: <input name="zip" type="text" size="10" />
E-mail Address: <input name="email" type="text" size="25" />
</fieldset>

<fieldset><legend align="right">About Your Order</legend>
Select the types of jewelry that you are interested in purchasing:
<br /><input name="pictype" type="checkbox" value="necklaces" />Necklaces
<input name="pictype" type="checkbox" value="bracelets" />Bracelets
<input name="pictype" type="checkbox" value="watches" />Watches

<p>Credit card type:
<select name="payment">
<option>Visa</option>
<option>MasterCard</option>
<option>American Express</option>
</select>

Credit card number:
<input name="cardnum" type="text" size="20" maxlength="20" />

Expiration date:
<input name="cardexp" type="text" size="4" maxlength="4" /></p>
</fieldset>

<br /><fieldset><legend align="right">Additional Comments</legend>
Would you like to receive our e-mail newsletter with valuable coupons?
<input name="attend" type="radio" value="yes" />Yes
<input name="attend" type="radio" value="no" />No

<p>What other types of jewelry, in addition to those shown, would you be
interested in purchasing?
<br /><textarea name="other" rows="3" cols="100"></textarea></p>
</fieldset>

<p><input type="submit" value="Submit" />
<input type="reset" value="Reset" /></p>

<p>Thank you for your order.
<br /><b><font color="#590d8e">Jana's Jewels</font></b></p>

</form>
</body>
</html>
```

Figure 7–25

To Quit Notepad and a Browser

- Click the Close button on the browser title bar.
- Click the Close button on the Notepad window title bar.

Chapter Summary

In this chapter, you have learned how to convert a text-based Web page to a Web page form with various controls for user input. The items listed below include all the new HTML skills you have learned in this chapter.

1. Create a Form and Identify the Form Process (HTML 312)
2. Change the Text Message (HTML 312)
3. Add Text Boxes (HTML 314)
4. Add Check Boxes (HTML 316)
5. Add a Selection Menu (HTML 317)
6. Add Additional Text Boxes (HTML 320)
7. Add Radio Buttons (HTML 321)
8. Add a Textarea (HTML 322)
9. Add Submit and Reset Buttons (HTML 324)
10. Add Fieldset Controls to Create Form Groupings (HTML 327)

Learn It Online

Test your knowledge of chapter content and key terms.

Instructions: To complete the Learn It Online exercises, start your browser, click the Address bar, and then enter the Web address `scsite.com/html5e/learn`. When the HTML Learn It Online page is displayed, click the link for the exercise you want to complete and read the instructions.

Chapter Reinforcement TF, MC, and SA

A series of true/false, multiple choice, and short answer questions that test your knowledge of the chapter content.

Flash Cards

An interactive learning environment where you identify chapter key terms associated with displayed definitions.

Practice Test

A series of multiple choice questions that test your knowledge of chapter content and key terms.

Who Wants To Be a Computer Genius?

An interactive game that challenges your knowledge of chapter content in the style of a television quiz show.

Wheel of Terms

An interactive game that challenges your knowledge of chapter key terms in the style of the television show, *Wheel of Fortune*.

Crossword Puzzle Challenge

A crossword puzzle that challenges your knowledge of key terms presented in the chapter.

STUDENT ASSIGNMENTS

Apply Your Knowledge

Reinforce the skills and apply the concepts you learned in this chapter.

Creating a Web Page Restaurant Questionnaire

Instructions: Start Notepad. Open the file apply7-1.html from the Chapter07\Apply folder in the Data Files for Students. See the inside back cover of this book for instructions for downloading the Data Files for Students, or contact your instructor for information about accessing the files in this book. The apply7-1.html file is a partially completed HTML file that contains a questionnaire for a restaurant. Figure 7–26 shows the Apply Your Knowledge Web page as it should appear in your browser after adding the necessary HTML code for the controls shown.

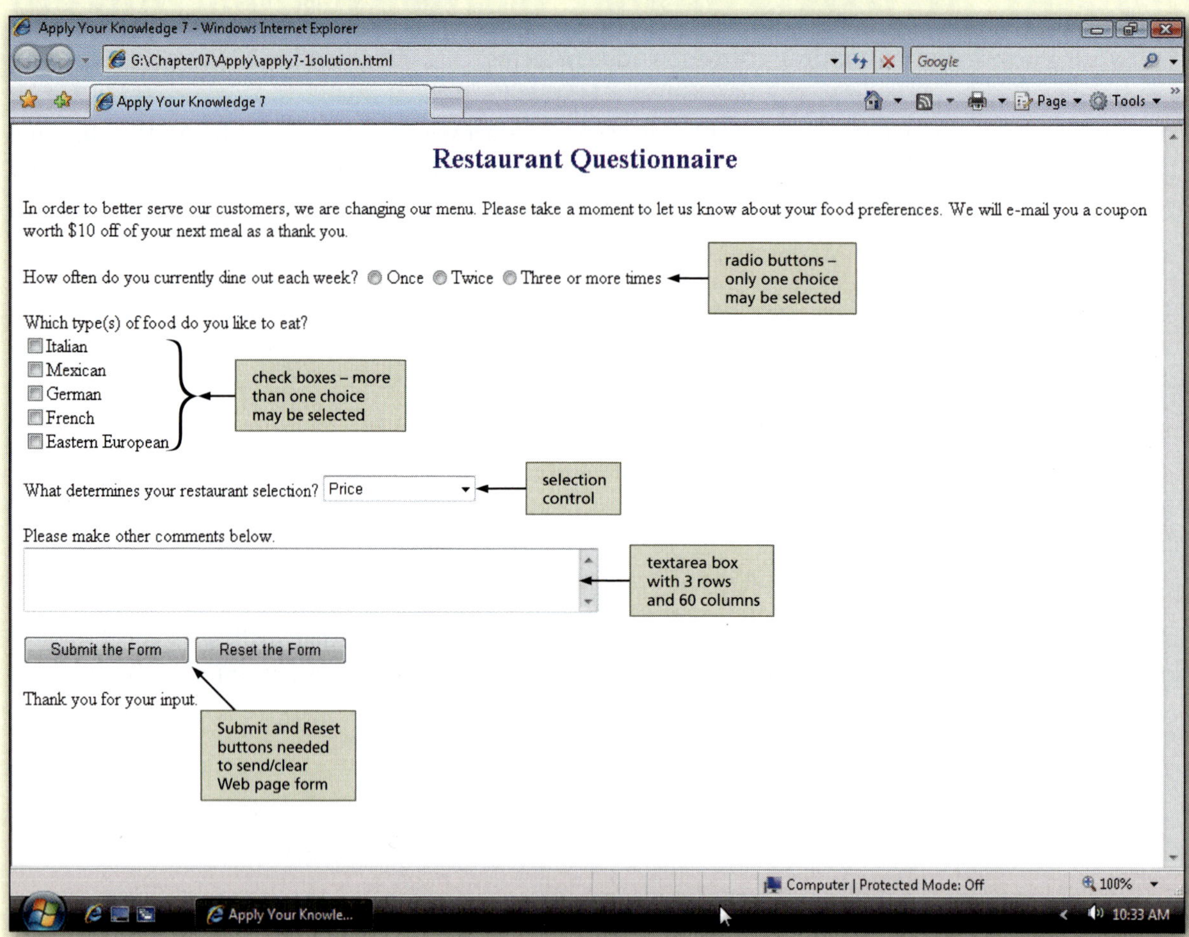

Figure 7–26

Perform the following steps:

1. Open your browser and then enter the URL, G:\Chapter07\Apply\apply7-1.html, to view the Web page.
2. Examine the HTML file and its appearance in the browser.

3. Using Notepad, add any HTML code necessary to make the Web page look similar to the one shown in Figure 7–26, including:
   a. Three radio buttons for number of times the visitor eats out
   b. Five check boxes for types of food the visitor eats
   c. A selection box with three options for factors that determine where they eat
   d. A textarea box with three rows and 60 columns
4. Add the HTML code necessary to add Submit and Reset buttons.
5. Save the revised file using the file name apply7-1solution.html.
6. Print the revised HTML file.
7. Enter the URL, G:\Chapter07\Apply\apply7-1solution.html, to view the Web page in your browser. Validate your HTML code and test all controls.
8. Print the Web page.
9. Submit the files in the format specified by your instructor.

Extend Your Knowledge

Extend the skills you learned in this chapter and experiment with new skills.

Creating a Community College Web Page Form

Instructions: Start Notepad. Open the file extend7-1.html from the Chapter07\Extend folder of the Data Files for Students. See the inside back cover of this book for instructions on downloading the Data Files for Students, or contact your instructor for information about accessing the required files. This sample HTML file contains all of the text for the Community College Survey Web page shown in Figure 7–27. You will add the necessary tags to make the Web page form as shown in Figure 7–27.

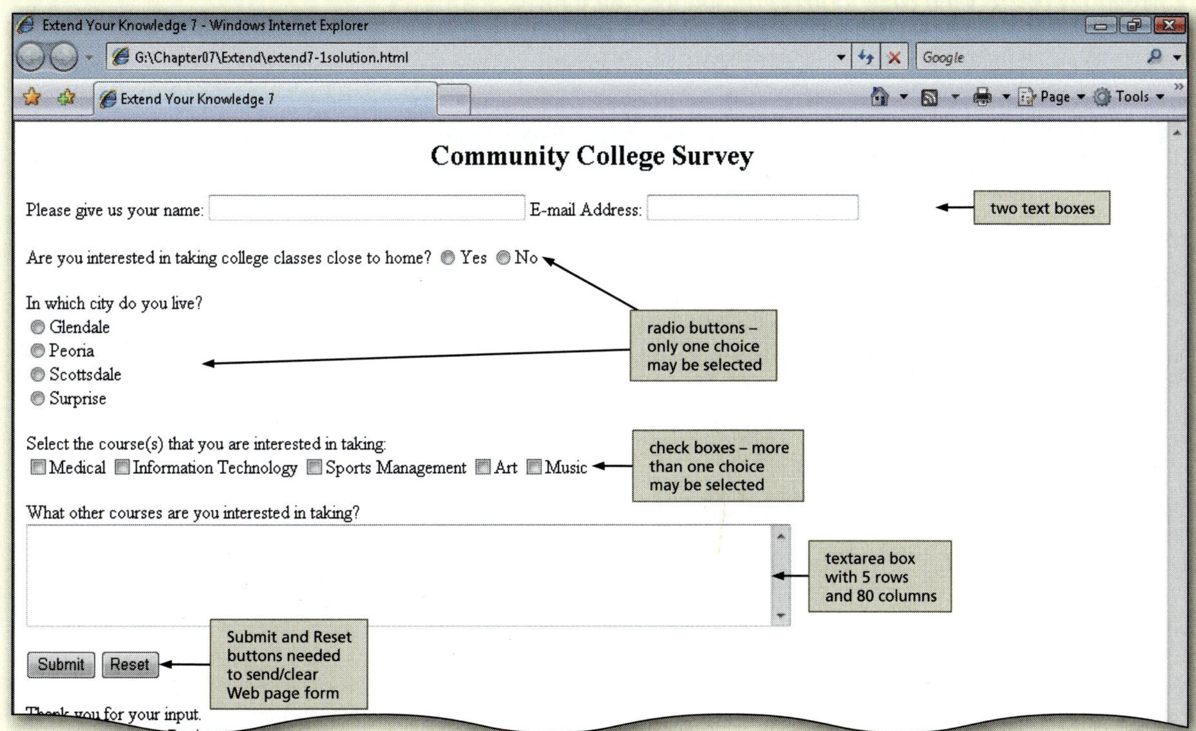

Figure 7–27

Continued >

Extend Your Knowledge *continued*

Perform the following tasks:

1. Using Notepad, add the HTML code necessary to make the Web page look similar to the one shown in Figure 7–27. Controls used in the form include:
   a. Two text boxes for name and e-mail information
   b. One set of radio buttons with two options (Yes and No); a second set of radio buttons with four options for city of residence information
   c. Five check boxes for course information
   d. A textarea box with 5 rows and 80 columns
2. Add the HTML code to add Submit and Reset buttons.
3. Save the revised document as extend7-1solution.html.
4. Validate your HTML code and test all controls.
5. Print the Web page and HTML.
6. Submit the solution in the format specified by your instructor.

Make It Right

Analyze a document and correct all errors and/or improve the design.

Correcting the Golf Survey Web Page

Instructions: Start Notepad. Open the file makeitright7-1.html from the Chapter07\MakeItRight folder of the Data Files for Students. See the inside back cover of this book for instructions on downloading the Data Files for Students, or contact your instructor for information about accessing the required files. The Web page is a modified version of what you see in Figure 7–28. Make the necessary corrections to the Web page to make it look like the figure.

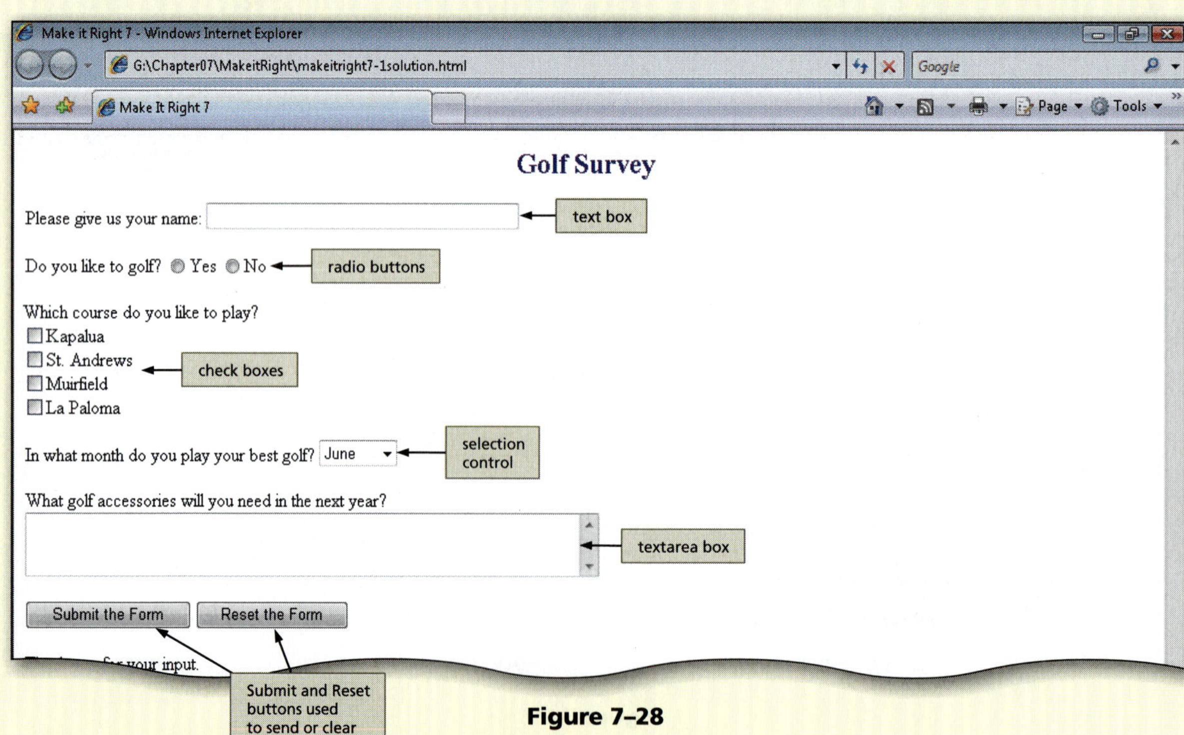

Figure 7–28

In the Lab

Lab 1: Creating a School Bookstore Survey

Problem: The staff of the school bookstore want to survey the students about their book-buying habits to determine where they purchase their books. The staff have asked you to create a Web page form that contains the questions shown in Figure 7–29.

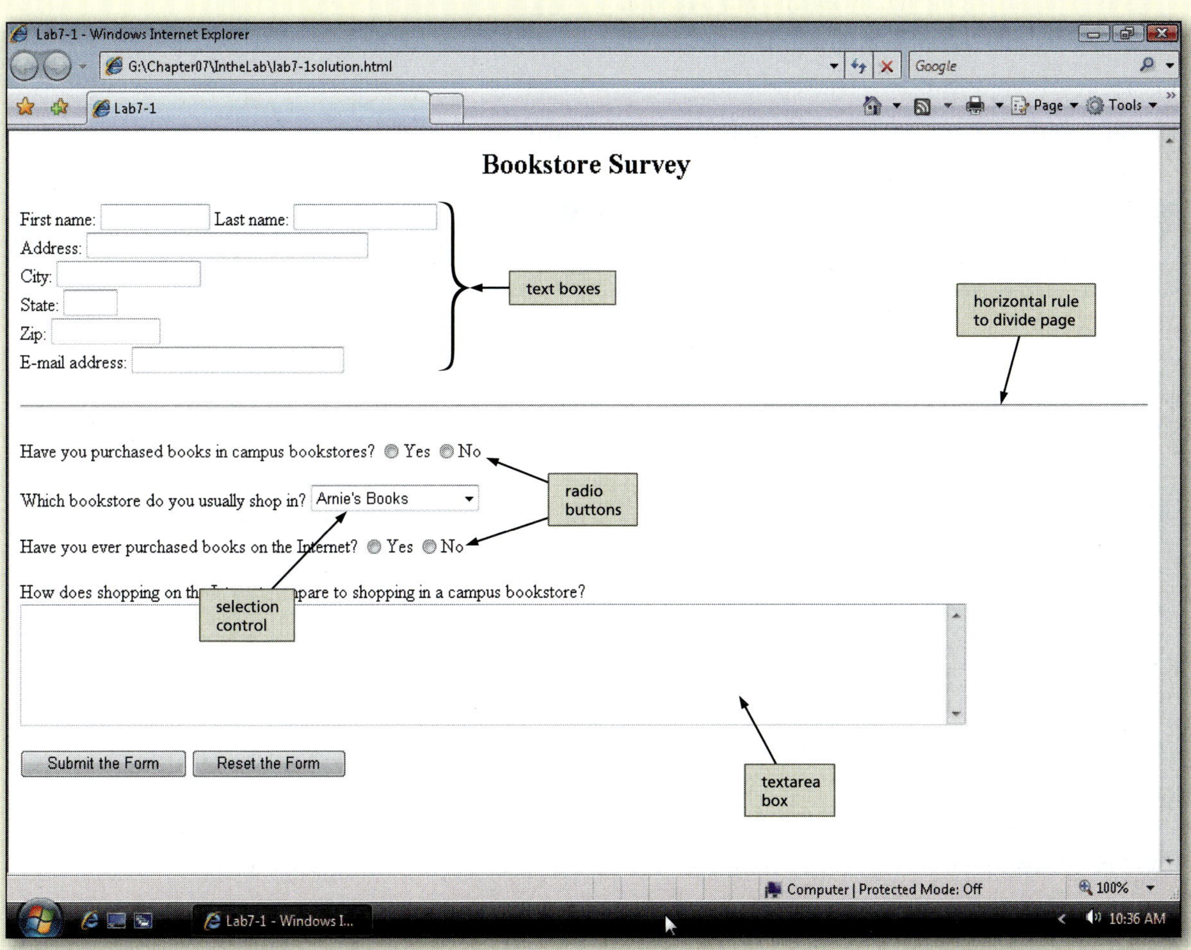

Figure 7–29

Instructions: Perform the following steps:

1. Using Notepad, create a new HTML file with the title Lab 7-1 in the main heading section. Add the Web page heading Bookstore Survey at the top of the page.
2. Create a form and identify the form process using the post method with the action attribute set to mailto:email@isp.com.
3. Add seven text boxes for first name, last name, home or school address, city, state, ZIP, plus e-mail address.
4. Add two radio buttons for users to say whether or not they use the campus bookstore.
5. Add a selection menu with three options of your choosing (or use Arnie's Books, Lafollet Shops, and University Bookstore) for users to select the bookstore in which they shop, as shown in Figure 7–29.

Continued >

In the Lab *continued*

6. Create a second set of radio buttons for users to say whether they have purchased books on the Internet, as shown in Figure 7–29.
7. Create a textarea for additional comments and set it to 6 rows and 100 columns.
8. Add Submit and Reset buttons at the bottom of the Web page form.
9. Save the HTML file in the Chapter07\IntheLab folder using the file name lab7-1solution.html. Validate the Web page. Print the HTML file.
10. Open the lab7-1solution.html file in your browser and test all controls (except the Submit button).
11. Print the Web page.
12. Submit the files in the format specified by your instructor.

In the Lab

Lab 2: Record Store Questionnaire

Problem: County Line Records is looking for information on their listeners' musical tastes. They want to know what type of music and radio stations you listen to. The company has asked you to create the survey as a Web page form, as shown in Figure 7–30.

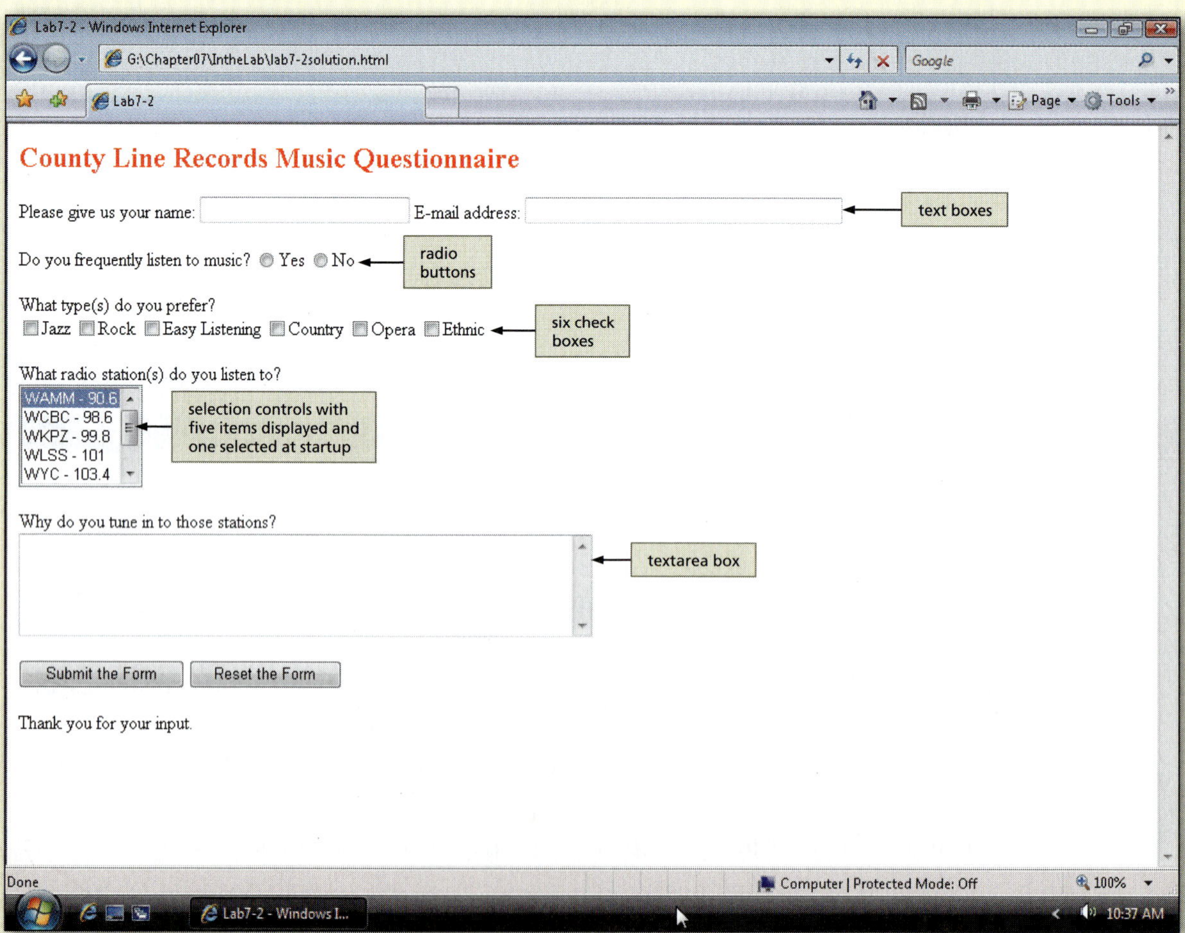

Figure 7–30

Instructions: Perform the following steps:

1. Using Notepad, create a new HTML file with the title, Lab 7-2, in the main heading section.
2. Create a form and identify the form process using the post method with the action attribute set to mailto your e-mail address (if you do not have an e-mail address, use email@isp.com).
3. Add two text boxes for name and e-mail address, as shown in Figure 7–30.
4. Add a set of radio buttons and six check boxes for users to select their musical preferences.
5. Add a selection menu that initially displays five rows and allows multiple input. One of the menu options should be selected at startup. Use local radio stations' call letters and numbers as your options.
6. Insert a 5-row, 60-column textarea for users to provide additional suggestions.
7. Add a Submit button and a Reset button at the bottom of the Web page form.
8. Save the HTML file in the Chapter07\IntheLab folder using the file name lab7-2solution.html. Validate the Web page. Print the HTML file.
9. Open the lab7-2solution.html file in your browser and test all controls. Test the Submit button only if you used your own e-mail address as the value for the form action attribute.
10. Print the Web page.
11. Submit the files in the format specified by your instructor.

In the Lab

Lab 3: Using Fieldset Controls to Organize a Form

Problem: Your manager at Horizon Learning has asked you to create a Web page form that newer HTML developers can use as a model for a well-designed, user-friendly form. Having created forms for several different Web sites, you have learned that using fieldset controls to group form controls results in a well-organized, easily readable form. Create a Web page form that utilizes three fieldset controls, like the one shown in Figure 7–31.

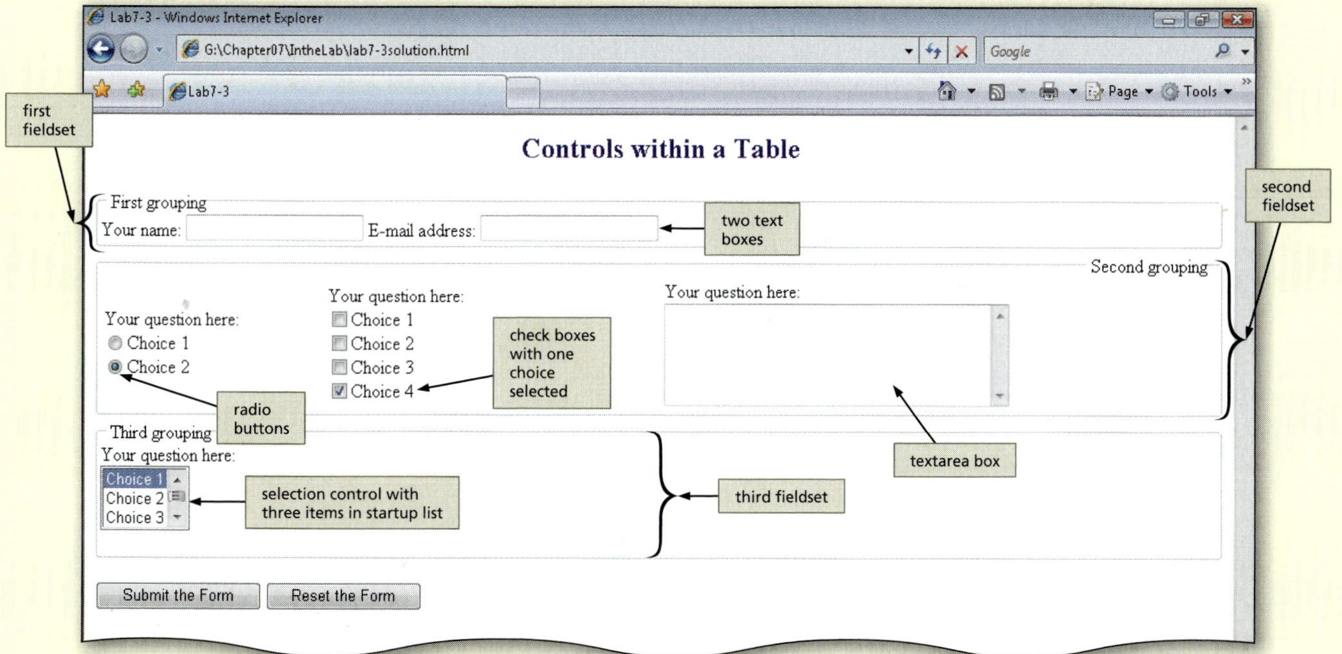

Figure 7–31

Continued >

In the Lab *continued*

Instructions: Perform the following steps:

1. Using Notepad, create a new HTML file with the title Lab 7-3 in the main heading section.
2. Add the Web page heading Controls within a Table.
3. Create a form and identify the form process using the post method with the action attribute set to mailto your e-mail address (if you do not have an e-mail address, use email@isp.com).
4. Add two text boxes for name and e-mail address.
5. Add two radio buttons, with Choice 2 preselected, as shown in Figure 7–31, together with four check boxes with Choice 4 selected.
6. Add a 5-row, 35-column textarea, as shown in Figure 7–31.
7. Insert a selection menu with options of Choice 1 through Choice 4. Set the selection menu to display three rows and have Choice 1 preselected as the default option.
8. Add a Submit button that says Submit the Form and a Reset button that says Reset the Form at the bottom of the Web page form.
9. Add three fieldset controls to group the other form controls, as shown in Figure 7–31.
10. Save the HTML file in the Chapter07\IntheLab folder using the file name lab7-3solution.html. Validate the Web page. Print the HTML file.
11. Open the lab7-3solution.html file in your browser and test all controls. Test the Submit button only if you used your own e-mail address as the value for the form action attribute.
12. Print the Web page.
13. Submit the files in the format specified by your instructor.

Cases and Places

Apply your creative thinking and problem solving skills to design and implement a solution.

• Easier ••More Difficult

• 1: Creating a Travel Form

The marketing director at Getaway Travel asked you to create a Web page form to allow customers to request information on the four travel packages offered by the agency: ski & snow, surf & sun, golf & spa, and adventure. Using the techniques learned in this chapter, create a Web page form with input controls to allow customers to request information on one or more travel packages. By default, have all of the travel packages selected on the form. In addition, include input controls for customers to provide a mailing address, an e-mail address, and any suggestions for new travel packages. Include a Submit and Reset button and use your e-mail address in the action attribute for the form. After creating the Web page, enter information and submit the form. Print the data file with the information and indicate which name-value pairs are related to which controls on the form.

• 2: Changing a Paper Form to an Online Form

As part of your Web development project, your instructor has asked you to find a text-based form that is currently in use by your school, a club, or another organization. Convert this text-based form to a Web page form. Start by designing the form on paper, taking into consideration the fields that are the most appropriate to use for each input area. Once your design is complete, use HTML to develop the Web page form. Test the form, and once testing is done, show the form to several people from the organization that controls the form. Explain to them why it is better to collect information using a Web page form, rather than a printed, text-based form.

• • 3: Collecting Information with a Form

Your friends recently opened a new business that provides tutoring to high school and college-aged students. The company has some great ideas about using Web pages to display information, but it is not as familiar with using the Web to collect information. The owners think it is a good idea to use paper form mailings to determine staffing needs. You want to convince the head of the company that Web page forms can be used to collect important information from the visitors to companies' Web sites. Search the Internet for two or three examples of Web page forms used in business. Print the forms as examples. If you were the Web developer for these Web sites, how would you update the forms to gather more information or make the forms easier to use? Using the example Web pages that you have found, draw a sketch of a Web page form design for a tutoring business. Develop the Web page form as an example to share with the head of the company.

• • 4: Making a Form Easier to Use

Make It Personal

Your manager at Cards and Such has asked you to update the order form on the Web site to make it easier to use. In Chapter 3, tables were used to lay out information in a more controlled manner. In this chapter, you used fieldset controls to group information so it was more readable and, thereby, easier to use. Forms also can be combined with tables to provide more control over the placement of the form controls. Create a Web page form that utilizes a table (either borderless or with borders) to structure the placement of controls and includes at least two fieldset controls that group other controls on a form.

Continued >

Cases and Places *continued*

•• 5: Creating a Travel Journal

Working Together

Your team works in the Web development department for a small company in your community. You are interested in learning the latest programming techniques so you can stay current with the technology. In this chapter, data from a form was sent in a file to an e-mail address. The chapter mentioned CGI scripts and the PHP and Perl programming languages as a better, more secure method to use for processing the information submitted in a form. While CGI scripts and Perl programming are beyond the scope of this book, they are important topics to study. Search the Web to find additional information about CGI scripts, PHP, and Perl used in conjunction with forms. Try to find online tutorials that explain how to use these techniques. What other options are available for collecting information online? Develop a Web page that lists links to various Web sites that discuss these topics. Under each link, write a brief paragraph explaining the purpose of each Web site and why it is important to review.

8 Creating Style Sheets

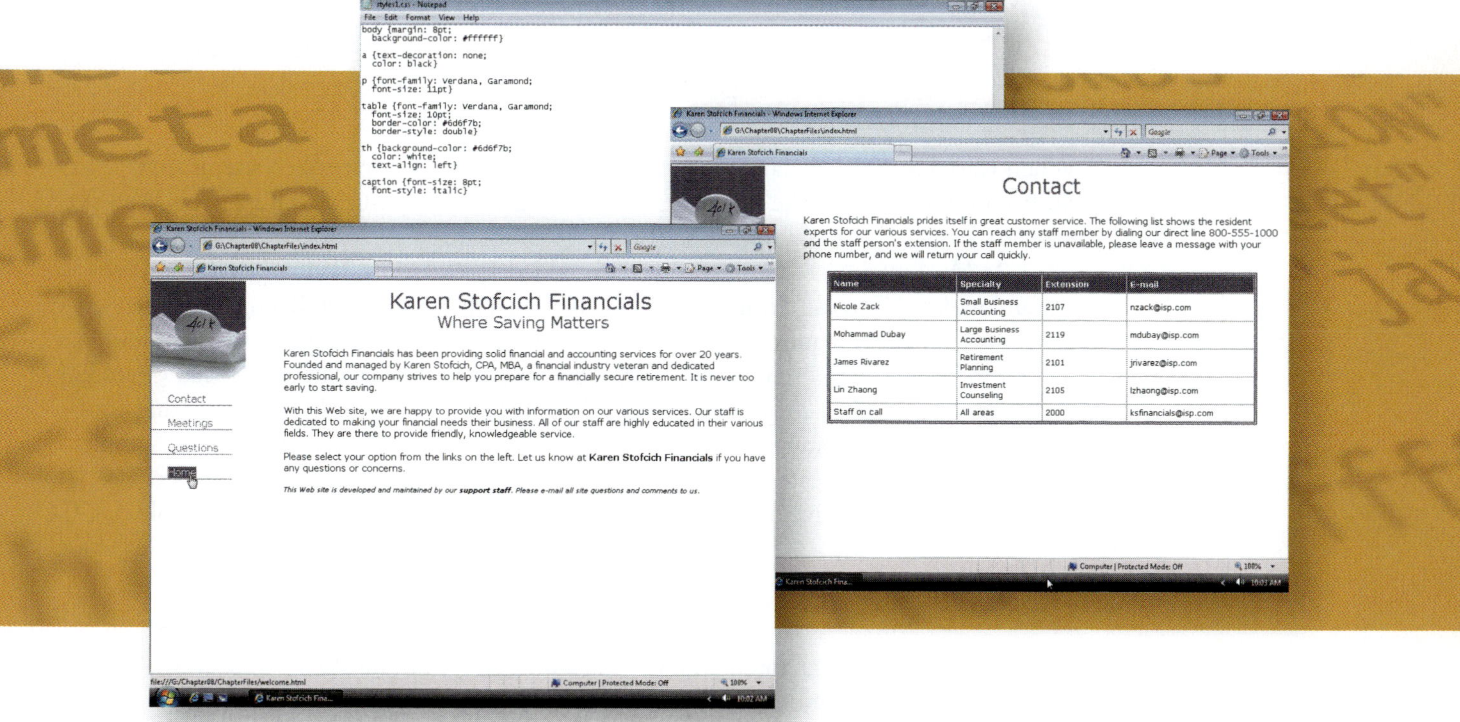

Objectives

You will have mastered the material in this chapter when you can:

- Describe the three different types of Cascading Style Sheets
- Add an embedded style sheet to a Web page
- Change the margin and link styles using an embedded style sheet
- Create an external style sheet
- Change the body margins and background using an external style sheet
- Change the link decoration and color using an external style sheet
- Change the font family and size for all paragraphs using an external style sheet
- Change table styles using an external style sheet
- Use the <link /> tag to insert a link to an external style sheet
- Add an inline style sheet to a Web page
- Change the text style of a single paragraph using an inline style sheet

8 | Creating Style Sheets

Introduction

In previous chapters, you used HTML tags to change the way a Web page is displayed in a Web browser, such as adding italics, bold, colors, headings, and tables. In this chapter, you learn an easier way to give your Web pages a consistent format and look: using style sheets.

Project — Using Style Sheets in the Stofcich Financials Web Site

When Karen Stofcich Financials decided to upgrade its corporate Web site, Karen Stofcich hired you to make the changes. The original Karen Stofcich Financials Web site was very basic, with a few simple pages of text information.

At Ms. Stofcich's request, you recently added several more Web pages to the Web site and updated it to use a frame structure, as shown in Figure 8–1a. Recognizing that the Karen Stofcich Financials Web site will continue to grow, you suggest that you should modify the Web site to use Cascading Style Sheets (CSS). You explain to her that Cascading Style Sheets maintain a consistent look across a Web site — especially Web sites that contain many pages, and can give the pages a more polished look. You show her some sample Web pages you have created using CSS (Figure 8–1b), so she can see the difference. Ms. Stofcich is supportive of the plan and encourages you to start as soon as possible.

Overview

As you read this chapter, you will learn how to create the Web pages shown in Figure 8–1b by performing these general tasks:

- Plan the CSS structure
- Enter HTML code into the Notepad window
- Save the file as an HTML file
- Enter basic HTML tags and add text to the file
- Create an external CSS file
- Use the <style> tag in an embedded style sheet
- Use the <style> attribute in an inline style sheet
- View the Web pages and HTML code in your browser
- Validate the Web pages
- Test and print the Web pages

(a) Web Pages without Style Sheets. **(b) Web Pages with Style Sheets.**

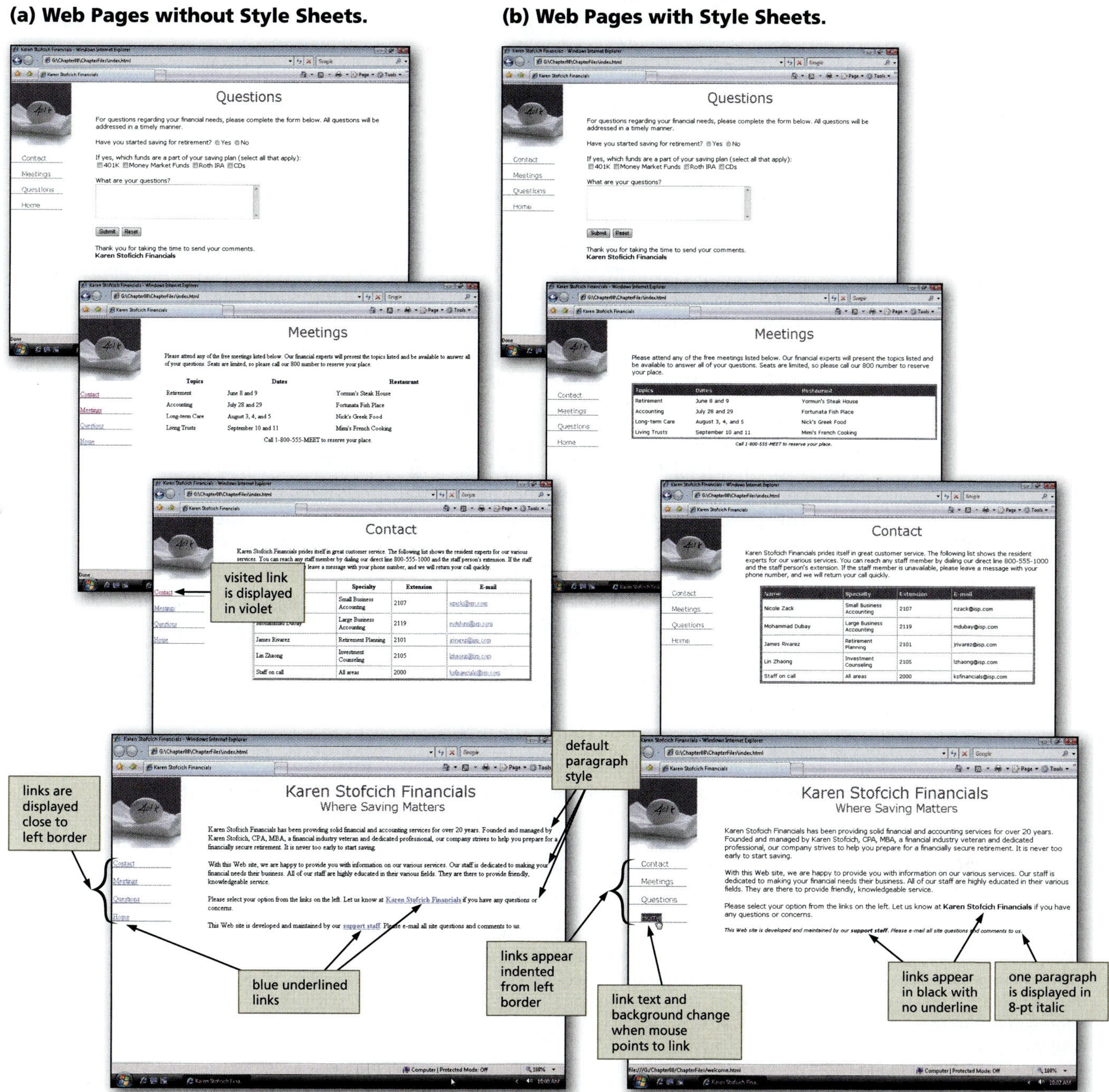

Figure 8–1

Plan Ahead

General Project Guidelines

As you create Web pages, such as the chapter project shown in Figure 8–1 on page HTML 343, you should follow these general guidelines:

1. **Plan the Web site**. First, you should determine if using Cascading Style Sheets (CSS) is appropriate for your Web site. If you have several Web pages and need a consistent style that can be easily updated, CSS is a good choice. If you have a single page with mostly static content and formatting, CSS might not be needed.
2. **Analyze the need**. In the analysis phase of the Web Development Life Cycle, you should analyze what content to include on the Web page. Chapter 8 introduces a new Web development technique. Using style sheets can eliminate the need to edit multiple Web pages for simple changes. An external style sheet can be edited to make changes across a Web site. Part of the analysis phase then includes determining how the multiple Web pages work together using CSS.
3. **Choose the content for the Web page**. With a multiple-page Web site, you can distribute the content as needed throughout the Web site.
4. **Determine the type of style sheets to use for the pages and their precedence**. If you determine that CSS is appropriate, then you must decide which type or types of style sheet described in this chapter is best. For Web sites with many Web pages that have a common look, the best option may be to utilize an external style sheet. For Web sites with fewer similarities among pages, using embedded or inline style sheets may be a better option. Also, knowing style sheet precedence (described later in this chapter) helps you to understand how each style reacts with the others.
5. **Create the style sheets**. Once the analysis and design is complete, the Web developer creates the Web page using HTML. Good Web development standard practices should be followed in this step. Embedded and inline style sheets are used within particular Web pages. External style sheets require a two-step process. First, an external style sheet must be created and saved as a .css file. Then, a link statement must be inserted into all Web pages in which you want to use the external style sheet.
6. **Test all Web pages within the Web site**. An important part of Web development is testing to assure that you are following XHTML standards. In this book, we use the World Wide Web Consortium (W3C) validator that allows you to test your Web page and clearly explains any errors you have. When testing, you should check all content for accuracy. Finally, all of the Web pages with style sheets (external, embedded, and inline) should be validated per the standard set throughout this book.

When necessary, more specific details concerning the above guidelines are presented at appropriate points in the chapter. The chapter also will identify the actions performed and decisions made regarding these guidelines during the creation of the Web page shown in Figure 8–1 on page HTML 343.

BTW

CSS

The World Wide Web Consortium (W3C) has a wealth of information about Cascading Style Sheets (CSS). You can find out what is new with CSS, access CSS testing suites, and find links to CSS authoring tools from this Web site. For more information, visit the W3C Web site and search for CSS.

Using Style Sheets

Although HTML allows Web developers to make changes to the structure, design, and content of a Web page, HTML is limited in its ability to define the appearance, or style, across one or more Web pages. As a result, style sheets were created.

A **style** is a rule that defines the appearance of an element on a Web page. A **style sheet** is a series of rules that defines the style for a Web page or an entire Web site. With a style sheet, you can alter the appearance of a Web page or pages by changing characteristics such as font family, font size, margins, and link specifications.

Like HTML, style sheets adhere to a common language with set standards and rules. This language, called **Cascading Style Sheets**, or CSS, allows a Web developer to write code statements that control the style of elements on a Web page. CSS is not HTML; it is a separate language used to enhance the display capabilities of HTML. The World Wide Web Consortium (W3C), the same organization that defines HTML standards, defines the specifications for CSS.

With CSS you can add visual elements such as colors, borders, margins, and font styles to your Web pages. CSS is not used to add any content to your Web site; it just makes your content look more stylish. For example, if you want all text paragraphs on a Web page to be indented by five spaces, you can use a style sheet to handle the indenting, rather than coding each paragraph. Style sheets allow you to change the style for a single element on a Web page, such as a paragraph, or to change the style of elements on all of the pages in a Web site.

BTW **CSS Benefits**
With CSS, you can establish a standard look for all Web pages in a Web site. Using CSS, you avoid the tedious steps of adding repetitive codes to format the same types of information. Instead of making all paragraphs of text 10pt Verdana in individual <p> tags, you can define that in a .css file and link that external file to all Web pages.

CSS provides support for three types of style sheets: inline, embedded, and external (or linked). With an **inline style sheet**, you add a style to an individual HTML tag, such as a heading or paragraph. The style changes that specific tag, but does not affect other tags in the document. With an **embedded style sheet**, you add the style sheet within the <head> tags of the HTML document to define the style for an entire Web page. With a linked style sheet, or **external style sheet**, you create a text file that contains all of the styles you want to apply, and then you save the text file with the file extension .css. You then add a link to this external style sheet on any Web page in the Web site. External style sheets give you the most flexibility and are ideal to apply the same formats to all of the Web pages in a Web site. External style sheets also make it easy to change formats quickly across Web pages. For example, if you decide to change from the Verdana font to Arial for all Web pages in a Web site, using an external style sheet you only need to change the font in one place — the style sheet.

In this chapter, you learn to implement all three types of style sheets. First, an embedded style sheet is used to change the link styles in the menu in the left frame (Figure 8–2a on the next page). An inline style sheet is used to change the style for a single paragraph on the Welcome page (Figure 8–2b on the next page). An external style sheet is used to change the body, link, paragraph, and table styles in the main pages in the right frame (Figure 8–2c on page HTML 347). After the three different style sheets are added to the Karen Stofcich Financials Web site, the finished Web pages appear using styles that make them more attractive, polished, and professional-looking than the original Web pages (Figure 8–2d on page HTML 347).

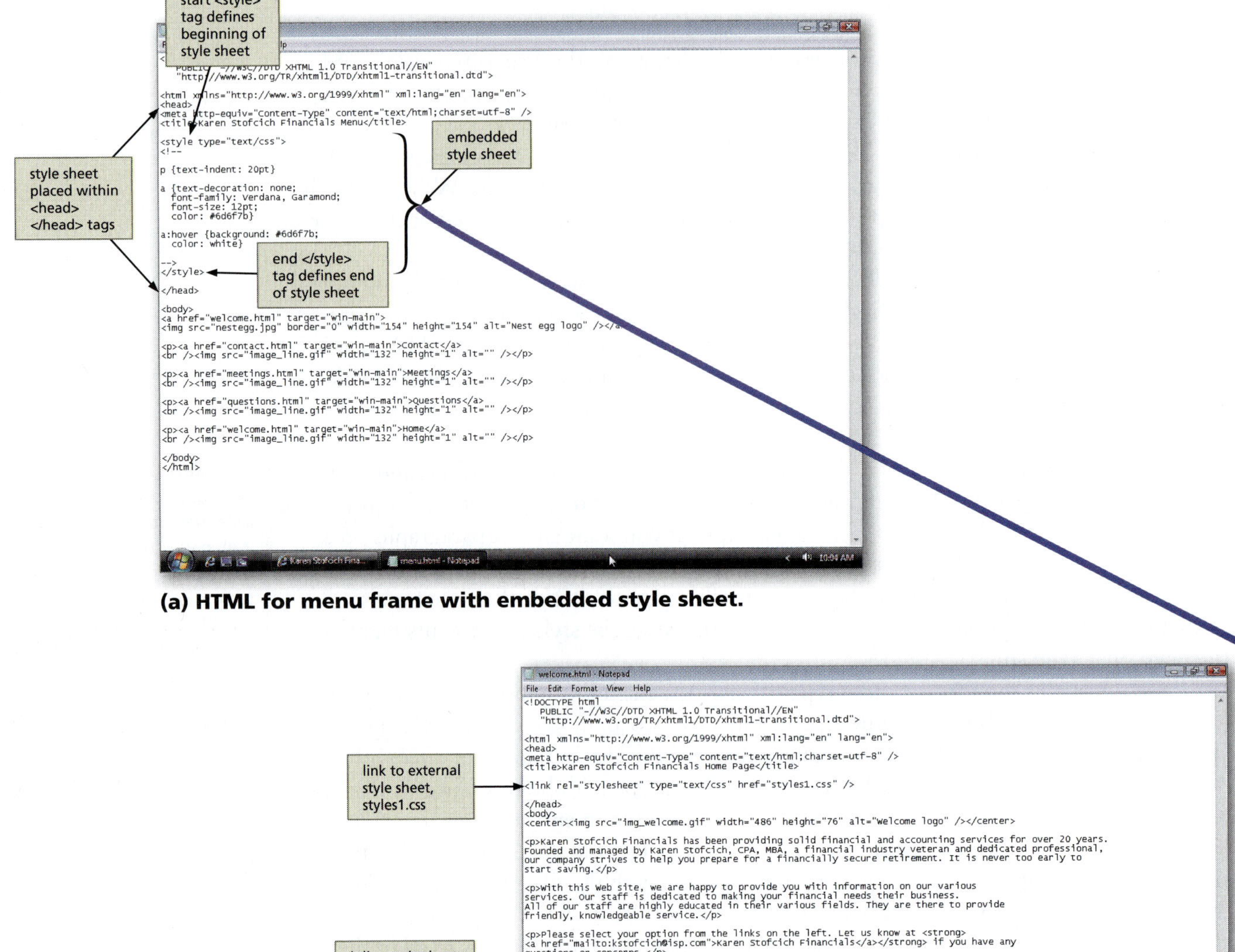

(a) HTML for menu frame with embedded style sheet.

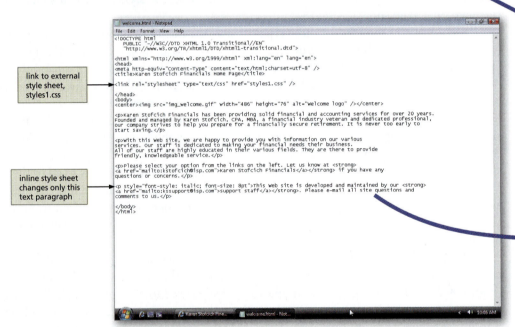

(b) HTML for welcome page with external style sheet link and inline style sheet.

Figure 8–2

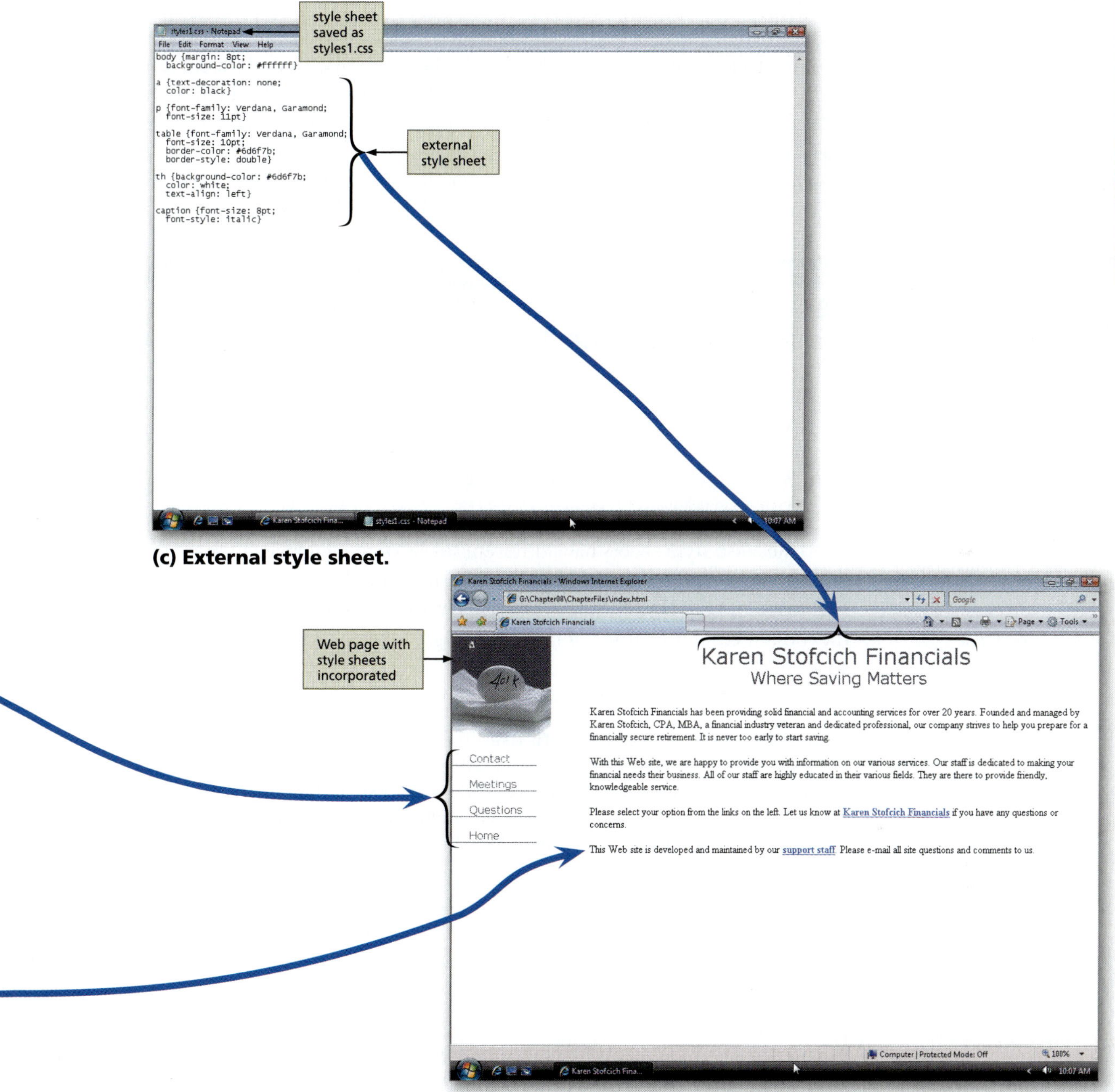

(c) External style sheet.

(d) Welcome page formatted using the three types of style sheets.

Figure 8–2 *(continued)*

Style Sheet Precedence

As shown in Table 8–1, the three style sheets supported by CSS control the appearance of a Web page at different levels. Each style sheet type also has a different level of **precedence** or priority in relationship to the others. An external style sheet, for example, is used to define styles for multiple pages in a Web site. An embedded style sheet is used to change the style of one Web page, but overrides or takes precedence over any styles defined in an external style sheet. An inline style sheet is used to control the style within an individual HTML tag and takes precedence over the styles defined in both embedded and external style sheets.

BTW

CSS Precedence
Although the three types of CSS (inline, embedded, and external) can co-exist, an inline style sheet takes precedence over any other style sheet, and an embedded style sheet overrides an external style sheet. So if you specify the style for your paragraphs in both embedded and inline style sheets, the style of the inline style sheet would override the embedded style.

Table 8–1 Style Sheet Precedence

Type	Level and Precedence
Inline	• To change the style within an individual HTML tag • Overrides embedded and external style sheets
Embedded	• To change the style of one Web page • Overrides external style sheets
External	• To change the style of multiple pages in a Web site

Because style sheets have different levels of precedence, all three types of style sheets can be used on a single Web page. For example, you may want some elements of a Web page to match the other Web pages in the Web site, but you also may want to vary the look of certain sections of that Web page. You can do this by using the three types of style sheets.

Plan Ahead

Identify what style sheets to use.
The first step to consider when using style sheets is to lay out a plan that takes style sheet precedence rules into account. Three different types of style sheets exist, and as discussed, one takes precedence over the next. An inline style sheet takes precedence over either of the other two, and the embedded style sheet takes precedence over the external style sheet.

- **Use external style sheets for styles that you want across the Web site.** As mentioned, the greatest benefit of CSS is the ability to identify a style across a Web site. For Web pages in which you want a common look, use external style sheets.
- **Use embedded style sheets for single Web page styles.** This type of style sheet is good to use if you want the style to affect just one (or a few) Web pages, and not all pages across the Web site.
- **Use inline style sheets for individual styles.** If you want to change the style of one or a few sections of one Web page, then using inline style sheets is the most appropriate. Once the style is intended for most (or all) of the Web page though, you may want to switch to embedded or external style sheets.

Style Statement Format

No matter what type of style sheet you use, you must use a **style statement** to define the style. The following code shows an example of a style statement used in an inline style sheet:

```
<h1 style ="font-family: Garamond; font-color: navy">
```

A style statement is made up of a selector and a declaration. The part of the style statement that identifies the page elements is called the **selector**. In this example, the selector is h1 (header size 1). The part of the style statement that identifies how the element(s) should appear is called the **declaration**. In this example, the declaration is everything between the quotation marks: the font-family and font-color properties and their values (Garamond and navy, respectively). A declaration includes at least one type of style, or **property**, to apply to the selected element. Examples of properties include color, text-indent, border-width, and font-style. For each property, the declaration includes a related **value**, which specifies the display parameters for that specific property.

Each property accepts specific values, based on the styles that property can define. The property, font-color, for example, can accept the value, navy, but cannot accept the value, 10%, because that is not a valid color value.

The following code shows an example of style statements used in an embedded style sheet:

```
h1 {font-family: Garamond;
 font-size: 32pt}
```

In this style statement, the h1 (header size 1) element is the selector, and the remainder of the code is the declaration. The declaration sets the values for two different properties. The first property-value statement sets the h1 font family to Garamond. The second property-value statement sets the font size to 32 point. This means that the browser will display all h1 headers in 32-point Garamond font.

Style sheets allow you to control many different property values for various elements on a Web page. Table 8–2 lists six main properties and related options that are used in style sheets. A complete list of properties and property values that can be used in style sheets is included in Appendix D.

BTW

CSS Tutorials

Many good CSS tutorials also can be found on the Web. Most sites start with CSS basics and then move to more advanced topics. CSS examples and quizzes are available along with many CSS references. Search for the term "CSS tutorial" to find great learning tools.

Table 8–2 Properties and Values

Property Name	Options That Can Be Controlled
background	• color • image • position
border	• color • style • width
font	• family • size • style • variant • weight
list	• image • position • type
margin	• length • percentage
text	• alignment • decoration • indentation • spacing • white space

The next sections discuss each type of style sheet in more detail and give examples.

BTW

Inline Style Sheets
Inline style sheets give you a great amount of flexibility in Web page styling. Inline style sheets override both embedded and external style sheets. This means if you want all paragraph styles throughout the Web site to be 10pt Garamond except for one, for that one paragraph you can use an inline style sheet to alter its style.

Inline Style Sheets

An inline style sheet is used to define the style of an individual HTML tag. For example, to change the style of a single paragraph, you could add an inline style sheet with the <p> (paragraph) tag as the selector and a declaration that defines new font style and color values for that paragraph, as shown here:

```
<p style="font-style: italic; font-size: 8pt">
```

Because they take precedence over the other types of style sheets and affect the style for individual HTML tags, inline style sheets are helpful when one section of a Web page needs to have a style different from the rest of the Web page.

BTW

Embedded Style Sheets
When you want to change the style of one Web page, you easily can do that with an embedded style sheet. The embedded style sheet needs to be put within the start <head> and end </head> tags. When you want to change the style of more than one Web page, using an external style sheet (a .css file) and linking to that style sheet is a more efficient method.

Embedded Style Sheets

An embedded style sheet is used to control the style of a single Web page. To add an embedded style sheet to a Web page, you insert a start <style> tag at the top of the Web page within the <head> tags that define the header section. After adding the desired style statements, you end the embedded style sheet by adding an end </style> tag. The following code shows an example of an embedded style sheet:

```
<style type="text/css">
<!--
p {text-indent: 8pt}
a {text-decoration: none;
 font-family: Verdana;
 font-size: 14pt;
 color: navy}
a:hover {background: navy;
 color: white}
-->
</style>
```

This embedded style sheet defines the style for three elements on the page: paragraphs, links, and the link-hover property. The first style statement uses the selector p to specify that all text in a paragraph should be indented by 8 points. Adding space to indent the text ensures that the text does not run up against the left side of the Web page, thus giving the Web page a cleaner look.

The second style statement defines four properties of the link element. The selector **a** is used to indicate the link element. The property-value statement *text-decoration: none* changes the default, so that no line will appear under the links. The next two property-value statements change the font family and font size to 14-point Verdana. The final property-value statement changes the color of all link text to navy. Because the style statement uses **a** as the selector, it changes all link states (normal, visited, active) to these property values. You also can define a unique style for normal, visited, and active links by creating three separate style statements with **a:link**, **a:visited**, and **a:active** as the selectors.

The last style statement uses the **a:hover** selector to define the style of a link when the mouse pointer points to, or **hovers** over, a link. This statement tells the browser to display white link text on a navy background when the mouse hovers over the link (see the preceding sample code). Adding a link hover style significantly changes the look of the links and adds a dimension of interactivity to the Web page.

Recall that an embedded style sheet has the second-highest level of precedence of the three types of style sheets. Although an inline style sheet overrides the properties of an embedded style sheet, the embedded style sheet takes precedence over an external style sheet.

External Style Sheets

External style sheets are the most comprehensive form of style sheet and can be used to control the consistency and look of many Web pages within a Web site. Adding an external style sheet to a Web page involves a two-step process of creating an external style sheet and then linking this style sheet onto the desired Web pages.

An external style sheet is a text file that contains style statements for all of the styles you want to define. The sample code that follows shows an example of an external style sheet:

```
a {text-decoration: none;
 color: blue}
p {font-family: Verdana, Garamond;
 font-size: 11pt}
table {font-family: Verdana, Garamond;
 font-size: 11pt}
th {color: white;
 background-color: blue;
 font-size: 11pt;
 text-align: left}
```

The format of the external style sheet is very similar to the format of the embedded style sheet. An external style sheet, however, does not need <style> tags to start and end the style sheet; it includes just the style statements.

To create an external style sheet, enter all of the style statements in a text file using Notepad or another text editor, and then save the text file with a **.css extension**. The code shown above, for example, can be saved with the file name styles1.css and then linked onto multiple Web pages.

For each Web page to which you want to apply the styles in an external style sheet, a <link /> tag similar to the sample code below must be inserted within the <head> tags of the Web page:

```
<link rel="stylesheet" type="text/css" href="styles1.css" />
```

The <link /> tag indicates that the style sheet styles1.css should be applied to this Web page. The property-value statement rel="stylesheet" defines the relationship of the linked document (that is, that it is a style sheet). The property-value statement type="text/css" indicates the content and language used in the linked document. The property-value statement href="styles1.css" indicates the name and location of the linked style sheet, styles1.css. To apply this style sheet to other pages in the Web site, you would insert the same <link /> tag within the <head> tag of each Web page.

Adding Style Sheets to the Karen Stofcich Financials Site

The Karen Stofcich Financials Web site for this chapter consists of seven files, as shown in Table 8–3. The first Web page, index.html, is the frame definition file, which contains the frame layout for the Web site. The frame definition file designates the Web page, menu.html, to always appear as the navigation menu in the left frame and sets the right frame to display various Web pages, depending on the link that the user chooses. When you first open the frame definition file index.html, the Web page menu.html appears as the navigation menu in the left frame and the Web page welcome.html appears in the right frame.

Table 8–3 Files Used for Chapter 8

File Name	Purpose and Display Specifics	Changes Made in Chapter 8
index.html	• Frame definition file • Defines layout of frames on the Web page	• None
menu.html	• Provides links to all other Web pages in the Web site • Is displayed in left frame	• Add an embedded style sheet
styles1.css	• External style sheet that is linked to next four pages	• Create as external style sheet • Save as a .css file
welcome.html	• Provides welcome to Web site • Is displayed in right frame	• Add link to external style sheet • Add inline style sheet
contact.html	• Lists contact information • Is displayed in right frame	• Add link to external style sheet
meetings.html	• Lists meeting dates/topics available • Is displayed in right frame	• Add link to external style sheet
questions.html	• Displays form for questions • Is displayed in right frame	• Add link to external style sheet

In this chapter project, you will add different types of style sheets to the Web pages in the Karen Stofcich Financials Web site, to update them from the style shown in Figure 8–1a on page HTML 343 to the style shown in Figure 8–1b on the same page. To add the style sheets, you will make changes to five Web pages stored in the Chapter08/ChapterFiles folder of the Data Files for Students: welcome.html, menu.html, contact.html, meetings.html, and questions.html. You also will create an external style sheet file, styles1.css.

Plan Ahead

Creating an embedded style sheet.

You would use an embedded style sheet if you want to set the styles within a Web page. In the case of this Web site, we wanted to set the link colors and hover effect in the menu.html file only.

- **Determine which Web pages vary enough that an embedded style sheet makes sense.** You may have only one, or even just a few, Web pages in a Web site that will vary slightly from all other pages. In this case, an embedded style sheet makes sense. If there are styles that are to be repeated on that one (or a few) Web page(s), you would be better off using an embedded style sheet rather than a series of inline style sheets. For instance, if you want all paragraphs of text to have the same style within one Web page, then it makes more sense to embed that style rather than adding the style to each paragraph tag within the Web page.
- **Copy an embedded style sheet onto other Web pages.** If you have a few Web pages that should have the same style, insert the embedded sheet on one Web page, and then save, validate, and test it. Once you have verified that it works as you intend, then you can copy/paste the embedded style sheet onto the other Web pages.

(continued)

(continued)

- **Change to an external style sheet when necessary.** If you find that the style from the embedded style sheet is used on more Web pages as time goes on, you should create an external style sheet and link that onto all Web pages in which you had previously inserted an embedded style sheet.

Plan Ahead

Adding an Embedded Style Sheet

The first step in adding style sheets to the Karen Stofcich Financials Web site is to add an embedded style sheet to the navigation menu, menu.html. First, you look at the original Web pages provided in the Data Files for Students that do not use an embedded style sheet. To add an embedded style sheet, you open the file menu.html in Notepad and add the necessary code. Figure 8–3a shows the navigation menu in the default style without a style sheet, and after the embedded style sheet has been added (Figure 8–3b).

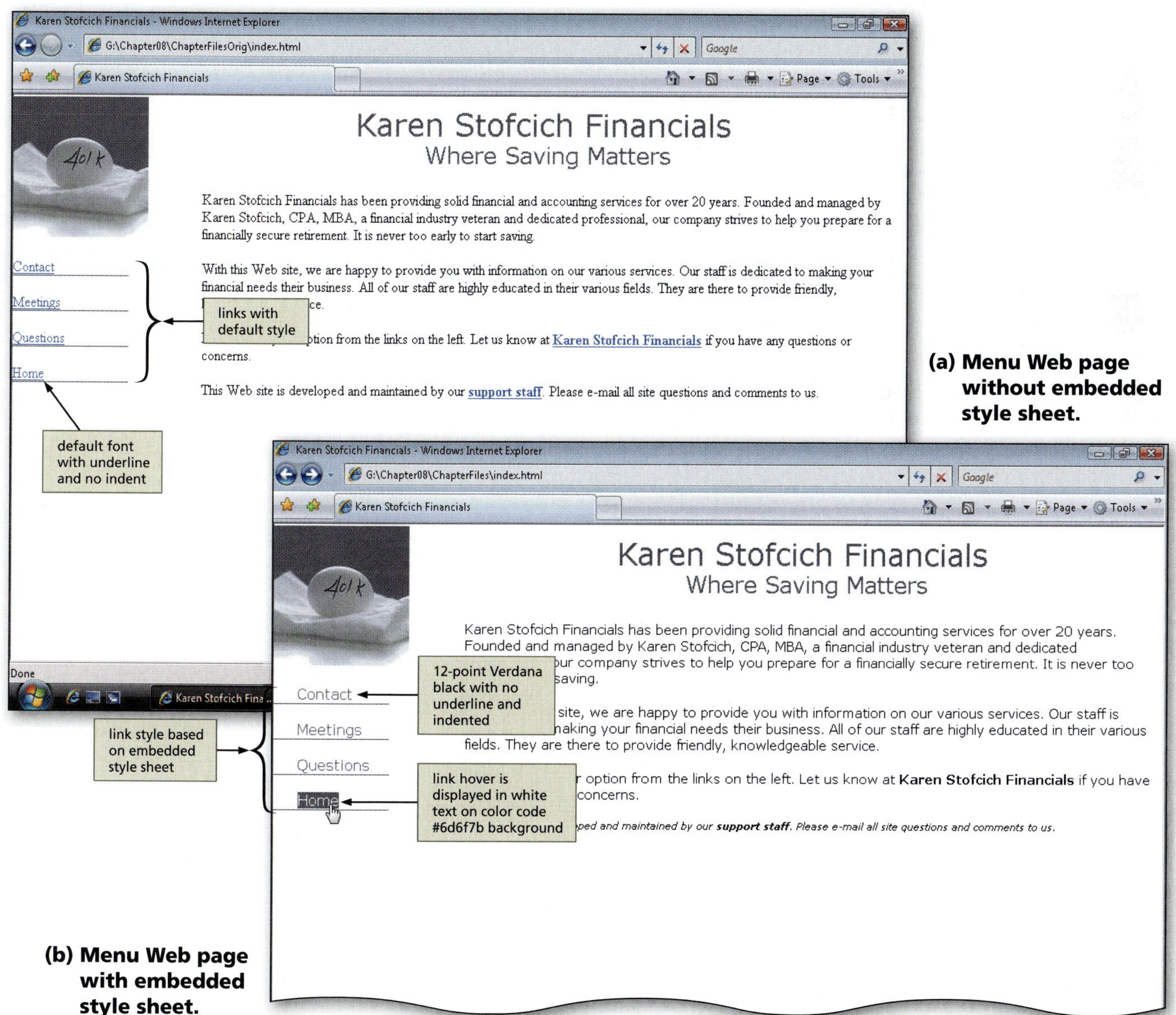

(a) Menu Web page without embedded style sheet.

(b) Menu Web page with embedded style sheet.

Figure 8–3

To Start Notepad and Open an HTML File

1

- With the USB drive plugged into your computer, start the Web browser and enter G:\Chapter08\ChapterFiles\index.html on the Address bar. Click the Contact, Meetings, Questions, and Home links to view the original Web pages provided in the Data Files for Students.
- Start Notepad and, if necessary, maximize the window.
- Navigate to the G:\Chapter08\ChapterFiles folder. If necessary, click the Files of type list arrow and then click All Files to display the menu.html file.

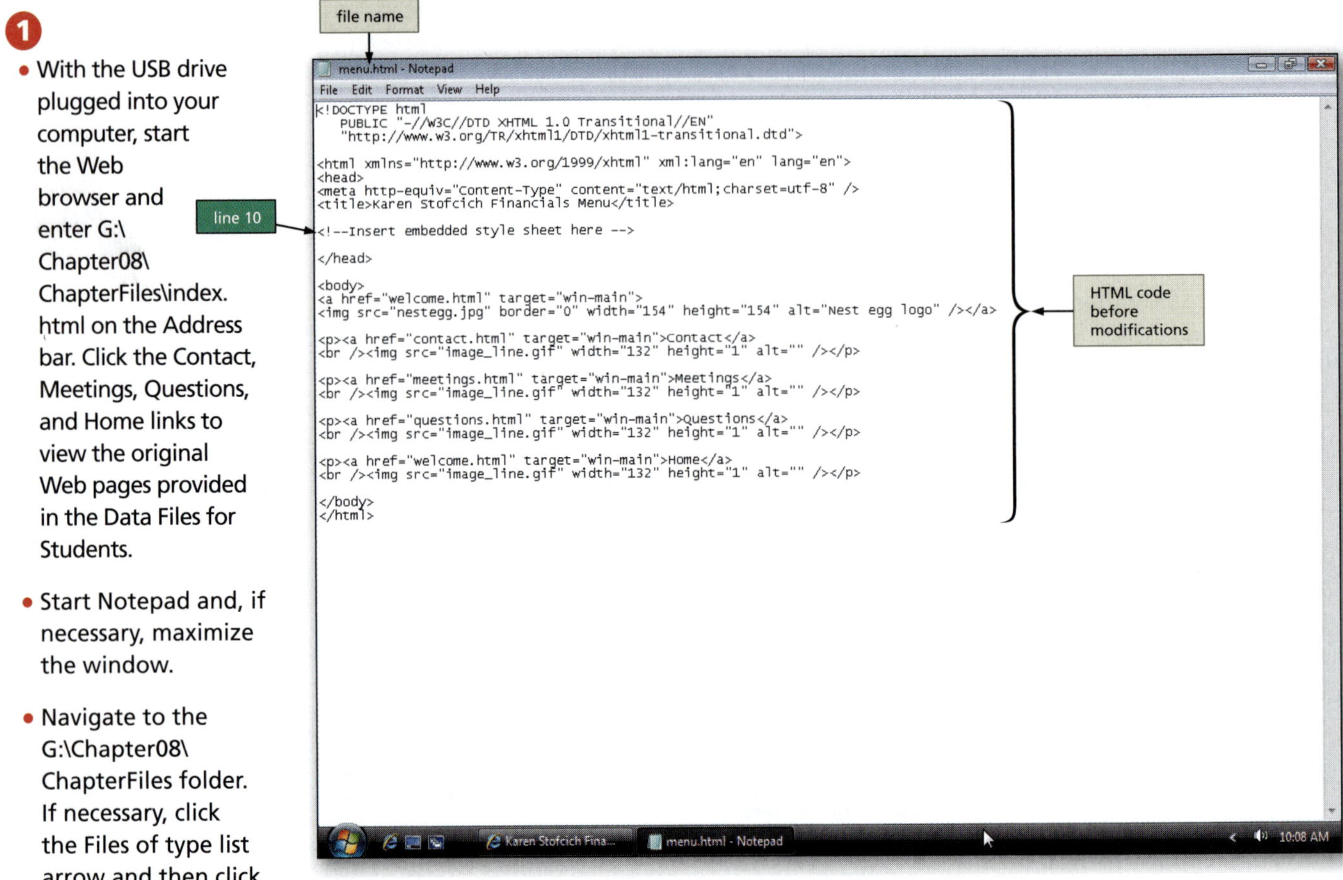

Figure 8–4

- Double-click menu.html in the list of files to open the file shown in Figure 8–4.

Setting the Paragraph Style, Link Style, and Link Hover Style

The code you will be entering for the embedded style sheet is shown in Table 8–4. Before entering the code, however, you should understand a little more about the styles you are setting.

Table 8–4 Code for an Embedded Style Sheet

Line	HTML Tag and Text
10	`<style type="text/css">`
11	`<!--`
12	
13	`p {text-indent: 20pt}`
14	
15	`a {text-decoration: none;`
16	`font-family: Verdana, Garamond;`
17	`font-size: 12pt;`
18	`color: #6d6f7b}`
19	
20	`a:hover {background: #6d6f7b;`
21	`color: white}`
22	
23	`-->`
24	`</style>`

The code for an embedded style sheet must be inserted between a start <style> tag (line 10) and an end </style> tag (line 24), which are positioned within the head element. Within the style tag container, Web developers generally follow the coding practice to add an HTML start comment code (line 11) and end comment code (line 23). The beginning and ending HTML comment lines hide any script language that a browser cannot interpret. Inserting these comment lines ensures that, if a browser does not support CSS, the browser will not try to interpret the code within the beginning and ending comment lines.

The first style statement is in line 13. This statement,

```
p {text-indent: 20pt}
```

indents the first word of each paragraph 20 points from the left edge of the browser window to make the navigation menu page look less cramped and unattractive. In addition to the points value used here, the text-indent property allows you to specify a fixed value in inches, centimeters, or pixels. You also can specify a relative value for a text indent using a percentage as the value. For example, the style statement

```
p {text-indent: 10%}
```

indents the first line of each paragraph 10 percent of the total width of the screen. Because the percentage indent is based on the total width of the screen, the indent widens when the screen is widened.

In general, paragraphs stand out better when they are indented from the rest of the text. In standard text applications, paragraphs generally are indented five spaces. On a Web page, you can use the text-indent declaration to set the value for the indent.

The next section of code in the embedded style sheet (lines 15 through 18 in Table 8–4) changes the style of the links in the menu page. The style statement uses the selector a and a series of property-value statements in the declaration to define the text decoration, font family, font size, and font color for all links.

As you have learned, links have three states (normal, visited, and active). You can change the style of the three states individually by using the selectors a:link, a:visited, or a:active, or use the selector a to set a style for all link states. In this chapter project, the selector a is used to change all link states to the same style.

BTW Word Spacing
The word-spacing property is a good way to add additional space between words. You can use any of the length units including inches, centimeters, millimeters, points, picas, ems, x-height, and pixels.

Setting the text-decoration property to a value of none (line 15) will remove the underline from all links. You also can set the text-decoration property to the following:

- **blink** — causes the text to blink on and off
- **line-through** — places a line through the middle of the text
- **overline** — places a line above the text
- **underline** — places a line below the text

If you want to apply two different text styles to a link, you can specify two text-decoration values, separating the choices with a space. For example, to give links a style with both an underline and an overline, you would add the property-value statement:

```
{text-decoration: underline overline}
```

to the embedded style sheet.

The font-family property (line 16) allows you to define a font for use on a Web page. In this embedded style sheet, the font-family property is set to two different values: Verdana and Garamond. Line 17 sets the size of all links to a 12-point font. Line 18 sets the color of all links to #6d6f7b.

In general, it is good practice to specify more than one font-family value. If the first font is not available on the user's computer, the browser will display text in the second font. If neither of the fonts is available, the browser will display text in the default font.

BTW Font Families
You also can specify font-weight using numerical values from 100 to 900. Normal text that is not bold has a value of 400. Each larger number is at least as bold as the one above it, and 900 is the boldest option of the font. The browser determines how bold each value is as it is displaying the Web page.

To specify more than one value for a font-family property, separate the font-family values with commas. Also, if you want to use a font family with a name that has spaces (such as Times New Roman or Courier New), you must put the font-family name in quotation marks. The resulting code would have

```
{font-family: "Times New Roman", Verdana}
```

as the style statement.

The final section of the embedded style sheet (lines 20 and 21) defines the style of the link:hover property. As you have learned, the link:hover property defines the way a link appears when a mouse pointer points to, or hovers over, the link. In this chapter project, the selector a:hover is used to change the hover state of all links. The code in lines 20 and 21 of Table 8–4 sets the link background to appear in color code `#6d6f7b` and the text to appear in white when the mouse hovers over the link. Using a link:hover style gives the menu page an aspect of interactivity.

To Add an Embedded Style Sheet

To add the embedded style sheet shown in Table 8–4 to the Web page, menu.html, the CSS code for the style sheet is entered directly in the header section of the HTML code for the Web page.

The following step illustrates how to add an embedded style sheet to the Web page menu.html.

1

- Highlight the comment <!-- Insert embedded style sheet here -->, on line 10 and then press the DELETE key.
- Enter the CSS code shown in Table 8–4 (Figure 8–5).

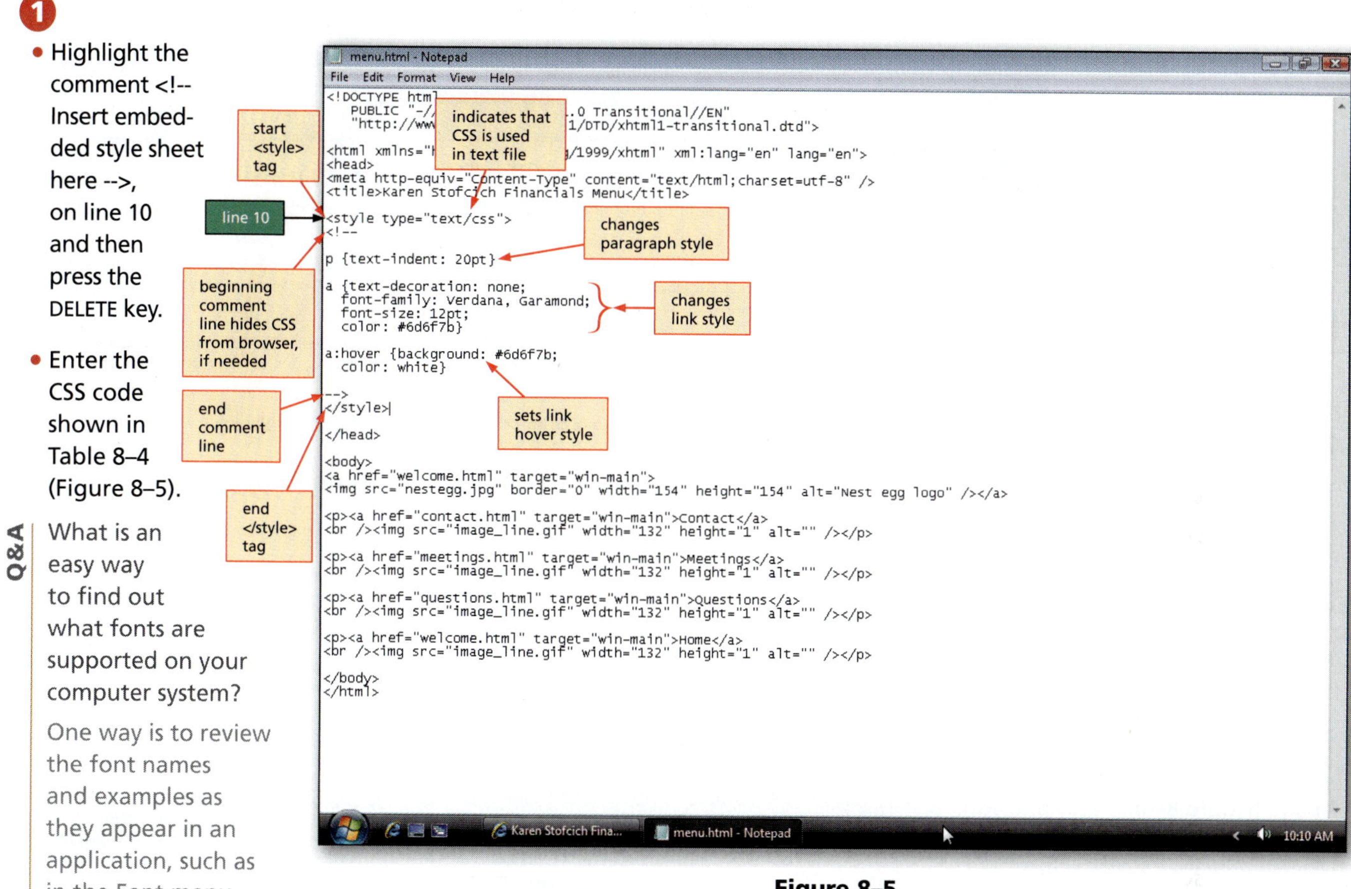

Figure 8–5

Q&A

What is an easy way to find out what fonts are supported on your computer system?

One way is to review the font names and examples as they appear in an application, such as in the Font menu in Microsoft Word. You may want to try different fonts and sizes in an application such as Word to see what they look like. You can save a document as a Web page from Word and view it in the browser as well.

Q&A

Why would I want to use the "hover" technique for links?

It adds a bit of interactivity and a different look when the background and font changes colors as the mouse hovers over a link.

Q&A

I notice that the borders of the table and the background of the hover are the same gray color as in the company "nestegg" logo. How did you figure out which color code to use?

To find a specific color, open the image file in a graphic editing software product such as Adobe Photoshop. Click a tool that allows you to select a color to use, such as the Text tool. Once the tool color selection is picked, click the color you want in the graphic image. In Photoshop, the Color Picker dialog box shows you the color code for the color you have clicked.

To Save, Validate, and View an HTML File

After you have added the embedded style sheet to the menu.html Web page, you should save the HTML file, and view the Web page to review the style changes. Before you can view the Web page to review the style changes, you must save the HTML file with the embedded style sheet.

1

- With the USB drive plugged into your computer click File on the menu bar and then click Save. If necessary, type `menu.html` in the File name text box.
- Validate the Web page using the W3C validation service.
- Open the index.html file in the Web browser to show the completed navigation menu as shown on the left side of the index.html Web page (Figure 8–6).

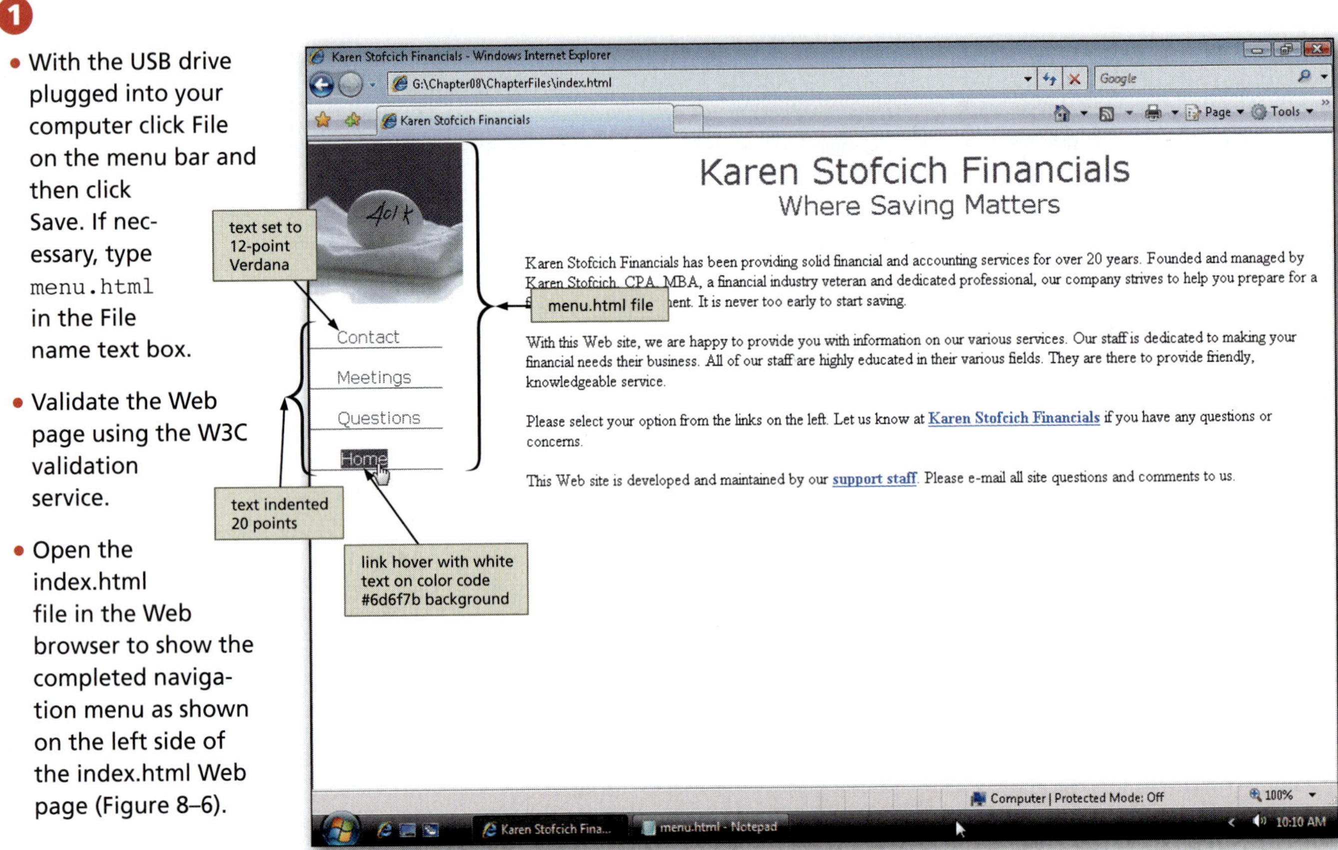

Figure 8–6

To Print an HTML File and Web Page

- Print the Web page from the browser.
- Click the menu.html - Notepad button on the taskbar.
- Click File on the menu bar and then click Print on the File menu.
- Click the Print button in the Print dialog box to print the HTML code (Figure 8–7).

```
<!DOCTYPE html
  PUBLIC "-//W3C//DTD XHTML 1.0 Transitional//EN"
  "http://www.w3.org/TR/xhtml1/DTD/xhtml1transitional.dtd">

<html xmlns="http://www.w3.org/1999/xhtml" xml:lang="en" lang="en">
<head>
<meta http-equiv="Content-Type" content="text/html;charset=utf-8" />
<title>Karen Stofcich Financials Menu</title>

<style type="text/css">
<!--

p {text-indent: 20pt}

a {text-decoration: none;
  font-family: Verdana, Garamond;
  font-size: 12pt;
  color: #6d6f7b}

a:hover {background: #6d6f7b;
  color: white}

-->
</style>

</head>

<body>
<a href="welcome.html" target="win-main">
<img src="nestegg.jpg" border="0" width="154" height="154" alt="Nest egg logo" /></a>

<p><a href="contact.html" target="win-main">Contact</a>
<br /><img src="image_line.gif" width="132" height="1" alt="" /></p>

<p><a href="meetings.html" target="win-main">Meetings</a>
<br /><img src="image_line.gif" width="132" height="1" alt="" /></p>

<p><a href="questions.html" target="win-main">Questions</a>
<br /><img src="image_line.gif" width="132" height="1" alt="" /></p>

<p><a href="welcome.html" target="win-main">Home</a>
<br /><img src="image_line.gif" width="132" height="1" alt="" /></p>

</body>
</html>
```

Figure 8–7

Plan Ahead

Creating an external style sheet.

The external style sheet is the most powerful and lowest precedence style sheet. With this style sheet, you can easily create a common look across a Web site by creating the external (.css) style sheet and linking it onto all other Web pages.

- **Create the external style sheet.** The first step is to create the file itself. This file, which contains all of the style statements that you want, has to be saved with a file name extension of .css. Make sure to store this file in the same folder as the other Web pages.
- **Link the external style sheet onto the Web pages.** The second step is to link the external style sheet (.css file) onto the Web pages where you want it. The link statement is placed between the <head> and </head> tags.

Adding an External Style Sheet

External style sheets are ideal for giving multiple pages in a Web site a common look or style. Instead of displaying styles based on an embedded style sheet added to each Web page, each Web page in the Web site references the same external style sheet for style information, thus ensuring each Web page uses a consistent style. In the Karen Stofcich Financials Web site, for example, each of the four main pages (welcome.html, contact.html, meetings.html, and questions.html) can be linked to the same external style sheet to define a common style.

An external style sheet is a separate text file that contains the style statements that define how the Web page elements will appear. Table 8–5 shows the style statements for an external style sheet for the Karen Stofcich Financials Web site. After you create the text file with all of the desired style statements, you save the file with the file extension .css to identify it as a CSS file. You then use a <link /> tag to link the external style sheet to any Web pages to which you want to apply the style.

Table 8–5 Code for an External Style Sheet

Line	HTML Tag and Text
1	`body {margin: 8pt;`
2	`background-color: #ffffff}`
3	
4	`a {text-decoration: none;`
5	`color: black}`
6	
7	`p {font-family: Verdana, Garamond;`
8	`font-size: 11pt}`
9	
10	`table {font-family: Verdana, Garamond;`
11	`font-size: 10pt;`
12	`border-color: #6d6f7b;`
13	`border-style: double}`
14	
15	`th {background-color: #6d6f7b;`
16	`color: white;`
17	`text-align: left}`
18	
19	`caption {font-size: 8pt;`
20	`font-style: italic}`

Setting the Body, Link, Paragraph, and Table Styles

The CSS code for the external style sheet shown in Table 8–5 defines a new style for four main elements on a Web page: body, links, paragraphs, and tables. For example, the first style statement on line 1 is entered as:

```
body {margin: 8pt}
```

to change the margin of the Web page body to 8 points. The margin is the amount of transparent space between elements on the page. Because it uses the margin property, the style statement sets the margin for all sides of the Web page. If desired, you also can set the margins individually for the top, bottom, left, or right of a page by using the properties margin-top, margin-bottom, margin-left, or margin-right, respectively. Like the text-indent property, the margin property can be set as a fixed length in points, pixels, inches, or centimeters, or as a relative length based on a percentage. Line 2 sets the color of the background to #ffffff.

Lines 4 and 5 of the external style sheet set the style for all link states to have no text decoration (that is, no underline) and to be displayed in the color black. The style statement in line 7 changes the style of all paragraph text to the font family Verdana or Garamond, depending on the fonts available on the user's computer. Line 8 sets the font size to 11 point, which is slightly smaller than the font selected for the link text in the navigation menu.

The next section of CSS code, lines 10 through 20, define the styles to be applied to tables. The style statement in lines 10 through 13 is entered as:

```
table {font-family: Verdana, Garamond;
  font-size: 10pt;
  border-color: #6d6f7b;
  border-color: double}
```

to set the style for table text to complement the style used for paragraph text. The border-color is set to color code #6d6f7b with a double-line style. The style statement in lines 15 through 17 sets the table header styles. Recall that table headers are bold and centered by default. In this code, all table headers are displayed with a background color of #6d6f7b and white text. The text also will be left-aligned, rather than the default center alignment.

Finally, lines 19 and 20 set the style of all table captions to appear in an 8pt italic font. Setting the caption to italic makes the table caption text different from the text in the table itself. The font-style property also can be set to values of normal (the default style) or oblique. An oblique font — one that is slanted to the right by the browser — can be used when the font itself does not provide an italic version. If you want to change italic or oblique text back to appear in the default or normal style, you insert a property-value statement font-style: normal in the style sheet.

BTW

Line Height
Another useful CSS property gives you the ability to control line height. With the line-height property, you can control the vertical spacing between lines of text. There are three ways to add the line-height value: by number, by length unit, and by percentage. If you specify by number, the browser uses the font-size property to determine the space. You also can use em and pt to set the height by unit. Finally, you can determine the line spacing by a percentage.

To Create an External Style Sheet

After you have defined the styles you want to use for various page elements, you can create the external style sheet. To create an external style sheet, you open a new text file and enter CSS code for the style statements that define the Web page style. After coding the style statements, you save the file with the file extension .css, to identify it as a CSS file.

The following step illustrates how to create an external style sheet.

1

- If necessary, click the menu.html - Notepad button on the taskbar. Click File on the menu bar and then click New.
- Enter the CSS code as shown in Table 8–5 on page HTML 360.
- With the USB drive plugged into your computer, click File on the menu bar and then click Save As. Type `styles1.css` in the File name text box. If necessary, navigate to the G:\Chapter08\ChapterFiles folder. Click the Save button in the Save As dialog box to save the file as styles1.css (Figure 8–8).

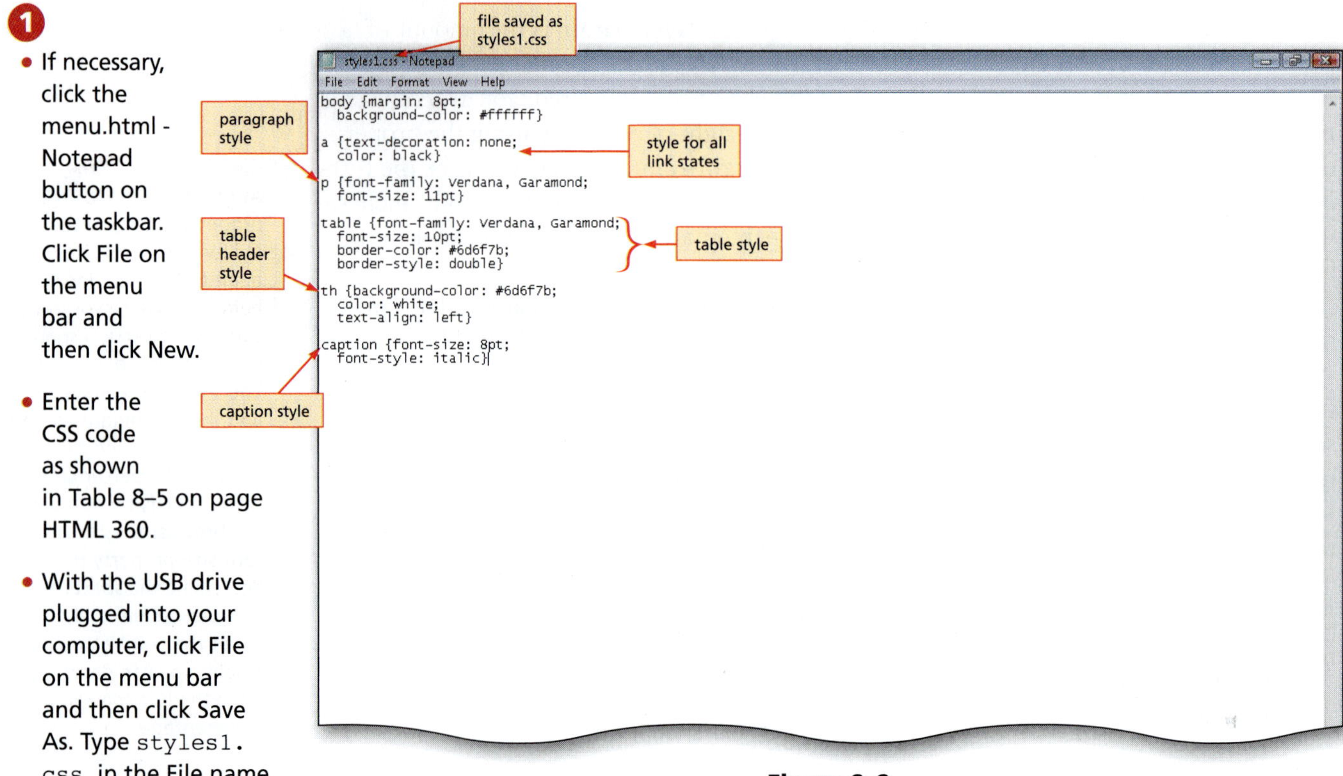

Figure 8–8

- Click the File menu, click Print on the File menu, and then click the Print button in the Print dialog box.

Q&A

What is the real benefit of using CSS?

With CSS, you can establish a standard look for all Web pages in a Web site. Using CSS, you avoid the tedious steps of adding repetitive codes to format the same types of information. Instead of making all paragraphs of text 10pt Verdana in individual <p> tags, you can define that in a .css file and link that external file to all Web pages.

Linking to an External Style Sheet

Four Web pages in the Karen Stofcich Financials Web site require the same style: welcome.html, contact.html, meetings.html, and questions.html. Linking the external style sheet to each of these Web pages gives them the same styles for margins, paragraph text, links, and tables.

To link to the external style sheet, a <link /> tag must be inserted onto each of these four Web pages. The <link /> tag used to link an external style sheet is added within the <head> tag of the Web page HTML. The general format of the <link /> tag is:

```
<link rel="stylesheet" type="text/css" href="styles1.css" />
```

where rel="stylesheet" establishes that the linked document is a style sheet, type="text/css" indicates that the CSS language is used in the text file containing the style sheet, and href="styles1.css" provides the name and location (URL) of the linked style sheet. To link a style sheet to a Web page, the <link /> tag must use "stylesheet" as the value for the rel property and text/css as the value for the type property. The URL used as the value for the href property varies, based on the name and location of the file used as the external style sheet. The URL used here indicates that the external style sheet, styles1.css, is located in the main or root directory of the Web site.

To Link to an External Style Sheet

The following steps illustrate how to add a link to an external style sheet using a <link /> tag and then save the HTML file.

- If necessary, click the styles1.css - Notepad button on the taskbar.
- With the USB drive plugged into your computer, click File on the menu bar and then click Open on the File menu.
- If necessary, navigate to the G:\Chapter08\ChapterFiles folder. Click the Files of type box arrow, and then click All Files to show all files in the Chapter08\ChapterFiles folder. Click the `contact.html` file.
- Click the Open button in the Open dialog box.

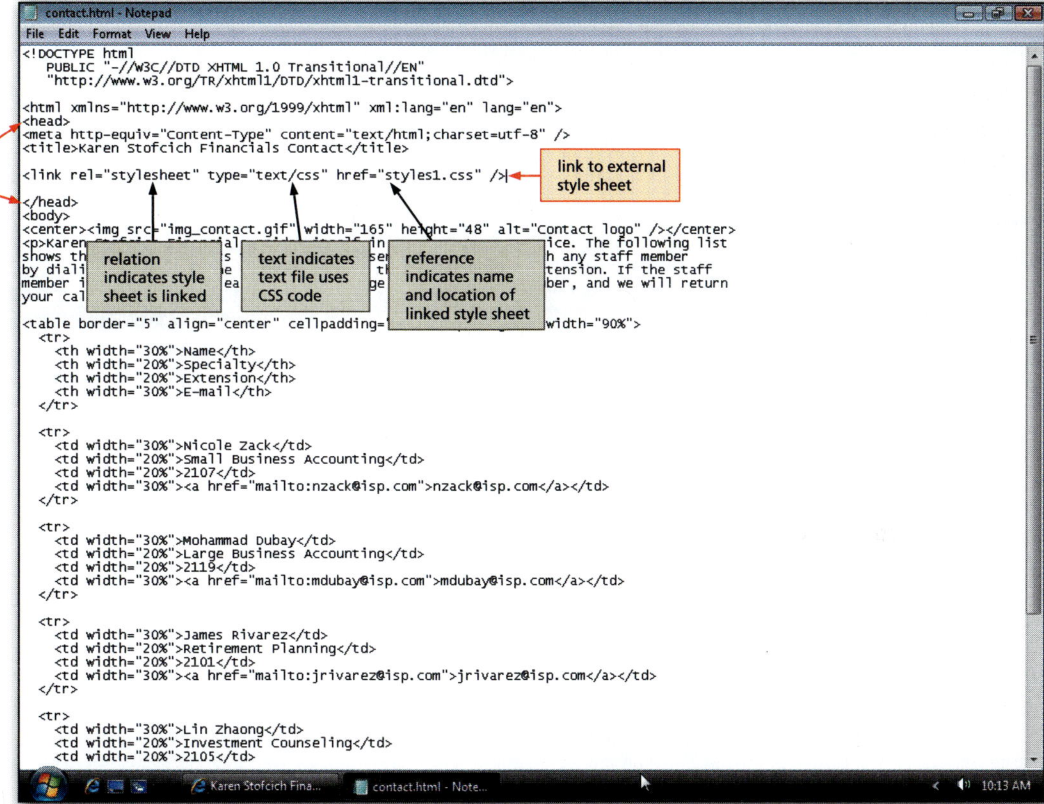

Figure 8–9

- Highlight the text, <!--Insert link statement here -->, in line 10.
- Type `<link rel="stylesheet" type="text/css" href="styles1.css" />` to enter the link to the external style sheet (Figure 8–9).

- Click File on the menu bar and then click Save on the File menu.
- Validate the Web page using the W3C service.
- Open the index.html file in the browser and click the Contact link (Figure 8–10) to see the change on the Web page.

Q&A

Is that all it takes to use an external style sheet — to insert that link statement?

Yes, that is all you need to do to use the styles identified in the external style sheet. The styles specified in the external style sheet will apply to that page, unless an embedded or inline style sheet takes precedence.

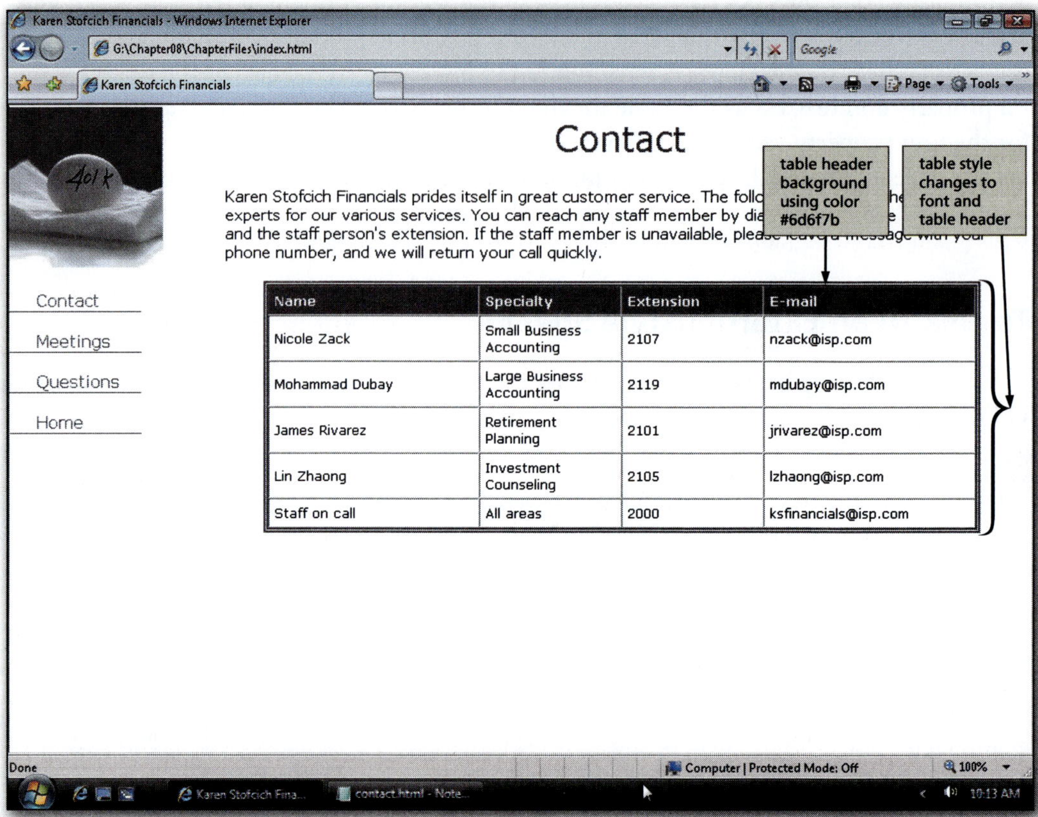

Figure 8–10

To Link the Remaining HTML Files to an External Style Sheet

You have linked the contact.html page to the external style sheet styles1.css. Now you need to link the meetings.html, questions.html, and welcome.html Web pages to the same style sheet. The following step shows how to add a <link /> tag to the remaining three Web pages and then save the files.

- If necessary, click the contact.html - Notepad button on the taskbar.
- With the USB drive plugged into your computer, click File on the menu bar and then click Open on the File menu.
- If necessary, navigate to the G:\Chapter08\ChapterFiles folder. Click the Files of type box arrow, and then click All Files to show all files in the Chapter08\ChapterFiles folder. Click the `meetings.html` file.
- Click the Open button in the Open dialog box.
- Highlight the text, <!--Insert link statement here --> on line 10.
- Type `<link rel="stylesheet" type="text/css" href="styles1.css" />` to enter the link to the external style sheet.
- Click File on the menu bar and then click Save on the File menu.
- Validate the Web page.
- One at a time, open the HTML files questions.html and welcome.html, and repeat bullets 5 through 8 to replace the placeholder text with the link tag, then save and validate the code.

Q&A

Will the table styles from the styles1.css take effect for all tables within the Web site?

As long as you insert the style sheet link statement onto the Web page, then the table styles will take effect. Remember that you can override those styles with either an embedded or an inline style sheet. You would do this if there is a table that you want to vary from all other tables in the Web site. Note that you already added an embedded style sheet to the menu.html file. If you had added table tag modifications within that embedded style sheet, those styles would have taken precedence over this external style sheet.

Working with Classes in Style Sheets

In some Web sites, you might need to have more control over the style on a Web page. For example, rather than having all paragraphs of text appear in the same style, you might want the style of the first paragraph on a page to be different from the other paragraphs of text. To gain more control for these purposes, you can define specific elements of an HTML file as a category, or **class**. You then can create a specific style for each class. Using classes in style sheets thus allows you to apply styles to HTML tags selectively. Using a class, for example, you could apply one style to a beginning paragraph and a different style to a closing paragraph on the same Web page.

Defining and using classes in a style sheet is a two-step process. First, any elements that belong to the class are marked by adding the tag:

```
class="classname"
```

where classname is the identifier or name of the class. To define a class that includes any beginning paragraphs, for example, you would enter the code:

```
<p class="beginning">
```

where beginning is the classname and the <p> tag indicates that the class is a specific type of paragraph style. Any word can be used as a classname, as long as it does not contain spaces. In general, however, you should use descriptive names that illustrate the purpose of a class (for example, beginning, legallanguage, or copyrighttext), rather than names that describe the appearance of the class (for example, bluetext, largereditalic, or boldsmallarial). Using names that describe the purpose makes the code easier to read and more flexible.

After you have named the classes, you can use the names in a selector and define a specific style for the class. For example, within the <style> tags in an embedded or external style sheet, you enter a style statement in the format:

```
p.beginning {color: red;
 font: 20pt}
```

where the p indicates that the class applies to a specific category of the paragraph tag and beginning is the classname. The tag and the classname are separated by a period. Together, the tag and the classname make up the selector for the style statement. The declaration then lists the property-value statements that should be applied to elements in the class.

For instance, if you want to display the beginning paragraph text in a 20-point red font, you would add a style statement like the one shown in the sample code in Figure 8–11a and then use the tag, <p class="beginning">, to apply the style defined by the declaration associated with the p.beginning selector. If the paragraph <p> tag is used without the classname, the paragraph appears in the default style or other style as defined by a style sheet.

In addition to the style for the beginning paragraphs, Figure 8–11a shows an example of HTML code with classes defined for and applied to the middle and end paragraphs. Figure 8–11b shows how the resulting Web page appears in the browser.

Classes allow you to have more control over the style used for different sections of a Web page. One drawback is that classes can be defined for use only in embedded or external style sheets. Because the purpose of using classes is to format a group of elements at once, not individual elements, classes do not work in inline style sheets.

BTW

Classes
One very important advanced CSS topic is classes. With classes, you can create several variations for any one tag. You might utilize three different classes of paragraphs, and each one can have a different style sheet declaration. You can name classes anything that you want, but make sure to use a period before the class name in the style sheets rule.

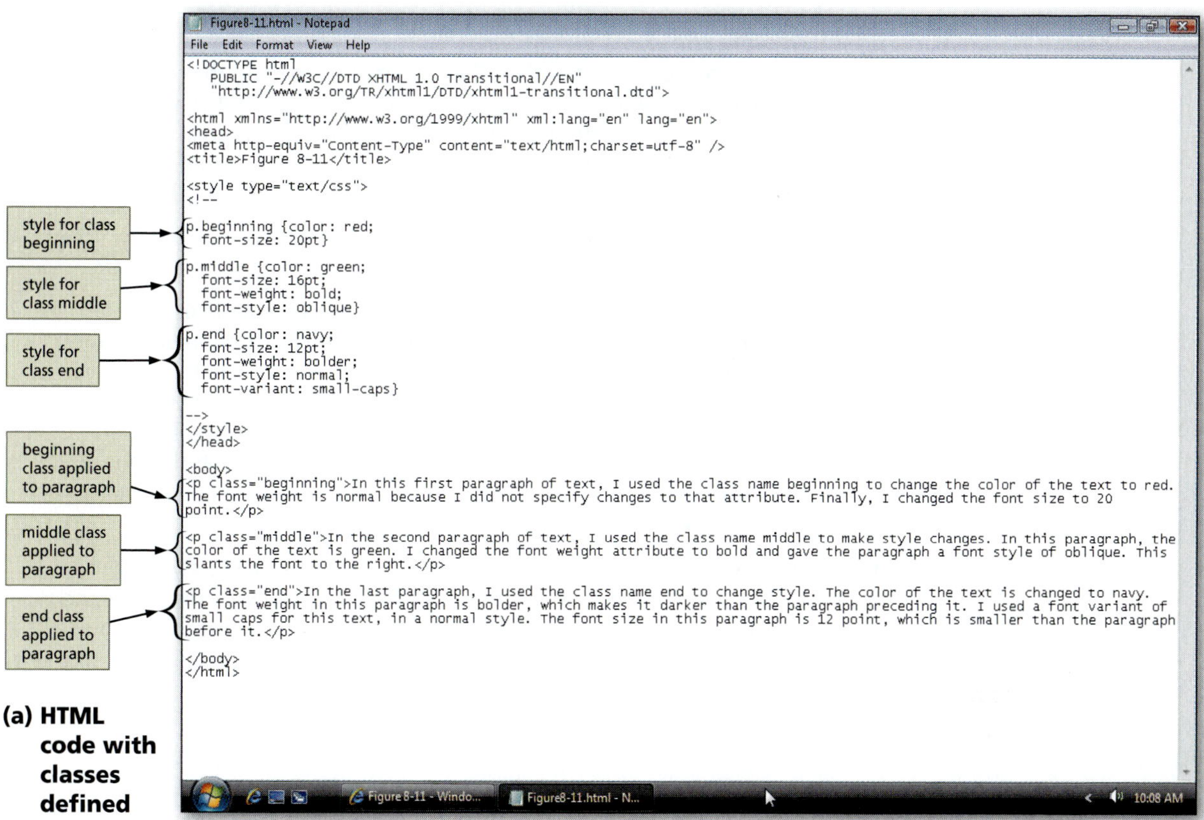


```
<!DOCTYPE html
   PUBLIC "-//W3C//DTD XHTML 1.0 Transitional//EN"
   "http://www.w3.org/TR/xhtml1/DTD/xhtml1-transitional.dtd">

<html xmlns="http://www.w3.org/1999/xhtml" xml:lang="en" lang="en">
<head>
<meta http-equiv="Content-Type" content="text/html;charset=utf-8" />
<title>Figure 8-11</title>

<style type="text/css">
<!--

p.beginning {color: red;
   font-size: 20pt}

p.middle {color: green;
   font-size: 16pt;
   font-weight: bold;
   font-style: oblique}

p.end {color: navy;
   font-size: 12pt;
   font-weight: bolder;
   font-style: normal;
   font-variant: small-caps}

-->
</style>
</head>

<body>
<p class="beginning">In this first paragraph of text, I used the class name beginning to change the color of the text to red.
The font weight is normal because I did not specify changes to that attribute. Finally, I changed the font size to 20
point.</p>

<p class="middle">In the second paragraph of text, I used the class name middle to make style changes. In this paragraph, the
color of the text is green. I changed the font weight attribute to bold and gave the paragraph a font style of oblique. This
slants the font to the right.</p>

<p class="end">In the last paragraph, I used the class name end to change style. The color of the text is changed to navy.
The font weight in this paragraph is bolder, which makes it darker than the paragraph preceding it. I used a font variant of
small caps for this text, in a normal style. The font size in this paragraph is 12 point, which is smaller than the paragraph
before it.</p>

</body>
</html>
```

(a) HTML code with classes defined

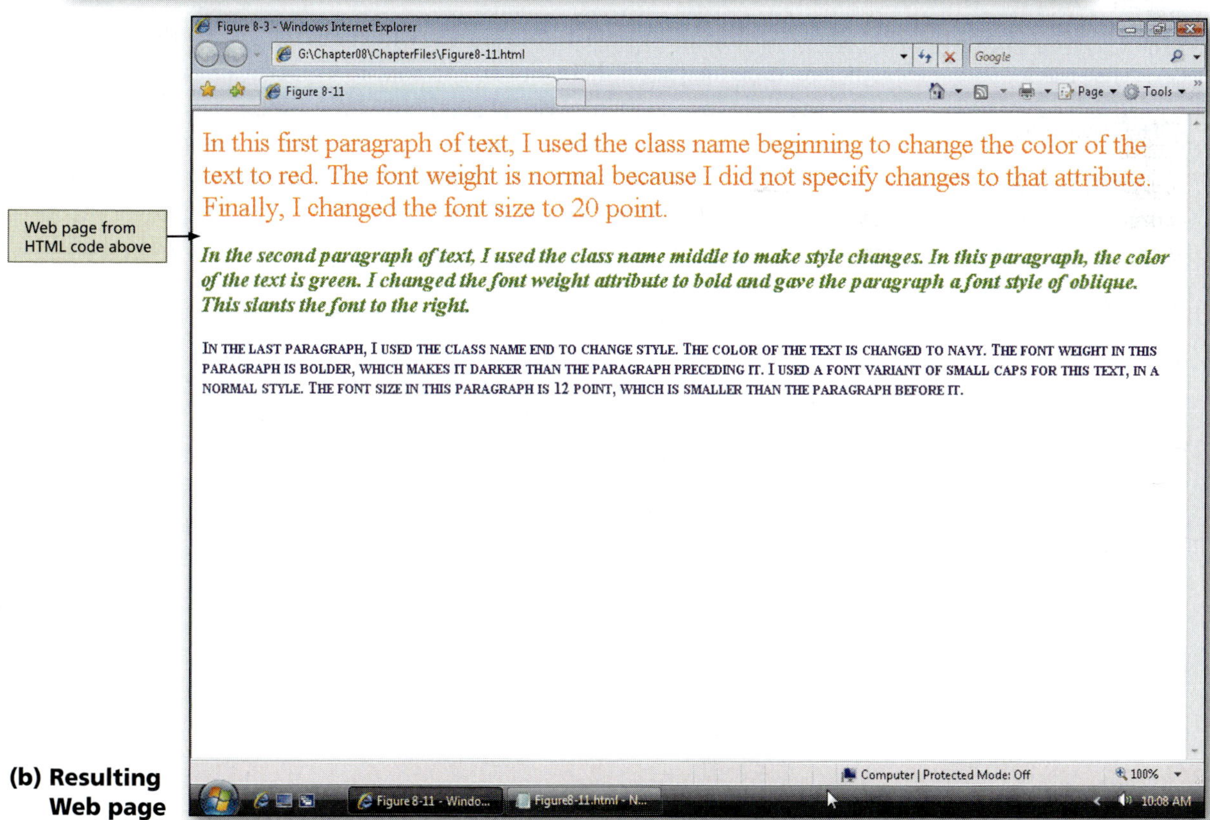

(b) Resulting Web page

Figure 8–11

Plan Ahead

Creating an inline style sheet.

An inline style sheet takes precedence over the other two styles, meaning that even if you have an external style sheet that is linked to a Web page, or a paragraph style in an embedded style sheet, the inline style would be the style that is displayed. Inline style sheets are used within individual tags, so you have to make sure that you use them when needed.

- **Utilize inline style sheets to set pieces of a Web page apart from the rest.** If you have a component of a Web page that needs to be different than all others, an inline style sheet is a good option.
- **Graduate to embedded or external style sheets when necessary.** Sometimes you find that the inline style that you used for one component of a Web page is something that you want throughout the Web page or even throughout the Web site. In that case, you should change from the inline style sheet to an embedded or even external style sheet. For instance, if you utilize a particular font for one paragraph of one page, and you determine that it is a style that you would like to see throughout the Web site, you could make that an external style sheet rather than copying/pasting the same inline style to all paragraphs on a Web page.
- **Use inline style sheets to test styles.** When you are first beginning to use style sheets, it might be helpful to use inline style sheets to test different styles. You can change the look of certain tags (i.e., paragraphs or tables) with inline style sheets just to see how they look.

BTW

CSS Negative

The only bad news about using CSS is that not all browsers support Cascading Style Sheets. Therefore, not all users will be viewing the same style on your Web pages. The good news is, over 90% of users use a browser that does support CSS. For specific details, you need to test your Web pages with multiple browsers.

Adding an Inline Style Sheet

The Karen Stofcich Financials Web site now includes two of the three types of style sheets: an embedded style sheet and an external style sheet. The embedded style sheet defines the style for the menu Web page, menu.html, which is displayed in the left frame. The external style sheet is linked to and defines the style of the main Web pages that are displayed in the right frame. To complete the new design for the Karen Stofcich Financials Web site, one additional type of style sheet — an inline style sheet — is needed to define a paragraph style that will appear only on the Welcome page that users see when they first visit the site.

The last paragraph on the welcome.html Web page provides basic information about Web site development and support. You would like the style for this paragraph to use a smaller font size with an italic style, so that it does not distract users from the more important information on the Welcome page.

An inline style sheet allows you to add a style to an individual HTML tag, such as a heading or paragraph. The style changes only that specific tag and does not affect other tags in the document. Because an inline style sheet also overrides the styles defined in embedded and external style sheets, it is ideal to use inline style sheets for making style changes to a single paragraph. For example, based on the external style sheet linked to the page, all text is displayed in 11-point normal font (Figure 8–12a). Using an inline style sheet, the external style sheet can be overridden to set the style of that one paragraph to be displayed with a font style of italic and a font size of 8 points, as shown in Figure 8–12b.

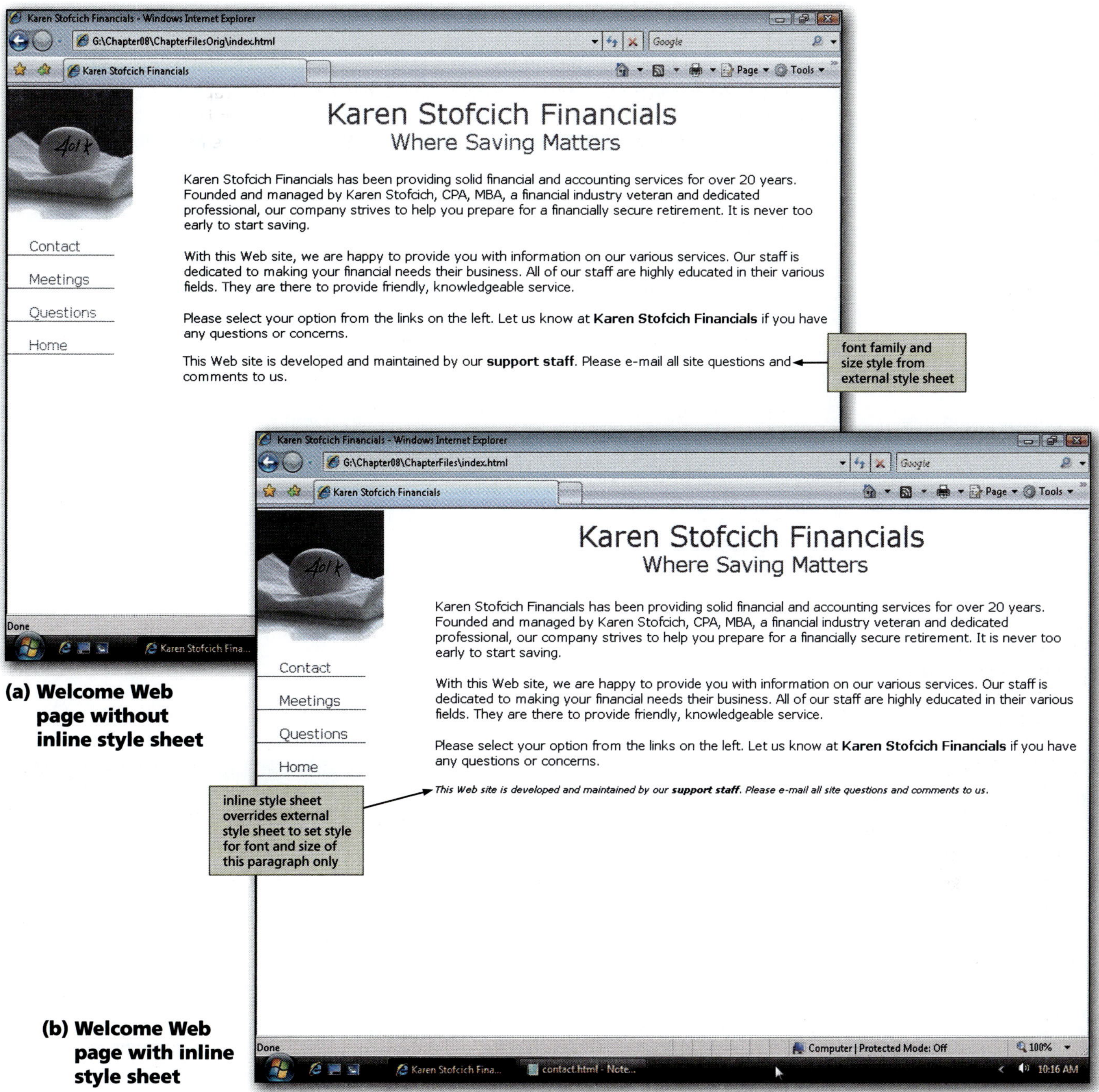

Figure 8–12

To add an inline style sheet, you enter the declaration within the HTML tag to which you want to apply the style. For example, for the Welcome Web page, the format of the inline style sheet is:

```
<p style="font-style: italic; font-size: 8pt">
```

with the HTML tag <p> functioning as the selector and the remainder of the style sheet functioning as the declaration.

To Add an Inline Style Sheet

The following step shows how to add an inline style sheet to the Welcome Web page.

1

- If necessary, click the welcome.html - Notepad button on the taskbar so the file welcome.html is displayed.
- Click immediately to the right of the p in the <p> tag on line 30. Press the SPACEBAR and then type `style="font-style: italic; font-size: 8pt"` to insert the inline style sheet (Figure 8–13).
- Click File on the menu bar and then click Save.
- Validate the Web page.

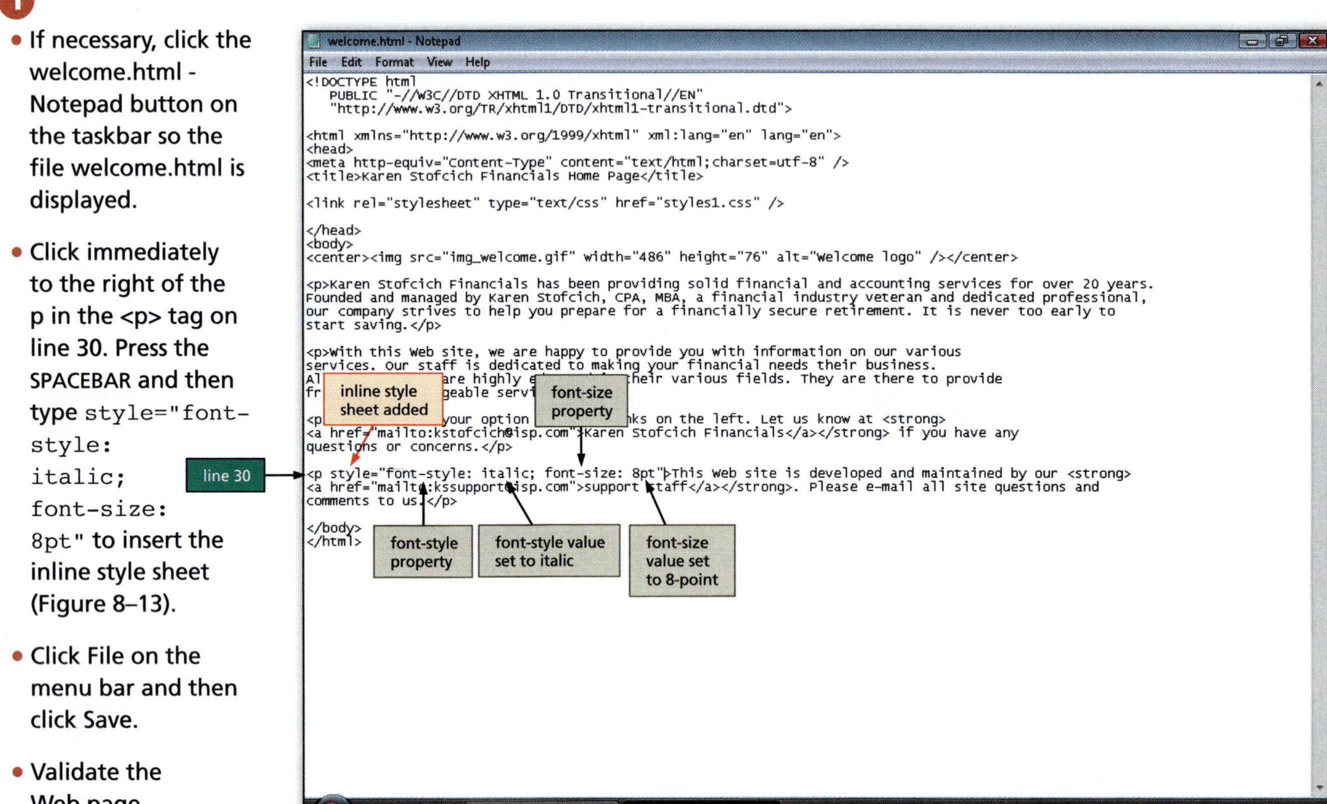

Figure 8–13

Q&A What is a good rule of thumb to use when determining whether to use an inline, embedded, or external style sheet?

If you want to change the style of all of the paragraphs on a Web page, it makes more sense to use an embedded style sheet. If you want that same style throughout the entire Web site (i.e., all paragraphs on all Web pages), then you should use an external style sheet. If you want to change a single feature on one page, an inline style sheet might be best.

Q&A Can I use an inline style sheet for most HTML tags?

The inline style sheet can be used on most HTML tags in which style is appropriate, such as tags for paragraphs and tables.

Viewing and Printing Framed Web Pages

Having added links to the external style sheet to all of the Web pages and an inline style sheet to the Welcome Web page, you should view the HTML files in your browser to confirm that the styles defined in the style sheets appear correctly on the Web page. To view the style changes in the menu.html Web page, you must open the frame definition file, index.html.

After viewing the Web page in the browser, you should print a copy of each Web page for reference. Because the Web pages are displayed in frames defined by the frame definition file index.html, several printing options are available. The Print dialog box default is to print all frames individually. To print the Web pages as they are displayed in the browser, select the As laid out on screen option.

To View and Print Framed Web Pages

By clicking the links to display the four Web pages in the main frame on the right, you can verify that the styles defined by the external style sheet styles1.css appear correctly on each of the four Web pages with the <link /> tag. You also can confirm that the paragraph style defined by the inline style sheet is displayed correctly on the Web page welcome.html. Perform the following step to view and print all of the framed Web pages in the Web site as laid out on screen.

1

- Click the browser button on the taskbar.
- Open the index.html file in the browser (Figure 8–14).
- Click the File menu, and then click Print.
- When the Print dialog box is displayed, click the Options tab.
- Click As laid out on screen and then click the Print button.
- One at a time, click the links, Contact, Meetings, and Questions, and repeat bullets 3 through 5.

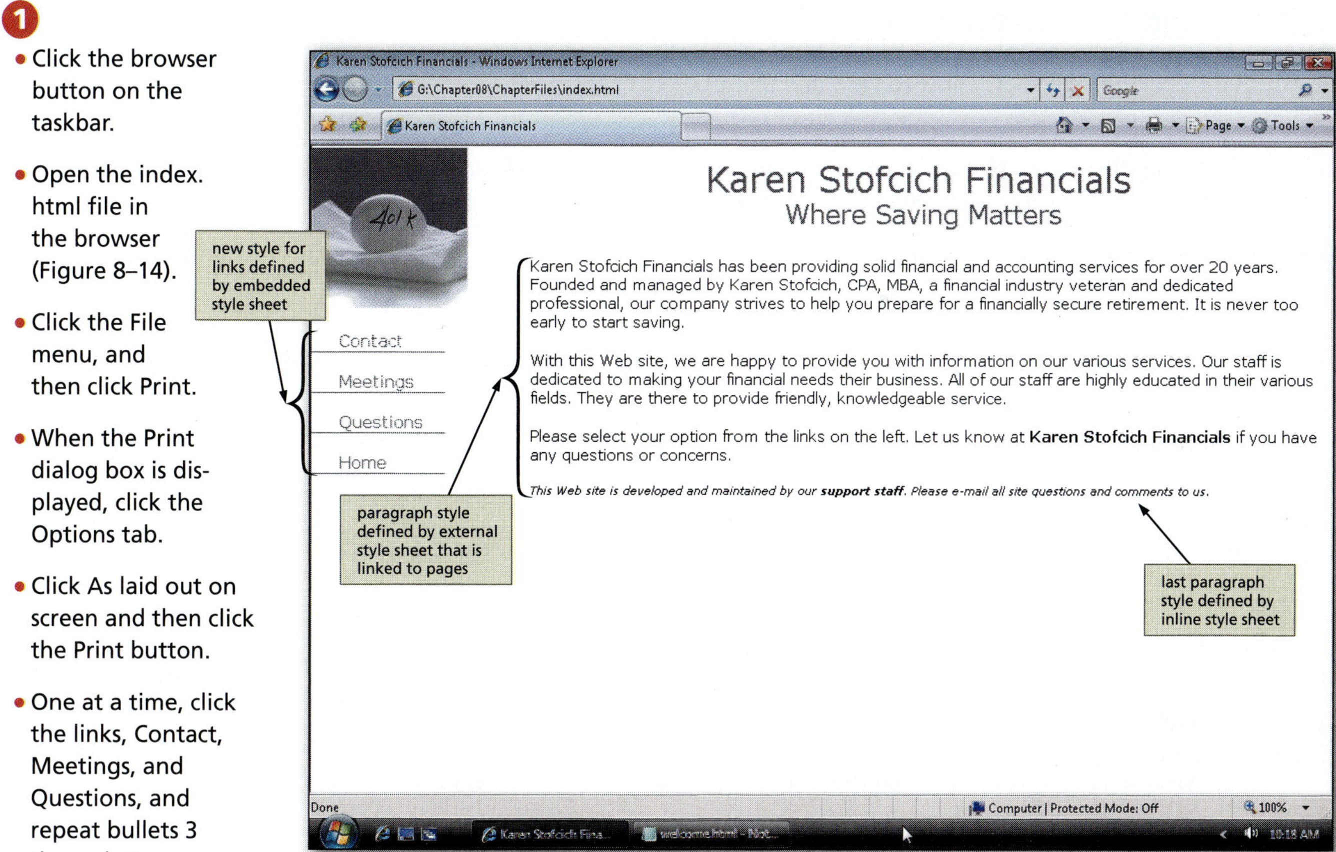

Figure 8–14

Q&A

My external style sheet does not work. What have I done wrong?

Make sure that you saved the external style sheet (the .css file) in the same folder in which you have stored the .html files. Also make sure that you have used straight (not curly) quotation marks to enclose your style definitions, and check that you have separated multiple property definitions with a semicolon.

Viewing and Printing HTML Files

After verifying that each Web page is displayed correctly in the browser window, you should print the HTML file for each Web page for reference. Because these Web pages are in a frame structure, printing the HTML source code requires you to right-click the Web page that you want to print in the frame and then click View Source on the shortcut menu to open the Web page file in Notepad. After the file is open in Notepad, you then can print the HTML file.

To print the HTML files for all the Web pages that are displayed in the right frame — Contact, Meetings, Questions, and Home (Welcome) — you must click each of the four menu links to display the page in the browser and then follow the steps outlined below. If you discover a problem with the Web page when you view it in the browser or when you view the HTML source code in Notepad, use Notepad to make the necessary changes in the HTML file and then save it before you print the HTML code. After the HTML files are printed, you can use the printed HTML files as a reference for style sheet formatting, selectors, and declarations.

To View and Print HTML Files

The following step shows how to view and print the HTML files.

- If necessary, click the Karen Stofcich Financials browser button on the taskbar. If necessary, click the Home link in the menu frame so the Welcome Web page (welcome.html) is displayed in the right frame.
- Right-click anywhere in the right frame except on a link.
- Click View Source on the shortcut menu.
- After the file welcome.html is opened in Notepad, click the File menu, then click Print. Click the Print button in the Print dialog box.
- Click the browser button on the taskbar, click the Contact link, and then repeat bullets 2 through 4.
- Click the browser button on the taskbar, click the Meetings link, and then repeat bullets 2 through 4.
- Click the browser button on the taskbar, click the Questions link, and then repeat bullets 2 through 4.

To Quit Notepad and a Browser

After you have viewed and printed the HTML files, the chapter project is complete.

- Close all open browser windows.
- Click the Close button on the Notepad window title bar.

Chapter Summary

In this chapter, you have learned how to add embedded, external, and inline style sheets to give your Web pages a consistent and polished look, and to make formatting changes easier and faster across Web pages. The items listed below include all the new HTML skills you have learned in this chapter.

1. Add an Embedded Style Sheet (HTML 357)
2. Create an External Style Sheet (HTML 362)
3. Link to an External Style Sheet (HTML 363)
4. Link the Remaining HTML Files to an External Style Sheet (HTML 365)
5. Add an Inline Style Sheet (HTML 370)

Learn It Online

Test your knowledge of chapter content and key terms.

Instructions: To complete the Learn It Online exercises, start your browser, click the Address bar, and then enter the Web address `scsite.com/html5e/learn`. When the HTML Learn It Online page is displayed, click the link for the exercise you want to complete and read the instructions.

Chapter Reinforcement TF, MC, and SA

A series of true/false, multiple choice, and short answer questions that test your knowledge of the chapter content.

Flash Cards

An interactive learning environment where you identify chapter key terms associated with displayed definitions.

Practice Test

A series of multiple choice questions that test your knowledge of chapter content and key terms.

Who Wants To Be a Computer Genius?

An interactive game that challenges your knowledge of chapter content in the style of a television quiz show.

Wheel of Terms

An interactive game that challenges your knowledge of chapter key terms in the style of the television show *Wheel of Fortune*.

Crossword Puzzle Challenge

A crossword puzzle that challenges your knowledge of key terms presented in the chapter.

Apply Your Knowledge

Reinforce the skills and apply the concepts you learned in this chapter.

Creating a Sign Web Site

Instructions: Start Notepad and a browser. Using your browser, open the apply8-1.html file from the Chapter08\Apply folder of the Data Files for Students. See the inside back cover of this book for instructions on downloading the Data Files for Students, or contact your instructor for information about accessing the required files. The apply8-1.html file is the frame definition file that will display the apply8-1menu.html file in the upper frame and the apply8-1home.html file in the lower frame. The apply8-1menu.html and apply8-1home.html files are partially completed HTML files. Figure 8–15 on the next page shows the Apply Your Knowledge Web page as it should appear in the browser after the necessary code is added.

Continued >

Apply Your Knowledge *continued*

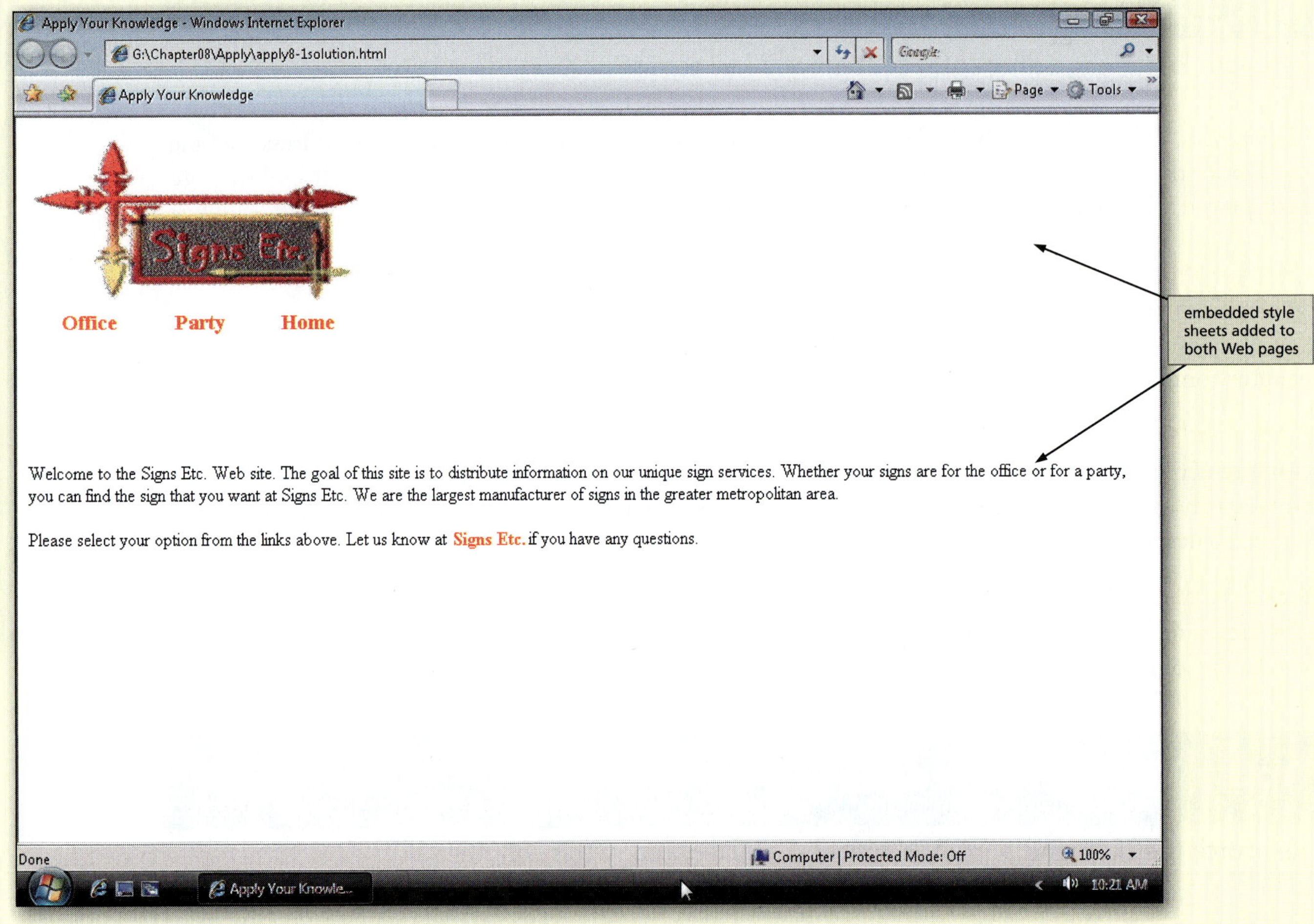

Figure 8–15

Perform the following tasks:

1. Open the apply8-1.html file in Notepad. Save the apply8-1.html file as apply8-1solution.html. Examine the HTML files within the frames and their appearance in the browser.
2. Right-click the menu page (top frame) and click View Source to view the HTML code of apply8-1menu.html in Notepad. Embed a style sheet into this file with:

```
a   {color: red;
  font-weight: bolder;
  text-decoration: none}

table {margin-left: 10;
 color: red;
 font-size: 14pt}

a:hover   {color: yellow;
 font-weight: bold;
 background: red}
```

3. Save the file, validate the code, and print the file.
4. Open the apply8-1home.html file and add an embedded style sheet with the following:

```
a  {color: red;
 font-weight: bolder;
 text-decoration: none}

a:hover   {color: yellow;
 font-weight: bold;
 background: red}
```

5. Save the revised files and validate the code.
6. Print the revised HTML files.
7. View the Web page in your browser.
8. Print the Web page as laid out on screen.
9. Submit the solution in the format specified by your instructor.

Extend Your Knowledge

Extend the skills you learned in this chapter and experiment with new skills.

Creating a Web Page with Style Sheets

Instructions: Start Notepad. Open the file extend8-1menu.html from the Chapter08\Extend folder of the Data Files for Students. See the inside back cover of this book for instructions on downloading the Data Files for Students, or contact your instructor for information about accessing the required files. This sample HTML file contains the text for the Web page shown in Figure 8–16 on the next page.

Continued >

STUDENT ASSIGNMENTS

Extend Your Knowledge *continued*

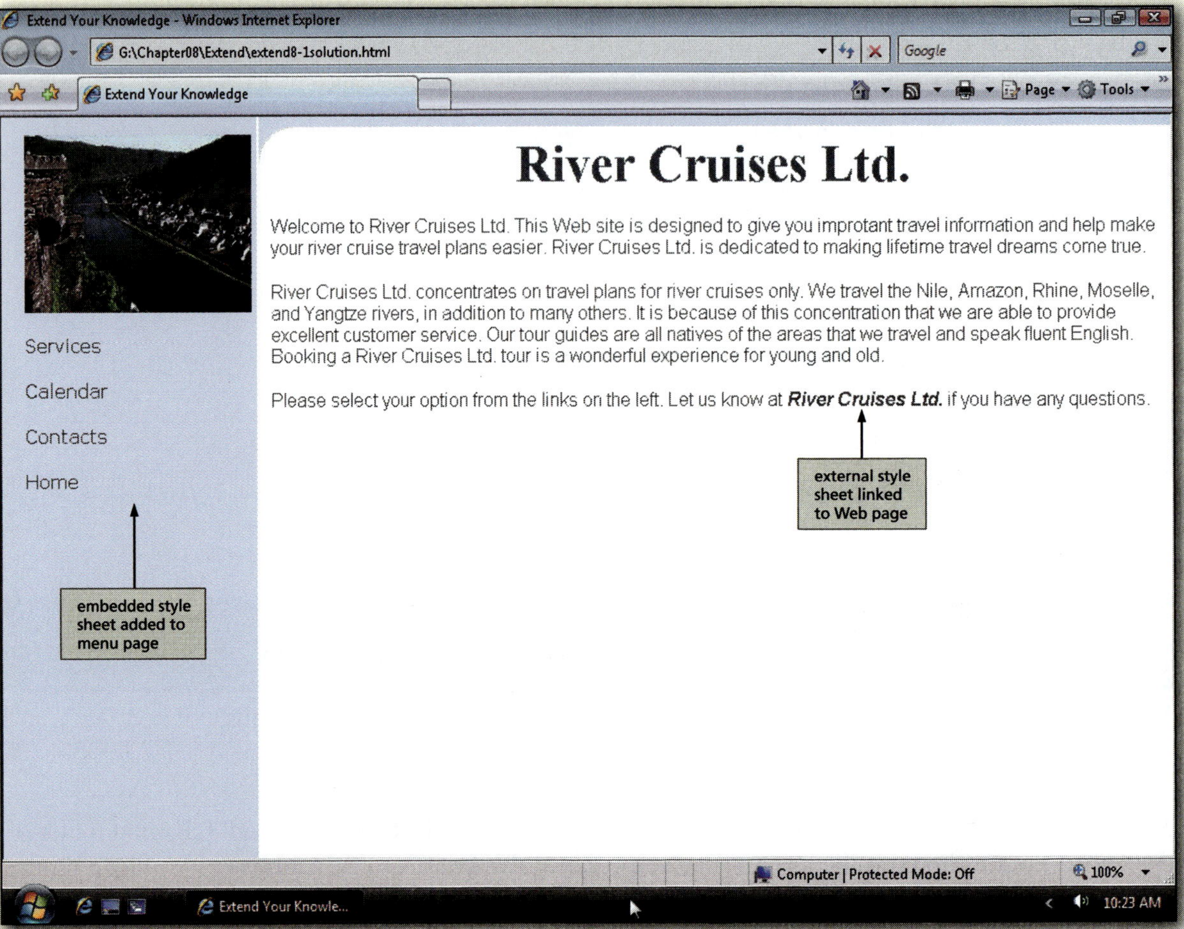

Figure 8–16

Perform the following tasks:

1. With the extend8-1menu.html file open in Notepad, add an embedded style sheet with the following:
   a. paragraphs with text indented 8 points
   b. links with no text decoration, the Verdana font in size 12 point, and color #808080
   c. link hover with a background color of #58778b and white text
2. Save the file; validate the code; print the file.
3. Create an external style sheet with the following:
   a. h1 headers with font Broadway, Forte in size 32, weight bolder, and color #58778b
   b. paragraphs with font family Arial, then Boulder; 20 point left margin; and color #808080
   c. set the links to no text decoration, their color to #808080, font weight to bold, and font style to italic
   d. margin of 15 points on all images
4. Save the file as styles5.css; validate the code; and print the file.
5. Open the extend8-1home.html file in Notepad. Add the HTML code necessary to link in the external style sheet created in Steps 3 and 4.
6. Save the revised document, validate the code, and print the file.
7. Test all links by opening the extend8-1.html file in your browser.
8. Submit the solution in the format specified by your instructor.

Make It Right

Analyze a document and correct all errors and/or improve the design.

Correcting the Halloween Dinner and Dance Web Page

Instructions: Start Notepad. Open the file makeitright8-1.html from the Chapter08\MakeitRight folder of the Data Files for Students and save it as makeitright8-1solution.html. See the inside back cover of this book for instructions on downloading the Data Files for Students, or contact your instructor for information about accessing the required files. The Web page is a modified version of what you see in Figure 8–17, but it contains some errors. Although the code in the two inline style sheets is correct, the format of the style sheet is not. Make the necessary corrections to the Web page to make it look like the figure. [*Hint*: check the spelling and punctuation for all inline style sheets.]

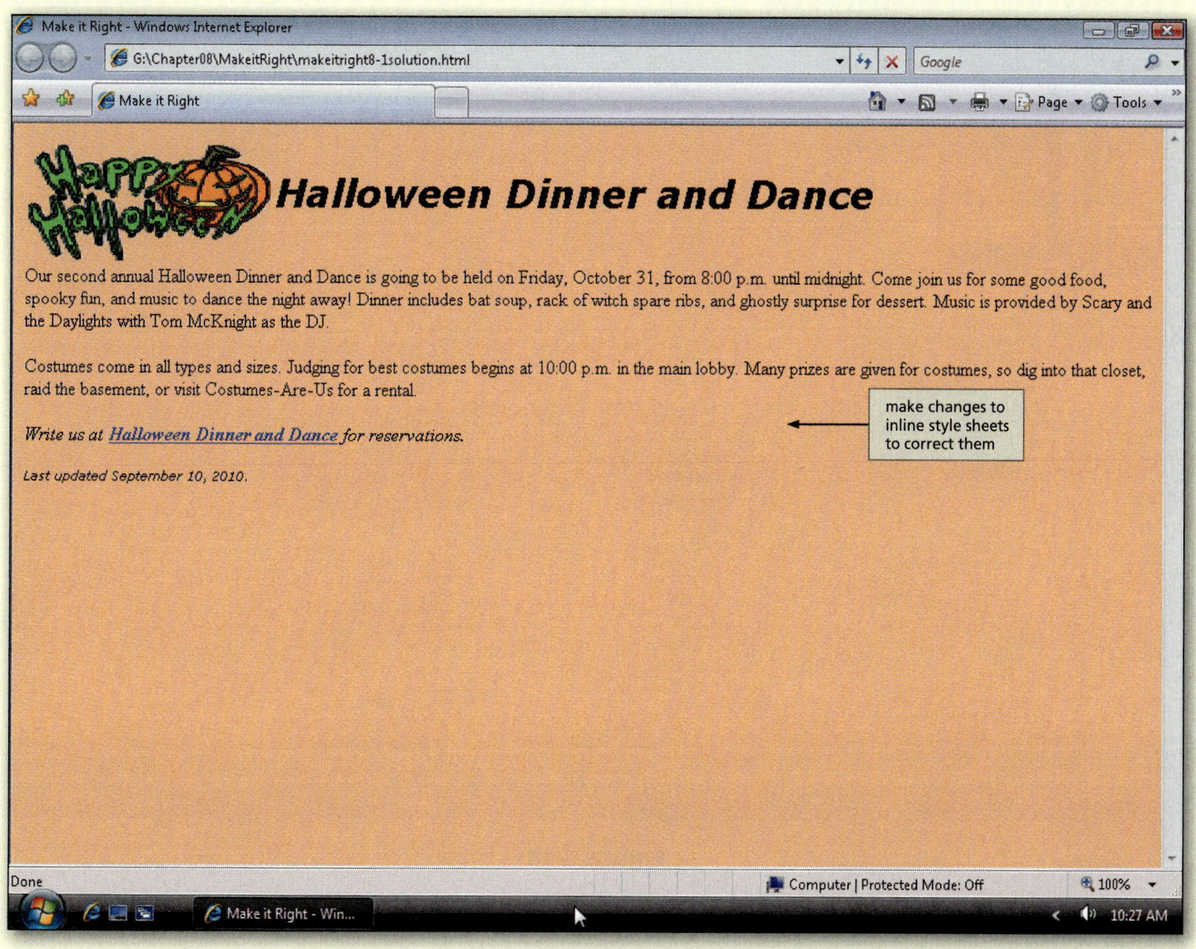

Figure 8–17

In the Lab

Lab 1: Using External and Internal Styles

Problem: Your father's business, Bold Ones Painting, is participating in the Home and Garden Show and wants to create a Web page to notify people about the event. The event coordinator asks you to create a Web page that contains information about the business and an e-mail address link, as shown in Figure 8–18. The Web page should have a link to the external style sheet, styles2.css, which is in the Chapter08\IntheLab folder of the Data Files for Students. The external style sheet is not complete, so you must add some selectors and declarations to complete it.

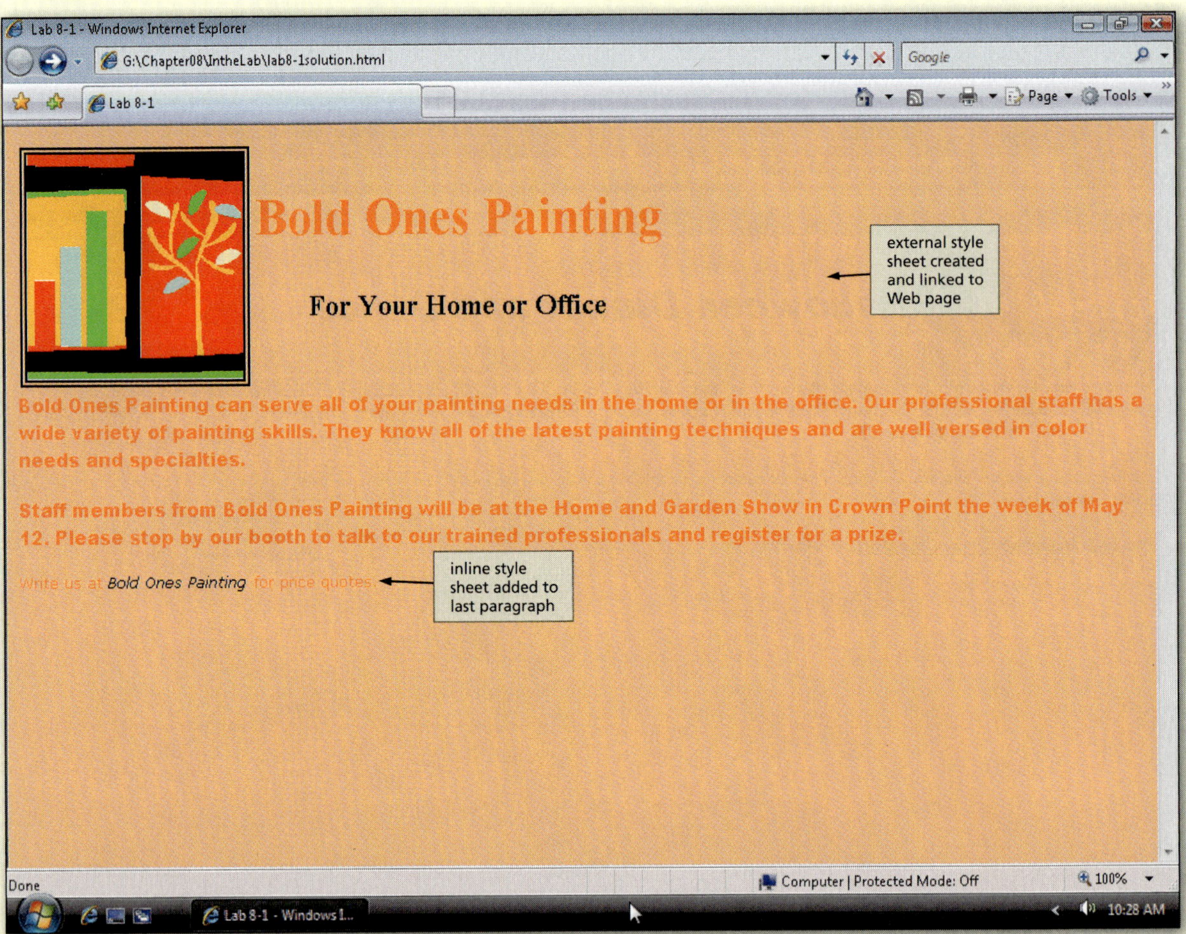

Figure 8–18

Instructions: Perform the following steps.

1. Using Notepad, open the HTML file lab8-1.html in the Chapter08\IntheLab folder of the Data Files for Students.
2. Add a link to the external style sheet, styles2.css.
3. Insert the image boldones.jpg as the image in the first table data cell. Add h1 and h2 headings in the second table data cell as shown in Figure 8–18.
4. Add an inline style sheet to the last paragraph with the declarations:
   ```
   style="font-style:strong; font-family:Verdana; font-size:10pt"
   ```
5. Save the HTML file in the Chapter08\IntheLab folder as lab8-1solution.html. Validate the file and then print it.
6. Open the file, styles2.css, in Notepad. This is a partially completed external style sheet.
7. Enter the following code to define styles for any h1 heading:
   ```
   h1 {font size: 32 pt;
    font-family: Calligrapher, Magneto;
    font-weight: bolder;
    color: #ff8429}
   ```
8. Enter the following code to define paragraph styles:
   ```
   p {font-family: "Arial Black", Boulder;
    color: #ff8429;
    margin-left: 10}
   ```
9. Enter the following code to define the style for image borders and margins:
   ```
   img {border-style: double;
    border-width: thick;
    margin: 10}
   ```
10. Save the styles2.css file.
11. Print the lab8-1solution.html file.
12. Print the styles2.css file.
13. Open the lab8-1solution.html file in your browser and test all styles to ensure they are displayed as shown in Figure 8–18.
14. Print the Web page.
15. Submit the solution in the format specified by your instructor.

STUDENT ASSIGNMENTS

In the Lab

Lab 2: Creating Embedded Style Sheets

Problem: Cogs in the Wheel, a small company that provides support services for both office and party use, is planning to advertise its business on the Internet. You will use inline, embedded, and external style sheets to create the framed Web pages shown in Figure 8–19. The lab8-2.html file included in the Chapter08\IntheLab folder in the Data Files for Students is the frame definition file that will display the lab8-2menu.html in the top frame and lab8-2home.html in the bottom frame. You will change those two files by adding embedded style sheets to define the styles in the pages.

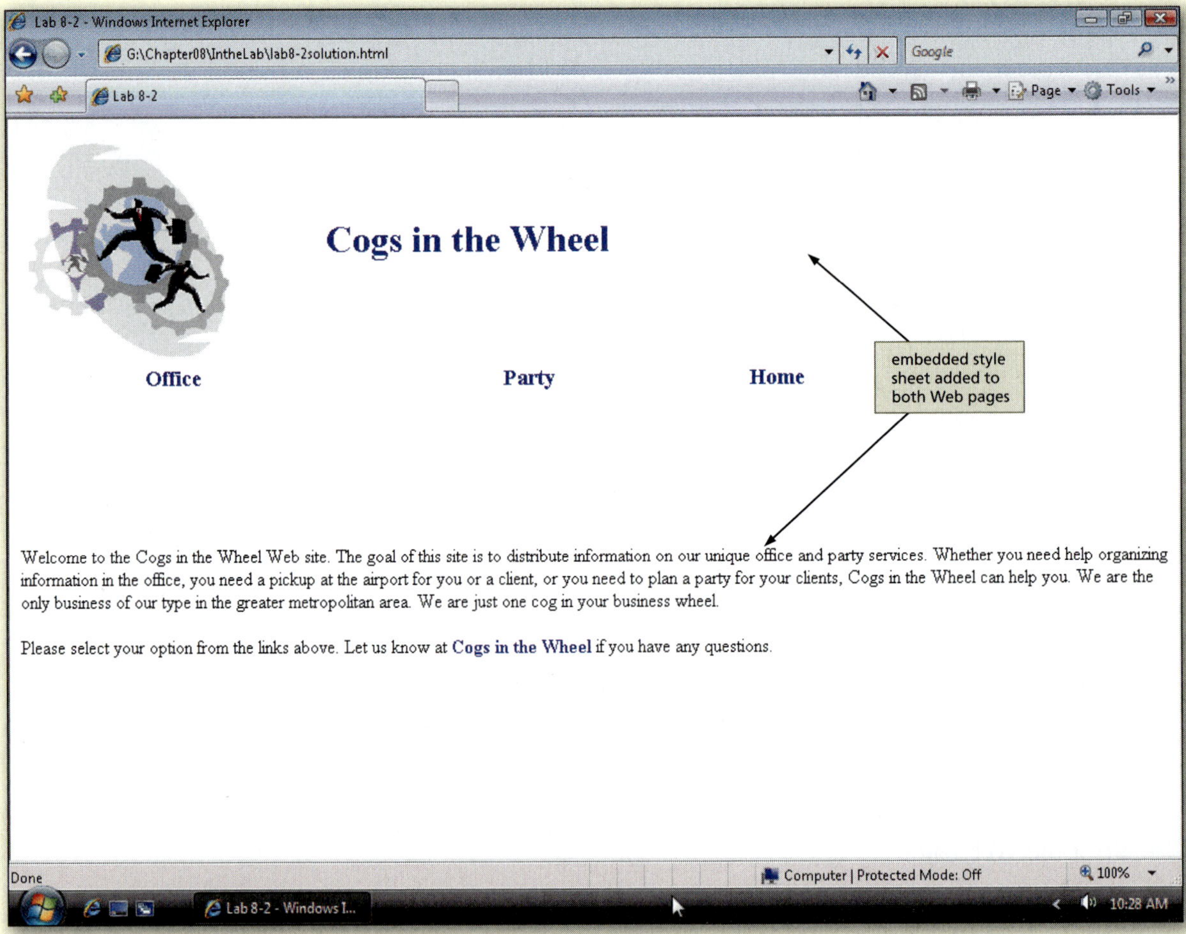

Figure 8–19

Instructions: Perform the following steps.

1. Using Notepad, open the HTML file lab8-2menu.html in the Chapter08\IntheLab folder of the Data Files for Students.
2. Add an embedded style sheet that defines the following styles:
   a. links: color blue, font weight of bolder, and no text decoration
   b. tables: left margin of 10, color blue, and a font size of 14 point
   c. link:hover: gray background, font weight of bold, and blue text
3. Create a borderless table with the image cogs.jpg in the top data cell of the Web page. Insert an <h1> heading tag next to the image.

4. Insert a second row in which you will enter three links (which open in the main frame) using bold font style:
   a. Office: links to file lab8-2office.html
   b. Party: links to the file lab8-2party.html
   c. Home: links to the file lab8-2home.html
5. Save the lab8-2menu.html file.
6. Using Notepad, open the HTML file Chapter08\IntheLab\lab8-2home.html in the Data Files for Students.
7. Copy and paste the embedded style sheet from Chapter08\IntheLab\lab8-2menu.html into this file. Change the left margin to 140 and the color for the table selector to red.
8. Save the file in the Chapter08\IntheLab folder as lab8-2home.html.
9. Open the Chapter08\IntheLab\lab8-2.html file in Notepad and save it as lab8-2solution.html. Open the lab8-2solution.html file in your browser.
10. Print the Web page using the option to print frames as laid out on screen.
11. Right-click each frame individually to view the HTML source code for lab8-2menu.html and lab8-2home.html. Print the HTML files from Notepad.
12. Submit the solution in the format specified by your instructor.

In the Lab

Lab 3: Developing External, Embedded, and Inline Style Sheets

Problem: You want to create a Web site that uses all three types of style sheets to give the look shown in Figure 8–20. The file lab8-3.html is a frame definition file that defines a menu frame on the left and a main page frame on the right. The file, lab8-3.html, is included in the Chapter08\IntheLab folder of the Data Files for Students. In this exercise, you will create a menu Web page for the left menu frame and a main Web page for the right main frame, both of which use style sheets to give them a specific look.

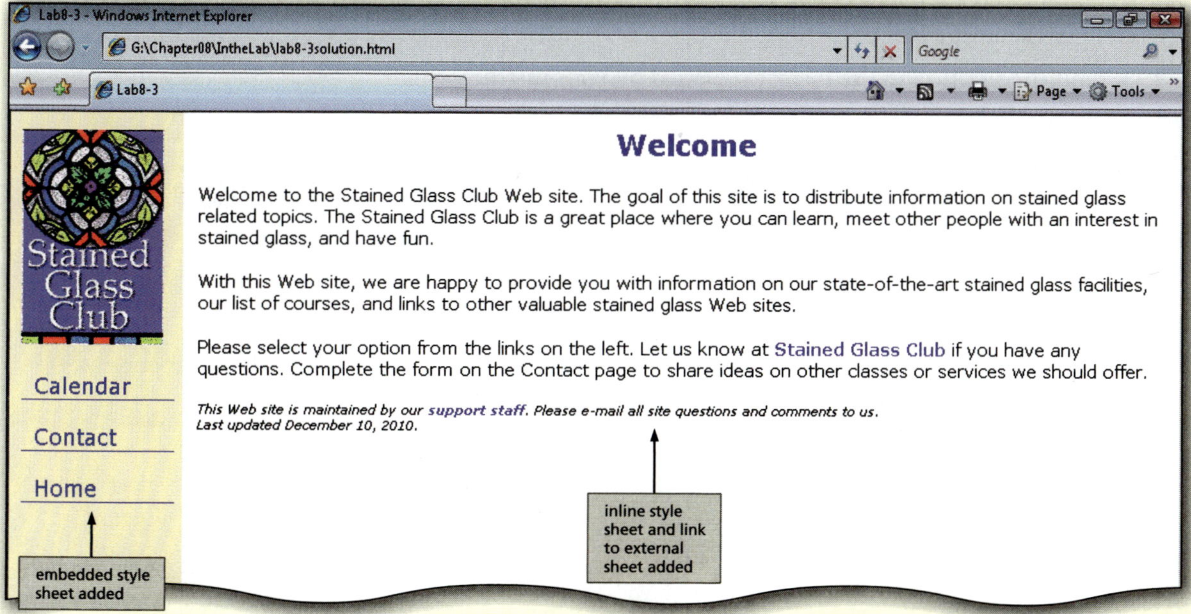

Figure 8–20

Continued >

In the Lab *continued*

Instructions: Perform the following steps.

1. Open the file lab8-3.html in Notepad. Save the file as lab8-3solution.html. Create a Web page with frames similar to the one shown in Figure 8–20. Use two columns with 150 pixel width in the first column. Let the browser determine the second column width. Save the file again. The Web page on the left side is lab3menu.html, while the Web page on the right should be lab3welcome.html at startup.
2. In the lab3menu.html file, insert the image ovalglass3.gif and link it to the lab8-3welcome.html file. Then insert three text links: Calendar, Contact, and Home, which point to the files lab8-3calendar.html, lab8-3contact.html, and lab8-3welcome.html, respectively. Use an embedded style sheet to set the following:
   a. paragraphs should be indented by 8 points
   b. links should be Verdana and Garamond as the font in size 14 point with no text decoration
   c. the link hover should have a blue background with white text
3. Save the file, validate it, and then print the HTML code.
4. Create a new external style sheet named styles3.css that has the following:
   a. body with a margin of 8pt
   b. links with no text-decoration and the color blue
   c. a paragraph style with Verdana first and Garamond second and font size of 11 point
   d. use the font families Verdana and Garamond in font size 11 point for all tables
   e. table headers should have white 11 point text on a blue background and left-aligned
   f. the caption color should be blue and italics
5. Save the file and then print it.
6. In the lab8-3welcome.html file, add a link to the styles3.css style sheet. Also add an inline style sheet to the last paragraph in which the font style is italics with a size of 8 point.
7. Save the welcome page, validate it, and then print it.
8. As a bonus, create the calendar Web page (see instructor for Web page information) and the contact Web page form.
9. Submit the solution in the format specified by your instructor.

Cases and Places

Apply your creative thinking and problem-solving skills to design and implement a solution.

• Easier ••More Difficult

• 1: Finding CSS Information Online

Browse the Internet to find two Web sites that discuss Cascading Style Sheets (CSS). How do these sites describe the three types of style sheets (inline, embedded, and external)? Are their definitions different or similar? Some sources refer to external style sheets as linked style sheets. What terminology do these two Web sites use when describing CSS? What determines which type of style sheet should be used? When would an embedded style sheet be more appropriate than an external style sheet? In what cases would you use an inline style sheet?

• 2: Presentation on CSS Classes

Your manager at WebSource has asked you to prepare a brief presentation on the use of classes in style sheets, as described in this chapter. He asked you to find at least two Web sites that describe the use of classes in style sheets and then review how the techniques discussed in the Web sites compare to the style sheet methods described and used in this chapter. The presentation also should discuss how the use of classes can help make Web development more effective — both in the development of one Web page and the development of an entire Web site.

•• 3: Trying More Styles

Ms. Stofcich is very impressed by the use of style sheets in the Karen Stofcich Financials Web site and would like to explore additional styles that can be applied to the Web pages. Using Appendix D, find three CSS properties that were not used in Chapter 8, modify the styles1.css style sheet that you used in the chapter project to include these properties and values, and then save the style sheet as styles1new.css in the Chapter08\CasesandPlaces folder. Update the link on the Web page, welcome.html, and then view the Web page in the browser using the new style sheet. How did the use of these new properties improve the appearance of the Web page?

•• 4: Using CSS in the Chapter 4 Project

Make It Personal

As a student in this class, you should have already completed the chapter project in Chapter 4. Review the chapter project that you did in Chapter 4 and determine how you can use the information provided in Chapter 8 to make the Web site more efficient. Many styles exist that you added to individual HTML tags that could be combined into inline, embedded, or external style sheets. Analyze the need for CSS in the Chapter 4 project and write up an action plan to convert the project to use CSS. What things should you consider when trying to convert separate styles to a more comprehensive plan? What are the benefits of using CSS for this project? If you do not see any benefits, then explain your reasoning. While doing your analysis, include Web sites in which CSS are used and not used.

•• 5: Creating Style Sheets for an Existing Web Site

Working Together

Your design team at Triple-D Design has been asked to create a proposal for an existing customer, to explain the value of using Cascading Style Sheets. Select a Web site with which you are familiar. Verify that the Web site does not utilize any of the three types of style sheets. Develop a graphic of the Web site hierarchy. Determine how the three types of style sheets could be utilized in this Web site and develop an outline explaining how they would help enhance pages or sections of the site, add style consistency, or make the site easier to maintain. Write a proposal to the owners of the Web site

Continued >

Cases and Places *continued*

that describes the features you could add with style sheets and the benefits of doing so, relative to the formatting techniques currently used in the Web site. As an example, you might want to address the number of times that a particular <font> tag is used in the site and contrast that with the ease of using one external style sheet and a link statement per page. Use other ideas as discussed in the chapter project to stress the other benefits of style sheets. Write the proposal in the form of a bid, giving time estimates and costs associated with the development effort. Include your hierarchy chart and style sheet outline as appendices to the proposal.

9 Integrating JavaScript and HTML

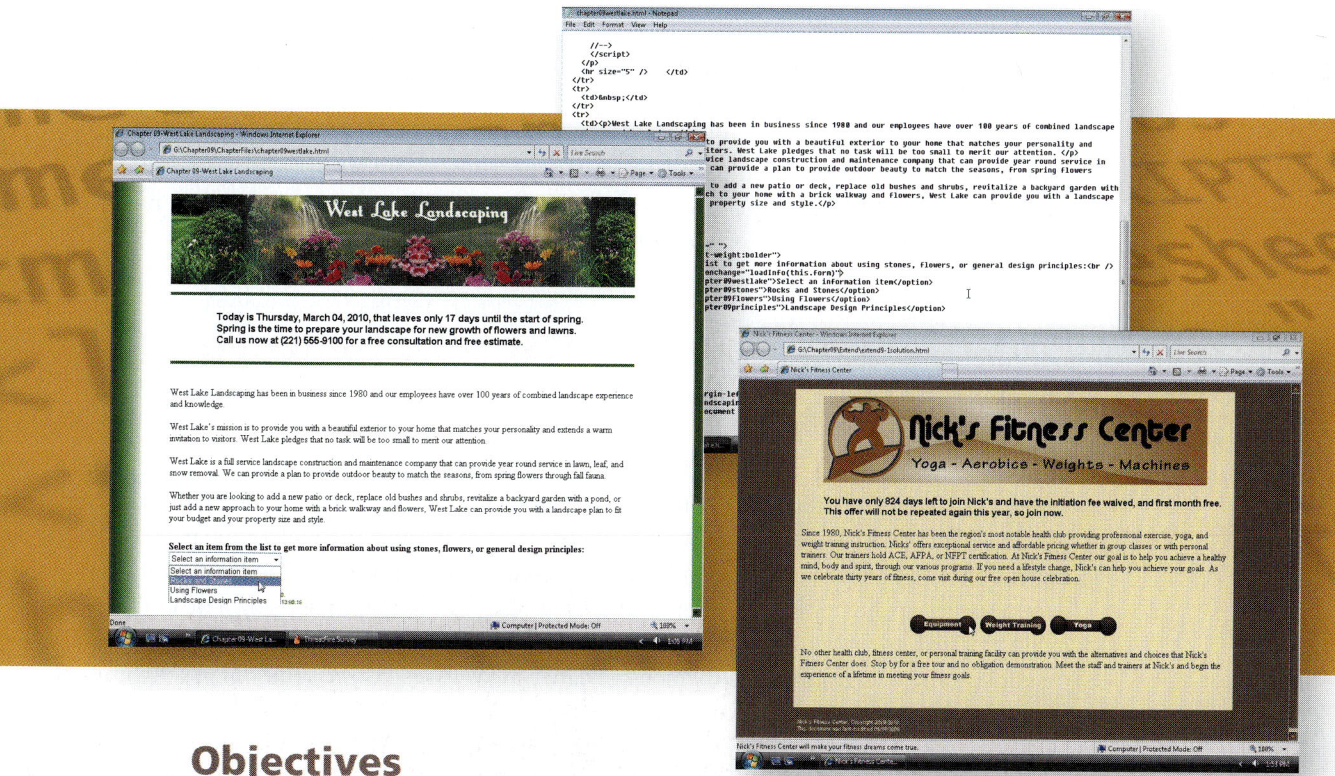

Objectives

You will have mastered the material in this chapter when you can:

- Discuss how to integrate JavaScript and HTML
- Insert <script> tags on a Web page
- Define and describe JavaScript variables
- Extract the current system date
- Calculate the number of days from the current date to a future date
- Describe the write() method of the document object
- Save the HTML file and test the Web page
- Write a dynamic message to a Web page
- Write a user-defined function that changes the color of the browser's scroll bar
- Construct a URL from a select list option choice
- Use the document's location property to link to a new Web page
- Use the lastModified property to display the last modified document date

9 Integrating JavaScript and HTML

Introduction

Many individuals, companies, and organizations rely on their Web sites as a key vehicle to communicate with friends, members, and current and future clients. Web pages often announce upcoming events, provide updated information, or act as a sales tool or catalog. Regardless of the content, Web page features should spark visitors' interests and entice them to return to the Web site. As with an advertisement, a Web page has six to seven seconds to attract and retain someone's attention.

An effective way to make Web pages interesting and useful is to include dynamic content and to make the Web page interactive. One way to add dynamic content to a Web page is to integrate JavaScript code onto the Web page. This chapter shows you how to add JavaScript code to a Web page to make it more dynamic and attractive.

Project — Creating the West Lake Landscaping Web Page

West Lake Landscaping has asked you to create a Web page that is dynamic and interactive with users, that is colorful and easy to navigate, and which showcases its landscaping skills and offerings. You have suggested a colored scroll bar to help balance the look of the page with the margin and banner colors, and a dynamic message that can be easily modified to address current issues or themes in landscaping or user needs. You also feel that using a drop-down menu will make the Web page more interactive for users, and keep the home page simple in its design. Another suggestion is to include the date the Web page was last modified so that users know the Web page content is current.

Chapter 9 shows how to add JavaScript code to an HTML file using these dynamic and interactive features to create the Web pages shown in Figure 9–1. The West Lake Landscaping home page includes a greeting that indicates the number of days until spring (Figure 9–1a). The home page also includes a select list (drop-down menu) containing items that link to three Web pages: a Web page with information about stones and rocks in landscaping (Figure 9–1b), a Web page with information on using flowers (Figure 9–1c), and a Web page with information about the principles of landscape design (Figure 9–1d).

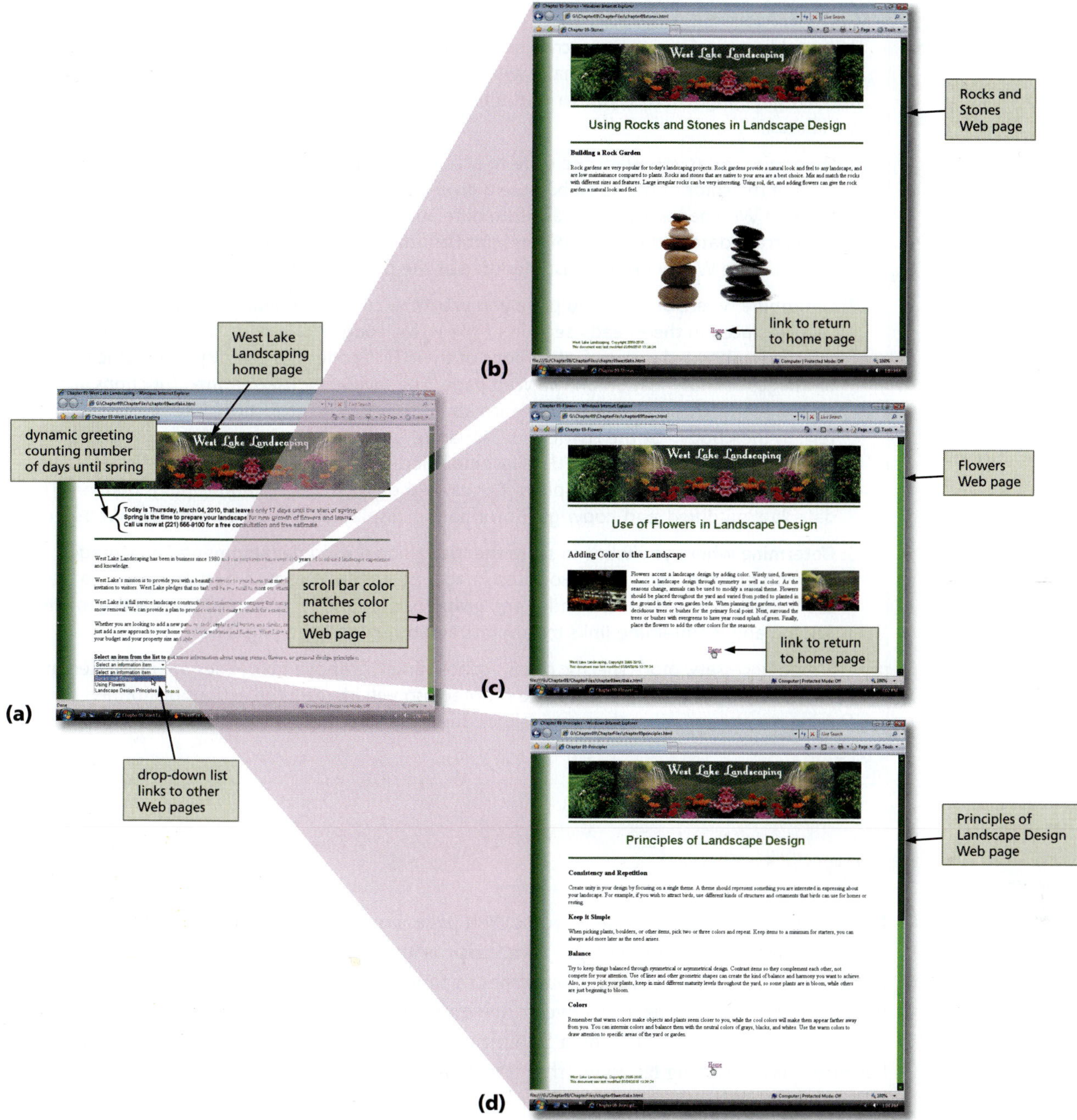

Figure 9–1

Overview

As you read through this chapter, you will learn how to integrate JavaScript onto a Web page as shown in Figure 9–1 by performing these general tasks:

- Write the embedded JavaScript code to display a countdown message
- Write a JavaScript function to change the color of the scroll bar
- Write a JavaScript function that uses a drop-down menu object to link to a new Web page
- Write the embedded JavaScript code to display the date the Web page was last modified and a copyright message

Plan Ahead

General Project Guidelines

When adding JavaScript or any scripting language to a Web page document, the actions you perform and decisions you make will affect the appearance and characteristics of the finished Web page. Before you write the JavaScript code, you should follow these general guidelines:

1. **Determine what you want the code to accomplish.** The JavaScript tasks in this chapter change the color of the scroll bar, use a drop-down menu (HTML <select/options>) to link to other Web pages, calculate a future date and display a dynamic message that includes the current date and number of days until another date, and display a copyright notice and date the Web page was last modified at the bottom of the Web page.
2. **Determine where on the Web page you want the code to appear.** JavaScript code is usually placed in the <head> section of the HTML code. When necessary, JavaScript must be embedded in specific locations of the HTML code so it can display specific text or images at that location on the Web page. The JavaScript user-defined functions are placed in the <head> section (you learn about user-defined functions later in the chapter). In the <body> of the HTML code, separate JavaScript <script> sections will display the dynamic message and the date last modified with the copyright information.

   The dynamic message displays beneath the West Lake Landscaping banner. The date last modified and copyright information display at the bottom of the Web page.
3. **Determine where you want to store the Web page during development.** The storage location of HTML code and associated images is very important. A best practice is to create folders to organize HTML files and graphics in a specific location. This practice makes finding and maintaining links to graphics and other Web site pages easy.

When necessary, more specific details concerning the above guidelines are presented at appropriate points in the chapter. The chapter also will identify the actions performed and decisions made regarding these guidelines during the creation of the Web page shown in Figure 9–1 on the previous page.

BTW

JavaScript Tutorials
Many Web sites provide help for JavaScript developers. For more information about links, search for key words such as "JavaScript Tutorials" or "JavaScript Help" in any good search engine.

JavaScript

Before adding JavaScript code to your Web page, you should understand some basics about the programming language. **JavaScript** is an event driven, object-based, programming language that provides various types of functionality to Web pages, such as the ability to interact with the user. An **event driven** programming language is one that responds to events, such as a user clicking a Submit or Calculate button. JavaScript is **object-based** because it is a scripting language that uses built-in objects that belong to the browser.

Built-in objects are values that are common to a browser (arrays, dates, strings, etc.), and neither depend on nor belong to another object. Table 9–1 contains a general list of the built-in JavaScript objects common to many browsers. JavaScript developers can create new objects based on the built-in objects and the new objects inherit properties from the original objects. For more information about these objects, see the JavaScript Quick Reference in Appendix E.

Table 9–1 Built-in JavaScript Objects

Object	Description
Array	Returns an ordered set of values
Boolean	Converts objects to Boolean values
Date	Accesses the system time and date
Document	Represents the content of a browser's window
Form	Represents forms created with the <form> tag
Function	Accesses information about specific functions
History	Keeps track of Web pages visited
Image	Represents images created with the <img> tag
Location	Switches to a new Web page
Math	Performs calculations
Navigator	Obtains information about the current Web browser
Number	Supports special constants
Screen	Gives platform-specific information about the user's screen
String	Represents a set of characters
Window and Frame	Represents a browser window or every frame within a browser window; every frame is a window and uses the same properties and methods as the window object

JavaScript objects have properties and methods. **Properties** are attributes that describe an object's characteristics. As shown in Table 9–2, an object and its property are written by separating the object from its property with a period. A specific value can be assigned to a property as shown in the following example:

```
dog.breed="terrier"
```

where the dog is the object, breed is the property, and terrier is the value assigned to the property.

BTW

Object Oriented Programming (OOP)
Object-oriented programming is an approach to programming in which the data and the code that operates on the data are packaged into a single unit called an object.

Table 9–2 Object and Property

General form:	object.property
Comment:	where the object is stated first, then a period, then the descriptive property. A value can be assigned to the property, or the property can return a value as shown in the examples below.
Examples:	document.bgColor="lightblue" browser=navigator.appName

Methods are actions that an object can perform. For example, methods associated with the dog object might be eat, fetch, and sit up. An object and one of its methods would be written as:

```
dog.fetch()
```

where dog is the object and fetch is a method of the dog object. Methods are followed by parentheses, which may be empty, or may contain an argument.

BTW

JavaScript Methods and Arguments
Not all JavaScript methods require an argument. With some methods, if an argument is used, it generates an error.

An **argument** is a value given to a method. Some methods require arguments, and others do not. For example, given a dog object and the fetch() method, a statement could be written as:

```
dog.fetch("ball")
```

where the argument "ball" describes what the dog fetches.

As shown in Table 9–3, the general form of writing an object with its method is similar to writing objects and properties.

Table 9–3 Object and Method

General form:	objectname.method(argument value)
Comment:	where objectname is the object, method is the action, and parameters are optional items or instructions the method should use. A period separates the object name from the property or method name.
Examples:	document.write("Some text") window.alert("This is a message") var ToDayDate=Date.toString( )

User-Defined Functions

A **user-defined function** is JavaScript code written by a Web developer to perform a particular task. The function can be used whenever that task is needed, eliminating the need to repeat the code several times throughout an application. JavaScript also contains a number of built-in functions called **global functions**, such as close() to close a window, open() to open a window, and print() to print the contents of a window. Most of these functions actually belong to the window object, but because the window object is assumed, they are called built-in functions. For a complete list of built-in functions, see the JavaScript Quick Reference in Appendix E.

Most JavaScript user-defined functions are called or activated using event handlers. An **event** is the result of an action, such as a mouse click or a document loading. An **event handler** is JavaScript's way to associate an action with a function. In this project, you first write the functions, and then the event handlers that will associate the functions with specific events, such as loading the Web page.

BTW

Other Scripting Languages
JavaScript and VBScript are the two main client-side script languages used today. There are over a dozen other scripting languages that work on specific platforms or operating systems. Perl and PHP are other popular scripting languages.

Adding JavaScript to a Web Page

Now that you have planned what you need the JavaScript to accomplish and where it should appear, you can begin modifying the Web page using a text editor.

To Open an Existing HTML File

The following step shows how to open the chapter09.html file included in the Data Files for Students.

1

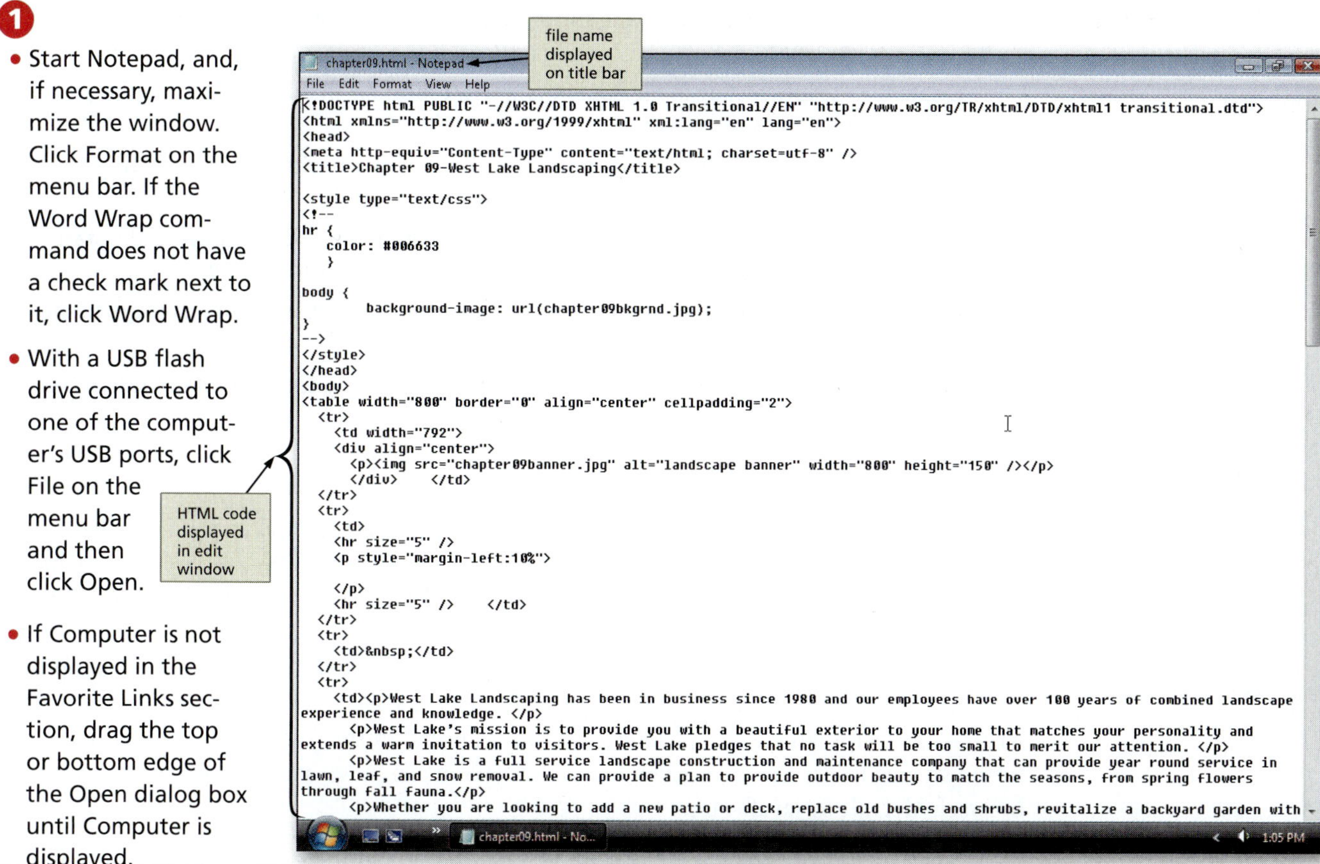

Figure 9–2

- Start Notepad, and, if necessary, maximize the window. Click Format on the menu bar. If the Word Wrap command does not have a check mark next to it, click Word Wrap.
- With a USB flash drive connected to one of the computer's USB ports, click File on the menu bar and then click Open.
- If Computer is not displayed in the Favorite Links section, drag the top or bottom edge of the Open dialog box until Computer is displayed.
- Click Computer in the Favorite Links section to display a list of available drives.
- If necessary, scroll until UDISK 2.0 (G:) appears in the list of available drives.
- Double-click USB drive (G:). Open the Chapter09 folder, and then double-click the ChapterFiles folder in the list of available folders.
- If necessary, click the Files of type box arrow, and then click All Files. Click chapter09.html in the list of files.
- Click the Open button in the Open dialog box to display the HTML code for the chapter09.html Web page as shown in Figure 9–2.

Inserting <script> Tags in HTML Code

JavaScript code can be placed anywhere in the HTML code in a <script> section. A standard JavaScript coding practice is to place variables and user-defined functions in the <head> section and other JavaScript code sections in the <body> section. JavaScript code sections placed in the <body> section are used to embed JavaScript code at specific locations on the Web page, such as to display dynamic messages.

Plan Ahead

Some JavaScript code must be embedded in the HTML code so it will display text at that location. Such code must be placed in a <script> section. To display a dynamic message on a Web page, you must find the location in the HTML code where you want the message to display. To display a message with the current date and the number of days until a specific future date, you must:

- **Create the <script> section in the appropriate HTML location.** In this project, the appropriate location is in a table cell.
- **Define variables.** A set of variables must be defined to work with the system date to calculate the number of days from today to the start of spring.
- **Calculate the number of days until spring.** To calculate the number of days to the start of spring, you write code to subtract the current date from the future date.
- **Display a message string.** Using the document.write() method, write the message to the Web page.
- **Close the <script> section.** All HTML tags must have a closing tag. If you fail to close the <script> section, you will have undesired results.

BTW

Script Tag Attributes
Although the language attribute has been deprecated, many browsers still accept it, and many JavaScript coders still use it. The type attribute is supported by the XHTML and XML standards.

In this chapter, you will use only JavaScript features that work in the latest versions of Microsoft Internet Explorer. JavaScript sections always start with a <script> tag, which indicates the language being used. Similar to other HTML tags, the JavaScript <script> tag has a start <script> tag and an end </script> tag.

The general form of the script tag is shown in Table 9–4. The <script> tag supports several attributes, including src, type, and defer. In the past, the start <script> tag was written as <script language="JavaScript">, but as noted in the Table 9–4 example, the preferred style is to use the type attribute. If the type or language attribute is omitted, most browsers default to JavaScript.

Table 9–4 JavaScript Section

General form:	<script src="url" type="content-type" language="language" defer>
Comments:	where script is the script tag, src specifies the location of an external script URL, type indicates the content-type or specific scripting language, language is a deprecated attribute, and defer is a Boolean attribute that indicates whether the script is going to generate any document content. The src, language, and defer attributes are optional.
Example:	<script type="text/javascript"> <!- -Hide from old browsers miscellaneous JavaScript code //--> </script>

BTW

JavaScript Comments
Comments can be added to JavaScript in two ways. The double slash [//] is used to indicate a comment for a single line. To comment multiple lines, begin a comment with a slash and asterisk [/*] and end the comment with an asterisk and slash [*/].

To Enter the Start <script> and Comment Tags

The following steps illustrate how to enter the <script> and HTML comment tags.

1

- Click the blank line (line 32) press the spacebar to indent as shown below the <p style="margin-left:10%"> tag, as shown in Figure 9–3.

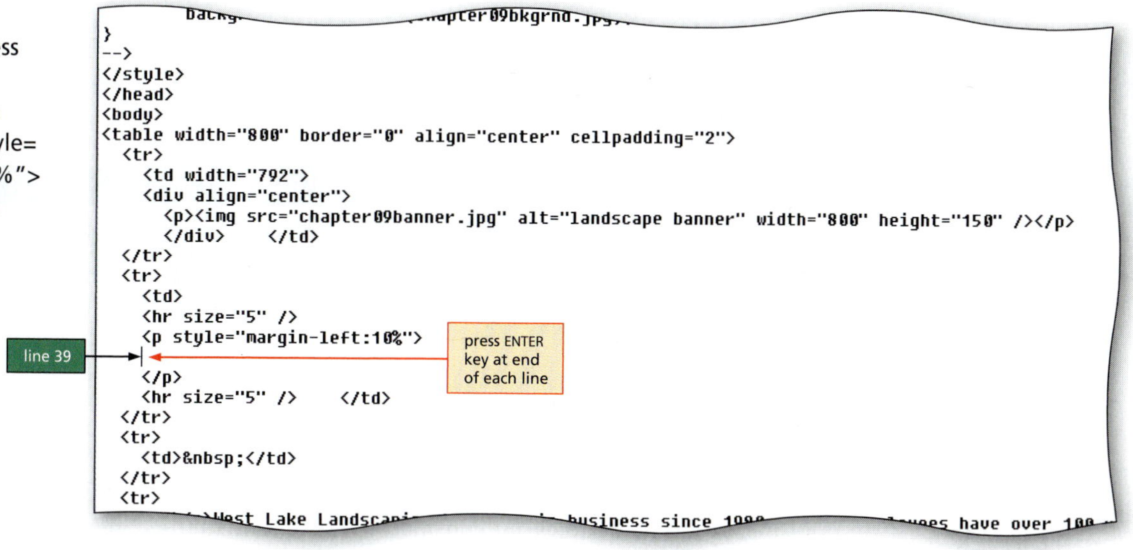

```
}
-->
</style>
</head>
<body>
<table width="800" border="0" align="center" cellpadding="2">
  <tr>
    <td width="792">
    <div align="center">
      <p><img src="chapter09banner.jpg" alt="landscape banner" width="800" height="150" /></p>
      </div>    </td>
  </tr>
  <tr>
    <td>
    <hr size="5" />
    <p style="margin-left:10%">
     |
    </p>
    <hr size="5" />    </td>
  </tr>
  <tr>
    <td> </td>
  </tr>
  <tr>
```

line 39

press ENTER key at end of each line

Figure 9–3

2

- Type `<script type="text/javascript">` as the beginning of the script and then press the ENTER key.
- Type `<!--Hide from old browsers` and then press the ENTER key (Figure 9–4).

Q&A

Why is an > end bracket not included on the HTML comment line?

Because the comment does not actually end until after the JavaScript code that you do not want to display in an older browser. The end comment tag (//-->) follows the JavaScript code.

```
</style>
</head>
<body>
<table width="800" border="0" align="center" cellpadding="2">
  <tr>
    <td width="792">
    <div align="center">
      <p><img src="chapter09banner.jpg" alt="landscape banner" width="800" height="150" /></p>
      </div>    </td>
  </tr>
  <tr>
    <td>
    <hr size="5" />
    <p style="margin-left:10%">
    <script type="text/javascript">
    <!--Hide from old browsers
     |
    </p>
    <hr size="5" />    </td>
  </tr>
  <tr>
    <td> </td>
  </tr>
  <tr>
    <td><p>West Lake Landscaping has been in business since 1980 and our employees have over 100
experience and knowledge. </p>
      <p>West Lake's mission is to provide you with a beautiful exterior to your home that matche
extends a warm invitation to visitors. West Lake pledges that no task will be too small to merit
      <p>West Lake is a full service landscape construction and maintenance company that can provi
lawn, leaf, and snow removal. We can provide a plan to provide outdoor beauty to match the seasons
through fall fauna.</p>
      <p>Whether you are looking to add a new patio or deck, replace old bushes and shrubs, revita
a pond, or just add a new approach to your home with a brick walkway and flowers, West Lake can pr
```

code to begin JavaScript section embedded in body of HTML code and end </script> and comment tags will be entered when script section code is completed

insertion point

Figure 9–4

JavaScript Variables

As in other programming languages, JavaScript uses **variables** to store values temporarily in internal memory. A variable's value can change, depending on the results of an expression or data entered by a user from a form. Variables must have a unique name, which must adhere to the naming conventions outlined in Table 9–5. JavaScript variable names are case sensitive, which means the variable name months is different from the variable name Months.

Table 9–5 Naming Conventions for JavaScript Variables

Rule	Valid Name Examples	Invalid Name Examples
Name must begin with a letter or underscore	menu	$menu
Rest of name must be letters, numerals, or underscores	Last_Name	Last-name
Name may not use spaces, hyphens, or punctuation	ZipCode	zip.code or zip code
Name may not contain JavaScript objects, properties, and reserved words	xNow	Date

JavaScript variables are considered global, unless the variable is defined within a user-defined function, in which case it is considered a local variable. **Global** means that the variable value is available for use anywhere inside the HTML file Web page. To define a variable as global, it must be declared in the <script> section before any of the user-defined functions. **Local** means that the variable's value is available only in the function in which it is defined.

A variable's **data type**, the type of data it stores, such as text or numbers, must be known so the computer knows how to store the data. JavaScript has four data types: numeric, string, date, or Boolean. **Numeric data types** hold numbers. **String data types** are variables that hold characters or a combination of letters, numbers, or symbols. **Date data types** contain a date and time. **Boolean data types** contain logical data that can be one of two values, such as True/False or Yes/No.

JavaScript variables are **loosely typed**, which means they do not have to be assigned an initial specific data type as in other programming languages. Instead, JavaScript indicates the data type by declaring the variable with an initial value. This feature allows variables to be flexible and store any data type. Web developers, however, do not recommend changing a variable's data type in the middle of JavaScript code. This action may create an error, which can be very difficult to find. Table 9–6 shows the general form of declaring a variable and assigning a value to it.

BTW

Undefined Variables
If a variable's value, which has not been defined or declared previously, is used or displayed on the Web page, JavaScript assigns the value "undefined" to that variable. An undefined variable can cause errors in mathematical calculations.

Table 9–6 Assigning Values to Variables

General form:	var variableName=value
Comment:	where var is an optional keyword to designate a variable; variableName is a valid variable name; and value is the string, numeric, date, or Boolean value being assigned to the variable.
Examples:	var NickName="Jasper" // This variable is a string data type var lineCnt=1 // This variable is a numeric data type var Continue=false // This variable is a Boolean data type

In the examples in Table 9–6, the keyword var, meaning variable, appears before the variable name. A **keyword**, or **reserved word**, is a word with special meaning in a programming language. The JavaScript var keyword is optional for global variables; however, it is good programming practice to precede the variable name with the var keyword. In addition, the var keyword is required for local variables defined within a function.

Extracting the Current System Date

The built-in Date() object accesses the current system date and time. On the West Lake Landscaping Web page, the Date() object and several of its methods are used to extract the current system date and then display it on the Web page as part of the greeting.

Plan Ahead

For the dynamic greeting on the home page, you need to calculate the number of days between two dates. First, you must extract information about the current date using the following steps:

- Obtain the current system date with the Date() object and create a new object instance
- Use the toLocaleString() method to convert the date to a string to be manipulated
- Use the substring() method to extract the month from the string
- Use the substring() method to extract the day of the week from the string
- Use the indexOf() method to locate the position of the year in the string
- Use the substr() method to extract the year from the string

To manipulate the Date() object, a new object instance must be created. Table 9–7 shows the general form of the JavaScript statement to create a new object instance, which uses the new keyword and assigns the built-in object to a variable. This variable is referred to as an **object instance variable**.

BTW

The Date() Object
The Date() object can use three other methods to build a string for a current date: getDate(), getMonth(), or getFullYear(). The getDate() method returns the date in the month; the getMonth() returns the value of the month as a number from 0 to 11 with 0 representing January; and the getFullYear() method returns the four digit year. Because the getMonth() method returns an integer that represents the month, the developer must add 1 to the result to get the current month.

Table 9–7 Creating a New Object Instance

General form:	var variableName=new Builtin_Object
Comments:	where variableName is the name of the new object instance, new is the required keyword, and Builtin_Object is the name of the object from which the new object instance is to be created.
Examples:	var sysDate=new Date() var sysDate=new Date("March 21, 2010")

The parentheses in the Date() object means a specified date and time other than the current system date and time can be used. The first example shown in Table 9–7 has no specific date value provided, thus the current system date and time from the computer is stored in the variable sysDate. The second example in Table 9–7 has a specific date value enclosed within quotation marks inside the parentheses. That value, March 21, 2010, is assigned to the object instance variable sysDate.

Converting the System Date to a String To use the date and time value stored in the variable sysDate, the variable first must be converted to a string using the toLocaleString() method. Table 9–8 shows the general form of the toLocaleString() method.

Table 9–8 toLocaleString() Method

General form:	var variable=dateString.toLocaleString()
Comment:	where dateString is an object instance and the toLocaleString() method converts an object instance of the Date() to a string using the default display format used on the client computer.
Example:	var curDate=sysDate.toLocaleString()
Result:	curDate contains the date and time stored as: Day of the Week, Month, Date, Year HH:MM:SS

Once the current system date has been converted to a string, the JavaScript indexOf(), substring(), and substr() methods can be used to extract the day, the month, the date, the year, and the hours (HH), minutes (MM), and seconds (SS) to be displayed on the Web page.

BTW

The IndexOf() Method
Items in a select list are indexed in the order in which they appear in the list. The first item is indexed as 0 (zero). Set the selectedIndex property to 0 (zero) to clear any existing selected items.

Using the indexOf() Method Table 9–9 explains how the indexOf() method searches a string for a particular value, which is enclosed within the quotation marks, and then returns the relative location of the parameter value within the string. If the search finds the value in the search string object, the indexOf() method returns the relative position of the value within the string object. If the search value is not found, the indexOf() method returns a negative one (-1).

Table 9–9 indexOf() Method

General form:	var position=stringValue.indexOf("x")
Comment:	where stringValue is a string in which a search is conducted, x is the value to be searched for within the stringValue, and position is the location of x in the string. The value x must be a literal value.
Examples:	curDate="March 21, 2010" dateLocate=curDate.indexOf(",")
Result:	returns the relative position of the comma found in the string value of curDate: 8

Using the substring() Method to Extract the Month from a String The substring() method uses two parameters (x,y), where x is the starting point of the string and y is the location of the last character needed. If only an x parameter is given, the substring() method returns all the characters starting at that position through the end of the string. Table 9–10 describes the general form of the substring() method.

Table 9–10 substring() Method

General form:	var variable=string.substring(x,y)
Comment:	where string is any string object. The substring method extracts a portion of a string, starting at location x and ending at location y. x and y may be constants or variables.
Example:	weekDay=dayofweek.substring(0, dateLocate)
Result:	the variable weekDay contains the substring

Using the substr() Method Table 9–11 describes the substr() method. The substr() method is similar to the substring() method, in that it extracts part of a string. Although the methods perform similar functions in JavaScript, they differ in how they use parameter values. The substring() method uses the exact byte locations in a string to extract part of the string between the x and y locations, whereas the substr() method uses a length value to extract y number of characters starting at x location.

Table 9–11 substr() Method

General form:	var variable=string.substr(x,y)
Comment:	where string is any string object instance. This method extracts a portion of a string, starting at location x for a length of y. x and y may be constants or variables.
Example:	year=dayofweek.substr(yearLocate, 4)
Result:	the variable year contains the four-digit year

Both the substring() and substr() methods use relative addressing as a means of locating characters in a string. A **relative address** is the location of a byte in a string of bytes, as defined by its position relative to the first byte in that string. As an example, assume the data in Table 9–12 is a string value stored in the variable birthDay. The address of the first byte in a string of characters is zero (0). To extract the year 2010 from the string using the substring() method, the JavaScript code would be written as:

```
birthDay.substring(17,20)
```

Table 9–12 Relative Addressing

S	u	n	d	a	y	,		M	a	r	c	h		7	,		2	0	1	0
0	1	2	3	4	5	6	7	8	9	10	11	12	13	14	15	16	17	18	19	20

Table 9–13 shows the JavaScript code used to extract the system date for the West Lake Landscaping Web page. The JavaScript code uses the toLocaleString(), substr(), substring(), and indexOf() methods of the Date() object to obtain the current system date and then extract the weekday, the date, the month, and the year. Once these values have been extracted and assigned to variables, they can be displayed on the Web page.

Table 9–13 Code to Extract the System Date

Line	Code
41	`var today = new Date()`
42	`var dayofweek = today.toLocaleString()`
43	`dayLocate = dayofweek.indexOf(" ")`
44	`weekDay = dayofweek.substring(0, dayLocate)`
45	`newDay = dayofweek.substring(dayLocate)`
46	`dateLocate = newDay.indexOf(",")`
47	`monthDate = newDay.substring(0, dateLocate+1)`
48	`yearLocate = dayofweek.indexOf("2010")`
49	`year = dayofweek.substr(yearLocate, 4)`

Line 41 creates the new date object instance variable, today, and assigns the current system date and time to the variable. Line 42 converts the date and time value stored in the today variable to a string, using the toLocaleString() method and assigns it to the dayofweek variable. To find the day of the week in the string, the indexOf() method in line 43 looks for the first blank space in the string. Line 44 uses the substring() method to extract the day of the week, while line 45 extracts the remainder of the string, which includes the month, day, year, and time. Line 46 looks for the comma that separates the date from the year using the indexOf() method. Using the address of the comma, the substring() method in line 47 extracts the date. To find the year, line 48 uses the indexOf() method and the current system year to determine the starting address of the year. Line 49 uses the substr() method, using the starting address from the indexOf() method and length of the year, which is four characters long.

To Extract the Current System Date Using the Date() Object

The step on the next page illustrates how to write JavaScript code that uses the Date() object and its methods to extract the current system date.

1

- If necessary, click the chapter 09 - Notepad button on the taskbar to activate the Notepad window.
- Click line 41 below the <!--Hide from old browsers statement.
- Enter the JavaScript code shown in Table 9–13. Press ENTER at the end of each complete line of code. Enter the current year in the indexOf() method on line 48.

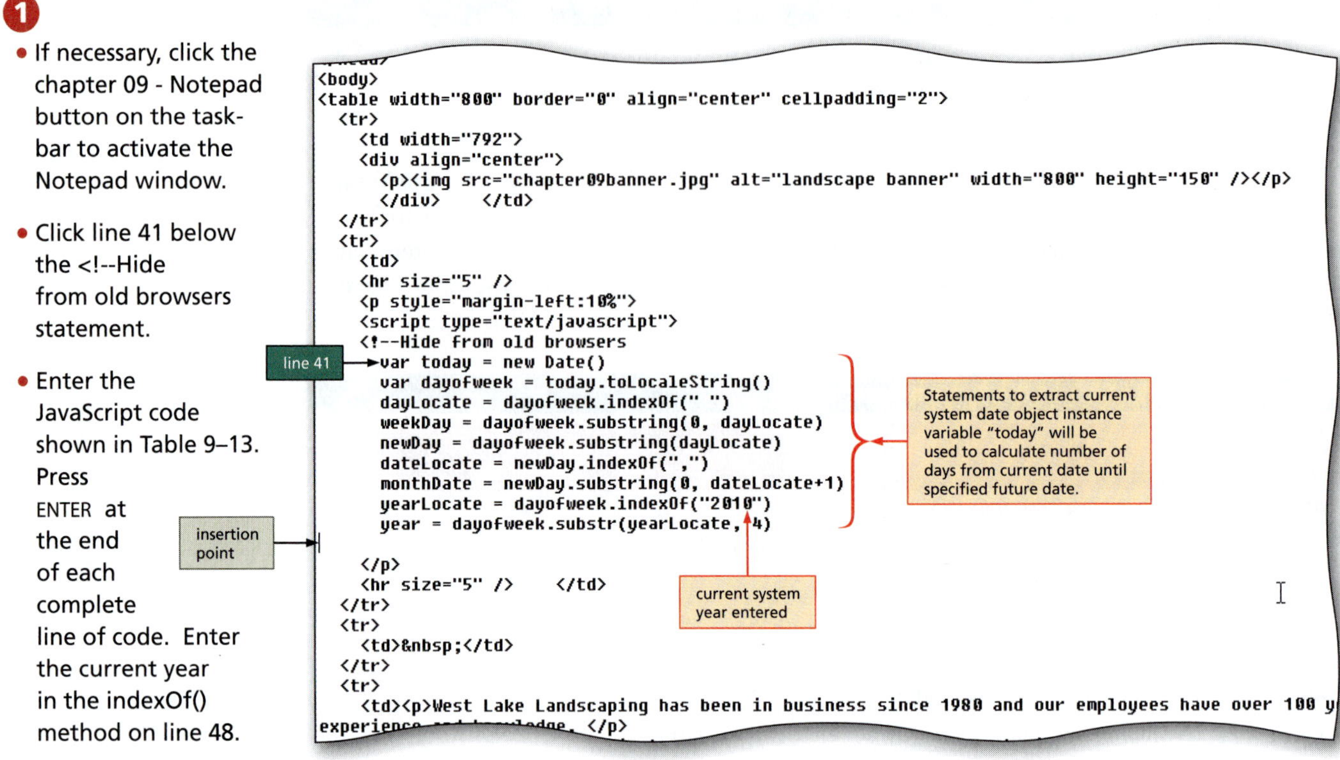

```
<body>
<table width="800" border="0" align="center" cellpadding="2">
  <tr>
    <td width="792">
    <div align="center">
      <p><img src="chapter09banner.jpg" alt="landscape banner" width="800" height="150" /></p>
      </div>    </td>
  </tr>
  <tr>
    <td>
    <hr size="5" />
    <p style="margin-left:10%">
    <script type="text/javascript">
    <!--Hide from old browsers
      var today = new Date()
      var dayofweek = today.toLocaleString()
      dayLocate = dayofweek.indexOf(" ")
      weekDay = dayofweek.substring(0, dayLocate)
      newDay = dayofweek.substring(dayLocate)
      dateLocate = newDay.indexOf(",")
      monthDate = newDay.substring(0, dateLocate+1)
      yearLocate = dayofweek.indexOf("2010")
      year = dayofweek.substr(yearLocate, 4)

    </p>
    <hr size="5" />    </td>
  </tr>
  <tr>
    <td> </td>
  </tr>
  <tr>
    <td><p>West Lake Landscaping has been in business since 1980 and our employees have over 100 y
experience and knowledge. </p>
```

line 41
insertion point
Statements to extract current system date object instance variable "today" will be used to calculate number of days from current date until specified future date.
current system year entered

Figure 9–5

- After typing the last line in Table 9–13, press the ENTER key once more to leave space for additional JavaScript code.
- Compare what you typed to Figure 9–5. Correct any errors before proceeding.

Q&A Why is some of the code in Figure 9–5 indented?

The code is indented with the SPACEBAR for ease of reading. It does not affect the execution of the code. You may want to indent sections of code two or three spaces to make it easier to identify.

Q&A Can a date only be entered as, "March 21, 2010" in the Date() object?

The date can be entered as 2010, 2, 21 in the Date object. Because the Date() object starts numbering the months with 0, that means March is 2.

Calculating the Number of Days until a Future Event

Calculating the number of days until a future date can be useful for a dynamic greeting. With the West Lake Landscaping Web page, each time users view the Web page in a browser, the Web page displays a greeting that notifies them of the number of days until the start of spring.

Plan Ahead

The steps required to calculate a future date for a dynamic greeting include:

- Creating a Date() object instance with the future date and the current date
- Calculating the milliseconds between the current date and the future date using the getTime() method
- Subtracting to determine the total number of milliseconds between the current date and the future date
- Converting the number of milliseconds to days
- Eliminating any decimal portions of a day to make the number of days an integer

Creating a Date() Object Instance to Store a Future Date To calculate the number of days until a future date, an object instance of the Date() object must be created using the future date. As previously discussed, the Date() object can have a specific literal date as a value, which is assigned to an object instance variable. For example, the JavaScript code to set the date to the first day of spring, which is March 21, 2010, is written as follows:

```
var springDate = new Date("March 21, 2010")
```

The object instance variable springDate now will contain the future date of March 21, 2010.

To Create a Date() Object Instance to Store a Future Date

The following step illustrates how to enter code to create an object instance of the Date() object that stores a future date for the start of spring.

1

- Click line 51.
- Substituting the current year for the spring date March 21, 2010, type `var springDate = new Date("March 21, 2010")` to set the date to the start of spring and then press the ENTER key (Figure 9–6).

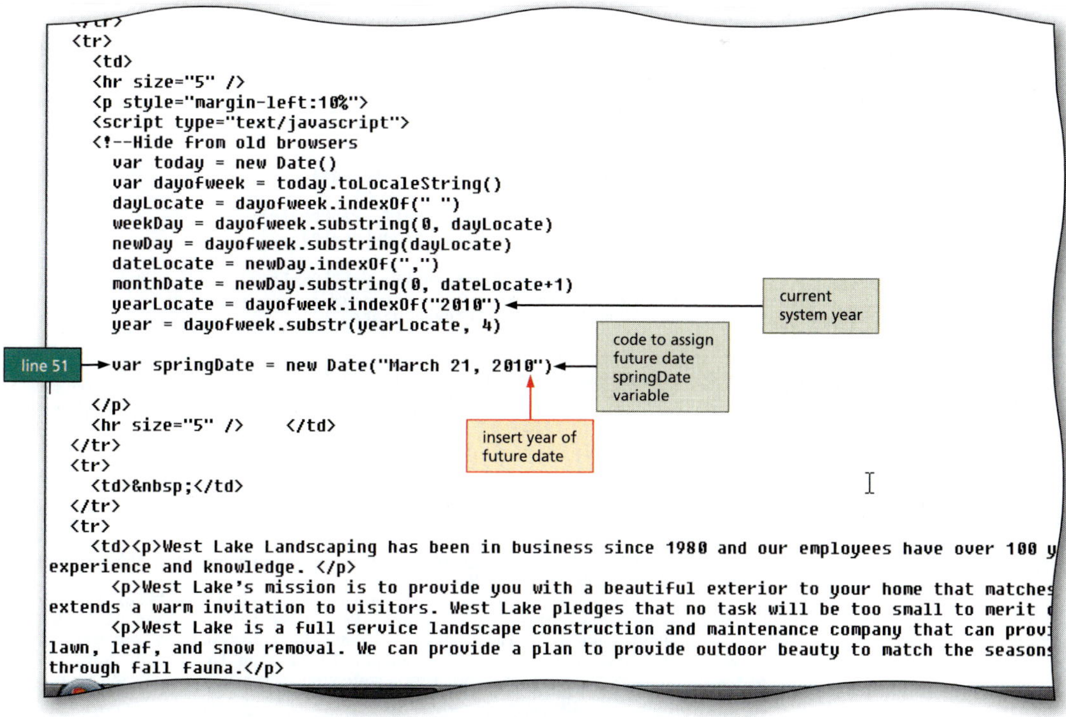

```
<tr>
  <td>
  <hr size="5" />
  <p style="margin-left:10%">
  <script type="text/javascript">
  <!--Hide from old browsers
    var today = new Date()
    var dayofweek = today.toLocaleString()
    dayLocate = dayofweek.indexOf(" ")
    weekDay = dayofweek.substring(0, dayLocate)
    newDay = dayofweek.substring(dayLocate)
    dateLocate = newDay.indexOf(",")
    monthDate = newDay.substring(0, dateLocate+1)
    yearLocate = dayofweek.indexOf("2010")
    year = dayofweek.substr(yearLocate, 4)
    var springDate = new Date("March 21, 2010")

  </p>
  <hr size="5" />    </td>
</tr>
<tr>
  <td> </td>
</tr>
<tr>
  <td><p>West Lake Landscaping has been in business since 1980 and our employees have over 100 y
experience and knowledge. </p>
    <p>West Lake's mission is to provide you with a beautiful exterior to your home that matches
extends a warm invitation to visitors. West Lake pledges that no task will be too small to merit
    <p>West Lake is a full service landscape construction and maintenance company that can prov
lawn, leaf, and snow removal. We can provide a plan to provide outdoor beauty to match the seasons
through fall fauna.</p>
```


Figure 9–6

Calculating Milliseconds Between Two Dates Using the getTime() Method The next step is to calculate the milliseconds between the current date and the actual date of the first day of spring using the getTime() method of the Date() object. The getTime() method returns the number of milliseconds that have elapsed since January 1, 1970 at 00:00:00 and another date. Calculating the number of milliseconds between two dates is easier than trying to count actual days, because each month has a different number of days and it may be necessary to take leap years into account. After determining the number of milliseconds, you then can convert that value to days.

To determine the number of milliseconds between a current date and another date, the JavaScript code should be written to subtract the value returned by the getTime() method of the future date and the value returned by the getTime() method of the current system date. For example, in this chapter, the JavaScript code is written as follows:

```
var daysToGo = springDate.getTime()-today.getTime()
```

To Calculate Milliseconds Between Two Dates Using the getTime() Method

The variable daysToGo will contain the number of milliseconds between the future spring date and the current system date. The following step shows how to enter the JavaScript code to calculate the milliseconds between the future spring date and the current system date.

1

- Click line 52, if necessary.
- Type `var daysToGo = springDate.getTime()-today.getTime()` to calculate the number of milliseconds and then press the ENTER key (Figure 9–7).

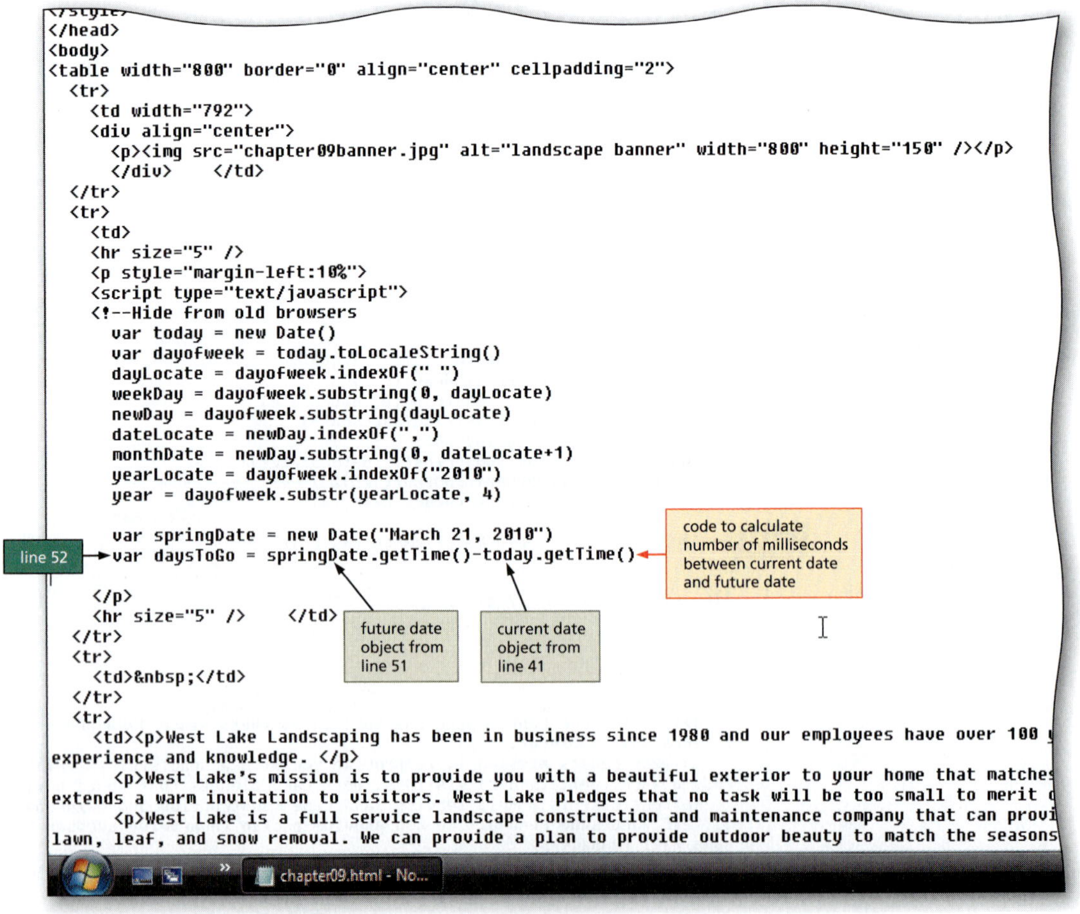

```
</head>
<body>
<table width="800" border="0" align="center" cellpadding="2">
  <tr>
    <td width="792">
    <div align="center">
      <p><img src="chapter09banner.jpg" alt="landscape banner" width="800" height="150" /></p>
      </div>    </td>
  </tr>
  <tr>
    <td>
    <hr size="5" />
    <p style="margin-left:10%">
    <script type="text/javascript">
    <!--Hide from old browsers
      var today = new Date()
      var dayofweek = today.toLocaleString()
      dayLocate = dayofweek.indexOf(" ")
      weekDay = dayofweek.substring(0, dayLocate)
      newDay = dayofweek.substring(dayLocate)
      dateLocate = newDay.indexOf(",")
      monthDate = newDay.substring(0, dateLocate+1)
      yearLocate = dayofweek.indexOf("2010")
      year = dayofweek.substr(yearLocate, 4)

      var springDate = new Date("March 21, 2010")
      var daysToGo = springDate.getTime()-today.getTime()

    </p>
    <hr size="5" />    </td>
  </tr>
  <tr>
    <td> </td>
  </tr>
  <tr>
    <td><p>West Lake Landscaping has been in business since 1980 and our employees have over 100 y
experience and knowledge. </p>
      <p>West Lake's mission is to provide you with a beautiful exterior to your home that matches
extends a warm invitation to visitors. West Lake pledges that no task will be too small to merit o
      <p>West Lake is a full service landscape construction and maintenance company that can provi
lawn, leaf, and snow removal. We can provide a plan to provide outdoor beauty to match the seasons
```


Figure 9–7

Converting Milliseconds to Days and Rounding Up Using the ceil() Method After calculating the number of milliseconds between the current date and the first day of spring, the next step is to convert the milliseconds to days. To convert milliseconds to days, the JavaScript code is written to divide the number of milliseconds stored in the daysToGo variable by the product of 1000*60*60*24. This expression represents the 1,000 milliseconds in a second, the 60 seconds in a minute, the 60 minutes in an hour, and the 24 hours in a day.

The value returned from the calculation daysToGo/(1000*60*60*24) probably will contain a decimal value. The West Lake Landscaping Web page, however, should display the number of days to the first day of spring as an integer value. The ceil() method of the Math object is used to round up to the nearest integer (for example, if the result is 12.843 days, 13 will display because of the ceil() method). The general form of the ceil() method is shown in Table 9–14.

Table 9–14 Math ceil() Method

General form:	var variable=ceil(value)
Comment:	where value may be the result of any calculation. The ceil() method returns a value that rounds the value up to the next highest integer.
Examples:	var myResult=ceil(-3.8) var myNumber=ceil(4.179)
Result:	myResult is -3 myNumber is 5

The JavaScript code for the West Lake Landscaping Web page is written as follows:

```
var daysToSpring = Math.ceil(daysToGo/(1000*60*60*24))
```

which first finds the product of 1000*60*60*24, then divides the value stored in the daysToGo variable by this product, and then raises the result (rounds up) to the next highest integer.

To Convert Milliseconds to Days and Round Up Using the ceil() Method

The following step illustrates how to enter the JavaScript code to convert the number of milliseconds to days.

1

- Click line 53, if necessary.
- Type `var daysToSpring = Math.ceil(daysToGo/(1000*60*60*24))` to convert milliseconds to days and then press the ENTER key twice (Figure 9–8).

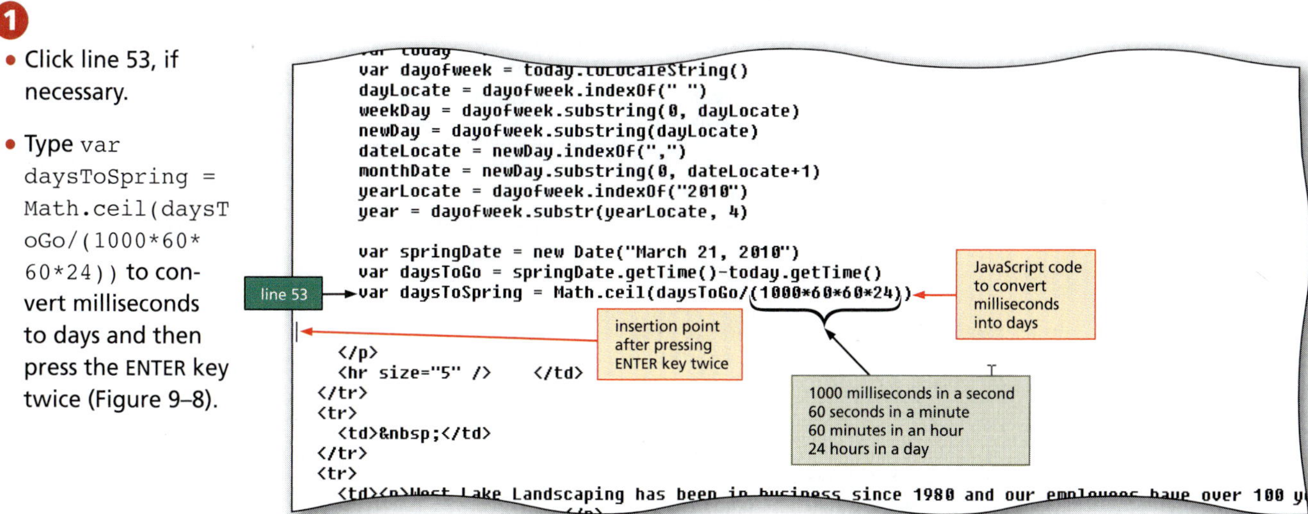

Figure 9–8

Plan Ahead

Using JavaScript to write dynamic text to a Web page.
Before writing dynamic text to a Web page, you need to determine what your message will say and how you will format it for display. Most messages will be a combination of text strings and variables. Text can be formatted using standard HTML tags or using embedded styles. Embedded styles can be placed in <p> or <span> tags to format text.

Writing Text and Variable Values to a Web Page

After the number of days until the first day of spring has been calculated, this data can be written on the Web page using JavaScript. To write data directly to the Web page, JavaScript uses the write() or writeln() methods of the document object. These methods use a string value, with any embedded HTML formatting tags, as a parameter inside the parentheses. Table 9–15 shows the general form of the write() and writeln() methods.

Table 9–15 write() and writeln() Methods

General form:	document.write("text string") document.writeln("text string")
Comment:	where text string is any combination of HTML tags, text, and variables.
Examples:	document.write("<p><h1 align="center">Welcome to my Web page</h1></p>") document.writeln("<center>Welcome to my Web page</center>")

BTW

JavaScript writeln() Method
The writeln() method works only in HTML tags that are sensitive to the new line character ("/n") or the carriage return, line feed, such as the <textarea> tag.

The write() and writeln() methods can embed any HTML tag for formatting the text string. Notice in the first example that the embedded tag has an attribute. The values for attributes must be enclosed in single quotation marks, not double quotation marks, because double quotation marks are used to enclose the entire string content.

To display the contents of a variable as part of a text string, JavaScript code can be written to concatenate the text and the variable. **Concatenate** means to join or link together. The symbol for concatenation is the plus sign (+). Table 9–16 shows the code to write a simple welcome message that concatenates text with the values stored in several variables.

Table 9–16 Code to Write a Message to the Web Page

Code
document.write("<p style='margin-left:10%; font-family:Arial, sans-serif; font-weight:bold; font-size:14'>Today is "+weekDay+" "+monthDate+" "+year+", that leaves only "+ daysToSpring + " days until the start of spring.")
document.write(" Spring is the time to prepare your landscape for new growth of flowers and lawns. ")
document.write(" Call us now at (221) 555-9100 for a free consultation and free estimate.</p>")

In line 55, the write() method is used to write data directly to a Web page. The text message string encloses the HTML tags in quotation marks within the text message string. The plus sign (+) concatenates the three variables weekDay, monthDate, and year together, along with the text message and variable daysToSpring. Placement of quotation marks is important and you must include closing HTML tags. Lines 56 and 57 complete the message.

To Write Text and Variable Values to a Web Page

The following step illustrates how to display text and variables using the write() method.

1

- Click line 55, if necessary.
- Enter the JavaScript code shown in Table 9–16 to concatenate the message text with the stored values. Press the ENTER key only at the end of each complete line of code.
- Press the ENTER key an additional time after line 57 (Figure 9–9).

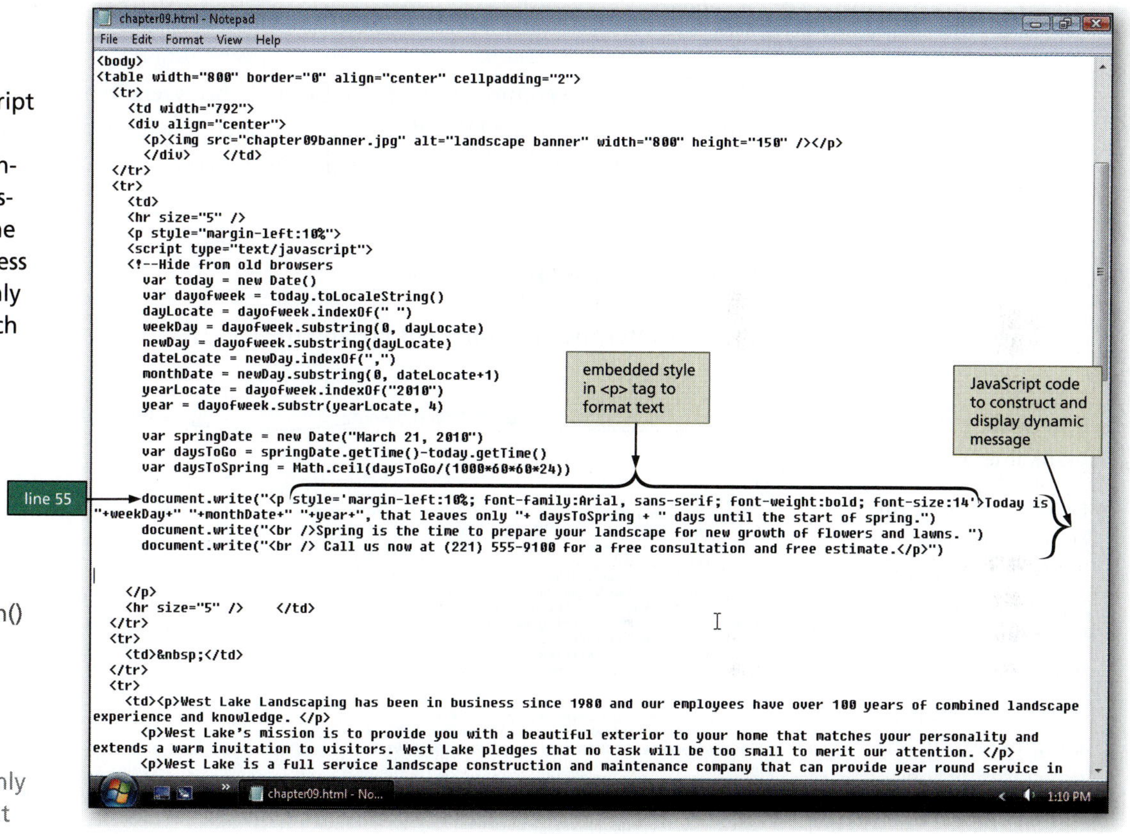

chapter09.html - Notepad

File Edit Format View Help

```
<body>
<table width="800" border="0" align="center" cellpadding="2">
  <tr>
    <td width="792">
    <div align="center">
      <p><img src="chapter09banner.jpg" alt="landscape banner" width="800" height="150" /></p>
      </div>    </td>
  </tr>
  <tr>
    <td>
    <hr size="5" />
    <p style="margin-left:10%">
    <script type="text/javascript">
    <!--Hide from old browsers
      var today = new Date()
      var dayofweek = today.toLocaleString()
      dayLocate = dayofweek.indexOf(" ")
      weekDay = dayofweek.substring(0, dayLocate)
      newDay = dayofweek.substring(dayLocate)
      dateLocate = newDay.indexOf(",")
      monthDate = newDay.substring(0, dateLocate+1)
      yearLocate = dayofweek.indexOf("2010")
      year = dayofweek.substr(yearLocate, 4)

      var springDate = new Date("March 21, 2010")
      var daysToGo = springDate.getTime()-today.getTime()
      var daysToSpring = Math.ceil(daysToGo/(1000*60*60*24))

      document.write("<p style='margin-left:10%; font-family:Arial, sans-serif; font-weight:bold; font-size:14'>Today is
"+weekDay+" "+monthDate+" "+year+", that leaves only "+ daysToSpring + " days until the start of spring.")
      document.write("<br />Spring is the time to prepare your landscape for new growth of flowers and lawns. ")
      document.write("<br /> Call us now at (221) 555-9100 for a free consultation and free estimate.</p>")


    </p>
    <hr size="5" />    </td>
  </tr>
  <tr>
    <td> </td>
  </tr>
  <tr>
    <td><p>West Lake Landscaping has been in business since 1980 and our employees have over 100 years of combined landscape
experience and knowledge. </p>
      <p>West Lake's mission is to provide you with a beautiful exterior to your home that matches your personality and
extends a warm invitation to visitors. West Lake pledges that no task will be too small to merit our attention. </p>
      <p>West Lake is a full service landscape construction and maintenance company that can provide year round service in
```

chapter09.html - No... 1:10 PM

line 55

embedded style in <p> tag to format text

JavaScript code to construct and display dynamic message

Figure 9–9

Q&A Why does writeln() not place a new line in an HTML document?

The writeln() method works only in HTML tags that either are sensitive to the new line character ("\n") or the carriage return, line feed, such as the <textarea> tag.

Q&A How does JavaScript know to concatenate instead of add when it sees the plus sign (+)?

When the JavaScript interpreter identifies the values surrounding a plus sign (+) and they are not numeric values, it will attempt to join them together.

BTW

HTML Comments within JavaScript

Within a <script> section, an HTML comment often is added to hide the JavaScript from old browsers. This comment is a tag that begins with <!-- and ends with //-->. If you fail to close the HTML comment properly, the remainder of your Web page will not be visible.

Completing the JavaScript Section

As you know, all HTML tags must have start and end tags to separate them from other page elements. To complete this section of JavaScript code, it is necessary to add the end comment tag and the end </script> tag. Table 9–17 shows the code used to close the start <script> tag on line 39 and the comment tag on line 40, as entered in Figure 9–4 on page HTML 393.

Table 9–17 Closing the Script Section

Line	Code
59	//-->
60	</script>

Line 59 ends the comment, <!--Hide from old browsers, that was started on line 39. The end </script> tag on line 60 ends the JavaScript code section and prevents the HTML code that follows from being interpreted as JavaScript code.

To Enter the End Comment and </script> Tags

The following step shows how to enter the end comment tag and the end </script> tag.

1

- If necessary, click blank line 59.
- Enter the JavaScript code shown in Table 9–17 and do not press the ENTER key after the last line (Figure 9–10).

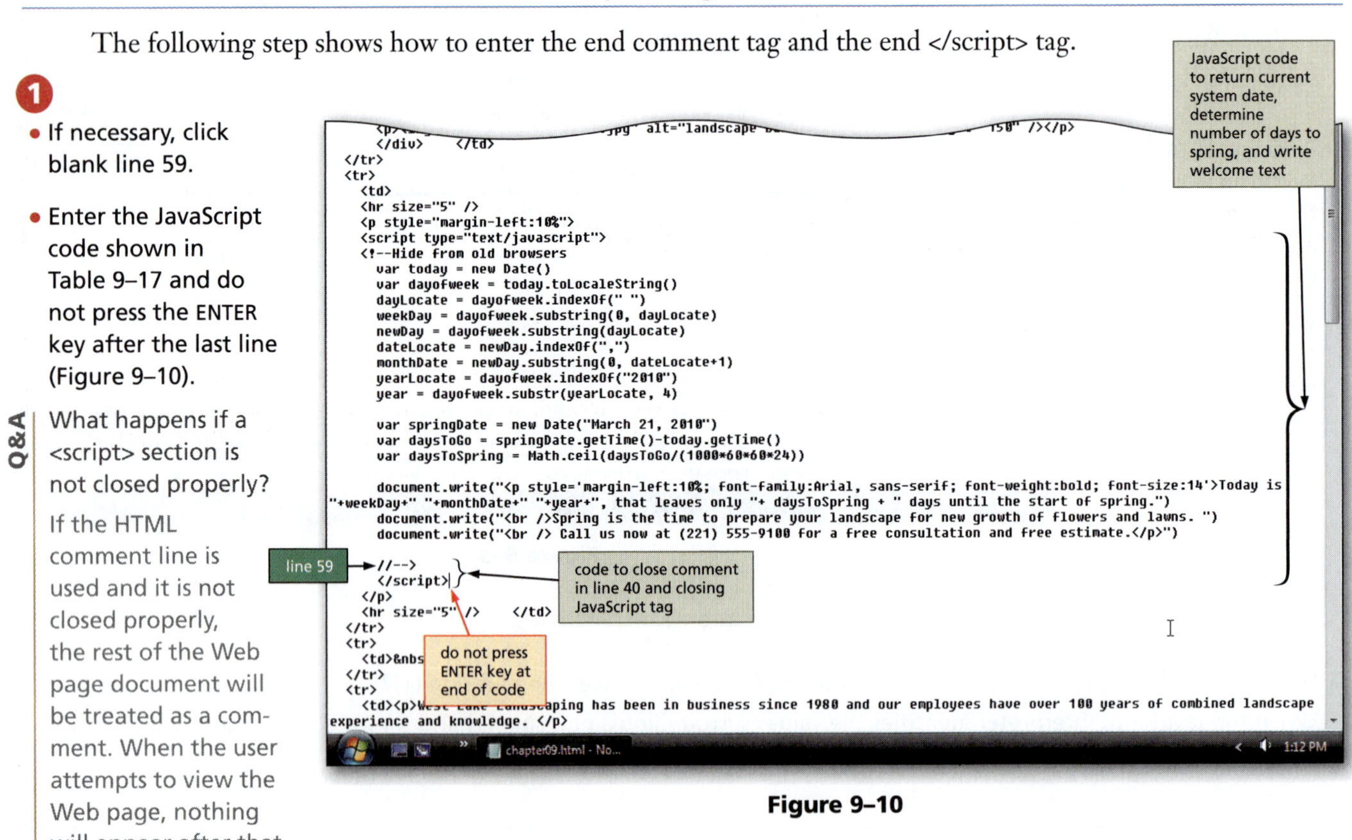

Figure 9–10

Q&A

What happens if a <script> section is not closed properly?

If the HTML comment line is used and it is not closed properly, the rest of the Web page document will be treated as a comment. When the user attempts to view the Web page, nothing will appear after that comment line.

Q&A

Why is the comment needed in <script> sections?

Some browsers or mobile Web devices do not interpret JavaScript code correctly, so the comment hides the JavaScript code. If the comment line is not closed properly, the Web page may not display from the point of the comment forward, thus giving the impression the Web page is blank. If this occurs, always check to ensure the end comment tag was included.

Saving the HTML File and Testing the Web Page

With the first section of JavaScript code for the West Lake Landscaping Web page complete, you should save the file and test the Web page in a browser.

To Save an HTML File

- With a USB flash drive connected to one of the computer's USB ports, click File on the Notepad menu bar and then click Save As. Type `chapter09westlake.html` in the File name text box (do not press the ENTER key).
- If Computer is not displayed in the Favorite Links section, drag the top or bottom edge of the Save As dialog box until Computer is displayed.
- Click Computer in the Favorite Links section to display a list of available drives.
- If necessary, scroll until UDISK 2.0 (G:) appears in the list of available drives.
- If necessary, open the Chapter09\ChapterFiles folder.
- Click the Save button in the Save As dialog box to save the file on the USB flash drive with the name chapter09westlake.html (Figure 9–11).

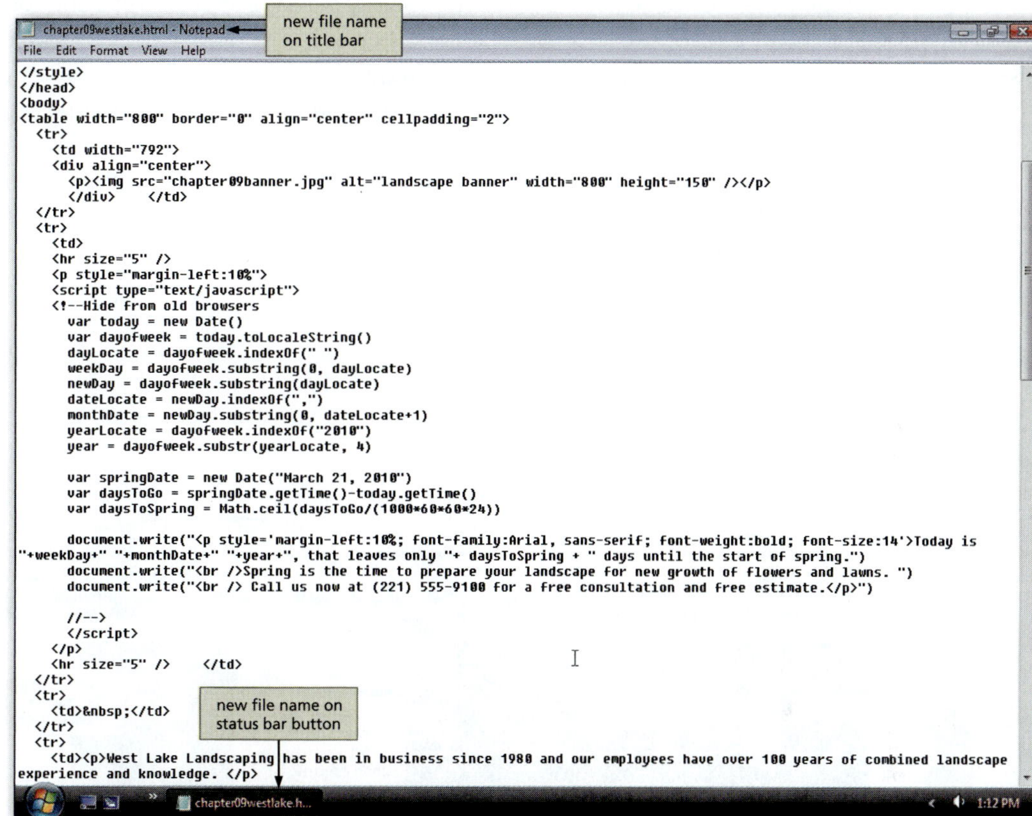

Figure 9–11

To Test the JavaScript on a Web Page

Once you complete your JavaScript code, you should test the code in a browser. The step on the next page illustrates how to open a browser, such as Internet Explorer, and load the chapter09westlake.html Web page to test if the JavaScript works correctly.

- Click the Start button on the Windows Vista taskbar to display the Start menu.
- Click Internet Explorer (or another browser icon) on the Start menu. If necessary, click the Maximize button to maximize the browser window.
- Click the Address bar to select the URL on the Address bar.
- Type `g:\Chapter09\ChapterFiles\chapter09westlake.html` in the Address box.
- Press ENTER to display the Web page (Figure 9–12). If a security message appears, read and follow the instructions in the following Q&A.

Q&A

When I started my Web page in Internet Explorer, a bar displayed across the top that said, "To help protect your security, Internet Explorer has restricted this webpage from running scripts or ActiveX controls that could access your computer. Click here for options…" What should I do?

For the Web page you just created, you can click that bar, and then click the Allow Blocked Content option that displays and then click Yes in the confirmation dialog box. With other Web pages that you are not familiar with, however, it is not advisable to let them run.

Q&A

What should I do if the Web page is not displayed properly?

If your Web page is not displayed correctly, close any error message and then click the Notepad button on the taskbar. Check your JavaScript code according to Figures 9–3 through 9–10 on pages HTML 393 through HTML 404. Correct any errors, save the file, click the Internet Explorer taskbar button to activate the browser, and then click the Refresh button on the Standard Buttons toolbar.

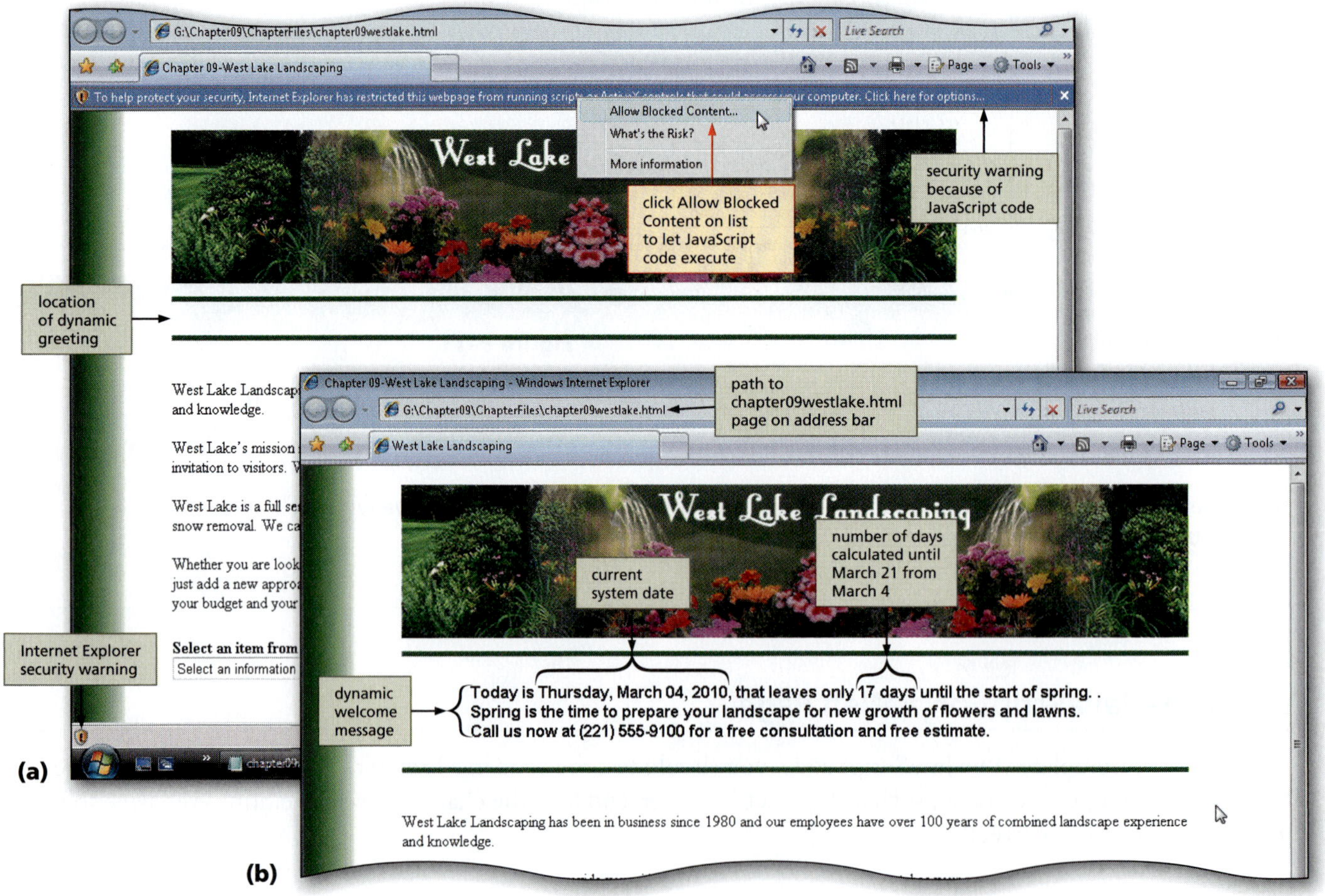

Figure 9–12

Displaying the Last Modified Document Date

Most Web developers agree that a Web page should display the date the Web page was last modified, so visitors are aware of how current the Web page content is. For the West Lake Landscaping Web page, the date last modified should appear at the bottom of the page in a smaller font to keep the message from distracting the user (see Figure 9–1 on page HTML 387).

Plan Ahead

Writing the date last modified on the Web page.
The purpose of displaying the date a Web page was last modified is to make sure the user knows how current the information is contained within the Web page. When writing this content you should follow these guidelines:

- Determine what your message will be. Many Web pages display a copyright notice with the date last modified.
- Create a text message string enclosed in quotation marks and include the document.lastModified property with the text string.
- To write directly to the Web page requires the use of the document write() method written in its own <script> section before the closing </body> tag.

JavaScript provides an easy way to display the date by using the lastModified property of the document object. The lastModified property displays the date in the form of mm/dd/yyyy followed by the time in the form of hh:mm:ss. Table 9–18 shows the general form of the lastModified property of the document.

BTW

Using document. lastModified
The lastModified property might return different values than expected with older browsers and unknown Web servers.

Table 9–18 lastModified Property

General form:	document.lastModified
Comment:	where lastModified is a property of the document object that returns the date the document was last saved.
Example:	document.write("This Web page was last modified " + document.lastModified)

Table 9–19 shows the JavaScript code to create a <script> section to display the date and time the document was last modified and a copyright message.

Table 9–19 Code to Display the lastModified Date

Line	Code
91	`<script type="text/javascript">`
92	`<!--Hide from old browsers`
93	`document.write("<p style='margin-left:10%; font-family:Arial, sans-serif; font-size:xx-small; color:#006600'>")`
94	`document.write("West Lake Landscaping, Copyright 2009-2010. ")`
95	`document.write(" This document was last modified "+document.lastModified+"</p>")`
96	`//-->`
97	`</script>`

Lines 91 and 92 include the required start <script> tag and start comment tag. Lines 93 through 95 are document.write() statements that display the copyright information and the date the document was last modified. Line 94 writes the copyright message and line 95 uses the document.lastModified property with a text string. Lines 96 and 97 close the <script> section.

To Include the Date Last Modified in a Text String

The following step shows how to enter JavaScript code to include the date last modified and a copyright message in a text string.

- If necessary, click the Notepad button on the taskbar to activate the Notepad window.
- Click blank line 91 below the second <p> </p> paragraph tag after the closing </table> tag.
- Enter the JavaScript code shown in Table 9–19 on the previous page. Press the ENTER key after each line but not after the last </script> line (Figure 9–13).

```
chapter09westlake.html - Notepad
File  Edit  Format  View  Help
  <tr>
    <td> </td>
  </tr>
  <tr>
    <td><p>West Lake Landscaping has been in business since 1980 and our employees have over 100 years of combined landscape
experience and knowledge. </p>
      <p>West Lake's mission is to provide you with a beautiful exterior to your home that matches your personality and
extends a warm invitation to visitors. West Lake pledges that no task will be too small to merit our attention. </p>
      <p>West Lake is a full service landscape construction and maintenance company that can provide year round service in
lawn, leaf, and snow removal. We can provide a plan to provide outdoor beauty to match the seasons, from spring flowers
through fall fauna.</p>
      <p>Whether you are looking to add a new patio or deck, replace old bushes and shrubs, revitalize a backyard garden with
a pond, or just add a new approach to your home with a brick walkway and flowers, West Lake can provide you with a landscape
plan to fit your budget and your property size and style.</p>
      <p></p></td>
  </tr>
  <tr>
    <td>
    <form name="infoMenu" action=" ">
      <p align="left" style="font-weight:bolder">
       Select an item from the list to get more information about using stones, flowers, or general design principles:<br />
            <select name="Menu" onchange="loadInfo(this.form)">
              <option value="chapter09westlake">Select an information item</option>
              <option value="chapter09stones">Rocks and Stones</option>
              <option value="chapter09flowers">Using Flowers</option>
              <option value="chapter09principles">Landscape Design Principles</option>
            </select>
        </p>
        </form>    </td>
  </tr>
</table>
<p> </p>
<p> </p>
<script type="text/javascript">
<!--Hide from old browsers
    document.write("<p style='margin-left:10%; font-family:Arial, sans-serif; font-size:xx-small; color:#006600'>")
    document.write("West Lake Landscaping, Copyright 2009-2010. ")
    document.write("<br />This document was last modified "+document.lastModified+"</p>")
//-->
</script>
</body>
</html>
```


Figure 9–13

Writing a JavaScript User-Defined Function

As previously discussed, a function is JavaScript code that is written to perform certain tasks repeatedly. Web developers use user-defined functions to perform specific tasks. Functions replace large sets of JavaScript codes that are too large to fit within an HTML attribute. Instead, functions are placed anywhere in a JavaScript section in the HTML code.

Plan Ahead

Writing user-defined functions.

User-defined functions are normally written in the <head> section so that this code is loaded before the remainder of the Web page. The user-defined functions in the West Lake Landscaping Web page do the following:

- Change the color of the scroll bar to match the Web page colors.
- Use a <select> list as a drop-down menu to link to other Web pages.

The code in the user-defined function in the <head> section is not executed until a JavaScript statement calls the function. To **call** a function means to have JavaScript execute the function. The general form of a user-defined function is shown in Table 9–20.

Table 9–20 User-Defined Functions

General form:	function functionName(optional parameters) {
	JavaScript Code
	}

Comment:	where functionName is the name of the user-defined function, the optional parameters represent values or properties passed to the function that will be used by the function in the JavaScript code. JavaScript code is the statements that execute.

Examples:	function showBrowserName() {
	alert("You are using " +navigator.appname)
	}
	
	function getSum(myform) {
	var sum= document.Calculator.Amount1.value+document.Calculator.Amount2.value
	}

The naming conventions for user-defined functions are similar to those for variables. A function name must begin with a letter, may contain numerals and an underscore, but may not contain any spaces, punctuation (such as periods or commas), or reserved words. Table 9–21 shows valid and invalid user-defined function names. Values or parameters are passed to the function by placing a variable name between the parentheses.

BTW

Placing JavaScript Functions
Always place your JavaScript function definitions in the <head> section to ensure they are loaded completely before they are called.

Table 9–21 Valid Function Names

Valid Function Names	Invalid Function Names	Reason
verifyForm()	3Ddisplay()	Starts with a number
get_Cookie()	make.cookie()	No periods allowed
calcPayment()	calc payment()	No spaces allowed
popWind()	pop-upWindow()	No hyphens allowed

Changing the Color of the Browser Scroll Bar

Plan Ahead

Changing the color of the browser scroll bar.
Because cascading style sheets (CSS) does not have an official standard style for changing colors of the browser scroll bar, the scroll bar color can be changed with a JavaScript user-defined function. To change the scroll bar color, follow these guidelines:

- JavaScript must have access to the object (the scroll bar). Use the getElementsByTagName() method of the document object to assign the "HTML" object to a variable. The getElementsByTagName() method returns an array of elements belonging to the identified object and all associated properties to that object.
- Using the variable as an object, JavaScript can set values to the various scroll bar properties: FaceColor, ArrowColor, HighlightColor, 3DlightColor, DarkshadowColor, TrackColor, and ShadowColor.
- Assign a color that matches or compliments the colors on the Web page to at least the FaceColor and TrackColor.

Table 9–22 describes the general form of the JavaScript getElementsByTagName() method. For more information about the getElementsBy methods, see the JavaScript Quick Reference in Appendix E.

Table 9–22 getElementsByTagName()

General form:	getElementsByTagName('html')
Comments:	where getElementsByTagName() is a method of the document object and 'html' is the object to be returned. Tag element must be entered as a string in single quotation marks and is case sensitive. The returning values are returned in an array format, so that each element can be referenced individually by an array value. The returned value also can use any properties associated with that value. The example shows the method to create an object of the html tag styles named styleObject.
Example:	styleObject=document.getElementsByTagName('html')[0].style

To modify the colors of the scroll bar, use the styleObject object name with the standard scroll bar properties: FaceColor, ArrowColor, HighlightColor, 3DlightColor, DarkshadowColor, TrackColor, and ShadowColor. For example, to change the FaceColor of the scroll bar write

```
styleObject.scrollbarFaceColor="#006600"
```

where the color must be written as a standard color name, a hexadecimal value, or using the rgb() values method.

On the West Lake Landscaping Web page, the scroll bar colors should be changed so the scroll bar appears in green and the scroll bar track appears in light green. Table 9–23 shows the code to change the scroll bar colors.

BTW

Color Values

For the most flexibility in using colors, Web developers suggest using either the hexadecimal version or the rgb() method version to assign a color. Be careful in using a standard color name. Color names like "lightblueaqua" might not be recognized by the style property.

Table 9–23 Code to Change the Browser Scroll Bar Color

Line	Code
6	`<script type="text/javascript">`
7	`<!--Hide from old browsers`
8	`function scrollColor() {`
9	`styleObject=document.getElementsByTagName('html')[0].style`
10	`styleObject.scrollbarFaceColor="#006600"`
11	`styleObject.scrollbarTrackColor="#00aa00"`
12	`}`

Lines 6 and 7 include the required start <script> tag and start comment tag. Line 8 defines the function name as scrollColor(). Line 9 defines the style property of the <html> tag and assigns it to an object, so face color and track color can be changed in lines 10 and 11. Line 10 changes the color of the scroll bar face to green using a hexadecimal value. Line 11 changes the scroll bar track color to light green using a hexadecimal value. Line 12 closes the scrollColor() function.

To Enter User-defined Functions in the <head> Section

The following step illustrates how to enter the user-defined function to change the browser scroll bar color in the <head> section.

- If necessary, click the chapter09westlake.html – Notepad icon on the taskbar.
- Click blank line 6 directly below the <title> tags.
- Enter the JavaScript code shown in Table 9–23.
- Press the ENTER key twice after the last } to leave a blank line between user-defined functions (Figure 9–14).

chapter09westlake.html - Notepad

File Edit Format View Help

```
<!DOCTYPE html PUBLIC "-//W3C//DTD XHTML 1.0 Transitional//EN" "http://www.w3.org/TR/xhtml/DTD/xht
<html xmlns="http://www.w3.org/1999/xhtml" xml:lang="en" lang="en">
<head>
<meta http-equiv="Content-Type" content="text/html; charset=utf-8" />
<title>Chapter 09-West Lake Landscaping</title>
<script type="text/javascript">
<!--Hide from old browsers
function scrollColor() {
   styleObject=document.getElementsByTagName('html')[0].style
   styleObject.scrollbarFaceColor="#006600"
   styleObject.scrollbarTrackColor="#00aa00"
}

<style type="text/css">
<!--
hr {
   color: #006633
   }

body {
        background-image: url(chapter09bkgrnd.jpg);
}
-->
</style>
</head>
<body>
<table width="800" border="0" align="center" cellpadding="2">
  <tr>
    <td width="792">
    <div align="center">
      <p><img src="chapter09banner.jpg" alt="landscape banner" width="800" height="150" /></p>
      </div>    </td>
  </tr>
  <tr>
    <td>
    <hr size="5" />
    <p style="margin-left:10%">
    <script type="text/javascript">
    <!--Hide from old browsers
```

line 6
scrollColor() function changes color of browser scroll bar and scroll bar track to green and light green, respectively
insertion point after pressing ENTER key twice

Figure 9–14

Using the Location Object and selectedIndex Property to Link to a New URL

As shown in Figure 9–1 on page HTML 387, the West Lake Landscaping Web page also includes a drop-down list object that allows users to select items from a drop-down menu. Depending on the item selected in the select list, the code will link users to one of three Web pages containing information about using rocks and stones, landscaping with flowers, or landscape design principles.

Plan Ahead

Using the select list as a drop-down menu.

To use a <select> list as a drop-down menu, a user-defined function must make use of the following:

- The window's location property (window.location), to which a URL can be assigned, and which changes the location of the Web page in the browser.
- The selectedIndex property to identify which item was selected in the drop-down menu list.

BTW

The selectedIndex Property

The selectedIndex property cannot be used alone: it must be used in full reference to the particular select list, the form it belongs to, and its options.

When a user selects an item in the select list, the **selectedIndex** property of the select list returns the value of the selected item. The selectedIndex values of the items in a select list are considered to be numbered, starting with zero for the first item. The second item is number one, and so on. The value returned by the selectedIndex property is an integer, starting with zero for the first item in the list. Table 9–24 shows the general form of the selectedIndex property.

Table 9–24 selectedIndex Property

General form:	var varname=formName.SelectListName.selectedIndex
Comments:	where varname is a variable, formName is the identifier of the form that holds the select list, SelectListName is the name of the select list, and selectedIndex is a property that returns an integer corresponding to the position of the item in the list.
Example:	var menuSelect=myForm.Menu.selectedIndex

As you learned in Chapter 7, the text that appears for each item in a select list is enclosed in <option> tags. The option tag also supports a value attribute, as shown in the code in Figure 9–15. The value in the value attribute describes the item and can be assigned to a variable.

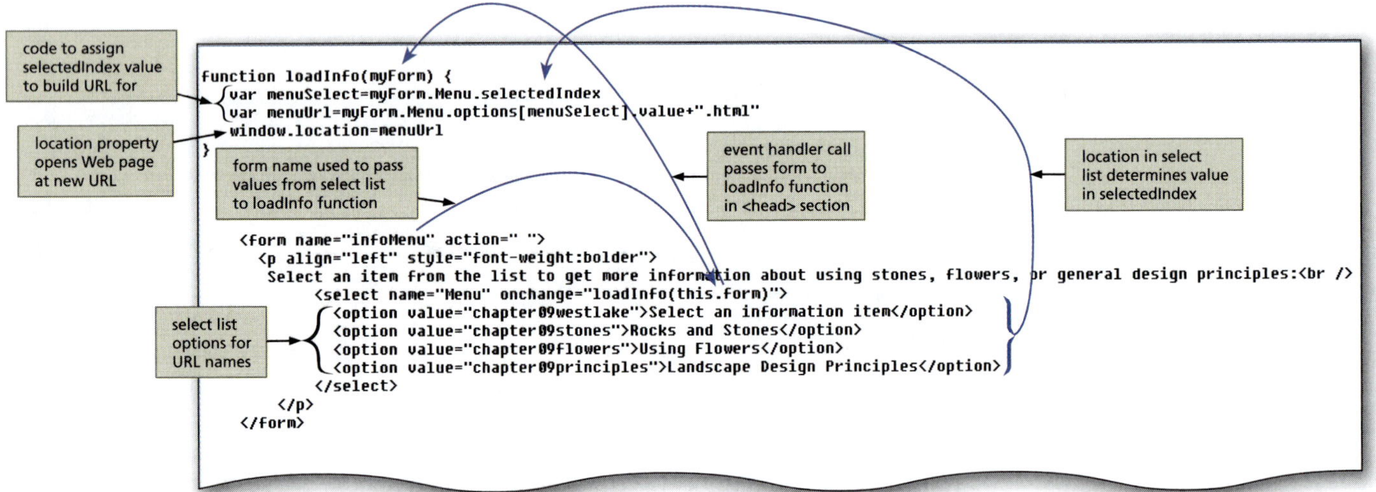

Figure 9–15

This variable can then be used to assign the new Web page location to the window's location property. This statement will load a new URL into the browser. Table 9–25 shows the general form of the location property.

Table 9–25 Location Property

General form:	object=window.location or window.location=URL
Comments:	where object is a variable or some other object that can display the URL of the current window, and URL is the address of the Web page to display. The use of the window object is optional.
Examples:	myform.textbox.value=window.location window.location="http://www.scsite.com"

Table 9–26 shows the JavaScript code for a loadInfo() function that uses the selectedIndex value to determine which item in a list was selected, assigns the value attribute for that item, and then uses that variable to create a URL.

Table 9–26 Code to Change Location

Line	Code
14	`function loadInfo(myForm) {`
15	`var menuSelect=myForm.Menu.selectedIndex`
16	`var menuUrl=myForm.Menu.options[menuSelect].value+".html"`
17	`window.location=menuUrl`
18	`}`
19	
20	`//-->`
21	`</script>`

The selectedIndex property then is used on the object name of the select list and the form. Line 14 defines the function name. The form object, myForm, is passed to the function from the select list name attribute. In line 15, the selectedIndex statement assigns the numerical value of the item selected from the list to the variable menuSelect. In this line, menuSelect is a variable name, myForm is the identifier of the form that holds the select list, and Menu is the name of the select list. The options property of Menu refers to the <option> tag in the select list, while selectedIndex indicates the integer value of the item selected in the select list. Line 16 concatenates the value attribute of the selected item (menuSelect) with the file extension .html to create a URL. The URL name is concatenated to the .html file name extension using the plus sign (+). Line 17 uses that URL to load that Web page into the browser window. Line 18 closes the function. Lines 20 and 21 close the <script> section for these two user-defined functions.

To Enter the User-defined Function to Link to a New URL using the Drop-Down Menu List

The following step illustrates how to enter the user-defined function to link to a new URL using the drop-down menu.

1

- Click line 14 if necessary.
- Enter the JavaScript code shown in Table 9–26 to enter the options and links for the drop-down menu list.
- Do not press the ENTER key after the last line (Figure 9–16).

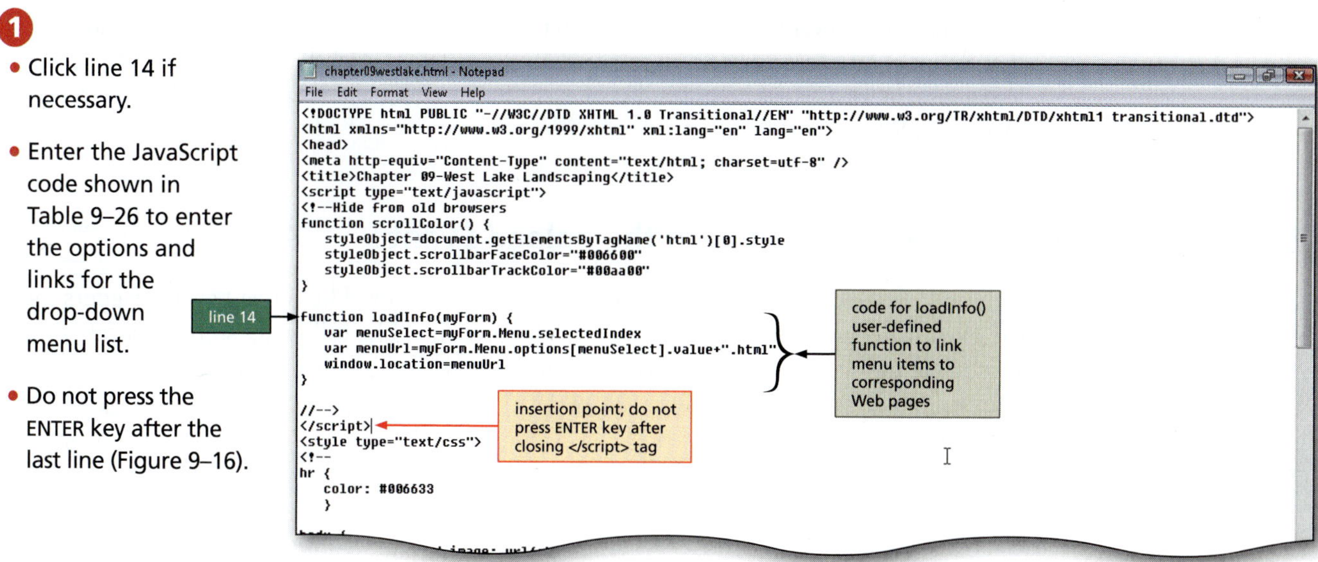

Figure 9–16

Calling JavaScript Functions Using Event Handlers

Now that you have added user-defined functions to change the scroll bar color and create a drop-down menu list, you need to add code that tells when these functions are to be called. JavaScript has two basic methods to call functions. One method to call a function is to use event handlers and object methods. The other method is to code the function name in a JavaScript section at the logical point of execution. The user-defined functions written in this chapter execute using event handlers.

Plan Ahead

Using event handlers to call user-defined functions.
Event handlers must be placed with the object (such as a button, drop-down list, or HTML tag) that controls the event. In this chapter, the events are load and change, so you use the event handlers onload and onchange to call the user-defined functions. In this chapter, you will:

- Place the onload event handler in the <body> tag.
- Place the onchange event handler in the <select> tag that starts the drop-down menu list.

As you have learned, an event is the result of an action, such as a mouse click or a window loading. An event handler is a way to associate that action with a function. For example, when a user clicks a button or a check box, a JavaScript user-defined function may be associated with that event. The associated function will execute if the event is captured and then **triggers**, or calls, the JavaScript user-defined function. The general form of an event handler is shown in Table 9–27.

Table 9–27 Event Handlers	
General form:	<tag attribute eventhandler="JavaScript code">
Comment:	where tag is the HTML tag; attribute is a property of the tag that can have a value assigned to it, eventhandler is the name of the JavaScript event handler, and JavaScript code is the instruction to execute, usually in the form of a function name.
Example:	<body onload="scrollColor()">

JavaScript event handlers make Web pages more dynamic and interactive by allowing JavaScript code to execute only in response to a user action, such as a mouse click or selection of an item in a list. For a complete list of event handlers, see the JavaScript Quick Reference in Appendix E.

To Associate a User-defined Function with the onload Event

An event handler not directly associated with a user action is the onload event. The onload event triggers the associated function when the Web page has completed loading into the browser. The following steps illustrate how to enter JavaScript code to associate the scrollColor() user-defined function with the onload event.

1

- Click to the right of the y in the <body> tag in line 34, as shown in Figure 9–17.

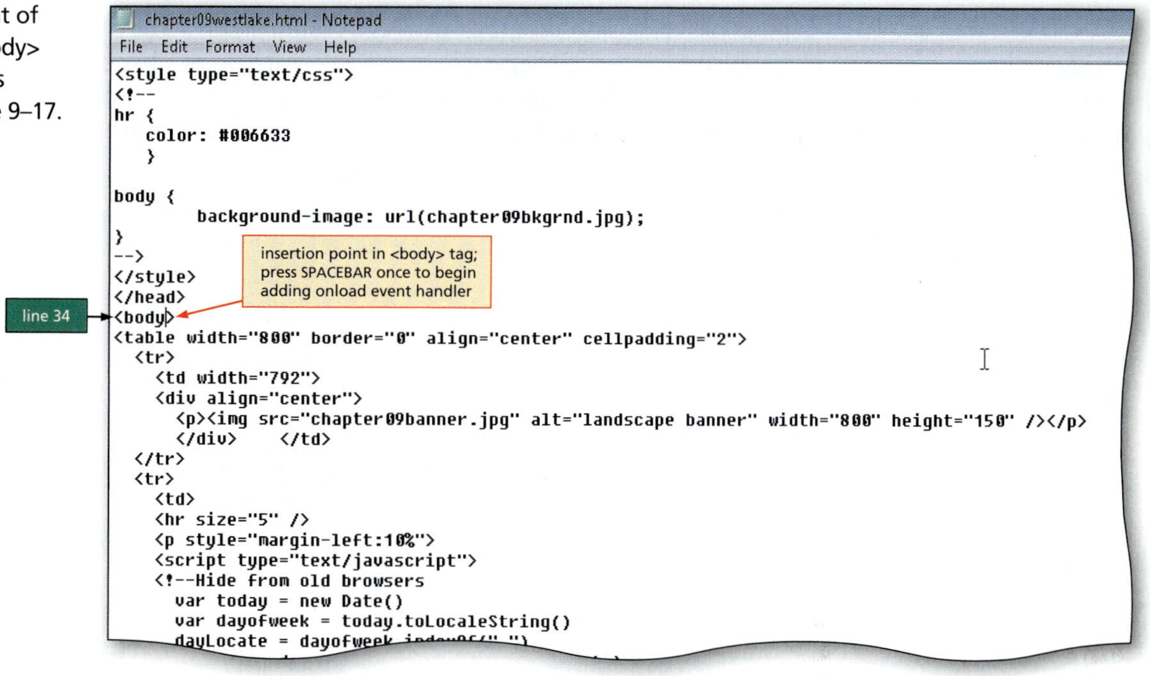

```
<style type="text/css">
<!--
hr {
   color: #006633
   }

body {
        background-image: url(chapter09bkgrnd.jpg);
}
-->
</style>
</head>
<body>
<table width="800" border="0" align="center" cellpadding="2">
  <tr>
    <td width="792">
    <div align="center">
      <p><img src="chapter09banner.jpg" alt="landscape banner" width="800" height="150" /></p>
      </div>    </td>
  </tr>
  <tr>
    <td>
    <hr size="5" />
    <p style="margin-left:10%">
    <script type="text/javascript">
    <!--Hide from old browsers
      var today = new Date()
      var dayofweek = today.toLocaleString()
      dayLocate = dayofweek.indexOf(" ")
```

line 34

insertion point in <body> tag; press SPACEBAR once to begin adding onload event handler

Figure 9–17

2

- Press the SPACEBAR once and then type `onload="scrollColor()"` within the <body> tag. Do not press the ENTER key (Figure 9–18).

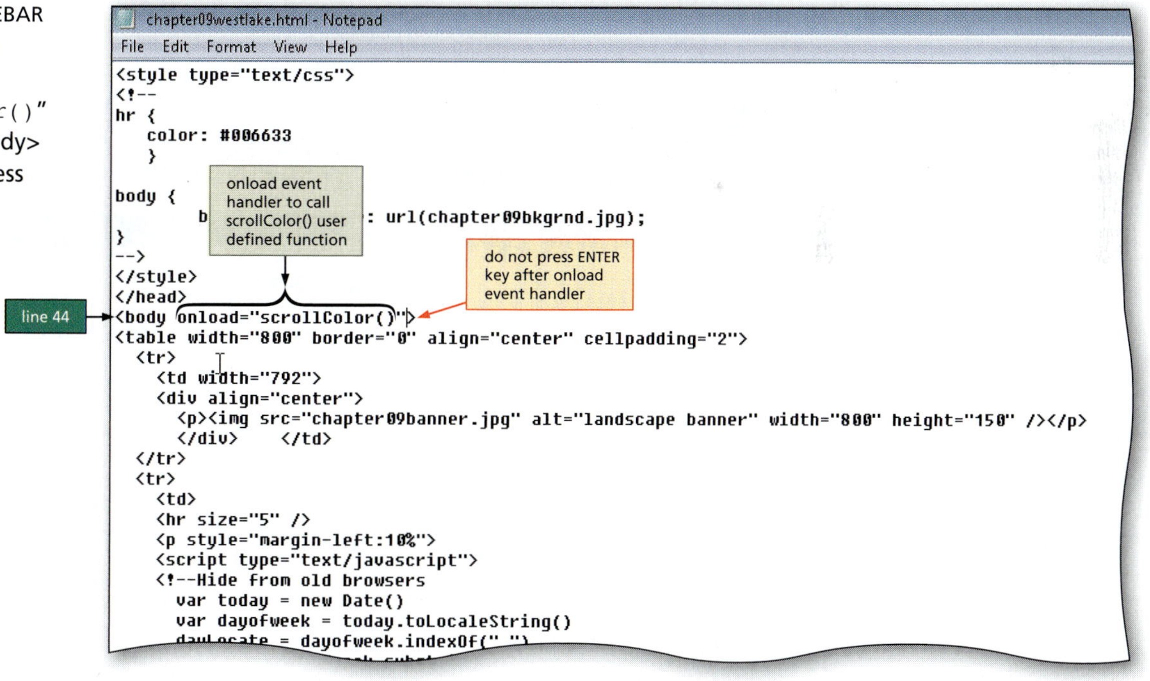

```
<style type="text/css">
<!--
hr {
   color: #006633
   }

body {
        background-image: url(chapter09bkgrnd.jpg);
}
-->
</style>
</head>
<body onload="scrollColor()">
<table width="800" border="0" align="center" cellpadding="2">
  <tr>
    <td width="792">
    <div align="center">
      <p><img src="chapter09banner.jpg" alt="landscape banner" width="800" height="150" /></p>
      </div>    </td>
  </tr>
  <tr>
    <td>
    <hr size="5" />
    <p style="margin-left:10%">
    <script type="text/javascript">
    <!--Hide from old browsers
      var today = new Date()
      var dayofweek = today.toLocaleString()
      dayLocate = dayofweek.indexOf(" ")
```

line 44

onload event handler to call scrollColor() user defined function

do not press ENTER key after onload event handler

Figure 9–18

To Associate a User-defined Function with the Select List

The West Lake Landscaping Web page also uses the onchange event handler. The onchange event handler is triggered when the value of an object changes. For example, when the user selects a list item in the select list, the value of the select list is changed. This change triggers the associated user-defined function loadInfo(). The following step illustrates how to associate the user-defined function loadInfo() with the select list.

- Click to the right of "Menu" in line 85.
- Press the SPACEBAR once and then type `onchange="loadInfo(this.form)"` within the <select> tag. Do not press the ENTER key (Figure 9–19).

chapter09westlake.html - Notepad

File Edit Format View Help

```
      //-->
      </script>
    </p>
    <hr size="5" />    </td>
  </tr>
  <tr>
    <td> </td>
  </tr>
  <tr>
    <td><p>West Lake Landscaping has been in business since 1980 and our employees have over 100 years of combined landscape experience and knowledge. </p>
      <p>West Lake's mission is to provide you with a beautiful exterior to your home that matches your personality and extends a warm invitation to visitors. West Lake pledges that no task will be too small to merit our attention. </p>
      <p>West Lake is a full service landscape construction and maintenance company that can provide year round service in lawn, leaf, and snow removal. We can provide a plan to provide outdoor beauty to match the seasons, from spring flowers through fall fauna.</p>
      <p>Whether you are looking to add a new patio or deck, replace old bushes and shrubs, revitalize a backyard garden with a pond, or just add a new approach to your home with a brick walkway and flowers, West Lake can provide you with a landscape plan to fit your budget and your property size and style.</p>
      <p></p></td>
  </tr>
  <tr>
    <td>
    <form name="infoMenu" action=" ">
      <p align="left" style="font-weight:bolder">
       Select an item from the list to get more information about u  or general design principles:<br />
        <select name="Menu" onchange="loadInfo(this.form)">
          <option value="chapter09westlake">Select an informati
          <option value="chapter09stones">Rocks and Stones</opt
          <option value="chapter09flowers">Using Flowers</option>
          <option value="chapter09principles">Landscape Design Principles</option>
        </select>
      </p>
      </form>    </td>
  </tr>
</table>
<p> </p>
<p> </p>
<script type="text/javascript">
<!--Hide from old browsers
   document.write("<p style='margin-left:10%; font-family:Arial, sans-serif; font-size:xx-small; color:#006600'>")
   document.write("West Lake Landscaping, Copyright 2009-2010. ")
   document.write("<br />This document was last modified "+document.lastModified+"</p>")
//-->
</script>
```

line 85

do not press ENTER key after entering event handler

enter onchange event handler to call loadInfo() user-defined function

chapter09westlake.h... Chapter 09-West La... 1:21 PM

Figure 9–19

To Save an HTML File and View and Test the Completed Web Page

With the code for the West Lake Landscaping Web page complete, you should save the HTML file and view the Web page in a browser to confirm the Web page is displayed and functioning as desired. The following step shows how to save an HTML file and then view and test the Web page in a browser.

1

- With the USB drive plugged into your computer, click File on the menu bar.
- Click Save on the File menu.
- Click the chapter 09-WestLake Landscaping – Windows Internet Explorer button on the taskbar.
- Click the Refresh button on the Standard Buttons toolbar.
- Select Rocks and Stones in the drop-down menu list (Figure 9–20a) to display the Rocks and Stones page.
- Click the Back button on the Standard Buttons toolbar to return to the West Lake Landscaping page.

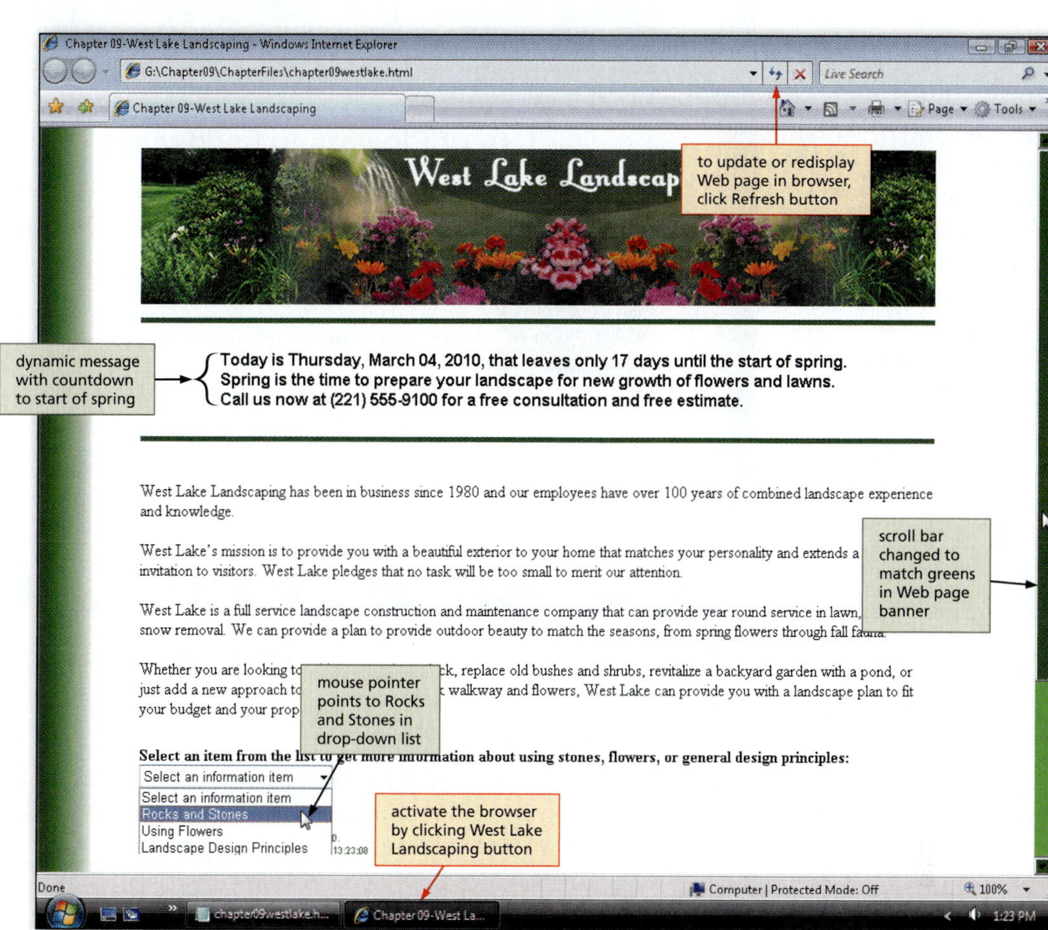

Figure 9–20a

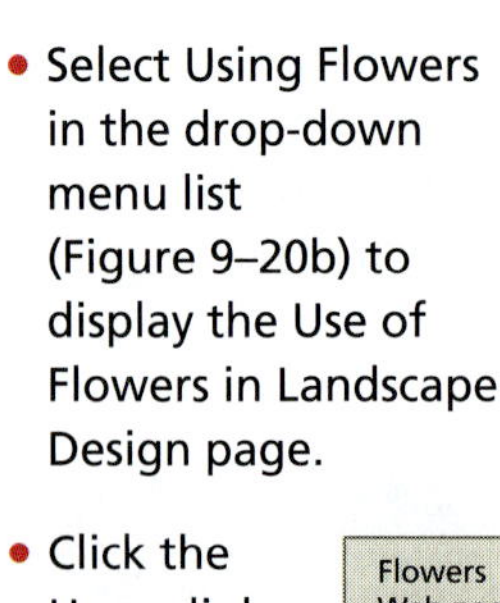

- Select Using Flowers in the drop-down menu list (Figure 9–20b) to display the Use of Flowers in Landscape Design page.
- Click the Home link at the bottom of the page to return to the West Lake Landscaping home page, and select Landscape Design Principles from the drop-down menu list to display the Design Principles page.
- Click the Home link at the bottom of the page to return to the West Lake Landscaping home page.

Figure 9–20b

Q&A Is there any way to display all the errors on a Web page at once?

Internet Explorer does not offer this feature. If the JavaScript code is missing periods, is missing quotation marks, or has misspelled words, the Web page displays with errors. To continue loading the Web page, click the OK button in the dialog box. The browser will cease to process any more JavaScript code, but will load what it can of the Web page. After you fix the errors, refresh the Web page to see if any other errors are found.

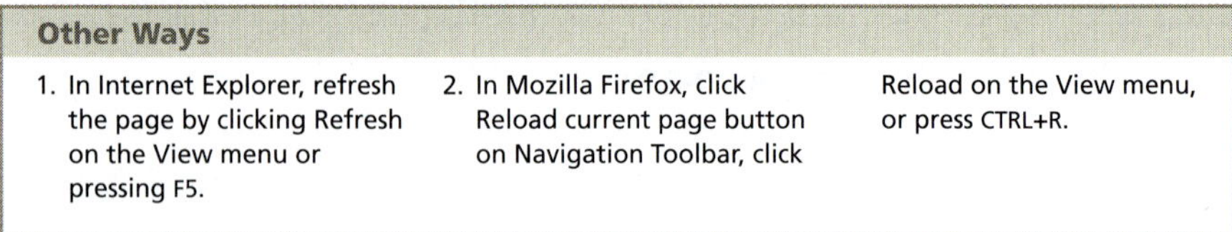

Other Ways

1. In Internet Explorer, refresh the page by clicking Refresh on the View menu or pressing F5.
2. In Mozilla Firefox, click Reload current page button on Navigation Toolbar, click Reload on the View menu, or press CTRL+R.

To Validate a Web Page

Now that you have tested the Web page and made sure the JavaScript works as desired, you should validate the page at the w3.org Web site. The following step illustrates how to validate an HTML file.

1

- Open Internet Explorer and navigate to the Web site `validator.w3.org`.
- Click the Validate by File Upload tab.
- Click the Browse button.
- Locate the chapter09westlake.html file on your storage device and click the file name.
- Click the Open button on the Choose file dialog box and the file name will be inserted into the File box.
- Click the Check button.

To Print an HTML File

After completing and testing the Web page, you should print the HTML file using Notepad for future reference. The following step shows how to print the chapter09westlake.html file using Notepad.

- If necessary, click the chapter09westlake.html - Notepad button on the taskbar.
- Click File on the menu bar and then click Print. Click the Print button in the Print dialog box.

To Quit Notepad and a Browser

- Click the Close button on the browser title bar.
- Click the Close button on the Notepad window title bar.

Chapter Summary

In this chapter, you learned basic JavaScript concepts and how to write and insert JavaScript code to make your Web page more dynamic and interactive. The items listed below include all the new HTML and JavaScript skills you have learned in this chapter.

1. Enter the Start <script> and Comment Tags (HTML 393)
2. Extract the Current System Date Using the Date() Object (HTML 397)
3. Create a Date() Object Instance to Store a Future Date (HTML 399)
4. Calculate Milliseconds Between Two Dates Using the getTime() Method (HTML 400)
5. Convert Milliseconds to Days and Round Up Using the ceil() Method (HTML 401)
6. Write Text and Variable Values to a Web Page (HTML 403)
7. Enter the End Comment and </script> Tags (HTML 404)
8. Test the JavaScript on a Web Page (HTML 405)
9. Include the Date Last Modified in a Text String (HTML 408)
10. Enter User-defined Functions in the <head> Section (HTML 411)
11. Enter the User-defined Function to Link to a New URL using the Drop-Down Menu List (HTML 413)
12. Associate a User-defined Function with the onload Event (HTML 414)
13. Associate a User-defined Function with the Select List (HTML 416)

BTW

Quick Reference
For a list of JavaScript statements and their associated attributes, see the JavaScript Quick Reference (Appendix E) at the back of this book, or visit the HTML Quick Reference Web page (scsite.com/HTML5e/qr).

Learn It Online

Test your knowledge of chapter content and key terms.

Instructions: To complete the Learn It Online exercises, start your browser, click the Address bar, and then enter the Web address `scsite.com/html5e/learn`. When the HTML Learn It Online page is displayed, click the link for the exercise you want to complete and read the instructions.

Chapter Reinforcement TF, MC, and SA

A series of true/false, multiple choice, and short answer questions that test your knowledge of the chapter content.

Flash Cards

An interactive learning environment where you identify chapter key terms associated with displayed definitions.

Practice Test

A series of multiple choice questions that test your knowledge of chapter content and key terms.

Who Wants To Be a Computer Genius?

An interactive game that challenges your knowledge of chapter content in the style of a television quiz show.

Wheel of Terms

An interactive game that challenges your knowledge of chapter key terms in the style of the television show, *Wheel of Fortune*.

Crossword Puzzle Challenge

A crossword puzzle that challenges your knowledge of key terms presented in the chapter.

Apply Your Knowledge

Reinforce the skills and apply the concepts you learned in this chapter.

Adding User-Defined Functions

Instructions: Start Notepad. Open the file apply9-1.html from the Chapter09\Apply folder of the Data Files for Students. See the inside back cover of this book for instructions on downloading the Data Files for Students, or contact your instructor for information about accessing the required files.

The apply9-1.html file is a partially completed HTML file that you will use for this exercise. Figure 9–21 shows the Apply Your Knowledge Web page as it should be displayed in a browser after the JavaScript has been added. This problem requires changing the scroll bar color with a user-defined function, using JavaScript to display a dynamic message, using JavaScript to display a copyright and date last modified at the bottom of the Web page, and adding an event handler in the <body> to activate the user-defined function.

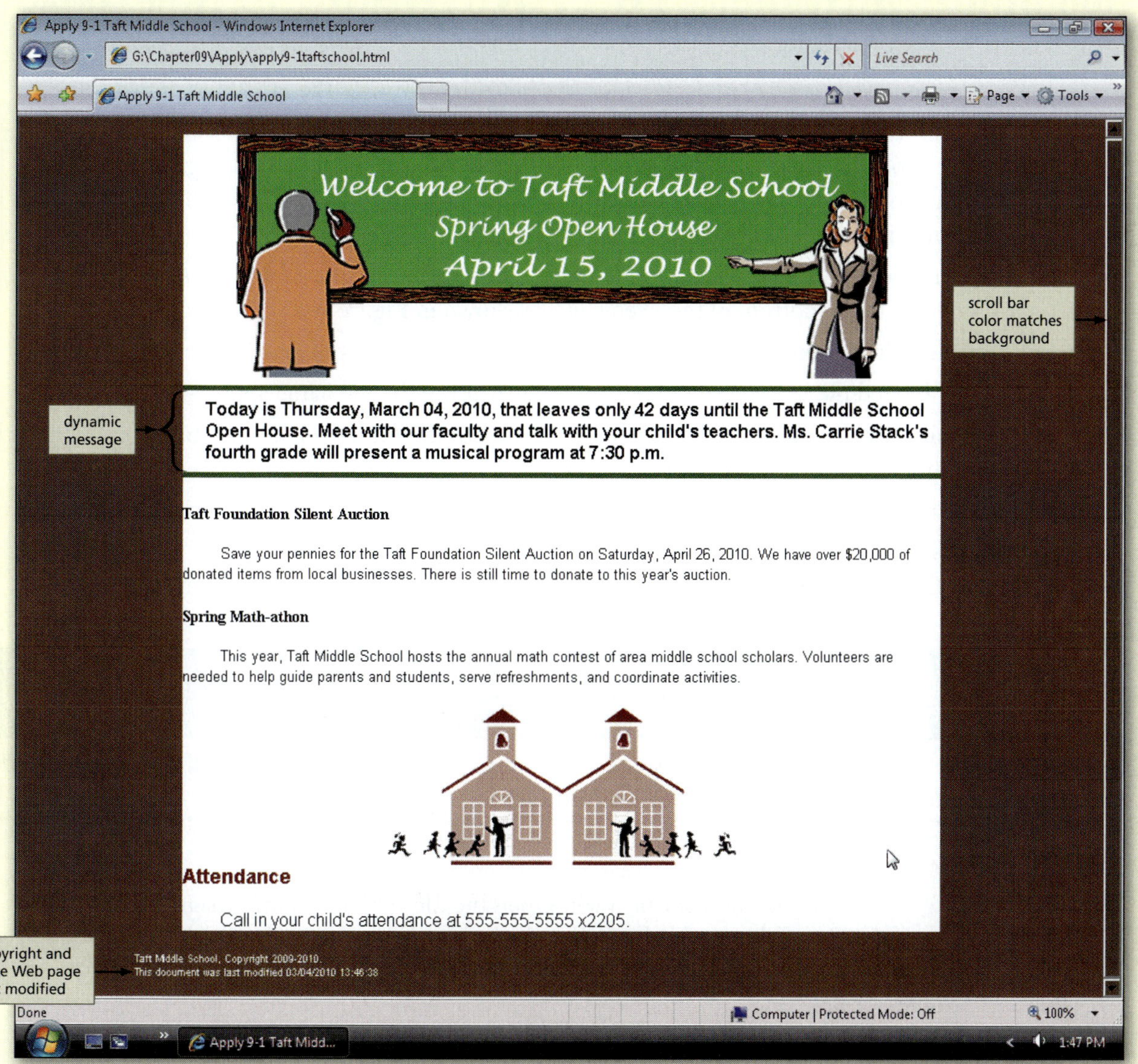

Figure 9–21

Perform the following tasks:

1. Enter the beginning of a JavaScript code section for a user-defined function in the <head> section of the Web page before the <style> tag. Be sure to include a comment line to hide the JavaScript from old browsers.
2. Using the code in Table 9–23 on page HTML 410 as a guide, enter the code for a user-defined function called scrollColor() to change the scroll bar face color and scroll bar track color to the hexadecimal values shown in Table 9–28.

Table 9–28 Scroll Bar Colors
scroll bar face color: #655028
scroll bar track color: #d2af7d

3. Be sure to enter the closing brace for the function, followed by the closing HTML tags to close the <script> section.

Continued >

Apply Your Knowledge *continued*

4. Write code to start a new JavaScript code section at line 50 after the HTML comment line 49: <!--JavaScript code-->.
5. Using the code in Table 9–13, Figures 9–6, 9–7, and 9–8 and Table 9–16 as a guide, enter the JavaScript code to display the countdown message shown in Figure 9–21 on the previous page. Use your own current and future dates for this Web page.
6. Using the code in Table 9–19 as a guide, write a copyright message and the date the document was last modified at the bottom of the Web page, as shown in Figure 9–21.
7. Enter the onload event handler in the <body> tag to call the scrollColor() function.
8. Save the revised file in the chapter09\Apply folder using the file name apply9-1solution.html.
9. Start your browser. Enter the URL g:\Chapter09\Apply\apply9-1solution.html in the address box to view and test the Web page in your browser.
10. If any errors occur, check the code against Steps 1 through 7, make any required changes, save the file using the same file name, and then refresh the Web page in the browser.
11. Submit the revised HTML file and Web page in the format specified by your instructor.

Extend Your Knowledge

Extend the skills you learned in this chapter and experiment with new skills. You will need to search the Internet to complete the assignment.

Learning More about Displaying Messages

Instructions: Start Notepad and your browser. Open the file extend9-1.html from the Chapter09\Extend folder of the Data Files for Students. See the inside back cover of this book for instructions on downloading the Data Files for Students, or contact your instructor for information about accessing the required files.

Perform the following tasks:

1. Search the Internet for the JavaScript instructions on how to display a message on the status bar of your browser. (*Hint*: Look for properties of the Windows object.)
2. Write the code for a user-defined function that assigns the message "Nick's Fitness Center will make your fitness dreams come true." on the status bar.
3. Using the code in Table 9–23 on page HTML 410 as a guide, enter the code for a user-defined function called scrollColor() to change the scroll bar colors to the hexadecimal values shown in Table 9–29.

Table 9–29 Scroll Bar Colors

scroll bar face color: #715a2d	scroll bar track color: #dfcfae
scroll bar arrow color: #d29117	scroll bar highlight color: #000000

4. In the second row of the table in the HTML code, add the code for the dynamic message. Pick a date about 30 days from the current date to use in the calculation. Embed a style in the document write() method that sets the left margin to 5 percent, the font family to Arial, sans-serif, the font-weight to bold, and the font size of 14 point.
5. The message should display similar to the Web page shown in Figure 9–22.
6. Add the onload event handler to the <body> tag to call this function when the Web page loads.

7. Use a JavaScript section to display the copyright and the date last modified for Nick's Fitness Center. Use the substr() or substring() method as discussed in Tables 9–10 and 9–11. Use one of these methods to display only the year portion of the date last modified message.
8. Save the revised file in the Chapter09\Extend folder using the file name extend9-1solution.html.
9. Start your browser. Enter the URL g:\Chapter09\Extend\extend9-1solution.html in the address box to view and test the Web page in your browser.
10. If any errors occur, check the code against Steps 1 through 7, make any required changes, save the file using the same file name, and then refresh the Web page in the browser.
11. Submit the revised HTML file and Web page in the format specified by your instructor.

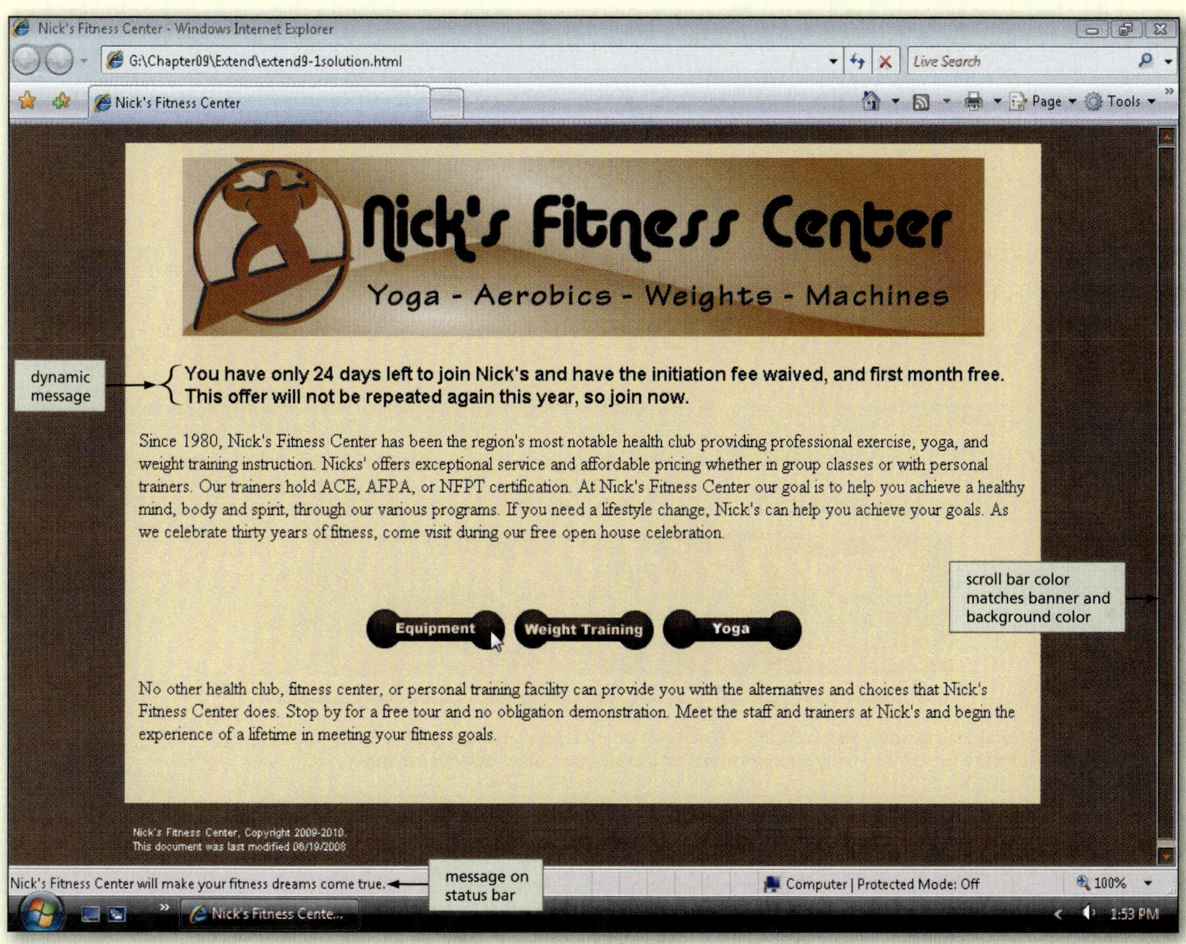

Figure 9–22

Make It Right

Analyze the JavaScript code on a Web page and correct all errors.

Correcting Syntax Errors and Inserting Missing Code

Instructions: Start your browser. Open the file makeitright9-1.html from the Chapter09\MakeItRight folder of the Data Files for Students. See the inside back cover of this book for instructions for downloading the Data Files for Students, or see your instructor for information on accessing the files required in this book.

Continued >

Make It Right *continued*

The Web page is an announcement for a fall event called Bayfield Days. This Web page has four errors that you are to find and correct.

Perform the following tasks:

1. When you open the makeitright9-1.html file in the browser, you will notice that the scroll bar did not change color and that the dynamic message did not display between the horizontal lines.
2. Save the HTML file in the Chapter09\MakeItRight folder using the file name makeitright9-1solution.html.
3. Compare the code in the user-defined function to the code to change the scroll bar color in Table 9–23 on page HTML 410. Make the changes necessary to change the scroll bar color on the Bayfield Days Web page.
4. Compare the code in Tables 9–13 and 9–16 to the code in the dynamic message in the Bayfield Days Web page. Make corrections as necessary.
5. Make sure the user-defined functions are called properly by the correct event handlers, and that they are in the correct locations.
6. Save the corrected HTML file and test it using your browser. If errors occur, check your code and save again. Your Web page should look similar to Figure 9–23.
7. Submit the revised HTML file and Web page in the format specified by your instructor.

Figure 9–23

In the Lab

Design and/or create a Web page using the guidelines, concepts, and skills presented in this chapter. Labs are listed in order of increasing difficulty.

Lab 1: Creating a Web Page for the College Theater

Problem: You belong to the Huysken College Theater Club and have offered to create a Web site to promote the campus theater. You create the Web page shown in Figure 9–24, which includes changing the color of the scroll bar, using a drop-down menu to link to related Web pages, and add the copyright and date last modified at the bottom of the Web page.

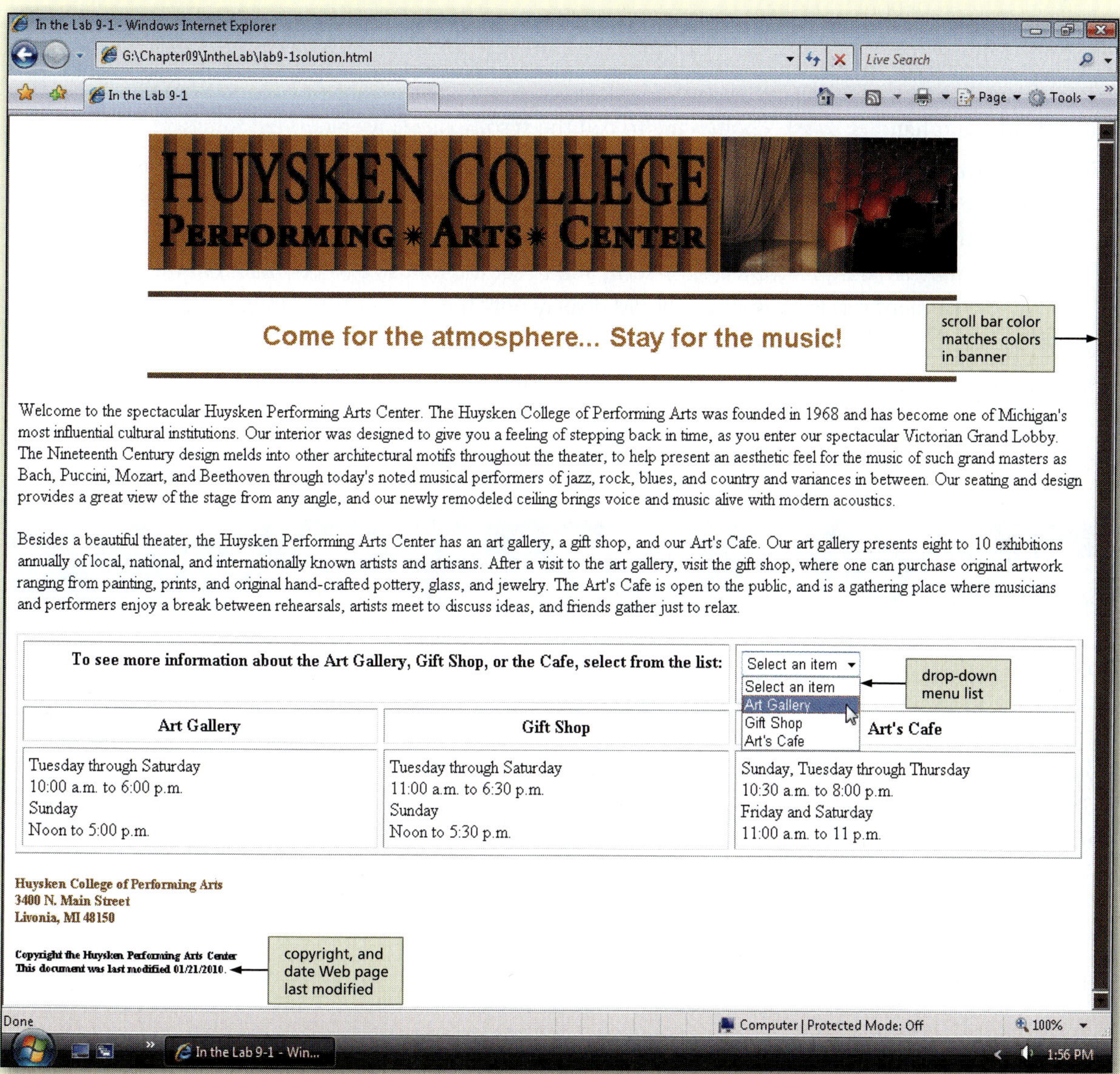

Figure 9–24

Continued >

In the Lab *continued*

Instructions: Perform the following tasks.

1. Start Notepad and open the lab9-1.html file from the Chapter09\IntheLab folder of the Data Files for Students.
2. Save the file as lab9-1solution.html.
3. Start a new <script> section in the <head> section under the <title> tag.
4. Write a JavaScript function called infoMenu() that uses the selectedIndex value of the moreInfo <select> list in the menuInfo <form>. Use the code in Table 9–26 as a guide.
5. Write another JavaScript function to change the scroll bar colors called scrollColor(). Use the code in Table 9–23 as a guide, and use the following color values for the scroll bar face and track colors:

   face color: #604000

   track color: #bf8a20
6. Add the onchange event handler in the <select> tag to call the loadMenu() function. Then, add the onload event handler to the <body> tag to call the scrollColor() user-defined function.
7. At the bottom of the Web page, after the HTML comment <!-- copyright and date last modified --> and before the closing </body> tag, write the JavaScript code to display the copyright and date last modified message as shown in Figure 9–24. Embed a style in the document write() method to set the font family to Arial, Helvetica, sans-serif, and to set the font size to xx-small. On the second line, the date document was last modified should display only the date, not the time, using a substring() method on the lastModified property.
8. Save the completed HTML file and test it using your browser. If an error occurs, check your code and save and test again.
9. Submit the completed HTML file and Web page in the format specified by your instructor.

In the Lab

Lab 2: Mountain Valley Recycling

Problem: You are an intern at Mountain Valley Recycling. Your supervisor knows of your Web page development experience and asks you to modify the company's Web page to include links to other pages of information using a drop-down menu. In addition, your supervisor wants to add a countdown in a dynamic announcement that Mountain Valley Recycling will be at the county fair grounds to collect any household hazardous materials. You suggest adding some color to the scroll bar, and copyright and the date last modified information. You add the JavaScript to make the Web page appear as in Figure 9–25.

Figure 9–25

Instructions: Perform the following tasks:

1. Start Notepad and open the lab9-2.html file from the Chapter09\IntheLab folder of the Data Files for Students.
2. Save the file as lab9-2solution.html.
3. Start a new <script> section in the <head> section, on the line following the <title> tag, for two user-defined functions.
4. Write a JavaScript function to change the scroll bar colors called valleyScroll(). Use the code in Table 9–23 as a guide, and use the following color values for the scroll bar face and track colors:

   face color: #0000cc

   track color: #6daff0
5. Write a JavaScript function called menuLinks() that uses the selectedIndex value of the menuList <select> list in the recycleMenu <form>. Use the code in Table 9–26 as a guide.
6. In the table cell beneath the blue divider line, write the JavaScript script code to take the current date and calculate the number of days until the fair. Use a future date associated with the current date in your code. The script code should display a dynamic message as shown in Figure 9–25.
7. Before the closing </body> tag, write the JavaScript code to display the copyright and the date the Web page was last modified.

Continued >

In the Lab *continued*

8. Add the event handler to call the valleyScroll() function and the event handler to call the menuLinks() function. Place these event handlers in the appropriate HTML tags.
9. Save the completed HTML file and test it using your browser. If an error occurs, check your code and save and test again.
10. Submit the completed HTML file and Web page in the format specified by your instructor.

In the Lab

Lab 3: The Rocky Mountain Outdoor Sportsmens Show

Problem: You work as an event planner for the Rocky Mountain Arena. The annual Outdoor Sportsmens show is coming soon. Your assignment is to create a Web page that announces the upcoming event (Figure 9–26).

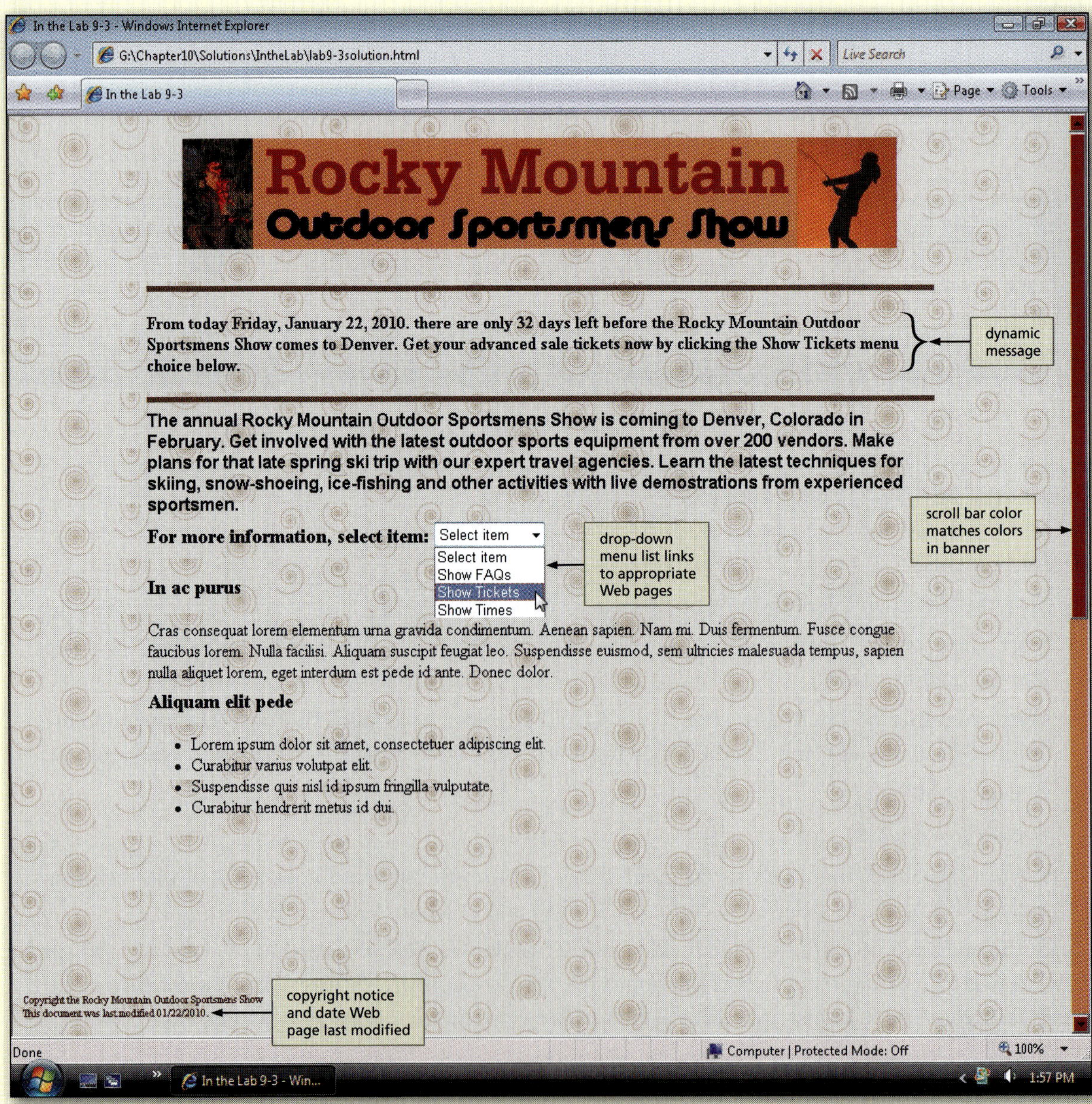

Figure 9–26

Instructions: Perform the following tasks:

1. Start Notepad and open the lab9-3.html file from the Chapter09\IntheLab folder. Save the file as lab9-3solution.html.
2. Using the techniques learned in this chapter, write the JavaScript code to create a dynamic message with a countdown, change the scroll bar color, and use the selectedIndex in the <select> tag to link to new Web pages. The menu links are Show FAQs, Show Tickets, and Show Times. Add a copyright notice and the date the Web page was last modified. Use a future date near the current date for this lab. For the scroll bar face color use #990000 and for scroll bar track color use #dc9b60.
3. Save the completed HTML file and test it using your browser. If an error occurs, check your code, and save and test again.
4. Submit the completed HTML file and Web page in the format specified by your instructor.

Cases and Places

Apply your creative thinking and problem solving skills to design and implement a solution.

• Easier ••More Difficult

• 1: Expanding the Chapter Web Page

West Lake Landscaping has received numerous requests for more information to be added to its Web site. One of the most common requests has been more information about decks. Using the material presented in this chapter, modify your chapter09westlake.html file to add two additional links in the drop-down menu list.

One link should be to a Web page about decks and the other is a link to garden design organizations (http://www.apld.com/). Use the file case9-1deck.html in the CasesPlaces folder of the Data Files for Students for the deck link and modify this page by replacing the simple greeting with a dynamic greeting announcing the deck exposition, change the color of the scroll bar, and add the copyright and date last modified information on the bottom of this Web page. Save as case9-1decksolution.html.

•• 2: Create the Shopper Newspaper Web Site

As a summer intern for the East San Alameda Heights Crosstown Shopper you have been asked to create the online version of the shopper. The page should have a drop-down menu list with links to coupons, real estate ads, and personal classified Web pages. The shopper page should change the scroll bar face color to #999999 and the track color to #cccccc. Make up an event the Crosstown Shopper might advertise. Create a dynamic message indicating the number of days to that event. Be sure to add the copyright, the URL, and the date last modified in a JavaScript section at the end of the shopper page and at the end of the case9-2coupons.html, case9-2personals.html, case9-2realestate.html pages found in the data files folder.

•• 3: Create the Tri City Community College Web Site

As the newly hired webmaster for Tri City Community College, you are going to redesign its Web site. You want to add a dynamic message to announce the number of days until the upcoming Job Fair. You use a drop-down menu to link to financial aid, student housing, and student life Web pages, and write a JavaScript user-defined function to change the URL location.

Because CSS does not have a standard for changing scroll bar colors, you add a JavaScript user-defined function to change the face color to #cb5b30, and the track color to #6b5030. You want a dynamic message that displays the current date and then calculates the number of days to the upcoming job fair. At the bottom of the Web page you display the copyright information and the date the Web page was last modified. Display only the date, not the time, with the lastModified property. Be sure to add the proper event handlers in the correct locations to call the user-defined functions. Use files from the Chapter09\CasesPlaces folder of the Data Files for Students to help build your Web page.

•• 4: Create a Family Web Page

Make It Personal

Many families have begun sharing information via the Internet. Many people use MySpace® and Facebook® to share photos and other information. Carefully consider your own family and then use the concepts and techniques presented in this chapter to create a Web page that announces a birthday, wedding, anniversary, or some other special family event. Use a dynamic message to display the current date and the number of days to the event. Make your page long enough so that the scroll bar is active and write the JavaScript user-defined function to change the scroll bar color. Create a drop-down menu list to link to other Web pages that you have created or that already exist, such as links to family or friends on MySpace or Facebook. Add a copyright notice and add the date the page was last modified at the bottom in small print. Be sure to check spelling and grammar on the Web pages that you create.

• • 5: Critique an Existing Web Site

Working Together

Many organizations in your community have Web pages. Each team member should search for these organization Web pages. Your team should find at least eight to ten Web sites. Print the Web pages and critique the layout and information presented on the page. Try to determine if the Web site has used JavaScript or some other scripting method (you can look at the source code). As a group, list four to five features that you like on each page, and four to five features you think could be improved on each page. If you find that a page used JavaScript, make note of how JavaScript was used for future reference in this text. Write up your evaluation and critique as a team and hand in the printed Web pages with the critique report.

10 Creating Pop-Up Windows, Adding Scrolling Messages, and Validating Forms

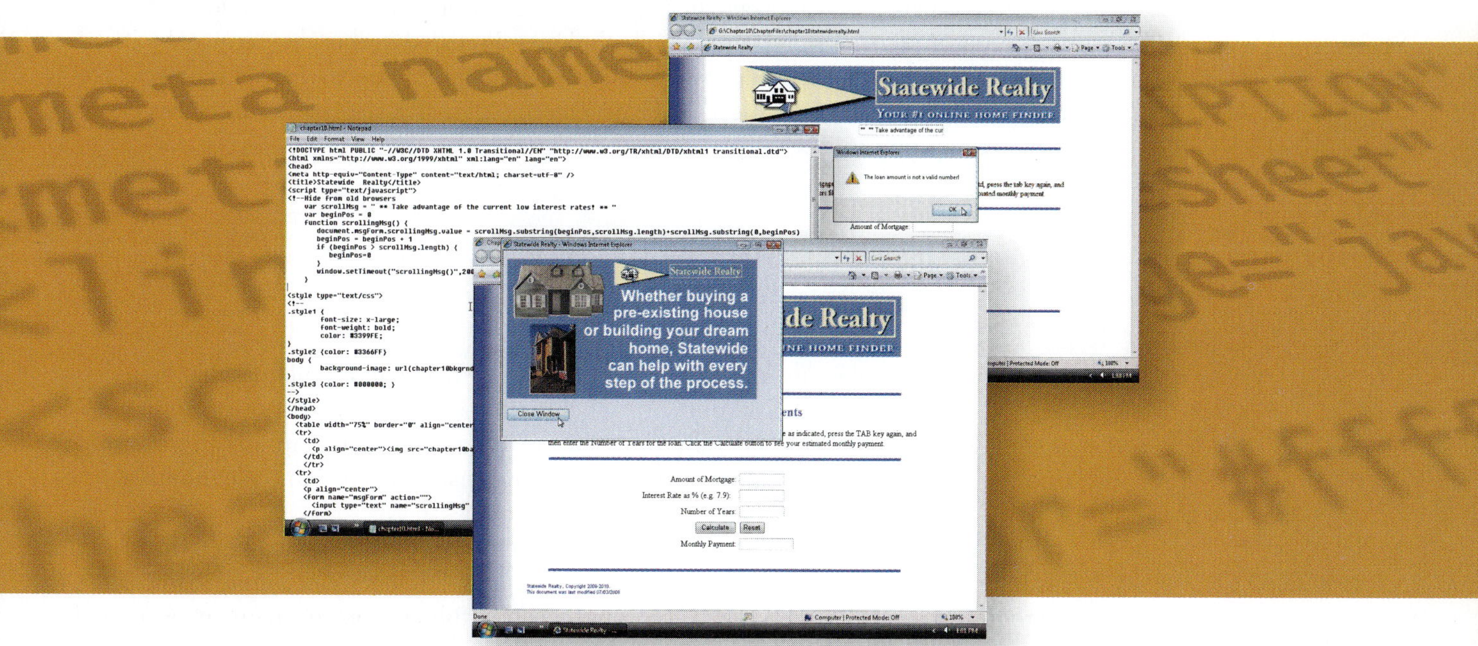

Objectives

You will have mastered the material in this chapter when you can:

- Write a JavaScript user-defined function to display a scrolling message
- Write a JavaScript user-defined function to validate form data
- Write a JavaScript user-defined function to calculate loan payments
- Define if and if...else statements, conditionals, and operands
- Write a JavaScript user-defined function to format output in a text field
- Describe how to display a pop-up window

10 Creating Pop-Up Windows, Adding Scrolling Messages, and Validating Forms

Introduction

In Chapter 9, you learned how to integrate JavaScript into an HTML document using variables and objects, and how to write JavaScript user-defined functions called by event handlers. This chapter reinforces these skills and shows you how to create a scrolling message that displays a text message in a form text field, using JavaScript to validate the data users enter into forms. The validation techniques discussed in this chapter use the if…else statement; parseInt(), parseFloat(), and isNaN() built-in functions; the Math object's pow() method; and the Number object's toFixed() method. Finally, the chapter discusses how to display a pop-up window.

Project — Statewide Realty Mortgage Loan Calculator

Many bank and real estate Web sites include monthly payment calculators that help buyers determine what their monthly payments will be for a car, mortgage, or other type of loan. These calculators generally allow buyers to input basic loan information — total amount, interest rate, and number of years — that is used to determine the monthly payment.

Recently, Statewide Realty has decided to improve their Web site based on a recent customer-satisfaction survey. One of the most-requested items was a simple loan calculator that would allow customers to estimate their monthly mortgage payments. As one of the Web developers, you have been assigned to create this new Web page.

You decide to create an interactive form that allows customers to enter the mortgage amount, interest rate, and number of years for the loan. After entering the information, users click a Calculate button to display the monthly mortgage payment or the Reset button to clear the text boxes. You suggest adding a simple scrolling message box that urges customers to take advantage of current low mortgage rates. You also suggest adding a pop-up window to promote Statewide's online home finder service. Figure 10–1 shows the pop-up window, the scrolling message, and the user input form for the mortgage calculator.

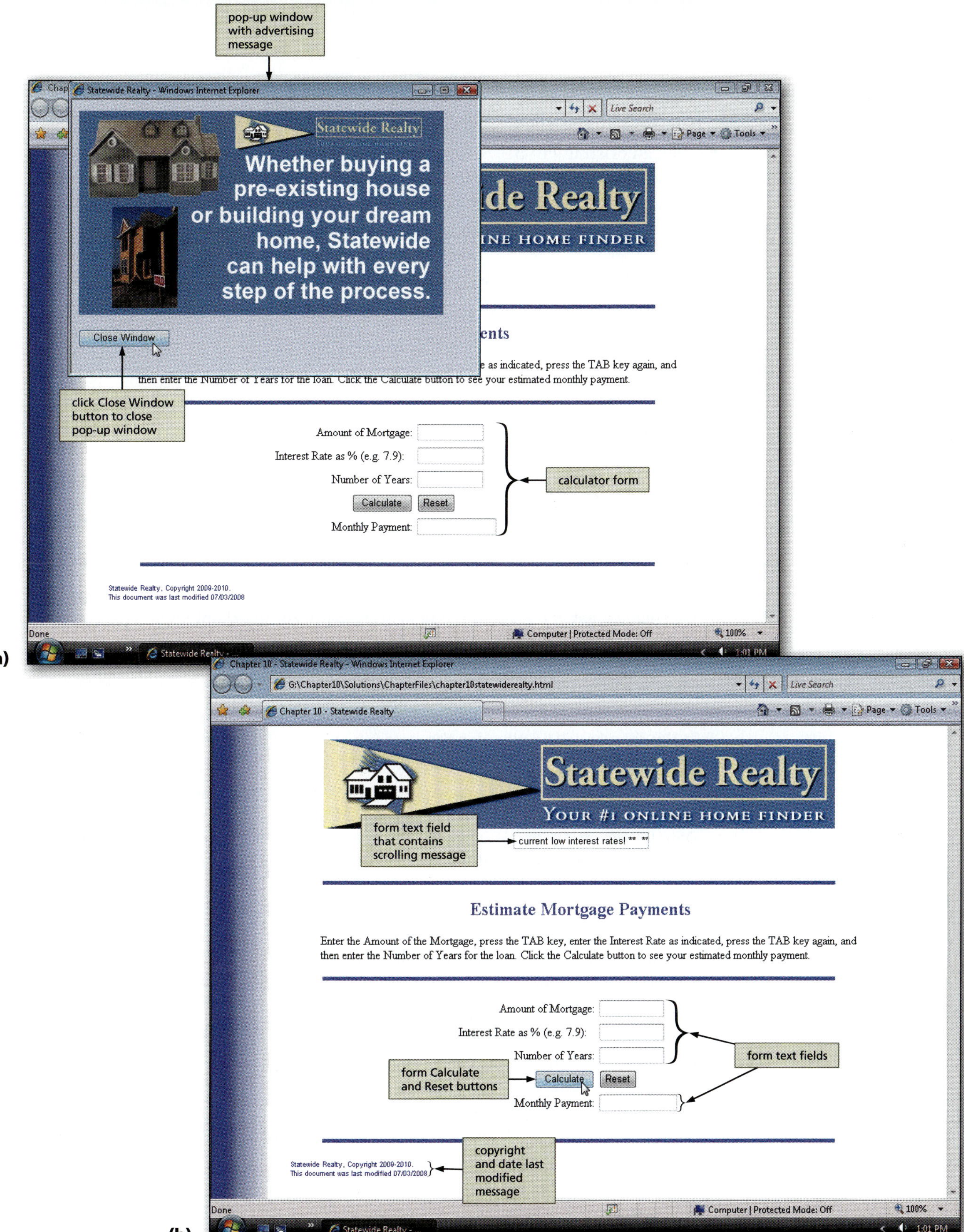
pop-up window with advertising message
Statewide Realty - Windows Internet Explorer
Statewide Realty
Whether buying a pre-existing house or building your dream home, Statewide can help with every step of the process.
Close Window
click Close Window button to close pop-up window
Amount of Mortgage:
Interest Rate as % (e.g. 7.9):
Number of Years:
Calculate
Reset
Monthly Payment:
calculator form
(a)
Chapter 10 - Statewide Realty - Windows Internet Explorer
G:\Chapter10\Solutions\ChapterFiles\chapter10statewiderealty.html
Statewide Realty
Your #1 online home finder
form text field that contains scrolling message
current low interest rates! ** **
Estimate Mortgage Payments
Enter the Amount of the Mortgage, press the TAB key, enter the Interest Rate as indicated, press the TAB key again, and then enter the Number of Years for the loan. Click the Calculate button to see your estimated monthly payment.
form text fields
form Calculate and Reset buttons
Statewide Realty, Copyright 2009-2010.
This document was last modified 07/03/2008
copyright and date last modified message
(b)

Figure 10–1

Overview

As you read this chapter, you will learn how to write embedded JavaScript code to create the Web pages shown in Figures 10–1a and 10–1b by performing these general tasks:

- Open an existing HTML file and add JavaScript code.
- Create a scrolling message in a text field.
- Calculate a mortgage payment based on loan amount, interest rate, and number of years.
- Validate data entered into a form.
- Format the monthly payment to display as currency.
- Open a pop-up window when the Web page initially loads.
- Convert text to numeric values using built-in functions.
- Display the date the Web page was last modified.
- Save, validate, and test the Web pages.
- Print the HTML code and Web pages.

Plan Ahead

General Project Guidelines

When adding JavaScript or any scripting language to a Web page document, the actions you perform and decisions you make will affect the appearance and characteristics of the finished Web page. Before you write the JavaScript code, you should follow these general guidelines:

- **Determine what you want the code to accomplish.** For this chapter's project, you want to create a scrolling message in a text field, add a pop-up window, create a form for user input, validate the user input, perform a calculation based on the user input, output a result formatted as currency, and display the date the Web page was last modified.
- **Determine where in the Web page you want the code to appear.** All the JavaScript code in this chapter will be placed in the <head> section of the HTML code in user-defined functions. Event handlers will call these functions as needed.
- **Determine the overall Web page appearance.** When the Web page first loads, a pop-up window is displayed. The Web page also includes a text message that scrolls continuously. Data for the mortgage calculation is entered in a form, validated, and the results are displayed in currency format. The date the page was last modified displays at the bottom of the page.
- **Determine the data validation requirements.** Before the monthly payment can be calculated, the data entered in the form must be validated. The loan amount, interest rate, and the number of years for the loan must be numeric, not blank, and greater than zero. If the data does not meet these criteria, an alert message box notifies the user and positions the insertion point in the appropriate text field.
- **Determine the calculations needed.** You will need a formula for calculating the monthly payment. This formula is given later in the chapter.

When necessary, more specific details concerning the above guidelines are presented at appropriate points in the chapter. The chapter also will identify the actions performed and decisions made regarding these guidelines during the creation of the Web page shown in Figure 10–1 on the previous page.

Inserting a Scrolling Message on a Web Page

A simple way to provide a Web site visitor with information is to add a scrolling text message to a Web page. Companies often use scrolling messages on their Web sites to highlight breaking news, key products, or special promotions. A scrolling text message can appear either in a text field within the Web page or on the status bar in the browser window. Because visitors to a Web page often do not look at the status bar, most Web developers agree that a scrolling message in a text field on the Web page is a better location.

A scrolling message has four basic components:

- The display object (a form text field)
- The text message to scroll in the text field
- The position of the next character in the text message
- A time delay

The **display object** identifies where the scrolling message is displayed, which, in this project, is in a form text field. The scrolling **message** is a text string assigned to a variable. The text string is what the user sees when the message is displayed. The **position** is the location of the next character in the text string. The **delay** regulates the speed in which the characters display in the text field.

Placement of Scrolling Text
Another reason to avoid placing scrolling text on the status bar is that it can be missed easily by the visitor.

The first step in creating the scrolling message for the Statewide Realty Web page is to create the display object (the text field). The text field is part of a simple form containing only the text field to display the scrolling message. The form and text field for the scrolling message are positioned below the title image. You begin by opening an existing HTML document, and adding the code to create a form and text field.

You must name the form and the form text field objects. These names serve as the object and properties used in the JavaScript code to assign the message string to the text field. The size attribute of the text field indicates the display width of the text field. Table 10–1 shows the HTML code to create the form and a text field for the scrolling message.

Table 10–1 Code to Create a Form and a Text Field

Line	Code
32	`<form name="msgForm" action="">`
33	`<input type="text" name="scrollingMsg" size="25" />`
34	`</form>`

Line 32 starts the form and uses the name attribute to give the form the unique name, msgForm. Line 33 indicates the input box is a text type, which means it can receive data. The text field is named scrollingMsg and is set to a size of 25. Line 34 is the closing <form> tag.

To Open an Existing HTML File

As in Chapter 9, you will integrate JavaScript into an existing HTML document. The following step shows how to open the chapter10.html file included in the Data Files for Students.

- Start Notepad, and, if necessary, maximize the window. If Word Wrap is not enabled, click Format on the menu bar and then click Word Wrap to enable it.
- With a USB drive plugged in to your computer, click File on the menu bar and then click Open.
- If necessary, navigate to the Chapter10\ChapterFiles folder on the USB drive.
- If necessary, click the Look in box arrow, and then click All Files to display all files in the Chapter10\ChapterFiles folder.
- Click chapter10.html in the list of files.
- Click the Open button to open the chapter10.html file in Notepad (Figure 10–2).

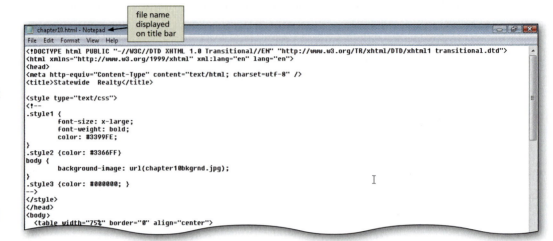

Figure 10–2

To Create a Form Text Field to Display a Scrolling Message

The following step illustrates how to create a form and a form text field to display a scrolling message.

- Click line 32 below the closing <p align="center"> tag.
- Enter the JavaScript code shown in Table 10–1 to enter the HTML code to create the form and text field (Figure 10–3).

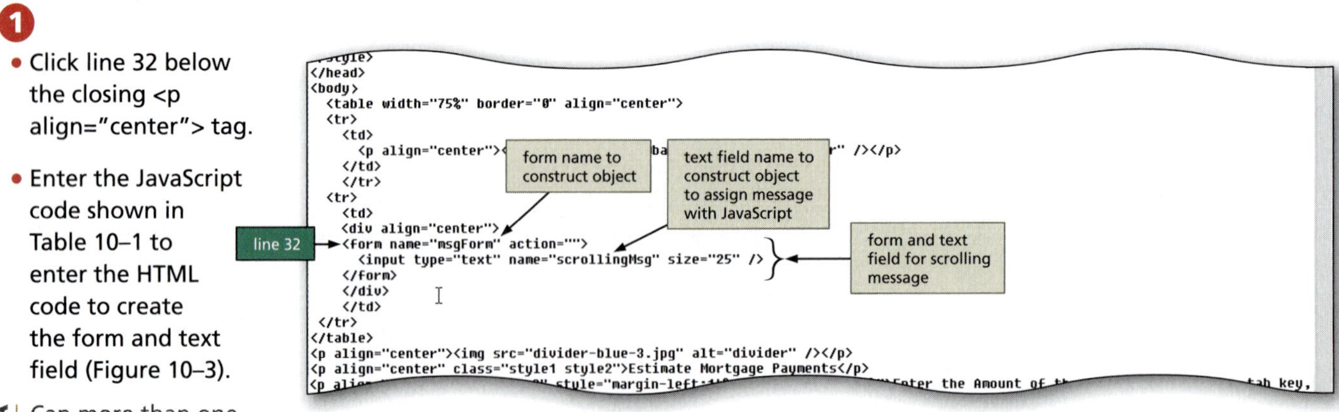

Figure 10–3

Q&A

Can more than one scrolling message be placed on a Web page?

Generally not, especially with older browsers. Too many recursive calls can overflow the programming stack and crash the browser.

Creating the scrollingMsg() User-defined Function

The scrollingMsg() function requires two variables and performs five tasks. The two variables are:

- The scrollMsg variable represents the message
- The beginPos variable represents the current character in the text message.

The five tasks the scrollingMsg() function performs are:

- Assigns the string message to the display object (which, in this project, is the text field)
- Increments the position variable by 1 to place the next character in the text message in the display object
- Uses an if statement to test for the end of the message
- If the text has scrolled to the end of the message, starts over with the first character
- Makes the display continuous and regulates the speed of the display using the setTimeout() method set to 200 milliseconds

Table 10–2 shows the code to begin the JavaScript section, declare and initialize the scrollMsg and beginPos variables, declare the scrollingMsg() function, and assign the first characters of the message to the text field. *Note: Because of the limitations of this textbook page, Lines 8 and 11 look like more than one line. However, each will be entered as a single line, pressing Enter only at the end of the entire numbered line.*

Table 10–2 Code to Begin the scrollingMsg() Function

Line	Code
6	`<script type="text/javascript">`
7	`<!--Hide from old browsers`
8	`var scrollMsg = " ** Take advantage of the current low interest rates! ** "`
9	`var beginPos = 0`
10	`function scrollingMsg() {`
11	`document.msgForm.scrollingMsg.value = scrollMsg.substring(beginPos,scrollMsg.length)+scrollMsg.substring(0,beginPos)`

Lines 6 and 7 start the <script> section of the Web page file. Line 8 declares the scrollMsg variable and assigns the message string, ** Take advantage of the current low interest rates! **, to it. The spaces at the beginning and end of the message string ensure that spaces appear at both ends of the message. Line 9 declares the beginPos variable, used to indicate the beginning position of the text string, and initializes it to zero. Line 10 declares the function scrollingMsg(). Line 11 assigns the message string to the text field using the object document.msgForm.scrollingMsg.value, which is derived from the form object and the input object. Figure 10–4 illustrates the relationship between these objects and how the statement is derived.

BTW

The Marquee <marquee> Tag
To make it easier to build scrolling messages, Microsoft developed the <marquee> tag. The direction attribute in the <marquee> tag controls scrolling up, down, left, or right. Internet Explorer recognizes the <marquee> tag, but other browsers do not. To create a scrolling message that works with Internet Explorer and other browsers, use a form text field, as discussed in this chapter.

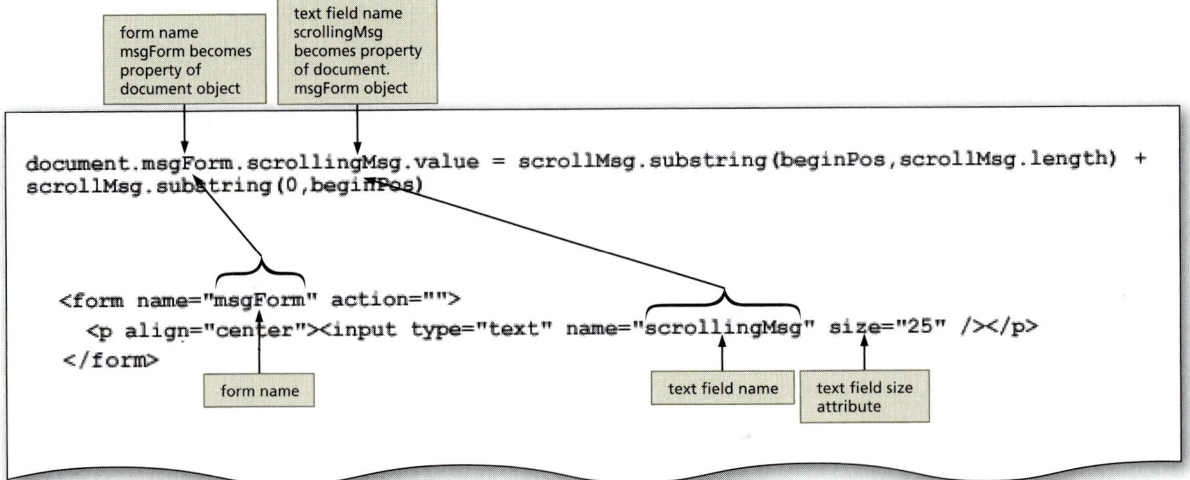

Figure 10–4

Line 11 also assigns the next character to the form text field object. The text field object is constructed using the form (msgForm) as an attribute of the document and the text field object (scrollingMsg) as an attribute of the msgForm object. The JavaScript code then assigns the string message to the input text field object (scrollingMsg) using the value attribute.

The rest of the assignment statement in line 11 uses the substring() method and concatenates the remainder of the scrollMsg variable to the beginning of the scrollMsg variable. As you learned in Chapter 9, the substring() method needs two parameters (x,y), where x is the starting point of the string and y is the location of the last character needed. This statement tells the scrollingMsg() function to assign the next character in the string message to the text field, to make the message appear as if it is scrolling.

To Create the scrollingMsg() User-Defined Function

The following step shows how to create the scrollingMsg() user-defined function and define its variables.

1

- Click line 6, the blank line below the <title> tag.
- Enter the JavaScript code shown in Table 10–2 to enter the beginning script tags and define the variables used in the scrolling message, using the SPACEBAR to indent as shown, and then press the ENTER key (Figure 10–5).

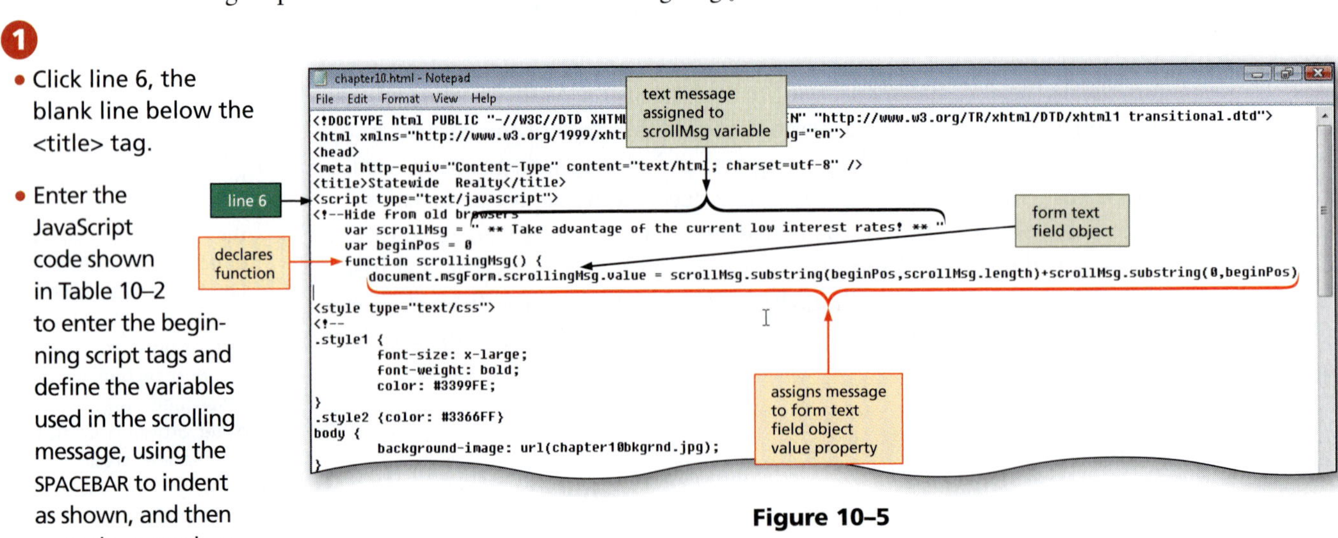

Figure 10–5

Incrementing the Position Locator Variable After declaring the scrollingMsg() function, the next step is to increment the beginPos variable and append the next character from the message string to the text field. To cause the message to scroll in the text field, the position locator variable (beginPos) must be incremented by one. Table 10–3 describes the various ways JavaScript statements can be used to increment variables.

Table 10–3 Incrementing a Variable

Statement	Explanation
`variable=variable+1`	Executes the expression on the right side of the equal sign and assigns the result to a variable on the left side
`variable+=1`	Adds the number after the equal sign to a variable
`variable++`	Adds 1 to a variable, increments after the assignment
`++variable`	Adds 1 to a variable before the assignment

Once incremented, the new value of the position locator variable, beginPos, allows the substring() method in line 11 to extract the next character in the message string and append it to the end of the message in the text field.

To Enter the Code to Increment the Position Locator Variable

The following step illustrates how to enter the code to increment the position counter.

1

- Click line 12.
- Press SPACEBAR to indent under the previous line, then type `beginPos = beginPos + 1` to increment the position locator by one, and then press the ENTER key (Figure 10–6).

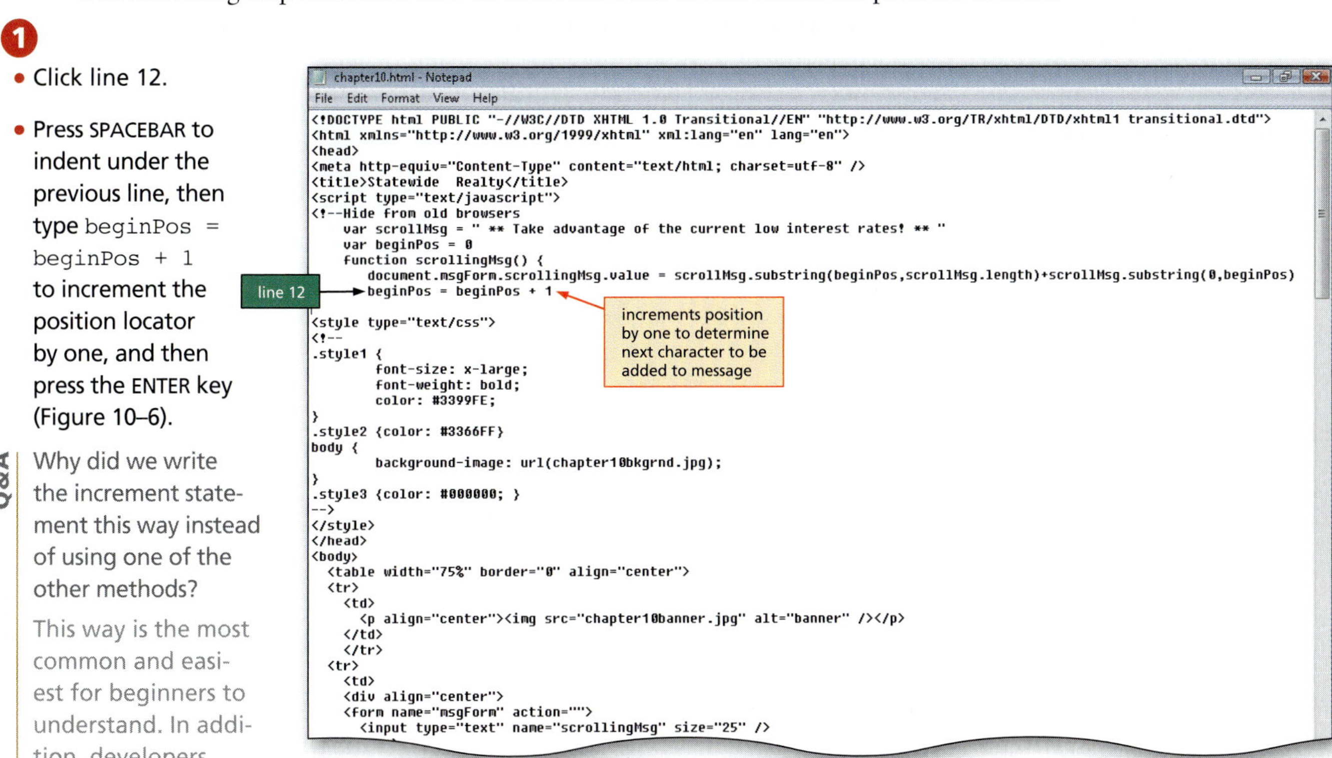

Figure 10–6

Q&A

Why did we write the increment statement this way instead of using one of the other methods?

This way is the most common and easiest for beginners to understand. In addition, developers should use a format that can be recognized by anyone who might have to modify their code after the initial implementation.

Entering an if Statement After incrementing the position location variable (beginPos) by one, the JavaScript code must determine if the current value of beginPos exceeds the length of the message string. The loan payment calculator will use an if statement to determine if the current value of the beginPos variable is greater than the length of the message. An **if statement** is used to test a condition and then take one or more actions, based on the results of the test. The general form of the if statement is shown in Table 10–4. The if statement tests a **condition**, which is any comparison of values that evaluates to true or false. If the result of the comparison is true, the JavaScript code within the braces is executed. If the result of the comparison is false, the code after the closing brace is executed. Figure 10–7 shows the flowchart that corresponds to an if statement.

Table 10–4 If Statement

General form:	`if (condition) {`
	`JavaScript statements if condition true`
	`}`

Comment:	where condition is the comparison of values. All conditions must be placed in parentheses. If the result of the comparison is true, JavaScript executes the statements between the curly braces. If the result of the comparison is false, the JavaScript statements after the closing brace are executed.

Example:	`if (beginPos>scrollMsg.length) {`
	`beginPos=0`
	`}`

BTW

The if Statement
JavaScript if statements are an integral part of the programming language. They are used to define one or more statements that only should be executed based on the result of a conditional test, which controls the flow of logic.

As shown in the example in Table 10–4, the conditions use symbols called operators to indicate what type of comparisons should be made between the values. Table 10–5 shows the conditional operands used for comparisons. For more information about conditional operands, see the JavaScript Quick Reference in Appendix E.

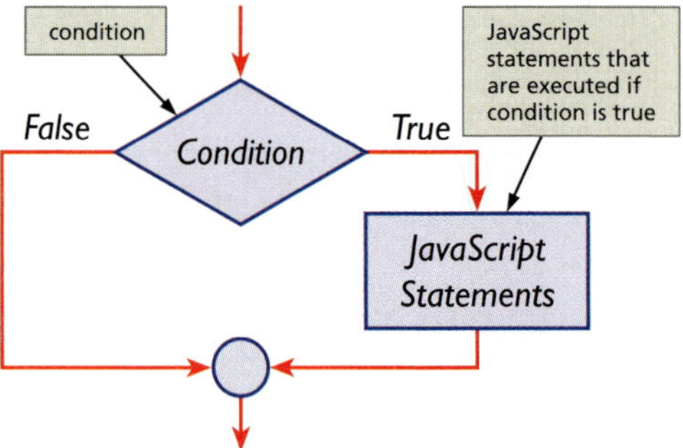

Figure 10–7

Table 10–5 Conditional Operators

Operand	Example	Results
==	(a==b)	True if a equals b
===	(a=== b)	True if a equals b and the data are of the same type
!=	(a!=b)	True if a does not equal b
!==	(a!==b)	True if a does not equal b and/or the data are not of the same type
>	(a>b)	True if a is greater than b
<	(a<b)	True if a is less than b
>=	(a>=b)	True if a is greater than or equal to b
<=	(a<=b)	True if a is less than or equal to b
&&	(a==b) && (x<y)	True if both conditions are true (a equals b and x is less than y)
||	(a!=b) || (x>=a)	True if either condition is true (a does not equal b or x is greater than or equal to a)

BTW

Conditional Operators
Conditional operators are symbols used to compare two values, called operands. The operator compares the two operands and returns a logical value based on whether the comparison is true.

To make the scrolling message work properly, an if statement is used to determine if the current value of beginPos is greater than the number of characters in the message string. The flowchart and sample code shown in Figure 10–8 illustrate how the if statement compares the beginning position variable (beginPos) with the overall length of the message (scrollMsg.length).

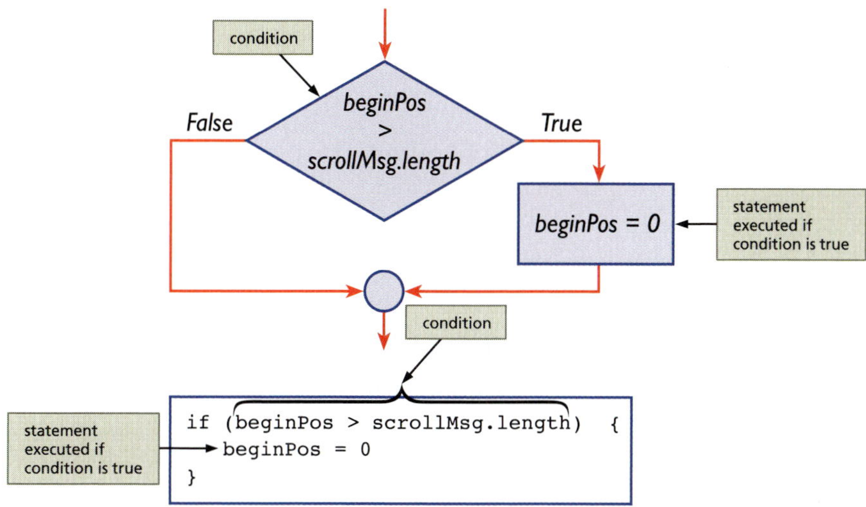

Figure 10–8

BTW

Operands
An operand is a numerical, string, logical, or object data type or value. Operands must be of the same data type, or you will not get a true comparison result.

If the current value of the beginPos variable exceeds the length of the scrollMsg variable, the statement assigns the value zero to the beginPos variable. By setting beginPos to zero, the code sets the string message so the first character of the string appears in the text field.

To Enter an if Statement

The following step illustrates how to enter an if statement.

1

- Click line 13.
- Press the SPACEBAR to indent under the line above.
- Type `if (beginPos > scrollMsg.length) {` to enter the if statement and then press the ENTER key.
- Press the SPACEBAR to indent under the open parenthesis in (beginPos.
- Type `beginPos=0` to reset the variable to zero if the condition is true, and then press the ENTER key.
- Press the SPACEBAR to indent under and line up with the if statement.

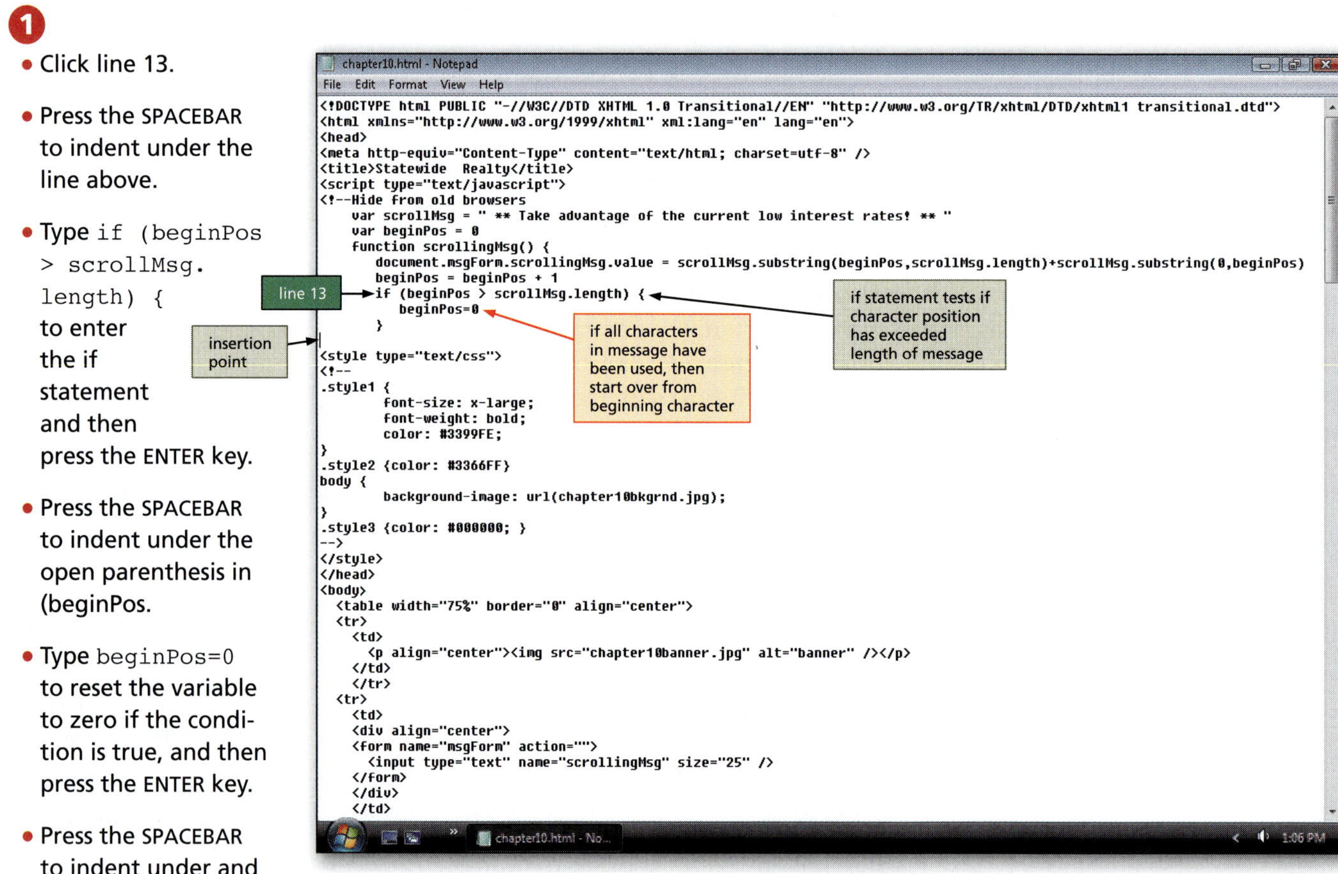

Figure 10–9

- Type } to close the if statement and then press the ENTER key (Figure 10–9).

Q&A Do all JavaScript if statements have to be written in this format?

When only one statement follows the condition, like in this example, the statement could have been written as follows: `if (beginPos > scrollMsg.length) beginPos=0`. Note that the braces have been dropped for just one statement to be executed if the condition is true. If more than one statement needs to be executed, then the braces must be used to create the block of statements.

Using the setTimeout() Method to Create a Recursive Call To have the message text scroll continuously in the text field, you use a programming technique called **recursion**, in which a function is called within itself, creating an "endless loop." The set-Timeout() method calls a function or evaluates an expression after a specified amount of time has elapsed, which is measured in milliseconds. The general form of the setTimeout() method is shown in Table 10–6.

BTW

Recursion
In this chapter's project, recursion is used to keep a routine going indefinitely or until some other function is called to stop it. Normally, recursive functions should have a mechanism that terminates the function when it completes its task.

Table 10–6 setTimeout() Method

General form:	`setTimeout("instruction", time delay in milliseconds)`
Comment:	where instruction is any valid JavaScript statement and time delay is expressed in number of milliseconds
Example:	`window.setTimeout("scrollingMsg()",200)`

In the scrollingMsg() user-defined function, the setTimeout() method continuously displays characters and regulates the speed of the characters displaying in the text field. The setTimeout() method calls the scrollingMsg() user-defined function from within the scrollingMsg() user-defined function. This recursive call to the scrollingMsg() function is what makes the message scroll in the text field continually.

To Add the setTimeout() Method to Create a Recursive Call

The following step illustrates how to add the setTimeout() method to create a recursive call to the scrollingMsg() function.

1

- If necessary, click line 16.
- Press the SPACEBAR to indent under the closing brace, then type `window.setTimeout("scrollingMsg()",200)` to call scrollingMsg() from within itself and then press the ENTER key.
- Press the SPACEBAR to indent and then type } to close the function and then press the ENTER key two times (Figure 10–10).

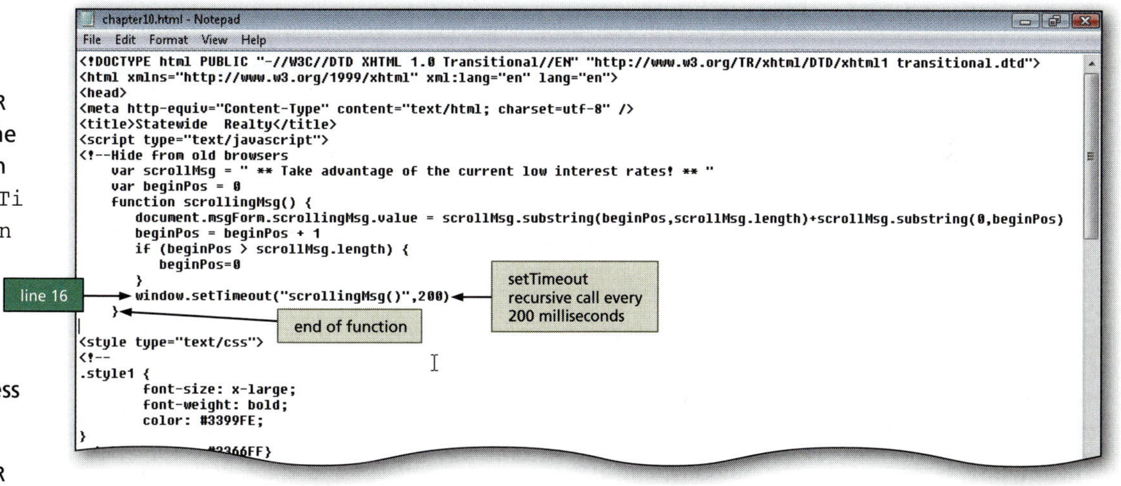

```
chapter10.html - Notepad
File  Edit  Format  View  Help
<!DOCTYPE html PUBLIC "-//W3C//DTD XHTML 1.0 Transitional//EN" "http://www.w3.org/TR/xhtml/DTD/xhtml1 transitional.dtd">
<html xmlns="http://www.w3.org/1999/xhtml" xml:lang="en" lang="en">
<head>
<meta http-equiv="Content-Type" content="text/html; charset=utf-8" />
<title>Statewide  Realty</title>
<script type="text/javascript">
<!--Hide from old browsers
    var scrollMsg = " ** Take advantage of the current low interest rates! ** "
    var beginPos = 0
    function scrollingMsg() {
        document.msgForm.scrollingMsg.value = scrollMsg.substring(beginPos,scrollMsg.length)+scrollMsg.substring(0,beginPos)
        beginPos = beginPos + 1
        if (beginPos > scrollMsg.length) {
            beginPos=0
        }
        window.setTimeout("scrollingMsg()",200)
    }

<style type="text/css">
<!--
.style1 {
        font-size: x-large;
        font-weight: bold;
        color: #3399FE;
}
               #3366FF}
```


Figure 10–10

Q&A

How do we know how fast to make the scrolling?

The best way is to try several different speeds and ask potential users to look at it and indicate their preference.

Q&A

What if we changed the number from 200 to 2000?

The text would display one character every two seconds and would be so boring to watch, you would lose the interest of your user.

To Complete a JavaScript Section

The following step shows how to enter the JavaScript code to complete the <script> section.

- If necessary, click line 19.
- Type `//-->` to close the comment to hide the JavaScript and then press the ENTER key.
- Type `</script>` to close the <script> section and then do not press the ENTER key (Figure 10–11).

Q&A

Can I use one hyphen and the greater than sign to end the comment?

No, it must be two hyphens and the greater than sign to close the comment started above.

```
<!DOCTYPE html PUBLIC "-//W3C//DTD XHTML 1.0 Transitional//EN" "http://www.w3.org/TR/xhtml/DTD/xh
<html xmlns="http://www.w3.org/1999/xhtml" xml:lang="en" lang="en">
<head>
<meta http-equiv="Content-Type" content="text/html; charset=utf-8" />
<title>Statewide  Realty</title>
<script type="text/javascript">
<!--Hide from old browsers
    var scrollMsg = " ** Take advantage of the current low interest rates! ** "
    var beginPos = 0
    function scrollingMsg() {
       document.msgForm.scrollingMsg.value = scrollMsg.substring(beginPos,scrollMsg.length)+scroll
       beginPos = beginPos + 1
       if (beginPos > scrollMsg.length) {
          beginPos=0
       }
       window.setTimeout("scrollingMsg()",200)
    }
//-->
</script>
<style type="text/css">
<!--
.style1 {
        font-size: x-large;
        font-weight: bold;
        color: #3399FE;
}
.style2 {color: #3366FF}
body {
        background-image: url(chapter10bkgrnd.jpg);
}
.style3 {color: #000000; }
-->
</style>
</head>
<body>
  <table width="75%" border="0" align="center">
  <tr>
```


Figure 10–11

Adding an Onload Event Handler

BTW

Event Handlers
Some older browsers have a problem recognizing mixed case event handlers. Although the newer versions of Web browsers have fixed the problem, they still recognize event handlers using all lowercase characters.

The last step in adding a scrolling message to a Web page is to add an event handler to start the scrolling message when the Web page loads. As discussed in Chapter 9, an event is an action, such as a mouse click or a window loading. An event handler is a way to associate that action with a function. The event handler to start the scrolling message is the onload event handler.

The JavaScript standard uses both upper- and lowercase in spelling event handlers, as shown in Table 10–7. In this text, however, to be XHTML-compliant and to pass XML validation, developers spell the event handlers in all lowercase characters because XHTML treats event handlers as tag attributes. The XHTML standard requires all tag attributes to be lowercase.

Table 10–7 shows some of the event handlers and the associated objects. As the table indicates, event handlers can be used only with certain objects. For example, the onclick event handler is used to trigger JavaScript code when a user clicks a button or link, while the onload event handler is used to trigger JavaScript code when a document is loaded into the browser window. For more information about event handlers, see the JavaScript Quick Reference in Appendix E.

Table 10–7 Objects and Associated Event Handlers

Object	Event Handler
button	`onClick, onDblClick`
document	`onLoad, onUnload`
form	`onSubmit, onReset, onBlur, onKeydown, onKeypress, onKeyup`
hyperlink	`onClick, onMouseover, onMouseout, onDblClick, onMousemove, onMousedown`
image	`onLoad, onAbort, onError, onMousemove, onMousedown`
input box	`onBlur, onChange, onFocus, onKeypress, onKeyup, onKeydown`
Submit button	`onClick`
window	onLoad, `onUnload, onBlur, onFocus`

In this chapter, the onload event handler calls the scrollingMsg() function, using the following statement:

```
onload="scrollingMsg()"
```

where onload is the event handler and the scrollingMsg() function is the code that is executed as the result of the event. The statement is entered in the <body> tag to indicate that the onload event handler should call the scrollingMsg() function when the Web page loads.

To Enter the onload Event Handler to Call the scrollingMsg() Function

The following step illustrates how to enter the onload event handler to call the scrollingMsg() function.

1

- Click to the right of the y in the body in line 36.
- Press the SPACEBAR once.
- Type `onload="scrollingMsg()"` to add the event handler and do not press the ENTER key (Figure 10–12).

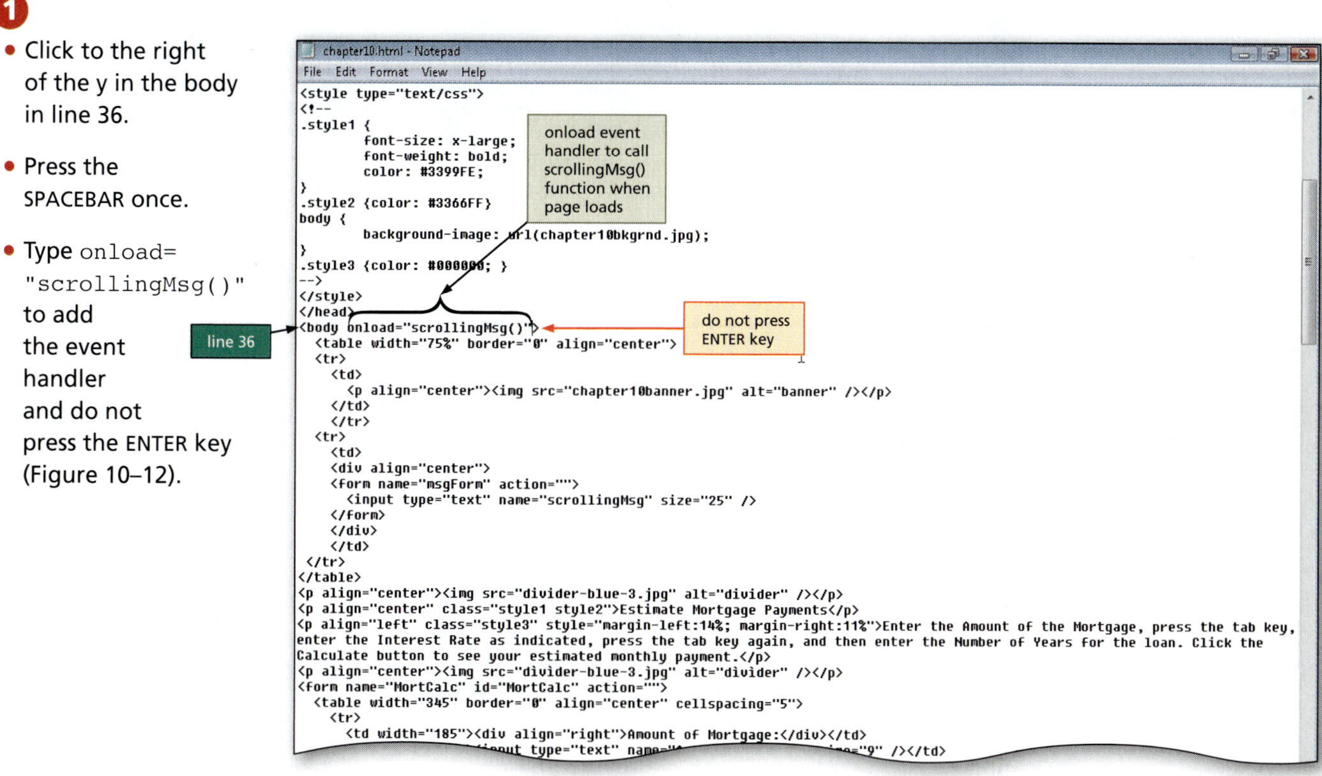

Figure 10–12

To Save an HTML File and Test a Web Page

With the code for the scrollingMsg() function complete and the onload event handler added to call the function when the Web page loads, you should save the HTML file and test the Web page. The following step illustrates how to save the HTML file and then test the Web page.

- With a USB drive plugged into your computer, click File on the Notepad menu bar and then click Save As. Type `chapter10statewiderealty.html` in the File name text box (do not press the ENTER key).
- If necessary, browse to the USB drive and open the Chapter10\ChapterFiles folder.
- Click the Save button in the Save As dialog box to save the file on the USB drive with the name chapter10statewiderealty.html.
- Start your browser. If necessary, click the Maximize button.
- Type `g:\chapter10\ChapterFiles\chapter10statewiderealty.html` in the Address box and then press the ENTER key.
- If necessary, click the security bar under the tabs, click Allow Blocked Content... (Figure 10–13a), and if necessary click Yes in the Security Warning dialog box to display the scrolling message (Figure 10–13b).

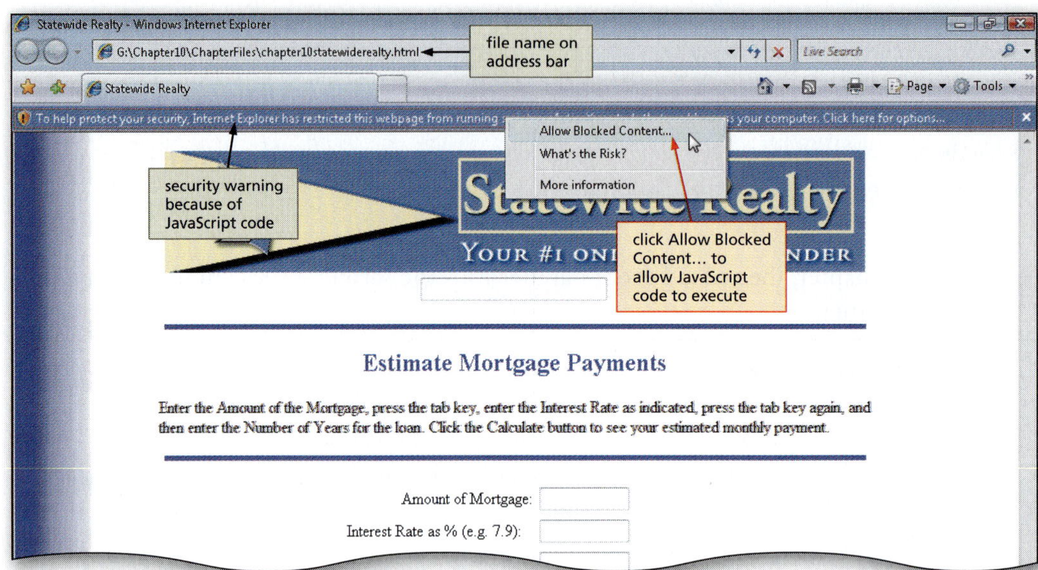

(a)

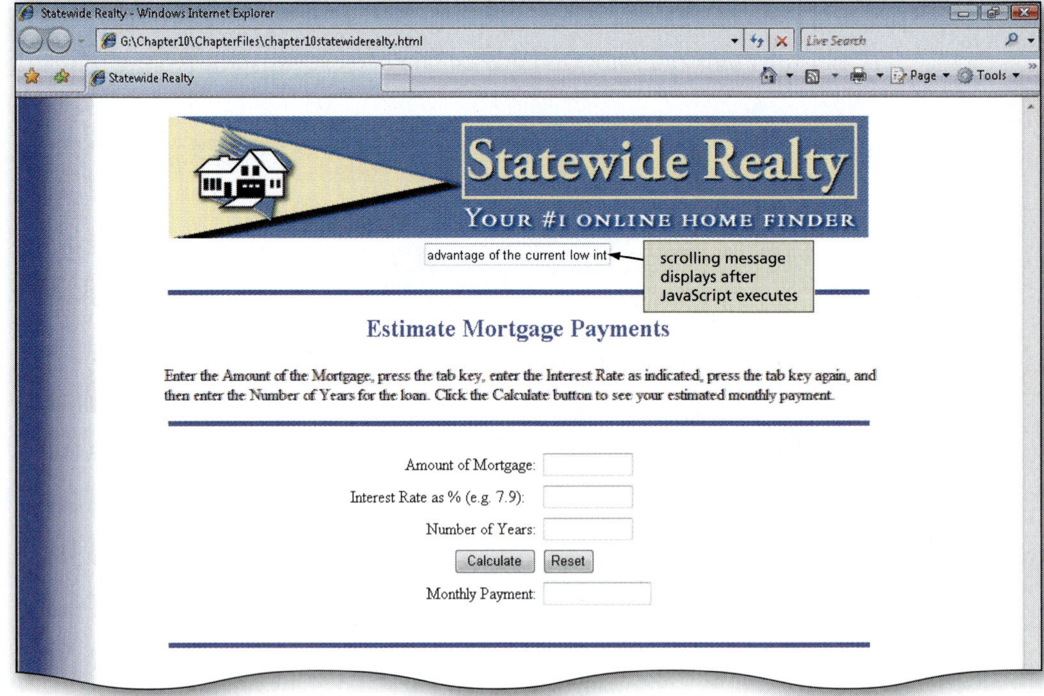

(b)

Figure 10–13

Q&A What if I do not see a security bar?

That simply means that tight restrictions and security are not set on your browser.

Plan Ahead

Validating a form.
In order to calculate the monthly payment, the values entered into the text fields must be valid numbers. A user-defined function called Calc() follows these steps to validate the text field entries:

- Convert the text field value to a numeric value using the parseInt() or parseFloat() function
- Test the value to be numeric using the isNaN (is Not a Number) function and checking that the value is greater than zero
- If the value is not a number or is zero or less, display a message, clear the text field, and position the insertion point in that text field

To call the Calc() validation function, an onClick event handler is added to the form.

Adding a Loan Payment Calculator

The mortgage loan payment calculator form shown in Figure 10–14 requests user input. The form, which is named MortCalc, already has been created in the HTML file. JavaScript code must be added to validate the input, calculate the monthly payment, and display the results in the MortCalc form. In order for the calculator to work, each text field must have a valid data entry. You will write a user-defined function called Calc() to perform these three tasks.

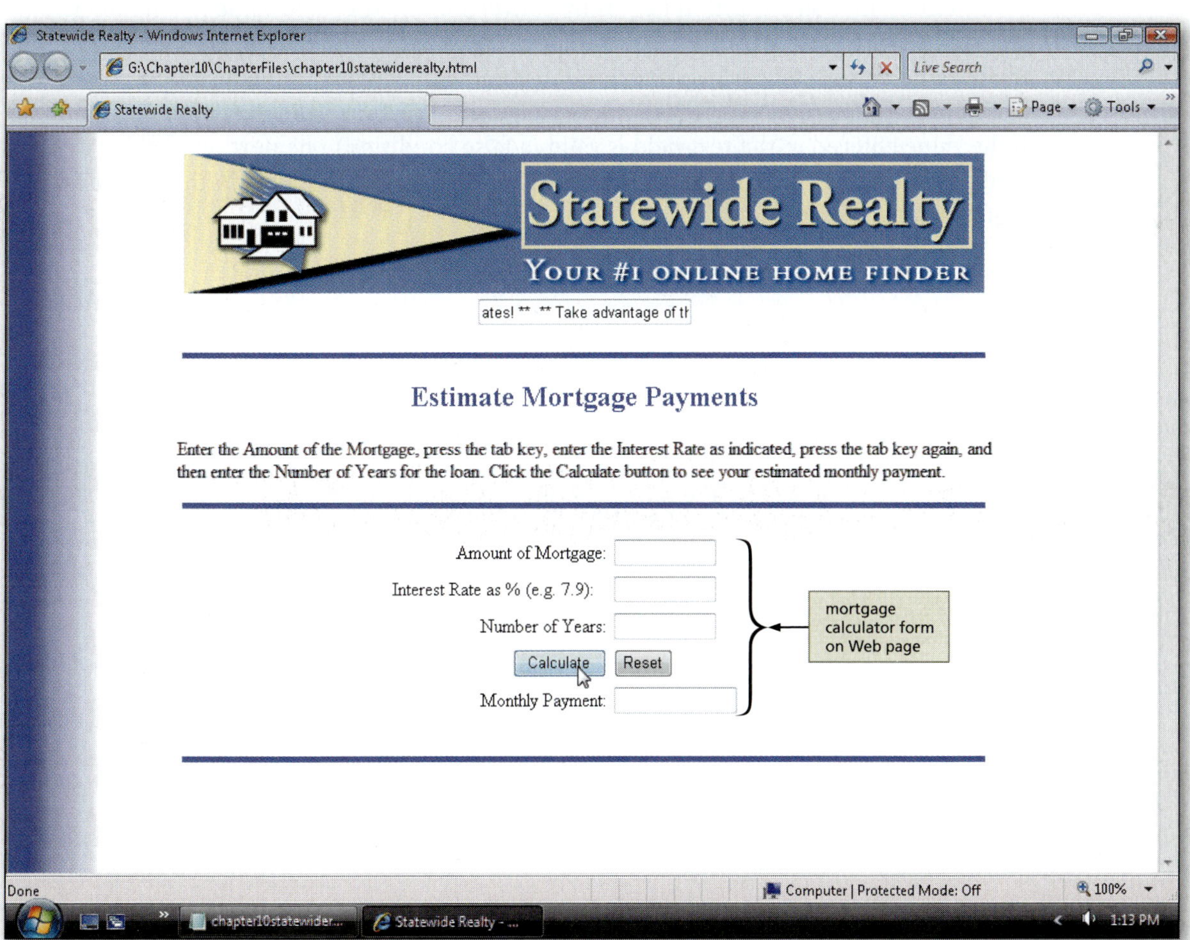

Figure 10–14

Validating Forms Using Nested if...else Statements

You can use different techniques to validate forms. This chapter uses a series of nested if...else statements, which is like the if statement except that it specifies statements to execute if the condition is false, as shown in the flowchart in Figure 10–15. Much like the if statement, an if...else statement tests a condition. If the condition is true, the statements between the curly braces after the if statement execute. If the condition is false, the statements between the braces after the else statement execute.

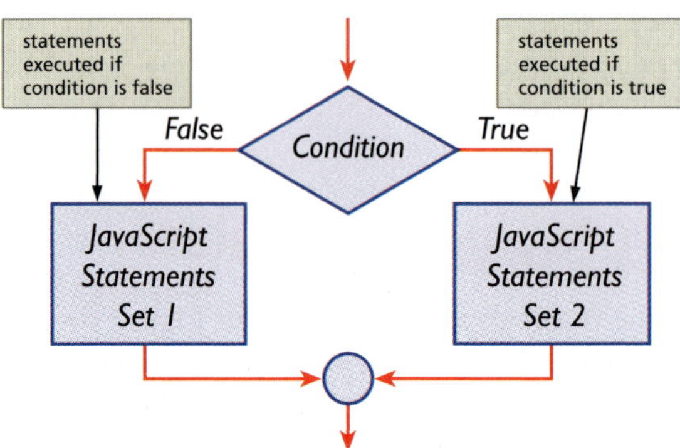

Figure 10–15

The validation algorithm begins by converting the text field value to a number. The if...else statement tests if the value entered in a text field is invalid (a true condition). If true, an error message is displayed, the text field is cleared, and the insertion point is placed back in the text field. This occurs until the user enters valid data in the text field. If the value entered in the text field is valid (a false condition), the next text field is examined until all text fields are validated. The validation process is shown in the flowchart in Figure 10–16.

BTW

Validating Web Form Data

Web developers use multiple techniques to validate Web forms using JavaScript. Some developers choose to validate each item as it is entered by using a combination of onchange event handlers and user-defined functions. It is important to validate Web forms because some Web databases are sensitive to invalid data and may crash, or mathematical formulas may cease to function when using invalid data.

BTW

Domains

A domain is a range of acceptable values for a field or column in a database. Using an HTML select list can ensure that accurate values are entered.

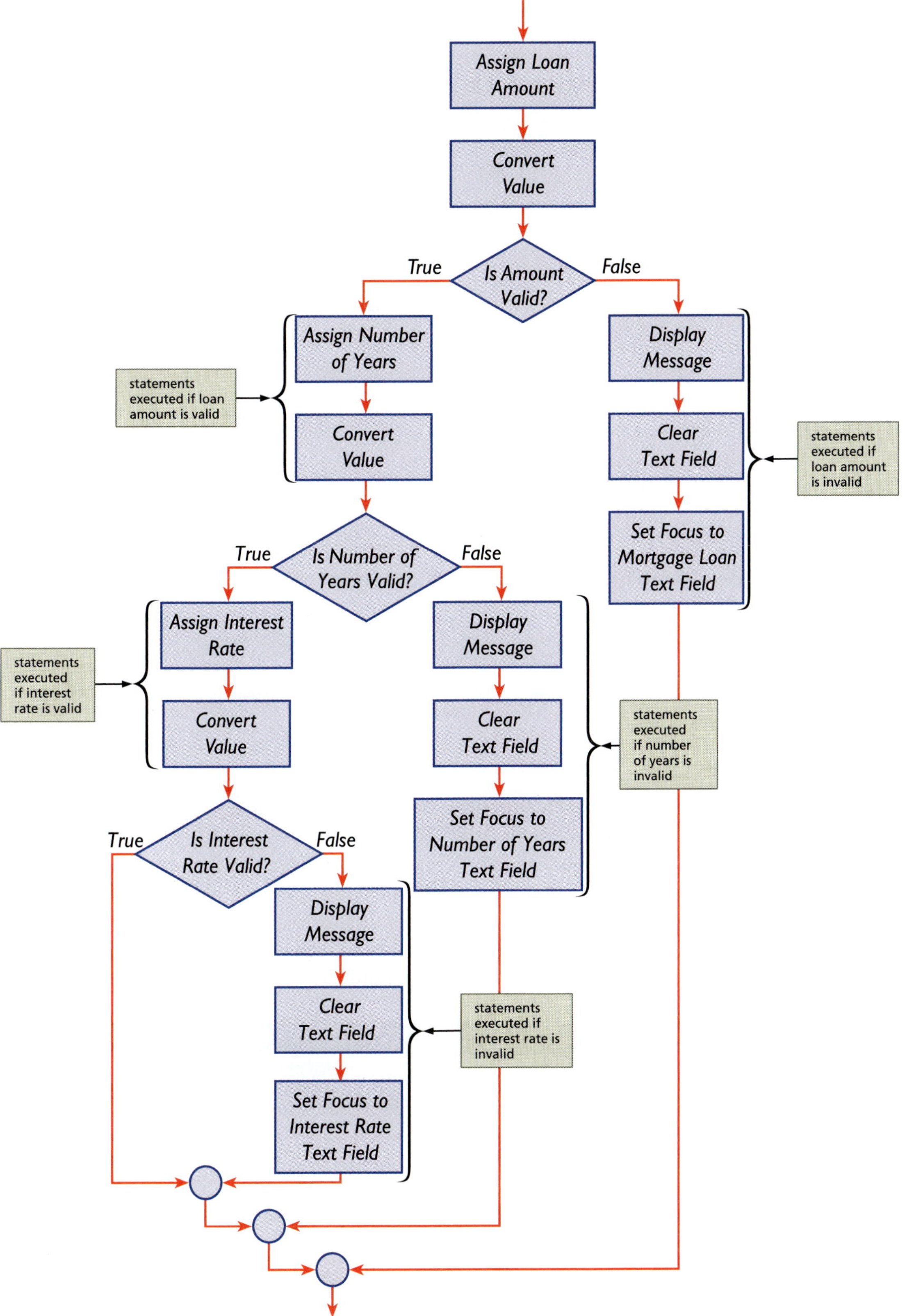
Assign Loan Amount
Convert Value
Is Amount Valid?
True
False
Assign Number of Years
Convert Value
statements executed if loan amount is valid
Display Message
Clear Text Field
Set Focus to Mortgage Loan Text Field
statements executed if loan amount is invalid
Is Number of Years Valid?
True
False
Assign Interest Rate
Convert Value
statements executed if interest rate is valid
Display Message
Clear Text Field
Set Focus to Number of Years Text Field
statements executed if number of years is invalid
Is Interest Rate Valid?
True
False
Display Message
Clear Text Field
Set Focus to Interest Rate Text Field
statements executed if interest rate is invalid

Figure 10–16

This validation design is necessary because of the event-driven nature of JavaScript. When a user triggers an event that calls a function, processing stays within that function until all statements execute. Because all the statements execute in a function, the form validation routine uses nested if...else statements to ensure each text field is validated correctly. By nesting if...else statements, you can place an if...else statement inside another as shown in Figure 10–17.

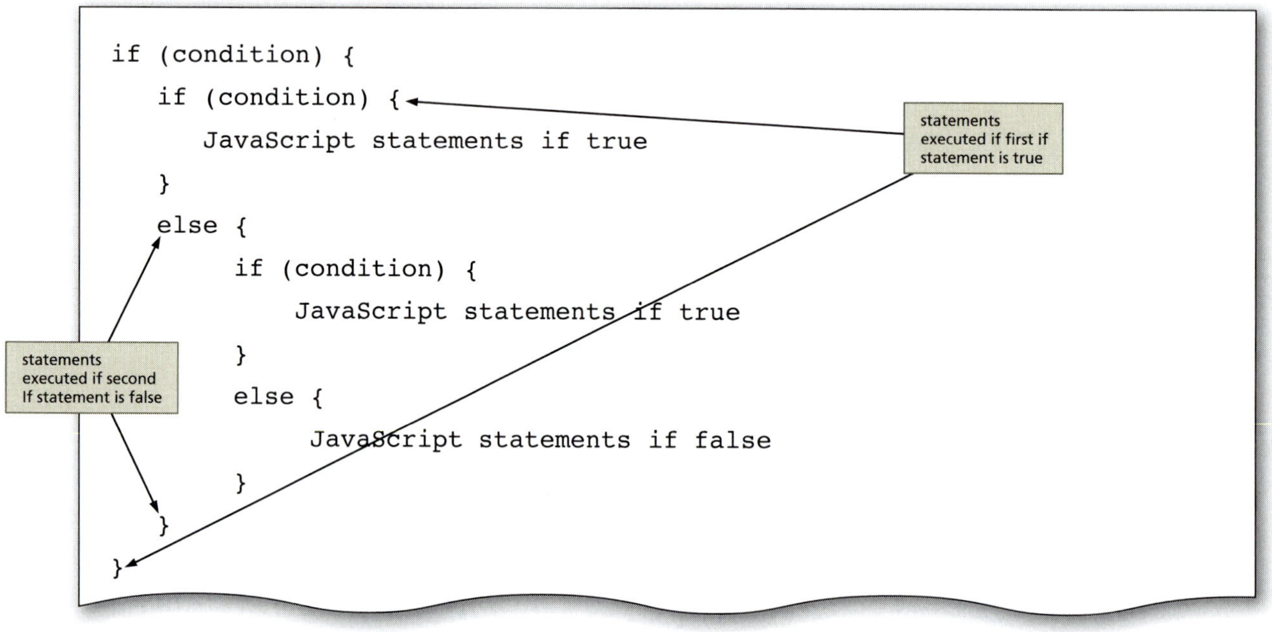

```
if (condition) {
   if (condition) {
      JavaScript statements if true
   }
   else {
       if (condition) {
           JavaScript statements if true
       }
       else {
           JavaScript statements if false
       }
   }
}
```


Figure 10–17

BTW

Radix or Number Base
Radix is the number base to which the integer value should be converted. The use of the numeral 2 represents binary, 8 represents octal, and 16 represents hexadecimal.

BTW

The parseFloat() Function
The parseFloat() built-in function parses a string argument and converts the value into a decimal floating-point number. If the first character cannot be converted to a number, the result is NaN, which means "not a number."

Using Built-In Functions to Validate Data When validating data, the JavaScript code may have to evaluate several criteria — for example, to ensure that a text field is not blank or that it contains numeric data (not text or characters). JavaScript accepts data entered into a text field as text character data, which means that the values must be converted to a number before they can be tested or validated. Table 10–8 describes the two built-in functions (parseInt() and parseFloat()) used to convert values and one function (isNaN()) used to test if the converted value is a number.

Table 10–8 Built-In Functions: parseInt(), parseFloat(), isNaN()

General form:	`variable = parseInt(value, base)`
Comment:	converts to an integer. Value is any string, which can be a variable or literal; base is the number base to which you want the string converted. A base of 2 means binary base number, an 8 means octal, and a 10 means decimal. The function returns an integer value, stripping the value after the decimal point.
Example:	`parseInt(loanAmount,10)`
General form:	`variable = parseFloat(value)`
Comment:	converts to a floating point number. Value is any string, which can be a variable or literal, representing a floating-point number. A floating-point number is one with a fractional or decimal value (including percentages). The function returns the value as a floating-point number.
Example:	`parseFloat(loanAmount)`
General form:	`isNaN(value)`
Comment:	isNaN means is Not a Number. Value is any value, which can be a variable or literal. The function returns a Boolean condition of true or false.
Example:	`isNaN(loanAmount)`

Figure 10–18 shows how the values of the form are passed to the Calc() user-defined function. Table 10–9 shows the general form of the JavaScript statement used to assign a null, or other, value to a text field object within a form.

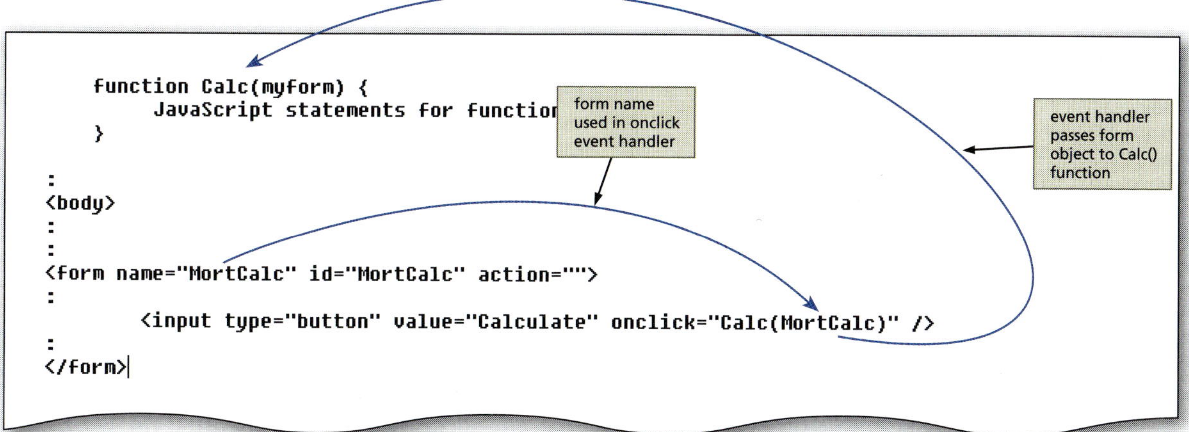

Figure 10–18

Table 10–9 Assignment Statement	
General form:	`document.formname.textfieldname.value=variable_or_literal`
Comment:	where formname is the name of the form; textfieldname is the name of a text field in the form; value is the attribute; and the variable_or_literal is the value assigned to the text field.

Examples:	`document.MortCalc.Amount.value=LoanAmt`
	`document.MortCalc.Amount.value="12500"`
	`document.MortCalc.Amount.value=""`

To place the insertion point back in a specific text field in the form, the focus must be set for that text field. Setting the focus means giving attention to an object. JavaScript uses the **focus() method** to give attention to an object. When the focus is set to an object, such as the Amount text field, the JavaScript statement automatically positions the insertion point in the text field. Table 10–10 shows the general form of the focus() method.

Table 10–10 focus() Method	
General form:	`document.formname.objectname.focus()`
Comment:	where formname is the name of the form that contains the object; and objectname identifies the object to which focus should be set.
Examples:	`document.MortCalc.Amount.focus()`

Table 10–11 shows the code to enter the Calc() user-defined function and the statements necessary to validate the mortgage loan amount using the parseInt() and isNaN() functions.

BTW

The isNaN() Built-in Function

The isNaN() function to test whether a value is not a number is the only function that tests a numeric value as the argument. The test uses the NOT operator and returns a Boolean value of true or false.

Table 10–11 Code for Calc() Function to Validate the Loan Amount

Line	Code
19	`function Calc(myForm) {`
20	`  var mortAmount=document.MortCalc.Amount.value`
21	`  var mortAmount=parseInt(mortAmount,10)`
22	`    if (isNaN(mortAmount) || (mortAmount<=0)) {`
23	`      alert("The loan amount is not a valid number!")`
24	`      document.MortCalc.Amount.value=" "`
25	`      document.MortCalc.Amount.focus()`
26	`    }`

Line 19 declares the Calc() function and passes any values entered or selected in the MortCalc form to the function. Line 20 can assign the data entered in the Amount of Mortgage text field to the mortAmount variable. Line 21 converts that value to an integer. The if statement beginning on line 22 checks the condition to see if the value for the mortAmount variable is not a number or if the value entered is less than or equal to zero. If the result of the condition is true (that is, the value entered is not a number or it is a negative number), the function notifies the user with an alert message (line 23) that the loan amount is not valid; clears the data entered in the Amount of Mortgage text field (line 24); and then sets the focus back to the Amount of Mortgage text field (line 25). The brace in line 26 closes the if statement.

To Start the Calc() Function and Nested if...else Statements to Validate Form Data

The following step illustrates how to enter the Calc() user-defined function and the if statement that validates the loan amount value entered in the Amount of Mortgage text field.

1

- If necessary, click the chapter10 statewiderealty.html - Notepad button on the taskbar to display the Notepad window.
- Click line 19.
- Press the ENTER key once to create a blank line, and then position the insertion point on the blank line (line 19).

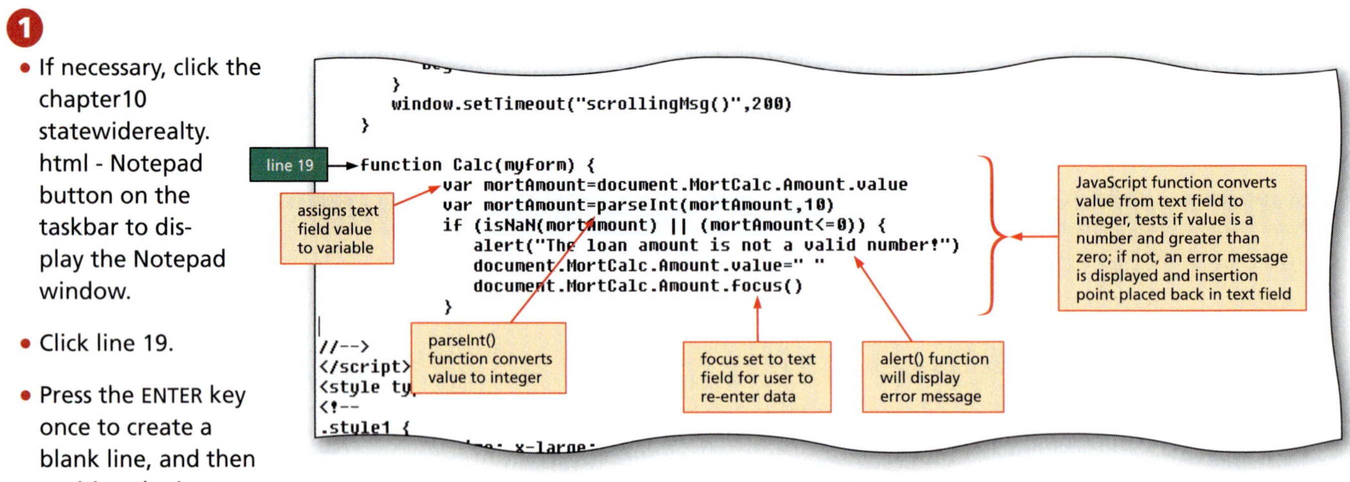

Figure 10–19

- Enter the JavaScript code shown in Table 10–11 using the SPACEBAR to indent as shown to start the Calc() user-defined function, define the variables for the loan amount, convert the loan amount to numeric values, and validate that the values are numeric (Figure 10–19).

Completing the Validation and Adding the Event Handler

Because an event must be executed until completion, the Calc() function validates all the entered values. Table 10–12 shows the code to validate the Interest Rate as % text field using the parseFloat() and isNaN() functions. If the interest rate data is valid, the function proceeds to validate the value in the Number of Years field and convert it to a floating-point number.

Table 10–12 Code to Validate the Interest Rate

<table>
<tr><th>Line</th><th>Code</th></tr>
<tr><td>27</td><td>else {</td></tr>
<tr><td>28</td><td>var mortRate=document.MortCalc.Rate.value</td></tr>
<tr><td>29</td><td>var mortRate=parseFloat(mortRate)</td></tr>
<tr><td>30</td><td>if (isNaN(mortRate) || (mortRate<=0)) {</td></tr>
<tr><td>31</td><td>alert("The interest rate is not a valid number!")</td></tr>
<tr><td>32</td><td>document.MortCalc.Rate.value=" "</td></tr>
<tr><td>33</td><td>document.MortCalc.Rate.focus()</td></tr>
<tr><td>34</td><td>}</td></tr>
</table>

Line 27 is an else statement that executes if the mortAmount data is valid and the function should proceed to validate the data entered in the Interest Rate as % text field. Line 29 passes the value in the Interest Rate as % text field to the mortRate variable, and converts it to a floating-point number using the parseFloat() function. Because the interest rate is a floating-point number, you must use the parseFloat() function to keep the interest rate a floating-point number.

The if statement in line 30 tests the mortRate variable to determine if it is a number or if the value is less than or equal to zero. If the result of the condition is true, an alert message (line 31) notifies the user that the interest rate is not valid. Line 32 clears the data entered in the Interest Rate as % text field, and then line 33 sets the focus back to the Interest Rate as % text field. The brace in line 34 closes the if statement. If the mortRate data is valid, the function then proceeds to validate the Number of Years.

Table 10–13 shows the code used to validate the value entered in the Number of Years text field.

Table 10–13 Code to Convert and Validate the Years Entered Value

<table>
<tr><th>Line</th><th>Code</th></tr>
<tr><td>35</td><td>else {</td></tr>
<tr><td>36</td><td>var mortYears=document.MortCalc.Years.value</td></tr>
<tr><td>37</td><td>var mortYears=parseInt(mortYears,10)</td></tr>
<tr><td>38</td><td>if (isNaN(mortYears) || (mortYears<=0)) {</td></tr>
<tr><td>39</td><td>alert("The number of years is not a valid number!")</td></tr>
<tr><td>40</td><td>document.MortCalc.Years.value=" "</td></tr>
<tr><td>41</td><td>document.MortCalc.Years.focus()</td></tr>
<tr><td>42</td><td>}</td></tr>
<tr><td>43</td><td>}</td></tr>
<tr><td>44</td><td>}</td></tr>
<tr><td>45</td><td>}</td></tr>
</table>

Line 35 is an else statement that executes the statements if the if condition on line 30 is false. Line 37 converts years to an integer, using the parseInt() function. The if statement beginning in line 38 checks the condition to determine if the mortYears value is greater than zero. If the number of years is not valid, line 39 displays a message and line 40 places the focus back in the Years text field. The braces in lines 42 through 45 close the nested if...else statements and the function.

To End the Nested if...else Statements to Validate Form Data

The following step shows how to enter the else portions of the nested if...else statements in the Calc() function to validate the Interest Rate as % text field and the Number of Years.

- If necessary, click line 27.
- Enter the JavaScript code shown in Table 10–12 to validate the interest rate, using the SPACEBAR to indent the code as shown in Figure 10–20.
- Press the ENTER key.
- Continue on line 35.
- Enter the JavaScript code shown in Table 10–13 to validate the number of years for the loan, using the SPACEBAR to align the code as shown.
- Press the ENTER key to finish the else portions of the nested if...else statements (Figure 10–20).

```
<script type="text/javascript">
<!--Hide from old browsers
    var scrollMsg = " ** Take advantage of the current low interest rates! ** "
    var beginPos = 0
    function scrollingMsg() {
       document.msgForm.scrollingMsg.value = scrollMsg.substring(beginPos,scrollMsg.length)+scrol
       beginPos = beginPos + 1
       if (beginPos > scrollMsg.length) {
          beginPos=0
       }
       window.setTimeout("scrollingMsg()",200)
    }

    function Calc(myForm) {
            var mortAmount=document.MortCalc.Amount.value
            var mortAmount=parseInt(mortAmount,10)
            if (isNaN(mortAmount) || (mortAmount<=0)) {
               alert("The loan amount is not a valid number!")
               document.MortCalc.Amount.value=" "
               document.MortCalc.Amount.focus()
            }
            else {
                var mortRate=document.MortCalc.Rate.value
                var mortRate=parseFloat(mortRate)
                if (isNaN(mortRate) || (mortRate<=0)) {
                   alert("The interest rate is not a valid number!")
                   document.MortCalc.Rate.value=" "
                   document.MortCalc.Rate.focus()
                }
                else {
                     var mortYears=document.MortCalc.Years.value
                     var mortYears=parseInt(mortYears,10)
                     if (isNaN(mortYears) || (mortYears<=0)) {
                        alert("The number of years is not a valid number!")
                        document.MortCalc.Years.value=" "
                        document.MortCalc.Years.focus()
                     }
                }
            }
    }

//-->
</script>
<style type="text/css">
<!--
```


Figure 10–20

Q&A Why is the year not converted to a floating point number?

Most loans, especially mortgage loans, are NOT made on part of a year, so the number of years should be an integer.

To Enter an onclick Event Handler to Call the Calc() Function

The last step in adding form validation to the mortgage loan payment calculator is to add an event handler to trigger the Calc() function when the user clicks the Calculate button. After entering data in the form, a user clicks the Calculate button, which triggers the Calc() function to validate the data entered in the form, using the if…else statements and built-in functions entered in previous steps. The following step shows how to enter the onclick event handler to call the Calc() function.

- Scroll down to the HTML code for the form and then click line 101, right after the closing quote in "Calculate" and before the rightmost /> bracket.
- Press the SPACEBAR once.
- Type `onclick="Calc(MortCalc)"` to add the event handler to the Calculate button, but do not press the ENTER key (Figure 10–21).

chapter10statewiderealty.html - Notepad

File Edit Format View Help

```
</table>
<p align="center"><img src="divider-blue-3.jpg" alt="divider" /></p>
<p align="center" class="style1 style2">Estimate Mortgage Payments</p>
<p align="left" class="style3" style="margin-left:14%; margin-right:11%">Enter the Amount of the M
enter the Interest Rate as indicated, press the tab key again, and then enter the Number of Years
Calculate button to see your estimated monthly payment.</p>
<p align="center"><img src="divider-blue-3.jpg" alt="divider" /></p>
<form name="MortCalc" id="MortCalc" action="">
  <table width="345" border="0" align="center" cellspacing="5">
    <tr>
      <td width="185"><div align="right">Amount of Mortgage:</div></td>
      <td width="141"><input type="text" name="Amount" value=" " size="9" /></td>
    </tr>
    <tr>
      <td>Interest Rate as % (e.g. 7.9):</td>
      <td><input type="text" name="Rate" value=" " size="9" /></td>
    </tr>
    <tr>
      <td><div align="right">Number of Years:</div></td>
      <td><input type="text" name="Years" value=" " size="9" /></td>
    </tr>
    <tr>
      <td><div align="right">
      <input type="button" value="Calculate" onclick="Calc(MortCalc)" />
      </div></td>
      <td><input type="reset" name="reset" id="reset" value="Reset" /></td>
    </tr>
    <tr>
      <td><div align="right">Monthly Payment:</div></td>
      <td><input type="text" name="Payment" value=" " size="12" /></td>
    </tr>
  </table>
</form>
</div>
<div align="center">
  <img src="divider-blue-3.jpg" alt="divider" width="700" height="5" />
</div>

</body>
</html>
```


Figure 10–21

To Save an HTML File and Test a Web Page

With the JavaScript code for the form validation entered, the Web page can be saved and tested in a browser. The Calc() function will validate the text field entries, but will not yet calculate the monthly payment. The following step shows how to save the HTML file and test the Web page.

- With the USB drive plugged into your computer, click File on the menu bar and then click Save.
- Click the browser button on the taskbar.
- Click the Refresh button on the browser toolbar.
- When the Web page is displayed, click the Amount of Mortgage text field.
- Enter test data set 1, as shown in Table 10–14.
- Press the TAB key to move the insertion point to the next text field.
- When you have entered test data set 1, click the Calculate button at the bottom of the form (Figure 10–22).

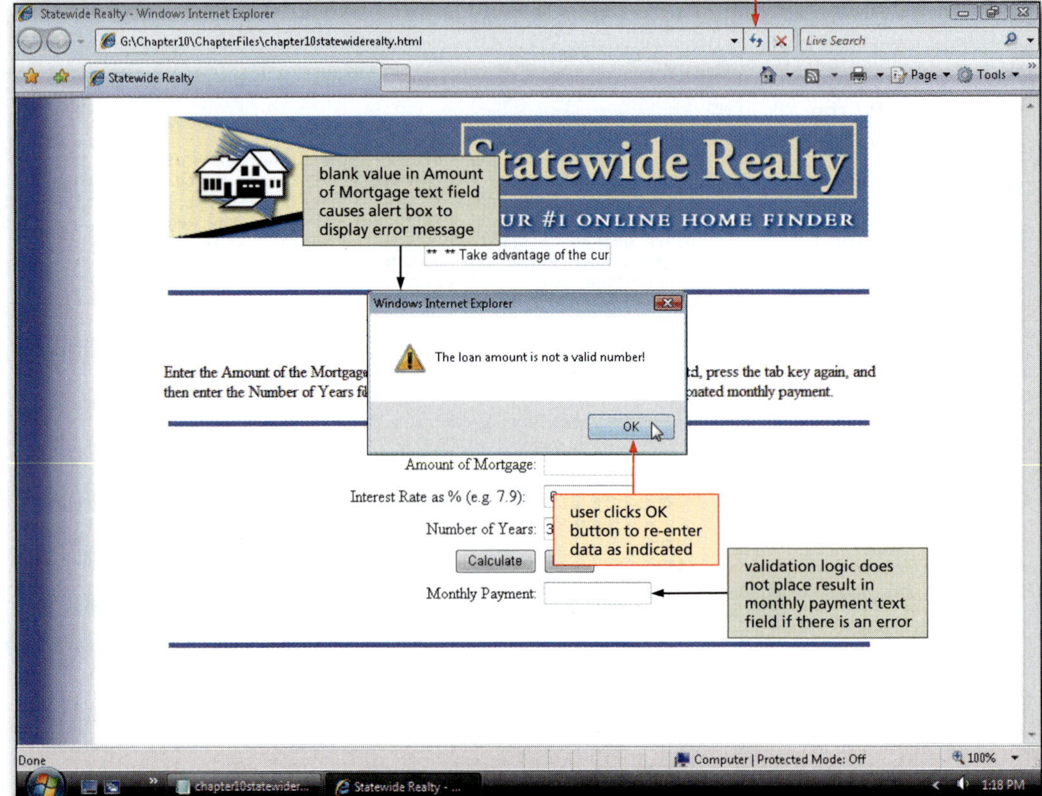

Figure 10–22

- When the message box is displayed, click the OK button.
- Click the Reset button at the bottom of the form.
- Repeat Steps 5 through 9, using test data sets 2, 3, and 4, as shown in Table 10–14.

Table 10–14 Test Data Set

Data Set	Amount of Mortgage	Interest Rate %	Number of Years	Comment
1		6	30	The loan amount is not a valid number!
2	109000	A	4	The interest rate is not a valid number!
3	99000	6	30	No error messages
4	193000	5.9	-30	The number of years is not a valid number!

Plan Ahead

Calculating the monthly payment.

The monthly() function requires three parameters: the mortgage loan amount (mortAmount), the interest rate (mortRate), and the number of years that the payments will be made (mortYears). These values are passed from the Calc() user-defined function to the monthly() function. The steps to calculate the monthly payment are as follows:

- The function call statement passes the three variables — mortAmount, mortRate, and mortYears — to the monthly() function.
- Convert the monthly interest rate to Irate by dividing mortRate by 1200
- Convert the number of years to Pmts by multiplying mortYears by 12
- Calculate the monthly payment with the following formula:

  mortAmount * (Irate / (1 - (1 / Math.pow(1+Irate,Pmts))))
- Return the monthly payment as a fixed decimal value to two decimal places using the toFixed(2) method.

Adding the Monthly Payment Calculation

With the JavaScript code for the form validation complete, the next step is to add code to the Calc() function to calculate the monthly payment. First, a statement must be added to the Calc() function to call a user-defined function, named monthly(), which calculates the monthly payment. The monthly() function uses the valid data in the form and calculates the monthly payment. The result is the monthly payment, which is returned as a floating-point value.

The placement of the monthly() function within the Calc() function is important so that, if a value in a text field is invalid, the function does not attempt to process invalid data and return an undefined result. To place this function properly, one more else statement must be added to the Calc() function, as shown in Table 10–15.

Table 10–15 Code to Call the monthly() Function

Line	Code
43	`else {`
44	`    var mortPayment=monthly(mortAmount,mortRate,mortYears)`
45	`    document.MortCalc.Payment.value=mortPayment`
46	`}`

Line 43 adds an additional else statement to the nested if...else statements. Line 44 calls the monthly() function and passes the loan amount, interest rate, and number of years for the loan as variables: mortAmount, mortRate, and mortYears. The result is stored in a temporary variable named monthlyPmt. Line 45 assigns the result to the Monthly Payment text field on the form. Line 46 is the closing brace for the additional else statement.

To Enter Code to Call the monthly() Function

The following step illustrates how to enter the final else statement and the function call that passes the required values to the monthly() function.

- Click line 43 and then press the ENTER key to insert a blank line.
- Click the blank line just inserted (line 43).
- Press the SPACEBAR to indent under the closing brace in line 42, then enter the JavaScript code shown in Table 10–15 to call the monthly user-defined function and assign the result to the payment text field but do not press the ENTER key (Figure 10–23).

Q&A If I try to execute this Web page now, will an error occur?

Yes, because the monthly() user-defined function has not been written and entered.

chapter10statewiderealty.html - Notepad

File Edit Format View Help

```
function Calc(myForm) {
        var mortAmount=document.MortCalc.Amount.value
        var mortAmount=parseInt(mortAmount,10)
        if (isNaN(mortAmount) || (mortAmount<=0)) {
           alert("The loan amount is not a valid number!")
           document.MortCalc.Amount.value=" "
           document.MortCalc.Amount.focus()
        }
        else {
            var mortRate=document.MortCalc.Rate.value
            var mortRate=parseFloat(mortRate)
            if (isNaN(mortRate) || (mortRate<=0)) {
               alert("The interest rate is not a valid number!")
               document.MortCalc.Rate.value=" "
               document.MortCalc.Rate.focus()
            }
            else {
                 var mortYears=document.MortCalc.Years.value
                 var mortYears=parseInt(mortYears,10)
                 if (isNaN(mortYears) || (mortYears<=0)) {
                    alert("The number of years is not a valid number!")
                    document.MortCalc.Years.value=" "
                    document.MortCalc.Years.focus()
                 }
                 else {
                       var mortPayment=monthly(mortAmount,mortRate,mortYears)
                       document.MortCalc.Payment.value=mortPayment
                 }
            }
        }
}

//-->
</script>
<style type="text/css">
<!--
.style1 {
        font-size: x-large;
        font-weight: bold;
        color: #3399FE;
}
.style2 {color: #3366FF}
body {
        background-image: url(chapter10bkgrnd.jpg);
```


Figure 10–23

Creating the monthly() User-Defined Function The monthly() function is a user-defined function to calculate the monthly payment amount. The JavaScript code for the monthly() function is shown in Table 10–16.

Table 10–16 Code for monthly() User-Defined Function

Line	Code
51	`function monthly(mortAmount,mortRate,mortYears) {`
52	`var Irate=mortRate/1200`
53	`var Pmts=mortYears*12`
54	`var Amnt=mortAmount * (Irate / (1 - (1 / Math.pow(1+Irate,Pmts))))`
55	`return Amnt.toFixed(2)`
56	`}`

Line 51 declares the monthly() function. Line 52 determines the monthly interest rate percentage by dividing the annual rate by 1200. The result is assigned to the Irate (interest rate) variable. Line 53 determines the number of monthly payments on the loan, by multiplying the number of years in the loan by 12. The resulting value is assigned to the Pmts variable.

Line 54 is the formula for calculating a monthly payment based on the amount of the loan, the monthly interest percentage, and the number of monthly payments. The mathematical representation of the formula is:

loan amount * (monthly interest rate / (1 - (1 /(1 + monthly interest rate)$^{\text{number of payments}}$)))

JavaScript, however, does not use typical programming language symbols to represent exponentiation in code. Instead, to calculate the expression (1 + monthly interest rate)$^{\text{number of payments}}$, JavaScript uses the pow() method associated with the Math object. Table 10–17 shows the general form of the pow() method.

Table 10–17 Math.pow() Method

General form:	`Math.pow(number, exponent)`
Comment:	where number is the value raised to the power of the exponent value. The pow() method accepts variables (X,n), constants (2,3), or both (Sidelength,2).

Examples:	`Math.pow(2,3)`
	`Math.pow(X,n)`
	`Math.pow(Sidelength,2)`

BTW

The Math Object
The Math object cannot be used to create other objects. Most of the properties of the Math object return preset values. Other properties really are methods and act as functions.

The return statement in line 55 tells the function to send the results of the expression back as a fixed decimal value with a length of two. The Number object's toFixed() method returns a value set to a specific decimal length, as shown in Table 10–18.

Table 10–18 Number.toFixed() Method

General form:	`Number.toFixed(digits)`		
Comment:	where digits is the exact number of digits after the decimal point. The number is rounded or padded with zeros if necessary.		
Examples:	Pmt = 234.8932	Pmt.toFixed(3)	Result: 234.893
	Amt = 843.6778	Amt.toFixed(2)	Result: 843.68

To Create the monthly() Function

The following step illustrates how to enter the monthly() user-defined function to calculate the monthly payment on a mortgage loan.

- Click line 51.
- Position the insertion point on the blank line directly above the //--> tag. (If necessary, insert a blank line above the tag.)
- Enter the JavaScript code shown in Table 10–16 to write the code to calculate the monthly payment and then press the ENTER key twice (Figure 10–24).

```
chapter10statewiderealty.html - Notepad
File  Edit  Format  View  Help
                    else {
                         var mortYears=document.MortCalc.Years.value
                         var mortYears=parseInt(mortYears,10)
                         if (isNaN(mortYears) || (mortYears<=0)) {
                            alert("The number of years is not a valid number!")
                            document.MortCalc.Years.value=" "
                            document.MortCalc.Years.focus()
                         }
                         else {
                               var mortPayment=monthly(mortAmount,mortRate,mortYears)
                               document.MortCalc.Payment.value=mortPayment
                         }

                    }
               }
      }
   function monthly(mortAmount,mortRate,mortYears) {
            var Irate=mortRate/1200
            var Pmts=mortYears*12
            var Amnt=mortAmount * (Irate / (1 - (1 / Math.pow(1+Irate,Pmts))))
            return Amnt.toFixed(2)
      }

//-->
</script>
<style type="te
<!--
.style1 {
        font-size: x-large;
        font-weight: bold;
        color: #3399FE;
}
.style2 {color: #3366FF}
body {
        background-image: url(chapter10bkgrnd.jpg);
}
.style3 {color: #000000; }
-->
</style>
</head>
<body onload="scrollingMsg()">
  <table width="75%" border="0" align="center">
  <tr>
    <td>
```


Figure 10–24

BTW

Math.round() Method

The Math.round() method returns the nearest integer value of a floating-point number. Thus, 28.453 will return 28. By multiplying the original number by 10 raised to the power of the number of decimals needed and then dividing by the same number, an original floating-point number also can be changed. For example, Math.round(9.453*100)/100 returns 9.45 and Math.round(9.454*10)/10 returns 9.5.

To Save an HTML File and Test a Web Page

Now that the monthly payment can be calculated, this is a good place to test the Web page. The following step shows how to save the HTML file and test the Web page.

1

- With the USB drive plugged into the computer, click File on the menu bar and then click Save.
- Click the browser button on the taskbar.
- Click the Refresh button on the browser toolbar.
- If necessary, click the Amount of Mortgage text field to place the insertion point in the text field.
- Type 73000 in the Amount of Mortgage text field and then press the TAB key.
- Type 6 in the Interest Rate as % (e.g. 7.9) text field and then press the TAB key.

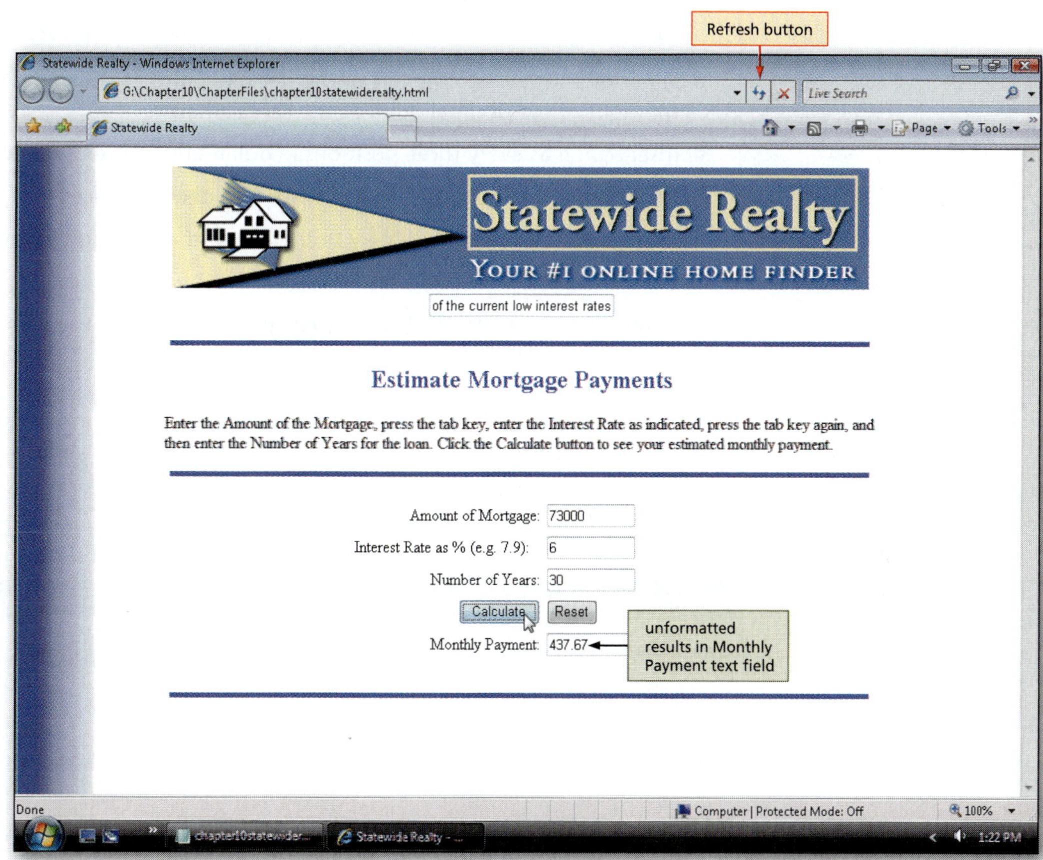

Figure 10–25

- Type 30 in the Number of Years text field and then click the Calculate button (Figure 10–25).

Q&A

What if my result was slightly different? Did I do something wrong?

If your result is only a few pennies different, it is probably just a difference in the math processor on your computer. If the value is hundreds or even thousands of dollars off, check your formulas on lines 52 through 54.

Formatting the Monthly Payment Output as Currency

As shown in Figure 10–25, the mortgage loan payment calculator currently displays the monthly payment amount as a value with two decimal places. To set the form to display the monthly payment amount in a currency format with a dollar sign, the dollarFormat() function is used. First, you must enter a statement that passes the resulting string object of the monthly payment Calc() function to the dollarFormat() function. The dollarFormat() function then analyzes the string, adds commas, and returns the number with a dollar sign and two decimal places.

Plan Ahead

Formatting output results.

To format the result, the dollarFormat() function performs these seven basic steps:

1. Use the string value passed to the function, which separates the dollars from the cents based on the position of the decimal point
2. Determine the location of the decimal point using the indexOf() method
3. Separate the value to the left of the decimal point as the dollar amount and the value to the right of the decimal point as the cents amount
4. Insert commas every three positions in dollar amounts exceeding 999
5. Reconstruct the result string value with two decimal places
6. Insert a dollar sign immediately to the left of the first digit without spaces
7. Return the completed formatted value

The value is assigned to the Monthly Payment text field in the form.

Using the indexOf() Method The **indexOf()** method is used to search a string for a particular value and returns the relative location of that value within the string. The indexOf() method searches the string object for the desired value, which is enclosed within the quotation marks. Table 10–19 shows the general form of the indexOf() method.

Table 10–19 indexOf() Method

General form:	`var position = stringname.indexOf("c")`
Comment:	where position is a variable; stringname is any string object; and "c" is the value for which the function searches.
Example:	`var decipos = valuein.indexOf(".")`

If the search value is found in the string object, the indexOf() method returns the relative position of the value within the string object. If the search value is not found, the indexOf() method returns a negative one (–1). In this chapter, the indexOf() method is used to search for a decimal point in the monthly payment amount. Figure 10–26 provides an example of how the indexOf() method works.

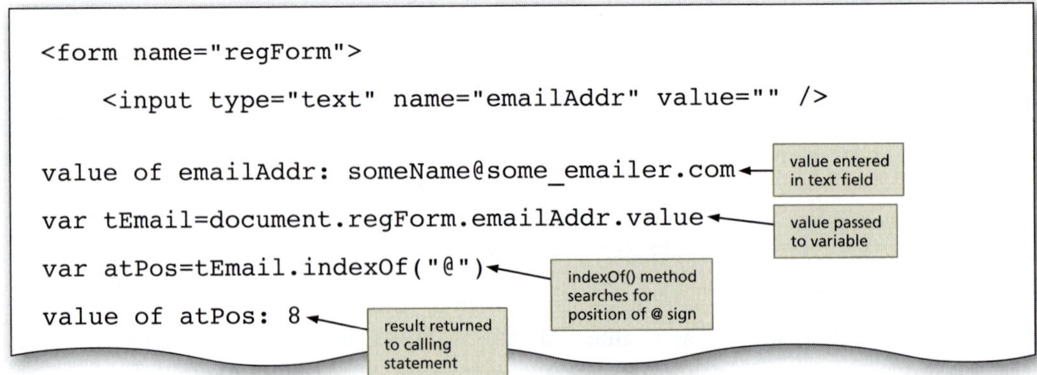
<form name="regForm">
<input type="text" name="emailAddr" value="" />
value of emailAddr: someName@some_emailer.com
value entered in text field
var tEmail=document.regForm.emailAddr.value
value passed to variable
var atPos=tEmail.indexOf("@")
indexOf() method searches for position of @ sign
value of atPos: 8
result returned to calling statement

Figure 10–26

Beginning the dollarFormat() Function and Formatting the Dollars Portion The dollarFormat() function initializes the variable that will return the formatted value and the variable used to manipulate the unformatted value. Most programmers agree it is a good programming practice to clear and initialize variables to ensure the data is valid. Table 10–20 shows the JavaScript code used to add the dollarFormat() function.

Table 10–20 Code for the dollarFormat() Function

Line	Code
58	`function dollarFormat(valuein) {`
59	`var formatStr=""`
60	`var Outdollars=""`
61	`var decipos=valuein.indexOf(".")`
62	`if (decipos==-1)`
63	`decipos=valuein.length`

Line 58 declares the dollarFormat() function and the valuein variable. Lines 59 and 60 clear the variables used to assemble the formatted output by assigning null (or empty) values. The indexOf() method in line 61 returns a value indicating the location of the decimal point — a value stored in the decipos variable. This value indicates at what position to concatenate the decimal values. Line 62 tests the condition of the decipos variable. If the value of decipos is –1, then decipos is set equal to the length of the string, as shown in line 63. If the value of decipos is 0, then the input value (valuein) is an integer and no decimal values need to be modified.

To Enter the dollarFormat() Function

The following step shows how to enter the dollarFormat() function and initialize the variables.

1

- Click line 58 above the closing comment //-->.
- Enter the JavaScript code from Table 10–20 to begin the dollarFormat() function and then press the ENTER key (Figure 10–27).

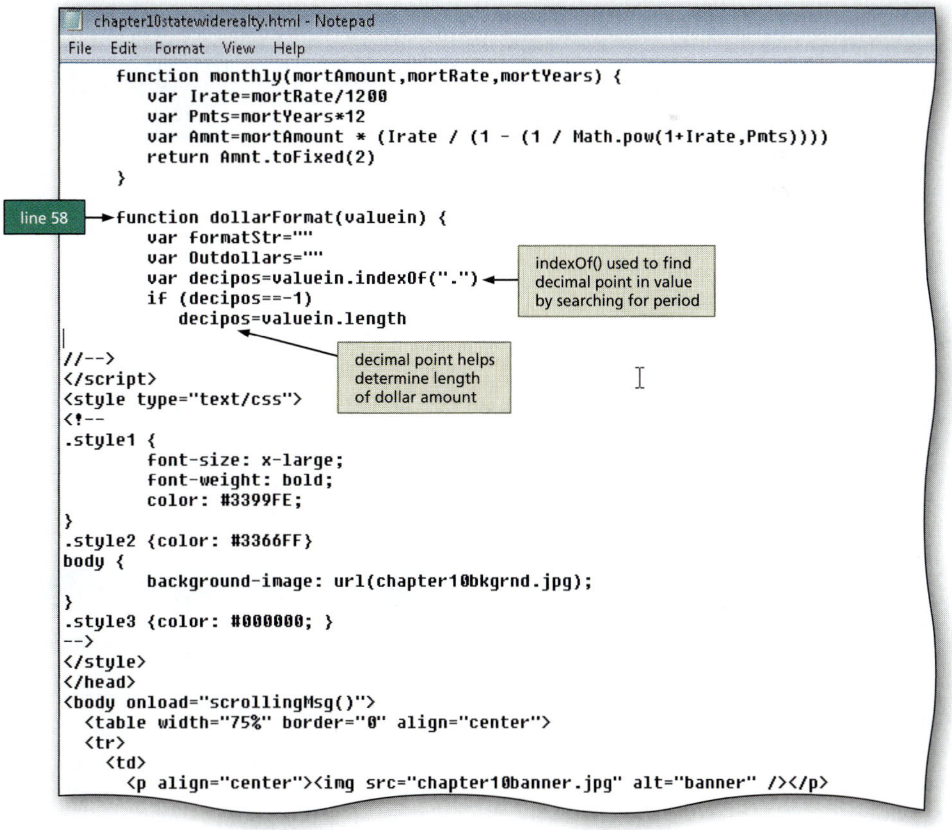

Figure 10–27

Plan Ahead

Using a while loop to insert commas every three digits in a number.
To place a comma every three digits, use a while loop. The following steps describe the logic of the while loop:

1. Extract three digits from the dollar value, starting from the right by subtracting 3 from the length of the dollar value (dollen).
2. Verify three digits have been subtracted and then insert a comma in the output string.
3. Decrement the length of the dollar value to look for the next group of three digits.
4. The process (loop) is complete when no more groups of three digits exist and the length of dollen is zero.

Using an if...else Statement and while Loop to Extract the Dollars Portion and Insert Commas A **loop** is a series of statements that executes repeatedly until it satisfies a condition. JavaScript has two types of loops: for loops and while loops. Both types of loops use the logic illustrated by the flowchart in Figure 10–28. Both loops first test a condition to determine if the instructions in the loop are to be executed.

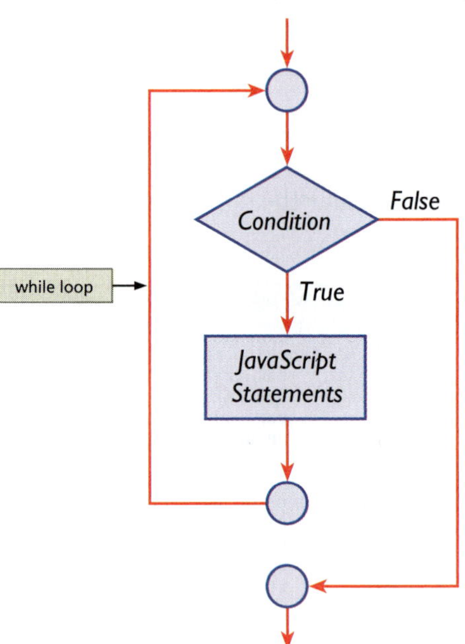

Figure 10–28

The **for loop** relies on a conditional statement using numeric values and thus often is referred to as a counter-controlled loop. Table 10–21 shows the general form of the for loop.

Table 10–21 for Loop

General form:	`for (start; stop; counter-control) {`
	`JavaScript statements`
	`}`

Comment:	where start is a variable initialized to a beginning value; stop is an expression indicating the condition at which the loop should terminate; and the counter-control is an expression indicating how to increment or decrement the counter. Semicolons separate the three variables.

Examples:	`for (j=1; j<5; j++) {`
	`for (ctr=6; ctr>0; ctr--) {`
	`for (itemx=1; itemx<10; itemx=itemx+2) {`

The while loop relies on a conditional statement that either can use a numeric value or a string. Table 10–22 shows the general form of the while loop.

Table 10–22 while Loop

General form:	`while (condition) {`
	`JavaScript statements`
	`}`

Comment:	where condition is either a numeric value or a string; and the JavaScript statements execute while the result of the condition is true.

Examples:	`while (ctr < 6) {`
	`while (isNaN(temp)) {`
	`while (Response != "Done") {`

In this chapter, the while loop is used in formatting the dollar value of the Monthly Payment value. The dollars portion is represented by the digits to the left of the decimal point. If the dollars portion of the mortgage loan payment contains more than three digits, commas need to be inserted. Table 10–23 shows the JavaScript statements used to determine the length of the dollar value and placement of the commas.

Table 10–23 Code for Determining the Length of the Dollar Value and Comma Placement

Line	Code
64	`var dollars=valuein.substring(0,decipos)`
65	`var dollen=dollars.length`
66	`if (dollen>3) {`
67	`while (dollen>0) {`
68	`tDollars=dollars.substring(dollen-3,dollen)`
69	`if (tDollars.length==3) {`
70	`Outdollars=","+tDollars+Outdollars`
71	`dollen=dollen-3`
72	`} else {`
73	`Outdollars=tDollars+Outdollars`
74	`dollen=0`
75	`}`
76	`}`
77	`if (Outdollars.substring(0,1)==",")`
78	`dollars=Outdollars.substring(1,Outdollars.length)`
79	`else`
80	`dollars=Outdollars`
81	`}`

The substring() method in line 64 uses the decipos value (the location of the decimal point) to extract the dollar value (the variable dollars). Next, a series of statements determines the length of the dollar value and then assigns the length to the variable dollen (line 65). Line 66 begins the if statement that determines if the dollar portion of the value is longer than three digits. The while loop routine (lines 67 through 76) places a comma every three digits, while the length of the dollar value is greater than three digits. Line 68 extracts three digits starting from the right by subtracting 3 from the length of the dollar value (dollen). Line 69 verifies three digits and line 70 inserts a comma in the output string. Line 71 decrements the length of the dollar value to look for the next group of three digits. When no more groups of three digits exist, the length of dollen is set to zero (line 74) and the loop terminates at line 76. The statements in lines 77 through 80 prevent the code from inserting a comma if only three digits are to the left of the decimal point.

To Enter an if...else Statement and while Loop to Extract the Dollar Portion of the Output and Insert Commas

The following step illustrates how to enter the if...else statement and while loop to extract the dollar portion of the output and insert commas into the output if needed.

- If necessary, click line 64, the line directly below the statement, decipos=valuein.length.
- Enter the JavaScript code as shown in Table 10–23 on the previous page using the SPACEBAR to indent as shown to extract the dollar portion of the output and insert the appropriate commas and then press the ENTER key (Figure 10–29).


```
function monthly(mortAmount,mortRate,mortYears) {
   var Irate=mortRate/1200
   var Pmts=mortYears*12
   var Amnt=mortAmount * (Irate / (1 - (1 / Math.pow(1+Irate,Pmts))))
   return Amnt.toFixed(2)
}

function dollarFormat(valuein) {
   var formatStr=""
   var Outdollars=""
   var decipos=valuein.indexOf(".")
   if (decipos==-1)
      decipos=valuein.length
   var dollars=valuein.substring(0,decipos)
   var dollen=dollars.length
   if (dollen>3) {
      while (dollen>0) {
            tDollars=dollars.substring(dollen-3,dollen)
            if (tDollars.length==3) {
               Outdollars=","+tDollars+Outdollars
               dollen=dollen-3
            } else {
                   Outdollars=tDollars+Outdollars
                   dollen=0
            }
      }
    if (Outdollars.substring(0,1)==",")
       dollars=Outdollars.substring(1,Outdollars.length)
    else
       dollars=Outdollars
    }

//-->
```

Figure 10–29

Reconstructing the Formatted Output and Returning the Formatted Value Next, the JavaScript statements must be written to reconstruct (concatenate) the formatted dollars and cents output into a formatted payment amount value, store the payment amount value in the formatStr variable, and return the formatStr value. Table 10–24 shows the statements needed to complete this task.

Table 10–24 Code for Reconstructing the Formatted Output and Returning the Formatted Value

Line	Code
82	`var cents=valuein.substring(decipos+1,decipos+3)`
83	`var formatStr="$"+dollars+"."+cents`
84	`return formatStr`
85	`}`

Line 82 extracts the two decimal places and assigns them to a variable to be used to reconstruct the formatted value. Line 83 reconstructs the values, concatenating a dollar sign ($) and the decimal value, and assigns the value to the formatStr variable. Line 84 returns the formatted value to the dollarFormat() function.

To Reconstruct the Formatted Output and Return the Formatted Value

The following step illustrates how to reconstruct the formatted output and return the formatted value to the calling function.

- If necessary, click line 82.
- Enter the JavaScript code from Table 10–24 using the SPACEBAR to indent as shown to reconstruct the formatted output and return the formatted value and then press the ENTER key (Figure 10–30).

```
chapter10statewiderealty.html - Notepad
File  Edit  Format  View  Help

    function dollarFormat(valuein) {
       var formatStr=""
       var Outdollars=""
       var decipos=valuein.indexOf(".")
       if (decipos==-1)
          decipos=valuein.length
       var dollars=valuein.substring(0,decipos)
       var dollen=dollars.length
       if (dollen>3) {
          while (dollen>0) {
                tDollars=dollars.substring(dollen-3,dollen)
                if (tDollars.length==3) {
                   Outdollars=","+tDollars+Outdollars
                   dollen=dollen-3
                } else {
                       Outdollars=tDollars+Outdollars
                       dollen=0
                   }
          }
         if (Outdollars.substring(0,1)==",")
            dollars=Outdollars.substring(1,Outdollars.length)
         else
            dollars=Outdollars
         }
         var cents=valuein.substring(decipos+1,decipos+3)
         var formatStr="$"+dollars+"."+cents
         return formatStr
    }

//-->
</script>
<style type="text/css">
<!--
.style1 {
        font-size: x-large;
        font-weight: bold;
        color: #3399FE;
}
.style2 {color: #3366FF}
body {
        background-image: url(chapter10bkgrnd.jpg);
}
.style3 {color: #000000; }
-->
</style>
```


Figure 10–30

To Pass the Monthly Payment Value to the dollarFormat() Function

To have the monthly payment value appear in the Monthly Payment text field formatted as currency, it must be passed to the dollarFormat() function. Because the dollarFormat() function manipulates a string value, the monthly payment result first must be converted to a string using the toString() method. In Chapter 9, the toString() method was used to convert a date value to a string. In this chapter, the toString() method is used to convert the monthly payment to a string that the dollarFormat() function can manipulate.

The following step shows how to enter the JavaScript statements needed to pass the monthly payment as a string object to the dollarFormat() function.

1

- Scroll up to and click line 45 (the line that starts document. MortCalc).
- Highlight and delete the variable, mortPayment, after the = symbol.
- Type `dollarFormat (mortPayment. toString())` to replace mortPayment with the dollarFormat() function using the mortPayment value. Do not press the ENTER key (Figure 10–31).

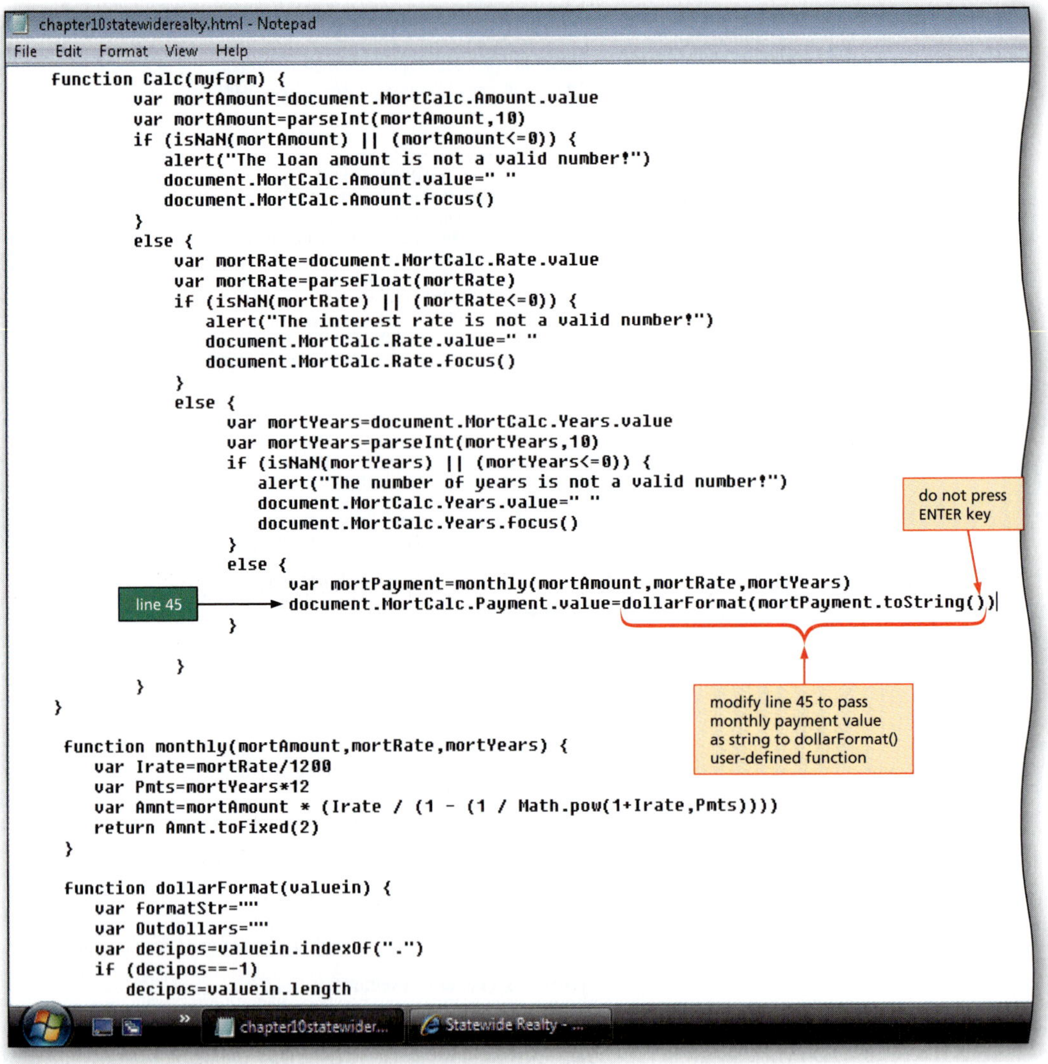

```
chapter10statewiderealty.html - Notepad
File Edit Format View Help
function Calc(myform) {
        var mortAmount=document.MortCalc.Amount.value
        var mortAmount=parseInt(mortAmount,10)
        if (isNaN(mortAmount) || (mortAmount<=0)) {
           alert("The loan amount is not a valid number!")
           document.MortCalc.Amount.value=" "
           document.MortCalc.Amount.focus()
        }
        else {
            var mortRate=document.MortCalc.Rate.value
            var mortRate=parseFloat(mortRate)
            if (isNaN(mortRate) || (mortRate<=0)) {
               alert("The interest rate is not a valid number!")
               document.MortCalc.Rate.value=" "
               document.MortCalc.Rate.focus()
            }
            else {
                 var mortYears=document.MortCalc.Years.value
                 var mortYears=parseInt(mortYears,10)
                 if (isNaN(mortYears) || (mortYears<=0)) {
                    alert("The number of years is not a valid number!")
                    document.MortCalc.Years.value=" "
                    document.MortCalc.Years.focus()
                 }
                 else {
                       var mortPayment=monthly(mortAmount,mortRate,mortYears)
                       document.MortCalc.Payment.value=dollarFormat(mortPayment.toString())
                 }

            }
        }
}

 function monthly(mortAmount,mortRate,mortYears) {
    var Irate=mortRate/1200
    var Pmts=mortYears*12
    var Amnt=mortAmount * (Irate / (1 - (1 / Math.pow(1+Irate,Pmts))))
    return Amnt.toFixed(2)
 }

 function dollarFormat(valuein) {
    var formatStr=""
    var Outdollars=""
    var decipos=valuein.indexOf(".")
    if (decipos==-1)
       decipos=valuein.length
```


Figure 10–31

To Save an HTML File and Test a Web Page

The following step shows how to save the HTML file and test the Web page.

- With the USB drive plugged into your computer, click File on the menu bar and then click Save.
- Click the browser button on the taskbar.
- Click the Refresh button on the browser toolbar.
- Enter the test data as follows: Amount of Mortgage: `173000`; Interest Rate as % (for example, 7.9): `6`; and Number of Years: `30`.
- Click the Calculate button. The result should be formatted as shown in Figure 10–32.

Figure 10–32

> **Plan Ahead**
>
> **Planning pop-up windows.**
> A pop-up window is used to add additional information to Web page. You must decide what features you want the pop-up window to utilize. Ask yourself these questions:
>
> - Do you want to include the status bar, title bar, address bar, scroll bars, toolbars, and menu bar?
> - Do you want the user to be able to resize the window?
> - What width and height should the window be?
>
> Each of these properties can be set as properties in the open() method, creating a customized look for that particular pop-up window.

Adding a Pop-Up Window

As you have learned in this chapter, the alert() method is one way to display messages to a user. These message boxes, however, only display text on a gray background. To create more visually interesting messages, you can use JavaScript to open and display another HTML file in a separate window that displays colors, graphics, animations, and other media. Such a window is called a **pop-up window**, because it appears over the previously opened browser window.

The **open() method** is used to create a pop-up window. Table 10–25 shows the general form of the open() method.

Table 10–25 open() Method

General form:	`var windowname=open("window file name(URL)", "object name", "window features")`
Comment:	where windowname is an optional name of a window object (required only if you need to refer to the pop-up window in any other Web page); window file name is the name of the HTML file; and window features describe how the window should appear.
Examples:	`open("Adwindow.htm", "AdWin", "resize=off,titlebar=false")`

BTW

Pop-up Windows
In addition to alert() message boxes, Web developers use pop-up windows to display more information to gain attention. Use pop-up windows sparingly, because having many pop-up windows can annoy visitors.

As shown in Table 10–25, when adding the open() method to create a pop-up window, all of the pop-up window features must be enclosed within one set of quotation marks. Table 10–26 describes the more commonly used attributes of the open() method, which are used to define pop-up window features. For more information about the open() method, see the JavaScript Quick Reference in Appendix E.

Table 10–26 open() Method Attributes

Feature	Description	Written As	Comments
location	Includes address bar	"location=yes"	
menubar	Includes menu bar	"menubar=yes"	
resize	Allows user to resize	"resizeable=yes"	
scrollbars	Includes scroll bars	"scrollbars=yes"	
status	Includes status bar	"status=yes"	
titlebar	Removes title bar	"titlebar=false"	Default is true
toolbar	Includes toolbar	"toolbar=yes"	
width	States width in pixels	"width=220"	
height	States height in pixels	"height=450"	

In this chapter, the open() method is used to open a pop-up window that will display information about Statewide Realty services. You insert code for the popupAd function and open() method, and then add an event handler to call the popupAd() function when the page is loaded. Earlier in the chapter, the onload event handler was associated with the scrollingMsg() function. You also will use the onload event handler for the popupAd() function. Multiple functions can be associated with the same event handler.

Table 10–27 shows the code to create the user-defined function popupAd(). The chapter10notice.html file already has been created and is stored in the Chapter10\ChapterFiles folder of the Data Files for Students.

Table 10–27 Code to Open chapter10notice.html Pop-Up Window

```
function popupAd() {
     open("chapter10notice.html","noticeWin","width=550,height=360")
}
```

Line 85 declares the popupAd() function. The statement in line 86 opens the chapter10notice.html Web page as a pop-up window that is 550 pixels wide and 360 pixels high.

To Enter the popupAd() Function to Open a Pop-Up Window

The following step illustrates how to enter the popupAd() user-defined function that contains the open() method to open the chapter10notice.html file in a pop-up window.

1

- Click line 85, the line directly above the //--> tag.
- Enter the JavaScript code from Table 10–27 to open a pop-up window and press the ENTER key (Figure 10–33).

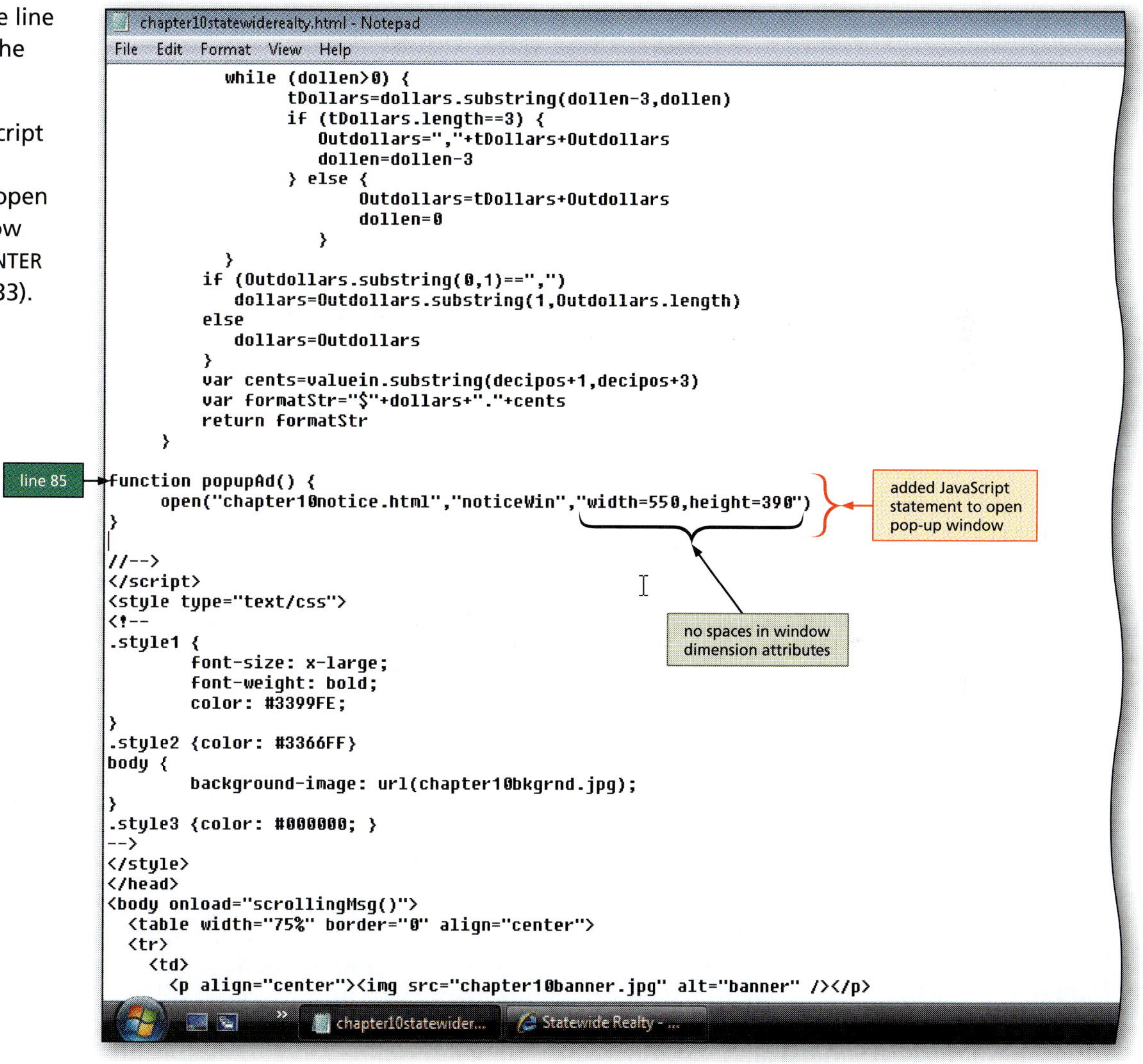

```
chapter10statewiderealty.html - Notepad
File  Edit  Format  View  Help
                 while (dollen>0) {
                         tDollars=dollars.substring(dollen-3,dollen)
                         if (tDollars.length==3) {
                            Outdollars=","+tDollars+Outdollars
                            dollen=dollen-3
                         } else {
                                Outdollars=tDollars+Outdollars
                                dollen=0
                            }
                 }
             if (Outdollars.substring(0,1)==",")
                 dollars=Outdollars.substring(1,Outdollars.length)
             else
                 dollars=Outdollars
             }
             var cents=valuein.substring(decipos+1,decipos+3)
             var formatStr="$"+dollars+"."+cents
             return formatStr
         }
function popupAd() {
        open("chapter10notice.html","noticeWin","width=550,height=390")
}

//-->
</script>
<style type="text/css">
<!--
.style1 {
        font-size: x-large;
        font-weight: bold;
        color: #3399FE;
}
.style2 {color: #3366FF}
body {
        background-image: url(chapter10bkgrnd.jpg);
}
.style3 {color: #000000; }
-->
</style>
</head>
<body onload="scrollingMsg()">
  <table width="75%" border="0" align="center">
  <tr>
    <td>
      <p align="center"><img src="chapter10banner.jpg" alt="banner" /></p>
```

line 85

added JavaScript statement to open pop-up window

no spaces in window dimension attributes

Figure 10–33

To Add the Event Handler to Call the popupAd()Function

Now we need to add the onload event handler to open the pop-up window when the Web page loads. Each function name is enclosed in one set of quotation marks and separated by a semicolon. The following step illustrates how to add the second function call to the onload() event handler.

1

- Position the insertion point in front of the "> at the end of line 106 (the line that begins <body onload=) (Figure 10–34).

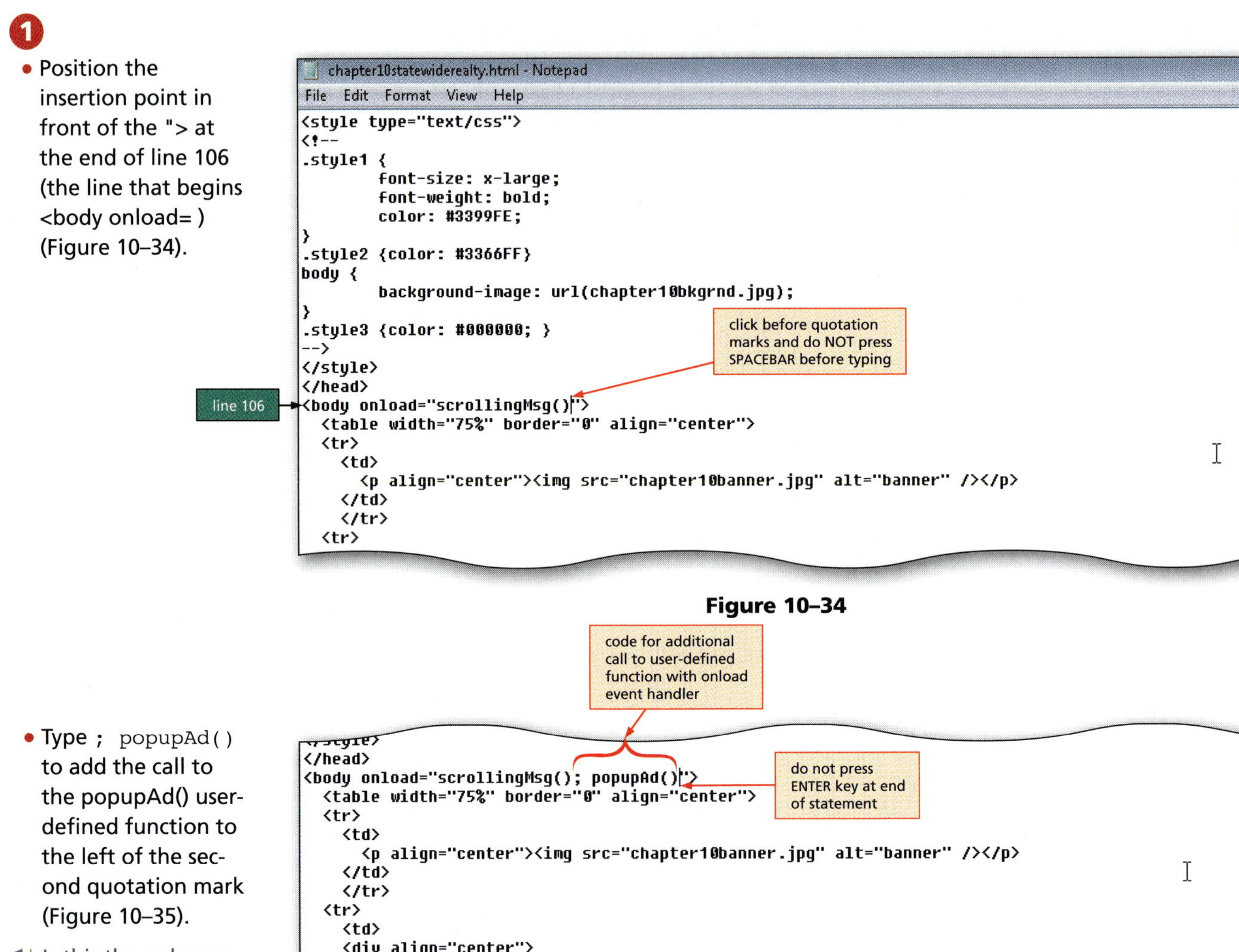

Figure 10–34

- Type ; popupAd() to add the call to the popupAd() user-defined function to the left of the second quotation mark (Figure 10–35).

Figure 10–35

Q&A

Is this the only way to open a pop-up window?

An open() method can be placed anywhere in the <script> section in the <head> section. Once the <head> section loads in the browser, it will execute the "stand-alone" open() method, opening a pop-up window. The code must be in the <head> section, however, in order for this to work properly.

Adding the Date Last Modified

As you learned in Chapter 9, the purpose of displaying the date a Web page was last modified is to make sure the user knows how current the information is contained on the Web page. You added JavaScript code to the Westlake Landscaping Web page to display the date and time a file was last modified. The Statewide Realty Web page should include similar JavaScript code to display just the date the Web page was modified, not the time. To display just the date, the code in Table 10–28 uses the substring() method to grab just the date. The parameters used in the substring() method only return the date for Microsoft Internet Explorer properly.

Table 10–28 Code to Display the Date Last Modified Using the substring() Method

Line	Code
157	<script type="text/javascript">
158	<!--Hide from old browsers
159	document.write("<p style='margin-left:10%; font-family:Arial, sans-serif; font-size:xx-small; color:#0000ff'>")
160	document.write("Statewide Realty, Copyright 2009-2010. ")
161	document.write(" This document was last modified "+document.lastModified.substring(0,10)+"</p>")
162	//-->
163	</script>

Lines 157 and 158 are the beginning <script> section tags. Line 159 is the document.write() method with an embedded style in a <p> tag. Line 160 writes the copyright statement and line 161 writes the date last modified. The substring(0,10) method in line 161 extracts the first 10 characters of the date and time — mm/dd/yyyy — so only the date is displayed, not the time. Lines 162 and 163 complete the JavaScript section.

To Display the Date Last Modified Using the substring() Method

The following step illustrates how to enter the JavaScript code to display the date the file was last modified using the substring() method.

1

- Click line 157 (the blank line between the </div> and </body> tags).
- Enter the JavaScript code from Table 10–28 to enter the copyright and date last modified code, pressing the ENTER key only at the end of each complete line. Do not press ENTER after the last </script> line (Figure 10–36).

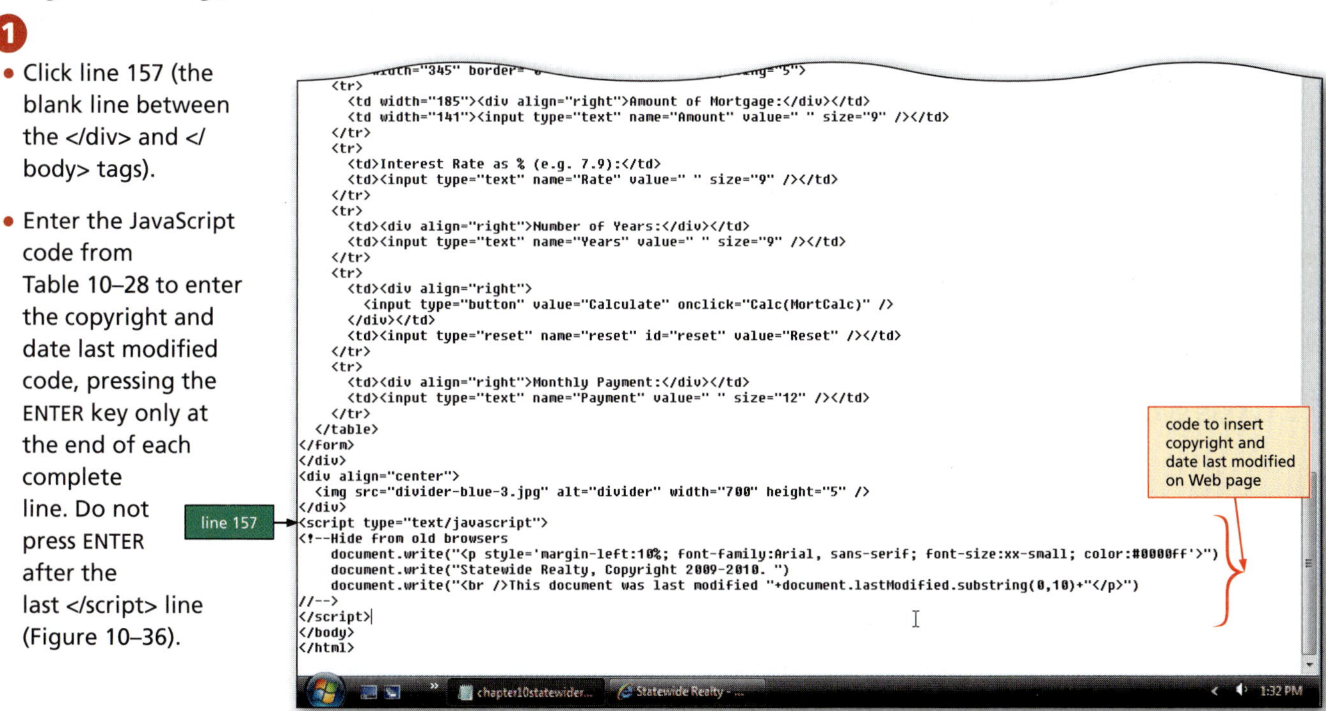

Figure 10–36

To Save and Validate an HTML File, Test a Web Page, and Print the HTML File

The code for the Statewide Realty Web page with a mortgage loan payment calculator and pop-up window is complete. Now you should save the HTML file, test the JavaScript code using a Web browser, and then print the HTML file.

- With the USB drive plugged into your computer, click File on the menu bar and then click Save.
- Validate the Web page.
- Click the browser button on the taskbar.
- Click the Refresh button on the browser toolbar.
- Click the Close Window button to close the pop-up window.
- If necessary, scroll down to verify that the bottom of the Web page displays the date the page was last modified (the date the file was saved) as shown in Figure 10–37.

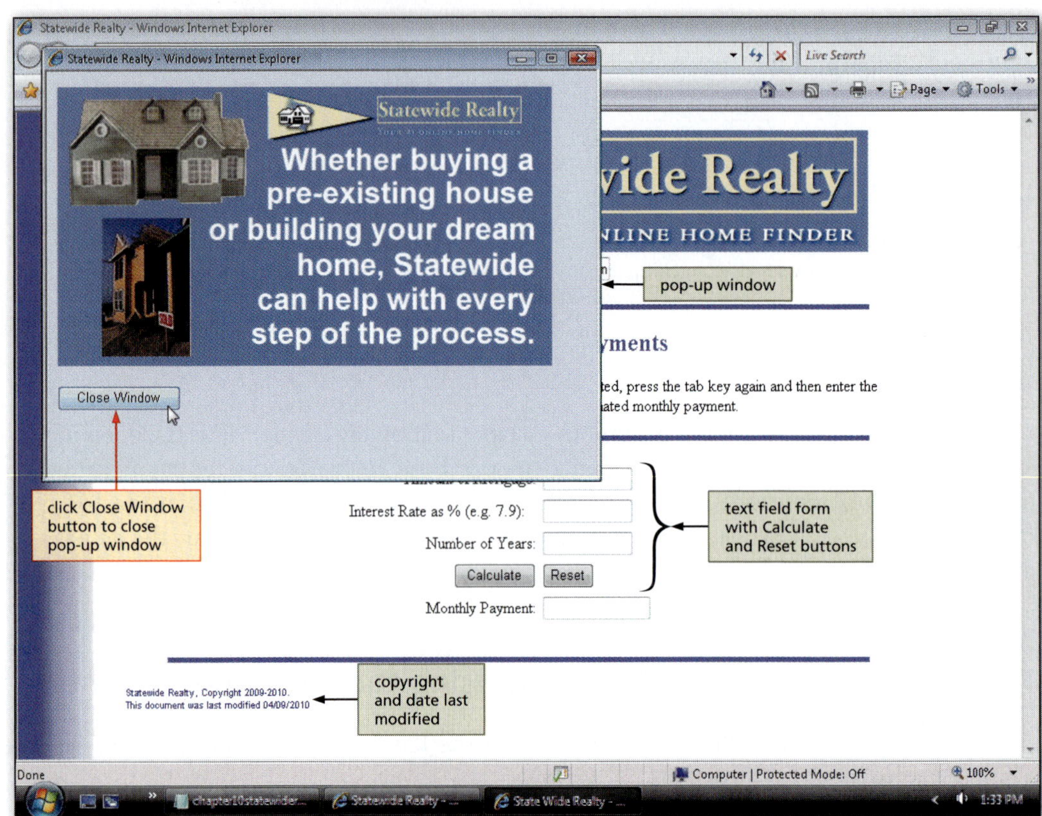

Figure 10–37

- If necessary, click the chapter10statewiderealty - Notepad button on the taskbar to activate the Notepad window.
- Click Print on the File menu to print the HTML file.

To Close Notepad and a Browser

- Click the Close button on the browser title bar.
- Click the Close button on the Notepad window title bar.

BTW

Quick Reference
For a list of JavaScript statements and their associated attributes, see the JavaScript Quick Reference (Appendix E) at the back of this book, or visit the HTML Quick Reference Web page (scsite.com/HTML5e/qr).

Chapter Summary

This chapter described how to write JavaScript to create a scrolling message, a pop-up window, if and if…else statements, pass values to a user-defined function, how to validate the data entered into a form and convert text to numeric values using the parseInt(), parseFloat(), and isNaN() built-in functions, and how to format string output results to display as currency. The items listed below include all the new JavaScript skills you have learned in this chapter.

1. Create a Form Text Field to Display a Scrolling Message (HTML 438)
2. Create the scrollingMsg() User-Defined Function (HTML 440)
3. Enter the Code to Increment the Position Locator Variable (HTML 441)
4. Enter an if Statement (HTML 444)
5. Add the setTimeout() Method to Create a Recursive Call (HTML 445)
6. Enter the onload Event Handler to Call the scrollingMsg() Function (HTML 447)
7. Start the Calc() Function and Nested if…else Statements to Validate Form Data (HTML 454)
8. End the Nested if...else Statements to Validate Form Data (HTML 456)
9. Enter an onclick() Event Handler to Call the Calc() Function (HTML 457)
10. Enter Code to Call the monthly() Function (HTML 460)
11. Create the monthly() Function (HTML 462)
12. Enter the dollarFormat() Function (HTML 465)
13. Enter an if…else Statement and while Loop to Extract the Dollar Portion of the Output and Insert Commas (HTML 468)
14. Reconstruct the Formatted Output and Return the Formatted Value (HTML 469)
15. Pass the Monthly Payment Value to the dollarFormat() Function (HTML 470)
16. Enter the popupAd() Function to Open a Pop-Up Window (HTML 473)
17. Add the Event Handler to Call the popupAd() Function (HTML 474)
18. Display the Date Last Modified Using the substring() Method (HTML 475)

Learn It Online

Test your knowledge of chapter content and key terms.

Instructions: To complete the Learn It Online exercises, start your browser, click the address bar, and then enter the Web address `scsite.com/html5e/learn`. When the HTML Learn It Online page is displayed, click the link for the exercise you want to complete and read the instructions.

Chapter Reinforcement TF, MC, and SA

A series of true/false, multiple choice, and short answer questions that test your knowledge of the chapter content.

Flash Cards

An interactive learning environment where you identify chapter key terms associated with displayed definitions.

Practice Test

A series of multiple choice questions that test your knowledge of chapter content and key terms.

Who Wants To Be a Computer Genius?

An interactive game that challenges your knowledge of chapter content in the style of a television quiz show.

Wheel of Terms

An interactive game that challenges your knowledge of chapter key terms in the style of the television show, *Wheel of Fortune*.

Crossword Puzzle Challenge

A crossword puzzle that challenges your knowledge of key terms presented in the chapter.

Apply Your Knowledge

Reinforce the skills and apply the concepts you learned in this chapter.

Instructions: Start Notepad. Open the file apply10-1.html from the Chapter10\Apply folder of the Data Files for Students. See the inside back cover of this book for instructions on downloading the Data Files for Students, or contact your instructor for information about accessing the required files.

The apply10-1.html file is a partially completed HTML file for the Cascade Mt. Front Range Resort that you will use for this exercise. You will use JavaScript to create a scrolling message and validate a text field entry for an e-mail address. You must add the event handler in the <body> tag to call the scrolling message function and the event handler in the Submit button to call the validate function. Figure 10–38 shows the Apply Your Knowledge Web page as it should be displayed in a browser after the JavaScript has been added.

Figure 10–38

Perform the following tasks:

1. Enter the beginning of a JavaScript code section for a user-defined function in the <head> section of the Web page.
2. Using the code presented in Figures 10-5 through 10-10 on pages HTML 440 through 445 as a guide, write a JavaScript user defined function called scrollingMsg() to display the following text string, **Specially Priced Family Weekend Packages Available**. Be sure to leave a space before and after the text string message.

3. Assign this text string to a variable named Msg.
4. Use the variable name beginWith as the position locator for the message.
5. Use Message as the name of the form and msgBox as the name of the text field.
6. In the setTimeout() method used to call the scrollingMsg() function, use 500 milliseconds as the time delay.
7. Declare a new user-defined function named emailValidate(emailForm).
8. Use the indexOf() method to determine if an @ sign is in the e-mail text field. Assign the result of the indexOf() method to a variable named atSign.
9. Enter an if statement to test the value of atSign. If atSign is less than 0, then use an alert() method to display the message, "Sorry, that e-mail address is not valid. Please re-enter your e-mail address."
10. Enter the else statement so that, if the e-mail address is in proper form, an alert() method will display the message, "Thank you. Your e-mail address will be added to our mailing list." Be sure to close the JavaScript <script> section properly.
11. Enter the proper event handler in the <body> tag to call the scrolling message function.
12. Enter the proper event handler in the <input> tag for the Submit button to call the emailValidate() user-defined function in the <head> section.
13. Save the revised file in the Chapter10\Apply folder using the file name apply10-1solution.html.
14. Start your browser. Enter the URL g:\Chapter10\Apply\apply10-1solution.html to view and test the Web page in your browser.
15. If any errors occur, check the code against Steps 1 through 13, make any required changes, save the file using the same file name, and then refresh the Web page in the browser.
16. Submit the revised HTML file and Web page in the format specified by your instructor.

Extend Your Knowledge

Extend the skills you learned in this chapter and experiment with new skills. You will need to search the Internet to complete the assignment.

Learning More About Displaying Messages

Instructions: Start Notepad and your browser. Open the file, extend10-1.html from the Chapter10\ Extend folder of the Data Files for Students. See the inside back cover of this book for instructions on downloading the Data Files for Students, or contact your instructor for information about accessing the required files.

The extend10-1.html file is a partially completed HTML file that you will use for this exercise. Figure 10–39 shows the Extend Your Knowledge Web page as it should be displayed in a browser after the JavaScript has been added.

Continued >

Extend Your Knowledge *continued*

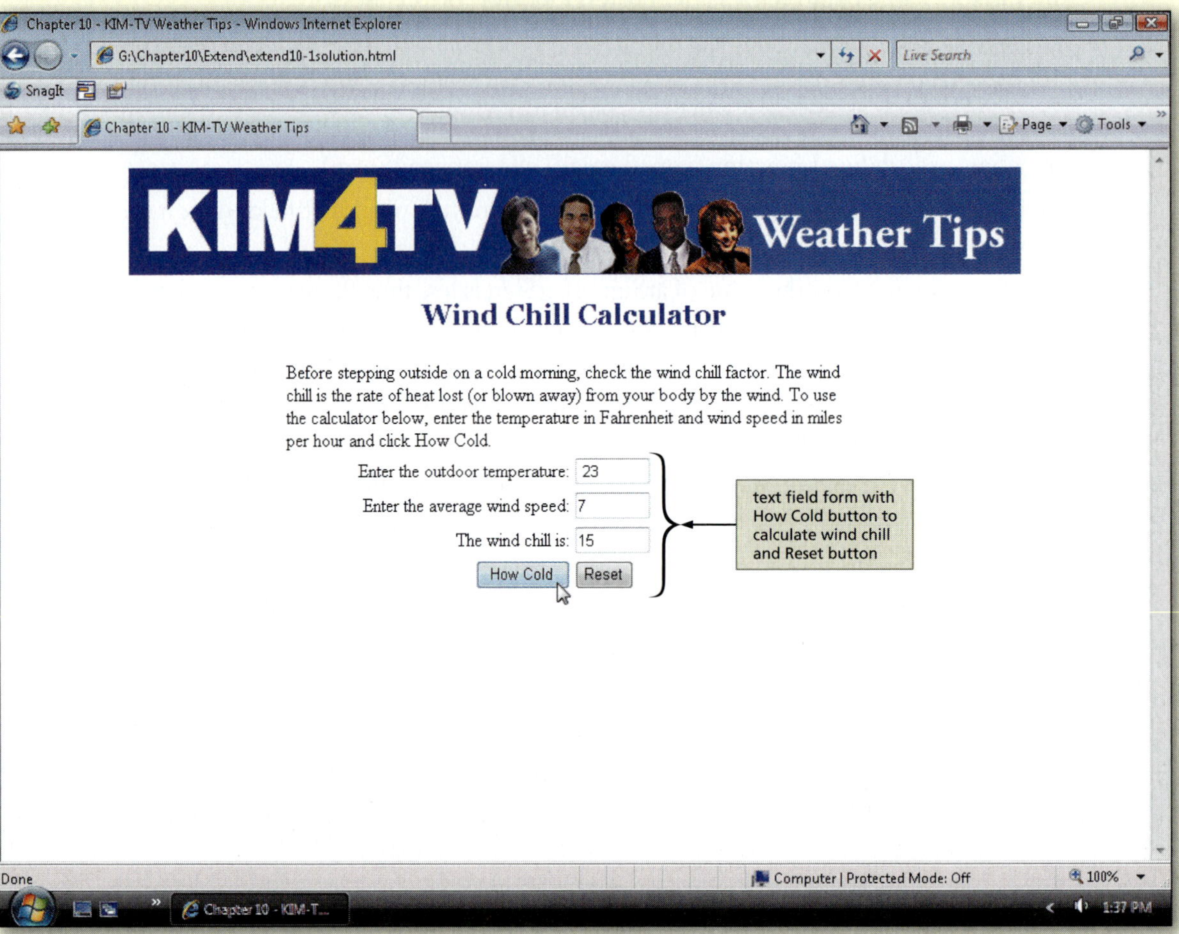

Figure 10–39

Perform the following tasks:

1. Search the Internet for the formula to calculate the wind chill factor given any temperature (Fahrenheit).
2. Using the form named Chill, write the JavaScript code to validate the two text field values in the form.
3. Write the if statements to validate that the OutdoorTemp and windSpeed are valid numeric values.
4. Display a message if the values are not numeric, clear the text field, and use the focus() method to position the insertion point back in that text field.
5. If the values are valid, compute the wind chill and place the result in the WindChill text field.
6. Save the revised file in the Chapter10\Extend folder using the file name extend10-1solution.html.
7. Start your browser. Enter the URL g:\Chapter10\Extend\extend10-1solution.html to view and test the Web page in your browser.
8. If any errors occur, check the code against Steps 1 through 5, make any required changes, save the file using the same file name, and then refresh the Web page in the browser.
9. Submit the revised HTML file and Web page in the format specified by your instructor.

Make It Right

Analyze the JavaScript code on a Web page and correct all errors.

Correcting Syntax Errors and Inserting Missing Code

Instructions: Start your browser. Open the file makeitright10-1.html from the Chapter10\MakeItRight folder of the Data Files for Students. See the inside back cover of this book for instructions for downloading the Data Files for Students, or contact your instructor for information about accessing the required files.

The makeitright10-1.html Web page is from Nick's Fitness Center. This page contains four errors. Use the following information as background for your corrections. Calories in our food come from the proteins, carbohydrates, and fats. A gram of fat contains 9 calories. A half cup of ice cream can have 12 grams of fat. At 9 calories a gram that is 108 calories. If the total calories are 180, that is over 60 percent of the calories from fat. The corrected Web page is shown in Figure 10–40.

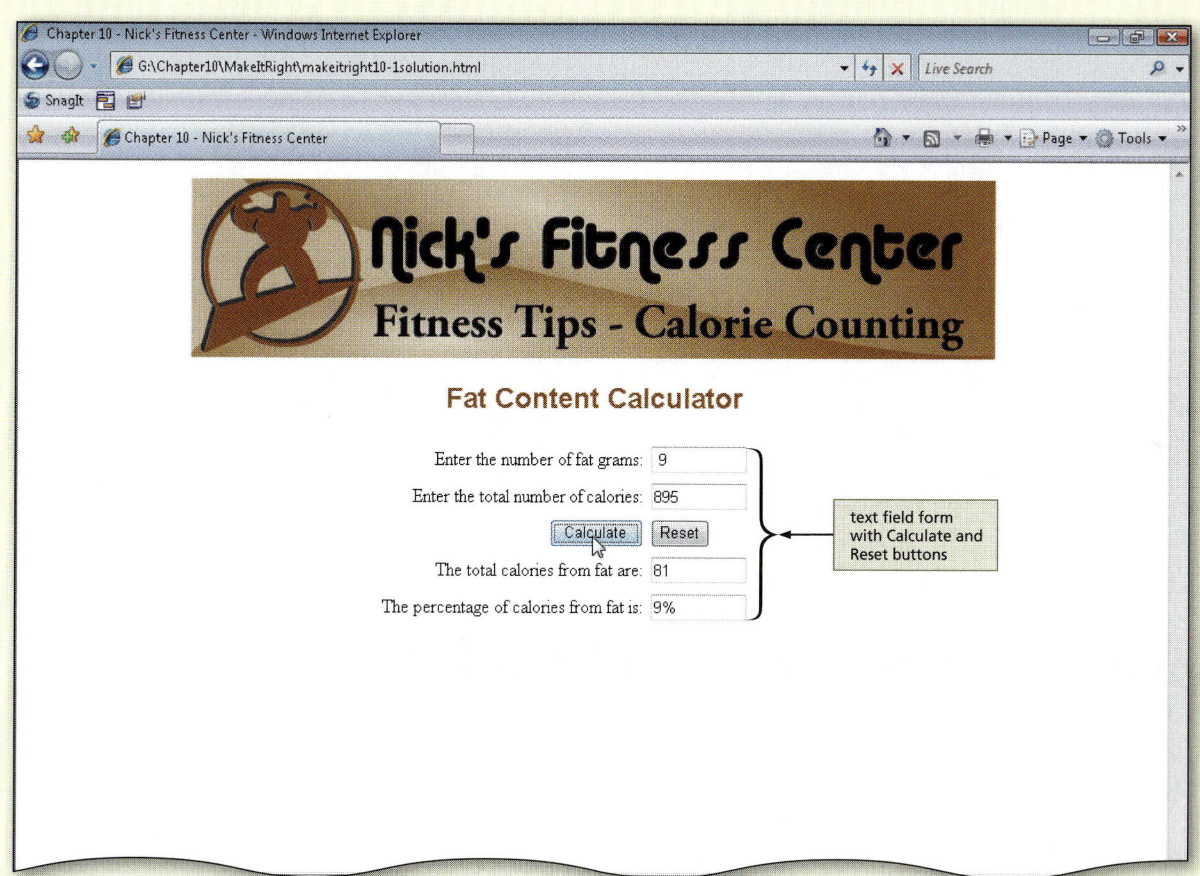

Figure 10–40

Perform the following tasks:

1. Refresh the Web page in the browser and look at the error message.
2. Correct the misspelled object names in the validation function and the event handler in the form.
3. Insert the missing line of code in the validation function to calculate the percentage.
4. Save the corrected HTML file and test using your browser. If an error still occurs, check your code from Steps 1 through 3 and save again.
5. Submit the revised HTML file and Web page in the format specified by your instructor.

In the Lab

Design and/or create a Web page using the guidelines, concepts, and skills presented in this chapter. Labs are listed in order of increasing difficulty.

Lab 1: Creating a Sports Web Page

Problem: You have an internship with a local newspaper, the *Hammond Daily News*. The sports editor asks you to create an interactive Web page that would allow users to enter in the number of at bats, walks, sacrifices, and hits into a form; validate the entries as numeric; and calculate the batting average. A batting average is calculated by dividing the number of hits by the number of at bats, minus the sum of the number of walks and sacrifice outs made: hits/bats-(walks+sacrifices). The form can do either one game or use accumulated totals as shown in Figure 10–41.

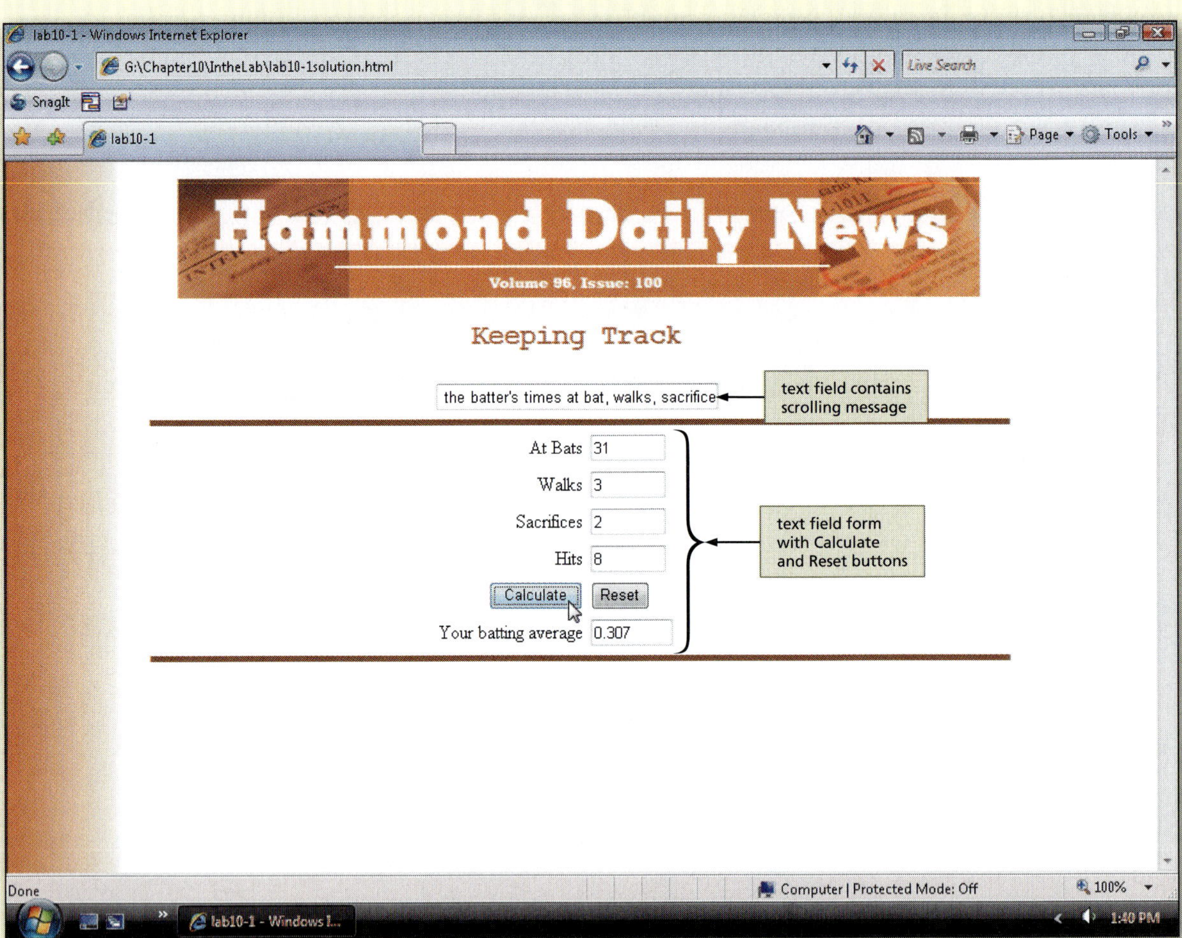

Figure 10–41

Instructions: Perform the following steps:

1. Start Notepad and open the lab10-1.html file from the Chapter10\IntheLab folder of the Data Files for Students.
2. Save the file as lab10-1solution.html.
3. Create a <script> section in the <head> section for the user-defined functions.

4. Using the code presented in Figures 10-5 through 10-10 on pages HTML 440 through 445 as a guide, write the user-defined function called scrollingMsg(). Use the message string ** Enter the batter's times at bat, walks, sacrifices, and hits. Then click the Calculate button. ** for the scrolling message.

   The form for the text field for scrolling message is named batAvg and has already been added to the data file. The text field for the scrolling message is msgScroller. Use these names when creating your user-defined function, scrollingMsg().
5. Use 200 for the setTimeout() method to recursively call the scrollingMsg() function.
6. Enter the appropriate event handler in the <body> tag to call the scrollingMsg() function when the Web page is loaded.
7. Using the code in Tables 10–11 through 10–13 on pages HTML 454 through 455 as a guide, write the JavaScript user-defined function calcBatAvg() to validate the data entered into the form as numeric. Be sure to enter the appropriate event handler to call the calcBatAvg() function when the user clicks the Calculate button on the form.
8. Once the data is validated as numeric, write the JavaScript equation to calculate the batting average.
9. Because the batting average will have more than three decimal places, pass the batting average to a user-defined function called fixDecimal() and assign the result to the batAverage text field.
10. Use the code in Table 10–29 to format the batting average to 3 decimal places.

Table 10–29

```
function fixDecimal(battingAvg) {
   var strBatAvg
   var valuein = battingAvg
   if (valuein.length>5) {
               strBatAvg=valuein.substring(0,5)
   }
   else {
                  strBatAvg=valuein+"00"
   }
   return strBatAvg.substring(0,5)
}
```

11. Save the completed HTML file and test it using your browser. If an error occurs, check your code from Steps 3 through 10 and save and test again.
12. Submit the completed HTML file and Web page in the format specified by your instructor.

STUDENT ASSIGNMENTS

In the Lab

Lab 2: Calculating Simple Property Tax Values

Problem: You are the Webmaster for the Lake County Assessor's office. You have been asked to create an interactive Web page that will allow home owners to enter their assessed home value, homestead discount, and any senior citizen discount to calculate property taxes. The Web page has a scrolling message, and validates the data entered into the form as numeric. The calculated tax is formatted as dollars and cents and is displayed in the propTax text field. Add the JavaScript to make the Web page appear as in Figure 10–42.

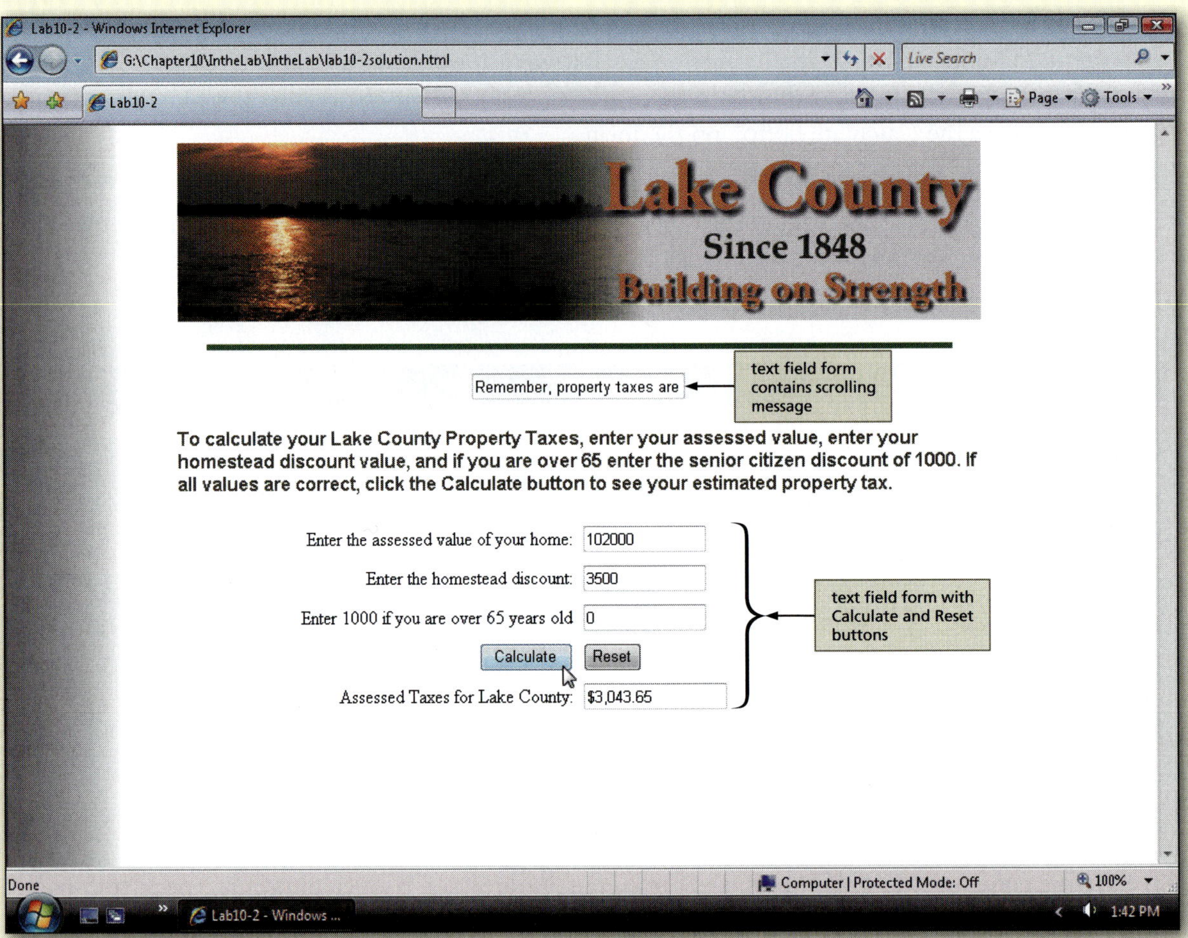

Figure 10–42

Instructions: Perform the following steps:

1. Start Notepad and open the file lab10-2.html from the Chapter10\IntheLab folder of the Data Files for Students.
2. Save the file as lab10-2solution.html.
3. Using the code from Table 10–1 on page HTML 437 as a guide, create a form with one text field for a scrolling message. Name the form msgForm, the input text field scrollingMsg, and make the size 25. Enter the form below the comment <!-- Enter form here --> above the <Table> tag.
4. Create a <script> section in the <head> section for the user-defined functions.
5. Using the code presented in Figures 10–5 through 10–10 on pages HTML 440 through 445 as a guide, write the user-defined function called scrollingMsg(). Use the message string ** Remember, property taxes are due on June 15 ** for the scrolling message.

6. Use 200 for the setTimeout() method to recursively call the scrollingMsg() function.
7. Using the code in Tables 10–11 through 10–13 on pages HTML 454 through 455 as a guide, write the JavaScript user-defined function validateInput() to validate the data entered into the form as numeric.
8. Once the data is validated as numeric, use the code in Table 10–30 to write the JavaScript equation to calculate property taxes and assign the result to the propTax text field.

Table 10–30

```
function CalcTaxes(assessedValue,HomeDisc,Seniors) {
   var newAssessedValue = assessedValue - HomeDisc - Seniors
   var propTaxes = newassessedValue * .0309
   propTaxes = Math.round(propTaxes*100)/100
   return propTaxes.toFixed(2)
}
```

9. Use the code in Tables 10–20, 10–23, and 10–24 on pages HTML 465 through 468 as a guide, to format the tax amount as currency.
10. Save the completed HTML file and test the Web page using your browser with the following data: Assessed value: 142000, Homestead Discount: 30000, Senior Citizen Discount: 0.
11. If an error occurs, check your code from Steps 3 through 9 and save and test again.
12. Submit the completed HTML file and Web page in the format specified by your instructor.

In the Lab

Lab 3: Shoreline Bank Car Loan Calculator

Problem: You are a summer Intern at Shoreline Bank. The bank recently completed a customer satisfaction survey and one item customers wanted was a monthly payment calculation Web page. Your assignment is to create a Web page that allows customers to calculate monthly payments on a car loan (Figure 10–43). This Web page has a scrolling message, ** Lock in on our low loan rates now!!! **. When the Web page loads, a pop-up window displays providing instructions on how to use the interactive form. Validate the form for numeric values. No value may be blank. Display the monthly payment formatted as currency.

Continued >

In the Lab *continued*

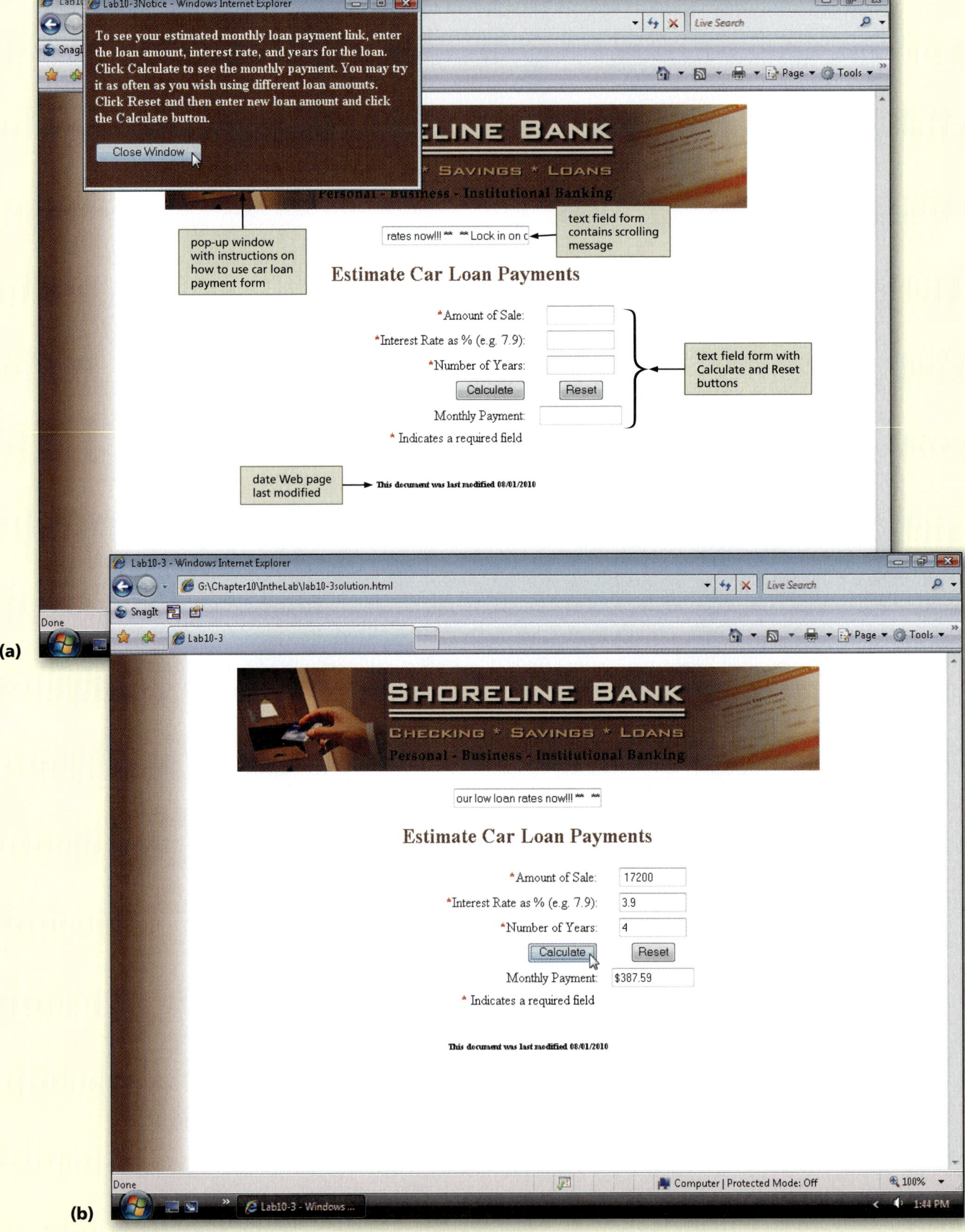

Figure 10–43

Instructions: Perform the following steps:

1. Start Notepad and open the lab10-3.html file from the Chapter10\IntheLab folder of the Data Files for Students. Save immediately as lab10-3solution.html.
2. Using the techniques learned in this chapter, write the JavaScript code to create a scrolling message, validate the data entered into the form, and calculate the monthly payment on a car loan. Place the scrolling message form text field where the HTML comment line indicates after the banner image. Add the date the Web page was last modified before the closing </body> tag as indicated by the HTML comment. A pop-up window should display with a message as indicated in Figure 10–43a.
3. Save the completed HTML file and test it using your browser. If an error occurs, check your code, save, and test again.
4. Submit the completed HTML file and Web page in the format specified by your instructor.

STUDENT ASSIGNMENTS

Cases and Places

Apply your creative thinking and problem solving skills to design and implement a solution.

• EASIER ••MORE DIFFICULT

• 1: Expanding the Chapter Web Page

Statewide Realty has received numerous questions about the loan calculator Web page. Customers want to be able to enter the sale price, a down payment percentage, and calculate the mortgage amount based on the down payment. In addition, they wish to have the amount of Personal Mortgage Insurance calculated and added to the form.

Using your completed chapter project files, add an additional form to the chapter Web page named getMortgage to add a Home Selling Price text field, Percent Down text field, and a Final Mortgage price text field. Add an Amount of PMI text field above the Monthly Payment text field to the MortCalc form.

Create a separate function to validate all the Selling Price and Percent Down (for Down Payment) text fields as valid numbers. Calculate the down payment by multiplying the down payment percentage times the selling price and subtracting that value from the selling price. Use an onblur event handler to call this function after the percent down value is entered. Use the results of this calculation for the MortAmount text field.
Hint: Selling Price – (Selling Price * (Percent Down/100)).

Using the remainder of the original form, use the original event handler to call the Calc() user-defined function. Add the calculation to test if the percent down is less than 20% to calculate the PMI. The monthly PMI is calculated by taking the mortgage amount * .005 and dividing the product by 12 to get the monthly amount.

• 2: Create the Shoreline Cinema Registration Page

Shoreline Cinema is a local theater that runs classic, foreign, and art films. The owner has asked you to develop a Web page for the theater so patrons can sign up for weekly e-mail announcements of films. The movie house is promoting its new movie club. To help gain attention to the Web site, you create a scrolling message, ** Enter your e-mail address below to subscribe to Shoreline Movie Club! **. Using data file provided, insert a simple form that asks for an e-mail address in a text field. Write the JavaScript code to validate the e-mail address by checking to make sure an @ sign is entered. Be sure to add the proper event handlers in the correct locations to call the user-defined functions.

•• 3: Create the Globe Financial Investment Strategy Planner Web Page

As the newly hired Webmaster for Globe Financial, using case10-3.html you are asked to create a Web page to allow patrons to calculate a monthly savings amount for a future value, such as a retirement goal. The form has a drop-down list for selecting the number of years, a text field for an estimated average interest, and a text field to enter a goal savings amount. The form should validate the values entered as numeric and calculate the future value to determine the monthly savings amount. In addition, the Web page should include a text field for a scrolling message: ** -Make an appointment with a Globe Financial planner today!- **. The Web page has a pop-up window ad that should display when the Web page is loaded. Be sure to add the proper event handlers in the correct locations to call the user-defined functions and to display the pop-up window provided.

•• 4: Exploring Alternative Form and Calculator Validation Methods

Make It Personal

Search the Internet to find a Web site that has a mortgage or car loan calculator. Use the Web site to find the monthly payment on a loan. For a car loan, use the following data:

Loan: $13,000.00, Interest Rate: 4.9%, Years: 5

For a mortgage loan, use the following data:

Loan: $120,000.00, Interest Rate: 5.75%, Years: 20

Leave a field blank to see how the loan calculator responds. Capture the screen using Print Screen and paste the screen into a Word document. Write a paragraph or two that compare the Web site calculator to the project you completed in this chapter, discussing the similarities or differences between the two forms. Next, search the Internet for various JavaScript routines that validate forms. Cut and paste this code into a Word document, indicating the Web site from which you copied the code. Write a paragraph or two describing how this validation method is different or similar to the method presented in the chapter project.

•• 5: Analyzing Financial Calculators on the Web

Working Together

As a team, search the Web for various forms with calculators. Each member should find at least two. Some types of calculators are for taxes, loans, savings plans, student financial aid, insurance, and many others. Collect and summarize these calculators. Write a description of how the calculator in the chapter project could be improved based on the different calculators you have discovered on the Internet. Redo the chapter project to improve it based on your recommendations.

11 Using DOM to Enhance Web Pages

Objectives

You will have mastered the material in this chapter when you can:

- Define the Document Object Model (DOM)
- Integrate Cascading Style Sheets (CSS) with JavaScript statements to position elements on a Web page
- Create a vertically scrolling menu
- Use the JavaScript setTimeout() and clearTimeout() methods to control a scrolling object
- Call JavaScript functions directly using the *JavaScript* command
- Use onmouseover and onmouseout event handlers to execute pop-up ScreenTips
- Integrate the <span> tag in JavaScript statements for ScreenTips
- Use the JavaScript write() method to write text directly to the document
- Define an array and describe how to create an array instance
- Define a rotating banner
- Create and use image objects for rotating banners

11 Using DOM to Enhance Web Pages

Introduction

In Chapter 10 you learned to write JavaScript user-defined functions to add scrolling messages and pop-up windows to your Web site, to validate user entries on Web forms, to make calculations from user input, and to format output to a text field. This chapter builds on those skills and others you have learned so far by introducing the **Document Object Model (DOM)**, a combination of technologies that include HTML, Cascading Style Sheets (CSS), and a scripting language, such as JavaScript, to make your Web pages even more dynamic. In this chapter you will use DOM to create Web pages with scrolling menus, ScreenTips, a rotating banner, and a scrolling image.

Project — The Lake Michigan Community College Web Site

You are on the Web development team for Lake Michigan Community College, which is redesigning its Web site to incorporate DOM technology. The new design includes a scrolling menu on the home page that scrolls down the page as the user scrolls down the page. The home page also includes links to the mission statement and annual blood drive pages that act as pop-up windows so they can be closed easily without the user having to navigate back and forth among several pages.

In addition, for an animation effect, you suggest the Blood Drive Web page use a rotating banner, and the Academic Assistance Web page use a scrolling image that also is a link to the Student Life pop-up window. You also want to add some pop-up ScreenTips to the Counseling Services page. A **ScreenTip** is text that appears in a small pop-up box on the screen and provides additional information about an item.

Figures 11–1a through 11–1g show the completed Lake Michigan Community College home page and six supporting Web pages and dynamic elements. The DOM techniques used to create these Web pages are designed for use in Microsoft Internet Explorer 7.x.

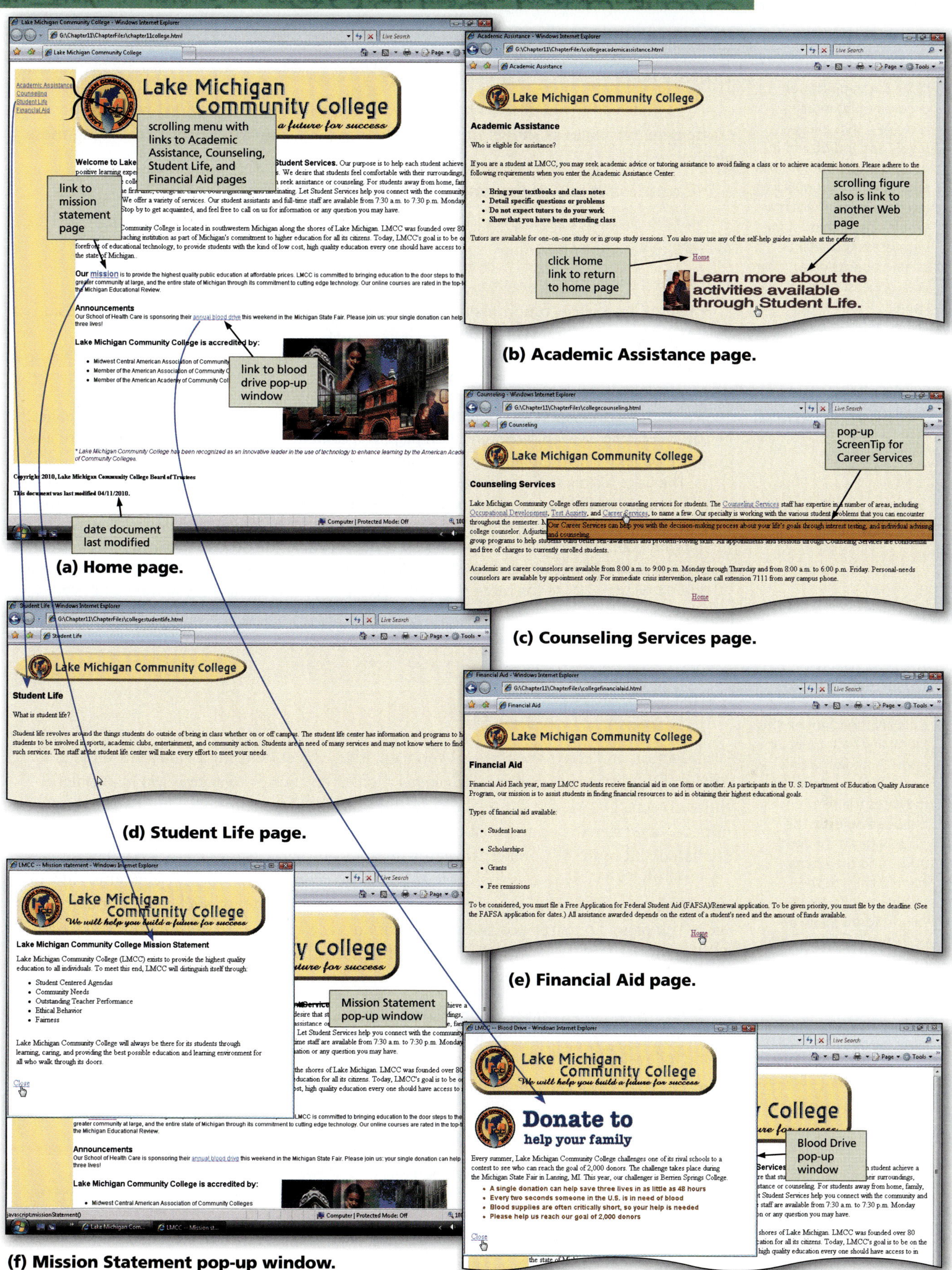

(a) Home page.

(b) Academic Assistance page.

(c) Counseling Services page.

(d) Student Life page.

(e) Financial Aid page.

(f) Mission Statement pop-up window.

(g) Blood Drive pop-up window.

Figure 11–1

BTW **DOM**
DOM is an application programming interface (API) that allows JavaScript and other languages to manipulate the structure of the underlying document. DOM is a simple, hierarchical naming system that makes certain objects on a Web page, such as images, forms, and layers, accessible to scripting languages.

Overview

As you read through this chapter, you will learn how to use DOM with JavaScript to create dynamic pages as shown in Figure 11–1 on page HTML 493 by performing these general tasks:

- Create a vertical scrolling menu
- Create ScreenTips to provide additional information about selected terms
- Create a rotating banner
- Create a scrolling image
- Create JavaScript functions that open the pop-up windows of the Blood Drive and Mission Statement Web pages

Plan Ahead

General Project Guidelines
In creating a complex Web site with multiple Web pages, you should determine what pages will be created and what content each page will contain. In addition, you should determine which pages will contain links to other pages.

The Lake Michigan Community College Web site contains several Web pages. The main home page has links to six other pages: Academic Assistance, Counseling Services, Student Life, Financial Aid, the college's mission statement, and the annual blood drive. The mission statement and blood drive will be pop-up windows while the other pages will open in their own windows. The Academic Assistance Web page will open the Student Life Web page as a pop-up window. Once the hierarchy of the Web pages is determined, you can begin work on each page.

BTW **DOM Nodes**
The DOM naming system uses a tree-like hierarchy of parent and child relationships. In this hierarchy, each object is a node. A **node** is a point in a tree-like structure that indicates the relationship between objects. The <html> tag is the root node, and the <body> tag is a child to the <html> tag node. These relationships allow an object to become a child of another object.

The Document Object Model (DOM)

Each section and component on a Web page is an object, and the Document Object Model (DOM) allows scripting languages such as JavaScript to access and manipulate those objects. DOM, similar to the older DHTML, uses a combination of HTML tags, options, style sheet properties, and scripting languages to create Web pages that are more animated and more responsive to visitor interaction than basic HTML Web pages.

With DOM, a developer is able to position, group, or move page elements anywhere on a Web page. **Positioning** specifies the placement of elements, such as text and graphics, on a Web page. Dynamic positioning of elements is a key feature of modern Web pages and makes the Web page more appealing and interactive.

Plan Ahead

Creating the vertical scrolling menu.
To create the vertical scrolling menu on the Lake Michigan Community College Web page, the following three items must be created:

- An HTML table with the menu text in a division (layer) that will be used to move the menu
- Style sheet class selectors to modify the menu links
- A JavaScript function that continually checks the location of the menu object

Creating the Vertical Scrolling Menu and Pop-up Windows

The first step in updating the Lake Michigan Community College Web site is to create the vertical scrolling menu on the home page. The vertical scrolling menu is a four-row, one-column table that contains links to four Web pages. The table's position is determined relative to the top of the document. As the visitor scrolls down the Web page document, the position of the table changes relative to the position of the top of the document.

Table 11–1 shows the code to enter the HTML division and create a menu object in an HTML table. The style attribute of the <div> tag sets the initial position of the table (menu object). Each table cell contains a menu text link to a specific Web page, and is formatted using a style sheet class selector. Class selectors will be discussed in more detail later in the chapter.

BTW

The <div> Tag

The <div> tag is called a container, and is used to format the layout of sections or divisions of text needing the same style. Web developers often describe divisions as layers, because they can be placed on top of each other and be revealed dynamically as needed.

Table 11–1 HTML Code to Create the HTML Division and Table to Contain a Menu Object

Line	Code
10	<div id="moveMenu" style="left: 13px; width: 125px; position: absolute; top: 10px; z-index: 0; background-color: #ffeba6; layer-background-color: #feeaa5; border: 1px none #000000;">
11	<table width="110%" border="0" style="border-collapse: collapse">
12	<tr>
13	<td class="menubg" width="20%">
14	<p align="left"><a href="collegeacademicassistance.html">Academic Assistance</a></p></td></tr>
15	<tr>
16	<td class="menubg" width="20%">
17	<p align="left"><a href="collegecounseling.html">Counseling</a></p></td></tr>
18	<tr>
19	<td class="menubg" width="20%">
20	<p align="left"><a href="collegestudentlife.html">Student Life</a></p></td></tr>
21	<tr>
22	<td class="menubg" width="20%">
23	<p align="left"><a href="collegefinancialaid.html">Financial Aid</a></p></td>
24	</tr>
25	</table>
26	</div>

Line 10 starts the HTML division in which the table (menu object) that holds the vertical scrolling menu is contained. The id attribute identifies the division as an object called moveMenu, so the division can be referenced by that name later in JavaScript code. The style attribute indicates the position of this division is absolute; meaning the table always shows the set number of pixels from the top of the screen, even as the user scrolls down the page. Lines 12, 15, 18, and 21 start a new row in the column, and lines 14, 17, 20, and 23 add a link to each of the four Web pages. Each table data cell (lines 13, 16, 19, and 22) includes a style class, menubg, which formats the link. A standard anchor hover style modifies the link when the mouse pointer is placed over the hyperlink. The </div> tag in line 26 closes the HTML division.

BTW

Moving Objects

Object positions can be changed within a division <div> or a span <span> tag. These are called layers (not to be confused with the deprecated <layer> tag in Netscape). Differences in browsers can cause a division to appear slightly lower or higher than originally intended by the developer.

To Open an Existing HTML File

The following step shows how to open the chapter11.html file included in the Data Files for Students.

- Start Notepad, and, if necessary, maximize the window. If Word Wrap is not enabled, click Format on the menu bar and then click Word Wrap to enable it.
- With a USB drive plugged in to your computer, click File on the menu bar and then click Open.

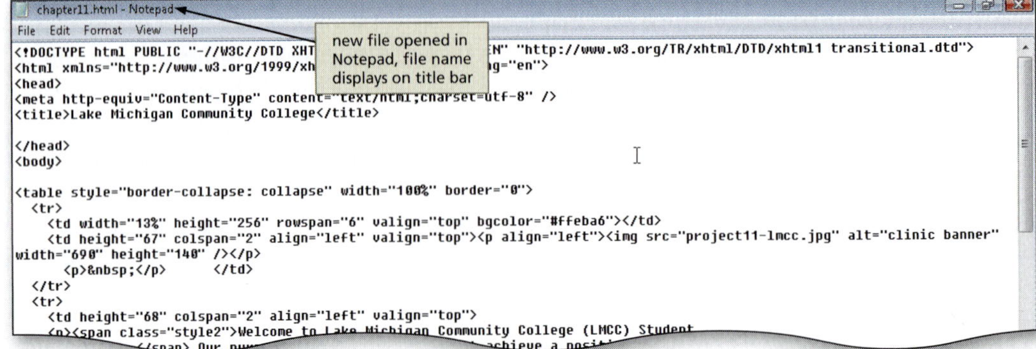

Figure 11–2

- If necessary, navigate to the Chapter11\ChapterFiles folder on the USB drive.
- If necessary, click the Files of type box arrow, and then click All Files to show all files in the Chapter11\ChapterFiles folder.
- Click chapter11.html in the list of files.
- Click the Open button to open the chapter11.html file in Notepad (Figure 11–2).

To Create an HTML Division and Table to Contain a Menu Object

The following step illustrates how to enter the HTML code to create the HTML division and an HTML table to contain the menu object.

1

- Click line 10.
- Enter the HTML code shown in Table 11–1 to create the division and HTML table. Note that in this chapter, many of the lines of code wrap to a second line in Notepad. When entering code, press the SPACEBAR to indent as shown, but do not press the ENTER key until you reach the end of the line of code (Figure 11–3).

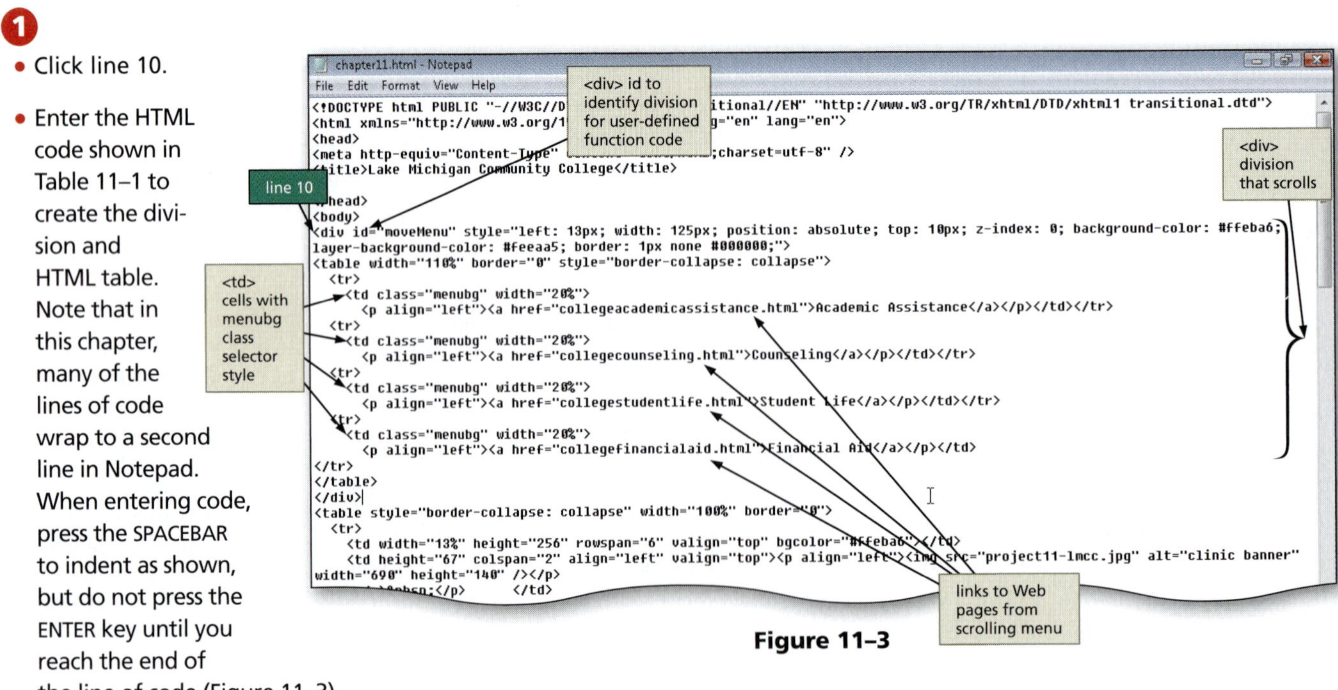

Figure 11–3

Creating an Embedded Style Sheet

The next step is to create the style sheet that is used to format the appearance of the text on the Web page and the menu, so the link text appears in dark red, italic font when the user points to a link. This chapter uses the class and pseudo-class elements to format text. A **class selector**, also called class name, defines specific style elements. These elements either can be applied to a specific tag type or can be independent and used in any tag within the <body> section.

As you learned in Chapter 8, the part of the style statement that identifies the page elements is called the selector. The part of the style statement that identifies how the elements should appear is called the declaration. In addition, a class selector can be used in a number of different HTML tags. An HTML tag can have multiple rules defined by creating different class selectors. To define a class, you would enter the code:

```
.menubg {font-family: arial; color: red;}
```

The class selector is applied to any HTML tag by using the class attribute in the HTML tag. To use the previous class selector in an HTML tag, like a table cell, you would enter:

```
<td class="menubg">table text formatted</td>
```

In addition to class selectors, CSS has **pseudo-class selectors**, which are used to apply a style or format to a specific characteristic of a tag or element. These format characteristics apply only for special circumstances. The a:hover pseudo-class selector is a popular example for hyperlinks. When the mouse hovers over a link, the style sheet elements modify the text. To define a hover pseudo-class selector, you would code a style sheet as follows:

```
a:hover {color: red; font-style: italic}
```

In this example, the text link appears in red italic font and then changes back to the default font when a user points off the link. Note that the pseudo-class selector name does not have a period in front of it, as does the class selector, menubg. Also, recall from Chapter 8 that each style must be enclosed in braces.

Table 11–2 shows code to create the embedded style sheet for the Lake Michigan Community College home page, using class and pseudo-class selectors.

Table 11–2 CSS Code for Embedded Style Sheet

Line	Code
7	`<style type="text/css">`
8	`.menubg {`
9	`font-size: 12px; font-family: arial, helvetica, sans-serif; color: #ffffff;`
10	`}`
11	`a:hover {`
12	`color: #cc3333; font-style: italic`
13	`}`
14	`.style1 {`
15	`font-size: 12px; font-family: arial, helvetica, sans-serif`
16	`}`
17	`.style2 {`
18	`font-weight: bold; font-family: arial, helvetica, sans-serif; font-size: 16px;`

Table 11–2 CSS Code for Embedded Style Sheet *(continued)*

Line	Code
19	`}`
20	`.style3 {`
21	`font-size: 12px; color: #333366; font-style: italic; font-family: arial, helvetica, sans-serif`
22	`}`
23	`</style>`

Line 7 starts the embedded style sheet with a <style> tag. Lines 8 through 10 define the .menubg class that will modify the table cell text for the scrolling menu. Lines 11 through 13 define the a:hover pseudo-class, which changes the font appearance only when the mouse is placed over the table menu text. Lines 14 through 22 define three additional classes — style1, style2, and style3 — which are used to format the body of the text on the home page. Line 23 includes the end </style> tag to end the embedded style sheet.

To Create an Embedded Style Sheet

The following step shows how to enter the style sheet to format the link text on the menu, including the hover pseudo-class, as well as to define formats for three different body text styles.

1

- Click line 7.
- Enter the code from Table 11–2 on the blank line to create the embedded style sheet, pressing the SPACEBAR to indent as shown. Do not press the ENTER key after the last line (Figure 11–4).

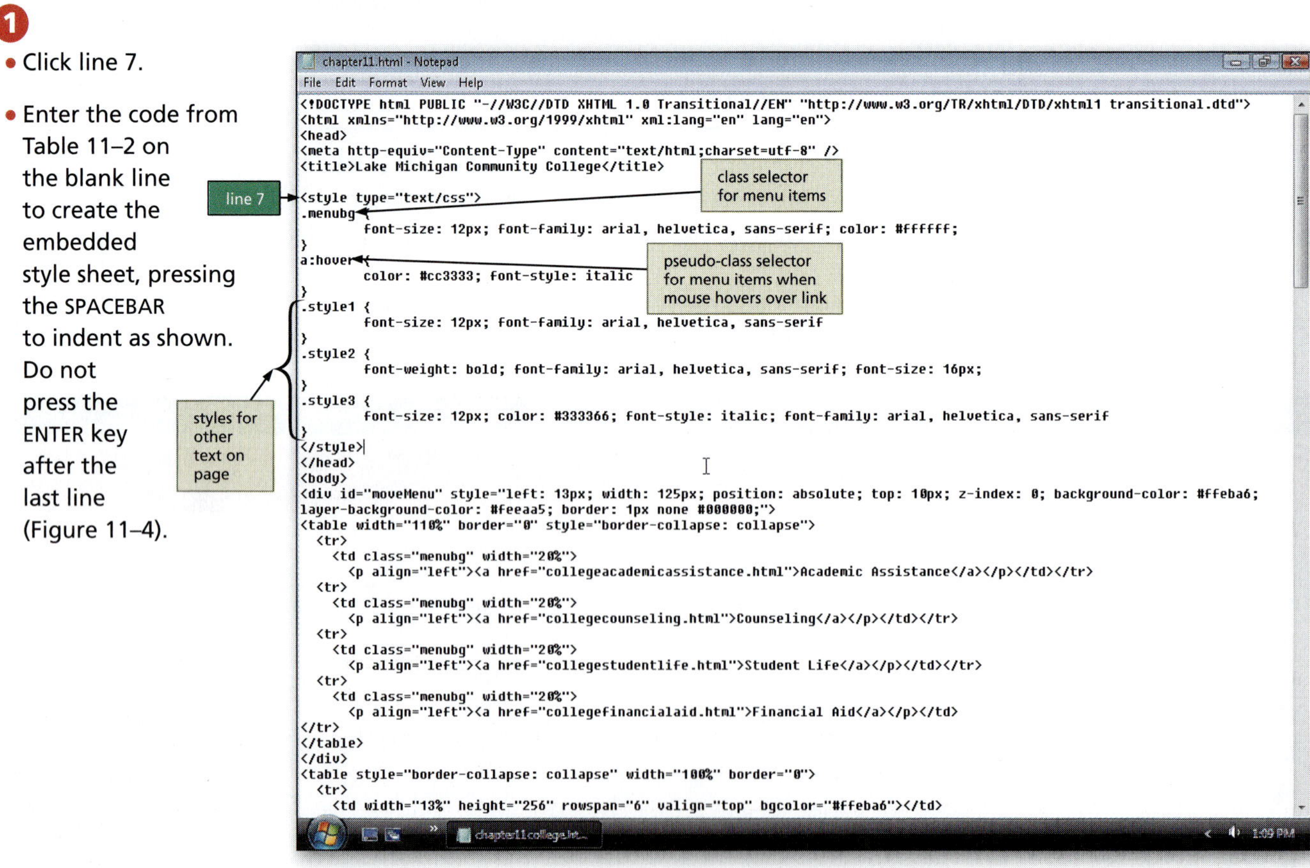

Figure 11–4

Plan Ahead

Creating the checkLocation() user-defined function to scroll an object.
To scroll the menu vertically as a user scrolls up or down the Web page, the checkLocation() function must complete the following tasks:

- Assign the width of the document to a variable
- Assign the height of the document to a variable
- Assign the distance from the top of the document window to a variable
- Assign the current scroll positions to variables
- Calculate the new positions of the document vertically and horizontally
- Assign the new positions to the menu object

Creating the checkLocation() Function to Scroll the Menu Vertically

The next step is to enter the JavaScript user-defined function called checkLocation(), which continually checks the location of the menu as the document is scrolled up or down. The checkLocation() function repositions the menu so it appears to scroll with the Web page.

Table 11–3 shows the code to create the checkLocation() user-defined function to scroll the vertical menu.

BTW

Making Web Pages Dynamic with DOM
Using JavaScript takes away the dependence on the server to produce interesting effects and animation on a Web page. As the content of the Web page grows or changes, so does the Web page's appearance and presentation.

Table 11–3 Code for the checkLocation() Function

Line	Code
6	<script type="text/javascript">
7	<!-- Hide from old browsers
8	function checkLocation() {
9	var availableX=document.body.clientWidth
10	var availableY=document.body.clientHeight
11	var currentX=document.body.scrollRight
12	var y=window.screenTop-50
13	moveMenu.style.pixelTop=document.documentElement.scrollTop+y
14	setTimeout("checkLocation()",100);
15	}
16	
17	//-->
18	</script>

Lines 6 and 7 start the script section with the beginning <script> tag and HTML comment to hide the JavaScript from older browsers. Line 8 declares the user-defined function, checkLocation(). Lines 9 and 10 assign the width and height of the browser window to the variables availableX and availableY. Line 11 assigns the current left position. Line 12 calculates a new top position using the screenTop property of the window less 50 pixels, so it is not so far down. Line 13 assigns the new position to the style attributes for the menu object in the HTML division, moveMenu. If the user has scrolled the Web page, the menu moves to the new position.

BTW

Scrolling Menus
JavaScript and style sheet code places the scrolling menus dynamically in a relative position based on the screen resolution. A vertically scrolling menu may not be necessary with high screen resolution, because the Web page may fit completely in the browser window.

Line 14 is the setTimeout() method used to call the checkLocation() function recursively, so it continually checks the current location. Line 15 is a brace that closes the function. Line 16 is blank to allow additional JavaScript functions to be entered within the script section, and lines 17 and 18 close the script section.

To Create the checkLocation() User-Defined Function

The following step illustrates how to enter the code for the checkLocation() function that checks the location of the menu object and keeps positioning it in the same location as the user scrolls up or down the Web page.

1

- Click line 6.
- Enter the code shown in Table 11–3 to create the checkLocation() user-defined function, pressing the SPACEBAR to indent as shown (Figure 11–5). Do not press the ENTER key after the last line.

Q&A How is the checkLocation() function initialized?

To position the vertical scrolling menu initially, an onload event handler must be placed in the <body> tag to call the checkLocation() user-defined function when the Web page first loads.

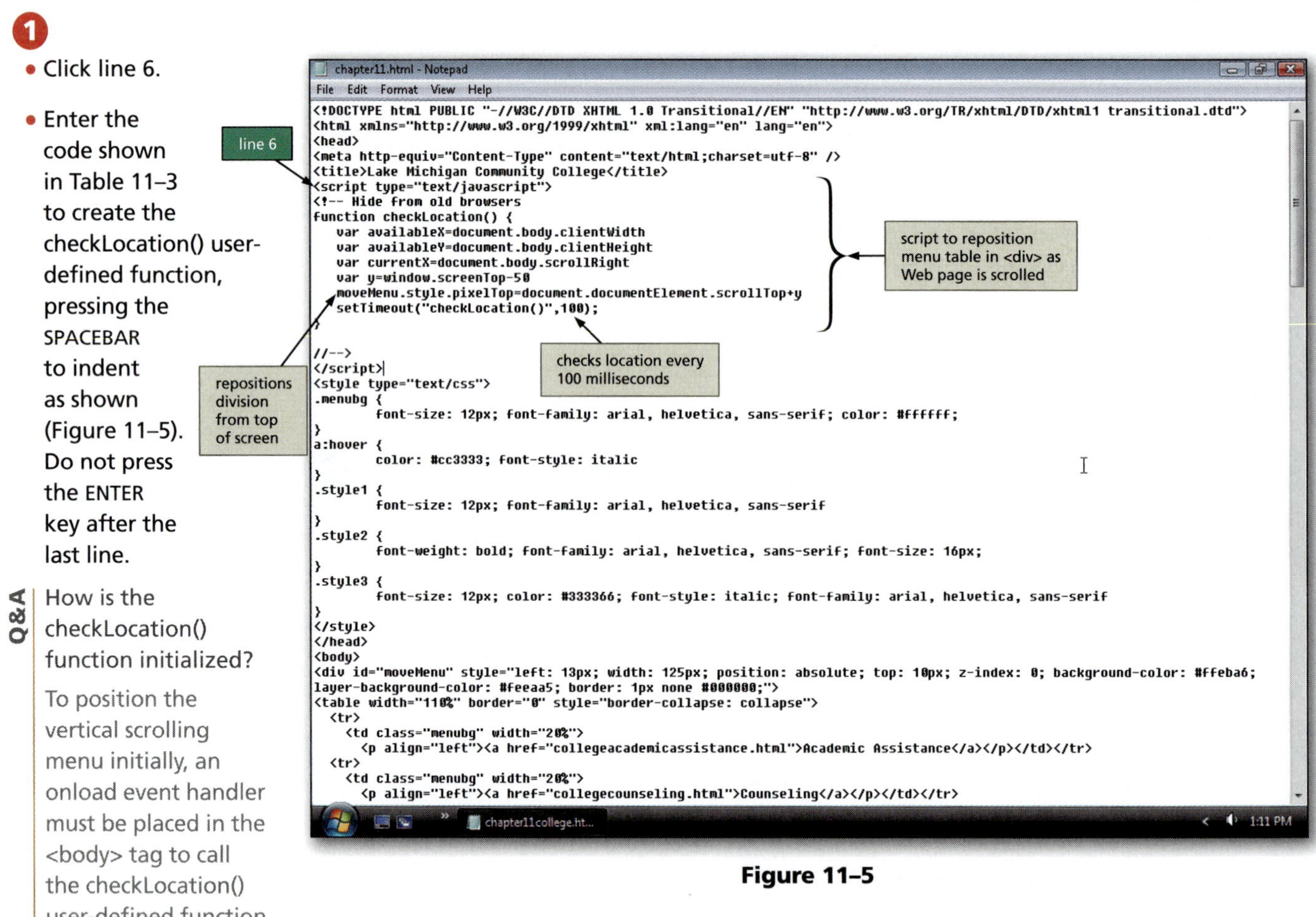

Figure 11–5

To Write the onload Event Handler to Call the checkLocation() Function

The following step shows how to write the onload event handler to call the checkLocation() user-defined function.

1

- Position the insertion point on line 37, before the right > symbol in the <body> tag.
- Press the SPACEBAR once.

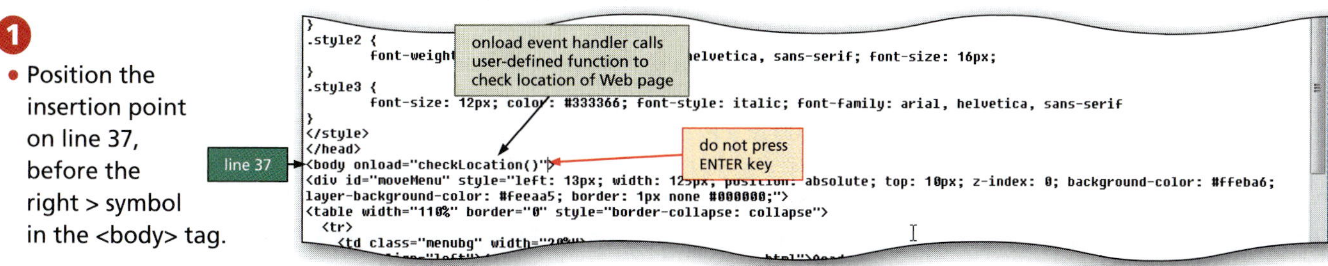

Figure 11–6

- Type `onload="checkLocation()"` to enter the onload event handler to call the checkLocation() user-defined function and do not press the ENTER key (Figure 11–6).

Plan Ahead

> **Creating the bloodDrive() and missionStatement() user-defined functions to open pop-up windows.**
>
> A pop-up window is used to add additional information to a Web page. You must decide what features you want the pop-up window to utilize. Ask yourself these questions:
>
> - Do you want to include the status bar, title bar, Address bar, scroll bars, toolbars, and menu bar?
> - Do you want the user to be able to resize the window?
> - What width and height should the window be?
>
> Each of these properties can be set as properties in the open() method, creating a customized look for that particular pop-up window.

Creating the Functions to Open the Blood Drive and Mission Statement Pop-up Windows

The next step in updating the Lake Michigan Community College home page is to create the functions to open the pop-up windows for the Blood Drive and Mission Statement Web pages. As you learned in Chapter 10, the open() method is used to open a new window and display a new Web page. Table 11–4 shows the code for the two user-defined functions to open the Blood Drive and Mission Statement pop-up windows. Both functions use the open() method to open a new pop-up window.

Table 11–4 Code for User-Defined Functions to Open Pop-up Windows

Line	Code
17	`function bloodDrive() {`
18	`window.open("collegeblooddrive.html", "BloodDrive", "width=620,height=450")`
19	`}`
20	
21	`function missionStatement() {`
22	`window.open("collegemission.html", "Mission", "width=600,height=500")`
23	`}`

Line 17 declares the user-defined function, bloodDrive(). The open() method on line 18 tells the function to open the Web page, collegeblooddrive.html, in a new window that is 620 pixels wide by 450 pixels high. No other window parameters are given. Recall from Chapter 10 that spaces are not allowed between any of the window parameters properties. Line 19 closes the function.

Line 21 declares the missionStatement() function. The open() method on line 22 tells the function to open the Web page, collegemission.html, in a new window that is 600 pixels wide by 500 pixels high. Line 23 closes the function.

To Enter the bloodDrive() and missionStatement() User-Defined Functions to Open Pop-up Windows

The following step shows how to enter two user-defined functions, bloodDrive() and missionStatement(), to open two pop-up windows.

1

- Click line 16 and press the ENTER key once.
- On line 17, enter the JavaScript code shown in Table 11–4 to create the user-defined functions to open the pop-up windows, pressing the SPACEBAR to indent as shown (Figure 11–7).

Figure 11–7

Calling Built-in Functions with the JavaScript Command
Some built-in functions can be used in a Web page without having to construct a JavaScript section. The method is to use the javascript: command before the function name. For example, javascript:open("scseries.com", "SC", "width=600, height=400") would open a pop-up window of the Shelly Cashman Series Web site.

Using JavaScript to Call a User-Defined Function from an Anchor Tag Link

The bloodDrive() and missionStatement() user-defined functions are called when a user clicks the annual blood drive or mission statement links on the home page. Each event causes a pop-up window to open. Because the pop-up windows are opened with the Window.open() method in a user-defined function, the anchor <a> tag used to create the link must include a JavaScript command to call the related user-defined function. The general form of the JavaScript command that calls the user-defined function is shown in Table 11–5.

Table 11–5 Using the JavaScript Command to Call the User-Defined Function

General form:	JavaScript:userdefinedFunction()
Comment:	where JavaScript indicates a direct call to a user-defined function and userdefinedFunction() is the name of a user-defined function defined in the <head> section. The value of the href attribute may be enclosed in either single or double quotation marks.
Example:	<a href='javascript:bloodDrive()'>annual blood drive</a>

To Enter Links with a JavaScript Method to Open the Pop-up Windows

The following step shows how to enter the two text links that include a JavaScript command to call the bloodDrive() and missionStatement() functions.

1

- Find the <p> and <span class="style2"> tags preceding the words Our mission, on line 85.
- Position the insertion point before the word mission.
- Type `<a href='javascript:missionStatement()'>` to enter the <a> tag link for the missionStatement() user-defined function, and do not press the ENTER key.
- Position the insertion point after the word mission.
- Type `</a>` to enter the closing <a> tag and do not press the ENTER key.
- Scroll down to line 91 and find the <span class="style1"> tag preceding the words: Our School of Health Care is sponsoring their.
- Position the insertion point before the word annual.
- Type `<a href='javascript:bloodDrive()'>` to enter the <a> tag link for the bloodDrive() user-defined function, and do not press the ENTER key.
- Position the insertion point after the word drive.
- Type `</a>` to enter the closing <a> tag and do not press the ENTER key (Figure 11–8).

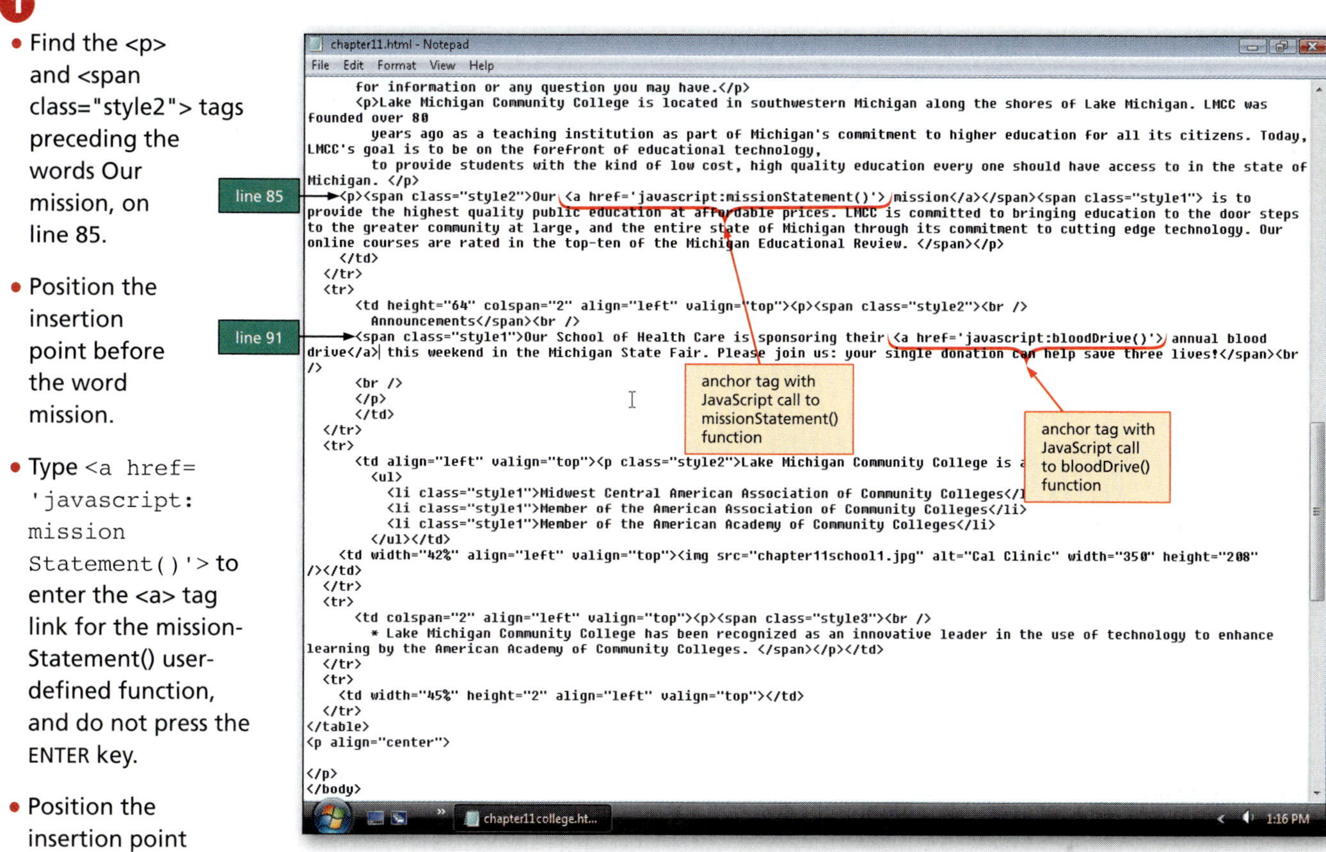

Figure 11–8

Q&A

Why not use a normal <a href> with a URL link to open the windows?

A normal link to a URL would open the Web page in the same window or a new tab, depending on the browser. By using the JavaScript call to a user-defined function, a new window with specific attributes is opened as a pop-up window.

To Enter Code to Show Copyright Information and Date Last Modified

As shown in Figure 11–1a on page HTML 493, the Lake Michigan Community College Web page is displayed with copyright information and the date the file was last modified at the bottom of the Web page. To show just the date, without the time, the JavaScript code uses the substring() method, which was introduced in Chapter 10. Table 11–6 shows the JavaScript code for the <script> section to show the copyright information and date the Web page was last modified.

Table 11–6 Code to Show the Date Last Modified

Line	Code
114	`<script type="text/javascript">`
115	`<!--Hide from old browsers`
116	`document.write("<p><h5>Copyright 2010, Lake Michigan Community College Board of Trustees</p>")`
117	`document.write("This document was last modified "+document.lastModified.substring(0,10)+".</h5>")`
118	`//-->`
119	`</script>`

The following step illustrates how to enter JavaScript code to show copyright information and the date the file was last modified using the substring() method so it is displayed at the bottom of the Web page.

- Click line 114.
- Enter the JavaScript code shown in Table 11–6 to show the copyright information and date last modified (Figure 11–9).

chapter11.html - Notepad

File Edit Format View Help

```
Michigan. </p>
    <p><span class="style2">Our <a href='javascript:missionStatement()'> mission</a></span><span class="style1"> is to
provide the highest quality public education at affordable prices. LMCC is committed to bringing education to the door steps
to the greater community at large, and the entire state of Michigan through its commitment to cutting edge technology. Our
online courses are rated in the top-ten of the Michigan Educational Review. </span></p>
    </td>
  </tr>
  <tr>
      <td height="64" colspan="2" align="left" valign="top"><p><span class="style2"><br />
        Announcements</span><br />
      <span class="style1">Our School of Health Care is sponsoring their <a href='javascript:bloodDrive()'> annual blood
drive</a> this weekend in the Michigan State Fair. Please join us: your single donation can help save three lives!</span><br
/>
      <br />
      </p>
      </td>
  </tr>
  <tr>
      <td align="left" valign="top"><p class="style2">Lake Michigan Community College is accredited by:</p>
        <ul>
          <li class="style1">Midwest Central American Association of Community Colleges</li>
          <li class="style1">Member of the American Association of Community Colleges</li>
          <li class="style1">Member of the American Academy of Community Colleges</li>
        </ul></td>
    <td width="42%" align="left" valign="top"><img src="chapter11school1.jpg" alt="Cal Clinic" width="350" height="208"
/></td>
  </tr>
  <tr>
      <td col                t" valign="top"><p><span class="style3"><br />
        * Lak                y College has been recognized as an innovative leader in the use of technology to enhance
learning by t               of Community Colleges. </span></p></td>
  </tr>
  <tr>
    <td width="45%" height="2" align="left" valign="top"></td>
  </tr>
</table>
<p align="center">
<script type="text/javascript">
<!--Hide from old browsers
document.write("<p><h5>Copyright 2010, Lake Michigan Community College Board of Trustees</p>")
document.write("This document was last modified "+document.lastModified.substring(0,10)+".</h5>")
//-->
</script>
</p>
</body>
</html>
```


Figure 11–9

To Save an HTML File and Test a Web Page

With the code for the user-defined functions and the JavaScript section for the copyright information and the date last modified complete, you should save the HTML file and test the Web page. The following steps illustrate how to save the HTML file and then test the Lake Michigan Community College Web page.

- With a USB drive plugged into your computer, click File on the menu bar and then click Save As. Type `chapter11college.html` in the File name text box.
- If necessary, browse to the USB drive and open the Chapter11\ChapterFiles folder.
- Click the Save button in the Save As dialog box.
- Start your browser. If necessary, click the Maximize button.

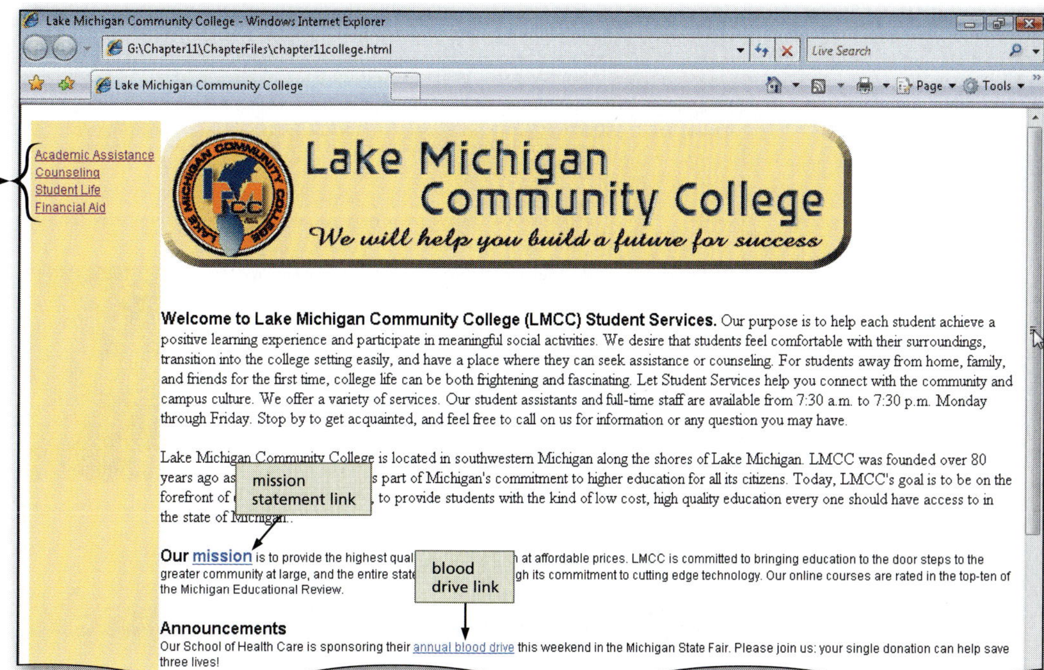

Figure 11–10

- Type `g:\Chapter11\ChapterFiles\chapter11college.html` on the Address bar and then press the ENTER key (Figure 11–10). If necessary, click the information bar, click Allow Blocked Content, and click Yes in the Security Warning dialog box.

2

- Use the mouse and drag the scroll box down to view more of the page. Notice how the menu scrolls with the page (Figure 11–11).

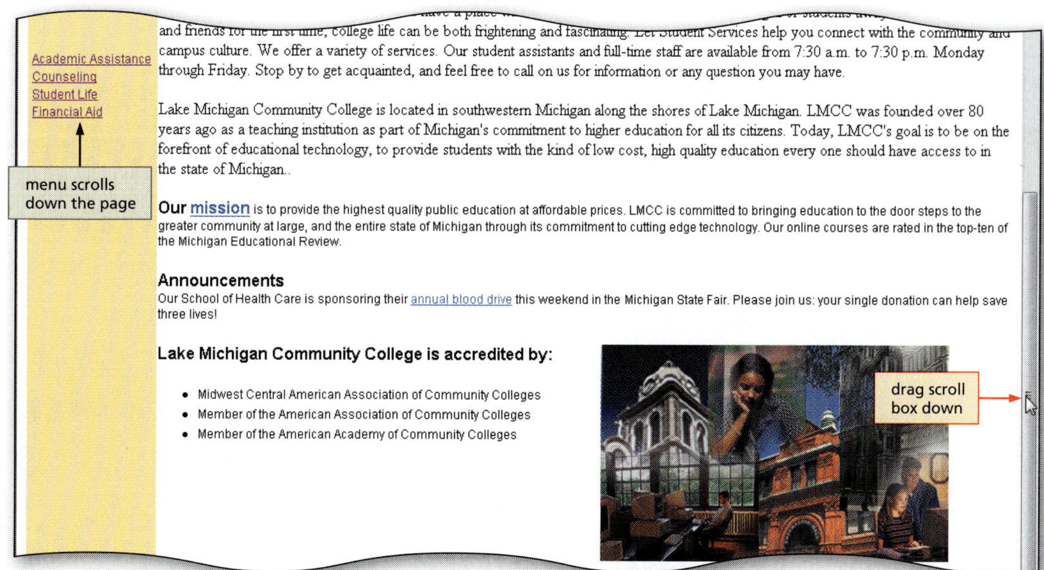

Figure 11–11

- Click the Financial Aid menu link (Figure 11–12) to show the Financial Aid page.

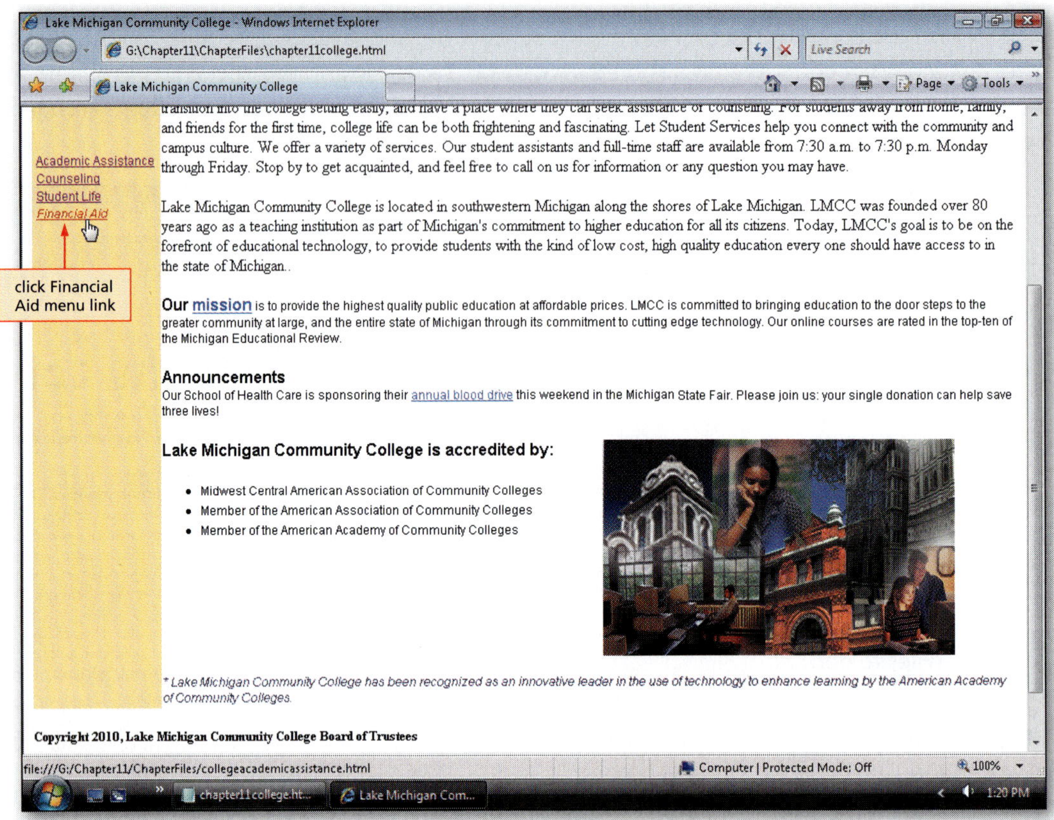

Figure 11–12

4

- Click the Home link at the bottom of the page (Figure 11–13) or click the Back button on the Standard toolbar to return to the Lake Michigan Community College home page.

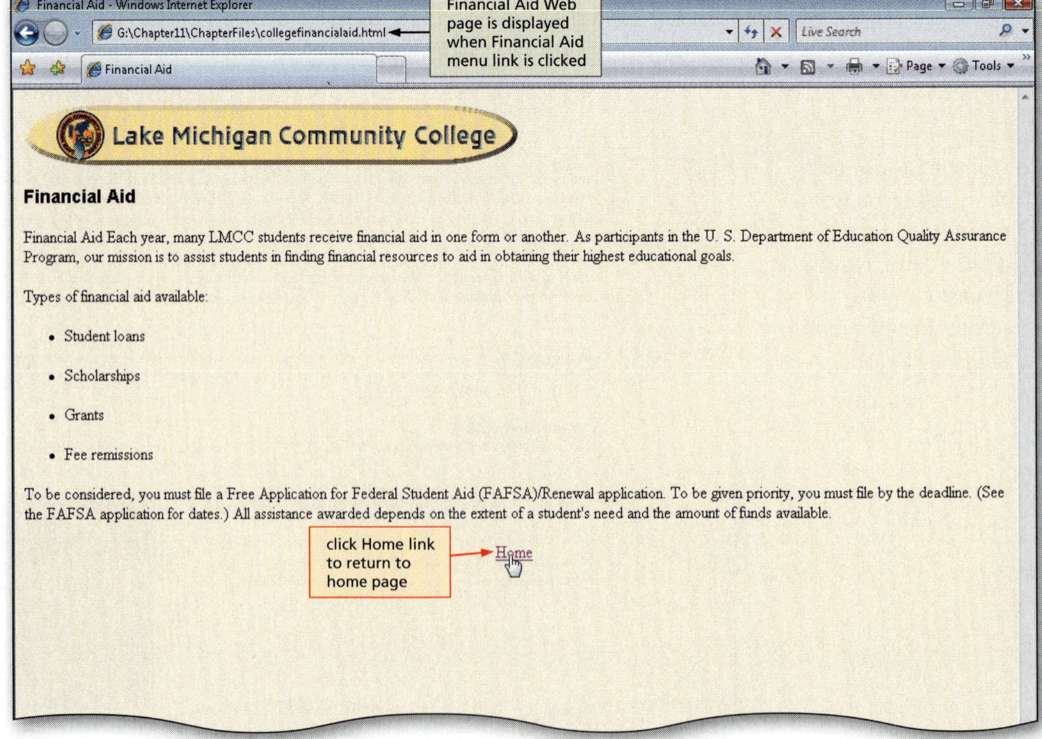

Figure 11–13

Plan Ahead

Creating a rotating banner.

- Determine the location for an image object
- Determine the images to be used
- Write the user-defined JavaScript function using the following logic:
  1 Define a list of images in an array object
  2 Establish a counter
  3 Increment the counter by 1
  4 Test the counter against the number of items in the list
  5 Assign the list element, based on the current counter value, to the image object
  6 Call the function again using the setTimeout() method
- Add the event handler to call the function

Creating a Rotating Banner on the Blood Drive Web Page

As shown in Figure 11–1g on page HTML 493, the Web page that appears in the Blood Drive pop-up window contains a rotating banner. A **rotating banner** is a set of images, all the same size, that are displayed in the same location for a few seconds, one after the other, to create the appearance that the images are rotating. A rotating banner often includes the company name followed by additional information. Other rotating banners may just be simple messages or ads.

BTW

Rotating Banners
On most Web sites, rotating banners are a series of different ads with a hyperlink to a matching URL for that ad. Because advertisers pay money to have their ad shown, Web sites have to have a way to track who clicks on what ad.

To Open an Existing HTML File in Notepad

In this chapter, the partially completed HTML code for the Blood Drive Web page is provided in the Data Files for Students. To modify this Web page, the file blooddrive.html must be opened in a new Notepad window.

- If necessary, click the Notepad button on the Windows taskbar. With a USB drive plugged into your computer, click File on the menu bar and then click Open on the File menu.
- If necessary, navigate to the Chapter11\ChapterFiles folder on the USB drive.
- If necessary, click the Files of type box arrow, and then click All Files to display all files in the Chapter11\ChapterFiles folder.
- Double-click blooddrive.html in the list of files (Figure 11–14).


```
<!DOCTYPE html PUBLIC "-//W3C//DTD XHTML 1.0 Transitional//EN" "http://www.w3.org/TR/xhtml/DTD/xhtml1 transitional.dtd">
<html xmlns="http://www.w3.org/1999/xhtml" xml:lang="en" lang="en">
<head>
<meta http-equiv="Content-Type" content="text/html;charset=utf-8" />
<title>LMCC -- Blood Drive</title>

<style type="text/css">
body
   {background: url(clinicbckgrnd.gif) }
.style1 {color: #996600;
         font-size:14px;}
</style>
</head>
<body>
<p> </p>
<table width="50%" height="249" border="0">
   <tr>
      <td width="53%" height="90">

      </td>
      <td width="47%"></td>
  </tr>
   <tr align="left">
     <td colspan="2" nowrap="nowrap">Every summer, Lake Michigan Community College challenges one of its rival schools to
```

Figure 11–14

Creating and Placing an Image Object

The first step in creating a rotating banner is to determine the location of the initial image. To define the image for the user-defined function, you must add the name attribute and value. The name attribute allows JavaScript to assign a new graphic image to the same location as the original image. Table 11–7 shows the general form of the <img> tag with the src and name attributes.

> BTW
> **Simple Animation with JavaScript**
> Animation can be created by moving objects associated with a division (layer). By repeatedly changing the position and placement of the division in a recursive user-defined function, the object moves.

Table 11–7 General Form of <img> Tag to Create Image Object

General form:	<img src="img_Filename" name="Object_Name" alt="alternative text" />
Comment:	where the source (img_Filename) represents the file name of the image that initially is displayed at the location where the tag appears. The name attribute identifies the object for JavaScript. To be XHTML compliant, <img> tags need an alt attribute, which is alternative text that appears if the graphic does not load. In addition, all tags must have a closing tag. Empty tags like <img> may place the closing / within the tag.
Example:	<img src="blooddriveimg1.gif" name="Rotate" alt="blood drive" />

Table 11–8 shows the general form of the JavaScript statement to assign a new image to the defined location, using the <img> name attribute as part of the object.

Table 11–8 Assign Image to Defined Location

General form:	document.objectname.src="newimg_filename"
Comment:	where the new image appears in the same location as the original by assigning a new file name to the image object source (src) property. The object name in the JavaScript code must match the object name in the image tag.
Example:	document.Rotate.src="blooddriveimg1.gif"

To Create an Image Object

The following step shows how to create an image object at a specific location on a Web page. In this project, the image is positioned at the top of the Blood Drive Web page.

- Position the insertion point on line 19.
- Using the SPACEBAR to indent as shown, type `<img src="blooddriveimg1.gif" alt="Be a Hero" name="Rotate" />` to define and place the initial image and then do not press the ENTER key (Figure 11–15).

```
</head>
<body>
<p><img src="project11-lmccpopup.jpg" alt="Logo" width="527" height="110" /> </p>
<table width="50%" height="249" border="0">
  <tr>
    <td width="53%" height="90">
      <img src="blooddriveimg1.gif" alt="Be a Hero" name="Rotate" />
    </td>
    <td width="47%"></td>
  </tr>
  <tr align="left">
    <td colspan="2" nowrap="nowrap">Every summer, Lake Mic... challenges one of its rival schools to
a<br />
     contest to see who can reach the goal of 2,000 donors... place during <br />
     the Michigan State Fair in Lansing, MI. This year, ou... n Springs College.</td>
  </tr>
  <tr align="left">
    <td colspan="2" nowrap="nowrap">
      <ul class="style1">
        <li><strong><font face="Geneva, Arial, Helvetica, sans-serif">A single donation can help save three lives in as
little as 48 hours </font></strong></li>
        <li><strong><font face="Geneva, Arial, Helvetica, sans-serif">Every two seconds someone in the U.S. is in need of
blood </font></strong></li>
        <li><strong><font face="Geneva, Arial, Helvetica, sans-serif">Blood supplies are often critically short, so your
help is needed</font></strong></li>
        <li><strong><font face="Geneva, Arial, Helvetica, sans-serif">Please help us reach our goal of 2,000
donors</font></strong></li>
      </ul>    </td>
  </tr>
  <tr>
```


Figure 11–15

Creating the Rotating Banner User-Defined Function

The first step in creating the rotating banner is to create a list in which to store the file names of the images that will rotate through the banner: blooddriveimg1.gif, blooddriveimg2.gif, blooddriveimg3.gif, and blooddriveimg4.gif . JavaScript, like other programming languages, uses a data structure called an array to work with lists of data. An **array** is a collection of data items, represented by one variable name. This variable is called the **array name**. Each of the individual data items is called an element, and a subscript references the individual data items in the array. A **subscript** is a number that designates a single occurrence of an array element.

Arrays are built-in objects. To create an array and fill that array with data, create an object instance of the Array object. Recall from Chapter 9 that an **object instance** is a new JavaScript object created from a built-in object. Table 11–9 shows the general form for creating an array object instance from the Array object.

Table 11–9 Create an Array

General form:	var myarrayname=new Array()
Comment:	where Array is a built-in object and the new command creates a new object instance of the array. Data items may fill an array in one of two ways: (1) by placing the data directly in the array object; or (2) by assigning the items separately.
Examples:	var rotatorMsg=new Array("graphic1.jpg", "graphic2.jpg", "graphic3.jpg", "graphic4.jpg") or var rotatorMsg=new Array() rotatorMsg[0]="graphic1.jpg" rotatorMsg[1]="graphic2.jpg" rotatorMsg[2]="graphic3.jpg" rotatorMsg[3]="graphic4.jpg"

The first item of a JavaScript array is element zero. Subscripts are placed after the array name in square [ ] brackets, as shown in the examples in Table 11–9. A subscript must be any valid JavaScript variable or numeric literal value.

After the data elements are assigned to the array, the JavaScript code can retrieve or use the data by referencing the array name with the subscript. As shown in Figure 11–16, the data in an array is stored sequentially. For example, to reference the first element (blooddriveimg1.gif), the JavaScript code uses the contents of rotatorMsg[0]. To reference the third element in the array, the JavaScript code uses the contents of rotatorMsg[2].

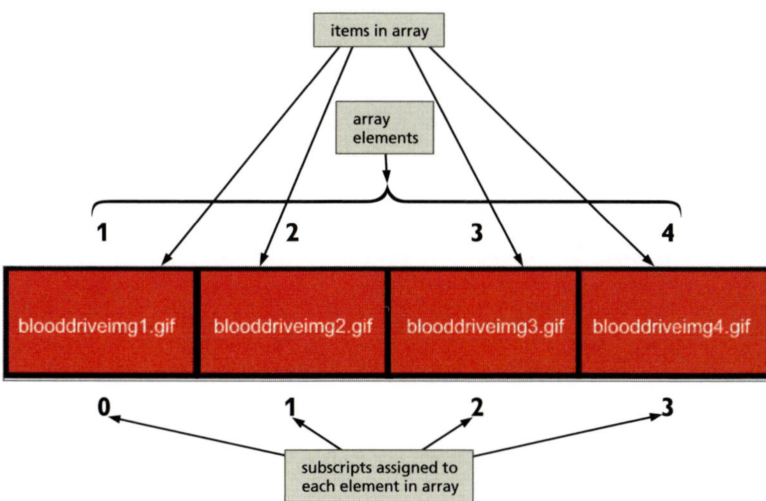

Figure 11–16

BTW

Arrays

JavaScript arrays are not a fixed length as in other programming languages. New elements can be added to the array without having to redefine the structure. JavaScript is a loosely-typed language and does not require variables to be declared a data type. Thus, you can store string, numeric, or Boolean values to the same array.

Table 11–10 shows the JavaScript code for the user-defined function RotateIt(), which creates the array and the rotating banner.

Table 11–10 Code to Create the RotateIt() Function

Line	Code
6	<script type="text/javascript">
7	<!--Hide from old browsers
8	var rotatorMsg=new Array("blooddriveimg1.gif","blooddriveimg2.gif", "blooddriveimg3.gif","blooddriveimg4.gif")
9	var rotatorCntr=3
10	
11	function RotateIt() {
12	rotatorCntr+=1
13	if (rotatorCntr==4) rotatorCntr=0
14	document.Rotate.src = rotatorMsg[rotatorCntr]
15	setTimeout("RotateIt()",2000)
16	}
17	
18	//-->
19	</script>

Lines 6 and 7 begin the JavaScript section. Line 8 begins by creating an array named rotatorMsg, with four image file names set as the data elements. Line 9 initializes the counter variable named rotatorCntr to 3, which represents the last element in the rotatorMsg array. Setting the counter variable to 3 forces the array to start at the first element, which is zero. This means that, when the page is displayed, the first image to appear is the first element in the array, blooddriveimg1.gif. Line 11 declares the user-defined function RotateIt(). Line 12 increments the rotatorCntr by one, and line 13 tests the counter against the number of items in the array, which is four. If rotatorCntr is equal to four, line 13 assigns a zero (0) to rotatorCntr, which reinitializes the counter to the first element of the array. Line 14 assigns the contents of rotatorMsg[rotatorCntr] to the image object, so the new image is displayed. The function then uses the setTimeout() method on line 15 to make a recursive call to itself after a two-second delay. The brace (line 16) completes the RotateIt() function. Lines 18 and 19 complete the JavaScript section.

To Create the User-Defined Function to Add a Rotating Banner

The following step illustrates how to enter the RotateIt() function to create a rotating banner.

1

- Click line 6.
- Enter the JavaScript code shown in Table 11–10 to create the RotateIt() user-defined function, pressing the SPACEBAR to indent as shown and then pressing the ENTER key only at the end of a line (Figure 11–17). Do not press the ENTER key after the last line.

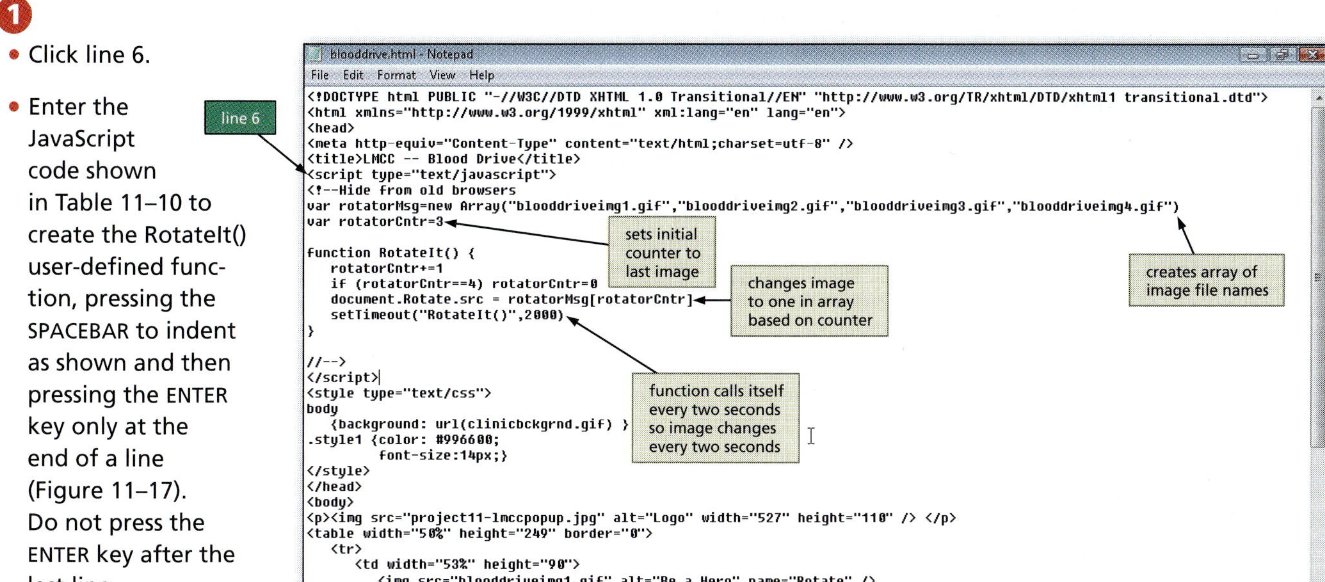

Figure 11–17

To Enter the onload Event Handler to Call a Function

The next step is to enter the onload event handler that calls the RotateIt() function when the Blood Drive Web page loads in the pop-up window. To call the RotateIt() user-defined function initially, an onload event handler is placed in the <body> tag. The following steps show how to enter the onload event handler to call the RotateIt() function.

- Position the insertion point between the y and the > symbol in the <body> tag on line 27 (Figure 11–18).

```
//-->
</script>
<style type="text/css">
body
   {background: url(clinicbckgrnd.gif) }
.style1 {color: #996600;
         font-size:14px;}
</style>
</head>
<body>
<p><img src="project11-lmccpopup.jpg" alt="Logo" width="527" height="110" /> </p>
<table width="50%" height="249" border="0">
   <tr>
      <td width="53%" height="90">
         <img src="blooddriveimg1.gif" alt="Be a Hero" name="Rotate" />
      </td>
      <td width="47%"></td>
  </tr>
   <tr align="left">
     <td colspan="2" nowrap="nowrap">Every summer, Lake Michigan Community College c
a<br />
       contest to see who can reach the goal of 2,000 donors. The challenge takes pl
       the Michigan State Fair in Lansing, MI. This year, our challenger is Berrien
   </tr>
  <tr align="left">
     <td colspan="2" nowrap="nowrap">
        <ul class="style1">
```

line 27

position insertion point between y and >

Figure 11–18

- Press the SPACEBAR once.
- Type `onload="RotateIt()"` to enter the onload event handler in the <body> tag and then do not press the ENTER key (Figure 11–19).

```
body
   {background: url(clini                    }
.style1 {color: #996600;
        font-size:14px;}
</style>
</head>
<body onload="RotateIt()">
<p><img src="project11-lmccpopup.jpg" alt="Logo" width="527" height="110" /> </p>
<table width="50%" height="249" border="0">
  <tr>
    <td width="53%" height="90">
      <img src="blooddriveimg1.gif" alt="Be a Hero" name="Rotate" />
    </td>
    <td width="47%"></td>
  </tr>
  <tr align="left">
```

onload event handler calls RotateIt() when Web page loads

do not press ENTER key

Figure 11–19

To Save an HTML File and Test a Web Page

With the code for the Blood Drive Web page complete, the HTML file should be saved and the Web page should be viewed in a browser to confirm the Web page appears and functions as desired. The following step shows how to save an HTML file and then view and test the Web page in a browser.

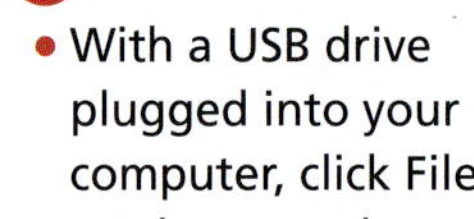

- With a USB drive plugged into your computer, click File on the menu bar and then click Save As on the File menu.
- Type `collegeblood drive.html` in the File name text box to save the file with a new name, and then click the Save button in the Save As dialog box.
- Click the Internet Explorer button on the taskbar.
- Click the Refresh button on the Standard toolbar to refresh the Lake Michigan Community College Web page.
- Click the annual blood drive link on the home page to show the rotating banner images (Figure 11–20). If necessary, click the Information Bar and Allow Blocked Content.
- Click the Close link on the Blood Drive pop-up window.

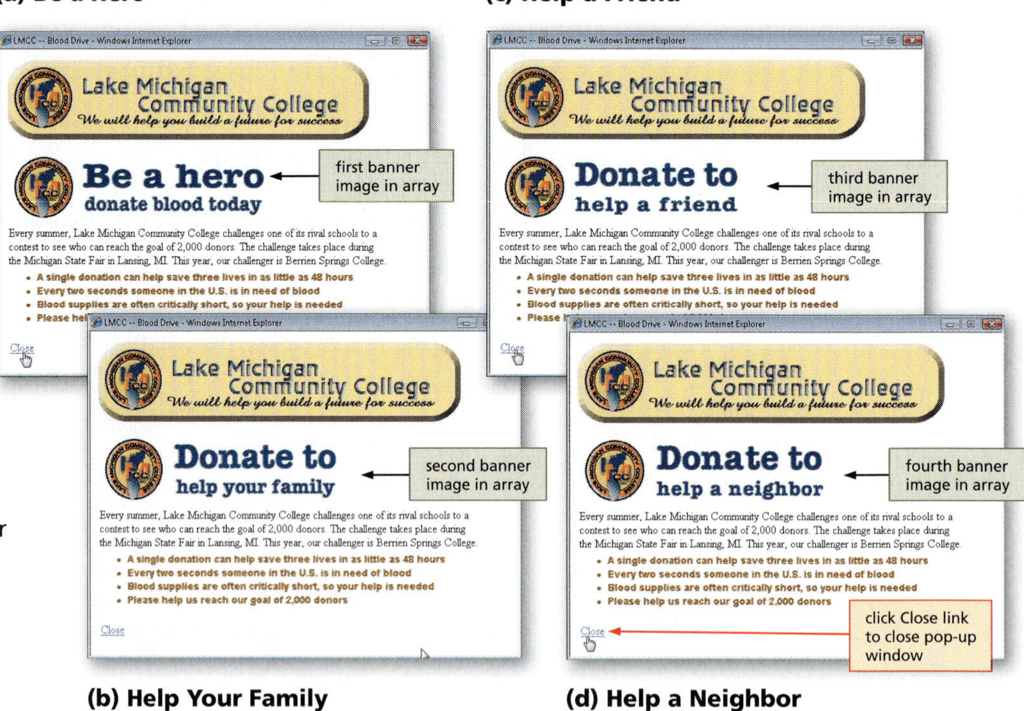

Figure 11–20

Plan Ahead

Creating ScreenTips.

Creating a ScreenTip requires four steps:

- Entering the JavaScript code for the user-defined function, popUp()
- Entering the embedded style sheet
- Entering the <a> tags and event handlers for each of the four terms
- Entering the <span> tags containing the ScreenTip text and style sheet attributes that format the appearance of the ScreenTip text

Creating ScreenTips on the Counseling Services Web Page

The Counseling Services Web page includes four terms that appear as hyperlinks on the Web page: Counseling Services, Occupational Development, Test Anxiety, and Career Services. When the user places the mouse over these hyperlinks, ScreenTips will display with more information about the various services. Figure 11–1c on page HTML 493 shows an example of a ScreenTip.

The four terms appear as hyperlinks by using the anchor tag <a> embedded with JavaScript statements and event handlers to call the user-defined function popUp(). The popUp() user-defined function uses a combination of JavaScript objects and properties, in conjunction with associated style sheet definitions, to show the ScreenTip text. Each ScreenTip is defined by <span> tags that work in conjunction with the style sheet.

To Open an Existing HTML File in Notepad

Now you will open the counseling.html file in Notepad to enter the JavaScript user-defined function, the style sheet information, the <a> tag, the event handlers to call the JavaScript function, and the <span> tags containing the ScreenTip text. The following step shows how to open the counseling file in Notepad.

- If necessary, click the Notepad button on the Windows taskbar. With a USB drive plugged into your computer, click File on the menu bar and then click Open on the File menu.
- If necessary, navigate to the Chapter11\ChapterFiles folder on the USB drive.
- If necessary, click the Files of type box arrow, and then click All Files to show all files in the Chapter11\ChapterFiles folder.
- Double-click counseling.html in the list of files (Figure 11–21).

counseling.html - Notepad

counseling file open in Notepad

File Edit Format View Help

```
<!DOCTYPE html PUBLIC "-//W3C//DTD XHTML 1.0 Transitional//EN" "http://www.w3.org/TR/xhtml/DTD/xh
<html xmlns="http://www.w3.org/1999/xhtml" xml:lang="en" lang="en">
<head>
<meta http-equiv="Content-Type" content="text/html; charset=utf-8" />
<title>Counseling</title>

<style type="text/css">


body {
        background-color: #fffbe8;
}
.style1 {
        font-family: Arial, Helvetica, sans-serif;
        font-size: large;
        font-weight: bold;
```

Figure 11–21

Creating the popUp() User-Defined Function

The JavaScript code for the popUp() user-defined function is written in such a way that it can be used for all ScreenTips. The function will accept two parameters from the event handlers and display the appropriate ScreenTip. Table 11–11 shows the JavaScript code used to create the popUp() function.

Table 11–11 Code to Create popUp() Function

```
Line  Code
6     <script type="text/javascript">
7     <!--Hide from the old browsers
8        function popUp(evnt,currElement){
9           documentObj="document.all"
10          styleObj=".style"
11          if (currElement!=0) {
12             var DOMobj=eval(documentObj+'.'+currElement+styleObj)
13             var state=DOMobj.visibility
14             if (state=="visible" || state=="show") {
15                DOMobj.visibility="hidden"
16             }
17          else {
18               topVal=eval(event.y+10)
19               leftVal=eval(event.x-125)
20               if (leftVal<2) leftVal=2
21               DOMobj.top=topVal
22               DOMobj.left=leftVal
23               DOMobj.visibility="visible"
24             }
25          }
26       }
27
28    //-->
29    </script>
```

Lines 6 and 7 begin the <script> section with standard JavaScript and comment tags. Line 8 declares the popUp() user-defined function and assigns two parameter values: the event value (evnt), and the element name or id (currElement). Later in the chapter, the code for the onmouseover and onmouseout event handlers, which pass values to the function for these parameters, will be entered. The event value indicates if the mouse pointer is moved over or off the hyperlink or if the hyperlink is clicked. If the visitor clicks the mouse, the function receives the null parameter as the event value, which does not trigger an event. The name or id parameter passed to the function indicates the style sheet selector to be used with the associated text in the <span> tags.

Lines 9 and 10 define two local variables — documentObj and styleObj — that will be used to create statements using the eval() function in the popUp() user-defined function. The **eval() function** is a global function that accepts a string or command and returns the result of an executed statement. Line 11 tests the value of currElement to determine which ScreenTip to show. If the value is greater than 0, lines 12 and 13 construct the strings to show the correct ScreenTip using the document.all, the currElement, and style properties. The **document.all object** is used to reference elements by their id, which is necessary when multiple <div> or <span> containers exist. Line 12 assigns the result of the eval() method, which combines and executes the constructed statement, to the DOMobj variable. The DOMobj variable can be used with the visibility property on line 13 to assign the current state of the object. Line 14 tests the state of the object to determine if another ScreenTip already is showing. If the test is true, line 15 hides any ScreenTips already visible, so the new ScreenTip can be displayed.

Lines 17 through 23 cause the ScreenTip to appear and ensure that the ScreenTip does not appear too far to the left. Line 17 begins the else portion of the if statement (for lines 18 through 23), which calculates the display position of ScreenTip. Lines 18 and 19 set the topVal position and the leftVal position of the ScreenTip. These position values are set using the eval() function and the x and y properties of the event object. The x and y properties are the x- and y-axis coordinates defined by Microsoft Internet Explorer. The if statement on line 20 tests the value of leftVal to determine whether the ScreenTip is too close to the left edge of the browser window; if so, it sets leftVal to 2. Lines 21, 22, and 23 set the top, left, and visibility properties of the DOMobj to define where the ScreenTip is displayed.

The braces on lines 24 and 25 close the if and else statements on lines 11 and 17, and the brace on line 26 closes the function. Lines 28 and 29 close the <script> section.

BTW

The eval() Function

The eval() function, short for evaluator, executes an expression as if it were originally written as language code. The eval() statement is useful in executing JavaScript statements using data, whose value is not known at the time the Web page loads, such as the size of a window.

To Enter the popUp() Function

The following step shows how to enter the code for the popUp() user-defined function.

1

- Click line 6.
- Enter the code shown in Table 11–11 to create the popUp() function, pressing the SPACEBAR to indent as shown, and then do not press the ENTER key at the end of the </script> tag (Figure 11–22).

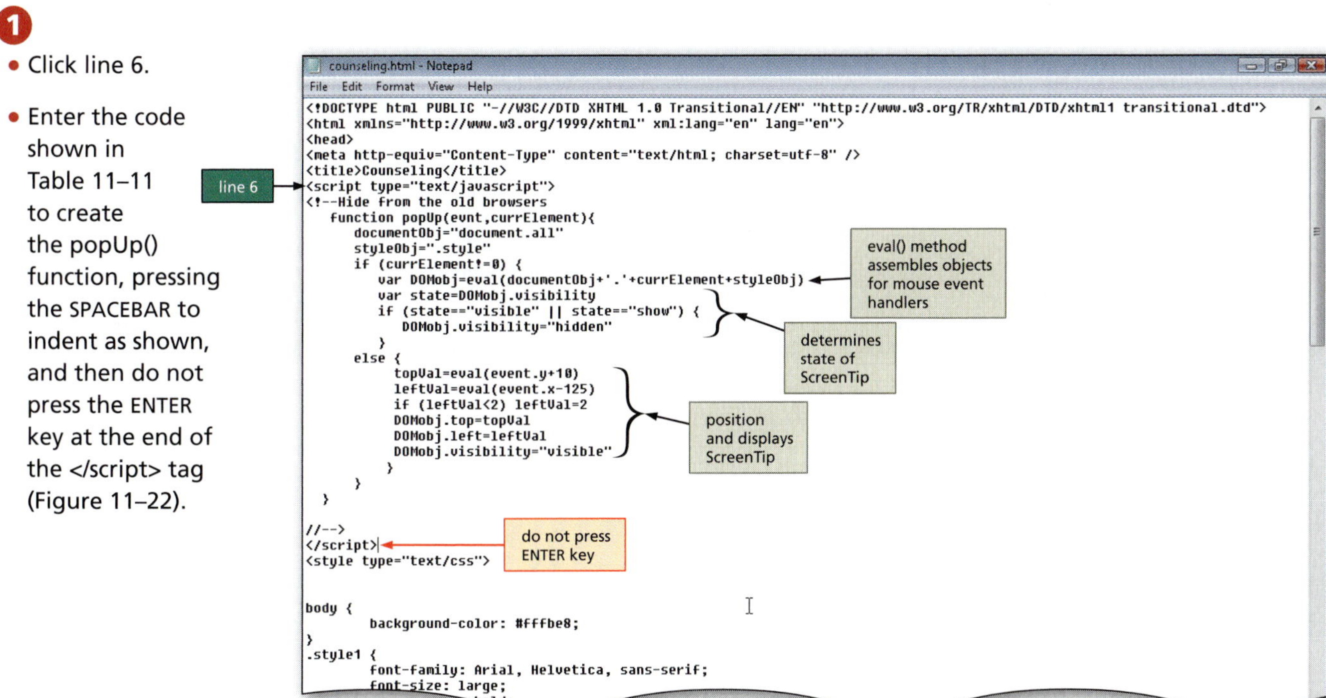

Figure 11–22

BTW

ID and Class Selector
An id selector is used to identify one element, and the class can be used to identify more than one. The class selector must be notated by the class attribute in the HTML tag. In the normal hierarchy of cascading selectors, the id selector has a higher priority than attribute selectors. When used with XML documents, however, id selectors are discouraged to prevent confusion.

BTW

Inline Styles
Inline styles are placed directly in the HTML tag of a Web page. The inline style affects only that tag. Inline styles are used to override default or embedded styles for a particular tag for a special reason. Inline styles are interpreted before embedded styles.

Adding an Embedded Style Sheet Using id and class Properties

The embedded style sheets used on the Counseling Services Web page employ the id and class selectors to define the style for each of the four ScreenTips. Each ScreenTip is identified uniquely using an id attribute and value, so the popUp() function can ensure only one ScreenTip appears at a time. An id selector is used in a style sheet much like a class selector — except that the id selector is entered with a preceding pound sign (#).

In the Counseling Services Web page, the <span> tag is used to enclose the text that appears in the ScreenTips. In this use, the <span> tag is referred to as a container. A **container** means that the text is grouped together. Text enclosed within the <span> tag is referred to as **inline**. The id and class attributes are used in the <span> tag to associate the selectors in the embedded style sheet with each of the four ScreenTips.

The popUp() user-defined function needs two parameters: evnt and currElement. For each ScreenTip, the evnt parameter indicates the type of event, using an onmouseover or onmouseout event handler, and the currElement parameter passes the style sheet id selector. Figure 11–23 illustrates the relationship between the event handler function call, the associated selector in the style sheet, and the text in the <span> tag. The <span> tag contains an id attribute, which is the style sheet selector, and the style sheet class, which indicates how to format the displayed ScreenTip text. To apply a style to the ScreenTips, the embedded style sheet thus uses the id attribute value as the selector.

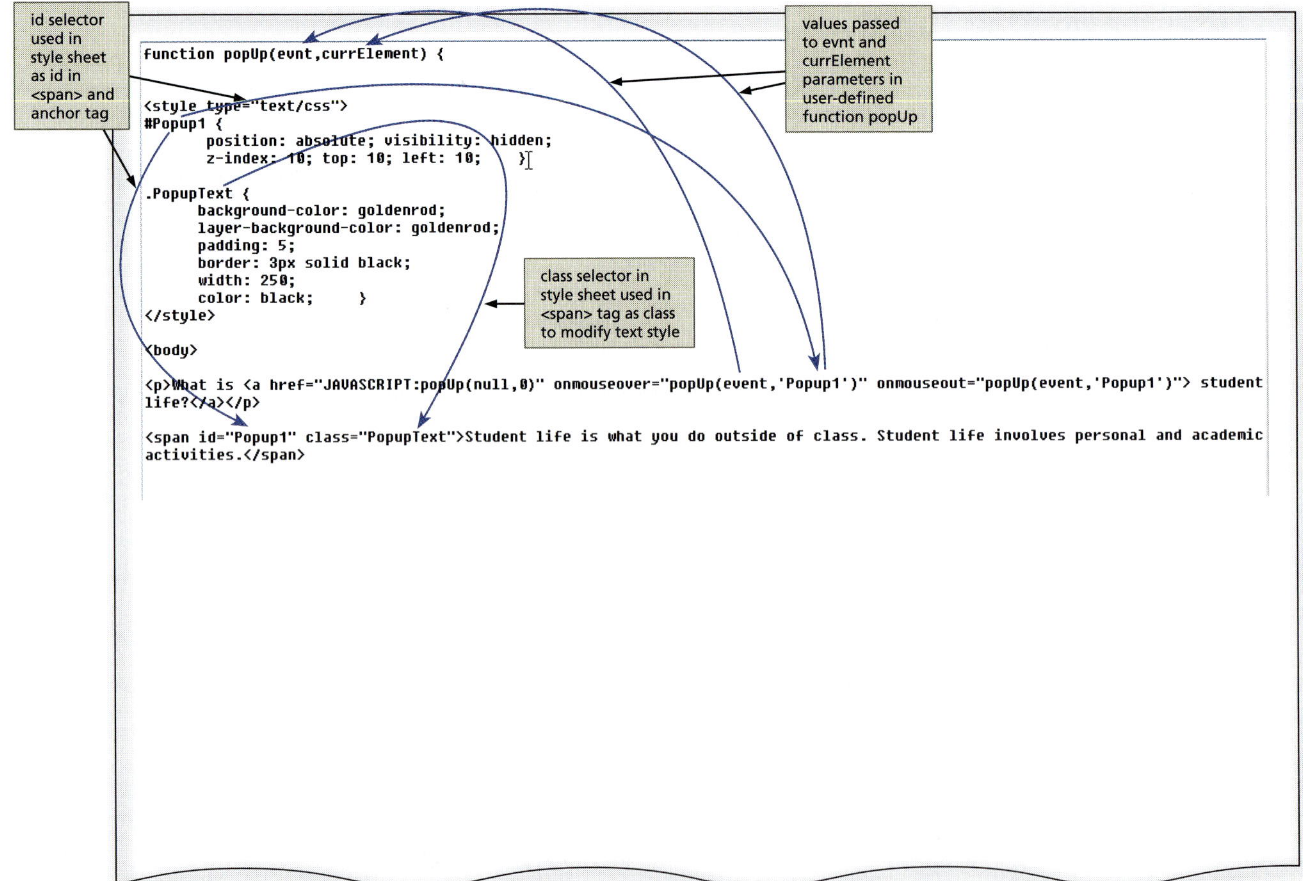

Figure 11–23

The popUp() function code uses these values to show the ScreenTip at the position defined by the Popup1 selector in the style sheet. The embedded style sheet on the Counseling Services Web page has four id selectors — Popup1 through Popup4 — one to set the position at which each ScreenTip appears. It also defines a style for the class PopupText, which defines the format of the ScreenTip text. Table 11–12 shows the embedded style sheet code used to set the position of the ScreenTips and format the ScreenTip text.

Table 11–12 Code to Use Selectors in a Style Sheet

Line	Code
31	`#Popup1`
32	`{position: absolute; visibility: hidden;`
33	`z-index: 10; top: 10px; left: 10;`
34	`}`
35	
36	`#Popup2`
37	`{position: absolute; visibility: hidden;`
38	`z-index: 10; top: 10px; left: 10;`
39	`}`
40	
41	`#Popup3`
42	`{position: absolute; visibility: hidden;`
43	`z-index: 10; top: 10px; left: 10;`
44	`}`
45	
46	`#Popup4`
47	`{position: absolute; visibility: hidden;`
48	`z-index: 10; top: 10px; left: 10;`
49	`}`
50	
51	`.PopupText`
52	`{background-color: goldenrod;`
53	`layer-background-color: goldenrod;`
54	`padding: 5;`
55	`border: 3px solid black;`
56	`width: 250;`
57	`color: black;`
58	`}`

Line 31 is the first style statement with the id selector, Popup1. The declarations on lines 32 and 33 define the positioning for the Popup1 style. Line 34 closes the declaration for Popup1. Lines 36 through 49 define the remaining selectors for Popup2, Popup3, and Popup4.

Line 51 starts the style statement with the class selector, PopupText. The declarations on lines 52 through 57 define the style of the ScreenTips text. The background color and layer background are goldenrod. The padding declaration sets 5 pixels around the text in the pop-up ScreenTip. The border declaration sets the border thickness to 3 pixels, the line type to solid, and the color to black. The width of the pop-up ScreenTip is 250 pixels, and the color of the text font is black. Line 58 closes the declarations.

To Enter a Cascading Style Sheet Using id and class Selectors

The following steps illustrate how to enter the cascading style sheet using id and class selectors.

- Click line 31.
- Enter the code shown in Table 11–12 from lines 31 to 49 to enter the class id and selectors for the ScreenTip style sheet pressing the SPACEBAR to indent as shown, and then press the ENTER key twice (Figure 11–24).

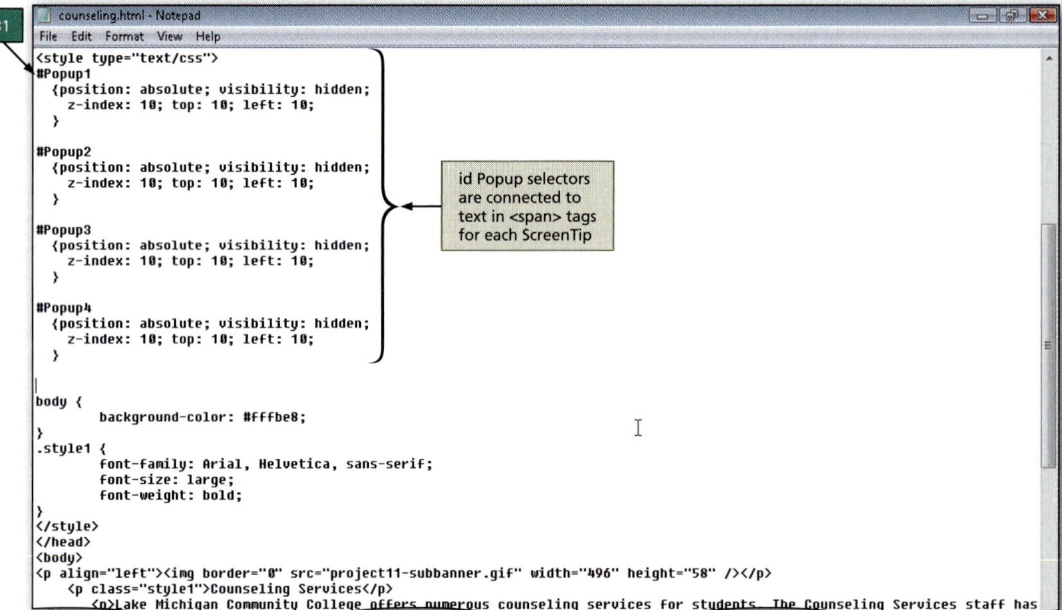

Figure 11–24

2

- Continuing on line 51, enter the code shown in Table 11–12 from lines 51 through 58 to enter the format style for the ScreenTip text, pressing the SPACEBAR to indent as shown, and then press the ENTER key after line 58 (Figure 11–25).

```
}

#Popup4
  {position: absolute; visibility: hidden;
    z-index: 10; top: 10; left: 10;
  }

.PopupText
  {background-color: goldenrod;
   layer-background-color: goldenrod;
   padding: 5;
   border: 3px solid black;
   width: 250;
   color: black;
  }

body {
        background-color: #fffbe8;
```

line 51

selector for ScreenTip text so all text is formatted the same

Figure 11–25

Q&A In this code for the style sheet, actual color names are used. Why not use the hex representations? What is the difference?

No difference exists. Most browsers will recognize the standard Web-safe colors by name. Non-Web-safe colors must be entered using the hex value. Using Web-safe color names makes it easier for another person to maintain the Web site.

Adding Links and Event Handlers to Call the popUp() Function

The Counseling Services Web page includes four terms — Counseling Services, Occupational Development, Test Anxiety, and Career Services — that show ScreenTips when the mouse pointer points to them. As shown in Figure 11–23 on page HTML 517, making these terms link allows the onmouseover and onmouseout event handlers associated with these links to call the popUp() user-defined function to show the appropriate ScreenTips. When the visitor places the mouse over the hyperlink, a ScreenTip is displayed just below the link. When the visitor removes the mouse, the ScreenTip disappears.

Normally, a link is associated with a URL, so when the visitor clicks the hyperlink, the browser shows a new Web page. In this chapter, the links are associated with the onmouseover and onmouseout event handlers to show a ScreenTip when a user points to the link. If a user accidentally clicks the link, the browser will not show a new Web page.

To Add Links and Event Handlers to Call the popUp() Function

The following steps describe how to enter the ScreenTip links and the onmouseover and onmouseout event handlers to call the popUp() function.

1

- In line 74, position the insertion point before the words Counseling Services and after the word the in the second sentence.
- Type `<a href="JAVASCRIPT:popUp(null,0)" onmouseover="popUp(event,'Popup1')" onmouseout="popUp(event,'Popup1')">` to enter the link for the Counseling Services ScreenTip and then do not press the ENTER key.
- Click to the right of the word Services and before the word staff. 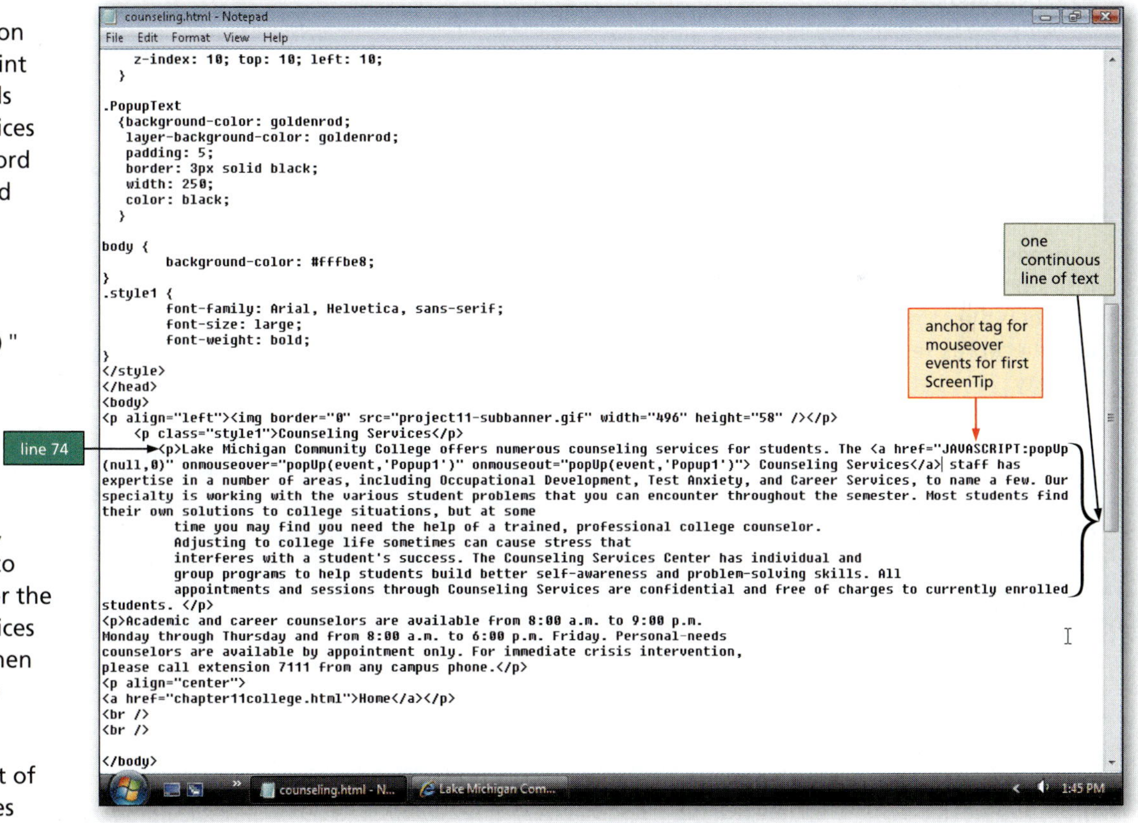
- Type `</a>` to close the <a> anchor tag and then do not press the ENTER key (Figure 11–26).

```
counseling.html - Notepad
File  Edit  Format  View  Help
   z-index: 10; top: 10; left: 10;
  }

.PopupText
  {background-color: goldenrod;
   layer-background-color: goldenrod;
   padding: 5;
   border: 3px solid black;
   width: 250;
   color: black;
  }

body {
        background-color: #fffbe8;
}
.style1 {
        font-family: Arial, Helvetica, sans-serif;
        font-size: large;
        font-weight: bold;
}
</style>
</head>
<body>
<p align="left"><img border="0" src="project11-subbanner.gif" width="496" height="58" /></p>
    <p class="style1">Counseling Services</p>
      <p>Lake Michigan Community College offers numerous counseling services for students. The <a href="JAVASCRIPT:popUp
(null,0)" onmouseover="popUp(event,'Popup1')" onmouseout="popUp(event,'Popup1')"> Counseling Services</a> staff has
expertise in a number of areas, including Occupational Development, Test Anxiety, and Career Services, to name a few. Our
specialty is working with the various student problems that you can encounter throughout the semester. Most students find
their own solutions to college situations, but at some
         time you may find you need the help of a trained, professional college counselor.
         Adjusting to college life sometimes can cause stress that
         interferes with a student's success. The Counseling Services Center has individual and
         group programs to help students build better self-awareness and problem-solving skills. All
         appointments and sessions through Counseling Services are confidential and free of charges to currently enrolled
students. </p>
<p>Academic and career counselors are available from 8:00 a.m. to 9:00 p.m.
Monday through Thursday and from 8:00 a.m. to 6:00 p.m. Friday. Personal-needs
counselors are available by appointment only. For immediate crisis intervention,
please call extension 7111 from any campus phone.</p>
<p align="center">
<a href="chapter11college.html">Home</a></p>
<br />
<br />

</body>
```


Figure 11–26

- Further in the same line, position the insertion point between the words including and Occupational Development in the same sentence.
- Type `<a href="JAVASCRIPT:popUp(null,0)" onmouseover="popUp(event,'Popup2')" onmouseout="popUp(event,'Popup2')">` to enter the link for the Occupational Development ScreenTip and then do not press the ENTER key.
- Click to the right of the word Development and before the comma.
- Type `</a>` to close the <a> anchor tag and then do not press the ENTER key (Figure 11–27).


```
        background-color: #fffbe8;
}
.style1 {
        font-family: Arial, Helvetica, sans-serif;
        font-size: large;
        font-weight: bold;
}
</style>
</head>
<body>
<p align="left"><img border="0" src="project11-subbanner.gif" width="496" height="58" /></p>
    <p class="style1">Counseling Services</p>
       <p>Lake Michigan Community College offers numerous counseling services for students. The <a href="JAVASCRIPT:popUp
(null,0)" onmouseover="popUp(event,'Popup1')" onmouseout="popUp(event,'Popup1')"> Counseling Services</a> staff has
expertise in a number of areas, including <a href="JAVASCRIPT:popUp(null,0)" onmouseover="popUp(event,'Popup2')"
onmouseout="popUp(event,'Popup2')">Occupational Development</a>, Test Anxiety, and Career Services, to name a few. Our
specialty is working with the various student problems that you can encounter throughout the semester. Most students find
their own solutions to college situations, but at some
          time you may find you need the help of a trained, professional college counselor.
          Adjusting to college life sometimes can cause stress that
          interferes with a student's success. The Counseling Services Center has individual and
          group programs to help students build better self-awareness and problem-solving skills. All
          appointments and sessions through Counseling Services are confidential and free of charges to currently enrolled
students. </p>
<p>Academic and career counselors are available from 8:00 a.m. to 9:00 p.m.
Monday through Thursday and from 8:00 a.m. to 6:00 p.m. Friday. Personal-needs
counselors are available by appointment only. For immediate crisis intervention,
please call extension 7111 from any campus phone.</p>
<p align="center">
<a href="chapter11college.html">Home</a></p>
<br />
<br />

</body>
</html>
```

counseling.html - N... Lake Michigan Com... 1:46 PM

Figure 11–27

3

- Further in the same line, position the insertion point between the comma and the words Test Anxiety.
- Type `<a href="JAVASCRIPT:popUp(null,0)" onmouseover="popUp(event,'Popup3')" onmouseout="popUp(event,'Popup3')">` to enter the link for the Test Anxiety ScreenTip and then do not press the ENTER key.


```
        background-color: #fffbe8;
}
.style1 {
        font-family: Arial, Helvetica, sans-serif;
        font-size: large;
        font-weight: bold;
}
</style>
</head>
<body>
<p align="left"><img border="0" src="project11-subbanner.gif" width="496" height="58" /></p>
    <p class="style1">Counseling Services</p>
       <p>Lake Michigan Community College offers numerous counseling services for students. The <a href="JAVASCRIPT:popUp
(null,0)" onmouseover="popUp(event,'Popup1')" onmouseout="popUp(event,'Popup1')"> Counseling Services</a> staff has
expertise in a number of areas, including <a href="JAVASCRIPT:popUp(null,0)" onmouseover="popUp(event,'Popup2')"
onmouseout="popUp(event,'Popup2')">Occupational Development</a>, <a href="JAVASCRIPT:popUp(null,0)" onmouseover="popUp
(event,'Popup3')" onmouseout="popUp(event,'Popup3')">Test Anxiety</a>, and Career Services, to name a few. Our
specialty is working with the various student problems that you can encounter throughout the semester. Most students find
their own solutions to college situations, but at some
          time you may find you need the help of a trained, professional college counselor.
          Adjusting to college life sometimes can cause stress that
          interferes with a student's success. The Counseling Services Center has individual and
          group programs to help students build better self-awareness and problem-solving skills. All
          appointments and sessions through Counseling Services are confidential and free of charges to currently enrolled
students. </p>
<p>Academic and career counselors are available from 8:00 a.m. to 9:00 p.m.
Monday through Thursday and from 8:00 a.m. to 6:00 p.m. Friday. Personal-needs
counselors are available by appointment only. For immediate crisis intervention,
please call extension 7111 from any campus phone.</p>
<p align="center">
<a href="chapter11college.html">Home</a></p>
<br />
<br />

</body>
</html>
```

counseling.html - N... Lake Michigan Com... 1:47 PM

Figure 11–28

- Click to the right of the word Anxiety and before the comma.
- Type `</a>` to close the <a> anchor tag and then do not press the ENTER key (Figure 11–28).

4

- In the same line, position the insertion point before the words Career Services.
- Type `<a href="JAVASCRIPT:popUp(null,0)" onmouseover="popUp(event,'Popup4')" onmouseout="popUp(event,'Popup4')">` to enter the link for the Career Services ScreenTip and then do not press the ENTER key.
- Click to the right of the word Services and before the comma.
- Type `</a>` to close the <a> anchor tag and then do not press the ENTER key (Figure 11–29).

counseling.html - Notepad

File Edit Format View Help

```
.PopupText
  {background-color: goldenrod;
   layer-background-color: goldenrod;
   padding: 5;
   border: 3px solid black;
   width: 250;
   color: black;
  }

body {
        background-color: #fffbe8;
}
.style1 {
        font-family: Arial, Helvetica, sans-serif;
        font-size: large;
        font-weight: bold;
}
</style>
</head>
<body>
<p align="left"><img border="0" src="project11-subbanner.gif" width="496" height="58" /></p>
    <p class="style1">Counseling Services</p>
        <p>Lake Michigan Community College offers numerous counseling services for students. The <a href="JAVASCRIPT:popUp
(null,0)" onmouseover="popUp(event,'Popup1')" onmouseout="popUp(event,'Popup1')"> Counseling Services</a> staff has
expertise in a number of areas, including <a href="JAVASCRIPT:popUp(null,0)" onmouseover="popUp(event,'Popup2')"
onmouseout="popUp(event,'Popup2')">Occupational Development</a>, <a href="JAVASCRIPT:popUp(null,0)" onmouseover="popUp
(event,'Popup3')" onmouseout="popUp(event,'Popup3')">Test Anxiety</a>, and <a href="JAVASCRIPT:popUp(null,0)"
onmouseover="popUp(event,'Popup4')" onmouseout="popUp(event,'Popup4')">Career Services</a>, to name a few. Our
specialty is working with the various student problems that you can encounter throughout the semester. Most students find
their own solutions to college situations, but at some
         time you may find you need the help of a trained, professional college counselor.
         Adjusting to college life sometimes can cause stress that
         interferes with a student's success. The Counseling Services Center has individual and
         group programs to help students build better self-awareness and problem-solving skills. All
         appointments and s               ounseling Services are confidential and free of charges to currently enrolled
students. </p>
<p>Academic and career coun               ble from 8:00 a.m. to 9:00 p.m.
Monday through Thursday and               o 6:00 p.m. Friday. Personal-needs
counselors are available by appointment only. For immediate crisis intervention,
please call extension 7111 from any campus phone.</p>
<p align="center">
<a href="chapter11college.html">Home</a></p>
<br />
<br />

</body>
```

anchor tag for fourth pop-up ScreenTip

counseling.html - N... Lake Michigan Com... 1:48 PM

Figure 11–29

Q&A The PopupTip selectors all have the same features. Why must we use so many?

Each pop-up ScreenTip must have its own selector to be identified by the ScreenTip code and to match the text in the <span> containers.

Entering the <span> Tags Containing ScreenTip Text

The text then appears in each of the four ScreenTips on the Counseling Services Web page enclosed in <span> tags. The <span> tags use the id and class attributes to associate the ScreenTips with the embedded style sheet declarations that control the appearance of the text in the ScreenTip. Table 11–13 shows the HTML code used to enter the <span> tags that define the ScreenTip text.

Table 11–13 Code for <span> Tags Containing ScreenTip Text

Line	Code
88	`<span id="Popup1" class="PopupText">Academic and personal-needs counselors are available to guide you through your time on campus. </span>`
89	`<span id="Popup2" class="PopupText">The ODP personnel address the needs of students pursuing degrees certification in the various health related fields, such as Nursing. </span>`
90	`<span id="Popup3" class="PopupText">If you suffer from test anxiety, attend one of our classes to help you overcome your fears. </span>`
91	`<span id="Popup4" class="PopupText">Our Career Services can help you with the decision-making process about your life's goals through interest testing, and individual advising and counseling. </span>`

BTW

When To Use <div> and <span>
The <div> tag groups things as a block, and the <span> tag operates inline. Inline refers to the fact that the <span> tag does not do any formatting of its own. For example, the <div> tag will cause a paragraph break, and the <span> tag will not. Thus, it allows changing styles within a single line or group of text.

Line 88 contains the ScreenTip text that appears when the mouse pointer points to the link for the words Counseling Services. The id property value, Popup1, associates the ScreenTip text with the Counseling Services link defined on line 74 in Figure 11–26 on page HTML 520, which sets Popup1 as a parameter of the popUp() function. The id property value, Popup1, also sets the ScreenTip text to appear using the position defined by the style statements for the id. The class property value, PopupText, sets the ScreenTip text to appear using the background, font colors, borders, and width defined by the style statements in the embedded style sheets.

The <span> tag on line 89 associates the ScreenTip text with the Occupational Development link. The <span> tag on line 90 associates the ScreenTip with the Test Anxiety link. The <span> tag on line 91 begins the last <span> container to associate the ScreenTip text with the Career Services link.

To Enter <span> Tags Containing ScreenTip Text

The following step shows how to enter the <span> tags containing the ScreenTip text.

- Click line 88, between the second break <br /> tag and the closing </body> tag.
- Enter the code shown in Table 11–13 to create <span> containers for the ScreenTip text (Figure 11–30).

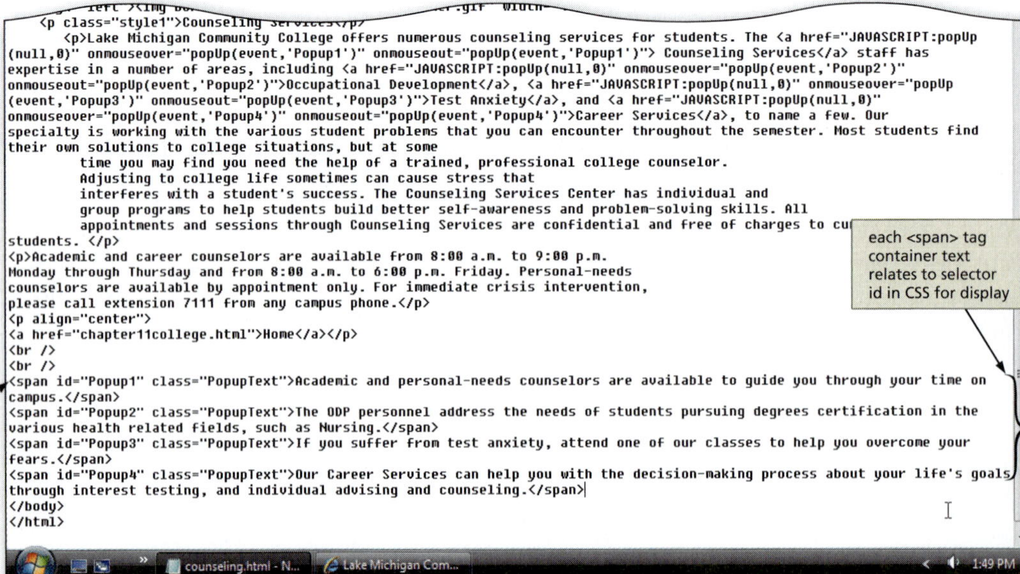

Figure 11–30

To Save an HTML File and Test the Counseling Services Web Page

After the JavaScript code for the Counseling Services Web page is complete, the HTML file should be saved and the Web page should be viewed in a browser to confirm the Web page appears as desired and that ScreenTip text is displayed correctly. The following step shows how to save and test the Counseling Services Web page.

- With a USB drive plugged into your computer, click File on the menu bar and then click Save As.
- Type `collegecounseling.html` in the File name text box and then click the Save button.
- Click the browser button on the taskbar and then click the Refresh button on the Standard toolbar to view the Lake Michigan Community College home page.
- Click Counseling on the vertically scrolling menu.

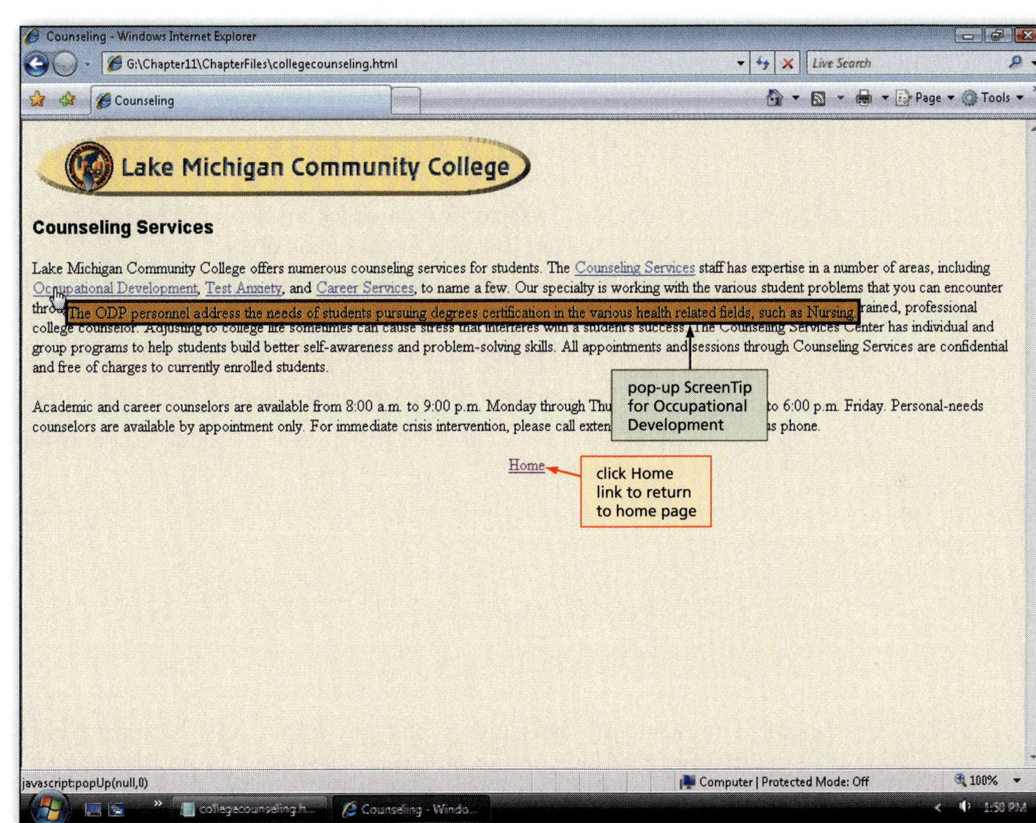

Figure 11–31

- When the Counseling Services Web page is displayed, move the mouse pointer over the linked words Test Anxiety to view the ScreenTip.
- Next, move the mouse pointer over the linked words Career Services to view the ScreenTip.
- Next, move the mouse pointer over the linked words Occupational Development to view the ScreenTip, as shown in Figure 11–31.
- Click the Home link at the bottom of the Counseling Services Web page to return to the Lake Michigan Community College home page.

Plan Ahead

Creating a scrolling image.

The position of the image on the Web page is based on a screen resolution of 1024 × 768. Different screen resolutions will need to adjust the positioning values.

In this chapter, the JavaScript code used to create a scrolling image includes four user-defined functions that do the following:

- Have an image scroll from right to left (scrollImage() function)

  The following steps detail the programming logic for the scrollImage() function:

  1 Decrement the left pixel position by 10
  2 Test left pixel position to determine if it is off the screen
  3 If left pixel < 250, reset to the right side of the screen (950) based on the screen resolution of 1024 × 768
  4 Use the id selector for the <div> tag to assign the calculated value of the left pixel to the pixelLeft property of the image object
  5 Assign the setTimeout() method used to call the scrollImage() function to a variable so the clearTimeout() method can be used to stop the scrolling
- Stop the image from scrolling (stopScroll() function) with the clearTimeout() method
- Restart the image scrolling (restartScroll() function) using the setTimeout() method
- Open a pop-up window for the Student Life page (studentLife() function) using the open() method

Adding a Scrolling Image to the Academic Assistance Web Page

The Academic Assistance Web page (Figure 11–1b on page HTML 493) has an image that scrolls from right to left, and serves as a link to the Student Life Web page. When a visitor places the mouse over the image, it stops scrolling so the user can click the image link; when the mouse is moved off the image, it starts scrolling again. The image stops by using the clearTimeout() method and the mouse pointer becomes a hand by using an embedded style in the <img> tag. The scrolling image is a link to the Student Life Web page that is displayed as a pop-up window.

To Open an Existing HTML File in Notepad

To scroll an image, it is placed in a <div> tag layer that is referenced by the user-defined functions. The scrolling image is positioned at the bottom of the page to fill some of the blank space and to avoid overlaying any other text.

To begin, the Academic Assistance Web page must be opened.

1

- Activate the Notepad Window.
- With a USB drive plugged into your computer, click File on the menu bar and then click Open on the File menu.
- If necessary, navigate to the Chapter11\ChapterFiles folder on the USB drive.
- If necessary, click the Files of type box arrow, and then click All Files to show all files in the Chapter11\ChapterFiles folder.

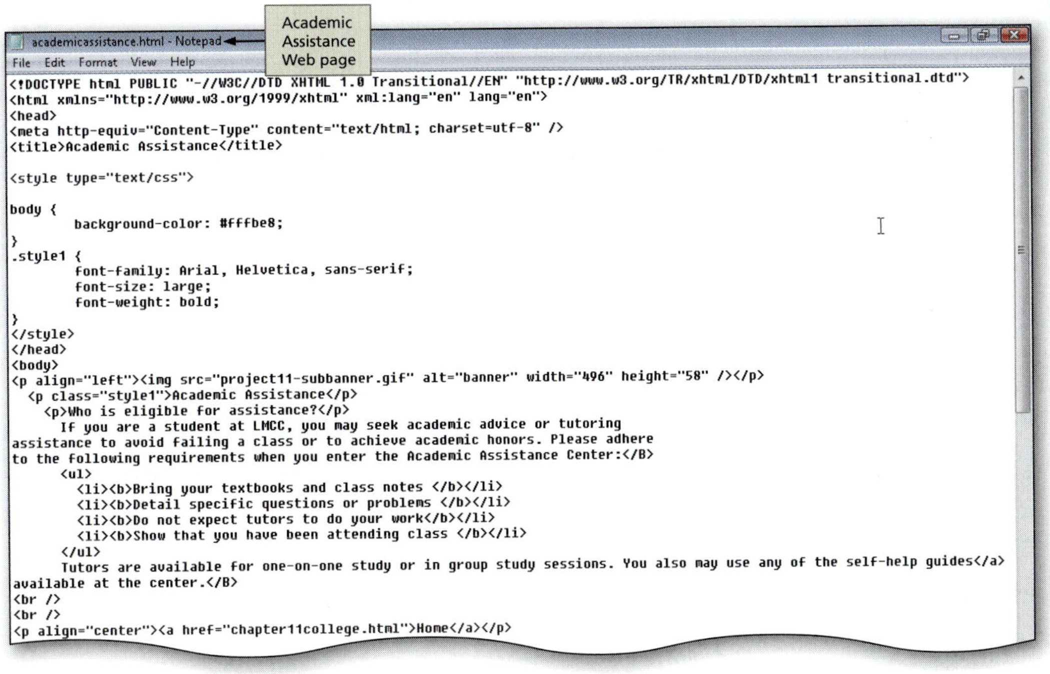

academicassistance.html - Notepad

File Edit Format View Help

Academic Assistance Web page

```
<!DOCTYPE html PUBLIC "-//W3C//DTD XHTML 1.0 Transitional//EN" "http://www.w3.org/TR/xhtml/DTD/xhtml1 transitional.dtd">
<html xmlns="http://www.w3.org/1999/xhtml" xml:lang="en" lang="en">
<head>
<meta http-equiv="Content-Type" content="text/html; charset=utf-8" />
<title>Academic Assistance</title>

<style type="text/css">

body {
        background-color: #fffbe8;
}
.style1 {
        font-family: Arial, Helvetica, sans-serif;
        font-size: large;
        font-weight: bold;
}
</style>
</head>
<body>
<p align="left"><img src="project11-subbanner.gif" alt="banner" width="496" height="58" /></p>
  <p class="style1">Academic Assistance</p>
    <p>Who is eligible for assistance?</p>
      If you are a student at LMCC, you may seek academic advice or tutoring
assistance to avoid failing a class or to achieve academic honors. Please adhere
to the following requirements when you enter the Academic Assistance Center:</B>
      <ul>
        <li><b>Bring your textbooks and class notes </b></li>
        <li><b>Detail specific questions or problems </b></li>
        <li><b>Do not expect tutors to do your work</b></li>
        <li><b>Show that you have been attending class </b></li>
      </ul>
      Tutors are available for one-on-one study or in group study sessions. You also may use any of the self-help guides</a>
available at the center.</B>
<br />
<br />
<p align="center"><a href="chapter11college.html">Home</a></p>
```

Figure 11–32

- Double-click academicassistance.html in the list of files so the HTML code for the Academic Assistance Web page is displayed as shown in Figure 11–32.

Entering the scrollImage(), stopScroll(), and restartScroll()Functions

The next step is to enter the code to have the image scroll from right to left, then to stop scrolling, and finally to restart scrolling. Table 11–14 shows the code for the scrollImage() function.

Table 11–14 Code for the scrollImage() Function

Code
`<script type="text/javascript">`
`<!--Hide from old browsers`
`var leftPX=950`
`function scrollImage() {`
`leftPX-=10`
`if (leftPX<-250) leftPX=950`
`document.all['Img1'].style.pixelLeft=leftPX`
`imager=setTimeout("scrollImage()",100)`
`}`

Lines 6 and 7 start a standard <script> section. Line 8 assigns 950 to the variable leftPX to represent the right side of the screen for the screen resolution 1024 × 768. Line 9 declares the function, scrollImage(). Line 10 decrements the leftPX variable by 10 pixels. Line 11 tests the value of leftPX to see if it has extended past the end of the screen. The value -250 was chosen to allow most of the image to scroll off the screen before starting over at the right. If the value is less than -250, leftPX is assigned 950 so the image can start from the right again.

Line 12 assigns the value of leftPX to the pixelLeft property of the image object, identified by the Img1 name. Line 13 assigns the recursive call of the setTimeout() method to a variable so the image scrolling can be stopped with an onmouseover event handler calling a different function. Line 14 closes the function code.

To Enter the scrollImage() Function

The following step illustrates how to enter the scrollImage() function.

1

- Click line 6.
- Enter the JavaScript code as shown in Table 11–14 to enter the scrollImage() user-defined function, pressing the SPACEBAR to indent as shown.
- Press the ENTER key twice (Figure 11–33).

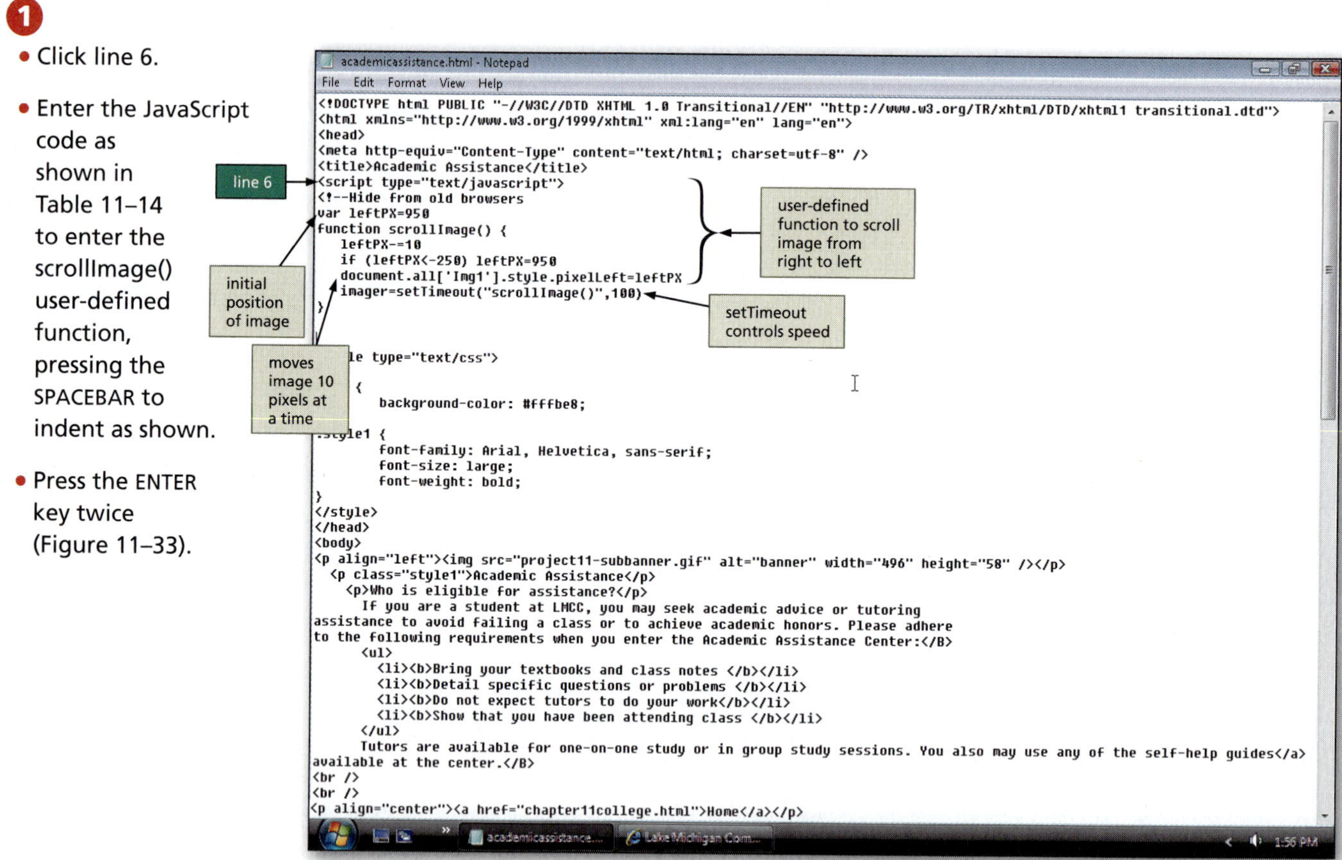

Figure 11–33

To Enter the stopScroll() Function

The stopScroll() function stops the image from scrolling when the visitor moves the mouse over the image. The function, stopScroll(), responds to an onmouseover event handler. Table 11–15 shows the JavaScript code for the stopScroll() function.

Table 11–15 Code for the stopScroll() Function

Line	Code
15	`function stopScroll() {`
16	`        clearTimeout(imager)`
17	`}`

Line 15 defines the stopScroll() user-defined function. The clearTimeout() method on line 16 stops the scrolling image by clearing the imager variable used in the recursive call made by the setTimeout() method on line 13 in Table 11–14 on page HTML 525. Line 17 ends the stopScroll() function.

The following step illustrates how to enter the stopScroll() user-defined function.

1

- If necessary, click line 15.
- Enter the code shown in Table 11–15 to create the stopScroll() user-defined function, pressing the SPACEBAR to indent as shown.
- Press the ENTER key twice (Figure 11–34).

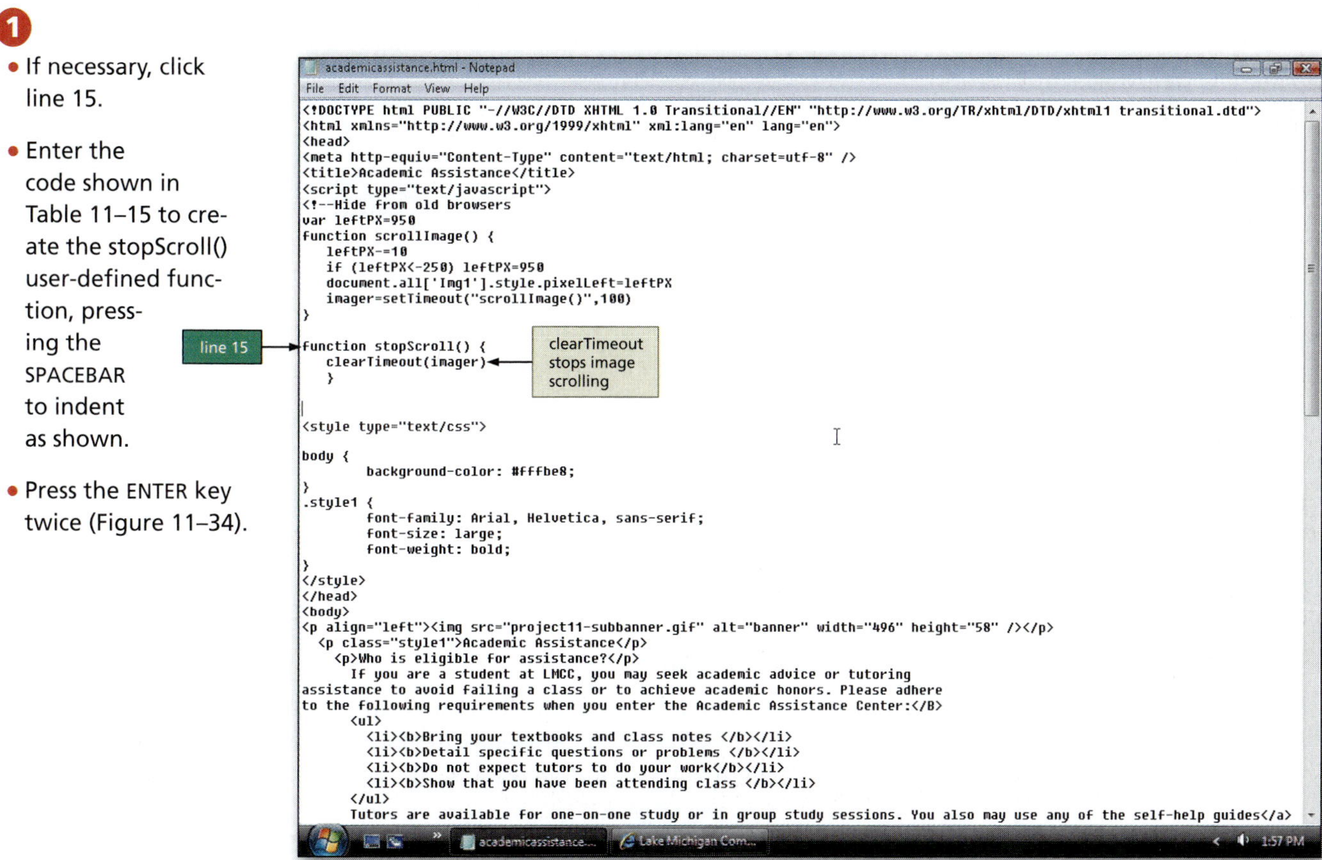

Figure 11–34

To Enter the restartScroll() Function

The restartScroll() function restarts the image scrolling when the visitor moves the mouse off the scrolling image. This function, restartScroll(), responds to an onmouseout event handler. Table 11–16 shows the code for the restartScroll() user-defined function.

Table 11–16 Code for the restartScroll() Function

Line	Code
19	`function restartScroll() {`
20	`        setTimeout("scrollImage()",100)`
21	`}`

Line 19 declares the function. Line 20 uses the setTimeout() method to call the scrollImage() user-defined function. Line 21 ends the restartScroll() function code.

The following step shows how to enter the user-defined function restartScroll().

1

- If necessary, click line 19.
- Enter the code shown in Table 11–16 to create the restartScroll() user-defined function, pressing the SPACEBAR to indent as shown.
- Press the ENTER key twice (Figure 11–35).

Figure 11–35

Entering the studentLife() Function to the Academic Assistance Web Page

The fourth user-defined function added to the Academic Assistance Web page is the studentLife() function, which opens the Student Life pop-up window when the user clicks the scrolling image. Table 11–17 shows the code for the studentLife() function.

Table 11–17 Code for the studentLife() Function

Line	Code
23	`function studentLife() {`
24	`   window.open("collegestudentlife.html", "studentLife", "scrollbar=yes,width=600,height=350")`
25	`}`
26	
27	`//-->`
28	`</script>`

Line 23 declares the function. Line 24 uses the open() method to open the Student Life Web page as a pop-up window. The attributes settings display the scroll bar, and set the window to a width of 600 pixels and a height of 350 pixels. Lines 27 and 28 complete the user-defined functions <script> section in the <head> section.

To Enter the studentLife() Function

The following step shows how to enter the studentLife() user-defined function.

1

- If necessary, click line 23.
- Enter the code shown in Table 11–17 to create the studentLife() user-defined function, pressing the SPACEBAR to indent as shown (Figure 11–36).

```
<!DOCTYPE html PUBLIC "-//W3C//DTD XHTML 1.0 Transitional//EN" "http://www.w3.org/TR/xhtml1/DTD/xhtml
<html xmlns="http://www.w3.org/1999/xhtml" xml:lang="en" lang="en">
<head>
<meta http-equiv="Content-Type" content="text/html; charset=utf-8" />
<title>Academic Assistance</title>
<script type="text/javascript">
<!--Hide from old browsers
var leftPX=950
function scrollImage() {
   leftPX-=10
   if (leftPX<-250) leftPX=950
   document.all['Img1'].style.pixelLeft=leftPX
   imager=setTimeout("scrollImage()",100)
}

function stopScroll() {
   clearTimeout(imager)
   }

function restartScroll() {
   setTimeout("scrollImage()",100)
}

function studentLife() {
   window.open("collegestudentlife.html", "studentLife", "scrollbar=yes,width=600,height=350")
}

//-->
</script>
<style type="text/css">

body {
        background-color: #fffbe8;
}
.style1 {
        font-family: Arial, Helvetica, sans-serif;
        font-size: large;
        font-weight: bold;
}
</style>
</head>
<body>
<p align="left"><img src="project11-subbanner.gif" alt="banner" width="496" height="58" /></p>
  <p class="style1">Academic Assistance</p>
    <p>Who is eligible for assistance?</p>
      If you are a student at LMCC, you may seek academic advice or tutoring
```

line 23

no spaces between attribute values

pop-up window displays when scrolling image is clicked

academicassistance....

Lake Michigan Com...

Figure 11–36

Adding an id Selector to the Style Sheet for the Scrolling Image

The next step is to add an id selector to the embedded style sheet to place the scrolling image. The style sheet uses the id selector, Img1, which later will be associated with the <span> tag container used to position the image. The embedded style sheet sets the initial position of the scrolling image to appear 420 pixels from the top of the window and 950 pixels from the left side of the screen.

To Enter the Embedded Style Sheet Used to Format the Scrolling Image

The following step shows how to enter the id selector in the embedded style sheet used to position the scrolling image on the Academic Assistance Web page.

1

- Click line 30.
- Type `#Img1 {` to create the id selector and then press the ENTER key.
- Type `position: absolute; top=420; left=950;` to define the initial position of the image and then press the ENTER key.
- Type `}` to close the #img id selector and then press the ENTER key (Figure 11–37).

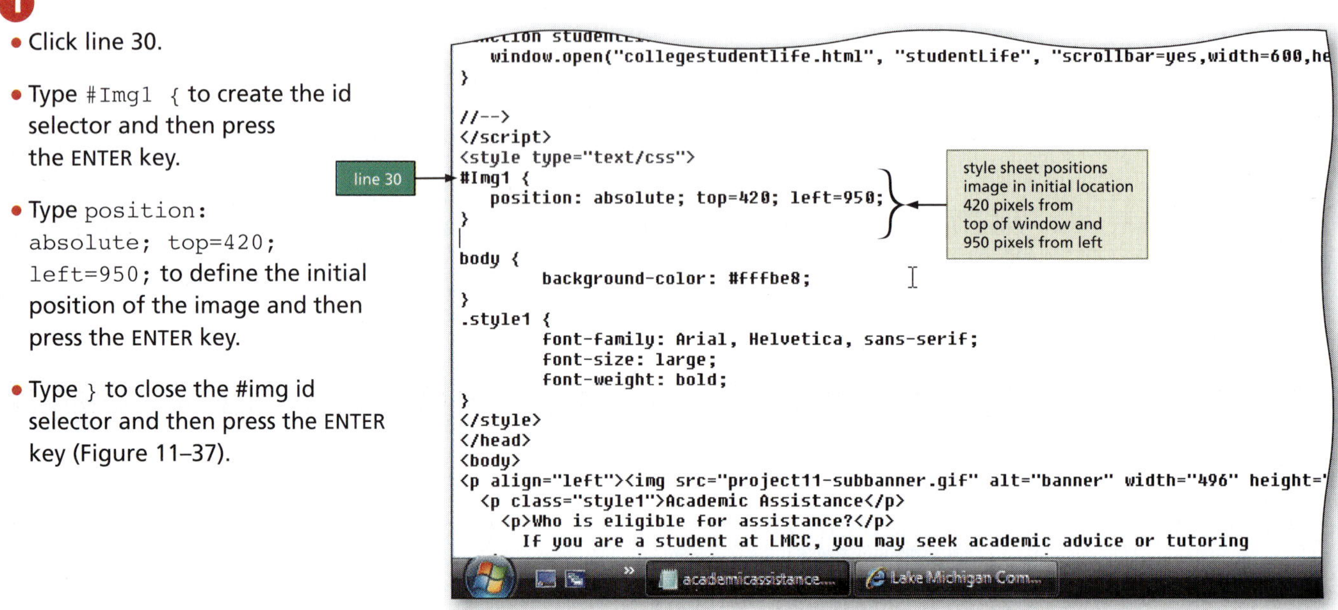

Figure 11–37

Entering an Image Object for the Scrolling Image Using the <div> and <img> Tags

The next step is to add the scrolling image. First, a <div> tag layer must be added on the Web page. The <div> tag uses the id selector, Img1, to indicate that the image initially should be positioned based on the parameters for that selector in the embedded style sheet. The <div> tag layer becomes the image object whose pixelLeft property is modified to scroll the image. Table 11–18 shows the HTML code for the <div> tag and image tags that must be added to the Web page table.

Table 11–18 Code to Add Scrolling Image

Line	Code
60	`<div id="Img1">`
61	`<img src="academicassistance.gif" alt="scrolling banner" style="cursor:hand" onmouseover="stopScroll()" onmouseout="restartScroll()" onclick="studentLife()" />`
62	`</div>`

Line 60 starts the <div> tag with the Img1 id selector attribute (id="Img1"). Line 61 is the <img> image tag with three event handlers and one embedded style. This line must be typed without any line breaks. The onmouseover event handler calls the stopScroll() user-defined function to stop the scrolling. When the visitor takes the mouse off the image, the onmouseout event handler calls the restartScroll() user-defined function. The onclick event handler calls the studentLife() user-defined function. To make the image appear as any other link, a style sheet element, cursor:hand, was embedded in the <img> tag.

To Enter the <div> and <img> Tags for the Scrolling Image

The following steps illustrate how to enter the <div> and <img> tags.

1

- Click line 60 to position the insertion point before the </body> tag.
- Enter the HTML code shown in Table 11–18 to create the <div> and <img> tags for the scrolling image at this position on the Web page (Figure 11–38).

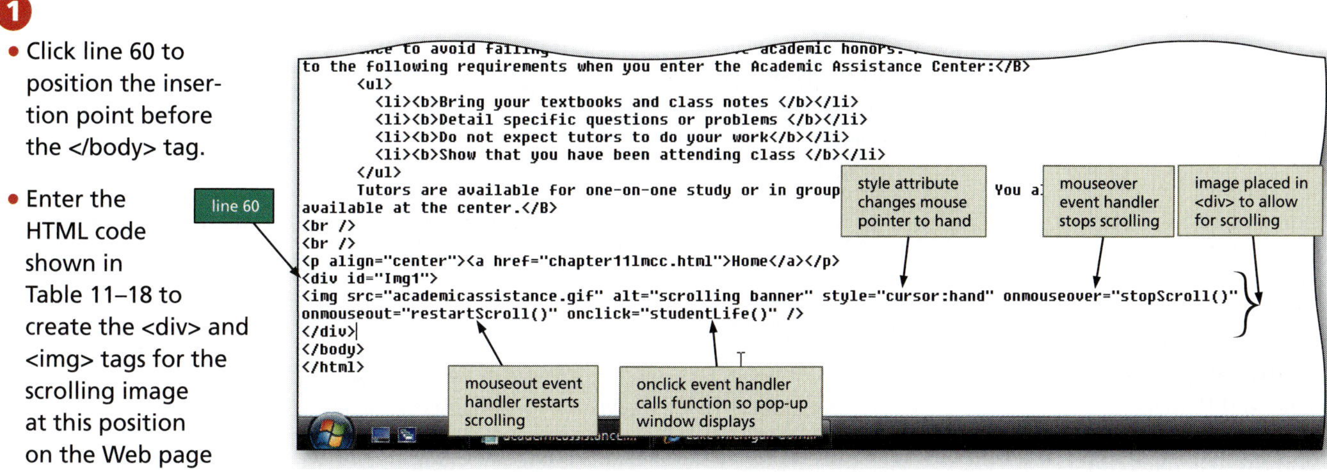

Figure 11–38

To Add the onload Event Handler to Call the scrollImage() Function

The final step in modifying the Academic Assistance Web page is to enter the onload event handler to call the scrollImage() user-defined function as soon as the Web page is loaded. The following steps show how to add the onload event handler to the <body> tag.

1

- Click line 44.
- Position the insertion point between the y in body and the > symbol and press the SPACEBAR once.
- Type `onload="scrollImage()"` and do not press the ENTER key (Figure 11–39).

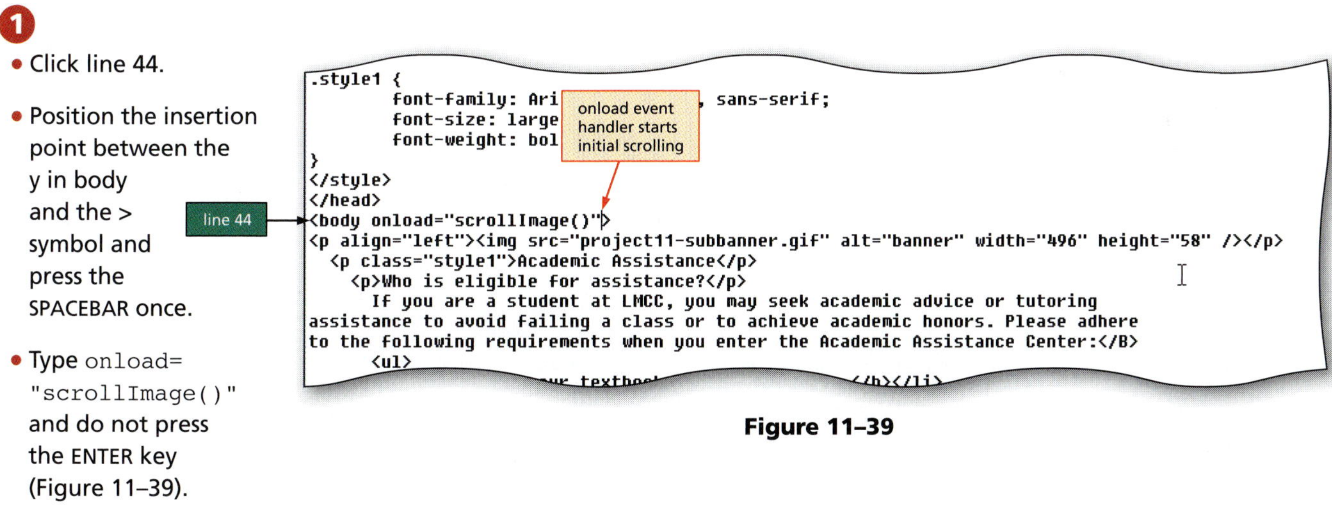

Figure 11–39

To Save an HTML File and Test a Web Page

With the JavaScript, style sheet, and <div> tag code complete for the Lake Michigan Community College Academic Assistance Web page, the file should be saved and the Web page tested in a browser. The following steps show how to save and test the Academic Assistance Web page.

- With the USB drive plugged into your computer, click File on the menu bar and then click Save As.
- Type `collegeacademicassistance.html` in the File name text box and then click the Save button.
- Click the browser button on the taskbar and then click the Refresh button on the Standard toolbar to view the Lake Michigan Community College home page.
- Click Academic Assistance on the vertically scrolling menu.
- Position the mouse pointer over the scrolling image (Figure 11–40).

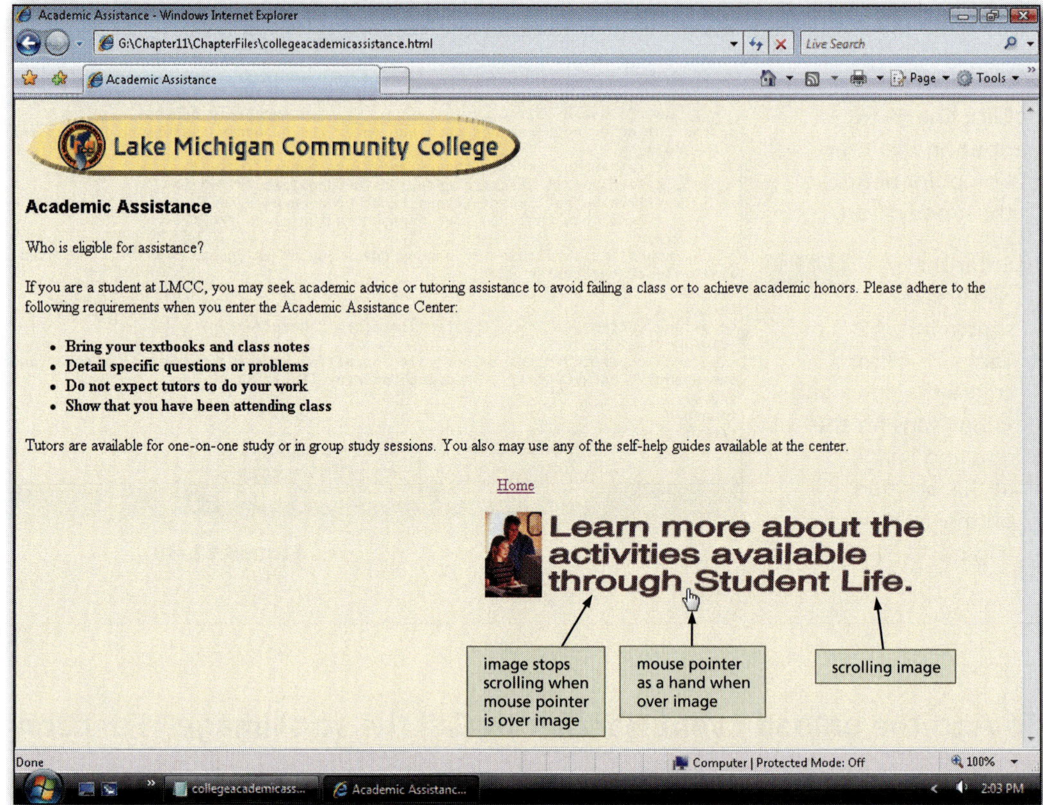

Academic Assistance - Windows Internet Explorer
G:\Chapter11\ChapterFiles\collegeacademicassistance.html
Lake Michigan Community College
Academic Assistance
Who is eligible for assistance?
If you are a student at LMCC, you may seek academic advice or tutoring assistance to avoid failing a class or to achieve academic honors. Please adhere to the following requirements when you enter the Academic Assistance Center:
Bring your textbooks and class notes
Detail specific questions or problems
Do not expect tutors to do your work
Show that you have been attending class
Tutors are available for one-on-one study or in group study sessions. You also may use any of the self-help guides available at the center.
Home
Learn more about the activities available through Student Life.
image stops scrolling when mouse pointer is over image
mouse pointer as a hand when over image
scrolling image

Figure 11–40

- Click the scrolling image.
- Close the Student Life pop-up window.
- Click the Home link on the bottom of the Academic Assistance Web page to return to the home page (Figure 11–41).

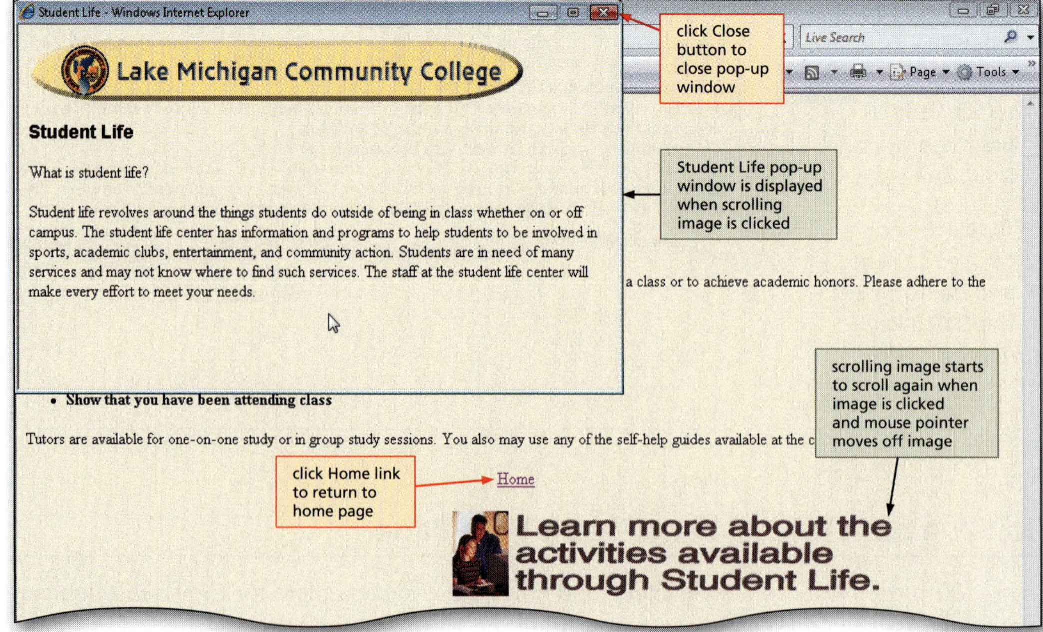

Figure 11–41

To Test and Validate the Lake Michigan Community College Web Pages

The final step in developing a Web site is to test all the Web pages and links. The following step illustrates how to test the Lake Michigan Community College Web pages.

- Click the Internet Explorer button on the status bar.
- Drag the vertical scroll bar down to reveal more of the page and watch the scrolling menu on the left side.
- Click the Student Life menu item.
- Position the mouse over any of the hyperlink items.
- Click the Home link.
- Click the Mission Statement link.
- Click the Close link.
- Click the Counseling menu link.
- Drag the mouse over any of the links to verify the pop-up ScreenTips are displayed, and then click the Home link.
- Click the annual blood drive link.
- Click the Close link on the Blood Drive Web page.
- Validate the Lake Michigan College Web pages.

To Close Notepad and a Browser

- Click the Close button on the browser title bar.
- Click the Close button on the Notepad title bar.

BTW

Quick Reference
For a list of JavaScript statements and their associated attributes, see the JavaScript Quick Reference (Appendix E) at the back of this book, or visit the HTML Quick Reference Web page (**scsite.com/HTML5e/qr**).

Chapter Summary

Chapter 11 introduced the concepts of the Document Object Model (DOM), a combination of technologies that include HTML, Cascading Style Sheets (CSS), and a scripting language, such as JavaScript. Using the DOM, you learned how to create scrolling menus and images. The items listed below include all the new skills you have learned in this chapter.

1. Create an HTML Division and Table to Contain a Menu Object (HTML 496)
2. Create an Embedded Style Sheet (HTML 498)
3. Create the checkLocation() User-Defined Function (HTML 500)
4. Write the onload Event Handler to Call the checkLocation() Function (HTML 501)
5. Enter the bloodDrive() and missionStatement() User-Defined Functions to Open Pop-up Windows (HTML 502)
6. Enter Links with a JavaScript Method to Open the Pop-up Windows (HTML 503)
7. Create an Image Object (HTML 508)
8. Create the User-Defined Function to Add a Rotating Banner (HTML 511)
9. Enter the onload Event Handler to Call a Function (HTML 511)
10. Enter the popUp() Function (HTML 515)
11. Enter a Cascading Style Sheet Using id and class Selectors (HTML 518)

12. Add Links and Event Handlers to Call the popUp() Function (HTML 519)
13. Enter <span> Tags Containing ScreenTip Text (HTML 522)
14. Enter the scrollImage() Function (HTML 526)
15. Enter the stopScroll() Function (HTML 527)
16. Enter the restartScroll() Function (HTML 528)
17. Enter the studentLife() Function (HTML 529)
18. Enter the Embedded Style Sheet Used to Format the Scrolling Image (HTML 530)
19. Enter the <div> and <img> Tags for the Scrolling Image (HTML 531)
20. Add the onload Event Handler to Call the scrollImage() Function (HTML 531)

Learn It Online

Test your knowledge of chapter content and key terms.

Instructions: To complete the Learn It Online exercises, start your browser, click the Address bar, and then enter the Web address `scsite.com/html5e/learn`. When the HTML Learn It Online page is displayed, click the link for the exercise you want to complete and read the instructions.

Chapter Reinforcement TF, MC, and SA

A series of true/false, multiple choice, and short answer questions that test your knowledge of the chapter content.

Flash Cards

An interactive learning environment where you identify chapter key terms associated with displayed definitions.

Practice Test

A series of multiple choice questions that test your knowledge of chapter content and key terms.

Who Wants To Be a Computer Genius?

An interactive game that challenges your knowledge of chapter content in the style of a television quiz show.

Wheel of Terms

An interactive game that challenges your knowledge of chapter key terms in the style of the television show, *Wheel of Fortune*.

Crossword Puzzle Challenge

A crossword puzzle that challenges your knowledge of key terms presented in the chapter.

Apply Your Knowledge

Reinforce the skills and apply the concepts you learned in this chapter.

Instructions: Start Notepad. Open the file apply11-1.html from the Chapter11\Apply folder of the Data Files for Students. See the inside back cover of this book for instructions on downloading the Data Files for Students, or contact your instructor for information about accessing the required files.

The apply11-1.html file is a partially completed HTML file that you will use for this exercise. Figure 11–42 shows the Apply Your Knowledge Web page as it should be displayed in a browser after the JavaScript code has been added.

Figure 11–42

Perform the following tasks:

1. Using the JavaScript code in Table 11–10 on page HTML 510 and the names of the .jpg files in the Apply data folder of candles and flowers, create two arrays. One array should be named rotatePicsLeft using the candles images, and the other should be named rotatePicsRight using the flowers images.

Continued >

STUDENT ASSIGNMENTS

Apply Your Knowledge *continued*

2. Using the logic presented in the code in Table 11–10 on page HTML 510, change the image in picture1.src with the rotatePicsLeft array item, and the image in picture2.src with the rotatePicsRight array item for the current counter.
3. Find the word candles in the paragraph (indicated as a link in Figure 11–42).
4. Using the code described in the steps for Figure 11–25, write the HTML <a href> tag with the JavaScript event handlers to show the ScreenTip for the candles. Be sure to close the <a href> tag after the word candles. Use the id selector Tip1 in the event handlers.
5. Using the code in Table 11–11 on page HTML 514 as a guide, write the JavaScript code to make the ScreenTip show when the mouse is placed over the word candles in the paragraph.
6. Using the code in Table 11–12 on page HTML 517 as a guide, write the Cascading Style Sheet for the ScreenTips. Use the id selector Tip1 and the class selector TipText.
7. Use the following attribute values for id: "Tip1" position: absolute; visibility: hidden; z-index: 10; top: 10px; left: 10px. Use the following attributes value for class: "TipText" background-color: #006600; padding: 3px; border: 3px solid black; width: 250px; font-weight: bolder; color: white.
8. Following the style of the code in Table 11–13 on page HTML 522, write the <span> tag and place it in the blank line after the HTML comment <!-- span tag for ScreenTip -->.
9. The ScreenTip message should read: "We carry a wide array of candles made from bee's and paraffin wax to specially scented oils for decoration or ceremonial use." Be sure to close the <span> tag.
10. Save the revised file in the Chapter11\Apply folder using the file name apply11-1solution.html.
11. Start your browser. Enter the URL g:\Chapter11\Apply\apply11-1solution.html to view and test the Web page in your browser. Validate the Web page.
12. If any errors occur, check the code against Steps 1 through 9, make any required changes, save the file using the same file name, and then refresh the Web page in the browser.
13. Submit the revised HTML file and Web page in the format specified by your instructor.

Extend Your Knowledge

Extend the skills you learned in this chapter and experiment with new skills. You will need to search the Internet to complete the assignment.

Learning More About Moving or Scrolling Images

Instructions: Start Notepad and your browser. Open the file, extend11-1.html from the Chapter11\ Extend folder of the Data Files for Students. See the inside back cover of this book for instructions on downloading the Data Files for Students, or contact your instructor for information about accessing the required files.

Search the Internet at JavaScript sites and find some code that explains how to move an image object from one side of the Web page to another using a mouseover event handler. The technique for moving objects is to use the positioning of the object with Cascading Style Sheets and then using the document object with the style property to change the pixelLeft and pixelTop properties. The style. pixelLeft property should be set to 850 to move the image object (#inoculateImg) from left to right and then set to 10 to return the object to the original position (Figure 11–43).

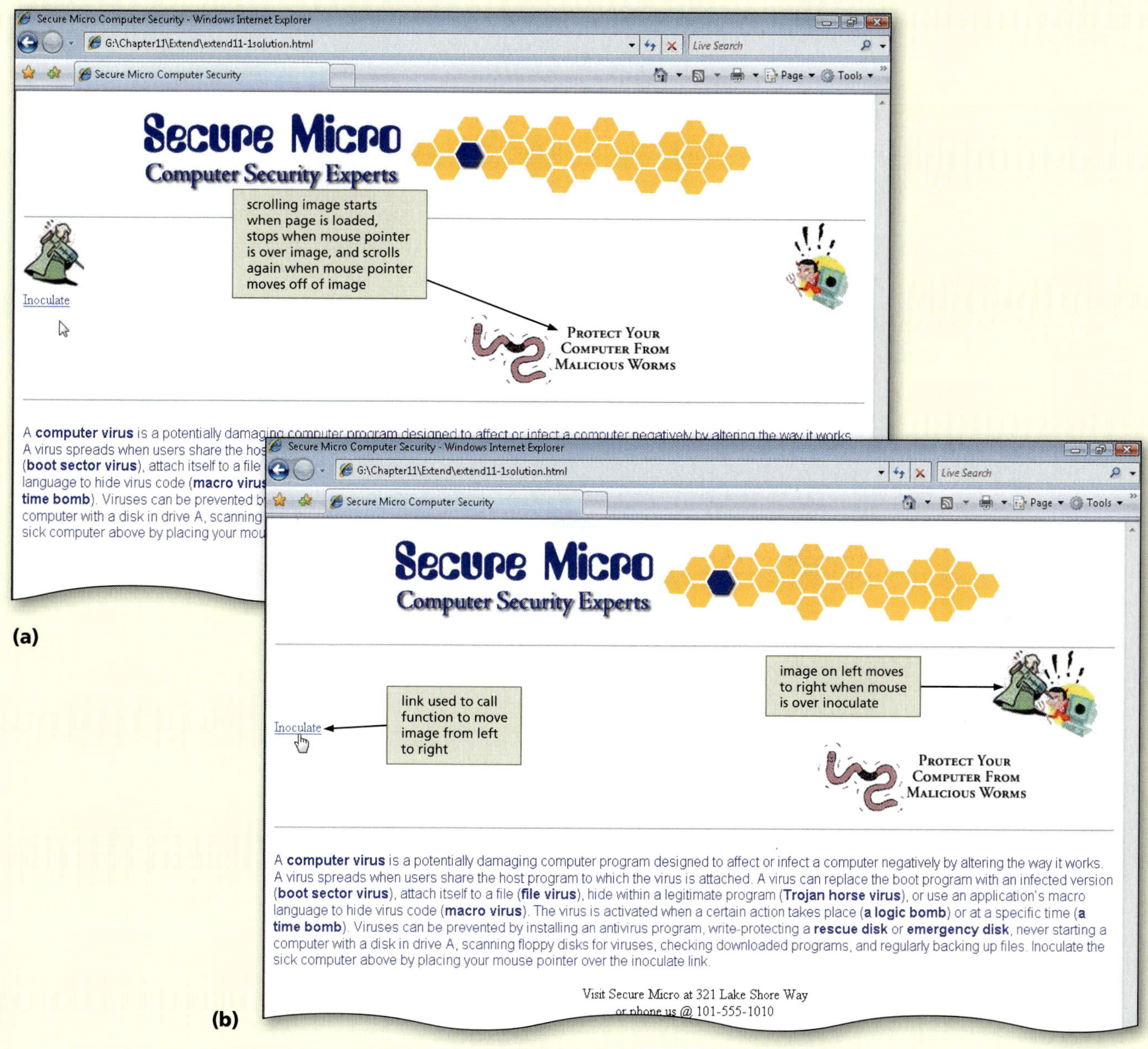

Figure 11–43

Perform the following tasks:

1. Save the extend11-1.html file as extend11-1solution.html.
2. Write a JavaScript function called IEmoveIT() to move the left image on the screen to the virus-infected computer on the right, when the onMouseover event handler is activated on the Inoculate link.
3. Write a JavaScript function called IEmoveBack() to move the image back to its original position on the left, when the onMouseout event handler is activated by moving the mouse off the Inoculate link.
4. Using the code in Table 11–14 on page HTML 525 as a guide, write a JavaScript function that scrolls the worm image from the right of the Web page to the left. Use a variable named leftPX to adjust the style.pixelLeft of the scrolling image. Set the initial value of leftPX to 1024. Decrement the value by 10 each time the function is called. If leftPX < –250, then set leftPX to 1024 to set the scrolling image back on the right side of the screen. Call the function recursively with the setTimeout() method every 100 milliseconds. When calling the function recursively, assign the setTimeout() method to an identifier called imager. Set the time for the setTimeout() function to 100 milliseconds.

Continued >

Extend Your Knowledge *continued*

5. Write a function called stopScroll() using the clearTimeout(imager) that is called when the user puts the mouse over the scrolling image.
6. Write a function called restartScroll() to call the scrollImage() function using the setTimeout method.
7. Save the revised file in the Chapter11\Extend folder.
8. Start your browser. Enter the URL g:\Chapter11\Extend\extend11-1solution.html to view and test the Web page in your browser.
9. If any errors occur, check the code against Steps 1 through 7, make any required changes, save the file using the same file name, and then refresh the Web page in the browser.
10. Submit the revised HTML file and Web page in the format specified by your instructor.

Make It Right

Analyze the JavaScript code on a Web page and correct all errors.

Correcting Syntax Errors and Inserting Missing Code

Instructions: Start your browser. Open the file makeitright11-1.html from the Chapter11\MakeItRight folder of the Data Files for Students. See the inside back cover of this book for instructions on downloading the Data Files for Students, or contact your instructor for information about accessing the required files. The file is a Web page for the Lincoln Pioneers Minor League team that includes some errors and omissions. The corrected page appears as shown in Figure 11–44.

Figure 11–44

Perform the following tasks:

1. Save the makeitright11-1.html file as makeitright11-1solution.html.
2. The image on the right should scroll the entire length of the Web page. Find the error in the scrollImage() function so that the image scrolls the entire length of the Web page.
3. The ScreenTips for the links Class A minor league team, Minor League Teams, Some History, and Winter Meetings are all the same ScreenTip. Find the error in the <a href> tags for the ScreenTips and correct them so the correct ScreenTip is displayed when the onMouseover event handler is used.
4. Save the corrected HTML file and test using your browser. If an error still occurs, check your code, save, and test again.
5. Submit the revised HTML file and Web page in the format specified by your instructor.

In the Lab

Design and/or create a Web page using the guidelines, concepts, and skills presented in this chapter. Labs are listed in order of increasing difficulty.

Lab 1: Creating the Duneland Country Club Web Page

Problem: Your aunt Felicia is the manager of the Duneland Country Club and she asks you to design a new Web page for them to announce the hiring of the WPGA golf pro, Selena Martinez, as shown in Figure 11–45. She asks you to create a scrolling text message, a slide show of golfers, and a ScreenTip promoting Selena's lessons. To extend your knowledge, you decide to try using the Microsoft <marquee> tag to scroll the message.

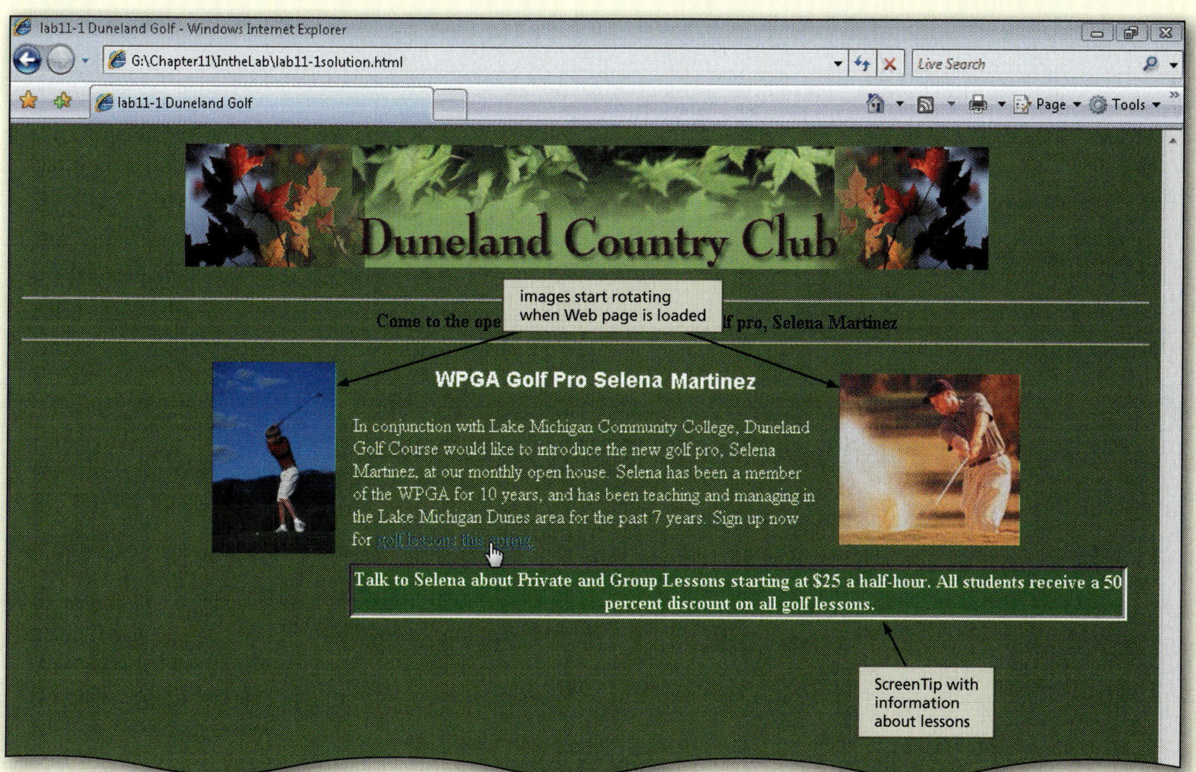

Figure 11–45

Continued >

STUDENT ASSIGNMENTS

In the Lab *continued*

Instructions: Perform the following steps:

1. Start Notepad and open the file lab11-1.html from the Chapter11\IntheLab folder of the Data Files for Students.
2. Save the file as lab11-1solution.html.
3. Using the code in Table 11–10 on page HTML 510 as a guide, write a JavaScript function called RotateIt() to have rotating images of golfers where the two original figures display on the Web page. Use the eight golf .jpg images in the Chapter11\IntheLab folder for the slide show. Use the first four images in an array named slideShow1 for the figures on the left, and images five through eight in an array named slideShow2 for the figures on the right.
4. Using the code in Table 11–11 on page HTML 514 as a guide, write a JavaScript function called popUp() to show a ScreenTip.
5. Using the code in Table 11–12 on page HTML 517 as a guide, add the id selector Popup1 and class selector ScreenTip to the Cascading Style Sheet. For id selector Popup1, use the following attributes: position: absolute; visibility: hidden; z-index: 10; top: 10px; left: 10px. For the class selector ScreenTip, use the following attributes: background-color: green; layer-background-color: green; padding: 5; border: medium inset white; width: 150; font-weight: bold; color: #ffffff.
6. The text for the ScreenTip should read: "Talk to Selena about Private and Group Lessons starting at $25 a half-hour. All students receive a 50 percent discount on all golf lessons." Place the text in a <span> tag with the Cascading Style Sheet id as Popup1, and the class as ScreenTip. Add the <a href> anchor tag to use the mouseover and mouseout event handlers to call the popUp() function written in step 4.
7. Between the two horizontal rule <hr> tags, write a <script> section that only works in Internet Explorer using the <marquee> tag.
8. Initialize a variable called marqueeMsg with the following message: "Come to the open house and meet our new golf pro, Selena Martinez." Make the message bold using the <strong> tag.
9. Use the document.write() method to write the <marquee> tag with these attributes set as follows: scrollAmount=3, scrolldelay=30, style=width:300.
10. Place the marqueeMsg between the beginning and ending <marquee> tags.
11. Save the completed HTML file and test it using your browser. If an error occurs, check your code from Steps 3 through 10, and then save and test again.
12. Submit the completed HTML file and Web page in the format specified by your instructor.

In the Lab

Lab 2: Creating Al's Home Hardware Web Site

Problem: Your neighbor owns and operates a local hardware store. He has been wanting to have a Web site that would be a place for customers to find home repair tips, energy savings tips, and to announce upcoming workshops for the do-it yourself person. Al would like the main page to link to the other items. For the home repair tips, he wants ScreenTips to pop up for the different items. The workshop page has a scrolling image that passes across the front of the Web page. Add the JavaScript code to make the Web page appear as shown in Figure 11–46.

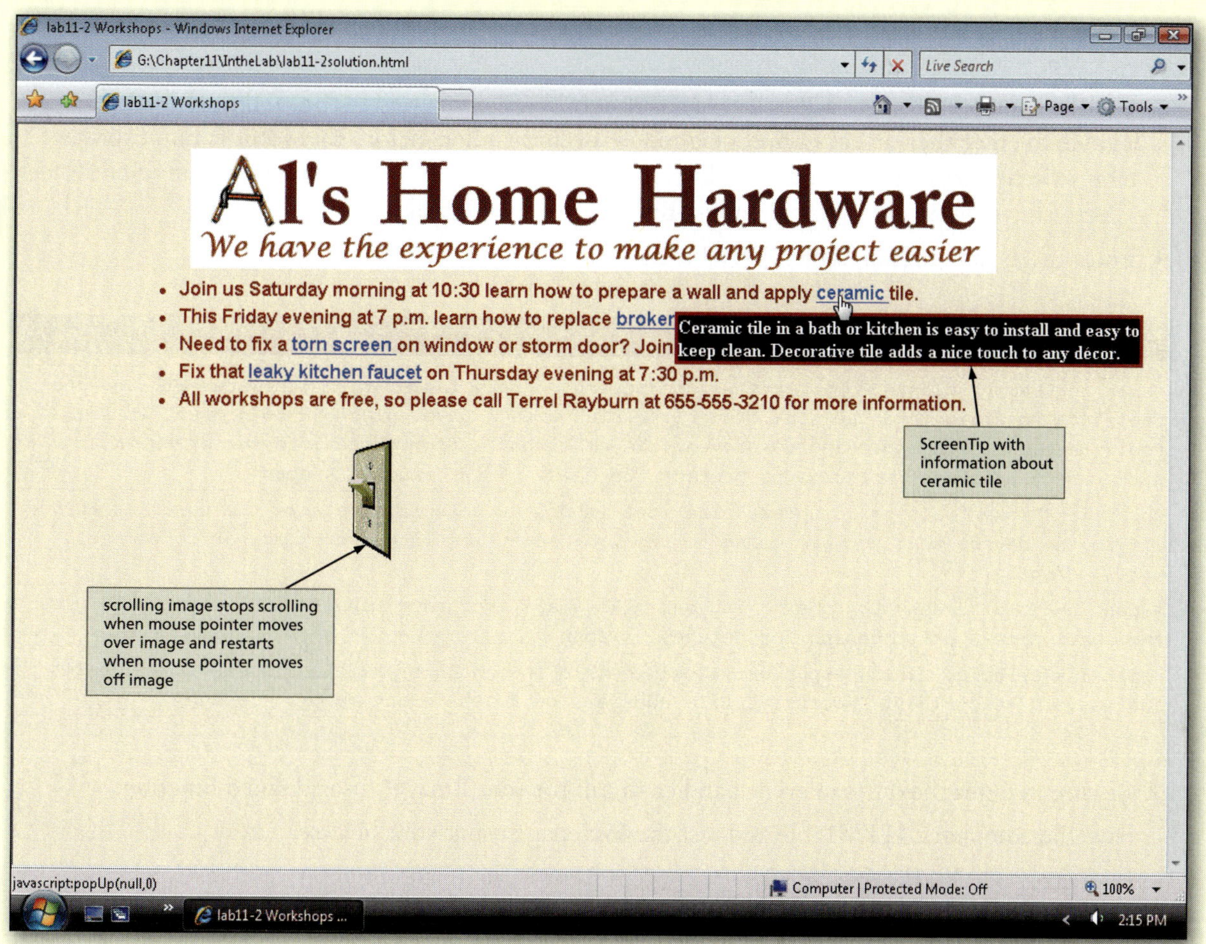

Figure 11–46

Instructions: Perform the following steps:

1. Start Notepad and open the file lab11-2.html from the Chapter11\IntheLab folder of the Data Files for Students.
2. Save the file as lab11-2workshopsolution.html.
3. Start a <script> section in the <head> section below the <title> tag as indicated.
4. Use the code in Table 11–14 on page HTML 525 as a guide to write the JavaScript user-defined function scrollImage() to make the image, lab11-2lightswitch.gif, scroll from right to left across the Web page. The Cascading Style Sheet selector for this image is Img1 and is identified with a <span> tag in the last row of the Web page table.
5. Use the code in Tables 11-15 and 11-16 on pages HTML 527 and HTML 528 to write the JavaScript user-defined functions stopScroll() and restartScroll(). These functions should be called by onMouseover and onMouseout event handlers in the <img> tag. Add the style attribute to change the cursor to a hand.
6. Use the code in Table 11–11 on page HTML 514 as guide to write the JavaScript user-defined function popUp().
7. Use the code in Table 11–12 on page HTML 517 as a guide to add the id selector Img1 and class selector list to the Cascading Style Sheet. For id selector Img1, use the following attributes: position: absolute; top: 263px; left: 764px. For the class selector list, use the following attributes: font-family: arial, helvetica, sans-serif; font-style: normal; font-weight: bolder; color: #993300; list-style-image: url(dot-tool.gif); padding: 2px; text-indent: 2px.

Continued >

In the Lab *continued*

8. Use the code presented in Figures 11–26 through 11–29 on pages HTML 520 to HTML 521 as a guide to enter the correct <a href> tag mouse event handlers before the words ceramic, broken light switches, torn screen, and leaky kitchen faucet. Use the corresponding Cascading Style Sheet selector for each mouse event: Ceramic, Broken, Torn, and Leaky.
9. Enter the <span> tags in Table 11–19 for the ScreenTip text.

Table 11–19 ScreenTip Text
`<span id="Leaky" class="PopupText">Before working on any faucet turn the water off and open the lines to drain into the sink. Cover the sink with a towel or cloth to protect it from tools that may be dropped and to prevent the small parts from going into the drain. Wrap with tape the jaws of wrenches to protect the finish of the faucet. </span>`
`<span id="Broken" class="PopupText">The most important rule is make sure the power is turned off to the device that you are going to repair. Use an insulated screw driver to remove wires. </span>`
`<span id="Torn" class="PopupText">You can make small emergency repairs with waterproof glue and small pieces of screening for patches. </span>`
`<span id="Ceramic" class="PopupText">Ceramic tile in a bath or kitchen is easy to install and easy to keep clean. Decorative tile adds a nice touch to any decor. </span>`

10. Be sure to enter the onLoad event handler to call the scrollImage() user-defined function.
11. Save the completed HTML file and test the Web page using your browser.
12. If an error occurs, check your code from Steps 3 through 10, and then save and test again.
13. Submit the completed HTML file and Web page in the format specified by your instructor.

In the Lab

Lab 3: The Global Charters and Travel Web Page

Problem: Your parents own a travel agency and have asked you to create a Web page that showcases the four tours they are promoting this month. The tours are to the Washington, D.C. area; the Rocky Mountains; Ireland, England and Scotland to visit ancient castles; and Southeast Asia. You decide to create a slide show, using rotating photos representing each of the tours: Mount Vernon in Virginia, a boat trip in the Rockies, a castle ruin from England, and a jungle village in Southeast Asia. To make the Web page more animated you add an image of a jet that scrolls across the bottom of the page (Figure 11–47).

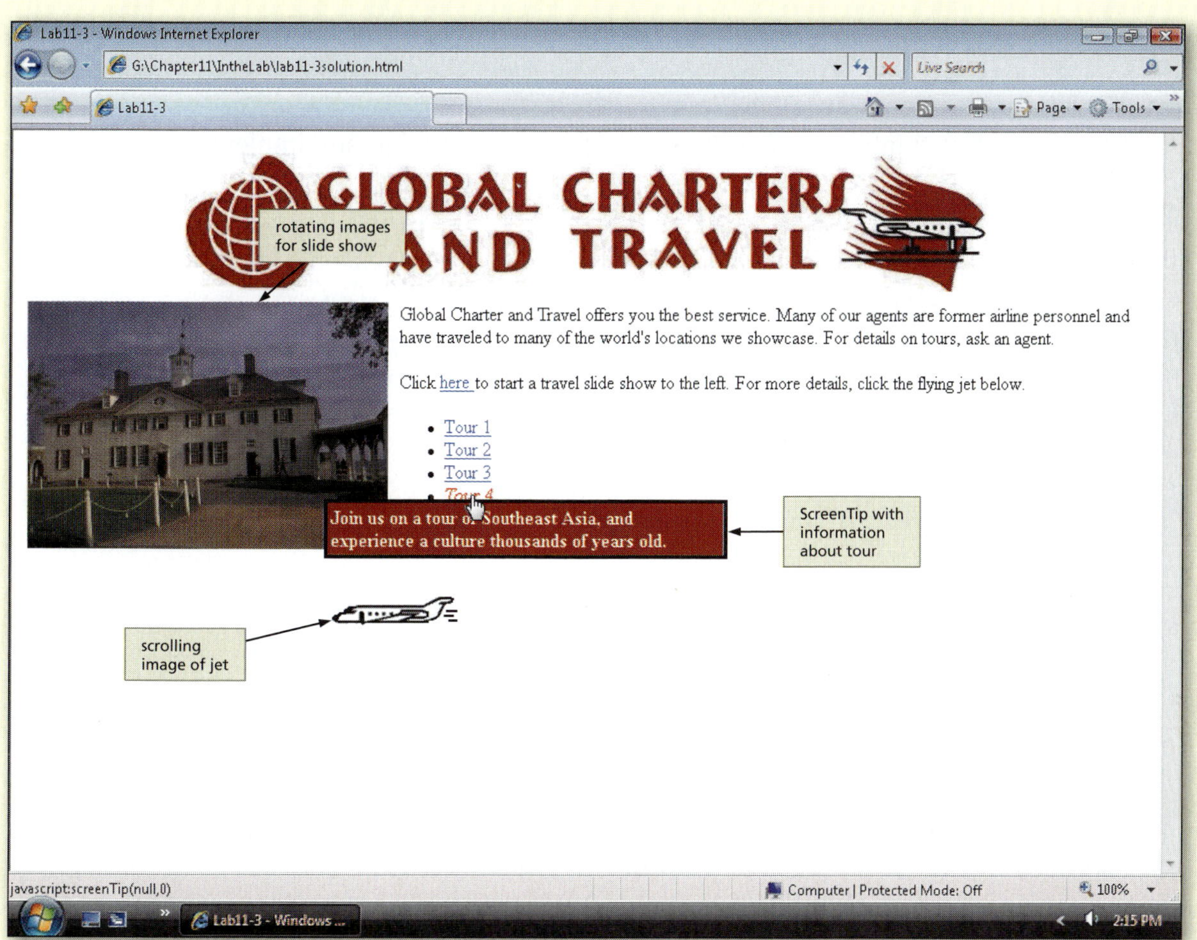

Figure 11–47

Instructions: Perform the following steps:

1. Start Notepad and open the lab11-3.html file. Save immediately as lab11-3solution.html.
2. Using the techniques learned in this chapter, write the JavaScript code to use the images provided in a rotating slide show, show ScreenTips for each of the tours, and use the jet image as a scrolling image from right to left.
3. The four tours are for the Washington D.C. area, the Rocky Mountains, ancient castles of Ireland, England, and Scotland, and exotic places in Southeast Asia. Search the Internet for brief descriptions to use in the ScreenTips for each area.
4. Add the following id selectors to the style sheet for ScreenTips: ieImg1, Tour1, Tour2, Tour3, Tour4. Add the class selector TipText. Use the same attributes as in the chapter.
5. Save the completed HTML file and test it using your browser. If an error occurs, check your code, save and test again.
6. Submit the completed HTML file and Web page in the format specified by your instructor.

STUDENT ASSIGNMENTS

Cases and Places

Apply your creative thinking and problem solving skills to design and implement a solution.

• Easier •• More Difficult

• 1: Expanding the Chapter Web Page

The collegefinancialaid.html file in the Chapter11\CasesPlaces folder of the Data Files for Students is the same as the collegefinancialaid.html file in the Chapter11\ChapterFiles folder. The file has four bullet items: Student loans, Scholarships, Grants, and Fee Remissions. Using the techniques discussed in this chapter add JavaScript to add a pop-up ScreenTip for each item. Use the following text for the pop-up ScreenTips.

Student Loans: Many various student loans are available. See a financial advisor or your local bank on which options are best for you.
Scholarships: Scholarships can be awarded for academic achievement, athletics, or musical ability. The money does not need to be repaid or earned through employment.
Grants: Grants are a form of financial aid that do not need to be repaid or earned through employment. To be awarded a grant, a student must demonstrate need and make reasonable academic progress.
Fee Remission: Certain part-time and all full-time employment within the college provides a fee remission for students. See the campus HR Department for information on jobs and benefits.

In addition, search the Internet and find the Web site for the FAFSA application. Add the <a href> anchor tag for a link on the word, FAFSA, to open as a pop-up window. Save as case11-1collegefinancialsolution.html. Modify the scrolling menu from the chapter file you created to link to this new file name.

•• 2: Create the Paw Prints Pet Supplies Web Page

As a summer intern for Paw Prints Pet Supplies you have been asked to create a Web page for the store. The owner, Waylon Lavis, wants to have a rotating set of pictures of various animals, from cats and dogs, to parrots, fish, and rodents. In addition, for each of the pet types, he would like to have a pop-up ScreenTip with some information about that type of pet. Use the images supplied in the Chapter11\CasesPlaces folder of the Data Files for Students to make the rotating slide show and the ScreenTip text to create the pop-up ScreenTips. ScreenTip text appears in the case11-2screentiptext .txt file.

•• 3: Create Kelly's Home Cookin' Catering Service Web Site

Your older sister, Kelly, has started a catering service. She asks you to create a Web site to showcase her abilities. On her home page (case11-3.html) she would like a menu that scrolls vertically as users scroll down the page. Her main menu lists Weddings, Event Catering, Corporate Meetings, and Picnics.

The Wedding page should contain a picture (case11-3food-weddingcake.jpg) of a wedding cake scrolling across the bottom. The picture should stop if the mouse is placed over it and should restart when the mouse is moved off the scrolling photo.

The events page should use a mouseover event handler to change the original breakfast image (case11-3food9.jpg) to a new breakfast image (case11-3food8.jpg) when the mouse pointer is over the word breakfast. When the mouse is placed over the word dinners, a new dinner image (case11-3food21 .jpg) should display. When the mouse is moved off either link the original images should display.

The Corporate Web page should have rotating images and a ScreenTip for the Wine and Cheese link. The images for the rotating images are case11-3food-dinner1.jpg, case11-3food-dinner2.jpg, case11-3food13.jpg, and case11-3food11.jpg. The text for the ScreenTip is "We have an assortment of imported wine and cheeses, please ask for list and prices."

The last Web page, Picnics, also has a rotating image. The images are case11-3food3.jpg, case11-3food12.jpg, case11-3food-hotdog.jpg, and case11-3food-grill.jpg.

• • 4: Create a Family Event Web Page

Make It Personal

Using a family event like a wedding, christening, bar mitzvah, or reunion, create one or more Web pages that detail events. Create at least one rotating image slide show with at least five photos from the event. Also, list the names of people being honored at the event. For each name, create a pop-up ScreenTip with a short comment about that person. The comment can be something from their life, or something that was amusing that happened at the family event.

• • 5: Creating Student Clubs and Organization Web Pages

Working Together

At your school there are many student clubs and organizations that have or sponsor different events. Depending on the number of members in your team, each one should take one club and meet with them. Ask permission to make a Web page about their group. Collect some information, photos, or other images they may have. Construct a home page that showcases the various clubs using a scrolling vertical menu to link to the other club Web pages each member created. Each team member's Web page should have a rotating slide show of images, and at least one pop-up ScreenTip highlighting some feature of the club.

12 Creating and Using XML Documents

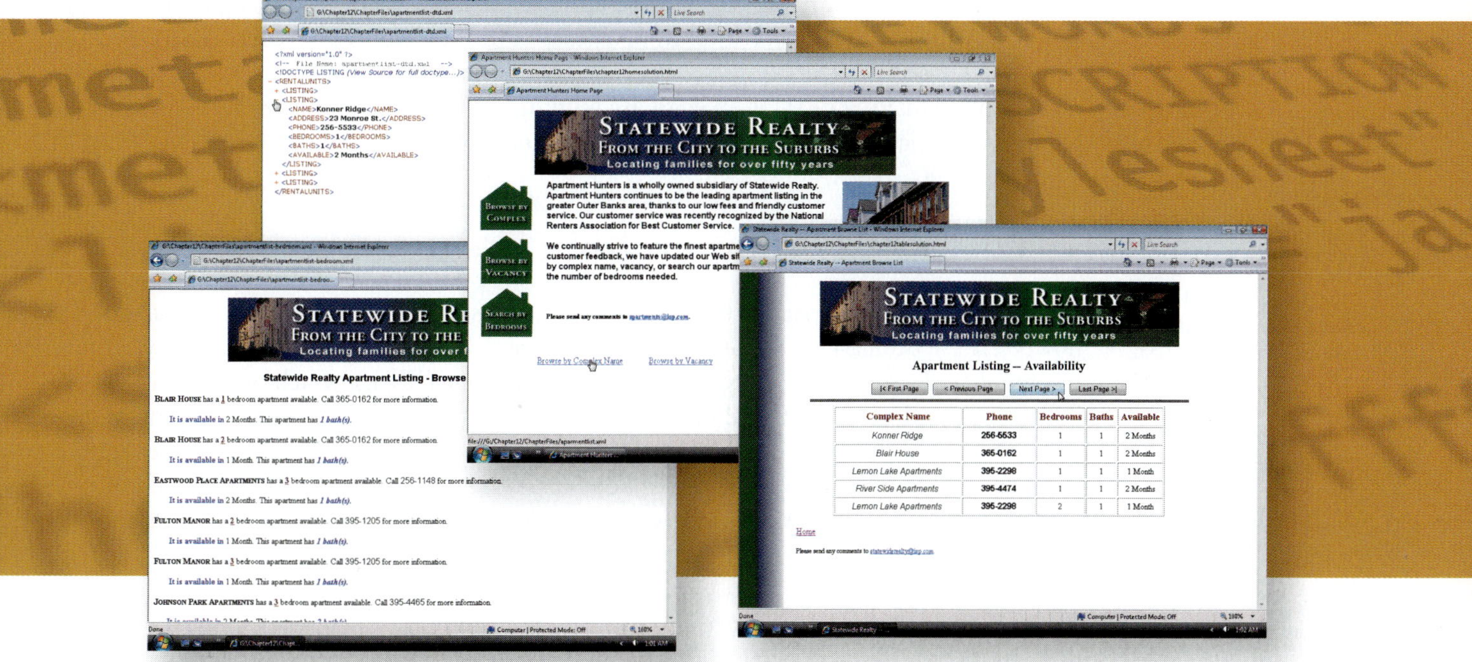

Objectives

You will have mastered the material in this chapter when you can:

- Describe an XML document, and rules for a well-formed and valid XML document
- Define the purpose of processing instructions, document prolog, and document instance
- Describe the purpose of a Document Type Definition (DTD)
- Create and bind CSS and XSL style sheet files to an XML document
- Discuss the uses of an XML data island
- Discuss the built-in table element methods for displaying an XML document in a table
- Create a JavaScript user-defined function to search an XML document

12 Creating and Using XML Documents

Introduction

In Chapter 4, you created a Web site using tables to present information in rows and columns. In this chapter, you learn to add functionality and interactivity to tables and to extend the capabilities of Web pages using XML. This chapter illustrates how to create and use XML documents for use as stand-alone Web pages, formatted using a style sheet, or bound with HTML Web pages. In particular, in this chapter you create an XML document that is used as a database or data island. A **data island** is a set of data elements separate from the main HTML Web page. By binding the XML data to an HTML Web page, the HTML objects can be manipulated to enhance usability.

BTW

XML

Like HTML, XML is a subset of Standard Generalized Markup Language (SGML). SGML gives developers the ability to create their own elements. XML inherits this ability from SGML. XML does not replace HTML, but it provides a means to extend and enhance the use and appearance of a document. Developers can create XML documents manually using any editor, or generate an XML document using existing tables in a Microsoft SQL Server or Microsoft Access database, and then bind them to their Web pages.

Project — Creating an XML Document

Statewide Realty's Web page with its apartment listings has been a great success. Customers, however, have been asking for other ways to browse or search the apartment offerings. You recently have learned about Extensible Markup Language (XML), which offers some flexibility not found with traditional HTML pages. You suggest the Web site offer clients various ways to view the apartment listings. The ways include using the Extensible Stylesheet Language (XSL) to transform the XML document into a readable, useful Web page to browse the apartment offerings in order by complex name, by the number of months until the apartment will be vacant, or to search by the number of bedrooms.

The Web pages shown in Figure 12–1 demonstrate three different applications of the same XML document. Figure 12–1a shows the Statewide Realty Web home page containing three links: one link opens an XML Web page (Figure 12–1b) displaying a list of all the available apartments formatted by an XSL style sheet in complex name order. The next link (Figure 12–1c) displays in an HTML table an XML document listing the number of months until the apartment is available. The last link (Figure 12–1d) displays a Web page to search for apartments based on the number of bedrooms.

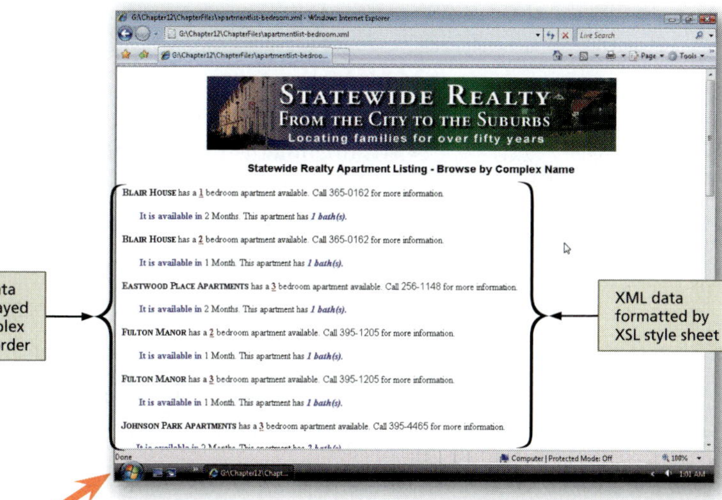
XML data is displayed in complex name order
XML data formatted by XSL style sheet
Statewide Realty Apartment Listing - Browse by Complex Name

(b) Statewide Realty – Browse by Complex Name.

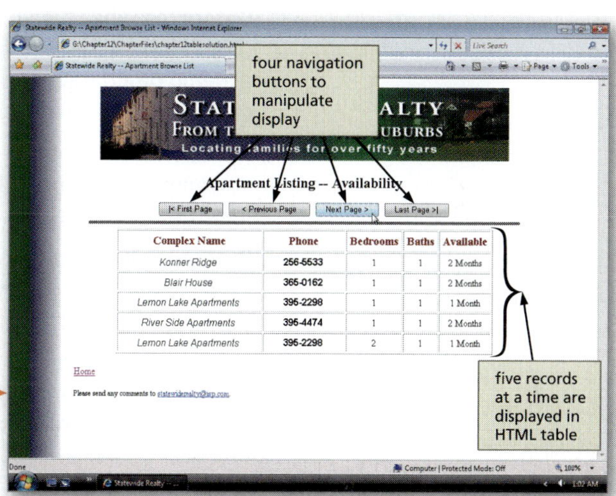
four navigation buttons to manipulate display
five records at a time are displayed in HTML table

(c) Statewide Realty – Browse by Vacancy.

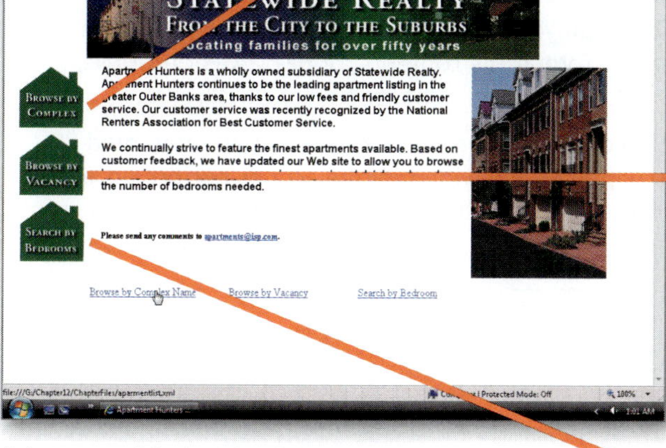

(a) Statewide Realty home page.

enter number of bedrooms desired in search
click Search button to find apartment listings
output area is displayed with apartment information
click Home link to return to Statewide Realty home page

(d) Statewide Realty – Search by Number of Bedrooms.

Figure 12–1

Overview

As you read through this chapter, you will learn how to create, format, and display XML documents using CSS and XSL style sheets, and how to create well-formed and valid XML documents. You will learn how to display an XML document in a Web page as shown in Figure 12–1 on the previous page by performing these general tasks:

- Create an XSL style sheet to format the output of an XML document
- Bind an XSL style sheet to an XML document
- Bind an XML document to an HTML document
- Create an HTML Web page, using a JavaScript function to search for items in an XML document

Plan Ahead

General Project Guidelines

When creating an XML document you should follow these general guidelines:

1. **Determine what type of XML document you are going to create.** An XML document should follow the form of the desired output. If you are creating a text document, like a memo or a database of inventory items, the XML document should conform to the general form of that type of document.
2. **Determine the contents of the document.** The contents may be created from an existing document or database. Many applications can create XML documents automatically, or it may have to be created manually.
3. **Determine how the document will be displayed.** If the document will be displayed on a Web page, you must think about how to format the contents for display. For example, the document may be formatted with CSS or XSL style sheets.

When necessary, more specific details concerning the above guidelines are presented at appropriate points in the chapter. The chapter also will identify the actions performed and decisions made regarding these guidelines during the creation of the Web pages shown in Figure 12–1 on page HTML 549.

Designing XML Documents

The **Extensible Markup Language (XML)** uses tags to describe the structure of a document and its content, not just the format for display as with an HTML document. XML provides a flexible way for organizations to share common data and to integrate databases with Web pages.

Formatting XML documents for display on a Web page requires binding or linking a style sheet to the XML document, which formats the elements of the XML document as they appear in a browser. An XML document can be formatted with a Cascading Style Sheet (CSS) or an Extensible Stylesheet Language (XSL) style sheet. **Extensible Stylesheet Language (XSL)** is used to create style sheets for formatting structured XML data. XSL style sheets provide more flexibility and control over XML documents than CSS. While CSS can format individual XML elements, XSL can control the order of elements or add other information.

The main XML document created in this chapter is an apartment listing available at Statewide Realty, and will serve as a database (or data island) formatted by XSL or bound to an HTML Web page for display in a table or a search using JavaScript.

BTW

XML as a Data Island
A data island has the capability of embedding XML documents in HTML pages. The process uses data source object technology. The disadvantage to using an XML data island is that the XML documents are static. Client-side processing does not allow real-time updates to the XML document on the server.

XML Standards

As you learned in Chapter 1, the World Wide Web Consortium (W3C) oversees and develops standards for Web development. To help ensure consistency among the discipline-specific tags created in XML, the W3C has defined a set of standards, or goals, for XML, shown in Table 12–1. The goals provide a framework for all future XML development and XML-related discipline-specific markup languages.

Table 12–1 Design Goals for XML

1.	XML shall be straightforwardly usable over the Internet.
2.	XML shall support a wide variety of applications.
3.	XML shall be compatible with SGML.
4.	It shall be easy to write programs, which process XML documents.
5.	The number of optional features in XML is to be kept to the absolute minimum, ideally zero.
6.	XML documents should be human-legible and reasonably clear.
7.	The XML design should be prepared quickly.
8.	The design of XML shall be formal and concise.
9.	XML documents shall be easy to create.
10.	Terseness in XML markup is of minimal importance.

Using XML documents as databases is just one of the many ways Web developers use XML. The creation and use of these databases is the central focus of this chapter. As the W3C group continues to develop XML standards, businesses and organizations find numerous new uses for XML. An important goal of XML is to allow the creation of discipline-specific markup language tags. Table 12–2 lists several of these uses and extended markup languages created using XML.

BTW

Real-World Uses of XML
XML is not limited to use in Web databases. There are over a hundred industries using some form of XML, ranging from accounting and finance to weather.

Table 12–2 Real-World Uses of XML

Use	Description of Extended Markup Languages
Define databases	Use labels and fields to store and display data in a variety of ways
Give structure to documents	Provide structure to elements in books and plays, such as indexes or scene directions
Define channels	Push Web pages to subscribers using Channel Definition Format (CDF)
Exchange financial information	Exchange information among various applications using Open Financial Exchange (OFX)
Store voice scripts	Store voice mail messages or regular daily messages
Store tracking information	Allow customers to track shipments and packages; used by courier services such as FedEx
Format mathematical formulas	Format math and science content markup with MathML
Encode weather reports	Define annotations for weather reports using Weather Observation Markup Format (OMF)
Define standard document format for businesses	Allow business partners to share a standard library of XML business documents, such as purchase orders and invoices; identify the documents exchanged in a particular context using Universal Business Language (UBL)
Create HTML pages that are valid XML	Transition to XHTML following XML standards and tools

BTW

The XML Parser

The XML parser is necessary to create, read, update, or manipulate an XML document. Most modern Web browsers contain various parsers for scripting languages and XML.

Syntax Rules

XML documents must be well-formed to be processed by an application. For an XML document to be **well-formed**, it must adhere to the basic syntax rules for XML, as listed in Table 12–3. Before an XML document is displayed in an application, the document must be parsed. A **parser** is an XML processor that verifies the document follows the syntax rules for a well-formed document and converts the document into a tree of elements. Modern Web browsers are XML parsers. For more information on XML syntax, see the XML Quick Reference in Appendix F.

Table 12–3 XML Syntax Rules

Rule	Comment	Example
XML is case-sensitive.	Use any case — uppercase, lowercase, or mixed — but be consistent.	Correct: <Root></Root> <root></root> <ROOT></ROOT> Incorrect: <Root></ROOT>
All tags must have a closing tag.	All tags, including empty tags, must have a closing tag. Empty tags are allowed a special form. Empty tags have no content, such as and <img> tags.	<p>This is a paragraph</p> <name>Susan</name>
All documents must have a root element.	Include the root or start tag that begins a document.	<root> <child></child> </root>
Elements must be nested.	Elements cannot stand alone unless they are the only root element.	<club> <name>Spanish</name> </club>
Attribute values must be enclosed in quotation marks.	Use single or double quotation marks, but be consistent.	<Image picture="icon.jpg" />
With XML, white space is preserved.	Spaces between words within tags are preserved.	No need for ASCII characters ( ) to add spaces

This chapter shows how to create well-formed documents manually. Figure 12–2a shows a simple XML document created in Notepad. When displayed in or parsed by a browser or application (Figure 12–2b), this XML document may have little meaning to a user. Linking the XML document to a style sheet such as a Cascading Style Sheet (Figure 12–2c) enables the browser to display the document in a more readable format (Figure 12–2d).

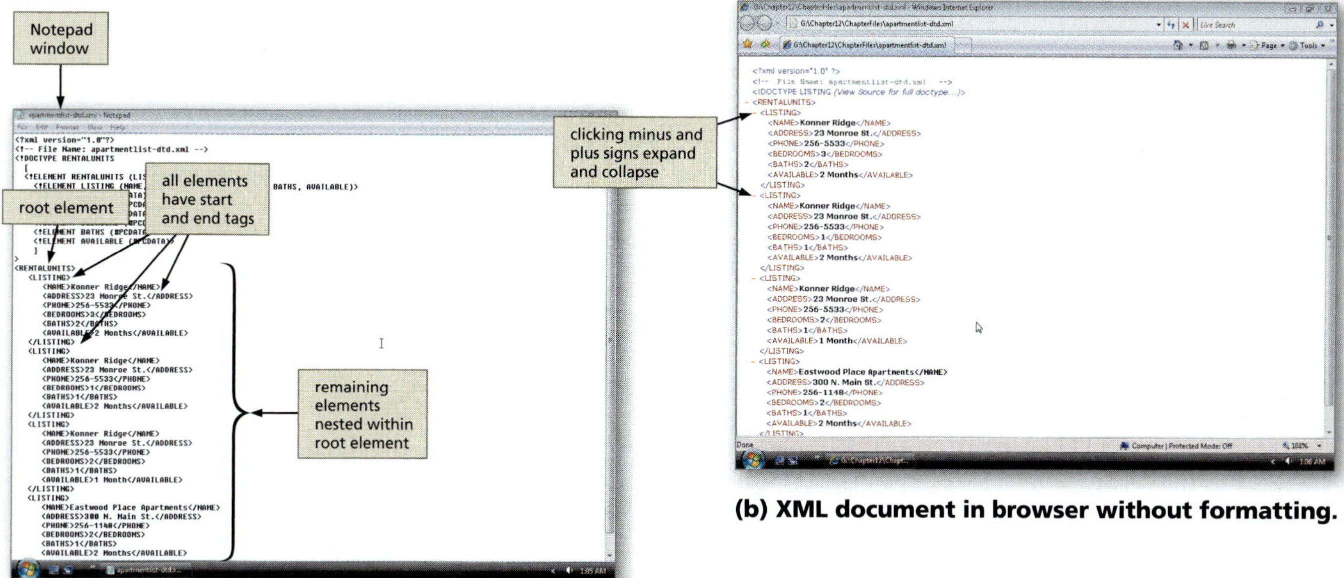
Notepad window
root element
all elements have start and end tags
remaining elements nested within root element
clicking minus and plus signs expand and collapse

(b) XML document in browser without formatting.

(a) Contents of XML document.

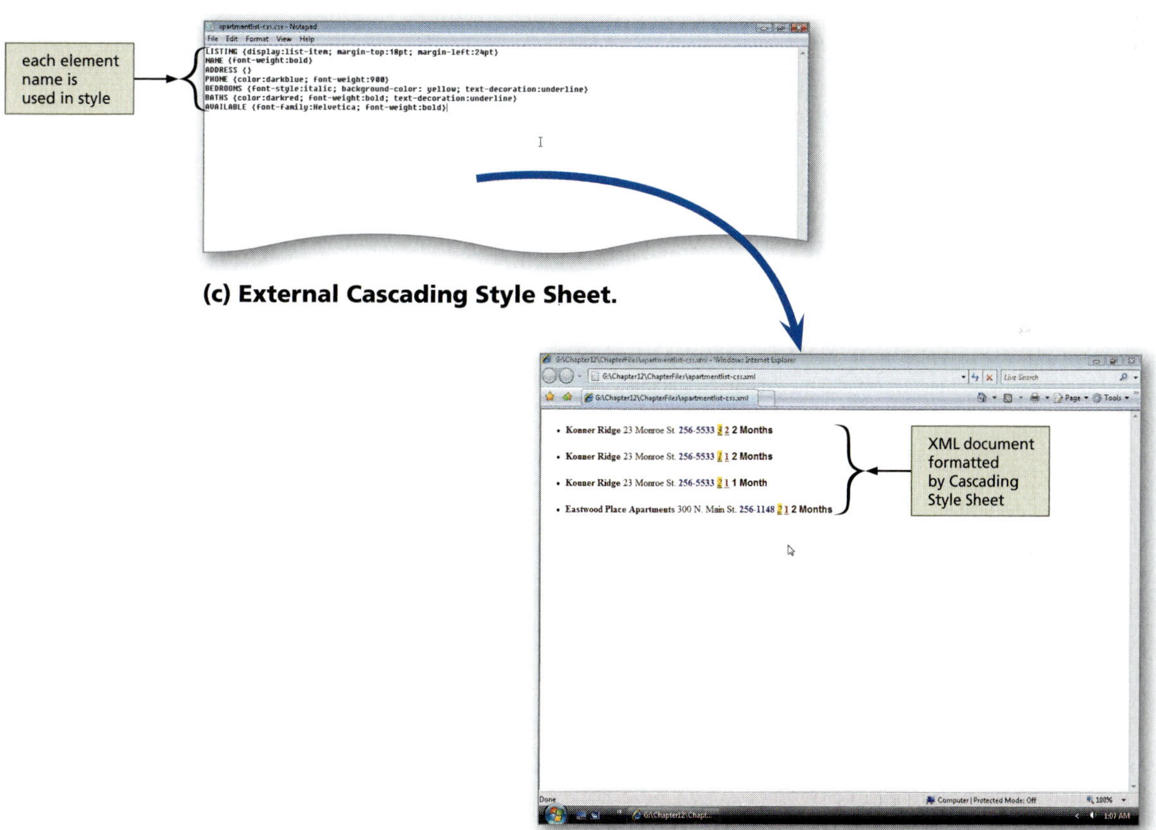
each element name is used in style
XML document formatted by Cascading Style Sheet

(c) External Cascading Style Sheet.

(d) XML document formatted by CSS in browser.

Figure 12–2

Plan Ahead

Creating a well-formed XML document.
The following tasks are necessary to create a well-formed XML document, as described in the next section:

1. Create the prolog.
2. Identify the tags to describe the document content and create the Document Type Definition (DTD).
3. Create the document instances.

BTW

The XML Prolog
Every XML document must have a prolog. The prolog must contain at least one line — a declaration statement — identifying the document as an XML document: <?xml version="1.0"?>.

Creating a Well-Formed XML Document

A well-formed XML document consists of two main parts: the prolog, and the document instance or elements (Figure 12–3). The **prolog** contains the processing instruction statements, any additional comments necessary to provide information about the document's content and structure, and the optional Document Type Definition (DTD) statements. The **document instance** contains the main content or elements of the XML document.

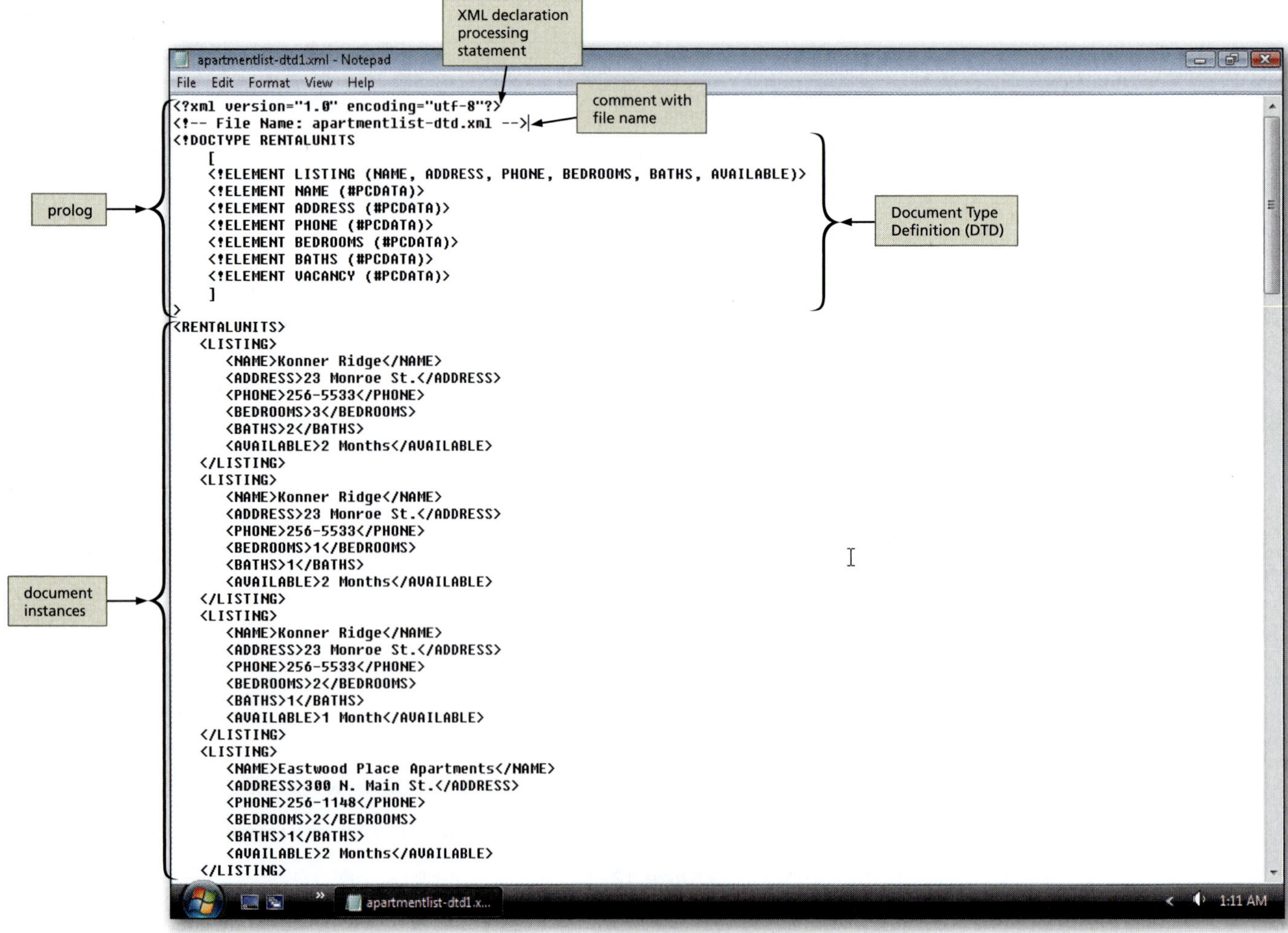

Figure 12–3

The prolog may contain processing instruction statements, declaration statements, or comments. A **processing instruction** is one or more instructions passed to the application using the XML document. The **XML declaration** is a processing instruction statement identifying the version of XML used in the document. The prolog shown in Figure 12–3 contains an XML declaration, a processing instruction on line 1, a comment on line 2 identifying the file, and a document type declaration on line 3.

A **document type declaration** is a processing instruction that tells the processor where to locate the Document Type Definition. A **Document Type Definition (DTD)** defines the elements and attributes in an XML document. A DTD also defines the order in which the elements and attributes appear. The DTD can be embedded within a document type declaration, as shown in Figure 12–3, or linked as an external document. Using a DTD allows the developer to confirm that an XML document is **valid**, meaning it conforms to the specified structure in the DTD.

The document instance contains the main content or elements of the XML document and provides a logical structure for the document. An **instance** is an occurrence of XML elements. The XML document must include at least one instance, or occurrence, of an element. The main element is the **root element** and may contain one or more sub- or child elements. This parent-child relationship between elements gives XML its hierarchical, tree-like structure, as shown in Figure 12–4.

BTW

Well-Formed Documents

A well-formed document meets certain criteria: the document must have at least one root element, and it must nest child elements in the root; every tag must have a beginning and closing tag, including empty tags; and all attribute values must be enclosed in quotation marks, either single or double, but they must be consistent.

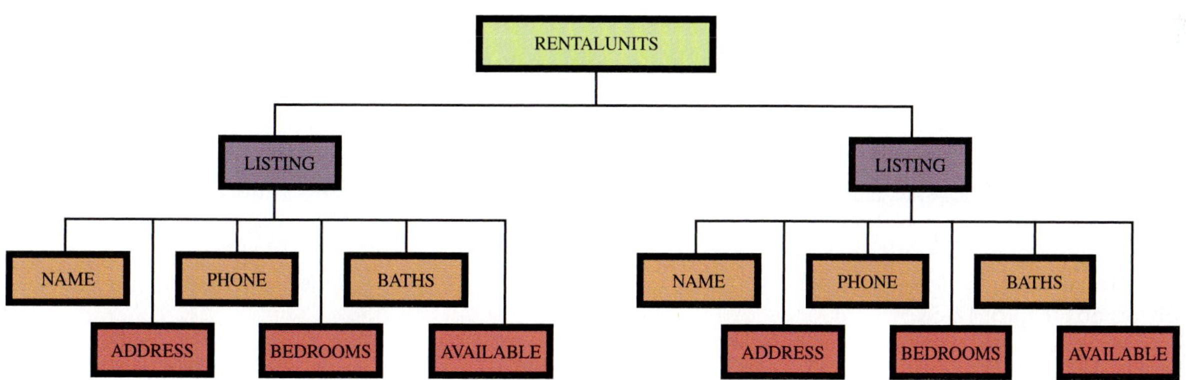

Figure 12–4

BTW

DTD Case Sensitivity

Like other items in XML, the DTD is case sensitive. In particular, key words such as DOCTYPE, ELEMENT, ENTITY, and PCDATA must be in upper case. The element items in the DTD must be the same case as the element item tags.

To Start Notepad and Create a New XML Document

The following step illustrates how to use Notepad to create a new XML document.

- Start Notepad, and, if necessary, maximize the Notepad window. If the Word Wrap feature is not enabled, click Format on the menu bar and then click Word Wrap to enable it.
- With the USB drive plugged into your computer, click File on the menu bar and then click Save As on the File menu.
- If necessary, navigate to the Chapter12\ChapterFiles folder on UDISK (G:).
- Type `apartmentlist-dtd.xml` in the File name text box.
- Click the Save button in the Save As dialog box (Figure 12–5).

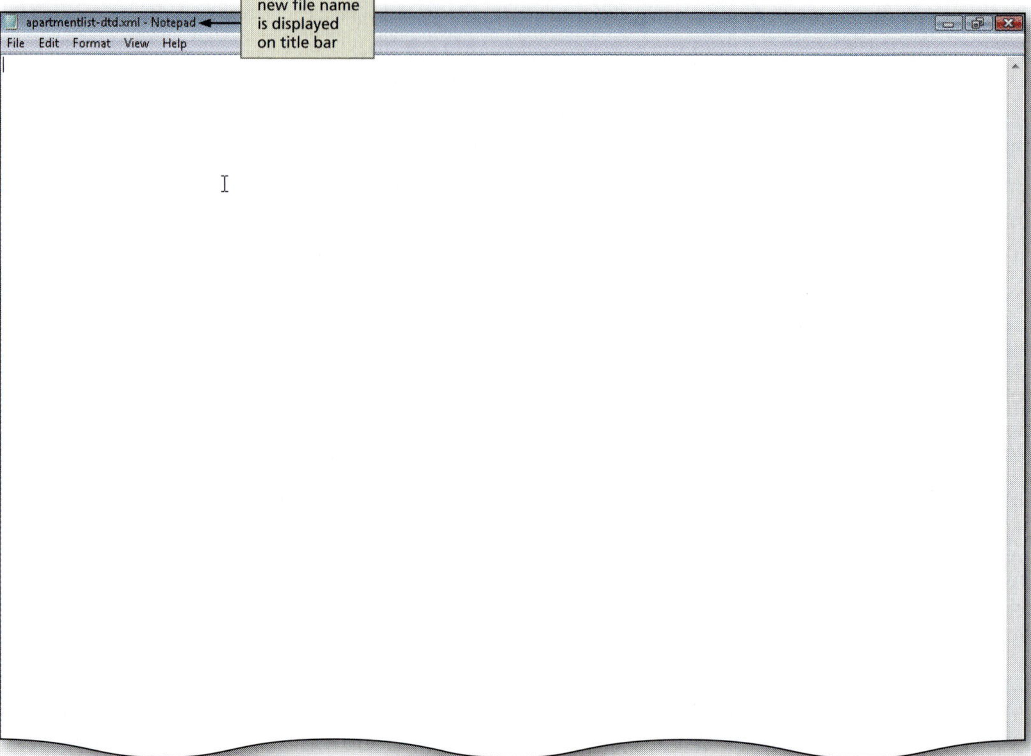

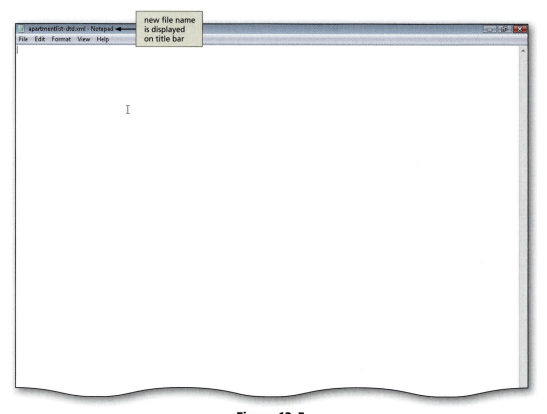

Figure 12–5

> **BTW**
> **Valid XML Documents and DTD**
> No specific XML validation exists, but you can submit an XML document to the standard HTML validation at w3.org. A document without a DTD will validate as well-formed. A character-set warning may display, but this is a warning and not an indication of an invalid XML file.

Creating the Prolog in an XML Document

The first statement in an XML prolog is the XML declaration. As previously discussed, the **XML declaration** is a processing instruction in the prolog that provides additional information to the application that will process the XML document. Although optional, the first processing instruction in most XML document prologs is the XML declaration. Table 12–4 shows the general form of a processing instruction.

Table 12–4 General Form of a Processing Instruction

General form:	<?target attribute1="value" attribute2="value"?>
Comment:	The ? identifies this as a processing instruction. The target is the name of the application. The attributes and values tell the processor how to handle the statement. The values assigned to the attributes can be enclosed in single or double quotation marks, as long as they are consistent.
Examples:	<?xml?> <?xml version="1.0"?> <?xml version="1.0" standalone="yes"?> <?xml version="1.0" encoding="UTF-8"?>

The prolog also can contain comments that provide a user or developer with information about the document. XML comments are very similar in form to HTML comments. As with HTML comments, the browser or parser ignores the XML comments. Table 12–5 discusses the general form of an XML comment.

Table 12–5 General Form of a Comment

General form:	<!- - comment statements -->
Comment:	Comments are optional and can be placed anywhere between, but not within, a tag. Comments must begin with the left angle bracket (<), an exclamation point (!), and double hyphens (--). The comment must terminate with the double hyphens (--) and the right angle bracket (>).
Valid example:	<!- - File Name: apartmentlist.xml - -> <Tag><!- - Comment about tag --></Tag>
Invalid example:	<Tag <!- - This tag is new -->>Data</Tag>

BTW

Generic Identifier

An element consists of tags based on names that a developer provides or defines. The name that a developer provides for the tags is called the **generic identifier (GI)**. When choosing generic identifiers to name document elements, a developer must follow two simple rules: 1) The name must begin with a letter or underscore (_) and may contain letters, numbers, periods, hyphens, or underscores, and 2) A prefix of XML or the use of colons is reserved for future anticipated standardization.

As explained, the prolog also can contain a document type declaration that tells the processor where to locate the DTD. The DTD can be an external file or embedded within the XML document. The DTD has two elements that indicate a relationship between the parent (RENTALUNITS) and the child (LISTING). Table 12–6 shows the general form of a document type declaration identifying an embedded DTD.

Table 12–6 General Form of a Document Type Declaration and an Embedded Document Type Definition

General form:	<!DOCTYPE Name [<!ELEMENT Parent Definition (Child Definition * | + | ?)> <!ELEMENT Child Definition (child element list) <!ELEMENT Child element Definition ANY|(#PCDATA)>] >
Comment:	!DOCTYPE is a reserved word that indicates the start of a document type declaration. Name is any valid name of an element and defines the name of the embedded DTD. The square bracket on line 2 indicates the beginning of the DTD. !ELEMENT is a reserved word that defines the type of elements in the document. The child definition qualifiers are an asterisk (*), a plus sign (+), or a question mark (?). The asterisk means zero to many, the plus sign means one to many, and the question mark means zero or one only. Definition is one or more valid element definitions. ANY indicates that any type of data may be associated with the element, (#PCDATA) indicates that the element contains parsed character data, which is text data. The square bracket in line 6 ends the DTD, and the right angle bracket on line 7 ends the document type declaration.
Example:	<!DOCTYPE RENTALUNITS [<!ELEMENT RENTALUNITS (LISTING*)> <!ELEMENT LISTING (NAME, ADDRESS, PHONE, BEDROOMS, BATHS, AVAILABLE)> <!ELEMENT NAME (#PCDATA)> <!ELEMENT ADDRESS (#PCDATA)> <!ELEMENT PHONE (#PCDATA)> <!ELEMENT BEDROOMS (#PCDATA)> <!ELEMENT BATHS (#PCDATA)> <!ELEMENT AVAILABLE (#PCDATA)>] >

BTW

Document Type Declarations

XML document type declarations (DTD) contain element types, attributes, entities, and notations, either internally or externally, that provide a structure for a document's schema.

In the example in Table 12–6 on the previous page, the first !ELEMENT definition contains the root element, RENTALUNITS, and the child element, LISTING. The asterisk indicates a zero to many relationship between RENTALUNITS and LISTING. The remaining six !ELEMENT definitions indicate that the child elements will contain parsed character data, or text: NAME, ADDRESS, PHONE, BEDROOMS, BATHS, AVAILABLE. These elements will be the tags for the XML document. Table 12–7 shows the prolog for the XML document, apartmentlist-dtd.xml.

Table 12–7 Code for Inserting the Prolog

Line	Code
1	<?xml version="1.0"?>
2	<!-- File Name: apartmentlist-dtd.xml -->
3	<!DOCTYPE RENTALUNITS
4	[
5	<!ELEMENT RENTALUNITS (LISTING*)>
6	<!ELEMENT LISTING (NAME, ADDRESS, PHONE, BEDROOMS, BATHS, AVAILABLE)>
7	<!ELEMENT NAME (#PCDATA)>
8	<!ELEMENT ADDRESS (#PCDATA)>
9	<!ELEMENT PHONE (#PCDATA)>
10	<!ELEMENT BEDROOMS (#PCDATA)>
11	<!ELEMENT BATHS (#PCDATA)>
12	<!ELEMENT AVAILABLE (#PCDATA)>
13	]
14	>

Line 1 is the XML declaration that identifies this as an XML document using XML version 1.0. Line 2 is a comment stating the name of the XML file. Line 3 begins the document type declaration, with <!DOCTYPE as the start tag and the root element, RENTALUNITS, as the name of the embedded DTD. Line 4 begins the DTD listing of ELEMENTS. Lines 5 through 12 are the actual DTD, listing the root element RENTALUNITS, the element LISTING, and the six child elements that belong to LISTING. The #PCDATA listed after each of the six child elements indicates that the child elements will contain parsed character data, or text. The] on line 13 ends the Document Type Definition, and the > on line 14 ends the document type declaration.

To Enter the Prolog in an XML Document

The following step shows how to enter the prolog for the XML document, apartmentlist-dtd.xml.

- Click line 1.
- Enter the XML code shown in Table 12–7 to create the prolog and press the ENTER key (Figure 12–6).

Q&A What is the purpose of the DTD?

The purpose of a DTD is to ensure that data in the XML document is valid. A valid XML document is one that adheres to the rules outlined in the DTD. If an XML document is not valid, the XML parser flags any errors where the XML document does not conform to the DTD.

Q&A Will an XML document be displayed if it is not valid?

Depending on how it is used, a Web browser or application parser may display part of the document. Some errors, though, entirely prevent the document being displayed.

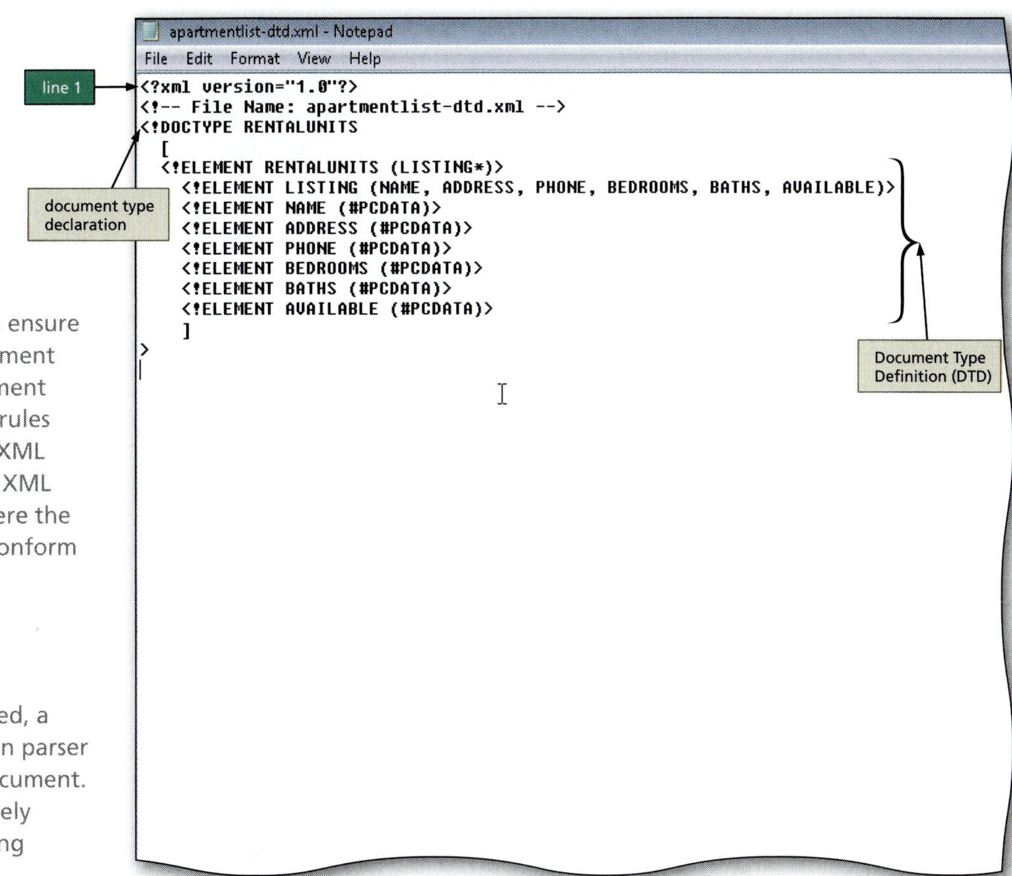


```
<?xml version="1.0"?>
<!-- File Name: apartmentlist-dtd.xml -->
<!DOCTYPE RENTALUNITS
 [
 <!ELEMENT RENTALUNITS (LISTING*)>
   <!ELEMENT LISTING (NAME, ADDRESS, PHONE, BEDROOMS, BATHS, AVAILABLE)>
   <!ELEMENT NAME (#PCDATA)>
   <!ELEMENT ADDRESS (#PCDATA)>
   <!ELEMENT PHONE (#PCDATA)>
   <!ELEMENT BEDROOMS (#PCDATA)>
   <!ELEMENT BATHS (#PCDATA)>
   <!ELEMENT AVAILABLE (#PCDATA)>
   ]
>
```

Figure 12–6

Plan Ahead

Creating document instances.

The main data of an XML document is the document instance. The document instance is all the components of the document, whether it is free-form text or a database. When creating the document instance a designer should complete the following tasks:

- Determine the names of identifiers or tags that describe document elements
- Determine if namespaces are necessary if duplicate identifier names are used
- Design the relation or logical schema with attributes

Creating the Document Instance in an XML Document

The second part of an XML document is the document instance, or elements. The document instance section contains the document elements and actual content or data. There must be one root element with all other elements nested inside the root. This format creates a hierarchical, tree-like structure. This structure defines the XML document as a well-formed document. Table 12–8 shows the general form of an element tag.

Table 12–8 General Form of an Element Tag

General form:	<element start tag>element contents</element end tag>
Comment:	XML documents require start and end element tags. The element tag name must be a valid name. The tag describes the type of content represented by the element (for example, Title, Year). Start and end tags must match exactly in spelling and case. The element contents or data are the text entered between the tags.
Examples:	<NAME>Konner Ridge</NAME> <ADDRESS>23 Monroe St.</ADDRESS> <PHONE>256-5533</PHONE>

Although colons cannot be used in element names, colons can be used to denote or declare a namespace. A **namespace** is a unique identifier or prefix used to identify tags that have the same name. The namespace prefix is associated with a Uniform Resource Identifier (URI) or a Uniform Resource Locator (URL). For example, two companies using the same element name tag, <Cost>, may need to identify their tags with a namespace so the browser does not confuse the data. Namespaces allow for the sharing of XML elements across documents and help eliminate possible confusion when two or more XML documents use the same element names.

Database analysts refer to a collection of data as a **relation**. To represent the attributes or fields in a relation, database analysts use a simple notation, called a schema. A database **schema** is a logical design to show relationships, and is written as the relation name followed by a list of attributes or fields in parentheses, in the form:

```
Relation_Name (attribute1, attribute2..., attributen)
```

The Relation_Name indicates the name of the collection of data, and *n* represents the total number of attributes. Following this notation, the schema for the XML document, apartmentlist-dtd.xml, is LISTING (NAME, ADDRESS, PHONE, BEDROOMS, BATHS, AVAILABLE). LISTING is the name of the relation; the attributes within the parentheses describe things about the apartment listing. As shown in Table 12–9, NAME, ADDRESS, PHONE, BEDROOMS, BATHS, AVAILABLE are all child elements within the LISTING element. LISTING is a child element nested within the RENTALUNITS root element.

Table 12–9 Code for Inserting the Document Instance

Line	Code
15	`<RENTALUNITS>`
16	`   <LISTING>`
17	`      <NAME>Konner Ridge</NAME>`
18	`      <ADDRESS>23 Monroe St.</ADDRESS>`
19	`      <PHONE>256-5533</PHONE>`
20	`      <BEDROOMS>3</BEDROOMS>`
21	`      <BATHS>2</BATHS>`
22	`      <AVAILABLE>2 Months</AVAILABLE>`
23	`   </LISTING>`

Line 15 represents the root element of the XML document, with the start <RENTALUNITS> tag. Line 16 defines the <LISTING> element. Lines 17 through 22 are the data child elements of the <LISTING> element, with one instance for each occurrence of a data item. Line 23 is the </LISTING> element end tag. If this completed the data, line 24 would be the location of the end tag </RENTALUNITS>.

To complete the document instance, the remaining elements for each apartment listing record in the apartment list are entered using the same format, as shown in Table 12–10.

Table 12–10 Code for Completing the Document Instance

Line	Code
24	<LISTING>
25	<NAME>Konner Ridge</NAME>
26	<ADDRESS>23 Monroe St.</ADDRESS>
27	<PHONE>256-5533</PHONE>
28	<BEDROOMS>1</BEDROOMS>
29	<BATHS>1</BATHS>
30	<AVAILABLE>2 Months</AVAILABLE>
31	</LISTING>
32	<LISTING>
33	<NAME>Konner Ridge</NAME>
34	<ADDRESS>23 Monroe St.</ADDRESS>
35	<PHONE>256-5533</PHONE>
36	<BEDROOMS>2</BEDROOMS>
37	<BATHS>1</BATHS>
38	<AVAILABLE>1 Month</AVAILABLE>
39	</listing>
40	<LISTING>
41	<NAME>Eastwood Place Apartments</NAME>
42	<ADDRESS>300 N. Main St.</ADDRESS>
43	<PHONE>256-1148</PHONE>
44	<BEDROOMS>2</BEDROOMS>
45	<BATHS>1</BATHS>
46	<AVAILABLE>2 Months</AVAILABLE>
47	</LISTING>
48	</RENTALUNITS>

Lines 24 through 47 repeat elements for each apartment listing, indicating the NAME, ADDRESS, PHONE, BEDROOMS, BATHS, and AVAILABLE for each instance. The end </listing> tag on line 39 is entered in lowercase characters intentionally to demonstrate an error when the XML document is displayed in the browser. Line 48 is the end tag for the root element, RENTALUNITS.

To Start Entering the Document Instance in an XML Document

The following step shows how to start entering the document instance in the XML document, apartmentlist-dtd.xml.

1

- If necessary, click line 15.
- Enter the XML code shown in Table 12–9 on page HTML 560 to create the first document instance (Figure 12–7).

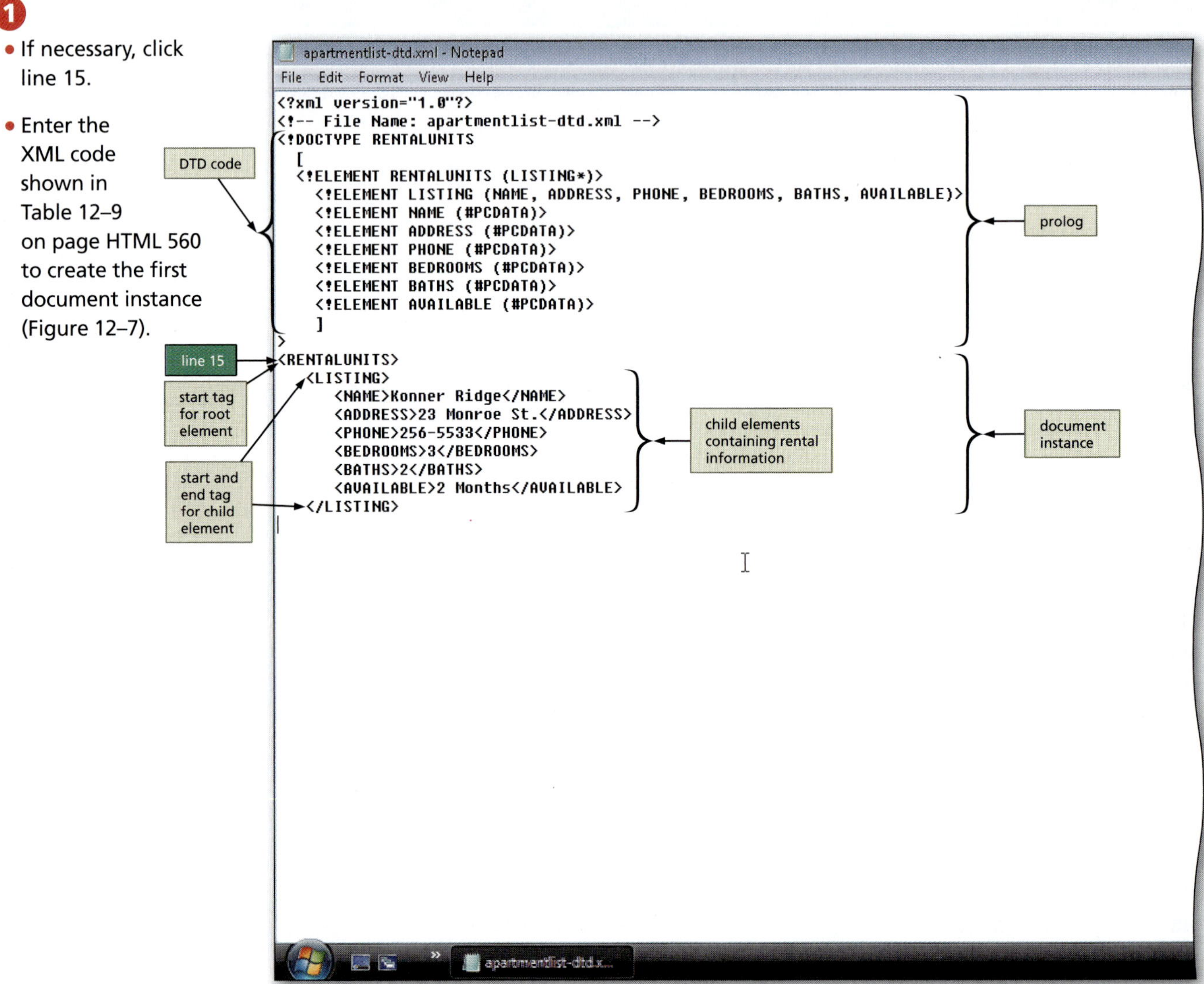

Figure 12–7

To Finish Entering the Document Instance in an XML Document

The following step illustrates how to enter the remainder of the document instance for the XML document, apartmentlist-dtd.xml.

- Click line 24.
- Enter the XML code shown in Table 12–10 on page HTML 561 with the error on line 39 to finish creating the document instance (Figure 12–8).

apartmentlist-dtd.xml - Notepad

File Edit Format View Help

```
<!DOCTYPE RENTALUNITS
  [
  <!ELEMENT RENTALUNITS (LISTING*)>
    <!ELEMENT LISTING (NAME, ADDRESS, PHONE, BEDROOMS, BATHS, AVAILABLE)>
    <!ELEMENT NAME (#PCDATA)>
    <!ELEMENT ADDRESS (#PCDATA)>
    <!ELEMENT PHONE (#PCDATA)>
    <!ELEMENT BEDROOMS (#PCDATA)>
    <!ELEMENT BATHS (#PCDATA)>
    <!ELEMENT AVAILABLE (#PCDATA)>
    ]
>
<RENTALUNITS>
   <LISTING>
      <NAME>Konner Ridge</NAME>
      <ADDRESS>23 Monroe St.</ADDRESS>
      <PHONE>256-5533</PHONE>
      <BEDROOMS>3</BEDROOMS>
      <BATHS>2</BATHS>
      <AVAILABLE>2 Months</AVAILABLE>
   </LISTING>
   <LISTING>
      <NAME>Konner Ridge</NAME>
      <ADDRESS>23 Monroe St.</ADDRESS>
      <PHONE>256-5533</PHONE>
      <BEDROOMS>1</BEDROOMS>
      <BATHS>1</BATHS>
      <AVAILABLE>2 Months</AVAILABLE>
   </LISTING>
   <LISTING>
      <NAME>Konner Ridge</NAME>
      <ADDRESS>23 Monroe St.</ADDRESS>
      <PHONE>256-5533</PHONE>
      <BEDROOMS>2</BEDROOMS>
      <BATHS>1</BATHS>
      <AVAILABLE>1 Month</AVAILABLE>
   </listing>
   <LISTING>
      <NAME>Eastwood Place Apartments</NAME>
      <ADDRESS>300 N. Main St.</ADDRESS>
      <PHONE>256-1148</PHONE>
      <BEDROOMS>2</BEDROOMS>
      <BATHS>1</BATHS>
      <AVAILABLE>2 Months</AVAILABLE>
   </LISTING>
</RENTALUNITS>
```


Figure 12–8

To Save and Test the XML Document

The following step shows how to save and test the XML document.

- With a USB drive plugged into your computer, click File on the menu bar and then click Save to save the completed apartmentlist-dtd.xml document.
- Start your browser. If necessary, click the Maximize button.
- Click the Address bar.
- Type `G:\Chapter12\ChapterFiles\apartmentlist-dtd.xml` and then press the ENTER key to display the completed document (Figure 12–9).

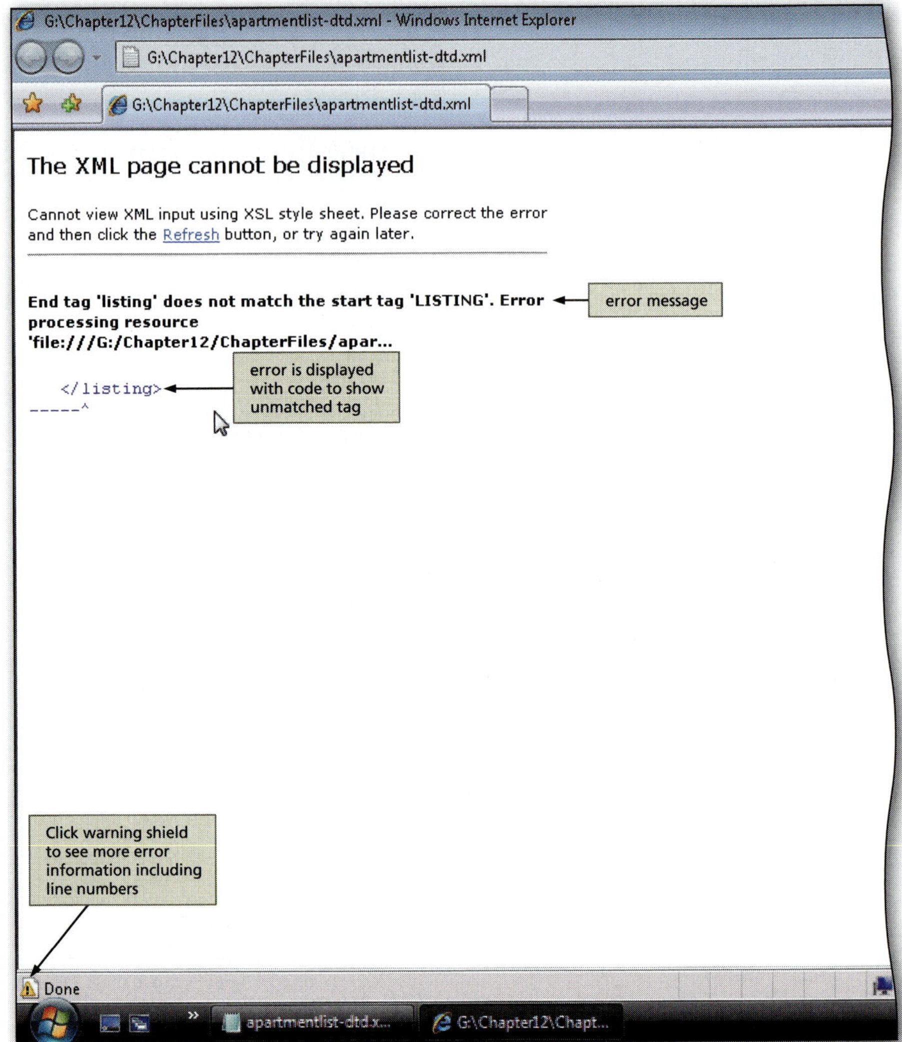

Figure 12–9

Q&A An error message occurred and the document did not display correctly. What happened?

The tag on line 39 is not correct and generates an error. The error message indicates that the error is located in the tag on line 39 of the XML document.

Q&A This error was made on purpose, so we know the line number. How do I find out what line number an error is on that is made accidentally?

Double-click the triangular warning shield in the lower-left corner next to Done, if necessary click OK, and an error dialog box will be displayed with the line number.

Q&A Will the browser show all the errors at one time?

No, as you correct each error, any remaining errors will display in the browser until all errors have been corrected.

To Correct the Tag Error and Retest the XML Document

The following steps show how to correct the tag error and retest the XML document.

- Click the Notepad button on the taskbar.
- Click line 39.
- Delete the lowercase </listing> tag.
- Type `</LISTING>` as the new tag in place of the deleted tag to correct the closing listing tag (Figure 12–10).

```
<!DOCTYPE RENTALUNITS
  [
  <!ELEMENT RENTALUNITS (LISTING*)>
    <!ELEMENT LISTING (NAME, ADDRESS, PHONE, BEDROOMS, BATHS, AVAILABLE)>
    <!ELEMENT NAME (#PCDATA)>
    <!ELEMENT ADDRESS (#PCDATA)>
    <!ELEMENT PHONE (#PCDATA)>
    <!ELEMENT BEDROOMS (#PCDATA)>
    <!ELEMENT BATHS (#PCDATA)>
    <!ELEMENT AVAILABLE (#PCDATA)>
    ]
>
<RENTALUNITS>
   <LISTING>
      <NAME>Konner Ridge</NAME>
      <ADDRESS>23 Monroe St.</ADDRESS>
      <PHONE>256-5533</PHONE>
      <BEDROOMS>3</BEDROOMS>
      <BATHS>2</BATHS>
      <AVAILABLE>2 Months</AVAILABLE>
   </LISTING>
   <LISTING>
      <NAME>Konner Ridge</NAME>
      <ADDRESS>23 Monroe St.</ADDRESS>
      <PHONE>256-5533</PHONE>
      <BEDROOMS>1</BEDROOMS>
      <BATHS>1</BATHS>
      <AVAILABLE>2 Months</AVAILABLE>
   </LISTING>
   <LISTING>
      <NAME>Konner Ridge</NAME>
      <ADDRESS>23 Monroe St.</ADDRESS>
      <PHONE>256-5533</PHONE>
      <BEDROOMS>2</BEDROOMS>
      <BATHS>1</BATHS>
      <AVAILABLE>1 Month</AVAILABLE>
   </LISTING>
   <LISTING>
      <NAME>Eastwood Place Apartments</NAME>
      <ADDRESS>300 N. Main St.</ADDRESS>
      <PHONE>256-1148</PHONE>
      <BEDROOMS>2</BEDROOMS>
      <BATHS>1</BATHS>
      <AVAILABLE>2 Months</AVAILABLE>
   </LISTING>
</RENTALUNITS>
```


Figure 12–10

2

- Click File on the menu bar and then click Save.
- Activate the browser.
- Click the Refresh button on the browser toolbar to display the corrected page (Figure 12–11).
- If necessary, click the security bar under the tabs, and then click Allow Blocked Content… on the menu.
- If necessary, click Yes in the Security Warning dialog box.

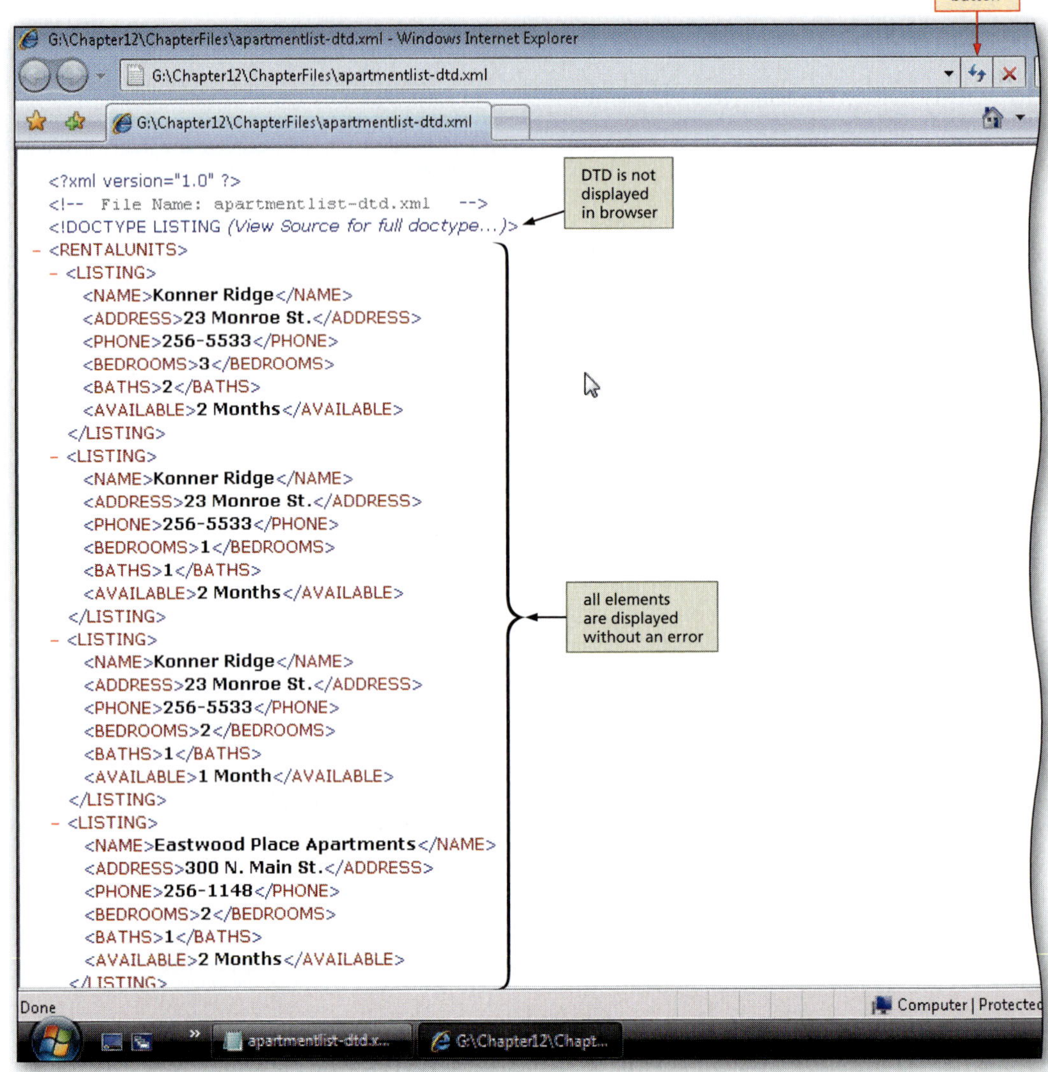
Refresh button
G:\Chapter12\ChapterFiles\apartmentlist-dtd.xml - Windows Internet Explorer
G:\Chapter12\ChapterFiles\apartmentlist-dtd.xml
G:\Chapter12\ChapterFiles\apartmentlist-dtd.xml
<?xml version="1.0" ?>
<!-- File Name: apartmentlist-dtd.xml -->
<!DOCTYPE LISTING (View Source for full doctype...)>
- <RENTALUNITS>
- <LISTING>
<NAME>Konner Ridge</NAME>
<ADDRESS>23 Monroe St.</ADDRESS>
<PHONE>256-5533</PHONE>
<BEDROOMS>3</BEDROOMS>
<BATHS>2</BATHS>
<AVAILABLE>2 Months</AVAILABLE>
</LISTING>
- <LISTING>
<NAME>Konner Ridge</NAME>
<ADDRESS>23 Monroe St.</ADDRESS>
<PHONE>256-5533</PHONE>
<BEDROOMS>1</BEDROOMS>
<BATHS>1</BATHS>
<AVAILABLE>2 Months</AVAILABLE>
</LISTING>
- <LISTING>
<NAME>Konner Ridge</NAME>
<ADDRESS>23 Monroe St.</ADDRESS>
<PHONE>256-5533</PHONE>
<BEDROOMS>2</BEDROOMS>
<BATHS>1</BATHS>
<AVAILABLE>1 Month</AVAILABLE>
</LISTING>
- <LISTING>
<NAME>Eastwood Place Apartments</NAME>
<ADDRESS>300 N. Main St.</ADDRESS>
<PHONE>256-1148</PHONE>
<BEDROOMS>2</BEDROOMS>
<BATHS>1</BATHS>
<AVAILABLE>2 Months</AVAILABLE>
DTD is not displayed in browser
all elements are displayed without an error
Done
Computer | Protected
apartmentlist-dtd.x...
G:\Chapter12\Chapt...

Figure 12–11

Q&A What are the plus and minus signs by the <RENTALUNITS> and <LISTING> tags?

The minus signs preceding the tags <RENTALUNITS> and <LISTING> indicate the level or node (root or child) of the data. A user can collapse or expand the levels of the document by clicking the plus sign to expand or the minus sign to collapse. An XML document, however, can be quite difficult to read as an unformatted Web page.

Q&A Why is the DTD code not displayed in the browser?

Because of the differences in browsers, and because the DTD is "optional," the DTD is treated as a Meta tag as in HTML. The purpose of the DTD is to help validate a well-formed document.

- Click the minus signs in front of the <LISTING> tags to collapse the individual instances in the list.
- Click the plus sign in front of the second <LISTING> tag to expand that instance (Figure 12–12).

Q&A What would happen if I clicked the minus sign in front of the first <RENTALUNITS> tag?

The entire list of instances would collapse and none of the child <LISTING> tags would be visible.

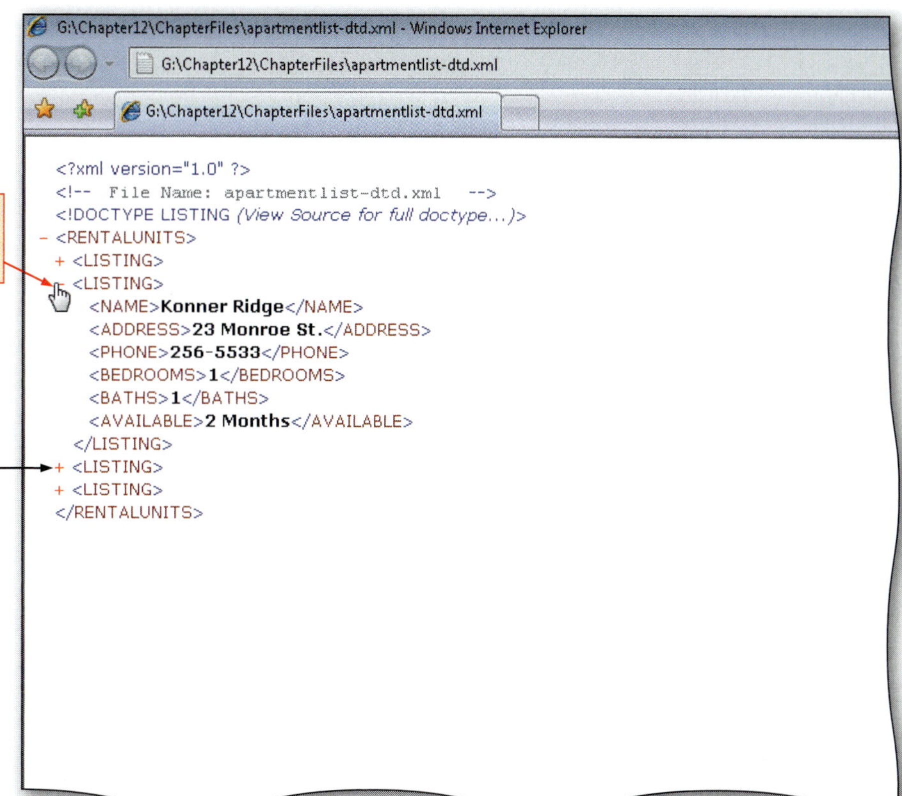

Figure 12–12

Plan Ahead

Formatting and linking an XML document with a style sheet.
Unformatted XML documents can be difficult to read, especially in a Web browser. One solution is to format the document with a CSS or XSL style sheet. To format an XML document with a style sheet, consider the following tasks:

- Determine what type of style sheet to use and how it will impact the output of the XML document.
- When using a CSS, each XML identifier tag must have a style defined.
- Format text in the same order as the XML tag hierarchy.
- Link the style sheet to the XML document.

Formatting an XML Document Using a Cascading Style Sheet

Because an unformatted XML document can be quite difficult to read, developers like to use a style sheet to format the XML document. Figure 12–13 on the next page shows the apartmentlist-css.xml document formatted using an external Cascading Style Sheet.

In Chapter 8, you learned how to create external style sheets using CSS and to link them to Web pages using the HTML <link> tag. Linking an external style sheet to an XML document follows a similar process. Table 12–11 on the next page shows the CSS code for the external style sheet used to format the XML document shown in Figure 12–13.

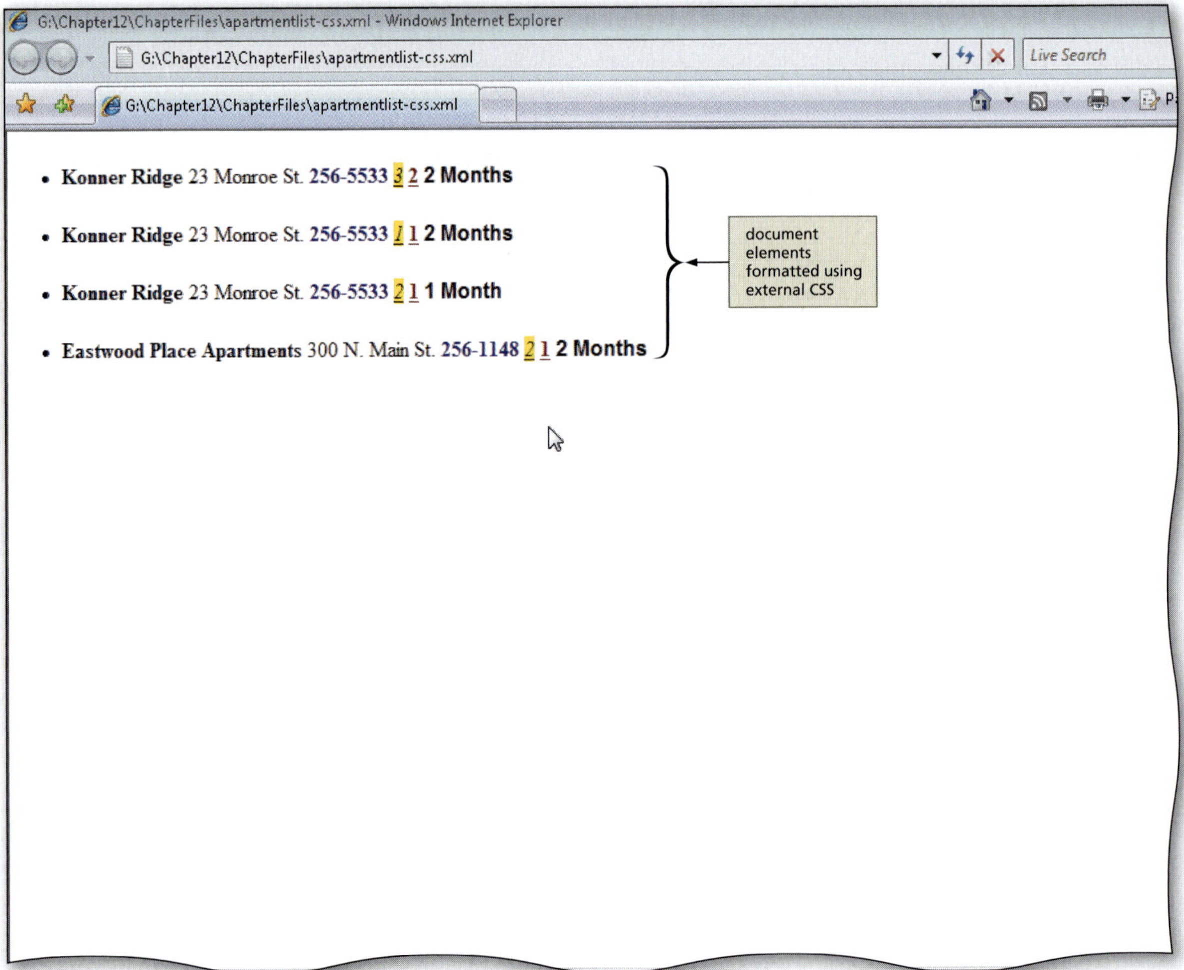

Figure 12–13

Table 12–11 CSS Code for Creating an External Cascading Style Sheet

Line	Code
1	`LISTING {display:list-item; margin-top:18pt; margin-left:24pt}`
2	`NAME  {font-weight:bold}`
3	`ADDRESS  {}`
4	`PHONE {color:darkblue; font-weight:900}`
5	`BEDROOMS {font-style:italic; background-color:yellow; text-decoration:underline}`
6	`BATHS {color:darkred; font-weight:bold; text-decoration:underline}`
7	`AVAILABLE {font-family:Helvetica; font-weight:bold}`

The style sheet code shown in Table 12–11 uses the element names in the XML document as selectors. Line 1 instructs the browser to display the data as an unordered list, with margins of 18 points from the top and 24 points from the left. Line 2 makes the NAME element font weight bold. In line 3, the ADDRESS is left blank. In line 4, the PHONE element is a dark blue color and also bold weight of 900. Line 5 changes the BEDROOMS element font style to italic, the background color to yellow, and underlines the data. In line 6, the BATHS element is dark red, font-weight is bold, and text is underlined. Line 7 changes the font family of the AVAILABLE element to Helvetica and bold.

To Create an External Style Sheet Using CSS

The following step illustrates how to create an external CSS to format an XML document.

- Start a new Notepad document, keeping the original Notepad document open. If necessary, maximize the new Notepad window. If the Word Wrap feature is not enabled, click Format on the menu bar and then click Word Wrap to enable it.
- Click line 1.
- Enter the code shown in Table 12–11 to create an external CSS.

apartmentlist-css.css - Notepad

File Edit Format View Help

line 1

```
LISTING {display:list-item; margin-top:18pt; margin-left:24pt}
NAME {font-weight:bold}
ADDRESS {}
PHONE {color:darkblue; font-weight:900}
BEDROOMS {font-style:italic; background-color: yellow; text-decoration:underline}
BATHS {color:darkred; font-weight:bold; text-decoration:underline}
AVAILABLE {font-family:Helvetica; font-weight:bold}
```

CSS code to format each tag in the document instance

Figure 12–14

- Click File on the menu bar and then click Save As.
- Type `apartmentlist-css.css` in the File name text box. If necessary, navigate to UDISK (G:). Double-click the Chapter12 folder and then double-click the ChapterFiles folder in the list of available folders.
- Click the Save button in the Save As dialog box (Figure 12–14).

Linking the Style Sheet and XML Document File

Next, the external CSS must be linked to the XML document. To link a style sheet to a document, you enter a processing instruction in the prolog of an XML document. Table 12–12 shows the XML processing instruction to link a CSS to an XML document.

Table 12–12 General Form of an XML Style Sheet Processing Instruction to Link an External CSS

General form:	<?xml-stylesheet type="text/css" href="file path"?>
Comment:	The type attribute indicates that this is a CSS file. The file path is the location of the style sheet, which generally is a URL.
Example:	<?xml-stylesheet type="text/css" href="apartmentlist-css.css"?>

To Link an External Cascading Style Sheet to an XML Document

The following step illustrates how to link a CSS to an XML document.

1

- Activate the Notepad window containing the XML document, apartmentlist-dtd.xml.
- Click line 2 and change the file name from apartmentlist-dtd.xml to apartmentlist-css.xml.
- Click the beginning of line 3.
- Press the ENTER key once. Position the insertion point on the blank line created, line 3.
- Type `<?xml-stylesheet type="text/css" href="apartmentlist-css.css"?>` on the blank line, but do not press the ENTER key (Figure 12–15).

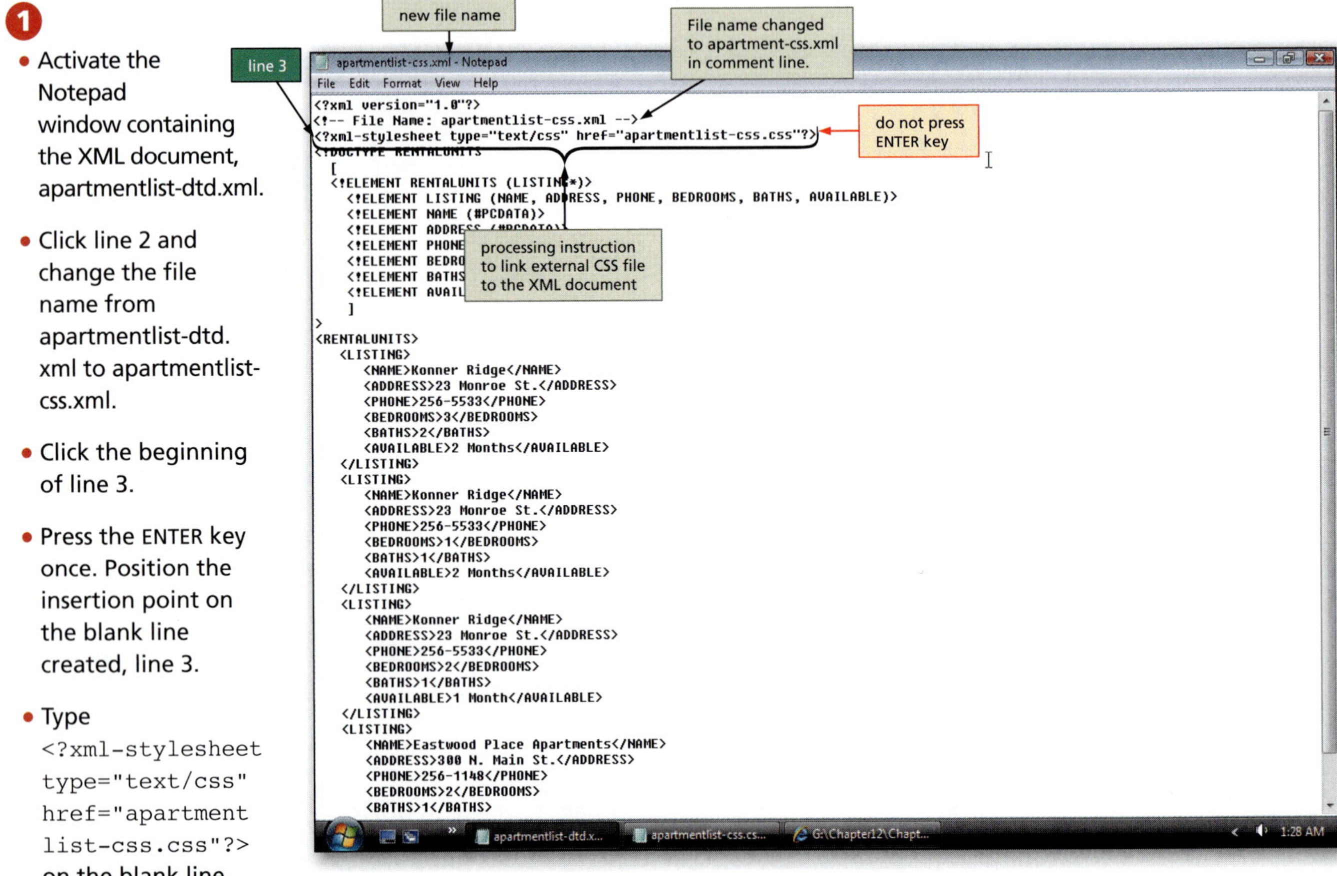
new file name
File name changed to apartment-css.xml in comment line.
line 3
do not press ENTER key
processing instruction to link external CSS file to the XML document
apartmentlist-css.xml - Notepad
File Edit Format View Help
<?xml version="1.0"?>
<!-- File Name: apartmentlist-css.xml -->
<?xml-stylesheet type="text/css" href="apartmentlist-css.css"?>
<RENTALUNITS>
<LISTING>
<NAME>Konner Ridge</NAME>
<ADDRESS>23 Monroe St.</ADDRESS>
<PHONE>256-5533</PHONE>
<BEDROOMS>3</BEDROOMS>
<BATHS>2</BATHS>
<AVAILABLE>2 Months</AVAILABLE>
</LISTING>
<NAME>Eastwood Place Apartments</NAME>
<ADDRESS>300 N. Main St.</ADDRESS>
<PHONE>256-1148</PHONE>

Figure 12–15

- Click File on the menu bar and then click Save As.
- Type `apartmentlist-css.xml` in the File name text box. If necessary, navigate to UDISK (G:). Double-click the Chapter12 folder and then double-click the ChapterFiles folder in the list of available folders.
- Click the Save button in the Save As dialog box.

Q&A

Why did we save the file with a new name?

So we do not destroy the original file and to help keep the different versions and uses separate. Future steps will use a different XML file and will be linked with an XSL style sheet.

To Test an XML Document Formatted Using an External CSS

The following step shows how to test the XML document formatted using an external Cascading Style Sheet.

- Activate the browser. Enter the URL `G:\Chapter12\ChapterFiles\apartmentlist-css.xml` to display the XML document formatted using an external style sheet (Figure 12–16).

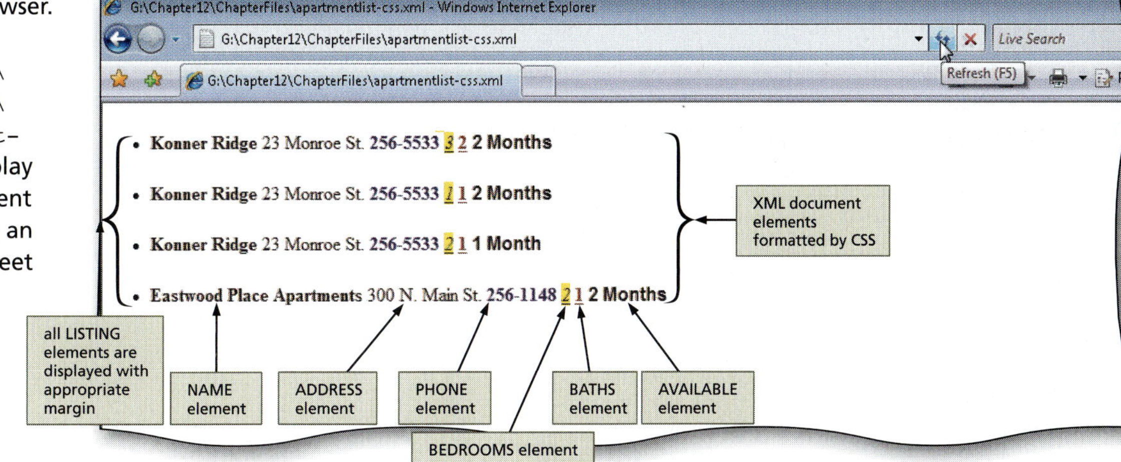

Figure 12–16

Plan Ahead

Formatting and linking an XSL style sheet to an XML document.
XSL style sheets are used to transform an XML document into a more stylized document. To create an XSL document perform these tasks:

- Determine the XML document elements that will be displayed and how you want them to appear.
- Determine the XSL elements:
  1. Determine if the <template> element will use all or only some elements.
  2. Determine the for-each elements.
  3. Determine the style for each XSL value-of element and format with <span> tags and inline styles.
  4. Determine if sorting is required and which XML element to use as a sort key.
  5. Determine any descriptive text that is needed.
- Link the XSL style sheet to the XML document.

Formatting an XML Document Using an XSL Style Sheet

This section outlines the techniques needed to format the display of an XML document using the Extensible Stylesheet Language (XSL) and how to bind XML documents to HTML Web pages. Recall that the Browse by Complex Name link on the Statewide Realty home page links to an XML document that will display the apartment complex names in ascending order by name order (Figure 12–1b on page HTML 549). The output and display of this XML document are defined using an XSL style sheet that sets each record to be displayed in a list, sorted in ascending order by the NAME element.

The remainder of the chapter uses the XML document, apartmentlist.xml, supplied in the Data Files for Students, which will be renamed. This XML document is similar to the XML document, apartmentlist-dtd.xml, but does not contain the DTD created in Table 12–7 on page HTML 558. This file does contain additional apartment records, and has been created in BEDROOMS order. Once the file is opened, it will be saved with a different name, to maintain an original version of the data file.

To Open and Save an XML Document with a New File Name

The following step illustrates how to open the XML document, apartmentlist.xml, and save it with a new file name, apartmentlist-bedroom.xml.

- Click the apartmentlist-css.xml Notepad button on the status bar to activate the Notepad window.
- With the USB drive plugged into your computer, click File on the menu bar and then click Open on the File menu.
- If necessary, navigate to the Chapter12\ChapterFiles folder on the USB drive. Click All Files in the Files of type drop-down list.
- Double-click apartmentlist.xml in the list of files.
- With the apartmentlist.xml file open, click File on the menu bar and then click Save As.
- Type `apartmentlist-bedroom.xml` in the File name text box.
- Click the Save button in the Save As dialog box to save the file with the new name.

BTW

XSL

XSL is three languages: one to transform XML (XSLT), one to define XML parts or patterns (XPath), and one to format objects and define the XML display (XSL). An XSL style sheet assumes that the associated XML document uses a hierarchical structure, which contains a root element, child elements, and any optional attributes, namespaces, processing statements, or comments. An XSL style sheet cannot transform any other type of document, such as Word, PDF, or PostScript files, into HTML documents.

Creating an XSL Style Sheet

As you learned previously, an XML document can be formatted with a style sheet created in CSS or XSL. Most Web developers agree that formatting with CSS is impractical and prefer to use the XSL style sheets. An XSL style sheet performs two actions: it formats and transforms XML documents. An XSL style sheet can **transform** an XML document by instructing the browser or parser to output the XML document in a completely different form. XSL takes the XML document, called a **source**, and produces completely different output, called a **result tree**.

An XSL style sheet uses syntax similar to the syntax used for XML documents and has the same hierarchical, tree-like structure as other XML documents. Each of the style sheet elements in an XSL style sheet must use the namespace prefix, **xsl**, to distinguish the XSL elements from XML elements. The general form of the stylesheet element in an XSL style sheet is shown in Table 12–13. For a complete list of XSL style sheet elements, see the XML Quick Reference in Appendix F.

Table 12–13 General Form of the stylesheet Element in an XSL Style Sheet

General form:	<xsl:stylesheet xmlns:prefix="URL" language="language"> ... *(other stylesheet code)* </xsl:stylesheet> or <xsl:transform version="v.x" xmlns:prefix="URL" language="language"> ... *(other stylesheet code)* </xsl:transform>
Comment:	The stylesheet element is the root element of an XSL style sheet. The prefix defines the xml namespace (xmlns). The namespace allows duplicate names to be used in a document. The URL indicates the official XSL specification as recommended by the W3C. The language attribute is optional. The stylesheet element must be closed at the end of the document by the end tag, </xsl:stylesheet>.
Examples:	(1) <xsl:stylesheet xmlns:xsl="http://www.w3.org/TR/WD-xsl"> (2) <xsl:transform version="1.0" xmlns:xsl="http://www.w3.org/1999/XSL/Transform">

BTW

The XSL Stylesheet Element
The xsl:stylesheet or xsl:transform element must have a version number and should be written as follows: <xsl:stylesheet version="1.0" xmlns:xsl="http://www.w3.org/1999/XSL/Transform"> or <xsl:transform version="1.0" xmlns:xsl="http://www.w3.org/1999/XSL/Transform">. The version number is required because the namespace code, xmlns:xsl="http://www.w3.org/1999/XSL/Transform", indicates the use of the official W3C specification.

The **stylesheet element** establishes a namespace, so the remaining elements, such as the template, can use names that will not be confused with other elements. A **template** is an instruction that identifies the elements in a document that should be transformed or converted and then specifies how the element should be transformed. The browser refers to the template when displaying a particular element in the XML document. The template is the most important part of the XSL style sheet, and the XSL style sheet must include at least one template element. Table 12–14 shows the general form of the template element.

Table 12–14 General Form of the template Element

General form:	<xsl:template match="pattern" language="language"> ... *(other stylesheet code)* </xsl:template>
Comment:	The pattern indicates the XML element or node. A pattern of "/" indicates that the entire document will be displayed. The template element needs an end element.
Example:	<xsl:template match="/"> ... *(other stylesheet code)* </xsl:template>

BTW

The XSL Template Element
The XSL template element associates each output with an input. The match="/" attribute defines the entire document.

To Start Creating an XSL Style Sheet

Table 12–15 shows the code for the processing instruction, an XML declaration, a stylesheet element, and a template element in an XSL style sheet. This XSL stylesheet will display the apartments in order by name, using the <NAME> tag element in the XML file.

Table 12–15 Code for Creating an XSL Style Sheet

Line	Code
1	`<?xml version="1.0"?>`
2	`<xsl:transform version="1.0" xmlns:xsl="http://www.w3.org/1999/XSL/Transform">`
3	`  <xsl:template match="/">`

Line 1 is the XML declaration that identifies this as an XML document using XML version 1.0. Line 2 is the XSL stylesheet element to define the namespace, xsl, for the remaining elements. Line 3 defines the template pattern, using a "/" to indicate that the template applies to the entire XML document. The following step illustrates how to start creating an XSL style sheet.

1

- Click the apartmentlist-css.css Notepad button to activate the Notepad window.
- Click File on the menu bar, and then New to start a new Notepad document.
- Enter the code shown in Table 12–15 to start the XSL style sheet and then press the ENTER key (Figure 12–17).

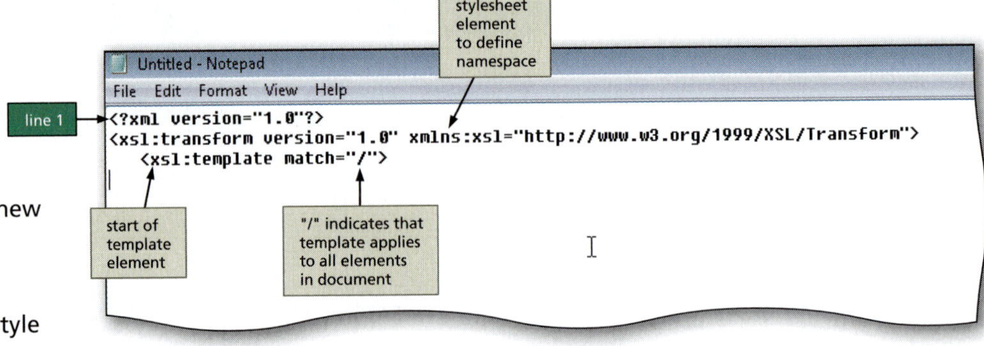

Figure 12–17

Q&A What happens if more than one XSL style sheet is linked to an XML document?

If more than one XSL style sheet is linked to an XML document, the first XSL style sheet the browser reads is used and the others are ignored.

Q&A Can an XSL style sheet and Cascading Style Sheet both be linked to an XML document?

If an XSL style sheet and a Cascading Style Sheet both are linked to an XML document, the XSL style sheet is used and the Cascading Style Sheet is ignored.

The **for-each** element makes each element appear in the list, and associates each child element <LISTING> related with the <RENTALUNITS>. This association identifies the XML elements that should appear in the apartment list on the Web page. Table 12–16 discusses the general form of the for-each element and shows two different ways to place items in order.

BTW

The XSL for-each Element

The for-each element allows a developer to do "looping" through a set of XML data. The use of the for-each will select every item in a set of nodes. In the event of multiple items, the first value is used.

Table 12–16 General Form of the for-each Element

General form:	<xsl:for-each select="pattern">
Comment:	The for-each element returns the associated child element's data identified by the select attribute pattern. As the for-each cycles through the data, each of the child nodes contained in the pattern name becomes the current node element or record.
Example:	<xsl:for-each select="RENTALUNITS/LISTING">

XSL style sheets allow for a more free-form, yet organized, display of data. To make the listings be displayed in order by apartment complex name, use the sort element as discussed in Table 12–17.

Table 12–17 General Form of the sort Element

General form:	<xsl:sort select="value" lang="token" data-type="value" order="ascending|descending" case-order="upper-first|lower-first" />
Comment:	The sort element has five attributes: select, lang, data-type, order, and case-order. The select attribute value indicates on which element to sort; lang indicates the language of the sort keys. The system default language is assumed. Data-type is used to indicate the data type of the select value (alphabetic or numeric). In an alphabetic sort, numbers are sorted alphabetically, meaning 100 comes before 99. Numeric data types sort numbers in their correct numeric order. Order indicates ascending (default) or descending. Case-order indicates if uppercase or lowercase order should be first.
Example:	<xsl:sort select="NAME" data-type="text" />

Table 12–18 shows the code to write the XSL tags to center the logo and heading, and sort the data by NAME in ascending order.

Table 12–18 Code for Adding XML Tags to a template Element

Line	Code
4	<p align="center">
5	<img border="0" src="chapter12banner.jpg" /></p>
6	<p align="center">
7	<span style="font-weight:bold; font-family:arial, helvetica, san-serif; font-size:18px">
8	Statewide Realty Apartment Listing - Browse by Complex Name</span></p>
9	<xsl:for-each select="RENTALUNITS/LISTING">
10	<xsl:sort select="NAME" data-type="text" />

Line 4 uses the paragraph tag with an align center attribute to center the image in the browser window. Line 6 starts a new <p> tag with an align center attribute to place the header text in the center of the page. Line 7 is a <span> tag with a style attribute to format the header text. Line 8 contains the header text and the closing </span> and </p> tags. Line 9 sets the pattern for the root and child elements with the for-each element. Line 10 uses the sort parameter to sort the data in NAME order.

To Add XML Tags to a template Element in an XSL Style Sheet

The following step illustrates how to use the XSL sort parameter to list the apartment data in NAME order.

1

- Click line 4.
- Enter the code shown in Table 12–18 to add the XML template element tags and then press the ENTER key (Figure 12–18).

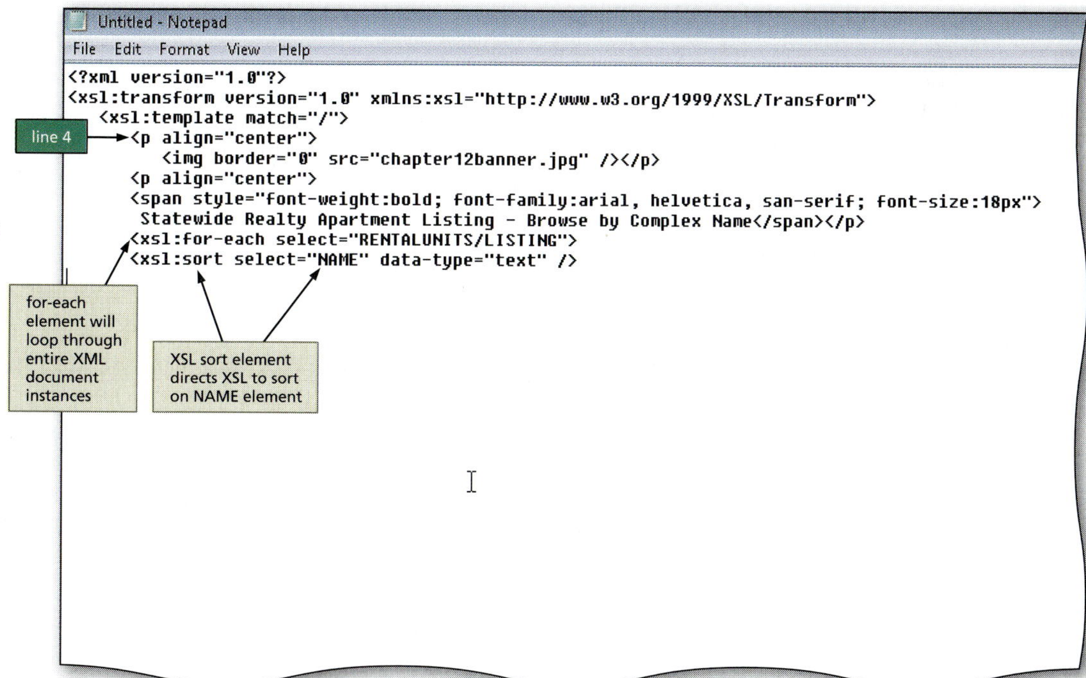

Figure 12–18

BTW

The XSL value-of Element

The value-of element transfers the value of the designated XML tag (field) to the output document.

Completing the XSL Style Sheet

In conjunction with the for-each element, the XSL style sheet uses the XSL value-of element to define the display for each instance within the apartment list. Table 12–19 shows the general form of the XSL value-of element.

Table 12–19 General Form of the value-of Element

General form:	<xsl:value-of select="pattern" />
Comment:	The value-of element indicates that the page should display the value for the specified element. The pattern value of the select attribute identifies the name of the specific element used in the output.
Example:	<xsl:value-of select = "PHONE" />

By combining the XSL elements and XML markup tags, the XSL style sheet tells the browser how to transform and format the XML document to display records in paragraph mode on the Web page. Table 12–20 shows the code for the remainder of the XSL style sheet, including the end tags for the for-each, template, and stylesheet elements.

Table 12–20 Code for Creating an XSL Style Sheet

```
            <p>
                <span style="font-variant:small-caps; font-weight:bold">
                   <xsl:value-of select="NAME" />
                </span>
                <xsl:text> has a </xsl:text>
                <span style="font-weight:bold; text-decoration:underline; color:#7f0000">
                   <xsl:value-of select="BEDROOMS" />
                </span>
                <xsl:text> bedroom apartment available. Call </xsl:text>
                <span style="font-family: arial, helvetica, sans-serif">
                   <xsl:value-of select="PHONE" />
                </span>
                <xsl:text> for more information.</xsl:text>
              </p>
              <p style="margin-left: 3%">
                <span style="font-weight:bold; color:#2f1fff">It is availabile in </span>
                <xsl:value-of select="AVAILABLE" />. This apartment has
                <span style="font-style:italic; font-weight: bold; color:#2f1fff">
                    <xsl:value-of select="BATHS" /> bath(s).
                </span>
              </p>
            </xsl:for-each>
            <p style="font-family:helvetica,arial; font-weight:bold"><a href="chapter12homesolution.html">Home</a></p>
        </xsl:template>
      </xsl:transform>
```

The paragraph <p> tag on line 11 will display each record on a separate line. Line 12 is a <span> tag with an embedded style sheet used to set the font weight to bold, set the font to small caps. Line 13 uses the value-of select attribute to display the value for the NAME element. Line 14 closes the <span> tag started on line 12, so the next text displayed does not use the same style.

Line 15 uses the text attribute to insert the text "has a" between the apartment complex name and the number of bedrooms. The <span> tag on line 16 uses an embedded style sheet to set the font of the bedrooms to bold, underline the text and the color to red. Line 17 uses the value-of select attribute to display the value for the BEDROOMS element. Line 18 closes the start <span> tag on line 16.

Line 19 adds additional descriptive text, "bedroom apartment available. Call " between the number of the bedrooms and the PHONE element. Line 20 uses a <span> tag with an embedded style sheet to set the style for the PHONE element displayed by line 21. Line 23 uses the xsl:text element to add the descriptive text, "for more information." Line 25 starts a new paragraph and the <span> tag on line 26 sets the style for the text, "It is available in " followed by the value-of select attribute for the AVAILABLE element in line 27, followed by a period and the descriptive text, "This apartment has". Lines 28 and 29 are a <span> tag setting the style for the BATHS element and the text, "bath(s)." Lines 30 and 31 close the <span> and <p> tags, and line 32 closes the <xsl:for-each> tag started on line 9. Line 33 is a <p> tag with an embedded style and an <a href> tag to return the user to the home page. Line 34 closes the <xsl:template> tag on line 3. Line 35 closes the <xsl:transform> tag on line 2, which began the XSL markup tag elements.

To Finish Creating an XSL Style Sheet

The following step shows how to enter the remaining code to complete the XSL style sheet.

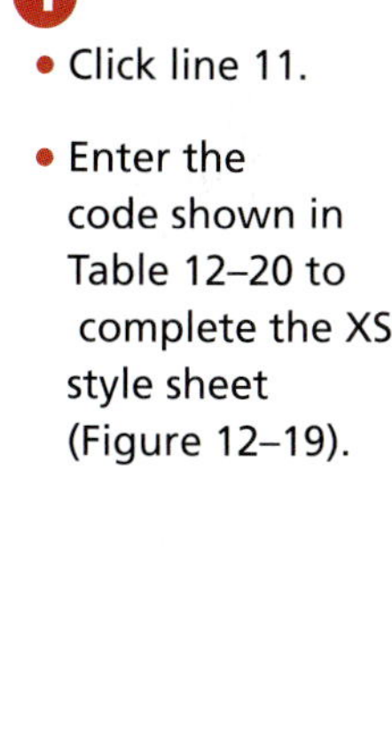

1

- Click line 11.
- Enter the code shown in Table 12–20 to complete the XSL style sheet (Figure 12–19).

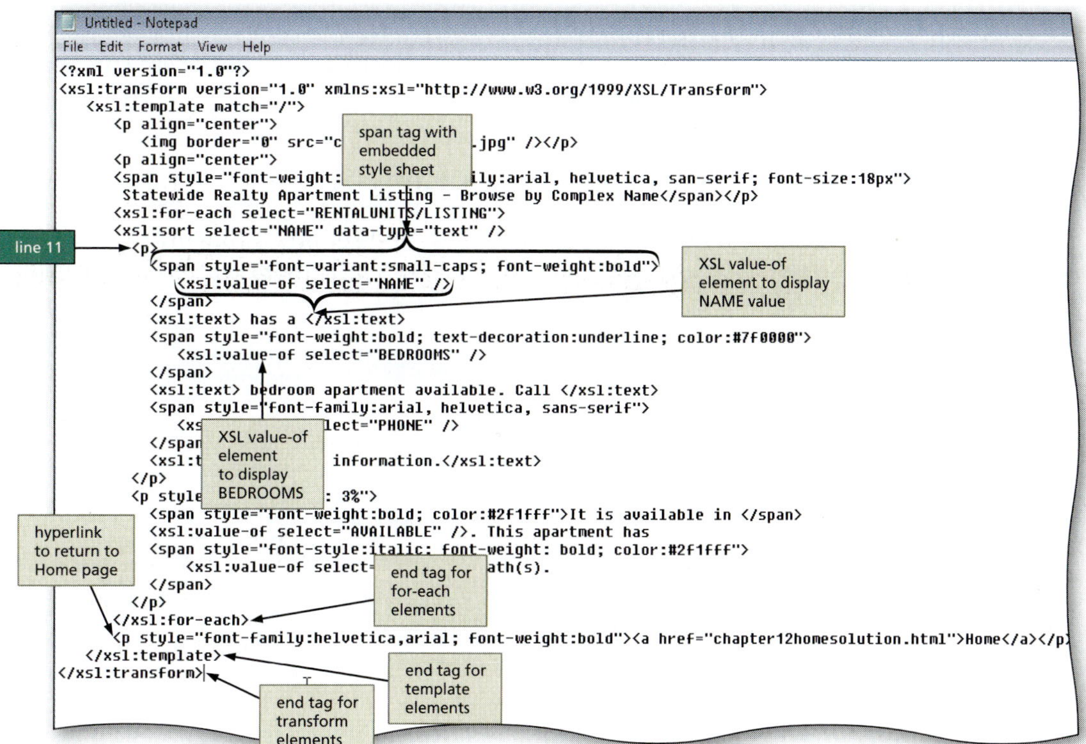

Figure 12–19

To Save an XSL Style Sheet

Once the XSL style sheet is complete, the file should be saved. The following step shows how to save the XSL style sheet as chapter12xslsolution.xsl.

- With your USB drive plugged into your computer, click File on the menu bar and then click Save As.
- If necessary, navigate to the Chapter12\ChapterFiles folder on UDISK (G:).
- Type chapter12xslsolution.xsl in the File name text box.
- Click the Save button in the Save As dialog box to save the chapter12xslsolution.xsl style sheet.

Linking an XSL Style Sheet to an XML Document

With the XSL file saved, the next step is to link the XSL style sheet to the XML document, apartmentlist-bedroom.xml. Linking an XSL style sheet to an XML document requires an xml-stylesheet processing instruction. Table 12–21 shows the general form of this xml-stylesheet processing instruction, which is similar to the processing instruction used to link the Cascading Style Sheet to an XML document.

Table 12–21 General Form of the xml-stylesheet Processing Instruction

General form:	<?xml-stylesheet type="text/xsl" href="file path"?>
Comment:	The processing instruction used to link an XSL style sheet is similar to the processing statement used to link a Cascading Style Sheet. The key difference is that the xml-stylesheet type attribute value contains text/xsl to indicate that this is an XSL file. The type indicates it is XSL, and href is the external path or URL.
Example:	<?xml-stylesheet type="text/xsl" href="chapter12xslsolution.xsl"?>

XSL style sheet processing instructions usually are entered in the prolog of the XML document.

To Link an XSL Style Sheet to an XML Document

The following step illustrates how to add an XSL style sheet processing instruction to link the XSL style sheet to the XML document, apartmentlist-bedroom.xml.

- Activate the Notepad window containing the XML document, apartmentlist-bedroom.xml.
- Click line 2 and change the file name, NAMElist.xml, to apartmentlist-bedroom-xml (Figure 12–20).
- Click at the beginning of line 3.
- Press the ENTER key to create a blank line, and then click the blank line.
- Type <?xml-stylesheet type="text/xsl" href="chapter12xslsolution.xsl"?> but do not press the ENTER key to enter the code to link the XSL style sheet to the XML document (Figure 12–20).

Corrected comment line for new file name

line 2

do not press ENTER key

processing statement to link the XSL style sheet to this XML document

```
apartmentlist-bedroom.xml - Notepad
File Edit Format View Help
<?xml version="1.0"?>
<!-- File Name: apartmentlist-bedroom.xml -->
<?xml-stylesheet type="text/xsl" href="chapter12xslsolution.xsl"?>
<RENTALUNITS>
   <LISTING>
      <NAME>Konner Ridge</NAME>
      <ADDRESS>23 Monroe St.</ADDRESS>
      <PHONE>256-5533</PHONE>
      <BEDROOMS>1</BEDROOMS>
```

Figure 12–20

To Save and Test an XML Document Formatted Using an XSL Style Sheet

Once the XSL style sheet is complete and the processing instruction is added to the XML document, you should save and test the changes to the XML document in a browser. The following step shows how to save and test the XML document formatted using an XSL style sheet.

- With the USB drive plugged into your computer, click File on the menu bar and then click Save.
- Activate the browser.
- Click the Address bar.
- Type `G:\Chapter12\ChapterFiles\apartmentlist-bedroom.xml` and then press the ENTER key to display the formatted XML document formatted by the XSL style sheet (Figure 12–21).

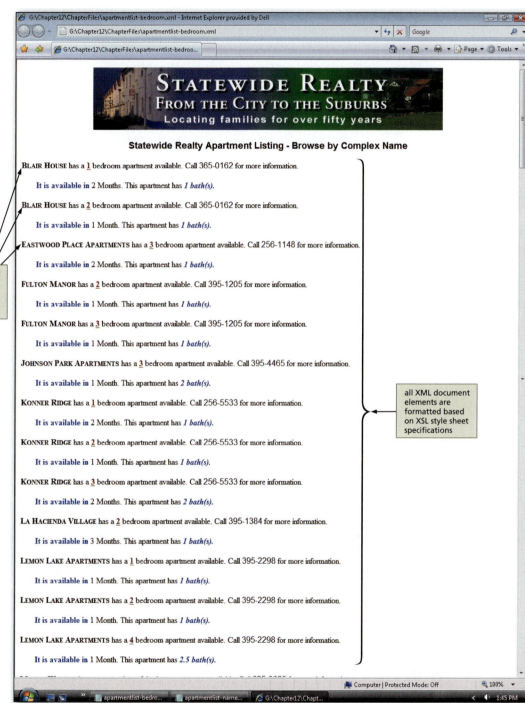

G:\Chapter12\ChapterFiles\apartmentlist-bedroom.xml - Internet Explorer provided by Dell

STATEWIDE REALTY
FROM THE CITY TO THE SUBURBS
Locating families for over fifty years

Statewide Realty Apartment Listing - Browse by Complex Name

BLAIR HOUSE has a 1 bedroom apartment available. Call 365-0162 for more information.
It is available in 2 Months. This apartment has *1 bath(s).*
BLAIR HOUSE has a 2 bedroom apartment available. Call 365-0162 for more information.
It is available in 1 Month. This apartment has *1 bath(s).*
EASTWOOD PLACE APARTMENTS has a 3 bedroom apartment available. Call 256-1148 for more information.
It is available in 2 Months. This apartment has *1 bath(s).*
FULTON MANOR has a 2 bedroom apartment available. Call 395-1205 for more information.
It is available in 1 Month. This apartment has *1 bath(s).*
FULTON MANOR has a 3 bedroom apartment available. Call 395-1205 for more information.
It is available in 1 Month. This apartment has *1 bath(s).*
JOHNSON PARK APARTMENTS has a 3 bedroom apartment available. Call 395-4465 for more information.
It is available in 1 Month. This apartment has *2 bath(s).*
KONNER RIDGE has a 1 bedroom apartment available. Call 256-5533 for more information.
It is available in 2 Months. This apartment has *1 bath(s).*
KONNER RIDGE has a 2 bedroom apartment available. Call 256-5533 for more information.
It is available in 1 Month. This apartment has *1 bath(s).*
KONNER RIDGE has a 3 bedroom apartment available. Call 256-5533 for more information.
It is available in 2 Months. This apartment has *2 bath(s).*
LA HACIENDA VILLAGE has a 2 bedroom apartment available. Call 395-1384 for more information.
It is available in 3 Months. This apartment has *1 bath(s).*
LEMON LAKE APARTMENTS has a 1 bedroom apartment available. Call 395-2298 for more information.
It is available in 1 Month. This apartment has *1 bath(s).*
LEMON LAKE APARTMENTS has a 2 bedroom apartment available. Call 395-2298 for more information.
It is available in 1 Month. This apartment has *1 bath(s).*
LEMON LAKE APARTMENTS has a 4 bedroom apartment available. Call 395-2298 for more information.
It is available in 1 Month. This apartment has *2.5 bath(s).*

apartment listing data in order by name

all XML document elements are formatted based on XSL style sheet specifications

Figure 12–21

To Close the Notepad Window and the XSL Style Sheet

- Activate the Notepad window containing the XSL style sheet, chapter12xslsolution.xsl.
- Click the Close button on the Notepad title bar.

Plan Ahead

Displaying XML data in an HTML table.
Displaying long lists of data can be tedious to look at. Dividing the list up into manageable pages using a table can make the data easier to read. To plan a table:

- Determine the number of rows to display on each Web page
- Determine the ID names to associate the objects properly with the table
- Determine the navigation control for the table
- Determine any style formatting for the data in the table

Using an HTML Table with Paging to Display XML Data

The second hyperlink on the Statewide Realty Web page, Browse by Vacancy, links to a Web page that displays a list of available apartments (Figure 12–22). The HTML Web page binds with the XML document and displays each record element in an HTML table. The table attribute, datapagesize, restricts the display to five rows at a time. The Web page has four buttons that use built-in browser functions allowing users to navigate forward and backward through the table rows or to move to the first or last page.

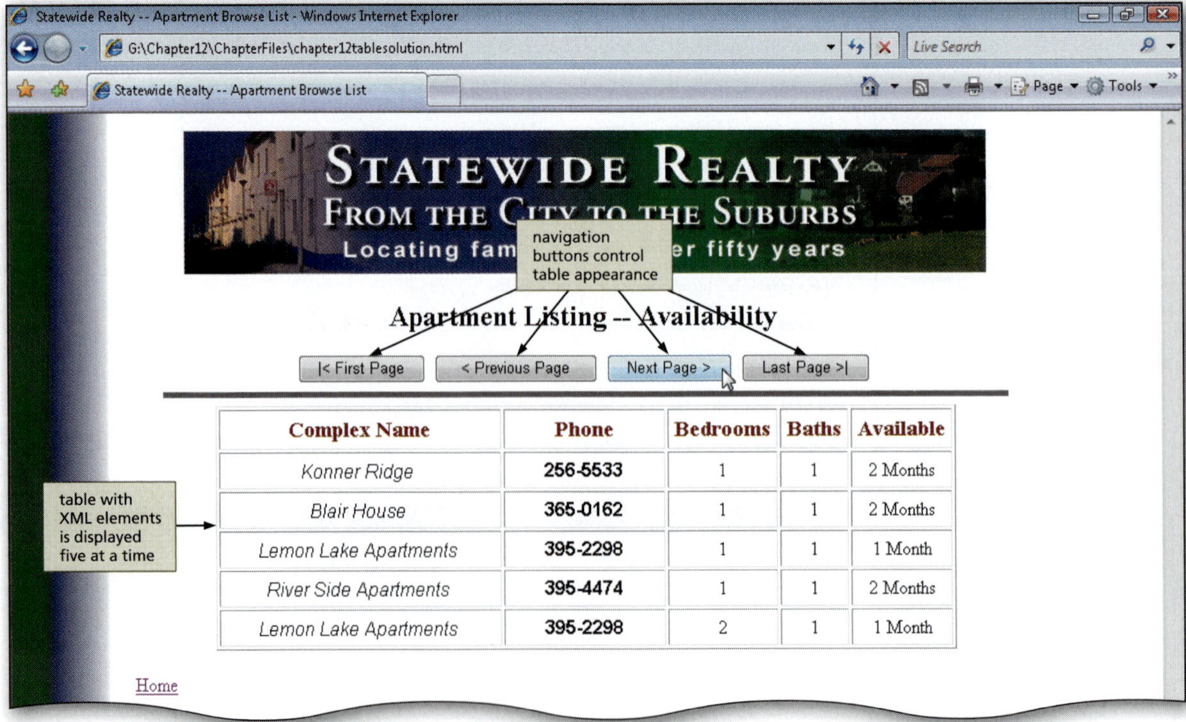

Figure 12–22

Data binding is the process of mapping XML elements to a data format that preserves the hierarchy of the data and allows the data to be manipulated using different methods. XML data binding requires two steps: linking an XML document to an HTML Web page and then binding the HTML elements to the XML elements.

Linking an XML document to an HTML Web page requires the use of the HTML element <xml> to create a data island. Recall that a data island is a set of data elements separate from the HTML Web page. A unique name represents the data island in the XML element, called a **data source object (dso)**. Table 12–22 shows the general form of the <xml> element.

> **BTW** **Data Binding**
> Data binding consists of four major pieces: the data source object (DSO), data consumers, the binding agent, and the table repetition agent.

Table 12–22 General Form of the HTML <xml> Element

General form:	<xml id="name" src="URL"></xml>
Comment:	The <xml> element is a Microsoft extension and may not be recognized by browsers other than Internet Explorer. The id attribute value, name, must be a unique name, and it must represent the data source. Web developers use the prefix dso before any name value to indicate that it is the data source object. The URL is the location and name of the XML data file. The <xml> element must have an end element.
Example:	<xml id="dsoApartment" src="apartmentlist-type.xml"></xml>

When the browser opens the HTML Web page, the XML parser reads and parses the XML data. The browser then creates a data island or data source object (dso), which handles and manipulates the XML data as a recordset. A **recordset** is a collection of data records and their fields. The Internet Explorer browser also contains several built-in methods, properties, and events that are automatically associated with the recordset.

> **BTW** **The <xml> Tag and Validation**
> The <xml> tag is unique to Microsoft Internet Explorer in HTML. This tag is what links or binds an XML document to the Web page. This tag is not recognized by other browsers, so when validating the HTML pages this tag will be identified as invalid.

To Create an HTML Document to Display XML Data in a Table

The following step illustrates how to create the HTML document to display the XML data in a table.

1

- Activate the open Notepad window.
- With a USB drive plugged into your computer, open the file chapter12table.html from the Chapter12\ChapterFiles folder.
- Click File on the menu bar and then click Save As.

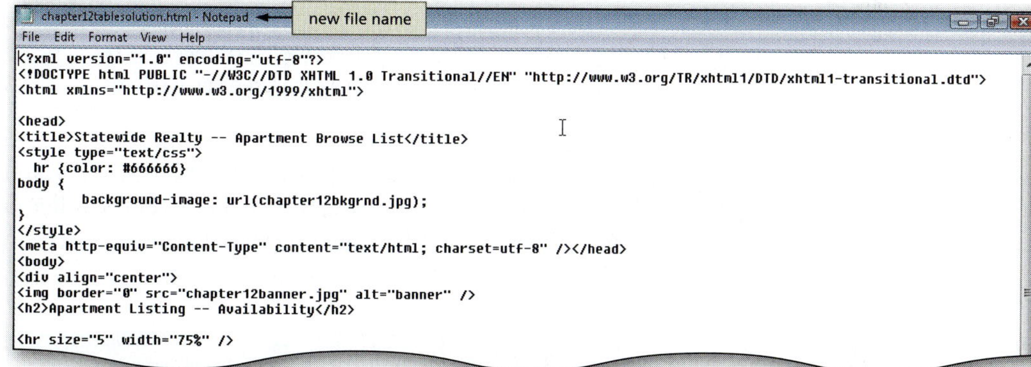

Figure 12–23

- Type `chapter12tablesolution.html` in the File name text box.
- Click the Save button in the Save As dialog box to save the file with a new name (Figure 12–23).

To Enter Code to Link an XML Document with an HTML Web Page

The following step illustrates how to bind the XML document, apartmentlist-bedroom.xml, with an HTML Web page.

1

- With the chapter12tablesolution.html Notepad window active, click line 4.
- Type <xml id="dsoApartments" src="apartmentlist-bedroom.xml"></xml> but do not press the ENTER key to link the XML document to the HTML Web page (Figure 12–24).

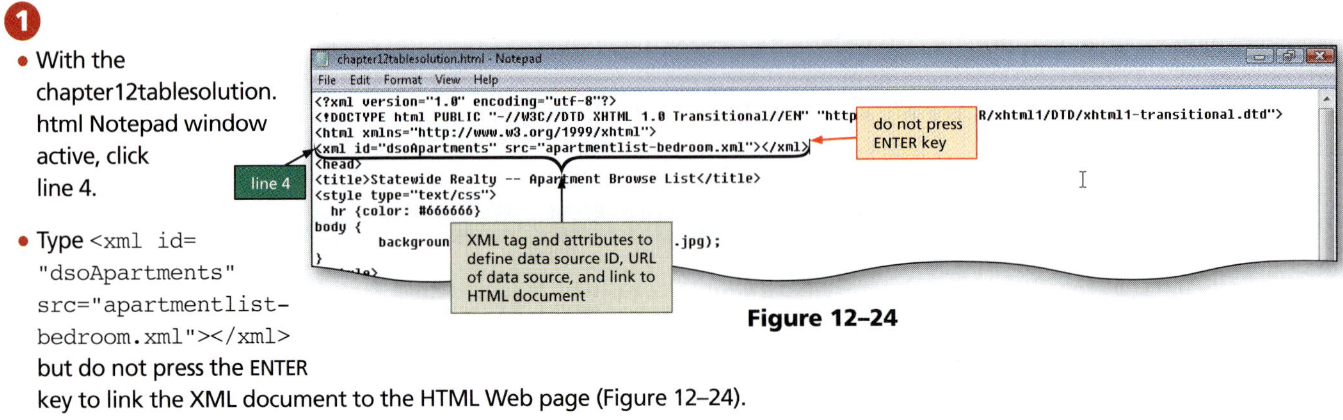

Figure 12–24

Adding Navigation Controls

The next step is to enter code to add the four navigation buttons that allow a user to manipulate the table appearance on the HTML Web page. Each of the four buttons calls an element method that will display the records in the table. Table 12–23 lists four table element methods.

Table 12–23 Table Element Methods

Method	Action	Example Code
firstPage	Displays the first page of records	TableName.firstPage()
previousPage	Displays the previous page of records	TableName.previousPage()
nextPage	Displays the next page of records	TableName.nextPage()
lastPage	Displays the last page of records	TableName.lastPage()

The buttons used to navigate through the records are standard HTML <form> buttons. When a user clicks a button, the onclick event handler calls the associated built-in method. Table 12–24 shows the code used to add the navigation buttons to the HTML Web page.

Table 12–24 Code for Adding Navigation Buttons

Line	Code
18	<button onclick="apartmentTable.firstPage()">|< First Page </button>
19	<button onclick="apartmentTable.previousPage()">< Previous Page </button>
20	<button onclick="apartmentTable.nextPage()"> Next Page > </button>
21	<button onclick="apartmentTable.lastPage()"> Last Page >| </button>

The apartmentTable object in each line associates the table, buttons, and the onclick event handlers for each button. The apartmentTable is the table ID, which will be entered in Table 12–25 on page HTML 584.

Line 18 creates the First Page button with the caption |< First Page. The code < is an ASCII character set that creates a less-than symbol (<), or angle bracket, on the button caption. The First Page button calls the firstPage() method, which tells the Web page to display the first set of records in the table. The code,   , is an ASCII character set to represent two spaces that separate the buttons. Line 19 creates the Previous Page button with the caption, < Previous Page. The Previous Page button calls the previousPage() method, which tells the Web page to display the previous set of records in the table. Line 20 creates the Next Page button with the caption, Next Page >. The > code is an ASCII character set that creates a greater than symbol (>), or angle bracket, on the button caption. The Next Page button calls the nextPage() method, which tells the Web page to display the next set of records in the table. Line 21 creates the Last Page button with the caption, Last Page >|. The Last Page button calls the lastPage() method, which tells the Web page to display the last set of records in the table. Each button uses the ASCII character set code,   , to place spaces between the buttons.

To Enter Code to Add Navigation Buttons

The following step illustrates how to enter the code to add the navigation buttons to the HTML Web page.

1

- Click line 18.
- Enter the code shown in Table 12–24 and do not press the ENTER key to enter the navigation buttons for the HTML table (Figure 12–25).

Q&A How do the built-in functions work?

All browsers have some ability to interpret client-side scripts, like JavaScript or PHP. The built-in functions are extensions of these scripts and can be utilized without specifically calling on a scripting language.

```
<title>Statewide Realty -- Apartment Browse List</title>
<style type="text/css">
  hr {color: #666666}
body {
        background-image: url(chapter12bkgrnd.jpg);
}
</style>
<meta http-equiv="Content-Type" content="text/html; charset=utf-8" /></head>
<body>
<div align="center">
<img border="0" src="chapter12banner.jpg" alt="banner" />
<h2>Apartment Listing -- Availability</h2>
<button onclick="apartmentTable.firstPage()">|&lt; First Page </button>  
<button onclick="apartmentTable.previousPage()">&lt; Previous Page </button>  
<button onclick="apartmentTable.nextPage()"> Next Page &gt; </button>  
<button onclick="apartmentTable.lastPage()"> Last Page &gt;| </button>
<hr size="5" width="75%" />

</div>
<p style="margin-left:10%"><a href="chapter12homesolution.html">Home</a></p>
<p style="font-size: 9pt; margin-left:10%">Please send any comments to <a
href="mailto:statewiderealty@isp.com">statewiderealty@isp.com</a>.</p>
</body>
</html>
```

line 18

code for navigation buttons with built-in methods

Figure 12–25

To Enter Code to Bind XML Elements to an HTML Table Header

Table 12–25 shows the <table> tag and the attributes needed to indicate the width of the table, indicate the number of rows to be displayed, and bind the data source object. The code in Table 12–25 includes the table heading <thead> and the individual column heading names. An inline style attribute formats the text of the column headings.

Table 12–25 Code for Binding XML Elements to an HTML Table — The Header

Line	Code
23	<table width="645" border="1" cellpadding="5" datapagesize="5" id="apartmentTable" datasrc="#dsoApartments">
24	<thead style="color:darkred; font-size:14pt; font-weight:900">
25	<th width="241">Complex Name</th>
26	<th width="132">Phone</th>
27	<th width="72">Bedrooms</th>
28	<th width="43">Baths</th>
29	<th width="72">Available</th>
30	</thead>

Line 23 starts the table definition with the <table> tag and includes an id attribute to name the table, apartmentTable, which relates to the onclick event handler for the buttons and built-in functions. The datasrc attribute must match the name of the data source object defined in the <xml> element on line 4 and be preceded by a pound sign (#) to read: #dsoApartments. The datapagesize attribute sets the size of the page to 5, so the table will be display with five records or rows at a time. The border and cellpadding attributes define the look of the HTML table. Lines 24 through 30 use the <thead> tag to create column headings.

The following step shows how to enter the code to start the HTML table.

- Click line 23.
- Enter the code shown in Table 12–25 and then press the ENTER key to bind the XML elements to the table header (Figure 12–26).

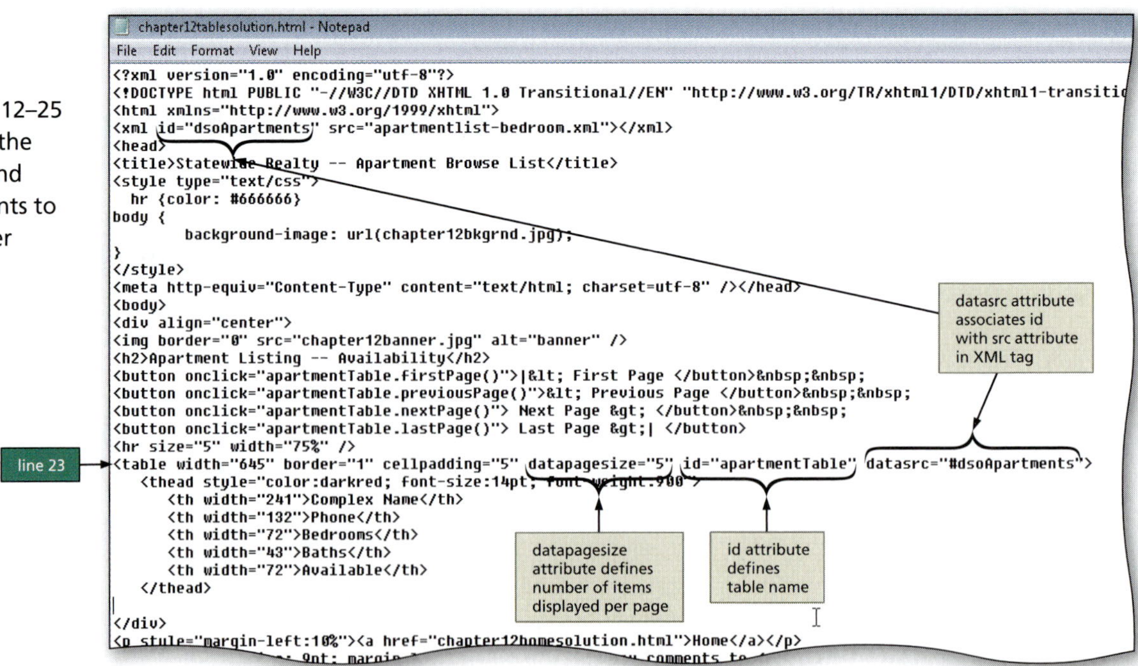

Figure 12–26

To Enter Code to Bind XML Elements to HTML Table Rows

Table 12–26 shows the code to complete the table that will display each row of data. The table contains one row and five cells of data. The <span> tag and the datafld attribute identify the XML element value to be displayed in each cell. Inline styles format the contents of the cells.

Table 12–26 Code for Binding XML Elements to an HTML Table — Table Rows

Line	Code
31	`<tr>`
32	`<td><span datafld="NAME" style="font-family:arial; font-style:italic"></span></td>`
33	`<td><span datafld="PHONE" style="font-family:arial; font-weight:900"></span></td>`
34	`<td><span datafld="BEDROOMS"></span></td>`
35	`<td><span datafld="BATHS"></span></td>`
36	`<td><span datafld="AVAILABLE"></span></td>`
37	`</tr>`
38	`</table>`

Line 31 creates a table row with the <tr> tag. Lines 32 through 36 create table cells using <td> tags. The datafld attribute of the <span> tags defines the specific XML element data value that appears in the cell. The <span> tag on line 32 also uses a style attribute to set the Name field to be displayed in italic font.

The following step illustrates how to enter the code to complete the table.

- If necessary, click line 31.
- Enter the code shown in Table 12–26 to bind the XML elements to the table rows (Figure 12–27).

```
<html xmlns="http                    html">
<xml id="dsoApartments" src="apartmentlist-bedroom.xml"></xml>
<head>
<title>Statewide Realty -- Apartment Browse List</title>
<style type="text/css">
  hr {color: #666666}
body {
        background-image: url(chapter12bkgrnd.jpg);
}
</style>
<meta http-equiv="Content-Type" content="text/html; charset=utf-8" /></head>
<body>
<div align="center">
<img border="0" src="chapter12banner.jpg" alt="banner" />
<h2>Apartment Listing -- Availability</h2>
<button onclick="apartmentTable.firstPage()">|&lt; First Page </button>  
<button onclick="apartmentTable.previousPage()">&lt; Previous Page </button>  
<button onclick="apartmentTable.nextPage()"> Next Page &gt; </button>  
<button onclick="apartmentTable.lastPage()"> Last Page &gt;| </button>
<hr size="5" width="75%" />
<table width="645" border="1" cellpadding="5" datapagesize="5" id="apartmentTable" datasrc="#dsoApartments">
   <thead style="color:darkred; font-size:14pt; font-weight:900">
      <th width="241">Complex Name</th>
      <th width="132">Phone</th>
      <th width="72">Bedrooms</th>
      <th width="43">Baths</th>
      <th width="72">Available</th>
   </thead>
   <tr>
       <td><span datafld="NAME" style="font-family:arial; font-style:italic"></span></td>
       <td><span datafld="PHONE" style="font-family:arial; font-weight:900"></span></td>
       <td><span datafld="BEDROOMS"></span></td>
       <td><span datafld="BATHS"></span></td>
       <td><span datafld="AVAILABLE"></span></td>
   </tr>
</table>
</div>
<p style="margin-left:10%"><a href="chapter12homesolution.html">Home</a></p>
<p style="font-size: 9pt; margin-left:10%">Please send any comments to <a
href="mailto:statewiderealty@isp.com">statewiderealty@isp.com</a>.</p>
</body>
```

line 31

span tags with datafld attribute to define XML elements to be displayed in each table cell

Figure 12–27

To Save the HTML File and Test the Web Page

Before proceeding, you should save and test the HTML Web page.

1

- With the USB drive plugged into your computer, click File on the menu bar and then click Save.
- Activate your browser. If necessary, maximize the window.
- Click the Address bar.
- Type `G:\Chapter12\ChapterFiles\chapter12tablesolution.html` and then press the ENTER key so the Web page is displayed in the browser.
- If necessary, click the security bar under the tabs, and then click Allow Blocked Content... on the menu.
- If necessary, click Yes in the Security Warning dialog box.
- Click the Next Page button.
- Click the First Page button and then click the Last Page button to scroll through the table (Figure 12–28).

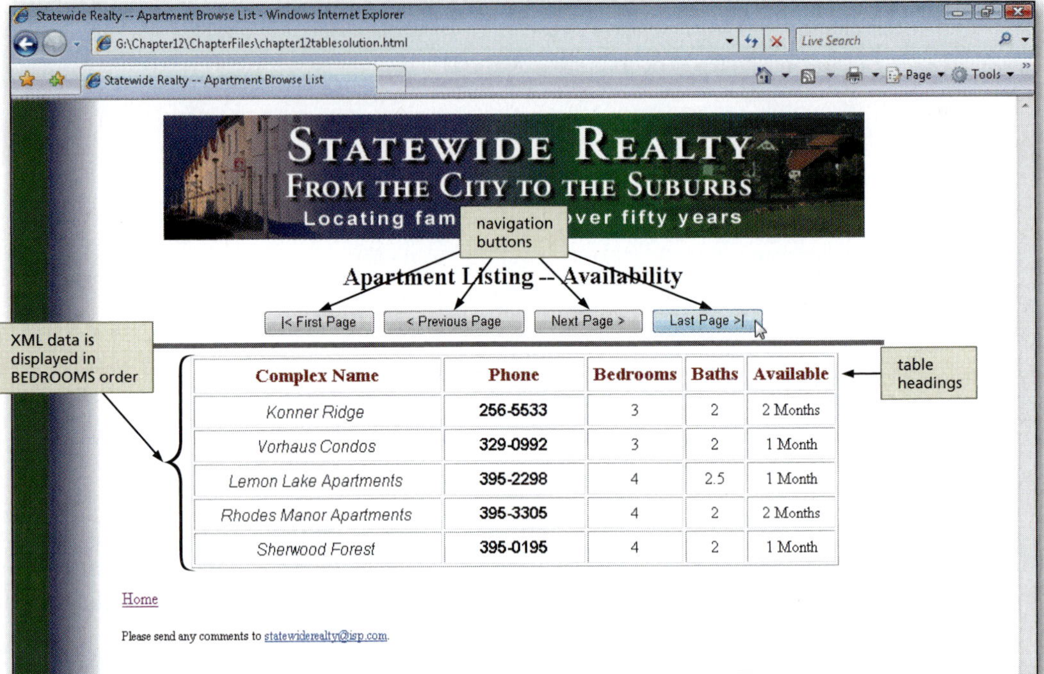

Figure 12–28

Q&A No JavaScript was actually entered into this HTML code. Where is the function that is associated with the buttons?

The firstPage(), nextPage(), previousPage(), and lastPage() functions are built into the Internet Explorer browser. These codes will not work with other browsers such as Firefox.

Plan Ahead

Creating an HTML document to search an XML document and display results.
The JavaScript code to find an apartment by number of bedrooms has four key components that you will create:

- The HTML element <xml> to create a data island
- An input text box and Search command button
- A <div> tag with an id attribute to identify the output area on the Web page
- A JavaScript function that cycles through the recordsets until it finds a match between the text box input value and the corresponding XML data element

(continued)

Plan Ahead

(continued)

After adding the four key elements, you will need to do the following:

- Bind the XML document to the HTML so the JavaScript user-defined function can find the data
- Add a form text field for input
- Add a button to activate the search
- Determine the output display area and format

Using JavaScript to Search an XML Document and Display Results on a Web Page

The third hyperlink on the Statewide Realty home page, Search by Bedrooms, links to a Web page that allows users to search for an apartment by the number of bedrooms (Figure 12–29). A common use for a database is providing a mechanism for users to search for specific data items. By creating data islands that bind with a Web page, a user can view records without conflicting with other database processes. A user can enter the number of bedrooms needed and then press the ENTER key or click the Search button. If a valid number of bedrooms are entered, the Web page will be displayed with all the available apartments matching that number of bedrooms. The HTML Web page is bound to the XML document, apartmentlist.xml, and uses a JavaScript function to search the XML recordsets for a match. The JavaScript code uses data source object properties and methods that are built-in functions of the Internet Explorer browser.

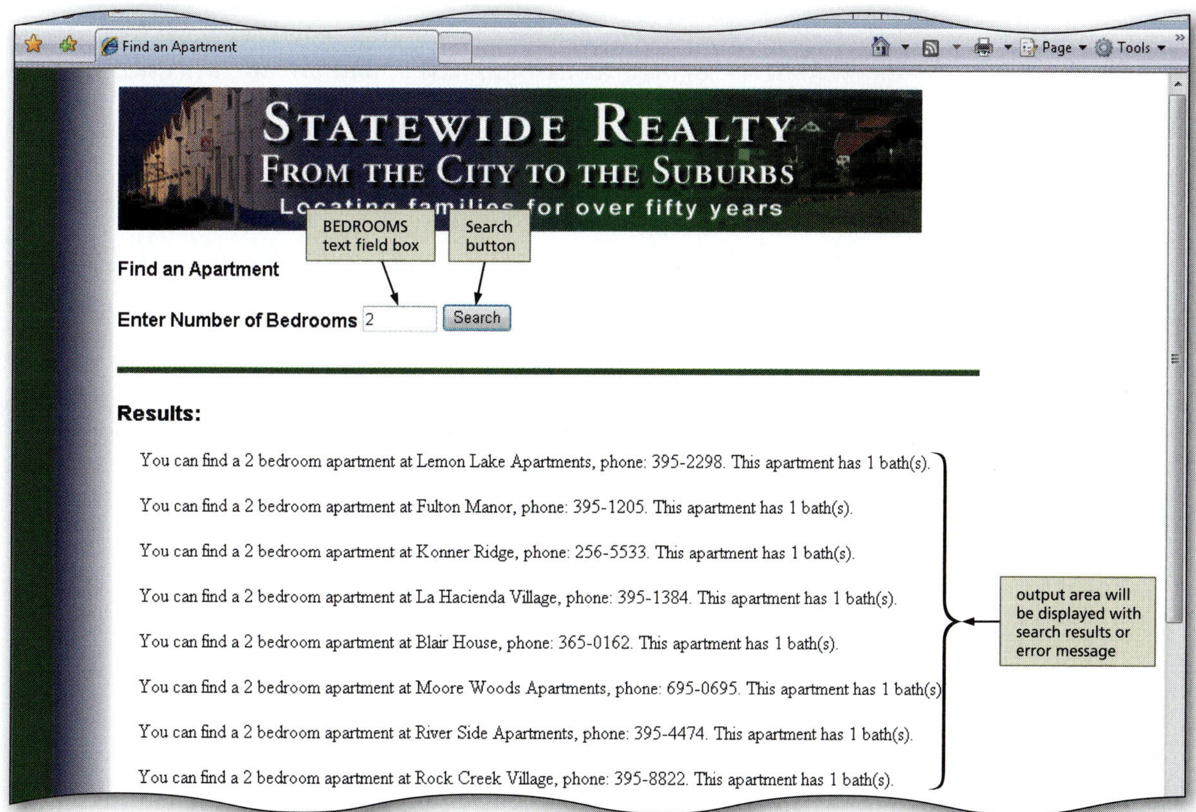

Figure 12–29

To Create an HTML Document to Search an XML Document and Display Results

The following step illustrates how to create the HTML Web page that allows users to search an XML document and view the results.

- If necessary, click the Notepad button on the taskbar to activate the Notepad window.
- With the USB drive plugged into your computer, open the file, chapter12findapartment.html, from the Chapter12\ChapterFiles folder.
- Click File on the menu bar and then click Save As.
- Type `chapter12findapartmentsolution.html` in the File name text box.
- If necessary, click UDISK (G:) and navigate to the Chapter12 folder, and then double-click the ChapterFiles folder in the list of available folders.
- Click the Save button in the Save As dialog box.

To Enter Code to Bind an XML Document with an HTML Web Page

To allow a user to search the XML document using the search function on this Web page, the XML document apartmentlist.xml must be bound to the HTML Web page by first linking the XML document to the HTML Web page and then binding the XML document with the HTML Web page. The following step shows how to enter the code that links the XML document, apartmentlist.xml, with the HTML Web page.

1

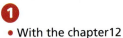

- With the chapter12findapartmentsolution.html Notepad window active, click line 4.
- Type `<xml id="dsoApartment" src="apartmentlist.xml"></xml>` but do not press the ENTER key to bind the XML document with the HTML code (Figure 12–30).

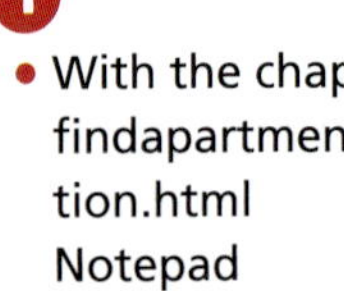

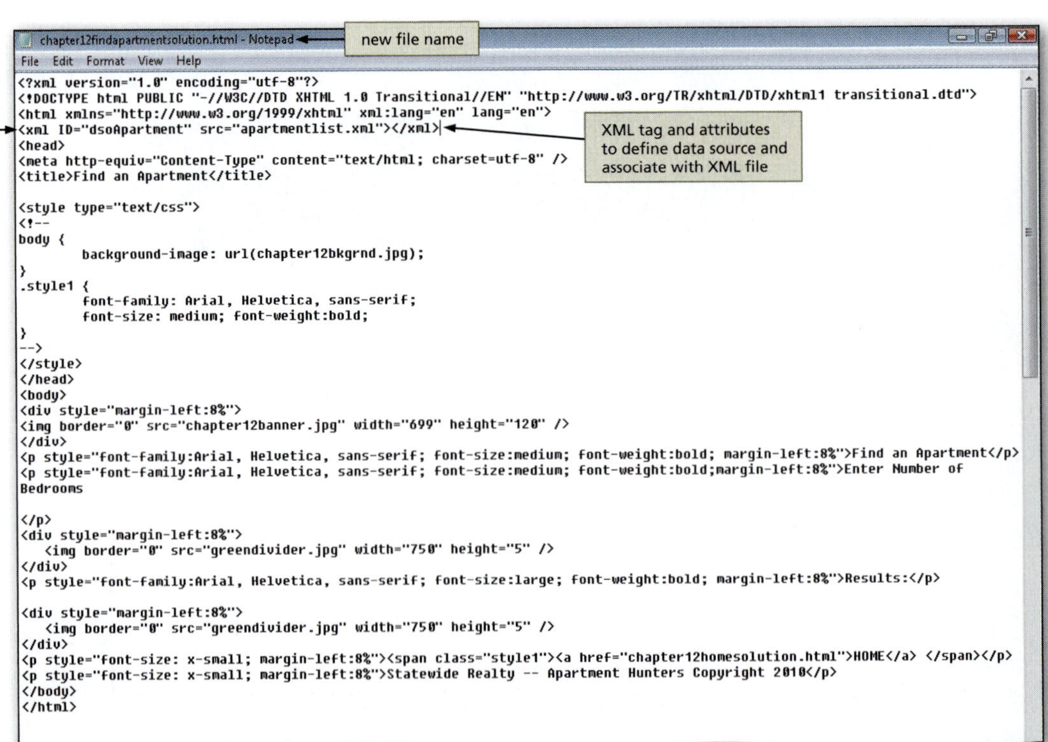


```
<?xml version="1.0" encoding="utf-8"?>
<!DOCTYPE html PUBLIC "-//W3C//DTD XHTML 1.0 Transitional//EN" "http://www.w3.org/TR/xhtml/DTD/xhtml1 transitional.dtd">
<html xmlns="http://www.w3.org/1999/xhtml" xml:lang="en" lang="en">
<xml ID="dsoApartment" src="apartmentlist.xml"></xml>
<head>
<meta http-equiv="Content-Type" content="text/html; charset=utf-8" />
<title>Find an Apartment</title>

<style type="text/css">
<!--
body {
        background-image: url(chapter12bkgrnd.jpg);
}
.style1 {
        font-family: Arial, Helvetica, sans-serif;
        font-size: medium; font-weight:bold;
}
-->
</style>
</head>
<body>
<div style="margin-left:8%">
<img border="0" src="chapter12banner.jpg" width="699" height="120" />
</div>
<p style="font-family:Arial, Helvetica, sans-serif; font-size:medium; font-weight:bold; margin-left:8%">Find an Apartment</p>
<p style="font-family:Arial, Helvetica, sans-serif; font-size:medium; font-weight:bold;margin-left:8%">Enter Number of
Bedrooms

</p>
<div style="margin-left:8%">
   <img border="0" src="greendivider.jpg" width="750" height="5" />
</div>
<p style="font-family:Arial, Helvetica, sans-serif; font-size:large; font-weight:bold; margin-left:8%">Results:</p>

<div style="margin-left:8%">
   <img border="0" src="greendivider.jpg" width="750" height="5" />
</div>
<p style="font-size: x-small; margin-left:8%"><span class="style1"><a href="chapter12homesolution.html">HOME</a> </span></p>
<p style="font-size: x-small; margin-left:8%">Statewide Realty -- Apartment Hunters Copyright 2010</p>
</body>
</html>
```

Figure 12–30

Adding the <input> and <button> Elements

The next step is to add the HTML <input> and <button> elements to create the input text box and Search command button. The code for the <input> element is entered as follows:

```
<input type="text" id="SearchText" size="5" onkeypress=
"keyPressed()" />
```

The type attribute defines the text box as text. The id attribute names the text box as SearchText, which becomes an object that the user-defined JavaScript function uses to access the input characters. The size attribute sets the width of the text box to 5 characters. The onkeypress event handler calls the keyPressed() user-defined function if the user pressed the ENTER key after typing in the data requested.

The code for the <button> element is written as follows:

```
<button onclick="findApartment()">Search</button>
```

An onclick event handler calls the user-defined JavaScript function, findApartment(). The text, Search, between the <button> elements defines the caption for the button. The two statements are entered on the same line, separated by the ASCII code, , representing a space.

To Enter Code to Add the <input> and <button> Elements

The following step shows how to enter the code to add the <input> and <button> elements to the Web page.

1

- Click line 27 and position the insertion point before the closing </p> paragraph tag.
- Type `<input type="text" id="SearchText" size="5" onkeypress="keyPressed()" /> ` and do not press the ENTER key to enter the search text field.
- On the same line, type `<button onclick="findApartment()">Search</button>` but do not press the ENTER key to enter the onclick event handler to call the user defined function (Figure 12–31).

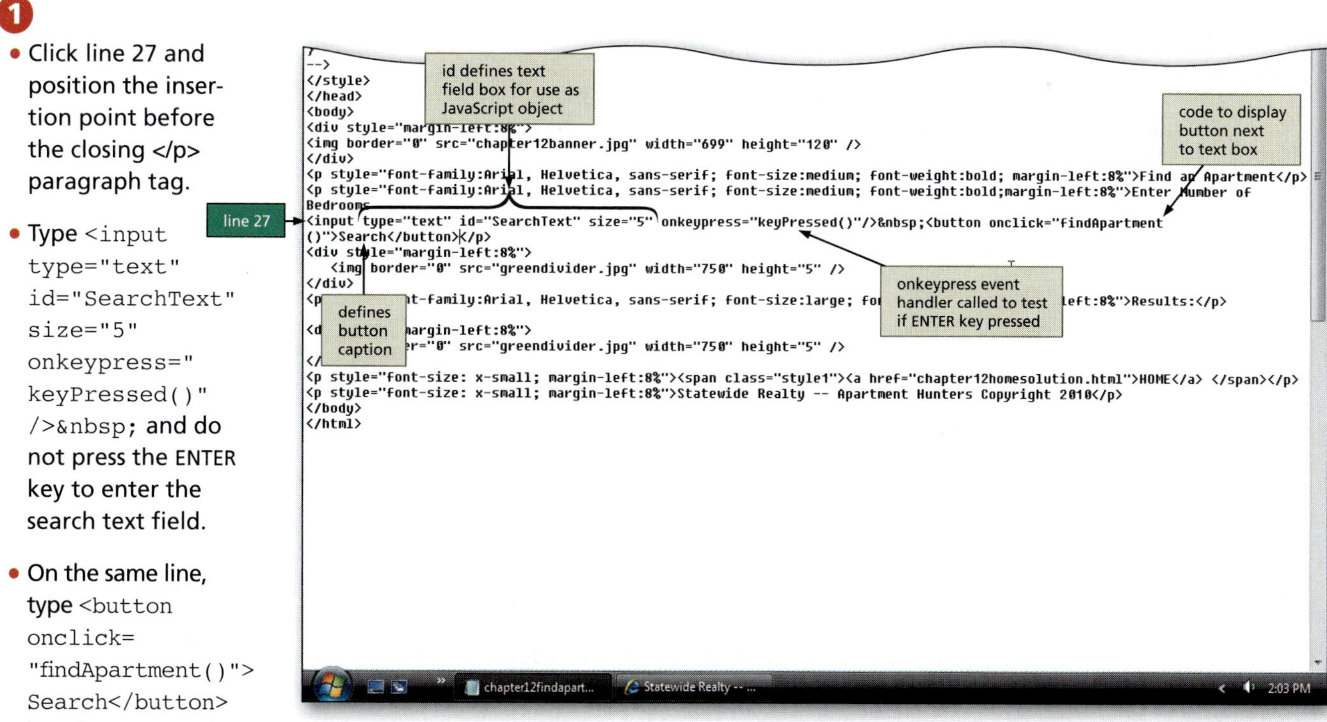

Figure 12–31

To Enter the <div> Element

The next step is to add the <div> element to define an output area of the Web page where search results will appear. To create the output area, the <div> tag uses the id attribute and value, SearchResult, to indicate that search results will be displayed in that area. The JavaScript user-defined function uses that id value to assign the search results to the output area of the Web page. The following step illustrates how to enter the <div> element to define the output area of the Web page.

- Click line 32.
- Type `<div id="SearchResult" style="margin-left:10%"></div>` and do not press the ENTER key to create the ouput area for the search results (Figure 12–32).

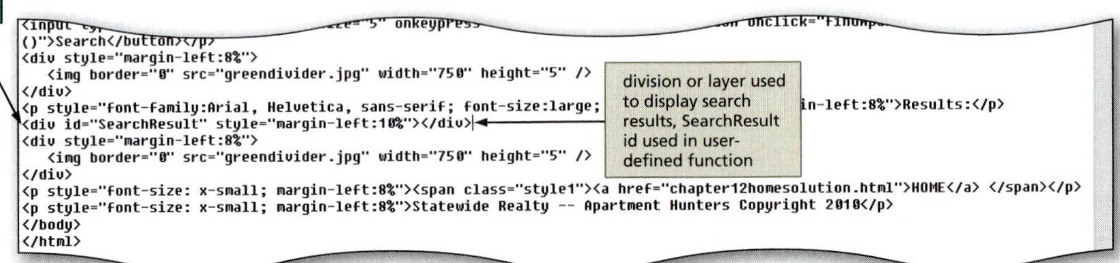

Figure 12–32

Plan Ahead

Writing the user-defined function findApartment().

The user-defined function, findApartment(), uses a combination of standard document object model (DOM) objects, properties, and methods and Internet Explorer's built-in XML parser methods to find an apartment in the XML document. The findApartment() function will accomplish the following activities to complete this action:

1. Convert the text field (search) input value into numbers (or in case of character data to uppercase characters).
2. Validate that the input value is a valid number (not blank, zero or negative).
3. Move to the first record in the XML document.
4. Compare each element in the XML document with the text box value until a match is found.
5. Construct an output text string with search results.

Creating the JavaScript User-Defined Functions, findApartment() and keyPressed()

The next step is to create the JavaScript user-defined function that takes a target value from the input search text box and compares it with the <BEDROOMS > elements in the XML document, apartmentlist.xml.

With the XML document linked to the HTML Web page, chapter12findap artmentsolution.html, the next step is to add the JavaScript user-defined functions, findApartment()and keyPressed(), to the HTML document. The findApartment() function is called when a user clicks the Submit button. The keyPressed() function is called when the user presses the ENTER key on the keyboard. The function's if statement examines the key to see if it was the ENTER key, by comparing the key to the number 13, which represents the ENTER key. If the ENTER key was pressed, the findApartment() function is called.

The code to begin the JavaScript section and create the findApartment() user-defined function is shown in Table 12–27.

Table 12–27 Code to Begin the JavaScript Section and Create the findApartment() Function

<table>
<tr><th>Line</th><th>Code</th></tr>
<tr><td>8</td><td><script type="text/javascript"></td></tr>
<tr><td>9</td><td><!--Hide from old browsers</td></tr>
<tr><td>10</td><td>function findApartment() {</td></tr>
<tr><td>11</td><td>SearchString = parseInt(SearchText.value,10)</td></tr>
<tr><td>12</td><td>if (isNaN(SearchString) || SearchString <= 0) {</td></tr>
<tr><td>13</td><td>SearchResult.innerHTML = "<Please enter a valid number for the bedrooms you need.>"</td></tr>
<tr><td>14</td><td>return</td></tr>
<tr><td>15</td><td>}</td></tr>
</table>

Lines 8 and 9 start the JavaScript <script> section. Line 11 converts the SearchText text box value to an integer value using the parseInt() method. The parseInt() method was used in Chapter 10 to convert text box values in a form to numbers. Line 12 is a standard if statement to determine if the resulting SearchString value is blank, or a negative number. If the string is not a number, the code assigns a message to the contents to <div> area innerHTML property. The return statement on line 14 stops the search and displays the error message. The brace on line 15 closes the if statement.

To Enter Code for the findApartment() User-Defined Function

The following step shows how to enter the conversion and validation statements for the findApartment() user-defined function.

1

- Click line 8.
- Enter the code shown in Table 12–27 and then press the ENTER key to enter the findApartment() user-defined function (Figure 12–33).

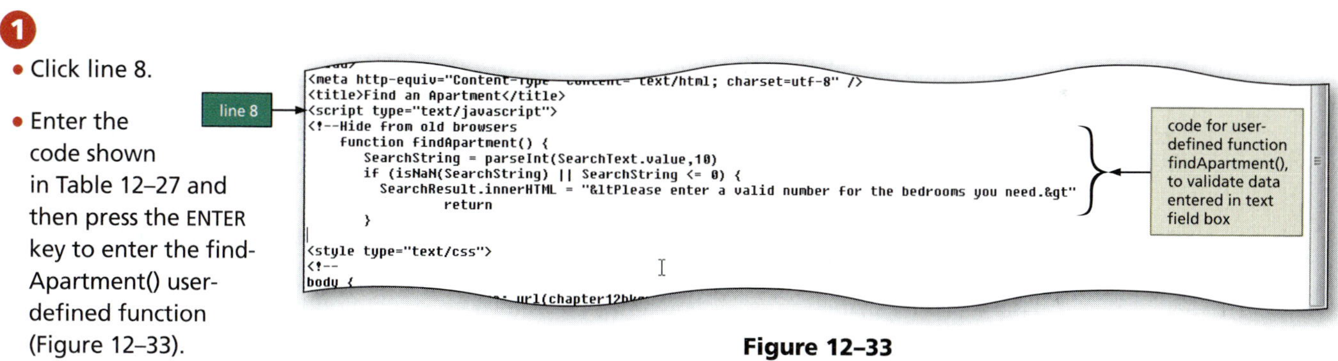

Figure 12–33

Searching the Recordset Values and Outputting Results

After converting the SearchText text box input value and validating that the value is a number, the findApartment() user-defined function sequentially searches through the data in the linked XML document, apartmentlist.xml, to find a match for the text box input value. The search uses the data source object, dsoApartment, and Internet Explorer's built-in methods to move through the records in the XML document. If a match is found, the function creates a results message that incorporates specific XML elements in the HTML string. Table 12–28 on the next page shows the JavaScript code that sequentially searches the XML document and creates the results message to be displayed in the output area.

Table 12–28 Code for Searching the Recordset Values and Building the Output String

Line	Code
16	dsoApartment.recordset.moveFirst()
17	var outputResult=""
18	while (!dsoApartment.recordset.EOF) {
19	BedString = dsoApartment.recordset("BEDROOMS").value
20	if (BedString.indexOf(SearchString)>=0)
21	outputResult += "You can find a " + dsoApartment.recordset("BEDROOMS")
22	+ " bedroom apartment at " + dsoApartment.recordset("NAME")
23	+ ", phone: "
24	+ dsoApartment.recordset("PHONE")
25	+ ". This apartment has "
26	+ dsoApartment.recordset("BATHS") + " bath(s).<p></p>"
27	dsoApartment.recordset.moveNext();
28	}

Recall that a recordset is a collection of data records. The built-in moveFirst() method on line 16 positions an internal pointer to the first record in the recordset of the data source object, dsoApartment. Line 17 initializes an output variable, outputResult, to a null or blank value. Line 18 starts a while processing loop. As you learned in Chapter 10, the while loop relies on a conditional statement to terminate. In this function, the while loop processes each record until the EOF property is true. **EOF** means end of file and signals that all XML document records have been read.

Line 19 assigns the values of the BEDROOMS element to the BedString variable of the current record. To determine if the value in the SearchString matches any part of the search text, line 20 uses the indexOf() method to look for a particular value in BedString. Recall from Chapter 10 that the indexOf() method returns the relative location of the value found. The if statement tests if the returned value is greater than 0, indicating a match was found. This method is used to allow this script to be changed easily and adapt to searching any text string.

Lines 21 through 27 construct the outputResult value. These lines concatenate the XML elements, the associated descriptive text, and the HTML tags together and assign the resulting string to the outputResult variable. The <p> tag on line 26 ensures that each outputResult string will appear on a separate line in the output area of the Web page. To read each of the records in the recordset, line 27 uses the built-in moveNext() method to tell the function to read the next record in the XML document. Line 28 closes the while loop.

To Enter Code to Search the Recordset Values and Build the Output String

The following step shows how to enter the code to search the apartmentlist XML file for an apartment.

1

- If necessary, click line 16.
- Enter the code shown in Table 12–28 to search the recordset values and build the output string. Press the ENTER key (Figure 12–34).

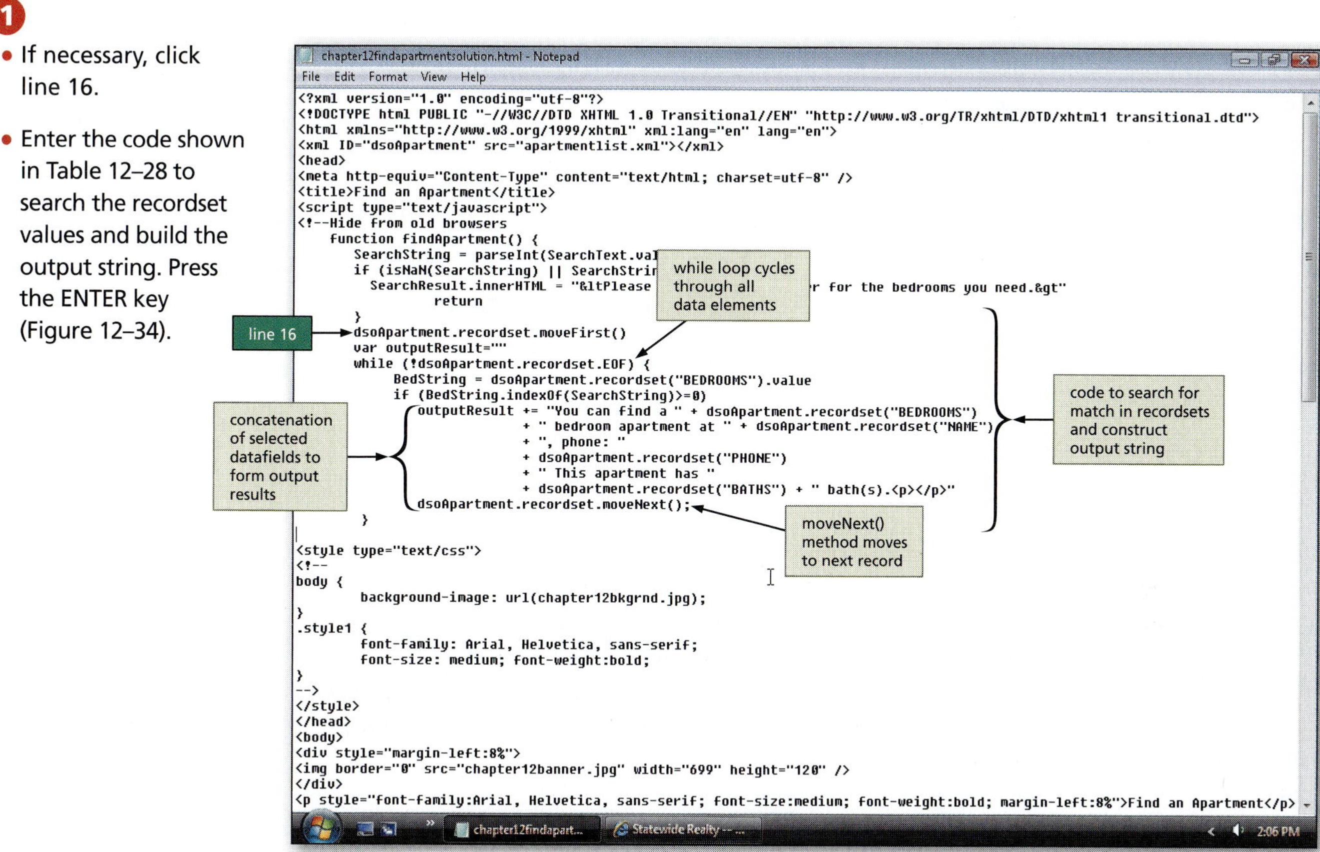

Figure 12–34

The next step is to test if the outputResult string has any content. If not, then a message to tell the users no results were found is assigned to the SearchResult.innerHTML object. Table 12–29 shows the code for building the no result found message.

Table 12–29 Completing the findApartment() function

Line	Code
29	`if (outputResult=="")`
30	`SearchResult.innerHTML = "<Sorry, we have no apartments that currently meet your needs. Call us for more information>";`
31	`else`
32	`SearchResult.innerHTML = outputResult`
33	`}`

Line 29 tests the outputResult variable. If the outputResult is blank because no match was found on line 20, then line 30 assigns a message to the SearchResult.innerHTML property that no record was found. If a match is found, the else portion of the if...else statement on line 31 displays the outputResult results message constructed on lines 21 through 26. Line 33 ends the user-defined function.

To Enter Code to Complete the findApartment() Function

1

- Click line 29.
- Enter the code shown in Table 12–29 on previous page and then press the ENTER key to enter the code to complete the findApartment() function (Figure 12–35).

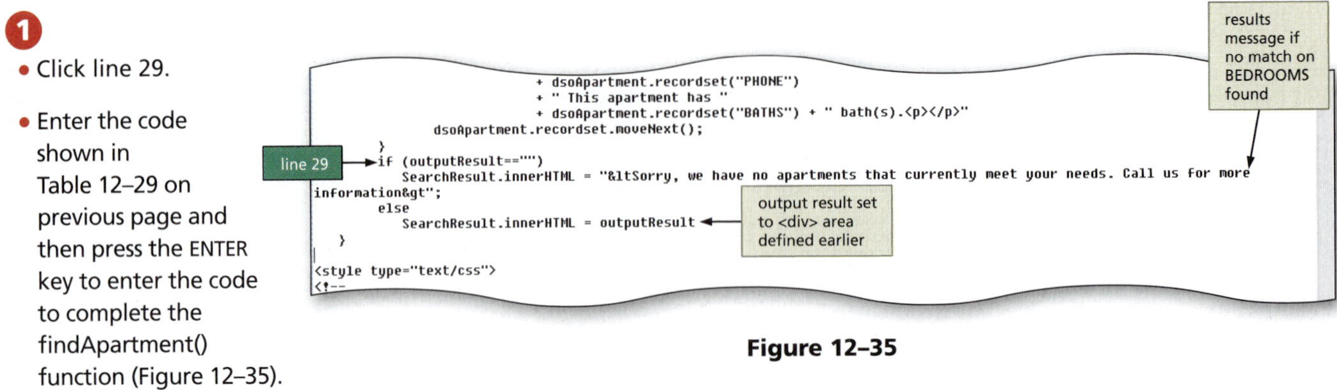

Figure 12–35

To Enter the Code for the keyPressed() Function

Table 12–30 shows the code to create a JavaScript user-defined function, called keyPressed(), so that if the ENTER key is pressed, it calls the findApartment() user-defined function.

Table 12–30 Code for the keyPressed() User-Defined Function

Line	Code
35	`function keyPressed(k) {`
36	`var hitEnter=event.keyCode`
37	`if (hitEnter==13) findApartment()`
38	`}`
39	
40	`//-->`
41	`</script>`

Line 35 declares the keyPressed() user-defined function and accepts a parameter value k, which represents the key pressed. Line 36 assigns the value of the keyCode property of the key pressed to a decimal value stored in the variable, hitEnter. The if statement on line 37 tests if the value of hitEnter is equal to 13, which is the decimal equivalent of the ENTER key. If hitEnter is equal to 13, meaning the ENTER key has been pressed, then the find-Apartment() user-defined function is called. The keyPressed() function is called with every press of a key until the ENTER key is pressed. Line 41 closes the JavaScript function.

The following step shows how to enter the keyPressed() user-defined function.

1

- Click line 35.
- Enter the code shown in Table 12–30 and then press the ENTER key to enter the code for the keyPressed() function (Figure 12–36).

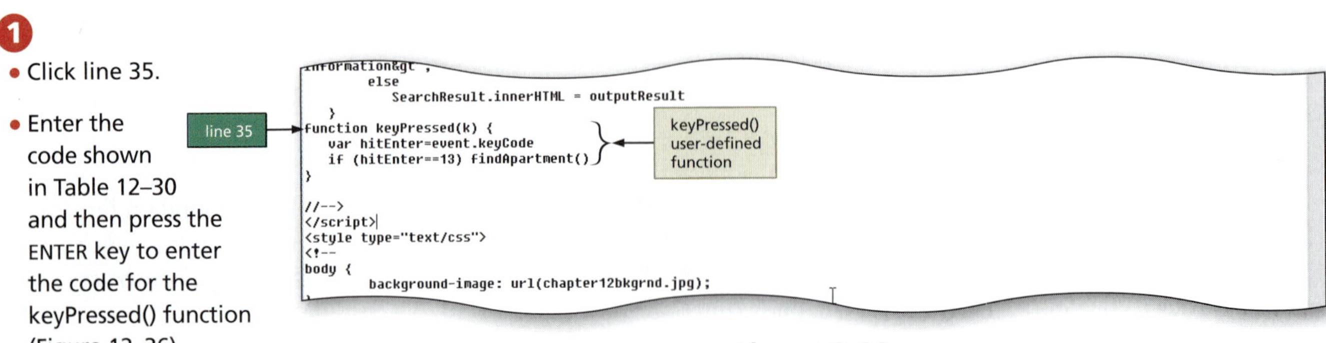

Figure 12–36

To Save and Test the HTML Document in the Browser

1

- With your USB drive plugged into your computer, click File on the menu bar and then click Save.
- Click the browser button on the taskbar to activate the browser.
- Click the Address bar. Type `G:\Chapter12\ChapterFiles\chapter12findapartmentsolution.html` and then press the ENTER key so the Web page is displayed in the browser.
- Enter the data values shown in Table 12–31 in the input text box and then click the Search button to test this Web page (Figure 12–37).

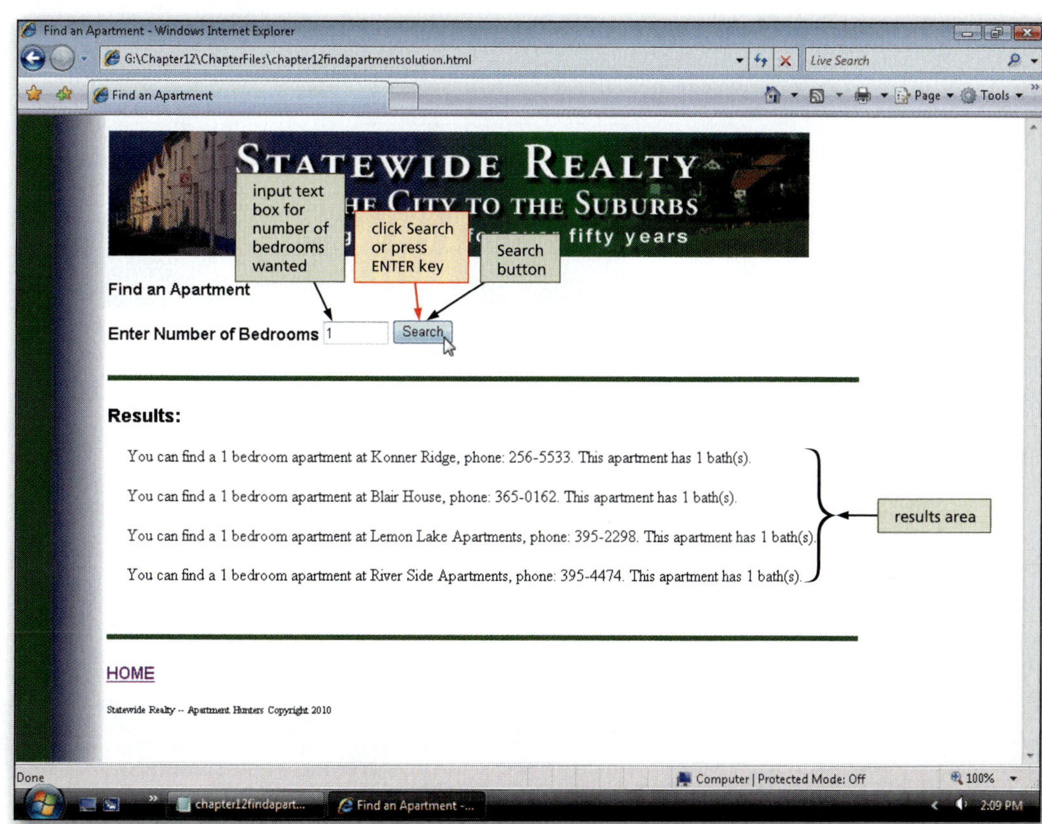

Figure 12–37

Table 12–31 Search Test Data

Test Data Set	Number of Bedrooms	Results Message
1	3	Five apartment complexes should be displayed with three bedrooms
2	blank	<Please enter a valid number for the bedrooms you need.>
3	-2	<Please enter a valid number for the bedrooms you need.>
4	1	Four apartment complexes should be displayed with one bedroom.

To Verify the Links on the Statewide Realty Web Page

A final test is necessary to verify that the links on chapter12homesolution.html, the main Statewide Realty Web page, are correct. The file, chapter12homesolution.html, is included in the Data Files for Students. The following step illustrates how to verify the links on the Statewide Realty Web page are correct.

1

- Click the Address bar. Type `G:\Chapter12\ChapterFiles\chapter12homesolution.html` and then press the ENTER key to display the Web page in the browser.
- Click the Browse by Complex image hot spot link (Figure 12–38a).
- After viewing the Web page, click the Back button on the browser toolbar to return to the Statewide Realty Web home page.
- Click the Browse by Vacancy image hot spot link (Figure 12–38b).
- After viewing the Vacancy Web page, click the Back button on the browser toolbar or click the Home link to return to the Statewide Realty Web page.
- Click the Search by Bedrooms image hot spot link.
- When the Statewide Realty – Search by Bedrooms page is displayed, enter a 2 in the search text field and then click Search to search for apartments with two bedrooms (Figure 12–38c).

Q&A What if the browser does not display the Web pages correctly?

Close any error message windows. Make sure the file names match the hyperlinks, and check the code associated with that Web page.

XML data formatted by XSL style sheet

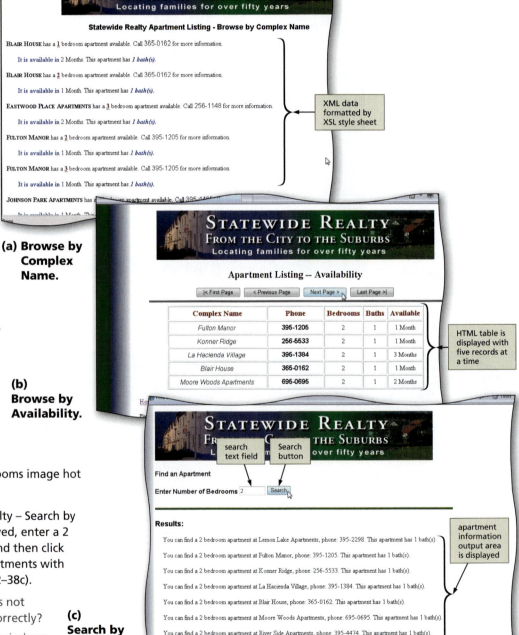

(a) Browse by Complex Name.

HTML table is displayed with five records at a time

(b) Browse by Availability.

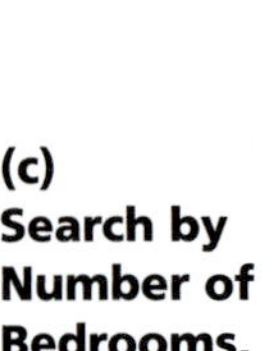

search text field

Search button

apartment information output area is displayed

(c) Search by Number of Bedrooms.

Figure 12–38

To Validate a Web Page

The following step illustrates how to validate an HTML file.

- Open Internet Explorer and navigate to the Web site `validator.w3.org`.
- Click the Validate by File Upload tab.
- Click the Browse button.
- Locate the chapter12homesolution.html file on your storage device and then click the file name.
- Click the Open button in the Choose file dialog box and the file name will be inserted into the File box.
- Click the Check button.
- Click the Browse button.
- Locate the apartmentlist-dtd.xml file on your storage device and then click the file name.
- Click the Open button in the Choose file dialog box and the file name will be inserted into the File box.
- Click the Revalidate button.

To Close Notepad and the Browser

After verifying the links on the main Statewide Realty Web page are correct and that Web page is valid, close Notepad and your browser.

- Click the Close button on the browser title bar.
- Click the Close button on the Notepad window title bar.

BTW **Quick Reference**
For more information on XML and XSL, see the XML Quick Reference (Appendix F) at the back of this book, or visit the HTML Quick Reference Web page (scsite.com/HTML5e/qr).

Chapter Summary

In Chapter 12, you learned how to create and use XML documents. You created a well-formed and valid XML document with a Document Type Definition, and formatted an XML document by linking both a CSS and an XSL style sheet. By binding an XML document with an HTML Web page, you created Web pages that displayed XML data in a table and you learned to code a JavaScript function to search for records in an XML document. The items listed below include all the new skills you have learned in this chapter.

1. Start Notepad and Create a New XML Document (HTML 556)
2. Enter the Prolog in an XML Document (HTML 559)
3. Start Entering the Document Instance in an XML Document (HTML 562)
4. Finish Entering the Document Instance in an XML Document (HTML 563)
5. Save and Test the XML Document (HTML 564)
6. Correct the Tag Error and Retest the XML Document (HTML 565)
7. Create an External Style Sheet Using CSS (HTML 569)
8. Link an External Cascading Style Sheet to an XML Document (HTML 570)
9. Test an XML Document Formatted Using an External CSS (HTML 571)

10. Open and Save an XML Document with a New File Name (HTML 572)
11. Start Creating an XSL Style Sheet (HTML 573)
12. Add XML Tags to a template Element in an XSL Style Sheet (HTML 575)
13. Finish Creating an XSL Style Sheet (HTML 577)
14. Save an XSL Style Sheet (HTML 578)
15. Link an XSL Style Sheet to an XML Document (HTML 578)
16. Save and Test an XML Document Formatted Using an XSL Style Sheet (HTML 579)
17. Create an HTML Document to Display XML Data in a Table (HTML 581)
18. Enter Code to Link an XML Document with an HTML Web Page (HTML 582)
19. Enter Code to Add Navigation Buttons (HTML 583)
20. Enter Code to Bind XML Elements to an HTML Table Header (HTML 584)
21. Enter Code to Bind XML Elements to HTML Table Rows (HTML 585)
22. Create an HTML Document to Search an XML Document and Display Results (HTML 588)
23. Enter Code to Bind an XML Document with an HTML Web Page (HTML 588)
24. Enter Code to Add the <input> and <button> Elements (HTML 589)
25. Enter the <div> Element (HTML 590)
26. Enter Code for the findApartment() User-defined Function (HTML 591)
27. Enter Code to Search the Recordset Values and Build the Output String (HTML 593)
28. Enter code to Complete the findApartment() Function (HTML 594)
29. Enter Code for the keyPressed() Function (HTML 594)
30. Verify the Links on the Statewide Realty Web Page (HTML 596)

Learn It Online

Test your knowledge of chapter content and key terms.

Instructions: To complete the Learn It Online exercises, start your browser, click the Address bar, and then enter the Web address `scsite.com/html5e/learn`. When the HTML Learn It Online page is displayed, click the link for the exercise you want to complete and read the instructions.

Chapter Reinforcement TF, MC, and SA

A series of true/false, multiple choice, and short answer questions that test your knowledge of the chapter content.

Flash Cards

An interactive learning environment where you identify chapter key terms associated with displayed definitions.

Practice Test

A series of multiple choice questions that test your knowledge of chapter content and key terms.

Who Wants To Be a Computer Genius?

An interactive game that challenges your knowledge of chapter content in the style of a television quiz show.

Wheel of Terms

An interactive game that challenges your knowledge of chapter key terms in the style of the television show, *Wheel of Fortune*.

Crossword Puzzle Challenge

A crossword puzzle that challenges your knowledge of key terms presented in the chapter.

Apply Your Knowledge

Reinforce the skills and apply the concepts you learned in this chapter.

Instructions: Start Notepad. Open the file apply12-1data.txt from the Chapter12\Apply folder of the Data Files for Students. See the inside back cover of this book for instructions on downloading the Data Files for Students, or contact your instructor for information about accessing the required files. Create an XML document with a DTD to make it a valid XML file. The database has the following schema: item (item-id, description, seller, est-value) as indicated by the title row in the text file. Use the identifier of sport-memorabilia for the DTD. Figure 12–39 shows the Apply Your Knowledge Web page as it should be displayed in a browser.

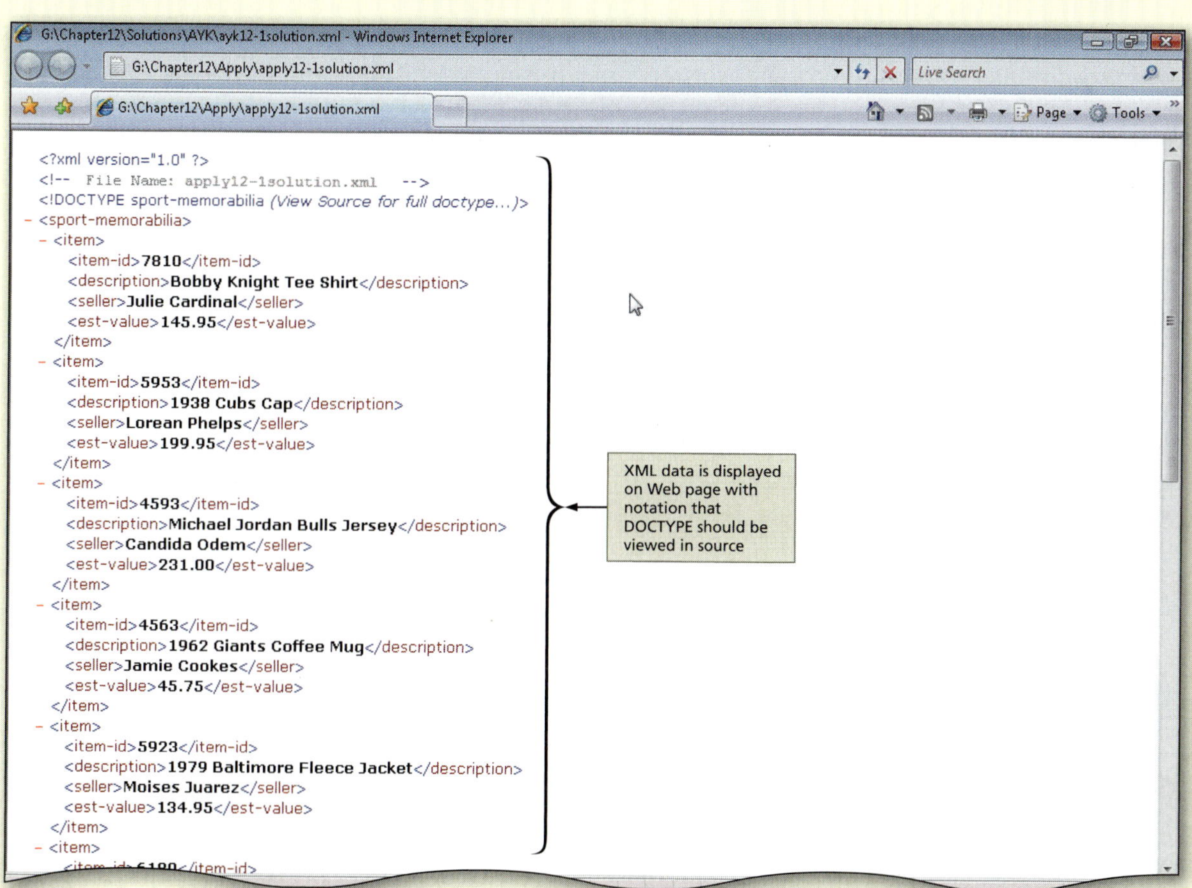

Figure 12–39

Perform the following tasks:

1. Create the first two lines of the prolog following the example in Tables 12-4 and 12-5 on pages HTML 556 and 557.
2. Using Table 12–6 on page HTML 557 as a guide, enter the document type declaration and Document Type Definition (DTD) for the XML document, starting on line 4.
3. Using Table 12–9 on page HTML 560 as a guide, enter the XML document instance elements using the item data in the apply12-1data.txt file.
4. Save the XML document in the Chapter12\Apply folder using the file name apply12-1solution.xml.

Continued >

Apply Your Knowledge *continued*

5. Start your browser. Enter G:\Chapter12\Apply\apply12-1solution.xml in the Address box to view the XML document in your browser. If an error occurs, check your code against the instructions in Steps 1 through 3 and then save and test the XML page again.
6. Submit the revised XML file and Web page in the format specified by your instructor.

Extend Your Knowledge

Extend the skills you learned in this chapter and experiment with new skills. You will need to search the Internet to complete the assignment.

Learning More about Displaying XML Data Islands

Instructions: Start Notepad and your browser. Open the file, extend12-1.html from the Chapter12\Extend folder of the Data Files for Students. See the inside back cover of this book for instructions on downloading the Data Files for Students, or contact your instructor for information about accessing the required files.

Images do not display in XML files. You need the help of HTML. Search the Internet for instructions on how to display an image in the HTML table. You may have to modify this code slightly. Using the concepts presented in Tables 12-24 through 12-26 on pages HTML 582 through 585 as a guide, modify the extend12-1.html Web page by adding a table, and the navigation buttons, so one car shows up with an image on each page. Figure 12–40 shows the completed page.

Perform the following tasks:

1. With the extend12-1.html file open in Notepad, save it immediately as extend12-1solution.html.
2. Start a new Notepad document and, using the data found in CarsXML.txt, create an XML document called extend12-1solution.xml.
3. With the extend12-1solution.html Notepad window active, use the steps described for Figure 12–24 on page HTML 582 as a guide, and add the <xml> tag to identify the source file extend12-1solution.xml.
4. Using the code in Table 12–24 on page HTML 582 as a guide, enter the code to create buttons with the following text values: First Car, Previous Car, Next Car, and Last Car.
5. Using the code in Tables 12-25 and 12-26 on pages HTML 584 and HTML 585 as a guide, enter the code to create HTML table cells, replacing the comment line : <!--Table contents go here-- > to display the XML contents in the table.
6. Save the completed HTML document in the Chapter12\Extend folder.
7. Start your browser. Enter G:\Chapter12\Extend\extend12-1solution.html in the Address box to view the XML document in a table in your browser. If an error occurs, check your code against the instructions in Steps 1 through 5 and then save and test the XML page again.
8. Submit the revised XML file and HTML Web page in the format specified by your instructor.

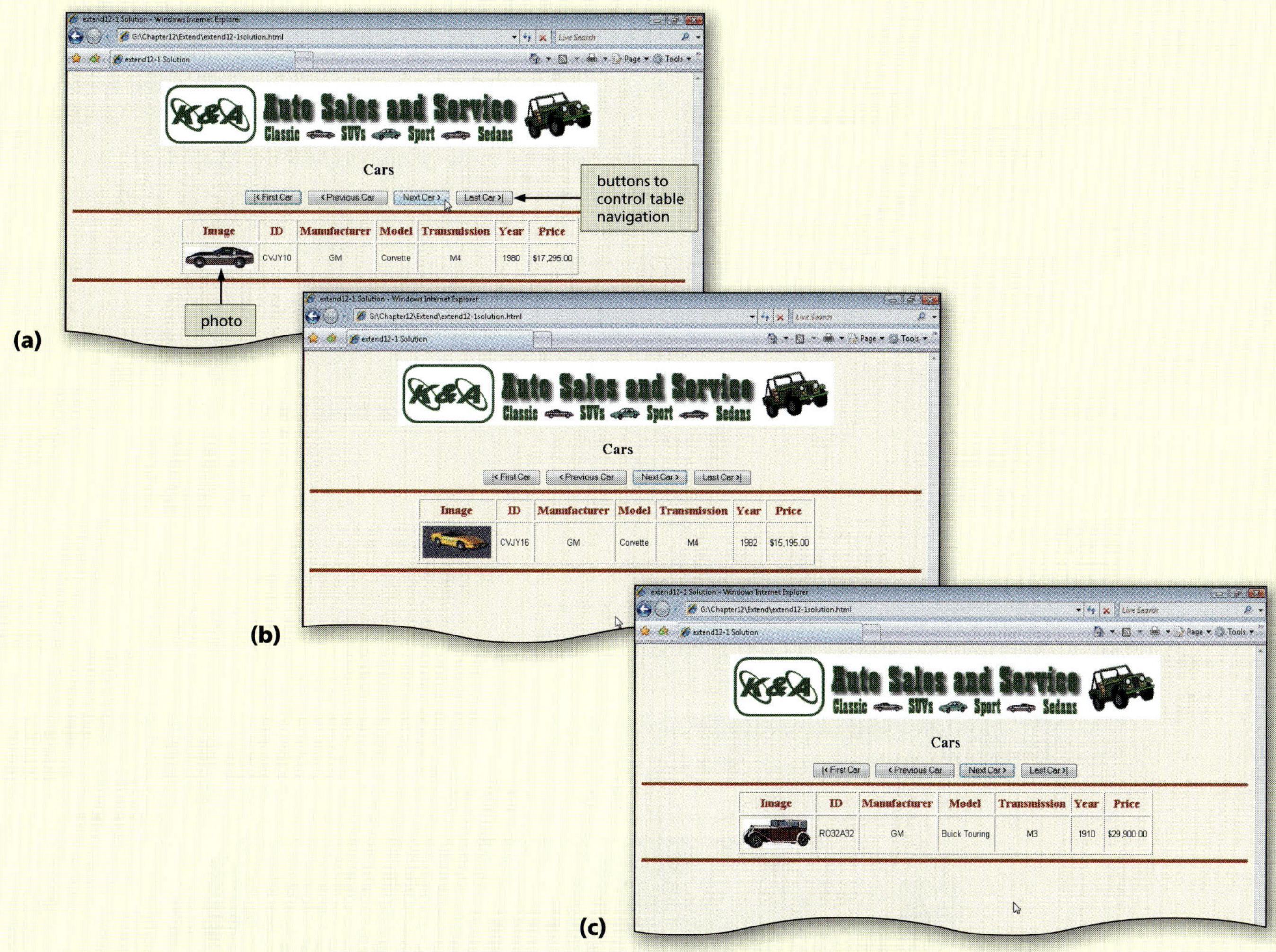

Figure 12–40

Make It Right

Analyze the XML code on a Web page and correct all errors.

Correcting Syntax Errors

Instructions: Start your browser. Open the file makeitright12-1.xml from the Chapter12\MakeItRight folder of the Data Files for Students. See the inside back cover of this book for instructions on downloading the Data Files for Students, or contact your instructor for information about accessing the required files.

The Web page is the Tampa Bay Area Transit morning commuter train schedule. This XML Web page will not display because it has four errors that you are to find and correct. In addition, the XSL page has one error that needs to be corrected before the Web page can display without error messages as shown in Figure 12–41.

Perform the following tasks:

1. Open makeitright12-1.xml in Notepad and immediately save as makeitright12-1solution.xml.
2. Open the makeitright12-1.xsl file in Notepad. Save it immediately as makeitright12-1solution.xsl.
3. Click the browser button on the taskbar. Enter G:\Chapter12\MakeItRight\makeitright12-1solution.xml in the Address box to view the XML document in your browser. Make note of the error message that appears.

Continued >

Make It Right *continued*

4. Correct the error and save the XML file. Activate the browser and refresh the Web page. A second error should be displayed.
5. Correct the error and save the XML file. Activate the browser and refresh the Web page. Make sure the XML file is error free before continuing. Correct the next error, refresh the Web page, and correct the fourth error in the XML file. Make sure all the XML file errors have been corrected before continuing.
6. In the second line of the makeitright12-1solution.xml file, using the code associated with Figure 12–20 on page HTML 578 as a guide,insert the style sheet processing instruction statement to link the XSL style sheet to the XML file.
7. Save the XML Notepad file, activate the browser, and refresh the Web page.
8. A fifth error will be displayed related to the XSL style sheet.
9. Activate the makeitright12-1solution.xsl file, correct the error indicated in the browser, then save the XSL Notepad file and refresh the Web page.
10. If an error still occurs, check your code from Steps 1 through 9, save the files, and test again in the browser.
11. Submit the revised XML and XSL files in the format specified by your instructor.

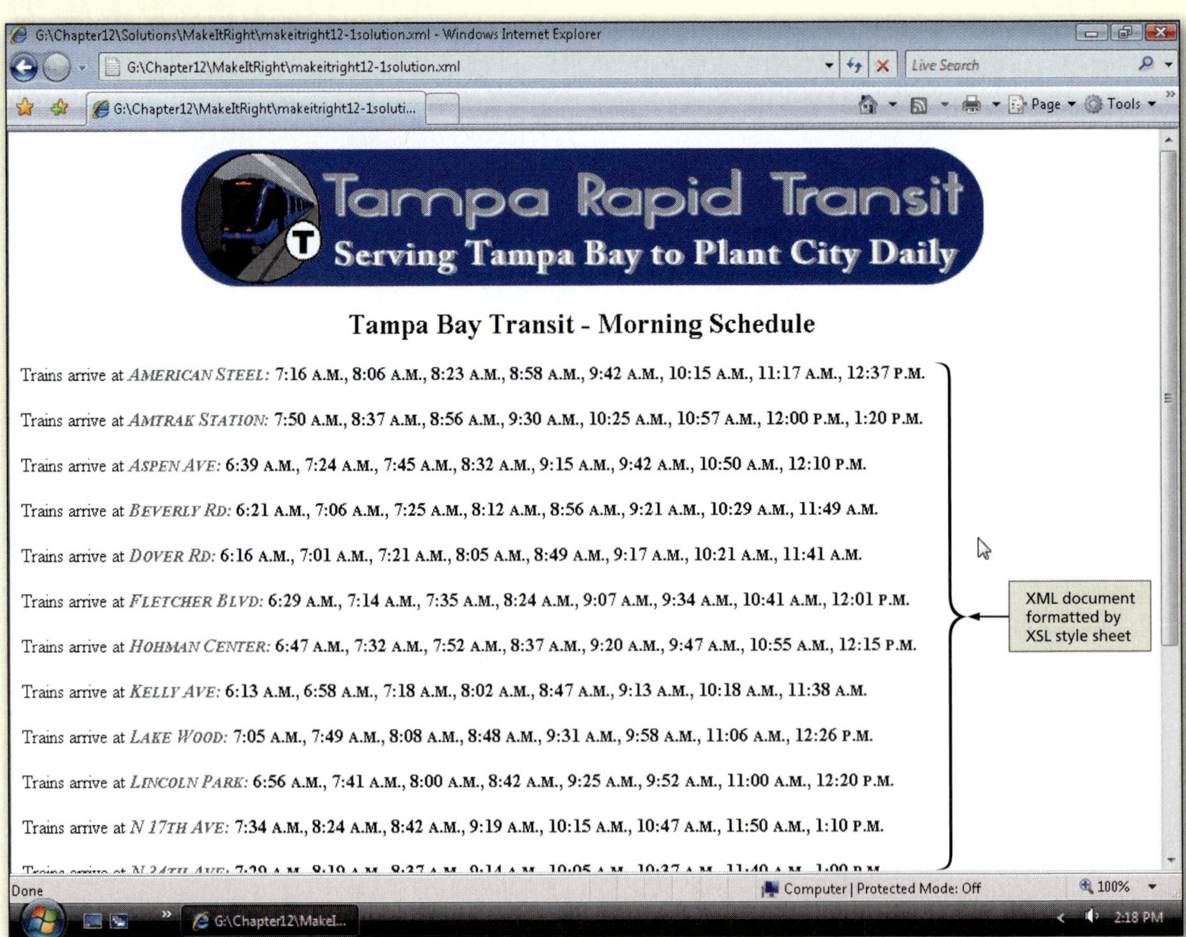

Figure 12–41

In the Lab

Design and/or create a Web page using the guidelines, concepts, and skills presented in this chapter. Labs are listed in order of increasing difficulty.

Lab 1: Creating the Taft Middle School Weekly Lunch Menu

Problem: You are the Webmaster for the Taft School District. The principal has asked you to create a Web page that will display the weekly lunch menu, one day at a time (Figure 12–42). Using an XML data island, you know you can create a Web page quickly that allows interaction and the ability to see individual days of the week.

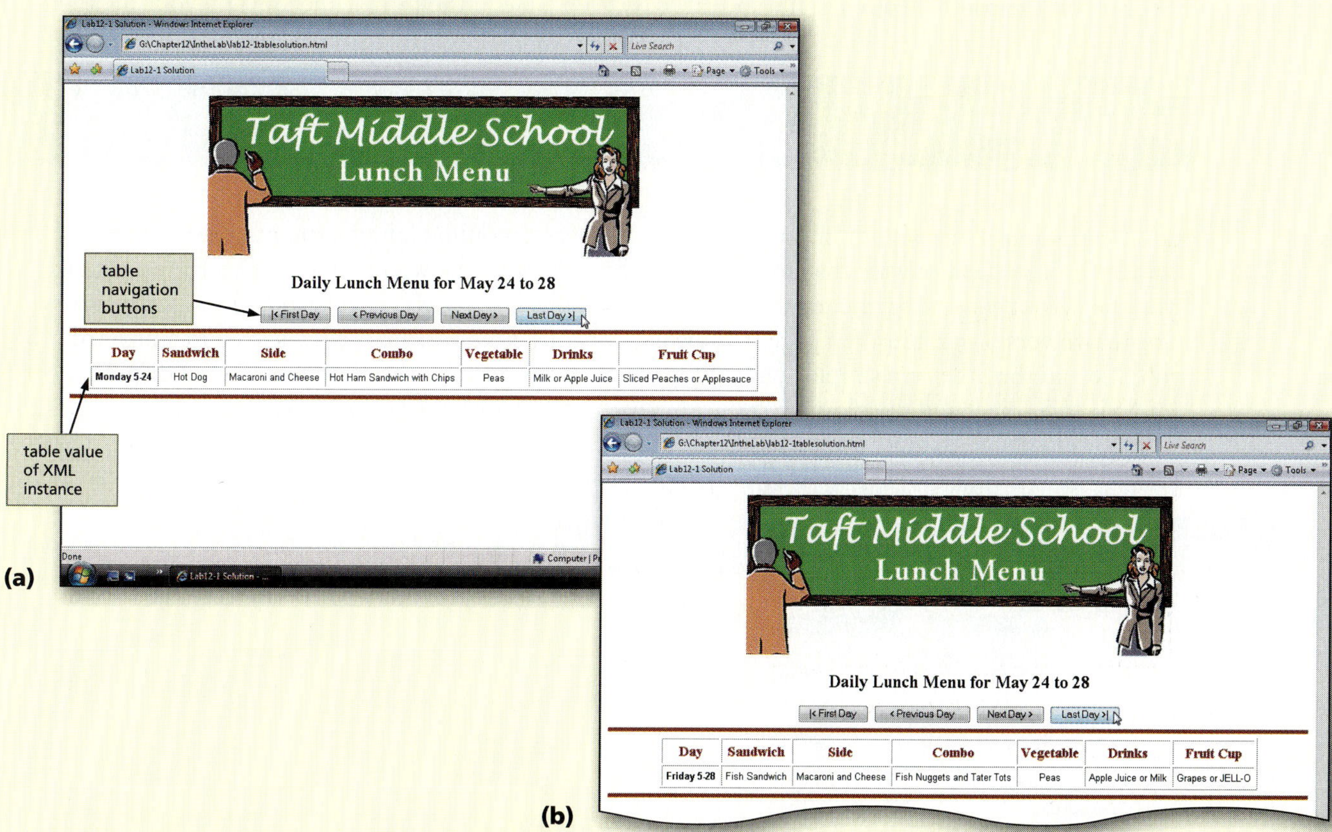

Figure 12–42

Instructions: Perform the following steps:

1. Start a new blank Notepad file.
2. Create the XML data island using the text found in lab12-1lunch.txt. Save the data island file as lab12-1solution.xml.
3. Start Notepad and open the file lab12-1table.html from the Chapter12\IntheLab folder of the Data Files for Students.
4. Save the file as lab12-1tablesolution.html.
5. Use the code presented in Figure 12–23 and Tables 12-24 through 12-26 on pages HTML 581 through HTML 585 as a guide to add the HTML to view lunch menu items in the XML data island. Use the <xml> tag id of dsoMenu to identify the data island in the remainder of the HTML page.

Continued >

In the Lab *continued*

6. On the buttons, use First Day, Previous Day, Next Day, and Last Day as button label text respectively.
7. In the <table> tag, use "LunchMenu" as the id, "#dsoMenu" as the datasrc, and use "1" as the datapagesize. Keep the border to 1, and cellpadding to 5.
8. Use Day, Sandwich, Side, Combo, Vegetable, Drinks, and Fruit Cup as the column headings in the table.
9. In the cells, use the appropriate XML data island tag names for the datafld attributes.
10. Save the completed HTML file and test it using your browser. If an error occurs, check your code from Steps 1 through 9 and save and test again.
11. Submit the completed XML file and HTML Web page in the format specified by your instructor.

In the Lab

Lab 2: Creating the Career Helpers XML Data Island

Problem: You are a summer intern for Career Helpers, an online job placement bureau. They list hundreds of jobs nationwide that are posted on the Internet. The webmaster, Darius Evans, assigns you the task of converting the text file version of the jobs to an XML data island. He wants you to create two versions of the Web page that display the jobs. One version is a list sorted in alpha order by job title and the other is a simple search Web page. You determine the sorted list can be displayed with an XSL style sheet and the search can be done with simple a JavaScript routine.

You add the XSL code and JavaScript to make the Web pages appear as shown in Figure 12–43.

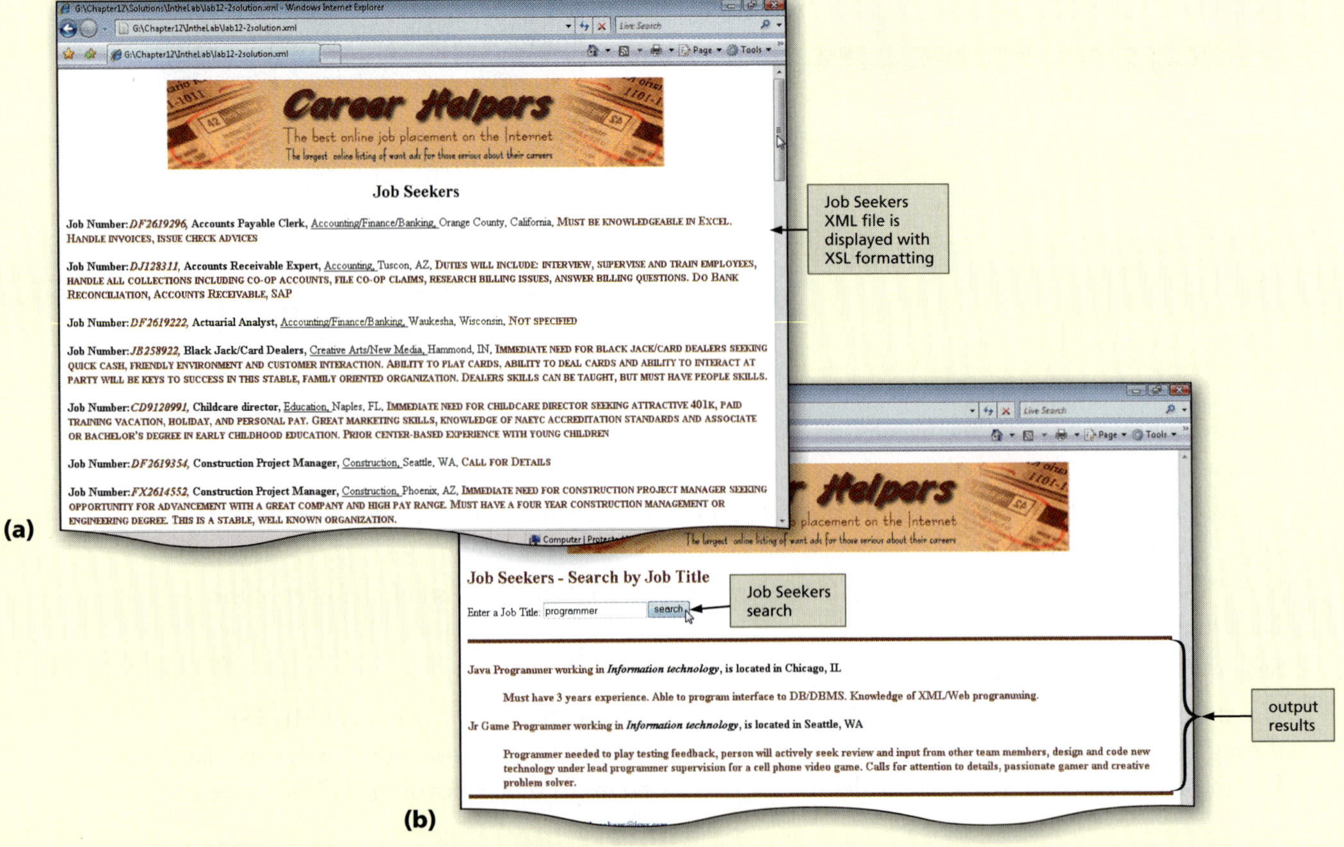

Figure 12–43

Instructions: Perform the following steps:

1. Use Notepad and open the lab12-2data.txt file from the Chapter12\IntheLab folder of the Data Files for Students.
2. Create an XML data file using this data and save the file as lab12-2solution.xml.
3. In a new Notepad session, open the lab12-2.xsl file and save immediately as lab12-2solution.xsl.
4. Use the code in Tables 12-18 through 12-20 on pages HTML 575 and 576 as a guide to complete the XSL style sheet to display the jobs list in alphabetic order by job title. Save the completed file. Use the style definitions in Table 12–32 to create the XSL style sheet.

Table 12–32 Lab 12-2 Style Definitions

text/Element items	Style
Job Number	font-weight:bolder
value-of select="reference"	font-variant:small-caps; font-style:italic; font-weight:bold; color:#834411
value-of select="title"	font-variant:normal; font-weight:bolder; color:#000000
value-of select="category"	font-variant:normal; font-weight:medium; color:#000000; text-decoration:underline
value-of select="location"	font-variant:normal; font-weight:medium; color:#000000
value-of select="description"	font-variant:small-caps; font-weight:bold; color:#834411

5. Activate the lab12-2solution.xml Notepad file and add the XML processing statement to link the XSL file with the XML data.
6. Start your browser and display your lab12-2solution.xml file in the browser to make sure it displays correctly.
7. Start another new Notepad session and open the lab12-2.html file and immediately save it as lab12-2solution.html.
8. Use the code presented in Figures 12-30 through 12-35 on pages HTML 588 through 594 as a guide to write the JavaScript code to search for a job based on Job Title.
9. Save the completed HTML file and test it using your browser. If an error occurs, check your code from Steps 1 through 8 and save and test again.
10. Submit the completed XML, XSL, and the HTML search Web page in the format specified by your instructor.

In the Lab

Lab 3: Creating the Lincoln Pioneers Web Site

Problem: You work for Lincoln Pioneers as the team publication relations leader. Part of your job is collecting and recording the team statistics and creating and maintaining the team Web site. You recently converted the team's stats to an XML data island to allow fans to browse or search information about the team or individual team members. Your assignment is to create a Web site that is depicted in Figure 12–44. This Web site allows fans to browse the database in batting average order, to browse a table of team players in player number order, and to search for individual team members by last name.

The lab12-3solutionindex.html home page is provided in the Data Files for Students. This page has links to the three pages you will finish: lab12-3xslsolution.xml, lab12-3tablesolution.html, and lab12-3searchsolution.html.

Continued >

In the Lab *continued*

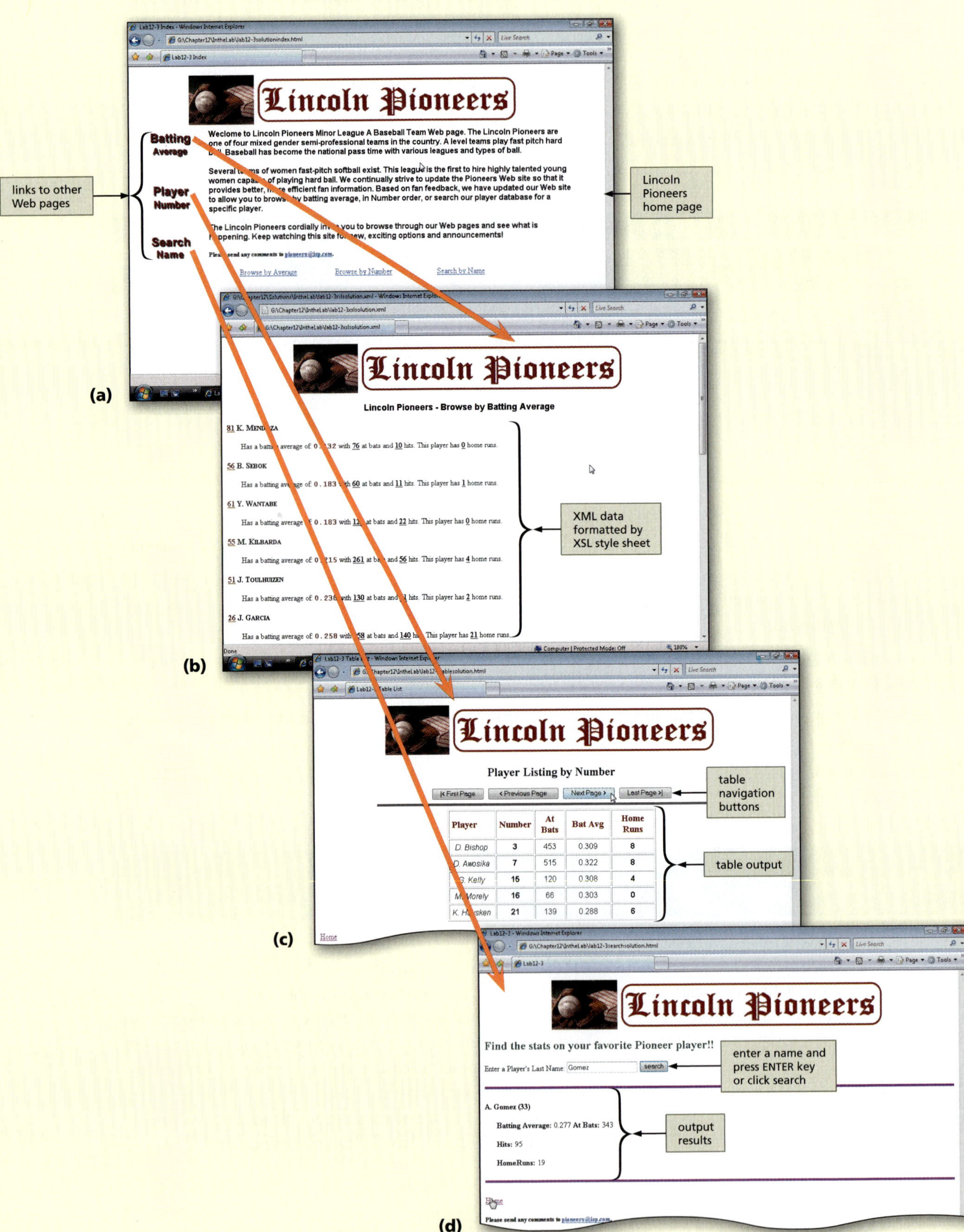

Figure 12–44

Instructions: Perform the following steps:

1. Using the techniques learned in this chapter, create an XML data island from the lab12-3playersdata.txt file. This XML file should be in player number order and include a DTD. Save this file as lab12-3xslsolution.xml. In addition, add the proper XML processing statement in your XML file to link lab12-3solution.xsl, which will be created in Step 2.
2. Using the techniques learned in this chapter, write XSL code to create an XSL style sheet that will display the data island in batting average order. Use the style definitions in Table 12–33 to create the XSL style sheet. Save this file as lab12-3solution.xsl.

Table 12–33 Lab 12-3 Style Definitions

Text/Element items	Style
Lincoln Pioneers - Browse by Batting Average	font-weight:bold; font-family:arial, helvetica, san-serif; font-size:18px
value-of select="PlayerNumber"	font-weight:bold; text-decoration:underline; color:#7f0000
value-of select=PlayerName	font-variant:small-caps; font-weight:bold
Has a batting average of:	margin-left: 3%
value-of select="BattingAvg"	font-family:Courier New; font-weight:bold; color:7f0000"
value-of select="AtBat"	font-weight:bold; text-decoration:underline;
value-of select="Hits"	font-weight:bold; text-decoration:underline
value-of select="HomeRuns	font-weight:bold; text-decoration:underline

3. Make a copy of lab12-3xslsolution.xml. Rename the copy file to lab12-3solution-number.xml. You must remove the DTD from this version of the XML file for use in the table to display the HTML page.
4. Starting with lab12-3table.html, use the techniques learned in this chapter to create an HTML Web page that will display the data island in a table. Show only five players at a time. Save this file as lab12-3tablesolution.html.
5. Starting with lab12-3search.html, use the techniques learned in this chapter create an HTML Web page that allows the fans to search the XML data file on last name. As in the chapter project, the user should be able to click the Search button or press the ENTER key to activate the search. Save this file as lab12-3searchsolution.html. Use lab12-3solution-number.xml as the XML data island for the JavaScript search function.
6. Make sure you save the completed XML, XSL, and HTML files. The HTML lab12-3solutionindex.html has been provided. It has links to each of these files. Start your browser and test the files. If an error occurs, check your code, save and test again.
7. Submit the completed XML, XSL, and HTML Web page files in the format specified by your instructor.

Cases and Places

Apply your creative thinking and problem solving skills to design and implement a solution.

• Easier •• More Difficult

• 1: Create a Web Page for Community Non-credit Courses

You have been a volunteer member of the Great Northern Community Center, which serves as your community's sponsor for community events, parks, and other activities. The president of the center has asked you if you could create a Web page that will display the various non-credit courses the

Continued >

Cases and Places *continued*

community center offers. He gives you a text file, case12-1data.txt in the Chapter12/CasesPlaces folder of the Data Files for Students, with the information about the courses. Create an XML data island and format the display using an XSL style sheet.

• • 2: Create a Restaurant Supply Web Site

As a summer intern for the Calumet Restaurant Supply company, you are given the task to create a Web site that allows customers to browse a list of inventory or to search the inventory for specific items. You have a file called case12-2index.html, which has two links: one to browse the data in a table (case12-2tablesolution.html) and the other to search for specific items by description.

Using the file, case12-2data.txt in Chapter12\CasesPlaces folder of the Data Files for Students, create an XML data island with a DTD. Save the XML document as case12-2solution.xml. Using the case12-2table.html file, create an HTML Web page that displays the data items, four to a page, in a table using the navigation buttons discussed in this chapter. Save this file as case12-2tablesolution.html. In addition, using case12-2search.html, create a Web page that allows the customer to search for items by entering in part or all of a description. Save this file as case12-2searchsolution.html.

• • 3: Create the Redstone Cinema Movie Database

As the newly hired Webmaster for Redstone Cinema, which maintains a database of information about movies, you are asked to create a Web site (use the graphics supplied) that allows users to view movies in genre order, in year order, and to search for movies by year. The movie data is supplied with the file case12-3data.txt in Chapter12\CasesPlaces folder of the Data Files for Students. You are to create an XML file with a DTD. Name the file case12-3movies-all.xml. Create an XSL file that will sort and display this file by year. Bind this XSL stylesheet to the file case12-3movies-all.xml. This XML file will be used in the search Web page. Make a copy of the original XML file and name it case12-3movies-all2.xml.

Using the case12-3solutionindex.html file, create a Web site that has a main page (index) with links to a Web page that lists all the movies in case12-3movies-all2.xml in a table in Genre (Type) order. Create another Web page that lists the movies in title order using case12-3movies-all.xml. Using the techniques learned in this chapter, create the XSL file that sorts the movies in Title order. Save this XSL file as case12-3movie-title.xsl and bind it to case12-3movies-all2.xml. Finally, create a Web page that allows the user to search movies by typing in a year. Use the file case12-3movies-all.xml as the data island. Save this file as case12-3searchsolution.html.

• • 4: Create a Club Roster

Make It Personal

Are you a member of a club? Perhaps they would like a club membership roster. Create the XML data island of a campus club. Display the list in a Web page using an XSL style sheet sorted by last name. Display the list using an HTML table. If you learned the techniques in the Extend Your Knowledge exercise, add member's photos to the Web page and data island.

• • 5: How to Create XML Files from Existing Database or Spreadsheet Files

Working Together

Each group member should find at least one Microsoft Access database file and one Microsoft Excel file (you can create your own). Using either Office 2003 or Office 2007, use the Help system to learn how to export these files to an XML file. Create the XML files with and without the schemas. If possible, the group members should use both versions of Office to create the XML files. As a group, write the instructions for each piece of software on how to export the files to XML. Finally, create a main index Web page that displays the XML files based on what you discovered.

Appendix A
HTML Quick Reference

HTML Tags and Attributes

HTML is the original language used for publishing hypertext on the World Wide Web. It is a nonproprietary format based on Standard Generalized Markup Language (SGML). HTML documents can be created with a wide variety of tools, from simple plain text editors such as Notepad, to sophisticated WYSIWYG authoring tools such as Adobe Dreamweaver. HTML uses tags such as <h1> and <p> to structure text into headings, paragraphs, lists, hypertext links, and so on.

Many HTML tags have attributes that can be defined in different ways to further modify the look of the Web page. Table A–1 lists HTML tags and their associated attributes. The list provides a brief description of each tag and its attributes. The default value for each attribute is indicated by bold text. For a comprehensive list, more thorough descriptions, and examples of all HTML tags, visit the World Wide Web Consortium Web site at *www.w3.org*.

As the World Wide Web Consortium updates the HTML specifications, HTML tags constantly are being added to, deleted, and replaced by newer tags. In the list in Table A–1, deprecated elements—tags that can be replaced with newer elements—are indicated with an asterisk. Deprecated elements still are available for use, and most browsers still support them. Default values are bolded. Obsolete elements are no longer in use and are not supported by common browsers. This appendix does not list obsolete elements.

Table A–1 HTML Tags and Attributes

HTML Tag and Attributes	Description
<!DOCTYPE	Indicates the version of XHTML used
<!-- Text here -->	Inserts invisible comments
<a>....</a>	Anchor; creates a hyperlink or fragment identifier
accesskey	Defines keyboard shortcut
charset=*character set*	Specifies the character encoding of the linked resource
href=*url*	Hyperlink reference that specifies the target URL
name=*text*	Specifies a name for enclosed text, allowing it to be the target of a hyperlink
rel=*relationship*	Indicates the relationship going from the current page to the target
rev=*relationship*	Indicates the relationship going from the target to the current page
tabindex	Defines order in which the Tab key moves
target=*name* *	Defines the name of the window or frame in which the linked resource will appear

Table A–1 HTML Tags and Attributes *(continued)*

HTML Tag and Attributes	Description
<abbr>...</abbr>	Explains the meaning of abbreviations
<acronym>...</acronym>	Explains the meaning of acronyms
<address>....</address>	Used for information such as authorship, e-mail addresses, or addresses; enclosed text appears italicized and indented in some browsers
No attributes	
<area>....</area>	Creates a clickable area, or hotspot, on a client-side image map
coords=*value1, value2*	Specifies the coordinates that define the edges of the hotspot; a comma-delimited list of values
href=*url*	Hyperlink reference that specifies the target URL
nohref	Indicates that no link is associated with the area
shape=*shape*	Identifies the shape of the area (poly, rect, circle)
target=*name* *	Defines the name of the window or frame in which the linked resource will appear
<b>....</b>	Specifies text to appear in bold
No attributes	
<base />	Identifies the base in all relative URLs in the document
href=*url*	Specifies the absolute URL used to resolve all relative URLs in the document
target=*name* *	Defines the name for the default window or frame in which the hyperlinked pages are displayed
<big>....</big>	Increases the size of the enclosed text to a type size bigger than the surrounding text; exact display size depends on the browser and default font
No attributes	
<blockquote>....</blockquote>	Sets enclosed text to appear as a quotation, indented on the right and left
No attributes	
<body>....</body>	Defines the start and end of a Web page
alink=*color*	Defines the color of an active link
background=*url*	Identifies the image to be used as a background
bgcolor=*color*	Sets the document's background color
link=*color*	Defines the color of links not yet visited
vlink=*color*	Defines the color of visited links
<b>....</b>	Sets enclosed text to appear in bold
No attributes	
** **	Inserts a line break
clear=*margin*	Sets the next line to start in a spot where the requested margin is clear (left, right, all, none); used to stop text wrap
<caption>....</caption>	Creates a caption for a table
align=*position* *	Sets caption position (top, bottom, left, right)

Table A–1 HTML Tags and Attributes *(continued)*

HTML Tag and Attributes	Description
<center>....</center> *	Centers the enclosed text horizontally on the page
No attributes	
<cite>....</cite>	Indicates that the enclosed text is a citation; text usually is displayed in italics
No attributes	
<code>....</code>	Indicates that the enclosed text is a code sample from a program; text usually is displayed in fixed width font such as Courier
No attributes	
<col>....</col>	Organizes columns in a table into column groups to share attribute values
align=*position*	Sets horizontal alignment of text within the column (char, center, top, bottom, left, right)
span=*value*	Sets the number of columns that span the <col> element
valign=*position*	Specifies vertical alignment of text within the column (top, middle, bottom)
width=*value*	Sets the width of each column in the column group
<colgroup>....</colgroup>	Encloses a group of <col> tags and groups the columns to set properties
align=*position*	Specifies horizontal alignment of text within the column (char, center, top, bottom, left, right)
char=*character*	Specifies a character on which to align column values (for example, a period is used to align monetary values)
charoff=*value*	Specifies a number of characters to offset data aligned with the character specified in the char property
span=*number*	Sets the number of columns the <col> element spans
valign=*position*	Specifies vertical alignment of text within the column (top, middle, bottom)
width=*value*	Sets the width of each column spanned by the colgroup statement
<dd>....</dd>	Indicates that the enclosed text is a definition in the definition list
No attributes	
<del>...</del>	Marks deleted text by striking it out
<div>....</div>	Defines block-level structure or division in the HTML document
align=*position* *	Specifies alignment of the content block (center, left, right)
class=*name*	Assigns the class name to each class of divisions
id=*name*	Assigns a unique name to a specific content block
<dl>....</dl>	Creates a definition list
No attributes	
<dt>....</dt>	Indicates that the enclosed text is a term in the definition list
No attributes	

Table A–1 HTML Tags and Attributes *(continued)*

HTML Tag and Attributes	Description
<em>....</em>	Indicates that the enclosed text should be emphasized; usually appears in italics
No attributes	
<fieldset>....</fieldset>	Groups related form controls and labels
align=*position*	Specifies alignment of a legend as related to the fieldset (top, bottom, middle, left, right)
<font>....</font> *	Defines the appearance of enclosed text
size=*value*	Sets the font size in absolute terms (1 through 7) or as a relative value (for example, +2)
color=*color*	Sets the font color; can be a hexadecimal value (#rrggbb) or a word for a predefined color value (for example, navy)
face=*list*	Identifies the font face; multiple entries should be separated by commas
point-size=*value*	Sets the point size of text for downloaded fonts
weight=*value*	Sets the weight of the font, ranging from 100 (lightest) to 900 (heaviest)
<form>....</form>	Marks the start and end of a Web page form
action=*url*	Specifies the URL of the application that will process the form; required attribute
enctype=*encoding*	Specifies how the form element values will be encoded
method=*method*	Specifies the method used to pass form parameters (data) to the server
target=*text*	Specifies the frame or window that displays the form's results
<frame>....</frame>	Delimits a frame within a frameset
frameborder=*option*	Specifies whether the frame border is displayed (1, 0)
marginheight=*value*	Adds *n* pixels of space above and below the frame contents
marginwidth=*value*	Adds *n* pixels of space to the left and the right of the frame contents
name=*text*	Specifies the name of the frame
noresize	Prevents the user from resizing the frame
scrolling=*option*	Defines the URL of the source document that is displayed in the frame
src=*url*	Adds scroll bars or not—always (yes), never (no), or add when needed (**auto**)
<frameset>....</frameset>	Defines a collection of frames in a frameset
cols=*value1*, *value2*,...	Defines the number and width of frames within a frameset
rows= *value1*, *value2*,...	Defines the number and height of frames within a frameset
frameborder=*option*	Specifies whether the frame border is displayed (1, 0)
<h*n*>....</h*n*>	Defines a header level *n*, ranging from the largest (h1) to the smallest (h6)
align=*position* *	Specifies the header alignment (**left**, center, right)
<head>....</head>	Delimits the start and end of the HTML document's head
No attributes	

Table A–1 HTML Tags and Attributes *(continued)*

HTML Tag and Attributes	Description
<hr /> *	Inserts a horizontal rule
align=*type* *	Specifies the alignment of the horizontal rule (left, **center**, right)
noshade *	Specifies to not use 3D shading and to round the ends of the rule
size=*value* *	Sets the thickness of the rule to a value in pixels
width=*value or %* *	Sets the width of the rule to a value in pixels or a percentage of the page width; percentage is preferred
<html>....</html>	Indicates the start and the end of the HTML document
version=*data*	Indicates the HTML version used; not usually used
<i>....</i>	Sets enclosed text to appear in italics
No attributes	
<iframe>....</iframe> *	Creates an inline frame, also called a floating frame or subwindow, within an HTML document
align=*position* *	Aligns the frame with respect to context (top, middle, **bottom**, left, right)
frameborder=*option* *	Specifies whether a frame border is displayed (1=yes; 0=no)
height=*value* *	Sets the frame height to a value in pixels
marginheight=*value* *	Sets the margin between the contents of the frame and its top and bottom borders to a value in pixels
marginwidth=*value* *	Sets the margin between the contents of the frame and its left and right borders to a value in pixels
name=*text* *	Assigns a name to the current frame
noresize *	Prevents the user from resizing the frame
src=*url* *	Defines the URL of the source document that is displayed in the frame
width=*value* *	Sets the frame width to a value in pixels
scrolling=*option* *	Adds scroll bars or not—always (yes), never (no), or add when needed (**auto**)
<img>....</img>	Inserts an image into the current Web page
align=*type* *	Defines image alignment in relation to the text or the page margin (top, middle, bottom, right, left)
alt=*text*	Provides a text description of an image if the browser cannot display the image; always should be used
border=*value* *	Sets the thickness of the border around the image to a value in pixels; default size is 3
height=*value*	Sets the height of the image to a value in pixels; always should be used
src=*url*	Specifies the URL of the image to be displayed; required
usemap=*url*	Specifies the map of coordinates and links that defines the href within this image
width=*value*	Sets the width of the image to a value in pixels; always should be used

Table A–1 HTML Tags and Attributes *(continued)*

HTML Tag and Attributes	Description
<input>....</input>	Defines controls used in forms
alt=*text*	Provides a short description of the control or image button; for browsers that do not support inline images
checked	Sets radio buttons and check boxes to the checked state
disabled	Disables the control
maxlength=*value*	Sets a value for the maximum number of characters allowed as input for a text or password control
name=*text*	Assigns a name to the control
readonly	Prevents changes to the control
size=*value*	Sets the initial size of the control to a value in characters
src=*url*	Identifies the location of the image if the control is set to an image
tabindex=*value*	Specifies the tab order between elements in the form, with 1 as the first element
type=*type*	Defines the type of control (**text**, password, check box, radio, submit, reset, file, hidden, image, button)
usemap=*url*	Associates an image map as defined by the <map> element
value=*data*	Sets the initial value of the control
<ins>....</ins>	Identifies and displays text as having been inserted in the document in relation to a previous version
cite=*url*	Specifies the URL of a document that has more information on the inserted text
datetime=*datetime*	Date and time of a change
<kbd>....</kbd>	Sets enclosed text to display as keyboard-like input
No attributes	
<label>....</label>	Creates a label for a form control
for=*data*	Indicates the name or ID of the element to which the label is applied
<legend>....</legend>	Assigns a caption to a fieldset element, as defined by the <fieldset> tags
No attributes	
<li>....</li>	Defines the enclosed text as a list item in a list
value=*value1*	Inserts or restarts counting with value1
<link>....</link>	Establishes a link between the HTML document and another document, such as an external style sheet
charset=*character set*	Specifies the character encoding of the linked resource
href=*url*	Defines the URL of the linked document
name=*text*	Names the current anchor so that it can be the destination to other links
rel=*relationship*	Indicates the relationship going from the current page to the target
rev=*relationship*	Indicates the relationship going from the target to the current page
target=*name*	Defines the name of the frame into which the linked resource will appear
type=*mime-type*	Indicates the data or media type of the linked document (for example, text/css for linked style sheets)

Table A–1 HTML Tags and Attributes *(continued)*

HTML Tag and Attributes	Description
<map>....</map>	Specifies a client-side image map; must enclose <area> tags
id=*text*	Assigns a name to the image map
name=*text*	Assigns a name to the image map
<meta />	Provides additional data (metadata) about an HTML document
content=*text*	Specifies the value for the <meta> information; required
http-equiv=*text*	Specifies the HTTP-equivalent name for metadata; tells the server to include that name and content in the HTTP header when the HTML document is sent to the client
name=*text*	Assigns a name to metadata
scheme=*text*	Provides additional context for interpreting the information in the content attribute
<noframes>....</noframes>	Defines content to be displayed in browsers that do not support frames; very important to include
No attributes	
<object>....</object>	Includes an external object in the HTML document such as an image, a Java applet, or other external object, not well-supported by most browsers
archive=*url*	Specifies the URL of the archive containing classes and other resources that will be preloaded for use by the object
classid=*url*	Specifies the URL of the embedded object
codebase=*url*	Sets the base URL for the object; helps resolve relative references
codetype=*type*	Identifies the content type of the data in the object
data=*url*	Identifies the location of the object's data
declare	Indicates the object will be declared only, not installed in the page
height=*value*	Sets the height of the object to a value in pixels
name=*text*	Assigns a control name to the object for use in forms
standby=*text*	Defines the message to display while the object loads
tabindex=*value*	Specifies the tab order between elements, with 1 as the first element
type=*type*	Specifies the content or media type of the object
usemap=*url*	Associates an image map as defined by the <map> element
width=*value*	Sets the width of the object to a value in pixels
<ol>....</ol>	Defines an ordered list that contains numbered list item elements (<li>)
type=*option* *	Sets or resets the numbering format for the list; options include: A=capital letters, a=lowercase letters, I=capital Roman numerals, i=lowercase Roman numerals, or **1**=Arabic numerals
<optgroup>....</optgroup>	Divides a menu into submenus
disabled	Grays out menu options until an event occurs
label	Specifies how option appears in the menu

Table A–1 HTML Tags and Attributes *(continued)*

HTML Tag and Attributes	Description
<option>....</option>	Defines individual options in a selection list, as defined by the <select> element
label=*text*	Provides a shorter label for the option than that specified in its content
selected	Sets the option to be the default or the selected option in a list
value=*value*	Sets a value returned to the server when the user selects the option
disabled	Disables the option items
<p>....</p>	Delimits a paragraph; automatically inserts a blank line between text
align=*position* *	Aligns text within the paragraph (left, center, right)
<param>....</param>	Passes a parameter to an object or applet, as defined by the <object> or <applet> element
id=*text*	Assigns an identifier to the element
name=*text*	Defines the name of the parameter required by an object
type=*type*	Specifies the content or media type of the object
value=*data*	Sets the value of the parameter
valuetype=*data*	Identifies the type of parameter used in the value attribute (data, ref, object)
<pre>....</pre>	Preserves the original format of the enclosed text; keeps line breaks and spacing the same as the original
No attributes	
<q>....</q>	Sets enclosed text as a short quotation
lang=*option*	Defines the language in which the quotation will appear
<samp>....</samp>	Sets enclosed text to appear as sample output from a computer program or script; usually appears in a monospace font
No attributes	
<script>....</script>	Inserts a client-side script into an HTML document
defer	Indicates that the browser should defer executing the script
src=*url*	Identifies the location of an external script
type=*mime-type*	Indicates the data or media type of the script language (for example, text/javascript for JavaScript commands)
<select>....</select>	Defines a form control to create a multiple-choice menu or scrolling list; encloses a set of <option> tags to define one or more options
name=*text*	Assigns a name to the selection list
multiple	Sets the list to allow multiple selections
size=*value*	Sets the number of visible options in the list
disabled	Disables the selection list
tabindex=*value*	Specifies the tab order between list items, with 1 as the first element
<small>....</small>	Sets enclosed text to appear in a smaller typeface
No attributes	

Table A–1 HTML Tags and Attributes *(continued)*

HTML Tag and Attributes	Description
<span>….</span>	Creates a user-defined container to add inline structure to the HTML document
No attributes	
<strike>...</strike> *	Displays text with a line through it
<strong>….</strong>	Sets enclosed text to appear with strong emphasis; usually displayed as bold text
No attributes	
<style>….</style>	Encloses embedded style sheet rules for use in the HTML document
media=*data*	Identifies the intended medium of the style (**screen**, tty, tv, projection, handheld, print, braille, aural, all)
title=*data*	Indicates the title of the style sheet
type=*data*	Specifies the content or media type of the style language (for example, text/css for linked style sheets)
_{….}	Sets enclosed text to appear in subscript
No attributes	
^{….}	Sets enclosed text to appear in superscript
No attributes	
<table>….</table>	Marks the start and end of a table
align=*position* *	Aligns the table text (left, right, center, justify, char)
border=*value*	Sets the border around a table to a value in pixels
cellpadding=*value*	Sets padding around each cell's contents to a value in pixels
cellspacing=*value*	Sets spacing between cells to a value in pixels
summary=*text*	Provides a summary of the table's purpose and structure
width=*value or %*	Sets table width in pixels or a percentage of the window
frame=*option*	Defines which parts of the outer border (frame) to display (void, above, below, hsides, lhs, rhs, vsides, box, border)
rules=*option*	Specifies which inner borders are to appear between the table cells (none, groups, rows, cols, all)
<tbody>….</tbody>	Defines a groups of rows in a table body
align=*option*	Aligns text (left, center, right, justify, char)
char=*character*	Specifies a character on which to align column values (for example, a period is used to align monetary values)
charoff=*value*	Specifies a number of characters to offset data aligned with the character specified in the char property
valign=*position*	Sets vertical alignment of cells in a group (top, middle, bottom, baseline)
<td>….</td>	Defines a data cell in a table; contents are left-aligned and normal text by default
bgcolor=*color* *	Defines the background color for the cell
colspan=*value*	Defines the number of adjacent columns spanned by the cell
rowspan=*value*	Defines the number of adjacent rows spanned by the cell

Table A–1 HTML Tags and Attributes *(continued)*

HTML Tag and Attributes	Description
<td>....</td> *(continued)*	
width=*n* or % *	Sets the width of the table in either pixels or a percentage of the whole table width
headers=*idrefs*	Defines the list of header cells for the current cell
abbr=*text*	Provides an abbreviated version of the cell's contents that browsers can use if space is limited
scope=*option*	Specifies cells for which the element defines header cells (row, col, rowgroup, colgroup)
align=*position*	Specifies horizontal alignment (left, center, right, justify, char)
char=*character*	Specifies a character on which to align column values (for example, a period is used to align monetary values)
charoff=*value*	Specifies a number of characters to offset data aligned with the character specified in the char property
valign=*position*	Sets vertical alignment of cells in the group (top, middle, bottom, baseline)
<textarea>....</textarea>	Creates a multiline text input area within a form
accesskey	Defines keyboard shortcut
cols=*value*	Defines the number of columns in the text input area
name=*data*	Assigns a name to the text area
rows=*value*	Defines the number of rows in the text input area
disabled	Disables the element
readonly	Prevents the user from editing content in the text area
tabindex=*value*	Specifies the tab order between elements, with 1 as the first element
<tfoot>....</tfoot>	Identifies and groups rows into a table footer
align=*position*	Specifies horizontal alignment (left, center, right, justify, char)
char=*character*	Specifies a character on which to align column values (for example, a period is used to align monetary values)
charoff=*value*	Specifies a number of characters to offset data aligned with the character specified in the char property
valign=*position*	Sets vertical alignment of cells in a group (top, middle, bottom, baseline)
<th>....</th>	Defines a table header cell; contents are bold and center-aligned by default
bgcolor=*color* *	Defines the background color for the cell
colspan=*value*	Defines the number of adjacent columns spanned by the cell
rowspan=*value*	Defines the number of adjacent rows spanned by the cell
width=*n* or % *	Sets the width of the table in either pixels or a percentage of the whole table width
<thead>....</thead>	Identifies and groups rows into a table header
align=*position*	Specifies horizontal alignment (left, center, right, justify, char)
char=*character*	Specifies a character on which to align column values (for example, a period is used to align monetary values)
charoff=*value*	Specifies a number of characters to offset data aligned with the character specified in the char property
valign=*position*	Sets vertical alignment of cells in a group (top, middle, bottom, baseline)

Table A–1 HTML Tags and Attributes *(continued)*

HTML Tag and Attributes	Description
<title>....</title>	Defines the title for the HTML document; always should be used
No attributes	
<tr>....</tr>	Defines a row of cells within a table
bgcolor=*color* *	Defines the background color for the cell
align=*position* *	Specifies horizontal alignment (left, center, right, justify, char)
char=*character*	Specifies a character on which to align column values (for example, a period is used to align monetary values)
charoff=*value*	Specifies a number of characters to offset data aligned with the character specified in the char property
valign=*position*	Sets vertical alignment of cells in a group (top, middle, bottom, baseline)
<tt>....</tt>	Formats the enclosed text in teletype- or computer-style monospace font
No attributes	
<u>....</u> *	Sets enclosed text to appear with an underline
No attributes	
<ul>....</ul>	Defines an unordered list that contains bulleted list item elements (<li>)
type=*option* *	Sets or resets the bullet format for the list; options include: circle, **disc**, square
<var>....</var>	Indicates the enclosed text is a variable's name; used to mark up variables or program arguments
No attributes	

Appendix B

Browser-Safe Color Palette

Browser-Safe Colors

Three hardware components help deliver color to a computer user: the processor, the video card, and the monitor. Because of the wide variety of components that exist, the color quality that users see varies greatly. The software on a user's computer, specifically the Web browser, also affects the way that color is displayed on a monitor. For Web developers, it is the browser that limits color significantly. It is very difficult, if not impossible, to plan for all possible color variations created by a Web browser. Using browser-safe colors allows for the browser variations, but it also limits the number of colors used on the Web page.

A total of 216 browser-safe colors appear well on different monitors, operating systems, and browsers—including both Windows and Macintosh operating systems and Internet Explorer and Mozilla Firefox browsers. When using color on your Web site, keep in mind that using only the 216 browser-safe colors can be very restrictive, especially for the approximately 10% of Web visitors who have 256-color monitors. On those monitors, only the browser-safe colors will be displayed. If you decide to use a non-browser-safe color, the visitor's browser will try to create the color by combining (a process called dithering) any number of the 216 acceptable colors. The resulting color could be slightly different from the color you had intended.

For a complete list of the 216 browser-safe colors, see Table B–1 on the next page or visit the Shelly Cashman Series HTML Web page (*scsite.com/html5e*) and click Color Chart. Links to other Web sites with information about browser-safe colors also are available.

Note that you can use the color name as well as the color number when identifying a particular color to use. For instance, you can use the number #000099 (see color sample on the following page) or the word "navy" to specify the same color. Also note that to comply with XHTML standards, color names such as "navy" or "silver" must be all lowercase letters.

Table B–1 Browser-Safe Colors

#ffffff	#ffffcc	#ffff99	#ffff66	#ffff33	#ffff00
#ffccff	#ffcccc	#ffcc99	#ffcc66	#ffcc33	#ffcc00
#ff99ff	#ff99cc	#ff9999	#ff9966	#ff9933	#ff9900
#ff66ff	#ff66cc	#ff6699	#ff6666	#ff6633	#ff6600
#ff33ff	#ff33cc	#ff3399	#ff3366	#ff3333	#ff3300
#ff00ff	#ff00cc	#ff0099	#ff0066	#ff0033	#ff0000
#ccffff	#ccffcc	#ccff99	#ccff66	#ccff33	#ccff00
#ccccff	#cccccc	#cccc99	#cccc66	#cccc33	#cccc00
#cc99ff	#cc99cc	#cc9999	#cc9966	#cc9933	#cc9900
#cc66ff	#cc66cc	#cc6699	#cc6666	#cc6633	#cc6600
#cc33ff	#cc33cc	#cc3399	#cc3366	#cc3333	#cc3300
#cc00ff	#cc00cc	#cc0099	#cc0066	#cc0033	#cc0000
#99ffff	#99ffcc	#99ff99	#99ff66	#99ff33	#99ff00
#99ccff	#99cccc	#99cc99	#99cc66	#99cc33	#99cc00
#9999ff	#9999cc	#999999	#999966	#999933	#999900
#9966ff	#9966cc	#996699	#996666	#996633	#996600
#9933ff	#9933cc	#993399	#993366	#993333	#993300
#9900ff	#9900cc	#990099	#990066	#990033	#990000
#66ffff	#66ffcc	#66ff99	#66ff66	#66ff33	#66ff00
#66ccff	#66cccc	#66cc99	#66cc66	#66cc33	#66cc00
#6699ff	#6699cc	#669999	#669966	#669933	#669900
#6666ff	#6666cc	#666699	#666666	#666633	#666600
#6633ff	#6633cc	#663399	#663366	#663333	#663300
#6600ff	#6600cc	#660099	#660066	#660033	#660000
#33ffff	#33ffcc	#33ff99	#33ff66	#33ff33	#33ff00
#33ccff	#33cccc	#33cc99	#33cc66	#33cc33	#33cc00
#3399ff	#3399cc	#339999	#339966	#339933	#339900
#3366ff	#3366cc	#336699	#336666	#336633	#336600
#3333ff	#3333cc	#333399	#333366	#333333	#333300
#3300ff	#3300cc	#330099	#330066	#330033	#330000
#00ffff	#00ffcc	#00ff99	#00ff66	#00ff33	#00ff00
#00ccff	#00cccc	#00cc99	#00cc66	#00cc33	#00cc00
#0099ff	#0099cc	#009999	#009966	#009933	#009900
#0066ff	#0066cc	#006699	#006666	#006633	#006600
#0033ff	#0033cc	#003399	#003366	#003333	#003300
#0000ff	#0000cc	#000099	#000066	#000033	#000000

Appendix C

Accessibility Standards and the Web

Making the Web Accessible

Nearly 20% of the world population has some sort of disability, a physical condition that limits the individual's ability to perform certain tasks. The U.S. Congress passed the Rehabilitation Act in 1973, which promotes economic independence for those with disabilities. In 1998, Congress amended this act to reflect the latest changes in information technology. Section 508 requires that any electronic information developed, procured, maintained, or used by the federal government be accessible to people with disabilities. Disabilities that inhibit a person's ability to use the Web fall into four main categories: visual, hearing, motor, and cognitive. This amendment has had a profound effect on how Web pages are designed and developed.

Although Section 508 is specific to Web sites created and maintained by the federal government, all competent Web developers adhere to the Section 508 guidelines. It is important to include everyone as a potential user of your Web site, including those with disabilities. To ignore the needs of nearly 20% of our population is just poor practice.

The World Wide Web Consortium (W3C) developed its own set of guidelines, called the Web Accessibility Initiative (WAI), for accessibility standards. These guidelines cover many of the same issues defined in the Section 508 rules and expand on them relative to superior Web site design.

Section 508 Guidelines Examples

The 13 parts of the Section 508 guidelines are as follows:

- Subpart A—General
  - 1194.1 Purpose.
  - 1194.2 Application.
  - 1194.3 General exceptions.
  - 1194.4 Definitions.
  - 1194.5 Equivalent facilitation.

- Subpart B—Technical Standards
  - 1194.21 Software applications and operating systems.
  - 1194.22 Web-based intranet and Internet information and applications. 16 rules.
  - 1194.23 Telecommunications products.
  - 1194.24 Video and multimedia products.
  - 1194.25 Self contained, closed products.
  - 1194.26 Desktop and portable computers.
- Subpart C—Functional Performance Criteria
  - 1194.31 Functional performance criteria.
- Subpart D—Information, Documentation, and Support
  - 1194.41 Information, documentation, and support.

Web developers should review these guidelines thoroughly. We focus on the specific guidelines for intranet and Internet development in the following sections.

Sub-section **§ 1194.22** of Section 508, **Web-based intranet and Internet information and applications**, is the segment of the amendment that impacts Web design. There are 16 paragraphs within § 1194.22, which are lettered (a) through (p). These 16 paragraphs describe how each component of a Web site should be designed to ensure accessibility. The following is a list of the 16 paragraphs:

§ 1194.22 (a) A text equivalent for every non-text element shall be provided (e.g., via "alt", "longdesc", or in element content).

Graphical images that contain Web page content should include a text alternative (for example, using the alt or longdesc attributes). For good Web development practice, all images should include the alt attribute to describe that image, as shown in Project 2.

§ 1194.22 (b) Equivalent alternatives for any multimedia presentation shall be synchronized with the presentation.

Audio clips should contain a transcript of the content; video clips need closed captioning.

§ 1194.22 (c) Web pages shall be designed so that all information conveyed with color is also available without color, for example from context or markup.

Although color is an important component of most Web pages, you need to consider those site visitors with forms of color blindness if the color contributes significantly to the Web site content.

§ 1194.22 (d) Documents shall be organized so they are readable without requiring an associated style sheet.

Style sheets have an important role in Web development. Some browsers, however, allow users to create their own customized style sheets, which could alter the style sheets that you have designated. When developing a Web site using style sheets, ensure that the site maintains its functionality, even if your specified style sheets have been turned off.

§ 1194.22 (e) Redundant text links shall be provided for each active region of a server-side image map.

and

§ 1194.22 (f) Client-side image maps shall be provided instead of server-side image maps except where the regions cannot be defined with an available geometric shape.

This means that it is preferable for the Web developer to use client-side image maps unless the map uses a shape that the client-side will not allow. If the Web developer chooses to use server-side image maps, the developer should provide text alternatives for each link on the image map.

§ 1194.22 (g) Row and column headers shall be identified for data tables.

and

§ 1194.22 (h) Markup shall be used to associate data cells and header cells for data tables that have two or more logical levels of row or column headers.

You should structure your tables so that they appear in a linear fashion. In other words, the table content should be displayed one cell at a time, working from left to right across each row before moving to the next row.

§ 1194.22 (i) Frames shall be titled with text that facilitates frame identification and navigation.

Nonvisual browsers open frame sites one frame at a time. It is therefore important that the Web developer gives a name to each frame, and that the name reflects the contents of that frame. You can use either the title or the name attribute, but because nonvisual browsers differ in which attribute they use, the Web developer should use both attributes.

§ 1194.22 (j) Pages shall be designed to avoid causing the screen to flicker with a frequency greater than 2 Hz and lower than 55 Hz.

Animations on a Web page can be irritating to many people. However, they also can be quite harmful to people who have certain cognitive or visual disabilities or seizure disorders. You should therefore ensure that animations fall within the ranges stated, and you should limit the use of animations when possible. You also should make certain that necessary page content is available without the animations.

§ 1194.22 (k) A text-only page, with equivalent information or functionality, shall be provided to make a Web site comply with the provisions of this part, when compliance cannot be accomplished in any other way. The content of the text-only pages shall be updated whenever the primary page changes.

If you cannot comply with the other 15 guidelines, you should provide a text-only page to display the content of the page. You should also provide an easily accessible link to that text-only Web page.

§ 1194.22 (l) When pages utilize scripting languages to display content, or to create interface elements, the information provided by the script shall be identified with functional text that can be read by adaptive technology.

Scripts are often used to create a more interesting and dynamic Web page. You should ensure that the functionality of the script is still available for any person using nonvisual browsers.

§ 1194.22 (m) When a Web page requires that an applet, plug-in, or other application be present on the client system to interpret page content, the page must provide a link to a plug-in or applet that complies with 1994.21 (a) through (i).

Any applet or plug-in that is used on your Web pages should also comply with Section 508. The Web developer should provide a link to the applet or plug-in that is compliant with Section 508.

§ 1194.22 (n) When electronic forms are designed to be completed on-line, the form shall allow people using assistive technology to access the information, field elements, and functionality required for completion and submission of the form, including all directions and cues.

Forms need to be accessible to anyone, including those using nonvisual browsers. You should therefore include value attributes or alternative text for buttons, input boxes, and text area boxes on any form included on your Web page.

§ 1194.22 (o) A method shall be provided that permits users to skip repetitive navigation links.

It can be helpful to provide text links at the very top of a Web page so that users of nonvisual browsers can quickly link to the content of the Web site. Some Web developers use a link that allows users to skip to the main content of the Web page immediately by using a transparent image.

§ 1194.22 (p) When a timed response is required, the user shall be alerted and given sufficient time to indicate that more time is required.

Users need to be given sufficient time to react to a time-out from inactivity by notifying users that the process will soon time out. The user should then be given a way to easily request additional time.

WAI Guidelines

The WAI identifies 14 guidelines for Web developers. Within each guideline is a collection of checkpoints that identifies how to apply the guideline to specific Web site features. Each checkpoint is given a priority score that shows how much importance the WAI places on that guideline. All Web developers should review the information at the official Web site at *www.w3c.org/WAI* for complete information on these guidelines, and should apply the guidelines, together with the following suggestions on the application of the guidelines, to their Web page development.

The three WAI priorities are:

Priority 1 A Web content developer **must** satisfy this checkpoint. Otherwise, one or more groups will find it impossible to access information in the document. Satisfying this checkpoint is a basic requirement for some groups to be able to use Web documents.

Priority 2 A Web content developer **should** satisfy this checkpoint. Otherwise, one or more groups will find it difficult to access information in the document. Satisfying this checkpoint will remove significant barriers to accessing Web documents.

Priority 3 A Web content developer **may** address this checkpoint. Otherwise, one or more groups will find it somewhat difficult to access information in the document. Satisfying this checkpoint will improve access to Web documents.

Table C-1 contains the WAI guidelines together with the checkpoints and corresponding priority value.

Table C-1

WAI Guidelines and Checkpoints	Priority
1. Provide equivalent alternatives to auditory and visual content.	
1.1 Provide a text equivalent for every non-text element (e.g., via "alt," "longdesc," or in element content). ***This includes***: images, graphical representations of text (including symbols), image map regions, animations (e.g., animated GIFs), applets and programmatic objects, ASCII art, frames, scripts, images used as list bullets, spacers, graphical buttons, sounds (played with or without user interaction), standalone audio files, audio tracks of video, and video.	1
1.2 Provide redundant text links for each active region of a server-side image map.	1
1.3 Until user agents can automatically read aloud the text equivalent of a visual track, provide an auditory description of the important information of the visual track of a multimedia presentation.	1
1.4 For any time-based multimedia presentation (e.g., a movie or animation), synchronize equivalent alternatives (e.g., captions or auditory descriptions of the visual track) with the presentation.	1
1.5 Until user agents render text equivalents for client-side image map links, provide redundant text links for each active region of a client-side image map.	3
2. Don't rely on color alone.	
2.1 Ensure that all information conveyed with color is also available without color; for example, from context or markup.	1
2.2 Ensure that foreground and background color combinations provide sufficient contrast when viewed by someone having color deficits or when viewed on a black and white screen.	2
3. Use markup and style sheets and do so properly.	
3.1 When an appropriate markup language exists, use markup rather than images to convey information.	2
3.2 Create documents that validate to published formal grammars.	2
3.3 Use style sheets to control layout and presentation.	2
3.4 Use relative rather than absolute units in markup language attribute values and style sheet property values.	2
3.5 Use header elements to convey document structure and use them according to specification.	2
3.6 Mark up lists and list items properly.	2
3.7 Mark up quotations. Do not use quotation markup for formatting effects such as indentation.	2

Table C-1 *(continued)*

WAI Guidelines and Checkpoints	Priority
4. Clarify natural language usage.	
4.1 Clearly identify changes in the natural language of a document's text and any text equivalents (e.g., captions).	1
4.2 Specify the expansion of each abbreviation or acronym in a document where it first occurs.	3
4.3 Identify the primary natural language of a document.	3
5. Create tables that transform gracefully.	
5.1 For data tables, identify row and column headers.	1
5.2 For data tables that have two or more logical levels of row or column headers, use markup to associate data cells and header cells.	1
5.3 Do not use tables for layout unless the table makes sense when linearized. Otherwise, if the table does not make sense, provide an alternative equivalent (which may be a linearized version).	2
5.4 If a table is used for layout, do not use any structural markup for the purpose of visual formatting.	2
5.5 Provide summaries for tables.	3
5.6 Provide abbreviations for header labels.	3
6. Ensure that pages featuring new technologies transform gracefully.	
6.1 Organize documents so they may be read without style sheets. For example, when an HTML document is rendered without associated style sheets, it must still be possible to read the document.	1
6.2 Ensure that equivalents for dynamic content are updated when the dynamic content changes.	1
6.3 Ensure that pages are usable when scripts, applets, or other programmatic objects are turned off or not supported. If this is not possible, provide equivalent information on an alternative accessible page.	1
6.4 For scripts and applets, ensure that event handlers are input device-independent.	2
6.5 Ensure that dynamic content is accessible or provide an alternative presentation or page.	2
7. Ensure user control of time-sensitive content changes.	
7.1 Until user agents allow users to control flickering, avoid causing the screen to flicker.	1
7.2 Until user agents allow users to control blinking, avoid causing content to blink (i.e., change presentation at a regular rate, such as turning on and off).	2
7.3 Until user agents allow users to freeze moving content, avoid movement in pages.	2
7.4 Until user agents provide the ability to stop the refresh, do not create periodically auto-refreshing pages.	2
7.5 Until user agents provide the ability to stop auto-redirect, do not use markup to redirect pages automatically. Instead, configure the server to perform redirects.	2
8. Ensure direct accessibility of embedded user interfaces.	
8.1 Make programmatic elements such as scripts and applets directly accessible or compatible with assistive technologies (Priority 1 if functionality is important and not presented elsewhere, otherwise Priority 2).	2

Table C-1 *(continued)*

WAI Guidelines and Checkpoints	Priority
9. Design for device-independence.	
9.1 Provide client-side image maps instead of server-side image maps except where the regions cannot be defined with an available geometric shape.	1
9.2 Ensure that any element that has its own interface can be operated in a device-independent manner.	2
9.3 For scripts, specify logical event handlers rather than device-dependent event handlers.	2
9.4 Create a logical tab order through links, form controls, and objects.	3
9.5 Provide keyboard shortcuts to important links (including those in client-side image maps), form controls, and groups of form controls.	3
10. Use interim solutions.	
10.1 Until user agents allow users to turn off spawned windows, do not cause pop-ups or other windows to appear and do not change the current window without informing the user.	2
10.2 Until user agents support explicit associations between labels and form controls, for all form controls with implicitly associated labels, ensure that the label is properly positioned.	2
10.3 Until user agents (including assistive technologies) render side-by-side text correctly, provide a linear text alternative (on the current page or some other) for ***all*** tables that lay out text in parallel, word-wrapped columns.	3
10.4 Until user agents handle empty controls correctly, include default, place-holding characters in edit boxes and text areas.	3
10.5 Until user agents (including assistive technologies) render adjacent links distinctly, include non-link, printable characters (surrounded by spaces) between adjacent links.	3
11. Use W3C technologies and guidelines.	
11.1 Use W3C technologies when they are available and appropriate for a task and use the latest versions when supported.	2
11.2 Avoid deprecated features of W3C technologies.	2
11.3 Provide information so that users may receive documents according to their preferences (e.g., language, content type, etc.).	3
11.4 If, after best efforts, you cannot create an accessible page, provide a link to an alternative page that uses W3C technologies, is accessible, has equivalent information (or functionality), and is updated as often as the inaccessible (original) page.	1
12. Provide context and orientation information.	
12.1 Title each frame to facilitate frame identification and navigation.	1
12.2 Describe the purpose of frames and how frames relate to each other if it is not obvious by frame titles alone.	2
12.3 Divide large blocks of information into more manageable groups where natural and appropriate.	2
12.4 Associate labels explicitly with their controls.	2
13. Provide clear navigation mechanisms.	
13.1 Clearly identify the target of each link.	2
13.2 Provide metadata to add semantic information to pages and sites.	2
13.3 Provide information about the general layout of a site (e.g., a site map or table of contents).	2

Table C-1 *(continued)*

WAI Guidelines and Checkpoints	Priority
13.4 Use navigation mechanisms in a consistent manner.	2
13.5 Provide navigation bars to highlight and give access to the navigation mechanism.	3
13.6 Group related links, identify the group (for user agents), and, until user agents do so, provide a way to bypass the group.	3
13.7 If search functions are provided, enable different types of searches for different skill levels and preferences.	3
13.8 Place distinguishing information at the beginning of headings, paragraphs, lists, etc.	3
13.9 Provide information about document collections (i.e., documents comprising multiple pages).	3
13.10 Provide a means to skip over multi-line ASCII art.	3
14. Ensure that documents are clear and simple.	
14.1 Use the clearest and simplest language appropriate for a site's content.	1
14.2 Supplement text with graphic or auditory presentations where they will facilitate comprehension of the page.	3
14.3 Create a style of presentation that is consistent across pages.	3

Appendix D

CSS Properties and Values

Style Sheet Properties and Values

This appendix provides a listing of the CSS (Cascading Style Sheets) level 1 and 2 properties and values supported by most browsers. Tables D–1 through D–6 show the property names, descriptions, and valid values for various categories of CSS properties. Values listed in bold are the default.

A newer version of Cascading Style Sheets, CSS3, is currently being defined. CSS3 is therefore not covered in this appendix. CSS3 utilizes a modularized approach to style sheets, which allows CSS to be updated in a more timely and flexible manner.

For a more comprehensive list of CSS properties and values, see the www.w3.org Web site. In addition to an abundance of information about CSS levels 1 and 2, the w3 site also has extensive information about CSS3, from its history to its use with browsers today. The Web site also includes many online tutorials available for learning CSS levels 1 and 2 as well as CSS3.

Background and Color Styles

Colors and subtle backgrounds can enhance the style of a Web page significantly. You can set the background or color of an element using these style sheet properties. Not all browser versions support these style attributes, however, so be aware that not all users will be able to see the background and color styles set by these properties. Table D–1 provides a list of background and color properties.

Table D–1 Background and Color Properties

Property Name	Description	Values
background-attachment	Sets the background image to fixed, or scrolls with the page	**scroll** fixed
background-color	Sets the background color of an element	**transparent** [color]
background-image	Sets an image as the background	**none** [url]
background-position	Sets the starting position of a background image	[length] [percentage] bottom center left right top
background-repeat	Sets if/how a background image will be repeated	**repeat** repeat-x repeat-y no-repeat
color	Sets the foreground color of an element	[color] transparent

Border Styles

Many changes can be made to the style, color, and width of any or all sides of a border using the border properties listed in Table D–2. Using the border-color, border-width, or border-style border properties allows you to set the style for all sides of a border. Using style properties such as border-top-width, border-right-color, or border-bottom-style gives you the option to set the width, color, or style for only the top, right, bottom, or left border of a table cell. If you do not make changes to the border style using style sheet properties, the default border will be displayed.

Table D–2 Border Properties

Property Name	Description	Values
border-color	Sets the color of the four borders; can have from one to four colors	[color] transparent
border-top-color border-right-color border-bottom-color border-left-color	Sets the respective color of the top, right, bottom, and left borders individually	[color]
border-style	Sets the style of the four borders; can have from one to four styles	**none** dashed dotted double groove inset outset ridge solid
border-top-style border-right-style border-bottom-style border-left-style	Sets the respective style of the top, right, bottom, and left borders individually	**none** dashed dotted double groove inset outset ridge solid
border-width	Shorthand property for setting the width of the four borders in one declaration; can have from one to four values	**medium** [length] thick thin
border-top-width border-right-width border-bottom-width border-left-width	Sets the respective width of the top, right, bottom, and left borders individually	**medium** [length] thick thin

Font Styles

An element's font can be changed using the font attribute and various font properties. When you set the font family for an element, you can set one or more fonts or font families by using a comma-delimited list. Each font family generally includes several font definitions. For example, the Arial font family includes Arial Black and Arial Narrow. If you specify more than one font, the browser assesses the user's system and finds the first font family installed on the system. If the system has none of the font families specified in the style sheet, the browser uses the default system font. Table D–3 lists common font properties.

Table D–3 Font Properties

Property Name	Description	Values
font-family	A prioritized list of font-family names and/or generic family names for an element	[family-name] cursive fantasy monospace sans-serif serif
font-size	Sets the size of a font	[length] [percentage] large medium small x-large x-small xx-large xx-small
font-style	Sets the style of a font	**normal** italic oblique
font-variant	Displays text in a small-caps font or a normal font	**normal** small-caps
font-weight	Sets the weight of a font	**normal** bold bolder lighter

List Styles

Using the properties associated with list styles allows you to set the kind of marker that identifies a list item. An unnumbered list marker, for example, can be a filled disc, an empty circle, or a square. A numbered list marker can be a decimal, lower-alpha, lower-roman numeral, upper-alpha, or upper-roman numeral. Table D–4 provides compatible browser list properties.

Table D–4 List Properties

Property Name	Description	Values
list-style-image	Sets an image as the list-item marker	**none** url
list-style-position	Indents or extends a list-item marker with respect to the item's content	**outside** inside
list-style-type	Sets the type of list-item marker	**disc** circle square decimal lower-alpha lower-roman upper-alpha upper-roman

Margin and Padding Styles

Many changes can be made to the width and spacing around an element using the margin and padding properties listed in Table D–5. Padding is the space that occurs between the edge of an element and the beginning of its border. If you increase padding around an element, you add space inside its border. The border, therefore, has a larger area to cover.

You can use the margin or padding property to set the widths of margins and padding amounts along all four sides of an element. Using margin and padding properties such as margin-top, margin-right, padding-left, or padding-bottom gives you the option to set the margin or padding for only the top, right, bottom, or left side of an element.

Table D–5 Margin and Padding Properties

Property Name	Description	Values
margin	Shorthand property for setting margin properties in one declaration	[length] [percentage] auto
margin-top margin-right margin-bottom margin-left	Sets the top, right, bottom, and left margin of an element individually	[length] [percentage] auto
padding	Shorthand property for setting padding properties in one declaration	[length] [percentage]
padding-top padding-right padding-bottom padding-left	Sets the top, right, bottom, and left padding of an element individually	[length] [percentage]

Text Styles

Text styles can be used to change the letter-spacing, alignment, line-height (not recommended), and text decoration, along with other text properties. The text-transform property can change text into all uppercase, all lowercase, or be used to change the first letter of each word to uppercase. With text-align, you can align text left, right, center, or justify the text. The text style properties are listed in Table D–6.

Table D–6 Text Properties

Property Name	Description	Values
letter-spacing	Increases or decreases the space between characters	**normal** [length]
line-height	Sets the spacing between text baselines	**normal** [length] [number] [percentage]
text-align	Aligns the text in an element	left right center justify
text-decoration	Adds decoration to text	**none** blink line-through overline underline

Table D–6 Text Properties *(continued)*

Property Name	Description	Values
text-indent	Indents the first line of text in an element	[length] [percentage]
text-transform	Controls text capitalization	**none** capitalize lowercase uppercase
vertical-align	Sets the vertical positioning of text	**baseline** [length] [percentage] bottom middle sub super text-bottom text-top top
white-space	Sets how white space inside an element is handled	**normal** pre nowrap
word-spacing	Increases or decreases the space between words	**normal** [length]

Appendix E
JavaScript Quick Reference

JavaScript Introduction

Webster's dictionary defines **script** in several ways: first, as a style of handwriting or font style, such as cursive; second, as a document; and third, as text for stage, film, or a radio or television show. A stage, movie, or television script also contains stage directions for actors. Computers, however, also use scripts, which are a set of instructions used by a program to perform a specific task or set of tasks. A **scripting language** follows a set of rules and has its own syntax. Scripting languages generally need to be interpreted by the program or utility using the script.

Scripting languages like JavaScript extend the power of **HTML** (Hypertext Markup Language) and allow Web pages to be interactive. Whereas HTML tells your browser how to display text and images, set up lists and option buttons, and establish hyperlinks, JavaScript brings Web pages to life by adding dynamic content and interactive elements. Using JavaScript, a Web page developer enhances a Web page by adding features such as:

- Scrolling messages
- Animation and dynamic images
- Pop-up windows
- Dynamic messages
- Data validation

JavaScript is a product of a joint venture between Sun Microsystems and Netscape. Netscape developed a script language called LiveScript, and Sun Microsystems was trying to simplify its Java programming language. The cooperation of those two efforts brought about JavaScript. The following reference guide applies to the JavaScript model version 1.5 standardized in 1999 and still in effect for all cross-browser applications. Later versions of JavaScript are browser-specific and are not detailed. For more detailed information about JavaScript 1.5, see http://developer.mozilla.org/En/Core_JavaScript_1.5_Reference.

Why Use JavaScript?

Using JavaScript enhances your Web page by adding interactivity to it. Users can receive instant feedback, without complicated Common Gateway Interferance (**CGI**) scripts and languages. A CGI script is any program that runs on a Web server for the purpose of processing data. The Web page sends the data to the server that processes the data and may return a result to the Web page. Along with server-side scripts and programs, many Web sites use CGI for searching databases or processing purchase orders on a server.

The disadvantage of using CGI scripts is they waste resources when the needed task can be processed on the user's computer. For example, with JavaScript you can validate a data-entry form, such as a purchase request, immediately on the user's computer. The need to send the data back to the server for validation is eliminated. The user receives feedback instantly and does not have to wait for a response during heavy Internet traffic times.

Reserved Words

Reserved words (also called **keywords**) are words with special meaning to a programming language. Most reserved words are used in program statements or in defining data. A **reserved word** should not be used as a JavaScript variable, function, method, or object name. The JavaScript reserved word list is summarized in Table E–1. Some of these reserved words have special meaning to JavaScript, some are reserved for future use, and, to be certain your code is compatible with Java, others should not be used.

Table E–1 Reserved Words

abstract	else	instanceof	super
boolean	enum	int	switch
break	export	interface	synchronized
byte	extends	label	this
case	false	long	throw
catch	final	native	throws
char	finally	new	transient
class	float	null	true
const	for	package	try
continue	function	private	typeof
debugger	goto	protected	var
default	if	public	void
delete	implements	return	volatile
do	import	short	while
double	in	static	with

Data Types

Data type refers to the category of data held by a variable. JavaScript supports several data types, including primitive data types (numbers, strings, and boolean values), compound types (objects and arrays), special types (null and undefined), regular expressions, and functions. Table E–2 summarizes the primitive and special data types.

Table E–2 Primitive and Special Data Types

Data Type	Form	Description	Example	Range
Boolean	True/False	Can represent yes or no, on or off, true or false	check_pt = true test_2 = false	true or false
Null	No value	Empty	val_hold = null	null
Numeric	Integer	Positive or negative numbers with no decimal places	count = 4	-2^{53} to 2^{53}

Table E–2 Primitive and Special Data Types *(continued)*

Data Type	Form	Description	Example	Range
	Floating-point	Positive or negative numbers, with decimal places, or numbers written using exponential notation	accum = 4.678 amt = –67.126 distance = 2e11	Approximately +1.79769e308 to –1.7e308
	Special numbers	NaN	ValType = NaN	NaN means Not a Number
		Infinity (or MAX_VALUE or POSITIVE_INFINITY)	highNum = Infinity	MAX_VALUE: +1.7976931348623157e308
		–Infinity (or MIN_VALUE or NEGATIVE_INFINITY)	highNegNum = –Infinity	MIN_VALUE: +5e-324
String	Text and non-numeric characters	A set of continuous characters surrounded by quotation marks	productName = "Router"	zero or more characters
Undefined	No value	A variable that has been declared but not yet assigned a value	var i	undefined

Variable Names

A **variable name** (also called an **identifier**) must begin with a letter or an underscore and cannot be a reserved word shown in Table E–1 on page APP 34. Variable names are case sensitive and may not contain a space. Variables can be declared with the var statement, where they also can be initialized.

Although the dollar sign ($) is a valid variable name character, most developers avoid using it because the dollar sign also can indicate machine-generated code to the interpreter. In addition, the number of characters in a variable is not subject to any specific limitation. Older browsers, however, do have a limitation of 255 characters for an entire statement.

A variable name cannot use a period because periods separate objects, properties, and methods. See Table E–3 for examples of valid and invalid variable names. In addition, you must remember that, in JavaScript, variable names are case sensitive. If you create a form and use mixed-case spelling, such as State, as a variable name, and later use the uppercase spelling, STATE, as a variable name, JavaScript will determine these spellings are two different variable names.

Table E–3 Valid and Invalid Variable Names

Valid Variable Names	Invalid Variable Names
cust_id	cust.id
Cust_Id	%Cust_Id
_cust_id	+cust_identifier
cust_id_number	Cust id number
CustIdNumber	9custIDNumber
Custid1	Cust ID
_case	case

Variables are declared the first time they are used by inserting the word **var**, then the variable name, followed by an equal sign (=), and then the value. For example, if you declare a variable named gpa by typing `var gpa`, this variable would be assigned no value. To assign a variable an initial value of zero, type `var gpa=0`. Current versions of Mozilla Firefox and Microsoft Internet Explorer indicate that a variable is **undefined** if the variable has not been assigned a value. In addition, a variable can have a **null** value.

Literals

While a variable is used to store data or values, a **literal** is a constant value that does not change. A literal is an actual number or text, rather than a calculated result or value input from a keyboard. If the literal is a number, it is called a numeric literal; if it is a character or text value, it is called a string literal.

A **string literal** is text enclosed in quotation marks. With string literals, you must place the text inside a pair of quotation marks. If numeric digits are enclosed within quotation marks, they will be treated as a string, not as a number. Think of the characters between quotation marks as a sequential group of characters, one after the other, forming a continuous string.

Escape Sequences in Strings

The **escape character** (\) indicates that the character that follows in a string has a special meaning. The escape character and its following character form an **escape sequence**. The escape sequences are summarized in Table E–4.

Table E–4 Escape Sequences

Escape Sequence	Meaning	Escape Sequence	Meaning
\'	Single quotation mark	\r	Carriage return
\"	Double quotation mark	\t	Horizontal tab
\\	Backslash	\ddd	Octal sequence (deprecated)
\b	Backspace	\xdd	Hexadecimal sequence
\f	Form feed	\udddd	Unicode sequence
\n	New line		

Operators

Operators are symbols used to manipulate operands in an expression.

Operator Types

Table E–5 summarizes the JavaScript operator types.

Table E–5 Operator Types

Type	Operator	Name	Description	Example
Arithmetic	+	Addition	Adds two operands	rtn = amt + 5.6
	–	Subtraction	Subtracts one operand from another	rtn = amt – disc
	*	Multiplication	Multiplies one operand by another	rtn = amt * .5
	/	Division	Divides one operand by another	rtn = amt / 4
	%	Modulo	Returns the remainder of a division operation	rtn = amt % 3
	++	Increment	Increases an operand by one	newAmt = ++oldAmt newAmt = oldAmt++
	– –	Decrement	Decreases an operand by one	newAmt = – –oldAmt newAmt = oldAmt– –
	–	Negation	Returns the opposite value of an operand	newAmt = –oldAmt
Assignment	=	Assigns	Assigns the value of the right operand to the left operand	discRate = 4
	+=	Combines	Adds the value of the right operand to the value of the left operand and assigns a new value to the left operand	discRate += 13
	– =	Subtracts	Subtracts the value of the right operand from the value of the left operand and assigns a new value to the left operand	discRate -= 3
	*=	Multiplies	Multiplies the value of the right operand by the value of the left operand and assigns a new value to the left operand	discRate *= .2
	/=	Divides	Divides the value of the left operand by the value of the right operand and assigns a new value to the left operand	discRate /= 10
	%=	Modulus	Divides the value of the left operand by the value of the right operand and assigns a remainder to the left operand	discRate %= 5
Bitwise	~	Complement	Performs a binary NOT	secur = ~rights
	<<	Shift left	Performs a binary shift left of the bits of an integer	Op = 15 << 1
	>>	Shift right	Performs a binary shift right of the bits of an integer	Op = 15 >> 1
	>>>	Shift right with zero extension	Performs a binary unsigned shift right on an integer	Op = 15 >>> 1
	&	AND	Performs a bitwise AND on an integer	Op = 01111 & 11111
	^	XOR	Performs a bitwise XOR on an integer	Op = 01111 ^ 11111
	|	OR	Performs a bitwise OR on an integer	Op = 01111 | 11111
Comparison	= =	Equal	Returns true if operands are equal	if (a = = b) {
	!=	Not Equal	Returns true if operands are not equal	if (a != b) {
	>	Greater Than	Returns true if the left operand is greater than the right operand	if (a > b) {

Table E–5 Operator Types *(continued)*

Type	Operator	Name	Description	Example
	<	Less Than	Returns true if the left operand is less than the right operand	if (a < b) {
	>=	Greater Than or Equal	Returns true if the left operand is greater than or equal to the right operand	if (a >= b) {
	<=	Less Than or Equal	Returns true if the left operand is less than or equal to the right operand	if (a <= b) {
	= = =	Equal (no type conversion done)	Returns true if operands are equal and their types are the same	if (a = = = b) {
	! = =	Not Equal (no type conversion done)	Returns true if operands are not equal or their types are the same	if (a ! = = b) {
	in	in	Returns true if the property is found as a property member of the object	(property in object)
	instanceof	instanceof	Returns true if the datatype matches the object	(datatype instanceof object)
Conditional	?:	If?then:else	Performs an inline if-then-else and assigns one of two possible values	Ret = (test = = true) ? "Its true" : "Its false"
Expression Control	void	Return a void	Sets a variable to an undefined state	ret = void
Logical	&&	And	Returns true if both the left operand and the right operand return a value of true, otherwise it returns a value of false	if ((a < b) && (c > d)) {
	||	Or	Returns true if either the left operand or the right operand returns a value of true; if neither operand returns a value of true, then the expression containing the || (or) operator returns a value of false	if ((a < b) || (c > d)) {
	!	Not	Returns true if an expression is false and returns false if an expression is true	if (!(a < b)) {
Multiple Evaluation	,	Evaluate/Return right+	Evaluates two expressions and returns the second one	Ret = (x- -, z) * (y- -, q)
Object	new	New object	Creates a new object	CD = new Album
	delete	Remove an object property	Removes a single property of an object	delete CD
String	+	Concatenation	Combines two strings	lang = "Java" + "Script"
	+=	Concatenates	Concatenates the value of the right operand to the value of the left operand and assigns a new value to the left operand	Lang += "Script"
Type Identification	typeof	Return type	Returns the data type of the operand	ret = typeof(CD)

Order of Precedence

Unless parentheses/brackets/dot dictates otherwise, reading from left to right in an expression, all negation/increment/misc are performed first, then all multiply/divide/modulo, then all addition/subtraction, then all comparison, then all equality/identity, then all logical and, then all logical or, and then all assignment operators. The **order of precedence** is summarized in Table E–6.

Table E-6 Order Of Precedence

Operator	Symbol	Precedence
Parentheses/brackets/dot	( ) [ ] .	highest
Negation/increment/misc	! – ++ – – ~ delete new typeof void	
Multiply/divide/modulo	* / %	
Addition/subtraction	+ –	
Shift	<< >> >>>	
Comparison	< <= > >=	
Equality/Identity	= = != = = ! = = != ===	
Bitwise AND	&	
Bitwise XOR	^	
Bitwise OR	|	
Logical and	&&	
Logical or	||	
Conditional	?:	
Assignment operators	= += –= *= /= %=	
Multiple evaluation	,	lowest

JavaScript Statements

Statements are used to write JavaScript instructions. Table E–7 summarizes the JavaScript statements.

Table E–7 JavaScript Statements

Statement	Description
block	A block of JavaScript statements delimited by a pair of braces { }
break	Exits switch statements and loops. Transfers program control to the statement line following the switch statement or following the terminated loop
comment	Notations that explain what a script does. Comments are ignored by the interpreter. Single-line comments begin with //. Multiple-line comments begin with /* and end with */
continue	Halts execution of a block of statements in a while or for loop and continues execution of the loop with the next iteration
do...while	Executes the block of statements in a loop until the test condition evaluates to false. Statements in a loop execute at least once
export	Makes functions and properties available to other windows (Navigator 4 and up). Statement not supported in version 1.5
finally	Executes a block of statements after the try and catch block of statements execute. The finally block of statements executes whether or not an exception is thrown. A good use for the finally block of statements is to allow a graceful failure
for	Creates a loop that consists of three optional expressions, enclosed in parentheses and separated by semicolons, followed by a block of statements executed in the loop. The test to terminate a loop is done before the block of statements in the loop executes
for...in	Iterates a specified variable over all the properties of an object. For each distinct property, JavaScript executes the specified statements
function	Defines a new function. Acceptable parameters include strings, numbers, and objects. For example, function myfunc() {
if...else	Executes one block of statements if the condition is true. Executes another block of statements if the condition is false
import	Allows use of other objects available at run-time (Navigator 4 and up). Not supported in version 1.5
label	Provides an identifier that can be used with break or continue to indicate where the program should continue execution
return	Causes the current function to halt and possibly returns a value to the caller. For example, return endingval
switch	Allows a program to evaluate an expression and attempts to match the expression's value to a case label
throw	Throws or sends an exception. The exception can be an expression or an object

Table E–7 JavaScript Statements *(continued)*

Statement	Description
try...catch	Executes a block of statements to try, and the statements to execute if an error occurs. Implemented in IE 5 and later versions of Navigator
var	Declares and possibly initializes new variables. For example, var retval
while	Creates a loop that evaluates an expression, and if it is true, executes a block of statements. The loop then repeats, as long as the specified condition is true
with	Establishes the default object for a block of statements

Event Handlers

JavaScript makes HTML documents dynamic through events. An **event** is an action that a user makes, such as clicking a button. Usually, when an event occurs, JavaScript code executes. Event handler names always begin with "on." In standard HTML, event handler names are in mixed case; the first letter after the word "on" is in uppercase. In XML, because all attributes must be in lowercase, they are spelled in all lowercase characters. Table E–8 summarizes the JavaScript event handlers.

Table E–8 Event Handlers

Event Handler	Triggered When	Handler For	Used in HTML Statement
onabort	The loading of an image is interrupted	Image	<img>
onblur	An element becomes inactive	Button, Checkbox, FileUpload, Layer, Password, Radio, Reset, Select, Submit, Text, Textarea, Window	<body> ... </body> <frameset> ... </frameset> <frame> ... </frame> <input type="text" /> <textarea> ... </textarea> <select> ... </select>
onchange	The value of an element changes	FileUpload, Select, Text, Textarea	<input type="text" /> <textarea> ... </textarea> <select> ... </select>
onclick	An element is clicked once	Button, Checkbox, Document, Link, Radio, Reset, Submit	<a> ... </a> <input type="submit" /> <input type="reset" /> <input type="radio" /> <input type="checkbox" /> <input type="text" />
ondblclick	An element is double-clicked	Document, Link	<a> ... </a> <input type="submit" /> <input type="reset" /> <input type="radio" /> <input type="checkbox" /> <input type="text" />
ondragdrop	An object is dragged and dropped into a window	Window (may not be available on all platforms)	<body> ... </body> <frameset> ... </frameset>
onerror	An error occurs when loading a document or image	Image, Window	<img /> <body> ... </body> <frameset> ... </frameset>

Document Object

The **Document object** represents the content of a browser's window. Table E–10 summarizes the Document object properties and methods. Note that all properties and methods may not work with all browsers, especially older versions.

Table E–10 Document Object

Property	Description
activeElement	Element that currently has focus
alinkColor	Color of an active link specified by the alink attribute of the <body> tag; recommend using style sheet in place of property
all[]	Array referring to all HTML elements in a document
anchors[]	Array referring to the document's anchors
applets[]	Array referring to the document's applets
bgColor	Background color of the document as specified by the bgColor attribute of the <body> tag; recommend using style sheet in place of property
charset	Character set currently in use
children[]	Array referring to child elements of the document
classes	Defines classes for style
cookie	Specifies a cookie for the current document
defaultCharset	Default character set of the document
domain	Domain name of the server where the current document is located
embeds[]	Array referring to the document's ActiveX controls and plug-ins
expando	Do not allow creation of new properties
fgColor	Foreground text color of the document as specified by the fgColor attribute of the <body> tag; recommend using style sheet in place of property
forms[]	Array referring to multiple forms within a document
height	Document height
ids	Styles for individual tags
images[]	Array referring to the document's images
lastModified	Date the document was last modified
layers[]	DHTML layers in a document; not supported in Navigator 6.x
linkColor	Color of the document's unvisited links as specified by the link attribute of the <body> tag; recommend using style sheet in place of property
links[]	Array referring to the document's links
location	URL of the document
parentWindow	Refers to the document's window
plugins[]	Array referring to objects used in the document, synonym for embeds[] array
readyState	State of the document as it loads
referrer	URL of the document that provided a link to the current document
tags	Styles for HTML tags
title	Title of the document as specified by the <title> ... </title> tag pair in the document's HEAD section
URL	URL of the current document
vlinkColor	Color of the document's visited links as specified by the vlink attribute of the <body> tag (deprecated)
width	Document width
captureEvents()	Names event types to be captured
clear()	Clears a document

Table E–10 Document Object *(continued)*	
Property	**Description**
close()	Notifies the Web browser you are finished writing to a window or frame and that the document should be displayed
contextual()	Defines the contextual style
elementFromPoint()	Specifies which HTML element is at a point
getElementByID()	Refers to an object by its specified id
getElementByName()	Refers to an object by its name value
getElementByTagName()	Refers to an object by its tag name
getSelection()	Returns selected text
open()	Opens a window or frame, other than the current window or frame, and is used to update its contents with the write() and writeln() methods
releaseEvents()	Stops the capturing of events
routeEvent()	Passes the captured events to the next event handler
write()	Creates new text on a Web page
writeln()	Creates new text on a Web page followed by a line break

Form Object

The **Form object** represents forms created with the <form> ... </form> tag pair. Table E–11 summarizes the Form object properties and methods.

Table E–11 Form Object	
Property	**Description**
action	URL to which a form's data will be submitted
method	Method in which a form's data will be submitted (GET or POST)
encoding	Format of data being submitted
target	Window in which any results returned from the server are displayed
name	Name of a form
elements[]	Array representing a form's elements
elements.length	Number of elements on a form
Method	**Function**
reset()	Clears any data entered into a form
submit()	Submits a form to a Web server

History Object

The **History object** keeps track of the pages that have been visited. Table E–12 summarizes the History object property and methods.

Table E–12 History Object	
Property	**Description**
current	URL of the current document
length	Contains the specific number of documents that have been opened during the current browser session

Table E-12 History Object *(continued)*	
Property	**Description**
next	URL of the next document in the history array
previous	URL of the previous document in the history array
Method	**Function**
back()	Equivalent to clicking a Web browser's Back button
forward()	Equivalent to clicking a Web browser's Forward button
go(n)	Opens a specific document in the history list indicated by n
toString()	Browsing history in the HTML format

Image Object

The **Image object** represents images created using the <img> tag. Table E–13 summarizes the Image object properties and events.

Table E–13 Image Object	
Property	**Description**
border	Read-only property containing border width, in pixels, as specified by border attribute of <img> tag, including if an error occurs during loading
complete	Boolean value that returns true when an image is completely loaded
height	Read-only property containing height of image as specified by height attribute of <img> tag
hspace	Read-only property containing amount of horizontal space, in pixels, to left and right of image, as specified by hspace attribute of <img> tag
lowsrc	URL of alternate image to display at low resolution
name	Name assigned to tag
src	URL of displayed image
vspace	Read-only property containing amount of vertical space, in pixels, above and below image, as specified by vspace attribute of <img> tag
width	Read-only property containing width of image as specified by width attribute of <img> tag
Event	**Description**
onLoad	Image finishes loading
onAbort	User cancels the loading of an image, usually by clicking the Stop button
onError	Error occurs while loading image

Math Object

The **Math object** provides the capability of performing calculations. Table E–14 summarizes the Math object properties and methods.

Table E–14 Math Object	
Property	**Description**
E	Base of a natural logarithm
LN10	Natural logarithm of 10
LN2	Natural logarithm of 2

Table E–14 Math Object *(continued)*

Property	Description
LOG2E	Base-2 logarithm of e
LOG10E	Base-10 logarithm of e
PI	Ratio of the circumference of a circle to its diameter
SQRT1_2	1 divided by the square root of 2
SQRT2	The square root of 2
Method	**Function**
abs(x)	Absolute value of x
acos(x)	Arc cosine of x
asin(x)	Arc sine of x
atan(x)	Arc tangent of x
atan2(y,x)	Angle from the x-axis
ceil(x)	Value of x rounded to the next highest integer
cos(x)	Cosine of x
exp(x)	Exponent of x
floor(x)	x rounded to the next lowest integer
log(x)	Natural logarithm of x
max(x,y)	Larger of two numbers
min(x,y)	Smaller of two numbers
pow(x,y)	x raised to the y power
random()	Random number between 0.0 and 1.0
round(x)	x rounded to the nearest integer
sin(x)	Sine of x
sqrt(x)	Square root of x
tan(x)	Tangent of x

Location Object

The **Location object** allows you to switch to a new Web page. Table E–15 summarizes the Location object properties and methods.

Table E–15 Location Object

Property	Description
hash	URL's anchor
host	Combination of URL's host name and port sections
hostname	URL's host name
href	Full URL address
pathname	URL's path
port	URL's port
protocol	URL's protocol
search	URL's search or query portion
Method	**Function**
reload()	Causes the page currently displayed in the Web browser to open again
replace()	Replaces the currently loaded URL with a different one

Navigator Object

The **Navigator object** is used to get information about the current Web browser. Table E–16 summarizes the Navigator object properties and methods.

Table E–16 Navigator Object

Property	Description
appCodeName	Web browser code name
appName	Web browser name
appVersion	Web browser version
cookieEnabled	Boolean result; Read only indicating cookie status
language	Language used by the Web browser
mimeTypes[]	Array containing MIME types supported by the client browser
platform	Operating system in use
plugins[]	Array containing installed plugins
systemLanguage	Default language of the client system
userAgent	User agent
userLanguage	Language currently in use on the client
Method	**Function**
javaEnabled()	Determines whether Java is enabled in the current browser
plugins.refresh()	Enables newly installed plugins on the client
preference()	Gets or sets a user preference
savePreferences()	Saves all user preferences
taintEnabled()	Boolean that determines whether data tainting is enabled

Window and Frame Objects

The **Window object** represents a browser's window or an individual frame within a window. Thus, every **Frame object** is a window object, and uses all the methods and properties of the Window object. Table E–17 summarizes the Window and Frame objects' properties, methods, and events.

Table E–17 Window and Frame Objects

Property	Description
closed	Boolean value to determine if window has been closed
defaultStatus	Default text that is written to the status bar
document	Reference to the Document object
frames[]	Array listing the Frame objects in the window
history	Reference to the History object
length	Number of frames in a window
location	Reference to the Location object
name	Name of a window
navigator	Points to the Navigator object for the browser
offscreenBuffering	Boolean to determine if updates for the window are buffered
opener	Window object that opens another window
parent	Parent frame that contains the current frame
screen	Screen information where the browser is running

Table E–17 Window and Frame Objects *(continued)*

Property	Description
self	Self-reference to the Window object
status	Temporary text that is written to the status bar
top	Topmost Window object that contains the current frame
window	Self-reference to the Window object
Method	**Function**
alert()	Displays a message dialog box with an OK button
blur()	Removes the focus from the window
clearTimeout()	Cancels a set timeout
close()	Closes the window
confirm()	Displays a confirmation dialog box with OK and Cancel buttons
focus()	Makes the Window object the active window
moveBy(x,y)	The moveBy() method moves the window horizontally or vertically by the number of pixels; positive numbers move right and down, negative move the opposite direction
moveTo(x,y)	The moveTo() method moves the window to the location specified by the numeric values
open()	Opens a new window
prompt()	Displays a dialog box prompting a user to enter information
setTimeout()	Executes a function after a specified number of milliseconds has elapsed
Event	**Triggered When**
onblur	Window becomes inactive
onerror	Error occurs when the window loads
onfocus	Window becomes active
onload	Document is completely loaded in the window
onresize	Window is resized
onunload	Current document in the window is unloaded

Number Object

The **Number object** gives support for special constants that may be platform specific and exposes one conversion method. Table E–18 summarizes the Number object properties and methods.

Table E–18 Number Object

Property	Description
MAX_VALUE	Maximum numeric value
MIN_VALUE	Minimum numeric value
NaN	Not a number value
NEGATIVE_INFINITY	Value for negative infinity
POSITIVE_INFINITY	Value for positive infinity
Method	**Description**
toExponential()	Returns a string representing the number in exponential notation
toFixed()	Returns a string representing the number in fixed-point notation
toLocaleString()	Returns a string representation of the number based on system setting

Table E–18 Number Object *(continued)*

Method	Description
toPrecision()	Returns a string representing the number to a specified precision in fixed-point notation
toString()	Converts a numeric value to a string value

Function Object

The **Function object** gives the programmer access to information about specific functions. Table E–19 summarizes the Function object properties and methods.

Table E–19 Function Object

Property	Description
arguments[]	Array containing arguments passed to the function
arity	Number of arguments declared for the function
caller	Name of the function that called the current one
length	Number of arguments declared for the function
prototype	Prototype for a class of objects
Method	**Description**
apply()	Uses a function as a method for an object
call()	Allows you to call (execute) a method of another object in the context of a different object (the calling object)
toSource()	Returns a string representing the source code of the function; overrides the Object.toSource method
toString()	Converts a function to a string value

Screen Object

The **Screen object** gives platform-specific information about the user's screen. Table E–20 summarizes the Screen object properties.

Table E–20 Screen Object

Property	Description
availHeight	Available height of the screen
availLeft	First horizontal pixel available
availTop	First vertical pixel available
availWidth	Available width of the screen
colorDepth	Depth of the client browser's color palette
height	Height of the client screen
pixelDepth	Depth of the client browser's screen
width	Width of the client screen

Boolean Object

The **Boolean object** converts other objects to Boolean values. A value of False is returned for values of undefined, null, 0, -0, false, NaN, or an empty string (""). All other values return a value of True. Table E–21 summarizes the methods for the Boolean object.

Table E–21 Boolean Object

Method	Function
toSource	Returns an object literal representing the specified Boolean object; you can use this value to create a new object. It overrides the Object.toSource method.
toString	Returns a string representing the specified object. It overrides the Object.toString method.

Array Object

An **array** is an ordered set of values associated with a single variable name. Table E–22 summarizes the properties and methods for the Array object.

Table E–22 Array Object

Property	Description
index	For an array created by a regular expression match, the zero-based index of the match in the string
input	For an array created by a regular expression match, reflects the original string against which the regular expression was matched
length	Reflects the number of elements in an array; can be changed to truncate or extend array
Method	**Function**
concat()	Joins two arrays and returns a new array
join()	Joins all elements of an array into a string
pop()	Removes the last element from an array and returns that element
push()	Adds one or more elements to the end of an array and returns the new length of the array
reverse()	Transposes the elements of an array; first array element becomes the last and the last becomes the first
shift()	Removes the first element from an array and returns that element
slice()	Extracts a section of an array and returns a new array
splice()	Adds and/or removes elements from an array
sort()	Sorts the elements of an array
toSource()	Returns an array literal representing the specified array; use this value to create a new array as it overrides the Object.toSource method
toLocaleString()	Returns a string representing the array and its elements
toString()	Returns a string representing the array and its elements; overrides the Object.toString method
unshift()	Adds one or more elements to the front of an array and returns the new length of the array

String Object

The **String object** represents a set of characters. Any object converted to the String object can use any of the string methods. Table E–23 summarizes the property and methods for the String object.

Table E–23 String Object

Property	Description
length	Specifies the length of the string
Method	**Function**
anchor()	Creates a hypertext target
big()	Displays text in a big font as if it were in a <big>... </big> tag
blink()	Blinks text as if it were in a <blink>... </blink> tag
bold()	Displays text as if it were in a <b>... </b> tag
charAt()	Returns the character at the specified location (relative index)
charCodeAt()	Returns a number indicating the Unicode value of the character at the given location (relative index)
concat()	Combines the text of two strings
fixed()	Displays text in a fixed-pitch font as if it were in a <tt>... </tt> tag
fontcolor()	Displays text in the specified color as if it were in a <font>...</font> tag
fontsize()	Displays text in the specified font size as if it were in a <font>... </font> tag
fromCharCode()	Creates a string by using the specified sequence of Unicode values
indexOf()	Returns the index within the calling String object of the first occurrence of the specified value, or –1 if not found
italics()	Displays a string to be italic as if it were in an <i>...</i> tag
lastIndexOf()	Returns the index within the calling String object of the last occurrence of the specified value, or –1 if not found
link()	Creates an HTML hypertext link that requests another URL
match()	Matches a regular expression against a string
replace()	Matches a regular expression and a string, and replaces the matched substring with a new substring
search()	Searches for a match between a regular expression and a specified string
slice()	Returns a new string from an existing string
small()	Displays text in a small font as if it were in a <small>... </small> tag
split()	Splits a String object into an array of substrings
strike()	Displays text as struck-out text as if it were in a <strike>...</strike> tag
sub()	Displays text as a subscript as if it were in a _{...} tag
substr()	Returns the characters in a string starting at a specific location for a specific length
substring()	Returns a substring of a string
sup()	Displays text as a superscript as if it were in a ^{...} tag
toLowerCase()	Displays a string value converted to lowercase
toSource()	Returns the source of the instance created; overrides the Object.toSource method
toString()	Returns the object type or name of the constructor that created the object; overrides the Object.toString method
toUpperCase()	Displays a string value converted to uppercase

Regular Expression

A Regular Expression (RegExp) is used for pattern matching. The special characters used for the patterns are described in Table E–24.

Table E–24 RegExp

Character	Description
/	Every pattern must begin with a slash
\d	Match any digit
\s	Match any space, newline, tab, return
\w	Match any alphanumeric character
^	Beginning of a string
$	End of a string
?	First of all characters (?xy) means x or xy
*	Multiple of characters (*xy) means x or xy or xyy
+	Multiple of all characters (xy+) means xy, or xyy, or xyyy
[xx]	Used in brackets for alternatives; (Adobe CS[234]) means Adobe CS2, Adobe CS3, or Adobe CS4
[x–x]	Used in brackets for sequence; (JavaScript 1.[1–5]) means JavaScript 1.1 or JavaScript 1.2 etc.
[^x–x]	Used in brackets to match anything BUT the selected characters; ([^x–y]) means any letter but x or y
(x)	Subpattern
.	The dot means any character
{min, max}	The minimum or maximum number of sequences; (x{1,3}) means x or xx or xxx

Global Functions

Table E–25 summarizes the **global functions** that always are available in JavaScript.

Table E–25 Global Functions

Function	Description
decodeURI()	Decodes or replaces an escape sequence in the encoded URI with the character that it represents; cannot decode escape sequence not coded by encoded URI
decodeURI	Decodes or replaces each escape sequence in the encoded URI Component() component with the character that it represents
escape()	Returns the hexadecimal code
eval()	Evaluates a string of JavaScript code without reference to a particular object
isFinite()	Evaluates an argument to determine whether it is a finite number
isNaN()	Evaluates an argument to determine if it is not a number
number()	Converts an object to a number
parseFloat()	Parses a string argument and returns a floating-point number
parseInt()	Parses a string argument and returns an integer
string()	Converts an object to a string
encodeURI()	Replaces all characters, except those with special meaning in a URI, with the appropriate UTF-8 escape sequences
encodeURI	Assumes that the URI is not complete, and does not treat reserved Component() characters as if they have special meaning and encodes them
unescape()	Returns the ASCII string for the specified hexadecimal encoding value

Appendix F

XML Quick Reference

What Is XML?

Extensible Markup Language (XML) is a subset of the Standard Generalized Markup Language (SGML). XML allows developers to create their own document elements or tags. The World Wide Web Consortium (W3C, *www.w3.org*) develops the standards for XML and other Web languages.

An XML document consists of two main parts: the prolog and the document instance. The prolog contains processing instructions and any additional comments necessary to provide information about the document's content and structure. An XML prolog can include any of the following:

- XML declaration statements and comments
- Document type declaration with an optional Document Type Definition (DTD) to define elements, attributes, and logical relationships of data
- Optional link to either a CSS or XSL style sheet

The document instance contains the main content or elements of the XML document and provides a logical structure for the document.

Well-Formed and Valid XML Documents

XML documents must be well-formed to be processed by an application. A valid XML document is one that adheres to the rules and structure specified in the DTD. Table F–1 shows the syntax rules that define well-formed and valid XML documents. An XML document must be at least well-formed. You can check the syntax of your XML document at *http://www.w3schools.com/dom/dom_validate.asp* or check for a valid DTD at *http://www.xmlvalidation.com/*. See the Web sites for instructions on how to use and validate XML documents.

Table F–1 Rules for Well-Formed and Valid XML Documents

Rule Number	Rules
1	XML is case-sensitive
2	Element tags must be nested correctly; the document must contain at least one root element and nest the child elements within the root
3	All elements include a start tag and end tag
4	Valid documents must include a Document Type Definition (DTD)
5	Element attribute values must be enclosed in quotation marks
6	Elements can be empty; empty elements must be formatted correctly to include a / (forward slash) before the end tag
7	Entity references use < and & characters, which must be used in entity references

XML Processing Instructions

Table F–2 shows the basic form of the declarations, statements, and comments found in the prolog section of an XML document.

Table F–2 XML Instructions

<table>
<tr><th>Instruction</th><th>General Form</th><th>Example</th><th>Comment</th></tr>
<tr><td>XML declaration</td><td><?xml version="#" encoding="encoding" standalone="yes|no" ?></td><td><?xml version="1.0" standalone="yes|no"?></td><td>Defines version, character encoding, and if DTD is required to parse XML document</td></tr>
<tr><td>Document type declaration</td><td><!DOCTYPE ROOT-ELEMENT PUBLIC/SYSTEM="URL-DTD.DTD"></td><td><!DOCTYPE PHONELIST SYSTEM="PHONELIST.DTD"></td><td>PUBLIC indicates location of public DTD; SYSTEM indicates location of private DTD</td></tr>
<tr><td>Processing Instruction</td><td><?target attribute="value" ?></td><td><?xml-stylesheet type="text/xsl" href="xslalphaclublist.xsl"?></td><td>Gives instruction to the application to access a document or file outside the application (in this example, a style sheet); can include one or more attributes</td></tr>
<tr><td>Comment</td><td><!--Comments --></td><td><!-- File Name: studentclubs.xml --></td><td>Provides a user or developer with information about the document; comments are ignored by application</td></tr>
<tr><td>Character Data Type</td><td><![CDATA [text]]></td><td><![CDATA [The <b> tag should always have an end </b> tag.]]</td><td>Special section of character data not interpreted as markup, as opposed to parsed character data (PCDATA), to which the XML syntax rules apply; CDATA sections often used to show XML or HTML syntax examples</td></tr>
</table>

XML Element and Attribute Rules

Elements must be bound by start and end tags or be an empty element. Elements may contain other elements, but they must be nested in the proper order. Table F–3 lists the syntax rules for creating valid XML elements. Table F–4 contains a list of element rules. Table F–5 shows examples of valid, invalid, and empty XML elements.

Table F–3 XML Element Syntax Rules

Rule Number	Rules
1	Must begin with a letter or an underscore
2	May contain letters, numbers, hyphens, periods, or underscores
3	May not contain spaces, commas, or symbols (@#$%^&*!)
4	May not begin with XML, which is reserved for future use
5	Names are case-sensitive; start and end tags must use same case
6	Colons are acceptable only for declaring namespaces
7	Empty elements have no text or values, but may contain attributes

Table F–4 XML Element Rules

Symbol	Meaning
#PCDATA	Element contains parsed character data or text and conforms to XML constraints (CDATA attributes are non-parsed character data.)
element name (by itself)	Element name may be used one time only
element name ?	Element is used either once or not at all
element name +	Element has a one-to-many (1:n) relationship
element name *	Element has a zero, or one-to-many (1:n) relationship
, (comma)	Used between elements to indicate order
| (bar)	Used between elements to indicate either or
( )	Used to group related elements together; may be nested

Table F–5 Valid and Invalid Examples of XML Elements

Example	Comment
<FirstName></FirstName>	Valid
<45Degree></45Degree>	Invalid (starts with a numeral)
<_Project></_Project>	Valid
<First-Name></First-Name>	Valid
<Hanger_41></Hanger_41>	Valid
<Java Script></Java Script>	Invalid (contains a space)
<xmlproject></xmlproject>	Invalid (may not begin with xml)
<Para></PARA>	Invalid (start and end tags use different case)
<Picture SRC="mypic.jpg" />	Valid empty element

Element attributes describe additional information about the element. Attribute values must be enclosed in quotation marks (either single or double quotation marks are acceptable). Attribute names follow the same rules as elements. Table F–6 shows the reserved attributes.

Table F–6 Reserved Attributes

Attribute	Comment	Example
xml:lang="code"	where code indicates language of element body	`<Greet xml:lang="en">Hey</Greet>`

xml:space="action"	where action is either default or preserve; preserve means preserve white space, default means treat white space based on default settings	`<Lines xml:space="preserve">This`
		`is`
		`one`
		`line`
		`</Lines>`

xml:link="type"	where type is simple, extended, locator, group, or document	`<a xml:link="simple"` `href=http://www.w3.org>W3C</A>`

Document Type Definition (DTD)

A Document Type Definition (DTD) is similar to a database schema and defines the elements and attributes in an XML document. A DTD indicates how elements of an XML document relate to each other. A DTD provides the grammar rules of a document. When an XML document adheres to a DTD, it is considered valid.

A DTD can include element declarations, attribute list declarations, entity declarations, and notation declarations. An element declaration defines the type of content contained in an element. Table F–7 describes the basic form of an element declaration.

Table F–7 General Form of an Element Declaration

General form:	<!ELEMENT element-name (rule)>
Comment:	!ELEMENT is the declaration element-name; is any valid XML element name (see rules in Table F–3 on page APP 54); rule is a keyword, such as ANY or #PCDATA. The ANY keyword means other valid tags and data can be displayed; #PCDATA means only parsed character data can be displayed.
Example:	<!ELEMENT SONG (Title, Singer)> <!ELEMENT Title (#PCDATA)> <!ELEMENT Singer (#PCDATA)>

Attribute List Declarations

A DTD also can contain an attribute list declaration. The items in the attribute list must correspond to any attributes declared within XML elements. Table F–8 shows the general form of an attribute list declaration.

Table F–8 General Form of an Attribute List Declaration

General form:	<!ATTLIST element-name attribute-name data-type default-value>
Comment:	element-name is the name of the XML element. The attribute-name is the name of the attribute. The data-type is the data type of the attribute (see Table F–9). The default-value is any default value of the attribute. In the example, width is an attribute, with a CDATA (character data) type and default value of 10.
Example:	<!ATTLIST txtBox width CDATA "10">

The data type in an attribute list declaration can be one of 10 different kinds of data type attributes, as shown in Table F–9.

Table F–9 DTD Data Type Attributes

Type	Description
CDATA	Character data; can include any character string as well as special symbols for ampersand (&), less than and greater than symbols or angle brackets (< or >), or quotation marks (")
Enumerated	List of possible values for an attribute; only one can be used
ENTITY	Single entity; either external data or declared DTD entity
ENTITIES	Multiple entities; either external data or declared in DTD
ID	Unique element identifier for an attribute that distinguishes one element from others
IDREF	Identifies the value of an attribute of a unique ID
IDREFS	Identifies multiple values for an attribute, separated by white space
NMTOKEN	XML name token; restricts the attribute value to any valid XML name (letters, number, hyphens, underscores, and periods)
NMTOKENS	Allows the attribute value to include multiple XML tokens, separated by white space
NOTATION	Allows the attribute value to be a value specified in a DTD notation declaration

The default value in an attribute list declaration must match the data type. If a specific value is noted, the value must be enclosed within quotation marks. A default value consists of one of the four options shown in Table F–10.

Table F–10 DTD Data Type Attributes

Modifier	Description
#REQUIRED	Attribute value must be specified with the element
#IMPLIED	Attribute value is optional; if used in an element type, no default value is supplied
#FIXED "value"	Attribute value is fixed and must always take the default value assigned
"value"	Specific value set at the default attribute value

Entity Declarations

As just discussed, a DTD also can include entity declarations, which assign a name to a block of text or other characters that can be interpreted as markup language and substituted in a document. The replacement text must begin with an ampersand (&) and end with a semicolon (;). Entity declarations can be internal or external. Table F–11 shows the general form of an internal entity declaration. Table F–12 shows the predefined symbols that can be used in an entity declaration.

Table F–11 General Form of Internal Entity Declaration

General form:	<!ENTITY name "replacement;"> <ELEMENT>text "&replacement;"</ELEMENT>
Comment:	name is a valid element name and the replacement is the entity characters to be substituted within the string. Circular references are not allowed.
Example:	`<!ENTITY copyright "©">` `<PUBLISHED>2010, Course Technology ©right;</PUBLISHED>`

Table F–12 Predefined Entity Symbols

Entity	Symbol	Explanation
&	&	Cannot be used in processing instructions
<	<	Use with attributes beginning with quotation marks
>	>	Use after]] in normal text and processing instructions
"	"	Use in attributes within double quotation marks
'	'	Use in attributes within single quotation marks
&#xhex		To use a hexadecimal value for a character, such as A9 for the copyright symbol (©)

XML allows the use of external entities to refer to the contents of another file. An external entity exists at a specified location or URL. The content of the external file is inserted at the point of reference and parsed as part of the referring document. Table F–13 shows the general form of an external entity.

Table F–13 General Form of an External Entity

General form:	<!ENTITY name PUBLIC/SYSTEM "identifier"> <ELEMENT>text "&replacement;" </ELEMENT>
Comment:	name is a valid element name; identifier is an identifier that points to a file on that system or a public file available via URL. ENTITY must be declared first.
Example:	<!ENTITY stockquotes SYSTEM "http://www.stockquotes.com/dowjones.xml"> <finances> <dowjones>Dow Jones Industrial Averages</dowjones> &stockquotes; </finances>

Unparsed Entities and Notation Declarations

A notation declaration tells a processor that an entity refers to non-XML content that should not be parsed. Unparsed entities are used most frequently on XML elements that incorporate graphics into a document.

A notation also has to be declared in an entity. An unparsed entity is indicated by the NDATA keyword. Ampersands and semicolons are not used with unparsed data. Table F–14 shows an example.

Table F–14 Unparsed Entity Example

<!ENTITY imageA SYSTEM http://www.mysite.com/myimage.gif NDATA GIF89a> <image src="imageA" />

XSL Style Sheets

Extensible Stylesheet Language (XSL), which is a language for expressing style sheets, incorporates three technologies:

- XSL Transformations (XSLT) is a language for transforming XML documents into other types of documents.
- XML Path Language (XPath) is a language used by XSLT to access or refer to parts of an XML document.
- XSL Formatting Objects is a language that defines XML formatting and display.

Table F–15 shows the XSLT elements specified by the W3C.

Table F–15 XSLT Elements

Element Name	Description	Attributes
xsl:apply-imports	Applies template rule from an imported style sheet	N/A
xsl:apply-templates	Applies a template to the current element	order-by="+|-pattern" select="pattern"
xsl:attribute	Adds a new attribute to the current output element	name="attribute-name"
xsl:attribute-set	Defines a named set of attributes	N/A
xsl:call-template	Provides a way to call a named template	name="template-name"
xsl:choose	Provides a selection mechanism based on conditions	N/A
xsl:comment	Adds a comment node to the output	N/A
xsl:copy	Copies the current node to the output	N/A
xsl:copy-of	Creates a copy of the current node	N/A
xsl:decimal-format	Defines the characters and symbols to be used when converting numbers into strings in conjunction with the format-number() function	N/A
xsl:element	Adds a new element node to the output	name="name"
xsl:fallback	Indicates code to execute if the processor does not support an XSLT element	N/A
xsl:for-each	Provides a mechanism to create a loop in the output stream	select="pattern" order-by="-|+ pattern"
xsl:if	Provides a conditional branch mechanism based on a condition	match="pattern"
xsl:import and xsl:include	Merges rules from different style sheets	N/A
xsl:key	Declares a named key that can be used in the style sheet with the key() function	N/A
xsl:message	Writes error message to the output	N/A
xsl:namespace-alias	Replaces namespaces in the style sheet with different namespaces in the output	N/A
xsl:number	Determines the integer position of the current node and formats a number	N/A
xsl:otherwise	Is part of the choose mechanism (see xsl:choose)	N/A
xsl:output	Defines the format of the output document	N/A
xsl:param	Declares a local or global parameter	N/A
xsl:preserve-space	Indicates elements to preserve white space	N/A
xsl:processing-instruction	Adds a processing statement or instruction to the output	name="name"
xsl:sort	Reorders input before copying to output	N/A
xsl:strip-space	Indicates elements to remove white space	N/A
xsl:stylesheet	Defines the root element of the style sheet	xmlns:xml="namespace" language="language" indent-result="yes|no"
xsl:template	Defines a template	match="pattern" language="language"
xsl:text	Writes literal text or spaces to the output	N/A
xsl:transform	The root element of a style sheet	N/A
xsl:value-of	Defines a node to insert into the output	select="pattern"
xsl:variable	Defines constants	N/A
xsl:when	Is part of the choose mechanism (see xsl:choose)	test="expression"
xsl:with-param	Defines the value of a parameter to be passed into a template	N/A

Index

D

E

F

G

H

I

J

K

L

Q

R

S

X

Y